Accolades for DB2 Developer's Guide:

"Once you've picked up and read *DB2 Developer's Guide* you will know why people on the DB2 List Serve forum refer to this book as the BIBLE. You will find that the *DB2 Developer's Guide* is a comprehensive guide for both the beginner and experienced in DB2 and relational database technology...I cannot say enough about the *DB2 Developer's Guide*."

—Troy Coleman
Data Administration Newsletter

"*DB2 Developer's Guide* has the potential to pay for itself many times over if you follow its useful design and performance advice. If you use DB2 in your workplace, the most recent edition of *DB2 Developer's Guide* should definitely be on your bookshelf. Read it to save yourself an enormous amount of pain and suffering."

—Ron Shirey
Relational Database Journal

"...the book is not only the size of a small encyclopedia, it is also just about as comprehensive."

Books & Bytes News & Reviews

"*DB2 Developer's Guide* is a must buy for both inexperienced and DB2 experts alike. I am amazed at the amount of information Craig covers in the *DB2 Developer's Guide*."

—Chris Foot
Data Administration Newsletter

"*DB2 Developer's Guide* is a complete reference for the DB2 professional. It is a perfect tool for finding the options available to the DB2 developer, and steering you to the right method."

—Gregory Amov
Computing News & Review

"*DB2 Developer's Guide* presents literally everything programmers and DBAs need to know about advanced DB2...This is an excellent book...It is chock full of DB2 technical information, design and tuning approaches, and database administration guidelines...In an organized and coherent way, Mullins seems to have dumped his entire DB2 life experience into *DB2 Developer's Guide*."

—Jonathon Sayles
Relational Database Journal

DB2
Developer's Guide

Craig S. Mullins

SAMS

800 East 96th Street, Indianapolis, Indiana 46240 USA

DB2 Developer's Guide

International Standard Book Number: 0-672-32613-2

Library of Congress Catalog Card Number: 2004091254

Printed in the United States of America

First Printing: May 2004

08 09   7 6 5

Trademarks

All terms mentioned in this book that are known to be trademarks or service marks have been appropriately capitalized. Sams Publishing cannot attest to the accuracy of this information. Use of a term in this book should not be regarded as affecting the validity of any trademark or service mark.

Warning and Disclaimer

Every effort has been made to make this book as complete and as accurate as possible, but no warranty or fitness is implied. The information provided is on an "as is" basis. The author and the publisher shall have neither liability nor responsibility to any person or entity with respect to any loss or damages arising from the information contained in this book.

Bulk Sales

Sams Publishing offers excellent discounts on this book when ordered in quantity for bulk purchases or special sales. For more information, please contact

U.S. Corporate and Government Sales
1-800-382-3419
corpsales@pearsontechgroup.com

For sales outside of the U.S., please contact

International Sales
international@pearsoned.com

Associate Publisher
Michael Stephens

Acquisitions Editor
Loretta Yates

Development Editor
Sean Dixon

Managing Editor
Charlotte Clapp

Project Editor
Elizabeth Finney

Copy Editor
Sean Dixon

Indexer
Heather McNeill

Proofreader
Juli Cook

Technical Editors
Chuck Kosin
Willie Favero

Publishing Coordinator
Cindy Teeters

Multimedia Developer
Dan Scherf

Book Designer
Gary Adair

Contents at a Glance

Table of Contents

About the Author

Craig S. Mullins is Director of DB2 Technology Planning for BMC Software, Inc. He has extensive experience in all facets of database systems development, including systems analysis and design, database and system administration, data analysis, and developing and teaching various courses (on DB2, Sybase, and database design). Craig has worked with DB2 since Version 1 and has experience in multiple roles, including programmer, DBA, instructor, and analyst. His experience spans industries, having worked for companies in the following fields: manufacturing (USX Corporation), banking (Mellon Bank), utilities (Duquesne Light Company), commercial software development (BMC Software, PLATINUM technology, inc.), consulting (ASSET, Inc.), and computer industry analysis (Gartner Group). Additionally, Craig authored many of the popular "Platinum Monthly DB2 Tips" and worked on Platinum's DB2 system catalog and access paths posters.

Craig is a regular lecturer at industry conferences. You may have seen him present at such events as the International DB2 Users Group (IDUG), the IBM DB2 Technical Conference, SHARE, DAMA, or at one of many regional DB2 user groups.

Craig is also a frequent contributor to computer industry publications, having published hundreds of articles during the past few years. His articles have been published in magazines such as *Byte*, *DB2 Update*, *DB2 Magazine*, *Database Programming & Design*, *DBMS*, *Data Management Review*, *Relational Database Journal*, *Enterprise Systems Journal*, *IDUG Solutions Journal*, *z/Journal*, and others. Craig writes four regular industry columns covering the database industry:

- "The DBA Corner" in *Database Trends & Applications*

- "The Database Report" in *The Data Administration Newsletter*

- "z/Data Perspectives" in *z/Journal*

- "The Buffer Pool" in *IDUG Solutions Journal*

Additionally, he is a consulting editor and regular contributor to www.dbazine.com. Complete information on Craig's published articles and books can be found on the Web at http://www.craigsmullins.com.

Craig has also written another book titled *Database Administration: The Complete Guide to Practices and Procedures* (Addison-Wesley, 2002; ISBN: 0201741296) that can be used as a complement to this book. It addresses heterogeneous database administration.

Craig graduated cum laude with a degree in Computer Science and Economics from the University of Pittsburgh.

Dedication

This book is dedicated to my mom, Donna Mullins, and to the memory of my father, Giles R. Mullins. Without the constant support and guidance my parents provided, I would not have the success I enjoy today.

Acknowledgments

The process of writing, editing and producing a technical book is time-consuming and laborious. Luckily, I had many understanding and helpful people to make the process much easier. First, I would like to thank the many folks who have reviewed and commented upon the text for each of the five editions. Chuck Kosin has served as technical editor for the last four editions of this book, and I know it is a much better text thanks to his eagle eye, technical acumen, and excellent suggestions. Willie Favero of IBM reviewed this fifth edition and his many excellent suggestions were tremendously helpful. Extra special thanks go out to my good friend Sheryl Larsen (www.smlsql.com) who not only reviewed all of the SQL portions of the book, but also allowed me to use several of her excellent access path diagrams. Bill Backs and Roger Miller have reviewed various past incarnations and editions of the manuscript and this book is much better thanks to their expert contributions, as well.

I would also like to thank the many people who provided suggestions for improvements on the first four editions of the book. I do read the email suggestions and comments sent to me by readers, so keep them coming.

Additionally, I'd like to extend my gratitude to the many understanding and patient folks at Sams who have worked with me on each of the five editions. And finally, a thank you to all of the people with whom I have worked at USX Corporation, Mellon Bank, ASSET, Inc., Barnett Technologies, Duquesne Light Company, Gartner Group, PLATINUM technology, inc. and BMC Software. This book is surely a better one due to the fine quality of my coworkers, each of whom has expanded my horizons in many different and satisfying ways.

If you have any questions or comments about this text, you can contact me at craig@craigsmullins.com or Craig_Mullins@BMC.com. For more DB2 information and news about future editions of this book, visit my Web site at http://www.CraigSMullins.com. You can also write to me in care of the publisher.

We Want to Hear from You!

As the reader of this book, *you* are our most important critic and commentator. We value your opinion and want to know what we're doing right, what we could do better, what areas you'd like to see us publish in, and any other words of wisdom you're willing to pass our way.

As an associate publisher for Sams Publishing, I welcome your comments. You can email or write me directly to let me know what you did or didn't like about this book—as well as what we can do to make our books better.

Please note that I cannot help you with technical problems related to the topic of this book. We do have a User Services group, however, where I will forward specific technical questions related to the book.

When you write, please be sure to include this book's title and author as well as your name, email address, and phone number. I will carefully review your comments and share them with the author and editors who worked on the book.

Email: feedback@samspublishing.com

Mail: Mike Stephens
           Associate Publisher
           Sams Publishing
           800 East 96th Street
           Indianapolis, IN 46240 USA

For more information about this book or another Sams Publishing title, visit our Web site at www.samspublishing.com. Type the ISBN (0672326132) or the title of a book in the Search field to find the page you're looking for.

What's New in This Edition?

This book is completely revised and updated for DB2 Versions 7 and 8, and it includes coverage of

- How to make changes to DB2 objects using online schema evolution features and the impact of doing so on your systems.

- New utilities and utility functionality, including UNLOAD, BACKUP SYSTEM, RESTORE SYSTEM, LISTDEF, historical RUNSTATS, templates, and wildcards. Also includes an analysis of the impact of IBM charging for DB2 utilities as of V7 (instead of providing them free of charge with DB2).

- Deploying the Real Time Statistics capability of DB2 to capture performance statistics and populate them into catalog-like tables, as DB2 runs—without the need to run an external utility. Also, guidance on how to use the new RTS tables.

- Using DB2 Type Extenders, including the XML Extender, to extend the functionality of DB2 into the object/relational realm.

- Capacity improvements, including support for the new IBM z/Architecture and 64-bit z/OS operating system.

- How to code recursive SQL queries using common table expressions. Recursive SQL is helpful for traversing hierarchies like bill-of-materials and reporting structures.

- Application development and SQL programming changes, such as the new XML and MQSeries built-in functions, larger SQL statements, long names, UNION and UNION ALL in views, FETCH FIRST n ROWS ONLY, SQL Procedure Language, and so on.

- Administration changes, such as deferred data set creation, multilevel security, padded indexes, and online DSNZPARMs.

- Information on migrating to DB2 V8, including the three modes of V8, new utilities for migrating, and basic migration guidance.

- How to effectively manage logic stored in DB2 databases in the form of stored procedures, user-defined functions, and triggers.

Additional revisions were made to the entire book to expand the techniques that were previously covered, and to add new tips, tricks, and techniques for developing performance-oriented, stable DB2 application systems. New and revised SQL and DDL tips, dynamic SQL usage considerations, and DB2 subsystem performance and reporting techniques will prove to be invaluable to DB2 Version 7 and 8 sites. The sections on DB2 tools and vendors were completely revised to take mergers and acquisitions and new products into account.

Three brand new chapters have been added. The first covers the DB2 V8 Online Schema Evolution functionality. The second new chapter covers indexing; it consolidates information from other sections, and adds new guidelines and tips on proper index creation strategies for DB2 applications. And the third new chapter covers how to use DB2 Connect to hook up workstations to mainframe DB2 databases.

With this edition, I have removed the appendixes covering SQLCODEs and DB2 Catalog tables. This reference information is easily obtained by downloading the appropriate manuals from IBM's Web site at:

`http://www-306.ibm.com/software/data/db2/library/`

A full list of the SQLCODEs can be found in the DB2 *Messages and Codes* manual, and the DB2 Catalog table descriptions can be found in the DB2 *SQL Reference* manual.

Introduction

Welcome to the fifth edition of *DB2 Developer's Guide*. I have been overwhelmed by the success of the first four editions of this book. The information technology community obviously needs a practitioner's view of DB2 development issues and concerns. The second edition covered DB2 through V3; the third edition expanded that coverage to include DB2 V4 and V5; the fourth edition updated the text to cover DB2 V6; and this fifth edition brings the book up-to-date with the information about DB2 Versions 7 and 8. For an overview of the changes made to DB2 for V7 please refer to Appendix F, while Appendix G provides an introduction to DB2 V8.

Other books about DB2 are available, but most of them discuss the same tired subjects: SQL syntax, basic relational database design, normalization and embedded SQL programming with COBOL. *DB2 Developer's Guide,* 5E unlocks the secrets of DB2, picking up where the DB2 tutorial books leave off. It delves into subjects not covered adequately elsewhere—sometimes not even in IBM's DB2 manuals. This book clarifies complex DB2 topics, provides performance and procedural advice for implementing well-designed DB2 applications, and describes what DB2 does behind the scenes. Using *DB2 Developer's Guide,* 5E as a blueprint, your administration and development staff can implement optimized DB2 application systems.

This is not an introductory text on DB2 and SQL, but much of the advice contained herein is useful to the beginner as well as to the advanced user. It does not teach SQL syntax, relational theory, normalization, or logical database design, but it does provide suggestions on how and when to use these and other techniques. If you are interested in the intricacies of complex SQL instead of syntax diagrams, this book is for you. Other areas covered include

- Comprehensive coverage of DB2 V8—the latest and greatest version of DB2. Some of the many V8 features explained herein include online schema evolution, data partitioned secondary indexes (DPSIs), sequences, recursive SQL, the latest SQL enhancements, long names, partitioning enhancements, dynamic scrollable cursors, multilevel security, new XML and MQSeries functions, new utilities (BACKUP SYSTEM and RESTORE SYSTEM), and much more.

- Extensive coverage of DB2 V7 features including Real Time Statistics (RTS), new utilities (UNLOAD), utility wildcarding and templates, utility packaging, identity columns, the XML extender, Stored Procedure Builder, scrollable cursors, external SAVEPOINTs, row expressions, declared temporary tables, and deferred data set creation.

- Tips, tricks, and guidelines for coding efficient SQL.

- Guidelines for building performance-oriented DB2 databases.

- Environmental options for developing DB2 applications using TSO, CICS, IMS/TM, CAF, and RRSAF.

- Description of what goes on in DB2 behind the scenes, including logging, locking, and a roadmap for using the System Catalog and Directory.

- Comprehensive techniques for achieving and maintaining optimal DB2 performance.

- In-depth performance monitoring and tuning guidelines from both an application and a system perspective.

- Using EXPLAIN and interpreting its output, including how to use optimizer hints and the V6 estimation and function resolution tables.

- Procedures for using the DB2 Catalog and RTS to monitor DB2.

- DB2 application development guidelines.

- In-depth advice on using the DB2 utilities.

- Guidelines for assigning buffer pool sizes and strategies for implementing multiple buffer pools.

- DB2 disaster recovery scenarios and recommendations.

- How and when to use DB2 views.

- How to use DB2 in a client/server environment including discussion of stored procedures, access to DB2 over the Internet, ODBC, and DB2 Connect.

- How to combine DBA skills and development skills to effectively manage logic stored in DB2 databases in the form of triggers, user-defined functions, and stored procedures.

- Coverage of DB2's support for distributed databases including a discussion of DRDA and distributed two-phase commit.

- In-depth coverage of how to deploy DB2-based data warehouses.

- Coverage of add-on tools for DB2, including a description of the types of tools and a listing of vendors and their offerings (useful if you must evaluate DB2 tools).

- Discussion of DB2 organizational issues including roles and responsibilities, design review guidelines, and political issues.

How To Use This Book

This book serves as a tour guide for your adventurous journey through the world of DB2. Of course, you can read the book from cover to cover. The book's usefulness does not diminish after your initial reading, however. It is probably best used as a reference text for your daily workings with DB2.

The book is organized to function in both capacities. Each chapter deals with a particular subject and references other chapters or DB2 manuals when appropriate. In short, the book is designed to optimize the performance of both planned and ad hoc access, much like DB2!

Supplementary chapters and appendixes not included in the printed book are available online. Go to www.samspublishing.com and type the book's ISBN (**0672326132**) into the Search field to go to the *DB2 Developer's Guide* page. In the Table of Contents, these chapters have the designation "PDF" along with their page numbers. The same format is used in the Index, to indicate page numbers from the chapters and appendixes on the Web.

So turn the page and let's begin our exploration of the inner depths of DB2 together.

CHAPTER 1

The Magic Words

IN THIS CHAPTER

- An Overview of SQL
- SQL Tools of the Trade
- Static SQL
- Dynamic SQL
- SQL Performance Factors

Once upon a time there was a kingdom called Userville. The people in the kingdom were impatient and wanted to know everything about everything—they could never get enough information. Life was difficult and the people were unhappy because data was often lost, and even when it was available, it was often inaccurate and not easy to access.

The King decided to purchase DB2, an advanced tool for storing and retrieving data. With DB2 the Users could process their data and turn it into information. "This," he thought, "should keep the people happy. DB2 will solve all my problems." But he soon found out that special knowledge was necessary to make DB2 work its wonders. Nobody in Userville knew how to use it properly.

Luckily, a grand Wizard living in a nearby kingdom knew many mystical secrets for retrieving data. These secrets were a form of magic called SQL. The King of Userville summoned the Wizard, offering him many great treasures if only he would help the poor Users in Userville.

The Wizard soon arrived, determined to please. Armed with nothing more than SQL and a smile, the Wizard strode to the terminal and uttered the magic words:

```
SELECT E.EMPNO, E.FIRSTNME, E.LASTNAME, D.DEPTNO, D.DEPTNAME
FROM   DSN8810.DEPT  D,
       DSN8810.EMP   E
WHERE  E.WORKDEPT = D.DEPTNO;
```

A crowd gathered and applauded as the desired information began pumping out of the terminal. "More, more," shouted the data-starved masses. The Wizard gazed into the screen, and with amazing speed effortlessly produced report after report. The King was overheard to say, "You know, this is just too good to be true!" Everybody was happy. The Users had their share of information, the King had a peaceful kingdom, and the Wizard had his treasures and the respect of the Users.

For many months, the Users were satisfied with the magic of the great Wizard. Then, one day, the Wizard disappeared...in a jet to the West Coast for 130 grand a year—and a bunch of stock options. The people of the kingdom began to worry. "How will we survive without the magic of the Wizard? Will we have to live, once again, without our precious information?" The Wizard's apprentice tried to silence the crowd by using his magic, but it wasn't the same. The information was still there, but it wasn't coming fast enough or as effortlessly. The apprentice was not yet as skilled as the great Wizard who had abandoned the kingdom. But, as luck would have it, one day he stumbled upon the great Wizard's diary. He quickly absorbed every page and soon was invoking the Wizard's magic words. And all was well again.

Well, life is not always that simple. Departing Wizards do not often leave behind documentation of their secrets. The first part of this book can be used as a "Wizard's diary" for efficient SQL. This chapter is an overview of SQL, not from a syntactic viewpoint, but from a functional viewpoint. This chapter is not intended to teach SQL, but to provide a framework for the advanced issues discussed in the remainder of this text. This framework delineates the differences between SQL and procedural languages and outlines the components and types of SQL. Chapters 2 through 10 delve into the performance and administrative issues surrounding the effective implementation of SQL for DB2.

So continue and take the next step toward becoming a DB2 Wizard...

An Overview of SQL

Structured Query Language, better known as *SQL* (and pronounced "sequel" or "ess-cue-el"), is a powerful tool for manipulating data. It is the de facto standard query language for *relational database management systems (RDBMSs)* and is used not just by DB2, but also by the other leading RDBMS products such as Oracle, Sybase, and Microsoft SQL Server. Indeed, every relational database management system—and many non-relational DBMS products—support SQL. Why is this so? What benefits are accrued by using SQL rather than some other language?

> **NOTE**
>
> Technically, there are no true commercially available *relational* DBMS products. By this I mean that no DBMS today fully supports the relational model as defined by Dr. E.F. Codd. Products such as DB2 and Oracle are more accurately called SQL DBMSs. However, due to common usage, the term RDBMS will be used in this book.

There are many reasons. Foremost is that SQL is a high-level language that provides a greater degree of abstraction than do procedural languages. Third-generation languages (3GLs), such as COBOL and C, and fourth-generation languages (4GLs), such as FOCUS and NOMAD, require the programmer to navigate data structures. Program logic must be coded to proceed record by record through the data stores in an order determined by the application programmer or systems analyst. This information is encoded in the high-level language and is difficult to change after it has been programmed.

SQL, on the other hand, is fashioned so that the programmer can specify what data is needed but cannot specify how to retrieve it. SQL is coded without embedded data-navigational instructions. The DBMS analyzes SQL and formulates data-navigational instructions "behind the scenes." These data-navigational instructions are called *access paths*. By forcing the DBMS to determine the optimal access path to the data, a heavy burden is removed from the programmer. In addition, the database can have a better understanding of the state of the data it stores, and thereby can produce a more efficient and dynamic access path to the data. The result is that SQL, used properly, provides a quicker application development and prototyping environment than is available with corresponding high-level languages.

Another feature of SQL is that it is not merely a query language. The same language used to query data is used also to define data structures, control access to the data, and insert, modify, and delete occurrences of the data. This consolidation of functions into a single language eases communication between different types of users. DBAs, systems programmers, application programmers, systems analysts, systems designers, and end users all speak a common language: SQL. When all the participants in a project are speaking the same language, a synergy is created that can reduce overall system-development time.

Arguably, though, the single most important feature of SQL that has solidified its success is its capability to retrieve data easily using English-like syntax. It is much easier to understand

```
SELECT    LASTNAME
FROM      EMP
WHERE     EMPNO = '000010';
```

than it is to understand pages and pages of COBOL, C, or Java source code or the archaic instructions of Assembler. Because SQL programming instructions are easier to understand, they are easier also to learn and maintain—thereby making users and programmers more productive in a shorter period of time.

The remainder of this chapter focuses more fully on the features and components of SQL touched on in this overview.

The Nature of SQL

SQL is, by nature, a flexible creature. It uses a free-form structure that gives the user the ability to develop SQL statements in a way best suited to the given user. Each SQL request is parsed by the DBMS before execution to check for proper syntax and to optimize the request. Therefore, SQL statements do not need to start in any given column and can be strung together on one line or broken apart on several lines. For example, the following SQL statement:

```
SELECT * FROM DSN8810.EMP WHERE SALARY < 25000;
```

is functionally equivalent to this SQL statement:

```
SELECT    *
FROM      DSN8810.EMP
WHERE     SALARY < 25000;
```

Another flexible feature of SQL is that a single request can be formulated in a number of different and functionally equivalent ways. This flexibility is possible because SQL provides the ability to code a single feature in several ways. One example of this SQL capability is that you can combine data from multiple tables either by joining or nesting queries. A nested query can be converted to an equivalent join. Other examples of this flexibility can be seen in the vast array of functions and predicates. Examples of features with equivalent functionality are:

- BETWEEN versus <= and >=

- IN versus a series of predicates tied together with AND

- INNER JOIN versus tables strung together using the FROM clause separated by commas

- OUTER JOIN versus a simple SELECT, with a UNION, and a correlated subselect

- CASE expressions versus complex UNION ALL statements

- Single-column function versus multiple-column functions (for example, AVG versus SUM and COUNT)

This flexibility exhibited by SQL is not always desirable as different but equivalent SQL formulations can result in extremely differing performance. The ramifications of this flexibility are discussed in the next few chapters, which provide guidelines for developing efficient SQL.

As mentioned, SQL specifies **what** data to retrieve or manipulate, but does not specify **how** you accomplish these tasks. This keeps SQL intrinsically simple. If you can remember the set-at-a-time orientation of the relational model, you will begin to grasp the essence and nature of SQL. The capability to act on a set of data coupled with the lack of need for establishing how to retrieve and manipulate data defines SQL as a non-procedural language.

A procedural language is based, appropriately enough, on procedures. One procedure is coded to retrieve data record-by-record. Another procedure is coded to calculate percentages based on the retrieved data. More procedures are coded to modify the data, rewrite the data, check for errors, and so on. A controlling procedure then ties together the other procedures and invokes them in a specific and non-changing order. COBOL is a good example of a procedural language.

SQL is a non-procedural language. A single statement can take the place of a series of procedures. Again, this is possible because SQL uses set-level processing and DB2 optimizes the query to determine the data-navigation logic. Sometimes one or two SQL statements can accomplish what entire procedural programs were required to do.

> **NOTE**
>
> Most of the major RDBMS vendors have extended SQL to support procedural logic over the years. Microsoft SQL Server provides procedural support in Transact-SQL; Oracle in PL/SQL. IBM too now supplies a stored procedure language for DB2.

Procedural SQL will look familiar to anyone who has ever written any type of SQL or coded using any type of programming language. Typically, procedural SQL dialects contain constructs to support looping (`while`), exiting (`return`), branching (`goto`), conditional processing (`if...then...else`), blocking (`begin...end`), and variable definition and usage. Procedural extensions enable more of the application to be written using only SQL.

The primary reason SQL was extended to support procedural structures was to enable stored procedures and triggers to be written and deployed using SQL alone. DB2 supports a subset of the ANSI standard version of SQL/PSM. More details on PSM and DB2 can be found in Chapter 15, "Using DB2 Stored Procedures."

Set-at-a-Time Processing

Every SQL manipulation statement operates on a table and results in another table. All operations native to SQL, therefore, are performed at a set level. One retrieval statement can return multiple rows; one modification statement can modify multiple rows. This feature of relational databases is called *relational closure*. Relational closure is the major reason that relational databases such as DB2 generally are easier to maintain and query.

Refer to Figure 1.1 for a further explanation of relational closure. A user of DB2 issues the SQL request, which is sent to the DBMS. (This request may need to access one or many DB2 tables.) The DBMS analyzes the SQL request and determines which pieces of information are necessary to resolve the user's request. This information then is presented to the user as a table: one or more columns in zero, one, or many rows. This is important. Set-level processing means that a set always is used for input and a set always is returned as output. Sometimes the set is empty or consists of only one row or column. This is appropriate and does not violate the rules of set-level processing. The relational model and set-level processing are based on the laws of the mathematics of *set theory*, which permits empty or single-valued sets.

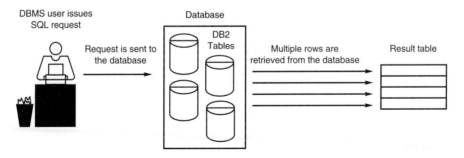

FIGURE 1.1   Relational closure.

Contrast the set-at-a-time processing of SQL with record-at-a-time processing as depicted in Figure 1.2. Record-level processing requires multiple reads to satisfy a request, which is hard-coded data navigation. Set-level processing, on the other hand, satisfies the same request with a single, non-navigational statement. Because fewer distinct operations (read, write, and so on) are required, set-level processing is simpler to implement.

The power of SQL becomes increasingly evident when you compare SQL to COBOL (and flat files to relational databases). Consider the following SQL statement:

```
UPDATE    DSN8810.EMP
SET       BONUS = 1000
WHERE     EMPNO = '000340';
```

This single SQL statement accomplishes the same job as the following, comparably complex COBOL pseudo-code program:

```
Must set up IDENTIFICATION and
    ENVIRONMENT DIVISIONS.
DATA DIVISION.
FILE-SECTION.
    Must define input and output files.
WORKING-STORAGE SECTION.
    Must declare all necessary variables.
01  EMPLOYEE-LAYOUT.
    05  EMPNO       PIC X(6).
    05  FIRSTNME    PIC X(12).
    05  MIDINIT     PIC X.
    05  LASTNAME    PIC X(15).
    05  WORKDEPT    PIC X(3).
    05  PHONENO     PIC X(4).
    05  HIREDATE    PIC X(10).
    05  JOB         PIC X(8).
    05  EDLEVEL     PIC S9(4) COMP.
    05  SEX         PIC X.
    05  BIRTHDATE   PIC X(10).
    05  SALARY      PIC S9(7)V99 COMP-3.
    05  BONUS       PIC S9(7)V99 COMP-3.
    05  COMM        PIC S9(7)V99 COMP-3.
77  EOF-FLAG        PIC X      VALUE 'N'.

PROCEDURE DIVISION.
MAIN-PARAGRAPH.
    PERFORM OPEN-FILES.
    PERFORM PROCESS-UPDATE
        UNTIL EOF-FLAG = 'Y'.
    PERFORM CLOSE-FILES.
    STOP RUN.
OPEN-FILES.
    OPEN INPUT INPUT-DATASET.
    OPEN OUTPUT OUTPUT-DATASET.
PROCESS-UPDATE.
    READ INPUT-DATASET
        INTO EMPLOYEE-LAYOUT
        AT END MOVE 'Y' TO EOF-FLAG.
    IF EOF-FLAG = 'Y'
        GO TO PROCESS-UPDATE-EXIT.
    IF EMPNO = '000340'
        MOVE +1000.00 TO BONUS.
    WRITE OUTPUT-DATASET
        FROM EMPLOYEE-LAYOUT.
PROCESS-UPDATE-EXIT.
```

```
        EXIT.
CLOSE-FILES.
        CLOSE INPUT-DATASET
                OUTPUT-DATASET.
```

Record-Level Processing

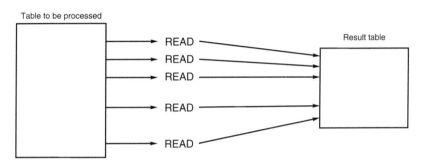

Many iterations of READ are necessary

Set-Level Processing

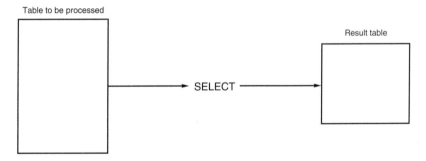

A single SELECT statement produces the desired results

FIGURE 1.2   Record-at-a-time processing versus set-at-a-time processing.

Indeed, many lines that are required in the COBOL program have been eliminated when using SQL. Both the SQL statement and the sample COBOL program change the bonus of employee number 000340 to $1,000.00. The SQL example obviously is easier to code and maintain because of the limited size of the statement and the set-level processing inherent in SQL. The COBOL example, though straightforward to a COBOL programmer, is more difficult for most beginning users to code and understand.

NOTE

Set-level processing differs from record-level processing because:

- All operations act on a complete set of rows
- Fewer operations are necessary to retrieve the desired information
- Data manipulation and retrieval instructions are simpler

The set-level processing capabilities of SQL have an immediate and favorable impact on DB2's capability to access and modify data. For example, a single SQL SELECT statement can produce an entire report. With the assistance of a query-formatting tool, such as QMF, a general SQL processor, such as DSNTEP2, or one of many Windows-based query tools, such as Crystal Reports or Business Objects, hours of coding report programs can be eliminated.

In addition, all of the data-modification capabilities of DB2 act also on a set of data, not row by row. So a single UPDATE or DELETE statement can impact zero, one, or many rows. For example, consider the following statement:

```
UPDATE DSN8810.PROJACT
    SET PROJNO = '222222'
WHERE  PROJNO = '111111';
```

This statement will change the PROJNO for every row where the PROJNO is currently set to the value 111111. The value will be changed whether there is only one row that applies or one million rows. If the WHERE clause were not specified, every row would be changed to the value 222222, regardless of its current value.

The set-level benefits of SQL provide great power to the SQL UPDATE and DELETE statements. Because UPDATE and DELETE can act on sets of data, a single SQL statement can be used to update or delete all rows meeting certain conditions. Great care must be taken always to provide the appropriate WHERE clause or more data may be changed than desired.

Another benefit of the set-level processing capabilities of DB2 is that SQL can append rows to one table based on data retrieved from another table. The following statement assigns every employee of department E21 to activity 1 of project 222222.

```
INSERT
INTO DSN8810.EMPPROJACT
    (SELECT  EMPNO, '222222', 1, 0.10,
             '1991-12-30', '1991-12-31'
     FROM    DSN8810.EMP
     WHERE   WORKDEPT = 'E21');
```

NOTE

Of course, if you tried to run this exact SQL statement on your system it would fail because it violates a referential constraint.

Therefore, a single INSERT statement can be used either to add multiple rows to a table or just to insert a single row.

Types of SQL

SQL is many things to many people. The flexibility of SQL can make it difficult to categorize. Definitive SQL types or categories, however, can be used to group the components of SQL.

Perhaps the most obvious categorization of SQL is based on its functionality. SQL can be used to control, define, and manipulate data, as follows:

- The *Data Control Language (DCL)* provides the control statements that govern data security with the GRANT and REVOKE verbs.

- The *Data Definition Language (DDL)* creates and maintains the physical data structure with the CREATE, DROP, and ALTER SQL verbs.

- The *Data Manipulation Language (DML)* accesses and modifies data with the SELECT, INSERT, DELETE, and UPDATE verbs.

Figure 1.3 depicts this breakdown of SQL statements by functionality.

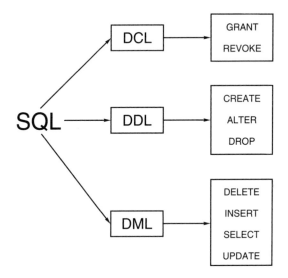

FIGURE 1.3   SQL statement types.

Another way to categorize SQL is by execution type. SQL can be planned and executed as embedded SQL in an application program, or it can be unplanned (ad hoc). The execution of planned SQL usually is referred to as a *production environment*. The production environment is stable and well-defined, and can be planned before the execution of the SQL. This approach to data processing is the traditional one, and SQL fits into it nicely. Batch processing, on-line transaction processing (OLTP), canned reporting, and administrative jobs typify the common production SQL environment. Typical applications in the production environment include accounts receivable, order entry, and inventory control systems.

Ad hoc SQL, on the other hand, usually is undefined until an immediate need is identified. Upon identification, an unplanned or, at best, hastily planned query is composed and executed. Decision-support processing, data warehouse queries, on-line analytical processing (OLAP), power user queries, new query testing, and critical unplanned reporting needs typify the common ad hoc SQL environment. The ad hoc environment is just as critical, if not more so in some cases, to the ongoing business of the organization as the production environment.

Another type of SQL can be thought of as existential SQL. SQL has an existence that relies on the vehicle that maintains and supports it. SQL statements can exist either embedded in an application program or as stand-alone entities.

Yet another way to categorize SQL is according to its dynamism. This fourth and final category is probably the most difficult to define, and provides the greatest flexibility of all the categories. SQL can be either static or dynamic. Static SQL is embedded in an application program written in a high-level language. Dynamic SQL is either typed in at a terminal for real-time execution or constructed in an application program's algorithms at run time. This complex type of SQL is examined in greater detail later in this chapter (and in Chapter 12, "Dynamic SQL Programming").

As you can see, categorization of SQL is not straightforward. Four categories define the nature of SQL. Every SQL statement belongs to a component in every one of these categories. For example, a given SQL statement can be used to manipulate data functionally in a planned production environment embedded in a COBOL program coded as static SQL. Or, it could be used to control data security in an ad hoc query environment as stand-alone dynamic SQL. At any rate, every SQL statement has four defining features, as shown in the following groupings:

Functionality

DCL	Control of data and security
DDL	Data definition
DML	Data manipulation

Execution Type

Production	Planned
Ad hoc	Unplanned

Existence

Embedded	Requires a program
Stand-alone	No program used

Dynamism

Dynamic SQL	Changeable at run time
Static SQL	Unchangeable at run time

SQL Tools of the Trade

SQL, as a "relational" data sublanguage, must support certain basic functions. These functions, or tools of the trade, implement the basic features of set-theory functions. You must have a basic understanding of the capabilities of SQL before you can explore the deeper issues of efficiency, development environments, performance, and tuning.

The basic functions of SQL are described in the following sections. Use these sections as a refresher course; they are not meant to teach SQL syntax or provide in-depth coverage of its use.

Selection and Projection

The *selection* operation retrieves a specified subset of rows from a DB2 table. You use predicates in a WHERE clause to specify the search criteria. The SQL implementation for selection is shown in the following example:

```
SELECT     *
FROM       DSN8810.PROJ
WHERE      DEPTNO = 'D01';
```

To retrieve all rows from the PROJ table, simply eliminate the WHERE clause from the statement.

The *projection* operation retrieves a specified subset of columns from a given DB2 table. A DB2 query can provide a list of column names to limit the columns that are retrieved. Projection retrieves all of the rows but only the specified columns. The following statement illustrates the SQL implementation for projection:

```
SELECT   DEPTNO, PROJNO, PROJNAME
FROM     DSN8810.PROJ;
```

Simply, the selection operation determines which rows are retrieved, and the projection operation determines which columns are retrieved. This is clearly depicted in Figure 1.4.

The SQL SELECT statement is used to implement both the selection and projection operations. In most cases, queries combine selection and projection to retrieve data. The following SQL statement combines the selection and projection operations of the preceding two examples:

```
SELECT  DEPTNO, PROJNO, PROJNAME
FROM    DSN8810.PROJ
WHERE   DEPTNO = 'D01';
```

Joins and Subqueries

The capability to query data from multiple tables using a single SQL statement is one of the nicer features of DB2. The more tables involved in a SELECT statement, however, the more complex the SQL. Complex SQL statements sometimes cause confusion. Therefore, a basic understanding of the multiple table capabilities of SQL is essential for all users.

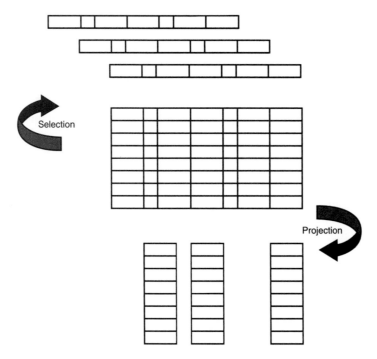

FIGURE 1.4   Selection and projection.

Joining Tables

The capability of DB2 to combine data from multiple tables is called *joining*. A standard join, also referred to as an inner join, matches the data from two or more tables, based on the values of one or more columns in each table. All matches are combined, creating a resulting row that is the concatenation of the columns from each table where the specified columns match.

The most common method of joining DB2 tables requires SQL SELECT statements having the following:

- A string of table names separated by commas in the FROM clause

- A WHERE clause comparing the value of a column in one of the joined tables to the value of a column in the other joined table (this is usually an equality comparison)

For example, to query employees and their department names, the EMP table is joined to the DEPT table as follows:

```
SELECT   EMPNO, LASTNAME, DEPTNO, DEPTNAME
FROM     DSN8810.EMP,
         DSN8810.DEPT
WHERE    WORKDEPT = DEPTNO;
```

This method of coding joins, however, has confused many novice SQL programmers. No join verb need be coded explicitly in the SQL SELECT statement to implement table joining. A join can be specified by the presence of more than one table in the FROM clause of the SELECT statement. It is sometimes difficult to grasp the concept of joining tables without a specific JOIN keyword being used in the SQL join statement.

DB2 V4 introduced the JOIN keyword and an alternate method of coding joins. The following two join statements are equivalent to the previous join statement:

```
SELECT  EMPNO, LASTNAME, DEPTNO, DEPTNAME
FROM    DSN8810.EMP JOIN DSN8810.DEPT
ON      WORKDEPT = DEPTNO;
```

or:

```
SELECT  EMPNO, LASTNAME, DEPTNO, DEPTNAME
FROM    DSN8810.EMP INNER JOIN DSN8810.DEPT
ON      WORKDEPT = DEPTNO;
```

Note that the comma-delimited list of tables is replaced with the keyword JOIN or INNER JOIN. The INNER keyword is used to differentiate a standard, or inner, join from an outer join. Outer joins will be discussed in a moment. The INNER keyword is implicit and will be assumed if not explicitly coded.

Likewise, note that when you use the JOIN keyword you must use ON (instead of WHERE) to specify the join condition. Additional local predicates can be applied with an additional WHERE clause if so desired.

> **NOTE**
>
> Although both types of joins are supported by DB2, consider adopting an SQL coding standard using the explicit [INNER] JOIN keyword. Using the JOIN keyword makes it more difficult to forget to code the join columns (because it requires the special ON clause). Furthermore, when using the JOIN keyword it is easier for novices to learn and effectively code join statements.

When coding joins, remember to keep in mind that SQL is a set-level language. If the value of the data in the columns being matched is not unique, multiple matches might be found for each row in each table. Even if the data is unique, many rows could still match if the operation specified in the join criteria is not an equality operation. For example

```
SELECT  EMPNO, LASTNAME
FROM    DSN8810.EMP INNER JOIN
        DSN8810.DEPT
ON      WORKDEPT > DEPTNO;
```

(Admittedly, this example is contrived.) Many rows will match, and could result in the join returning more rows than either table originally contained.

You do not have to join tables based only on equal values. Matching can be achieved with any of the following operations:

=	Equal to
>	Greater than
>=	Greater than or equal to

<>	Not equal to
<	Less than
<=	Less than or equal to

Take care to ensure that the proper join criteria are specified for the columns you are joining. Base the predicates of a join on columns drawn from the same logical domain. For example, consider the following join:

```
SELECT   EMPNO, LASTNAME, DEPTNO, DEPTNAME
FROM     DSN8810.EMP JOIN
         DSN8810.DEPT
ON       WORKDEPT = DEPTNO;
```

This is a good example of a join. The employee table is joined to the department table using a logical department code that exists physically as a column in both tables (WORKDEPT in the employee table and DEPTNO in the department table). Both these columns are pooled from the same domain: the set of valid departments for the organization. Remember, there are two ways of coding join statements and this join statement could alternately be coded as follows:

```
SELECT   EMPNO, LASTNAME, DEPTNO, DEPTNAME
FROM     DSN8810.EMP,
         DSN8810.DEPT
WHERE    WORKDEPT = DEPTNO;
```

You must consider the possible size of the results table before deciding to join tables. Generally, the more data that must be *accessed* to accomplish the join, the less efficient the join will be. Note that this does not necessarily mean that joining larger tables will result in poorer performance than joining smaller tables. It all depends on the formulation of the query, the design of the database, the amount of data that must be accessed, the organization of the data, and the amount of data that will be returned as the result set for the query. Guidelines for the efficient coding of SQL joins are presented in Chapter 2, "Data Manipulation Guidelines."

V8 More than two tables can be joined in a single SQL statement. As of Version 8, up to 225 DB2 tables can be joined in one SQL statement, but it is not usually practical to code such a large number of tables into a single statement. From both a performance and a maintainability standpoint, the practical limit is probably about a dozen or so tables, but it is *possible* to code very large SQL statements that access hundreds of tables. It is even possible to get acceptable performance when joining large numbers of tables.

The order of magnitude for the join is determined by the number of tables specified in the FROM clause; or by counting the number of JOIN keywords and adding 1. For example, the following join is a three-table join because three tables—EMP, DEPT, and PROJ—are specified:

```
SELECT   PROJNO, EMPNO, LASTNAME, DEPTNAME
FROM     DSN8810.EMP    E,
         DSN8810.DEPT   D,
```

```
            DSN8810.PROJ   P
WHERE       EMPNO = RESPEMP
AND         D.DEPTNO = E.WORKDEPT;
```

This example of an equijoin involves three tables. DB2 matches rows in the EMP table with rows in the PROJ table where the two rows match on employee number. Likewise, rows in the EMP table are matched with rows in the DEPT table where the department number is the same. This example produces a results table listing each project number along with information about the employee responsible for the project including his or her department name.

The following is an equivalent formulation of the prior statement using the [INNER] JOIN keyword (and it should perform similarly):

```
SELECT   PROJNO, EMPNO, LASTNAME, DEPTNAME
FROM     (DSN8810.EMP E JOIN
         DSN8810.DEPT D
ON       D.DEPTNO = E.WORKDEPT) JOIN
         DSN8810.PROJ P
ON       EMPNO = RESPEMP;
```

The join criteria are specified in the ON clause immediately following the table join specification. Contrast this with the looser, comma-delimited formulation. It is much easier to determine which predicate applies to which join specification when the INNER JOIN syntax is used. To determine the magnitude of the join in this example, count the JOIN keywords and add 1. There are two JOIN keywords specified, so the magnitude of the join is 2+1, or 3.

Tables can be joined to themselves also. Consider the following query:

```
SELECT   A.DEPTNO, A.DEPTNAME, A.ADMRDEPT, B.DEPTNAME
FROM     DSN8810.DEPT   A,
         DSN8810.DEPT   B
WHERE    A.ADMRDEPT = B.DEPTNO;
```

This join returns a listing of all department numbers and names, along with the associated department number and name to which the department reports. Self-referencing lists such as this one would not be possible without the capability to join a table to itself.

Joins are possible because all data relationships in DB2 are defined by values in columns instead of by other methods (such as pointers). DB2 can check for matches based solely on the data in the columns specified in the predicates of the WHERE clause in the SQL join statement. When coding a join, you must take extra care to code a proper matching predicate for each table being joined. Failure to do so can result in a *Cartesian product*, the subject of the next section.

Cartesian Products

A Cartesian product is the result of a join that does not specify matching columns. Consider the following query:

```
SELECT  *
FROM    DSN8810.DEPT,
        DSN8810.EMP;
```

This query lacks a WHERE clause. To satisfy the query DB2 combines every row from the DEPT table with every row in the EMP table. An example of the output from this statement follows:

```
DEPTNO DEPTNAME       MGRNO  ADMRDEPT EMPNO   FIRSTNAME MIDINIT LASTNAME WORKDEPT ...
A00    SPIFFY CO.     000010 A00      000010 CHRISTINE I        HAAS     A00      ...
A00    SPIFFY CO.     000010 A00      000020 MICHAEL   L        THOMPSON B01      ...
A00    SPIFFY CO.     000010 A00      000030 SALLY     A        KWAN     C01      ...
A00    SPIFFY CO.     000010 A00      000040 JOHN      B        GEYER    E01      ...
A00    SPIFFY CO.     000010 A00      000340 JASON     R        GOUNOT   E21      ...
B01    PLANNING       000020 A00      000010 CHRISTINE I        HAAS     A00      ...
B01    PLANNING       000020 A00      000020 MICHAEL   L        THOMPSON B01      ...
B01    PLANNING       000020 A00      000030 SALLY     A        KWAN     C01      ...
B01    PLANNING       000020 A00      000040 JOHN      B        GEYER    E01      ...
E21    SOFTWARE SUP.  000100 E01      000340 JASON     R        GOUNOT   E21      ...
```

All the columns of the DEPT table and all the columns of the EMP table are included in the Cartesian product. For brevity, the example output does not show all of the columns of the EMP table. The output shows the first four rows of the output followed by a break and then additional rows and breaks. A break indicates data that is missing but irrelevant for this discussion.

By analyzing this output, you can see some basic concepts about the Cartesian product. For example, the first row looks okay. Christine I. Haas works in department A00, and the information for department A00 is reported along with her employee information. This is a coincidence. Notice the other rows of the output. In each instance, the DEPTNO does not match the WORKDEPT because we did not specify this in the join statement.

When a table with 1,000 rows is joined as a Cartesian product with a table having 100 rows, the result is 1,000 * 100 rows, or 100,000 rows. These 100,000 rows, however, contain no more information than the original two tables because no criteria were specified for combining the table. In addition to containing no new information, the result of a Cartesian product is more difficult to understand because the information is now jumbled, whereas before it existed in two separate tables. In general, avoid Cartesian products.

> **NOTE**
>
> Although Cartesian products should be avoided in practice, there are certain circumstances where DB2 can use Cartesian products "behind the scenes" to practical benefit. These circumstances occur when the DB2 optimizer determines that better performance can be achieved using a Cartesian product. You, as a user, should not attempt to create and execute a Cartesian product because the performance is usually atrocious and no additional information is gained by running such a query.
>
> The DB2 optimizer may determine that a Cartesian product should be performed for a portion of a join. Such a situation usually happens in data warehousing queries where a star join is used to build a Cartesian product for dimension tables. (For details on star joins consult Chapter 45, "Data Warehousing with DB2.") The result of the dimension table Cartesian join is then joined

with the fact table. Because the fact table is usually many times larger than the dimension table, processing the fact table only once can significantly improve performance by reducing the size of intermediate results sets.

Subqueries

SQL provides the capability to nest SELECT statements. When one or more SELECT statements are nested in another SELECT statement, the query is referred to as a *subquery*. (Many SQL and DB2 users refer to subqueries as nested SELECTs.) A subquery enables a user to base the search criteria of one SELECT statement on the results of another SELECT statement.

> **CAUTION**
>
> Do not confuse a subquery with a subselect. The term subquery is used when one query is embedded in the WHERE clause of another query.
>
> The term subselect is used by IBM to define a particular component of a fullselect statement.

Although you can formulate subqueries in different fashions, they typically are expressed as one SELECT statement connected to another in one of four ways:

- Using the IN (or NOT IN) predicate

- Using the EXISTS (or NOT EXISTS) predicate

- Specifying the equality predicate (=) or the inequality predicate (<>)

- Specifying a predicate using a comparative operator (<, <=, >, or >=)

The following SELECT statement is an example of a subquery:

```
SELECT   DEPTNAME
FROM     DSN8810.DEPT
WHERE    DEPTNO IN
         (SELECT   WORKDEPT
          FROM     DSN8810.EMP
          WHERE    SALARY > 50000);
```

DB2 processes this SQL statement by first evaluating the nested SELECT statement to retrieve all WORKDEPTs where the SALARY is over $50,000. It then matches rows in the DEPT table that correspond to the WORKDEPT values retrieved by the nested SELECT. This match produces a results table that lists the name of all departments where any employee earns more than $50,000. Of course, if more than one employee earns over $50,000 per department, the same DEPTNAME may be listed multiple times in the results set. To eliminate duplicates, the DISTINCT clause must be used. For example:

```
SELECT   DISTINCT DEPTNAME
FROM     DSN8810.DEPT
WHERE    DEPTNO IN
         (SELECT   WORKDEPT
          FROM     DSN8810.EMP
          WHERE    SALARY > 50000);
```

The preceding statements use the IN operator to connect SELECT statements. The following example shows an alternative way of nesting SELECT statements, by means of an equality predicate:

```
SELECT  EMPNO, LASTNAME
FROM    DSN8810.EMP
WHERE   WORKDEPT =
        (SELECT  DEPTNO
         FROM    DSN8810.DEPT
         WHERE   DEPTNAME = 'PLANNING');
```

DB2 processes this SQL statement by retrieving the proper DEPTNO with the nested SELECT statement that is coded to search for the PLANNING department. It then matches rows in the EMP table that correspond to the DEPTNO of the PLANNING department. This match produces a results table that lists all employees in the PLANNING department. Of course, it also assumes that there is only one PLANNING department. If there were more, the SQL statement would fail because the nested SELECT statement can only return a single row when the = predicate is used. This type of failure can be avoided by using IN instead of the = predicate.

The capability to express retrieval criteria on nested SELECT statements gives the user of SQL additional flexibility for querying multiple tables. A specialized form of subquery, called a *correlated subquery*, provides a further level of flexibility by permitting the nested SELECT statement to refer back to columns in previous SELECT statements. As an example:

```
SELECT  A.WORKDEPT, A.EMPNO, A.FIRSTNME, A.MIDINIT,
        A.LASTNAME, A.SALARY
FROM    DSN8810.EMP  A
WHERE   A.SALARY >
        (SELECT  AVG(B.SALARY)
         FROM    DSN8810.EMP  B
         WHERE   A.WORKDEPT = B.WORKDEPT)
ORDER BY A.WORKDEPT, A.EMPNO;
```

Look closely at this correlated subquery. It differs from a normal subquery in that the nested SELECT statement refers back to the table in the first SELECT statement. The preceding query returns information for all employees who earn a SALARY greater than the average salary for that employee's given department. This is accomplished by the correlation of the WORKDEPT column in the nested SELECT statement to the WORKDEPT column in the first SELECT statement.

The following example illustrates an alternative form of correlated subquery using the EXISTS predicate:

```
SELECT  A.EMPNO, A.LASTNAME, A.FIRSTNME
FROM    DSN8810.EMP  A
WHERE   EXISTS
        (SELECT  '1'
         FROM    DSN8810.DEPT  B
         WHERE   B.DEPTNO = A.WORKDEPT
         AND     B.DEPTNAME = 'OPERATIONS');
```

This query returns the names of all employees who work in the OPERATIONS department.

A *non-correlated subquery* is processed in bottom-to-top fashion. The bottom-most query is executed and, based on the results, the top-most query is resolved. A correlated subquery works in a top-bottom-top fashion. The top-most query is analyzed, and based on the analysis, the bottom-most query is initiated. The bottom-most query, however, relies on the top-most query to evaluate its predicate. After processing for the first instance of the top-most query, therefore, DB2 must return to that query for another value and repeat the process until the results table is complete.

Both forms of subqueries enable you to base the qualifications of one retrieval on the results of another.

Joins Versus Subqueries

A subquery can be converted to an equivalent join. The concept behind both types of queries is to retrieve data by accessing multiple tables based on search criteria matching data in the tables.

Consider the following two SELECT statements. The first is a subquery:

```
SELECT   EMPNO, LASTNAME
FROM     DSN8810.EMP
WHERE    WORKDEPT IN
         (SELECT   DEPTNO
          FROM     DSN8810.DEPT
          WHERE    DEPTNAME = 'PLANNING');
```

The second SELECT statement is a join:

```
SELECT   EMPNO, LASTNAME
FROM     DSN8810.EMP,
         DSN8810.DEPT
WHERE    WORKDEPT = DEPTNO
AND      DEPTNAME = 'PLANNING';
```

Both of these queries return the employee numbers and last names of all employees who work in the PLANNING department.

Let's first discuss the subquery formulation of this request. The list of valid DEPTNOs is retrieved from the DEPT table for the DEPTNAME of 'PLANNING'. This DEPTNO list then is compared against the WORKDEPT column of the EMP table. Employees with a WORKDEPT that matches any DEPTNO are retrieved.

The join operates in a similar manner. In fact, the DB2 optimizer can be intelligent enough to transform a subquery into its corresponding join format before *optimization*; optimization is covered in depth in Chapter 21, "The Optimizer."

The decision to use a subquery, a correlated subquery, or a join usually is based on performance. In early releases of DB2, the performance of logically equivalent queries could vary greatly depending upon whether they were coded as a subquery or a join. With the performance changes made to DB2 in recent years, worrying about the performance of joins and subqueries is usually not worth the effort.

As a general rule of thumb, I suggest using joins over the other two types of multi-table data retrieval. This provides a consistent base from which to operate. By promoting joins over subqueries, you can meet the needs of most users and diminish confusion. If you need to squeeze the most performance from a system, however, try rewriting multi-table data retrieval SQL SELECT statements as both a join and a subquery. Test the performance of each SQL formulation and use the one that performs best.

Union

The *union* operation combines two sets of rows into a single result set composed of all the rows in both of the two original sets. The two original sets must be *union-compatible*. For union compatibility

- The two sets must contain the same number of columns.

- Each column of the first set must be either the same data type as the corresponding column of the second set *or* convertible to the same data type as the corresponding column of the second set.

In purest set-theory form, the union of two sets contains no duplicates, but DB2 provides the option of retaining or eliminating duplicates. The UNION verb eliminates duplicates; UNION ALL retains them.

An example SQL statement using UNION follows:

```
SELECT   CREATOR, NAME, 'TABLE  '
FROM     SYSIBM.SYSTABLES
WHERE    TYPE = 'T'
UNION
SELECT   CREATOR, NAME, 'VIEW   '
FROM     SYSIBM.SYSTABLES
WHERE    TYPE = 'V'
UNION
SELECT   CREATOR, NAME, 'ALIAS  '
FROM     SYSIBM.SYSTABLES
WHERE    TYPE = 'A'
UNION
SELECT   CREATOR, NAME, 'SYNONYM'
FROM     SYSIBM.SYSSYNONYMS;
```

This SQL UNION retrieves all the tables, views, aliases, and synonyms in the DB2 Catalog. Notice that each SELECT statement tied together using the UNION verb has the same number of columns, and each column has the same data type and length. This statement could be changed to use UNION ALL instead of UNION because you know that none of the SELECTs will return duplicate rows. (A table cannot be a view, a view cannot be an alias, and so on.)

The ability to use UNION to construct results data is essential to formulating some of the more complex forms of SQL. This is demonstrated in the next section.

When results from two SELECT statements accessing the **same table** are combined using UNION, remember that the same result can be achieved using the OR clause and CASE expressions. Moreover, the use of OR is preferable to the use of UNION because the OR formulation

- Is generally easier for most users to understand

- Tends to outperform UNION

Consider the following two queries:

```
SELECT  EMPNO
FROM    DSN8810.EMP
WHERE   LASTNAME = 'HAAS'
UNION
SELECT  EMPNO
FROM    DSN8810.EMP
WHERE   JOB = 'PRES';
```

and

```
SELECT  EMPNO
FROM    DSN8810.EMP
WHERE   LASTNAME = 'HAAS'
OR      JOB = 'PRES';
```

After scrutinizing these queries, you can see that the two statements are equivalent. If the two SELECT statements were accessing different tables, however, the UNION could not be changed to an equivalent form using OR.

NOTE

A literal can be used in the UNION query to indicate which predicate was satisfied for each particular row—for example:

```
SELECT  EMPNO, 'NAME=HAAS'
FROM    DSN8810.EMP
WHERE   LASTNAME = 'HAAS'
UNION ALL
SELECT  EMPNO, 'JOB =PRES'
FROM    DSN8810.EMP
WHERE   JOB = 'PRES';
```

The result set from the query using OR cannot include a literal. However, if rows exists that satisfy both predicates, the results of the UNION query will not match the results of the OR query because the literal will cause the duplicates to remain (when the literal is added, the row is no longer a duplicate).

A better-performing alternative is to use the following query with a CASE expression:

```
SELECT  EMPNO, (CASE WHEN LASTNAME = 'HAAS' THEN 'NAME=HAAS'
                     WHEN JOB = 'PRES' THEN 'NAME=PRES' END) AS NAMETAG
FROM    DSN8810.EMP
WHERE   LASTNAME = 'HAAS'
OR      JOB = 'PRES';
```

V7 In older versions of DB2, UNION was not permitted in views. As of DB2 Version 7, views can contain the UNION and UNION ALL clauses. This brings much more flexibility to views—and makes UNION more useful, too.

Outer Join

As discussed previously, when tables are joined, the rows that are returned contain matching values for the columns specified in the join predicates. Sometimes, however, it is desirable to return both matching and non-matching rows for one or more of the tables being joined. This is known as an *outer join*. Prior to V4, DB2 did not explicitly support outer joins. Instead, users were forced to accommodate outer join processing by combining a join and a correlated subquery with the UNION verb.

Before we progress to discussing how to code an outer join, let's first clarify the concept of an outer join. Suppose that you want a report on the departments in your organization, presented in department number (DEPTNO) order. This information is in the DEPT sample table. You also want the last name of the manager of each department. Your first attempt at this request might look like this:

```
SELECT  DISTINCT
        D.DEPTNO, D.DEPTNAME, D.MGRNO, E.LASTNAME
FROM    DSN8810.DEPT  D,
        DSN8810.EMP   E
WHERE   D.MGRNO = E.EMPNO;
```

This example, using an inner join, appears to satisfy your objective. However, if a department does not have a manager or if a department has been assigned a manager who is not recorded in the EMP table, your report would not list every department. The predicate D.MGRNO = E.EMPNO is not met for these types of rows. In addition, a MGRNO is not assigned to the DEVELOPMENT CENTER department in the DEPT sample table. That department therefore is not listed in the result set for the preceding query.

The following query corrects the problem by using UNION to concatenate the non-matching rows:

```
SELECT  DISTINCT
        D.DEPTNO, D.DEPTNAME, D.MGRNO, E.LASTNAME
FROM    DSN8810.DEPT  D,
        DSN8810.EMP   E
WHERE   D.MGRNO = E.EMPNO
UNION ALL
SELECT  DISTINCT
        D.DEPTNO, D.DEPTNAME, D.MGRNO, '* No Mgr Name *'
FROM    DSN8810.DEPT D
WHERE   NOT EXISTS
        (SELECT  EMPNO
         FROM    DSN8810.EMP E
         WHERE   D.MGRNO = E.EMPNO)
ORDER BY 1;
```

By providing the constant '* No Mgr Name *' in place of the nonexistent data, and by coding a correlated subquery with the NOT EXISTS operator, the rows that do not match are returned. UNION appends the two sets of data, returning a complete report of departments regardless of whether the department has a valid manager.

Using the OUTER JOIN syntax simplifies this query significantly:

```
SELECT  DEPTNO, DEPTNAME, MGRNO, LASTNAME
FROM    DSN8810.EMP LEFT OUTER JOIN DSN8810.DEPT
        ON EMPNO = MGRNO;
```

The keywords LEFT OUTER JOIN cause DB2 to invoke an outer join, returning rows that have matching values in the predicate columns, but also returning unmatched rows from the table on the left side of the join. In the case of the left outer join example shown, this would be the EMP table because it is on the left side of the join clause.

Note that the WHERE keyword is replaced with the ON keyword for the outer join statement. Additionally, the missing values in the result set are filled with nulls (not a sample default as shown in the previous example). Use the VALUE (or COALESCE) function to fill in the missing values with a default, as shown in the following SQL query:

```
SELECT  DEPTNO, DEPTNAME, MGRNO, VALUE(LASTNAME, '* No Mgr Name *')
FROM    DSN8810.EMP LEFT OUTER JOIN DSN8810.DEPT
        ON EMPNO = MGRNO;
```

Types of Outer Joins
There are three types of outer joins supported by DB2 for OS/390:

- LEFT OUTER JOIN

- RIGHT OUTER JOIN

- FULL OUTER JOIN

The keywords LEFT OUTER JOIN, RIGHT OUTER JOIN and FULL OUTER JOIN can be used in place of the INNER JOIN keyword to indicate an outer join.

As you might guess, the keywords RIGHT OUTER JOIN cause DB2 to return rows that have matching values in the predicate columns but also return unmatched rows from the table on the right side of the join. So the following outer join is 100% equivalent to the previous query:

```
SELECT  DEPTNO, DEPTNAME, MGRNO, LASTNAME
FROM    DSN8810.DEPT RIGHT OUTER JOIN DSN8810.EMP
        ON EMPNO = MGRNO;
```

The only code change was swapping the position of the DEPT and EMP table in the FROM clause and changing from a LEFT OUTER JOIN to a RIGHT OUTER JOIN. In general practice, consider limiting your usage of RIGHT OUTER JOIN statements, instead converting them to LEFT OUTER JOIN statements.

The remaining outer join option is the FULL OUTER JOIN. It, like all previous outer joins, returns matching rows from both tables, but it also returns non-matching rows from both tables; left and right. A FULL OUTER JOIN can use only the equal (=) comparison operator.

Left and right outer joins are able to use all the comparison operators. An example of the
FULL OUTER JOIN follows:

```
SELECT  EMPNO, WORKDEPT, DEPTNAME
FROM    DSN8810.EMP FULL OUTER JOIN DSN8810.DEPT
          ON WORKDEPT = DEPTNO;
```

In this example, all of the following will be returned in the results set:

- Rows where there are matches indicating that the employee works in a specific
  department (for example, where WORKDEPT in EMP matches DEPTNO in DEPT).

- Employee rows where there is no matching department in the DEPT table (for
  example, where a WORKDEPT in EMP has no matching DEPTNO in DEPT). This could
  occur when an employee is temporarily unassigned to a department or the employee
  is assigned to an invalid department (or if there are data integrity problems).

- Department rows where there is no matching work department in the EMP table (for
  example, where a DEPTNO in DEPT has no matching WORKDEPT in EMP). This could
  occur when a department has no employees assigned to it.

Coding appropriate outer join statements can be tricky. Outer joins become even more
confusing when local predicates need to be applied. Consider, for example, our previous
left outer join:

```
SELECT  DEPTNO, DEPTNAME, MGRNO, VALUE(LASTNAME, '* No Mgr Name *')
FROM    DSN8810.EMP LEFT OUTER JOIN DSN8810.DEPT
          ON EMPNO = MGRNO;
```

Now what happens if you need to apply a local predicate to this join? For example,
perhaps we only want to concern ourselves with department number "A00". The first reaction is just to add AND DEPTNO = "A00", but this might not be correct. It all depends on
what you are truly requesting. Adding this clause directly to the ON clause will cause DB2
to apply the predicate during the join. So, DB2 will retrieve all rows but only join the
"A00" rows. So, you will see other DEPTNO values in your result set. This is probably not the
result you intended.

Instead you would need to code a WHERE clause for this predicate, so it does not become
part of the join criteria in the ON clause. So, our right outer join SQL statement becomes

```
SELECT  DEPTNO, DEPTNAME, MGRNO, VALUE(LASTNAME, '* No Mgr Name *')
FROM    DSN8810.EMP LEFT OUTER JOIN DSN8810.DEPT
        ON EMPNO = MGRNO;
WHERE   DEPTNO = 'A00';
```

This section outlines the basics of the outer join. For suggestions on coding efficient outer
joins, refer to Chapter 2.

Sorting and Grouping

SQL also can sort and group retrieved data. The ORDER BY clause sorts the results of a
query in the specified order (ascending or descending) for each column. The GROUP BY

clause collates the resultant rows to apply functions that consolidate the data. By grouping data, users can use statistical functions on a column (discussed later) and eliminate non-pertinent groups of data with the HAVING clause.

For example, the following query groups employee data by department, returning the aggregate salary for each department:

```
SELECT   WORKDEPT, SUM(SALARY)
FROM     DSN8810.EMP
GROUP BY WORKDEPT;
```

By adding a HAVING clause to this query, you can eliminate aggregated data that is not required. For example, if you're interested in departments with an average salary of less than $19,500, you can code the following query:

```
SELECT   WORKDEPT, SUM(SALARY)
FROM     DSN8810.EMP
GROUP BY WORKDEPT
HAVING   AVG(SALARY) < 19500 ;
```

Note that the report is not necessarily returned in any specific order. The GROUP BY clause does not sort the data for the result set; it only consolidates the data values for grouping. To return the results of this query in a particular order, you must use the ORDER BY clause. For example, to order the resultant data into descending department number order, code the following:

```
SELECT   WORKDEPT, SUM(SALARY)
FROM     DSN8810.EMP
GROUP BY WORKDEPT
HAVING   AVG(SALARY) < 17500
ORDER BY WORKDEPT;
```

The ORDER BY, GROUP BY, and HAVING clauses are important SQL features that can increase productivity. They are the means by which you can sort and group data using SQL.

CAUTION

The only way to ensure the data is returned in a specific order is to use the ORDER BY clause. When DB2 uses an index to satisfy a query, your data might be returned in the specific order you desire. However, without an ORDER BY clause, there is no guarantee that the data will always be sorted in that particular order. Changes to the access path used to satisfy the query can change the order of your results.

Therefore, when the order of your results set is important, **always** specify an ORDER BY clause.

The Difference Between HAVING and WHERE

The WHERE and HAVING clauses are similar in terms of functionality. However, they operate on different types of data.

Any SQL statement can use a WHERE clause to indicate which rows of data are to be returned. The WHERE clause operates on "detail" data rows from tables, views, synonyms, and aliases.

The HAVING clause, on the other hand, operates on "aggregated" groups of information. Only SQL statements that specify the GROUP BY clause can use the HAVING clause. The predicates in the HAVING clause are applied after the GROUP BY has been applied.

If both a WHERE clause and a HAVING clause are coded on the same SQL statement, the following occurs:

- The WHERE clause is applied to the "detail" rows

- The GROUP BY is applied to aggregate the data

- The HAVING clause is applied to the "aggregate" rows

Consider the following SQL:

```
SELECT   WORKDEPT, AVG(BONUS), MAX(BONUS), MIN(BONUS)
FROM     DSN8810.EMP
WHERE    WORKDEPT NOT IN ('D11', 'D21')
GROUP BY WORKDEPT
HAVING   COUNT(*) > 1;
```

This query will return the average, maximum, and minimum bonus for each department except 'D11' and 'D12' as long as the department has more than 1 employee. The steps DB2 takes to satisfy this query are:

- Apply the WHERE clause to eliminate departments 'D11' and 'D12'.

- Apply the GROUP BY clause to aggregate the data by department.

- Apply the HAVING clause to eliminate any department groups consisting of only one employee.

Relational Division

A very useful, though somewhat complex SQL statement is relational division. Because of its complexity, developers often avoid relational division, but it is wise to understand relational division because of its power and usefulness. The *relational division* of two tables is the operation of returning rows whereby column values in one table match column values for *every* corresponding row in the other table.

For example, look at the following query:

```
SELECT   DISTINCT PROJNO
FROM     DSN8810.PROJACT   P1
WHERE    NOT EXISTS
         (SELECT ACTNO
          FROM   DSN8810.ACT   A
          WHERE  NOT EXISTS
                 (SELECT PROJNO
                  FROM   DSN8810.PROJACT   P2
                  WHERE  P1.PROJNO = P2.PROJNO
                  AND    A.ACTNO = P2.ACTNO));
```

Division is implemented in SQL using a combination of correlated subqueries. This query is accomplished by coding three correlated subqueries that match projects and activities. It retrieves all projects that require every activity listed in the activity table.

> **NOTE**
>
> If you execute this query, no rows are returned because no projects in the sample data require all activities.

Relational division is a powerful operation and should be utilized whenever practical. Implementing relational division using a complex query such as the one depicted above will *almost* always out-perform an equivalent application program using separate cursors processing three individual SELECT statements. However, this query is complicated and may be difficult for novice programmers to understand and maintain as your application changes.

CASE **Expressions**

The CASE expression, introduced to DB2 in V5, is similar to CASE statements used by many popular programming languages. A CASE statement uses the value of a specified expression to select one statement among several for execution. A common application of the CASE statement will be to eliminate a multi-table UNION statement; for example

```
SELECT  CREATOR, NAME, 'TABLE'
FROM    SYSIBM.SYSTABLES
WHERE   TYPE = 'T'
UNION ALL
SELECT  CREATOR, NAME, 'VIEW '
FROM    SYSIBM.SYSTABLES
WHERE   TYPE = 'V'
UNION ALL
SELECT  CREATOR, NAME, 'ALIAS'
FROM    SYSIBM.SYSTABLES
WHERE   TYPE = 'A';
```

it can be coded more simply as

```
SELECT CREATOR, NAME,
CASE TYPE
  WHEN 'T' THEN 'TABLE'
  WHEN 'V' THEN 'VIEW '
  WHEN 'A' THEN 'ALIAS'
END
FROM SYSIBM.SYSTABLES;
```

The WHEN clause of the CASE expression replaces the predicates from each of the SELECT statements in the UNION. When CASE is used in place of multiple UNIONs, performance most likely will be improved because DB2 will make fewer passes against the data to return a result set. In the preceding example, one pass is required instead of three.

There are two types of CASE expressions: those with a simple WHEN clause and those with a searched WHEN clause. The previous example depicts a simple WHEN clause. Simple WHEN clauses only test for equality of an expression. Searched `WHEN` clauses provide more complex expression testing. An example follows:

```
SELECT EMPNO, LASTNAME,
  CASE  WHEN SALARY < 0. THEN 'ERROR'
    WHEN SALARY = 0. THEN 'NONE '
    WHEN SALARY BETWEEN 1. AND 20000. THEN 'LOW  '
    WHEN SALARY BETWEEN 20001. AND 50000. THEN 'MID  '
    WHEN SALARY BETWEEN 50001. AND 99999. THEN 'HIGH '
    ELSE '100+ '
  END
FROM DSN8810.EMP;
```

In this case, the `SALARY` column is examined by the `CASE` expression to place it into a specific, predefined category. `CASE` expressions also can be specified in a `WHERE` clause, for example:

```
SELECT  EMPNO, PROJNO, ACTNO, EMPTIME
FROM    DSN8810.EMPPROJACT
WHERE   (CASE WHEN
           EMPTIME=0. THEN 0.
         ELSE
           40./EMPTIME
         END) > 25;
```

This query returns data for employees who are allocated to spend more than 25 hours (of a typical 40-hour work week) on a specific activity. The `CASE` expression is used to avoid division by zero. Values for the `EMPTIME` column range from 0.0 to 1.0 and indicate the ratio of time to be spent on an activity. When `EMPTIME` is zero, the `CASE` expression substitutes zero and avoids the calculation.

Another valuable usage of the `CASE` expression is to perform table pivoting. A common requirement is to take a normalized table and produce denormalized query results. For example, consider the following table containing monthly sales numbers:

```
CREATE TABLE SALES
  (SALES_MGR    INTEGER       NOT NULL,
   MONTH        INTEGER       NOT NULL,
   YEAR         CHAR(4)       NOT NULL,
   SALES_AMT    DECIMAL(11,2) NOT NULL WITH DEFAULT);
```

The table contains 12 rows, one for each month, detailing the amount of product sold by the specified sales manager. A standard query can be produced using a simple `SELECT` statement. However, many users prefer to see the months strung out as columns showing one row per sales manager with a bucket for each month. This is known as table pivoting and can be produced using the following SQL statement using the `CASE` expression in the `SELECT`-list:

```
SELECT SALES_MGR,
  MAX(CASE MONTH WHEN 1 THEN SALES_AMT ELSE NULL END) AS JAN,
  MAX(CASE MONTH WHEN 2 THEN SALES_AMT ELSE NULL END) AS FEB,
  MAX(CASE MONTH WHEN 3 THEN SALES_AMT ELSE NULL END) AS MAR,
  MAX(CASE MONTH WHEN 4 THEN SALES_AMT ELSE NULL END) AS APR,
```

```
      MAX(CASE MONTH WHEN 5 THEN SALES_AMT ELSE NULL END) AS MAY,
      MAX(CASE MONTH WHEN 6 THEN SALES_AMT ELSE NULL END) AS JUN,
      MAX(CASE MONTH WHEN 7 THEN SALES_AMT ELSE NULL END) AS JUL,
      MAX(CASE MONTH WHEN 8 THEN SALES_AMT ELSE NULL END) AS AUG,
      MAX(CASE MONTH WHEN 9 THEN SALES_AMT ELSE NULL END) AS SEP,
      MAX(CASE MONTH WHEN 10 THEN SALES_AMT ELSE NULL END) AS OCT,
      MAX(CASE MONTH WHEN 11 THEN SALES_AMT ELSE NULL END) AS NOV,
      MAX(CASE MONTH WHEN 12 THEN SALES_AMT ELSE NULL END) AS DEC
   FROM  SALES
   WHERE YEAR = ?
   GROUP BY SALES_MGR;
```

The results will be spread out across a single row for the year specified. Other uses for CASE include rounding numeric data (containing positive and negative numbers), performing different calculations based on type indicators, and converting two-digit dates.

CASE expressions can be used in an ORDER BY clause.

SQL Functions

Functions can be specified in SQL statements to transform data from one state to another. Two types of functions can be applied to data in a DB2 table using SQL: *column functions* and *scalar functions*. *Column functions* compute, from a group of rows, a single value for a designated column or expression. For example, the SUM function can be used to add, returning the sum of the values instead of each individual value. By contrast, *scalar functions* are applied to a column or expression and operate on a single value. For example, the CHAR function converts a single date or time value into its character representation.

As of Version 6, DB2 added support for user-defined functions in addition to the base, system-defined functions (referred to as built-in functions, or BIFs). With user-defined functions the user can develop customized functions that can then be specified in SQL. A user-defined function can be specified anywhere a system-defined function can be specified.

There are two categories of user-defined functions that can be created:

- User-defined scalar functions
- User-defined table functions

Similar to system-defined scalar functions, user-defined scalar functions return a single-value answer each time it is invoked. A user-defined table function returns a complete table to the SQL statement that references it. A user-defined table function can be referenced in SQL statements in place of a DB2 table.

Using SQL functions can simplify the requirements of complex data access. For more details on using functions in DB2, both user-defined and system-defined, column and scalar, refer to Chapter 3, "Using DB2 Functions" and Chapter 4, "Using DB2 User-Defined Functions and Data Types."

Definition of DB2 Data Structures

You can use SQL also to define DB2 data structures. DB2 data structures are referred to as *objects*. Each DB2 object is used to support the structure of the data being stored. There are DB2 objects to support groups of DASD volumes, VSAM data sets, table representations, and data order, among others. A description of each type of DB2 object follows:

ALIAS	A locally defined name for a table or view in the same local DB2 subsystem or in a remote DB2 subsystem. Aliases give DB2 location independence because an alias can be created for a table at a remote site, thereby freeing the user from specifying the site that contains the data. Aliases can be used also as a type of global synonym. This is so because they can be accessed by anyone, not only by their creator (as is the case with synonyms).
COLUMN	A single, non-decomposable data element in a DB2 table.
DATABASE	A logical grouping of DB2 objects related by common characteristics, such as logical functionality, relation to an application system or subsystem, or type of data. A database holds no data of its own, but exists to group DB2 objects. A database can function also as a unit of start and stop for the DB2 objects defined to it or as a unit of control for the administration of DB2 security.
INDEX	A DB2 object that consists of one or more VSAM data sets. To achieve more efficient access to DB2 tables, these data sets contain pointers ordered based on the value of data in specified columns of that table.
STOGROUP	A series of DASD volumes assigned a unique name and used to allocate VSAM data sets for DB2 objects.
SYNONYM	An alternative, private name for a table or view. A synonym can be used only by the individual who creates it.
TABLE	A DB2 object that consists of columns and rows that define the physical characteristics of the data to be stored.
TABLESPACE	A DB2 object that defines the physical structure of the data sets used to house the DB2 table data.
VIEW	A virtual table consisting of an SQL SELECT statement that accesses data from one or more tables or views. A view never stores data. When you access a view, the SQL statement that defines it is executed to derive the requested data.

These objects are created with the DDL verbs of SQL, and must be created in a specific order. See Figure 1.5 for the hierarchy of DB2 objects.

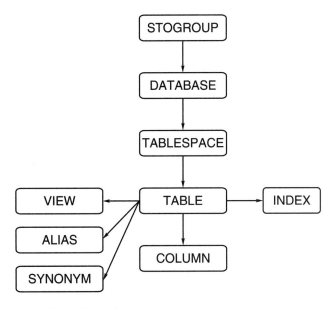

FIGURE 1.5   The DB2 object hierarchy.

Also, DB2 supports the ability to create user-defined data types. Each column of a DB2 table must be assigned to a data type. Appropriately enough, the data type defines the type of data that can be stored in the column. DB2 supports the following native data types:

CHAR	Fixed length alphanumeric data
VARCHAR	Variable length alphanumeric data
GRAPHIC	Fixed length graphical data
VARGRAPHIC	Variable length graphical data
SMALLINT	Small integer numbers
INTEGER	Larger integer numbers
DECIMAL(p,s)	Numeric data
FLOAT(n) or FLOAT	Single precision floating point (if n>21)
FLOAT(n) or REAL	Double precision floating point (if n<21)
DATE	Calendar date data
TIME	Time data
TIMESTAMP	Combination date and time data
ROWID	Unique row identifier (internally generated by DB2)
BLOB	Binary large object
CLOB	Character large object
DBCLOB	Double byte character large object

The last three data types, BLOB, CLOB, and DBCLOB, are used to store object/relational data. Using DB2 Extenders, rich data types such as audio, video, image, and character can be supported. Although there are many native DB2 data types, DB2 also supports user-defined DISTINCT data types. User-defined DISTINCT types are covered in detail in Chapter 4.

Security Control over DB2 Data Structures

The data-control feature of SQL provides security for DB2 objects, data, and resources with the GRANT and REVOKE verbs. The hierarchy of DB2 security types and levels is complicated, and can be confusing at first glance (see Figure 1.6).

You can administer group and individual levels of DB2 security. A group-level security specification is composed of other group-level and individual security specifications. Individual security is a single authorization for a single object or resource.

The group-level authorizations are enclosed in boxes in Figure 1.6. This list shows these authorizations:

INSTALL SYSADM	Authority for the entire system at installation time
SYSADM	Authority for the entire system
INSTALL SYSOPR	Authority for the entire system at installation time
SYSOPR	Authority for the entire system
SYSCTRL	Authority for the entire system, but with less access to end user data
BINDAGENT	Authority for the entire system
PACKADM	Authority for all packages in a specific collection or collections
DBADM	Authority for a specific database
DBCTRL	Authority for a specific database
DBMAINT	Authority for a specific database

Each group-level authorization is composed of the group and individual security levels connected by arrows in Figure 1.6. For example, INSTALL SYSOPR is composed of IMAGCOPY authority for the DB2 Catalog and SYSOPR authority, which in turn is composed of the DISPLAY, RECOVER, STOPALL, and TRACE authorities.

The effective administration of these levels of security often is a job in itself. Most organizations simplify authorization to DB2 objects using secondary authids. With secondary authids, sets of similar users can be assigned to an authorization group, and security can be granted to the group. In this way, fewer GRANT and REVOKE statements are required to administer DB2 security.

Guidelines for the efficient utilization and administration of DB2 security are covered in Chapter 10, "DB2 Security and Authorization."

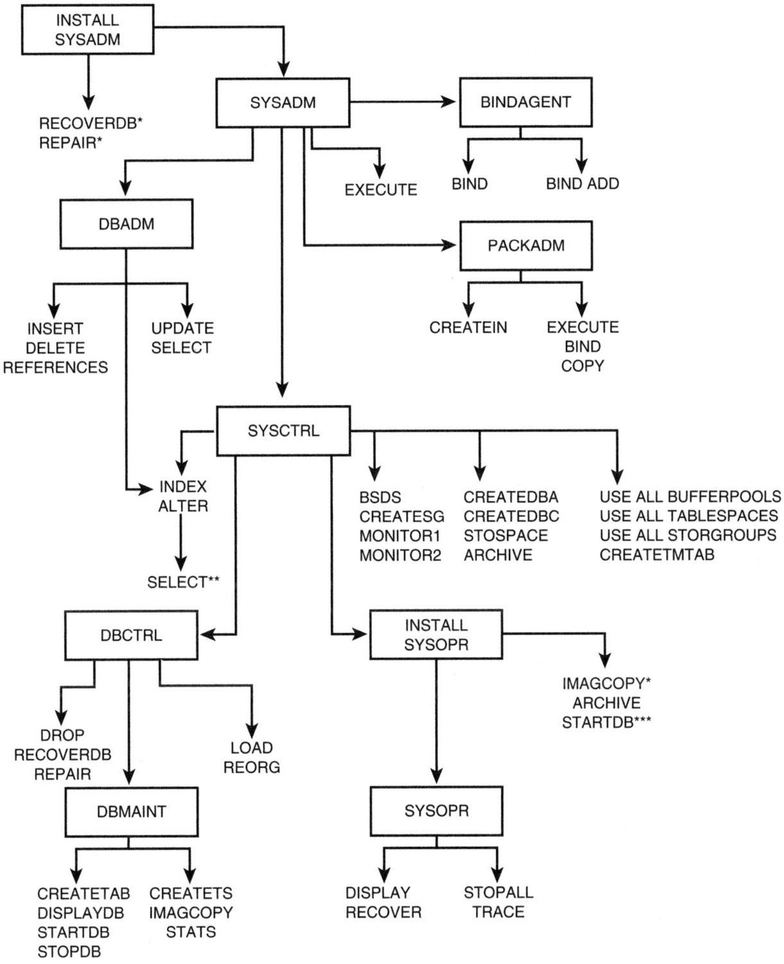

* This security applies to the DB2 Directory Database (DSNDB01) and the DB2 Catalog Database (DSNDB06). Install SYSADM can also run CATMAINT.

** This security applies only to the DB2 Catalog tables.

*** Cannot change ACCESS mode.

FIGURE 1.6 DB2 security levels.

Static SQL

Most DB2 application programs use static SQL to access DB2 tables. A *static SQL statement* is a complete, unchanging statement hard-coded into an application program. It cannot be modified during the program's execution except for changes to the values assigned to host variables.

Static SQL is powerful and more than adequate for most applications. Any SQL statement can be embedded in a program and executed as static SQL. The following listing shows several examples of static SQL statements embedded in a COBOL program.

```
WORKING-STORAGE SECTION.
        .
        .
        .
    EXEC SQL
      INCLUDE SQLCA
    END-EXEC.
    EXEC SQL                              TABLE
      INCLUDE EMP                         DECLARE
    END-EXEC.
        .
        .
        .
    EXEC SQL                              CURSOR
      DECLARE CSR1 FOR
        SELECT EMPNO, COMM                STATIC
        FROM   EMP                        SQL
        WHERE  SALARY > 60000             SELECT
        FOR UPDATE OF COMM                STATEMENT
    END-EXEC.
        .
        .
        .
PROCEDURE DIVISION.
        .
        .
        .
    PERFORM OPEN-CSR1.
    MOVE 'N' TO END-OF-DATA.
    PERFORM FETCH-AND-MODIFY
      UNTIL END-OF-DATA = 'Y'.
    STOP RUN.
FETCH-AND-MODIFY.
    EXEC SQL
      FETCH CSR1 INTO :HOST-EMPNO,        EMBEDDED
                      :HOST-COMM          FETCH
    END-EXEC.
    IF SQLCODE < +0
      PERFORM ERROR-ROUTINE
    ELSE
      IF SQLCODE = +100
        MOVE 'Y' TO END-OF-DATA
      ELSE
        PERFORM MODIFY-COMM.
MODIFY-COMM.
    IF HOST-COM < 1000
      COMPUTE HOST-COMM = HOST-COMM + 100.
    EXEC SQL
      UPDATE  EMP                         STATIC
        SET COMM = :HOST-COMM             SQL
      WHERE CURRENT OF CSR1               UPDATE
```

```
        END-EXEC.                       STATEMENT
        IF SQLCODE < 0
            PERFORM ERROR_ROUTINE.
OPEN-CSR.
        EXEC SQL
            OPEN CSR1
        END-EXEC.                       OPEN &
CLOSE-CSR.                              CLOSE
        EXEC SQL                        CURSOR
            CLOSE CSR1                  STATEMENTS
        END-EXEC.
```

To embed static SQL in a host program, you must prepare for the impedance mismatch between a high-level language and SQL. *Impedance mismatch* refers to the difference between set-at-a-time processing and record-at-a-time processing. High-level languages access data one record at a time, whereas SQL accesses data at a set level. Although DB2 always accesses data at the set level, the host program uses a structure called a *cursor* to access the set-level data one row at a time. SQL statements are coded with cursors that are opened, fetched from, and closed during the execution of the application program.

Static SQL is flexible enough that most application programmers never need to know any other means of embedding SQL in a program using a high-level language. Coding methods and guidelines are covered comprehensively in Chapter 11, "Using DB2 in an Application Program," where embedded SQL programming is discussed.

Sometimes, static SQL cannot satisfy an application's access requirements. For these types of dynamic applications, you can use another type of SQL: *dynamic SQL.*

Dynamic SQL

Dynamic SQL is embedded in an application program and can change during the program's execution. Dynamic SQL statements are coded explicitly in host-language variables, prepared by the application program, and then executed. QMF and SPUFI are two examples of programs that execute dynamic SQL statements.

Recall that the two types of SQL are static SQL and dynamic SQL. The primary difference between static and dynamic SQL is described capably by their names. A static SQL statement is hard-coded and unchanging. The columns, tables, and predicates are known beforehand and cannot be changed. Only host variables that provide values for the predicates can be changed.

A dynamic SQL statement, conversely, can change throughout a program's execution. The algorithms in the program can alter the SQL before issuing it. Based on the class of dynamic SQL being used, the columns, tables, and complete predicates can be changed "on the fly."

As might be expected, dynamic SQL is dramatically different from static SQL in the way you code it in the application program. Additionally, when dynamic SQL is bound, the application plan or package that is created does not contain the same information as a plan or package for a static SQL program.

The access path for dynamic SQL statements cannot be determined before execution. When you think about it, this statement makes sense. If the SQL is not completely known until the program executes, how can it be verified and optimized beforehand? For this reason, dynamic SQL statements are not bound, but are prepared at execution. The PREPARE statement is functionally equivalent to a dynamic BIND. The program issues a PREPARE statement before executing dynamic SQL (with the exception of EXECUTE IMMEDIATE, which implicitly prepares SQL statements). PREPARE verifies, validates, and determines access paths dynamically.

A program containing dynamic SQL statements still must be bound into an application plan or package. The plan or package, however, does not contain access paths for the dynamic SQL statements.

DB2 provides four classes of dynamic SQL: EXECUTE IMMEDIATE, non-SELECT PREPARE and EXECUTE, fixed-list SELECT, and varying-list SELECT. The first two classes do not allow SELECT statements, whereas the last two are geared for SELECT statements.

Dynamic SQL is a complex topic that can be difficult to comprehend and master. It is important that you understand all aspects of dynamic SQL before deciding whether to use it. Dynamic SQL is covered in depth in Chapter 12.

SQL Performance Factors

This first chapter discusses SQL basics, but little has been covered pertaining to SQL performance. You need at least a rudimentary knowledge of the factors affecting SQL performance before reading a discussion of the best ways to achieve optimum performance. This section is an introduction to DB2 optimization and some DB2 performance features. These topics are discussed in depth in Part V, "DB2 Performance Tuning."

Introduction to the Optimizer

The DB2 optimizer is integral to the operation of SQL statements. The optimizer, as its name implies, determines the optimal method of satisfying an SQL request. For example, consider the following statement:

```
SELECT  EMPNO, WORKDEPT, DEPTNAME
FROM    DSN8810.EMP,
        DSN8810.DEPT
WHERE   DEPTNO = WORKDEPT;
```

This statement, whether embedded statically in an application program or executed dynamically, must be passed through the DB2 optimizer before execution. The optimizer parses the statement and determines the following:

- Which tables must be accessed

- Whether the tables are in partitioned table spaces or not (to determine whether or not query I/O, CPU, and Sysplex parallelism is feasible)

- Which columns from those tables need to be returned

- Which columns participate in the SQL statement's predicates

- Whether there are any indexes for this combination of tables and columns

- The order in which to evaluate the query's predicates

- What statistics are available in the DB2 Catalog

Based on this information (and system information), the optimizer analyzes the possible access paths and chooses the best one for the given query. An access path is the navigation logic used by DB2 to access the requisite data. A "table space scan using sequential prefetch" is an example of a DB2 access path. Access paths are discussed in greater detail in Part V.

The optimizer acts like a complex expert system. Based on models developed by IBM for estimating the cost of CPU and I/O time, the impact of uniform and non-uniform data distribution, evaluation DB2 object statistics, and the state of table spaces and indexes, the optimizer usually arrives at a good estimate of the optimal access path. Remember, though, that it is only a "best guess." Several factors can cause the DB2 optimizer to choose the wrong access path, such as incorrect or outdated statistics in the DB2 Catalog, an improper physical or logical database design, an improper use of SQL (for example, record-at-a-time processing), or bugs in the logic of the optimizer (although this occurs infrequently).

The optimizer usually produces a better access path than a programmer or analyst could develop manually. Sometimes, the user knows more than DB2 about the nature of the data being accessed. If this is the case, there are ways to influence DB2's choice of access path. The best policy is to allow DB2 initially to choose all access paths automatically, then challenge its decision only when performance suffers. Although the DB2 optimizer does a good job for most queries, you might need to periodically examine, modify, or influence the access paths for some SQL statements.

> **NOTE**
>
> As a general rule of thumb, be sure to review and tune all SQL statements prior to migrating the SQL to the production environment.

Influencing the Access Path

DB2's optimizer determines the best access method based on the information discussed previously. However, users can influence the DB2 optimizer to choose a different access path if they know a few tricks.

To influence access path selection, users can tweak the SQL statement being optimized or update the statistics in the DB2 Catalog. Both of these methods are problematic and not recommended, but can be used as a last resort. If an SQL statement is causing severe performance degradation, you could consider using these options.

> **NOTE**
>
> As of DB2 V6, though, there is another option for bypassing the DB2 optimizer's access path choices. IBM calls the feature optimizer "hints." Optimizer hints are covered briefly in the next section, and in more depth in Chapter 28, "Tuning DB2's Components."
>
> Using "hints" to modify access paths usually is preferable to manually updating DB2 Catalog statistics.

One option is to change the SQL statement. Some SQL statements function more efficiently than others based on the version of DB2. As you learned previously, SQL is flexible; you can write functionally equivalent SQL in many ways. Sometimes, by altering the way in which an SQL statement is written, you can influence DB2 to choose a different access path.

The danger in coding SQL to take advantage of release-dependent features lies in the fact that DB2 continues to be enhanced and upgraded. If a future DB2 release changes the performance feature you took advantage of, your SQL statement may degrade. It usually is unwise to take advantage of a product's undocumented features, unless it is as a last resort. If this is done, be sure to document and retain information about the workaround. At a minimum, keep the following data:

- The reason for the workaround (for example, for performance or functionality).

- A description of the workaround (what exactly was changed and why).

- If SQL is modified, keep a copy of the old SQL statement and a copy of the new SQL statement.

- The version and release of DB2 at the time of the workaround.

The second method of influencing DB2's choice of access path is to update the statistics in the DB2 Catalog on which the optimizer relies. DB2 calculates a filter factor for each possible access path based on the values stored in the DB2 Catalog and the type of predicates in the SQL statement to be optimized. *Filter factors* estimate the number of accesses required to return the desired results. The lower the filter factor, the more rows filtered out by the access path and the more efficient the access path.

There are two methods of modifying DB2 Catalog statistics. The first is with the RUNSTATS utility. RUNSTATS can be executed for each table space that requires updated statistics. This approach is recommended because it populates the DB2 Catalog with accurate statistics based on a sampling of the data currently stored in the table spaces. Sometimes, however, accurate statistics produce an undesirable access path. To get around this, DB2 allows SYSADM users to modify the statistics stored in the DB2 Catalog. Most, but not all, of these statistical columns can be changed using SQL update statements. By changing the statistical information used by the optimization process, you can influence the access path chosen by DB2. This method can be used to

- Mimic production volumes in a test system to determine production access paths before migrating a system to production

- Favor certain access paths over others by specifying either lower or higher cardinality for specific tables or columns

- Favor indexed access by changing index statistics

Examples of this are shown in Chapter 21, along with additional information on access paths and influencing DB2.

Directly updating the DB2 Catalog, however, generally is not recommended. You may get unpredictable results because the values being changed will not accurately reflect the actual table space data. Additionally, if RUNSTATS is executed any time after the DB2 Catalog statistics are updated, the values placed in the DB2 Catalog by SQL update statements are overwritten. It usually is very difficult to maintain accurate statistics for some columns and inaccurate, tweaked values for other columns. To do so, you must reapply the SQL updates to the DB2 Catalog immediately after you run the RUNSTATS utility and before you run any binds or rebinds.

In order to update DB2 Catalog statistics, you must have been granted the authority to update the specific DB2 Catalog tables (or columns) or have SYSADM authority.

As a general rule, updating the DB2 Catalog outside the jurisdiction of RUNSTATS should be considered only as a last resort. If SQL is used to update DB2 Catalog statistics, be sure to record and maintain the following information:

- The reason for the DB2 Catalog updates

- A description of the updates applied:

  Applied once; RUNSTATS never runs again

  Applied initially; RUNSTATS runs without reapplying updates

  Applied initially; RUNSTATS runs and updates are immediately reapplied

- The version and release of DB2 when the updates were first applied

- The SQL UPDATE and INSERT statements used to modify the DB2 Catalog

- A report of the DB2 Catalog statistics overlaid by the UPDATE statements (must be produced before the initial updates)

DB2 Optimizer "Hints"

It is possible also to use optimizer "hints" to achieve more control over the access paths chosen by DB2. Similar to the techniques just discussed for influencing access paths, optimizer "hints" should be used only as a final approach when more traditional methods do not create optimal access paths. Optimizer "hints" are also useful when you need to temporarily choose an alternate access path, and later revert back to the access path chosen by DB2.

> **NOTE**
>
> IBM uses the term "hints," but I choose to place it in quotes because the technique is not literally a hint; instead it is a directive for DB2 to use a pre-determined specified access path. IBM probably chose the term "hints" because Oracle provides optimizer hints and IBM is competing quite heavily with Oracle these days. In Oracle, a hint is implemented by coding specific comments into SQL statements—such as USE NLJ to force use of a nested-loop join.

The typical scenario for using an optimizer "hint" follows. Over time, a query that was previously performing well begins to experience severe performance degradation. The performance problem occurs even though the DB2 Catalog statistics are kept up-to-date using RUNSTATS, and the package and/or plan containing the SQL is rebound using the new and accurate statistics. Upon further examination, the performance analyst determines that DB2 has chosen a new access path that does not perform as well as the old access path.

Faced with a choice between poor performance, modifying DB2 Catalogs statistics manually, and optimizer "hints," the performance analyst chooses to use "hints." Querying the PLAN_TABLE that contains the access path information for the offending statement, the analyst finds the older access path that performed well. The analyst then uses BIND to use the "hint" in the PLAN_TABLE, redirecting DB2 to use the old access path instead of calculating a new one. More details on access path "hints" are provided in Chapters 21 and 28.

> **NOTE**
>
> Be sure to thoroughly test and analyze the results of any query using optimizer "hints." If the environment has changed since the optimizer "hint" access path was chosen, the "hint" may be ignored by DB2, or only partially implemented.

DB2 Performance Features

Finally, it is important to understand the performance features that IBM has engineered into DB2. Performance features have been added with each successive release of DB2. This section is a short synopsis of some of the DB2 performance features discussed in depth throughout this book.

Sequential Prefetch

Sequential prefetch is a look-ahead *read engine* that enables DB2 to read many data pages in large chunks of pages, instead of one page at a time. It usually is invoked when a sequential scan of pages is needed. The overhead associated with I/O can be reduced with sequential prefetch because many pages are read before they must be used. When the pages are needed, they then are available without additional I/O.

Sequential prefetch can be invoked for both table space scans and index scans.

Sequential Detection

DB2 can dynamically detect sequential processing and invoke sequential prefetch even if the optimizer did not specify its use. DB2 can trigger sequential detection for a query that appears at first to be random, but instead begins to process data sequentially.

List Prefetch

When the DB2 optimizer determines that an index will increase the efficiency of access to data in a DB2 table, it may decide also to invoke *list prefetch*. List prefetch sorts the index entries into order by *record identifier* (*RID*). This sorting ensures that two index entries that must access the same page will require no more than one I/O because they now are accessed contiguously by record identifier. This reduction in I/O can increase performance.

Index Lookaside

The *index lookaside* feature is a method employed by DB2 to traverse indexes in an optimal manner. When using an index, DB2 normally traverses the b-tree structure of the index. This can involve significant overhead in checking root and nonleaf index pages when DB2 is looking for the appropriate leaf page for the given data. When using index lookaside, DB2 checks for the RID of the desired row on the current leaf page and the immediately higher nonleaf page. For repetitive index lookups, it is usually more efficient to check recently accessed pages (that are probably still in the bufferpool), than to traverse the b-tree from the root. Index lookaside, therefore, generally reduces the path length of locating rows.

Index Only Access

If all the data being retrieved is located in an index, DB2 can satisfy the query by accessing the index without accessing the table. Because additional reads of table pages are not required, I/O is reduced and performance is increased.

RDS Sorting

DB2 sorting occurs in the Relational Data Services (RDS) component of DB2. (See Part III for in-depth descriptions of DB2's components.) DB2's efficient sort algorithm uses a *tournament sort* technique. Additionally, with the proper hardware, DB2 can funnel sort requests to routines in microcode that significantly enhance the sort performance.

Operating System Exploitation

DB2 exploits many features of z/OS and OS/390, including cross memory services, efficient virtual storage use, data space usage with DB2 virtual pools, hiperspace usage with DB2 hiperpools, and effective use of expanded storage, enabling the use of very large buffer pool and EDM pool specifications. The dynamic statement cache also can be stored in a data space as of DB2 Version 6.

V8 One of the biggest impacts of DB2 Version 8 is the requirement that you first must be running a zSeries machine and z/OS v1.3. DB2 V8 does not support old hardware, nor will it support OS/390. Owing to these architectural requirements, DB2 will have the ability to support large virtual memory. DB2 V8 surmounts the limitation of 2GB real storage that was imposed due to S/390's 31-bit addressing. Theoretically, with 64-bit addressing DB2 could have up to 16 exabytes of virtual storage addressability to be used by a single DB2 address space. Now there is some room for growth!

> **CAUTION**
>
> Although z/OS V1.3 is the minimal requirement for DB2 V8, some features require z/OS V1.4 and even V1.5.

Stage 1 and Stage 2 Processing

Sometimes referred to as *sargable* and *nonsargable* processing, Stage 1 and Stage 2 processing effectively splits the processing of SQL into separate components of DB2. Stage 1 processing is more efficient than Stage 2 processing.

There is no magic regarding which SQL predicates are Stage 1 and which are Stage 2. Indeed, the stage in which a predicate is evaluated can change from version to version of DB2. Usually, IBM pushes predicates from Stage 2 to Stage 1 to make them more efficient. Consult Chapter 2 for more details on Stage 1 and Stage 2 predicates.

Join Methods

When tables must be joined, the DB2 optimizer chooses one of three methods based on many factors, including all the information referred to in the discussion on optimization. The join methods are a merge scan, a nested loop join, and a hybrid join. A *merge scan* requires reading sorted rows and merging them based on the join criteria. A *nested loop join* repeatedly reads from one table, matching rows from the other table based on the join criteria. A *hybrid join* uses list prefetch to create partial rows from one table with RIDs from an index on the other table. The partial rows are sorted, with list prefetch used to complete the partial rows.

Lock Escalation

During application processing, if DB2 determines that performance is suffering because an inordinate number of locks have been taken, the granularity of the lock taken by the application might be escalated. Simply stated, if a program is accessing DB2 tables using page locking, and too many page locks are being used, DB2 might change the locking strategy to table space locking. This reduces the concurrency of access to the tables being manipulated, but significantly reduces overhead and increases performance for the application that was the beneficiary of the lock escalation.

Lock Avoidance

With lock avoidance, DB2 can avoid taking locks under certain circumstances, while still maintaining data integrity. DB2 can test to see if a row or page has committed data on it. If it does then DB2 may not have to obtain a lock on the data at all. Lock avoidance reduces overhead and improves application performance for those programs that can take advantage of it.

Data Compression

DB2 provides Lempel Ziv data compression employing hardware-assist for specific high-end CPU models or software compression for other models. Additionally, data compression can be directly specified in the `CREATE TABLESPACE` and `ALTER TABLESPACE` DDL, thereby avoiding the overhead and restrictions of an `EDITPROC`.

Data Sharing

DB2 provides the ability to couple DB2 subsystems together enabling data to be shared between multiple DB2s. This allows applications running on more than one DB2 subsystem to read from and write to the same DB2 tables simultaneously. This was not possible in prior releases without using DB2's distributed data capabilities. Additionally, data sharing enables nonstop DB2 processing. If one subsystem becomes unavailable, workload can be shifted to other subsystems participating in the data sharing group. Refer to Chapter 19, "Data Sharing," for an in-depth discussion of data sharing.

Query Parallelism

DB2 can utilize multiple read tasks to satisfy a single SQL SELECT statement. By running multiple, simultaneous read engines the overall elapsed time for an individual query can be substantially reduced. This will aid I/O-bound queries.

DB2 V4 improved on query I/O parallelism by enabling queries to utilize CPU in parallel. When CPU parallelism is engaged, each concurrent read engine will utilize its own portion of the central processor. This will aid processor-bound queries.

DB2 V5 improved parallelism even further with Sysplex query parallelism. With Sysplex query parallelism DB2 can spread the work for a single query across multiple DB2 subsystems in a data sharing group. This will further aid intensive, processor-bound queries.

DB2 V6 further improved parallelism by enabling data accessed in a non-partitioned table space to use query parallelism.

Partition Independence

Using resource serialization, DB2 has the ability to process a single partition while permitting concurrent access to independent partitions of the same table space by utilities and SQL. This partition independence enhances overall data availability by enabling users concurrent access to data in separate partitions.

Limited Partition Scanning

When processing against a partitioned table space, DB2 can enhance the performance of table space scans by limiting the partitions that are read. A limited partition table space scan will only read the specific range of partitions required based on the specified predicates in the WHERE clause.

DB2 V5 further modified partition scanning to enable skipping partitions in the middle of a range.

Uncommitted Read, a.k.a. "Dirty" Read

When data integrity is not an issue, DB2 can bypass locking and enable readers to access data regardless of its state. The "UR" isolation level provides a dirty read by allowing a SELECT statement to access data that is locked, in the process of being deleted, inserted but not yet committed, or, indeed in *any* state. This can greatly enhance performance in certain situations.

> **CAUTION**
>
> Never use DB2's dirty read capability without a complete understanding of its ramifications on data integrity. For more information on uncommitted read processing refer to Chapter 2 for statement level usage; and Chapter 13, "Program Preparation," for plan and package level usage.

Run Time Reoptimization

DB2 can reoptimize static and dynamic SQL statements that rely on input variables in the WHERE clause during processing. This feature enables DB2 to optimize SQL statements after the host variable, parameter marker, and special register values are known. Run time reoptimization can result in better access paths (albeit at a cost).

V8 DB2 V8 adds the capability to reoptimize variables once—the first time the statement is executed, instead of every time.

Instrumentation Facility Interface (IFI)

DB2 provides the Instrumentation Facility Interface, better known to DB2 professionals as IFI. The IFI is a facility for gathering trace data enabling users to better monitor and tune the DB2 environment. Using the DB2 IFI users can submit DB2 commands, obtain trace information, and pass data to DB2.

V7 ### Dynamic System Parameters

Changing DB2 system parameters, commonly referred to as DSNZPARMs or simply ZPARMs, required DB2 to be stopped and restarted prior to Version 7. Due to rising availability requirements, in large part spurred by the Internet, many (but not all) ZPARMs can be changed on the fly—without requiring DB2 to be recycled. This capability offers DBAs and system administrators greater flexibility and adaptability to respond to system and performance problems.

V7 ### Historical and Real-Time Statistics

AS of V7 DB2 now stores historical statistical details in the DB2 Catalog. Previous DB2 versions simply overlaid old statistics with new whenever RUNSTATS was run. By keeping historical statistics DBAs can now compare current DB2 object characteristics with past statistics. Such comparisons can be helpful to tune queries and to predict performance results based on history.

IBM also added support for real-time statistics as a feature upgrade in between Version 7 and 8. Real-time stats are collected by DB2 during normal operations—without requiring a separate utility (such as RUNSTATS) to be run. The additional real-time statistics provide growth and performance information to help DBAs determine when maintenance tasks, such as reorganization, should be scheduled.

V8 ### Materialized Query Tables

Data warehousing queries regularly involve complex operations on large amounts of data. To reduce the amount of time required to respond to such queries, DB2 Version 8 introduced materialized query tables (or MQTs). Using an MQT, DB2 stores data derived from one or more source tables. This materialized data can be summarized, joined, and combined using SQL operations, but the data is stored so the data warehousing queries operate more efficiently. Consult Chapter 45 for more details on materialized query tables.

V8 ### Data Partitioned Secondary Indexes

One of the biggest problems faced by DBAs when they are managing large partitioned DB2 table spaces is contending with non-partitioned indexes. DB2 Version 8 helps to alleviate this problem with data partitioned secondary indexes (or DPSIs). A DPSI is basically a partitioned NPI. So, DPSIs are partitioned based on the data rows—similar to a partitioning index. The number of parts in the index will be equal to the number of parts in the table space—even though the DPSI is created based on columns different from those used to define the partitioning scheme for the table space. Therefore, partition 1 of the DPSI will be for the same rows as partition 1 of the table space and partition 1 of the partitioning index, and so on.

These changes to DB2 V8 provide many benefits, including

- The ability to cluster by a secondary index

- The ability to drop and rotate partitions easily

- Less data sharing overhead

Be careful though, because converting to a DPSI can require that your queries be rewritten in order to use the DPSI instead of a table space scan.

CHAPTER **2**

Data Manipulation Guidelines

In Chapter 1, "The Magic Words," you learned the basics of SQL, but you can gain a deeper body of knowledge on the proper way to code SQL statements. Any particular method of coding an SQL statement is not wrong, per se, as long as it returns the correct results. But, often, you can find a better way. By *better*, I mean

- SQL that understands and interacts appropriately with its environment

- SQL that executes more efficiently and therefore enhances performance

- SQL that is clearly documented and therefore easily understood

You should pursue each of these goals. The guidelines introduced in the following sections are based on these three goals. These guidelines enable you to write efficient SQL and thereby limit the time programmers, analysts, and DBAs must spend correcting performance problems and analyzing poorly documented SQL and application code.

A Bag of Tricks

Understanding the ins and outs of DB2 performance can be an overwhelming task. DB2 tuning options are numerous and constantly changing. Even the number of SQL tuning options is staggering. The differences in efficiency can be substantial. For example, coding a query as a join instead of as a correlated subquery sometimes results in a query that performs better. The same query, however, might result in degraded performance. Plus, to make matters worse, a new version or release of DB2 can cause completely different results.

> **NOTE**
>
> Although a new release rarely causes the results set of a query to change, the performance results can change dramatically. And sometimes even the query's answer can change if, for example, a default changes. IBM works diligently to make sure this does not happen, though.

The release level of DB2 is not the only factor that can cause performance problems. Changes to the z/OS or OS/390 operating system, the DB2 database environment, the application code, or the application database can cause performance fluctuations. The following is a sample list of system changes that can affect DB2 query performance:

- Enterprisewide changes

  Distributing data

  Moving data from site to site

  Replicating and propagating data

  Downsizing, upsizing, and rightsizing

  Integrating legacy applications to the web

  Changing to a new hardware environment

  Adding more users

- z/OS and OS/390 system-level changes

  Modifying DB2 dispatching priorities

  Modifying CICS, IMS/TM, or TSO dispatching priorities

  Modifying network parameters (TCP/IP, SNA, and so on)

  Implementing (or modifying) Workload Manager

  Installing a new release of OS/390 or z/OS

  Installing a new release of CICS, IMS/TM, or TSO

  Implementing parallel sysplex

  Modifying TSO parameters

  Adding or removing memory

  Installing additional hardware that consumes memory

  Increasing system throughput

- DB2 system-level changes

  Installing a new DB2 version or release

  Applying maintenance to the DB2 software

  Changing DSNZPARMs

Modifying IRLM parameters

Modifying buffer pool sizes or parameters

Incurring DB2 growth, causing the DB2 Catalog to grow without resizing or reorganizing

Ensuring proper placement of the active log data sets

Implementing data sharing

- Application-level changes

Increasing the application workload

Adding rows to a table

Deleting rows from a table

Increasing the volume of inserts, causing unclustered data or data set extents

Increasing the volume of updates to indexed columns

Updating variable character columns or compressed rows, possibly causing storage space to expand and additional I/O to be incurred

Changing the distribution of data values in the table

Updating RUNSTATS information (see Chapters 1 and 35 for more information on RUNSTATS)

Not running RUNSTATS at all

Rebinding application packages and plans

Implementing or changing stored procedures or user-defined functions

Enabling parallel processing

- Database-level changes

Adding or removing indexes

Changing the clustering index

Altering a table to add a column

Changing partitioning for a table space

Adding or removing triggers from a table

Reorganizing table spaces and indexes

Compressing data

Inserting data causing the table space to grow or to add an extent

Moving physical data sets for table spaces or indexes to different volumes

Luckily, you can prepare yourself to deal with performance problems by understanding the dynamic nature of DB2 performance features and keeping abreast of SQL tricks of the trade. Use caution when implementing these tips and tricks, though, because the cardinal rule of relational database development always applies—what is this cardinal rule?

> **NOTE**
>
> The cardinal rule of RDBMS development is **"It depends!"** Most DBAs and SQL experts resist giving a straight or simple answer to a general question because there is no simple and standard implementation that exists. Every situation is different, and every organization is unique in some way.
>
> Don't be discouraged when you ask the local expert which statement will perform better, and the answer is "It depends." The expert is just doing his or her job. The secret to optimizing DB2 performance is being able to answer the follow-up question to "It depends"—and that is "What does it depend on?"
>
> The key to effective SQL performance tuning is to document each SQL change along with the reason for the change. Follow up by monitoring the effectiveness of every change to your SQL statements before moving them into a production environment. Over time, trends will emerge that will help to clarify which types of SQL formulations perform best.

This chapter is divided into six major sections. In the first section, you learn SQL guidelines for simple SQL statements. The second section covers guidelines for complex SQL statements such as joins, subqueries, table expressions, and unions. Common table expressions and recursion are introduced in section three; these features are new to DB2 V8 and they require some effort to master. Section four introduces the concept of nulls. Section five deals with querying date, time, and timestamp values. The sixth section provides guidelines for the efficient use of the INSERT, DELETE, and UPDATE statements.

SQL Access Guidelines

The SQL access guidelines will help you develop efficient data retrieval SQL for DB2 applications. Test them to determine their usefulness and effectiveness in your environment.

Pretest All Embedded SQL   Before embedding SQL in an application program, you should test it using SPUFI, QMF, or whatever ad hoc query tool you have available. This way, you can reduce the amount of program testing by ensuring that all SQL code is syntactically correct and efficient. Only after the SQL statements have been thoroughly tested and debugged should they be placed in an application program.

Use EXPLAIN   Use the EXPLAIN command to gain further insight into the performance potential for each SQL statement in an application. When EXPLAIN is executed on an SQL statement or application plan, information about the access path chosen by the optimizer is provided. This information is inserted into a DB2 table called the PLAN_TABLE. By querying the PLAN_TABLE, an analyst can determine the potential efficiency of SQL queries. Part V, "DB2 Performance Tuning," provides a complete description of the EXPLAIN command and guidelines for interpreting its output. EXPLAIN also populates the DSN_STATEMNT_TABLE with statement cost information and the DSN_FUNCTION_TABLE table with information about user-defined function usage.

Use EXPLAIN and analyze the results for each SQL statement before it is migrated to the production application. Following this procedure is important not only for SQL statements in application programs, but also for canned QMF queries, and any other, predictable, dynamic SQL queries. For application programs, EXPLAIN can be used with the EXPLAIN option of the BIND command. Specifying EXPLAIN(YES) when you use BIND on an application plan or package provides the access path information necessary to determine the efficiency of the statements in the program. For a QMF (or ad hoc) query, use EXPLAIN on it before allowing the statement to be used in production procedures.

The following is an example of running EXPLAIN for a SELECT statement:

```
EXPLAIN PLAN SET QUERYNO = 1 FOR
     SELECT  *
     FROM    DSN8810.DEPT
     WHERE   DEPTNO = 'D21';
```

EXPLAIN enables a programmer or DBA to analyze the chosen access path by studying the PLAN_TABLE.

Because EXPLAIN provides access path information based on the statistics stored in the DB2 Catalog, you should keep these statistics current and accurate. Sometimes you must "fudge" the DB2 Catalog statistics to produce production access paths in a test environment. (See the section, "Influencing the Access Path," in Chapter 1 for more information.)

Use All PLAN_TABLE Columns Available   Each new release or version of DB2 adds new columns to the PLAN_TABLE. These new columns are used to report on new access paths and features. Sometimes shops fail to add the new PLAN_TABLE columns after a new release is installed. Be sure to verify that the PLAN_TABLE actually contains every column that is available for the current DB2 release being run. For more information on the PLAN_TABLE and the columns available for each DB2 release, refer to Chapter 25, "Using EXPLAIN."

V7 For DB2 V7, the following columns were added to the PLAN_TABLE to offer additional information on table functions, temporary intermediate result tables, and work files:

- PARENT_QBLOCK—SMALLINT

- TABLE_TYPE—CHAR(1)

V8 For DB2 V8, the following columns were added to the PLAN_TABLE:

- TABLE_ENCODE—CHAR(1)

- TABLE_SCCSID—SMALLINT

- TABLE_MCCSID—SMALLINT

- TABLE_DCCSID—SMALLINT

- ROUTINE_ID—INTEGER

Use the DSN_STATEMNT_TABLE   As of DB2 V6, EXPLAIN also can determine an estimated cost of executing SQL SELECT, INSERT, UPDATE, or DELETE statements. EXPLAIN will populate

DSN_STATEMNT_TABLE, also known as the statement table, at the same time it populates the PLAN_TABLE. After running EXPLAIN, the statement table will contain cost estimates, in service units and in milliseconds, for the SQL statements being bound or prepared (both static and dynamic SQL).

The estimates can be used to help determine the cost of running SQL statements. However, keep in mind that the cost numbers are just estimates. Factors that can cause the estimates to be inaccurate include cost adjustments caused by parallel processing, the use of triggers and user-defined functions, and inaccurate statistics.

For more information on statement tables and cost estimates, see Chapter 25.

Use DSN_FUNCTION_TABLE to Explain User-Defined Function Usage   If you have implemented user-defined functions (UDFs), be sure to create DSN_FUNCTION_TABLE, also known as the function table. DB2 inserts data into DSN_FUNCTION_TABLE for each function referenced in an SQL statement when EXPLAIN is executed on an SQL statement containing a UDF or when a program bound with EXPLAIN(YES) executes an SQL statement containing a UDF.

The data DB2 inserts to the function table contains information on how DB2 resolves the user-defined function references. This information can be quite useful when tuning or debugging SQL that specifies a UDF.

For more information on using EXPLAIN with the function table, see Chapter 4, "Using DB2 User-Defined Functions and Data Types."

Enable EXPLAIN for Auto Rebind   EXPLAIN during auto rebind can be enabled if you set an appropriate DSNZPARM. An auto rebind occurs when an authorized user attempts to execute an invalid plan or package. To revalidate the plan or package, DB2 will automatically rebind it. If EXPLAIN during auto rebind is not turned on, then you will not have a record of the new access paths that were created. The DSNZPARM for auto rebind is ABIND (the default is YES); the DSNZPARM for binding during auto rebind is ABEXP (the default is YES).

Plans and packages are invalidated when an object that an access path in the plan or package is using is dropped. Be sure that a proper PLAN_TABLE exists before enabling the EXPLAIN during auto rebind option.

When Data Sharing Specify COEXIST for Auto Rebind   If you are running in a data sharing environment, consider specifying COEXIST for ABIND. Doing so allows automatic rebind operations to be performed in a DB2 data sharing coexistence environment only when the plan or package is invalid, or when it was last bound on a new subsystem other than the one on which it is running. In this way, DB2 can keep the new access path even when a query is run in an older subsystem. Of course, DB2 will not magically use V7 features on a V6 subsystem (for example).

> **NOTE**
>
> When all members of a data sharing group have been migrated to the same DB2 version, ABIND COEXIST will be interpreted the same as ABIND YES.

Utilize Visual Explain and Query Analysis Tools   Visual Explain is a tool provided by IBM as a free feature of DB2 for z/OS. Visual Explain will display graphical representations of the DB2 access paths and advice on how to improve SQL performance. The display can be for access paths stored in a PLAN_TABLE or for EXPLAIN output from dynamic SQL statements.

One of the nice features of Visual Explain is its ability to display pertinent DB2 Catalog statistics for objects referenced in an access path. It is much easier to understand access paths from the visual representations of Visual Explain, than it is to interpret PLAN_TABLE output. Refer to Figure 2.1 for a sample Visual Explain screen shot.

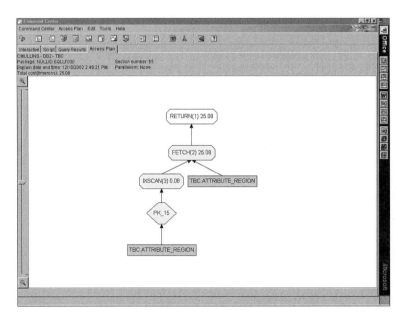

FIGURE 2.1   Visual Explain graphically depicts an EXPLAIN.

You must run Visual Explain from a client workstation (there is no TSO or ISPF interface).

V8   Significant improvements were made to the Visual Explain tool for DB2 Version 8. More detailed information is provided about access paths and more statistical details are available for each node in the query access graph. Furthermore, Visual Explain works with XML to document query access paths.

Even with all of the new functionality of Visual Explain, you may need to augment this tool with more in-depth SQL tuning options. To isolate potential performance problems in application plans or single SQL statements, utilize all available analysis tools, such as BMC Software's SQL Explorer or Computer Associates' Plan Analyzer. These products analyze the SQL code, provide a clear, textual description of the access path selected by the DB2 optimizer, and recommend alternative methods of coding your queries. They are similar in function to Visual Explain, but provide an ISPF interface and more in-depth tuning recommendations.

Avoid SELECT *   As a general rule, a query should *never* ask DB2 for anything more than is required to satisfy the desired task. Each query should access only the columns needed for the function to be performed. Following this dictum results in maximum flexibility and efficiency.

> **NOTE**
>
> Another cardinal rule of database performance is "never say *always* or *never*." Well, perhaps this rule is better stated as "*almost* never say always or never." There are very few times in this text where I will say "always" or "never," but there are a few, such as *never* asking DB2 for anything more than is required.

The gain in flexibility is the result of decreased maintenance on application programs. Consider a table in which columns are modified, deleted, or added. Only programs that access the affected columns need to be changed. When a program uses SELECT *, however, every column in the table is accessed. The program must be modified when any of the columns change, even if the program doesn't use the changed columns. This use complicates the maintenance process.

For example, consider a program that contains the following statement:

```
EXEC SQL
    SELECT  *
    INTO    :DEPTREC
    FROM    DSN8810.DEPT
    WHERE   DEPTNO = :HV-DEPT
END-EXEC.
```

Suppose that the program is developed, tested, and migrated to the production environment. You then add a column to the DEPT table. The program then fails to execute the preceding statement because the DEPTREC layout does not contain the new column. (This program was compiled with the old DCLGEN.) The program must be recompiled with the new DCLGEN, a step that is not required when the program asks for only the columns it needs.

Additionally, by limiting your query to only those columns necessary

- The programmer does not need extra time to code for the extraneous columns.

- You avoid the DB2 overhead required to retrieve the extraneous columns. Overhead will be incurred because there is work required to move each column.

- DB2 might be able to use an index-only access path that is unavailable for SELECT *.

Limit the Data Selected   Return the minimum number of columns and rows needed by your application program. Do not code generic queries (such as SELECT statements without a WHERE clause) that return more rows than necessary, and then filter the unnecessary rows with the application program. Doing so wastes disk I/O by retrieving useless data and wastes CPU and elapsed time returning the additional, unneeded rows to your program.

Allowing DB2 to use WHERE clauses to limit the data to be returned is more efficient than filtering data programmatically after it has been returned.

Do Not Ask for What You Already Know   This might sound obvious, but most programmers violate this rule at one time or another. For a typical example, consider what's wrong with this SQL statement:

```
SELECT   EMPNO, LASTNAME, SALARY
FROM     DSN8810.EMP
WHERE    EMPNO = '000010';
```

Give up? The problem is that EMPNO is included in the SELECT-list. You already know that EMPNO will be equal to the value '000010' because that is what the WHERE clause tells DB2 to do. But with EMPNO listed in the WHERE clause, DB2 will dutifully retrieve that column, too. This incurs additional overhead for each qualifying row, thereby degrading performance. So, this statement would be better coded this way:

```
SELECT   LASTNAME, SALARY
FROM     DSN8810.EMP
WHERE    EMPNO = '000010';
```

Singleton SELECT Versus the Cursor   To return a single row, an application program can use a cursor or a singleton SELECT. A cursor requires an OPEN, FETCH, and CLOSE to retrieve one row, whereas a singleton SELECT requires only SELECT...INTO. Usually, the singleton SELECT outperforms the cursor.

V7   This is especially true for DB2 V7 and later releases because the FETCH FIRST 1 ROW ONLY clause can be added to any SELECT statement (both singleton SELECTs and cursors) to ensure that only one row is ever returned. Historically, the biggest problem associated with using a singleton SELECT is managing what happens when more than one row can be returned. DB2 will return a SQLCODE of -811 if more than one row results from a singleton SELECT. By adding FETCH FIRST 1 ROW ONLY to the singleton SELECT, though, DB2 will never return more than one row.

Avoid Singleton SELECT When Modifying Data   When developing a program to retrieve data that must be subsequently modified, avoid using a singleton SELECT. When the selected row must be updated after it is retrieved, using a cursor with the FOR UPDATE OF clause is recommended over a singleton SELECT. The FOR UPDATE OF clause ensures the integrity of the data in the row because it causes DB2 to hold an X lock on the page containing the row to be updated. If you use a singleton SELECT, the row can be updated by someone else after the singleton SELECT but before the subsequent UPDATE, thereby causing the intermediate modification to be lost.

Use FOR READ ONLY   When a SELECT statement is used only for retrieval, code the FOR READ ONLY clause. This clause enables DB2 to use *block fetch*, which returns fetched rows more efficiently for distributed DB2 requests. Efficient row fetches are important for dynamic SQL in an application program or SPUFI. Furthermore, the FOR READ ONLY clause can be used to encourage DB2 to use lock avoidance techniques and parallelism.

QMF automatically appends `FOR READ ONLY` to `SELECT` statements. Static SQL embedded in an application program automatically uses block fetch if the `BIND` process determines it to be feasible.

Allowing block fetch is important in a distributed DB2 environment. If data is blocked, less overhead is required as data is sent over the communication lines.

> **NOTE**
>
> The `FOR FETCH ONLY` clause provides the same function as `FOR READ ONLY`, but `FOR READ ONLY` is preferable because it is ODBC-compliant.

V7 **Control Distributed Query Blocks Using** `OPTIMIZE FOR n ROWS`   Additionally, consider using the `OPTIMIZE FOR n ROWS` clause to optimize network traffic. If your application opens a cursor and downloads a great amount of data, specifying a large value for *n* increases the number of DRDA query blocks that a DB2 server returns in each network transmission for a non-scrollable cursor. If *n* is greater than the number of rows that fit in a DRDA query block, `OPTIMIZE FOR n ROWS` lets the DRDA client request multiple blocks of query data on each network transmission instead of requesting a new block when the first block is full.

Use `DISTINCT` **with Care**   The `DISTINCT` verb removes duplicate rows from an answer set. If duplicates will not cause a problem, do not code `DISTINCT` because it might add to overhead if it must invoke a sort to remove the duplicates.

However, do not avoid `DISTINCT` for performance reasons if you must remove duplicates from your result set. It is better for DB2 to remove the duplicates than for the results to be passed to the program and then having the duplicates removed by application logic. One major benefit is that DB2 will not make any mistakes, but the application logic could contain bugs.

For example, the following SQL will return a list of all departments to which an employee has been assigned with no duplicate `WORKDEPT` values returned:

```
SELECT   DISTINCT WORKDEPT
FROM     DSN8810.EMP;
```

Consider Using Multiple `DISTINCT` **Clauses**   The `DISTINCT` keyword can be used at the statement level or at the column level. When used at the statement level, for example

```
SELECT   DISTINCT LASTNAME, WORKDEPT
FROM     DSN8810.EMP;
```

duplicate rows are removed from the result set. So, only one `LASTNAME – WORKDEPT` combination will be returned even if multiple employees with the same last name work in the same department. When `DISTINCT` is used at the column level, for example

```
SELECT   AVG(SALARY), COUNT(DISTINCT EMPNO)
FROM     DSN8810.EMP;
```

duplicate values are removed for the column on which the `DISTINCT` keyword is used. Prior to DB2 V7 only one `DISTINCT` clause can be specified in a `SELECT` list.

V7 With DB2 V7 you can specify multiple DISTINCT clauses, but on the same column only. For example

```
SELECT  SUM(DISTINCT SALARY), COUNT(DISTINCT SALARY)
FROM    DSN8810.EMP;
```

However, for DB2 V7 and earlier releases, you cannot specify multiple DISTINCT clauses on different columns, or you get SQLCODE –127.

V8 DB2 Version 8 extends the functionality of the DISTINCT clause by enabling you to code multiple DISTINCTs in the SELECT or HAVING clause of SQL statements. The retriction limiting multiple DISTINCTs to the same column is lifted with DB2 V8. This enhancement is accomplished by performing multiple sorts on multiple distinct columns. For example, the following SQL statement uses two DISTINCT clauses on two different columns and is legal as of Version 8:

```
SELECT  COUNT(DISTINCT(ACTNO)),
        SUM(DISTINCT(ACSTAFF))
FROM    DSN8810.PROJACT
GROUP BY PROJNO;
```

You could even add a HAVING clause with a DISTINCT to this query as of V8, for example

```
HAVING AVG(DISTINCT ACSTAFF) < 2.0;
```

Code Predicates on Indexed Columns   DB2 usually performs more efficiently when it can satisfy a request using an existing index rather than no index. However, indexed access is not always the most efficient access method. For example, when you request most of the rows in a table or access by a non-clustered index, indexed access can result in a poorer performing query than non-indexed access. This is so because the number of I/Os is increased to access index pages. As a general rule of thumb, keep in mind that an index enhances performance when the total I/O required to access the index pages and the specific table space pages is less than simply accessing all of the table space pages.

You can find comprehensive guidelines for the efficient creation of DB2 indexes in Chapter 6, "DB2 Indexes."

Use ORDER BY When the Sequence Is Important   You cannot guarantee the order of the rows returned from a SELECT statement without an ORDER BY clause. At times SQL developers get confused when DB2 uses an index to satisfy a query and the results are returned in the desired order even without the ORDER BY clause. But, due to the nature of the DB2 optimizer, the access path by which the data is retrieved might change from execution to execution of an application program. If the access path changes (or parallelism kicks in), and ORDER BY is not specified, the results can be returned in a different (non-desired) order. For this reason, **always** code the ORDER BY clause when the sequence of rows being returned is important.

Limit the Columns Specified in ORDER BY   When you use ORDER BY to sequence retrieved data, DB2 ensures that the data is sorted in order by the specified columns. Doing so usually involves the invocation of a sort (unless an appropriate index is available). The more columns that are sorted, the less efficient the query will be. Therefore, use ORDER BY on only those columns that are absolutely necessary.

V7 Also, keep in mind that as of DB2 V6 you can ORDER BY columns that are not included in the SELECT list. And, as of Version 7, this feature is extended even if the item is an expression. So, be sure to prune the SELECT list to only the data required for the display.

Favor Stage 1 and Indexable Predicate   For SQL statements, you must consider at which stage the predicate is applied: Stage 1 or Stage 2.

> **NOTE**
>
> Stage 1 predicates were previously known as sargable predicates. *Sargable* is an IBM-defined term that stands for **s**earch **arguable**. The term simply defines in which portion of DB2 a predicate can be satisfied. The term *sargable* is ostensibly obsolete and has been replaced in the IBM literature by the term *Stage 1 processing*.

A predicate that can be satisfied by Stage 1 processing can be evaluated by the Data Manager portion of DB2, not the Relational Data System. The Data Manager component of DB2 is at a level closer to the data than the Relational Data System. You can find a more complete description of the components of DB2 in Chapter 20, "DB2 Behind the Scenes."

Because a Stage 1 predicate can be evaluated at an earlier Stage of data retrieval, you avoid the overhead of passing data from component to component of DB2. Try to use Stage 1 predicates rather than Stage 2 predicates because Stage 1 predicates are more efficient.

Additionally, a query that can use an index has more access path options, so it can be more efficient than a query that cannot use an index. The DB2 optimizer can use an index or indexes in a variety of ways to speed the retrieval of data from DB2 tables. For this reason, try to use indexable predicates rather than those that are not.

Of course, this raises the questions: "Which predicates are Stage 1 and which are Stage 2?" and "How do I know if a predicate is indexable or not?" This information is consolidated for you in Table 2.1.

TABLE 2.1   Predicate Stage and Indexability

Predicate Type	Stage	Indexable
COL = value	1	YES
COL = noncol expr	1	YES
COL IS NULL	1	YES
COL IS NOT NULL	1	YES
COL op value	1	YES
COL op noncol expr	1	YES
COL BETWEEN value1 AND value 2	1	YES
COL BETWEEN noncol expr1 AND noncol expr2	1	YES
COL BETWEEN expr1 and expr2	1	YES
COL LIKE 'pattern'	1	YES
COL IN (list)	1	YES

TABLE 2.1   Continued

Predicate Type	Stage	Indexable
COL LIKE :HV	1	YES
T1.COL = T2.COL	1	YES
T1.COL op T2.COL	1	YES
COL = (non subq)	1	YES
COL op (non subq)	1	YES
COL op ANY (non subq)	1	YES
COL op ALL (non subq)	1	YES
COL IN (non subq)	1	YES
COL = expression	1	YES
(COL1,…COLn) IN (non subq)	1	YES
(COL1,…COLn) = (val1,3…valn)	1	YES
T1.COL = T2.col expr	1	YES
COL <> value	1	NO
COL <> noncol expr	1	NO
COL NOT BETWEEN value1 AND value2	1	NO
COL NOT BETWEEN noncol expr1 AND noncol expr2	1	NO
COL NOT IN (list)	1	NO
COL NOT LIKE ' char'	1	NO
COL NOT LIKE '%char'	1	NO
COL NOT LIKE '_char'	1	NO
T1.COL <> T2.COL	1	NO
T1.COL1 = T1.COL2	1	NO
COL <> (non subq)	1	NO

If the predicate type is not listed in Table 2.1, then it is Stage 2 and non-indexable. Note that you can replace *op* with <=, >=, <, >, or <>. A noncol expr is a noncolumn expression; it refers to any expression in which a column of a table is not specified. Examples of such expressions include

```
CURRENT TIMESTAMP - 10 DAYS

:HOST-VARIABLE + 20

FLOAT(8.5)
```

Stage 1 predicates combined with AND, combined with OR, or preceded by NOT are also Stage 1. All others are Stage 2. Additionally, please note that a LIKE predicate ceases to be Stage 1 if the column is defined using a field procedure. Indexable predicates combined with AND or OR are also indexable. However, note that predicates preceded by NOT are not indexable.

> **NOTE**
>
> All indexable predicates are also Stage 1. The reverse, however, is not true: All Stage 1 predicates are not necessarily indexable.

V8 Keep in mind, too, that a predicate defined such that it conforms to the syntax specified for Stage 1 might in fact be changed to Stage 2 by DB2. Prior to V8, this can occur because the predicate contains constants whose data type or length does not match. As of Version 8, though, many Stage 1 predicates will remain Stage 1 even if the data types are not perfect.

Additionally, Stage 1 processing and indexability are only two aspects of efficient query writing and, as such, do not guarantee the most effective way to code your query. Follow the rest of the advice in this chapter to formulate efficient SQL code.

Finally, do not read more into this guideline than is intended. I am not saying you should never use Stage 2 predicates. Feel free to code Stage 2 predicates when necessary based on your application requirements. Using Stage 2 predicates is much preferable to returning the data to the program and filtering it there.

> **CAUTION**
>
> This information is accurate as of DB2 Version 8. Determine which predicates are Stage 1 and indexable with care because IBM tends to change certain predicates' stage and indexability with each release of DB2.

Reformulate SQL to Achieve Indexability   Remember that SQL is flexible and often the same results can be achieved using different SQL formulations. Sometimes one SQL statement will dramatically outperform a functionally equivalent SQL statement just because it is indexable and the other is not. For example, consider this SQL statement:

```
SELECT EMPNO, FIRSTNME, MIDINIT, LASTNAME
FROM   DSN8810.EMP
WHERE  MIDINIT NOT BETWEEN 'A' AND 'G';
```

It is not indexable because it uses the NOT BETWEEN predicate. However, if we understand the data in the table and the desired results, perhaps we can reformulate the SQL to use indexable predicates, such as

```
SELECT EMPNO, FIRSTNME, MIDINIT, LASTNAME
FROM   DSN8810.EMP
WHERE  MIDINIT >= 'H';
```

Or we could code MIDINIT BETWEEN 'H' AND 'Z' in place of MIDINIT >= 'H'. Of course, for either of these solutions to work correctly we would need to know that MIDINIT never contained values that collate lower than the value 'A'.

Try to Avoid Using NOT (Except with EXISTS)   In older versions of DB2, predicates using NOT were non-indexable and Stage 2. As of DB2 V4, predicates formed using NOT are evaluated at Stage 1, but they are still non-indexable. Therefore, whenever possible, you should recode queries to avoid the use of NOT (<>). Take advantage of your understanding of the data being accessed. For example, if you know that no values are less than the value that you are testing for inequality, you could recode

```
COLUMN1  <>  value
```

as

```
COLUMN1  >=  value
```

See the section on complex SQL guidelines for guidance in the use of the EXISTS predicate.

Use Equivalent Data Types   Use the same data types and lengths when comparing column values to host variables or literals. This way, you can eliminate the need for data conversion. Because the data type or length does not match, DB2 evaluates the predicate as Stage 2 (even if the predicate could be Stage 1 if the data type and length matched).

For example, comparing a column defined as INTEGER to another column defined as INTEGER is more efficient than comparing an INTEGER column to a column defined as DECIMAL(5,2). When DB2 must convert data, available indexes are not used.

DB2 also does not use an index if the host variable or literal is longer than the column being compared, or if the host variable has a greater precision or a different data type than the column being compared. This situation adversely affects performance and should be avoided.

V7 As of Version 7, you are allowed to CAST numeric equi-join columns to match in order to preserve Stage 1. But, if you can wait for Version 8, all you will have to do is REBIND because V8 resolves many of the data type mismatch problems. Until then, though, use CAST.

Use a CAST function to resolve data type mismatches for date and numeric values to avoid demotion to Stage 2. For example, if you need to compare a DECIMAL(9,2) column to a SMALLINT, cast the integer value to a decimal value as follows:

```
WHERE  DECIMAL(SMALLINTCOL, 9, 2) = DECIMALCOL
```

Be sure to CAST the column belonging to the larger result set if both columns are indexed. That is, the column that can take on more distinct values should be the one cast. However, if only one column is indexed, CAST the one that is not indexed. You will need to rebind in order to receive the promotion to Stage 1.

As of DB2 V6, and via a retrofit APAR to V5, DB2 partially alleviated the data type and length mismatch performance problem, but only for character data. When two character columns are specified in an equi-join predicate, they no longer need to be of the same length to be considered Stage 1 and indexable. Please note that this applies only to columns, not host variables or string literals. Also, note that the two columns being compared must be of CHAR or VARCHAR data type. For example, you cannot join an INTEGER column to a SMALLINT column and expect it to be Stage 1 or indexable (for DB2 V7 or earlier).

V8 DB2 V8 provides even more relief for this problem, but only within the data type family. This means that numbers can match numbers, characters match characters, and so on, without having to be an exact type and length match. In other words, as long as you are close to matching DB2 will evaluate the predicate in Stage 1 (if you are running DB2

Version 8 or greater). Even though this is now the case, it is still wise to exactly match up the data type and length of all column values, host variables, and literals within your predicates.

Consider BETWEEN **Instead of** <= **and** >=   The BETWEEN predicate is easier to understand and code than the equivalent combination of the *less than or equal to* predicate (<=) and the *greater than or equal to* predicate (>=). In past releases it was also more efficient, but now the optimizer recognizes the two formulations as equivalent and there usually is no performance benefit one way or the other. Performance reasons aside, one BETWEEN predicate is much easier to understand and maintain than multiple <= and >= predicates. For this reason, favor using BETWEEN.

However, there is one particular instance where this guidelines does not apply—when comparing a host variable to two columns. Usually BETWEEN is used to compare one column to two values, here shown using host variables:

```
WHERE COLUMN1 BETWEEN :HOST-VAR1 AND :HOST-VAR2
```

However, it is possible to use BETWEEN to compare one value to two columns, as shown:

```
WHERE :HOST-VAR BETWEEN COLUMN1 AND COLUMN2
```

This statement should be changed to

```
WHERE :HOST_VAR >= COLUMN1 and :HOST-VAR <= COLUMN2
```

The reason for this exception is that a BETWEEN formulation comparing a host variable to two columns is a Stage 2 predicate, whereas the preferred formulation is Stage 1.

Consider IN **Instead of** LIKE   Whenever feasible, use IN or BETWEEN instead of LIKE in the WHERE clause of a SELECT. If you know that only a certain number of occurrences exist, using IN with the specific list usually is more efficient than using LIKE. For example, use

```
IN ('VALUE1', 'VALUE2', 'VALUE3')
```

instead of

```
LIKE 'VALUE_'
```

The functionality of LIKE can be imitated using a range of values. For example, if you want a query to retrieve all employees with a last name beginning with *K*, you know that last names between *KAAAAAAAAAA* and *KZZZZZZZZZZ* also satisfy the request. To optimize performance, favor using

```
BETWEEN :VALUE_LO AND :VALUE_HI
```

instead of

```
LIKE 'VALUE%'
```

Formulate LIKE **Predicates with Care**   Avoid using the LIKE predicate when the percentage sign (%) or the underscore (_) appears at the beginning of the comparison string because they prevent DB2 from using a matching index. The LIKE predicate can produce efficient results, however, when you use the percentage sign or underscore at the end or in the middle of the comparison string.

Not Okay	Okay
LIKE %NAME	LIKE NAME%
LIKE _NAME	LIKE NA_ME

DB2 does not use direct index lookup when a wildcard character is supplied as the first character of a LIKE predicate. DB2 can determine when a host variable contains a wildcard character as the first character of a LIKE predicate. The optimizer therefore does not assume that an index cannot be used; rather, it indicates that an index might be used. At runtime, DB2 determines whether the index will be used based on the value supplied to the host variable. When a wildcard character is specified for the first character of a LIKE predicate, DB2 uses a non-matching index scan or a table space scan to satisfy the search.

Specify Appropriate Host Variable Values with LIKE   The LIKE predicate offers a great deal of flexibility and power to your SQL statements. Using LIKE you can quickly retrieve data based on patterns and wildcards. However, some uses of LIKE can be confusing to implement appropriately—especially when LIKE is used with host variables.

Let's assume that you need to create an application that retrieves employees by last name, but the supplied value for the last name can be either the entire name or just the first few bytes of that name. In that case, the following query can suffice:

```
SELECT EMPNO, FIRSTNME, LASTNAME
FROM   DSN8810.EMP
WHERE  LASTNAME LIKE :host_variable;
```

In order for this to work, when you enter the value for host_variable always append percent signs (%) to the end of the value. The percent sign specifies that DB2 should accept as a match any number of characters (including 0). This must be done programmatically. So, if the value entered is SM, the host_variable should contain SM%%%%%%% and if the value entered is SMITH, the host_variable should contain SMITH%%%%. Append as many percent signs as required to fill up the entire length of the host variable. Failure to do this will result in DB2 searching for blank spaces. Think about it—if you assign SMITH% to a 10-byte host variable, that host variable will think it should search for SMITH%, that is SMITH at the beginning, four blanks at the end, and anything in the middle.

So, for SMITH%%%%, SMITH will be returned, but so will SMITHLY (or any name beginning with SMITH). There is no way to magically determine if what was entered is a complete name or just a portion thereof. If this is not acceptable, then a single query will not likely be feasible. Instead, you would have to ask the user to enter whether a full name or just a portion is being entered.

Code Most Restrictive Predicate First (Within Predicate Type)   DB2 uses a predefined method for evaluating SQL predicates. The sequence in which predicates are evaluated is dependent upon four different factors:

- The indexes being used

- Whether the predicate is Stage 1 or Stage 2

- The type of predicate (for example, =, >, <, BETWEEN, and so on)

- The sequence in which the predicates are physically coded in the SQL statement

First, DB2 will apply the predicates that match the indexes selected in the access path. The sequence in which these predicates are applied is based on the order of the column in the index. So, you must design efficient indexes to impact performance (see Chapter 5, "Data Definition Guidelines," for more information on efficient index design).

After applying matching index predicates, DB2 then applies

1. Stage 1 predicates that were not chosen as matching predicates but still refer to index columns, followed by

2. Stage 1 predicates in columns that were not in the indexes being used, and then

3. any Stage 2 predicates

Within each of these three groups, the sequence in which predicates are evaluated is based on the predicate type and the sequence in which the predicate appears in the SQL statement.

Predicate types are applied in the following sequence:

1. All equality predicates (including column IN-list, where list has only one element)

2. All range predicates and predicates specifying *column* IS NOT NULL

3. All other predicate types, but non-correlated subqueries are processed before correlated subqueries

Due to the preceding set of rules, when you code predicates in your SELECT statement, place the predicate that will eliminate the greatest number of rows first (within predicate type). For example, consider the following statement:

```
SELECT  EMPNO, FIRSTNME, LASTNAME
FROM    DSN8810.EMP
WHERE   WORKDEPT = 'D21'
AND     SEX = 'F';
```

Suppose that the WORKDEPT has 10 distinct values. The SEX column obviously has only 2 distinct values. Because both are equality predicates, the predicate for the WORKDEPT column should be coded first (as shown) because it eliminates more rows than the predicate for the SEX column. The performance gain from predicate placement is usually minimal, but sometimes every little performance gain is significant.

> **CAUTION**
>
> Remember, this guideline is true only for like predicate types. If the predicates are not of the same type, the guideline is not applicable.

Use Predicates Wisely   By reducing the number of predicates on your SQL statements, you might be able to achieve better performance in two ways:

1. Reduced BIND time due to fewer options that must be examined by the DB2 optimizer.

2. Reduced execution time due to a smaller path length caused by the removal of redundant search criteria from the optimized access path. DB2 processes each predicate coded for the SQL statement. Removing predicates removes work, and less work equals less time to process the SQL.

However, if you remove predicates from SQL statements, you run the risk of changing the data access logic. So, remove predicates only when you're sure that their removal will not have an impact on the query results. For example, consider the following query:

```
SELECT  FIRSTNME, LASTNAME
FROM    DSN8810.EMP
WHERE   JOB = 'DESIGNER'
AND     EDLEVEL >= 16;
```

This statement retrieves all rows for designers who are at an education level of 16 or above. But what if you know that the starting education level for all designers in an organization is 16? No one with a lower education level can be hired as a designer. In this case, the second predicate is redundant. Removing this predicate does not logically change the results, but it might enhance performance.

On the other hand, performance possibly can degrade when you remove predicates. The DB2 optimizer analyzes correlation statistics when calculating filter factors. Examples of correlated columns include CITY and STATE (Chicago and Illinois are likely to occur together); FIRST_NAME and GENDER (Robert and male are likely to occur together).

Because the filter factor might change when a predicate is changed or removed, a different access path can be chosen. That access path might be more (or less) efficient than the one it replaces. The basic rule is to test the SQL both ways to determine which will perform better for each specific statement.

Truly "knowing your data," however, is imperative. For example, it is not sufficient to merely note that for current rows in the EMP table no designers are at an EDLEVEL below 16. This may just be a data coincidence. Do not base your knowledge of your data on the current state of the data, but on business requirements. You must truly *know* that a correlation between two columns (such as between JOB and EDLEVEL) actually exists before you modify your SQL to take advantage of this fact.

In any case, whenever you make changes to SQL statements based on your knowledge of the data, be sure to document the reason for the change in the actual SQL statement using

SQL comments. Good documentation practices make future tuning, maintenance, and debugging easier.

Be Careful with Arithmetic Precision   When you select columns using arithmetic expressions, be careful to ensure that the result of the expression has the correct precision. When an arithmetic expression operates on a column, DB2 determines the data type of the numbers in the expression and decides the correct data type for the result. Remember the following rules for performing arithmetic with DB2 columns:

- DB2 supports addition, subtraction, multiplication, and division.

- DATE, TIME, and TIMESTAMP columns can be operated on only by means of addition and subtraction. (See the section "Use Date and Time Arithmetic with Care" later in this chapter.)

- Floating-point numbers are displayed in scientific notation. Avoid using floating-point numbers because scientific notation is difficult for some users to comprehend. DECIMAL columns can contain as many as 31 bytes of precision, which is adequate for most users.

- When an arithmetic expression operates on two numbers of different data types, DB2 returns the result using the data type with the highest precision. The only exception to this rule is that an expression involving two SMALLINT columns is returned as an INTEGER result.

The last rule may require additional clarification. When DB2 operates on two numbers, the result of the operation must be returned as a valid DB2 data type. Consult the following chart to determine the result data type for operations on any two numbers in DB2:

Statement	Yields
SMALLINT *operator* SMALLINT	INTEGER
SMALLINT *operator* INTEGER	INTEGER
SMALLINT *operator* DECIMAL	DECIMAL
SMALLINT *operator* FLOAT	FLOAT
INTEGER *operator* SMALLINT	INTEGER
INTEGER *operator* INTEGER	INTEGER
INTEGER *operator* DECIMAL	DECIMAL
INTEGER *operator* FLOAT	FLOAT
DECIMAL *operator* SMALLINT	DECIMAL
DECIMAL *operator* INTEGER	DECIMAL
DECIMAL *operator* DECIMAL	DECIMAL
DECIMAL *operator* FLOAT	FLOAT
FLOAT *operator* ANY DATA TYPE	FLOAT

For example, consider the following SELECT:

```
SELECT  EMPNO, EDLEVEL/2, SALARY/2
FROM    DSN8810.EMP
WHERE   EMPNO BETWEEN '000250' AND '000290';
```

This statement returns the following results:

```
EMPNO           COL1            COL2
000250           7              9590.00000000
000260           8              8625.00000000
000270           7             13690.00000000
000280           8             13125.00000000
000290           6              7670.00000000
```

```
DSNE610I NUMBER OF ROWS DISPLAYED IS 5
```

Because EDLEVEL is an INTEGER and 2 is specified as an INTEGER, the result in COL1 is truncated and specified as an INTEGER. Because SALARY is a DECIMAL column and 2 is specified as an INTEGER, the result is a DECIMAL. If you must return a more precise number for COL1, consider specifying EDLEVEL/2.0. The result is a DECIMAL because 2.0 is specified as a DECIMAL.

V7 As of DB2 V7, you can use the MULTIPLY_ALT function to assure precision. MULTIPLY_ALT is preferable to the multiplication operator when performing decimal arithmetic where a scale of at least 3 is desired and the sum of the precisions exceeds 31. With MULTIPLY_ALT, DB2 performs the internal computation avoiding overflows. For example, the result of the following expression is the value of COL1 multiplied by the value of :HV2:

```
MULTIPLY_ALT(COL1, :HV2)
```

The precision of the result will be the precision of each argument added together (unless that is greater than 31, in which case, the precision will be 31). The scale of the result is determined as follows:

- If the scale of both arguments is 0, the scale of the result will be 0.

- If the sum of the two precisions added together is less than or equal to 31, the scale of the result will be either the two scales added together or 31, whichever is smaller.

- If the sum of the two precisions added together is greater than 31, the scale of the result will be determined using the following formula:

  ```
  MAX( MIN(3, s1+s2), 31-(p1-s1+p2-s2) )
  ```

  where s1 is the scale of the first argument, and so on.

Use Column Renaming with Arithmetic Expressions and Functions   You can use the AS clause to give arithmetic expressions a column name, as follows:

```
SELECT  EMPNO, EDLEVEL/2 AS HALF_EDLEVEL, SALARY/2 AS HALF_SALARY
FROM    DSN8810.EMP
WHERE   EMPNO BETWEEN '000250' AND '000290';
```

If you give expressions a descriptive name, SQL becomes easier to understand and maintain. Likewise, when specifying functions in the SELECT list, use the AS clause to give the new column a name.

Decimal Precision and Scale   The precision of a decimal number is the total number of digits in the number (do not count the decimal point). For example, the number 983.201 has a precision of 6. The scale of a decimal number is equal to the number of digits to the right of the decimal point. In the previous example, the scale is 3.

Avoid Arithmetic in Column Expressions   An index is not used for a column when the column participates in an arithmetic expression. For example, the predicate in the following statement is non-indexable:

```
SELECT  PROJNO
FROM    DSN8810.PROJ
WHERE   PRSTDATE - 10 DAYS = :HV-DATE;
```

You have two options to make the predicate indexable. You can switch the arithmetic to the non-column side of the predicate. For example

```
SELECT  PROJNO
FROM    DSN8810.PROJ
WHERE   PRSTDATE = DATE(:HV-DATE) + 10 DAYS;
```

It makes no logical difference whether you subtract 10 from the column on the left side of the predicate, or add 10 to the host variable on the right side of the predicate. However, it makes a big performance difference because DB2 can use an index to evaluate non-column arithmetic expressions.

Alternatively, you can perform calculations before the SQL statement and then use the result in the query. For example, you could recode the previous SQL statement as this sequence of COBOL and SQL:

```
ADD +10 TO HV-DATE.              COBOL

SELECT  PROJNO                   SQL
FROM    DSN8810.PROJ
WHERE   PRSTDATE = :HV-DATE;
```

In general, though, it is wise to avoid arithmetic in predicates altogether, if possible. In this case, however, we are dealing with date arithmetic, which can be difficult to emulate in a program.

The fewer arithmetic expressions in the SQL statement, the easier it is to understand the SQL. Furthermore, if arithmetic is avoided in SQL, you do not need to remember the exact formulations which are indexable and Stage 1. For these reasons, favor performing arithmetic outside of the SQL when possible.

Use the Dummy Table to Select Data not in a DB2 Table   Sometimes you will need to use DB2 facilities to retrieve data that is not stored in a DB2 table. This can be a challenge until you learn about the dummy table, SYSIBM.SYSDUMMY1.

Why would you want to SELECT data that is not stored in a DB2 table? Well, perhaps you need to use a function that does not require DB2 table data. One such function is RAND, which is used to return a random number. To use this function, you can select it from the dummy table as follows:

```
SELECT RAND(:HOSTVAR)
FROM   SYSIBM.SYSDUMMY1;
```

The dummy table is part of the DB2 Catalog and is available to all DB2 installations.

> **NOTE**
>
> Take care when using the RAND function to generate a random value. To get a random value every time, use RAND(), without the host variable. If using a host variable, supplying it with the same value will cause RAND always to return the same random value. Of course, this can be useful if you want consistent random values to be generated.

Use Date and Time Arithmetic with Care   DB2 enables you to add and subtract DATE, TIME, and TIMESTAMP columns. In addition, you can add date and time durations to or subtract them from these columns.

Use date and time arithmetic with care. If users understand the capabilities and features of date and time arithmetic, they should have few problems implementing it. Keep the following rules in mind:

- When you issue date arithmetic statements using durations, do not try to establish a common conversion factor between durations of different types. For example, the date arithmetic statement

    ```
    DATE('2004/04/03') - 1 MONTH
    ```

    is *not* equivalent to the statement

    ```
    DATE('2004/04/03') - 30 DAYS
    ```

    April has 30 days, so the normal response would be to subtract 30 days to subtract one month. The result of the first statement is 2004/03/03, but the result of the second statement is 2004/03/04. In general, use like durations (for example, use months or use days, but not both) when you issue date arithmetic.

- If one operand is a date, the other operand must be a date or a date duration. If one operand is a time, the other operand must be a time or a time duration. You cannot mix durations and data types with date and time arithmetic.

- If one operand is a timestamp, the other operand can be a time, a date, a time duration, or a date duration. The second operand cannot be a timestamp. You can mix date and time durations with timestamp data types.

- Date durations are expressed as a DECIMAL(8,0) number. The valid date durations are

DAY	DAYS
MONTH	MONTHS
YEAR	YEARS

- Time durations are expressed as a DECIMAL(6,0) number. The valid time durations are

HOUR	HOURS
MINUTE	MINUTES
SECOND	SECONDS
MICROSECOND	MICROSECONDS

Additional guidelines on handling date and time data in DB2 are provided in the "Date and Time Guidelines" section later in this chapter.

Use Built-in Functions Where Available   DB2 comes with more than 120 built-in functions that can be used in SQL statements to transform data from one state to another. Use the built-in functions instead of performing similar functionality in your application programs.

Prior to Version 6, DB2 provided only a minimal set of built-in functions. As such, developers needed to write their own work-arounds to achieve certain functionality. For example, previous editions of this book recommended using the following logic to return a day of the week

```
DAYS(CURRENT DATE) - (DAYS(CURRENT DATE)/7) * 7
```

However, DB2 now provides a DAYOFWEEK function that is easier to use and understand than this expression. I do not recommend going back to your old programs and retrofitting them to use the new functions because the manpower required would be excessive and the return would be marginal. However, for all new and future SQL, use the built-in functions. For more information on the built-in functions available to DB2 consult Chapter 3, "Using DB2 Functions."

V7

NOTE

As of V7, DB2 also provides the DAYOFWEEK_ISO function. This function is similar to the DAYOFWEEK function, but results in different numbers to represent the days of the week. For DAYOFWEEK_ISO, the result is a number where 1 represents Monday, 2 Tuesday, 3 Wednesday, 4 Thursday, 5 Friday, 6 Saturday, and 7 Sunday. For DAYOFWEEK, the resulting value is a number where 1 represents Sunday, 2 Monday, 3 Tuesday, 4 Wednesday, 5 Thursday, 6 Friday, and 7 Saturday.

Unfortunately, neither of the results matches the results of the old formula (0 for Sunday, 1 for Monday and so on), as returned by

```
DAYS(CURRENT DATE) - (DAYS(CURRENT DATE)/7) * 7
```

Limit the Use of Scalar Functions in WHERE **Clauses**   For performance reasons, you can try to avoid using scalar functions referencing columns in WHERE clauses, but do not read too much into this recommendation. It is still wise to use scalar functions to offload work from the application to DB2. But remember that an index is not used for columns to which scalar functions are applied. Scalar functions typically can be used in the SELECT list of SQL statements with no performance degradation.

Specify the Number of Rows to Be Returned   When you code a cursor to fetch a predictable number of rows, consider specifying the number of rows to be retrieved in the OPTIMIZE FOR n ROWS clause of the CURSOR. This way, DB2 can select the optimal access path for the statement based on actual use.

Coding the OPTIMIZE FOR n ROWS clause of the CURSOR does not limit your program from fetching more than the specified number of rows.

This statement can cause your program to be inefficient, however, when many more rows or many fewer rows than specified are retrieved. So be sure you specify a reasonable esti-mate for the number of rows to be returned if you code this clause.

Disable List Prefetch Using OPTIMIZE FOR 1 ROW   If a particular query experiences sub-optimal performance due to list prefetch, consider specifying OPTIMIZE FOR 1 ROW. Doing so makes it less likely that DB2 will choose an access path that uses list prefetch. This capability might be of particular use in an online environment in which data is displayed to the end user a screen at a time.

> **NOTE**
>
> Keep in mind that there is a difference between OPTIMIZE FOR 1 ROW and OPTIMIZE FOR n
> ROWS (were n is greater than 1). OPTIMIZE FOR 1 ROW tries to avoid sorts; OPTIMIZE FOR n ROWS
> will try to use the least cost access path for n.

Disable Index Access   During the tuning process, you can append OR 0 = 1 to a predicate to eliminate index access. For example, consider a query against the EMP table on which two indexes exist: one on EMPNO and one on WORKDEPT.

```
SELECT   EMPNO, WORKDEPT, EDLEVEL, SALARY
FROM     DSN8810.EMP
WHERE    EMPNO BETWEEN '000020' AND '000350'
AND      (WORKDEPT > 'A01' OR 0 = 1);
```

In this case, the 0 = 1 prohibits DB2 from choosing the WORKDEPT index by making the predicate Stage 2. This forces DB2 to use either the index on EMPNO or a table space scan. Similar techniques include adding 0 to a numeric column or appending a null string to a character column to avoid indexed access. The latter is preferred because it disables match-ing index access but leaves the predicate Stage 1. For example:

```
SELECT   EMPNO, WORKDEPT, EDLEVEL, SALARY
FROM     DSN8810.EMP
WHERE    EMPNO BETWEEN '000020' AND '000350'
AND      WORKDEPT > 'A01' CONCAT ' ';
```

Consider Other Forms of Query Tweaking   Both OPTIMIZE FOR 1 ROW and using OR 0=1 are valid query tweaks for specific types of tuning. The following techniques can be used to tweak queries to try to encourage DB2 to use different access paths:

OPTIMIZE FOR *n* ROWS: Note that the *n* can be any value.

FETCH FIRST *n* ROWS ONLY: Again, where *n* can be any value.

No Operation (+0, -0, /1, *1, CONCAT ''):   Adding or subtracting zero, dividing or multiplying by 1, or concatenating an empty string will not change the results of a query but might change the optimizer's decision.

These techniques can cause DB2 to choose a different access path. Consider using them when you are in a jam and need to try different types of access. Compare and contrast the results and costs of each scenario to determine which might be most useful to your particular situation.

Although non-column expressions are indexable (at least as of DB2 V5), IBM has made an exception for the "no operation" expressions because they are used as tricks to fool the optimizer. IBM did not include these expressions because these tricks were deployed by DB2 developers to avoid indexed access for more than a decade. An example SQL statement using one of these tricks follows:

```
SELECT  EMPNO, WORKDEPT, EDLEVEL, SALARY
FROM    DSN8810.EMP
WHERE   EMPNO < :HOST-VAR CONCAT '';
```

In this case, a table space scan is used because an empty string is concatenated to the host variable in the predicate and no other predicates are available for indexed access. However, the predicate remains Stage 1.

Consider Using REOPT to Change Access Paths   When SQL is bound into a plan or package you can specify whether to have DB2 determine an access path at runtime using values for host variables, parameter markers, and special registers. This is achieved using the REOPT (or NOREOPT) parameter.

Specifying NOREOPT(VARS) will cause DB2 to determine access paths at BIND time, and not at runtime. Instead, specifying REOPT(VARS) will cause DB2 to redetermine the access path at runtime. Consider choosing this option if performance fluctuates based on the values supplied to host variables and parameter markers when your program is run.

V8   DB2 V8 introduces another useful REOPT option, REOPT(ONCE). Consider choosing REOPT(ONCE) instead of REOPT(VARS) when you wish to avoid constantly recalculating access paths at a PREPARE. With REOPT(ONCE), access path selection will be deferred until the cursor is opened. The host variable and parameter marker values at cursor OPEN time will be used to determine the access path. The resultant access path will be cached in the global prepare cache.

Be Aware of Table Space Partitioning Key Ranges   When you access data in partitioned table spaces, be aware of the values used for the partitioning scheme. Prior to V4, DB2 scanned the entire table in a table space scan of a partitioned table. As of DB2 V4, you can limit a table space scan to accessing a subset of the partitions if the predicates of the WHERE clause can be used to limit the key ranges that need to be scanned. As of DB2 V5, the key ranges do not have to be contiguous.

For this technique to work with host variables you must BIND using the REOPT(VARS) parameter.

Specify Isolation Level for Individual SQL Statements   You can use the WITH clause to specify an explicit isolation level at the SQL statement level. Four options are available:

> WITH RR: Repeatable Read
>
> WITH RS: Read Stability
>
> WITH CS: Cursor Stability
>
> WITH UR: Uncommitted Read (can be specified only if the result table is read-only)

Sometimes it makes sense to change the isolation level of an SQL statement within a program, without changing the isolation level of the other SQL statements in the program. For example, one query might be able to tolerate a dirty read because the data is being aggregated and only an estimated result is required. In this case, that query can be specified as WITH UR, even though the package for the program is bound as ISOLATION(CS).

Use the WITH clause when you need to change the isolation level for specific SQL statements within a package or plan. More information on isolation levels is provided in Chapter 13, "Program Preparation."

V8

CAUTION

Do not confuse the use of WITH to specify isolation levels with the use of WITH to specify common table expressions. Common table expressions were introduced with DB2 Version 8 and are placed at the beginning of SQL statements. SQL statement isolation levels are placed at the end of SQL statements.

An example of a common table expression is given later in this chapter in the section titled "Common Table Expressions and Recursion."

Consider KEEP UPDATE LOCKS to Serialize Updates   The KEEP UPDATE LOCKS clause can be specified for RR and RS isolation levels. With KEEP UPDATE LOCKS, DB2 acquires X locks instead of U or S locks on all qualified rows or pages. Use this option to serialize updates when concurrency is not an issue.

V7 **Use SQL Assist to Help Build SQL Statements**   SQL Assist is a new feature of DB2 Version 7 that can greatly assist SQL developers. The SQL Assist feature is a GUI-driven tool to help you build SQL statements like SELECT, INSERT, UPDATE, and DELETE. Simply by picking and clicking SQL Assist will build syntactically correct SQL statements. Refer to Figure 2.2 for an example of SQL Assist. It is accessible from the following "products":

- Control Center
- DB2 Development Center (a.k.a Stored Procedure Builder)
- Data Warehouse Center

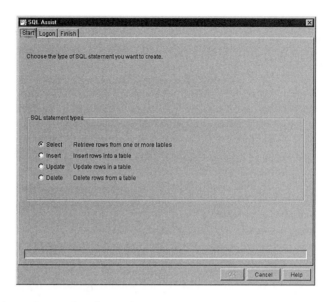

FIGURE 2.2   SQL Assist graphically guides SQL creation.

SQL Assist can be used to help developers build correct SQL statements, but it does not provide SQL performance advice. Using SQL Assist, however, can help to promote using a standard format for SQL statements within your organization.

Complex SQL Guidelines

The preceding section provided guidelines for simple SQL SELECT statements. These statements retrieve rows from a single table only. Complex SQL can use a single SQL SELECT statement to retrieve rows from different tables. There are five *basic* categories of complex SQL statements, namely

- Joins
- Subqueries
- Table Expressions (also known as in-line views)
- Unions
- Grouping

Other forms of complex SQL, such as common table expressions and recursion, are covered later in this chapter.

Before delving into each of the five basic categories let's first discuss a general approach to writing complex SQL. It is a good practice to build complex SQL in steps. Start with simple SQL, test it for accuracy, and slowly add any additional elements required to return the proper results. For example, if you need to access three tables do not start by trying to build a single SQL statement that references all three tables. Start with one table and code the local predicates for that table. Test it for accuracy. When that works, add any grouping, sorting, and functions that might be needed. Test again. Only when you are retrieving the proper data from the first table should you add an additional table and its join predicates to the statement. Repeating this process for each table allows you to slowly build complex SQL instead of just jumping in and starting off complex—which can be confusing and error-prone.

Retrieving Data From Multiple Tables

There are three basic ways to retrieve data from multiple tables in a single DB2 query: joins, subqueries, and table expressions.

A **join** references multiple tables in the FROM clause of a SELECT (or uses the JOIN keyword to combine tables). When joining tables, columns from any table in the join can be returned in the result set (simply by specifying the column names in the SELECT-list of the query).

A **subquery** is when one query references the results of another query. With subqueries, only those columns in the outermost table in the statement can be returned in the result set.

Table expressions are SQL statements that are used in place of a table in another SQL statement. As with joins, columns from any table in the statement can be returned in the result set.

Truthfully, there are four ways to access data from multiple tables in a single query if you include **unions**. A UNION, however, is fundamentally different from a join, subquery, or table expression because each SQL statement that is unioned returns a portion of the results set.

The following guidelines offer advice for complex SQL using joins, subqueries, table expressions, and unions.

UNION **Versus** UNION ALL   The UNION operator always results in a sort. When the UNION operator connects two SELECT statements, both SELECT statements are issued, the rows are sorted, and all duplicates are eliminated. If you want to avoid duplicates, use the UNION operator.

The UNION ALL operator, by contrast, does not invoke a sort. The SELECT statements connected by UNION ALL are executed, and all rows from the first SELECT statement are appended to all rows from the second SELECT statement. Duplicate rows might exist. Use UNION ALL when duplicate rows are required or, at least, are not a problem. Also use UNION ALL when you know that the SELECT statements will not return duplicates.

Use NOT EXISTS **Instead of** NOT IN   When you code a subquery using negation logic, try to use NOT EXISTS instead of NOT IN to increase the efficiency of your SQL statement. When you use NOT EXISTS, DB2 must verify only nonexistence. Doing so can reduce processing time significantly. With the NOT IN predicate, DB2 must materialize and sort the complete subquery results set.

Order the Elements in Your IN Lists   The order of elements in a SQL IN list can impact performance when an index is not used to process the IN list. DB2 will search the list of elements from left to right until a match is found or the end of the list is reached. For this reason, code the most commonly occurring values first in your IN lists. Doing so will cause DB2 to match as early as possible most of the time—thereby improving performance. For example, consider the following SQL statement:

```
SELECT  EMPNO, WORKDEPT, EDLEVEL, SALARY
FROM    DSN8810.EMP
WHERE   WORKDEPT IN ('A00', 'A01', 'E21');
```

This SQL statement demonstrates the natural tendency to order lists alphabetically or numerically. The statement is correctly coded only if A00 occurs more often than A01, which occurs more often than E21. But if A01 was most common, followed by E21 and then A00, the statement would be better coded (performance-wise) as

```
SELECT  EMPNO, WORKDEPT, EDLEVEL, SALARY
FROM    DSN8810.EMP
WHERE   WORKDEPT IN ('A01', 'E21', 'A00');
```

Remove Duplicates from Your IN Lists   When using the IN predicate with a list of values, DB2 sorts the IN-list into ascending sequence and removes duplicates if the column specified is indexed. The IN-list values are then used to probe the index to find the matching rows. However, if there is no index for the column, DB2 will not sort the IN-list and any duplicates will remain. Upon retrieval of a row, the column value is used to search the IN-list (duplicates and all).

Therefore, it makes sense to order the elements of the IN-list, code your most restrictive predicates first, and never code duplicates in the IN-list.

Be Aware of Predicate Transitive Closure Rules   *Predicate transitive closure* refers to the capability of the DB2 optimizer to use the rule of transitivity (if A=B and B=C, then A=C) to determine the most efficient access path for queries. The optimizer did not always have the capability to use the rule of transitivity.

In older releases of DB2, you produced a more efficient query by providing redundant information in the WHERE clause of a join statement, as in this example

```
SELECT  A.COL1, A.COL2, B.COL1
FROM    TABLEA A, TABLEB B
WHERE   A.COL1 = B.COL1
AND     A.COL1 = :HOSTVAR;
```

This query could process more efficiently in pre-V2.1 releases of DB2 by coding a redundant predicate, as follows:

```
SELECT  A.COL1, A.COL2, B.COL1
FROM    TABLEA A,
        TABLEB B
WHERE   A.COL1 = B.COL1
AND     A.COL1 = :HOSTVAR
AND     B.COL1 = :HOSTVAR;
```

The need to code redundant predicates for performance no longer exists for equality and range predicates. However, predicate transitive closure is not applied with LIKE or IN predicates. Consider this example:

```
SELECT  A.COL1, A.COL2, B.COL1
FROM    TABLEA A,
        TABLEB B
WHERE   A.COL1 = B.COL1
AND     A.COL1 LIKE 'ABC%';
```

The preceding can be more efficiently coded as follows:

```
SELECT  A.COL1, A.COL2, B.COL1
FROM    TABLEA A,
        TABLEB B
WHERE   A.COL1 = B.COL1
AND     A.COL1 LIKE 'ABC%'
AND     B.COL1 LIKE 'ABC%';
```

Unless you're using an IN or LIKE clause, or you are running on an ancient version of DB2 (pre V2.3) do not code redundant predicates; doing so is unnecessary and might cause the query to be less efficient.

Use SQL to Determine "Top Ten"   Application developers frequently wish to retrieve a limited number of qualifying rows from a table. For example, maybe you need to list the ten highest selling items from inventory or the top ten most expensive products (that is, the products with the highest price tags). There are several ways to accomplish this prior to DB2 V7 using SQL, but they are not necessarily efficient.

The basic question that arises frequently is how best to return only a portion of the actual result set for a query. This situation most frequently manifests itself in the "Top Ten" problem (for example, returning the top-ten highest salaries in the company).

The first reaction is to simply use the WHERE clause to eliminate non-qualifying rows. But this is simplistic, and often is not sufficient to produce the results desired in an optimal manner. What if the program only requires that the top ten results be returned? This can be a somewhat difficult request to formulate using SQL alone. Consider, for example, an application that needs to retrieve only the ten highest-paid employees from the EMP sample table. You could simply issue a SQL request that retrieves all of the employees in order by salary, but only use the first ten retrieved. That is easy, for example

```
SELECT  SALARY, EMPNO, LASTNAME
FROM    DSN8810.EMP
ORDER BY SALARY DESC;
```

It is imperative that you specify the ORDER BY clause with the DESC keyword. This sorts the results into descending order, instead of the default, which is ascending. Without the DESC key word, the "top ten" would be at the very end of the results set, not at the beginning.

But this "solution" does not really satisfy the requirement—retrieving only the top ten. It merely sorts the results into descending sequence. So the results would still be all employees in the table, but in the correct order so you can view the "top ten" salaries very easily.

The ideal solution should return **only** the ten employees with the highest salaries and not merely a sorted list of all employees. Consider the following SQL:

```
SELECT SALARY, EMPNO, LASTNAME
FROM    DSN8810.EMP  E1
WHERE  10 > (SELECT COUNT(*)
            FROM    DSN8810.EMP E2
            WHERE  E1.SALARY < E2.SALARY);
```

The ten highest salaries are returned. You can alter the actual number by changing the literal value 10 to whatever number you want. This particular SQL does not perform very well, but it will work with all versions of DB2.

V7 As of DB2 Version 7, the best way to perform this function is to use a query with the FETCH FIRST *n* ROWS ONLY clause. So, the query becomes:

```
SELECT SALARY, EMPNO, LASTNAME
FROM    DSN8810.EMP
ORDER BY SALARY DESC
FETCH FIRST 10 ROWS ONLY;
```

The ORDER BY clause will sort the data into descending order by SALARY values. The FETCH FIRST 10 ROWS ONLY clause will limit your output to 10 rows only. If duplicates are possible you can eliminate them by adding a DISTINCT clause after the SELECT and before the columns being selected.

V7 **Use FETCH FIRST *n* ROWS ONLY to Limit the Size of SQL Result Sets** The FETCH FIRST *n* ROWS ONLY clause can limit the number of qualifying rows for any SELECT statement. You can code FETCH FIRST *n* ROWS, which will limit the number of rows fetched and returned by a SELECT statement. So, for example, to limit your results to 371 rows, you could code

```
SELECT SALARY, EMPNO, LASTNAME
FROM    DSN8810.EMP
FETCH FIRST 371 ROWS ONLY;
```

The SQLCODE will be set to +100 when you try to FETCH row number 372, or at the end of the result set if there are fewer than 371 rows.

> **CAUTION**
>
> The FETCH FIRST *n* ROWS ONLY clause is not the same as the OPTIMIZE FOR *n* ROWS clause. The FETCH FIRST clause will cause your cursor to stop returning rows after *n* rows have been returned; the OPTIMIZE FOR clause will not (it just gives guidance to the DB2 optimizer for access path formulation).
>
> However, specifying FETCH FIRST causes DB2 to use an implicit OPTIMIZE FOR clause with the same number for *n*. So, specifying FETCH FIRST 12 ROWS ONLY causes DB2 to use an implicit OPTIMIZE FOR 12 ROWS; you do not need to code the OPTIMIZE FOR clause.

Keep in mind that this discussion differs from the previous guideline because we do not care about order (or the "top" so many rows), just limiting the number of rows to some preset number. That is why an ORDER BY is not required.

> **CAUTION**
>
> If you do not provide an ORDER BY clause on a query that uses the FETCH FIRST n ROWS ONLY clause, your results will be unpredictable. Remember, there is no inherent order to a DB2 table, so the order in which rows are returned is based on the access path chosen by the DB2 optimizer. So, although the FETCH FIRST n ROWS ONLY clause will limit your result set to n, you are **not** guaranteed to retrieve the same n rows every time.

Code Appropriate Existence Checking SQL   There are times when a program just needs to know that some given data exists and does not need to actually retrieve and use that data. For these situations you will need to develop the most efficient SQL possible that just checks if the specific data exists. But what is the best way to accomplish an existence check?

Prior to DB2 V7, the best way to check for existence is to use a correlated query against the SYSDUMMY1 table. For example, to check for the existence of an employee with the last name of Jones in the EMP table, the SQL would look like this:

```
SELECT 1
FROM    SYSIBM.SYSDUMMY1 A
WHERE   EXISTS (SELECT 1
               FROM    DSN8810.EMP B
               WHERE   LASTNAME = 'JONES'
               AND A.IBMREQD = A.IBMREQD);
```

Sometimes, though, we need more information. Perhaps we need to list all employees who are responsible for at least one project. That can be coded as follows:

```
SELECT  EMPNO
FROM    DSN8810.EMP    E
WHERE   EXISTS
        (SELECT  1
         FROM    DSN8810.PROJ    P
         WHERE   P.RESPEMP = E.EMPNO);
```

First, notice that we just SELECT the constant 1. Because the data does not need to be returned to the program, the SQL statement need not specify any columns in the SELECT-list. We simply check the SQLCODE. If the SQLCODE is zero, data exists; if not, the data does not exist.

If you do not use a correlated query with EXISTS, but instead simply issue the SELECT statement, performance can suffer as DB2 scans to find subsequent occurrences of the data—which might be many, especially for a common name such as Jones. Of course, if a unique index exists on the column(s) in question, then you can get by with the simple query.

V7   Which brings us to DB2 V7. In this version IBM added a new clause called FETCH FIRST n ROWS ONLY. This solves our problem for existence checking and should be the new standard after you move to DB2 V7. Going back to our example, the SQL for existence checking now becomes:

```
SELECT 1
FROM   DSN8810.EMP
WHERE  LASTNAME = 'JONES'
FETCH FIRST 1 ROW ONLY;
```

We still do not specify columns in the SELECT-list, but we no longer need the correlated query. DB2 will stop after 1 row has been checked—which is the desired result.

Minimize the Number of Tables in a Join   Joining many tables in one query can adversely affect performance. Although the maximum number of tables that can be joined in a single SQL statement is 225, the practical limit is usually fewer.

V8

> **CAUTION**
>
> Prior to DB2 V6, the limit for tables in a SQL statement was 15. DB2 V6 actually increased the limit for tables in a SQL statement from 15 to 225, but in a restricted manner: Each SQL statement can consist of up to 15 Query Blocks, each directly or indirectly identifying 15 base table references. The grand total number of tables for a single SQL statement is 225; however, no query block can exceed 15 base table references, whether direct or indirect.
>
> DB2 V8 removes this restriction; each SQL statement can reference up to 225 tables in total. The limit has been raised to such a high number to accommodate ERP vendors such as Peoplesoft and SAP, whose applications were designed originally for other RDBMS packages, such as Oracle, that have higher limits than DB2. Just because the limit has been increased does not mean you should write queries that access such a large number of tables. The performance of such queries will likely be poor and difficult to manage.

However, setting an artificial limit on the standard number of tables per join is not a wise course of action. In some situations, avoiding large, complex joins in an online environment may be necessary. But the same statement might be completely acceptable in a batch job or as an ad hoc request.

The number of tables to be joined in any application should be based on the following:

- The total number of rows participating in the join

- The results you want to obtain from the query

- The level of performance you want

- The anticipated throughput of the application

- The type of application (OLTP versus OLAP or DSS)

- The environment in which the application will operate (online versus batch)

- The availability you want (for example, 24×7)

In general, however, always eliminate unnecessary tables from your join statement.

Consider CASE Expressions to Optimize Counting   When you need to produce counts of rows in DB2 tables, consider using a CASE expression instead of using multiple SQL SELECT statements. For example, if you need to count the number of employees who earn different salary ranges, consider the following statement

```
SELECT SUM(CASE WHEN SALARY BETWEEN 0 AND 20000
                THEN 1 ELSE 0 END) AS UPTO20
      ,SUM(CASE WHEN SALARY BETWEEN 20001 AND 50000
                THEN 1 ELSE 0 END) AS FROM20TO50
      ,SUM(CASE WHEN SALARY BETWEEN 50001 AND 80000
                THEN 1 ELSE 0 END) AS FROM50TO80
      ,SUM(CASE WHEN SALARY > 80000
                THEN 1 ELSE 0 END) AS OVER80
      ,SUM(CASE WHEN SALARY < 0
                THEN 1 ELSE 0 END) AS NEGATIVESAL
FROM DSN8810.EMP;
```

This SELECT statement efficiently scans through the data and produces a sum for each range that is defined. The multiple CASE expressions return either a 0 or a 1. The SUM function just adds up the values and you get totals for employees within each range.

This outperforms multiple SELECT statements using COUNT(*) because DB2 can keep running totals as it passes once through the data using the CASE expressions.

CAUTION

The previous example shows the CASE expression returning either a 0 or a 1. If you did not include the ELSE portion of each CASE expression, DB2 would return either a 1 or a NULL. This can be more efficient than returning 1 or 0 for very large sets of data. This is so because DB2 will actually add the zeroes, but it can ignore the NULLs.

However, be careful, because if there are any categories where no rows apply, then DB2 will SUM up a bunch of NULLs—which returns NULL, not 0 as the result.

Consider Denormalizing to Reduce Joins   To minimize the need for joins, consider denormalization. Remember, however, that denormalization usually implies redundant data, dual updating, and extra DASD usage. Normalization optimizes data modification at the expense of data access; denormalization optimizes data access at the expense of data modification.

Whenever you denormalize be sure to document the specific reasons for the denormalization, as well as listing each specific change made to the database structure. Denormalization should be undertaken only as a last resort. You can find additional denormalization assistance in Chapter 5.

Reduce the Number of Rows to Be Joined   The number of rows participating in a join is the single most important determinant in predicting the response time of a join. To reduce join response time, reduce the number of rows to be joined in the join's predicates.

For example, when you try to determine which males in all departments reporting to department D01 make a salary of $40,000 or more, you can code the predicates for both SEX and SALARY as follows:

```
SELECT  E.LASTNAME, E.FIRSTNME
FROM    DSN8810.DEPT  D,
        DSN8810.EMP   E
WHERE   D.ADMRDEPT = 'D01'
```

```
AND     D.DEPTNO = E.WORKDEPT
AND     E.SEX = 'M'
AND     E.SALARY >= 40000.00;
```

The predicates on the SEX and SALARY columns can be used to reduce the amount of data that needs to be joined. If you fail to code either of the last two predicates, deciding instead to scan the results and pull out the information you need, more rows qualify for the join and the join is less efficient.

Join Using SQL Instead of Program Logic   Coding a join using SQL instead of COBOL or another high-level language is almost always more efficient. The DB2 optimizer has a vast array of tools in its arsenal to optimize the performance of SQL queries. Usually, a programmer will fail to consider the same number of possibilities as DB2.

If a specific SQL join is causing high overhead, consider the tuning options outlined in this chapter before deciding to implement the join using a program. To further emphasize the point, consider the results of a recent test. A three table join using GROUP BY and the COUNT(*) function similar to the one below was run:

```
SELECT    A.EMPNO, LASTNAME, COUNT(*)
FROM      DSN8810.EMP          E,
          DSN8810.EMPPROJACT   A,
          DSN8810.PROJ         P
WHERE     E.EMPNO = A.EMPNO
AND       P.PROJNAME IN ('PROJECT1', 'PROJECT7', 'PROJECT9')
AND       A.PROJNO = P.PROJNO
AND       A.EMPTIME > 40.0
GROUP BY A.EMPNO, LASTNAME;
```

Additionally, an equivalent program was coded using three cursors (one for each join), internal sorting (using Syncsort, DFSORT, or a similar utility), and programmatic counting. Performance reports were run on both, and the SQL statement outperformed the equivalent application program by several orders of magnitude in terms of both elapsed time and CPU time.

Programming your own application joins should *always* be a very last resort and should not be considered unless you have exhausted all other tuning techniques. In practice, application joins are almost never needed for performance reasons.

Use Joins Instead of Subqueries   A join can be more efficient than a correlated subquery or a subquery using IN. For example, this query joins two tables:

```
SELECT    EMPNO, LASTNAME
FROM      DSN8810.EMP,
          DSN8810.PROJ
WHERE     WORKDEPT = DEPTNO
AND       EMPNO = RESPEMP;
```

The preceding example is usually more efficient than the following query, which is formulated as a correlated subquery accessing the same two tables:

```
SELECT    EMPNO, LASTNAME
FROM      DSN8810.EMP X
```

```
WHERE    WORKDEPT IN
        (SELECT  DEPTNO
         FROM    DSN8810.PROJ
         WHERE   RESPEMP = X.EMPNO);
```

The preceding two queries demonstrate how to turn a correlated subquery into a join. You can translate non-correlated subqueries into joins in the same manner. For example, the join

```
SELECT   EMPNO, LASTNAME
FROM     DSN8810.EMP,
         DSN8810.DEPT
WHERE    WORKDEPT = DEPTNO
AND      DEPTNAME = 'PLANNING';
```

is usually more efficient than the subquery

```
SELECT   EMPNO, LASTNAME
FROM     DSN8810.EMP
WHERE    WORKDEPT IN
        (SELECT  DEPTNO
         FROM    DSN8810.DEPT
         WHERE   DEPTNAME = 'PLANNING');
```

Note that these two queries do not necessarily return the same results. If DEPTNO is not unique, the first SELECT statement could return more rows than the second SELECT statement, and some of the values for EMPNO could appear more than once in the results table.

Be aware, however, that with each new release of DB2, subqueries (both correlated and non-correlated) are becoming more and more efficient. Yet, performance concerns aside, standardizing on joins instead of subqueries (when possible) can make development and maintenance easier because fewer query formulations need to be considered during implementation, or modified during maintenance cycles. Additionally, in certain cases DB2 may transform subqueries into joins during optimization.

Join on Clustered Columns   When you join large tables, use clustered columns in the join criteria when possible. This way, you can reduce the need for intermediate sorts. Note that doing so might require clustering of the parent table by primary key and the child table by foreign key.

Join on Indexed Columns   The efficiency of your program improves when tables are joined based on indexed columns rather than on non-indexed ones. To increase the performance of joins, consider creating indexes specifically for the predicates being joined.

Use Caution When Specifying ORDER BY **with a Join**   When the results of a join must be sorted, limiting the ORDER BY to columns of a single table can cause DB2 to avoid a sort. Whenever you specify columns from multiple tables in the ORDER BY clause of a join statement, DB2 invokes a sort.

V8   In DB2 V8, you can alleviate the pain of the multi-table ORDER BY by using a Materialized Query Table, which is covered in detail in Chapter 45, "Data Warehousing with DB2."

Avoid Cartesian Products   Never use a join statement without a predicate. A join without a predicate generates a results table in which every row from the first table is joined with every row from the other table: a Cartesian product. For example, joining—without a predicate—a 1,000 row table with another 1,000 row table results in a table with 1,000,000 rows. No additional information is provided by this join, so a lot of machine resources are wasted.

> **NOTE**
>
> Although you should never specify a Cartesian product in your SQL queries, the DB2 optimizer may decide to use a Cartesian product for a portion, or portions of a join. For example, when a star join is being used, the DB2 optimizer will choose to implement Cartesian products for portions of the join. This may happen in data warehousing queries and other ad hoc queries where multiple dimension tables are joined to a very large fact table. Because the fact table is usually many times larger than the dimension tables, processing the fact table only once against the Cartesian product of the fact tables can enhance query performance. As many as six dimension tables (five prior to DB2 V6) can be joined as a Cartesian product for a star join in DB2.
>
> For more information on star joins consult Chapter 45.

Provide Adequate Search Criteria   When possible, provide additional search criteria in the WHERE clause for every table in a join. These criteria are in addition to the join criteria, which are mandatory to avoid Cartesian products. This information provides DB2 with the best opportunity for ranking the tables to be joined in the most efficient manner (that is, for reducing the size of intermediate results tables). In general, the more information you provide to DB2 for a query, the better the chances that the query will perform adequately.

Consider Using Explicit INNER JOINs   Instead of specifying joins by using a comma-delimited list of tables in the FROM clause, use INNER JOIN with the ON clause. Explicit INNER JOIN syntax might help when you're training new programmers in SQL because it provides a join keyword. Likewise, the join predicates must be isolated in the ON clause when you're using an explicit INNER JOIN. This way, reading, tuning, and maintaining the SQL code are easier.

Use Explicit OUTER JOINs   Avoid coding an outer join in the old style, which required a simple SELECT, a UNION, and a correlated subselect.

> **NOTE**
>
> Prior to DB2 V4, this was the only way to code an outer join.

Instead use the SQL outer join syntax which is easier to code, easier to maintain, and more efficient to execute. An explicit OUTER JOIN uses one pass against the tables and as such usually outperforms an outer join using UNION or UNION ALL. Using explicit OUTER JOIN statements reduces the number of bugs and speeds application development time due solely to the significant reduction in lines of code required. Furthermore, as IBM improves

---

1 This is one of those rare circumstances where saying "never" is appropriate.

the optimizer over time, techniques designed to make outer joins more efficient will most likely focus only on the new, explicit outer join syntax and not on the old, complex SQL formulation.

Exception Reporting   You can use the bottom half of the old style of outer join to report just the exceptions when you don't need a full-blown outer join. Consider this example:

```
SELECT  D.DEPTNO, D.DEPTNAME, D.MGRNO, '* No Mgr Name *'
FROM    DSN8810.DEPT  D
WHERE   NOT EXISTS
        (SELECT  1
         FROM    DSN8810.EMP  E
         WHERE   D.MGRNO = E.EMPNO)
ORDER BY 1;
```

This SQL returns only the departments without a manager name.

Favor LEFT **Over** RIGHT OUTER JOINs   Favor coding LEFT OUTER JOIN over RIGHT OUTER JOIN. The choice is truly arbitrary, but the manner in which DB2 shows EXPLAIN information makes left outer joins easier to tune. EXPLAIN populates the JOIN_TYPE column to describe the outer join method (FULL, RIGHT, or LEFT). The column contains the value F for a FULL OUTER JOIN, L for a LEFT OUTER JOIN or RIGHT OUTER JOIN, or a blank for an INNER JOIN or no join. DB2 always converts right outer joins to left outer joins, so there is no R value for JOIN_TYPE.

The right outer join syntax is only available to make the query easier to read and understand. Because deciphering the PLAN_TABLE data is more difficult for a RIGHT OUTER JOIN than for a LEFT OUTER JOIN, favor coding left outer joins whenever possible.

Use COALESCE **with** FULL OUTER JOINs   At times, you might need the COALESCE function to avoid nulls in the result columns of OUTER JOIN statements. To understand how COALESCE can be useful in an outer join, consider the following query:

```
SELECT  EMP.EMPNO, EMP.WORKDEPT, DEPT.DEPTNAME
FROM    DSN8810.EMP EMP FULL OUTER JOIN DSN8810.DEPT DEPT
ON      EMP.WORKDEPT = DEPT.DEPTNO;
```

A portion of the results for this query looks like the following:

EMPNO	WORKDEPT	DEPTNAME
200330	E21	SOFTWARE SUPPORT
200340	E21	SOFTWARE SUPPORT
- - - - - -	- - -	DEVELOPMENT CENTER

Note that the department code for DEVELOPMENT CENTER is not displayed, even though you know by simple browsing of the DEPT table that the code is D01. The value is not returned because the query selects the WORKDEPT column from EMP, not the DEPTNO column from DEPT. You can rectify this situation by using the COALESCE function. The COALESCE function notifies DB2 to look for a value in both of the listed columns, one from each table in the outer join (in this case, EMP and DEPT). If a value is found in either table, it can be returned in the result set. Consider the following example:

```
SELECT   EMP.EMPNO,
         COALESCE(EMP.WORKDEPT, DEPT.DEPTNO) AS DEPTNUM,
         DEPT.DEPTNAME
FROM     DSN8810.EMP EMP FULL OUTER JOIN DSN8810.DEPT DEPT
ON       EMP.WORKDEPT = DEPT.DEPTNO;
```

The results are changed as follows:

EMPNO	DEPTNUM	DEPTNAME
200330	E21	SOFTWARE SUPPORT
200340	E21	SOFTWARE SUPPORT
- - - - - -	D01	DEVELOPMENT CENTER

In this case, the last row of the result set contains the correct department code. The COALESCE function determines that the department code is stored in the DEPT.DEPTNO column and returns that value instead of the null because there is no corresponding WORKDEPT number.

> **NOTE**
>
> The VALUE function is a synonym for the COALESCE function. Favor using COALESCE though as it adheres to the ANSI standard.

OUTER JOINs and Inline Views   Be aware that you might need to combine inline views (also known as nested table expressions) with the COALESCE function to return the appropriate results. Consider adding a local predicate to the preceding example:

```
SELECT   EMP.EMPNO,
         COALESCE(EMP.WORKDEPT, DEPT.DEPTNO) AS DEPTNUM,
         DEPT.DEPTNAME
FROM     DSN8810.EMP EMP FULL OUTER JOIN DSN8810.DEPT DEPT
ON       EMP.WORKDEPT = DEPT.DEPTNO
WHERE    EMP.WORKDEPT = 'D01';
```

In this case, no rows are returned. The 'D01' department number is aligned with the "DEVELOPMENT CENTER" in the DEPT table as DEPTNO, not in the EMP table as WORKDEPT. The solution is to use an inline view as follows:

```
SELECT   EMPNO, DEPTNUM, DEPTNAME
FROM     (SELECT EMPNO,
                 COALESCE(EMP.WORKDEPT, DEPT.DEPTNO) AS DEPTNUM,
                 DEPT.DEPTNAME
          FROM   DSN8810.EMP EMP FULL OUTER JOIN DSN8810.DEPT DEPT
          ON     EMP.WORKDEPT = DEPT.DEPTNO) AS OJ_EMP_DEPT
WHERE    DEPTNUM = 'D01';
```

This example finds the row for 'D01' because COALESCE is applied to the inline view before the local predicate is applied.

OUTER JOINs and Predicate Placement   Prior to DB2 V6 inline views were required to achieve optimal outer join performance. This restriction no longer exists. Consider the following OUTER JOIN with a local predicate:

```
SELECT  EMP.EMPNO, EMP.LASTNAME, DEPT.DEPTNAME
FROM    DSN8810.EMP EMP LEFT OUTER JOIN DSN8810.DEPT DEPT
ON      EMP.WORKDEPT = DEPT.DEPTNO
WHERE   EMP.SALARY > 50000.00;
```

Running under DB2 V6 or later, this query will execute quite efficiently. However, in past releases, if thousands or millions of rows were filtered out by additional predicates, this method of coding outer joins performed quite poorly because the outer join was performed first, before any rows were filtered out. To resolve this problem in V5 and earlier DB2 subsystems, ensure that the local predicate is applied before the outer join takes place, using an inline view as follows:

```
SELECT  E.EMPNO, E.LASTNAME, DEPT.DEPTNAME
FROM    (SELECT EMPNO, LASTNAME
          FROM DSN8810.EMP
          WHERE SALARY > 50000.00) AS E
         LEFT OUTER JOIN DSN8810.DEPT DEPT
         ON E.WORKDEPT = DEPT.DEPTNO;
```

By moving the local predicate into the FROM clause as an inline view, the local predicate is evaluated before the outer join, thereby reducing the number of rows to be joined and enhancing performance.

If additional local predicates are required, you can specify additional inline views. If you want to return rows only for which a domestic resource has responsibility, you can change the sample query as shown:

```
SELECT  E.EMPNO, E.LASTNAME, DEPT.DEPTNAME
FROM    (SELECT EMPNO, LASTNAME, WORKDEPT
          FROM EMP
          WHERE SALARY > 50000.00) AS E
         LEFT OUTER JOIN
         (SELECT DEPTNO, DEPTNAME
          FROM DEPT
          WHERE MGRNO IS NOT NULL) AS D
         ON E.WORKDEPT = DEPT.DEPTNO;
```

CAUTION

To reiterate, this tuning technique is applicable only to DB2 V4 and V5. Do not code outer joins with inline views in the manner described for DB2 V6 and later because the query will be more difficult to code, explain, and maintain.

Limit the Columns Grouped   When you use a GROUP BY clause to achieve data aggregation, specify only the columns that need to be grouped. Do not provide extraneous columns in the SELECT list and GROUP BY list. To accomplish data grouping, DB2 must sort the retrieved data before displaying it. The more columns that need to be sorted, the more work DB2 must do, and the poorer the performance of the SQL statement.

GROUP BY and ORDER BY Are Not Equivalent   Although the GROUP BY clause typically sorts data to aggregate, the results are not necessarily ordered by the GROUP BY. If you want to ensure that the results are displayed in a specific order, you must use the ORDER BY clause.

When you specify both GROUP BY and ORDER BY, and the ordering requirements are compatible, DB2 can avoid the redundant sort.

ORDER BY **and Columns Selected**   As of DB2 V6, and via a retrofit APAR to V5, it became possible to ORDER BY columns not specified in the SELECT-list. However, you cannot eliminate columns from the SELECT-list if they are specified in an ORDER BY if you also are using a column function, UNION, UNION ALL, GROUP BY, or DISTINCT.

V7 Keep in mind that as of DB2 V7, you no longer need to SELECT what you GROUP BY.

Use Table Expressions to Your Advantage   Table Expressions, sometimes called *inline views*, allow the FROM clause of a SELECT statement to contain another SELECT statement. You can write any table expression in the FROM clause.

Why would you want to use an inline view instead of simply creating an actual view prior to issuing the SELECT statement? The first potential benefit is that an inline view expression can be easier to understand. Instead of attempting to query the DB2 Catalog to extract the SQL definition of a view, the SQL is clearly displayed in the body of the SELECT statement. Second, inline views do not require object management because no DB2 object is created. Finally, inline views provide direct SQL support for certain complex queries that required a view prior to DB2 V4.

Inline views are useful, for example, when detail and aggregated information from a single table must be returned by a single query. A prime example is reporting on column length information from the DB2 Catalog. Consider a request to provide column details for each table, and on each row also report the maximum, minimum, and average column lengths for that table. One solution is to create a view. Consider the COL_LENGTH view based on SYSIBM.SYSCOLUMNS, as shown here:

```
CREATE VIEW COL_LENGTH
    (TABLE_NAME, MAX_LENGTH,
     MIN_LENGTH, AVG_LENGTH)
AS SELECT   TBNAME, MAX(LENGTH),
            MIN(LENGTH), AVG(LENGTH)
    FROM     SYSIBM.SYSCOLUMNS
    GROUP BY TBNAME;
```

After the view is created, you can issue the following SELECT statement joining the view to the base table, thereby providing both detail and aggregate information on each report row:

```
SELECT   TBNAME, NAME, COLNO, LENGTH,
         MAX_LENGTH, MIN_LENGTH, AVG_LENGTH
FROM     SYSIBM.SYSCOLUMNS C,
         authid.COL_LENGTH V
WHERE    C.TBNAME = V.TABLE_NAME
ORDER BY 1, 3;
```

The solution using inline views is to skip the view-creation step and simply execute the following SQL statement:

```
SELECT TBNAME, NAME, COLNO, LENGTH,
       MAX_LENGTH, MIN_LENGTH, AVG_LENGTH
```

```
FROM    SYSIBM.SYSCOLUMNS C,
        (SELECT TBNAME AS TABLE_NAME,
                MAX(LENGTH) AS MAX_LENGTH,
                MIN(LENGTH) AS MIN_LENGTH,
                AVG(LENGTH) AS AVG_LENGTH
         FROM    SYSIBM.SYSCOLUMNS
         GROUP BY TBNAME) AS V
WHERE   C.TBNAME = V.TABLE_NAME
ORDER BY 1,3;
```

The same result is returned in a single SQL statement, but without using a view. You must enclose inline view expressions in parentheses and must use a correlation name. You cannot refer to the correlation name for the inline view expression elsewhere in the same FROM clause, but you can use it outside the FROM clause (just like any other table or view name) as the qualifier of a column name.

Consider Table Expressions to Improve Performance   Table expressions are frequently overlooked as a potential solution for resolving problems using only SQL.

One practical use for table expressions is to force the optimizer to choose a specific processing order. For example, consider the following query:

```
SELECT    D.DEPTNO, MIN(D.DEPTNAME) AS DEPT_NAME, MIN(D.LOCATION) AS DEPT_LOCATION,
          SUM(E.SALARY) AS TOTAL_SALARY
FROM      DSN8810.DEPT D,
          DSN8810.EMP  E
WHERE     D.DEPTNO = E.WORKDEPT
AND       E.BONUS BETWEEN 0.00 AND 1000.00
GROUP BY  D.DEPTNO;
```

In this query, the detail rows that qualify from each table are joined prior to the GROUP BY processing. In general, there will be more EMP rows than DEPT rows because a department comprises multiple employees. Suppose there were 200 DEPT rows joined to 75,000 EMP rows—then the GROUP BY is processed. Instead, you can use table expressions to force the optimizer to process the aggregations on a table-by-table basis:

```
SELECT  D.DEPTNO, D.DEPTNAME, D.LOCATION, TOTAL_SALARY
FROM    DSN8810.DEPT D,
        (SELECT WORKDEPT, SUM(SALARY) AS TOTAL_SALARY
         FROM    DSN8810.EMP  E
         WHERE   E.BONUS BETWEEN 0.00 and 1000.00
         GROUP BY E.WORKDEPT) AS E
WHERE   D.DEPTNO = E.WORKDEPT;
```

This will produce the same results with better performance. Use table expressions to pre-filter FULL JOIN tables, to pre-filter null supplying tables of LEFT/RIGHT joins, to separate GROUP BY work, and to generate or derive data.

Consider Table Expressions Instead of Views   Instead of creating views and using them in your application programs, consider using table expressions. By moving the SQL from the view into a table expression the full intent of the SQL becomes more apparent. Additionally, it is easier to debug SQL problems when the SQL is completely visible in the program.

When confronted with a problem in SQL that uses a view, you will have to query the DB2 Catalog to find the SQL that makes up the view. This information is in SYSIBM.SYSVIEWS. The SQL in this table can be difficult to read because it is not formatted. However, if the SQL were changed to include the view SQL too, it would be much easier to understand and debug or tune the query.

`V7` **Consider Row Expressions**   SQL becomes even more flexible under DB2 V7 with row expressions. Row expressions allow SQL statements to be coded using more than one set of comparisons in a single predicate using a subquery. The net result is that multiple columns can be compared within the scope of a single SQL predicate—possibly against multiple rows on the right side of the predicate. Perhaps the best way to understand this feature is by viewing an example:

```
SELECT *
FROM    SAMPLE_TABLE
WHERE   (COL1, COL2) IN (SELECT COLX, COLY
                        FROM    OTHER_TABLE);
```

The difference between this statement and a typical SQL statement is quite obvious: Two columns are coded on the left side of the predicate, thereby enabling two columns to be selected in the SELECT statement on the right side of the predicate. Of course, a row expression need not be limited to only two columns; any number of columns can be specified, so long as the number of columns on the left matches the number of columns on the right side of the predicate.

Row expressions bring more flexibility and can greatly simplify certain types of SQL statements. Additionally, they can be more efficient than an equivalent SQL statement using multiple subqueries. Consider

```
SELECT *
FROM    SAMPLE_TABLE
WHERE   COL1 IN (SELECT COLX
                FROM    OTHER_TABLE)
AND     COL2 IN (SELECT COLY
                FROM    OTHER_TABLE);
```

Although this SQL statement is functionally equivalent to the previous SQL statement, it contains two subquery predicates and requires two scans of OTHER_TABLE. The previous SQL statement can scan OTHER_TABLE once to achieve the same results.

`V8` **Use Scalar Fullselect to Your Advantage**   DB2 Version 8 extends the functionality of SQL to allow a scalar fullselect to be used almost anywhere an expression can be used. The term **scalar fullselect** basically means a SELECT statement that returns a single value (or a NULL). An example will help to clarify:

```
SELECT PROJNO, PROJNAME,
       (SELECT MIN(ACSTDATE)) FROM PROJACT),
       DEPTNO
FROM   DSN8810.PROJ;
```

The SELECT-list of this statement contains three columns and a scalar fullselect. For this SQL to work, it is important that only one value is returned to the fullselect embedded in the SELECT statement; this is what makes it a *scalar* fullselect.

V8 **Consider Using Multi-Row Fetches**   When you need to retrieve multiple rows, consider deploying a multi-row fetch to transfer more than one row using a single FETCH statement. This capability is new as of DB2 Version 8—basically, it allows you to FETCH multiple rows at one time into an array in your program. By fetching multiple rows at once your request can become more efficient, especially for distributed requests. More information on multi-row fetching is provided in Chapter 11, "Using DB2 in an Application Program."

Be Flexible and Adapt to Your Circumstances   When coding SQL, there are no rules that **always** apply. Adopt the basic tenet of almost never saying "always" or "never" and you will have grasped the zen of SQL coding.

Remember the cardinal rule of DBMS development that we discussed earlier—"It depends." To be successful with complex SQL, be sure to understand what can be done using SQL and have a good grasp on the fundamentals. Also, be sure to have the IBM DB2 SQL Reference manual readily available, too. With patience, willingness to experiment, and a sound understanding of your available options, you will be able to code efficient SQL statements—regardless of the complexity required.

Common Table Expressions and Recursion

V8 Common table expressions, or CTEs, are new to DB2 as of Version 8 and they greatly expand the useability of SQL. A common table expression can be thought of as a named temporary table within a SQL statement that is retained for the duration of a SQL statement. There can be many CTEs in a single SQL statement, but each must have a unique name and be defined only once.

CTEs can be used to decrease the number of views that are created. By using a CTE instead of a view, you can reduce the number of DB2 objects needed and perhaps clarify the purpose and intent of SQL statements. The SQL of the CTE is coded directly into the SQL statement. Of course, I do not mean to imply that CTEs always should be used instead of views, because CTEs make your SQL more complex and do not mask this complexity from end users the way that views can.

Nested table expressions, sometimes referred to as inline views, can be rewritten as CTEs. The CTE is written into your SQL using the WITH clause, as shown in this example:

```
WITH AVSAL (DEPT, AVG_SAL) AS
  (SELECT   WORKDEPT, AVG(SALARY)
   FROM     DSN8810.EMP
   GROUP BY WORKDEPT)
SELECT DEPT, MAX(AVG_SAL) FROM AVSAL;
```

The WITH statement defines the "table" from which the data in the SELECT statement is retrieved. More than one table can be specified in the CTE, but cyclic references are not legal. If more than one common table expression is specified, later ones can refer to the output from prior ones only.

> **CAUTION**
>
> Be careful when coding CTE names. A common table expression with the same name as a real table will replace the real table for that particular query. The table names used for CTEs must follow the standard DB2 table naming standards. Also, keep in mind that each temporary table name must be unique within a query.

A CTE can be easier to use than a regular table expression because it is defined once and then can be used multiple times throughout the query. However, if a nested table expression is needed more than once in the same query, it must be completely written into the query again.

Using CTEs for Recursion

V8 Recursion is implemented in DB2 using common table expressions, that is, using the WITH clause. But before we begin to understand how DB2 recursion works, let's first look at some data that would benefit from being read recursively. Figure 2.3 depicts an organization chart that constitutes a small hierarchy.

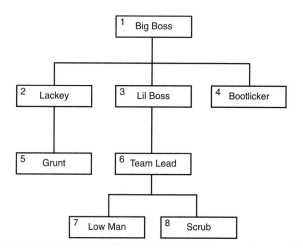

FIGURE 2.3   A sample hierarchy.

A DB2 table holding this data could be set up as follows:

```
CREATE TABLE ORG_CHART
    (MGR_ID        SMALLINT,
     EMP_ID        SMALLINT,
     EMP_NAME      CHAR(20))
  ;
```

Of course, this is a simple implementation and many more columns would likely be needed. But the simplicity of this table will suit our purposes for learning recursion. To make the data in this table match Figure 2.3, we would load the table as follows:

MGR_ID	EMP_ID	EMP_NAME
-1	1	BIG BOSS
1	2	LACKEY
1	3	LIL BOSS
1	4	BOOTLICKER
2	5	GRUNT
3	6	TEAM LEAD
6	7	LOW MAN
6	8	SCRUB

The MGR_ID for the top-most node is set to some value indicating that there is no parent for this row; in this case, -1 is used. Now that we have loaded the data, we can code a query to walk the hierarchy using recursive SQL. Suppose we need to report on the entire organizational structure under LIL BOSS. The following recursive SQL using a CTE will do the trick:

```
WITH EXPL (MGR_ID, EMP_ID, EMP_NAME) AS
(
 SELECT ROOT.MGR_ID, ROOT.EMP_ID, ROOT.EMP_NAME
 FROM   ORG_CHART   ROOT
 WHERE  ROOT.MGR_ID = 3

 UNION ALL

 SELECT CHILD.MGR_ID, CHILD.EMP_ID, CHILD.EMP_NAME
 FROM   EXPL PARENT, ORG_CHART CHILD
 WHERE  PARENT.EMP_ID = CHILD.MGR_ID
)

SELECT   DISTINCT MGR_ID, EMP_ID, EMP_NAME
FROM     EXPL
ORDER BY MGR_ID, EMP_ID;
```

The results of running this query would be:

1	3	LIL BOSS
3	6	TEAM LEAD
6	7	LOW MAN
6	8	SCRUB

Let's break this somewhat complex query down into its constituent pieces to help understand what is going on. First of all, a recursive query is implemented using the WITH clause (using a CTE). The CTE is named EXPL. The first SELECT primes the pump to initialize the "root" of the search. In our case, it starts with EMP_ID 3—LIL BOSS.

Now comes the tricky part. The next SELECT is an inner join combining the CTE with the table upon which the CTE is based. This is where the recursion comes in. A portion of the CTE definition refers to itself. Finally, we SELECT from the CTE.

Similar queries can be written to completely explode the hierarchy to retrieve all the descendants of any given node.

Use Recursion When Necessary   Recursion is a very powerful feature of DB2 SQL—and recursive SQL can be very elegant and efficient. However, because of the difficulty developers can have understanding recursion, recursive SQL is sometimes thought of as "too inefficient to use frequently."

But, if you have a business need to walk or explode hierarchies in DB2, recursive SQL is likely to be your most efficient option. Think about it: What else are you going to do? You can create pre-exploded tables (refer to Chapter 5 for more on this tactic), but this requires denormalization and a lot of pre-processing, which can be quite inefficient. Or, perhaps you might decide to write your own code to walk a hierarchy. This, too, is fraught with potential problems. You will likely retrieve more data than you need, causing inefficient I/O. Also, how will you assure more efficient access in your code than DB2?

If every row processed by the query is required in the answer set ("find all employees who work for LIL BOSS"), then recursion will most likely be quite efficient. If only a few of the rows processed by the query are actually needed ("find all flights from Houston to Pittsburgh, but show only the three fastest"), then a recursive query can be quite costly.

The bottom line is that you should consider coding recursive SQL when business requirements call for such processing. Be sure that suitable indexes are available and examine your access paths.

Specify Column Names in the CTE   You must specify column names for the CTE if the expression is recursive (or if the query returns duplicate column names). Column names are specified in parentheses immediately following the CTE name. For example:

```
WITH CTE_NAME (COL1, COL2). . .
```

In this example the CTE is named CTE_NAME and the columns for the CTE are COL1 and COL2.

Avoid Cyclic CTE References   If more than one CTE is defined in the same statement, cyclic references between the common table expressions are not permitted. A cyclic reference occurs when two CTEs refer to each other.

For example, consider two CTEs named CTE_A and CTE_B. If CTE_A refers to CTE_B and CTE_B also refers to CTE_A, then an error will be returned by DB2.

Use UNION ALL, not UNION for Recursion   When coding a recursive SQL query, you must use a UNION ALL between the two main parts of the statement. UNION ALL is required because it allows duplicates, whereas UNION does not. Duplicate output rows are needed for recursive processing.

Know How to Halt Recursion   Whenever you are writing recursive code, you must be aware of the potential for an infinite loop. Infinite loops can occur because of improper coding or because of the structure of the data being accessed.

The trick to preventing an infinite loop is to code a level into your CTE for recursion. For example, consider our previous example and the following query:

```
WITH EXPL (MGR_ID, EMP_ID, LVL, EMP_NAME) AS
(
SELECT ROOT.MGR_ID, ROOT.EMP_ID, 0, ROOT.EMP_NAME
FROM    ORG_CHART   ROOT
WHERE   ROOT.MGR_ID = 3

UNION ALL

SELECT CHILD.MGR_ID, CHILD.EMP_ID, PARENT.LVL+1 CHILD.EMP_NAME
FROM    EXPL PARENT, ORG_CHART CHILD
WHERE   PARENT.EMP_ID = CHILD.MGR_ID
AND     PARENT.LVL+1 < 3
)

SELECT   DISTINCT MGR_ID, EMP_ID, LVL, EMP_NAME
FROM     EXPL
ORDER BY MGR_ID, EMP_ID;
```

In this case we have coded the LVL column to count the levels of the organizational hierarchy. The bold predicate in the second SELECT statement will halt processing at 3 levels. Of course, you can make this however many levels you desire.

Keep in mind, though, that given our data we know that an infinite loop will not occur if the recursive SQL is written properly. However, if a lower-level row can be the parent of a higher-level row, then we can introduce an infinite loop. This is unlikely to occur in an organizational hierarchy, but could occur in other types of networks that need to be traversed using recursive SQL.

Know Your Data   It is very important to know your data when you are coding recursive SQL. Things to know about your data include:

- Whether it is a hierarchy or a network

- How many levels deep the structure goes

- The amount of data—overall, and at each level

- Existence of cycles

Only with in-depth knowledge of your data will you be able to write efficient and effective recursive SQL statements.

Working with NULLs

Writing queries against tables that can contain nulls can be a confusing endeavor. Nulls represent missing or unknown information at the column level. If a column "value" can be null, it can mean one of two things: The attribute is not applicable for certain occurrences of the entity, or the attribute applies to all entity occurrences, but the information may not always be known. Of course, it could be a combination of these two situations, too.

Nulls sometimes are inappropriately referred to as null "values." Using the term *value* to describe a null is inaccurate because the term *null* implies the *lack* of a value. Nulls would be better referred to as null "lack of values."

Problems with Nulls

Given that nulls are possible in DB2 tables, SQL must support three-valued logic (3VL) in order to retrieve data. To understand 3VL let's first define two-valued logic (2VL). With 2VL there are two possible answers to a query: true or false. Either the data was found or it was not found. However, if nulls exist, then there is a third possible answer: unknown.

Most of us are not accustomed to working with 3VL, and so handling nulls in DB2 queries can be difficult to master. Here are some basic rules to remember:

- NULL is the lack of a value—it means unknown or not applicable.
- A NULL is not less than, greater than, or equal to any value.
- A NULL is not less than, greater than, or equal to another NULL.
- When NULL is compared to any other column or value in a predicate the result is unknown.

The bottom line is that 3VL is hard to understand and hard to implement properly.

NULL Guidelines

The following guidelines are helpful to keep in mind as you design, build, and test your DB2 SQL statements.

Use the Special NULL Predicate   To test for the existence of nulls, use the special predicate IS NULL in the WHERE clause of the SELECT statement. For example, the following is not a valid SQL predicate:

```
WHERE column = NULL
```

Instead, you must code this as

```
WHERE column IS NULL.
```

Furthermore, it is not valid to test whether a column is < NULL, <= NULL, > NULL, or >= NULL. These are all meaningless because null is the absence of a value.

Do Not Try to Design Away the Null Issue   Because of the possible problems associated with nulls, it can be enticing to simply avoid using them. This simplistic thinking goes something like this: "If I create a database without using nulls then I do not need to worry about nulls in my queries." This is not true, though.

It is possible to code a statement against tables with no nullable columns and return NULL as a result. For example, consider the following query:

```
SELECT  SUM(SALARY)
FROM    DSN8810.EMP
WHERE   LASTNAME = 'RAINES';
```

What will be returned by this query if there are no employees with the last name of RAINES? The answer is NULL. The impact of applying a column function (other than COUNT) to no data is not zero, but NULL. This is true even if the column upon which the function is operating is not-nullable (as is the case with the SALARY column of the EMP sample table).

Understand Nulls and Collating   When a nullable column participates in an ORDER BY or GROUP BY clause, the returned nulls are grouped at the high end of the sort order.

Nulls are considered to be equal when duplicates are eliminated by SELECT DISTINCT or COUNT (DISTINCT column).

A unique index considers nulls to be equivalent and disallows duplicate entries because of the existence of nulls, unless the WHERE NOT NULL clause is specified in the index.

Consider Using IS NOT DISTINCT FROM   Two columns, each set to NULL, are not considered equivalent when compared in a predicate. In other words, as stated previously, a NULL does not equal another NULL. When a nullable column participates in a predicate in the WHERE or HAVING clause, the nulls encountered cause the comparison to evaluate to unknown.

V8 DB2 V8 provides a new comparison operator for handling NULL called IS NOT DISTINCT FROM. This comparison operator basically treats two nulls as equivalent. So, consider the following predicate:

```
WHERE COL IS NOT DISTINCT FROM :HOSTVAR
```

The predicate will be true when both COL and HOSTVAR are NULL, or when both COL and HOSTVAR are set to the same non-NULL value.

When only COL or only HOSTVAR is NULL, but the other is set to a value, the result is false. Of course, the result is false when both COL and HOSTVAR are set to different values.

Consider Nulls in Your Database Design   When you build your DB2 databases be sure to consider nulls and how they are used before setting any column as nullable. Keep in mind, too, that the default if nothing is specified is a nullable column.

More information on defining and using nulls in DB2 tables is provided in Chapter 5.

Date and Time Guidelines

DB2 provides sophisticated facilities for processing date and time data. First, DB2 provides native data types for storing date and time data. By storing date and time data directly using data types specifically designed for the data, the user does not need to transform the data to and from another data type. This simplifies program development and makes processing the data more efficient. Whenever you wish to store date and/or time data in a DB2 table, always use the appropriate date or time data type, instead of a character or numeric data type.

The date and time data types are:

DATE	a date stored as 4 bytes
TIME	a time stored as 3 bytes
TIMESTAMP	a combination of date and time stored as 10 bytes

Using TIMESTAMP Versus TIME and DATE   It is obvious when to use DATE and TIME data types: DATE for storing dates and TIME for storing times. But what if you must store both date and time information on a single row in DB2. Is it better to use a single TIMESTAMP column or two columns, one stored as DATE and the other as TIME?

The answer to this question depends on the specific situation. Consider the following points before making your decision:

- With DATE and TIME you must use two columns. TIMESTAMP uses one column, thereby simplifying data access and modification.

- The combination of DATE and TIME columns requires 7 bytes of storage, while a TIMESTAMP column requires 10 bytes of storage. Using the combination of DATE and TIME columns will save space.

- Index space requirements can be minimized when DATE and TIME are used separately, but only the date needs to be indexed. Additionally, indexing a DATE and TIME as separate columns provides the ability to assign an ascending sequence to the date and a descending sequence to the time (and visa versa).

- If you need to provide indexed access by date only (or time only) use two separate columns. Achieving indexed access for a TIMESTAMP column can be tricky when only the date value is supplied, and impossible when only the time value is supplied.

  For example, say TRACKING_TIMESTAMP is indexed. Most programmers would write code something like this:

  ```
  AND DATE(B.TRACKING_TIMESTAMP) < :WSDATE
  AND DATE(B.TRACKING_TIMESTAMP) - 7 DAYS  >= :WSDATE
  ```

  The index would not be used in this case. Instead, the programmers must be trained (and reminded) to write the SQL like this:

  ```
  AND B.TRACKING_TIMESTAMP < TIMESTAMP(:WSDATE,'00.00.00')
  AND B.TRACKING_TIMESTAMP >= TIMESTAMP(:WSDATE,'00.00.00') - 7 DAYS
  ```

- TIMESTAMP provides greater time accuracy, down to the microsecond level. TIME provides accuracy only to the second level. If precision is important, use TIMESTAMP. Use TIME if you do not need the time value stored to the microsecond level.

- Date and time arithmetic is easier to implement using TIMESTAMP data instead of a combination of DATE and TIME. Subtracting one TIMESTAMP from another results in a TIMESTAMP duration. To calculate a duration using DATE and TIME columns, two subtraction operations must occur: one for the DATE column and one for the TIME column.

- It is easier to format DATE and TIME columns via local DATE and TIME exits, the CHAR function, and the DATE and TIME precompiler options. These facilities are not available for TIMESTAMP columns. If the date and time information is to be extracted and displayed on a report or by an online application, the availability of these DB2-provided facilities for DATE and TIME columns should be considered when making your decision.

Displaying Dates and Times   DB2 provides four built-in options for displaying dates and times:

Format	Date Display	Time Display
ISO	YYYY-MM-DD	HH.MM.SS
USA	MM/DD/YYYY	HH:MM (AM or PM)
EUR	DD.MM.YYYY	HH.MM.SS
JIS	YYYY-MM-DD	HH:MM:SS

Date and time values will display, and be returned to your programs, as character string data formatted according to the format chosen by your site. The default is ISO. It is also possible to define your own installation-specific defined formats using a LOCAL format exit.

You can also change the display format by using built-in functions (to be discussed in Chapter 3).

Workaround Non-Standard Dates   What if you wish to work with a date in a format that does not fit into any of those supported by DB2? For example, you have a date stored in a character column using a format like YYYYMMDD (with no dashes or slashes), and you need to compare it to a DB2 date.

One potential solution to this problem is to convert the character column into a valid DB2 date format. You can use the SUBSTR function to break the character column into the separate components. For example, SUBSTR(column,1,4) returns the year component, SUBSTR(column,5,2) returns the month, and SUBSTR(column,7,2) returns the day.

Then you will need to concatenate all of these into a format that DB2 recognizes, for example, the USA format, which is MM/DD/YYYY. This can be done as follows:

```
SUBSTR(column,5,2) || "/" || SUBSTR(column,7,2) || "/" || SUBSTR(column,1,4)
```

Then you can use the DATE function to convert this character string into a date that DB2 will recognize. This is done as follows:

```
DATE(SUBSTR(column,5,2) || "/" || SUBSTR(column,7,2) || "/" || SUBSTR(column,1,4))
```

The result of this can be used in date arithmetic with other dates or date durations. Of course, it might not perform extremely well, but it should return the results you desire. Of course, all of these gyrations can be avoided by using DB2 DATE, TIME, and TIMESTAMP data types instead of forcing the data into CHAR or numeric data types.

Also, keep in mind that you can define your own installation-specific defined DATE and TIME formats using a LOCAL format exit.

Date and Time Arithmetic   Another nice feature of DATE and TIME data is the ability to perform arithmetic functions. The plus (+) and minus (-) operations can be used on date and time values and durations. A duration is a number used to represent an interval of time. DB2 recognizes four types of durations.

- A *labeled duration* explicitly specifies the type of duration. An example of a labeled duration is 15 MINUTES. Labeled durations can specify the duration in years, months, days, hours, minutes, seconds, or microseconds. A labeled duration can only be used as an operand of an arithmetic operator, and the other operand must have a data type of DATE, TIME, or TIMESTAMP.

- A DATE duration is a DECIMAL(8,0) number that has the format YYYYMMDD. The YYYY represents the number of years in the duration, MM the number of months, and DD the number of days. When you subtract one date from another, the result is a date duration in this format.

- Similar to DATE durations, DB2 also supports TIME durations. A TIME duration is a DECIMAL(6,0) number with the format HHMMSS. The HH represents the number of hours, MM the number of minutes, and SS the number of seconds. When you subtract one time from another, the result is a time duration in this format.

- A TIMESTAMP duration is more complex than date and time durations. The TIMESTAMP duration is a DECIMAL(20,6) number having the format YYYYXXDDHHMMSSZZZZZZ. The duration represents YYYY years, XX months, DD days, HH hours, MM minutes, SS seconds, and ZZZZZZ microseconds. When you subtract a TIMESTAMP from a TIMESTAMP, you get a TIMESTAMP duration.

> **CAUTION**
>
> The numeric component of a labeled duration cannot be substituted with a host variable or parameter marker—it must be a numeric literal.

The rules for date and time arithmetic are somewhat complex. Remember that only addition and subtraction can be performed on data and time data (no division or multiplication). For addition, one of the two operands must be a duration. This stands to reason. For example, two dates cannot be added together, but a duration can be added to a date. The same goes for two times.

For addition, use the matrix in Table 2.2 to determine what type of duration is valid for which data type. For example, for TIME data types, a labeled duration or a TIME duration can be specified in the addition expression.

TABLE 2.2   Date and Time Addition Table

Date Type	Labeled	Date	Time	Timestamp
DATE	YES	YES	NO	NO
TIME	YES	NO	NO	NO
TIMESTAMP	YES	YES	YES	YES

For labeled durations, they must be appropriate durations. For DATE, the labeled duration must specify years, months, or days only; for TIME, the label duration must specify hours, minutes, or seconds only. All of the preceding options for labeled durations are valid for TIMESTAMP data.

The result of adding a DATE and a duration is another DATE; a TIME and a duration is another TIME; and a TIMESTAMP and a duration is another TIMESTAMP.

For subtraction, the rules are different. Instead, the result of subtracting one date or time value from another date or time value results in a duration.

For DATE columns, you can subtract another DATE, a DATE duration, an appropriate labeled duration (years, months, or days), or a character representation of a DATE. The result is a DATE duration.

For TIME columns, you can subtract another TIME, a TIME duration, an appropriate labeled duration (hours, minutes, or seconds), or a character representation of a TIME. The result is a TIME duration.

For TIMESTAMP columns, you can subtract another TIMESTAMP, a TIMESTAMP duration, any labeled duration, or a character representation of a TIMESTAMP.

Do Not Mix DB2 Dates with Non-Dates in Arithmetic Expressions   Consider an example where you decide to store dates using a column defined as DECIMAL(8,0), instead of as a DATE. If you mix this column with a DATE column in arithmetic expressions, the results will be incorrect. For example, subtracting the column (in this example, DATE_COL) from a DB2 date (in this example, the current date), as follows

```
CURRENT DATE - DATE_COL
```

will not return a date duration, as you might expect. Instead, DB2 will interpret the DATE_COL value as a duration. Consider, for example, the value of DATE_COL being 19720212, which is meant to represent February 12, 1972. Instead, DB2 interprets it as a duration of 1,972 years, 2 months, and 12 days.

Use Functions to Return Total Number of Days   If you keep an open mind, most every problem is solvable in DB2. A common requirement when date arithmetic is involved is to return results in a common unit, for example, number of days. Let's examine using DB2 date subtraction to express the resulting duration as an exact total number of days. To illustrate, consider this query:

```
SELECT DATE('03/01/2004') - DATE('12/01/2003')
```

It will return a duration of `00000300` (that is, three months). We want total number of days. Now keep in mind that those three months encompass a 29-day February plus a 31-day January plus a 31-day December (total 91 days). How do we do this?

The answer lies in using the `DAYS` function. The following should return what you need:

```
SELECT DAYS('03/01/2004') - DAYS('12/01/2003')
```

This query will return to you the exact number of days between the two dates. More information on DB2 functions (like `DAYS`) can be found in Chapter 3.

Data Modification Guidelines

All of the guidelines thus far in this chapter have explored ways to make retrieving data more efficient. But data also must be modified, and you need to ensure that data modification is performed efficiently, too. Under normal circumstances, you can modify data in a DB2 table in six ways:

- Using an SQL `UPDATE` statement

- Using an SQL `INSERT` statement

- Using an SQL `DELETE` statement

- Because of a referential constraint specifying `ON DELETE CASCADE` or `ON DELETE SET NULL`

- Because a trigger is fired as the result of an `UPDATE`, `INSERT`, or `DELETE`, and the trigger issues a SQL data modification statement

- Using the DB2 `LOAD` utility

This section provides tips for the efficient implementation of the first three methods. You can find guidelines for the others as follows:

- For referential integrity, in Chapter 5

- For triggers, in Chapter 8, "Using DB2 Triggers for Integrity"

- For using the `LOAD` utility, as well as the other DB2 utilities, in Chapter 33, "Data Organization Utilities."

Limit Updating Indexed Columns   When you update columns in indexes, a corresponding update is applied to all indexes in which the columns participate. Updating can have a substantial impact on performance due to the additional I/O overhead.

Use `FOR UPDATE OF` Correctly   Specify only those columns that actually will or can be updated in the `FOR UPDATE OF` column list of a cursor. DB2 does not use any index that contains columns listed in the `FOR UPDATE OF` clause.

Consider Using `DELETE`/`INSERT` Instead of `FOR UPDATE OF`   If all columns in a row are being updated, use `DELETE` on the old row and use `INSERT` on the new one rather than the `FOR UPDATE OF` clause.

Update Multiple Rows   You have two options for updating data using the SQL UPDATE verb:

- A cursor UPDATE using WHERE CURRENT OF

- A direct SQL UPDATE

If the data does not have to be retrieved by the application before the update, use the direct SQL UPDATE statement.

A cursor UPDATE with the WHERE CURRENT OF option performs worse than a direct UPDATE for two reasons. First, the rows to be updated must be retrieved from the cursor a row at a time. Each row is fetched and then updated. A direct UPDATE affects multiple rows with one statement. Second, when using a cursor, you must add the overhead of the OPEN and CLOSE statement.

Update Only Changed Columns   UPDATE statements should specify only columns in which the value will be modified. For example, if only the ACSTAFF column of the DSN8810.PROJACT table should be changed, do not code the following:

```
EXEC SQL
    FETCH C1
    INTO :HV-PROJNO, :HV-ACTNO, :HV-ACSTAFF,
         :HV-ACSTDATE, :HV-ACENDATE
END-EXEC.
MOVE 4.5 TO HV-ACSTAFF.
UPDATE DSN8810.PROJACT
    SET PROJNO   = :HV-PROJNO,
        ACTNO    = :HV-ACTNO,
        ACSTAFF  = :HV-ACSTAFF,
        ACSTDATE = :HV-ACSTDATE,
        ACENDATE = :HV-ACENDATE
WHERE CURRENT OF C1;
```

Although the host variables contain the same data currently stored in the table, you should avoid this type of coding. DB2 checks to see whether the data is different before performing the update. If none of the values are different from those already stored in the table, the update does not take place. Performance may suffer, though, because DB2 has to perform the value checking. You can avoid this situation by coding the UPDATE statement as follows:

```
UPDATE DSN8810.PROJACT
    SET ACSTAFF = :HV-ACSTAFF
WHERE CURRENT OF C1;
```

Disregard this guideline when the application you are developing requires you to code a complicated check algorithm that DB2 can perform automatically. Because of the complexity of the code needed to check for current values, implementing this type of processing is not always feasible. Nevertheless, try to avoid specifying useless updates of this type when issuing interactive SQL.

Consider Dropping Indexes Before Large Insertions   When you execute a large number of INSERTs for a single table, every index must be updated with the columns and the appropriate RIDs (record IDs) for each inserted row. For very large insertions, the indexes can become disorganized, causing poor performance. Dropping all indexes for the table, performing the INSERTs, and then re-creating the indexes might be more efficient. The trade-offs to consider are

- The overhead of updating indexes must be weighed against the index re-creation plus the rebinding of all application plans that used the indexes.

- If indexes are required to enforce uniqueness, another method must be selected to enforce uniqueness before or after the indexes are rebuilt.

- After the indexes are rebuilt, RUNSTATS must be executed before any binds are executed or dynamic SQL is allowed. RI rules may need to be checked.

Exercise Caution When Issuing Ad Hoc DELETE Statements   Be extremely careful when issuing SQL DELETE statements outside the control of an application program. Remember that SQL acts on a set of data, not just one row. All rows that qualify based on the SQL WHERE clause are updated or deleted. For example, consider the following SQL statement:

```
DELETE
FROM DSN8810.DEPT;
```

This SQL statement, called a mass DELETE, effectively deletes every row from the DEPT table. Normally, this result is undesirable.

Exercise Caution When Issuing Ad Hoc UPDATE Statements   When issuing an ad hoc UPDATE, take care to specify an appropriate WHERE clause. Consider the following SQL statement:

```
UPDATE DSN8810.DEPT
SET DEPTNAME = 'NEW DEPARTMENT';
```

This SQL statement changes the value of the DEPTNAME column for every row in the table to the value 'NEW DEPARTMENT'. This result occurs because no WHERE clause is coded to limit the scope of the UPDATE. Requests of this nature are not usually desirable and should be avoided.

Mass DELETE Versus LOAD   Sometimes you need to empty a table. You can do so by issuing a mass DELETE or by loading an empty data set. A mass DELETE usually is more efficient when you're using segmented table spaces. Loading an empty data set usually is more efficient when you're using simple or partitioned table spaces.

V7 **Consider Using a Self-Referencing DELETE**   With DB2 Version 7 comes the ability to code a self-referencing sub-SELECT on searched UPDATE and DELETE statements. In previous releases of DB2, the WHERE clause cannot refer to the table (or view) being modified by the statement. For example, the following SQL is legitimate as of DB2 V7, and can be used to implement a 10% raise for employees who earn less than their department's average salary:

```
UPDATE DSN8710.EMP E1
SET SALARY = SALARY * 1.10
WHERE SALARY < (SELECT AVG(SALARY)
```

```
FROM    DSN8710.EMP E2
WHERE   E1.WORKDEPT = E2.WORKDEPT);
```

DB2 will evaluate the complete subquery before performing the requested UPDATE.

Use INSERT and UPDATE to Add Long Columns   The maximum length of a string literal that can be inserted into DB2 is 255 characters. This restriction poses a problem when you must insert a LONG VARCHAR column in an ad hoc environment.

To get around this limitation, issue an INSERT followed immediately by an UPDATE. For example, if you need to insert 260 bytes of data into a LONG VARCHAR column, begin by inserting the first 255 bytes as shown:

```
INSERT INTO your.table
COLUMNS    (LONG_COL,
            other columns)
VALUES     ('← first 255 bytes of LONG_COL →',
            other values);
```

Follow the INSERT with an UPDATE statement to add the rest of the data to the column, as in the following example:

```
UPDATE your.table
SET LONG_COL = LONG_COL || '← remaining 5 bytes of LONG_COL →',
WHERE KEY_COL = 'key value';
```

For this technique to be successful, a unique key column (or columns) must exist for the table. If each row cannot be uniquely identified, the UPDATE cannot be issued because it might update more data than you want.

> **CAUTION**
>
> Prior to DB2 V6 (and DB2 V5 with a retrofit APAR) the maximum length of a string literal that could be inserted into DB2 was limited to 254 characters, instead of 255.

V7 **Delete and Update with a Self-Referencing Sub-SELECT**   The ability to code a self-referencing sub-SELECT on searched UPDATE and DELETE statements was added to DB2 Version 7. In previous releases of DB2, the WHERE clause cannot refer to the table (or view) being modified by the statement. For example, the following SQL is legitimate as of DB2 V7, and can be used to implement a 10% raise for employees who earn less than their department's average salary:

```
UPDATE DSN8810.EMP E1
SET SALARY = SALARY * 1.10
WHERE SALARY < (SELECT AVG(SALARY)
                FROM    DSN8810.EMP E2
                WHERE   E1.WORKDEPT = E2.WORKDEPT);
```

DB2 will evaluate the complete subquery before performing the requested UPDATE.

V8 **SELECT from an INSERT to Retrieve Generated Values**   DB2 Version 8 offers the intriguing new ability to SELECT from an INSERT statement. To understand why we might need to do so, let's first review some background data. In some cases, it is possible to perform actions that generate new data for an inserted row before it gets saved to disk. For example, a BEFORE TRIGGER might change data before it is even recorded to disk, but the application program will not have any knowledge of this change that is made in the trigger. Using general registers, identity columns, and user-defined defaults can produce similar effects.

What can be done if the program needs to know the final column values? Prior to DB2 V8, this is difficult and inefficient to implement. For example, to retrieve that last identity column value, a separate singleton SELECT statement is needed to retrieve the result of IDENTITY_VAL_LOCAL() into a host variable. The SELECT FROM INSERT syntax solves this problem. It allows you to both insert the row and retrieve the values of the columns with a single SQL statement. It performs very well, because it performs both the INSERT and the SELECT as a single operation. Consider the following example:

```
SELECT PRSTDATE
FROM
 INSERT (PROJNO, DEPTNO, RESPEMP, PRSTDATE)
 INTO DSN8810.PROJ
 VALUES('000001', 'B01', '000020', CURRENT DATE);
```

The data is inserted as specified in the VALUES clause, and then retrieved as specified in the SELECT. Without the ability to select PRSTDATE, the program would have no knowledge of the value supplied to PRSTDATE, because it was assigned using CURRENT DATE. Instead, the program would have had to issue a separate SELECT statement to retrieve the actual date. With this new syntax, the program can retrieve the CURRENT DATE value that was just inserted into PRSTDATE without adding overhead.

List Columns for INSERT   When you are coding an INSERT statement in an application program, list the column names for each value you are inserting. Although you could merely align the values in the same order as the column names in the table, doing so leads only to confusion. Furthermore, if ALTER is used to add new columns to the table, every INSERT statement that does not explicitly list the columns being inserted will fail. The proper format is

```
INSERT INTO DSN8810.DEPT
        (DEPTNO,
         DEPTNAME,
         MGRNO,
         ADMRDEPT)
    VALUES
        ('077',
         'NEW DEPARTMENT',
         '123456',
         '123') ;
```

Consider Using Multi-Row INSERTs   When you need to INSERT multiple rows, consider deploying a multi-row INSERT to place more than one row at a time into the table. This capability is new as of DB2 Version 8. By inserting multiple rows at once, your request may become more efficient. More information on multi-row INSERTs is provided in Chapter 11.

CHAPTER **3**

Using DB2 Functions

Two types of built-in functions can be applied to data in a DB2 table using SQL: *column functions* and *scalar functions*. You can use these functions to further simplify the requirements of complex data access.

> **NOTE**
>
> DB2 also provides the capability for users to create their own functions. This capability, called user-defined functions, is discussed in-depth in Chapter 4, "Using DB2 User-Defined Functions and Data Types."

Functions are called by specifying the function name and any required operands. A built-in function can be used any place an expression can be used (with some exceptions).

Column Functions

Column functions compute, from a group of rows, a single value for a designated column or expression. This provides the capability to aggregate data, thereby enabling you to perform statistical calculations across many rows with one SQL statement. To fully appreciate the column functions, you must understand SQL's set-level processing capabilities.

This list shows some rules for the column functions:

- Column functions can be executed only in SELECT statements.

- A column function must be specified for an explicitly named column or expression.

- Each column function returns only one value for the set of selected rows.

- If you apply a column function to one column in a SELECT statement, you must apply column functions to any other columns specified in the same SELECT statement, unless you also use the GROUP BY clause.

- Use GROUP BY to apply a column function to a group of named columns. Any other column named in the SELECT statement must be operated on by a column function.

- The result of any column function (except the COUNT and COUNT_BIG functions) will have the same data type as the column to which it was applied. The COUNT function returns an integer number; COUNT_BIG returns a decimal number.

- The result of any column function (except the COUNT and COUNT_BIG functions) can be null. COUNT and COUNT_BIG always return a numeric result.

- Columns functions will not return a SQLCODE of +100 if the predicate specified in the WHERE clause finds no data. Instead, a null is returned. For example, consider the following SQL statement:

```
SELECT    MAX(SALARY)
FROM      DSN8810.EMP
WHERE     EMPNO = '999999';
```

There is no employee with an EMPNO of '999999' in the DSN8810.EMP table. This statement therefore returns a null for the MAX(SALARY). Of course, this does not apply to COUNT and COUNT_BIG, both of which always return a value, never a null.

- When using the AVG, MAX, MIN, STDDEV, SUM, and VARIANCE functions on nullable columns, all occurrences of null are eliminated before applying the function.

- You can use the DISTINCT keyword with all column functions to eliminate duplicates before applying the given function. DISTINCT has no effect, however, on the MAX and MIN functions.

- You can use the ALL keyword to indicate that duplicates should not be eliminated. ALL is the default.

A column function can be specified in a WHERE clause only if that clause is part of a subquery of a HAVING clause. Additionally, every column name specified in the expression of the column function must be a correlated reference to the same group.

The column functions are AVG, COUNT, COUNT_BIG, MAX, MIN, STDDEV, SUM, and VARIANCE.

The AVG Function

The AVG function computes the average of the values for the column or expression specified as an argument. This function operates only on numeric arguments. The following example calculates the average salary of each department:

```
SELECT    WORKDEPT, AVG(SALARY)
FROM      DSN8810.EMP
GROUP BY WORKDEPT;
```

The AVG function is the preferred method of calculating the average of a group of values. Although an average, in theory, is nothing more than a sum divided by a count, DB2 may not return equivalent values for AVG(COL_NAME) and SUM(COL_NAME)/COUNT(*). The reason is that the COUNT function will count all rows regardless of value, whereas SUM ignores nulls.

The COUNT Function

The COUNT function counts the number of rows in a table, or the number of distinct values for a given column. It can operate, therefore, at the column or row level. The syntax differs for each. To count the number of rows in the EMP table, issue this SQL statement:

```
SELECT    COUNT(*)
FROM      DSN8810.EMP;
```

It does not matter what values are stored in the rows being counted. DB2 will simply count the number of rows and return the result. To count the number of distinct departments represented in the EMP table, issue the following

```
SELECT    COUNT(DISTINCT WORKDEPT)
FROM      DSN8810.EMP;
```

The keyword DISTINCT is not considered an argument of the function. It simply specifies an operation to be performed before the function is applied. When DISTINCT is coded, duplicate values are eliminated.

If DISTINCT is not specified, then ALL is implicitly specified. ALL also can be explicitly specified in the COUNT function. When ALL is specified, duplicate values are not eliminated.

> **NOTE**
>
> The argument of the COUNT function can be of any built-in data type other than a large object: CLOB, DBCLOB, or BLOB. Character string arguments can be no longer 255 bytes and graphic string arguments can be no longer than 127 bytes.
>
> The result of the COUNT function cannot be null. COUNT always returns an INTEGER value greater than or equal to zero.

The COUNT_BIG Function

The COUNT_BIG function is similar to the COUNT function. It counts the number of rows in a table, or the number of distinct values for a given column. However, the COUNT_BIG function returns a result of data type DECIMAL(31,0), whereas COUNT can return a result only as large as the largest DB2 integer value, namely +2,147,483,647.

The COUNT_BIG function works the same as the COUNT function, except it returns a decimal value. Therefore, the example SQL for COUNT is applicable to COUNT_BIG. Simply substitute COUNT_BIG for COUNT. For example, the following statement counts the number of rows in the EMP table (returning a decimal value, instead of an integer):

```
SELECT    COUNT_BIG(*)
FROM      DSN8810.EMP;
```

> **NOTE**
>
> The COUNT_BIG function has the same restrictions as the COUNT function. The argument of the COUNT_BIG function can be of any built-in data type other than a large object: CLOB, DBCLOB, or BLOB. Character string arguments can be no longer than 255 bytes and graphic string arguments can be no longer than 127 bytes.
>
> The result of the COUNT_BIG function cannot be null. COUNT_BIG returns a decimal value greater than or equal to zero.

The MAX Function

The MAX function returns the largest value in the specified column or expression. The following SQL statement determines the project with the latest end date:

```
SELECT    MAX(ACENDATE)
FROM      DSN8810.PROJACT;
```

> **NOTE**
>
> The result of the MAX function is of the same data type as the column or expression on which it operates.
>
> The argument of the MAX function can be of any built-in data type other than a large object: CLOB, DBCLOB, or BLOB. Character string arguments can be no longer than 255 bytes and graphic string arguments can be no longer than 127 bytes.

A somewhat more complicated example using MAX is shown below. It returns the largest salary paid to a man in department D01:

```
SELECT    MAX(SALARY)
FROM      DSN8810.EMP
WHERE     WORKDEPT = 'D01'
AND       SEX = 'M';
```

The MIN Function

The MIN function returns the smallest value in the specified column or expression. To retrieve the smallest bonus given to any employee, issue this SQL statement:

```
SELECT    MIN(BONUS)
FROM      DSN8810.EMP;
```

> **NOTE**
>
> The result of the MIN function is of the same data type as the column or expression on which it operates.
>
> The argument of the MIN function can be of any built-in data type other than a large object: CLOB, DBCLOB, or BLOB. Character string arguments can be no longer than 255 bytes and graphic string arguments can be no longer than 127 bytes.

The STDDEV Function

The STDDEV function returns the standard deviation of a set of numbers. The standard deviation is calculated at the square root of the variance. For example

```
SELECT   STDDEV(SALARY)
FROM     DSN8810.EMP
WHERE    WORKDEPT = 'D01';
```

> **NOTE**
>
> The argument of the STDDEV function can be any built-in numeric data type. The resulting standard deviation is a double precision floating-point number.

The SUM Function

The accumulated total of all values in the specified column or expression are returned by the SUM column function. For example, the following SQL statement calculates the total yearly monetary output for the corporation:

```
SELECT   SUM(SALARY+COMM+BONUS)
FROM     DSN8810.EMP;
```

This SQL statement adds each employee's salary, commission, and bonus. It then aggregates these results into a single value representing the total amount of compensation paid to all employees.

> **NOTE**
>
> The argument of the SUM function can be any built-in numeric data type. The resulting sum must be within the range of acceptable values for the data type. For example, the sum of an INTEGER column must be within the range $-2,147,483,648$ to $+2,147,483,647$. This is because the data type of the result is the same as the data type of the argument values, except:
>
> - The sum of SMALLINT values returns an INTEGER result.
> - The sum of single precision floating point values returns a double precision floating-point result.

The VARIANCE Function

The VARIANCE function returns the variance of a set of numbers. The result is the biased variance of the set of numbers. The variance is calculated as follows:

```
VARIANCE = SUM(X**2)/COUNT(X) - (SUM(X)/COUNT(X))**2
```

> **NOTE**
>
> The argument of the VARIANCE function can be any built-in numeric data type. The resulting variance is a double precision floating-point number.
>
> For brevity and ease of coding, VARIANCE can be shortened to VAR.

Scalar Functions

Scalar functions are applied to a column or expression and operate on a single value. Contrast this with the column functions, which are applied to a set of data and return only a single result.

There are more than 110 scalar functions, each of which can be applied to a column value or expression.

> **NOTE**
>
> DB2 V6 significantly improved IBM's support for built-in scalar functions. Prior to DB2 V6 there were only 22 built-in scalar functions. Additional built-in functions were added for DB2 V7 and V8, as well.

The result of a scalar function is a transformed version of the column or expression being operated on. The transformation of the value is based on the scalar function being applied and the value itself. Consult the following descriptions of the DB2 scalar functions:

ABSVAL or ABS	Converts a value of any numeric data type to its absolute value.
ACOS	Returns the arc-cosine of the argument as an angle expressed in radians.
V7 ADD_MONTHS	Returns a date value that is the result of adding the second expression (which is a duration) to the first expression (which is a date).
ASIN	Returns the arc-sine of the argument as an angle expressed in radians.
ATAN	Returns the arc-tangent of the argument as an angle expressed in radians.
ATANH	Returns the hyperbolic arc-tangent of the argument as an angle expressed in radians.
ATAN2	Returns the arc-tangent of the specified x and y coordinates as an angle expressed in radians.
BLOB	Converts a string or ROWID data type into a value of data type BLOB.
V7 CCSID_ENCODING	Returns the encoding scheme of the specified CCSID. The result will be one of the following: ASCII, EBCDIC, UNICODE, or UNKNOWN.
CEILING or CEIL	Converts the argument, represented as any numeric data type, to the smallest integer value greater than or equal to the argument value.
CHAR	Converts a DB2 date, time, timestamp, ROWID, floating point, integer, or decimal value to a character value. For example

```
SELECT  CHAR(HIREDATE, USA)
FROM    DSN8810.EMP
WHERE   EMPNO = '000140';
```

This SQL statement returns the value for HIREDATE, in USA date format, of the employee with the EMPNO of '000140'.

CLOB	Converts a string or ROWID data type into a value of data type CLOB.

3

	COALESCE	For nullable columns, returns a value instead of a null (equivalent to VALUE function).
	CONCAT	Converts two strings into the concatenation of the two strings.
	COS	Returns the cosine of the argument as an angle expressed in radians.
	COSH	Returns the hyperbolic cosine of the argument as an angle expressed in radians.
	DATE	Converts a value representing a date to a DB2 date. The value to be converted can be a DB2 timestamp, a DB2 date, a positive integer, or a character string.
	DAY	Returns the day portion of a DB2 date or timestamp.
	DAYOFMONTH	Similar to DAY except DAYOFMONTH cannot accept a date duration or time duration as an argument.
	DAYOFWEEK	Converts a date, timestamp, or string representation of a date or timestamp into an integer that represents the day of the week. The value 1 represents Sunday, 2 Monday, 3 Tuesday, 4 Wednesday, 5 Thursday, 6 Friday, and 7 Saturday.
V7	DAYOFWEEK_ISO	Similar to the DAYOFWEEK function, but results in different numbers to represent the day of the week. Converts a date, timestamp, or string representation of a date or timestamp into an integer that represents the day of the week. The value 1 represents Monday, 2 Tuesday, 3 Wednesday, 4 Thursday, 5 Friday, 6 Saturday, and 7 Sunday.
	DAYOFYEAR	Converts a date, timestamp, or string representation of a date or timestamp into an integer that represents the day within the year. The value 1 represents January 1st, 2 January 2nd, and so on.
	DAYS	Converts a DB2 date or timestamp into an integer value representing one more than the number of days since January 1, 0001.
	DBCLOB	Converts a string or ROWID data type into a value of data type DBCLOB.
	DECIMAL or DEC	Converts any numeric value, or character representation of a numeric value, to a decimal value.
V8	DECRYPT_BIT	Decrypts an encrypted column into a binary value using a user-provided encryption password.
V8	DECRYPT_CHAR	Decrypts an encrypted column into a character value using a user-provided encryption password.
V8	DECRYPT_DB	Decrypts an encrypted column into a variable graphic value using a user-provided encryption password.
	DEGREES	Returns the number of degrees for the number of radians supplied as an argument.

	DIGITS	Converts a number to a character string of digits. Be aware that the DIGITS function will truncate the negative sign for negative numbers.
	DOUBLE or FLOAT	Converts any numeric value, or character representation of a numeric value, into a double precision floating point value. Another synonym for this function is DOUBLE-PRECISION.
V8	ENCRYPT_TDES	Uses the Triple DES encryption algorithm to encrypt a column in a table using a user-provided encryption password.
	EXP	Returns the exponential function of the numeric argument. The EXP and LOG functions are inverse operations.
	FLOOR	Converts the argument, represented as any numeric data type, to the largest integer value less than or equal to the argument value.
V8	GENERATE_UNIQUE	Generates a CHAR(13) FOR BIT DATA value that is unique across the Sysplex.
V8	GETHINT	Obtains a hint to help remember the encryption password.
V8	GETVARIABLE	Retrieves session variable values. Details on this function's operation can be found in Chapter 10, "DB2 Security and Authorization."
	GRAPHIC	Converts a string data type into a value of data type GRAPHIC.
V7	GREATEST	Returns the maximum value in a supplied set of values. The argument values can be of any built-in data type other than CLOB, DBCLOB, BLOB, or ROWID.
	HEX	Converts any value other than a long string to hexadecimal.
	HOUR	Returns the hour portion of a time, a timestamp, or a duration.
V7	IDENTITY_VAL_ LOCAL()	Returns the most recently assigned value for an identity column. (No input parameters are used by this function.)
	IFNULL	Returns the first argument in a set of two arguments that is not null. For example

```
SELECT   EMPNO, IFNULL(WORKDEPT, 'N/A')
FROM     DSN8810.EMP;
```

This SQL statement returns the value for WORKDEPT for all employees, unless WORKDEPT is null, in which case it returns the string 'N/A'.

	INSERT	Accepts four arguments. Returns a string with the first argument value inserted into the fourth argument value at the position specified by the second argument value. The third argument value indicates the number of bytes to delete (starting at the position indicated by the third argument value). For example

```
SELECT   INSERT('FLAMING', 2, 1, 'R')
FROM     SYSIBM.SYSDUMMY1;
```

3

This SQL statement returns the value `'FLAMING'`. Here is another example

```
SELECT  INSERT('BOSTON CHOWDER', 8, 0, 'CLAM ')
FROM    SYSIBM.SYSDUMMY1;
```

This SQL statement returns the value `'BOSTON CLAM CHOWDER'`.

CAUTION

Both the value of the argument being inserted into, and the value of the argument that is being inserted, must have the same string data type. That is, both expressions must be character strings, or both expressions must be graphic strings. If the expressions are character strings, neither can be a `CLOB`. If the expressions are graphic strings, neither can be a `DBCLOB`.

INTEGER or INT	Converts any number, or character representation of a number, to an integer by truncating the portion of the number to the right of the decimal point. If the whole number portion of the number is not a valid integer (for example, the value is out of range), an error results.
JULIAN_DAY	Converts a DB2 date or timestamp, or character representation of a date or timestamp, into an integer value representing the number of days from January 1, 4712 B.C. to the date specified in the argument.

NOTE

January 1, 4712 B.C. is the start date of the Julian calendar.

V7 LAST_DAY	Returns the last day of the month for the specified DB2 date or timestamp, or character representation of a date or timestamp.
V7 LEAST	Returns the minimum value in a supplied set of values. The argument values can be of any built-in data type other than `CLOB`, `DBCLOB`, `BLOB`, or `ROWID`.
LEFT	Returns a string containing only the leftmost characters of the string in the first argument, starting at the position indicated by the second argument. For example

```
SELECT  LEFT('THIS IS RETURNED', 4)
FROM    SYSIBM.SYSDUMMY1;
```

This SQL statement returns `'THIS'`, which is the four leftmost characters of the first argument.

LENGTH	Returns the length of any column, which may be null. Does not include the length of null indicators or variable character-length control values, but does include trailing blanks for character columns.
LOCATE	Returns the position of the first occurrence of the first string the second string. For example

```
SELECT  LOCATE('I', 'CRAIG MULLINS')
FROM    SYSIBM.SYSDUMMY1;
```

This SQL statement returns the value 4, because the value 'I' first appears in position four within the searched string. It also appears in the 11th position, but that is of no concern to the LOCATE function. Optionally, a third argument can be supplied indicating where the search should start. For example

```
SELECT  LOCATE('I', 'CRAIG MULLINS', 7)
FROM    SYSIBM.SYSDUMMY1;
```

This SQL statement returns the value 11, because after position 7, the value 'I' first appears in the 11th position. When the third argument is not specified, LOCATE defaults to the beginning of the second string.

LOG or LN	Returns the natural logarithm of the numeric argument. The EXP and LOG functions are inverse operations.
LOG10	Returns the base 10 logarithm of the numeric argument.
LOWER or LCASE	Converts a character string into all lowercase characters.
LTRIM	Removes the leading blanks from a character string.
V7 MAX	Returns the maximum value in a supplied set of values. The argument values can be of any built-in data type other than CLOB, DBCLOB, BLOB, or ROWID. (This scalar function is not the same as the MAX column function discussed earlier.) GREATEST is a synonym for the MAX scalar function.
MICROSECOND	Returns the microsecond component of a timestamp or the character representation of a timestamp.
MIDNIGHT_SECONDS	Returns the number of seconds since midnight for the specified argument, which must be a time, timestamp, or character representation of a time or timestamp.
V7 MIN	Returns the minimum value in a supplied set of values. The argument values can be of any built-in data type other than CLOB, DBCLOB, BLOB, or ROWID. (This scalar function is not the same as the MIN column function discussed earlier.) LEAST is a synonym for MIN.
MINUTE	Returns the minute portion of a time, a timestamp, a character representation of a time or timestamp, or a duration.
MOD	Returns the remainder of the division of the first argument by the second argument. Both arguments must be numeric.
MONTH	Returns the month portion of a date, a timestamp, a character representation of a date or timestamp, or a duration.
V7 MULTIPLY_ALT	Can be used as an alternative to the multiplication operator. This function returns a decimal value that is the product of multiplying the two arguments together.

V7	NEXT_DAY	Returns a timestamp indicating the first day of the week as specified in the second argument that is later than the date expression specified in the first argument. Valid values for the second argument are text representations of the days of the week; that is, MONDAY, TUESDAY, and so on. For example

```
SELECT  NEXT_DAY(CURRENT DATE, 'FRIDAY')
FROM    SYSIBM.SYSDUMMY1;
```

This SQL statement returns a timestamp specifying the first Friday after today.

NULLIF	Returns a null when two specified expressions are equal; if not equal, the first expression is returned.
POSSTR	Similar to the LOCATE function, but with the arguments reversed. POSSTR returns the position of the first occurrence of the second argument within the first argument. For example

```
SELECT  POSSTR('DATABASE ADMINISTRATION', 'ADMIN')
FROM    SYSIBM.SYSDUMMY1;
```

This SQL statement returns the value 10; the value 'ADMIN' first appears in the 10th position.

POWER	Returns the value of the first argument raised to the power of the second argument.
QUARTER	Converts a date, timestamp, or string representation of a date or timestamp into an integer that represents the quarter within the year. The value 1 represents first quarter, 2 second quarter, 3 third quarter, and 4 fourth quarter.
RADIANS	Returns the number of radians for the numeric argument expressed in degrees.
RAND	Returns a random floating-point number between 0 and 1. Optionally, an integer value can be supplied as a seed value for the random value generator. For example

```
SELECT  (RAND() * 100)
FROM    SYSIBM.SYSDUMMY1;
```

This SQL statement returns a random number between 0 and 100.

REAL	Converts any numeric value, or character representation of a numeric value, into a single precision floating point value.
REPEAT	Returns a character string that consists of the first argument repeated the number of times specified in the second argument. For example

```
SELECT  REPEAT('HO ', 3)
FROM    SYSIBM.SYSDUMMY1;
```

This SQL statement returns the character string 'HO HO HO '.

REPLACE | Returns a character string with the value of the second argument replaced by each instance of the third argument in the first argument. For example

```
SELECT  REPLACE('BATATA', 'TA', 'NA')
FROM    SYSIBM.SYSDUMMY1;
```

This SQL statement replaces all instances of 'TA' with 'NA' changing the character string 'BATATA' into 'BANANA'.

CAUTION

Neither the first nor the second argument may be empty strings. The third argument, however, can be an empty string. If the third argument is an empty string, the REPLACE function will simply replace each instance of the second argument with an empty string.

RIGHT | Returns a string containing only the rightmost characters of the string in the first argument, starting at the position indicated by the second argument. For example

```
SELECT  RIGHT('RETURN ONLY THIS', 4)
FROM    SYSIBM.SYSDUMMY1;
```

This SQL statement returns 'THIS', which is the four rightmost characters of the first argument.

ROUND | Rounds the first numeric argument to the number of places specified in the second argument.

V7 | ROUND_TIMESTAMP | Rounds the timestamp value specified in the first argument based on the unit specified in the second argument. The timestamp can be rounded to the nearest year, quarter, month, week, day, hour, minute, or second.

NOTE

Table 3.1 highlights the valid unit arguments for both the ROUND_TIMESTAMP and TRUNC_TIMESTAMP function.

ROWID | Casts the specified argument to a ROWID data type. Although the argument can be any character string, it should be a row ID value that was previously generated by DB2. Otherwise, the value may not be an accurate DB2 ROWID.

RTRIM | Removes the trailing blanks from a character string.

SECOND | Returns the seconds portion of a time, a timestamp, a character representation of a time or timestamp, or a duration.

SIGN | Returns a value that indicates the sign of the numeric argument. The returned value will be –1 if the argument is less than zero, +1 if the argument is greater than zero, and 0 if the argument equals zero.

SIN | Returns the sine of the argument as an angle expressed in radians.

SINH | Returns the hyperbolic sine of the argument as an angle expressed in radians.

SMALLINT	Converts any number, or character representation of a number, to an integer by truncating the portion of the number to the right of the decimal point. If the whole number portion of the number is not a valid integer (for example, the value is out of range), an error results.
SPACE	Returns a string of blanks whose length is specified by the numeric argument. The string of blanks is an SBCS character string.
SQRT	Returns the square root of the numeric argument.
STRIP	Removes leading, trailing, or both leading and trailing blanks (or any specific character) from a string expression.
SUBSTR	Returns the specified portion of a character column from any starting point to any ending point.
TAN	Returns the tangent of the argument as an angle expressed in radians.
TANH	Returns the hyperbolic tangent of the argument as an angle expressed in radians.
TIME	Converts a value representing a valid time to a DB2 time. The value to be converted can be a DB2 timestamp, a DB2 time, or a character string.
TIMESTAMP	Obtains a timestamp from another timestamp, a valid character-string representation of a timestamp, or a combination of date and time values.

V7　TIMESTAMP_FORMAT

Returns a DB2 timestamp for the data in the first argument (which must be a character expression) based on the formatting specified in the second argument. For example

```
SELECT  TIMESTAMP_FORMAT('2004-12-15 23:59:59', 'YYYY-MM-DD
HH24:MI:SS')
FROM    SYSIBM.SYSDUMMY1;
```

This SQL statement converts the non-standard timestamp representation into a standard DB2 timestamp.

TRANSLATE

Translates characters from one expression to another. There are two forms of the TRANSLATE function. If only one argument is specified, the character string is translated to uppercase. Alternately, three arguments can be supplied. In this case, the first argument is transformed by replacing the character string specified in the third argument with the character string specified in the second argument. For example

```
SELECT  TRANSLATE('BACK', 'R', 'C')
FROM    SYSIBM.SYSDUMMY1;
```

This SQL statement returns 'BARK', because the character string 'C' is replaced with the character string 'R'.

Optionally, a fourth argument can be specified. This is the pad character. If the length of the second argument is less than the length of the third argument, the second argument will be padded with the pad character (or blanks) to make up the difference in size. For example

```
SELECT   TRANSLATE('BACK', 'Y', 'ACK', '.')
FROM     SYSIBM.SYSDUMMY1;
```

This SQL statement returns 'BY..', because the character string 'ACK' is replaced with the character string 'Y', and is padded with '.' characters to make up the difference in size.

The string to be translated must be a character string not exceeding 255 bytes or a graphic string of no more than 127 bytes. The string cannot be a CLOB or DBCLOB.

TRUNCATE or TRUNC   Converts the first numeric argument by truncating it to the right of the decimal place by the integer number specified in the second numeric argument. For example

```
SELECT   TRUNC(3.014015,2)
FROM     SYSIBM.SYSDUMMY1;
```

This SQL statement returns the number 3.010000, because the second argument specified that only 2 significant digits are required. The rest was truncated.

V7   **TRUNC_TIMESTAMP**   Truncates the timestamp value specified in the first argument based on the unit specified in the second argument. The timestamp can be truncated by year, quarter, month, week, day, hour, minute, or second.

NOTE

Table 3.1 highlights the valid unit arguments for both the ROUND_TIMESTAMP and TRUNC_TIMESTAMP function.

UPPER or UCASE   Converts a character string into all uppercase characters.

VALUE   For nullable columns, returns a value instead of a null (equivalent to the COALESCE function).

VARCHAR   Converts a character string, date, time, timestamp, integer, decimal, floating point, or ROWID value into a corresponding variable character string representation.

V7   **VARCHAR_FORMAT**   Returns the character representation for the timestamp expression specified in the first argument based on the formatting specified in the second argument. For example

```
SELECT   VARCHAR_FORMAT(CURRENT TIMESTAMP,'YYYY-MM-DD HH24:MI:SS')
FROM     SYSIBM.SYSDUMMY1;
```

This SQL statement converts a standard timestamp into a non-standard character representation of that timestamp.

VARGRAPHIC	Converts a character string to a graphic string.
WEEK	Returns an integer between 1 and 54 based on the week of the year in which a date, timestamp, or string representation of a date or timestamp falls. The assumption is that a week begins on Sunday and ends on Saturday. The value 1 represents the first week, 2 the second week, and so on.
V7 WEEK_ISO	Returns an integer between 1 and 53 based on the week of the year in which a date, timestamp, or string representation of a date or timestamp falls. The assumption is that a week begins on Monday and ends on Sunday. Week 1 is the first week of the year to contain a Thursday. So, it is possible to have up to three days at the beginning of the year appear as the last week of the previous year, or to have up to three days at the end of a year appear as the first week of the next year.
YEAR	Returns the year portion of a date, a timestamp, or a duration.

TABLE 3.1   Units for Rounding and Truncating TIMESTAMPs

Unit	Definition	Explanation
CC	Century	Rounds up to the next century starting in the 50th year of the century or truncates to the first day of the current century. SCC can be used as a synonym for CC.
YYYY	Year	Rounds up to the next year starting on July 1st or truncates to the first day of the current year. The following can be used as synonyms in place of YYYY: SYYY, YEAR, SYEAR, YYY, YY, and Y.
IYYY	ISO Year	Provides the same functionality as YYYY. The following can be used as synonyms in place of IYYY: IYY, IY, and I.
Q	Quarter	Rounds up to the next quarter starting on the sixteenth day of the second month of the quarter or truncates to the first day of the current quarter.
MM	Month	Rounds up to the next month on the sixteenth day of the month or truncates to the first day of the current month. The following can be used as synonyms in place of MM: MONTH, MON, and RM.
WW	Week	Rounds up to the next week on the twelfth hour of the third day of the week (with respect to the first day of the year) or truncates to the first day of the current week.
IW	ISO Week	Rounds up to the next week on the twelfth hour of the third day of the week (with respect to the first day of the ISO year) or truncates to the first day of the current ISO week.
W	Week	Rounds up to the next week on the twelfth hour of the third day of the week (with respect to the first day of the month) or truncates to the first day of the current week (also with respect to the first day of the month).

TABLE 3.1   Continued

Unit	Definition	Explanation
DDD	Day	Rounds up to the next day on the twelfth hour of the day or truncates to the beginning of the current day. DD and J can be used as synonyms in place of DDD.
DAY	Start Day	Differs from DDD by rounding to the starting day of a week. Rounds up to the next week on the twelfth hour of the third day of the week, otherwise it truncates to the starting day of the current week. DY and D can be used as synonyms in place of DAY.
HH	Hour	Rounds up to the next hour at 30 minutes or truncates to the beginning of the current hour. HH12 and HH24 can be used as synonyms in place of HH.
MI	Minute	Rounds up to the next minute at 30 seconds or truncates to the beginning of the current minute.
SS	Second	Rounds up to the next second at 500000 microseconds or truncates to the beginning of the current second.

Some rules for the scalar functions follow:

- Scalar functions can be executed in the select-list of the SQL SELECT statement or as part of a WHERE or HAVING clause.

- A scalar function can be used wherever an expression can be used.

- The argument for a scalar function can be a column function.

The RAISE_ERROR Function

The RAISE_ERROR function is a different type of function than we have discussed so far. It is not a column function because it does not take a group of rows and return a single value. Nor is RAISE_ERROR truly a scalar function because it does not transform column data from one state to another.

Instead, the RAISE_ERROR function is used to raise an error condition in the SQLCA. The user supplies the SQLSTATE and error description for the error to be raised. The error will be raised with the specified SQLSTATE and a SQLCODE of –438.

The RAISE_ERROR function can be used to signal application program and data problems. One situation where RAISE_ERROR may prove useful is in a CASE statement such as

```
SELECT EMPNO,
  CASE WHEN SEX = 'M' THEN 'MALE  '
       WHEN SEX = 'F' THEN 'FEMALE'
 ELSE  RAISE_ERROR('70SX1', 'INVALID DATA, SEX IS NEITHER F NOR M.')
   END
   FROM DSN8810.EMP;
```

The value specified for SQLSTATE must conform to the following rules:

- The value must be a character string of exactly five characters in length.
- Only the characters '0' through '9' and uppercase 'A' through 'Z' may be used.
- The first two characters cannot be '00', '01', or '02'.
- If the first character is '0' through '6' or 'A' through 'H', the last three characters must start with a letter from 'I' through 'Z'.
- If the first character is '7', '8', '9', or 'I' though 'Z', the last three characters can be any valid character.

NOTE

Technically, the RAISE_ERROR function does return a value. It always returns NULL with an undefined data type. You must use the CAST function to cast it to a defined data type to return the value to a program.

MQSeries Built-in Functions

V7   DB2 Version 7 adds a number of new built-in scalar and table functions for use with IBM's message queuing software, MQSeries. These functions enable MQSeries messages to be received and sent. The MQSeries scalar functions are

MQREAD	Accepts two parameters; returns a message (as VARCHAR(4000)) from the MQSeries location specified in the first expression, using the quality of service policy defined in the second expression.
MQREADCLOB	Accepts two parameters; returns a message (as a CLOB) from the MQSeries location specified in the first expression, using the quality of service policy defined in the second expression.

NOTE

When performing either the MQREAD or MQREADCLOB function the operation does not remove the message from the queue specified in the first expression. Additionally, for both functions, if no messages are available a NULL is returned.

MQRECEIVE	Same as MQREAD, except the operation will remove the messages from the queue.
MQRECEIVECLOB	Same as MQREADCLOB, except the operation will remove the messages from the queue.

NOTE

When performing either the MQRECEIVE or MQRECEIVECLOB function, the operation will remove the message from the queue specified in the first expression. Additionally, for both functions, if no messages are available a NULL is returned.

MQSEND	This function is used to send messages to an MQSeries queue. It returns a value of 1 if successful; 0 if unsuccessful. It accepts three (possibly, four) parameters. The data contained in the first expression will be sent to the MQSeries location specified in the second expression, using the quality of service policy defined in the third expression. A user defined by the message correlation identifier may be specified as an optional fourth expression.

Using these scalar functions you can easily read, retrieve, and send information from and to MQSeries message queues. The scalar functions operate one message at a time. At times, though, you might want to operate on multiple MQSeries messages. This requires table functions, and DB2 Version 7 supplies several of these as well. The MQSeries table functions are

MQREADALL	Returns all of the messages (as VARCHAR) from the MQSeries location specified in the first expression, using the quality of service policy defined in the second expression. An optional third parameter can be used to limit the number of rows to return.
MQREADALLCLOB	Returns all of the messages (as CLOB) from the MQSeries location specified in the first expression, using the quality of service policy defined in the second expression. An optional third parameter can be used to limit the number of rows to return.
MQRECEIVEALL	Same as MQREADALL except the operation will remove the messages from the queue.
MQRECEIVECLOBALL	Same as MQREADALLCLOB except the operation will remove the messages from the queue.

NOTE

When performing any of the MQSeries functions that read or receive data, an operation returns a table with the following columns:

- MSG—Contains the contents of the MQSeries message, either a VARCHAR(4000) or CLOB based on which function was used.
- CORRELID—Correlation ID used to relate messages—VARCHAR(24).
- TOPIC—The topic that the message was published with, if available—VARCHAR(40).
- QNAME—The queue name where the message was received—VARCHAR(48).
- MSGID—The assigned MQSeries unique identifier for this message—CHAR(24).
- MSGFORMAT—The format (typically MQSTR) of the message, as defined by MQSeries—VARCHAR(8).

XML Publishing Built-in Functions

V8 DB2 Version 8 adds a number of new built-in scalar functions to allow applications to efficiently generate XML data from DB2 data. The XML publishing functions are

XMLELEMENT	Returns an XML element given an element name, an optional collection of attributes, and zero or more arguments that make up the contents of the element.
XMLATTRIBUTES	Used within the XMLELEMENT function to specify attributes of the XML element.
XMLFOREST	Returns a forest of XML elements that share a pattern from a list of expressions.
XMLCONCAT	Returns a forest of XML elements generated from a concatenation of two or more elements.
XMLAGG	Returns a concatenation of XML elements generated from a collection of XML elements.
XML2CLOB	Returns a CLOB representation of an XML expression.

Built-in Function Guidelines

Use the following guidelines to implement an effective strategy for deploying built-in functions in your DB2 applications.

Use Functions Instead of Program Logic

Use the built-in functions provided by DB2 instead of coding your own application logic to perform the same tasks. You can be sure the DB2 built-in functions will perform the correct tasks with no bugs. But you will have to take the time to code, debug, and test your application code. This is time you can better spend on developing application-specific functionality.

Avoid Function Synonyms

Several of the built-in functions have synonymous names that perform the same function. For example, VALUES and COALESCE perform the same exact function. You should standardize on one of the forms in your applications. By using only one of the forms your SQL will be easier to understand and maintain. Of course, your purchased applications may use any of the forms.

The following are my recommendations, but of course, yours may differ:

Use This	Instead of This
CEILING	CEIL
COALESCE	VALUES
DAY	DAYOFMONTH
DECIMAL	DEC
DOUBLE	FLOAT
GREATEST	MAX (scalar)
INTEGER	INT

Use This	Instead of This
LEAST	MIN (scalar)
LOG	LN
LOWER	LCASE
TIMESTAMP_FORMAT	TO_DATE
TRUNCATE	TRUNC
UPPER	UCASE
VARIANCE	VAR
VARIANCE_SAMP	VAR_SAMP

In general, it is better to use the long form of the function instead of the abbreviated form because it is easier to quickly understand the purpose of the function. For example, one might easily assume that VAR is short for the VARCHAR function, instead of the VARIANCE function.

I suggest using DAY instead of DAYOFMONTH because DAYOFMONTH does not support using a date duration or a timestamp duration as an argument. However, if you do not use durations in your applications you might want to standardize on DAYOFMONTH instead of DAY because it is similar in name to other related functions such as DAYOFWEEK and DAYOFYEAR.

I suggest using DOUBLE instead of FLOAT because one might confuse FLOAT with REAL. If there were a synonym for REAL, such as SINGLE, I would suggest using SINGLE. But there is not.

V7 I suggest using the scalar functions LEAST and GREATEST instead of the scalar functions MIN and MAX to avoid possible confusion with the column functions MIN and MAX.

Use UPPER instead of TRANSLATE

Using the TRANSLATE function with a single argument serves the same purpose as the UPPER function—to convert a character string into uppercase. However, the UPPER function should be used for this purpose instead of TRANSLATE because

- The UPPER function can be used only for the purpose of converting character strings to uppercase.

- The TRANSLATE function is not as easily identified by developers as converting text to uppercase and is therefore more difficult to debug, maintain, and test SQL changes.

Use HAVING to Search Column Function Results

When using column functions, remember that the WHERE clause applies to the data prior to modification. To remove results after the data has been modified by the function, you must use the HAVING clause in conjunction with a GROUP BY clause.

The GROUP BY clause collates the resultant rows after the column function(s) have been applied. When the data is grouped, users can eliminate non-pertinent groups of data with the HAVING clause.

For example, the following query groups employee data by department, returning the aggregate salary for each department, unless the average salary is $10,000 or less:

```
SELECT   WORKDEPT, SUM(SALARY)
FROM     DSN8810.EMP
GROUP BY WORKDEPT
HAVING   AVG(SALARY) > 10000 ;
```

The HAVING clause eliminates groups of non-required data after the data is summarized.

Be Aware of NULLs When Using Column Functions

Nulls can be one of the more difficult features of DB2 to understand and master. This is especially so when using certain built-in DB2 column functions. In some cases, you can write a query against a column using a built-in function and have the result be NULL— even if the column itself is defined as NOT NULL. Don't believe it? Run this query:

```
SELECT  SUM(ACTNO)
FROM    DSN8810.EMPPROJACT
WHERE   PROJNO = 'QRSTUV';
```

ACTNO is defined as NOT NULL, yet this query returns a NULL (unless someone inserted a row with the value of 'QRSTUV' for PROJNO). Why? The sum of all ACTNO values for project 'QRSTUV' is not zero, but is not applicable—at least as defined by DB2.

Basically, if there are no results that apply to the predicate, the result of using a function such as SUM or AVG is NULL because the sum or average of no rows is not zero, but undefined.

CHAPTER 4

Using DB2 User-Defined Functions and Data Types

As of DB2 Version 6, it became possible to create additional functions and data types to supplement the built-in function and data types supplied with DB2. User-defined functions and types give users the ability to effectively customize DB2 to their shop requirements. The ability to customize is potentially very powerful. It also can be quite complex and requires detailed knowledge, additional application development skills, and administrative dexterity.

What Is a User-Defined Function?

A user-defined function, or UDF for short, is procedural functionality added to DB2 by the user. The UDF, after coded and implemented, extends the functionality of DB2 SQL by enabling users to specify the UDF in SQL statements just like built-in SQL functions.

User-defined functions are ideal for organizations wanting to utilize DB2 and SQL to perform specialized, corporate routines performing business logic and data transformation.

Types of User-Defined Functions

There are two ways of creating a user-defined function: You can code your own function program from scratch, or you can edit an existing function.

Two types of user-defined functions can be written from scratch: *scalar functions* and *table functions*. Recall from Chapter 3, "Using DB2 Functions," that scalar functions are applied to a column or expression and operate on a single value. Table functions are a different type of function that, when invoked, return an entire table. A table function is specified in the WHERE clause of a SELECT statement taking the place of a table, view, synonym, or alias.

Scalar and table user-defined functions are referred to as *external functions* because they are written and developed outside of (or external to) DB2. External UDFs must be written in a host programming language. DB2 user-defined functions can be written in Assembler, C, C++, COBOL, Java, or PL/I.

A third type of user-defined function can be created from another existing function. This is a sourced function. A *sourced function* is based on a function that already exists—it can be based on a built-in function or another user-defined function that has already been created. A sourced function can be based on an existing scalar or column function. So, external functions are coded from scratch, whereas sourced functions are created based on a pre-existing function (see Figure 4.1).

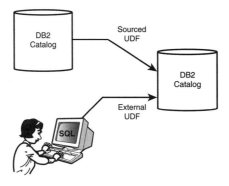

FIGURE 4.1   Sourced versus external UDFs.

User-defined functions are similar in functionality to application subroutines, but user-defined functions are different because they can be used inside SQL statements. In fact, the only way that user-defined functions can be executed is from within an SQL statement. This gives them great power. A user-defined function is not a substitute for an application subroutine, subprogram, or procedure. Instead, user-defined functions are used to extend the functionality of the SQL language.

The Schema

User-defined functions, user-defined distinct types, stored procedures, and triggers all are associated with a schema. By default, the schema name is the authid of the process that issues the CREATE FUNCTION, CREATE DISTINCT TYPE, CREATE PROCEDURE, or CREATE TRIGGER statement.

A schema, therefore, is simply a logical grouping of procedural database objects (user-defined functions, user-defined distinct types, stored procedures, and triggers).

You can specify a schema name when you create a user-defined function, type, or trigger. If the schema name is not the same as the SQL authorization ID, the issuer of the statement must have either SYSADM or SYSCTRL authority, or the authid of the issuing process must have the CREATEIN privilege on the schema.

For example, the following statement creates a user-defined function named NEWFUNC in the schema named MYSCHEMA:

```
CREATE FUNCTION MYSCHEMA.NEWFUNC ...
```

If the MYSCHEMA component was not included in the CREATE statement, the schema would default to the authid of the person (or process) that executed the CREATE statement. In short, the schema is set to the owner of the function. If the CREATE statement was embedded in a program, the owner is the authid of the owner of the plan or package; if the statement is dynamically prepared, the owner is the authid in the CURRENT SQLID special register.

Creating User-Defined Functions

Before using DDL to create a user-defined function, the function program should be coded and prepared. This requires the developer to write the program, precompile, compile, link-edit the program, BIND the DBRM for the program (if the function contains SQL statements), and then test the program to be sure it is free of bugs.

Then, before the user-defined function can be used, it must be registered to DB2 using the CREATE FUNCTION DDL statement. For example, assume that you have written a user-defined function program. Further assume that the program returns the number of days in the month for a given date. The following is a simplified version of the CREATE FUNCTION statement that could be used to register the UDF to DB2:

```
CREATE FUNCTION DAYSINMONTH(DATE)
    RETURNS INTEGER
    EXTERNAL NAME 'DAYMTH'
    LANGUAGE COBOL;
```

This statement creates a UDF named DAYSINMONTH, with one parameter of DATE data type, that returns a single value of INTEGER data type. The external name for the function program is DAYMTH and it is coded in COBOL.

> **NOTE**
>
> Most of the parameters have been omitted from this simple CREATE FUNCTION example. The parameters available for the CREATE FUNCTION statement are discussed in depth later in this chapter.

After the user-defined function has been created, and the appropriate authority has been GRANTed, the UDF can be used in an SQL statement as follows:

```
SELECT EMPNO, LASTNME, BIRTHDATE, DAYSINMONTH(BIRTHDATE)
FROM    DSN8810.EMP
WHERE   DAYSINMONTH(BIRTHDATE) < 31;
```

The result of this statement would be a list of employees whose birth date falls in a month having fewer than 31 days (that is, February, April, June, September, and November). This assumes that the program for the user-defined function DAYSINMONTH is correctly coded to examine the date specified as input and return the actual number of days in the month.

There are many different characteristics that need to be determined and specified when creating UDFs. Table 4.1 outlines the characteristics and whether each applies to external functions, sourced functions, or both.

TABLE 4.1   Characteristics of DB2 User-Defined Functions

Characteristic	Definition	Validity
UDF name (Input parameter types)	Name of the UDF and its B parameters.	B
RETURNS [TABLE]	Output parameter types.	B
SPECIFIC	Specific name.	B
PARAMETER CCSID	Encoding scheme for string parameters: ASCII, EBCDIC, or UNICODE.	B
EXTERNAL NAME	Name of the UDF program.	X
LANGUAGE	Programming language used to write the UDF program.	X
[NOT] DETERMINISTIC	Whether the UDF program is deterministic.	X
...SQL...	Whether or not SQL is issued in the UDF program and if SQL modifies or just reads DB2 data. Valid options are NO SQL, MODIFIES SQL DATA, READS SQL DATA, or CONTAINS SQL.	X
SOURCE	Name of the source function.	S
PARAMETER STYLE	The linkage convention used by the UDF program. DB2 SQL indicates parameters for indicator variables are associated with each input value and the return value to allow for NULLs.	X
FENCED	The UDF code cannot run in the DBMS address space.	X

V7 (marker beside PARAMETER CCSID row)

TABLE 4.1   Continued

Characteristic	Definition	Validity
...NULL...	Whether the function is called if any input arguments are NULL at execution time.	X
[NO] EXTERNAL ACTION	Whether the UDF performs an action that changes the state of objects that DB2 does not manage (such as files).	X
[NO] SCRATCHPAD	Whether or not a scratchpad is used to save information from one invocation of the UDF to the next.	X
[NO] FINAL CALL	Whether or not a final call is made to the UDF program to free system resources.	X
[DIS]ALLOW PARALLEL	Whether or not parallel processing is permitted.	X
[NO] COLLID	Package collection ID of UDF package. NO indicates same as calling program.	X
WLM ENVIRONMENT	The name of the WLM environment.	X
ASUTIME [NO] LIMIT	CPU resource limit for an invocation of a UDF.	X
STAY RESIDENT	Whether or not the UDF load module stays in memory.	X
PROGRAM TYPE	Whether the program runs as a main routine (MAIN) or as a subroutine (SUB).	X
SECURITY	Type of security to be used: DB2, USER, or DEFINER.	X
SPECIAL REGISTERS	Indicates whether values of special registers are inherited or defaulted.	X

V7

TABLE 4.1   Continued

Characteristic	Definition	Validity
STATIC DISPATCH	At function resolution time, DB2 chooses a function based on the static (or declared) types of the function parameters.	X
RUN OPTIONS	LE/370 runtime options.	X
CARDINALITY	An estimate of the expected number of rows returned by a table function.	X
[NO] DBINFO	Whether or not an additional argument is passed when the UDF is invoked.	X

> **NOTE**
>
> If the Validity column of Table 4.1 contains the value X, the characteristic applies to external functions only; S means it applies to sourced functions only; and B means it applies to both external and sourced functions.

UDF Programming Language Options   DB2 offers several application programming languages in which UDF programs can be written. The following languages are supported by DB2 for UDF creation:

- Assembler
- C
- C++
- COBOL
- Java (new as of DB2 V7)
- PL/I

DB2 also supports SQL scalar functions that are written using only SQL functionality.

Keep in mind, too, that all UDF programs must be designed to run in IBM's Language Environment (LE/370).

How Functions Are Executed

User-defined functions run in WLM-managed stored procedure address spaces. To execute a user-defined function, simply reference the function in an SQL statement. The SQL statement can be issued dynamically or statically, as part of an application program or via ad hoc SQL—anywhere SQL can be run, the UDF can be coded. External UDFs require WLM running in GOAL mode.

When a function is invoked in an SQL statement, DB2 must choose the correct function to run to satisfy the request. DB2 will check for candidate functions to satisfy the function request. The manner in which DB2 chooses which function to run is based on the following criteria:

- First of all, the schema must match. If the function being invoked is fully qualified, the schema must match for the function to be considered a candidate for execution. If the function being invoked is not fully qualified, DB2 will check the SQL path of the invoking process to find a function with a matching schema.

- Of course, the name must match the function being invoked for the user-defined function to be considered a candidate for execution.

- The number of parameters for the user-defined function must match the number of parameters specified by the invoked function. Additionally, the data type of each parameter must match, or be promotable to, the data types specified for each parameter in the function being invoked. Refer to Table 4.2 for a list of which data types are promotable to other data types. The data types in the first column can be promoted to the data types in the second column. When performing function resolution, the earlier the data type in the second column appears, the more preferable it is to the other promotable data types.

  To clarify this requirement, consider the following example:

  ```
  SELECT XSCHEMA.FUNCX(COLA)
  FROM    TABLE;
  ```

  The data type of COLA is SMALLINT. Furthermore, two user-defined functions have been created named FUNCX, both in the same schema, XSCHEMA. Both FUNCX UDFs require one parameter, but one is defined with an INTEGER data type and the other with a data type of REAL. The SMALLINT data type is promotable to both INTEGER and REAL, but, because INTEGER appears first in the promotion list, the FUNCX with the INTEGER parameter will be used instead of the one with the REAL parameter.

- The appropriate authority must exist. That is, the invoking authid must have the authority to execute the user-defined function.

- Finally, the timestamp of the BIND for the user-defined function must be older than the timestamp of the BIND for the package or plan that invokes the function.

> **NOTE**
>
> For a function that passes a transition table, the data type, length, precision, and scale of each column in the transition table must match the data type, length, precision, and scale of each column of the table specified in the function definition.

For unqualified UDFs, it is possible that two or more candidate functions will fit equally well. In this case, the user-defined function whose schema name is earliest in the SQL path will be chosen for execution.

For example, suppose functions XSCHEMA.FUNC1 and YSCHEMA2.FUNC1 both fit the function resolution criteria equally well. Both have the same function name but different schema names. Both also fit the rest of the criteria regarding number of parameters, parameter data types, and requisite authority. If the SQL path is

```
"ZSCHEMA"; "YSCHEMA"; "SYSPROC"; "SYSIBM"; "XSCHEMA";
```

DB2 will select function YSCHEMA.FUNC1 because YSCHEMA is before XSCHEMA in the SQL path.

The SQL path is specified to DB2 in one of two ways. The SQL path is determined by the CURRENT PATH special register for dynamically prepared SQL statements. For dynamic SQL, the SQL path can be set by issuing the SET CURRENT PATH statement. The PATH parameter of the BIND and REBIND commands is used to specify the SQL path for SQL containing UDFs in plans and packages.

DB2 supports function overloading. This means that multiple functions can have the same name and DB2 will decide which one to run based on the parameters. Consider an example where an application developer writes a UDF that overloads the addition operator +. The UDF is created to concatenate text strings together. The + function is overloaded because if it is acting on numbers it adds them together; if the function is acting on text it concatenates the text strings.

TABLE 4.2   Data Type Promotability

Data Type	Can Be Promoted to
CHAR or GRAPHIC	CHAR or GRAPHIC
	VARCHAR or VARGRAPHIC
	CLOB or DBCLOB
VARCHAR or VARGRAPHIC	VARCHAR or VARGRAPHIC
	CLOB or DBCLOB
CLOB or DBCLOB	CLOB or DBCLOB
BLOB	BLOB
SMALLINT	SMALLINT
	INTEGER
	DECIMAL
	REAL
	DOUBLE
INTEGER	INTEGER
	DECIMAL
	REAL
	DOUBLE
DECIMAL	DECIMAL
	REAL
	DOUBLE

TABLE 4.2   Continued

Data Type	Can Be Promoted to
REAL	REAL
	DOUBLE
DOUBLE	DOUBLE
DATE	DATE
TIME	TIME
TIMESTAMP	TIMESTAMP
ROWID	ROWID
UDT	UDT (with the same name)

The process of following these steps to determine which function to execute is called *function resolution*.

> **NOTE**
>
> When automatic rebind is invoked on a package or plan that contains UDFs, DB2 will not consider any UDF created after the original BIND or REBIND was issued. In other words, only those UDFs that existed at the time of the original BIND or REBIND are considered during function resolution for plans and packages bound as a result of automatic rebind.

DSN_FUNCTION_TABLE and EXPLAIN   You can use EXPLAIN to obtain information about DB2 function resolution. To use EXPLAIN to obtain function resolution information, you must create a special table called DSN_FUNCTION_TABLE. When EXPLAIN is executed and UDFs are used, DB2 will store function resolution details for each UDF in the statement, package, or plan, in DSN_FUNCTION_TABLE.

Information will be populated in DSN_FUNCTION_TABLE when you execute an EXPLAIN on an SQL statement that contains one or more UDFs, or when you run a program whose plan is bound with EXPLAIN(YES), and the program executes an SQL statement that contains one or more UDFs.

> **NOTE**
>
> EXPLAIN actually can be used to return a lot more information about SQL statements, including the actual access paths used by DB2 to run the SQL. Refer to Chapter 25, "Using EXPLAIN," for an in-depth exploration of using EXPLAIN and interpreting its results.

Remember, you must create a table named DSN_FUNCTION_TABLE before you can use EXPLAIN to obtain function resolution details. A sample CREATE statement for this table follows:

```
CREATE TABLE userid.DSN_FUNCTION_TABLE
    (QUERYNO        INTEGER      NOT NULL WITH DEFAULT,
     QBLOCKNO       INTEGER      NOT NULL WITH DEFAULT,
     APPLNAME       CHAR(8)      NOT NULL WITH DEFAULT,
     PROGNAME       CHAR(8)      NOT NULL WITH DEFAULT,
     COLLID         CHAR(18)     NOT NULL WITH DEFAULT,
     GROUP_MEMBER   CHAR(8)      NOT NULL WITH DEFAULT,
     EXPLAIN_TIME   TIMESTAMP    NOT NULL WITH DEFAULT,
```

4

```
SCHEMA_NAME     CHAR(8)       NOT NULL WITH DEFAULT,
FUNCTION_NAME   CHAR(18)      NOT NULL WITH DEFAULT,
SPEC_FUNC_NAME  CHAR(18)      NOT NULL WITH DEFAULT,
FUNCTION_TYPE   CHAR(2)       NOT NULL WITH DEFAULT,
VIEW_CREATOR    CHAR(8)       NOT NULL WITH DEFAULT,
VIEW_NAME       CHAR(18)      NOT NULL WITH DEFAULT,
PATH            VARCHAR(254)  NOT NULL WITH DEFAULT,
FUNCTION_TEXT   VARCHAR(254)  NOT NULL WITH DEFAULT
) IN database.tablespace;
```

After executing EXPLAIN for an SQL statement that uses a UDF, each of these columns will contain information about the UDF chosen during function resolution. The actual definition of the information contained in the columns of DSN_FUNCTION_TABLE is shown in Table 4.3.

TABLE 4.3   DSN_FUNCTION_TABLE Columns

Column Name	Description
QUERYNO	Indicates an integer value assigned by the user issuing the EXPLAIN or by DB2. Enables the user to differentiate between EXPLAIN statements.
QBLOCKNO	Indicates an integer value enabling the identification of subselects or a union in a given SQL statement. The first subselect is numbered 1; the second, 2; and so on.
APPLNAME	Contains the plan name for rows inserted as a result of running BIND PLAN specifying EXPLAIN(YES). Contains the package name for rows inserted as a result of running BIND PACKAGE with EXPLAIN(YES). Otherwise, contains blanks for rows inserted as a result of dynamic EXPLAIN statements.
PROGNAME	Contains the name of the program in which the SQL statement is embedded.
COLLID	Contains the collection ID for the package.
GROUP_MEMBER	Indicates the member name of the DB2 that executed EXPLAIN. The column is blank if the DB2 subsystem was not in a data sharing environment when EXPLAIN was executed.
EXPLAIN_TIME	Contains a TIMESTAMP value indicating when the EXPLAIN that created this row was executed.
SCHEMA_NAME	Contains the name of the schema for the invoked function.
FUNCTION_NAME	Contains the name of the UDF to be invoked.
SPEC_FUNC_NAME	Contains the specific name of the UDF to be invoked.
FUNCTION_TYPE	Contains a value indicating the type of function to be invoked: SU Scalar Function TU Table Function
VIEW_CREATOR	If the function is referenced in a CREATE VIEW statement, this column contains the creator name for the view. If not, the column is left blank.
VIEW_NAME	If the function is referenced in a CREATE VIEW statement, this column contains the name for the view. If not, the column is left blank.
PATH	Contains the value of the SQL path at the time DB2 performed function resolution for this statement.
FUNCTION_TEXT	Contains the first 100 bytes of the actual text used to invoke the UDF, including the function name and all parameters.

> **CAUTION**
>
> For UDFs specified in infix notation, the `FUNCTION_TEXT` column of `DSN_FUNCTION_TABLE` will contain the function name only. For example, suppose that * is UDF in the following reference:
>
> `COL1*COL6`
>
> In this case, the `FUNCTION_TEXT` column will contain only the value * and not the entire reference (`COL1*COL6`).

Table Functions

Table functions are different in nature from scalar functions. A table function is designed to return multiple columns and rows. Its output is a table. An example using a table function follows:

```
SELECT WINNER, WINNER_SCORE, LOSER, LOSER_SCORE
FROM   FOOTBALL_RESULTS(5)
WHERE  LOSER_SCORE = 0;
```

In this case, the table function `FOOTBALL_RESULTS()` is used to return the win/loss statistics for football games. The table function can be used in SQL statements, just like a regular DB2 table. The function program is designed to fill the rows and columns of the "table." The input parameter is an `INTEGER` value corresponding to the week the game was played; if 0 is entered, all weeks are considered. The previous query would return all results where the losing team was shut out (had 0 points) during the fifth week of the season.

The following or similar `CREATE FUNCTION` statement could be used to define the `FOOTBALL_RESULTS()` function:

```
CREATE FUNCTION FOOTBALL_RESULTS(INTEGER)
  RETURNS TABLE (WEEK INTEGER,
                 WINNER CHAR(20),
                 WINNER_SCORE INTEGER,
                 LOSER CHAR(20),
                 LOSER_SCORE INTEGER)
  EXTERNAL NAME FOOTBALL
    LANGUAGE C
  PARAMETER STYLE DB2SQL
    NO SQL
    DETERMINISTIC
  NO EXTERNAL ACTION
    FENCED
    SCRATCHPAD
    FINAL CALL
    DISALLOW PARALLEL
    CARDINALITY 300;
```

The key parameter is the `RETURNS TABLE` parameter, which is used to define the columns of the table function. The function program must create these rows itself or from another data source, such as a flat file.

The value supplied for the CARDINALITY parameter is only an estimate. It is provided to help DB2 optimize statements using the table function. It is possible to return more or fewer rows than is specified in CARDINALITY.

Sourced Functions

Sourced functions are created from already existing built-in (scalar and column) and user-defined (scalar) functions. The primary reason to create a sourced function is to enable functions for user-defined distinct data types. This is required because DB2 implements strong typing.

More information on sourced functions and strong typing is provided later in this chapter in the section "User-Defined Data Types and Strong Typing." For now, though, the following is an example of creating a sourced UDF:

```
CREATE FUNCTION FINDWORD (DOCUMENT, VARCHAR(50))
  RETURNS INTEGER
  SPECIFIC FINDWORDDOC
SOURCE SPECIFIC FINDWORDCLOB;
```

In this example, a new function, FINDWORD, is created from an existing function, FINDWORDCLOB. The function finds the location of the supplied word (expressed as a VARCHAR(50) value) in the supplied DOCUMENT. The function returns an INTEGER indicating the location of the word in the DOCUMENT. DOCUMENT is a user-defined type based on a CLOB data type.

User-Defined Function Guidelines

The following guidelines can be used to help you implement effective and efficient user-defined functions for your organization.

Naming User-Defined Functions   The rules for naming user-defined functions are somewhat complex. The UDF name can be the same as another UDF, even if it is in the same schema. However, to give one function the same name as another function in the same schema, the number of parameters and the data type of the parameters must differ. DB2 will not allow a UDF to be created if the schema, UDF name, number of parameters, and data type of each parameter match another existing UDF.

Furthermore, the name of the user-defined function cannot be any of the following system defined key words:

ALL	AND
ANY	BETWEEN
DISTINCT	EXCEPT
EXISTS	FALSE
FOR	FROM
IN	IS
LIKE	MATCH

NOT	NULL
ONLY	OR
OVERLAPS	SIMILAR
SOME	TABLE
TRUE	TYPE
UNIQUE	UNKNOWN
=	¬=
<	<=
>	>=
¬<	¬>
<>	

External UDF Program Restrictions   When you develop programs for external user-defined functions, DB2 places certain restrictions on the type of services and functions that can be used. Keep the following restrictions in mind as you code your external UDF programs:

- COMMIT and ROLLBACK statements cannot be issued in a user-defined function. The UDF is part of the unit of work of the issuing SQL statement.

- RRSAF calls cannot be used in user-defined functions. DB2 uses the RRSAF as its interface to user-defined functions. Therefore, any RRSAF calls made within the UDF code will be rejected.

- If your user-defined function does not specify either the EXTERNAL ACTION or SCRATCHPAD parameter, the UDF may not execute under the same task each time it is invoked.

- All open cursors in user-defined scalar functions must be closed before the function completes, or DB2 will return an SQL error.

- The host language that is used to write UDF programs can impose restrictions on UDF development as well. Each programming language has its own restrictions and limits on the number of parameters that can be passed to a routine in that language. Be sure to read the programming guide for the language being used (before you begin coding) to determine the number of parameters allowed.

- WLM running in GOAL mode is required for UDFs.

> **NOTE**
>
> The limitation on the number of parameters for the programming language to be used can impact table UDFs because table functions often require a large number of parameters (that is, at least one output parameter for every column of the table).

Starting and Stopping UDFs   Starting and stopping external UDFs can be an administrative burden. When UDFs fail, they will be stopped (unless you specify otherwise when the

UDF is created). In order for any application to call the UDF again, it must first be started again. You should develop administrative procedures such that appropriate personnel have the authority to start and stop UDFs.

To start a UDF, you must issue the following DB2 command:

```
-START FUNCTION SPECIFIC
```

This will cause the named UDF to be activated. You do not need to issue a START command for new UDFs; DB2 will automatically activate a new UDF the first time an SQL statement invokes the function. For example, the following command starts the function XFUNC in the schema XSCHEMA:

```
-START FUNCTION SPECIFIC(XCHEMA.XFUNC)
```

> **CAUTION**
>
> The -START FUNCTION SPECIFIC command will not refresh the Language Environment in the WLM-established stored procedure address space. In order to refresh the Language Environment to establish a new load module for a UDF, you must issue the following WLM command:
>
> ```
> VARY WLM, APPLENV=applenv,REFRESH
> ```

Similarly, you can issue the -STOP FUNCTION SPECIFIC command to stop a UDF. Stopping a UDF prevents DB2 from accepting SQL statements that invoke that function. Any SQL statements that have already been queued or scheduled by DB2 will continue to run. This command will not prevent these SQL statements from running.

UDF administration is complicated by the fact that only users with one of the following authorities (or qualities) can execute the START and STOP FUNCTION SPECIFIC commands:

- The owner of the UDF
- SYSOPR authority
- SYSCTRL authority
- SYSADM authority

> **CAUTION**
>
> Remember, these commands (both START FUNCTION SPECIFIC and STOP FUNCTION SPECIFIC) apply to external UDFs only; built-in functions and sourced UDFs cannot be stopped and started using DB2 commands.

Starting and Stopping All Functions   Issuing either the -START FUNCTION SPECIFIC or the –STOP FUNCTION SPECIFIC command without any arguments starts, or stops, all UDFs known to the system. For example

```
-START FUNCTION SPECIFIC
```

starts all UDFs for the DB2 subsystem on which the command was issued.

V8 **Exercise Control Over UDF Stopping**   In Version 8, DB2 for z/OS gives you greater control over UDF execution and utilization. You can now specify for each stored procedure or UDF the maximum number of failures that are allowed before DB2 stops the routine. Previously, when a UDF failed, DB2 stopped it, resulting in administrative overhead—particularly in a test environment.

By specifying the most appropriate value for an individual routine, you can let some routines continue to be invoked for development and debugging and stop other routines for maintenance before they cause problems in a production environment.

The available options that can be specified using CREATE or ALTER FUNCTION are

- STOP AFTER FAILURE:—Indicating that the UDF is to be stopped every time it fails

- STOP AFTER *n* FAILURES:—Indicating that the UDF is to be stopped only after every *n*th failure

- CONTINUE AFTER FAILURE:—Indicating that the UDF is not to be stopped when it fails

These options should only be specified on external UDFs, not on sourced UDFs.

Keep It Simple   Each user-defined function program should be coded to perform one and only one task. The UDF program should be as simple as possible while still performing the desired task. Do not create overly complex UDF programs that perform multiple tasks based on the input. It is far better to have multiple UDFs, each performing one simple task, than to have a single, very complex UDF that performs multiple tasks. The UDF program will be easier to code, debug, understand, and maintain when it needs to be modified.

Use DSN_FUNCTION_TABLE   To be sure that the right UDF is being chosen during function resolution, use EXPLAIN to populate DSN_FUNCTION_TABLE. It is only by reading the contents of DSN_FUNCTION_TABLE that you can ascertain which UDF was chosen for execution by DB2 during function resolution.

Promote UDF Reuseability   User-defined functions should be developed with reuseability in mind. After the UDF has been coded and registered to DB2, it can be shared by multiple applications. It is wise to code your UDFs such that they perform simple, useful tasks that can be used by many applications at your site.

Reusing UDFs in multiple applications is better than creating multiple UDFs having the same (or similar) functionality for each application. You should promote reuseability while at the same time keeping the UDF code as simple as possible.

Promote Consistent Enterprisewide SQL   Consider replicating UDFs across subsystems in order to keep the SQL language consistent across the enterprise. This might add a few maintenance steps; however, the gain is a more mobile development staff.

Handle UDF Abends   When an external UDF abends, the invoking statement in the calling program receives an error code, namely SQLCODE -430. The unit of work containing the invoking statement must be rolled back. The calling program should check for the –430 SQLCODE and issue a ROLLBACK when it is received.

Furthermore, the UDF might need to be restarted depending on the setting of the [STOP | CONTINUE] AFTER FAILURE option for the UDF.

Invoke UDFs Using Qualified Names   Use the qualified name of a function in the invoking SQL statement. By doing so, you simplify function resolution. DB2 will only search for functions in the specific schema you code. Therefore, DB2 is more likely to choose the function you intend, and the function resolution process will take less time to complete, because fewer functions will qualify as candidates.

V8   **Consider Using** SET CURRENT PACKAGE PATH   The new special register, CURRENT PACKAGE PATH, was added with DB2 Version 8. It is particularly useful for those organizations that use more than one collection for packages. In prior releases, applications that do not use plans must issue the SET CURRENT PACKAGE PATH statement each time a package from a different collection is used. With the CURRENT PACKAGE PATH special register, an application programmer can specify a list of package collections in one SET CURRENT PACKAGE PATH statement.

Using SET CURRENT PACKAGE PATH can reduce network traffic, simplify application coding, and result in improved processing and elapsed time.

CAST **Parameters to the Right Data Type**   Use the CAST function to cast the parameters of the invoked UDF to the data types specified in the user-defined function definition. This assists the function resolution process to choose the correct function for execution.

For example, consider a sample UDF named TAXAMT. It requires one input parameter, which is defined as DECIMAL(9,2). If you want to pass a column defined as INTEGER to the UDF, use the CAST function as follows to cast the value of the integer column to a DECIMAL(9,2) value:

```
SELECT TAXAMT(CAST (INT_COL AS DECIMAL(9,2)))
FROM    TABLE;
```

Define UDF Parameter Data Types Efficiently   Avoid defining UDF parameters using the following data types: CHAR, GRAPHIC, SMALLINT, and REAL. Instead, use VARCHAR, VARGRAPHIC, INTEGER, and DOUBLE, respectively.

To clarify this guideline, consider a UDF named FUNCX that is defined with a parameter of data type SMALLINT. To invoke this UDF, the parameter must be of data type SMALLINT. Using a data type of INTEGER will not suffice. For example, the following statement will not resolve to FUNCX, because the constant 500 is of type INTEGER, not SMALLINT:

```
SELECT FUNCX(500)
FROM    TABLE;
```

The same line of thinking applies to CHAR, GRAPHIC, and REAL data types. Of course, you could use the CAST function as described previously to resolve this problem. But it is better to avoid the problem altogether by specifying VARCHAR, VARGRAPHIC, INTEGER, and DOUBLE as parameter data types instead.

Choose Parameter Data Types for Portability   If you need to ensure that your UDFs are portable across platforms other than DB2 for z/OS, avoid defining UDFs with parameter data types of FLOAT or NUMERIC. Instead, use DOUBLE or REAL in place of FLOAT, and DECIMAL in place of NUMERIC.

UDFs Do Not Require Parameters   It is possible to code user-defined functions that have no parameters. However, when creating and executing the UDF, you still need to specify the parentheses with no value supplied for a parameter. For example, to create a procedure named FLOWERS() that requires no parameters, you should code the following:

```
CREATE FUNCTION FLOWERS(). . .
```

Similarly, to execute the UDF, you would code it in an SQL statement with the parentheses, but without specifying any parameter values, as shown in the following:

```
SELECT FLOWERS()
FROM   TABLE;
```

Use the Sample User-Defined Functions As Templates   IBM provides quite a few sample programs for user-defined functions. Examine these samples for examples of how to implement effective DB2 user-defined functions. There are sample function programs for

- Converting date and time formats

- Returning the name of the day or month for a specific date

- Formatting floating point data as a currency value

- Returning DB2 catalog information for DB2 objects

- Returning a table of weather data

These functions can be used as samples to learn how to code function programs for your specific needs and requirements.

SQL Usage Options Within External UDFs   There are four options for external functions regarding their usage of SQL:

- NO SQL   Indicates that the function cannot execute SQL statements. However, non-executable SQL statements, such as DECLARE CURSOR, are not restricted.

- MODIFIES SQL DATA   Indicates that the function can execute any legal SQL statement that can be issued by a UDF.

- READS SQL DATA   Indicates that the function can execute SQL statements that access data, but cannot modify data (this is the default SQL usage option for UDFs).

- CONTAINS SQL   Indicates that the function can execute SQL statements as long as data is neither read nor modified, and the SQL statement is legal for issuance by a UDF.

Table 4.4 indicates which SQL statements are valid for each type of SQL usage just described.

TABLE 4.4   Using SQL Within User-Defined Functions

SQL Statement	NO SQL	CONTAINS SQL	READS SQL	MODIFIES SQL
ALLOCATE CURSOR	N	N	Y	Y
ALTER	N	N	N	Y
ASSOCIATE LOCATORS	N	N	Y	Y
BEGIN DECLARE SECTION	Y	Y	Y	Y
CALL	N	Y	Y	Y
CLOSE	N	N	Y	Y
COMMENT ON	N	N	N	Y
COMMIT	N	N	N	N
CONNECT	N	N	N	N
CREATE	N	N	N	Y
DECLARE CURSOR	Y	Y	Y	Y
DECLARE GLOBAL TEMPORARY TABLE	N	Y	Y	Y
DECLARE STATEMENT	Y	Y	Y	Y
DECLARE TABLE	Y	Y	Y	Y
DELETE	N	N	N	Y
DESCRIBE	N	N	Y	Y
DESCRIBE CURSOR	N	N	Y	Y
DESCRIBE INPUT	N	N	Y	Y
DESCRIBE PROCEDURE	N	N	Y	Y
DROP	N	N	N	Y
END DECLARE SECTION	Y	Y	Y	Y
EXECUTE	N	Y	Y	Y
EXECUTE IMMEDIATE	N	Y	Y	Y
EXPLAIN	N	N	N	Y
FETCH	N	N	Y	Y
FREE LOCATOR	N	Y	Y	Y
GRANT	N	N	N	Y
HOLD LOCATOR	N	Y	Y	Y
INCLUDE	Y	Y	Y	Y
INSERT	N	N	N	Y
LABEL ON	N	N	N	Y
LOCK TABLE	N	Y	Y	Y
OPEN	N	N	Y	Y
PREPARE	N	Y	Y	Y
RELEASE	N	N	N	N
RENAME	N	N	N	Y
REVOKE	N	N	N	Y
ROLLBACK	N	N	N	N

TABLE 4.4   Continued

SQL Statement	NO SQL	CONTAINS SQL	READS SQL	MODIFIES SQL
SELECT	N	N	Y	Y
SELECT INTO	N	N	Y	Y
SET	N	Y	Y	Y
SET CONNECTION	N	N	N	N
SIGNAL SQLSTATE	N	Y	Y	Y
UPDATE	N	N	N	Y
VALUES	N	N	Y	Y
VALUES INTO	N	Y	Y	Y
WHENEVER	Y	Y	Y	Y

CAUTION

When a stored procedure is called from a user-defined function, it must allow for the same or more restrictive data access as the calling UDF. For example, a UDF defined as READS SQL DATA can call a procedure defined as READS SQL DATA or CONTAINS SQL. It cannot call a procedure defined as MODIFIES SQL DATA. The hierarchy of data access from least to most restrictive is

MODIFIES SQL DATA

READS SQL DATA

CONTAINS SQL

When to DISALLOW PARALLEL Operations   A table function cannot operate in parallel, so the DISABLE PARALLEL parameter should be specified when issuing a CREATE FUNCTION statement for a table UDF.

Some functions that are NOT DETERMINISTIC can receive incorrect results if the function is executed by parallel tasks. Specify the DISALLOW PARALLEL option for these functions.

Likewise, some functions that rely on a SCRATCHPAD to store data between UDF invocations might not function correctly in parallel. Specify the DISALLOW PARALLEL option for these functions, too.

DETERMINISTIC Versus NOT DETERMINISTIC   Be sure to specify accurately whether the UDF will always return the same result for identical input arguments. If the UDF always returns the same result for identical input arguments, the UDF is DETERMINISTIC. If not, the UDF should be identified as NOT DETERMINISTIC. Any UDF that relies on external data sources that can change should be specified as NOT DETERMINISTIC. Other examples of functions that are not deterministic include any UDF that contains SQL SELECT, INSERT, UPDATE, or DELETE statements or a random number generator.

DB2 uses the [NOT] DETERMINISTIC parameter to optimize view processing for SQL SELECT, INSERT, UPDATE, or DELETE statements that refer to the UDF. If the UDF is NOT DETERMINISTIC, view merge and parallelism will be disabled when the UDF is specified.

Choose the UDF SECURITY Option Wisely   The SECURITY parameter indicates how the UDF will interact with an external security product, such as ACF2 or RACF. If SECURITY

DB2 is specified, the UDF does not require an external security environment. This is the default value for SECURITY. If the UDF accesses resources protected by an external security product, the access is performed using the authid that is associated with the WLM-established stored procedure address space.

If SECURITY USER is specified, an external security environment should be established for the function. If the function accesses resources that the external security product protects, the access is performed using the primary authid of the process that invoked the UDF.

The third and final option for SECURITY is DEFINER. If this option is chosen and the UDF accesses resources protected by an external security product, the access is performed using the primary authid of the owner of the UDF.

Handling Null Input Arguments   There are two option for handling null input arguments in user-defined functions: RETURNS NULL ON NULL INPUT and CALLED ON NULL INPUT. If nulls are to be allowed to be specified as input to a UDF, the UDF must be programmed to test for and handle null inputs.

If RETURNS NULL ON INPUT is specified when the UDF is created, the function is not called if any of the input arguments are null. The result of the function call is null.

If CALLED ON NULL INPUT is specified when the UDF is created, the function is called whether any input arguments are null or not. In this case, the UDF must test for null input arguments in the function program.

UDF Scratchpads   The [NO] SCRATCHPAD clause should be specified to indicate whether DB2 provides a scratchpad for the UDF to utilize. In general, external UDFs should be coded as reentrant, and a scratchpad can help to store data between invocations of the UDF. A scratchpad provides a storage area for the UDF to use from one invocation to the next.

If a scratchpad is specified, a length should be provided. The length can be from 1 to 32,767; the default is 100, if no length is specified.

The first time the UDF is invoked, DB2 allocates memory for the scratchpad and initializes it to contain all binary zeroes. The scope of a scratchpad is a single SQL statement. A separate scratchpad is allocated for each reference to the UDF in the SQL statement. So, if the UDF is specified once in the SELECT-list and once in the WHERE clause, two scratchpads would be allocated. Furthermore, if the UDF is run in parallel, one scratchpad is allocated for each parallel task.

CAUTION

Take care when using SCRATCHPAD with ALLOW PARALLEL because results can be difficult to predict. Consider, for example, a UDF that uses the scratchpad to count the number of times it is invoked. The count would be thrown off if run in parallel because the count would be for the parallel task, not the UDF. For this reason, be sure to specify DISALLOW PARALLEL for UDFs that will not operate in parallel.

If the UDF acquires system resources, be sure to specify the FINAL CALL clause to make sure that DB2 calls the UDF one last time, so the UDF can free the system resources it acquired.

Specify EXTERNAL ACTION UDFs in SELECT-List to Ensure Processing   To make sure that DB2 executes a UDF with external actions for each row of the result set, the UDF should be in the SELECT-list of the SQL statement. The access path chosen by DB2 determines whether UDFs in predicates are executed. Therefore, to be sure the external actions in a UDF are processed, the UDF should be invoked in the SELECT-list, not just in a predicate.

V8 **Specify CARDINALITY Option to Guide Results for Table UDFs**   DB2 Version 8 adds the capability to override the expected cardinality of a table UDF on a case-by-case basis. The cardinality of the UDF is specified in the SYSIBM.SYSROUTINES catalog table when the UDF is registered to DB2. Consider overriding cardinality when you expect the results to be significantly greater than or less than the documented cardinality. Doing so enables DB2 to better gauge the access path for SQL queries against table UDFs.

There are two options for using the CARDINALITY keyword:

- CARDINALITY *n*   Indicates the expected number of rows to be returned by the table UDF. In this case, *n* must be an integer constant.

- CARDINALITY MULTIPLIER *n*   Indicates a multiplier for the cardinality (as stored in SYSIBM.SYSROUTINES); the result of multiplying the CARDINALITY column in the catalog by the multiplier *n* specifies the expected number of rows to be returned by the UDF. In this case, *n* can be any numeric constant.

Consider the following two examples:

```
SELECT * FROM TABLE(FOOTBALL_RESULTS(0) CARDINALITY 28) AS WEEK2;

SELECT * FROM TABLE(FOOTBALL_RESULTS(0) CARDINALITY MULTIPLIER 2) AS WEEK2;
```

For the sake of argument, let's assume that the CARDINALITY column in SYSIBM.SYSROUTINES for this UDF is 14 (the normal number of NFL games in a week). Either of the two SQL statements can be used to estimate the number of rows to be returned after two weeks of play.

For the MULTIPLIER option, we can specify non-integers. If only half a week's football results were available, we could change the cardinality using the multiplier as follows:

```
SELECT * FROM TABLE(FOOTBALL_RESULTS(0) CARDINALITY MULTIPLIER 0.5) AS HALFWEEK;
```

What Is a User-Defined Data Type?

A user-defined data type, or UDT for short, provides a mechanism for extending the type of data that can be stored in DB2 databases, and the way that the data is treated. The UDT, after defined and implemented, extends the functionality of DB2 by enabling users to specify the UDT in DDL CREATE TABLE statements, just like built-in DB2 data types.

User-Defined Data Types and Strong Typing

User-defined data types allow you to create custom data types based on existing DB2 data types. UDTs can be beneficial when you need specific data types geared toward your organization's data processing requirements. One example where UDTs may prove useful is to define new data types for foreign currencies, for example,

```
CREATE DISTINCT TYPE AUSTRALIAN_DOLLAR AS DECIMAL(11,2);

CREATE DISTINCT TYPE EURO AS DECIMAL(11,2);

CREATE DISTINCT TYPE US_DOLLAR AS DECIMAL(11,2);

CREATE DISTINCT TYPE JAPANESE_YEN AS DECIMAL(15,2);
```

DB2 enforces strong typing on user-defined data types. Strong typing prohibits non-defined operations between different types. For example, the following operation will not be allowed due to strong typing:

```
TOTAL = AUSTRALIAN_DOLLAR + EURO
```

Strong typing, in this case, helps us to avoid an error. Adding two different currencies together, without converting one currency to the other, will always result in nonsense data. Think about it: You cannot add a handful of Australian coins with a handful of U.S. coins and come up with anything meaningful (or, perhaps more importantly, spendable).

Consider another example where UDFs have been defined to convert currency amounts. If a specific conversion function is defined that accepts US_DOLLAR data types as input, you would not want to accept other currencies as input. Doing so would most likely cause the UDF to convert the currency amount incorrectly. For example, consider the UDF USDTOYEN( ) created as follows:

```
CREATE FUNCTION USDTOYEN(US_DOLLAR)
  RETURNS JAPANESE_YEN . . .
```

This function accepts a US_DOLLAR amount and converts it to JAPANESE_YEN. Consider the problems that could occur if, instead of a US_DOLLAR input, an AUSTRALIAN_DOLLAR amount was allowed to be specified. Without strong typing, the function would use the conversion routines for US_DOLLAR and arrive at the wrong JAPANESE_YEN amount for the input argument, which was actually specified as an AUSTRALIAN_DOLLAR. With strong typing, the function will reject the request as an error.

When using UDTs you can define only those operations that are pertinent for the UDT. For example, not all numbers should be available for math operations like addition, subtraction, multiplication, and division. A Social Security number, for instance, should always be numeric, but never needs to participate in mathematical equations. Other examples include credit card numbers, account numbers, and vehicle identification numbers. By assigning these types of data items to UDTs you can eliminate operations that do not make sense for the data type.

To summarize, strong typing ensures that only functions, procedures, comparisons, and assignments that are defined for a data type can be used.

User-Defined Distinct Types and LOBs

One of the most important uses for UDTs is to better define the contents of LOB columns. LOB columns allow large multimedia objects, such as audio, video, and large text documents, to be stored in DB2 columns. DB2 supports three types of LOB data types:

- `BLOB` Binary large object

- `CLOB` Character large object

- `DBCLOB` Double-byte character large object

For more details on DB2's object/relational support, refer to Chapter 9, "Large Objects and Object/Relational Databases." For the purposes of this chapter, it is sufficient to know that these types of columns can be created to house complex, unstructured data.

Let's look at a quick example. Suppose you want to create a DB2 table that contains an audio data column. You could define the column as a `BLOB`, such as in the following statement:

```
CREATE TABLE userid.MOVIE
  (MOVIE_ID       INTEGER      NOT NULL,
   MOVIE_NAME     VARCHAR(50)  NOT NULL,
   MOVIE_REVIEW   BLOB(1M),
   ROW_ID         ROWID GENERATED ALWAYS
  ) IN database.tablespace;
```

> **NOTE**
>
> A `ROWID` must appear in every table that contains a `BLOB` column or a UDT based on a `BLOB` data type. The role of the `ROWID` data type is explained further in Chapter 9.

However, this does not help us to know that the column contains audio. All we know is that the column contains a `BLOB`—which might be audio, video, graphic, and so on. We might surmise from the column name that the contents are audio, but it might be a video review. To rectify the potential confusion, you can create a UDT of type `AUDIO` as follows:

```
CREATE DISTINCT TYPE AUDIO AS BLOB(1M);
```

Then create the table specifying the column as the new UDT, instead of just as a `BLOB`. In fact, you could also create a video user-defined data type and store the actual video contents of the movie in the table as well, as shown in the following:

```
CREATE DISTINCT TYPE VIDEO AS BLOB(2G);

CREATE TABLE userid.MOVIE
  (MOVIE_ID       INTEGER      NOT NULL,
   MOVIE_NAME     VARCHAR(50)  NOT NULL,
   MOVIE_REVIEW   AUDIO,
   MOVIE          VIDEO
  ) IN database.tablespace;
```

This table DDL is much easier to read and understand than if both the `MOVIE_REVIEW` and the `MOVIE` columns were defined only as `BLOB`s.

The AUDIO and VIDEO UDTs that you created can now be used in the same way that you use DB2's built-in data types.

Using UDTs for Business Requirements

Another good use of UDTs is to take advantage of strong typing in applications. Remember that strong typing means that only those functions, comparisons, and assignments that are defined for a particular UDT can be executed. How is this an advantage? Consider the scenario where two table are defined, one containing an INTEGER column named SHOE_SIZE, and the other table containing an INTEGER column named IQ_RATING. Because both are defined as INTEGER data types, it is permissible to compare SHOE_SIZE to IQ_RATING. There really is no reason to permit this, and the results will be meaningless. To disable this ability, you could create two UDTs as follows:

```
CREATE DISTINCT TYPE SHOESIZE AS INTEGER;

CREATE DISTINCT TYPE IQ AS INTEGER DECIMAL(11,2);
```

The SHOE_SIZE column can then be created as a SHOESIZE data type, and the IQ_RATING column can be created as the IQ data type. Then it will be impossible to compare the two columns because they are of different data types and DB2 enforces strong typing. Furthermore, when UDTs are used as arguments to functions, that function must be defined to accept that UDT. For example, if you needed to determine average shoe sizes, the AVG function could not be used. But, you could create a sourced UDF that accepts the SHOESIZE data type as input, as shown in the following:

```
CREATE FUNCTION AVG(SHOESIZE)
    RETURNS INTEGER
    SOURCE SYSIBM.AVG(INTEGER);
```

> **NOTE**
>
> The built-in functions are within the SYSIBM schema.

An alternative to creating sourced functions is to use casting functions in your expressions. Casting allows you to convert a source data type into a target data type. Whenever a UDT is created, two casting functions are created: one to convert the UDT to the base data type, and another to convert the base data type to the new UDT. For example, when we created two UDTs named SHOESIZE and IQ, four casting functions were created as follows:

IQ(INTEGER)	Accepts an INTEGER and converts it to IQ
INTEGER(IQ)	Accepts an IQ and converts it to INTEGER
SHOESIZE(INTEGER)	Accepts an INTEGER and converts it to SHOESIZE
INTEGER(SHOESIZE)	Accepts a SHOESIZE and converts it to INTEGER

The casting functions have the same names as the target data types. These casting functions are created automatically by DB2 behind the scenes. You do not need to do anything in order for them to exist other than to create the UDT.

So, to use casting functions to provide an average SHOE_SIZE, you could code the following instead of creating a sourced AVG function:

```
SELECT AVG(INTEGER(SHOE_SIZE))...
```

You must understand, though, that strong typing applies not only to user-defined functions and built-in scalar and column functions, but also to DB2's built-in operators, also referred to as the *infix operators*. These are plus (+), minus (-), multiply (*), divide (/), and concatenation (|| or CONCAT). It is best to create sourced functions for these operations, instead of casting, if you want to use them with UDTs—for example

```
CREATE FUNCTION '+' (SHOESIZE, SHOESIZE)
  RETURNS SHOESIZE
  SOURCE SYSIBM. '+' (INTEGER, INTEGER);
```

> **NOTE**
>
> The built-in operators are within the SYSIBM schema.

Without this sourced function, it would not be possible to add two SHOESIZE columns using SQL. This is probably fine, because there is no real need to add two shoe sizes together in the real world. Of what possible value would the result be? So, it is best to create sourced functions only for those built-in infix operators that make sense and are required for business reasons.

For example, it would be wise to create sourced infix operator functions for the AUSTRALIAN_DOLLAR, EURO, US_DOLLAR, and JAPANESE_YEN data types we discussed earlier, because it makes sense to add, subtract, multiply, and divide currencies. Using sourced functions is easier and more effective than casting. Consider which is easier

```
USD_AMT1 * USD_AMT2
```

or

```
DECIMAL(USD_AMT1) * DECIMAL(USD_AMT2)
```

Clearly the first alternative is better.

This same problem does not exist for comparison operators, because the CREATE DISTINCT TYPE statement has a clause to automatically create comparison operators for UDTs. The clause is WITH COMPARISONS. For example, if the EURO UDT is defined as follows

```
CREATE DISTINCT TYPE EURO AS DECIMAL(11,2) WITH COMPARISONS
```

You will be able to use the following comparison operators on columns defined as the EURO data type:

```
BETWEEN

NOT BETWEEN

IN

NOT IN
```

```
IS NULL

IS NOT NULL

>    >=   ¬>

<    <=   ¬<

=    <>   ¬=
```

Always specify the `WITH COMPARISONS` clause when creating UDTs unless

- The UDT is based on a `BLOB`, `CLOB`, or `DBCLOB`.

    or

- The UDT is not based on `VARCHAR` or `VARGRAPHIC` and has a length greater than 255 bytes.

Assigning Values and UDTs

When assigning values to columns, the value must be of the data type of the column or of a compatible data type. For UDTs, you must use the casting functions to assign values to columns of a UDT.

For example, if you wanted to assign the value of a column named YEN_AMT, which is defined as a JAPANESE_YEN, to a column named EURO_AMT, which is defined as EURO, you must create a UDF that converts yen to euros. If one does not exist, you cannot assign a yen amount to the EURO column. Think about it: If the value of YEN_AMT was 50,000, simply assigning 50,000 to the EURO_AMT would result in a lot more value because 50,000 yen is a much smaller amount of money than is 50,000 euros.

The bottom line is that a conversion UDF is required for assignment of one UDT data type to another UDT data type.

If you are using host variables, DB2 makes the task a bit easier. You can assign the value of a column defined as a UDT to a host variable, if DB2 allows you to assign the underlying source data type to the host variable. For example, consider that a host variable, :HV-1, is defined in a COBOL program as a valid DECIMAL (that is PIC S9(7)V9(2) COMP-3). You can assign a column of type US_DOLLAR, USD_AMT, to a host variable underlying data type of US_DOLLAR is DECIMAL(9,2). For example,

```
SELECT  USD_AMT
INTO :HV-1
FROM    TAB-USD;
```

But, when you assign a value in a host variable to a column defined as a UDT, the type of the host variable can be cast to the UDT. So, a host variable defined as PIC S9(7)V9(2) COMP-3 in a COBOL program is fine for the USD_DOLLAR column. However, if the host variable were of a non-compatible data type, the assignment would fail. So the following statement is valid only if :HV-1 is defined appropriately:

```
INSERT INTO TAB-USD
VALUES (. . ., :HV-1, . . .) ;
```

User-Defined Distinct Type Guidelines

The following guidelines can be used to help you implement effective and efficient user-defined functions for your organization.

Naming User-Defined Functions   The rules for naming user-defined distinct types are similar to those for naming user-defined functions. However, the UDT name in combination with the schema name must be unique. DB2 will not allow a UDT to be created if the schema and UDT name matches another existing data type.

Furthermore, the name of the user-defined distinct type cannot be any of the following system defined key words:

ALL	AND
ANY	BETWEEN
DISTINCT	EXCEPT
EXISTS	FALSE
FOR	FROM
IN	IS
LIKE	MATCH
NOT	NULL
ONLY	OR
OVERLAPS	SIMILAR
SOME	TABLE
TRUE	TYPE
UNIQUE	UNKNOWN
=	¬=
<	<=
>	>=
¬<	¬>
<>	

Comparing UDTs to Base Data Types   DB2 does not let you compare data of a UDT to data of its source type. However, you can compare a UDT to its source data type by using a cast function. For example, to compare a US_DOLLAR column, namely USD_AMT, to a DECIMAL column, namely DEC_AMT, you could use the following SQL:

```
WHERE  USD_AMT > US_DOLLAR(DEC_AMT)
```

Cast Constants and Host Variables to UDTs   Constants and host variables will not be defined as user-defined distinct types. They will generally be specified in the underlying base data type of the UDT. For example, consider a UDF that is created to convert JAPANESE_YEN to EURO values. This UDF might look like the following:

```
CREATE FUNCTION CONVERT_YEN_EURO(JAPANESE_YEN)
    RETURNS EURO
    EXTERNAL NAME 'YENEURO'
    PARAMETER STYLE DB2SQL
    LANGUAGE C;
```

This UDF will accept only the JAPANESE_YEN data type as an input parameter. To use this UDF with a host variable or constant, you must use casting functions. For example, to convert 50,000 Japanese yen to euros, you could call the UDF with the following code:

```
CONVERT_YEN_EURO(JAPANESE_YEN(50000.00)
```

In this case, the underlying base data type as defined for JAPANESE_YEN is DECIMAL(11,2). The same basic idea can be used for host variables, substituting the host variable name for the constant 50000.00.

For dynamic SQL statements, if you want to use a parameter marker with a UDT, you can cast it to the data type of the UDT as follows:

```
WHERE CAST (? AS US_DOLLAR) > USD_AMT
```

Of course, you also could code the inverse of this operation as follows:

```
WHERE ? > DECIMAL(USD_AMT)
```

Using UNION with UDTs   DB2 enforces strong typing of UDTs in UNION statements. When you use a UNION to combine column values from several tables, the columns still must be UNION-compatible as described in Chapter 1, "The Magic Words." Recall that union compatibility means that for the two sets of columns being unioned

- The two sets must contain the same number of columns.

- Each column of the first set must be either the same data type as the corresponding column of the second set *or* convertible to the same data type as the corresponding column of the second set.

So, if you were to UNION data from a USD_SALES table and a YEN_SALES table, the following statement would not work because the data types are not compatible:

```
SELECT   YEN_AMT
FROM     YEN_SALES
UNION
SELECT   USD_AMT
FROM     USD_SALES;
```

Instead, you would have to ensure that the amounts were cast to the same data type. This can be done by using the automatic casting functions built by DB2 when the UDTs were created, or by using UDFs you may have created for converting currencies. A valid example using the casting functions follows:

```
SELECT  DECIMAL(YEN_AMT)
FROM    YEN_SALES
UNION
SELECT  DECIMAL(USD_AMT)
FROM    USD_SALES;
```

The results are all returned as decimal values. However, the results may not be useful because you will not know which amounts represent yen and which represent U.S. dollars. It would be better to use conversion functions to convert one currency to the other, for example, creating a UDF named CONVERT_YEN_USD to convert yen amounts to U.S. dollar amounts and using it as follows:

```
SELECT  CONVERT_YEN_USD(YEN_AMT)
FROM    YEN_SALES
UNION
SELECT  USD_AMT
FROM    USD_SALES;
```

In this case, the results are all returned in U.S. dollars. This makes the results easier to interpret and understand.

4

CHAPTER **5**

Data Definition Guidelines

You must make many choices when implementing DB2 objects. The large number of alternatives can intimidate the beginning user. By following the data definition guidelines in this chapter, you can ensure that you make the proper physical design decisions. Rules are provided for selecting the appropriate DB2 DDL parameters, choosing the proper DB2 objects for your application, and implementing a properly designed physical database.

An Overview of DB2 Database Objects

A DB2 database consists of multiple types of database objects. Each database object is designed for a specific purpose. The first database object is the *database* itself. A database is basically a collection of DB2 database objects. No disk storage is required to create a DB2 database.

DB2 data resides in a *table space*. The table space defines the storage and other physical characteristics for the data. Each table space can contain one or more *tables*. The table defines the actual data elements and constraints for the data. Each table will contain one or more *columns*.

You can also create virtual tables known as views. A *view* is basically a SELECT statement that acts as a table. No data is stored when a view is created; instead, when the view is accessed DB2 uses the SELECT statement that defines the view to materialize the virtual table. So a view is a way to turn a SELECT statement into a "table."

V8 *Materialized query tables* can be created, too. These are essentially views where the data has been physically stored instead of virtually accessed.

A *storage group* is a series of disk volumes that can be used by table spaces and indexes for allocating data sets on DASD devices.

A table can have indexes defined on it. A DB2 *index* is defined on one or more columns to enable more efficient access to DB2 tables.

Finally, DB2 allows users to create aliases and synonyms as alternative names for DB2 tables. An *alias* is defined to a local DB2 subsystem for either a local or remote table. A *synonym* is defined as a private name for a table or view; a synonym can be used only by its creator.

DB2 Databases

At the top of the DB2 object hierarchy is the DB2 database. Physically, a DB2 database is nothing more than a defined grouping of DB2 objects. A database contains no data, but acts as a high-level identifier for tracking other DB2 objects. The START and STOP commands can be issued at the database level, thereby affecting all objects grouped under that database.

Each DB2 database also has a *DBD*, or *database descriptor*, associated with it. A DBD is an internal structure used by DB2 to identify and manipulate DB2 objects defined to a database. DBDs are stored in the DB2 Directory and are loaded into the EDM Pool whenever an object in the associated database is accessed.

Logically, a database should be used to group like tables. You can do this for all tables in an application system or for tables in a logical subsystem of a larger application. It makes sense to combine tables with similar functions and uses in a single database, because doing so simplifies DB2 security and the starting and stopping of the application table spaces and indexes.

One database per logical application system (or subsystem) is a good starting point. As a general rule, though, limiting the number of objects defined to a database is smart, because this limits the size of the DBD. As the number of table spaces defined to a single database approaches 40 to 50, consider creating another database for subsequent database objects. More table spaces than this usually increases the difficulty of monitoring and administration.

When DDL is issued to CREATE, ALTER, and DROP objects in an existing database, the DBD for the affected database will be modified. For DB2 to modify the DBD, a lock must be taken. A DBD lock will cause contention, which can result in the failure of the DDL execution. If the DDL is submitted when there is little or no activity, however, application users might be locked out while the DDL is being executed. An X lock will be taken on the DBD while the DDL executes. For very active databases, there might not be a dormant window in which a lock of this kind can be taken. This can cause undue stress on the system when new objects must be added—a good reason to limit the number of objects defined to a single database.

An additional consideration is the size of the DBD. A DBD contains a mapping of the table spaces, tables, and indexes defined to a database. When a request for data is made, the DBD is loaded into an area of main storage called the *EDM pool*. The DBD should be small enough that it does not cause problems with EDM pool storage. Problems generally will not occur if your databases are not outrageously large and your EDM pool is well-defined. As of DB2 V6, loading DBDs into the EDM pool is less troublesome because the DBD can be loaded in 32K chunks and contiguous EDM pool pages are not required.

V8 DB2 V8 separates the EDM pool into separate storage areas as follows:

> The main *EDM pool* for managing CTs and PTs in use, SKCTs and SKPTs for the most frequently used applications, and cache blocks for your plans that have caches.
>
> The *EDM DBD cache* for the DBDs in use and DBDs referred to by the SKCTs and SKPTs for the most frequently used applications.
>
> The *EDM statement cache* for the skeletons of the most frequently used dynamic SQL statements, if your system has enabled the dynamic statement cache.

Separating DBDs from other EDM pool structures removes the possibility of inefficient DBDs causing problems for other plans and packages.

However, if you CREATE and DROP a lot of objects in a single database without running MODIFY RECOVERY or REPAIR to "clean up" the DBD, it can become too large to manage effectively in the EDM pool.

For a further discussion of DBDs and their effect on the EDM pool, see Chapters 22, "The Table-Based Infrastructure of DB2," and 28, "Tuning DB2's Components."

Furthermore, whenever a change is made to the DBD, DB2 must log the before and after image of the DBD. Such changes therefore tend to overburden log processing as the DBD's size increases.

Database Guidelines

The following guidelines apply to the creation and management of DB2 databases. By following these rules of thumb you can help to assure that you are creating efficient DB2 databases.

Specify Database Parameters   Specify a storage group and buffer pool for every database that you create. If you do not define a STOGROUP, the default DB2 storage group, SYSDEFLT, is assigned to the database. This is undesirable because the volumes assigned to SYSDEFLT become unmanageable if too many DB2 data sets are defined to them.

If you do not specify the BUFFERPOOL parameter, BP0 is used for the table spaces created in the database. As of DB2 V6, the INDEXBP parameter should be coded to specify the default buffer pool to use for indexes created in the database. If you do not specify INDEXBP on the CREATE DATABASE statement, the index buffer pool will default as defined on the installation panel DSNTIP1. The default for user indexes on the DSNTIP1 panel is BP0.

Depending on shop standards, defaults can be desirable, but explicitly coding the buffer pool is highly advisable in order to avoid confusion. This is especially so because it is a good rule of thumb to avoid placing user data in BP0. In-depth buffer pool guidelines can be found in Chapter 28.

> **NOTE**
>
> Actually, a good standard rule of thumb is to explicitly code *every* pertinent parameter for *every* DB2 statement. DB2's default values are rarely the best choice, and even when they are, the precision of explicitly coded parameters is preferable for debugging and tuning situations.

Avoid Use of DSNDB04   The default DB2 database is DSNDB04. DSNDB04 is created during installation and is used when a database is not explicitly stated in a table space CREATE statement, or when a database and table space combination is not explicitly stated in a table CREATE statement. I recommend that you never use DSNDB04. Objects created in DSNDB04 are hard to maintain and track. To limit the use of DSNDB04, grant its use only to SYSADMs.

An additional caveat regarding use of the default database—the REPAIR DROP DATABASE statement cannot be used on DSNDB04.

> **CAUTION**
>
> Some organizations choose to use DSNDB04 for QMF users to create objects. Even this use is discouraged. It is better to create a specific database for each QMF user needing to create objects. These databases can then be used, managed, and maintained more effectively without affecting other users.

Be Aware of the Impact of Drops on DBDs   When an object is dropped, the related entry in the DBD is marked as logically deleted, but not physically deleted. Certain types of changes, such as removing a column, reordering columns, or changing a data type, necessitate dropping and re-creating tables. Each time the table is dropped and re-created, the DBD will grow. Very large DBDs can result in -904 SQLCODEs specifying the unavailable resource as the EDM Pool (resource 0600).

To reduce the size of the DBD, you must follow these steps:

1. REORG the table spaces for tables that have been dropped and re-created. The log RBA recorded in SYSCOPY for this REORG will indicate to DB2 that the dropped tables are no longer in the table space.

2. Run MODIFY RECOVERY to remove the old image copy information for the dropped table. The preferred method with the least amount of down time is to run MODIFY RECOVERY DELETE AGE(*). This will shrink your DBD and delete all old SYSCOPY and SYSLGRNX information.

3. Run an image copy for each table space to ensure recoverability.

Creating and Using DB2 Table Spaces

Although DB2 data is accessed at the table level, the data itself is actually stored in a structure known as a table space. Each table space correlates to one or more individual physical VSAM linear data sets that are used to house the actual DB2 data.

Before any data can be physically stored in a DB2 database, a table space must first be created. If you attempt to create a table without specifying a table space, DB2 will create a default table space (unless you do not have authority to use the default database).

Types of Table Spaces

When designing DB2 databases, DBAs can choose from four types of table spaces, each one useful in different circumstances. The four types of table spaces are:

- Simple table spaces

- Segmented table spaces

- Partitioned table spaces

- LOB table spaces

Simple Table Spaces

Simple table spaces are found mostly in older DB2 applications. A simple table space can contain one or more tables. When multiple tables are defined to a simple table space, a single page can contain rows from all the tables defined to the table space.

Prior to DB2 V2.1, most DB2 table spaces were defined as simple table spaces because the only other option was a partitioned table space. However, most subsequent applications use segmented table spaces because of their enhanced performance and improved methods of handling multiple tables.

If an application must read rows from multiple tables in a predefined sequence, however, mixing the rows of these tables together in a single simple table space can prove to be beneficial. The rows should be mixed together on the page in a way that clusters the keys by which the rows will be accessed. This can be done by inserting the rows using a "round robin" approach, switching from table to table, as follows:

1. Create a simple table space; this is accomplished by issuing the CREATE TABLESPACE statement without specifying either the SEGSIZE or NUMPARTS clause.

2. Create the two tables (for example, Table1 and Table2), assigning them both to the simple table space you just created.

3. Sort the input data set of values to be inserted into Table1 into key sequence order.

4. Sort the input data set of values to be inserted into Table2 into sequence by the foreign key that refers to the primary key of Table1.

5. Code a program that inserts a row into Table1 and then immediately inserts all corresponding foreign key rows into Table2.

6. Continue this pattern until all of the primary keys have been inserted.

When the application reads the data in this predefined sequence, the data from these two tables will be clustered on the same (or a neighboring) page. Great care must be taken to ensure that the data is inserted in the proper sequence. Keep in mind that any subsequent data modification (INSERTs, UPDATEs that increase row size, and DELETEs) will cause the data to get out of sequence—and then performance will suffer. For this reason, this approach is more useful for static data than it is for dynamic, changing data.

Also, remember that mixing data rows from multiple tables on the same table space page adversely affects the performance of all queries, utilities, and applications that do not access the data in this manner. Be sure that the primary type of access to the data is by the predefined mixing sequence before implementing a simple table space in this manner.

Unless data-row mixing is being implemented, define no more than one table to each simple table space. Also, consider defining all your non-partitioned table spaces as segmented instead of simple.

Segmented Table Spaces

A segmented table space is the most common type of table space for most DB2 development efforts. A segmented table space provides most of the benefits of a simple table space, except multiple tables can be defined to one segmented table space without the problems encountered when using simple table spaces. Tables are stored in separate segments. Because data rows never are mixed on the same page, concurrent access to tables in the same segmented table space is not a problem.

For the segmented table space depicted in Figure 5.1, each box represents a segment. Notice how each segment is represented by a single pattern, signifying that only one table's data can be contained in the segment. Now look at the simple table space in the same figure. Each box represents a page. Notice how multiple patterns inter-mix on the same page.

Segmented table spaces have other benefits as well. For example,

- Segmented table spaces handle free space more efficiently, which results in less overhead for inserts and for variable-length row updates.

- Mass delete processing is more efficient because only the space map—not the data itself—is updated. A mass delete of rows from a table in a simple table space causes every row to be physically read and deleted. The following is an example of a mass delete:

```
DELETE
FROM DSN8810.DEPT;
```

If `DSN8810.DEPT` is defined in a simple table space, all of its rows are read, deleted, and logged. If it is defined in a segmented table space, however, only the space map is updated to indicate that all rows have been deleted.

- Space can be reclaimed from dropped tables immediately. This reduces the need for reorganization.

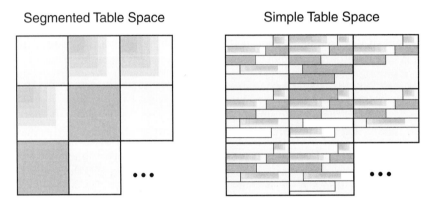

FIGURE 5.1   Simple versus segmented table spaces.

Most of your application table spaces should be segmented. All table spaces that contain multiple tables (and do not need to mix data from multiple tables on a page) should be segmented. Even when you're defining one table for each table space, the performance advantage of the more efficient space utilization should compel you to use segmented table spaces.

Choose the segment size carefully. Consider each of the following when selecting the segment size:

- `SEGSIZE` is defined as an integer representing the number of pages to be assigned to a segment. The size of a segment can be any multiple of 4, from 4 to 64, inclusive.

- DASD space is allocated based either on the `PRIQTY` and `SECQTY` specifications for `STOGROUP`-defined table spaces, or on the VSAM IDCAMS definition for user-defined VSAM table spaces. However, this space can never be smaller than a full segment. The primary extent and all secondary extents are rounded to the next full segment before being allocated.

- Space cannot be allocated at less than a full track. Consult the "`PRIQTY` and `SECQTY`" section later in this chapter for additional information.

- When defining multiple tables in a segmented table space, keep tables of like size in the same table space. Do not combine large tables with small tables in a single segmented table space. Defining small tables in a table space with a large segment size could result in wasted DASD space.

- When a segmented table space contains multiple tables large enough to be processed using sequential prefetch, be sure to define the SEGSIZE according to the following chart. The segment size should be at least as large as the maximum number of pages that can be read by sequential prefetch. Otherwise, sequential prefetch could read pages that do not apply to the table being accessed, causing inefficient sequential prefetch processing:

Bufferpool Range	Segment Size
1 through 500	16
501 through 999	32
1000 and over	64

Partitioned Table Spaces

A partitioned table space is divided into components called *partitions*. Each partition resides in a separate physical data set. Partitioned table spaces are designed to increase the availability of data in large tables by spreading the data across multiple physical disk devices.

Furthermore, data is assigned to a partition based on a partitioning limit key (see Figure 5.2). Each partition holds data only for the valid range of keys specified for the partition.

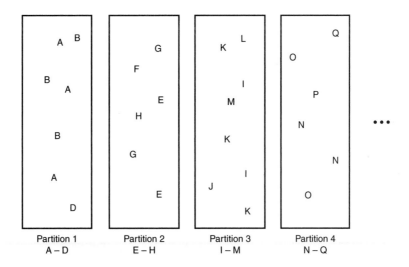

FIGURE 5.2   Partitioned table space.

V8 Prior to V8, the limit key was defined by a partitioning index. With DB2 V8, though, an index is not required to specify the partitioning limit key; instead, the partitioning limit key is specified in the table creation DDL.

In general, your larger table spaces should be partitioned in order to better control and manage your DB2 objects and data sets. As of DB2 V8, up to 4,096 partitions can be defined for a partitioned table space. For DB2 V6 and V7, the limit is 254 partitions for a LARGE table space. For a non-LARGE table space the limit is 64 partitions.

> **NOTE**
>
> As of DB2 V8, it is possible to create very large databases and table spaces. With up to 4,096 partitions, the maximum size of a partitioned table space is 128 terabytes. For example, a table space with a 4K page size and 4,096 partitions having a DSSIZE of 32GB would max out at 128TB. That is a lot of data! In fact, if you use one per partition for a single day's worth of data, then 4,096 partitions will provide for more than 11 years worth of data.
>
> For V6 and V7, a partitioned table space can hold up to 1TB of data (254 partitions each containing 4GB of data is approximately equal to 1TB). A LARGE partitioned table space can contain up to 16TB of data. (254 partitions, each containing 64GB of data, is approximately equal to 16TB.)
>
> So, even before V8 a partitioned table space could be used to store quite a bit of data.

There are two types of partitioned table space: LARGE and non-LARGE. Whether or not a partitioned table space is a LARGE table space is controlled using the DSSIZE parameter. The DSSIZE parameter specifies the maximum size, in gigabytes, for each partition of the table space. DB2 V8 continues to support the LARGE parameter for compatibility, but using DSSIZE is recommended over using LARGE.

When using the DSSIZE parameter, you will explicitly specify the maximum size of each partition. The following are valid DSSIZE values:

1GB (1 gigabyte)	2GB (2 gigabytes)
4GB (4 gigabytes)	8GB (8 gigabytes)
16GB (16 gigabytes)	32GB (32 gigabytes)
64GB (64 gigabytes)	

> **NOTE**
>
> To specify a value greater than 4GB, you must be running DB2 with DFSMS V1.5 or greater, and the data sets for the table space must be associated with a DFSMS data class defined with extended format and extended addressability. DFSMS's extended addressability function is necessary to create data sets larger than 4GB in size. The term used by IBM to define data sets that are enabled for extended addressability is *EA-enabled*.

V8 When the total table space size is 4TB or greater, DB2 will use a 5-byte RID instead of a 4-byte RID for record identifiers. Prior to DB2 V8, this restriction was more simply stated as whenever the DSSIZE is greater than 4GB, a 5-byte RID is used. But with the greater number of partitions supported as of DB2 V8, this restriction needs to be stated as a combination of NUMPARTS, page size, and DSSIZE. Table 5.1 outlines the table space parameter combinations and sizes requiring 5-byte RIDs.

TABLE 5.1 Large Table Space Combinations

NUMPARTS	Page Size	DSSIZE	Table Space Size
4096	4KB	1GB	4TB
4096	4KB	2GB	8TB
4096	4KB	4GB	16TB
2048	4KB	8GB	16TB

TABLE 5.1   Continued

NUMPARTS	Page Size	DSSIZE	Table Space Size
1024	4KB	16GB	16TB
512	4KB	32GB	16TB
256	4KB	64GB	16TB
4096	4KB	1GB	4TB
4096	4KB	2GB	8TB
4096	4KB	4GB	16TB
4096	4KB	8GB	32TB
2048	4KB	16GB	32TB
1024	4KB	32GB	32TB
512	4KB	64GB	32TB
4096	4KB	1GB	4TB
4096	4KB	2GB	8TB
4096	4KB	4GB	16TB
4096	4KB	8GB	32TB
4096	4KB	16GB	64TB
2048	4KB	32GB	64TB
1024	4KB	64GB	64TB
4096	4KB	1GB	4TB
4096	4KB	2GB	8TB
4096	4KB	4GB	16TB
4096	4KB	8GB	32TB
4096	4KB	16GB	64TB
4096	4KB	32GB	128TB
2048	4KB	64GB	128TB
4096	4KB	LARGE (4GB)	16TB

V8 As mentioned earlier, DB2 V8 partitioning is no longer dependent on indexing. For all previous releases, a partitioned table space required a partitioning index. It was the index that set up the specific limit keys that determined which data rows were placed in which partition. With DB2 V8, it is possible to specify the limit keys in the table DDL.

Keep the following terminology in mind:

- *Partitioned Table Space*—Any table space with multiple physical partitions.

- *Partitioned Index*—Any index with multiple physical partitions.

- *Partitioning Index*—Any index where the left-most columns match the partitioning limit key of the table space; the index might or might not be partitioned itself.

Furthermore, as of V8, the data in a partitioned table space need not be clustered by the partitioning limit key. So, it is now possible to create a partitioned table space without any indexes (but it is still not generally advisable to do so).

Another V8 partitioned table space improvement is the ability to modify partitions. With the online schema change capabilities of DB2 V8, you can add, remove, and rotate partitions easily using the facilities of DB2. Prior to V8, such changes required dropping and re-creating the table space—a difficult proposition for many large partitioned table spaces. For more information on the schema change capabilities of DB2 Version 8, refer to Chapter 7, "Database Change Management and Schema Evolution."

Partitioning, Size, and Data Distribution   Deciding to use a partitioned table space is not as simple as merely determining the size of the table. In the early days of DB2 (that is, pre-V4), size typically was the primary consideration for choosing a partitioned table space. However, as DB2 has matured and the applications written using DB2 have become modernized, additional considerations impact your partitioning decisions. Application-level details, such as data contention, performance requirements, degree of parallelism, and data access patterns, must factor into the decision to use partitioned table spaces.

A commonly held belief among DB2 DBAs is that partitioned table spaces should be defined with evenly distributed data across partitions. However, maintaining evenly distributed partitions might not be desirable when partitions are used to isolate data "hot spots." Indeed, it is better to design table space partitions with the needs of the application in mind. Therefore, the best approach is to define table space partitions based on the access requirements of the applications accessing the data. Keep in mind that parallel processing can benefit from properly partitioned table spaces placed on separate volumes.

Partitioning Versus Multiple Tables   Sometimes designers try to avoid partitioned table spaces by dividing a table into multiple tables, each with its own table space. Unless you have specific reasons for doing so, this approach is not wise. When proceeding in this manner, the designer usually places separate tables into each of the smaller table spaces. This can be problematic because it introduces an uncontrolled and unneeded denormalization. (See the "Denormalization" section later in this chapter for more information.)

Furthermore, when data that logically belongs in one table is separated into multiple tables, SQL operations to access the data as a logical whole are made needlessly complex. One example of this complexity is the difficulty in enforcing unique keys across multiple tables. Although partitioned table spaces can introduce additional complexities into your environment, these complexities rarely outweigh those introduced by mimicking partitioning with several smaller, identical table spaces. To clarify why this idea is usually not a good approach, consider these two different ways of implementing a three-"partition" solution:

The first, generally recommended way is to create the table in a single partitioned table space with three partitions. For example:

```
CREATE DATABASE DB_SAMP;

CREATE TABLESPACE TS_SAMPP
       IN DB_SAMP
       ERASE NO NUMPARTS 3
       (PART 1
        USING STOGROUP SG_SAMP1
```

```
            PRIQTY 2000 SECQTY 50
            COMPRESS NO,

            PART 2
            USING STOGROUP SG_SAMP2
            PRIQTY 4000 SECQTY 150
            COMPRESS YES,

            PART 3
            USING STOGROUP SG_SAMP3
            PRIQTY 1000 SECQTY 50
            COMPRESS YES)

        LOCKSIZE PAGE   BUFFERPOOL BP1   CLOSE NO;

CREATE TABLE TB_SAMP . . . IN DB_SAMP.TS_SAMPP;
```

The second, alternative approach is to create three table spaces, each with its own table, as follows:

```
CREATE DATABASE DB_SAMP2;

CREATE TABLESPACE TS_SAMP1 IN DB_SAMP2
        USING STOGROUP SG_SAMP1
        PRIQTY 2000   SECQTY 50
        ERASE NO COMPRESS NO
        LOCKSIZE PAGE   BUFFERPOOL BP1   CLOSE NO;

CREATE TABLESPACE TS_SAMP2 IN DB_SAMP2
        USING STOGROUP SG_SAMP2
        PRIQTY 4000   SECQTY 150
        ERASE NO COMPRESS YES
        LOCKSIZE PAGE   BUFFERPOOL BP1   CLOSE NO;

CREATE TABLESPACE TS_SAMP3 IN DB_SAMP2
        USING STOGROUP SG_SAMP3
        PRIQTY 1000   SECQTY 50
        ERASE NO COMPRESS YES
        LOCKSIZE PAGE   BUFFERPOOL BP1   CLOSE NO;

CREATE TABLE TB_SAMP1 . . . IN DB_SAMP2.TS_SAMP1;
CREATE TABLE TB_SAMP2 . . . IN DB_SAMP2.TS_SAMP2;
CREATE TABLE TB_SAMP3 . . . IN DB_SAMP2.TS_SAMP3;
```

Now consider how difficult it would be to retrieve data in the second implementation if you did not know which "partition" (table) the data resides in, or if the data could reside in multiple partitions. Using the first example, a simple SELECT will work:

```
SELECT   *
FROM     TB_SAMP
WHERE    COL1 = :HOST-VARIABLE;
```

In the second example, a UNION is required:

```
SELECT  *
FROM    TB_SAMP1
WHERE   COL1 = :HOST-VARIABLE
UNION ALL
SELECT  *
FROM    TB_SAMP2
WHERE   COL1 = :HOST-VARIABLE
UNION ALL
SELECT  *
FROM    TB_SAMP3
WHERE   COL1 = :HOST-VARIABLE;
```

If other tables need to be joined, the "solution" becomes even more complex. Likewise, if data must be updated, inserted, or deleted and you do not know which "partition" contains the affected data, it is difficult to code an efficient method to change the data.

V7   As of DB2 V7, it is possible to implement UNION in views, so the multi-table approach becomes a little easier. A view could be created so that all users and programs could access the view as if it were a table. The view would look something like this:

```
CREATE VIEW ALL_DATA
AS SELECT * FROM TB_SAMP1
   UNION ALL
   SELECT * FROM TB_SAMP2
   UNION ALL
   SELECT * FROM TB_SAMP3;
```

> **NOTE**
>
> Of course, the SELECT statements in the view should not use SELECT * but instead should list out all of the columns in the table. The example used the shorthand notation for simplicity.

Data integrity and modification poses an additional problem. Every UPDATE will need to "know" which table contains which ranges of values. Without this knowledge, valid data may be entered into the wrong table.

The bottom line is that you should avoid bypassing DB2 partitioning using your own pseudo-partitions unless the table is inordinately large and you are not running DB2 V7 or earlier. Using the multi-table approach can be viable for very, very large tables to get around non-partitioning index problems prior to V8.

V8   Prior to V8 only the partitioning index is partitioned like the underlying data.* Every other index will be a single, non-partitioned index (NPI), also known as a non-partitioned secondary index (NPSI). With DB2 V8 you can create data partitioned secondary indexes to alleviate NPI problems. NPSIs are unwieldy and difficult to manage, administer, backup, recover, and reorganize. These administration issues are somewhat alleviated by the multi-table approach—but keep in mind, additional administration issues are created. Such as:

As of DB2 V8 a partitioned index can have a superset of the partitioning key columns. For example, a table space partitioned on columns C1 and C2 can have a partitioned index on columns C1, C2, and C3.

- Assuring data integrity (as discussed above), including avoiding duplicate keys, ensuring key ranges are put in the proper table, and so on, is extremely difficult.

- Managing multiple indexes can be an administrative burden. Multiple indexes are required because each table will generally have to have the same indexes placed on them. That is, if you index on ACCT_TYPE, you will need to build that index on each of the individual tables; with partitioning, it is built once on the partitioned table.

- Creating and maintaining additional backup and recovery jobs for each of the table spaces is required when using the multi-table approach. Of course, you may have a similar number of backup jobs under the partitioned approach if you COPY by partition.

Partitioning Pros and Cons   Before deciding to partition a table space, weigh the pros and cons. Consult the following list of advantages and disadvantages before implementation:

Advantages of a partitioned table space are the following:

- Each partition can be placed on a different DASD volume to increase access efficiency.

- Partitioned table spaces can be used to store large amounts of data. They are the only type of table space that can hold more than 64GB of data (the maximum size of simple and segmented table spaces).

- START and STOP commands can be issued at the partition level. By stopping only specific partitions, the remaining partitions are available to be accessed thereby promoting higher availability.

- Free space (PCTFREE and FREEPAGE) can be specified at the partition level enabling the DBA to isolate data "hot spots" to a specific partition and tune accordingly.

- Query I/O, CPU, and Sysplex parallelism enable multiple engines to access different partitions in parallel, usually resulting in reduced elapsed time. DB2 can access non-partitioned table spaces in parallel, too, but partitioning can optimize parallelism by removing disk contention.

- Table space scans on partitioned table spaces can skip partitions that are excluded based on the query predicates. Skipping entire partitions can improve overall query performance for table space scans.

- By mixing clustering and partitioning you can design to decrease data contention. For example, if the table space will be partitioned by DEPTNO, each department (or range of compatible departments) could be placed in separate partitions. Each department is in a discrete physical data set, thereby reducing inter-departmental contention due to multiple departments coexisting on the same data page.

V8   As of DB2 V8 you can further reduce contention by creating data partitioned secondary indexes (DPSIs). Prior to V8, some contention will remain for data in non-partitioned indexes. Defining an NPSI on a table in a partitioned table space causes you to lose some of the benefits of partition-level independence for utility operations because access to an NPSI is sequential.

- DB2 creates a separate compression dictionary for each table space partition. Multiple dictionaries tend to cause better overall compression ratios. In addition, it is more likely that the partition-level compression dictionaries can be rebuilt more frequently than non-partitioned dictionaries. Frequent rebuilding of the compression dictionary can lead to a better overall compression ratio.

- The REORG, COPY, and RECOVER utilities can execute on table spaces at the partition level. If these utilities are set to execute on partitions instead of on the entire table space, valuable time can be saved by processing only the partitions that need to be reorganized, copied, or recovered. Partition independence and resource serialization further increase the availability of partitions during utility processing.

Disadvantages of a partitioned table space are as follows:

- Only one table can be defined in a partitioned table space. This is not really a disadvantage, merely a limitation.

- Prior to DB2 V8, updating the partitioning columns can be problematic. Although it is possible to UPDATE the columns of the partitioning index, it is not very efficient. First, the PARTKEYU DSNZPARM parameter must be set to enable portioning key modification. If this parameter is set to NO, then updates are not permitted. If updates are allowed, the actual UPDATE will in all likelihood run quite slowly. If the PARTKEYU previous ZPARM is not set, you must delete the row and then reinsert it with the new values in order change a value in a column of a partitioning index key. (As of V8, a partitioning index is no longer required.)

- The range of key values for which data will be inserted into the table should be known and stable before you create the partitioning index. To define a partition, a range of values must be hard coded either into the partitioning index definition or the table definition. These ranges should distribute the data throughout the partitions according to the access needs of the applications using the data. If you provide a stop-gap partition to catch all the values lower (or higher) than the defined range, monitor that partition to ensure that it does not grow dramatically or cause performance problems if it is smaller or larger than most other partitions.

CAUTION

For table spaces created with a large DSSIZE (or with the LARGE parameter), the values specified after the VALUES clause are strictly enforced. The highest value specified is the highest value that can be placed in the table. Any values greater than the value specified for the last partition are out of range and cannot be inserted.

> **NOTE**
>
> As of DB2 V6, you can change partition key ranges using ALTER INDEX without having to drop and redefine the partitioned table space and index. This capability greatly increases data availability when partition key ranges need to be changed.
>
> Of course, as of DB2 V8, partitioning becomes more flexible and modifying partitioning details becomes much easier with online schema changes.

Updating Partitioning Keys   Your organization must decide whether or not to allow updates to partitioning keys. This is controlled using the PARTKEYU DSNZPARM (which is set on the DSNTIP4 installation panel).

There are three valid settings for PARTKEYU:

- YES—The partitioning key columns may be updated. This is the default.

- NO—The partitioning key columns are not permitted to be updated.

- SAME—The partitioning key columns can be updated but only if the UPDATE results in the row staying in its current partition.

Partitioning and Data Set Sizes   For partitioned table spaces not specified as LARGE (or without the DSSIZE parameter), the number of partitions affects the maximum size of the data set partition as follows:

Number of Partitions	Maximum Data Set Size
1 to 16	4GB
17 to 32	2GB
33 to 64	1GB

V7 Prior to V7, table spaces that are defined with the LARGE parameter can have a maximum data set size of 4GB for 1 to 256 partitions.

For V7, table spaces that are defined with a DSSIZE of 4GB or greater can have a maximum data set size of 64GB; partitions can range from 1 to 256.

V8 For V8, table spaces that are defined with a DSSIZE of 4GB or greater can have a maximum data set size of 64GB; partitions can range from 1 to 4,096.

The preceding discussion of table space size is somewhat unclear, so let's clarify it. The maximum number of partitions a table space can have is dependent on the DSSIZE, the page size, and the total tablespace size. Page size affects table size because it affects the number of partitions allowed. Table 5.2 consolidates this information accurately as of DB2 V8.

TABLE 5.2   Table Space Size

Max Part	Page Size	DSSIZE	Max TS Size
4096	4KB	4GB	16TB
256	4KB	64GB	16TB

> **CAUTION**
>
> Use caution when creating very large table spaces with LOBs. You can only specify up to 5 LOBs per table if 4096 partitions are to be supported. This is so because one LOB table space is required for each LOB per partition. So one LOB on a table with 4,096 partitions would require 12,288 objects. The maximum number of objects per DB2 database is 65,535, hence the 5 LOB limit.

V8 **Table-Controlled Partitioning**   Consider favoring table-controlled partitioning over index-controlled partitioning. This option is available as of DB2 V8. By specifying the partitioning limit keys in the table DDL, DB2 will not have to rely on a partitioning index to keep the correct data in the proper partition.

The ability to ALTER a table-controlled partitioned scheme is made much simpler with the advent of online schema evolution. Online schema evolution is addressed in detail in Chapter 7.

In order to determine whether a given partitioned table space is index-controlled or table-controlled you will have to query the DB2 Catalog. The PARTKEYCOLUMN in SYSIBM.SYSTABLES will be set to zero if it is index-controlled, or to a particular value if it is table-controlled.

Index-controlled partitioning will be converted to table-controlled partitioning whenever a new DB2 V8 table-controlled partitioning feature is exploited. This includes

- Creating a data partitioned secondary index (DPSI)

- Creating a partitioning index without the CLUSTER keyword or altering the existing partitioning index to specify CLUSTER NO

- Dropping the partitioning index on an index-controlled partitioning table space

- Altering the table in a partitioned table space to add a partition, rotate a partition, or modify a partition parameter

LOB Table Spaces
LOB table spaces are to be used only in conjunction with LOB columns. One LOB table space is required per LOB column in a table. If the table space containing the LOB column is partitioned, one LOB table space per partition per column is required. The LOB table space is used to store the large object data.

Comprehensive coverage of LOB table spaces is provided in Chapter 9, "Large Objects and Object/Relational Databases."

Table Space Parameters
Many parameters must be considered when creating a table space. Each of these parameters is discussed in this section.

LARGE

The LARGE parameter is available for partitioned table spaces only. When LARGE is specified more than 64GB of data can be stored in the table space. A large table space can have up to 254 partitions, each containing up to 4GB; if EA-enabled, each containing up to 64GB. Refer to Table 5.3 for definitions of storage abbreviations such as GB and TB.

TABLE 5.3   Storage Abbreviations

Abbreviation	Term	Amount
KB	Kilobyte	1,024 bytes
GB	Gigabyte	1,024 KB
TB	Terabyte	1,024 GB
PB	Petabyte	1,024 TB
EB	Exabyte	1,024 PB
ZB	Zettabyte	1,024 EB
YB	Yottabyte	1,024 ZB

When LARGE (or DSSIZE) is not specified, the maximum storage amount is limited to 64GB; the maximum number of partitions to 64.

CAUTION

If the NUMPARTS parameter is defined to be greater than 64, the table space will automatically be defined as a large table space even if the LARGE parameter is omitted.

Create LARGE Table Spaces Sparingly

Although it may be tempting to define every table space as LARGE, space considerations and resource requirements need to be taken into account. RIDs in a large table space are 5 bytes instead of 4 bytes. As such, index space usage will increase. Additionally, large table spaces can use more data sets and increase resource consumption of utility processing. Therefore, a large table space should be used only under the following conditions:

- When more than 16 partitions are required and more than 1GB must be stored per partition; or

- More than 64 partitions are required; or

- More than 64GB of data must be stored in a single table space

CAUTION

Use the DSSIZE clause instead of LARGE to specify a maximum partition size of 4GB and larger. The LARGE clause is retained for compatibility with releases of DB2 prior to Version 6.

DSSIZE

The DSSIZE parameter is used to specify the maximum size for each partition or, for LOB table spaces, each data set. If you specify DSSIZE, you must also specify NUMPARTS or LOB. Remember that to specify a value greater than 4GB, the table space must be EA-enabled.

One way of determining whether a data set is EA-enabled is to view it using ISPF option 3.4. The DSORG column will show VS-E for a VSAM EA-enabled data set.

The same cautions regarding the use of LARGE should be adhered to regarding specifying a DSSIZE greater than 4GB.

LOCKSIZE
The LOCKSIZE parameter indicates the type of locking DB2 performs for the given table space. The choices are

ROW	Row-level locking
PAGE	Page-level locking
TABLE	Table-level locking (for segmented table spaces only)
TABLESPACE	Table space-level locking
LOB	LOB locking; valid only for LOB table spaces
ANY	Lets DB2 decide, starting with PAGE

In general, it is fine to let DB2 handle the level of locking required. DB2 will usually use LOCKSIZE PAGE and LOCKMAX SYSTEM unless it is a LOB table space, in which case DB2 will usually choose LOCKSIZE LOB and LOCKMAX SYSTEM. When the number of locks acquired for the table space exceeds the maximum number of locks allowed for a table space, locking escalates to the next higher level. If the table space is segmented, the next higher level is the table. If the table space is nonsegmented, the next higher level is the table space. Any page or LOB locks held are not released when lock escalation occurs.

A good general locking strategy would be to implement LOCKSIZE ANY, except in the following circumstances:

- A read-only table defined in a single table space should be specified as LOCKSIZE TABLESPACE. There rarely is a reason to update the table, so page locks should be avoided.

- A table that does not require shared access should be placed in a single table space specified as LOCKSIZE TABLESPACE. Shared access refers to multiple users (or jobs) accessing the table simultaneously.

- A grouping of tables in a segmented table space used by a single user (for example, a QMF user) should be specified as LOCKSIZE TABLE. If only one user can access the tables, there is no reason to take page-level locks.

- Specify LOCKSIZE PAGE for production systems that cannot tolerate a lock escalation, but for which row locking would be overkill. When many accesses are made consistently to the same data, you must maximize concurrency. If lock escalation can occur (that is, a change from page locks to table space locks), concurrency is eliminated. If a particular production system always must support concurrent access, use LOCKSIZE PAGE and set the LOCKMAX parameter for the table space to 0.

- For LOB table spaces, always specify LOCKSIZE LOB.

- Consider specifying LOCKSIZE ROW only when concurrency is of paramount importance. When multiple updates must occur to the same page at absolutely the same time, LOCKSIZE ROW might prove to be beneficial. But row locking can cause performance problems, because a row lock requires about the same amount of resources as a page lock. And, because there are usually multiple rows on a page, row locking will typically consume more resources. Do not implement LOCKSIZE ROW, though, unless you are experiencing a locking problem with page locking. Often, at design time, developers believe multiple transactions will be updating the same page simultaneously, but it is not very commonplace in practice. An alternative to LOCKSIZE ROW is LOCKSIZE PAGE with MAXROWS 1, which will achieve the same purpose by forcing one row per page.

Consider using LOCKSIZE ANY in situations other than those just outlined because it allows DB2 to determine the optimal locking strategy based on actual access patterns. Locking begins with PAGE locks and escalates to TABLE or TABLESPACE locks when too many page locks are being held. The LOCKMAX parameter controls the number of locks that can be taken before escalation occurs. LOCKSIZE ANY generally provides an efficient locking pattern because it allows the DBMS to actively monitor and manage the locking strategy.

Use LOCKSIZE ROW with Caution   The resources required to acquire, maintain, and release a lock at the row level are about the same as required for locking at the page level lock. When row locking is used and a table or table space scan is required, DB2 will lock every row on every page accessed. The number of locks required to successfully accomplish a scan can have a detrimental impact on performance. If a table has 100 rows per page, a table space scan could possibly require nearly 100 times as many resources for row locks as it would for page locks.

Switch Locking Strategies Based on Processing   Some tables have different access patterns based upon the time of day. For example, many applications are predominantly OLTP during work hours and predominantly batch during off hours. OLTP is usually characterized by short, indexed access to tables. Batch processing typically requires more intensive data access and table scans.

To take advantage of these situations, use the ALTER TABLESPACE statement to change the LOCKSIZE parameter to ROW for daylight processing. Before the nightly batch jobs and after online processing diminishes, alter the LOCKSIZE parameter back to ANY or PAGE.

By changing the locking strategy to conform to the type of processing, contention can be reduced thereby enhancing application performance.

Of course, in order to change each program's locking strategy you will need to rebind your static plans and packages after altering LOCKSIZE. For this approach to be successful you should consider assigning different plans and packages to online and batch, if you do not already do so.

LOCKMAX

The LOCKMAX parameter specifies the maximum number of page or row locks that any one process can hold at any one time for the table space. When the threshold is reached, the page or row locks are escalated to a table or table space lock.

Three options are available for setting the LOCKMAX parameter:

- The literal SYSTEM can be specified, indicating that LOCKMAX should default to the systemwide value as specified in DSNZPARMs.

- The value 0 can be specified, indicating that lock escalation should never occur for this table space.

- An integer value ranging from 1 to 2,147,483,647 can be specified, indicating the actual number of row or page locks to tolerate before lock escalation.

Use Caution Before Disabling Lock Escalation   Specify LOCKMAX 0 only when you are absolutely sure of the impact it will have on your processing mix. A very high value for LOCKMAX can have a similar effect to LOCKMAX 0, with the added benefit of an escape if the number of locks becomes intolerable. Large batch jobs running against a table space specified as LOCKMAX 0 can severely constrain concurrent access if a large number of locks are held without an intelligent commit strategy. When volumes fluctuate (for example, monthly processing cycles), lock patterns can deviate from the norm, potentially causing concurrency problems.

USING

The method of storage allocation for the table space is defined with the USING parameter. You can specify either a STOGROUP name combined with a primary and secondary quantity for space allocation or a VCAT indicating the high-level ICF catalog identifier for user-defined VSAM data sets.

In most cases, you should create the majority of your table spaces and indexes as STOGROUP-defined. This allows DB2 to do most of the work of creating and maintaining the underlying VSAM data sets, which contain the actual data. Another approach that reduces maintenance even more is to let SMS manage your page set allocations.

Table spaces and indexes defined using STOGROUPs provide the additional advantage of automatic data set creation as new data sets are needed. This is more beneficial than simply having DB2 create the initial data sets when the objects are defined. When a table space exceeds the maximum VSAM data set size, DB2 will automatically create additional data sets as needed to store the additional data. If you were using user-defined VSAM data sets instead, you would have to manually add new data sets when new VSAM data sets were needed. It is very difficult to predict when new data sets are needed, and even if you can predict this need, it is difficult to manage and create the data sets when they are needed.

Some DBAs believe that explicitly creating user-defined VSAM data sets for VCAT-defined table spaces gives them more control over the physical allocation, placement, and movement of the VSAM data sets. Similar allocation, placement, and movement techniques, however, can be achieved using STOGROUPs if the STOGROUPs are properly created and maintained and the table spaces are assigned to the STOGROUPs in a planned and orderly manner.

Another perceived advantage of user-defined VSAM data sets is the capability of recovering them if they inadvertently are dropped. The underlying, user-defined VSAM data sets for VCAT-defined objects are not deleted automatically when the corresponding object is dropped. You can recover the data for the table space using the DSN1COPY utility with the translate option. When you intentionally drop table spaces, however, additional work is required to manually delete the data sets.

There is one large exception to this scenario: If a segmented table space is dropped erroneously, the data cannot be recovered regardless of whether it was VCAT- or STOGROUP-defined. When a table is dropped from a segmented table space, DB2 updates the space map for the table space to indicate that the data previously in the table has been deleted, and the corresponding space is available immediately for use by other tables. When a table space is dropped, DB2 implicitly drops all tables in that table space.

A DBA can attempt to recover from an inadvertent drop of a segmented table space, and will appear to be successful with one glaring problem: DB2 will indicate that there is no data in the table space after the recovery. As you can see, the so-called advantage of easy DSN1COPY recovery of dropped tables disappears for user-defined VSAM data sets when you use segmented table spaces. This is crucial because more users are using segmented table spaces instead of simple table spaces to take advantage of their enhanced features.

Another perceived advantage of user-defined VSAM data sets was avoiding deleting and redefining the underlying data sets during utility processing. With STOGROUP-defined data sets, certain utilities, such as REORG, will delete and define the underlying data sets as part of the REORG process. As of DB2 V6, the REUSE option can be specified indicating that STOGROUP-defined data sets should be reused instead of being deleted and redefined. The utilities impacted are LOAD, REBUILD, RECOVER, and REORG.

See Table 5.4 for a comparison of VCAT- and STOGROUP-defined data sets.

TABLE 5.4   User-Defined VSAM Data Sets Versus STOGROUPs

	VCAT	STOGROUP
Need to know VSAM	Yes	No
User physically must create the underlying data sets	Yes	No
Can ALTER storage requirements using SQL	No	Yes
Can use AMS	Yes	No*
Confusing when data sets are defined on more than one DASD volume	No	Yes
After dropping the table or the table space, the underlying data set is not deleted	Yes	No**

*A table space initially created as a user-defined VSAM later can be altered to use STOGROUPs. A STOGROUP-defined table space can be altered to user-defined VSAM as well.

**Data in a segmented table space is unavailable after dropping the table space because the space map pages are modified to indicate that the table space is empty after a DROP.

> **NOTE**
>
> If you are using RAID storage devices do not try to explicitly place data sets. RAID storage devices will "mix" up the data anyway, so your placement efforts will be for naught.

PRIQTY and SECQTY

If you are defining your table spaces using the STOGROUP method, you must specify primary and secondary space allocations. The primary allocation is the amount of physical storage allocated when the table space is created. As the amount of data in the table space grows, secondary allocations of storage are taken. To accurately calculate the DASD space requirements, you must know the following:

Number of columns in each row

Data type for each column

Nullability of each column

Average size of variable columns

Number of rows in the table

Row overhead, such as RID size

Growth statistics

Growth horizon

Row compression statistics (if compression is used)

The values specified for PRIQTY and SECQTY are in kilobytes. Most DB2 pages are 4K in size, so you usually should specify PRIQTY and SECQTY in multiples of four. DB2 also supports page sizes of 8KB, 16KB, and 32KB. For table spaces with these page sizes, always specify the PRIQTY and SECQTY amounts in multiples of the page size: 8, 16, or 32, respectively.

Additionally, you should specify PRIQTY and SECQTY amounts in terms of the type of DASD defined to the STOGROUP being used. For example, a table space with 4KB pages defined on an IBM 3390 DASD device uses 48KB for each physical track of storage. This corresponds to 12 pages. A data set cannot be allocated at less than a track, so it is wise to specify the primary and secondary allocations to at least a track boundary. For an IBM 3390 DASD device, specify the primary and secondary quantities in multiples of 48. Here are the physical characteristics of the two most popular IBM DASD devices:

	Track	Cylinder	Cylinders/Device	Bytes/Track
3380 Device	40KB	600KB	885	47,476
3390 Device	48KB	720KB	1113	56,664

For segmented table spaces, be sure to specify these quantities such that neither the primary nor the secondary allocation is less than a full segment. If you indicate a SEGSIZE of 12, for instance, do not specify less than four times the SEGSIZE, or 48K, for PRIQTY or SECQTY. It is worth noting that a table space with a SEGSIZE of 12 will require 13 total pages, and thus two tracks to store: 1 page for the space map and 12 pages for the first segment.

If you are allocating multiple tables to a single table space, calculate the `PRIQTY` and `SECQTY` separately for each table using the formulas in Table 5.5. When the calculations have been completed, add the totals for `PRIQTY` to get one large `PRIQTY` for the table space. Do the same for the `SECQTY` numbers. You might want to add approximately 10% to both `PRIQTY` and `SECQTY` when defining multiple tables to a simple table space. This additional space offsets the space wasted when rows of different lengths from different tables are combined on the same table space page. (See the section in this chapter called "Avoid Wasted Space" for more information.) Remember, however, that the practice of defining multiple tables to a single, simple table space is not encouraged.

TABLE 5.5   Lengths for DB2 Data Types

Data Type	Internal Length	COBOL WORKING STORAGE		
CHAR(n)	n	01 identifier	PIC X(n)	
VARCHAR(n)	max=n+2	01 identifier		
		49 identifier	PIC S9(4) COMP	
		49 identifier	PIC X(n)	
LONG VARCHAR	*	01 identifier		
		49 identifier	PIC S9(4) COMP	
		49 identifier	PIC X(n)	
GRAPHIC(n)	2*n	01 identifier	PIC G(n) DISPLAY-1	
VARGRAPHIC(n)	(2*n)+2	01 identifier		
		49 identifier	PIC S9(4) COMP	
		49 identifier	PIC G(n) DISPLAY-1	
LONG VARGRAPHIC	*	01 identifier		
		49 identifier	PIC S9(4) COMP	
		49 identifier	PIC G(n) DISPLAY-1	
SMALLINT	2	01 identifier	PIC S9(4) COMP	
INTEGER	4	01 identifier	PIC S9(9) COMP	
DECIMAL(p,s)	INTEGER (p/2)+1	01 identifier	PIC S9(p)V9(s) COMP-3	
FLOAT(n) or REAL	8 (SINGLE PRECISION if n>21)	01 identifier	COMP-2	
FLOAT(n) or FLOAT	4 (DOUBLE PRECISION if n<21)	01 identifier	COMP-1	
DATE	4	01 identifier	PIC X(10)	
TIME	3	01 identifier	PIC X(8)	
TIMESTAMP	10	01 identifier	PIC X(26)	

* See text following this table to calculate this length.

To calculate the internal length of a long character column, use these formulas:

Modified row size = (max row size)–(size of all other cols)–(nullable long char cols)

Internal length = 2 * INTEGER((INTEGER((modified row size)/(long cols in table))/2))

Next, calculate the number of rows per page and the total number of pages necessary. To do this, use the following formula:

Rows per page = (((page size)–22) * ((100* PCTFREE)/100)/row length)

Total pages = (number of rows) / (rows per page)

Finally, the PRIQTY is calculated as follows:

PRIQTY = total pages * 4

To accurately calculate the primary quantity for a table, you must make a series of calculations.

First, calculate the row length. To do this, add the length of each column, using Table 5.5 to determine each column's internal stored length. Remember to add one byte for each nullable column and two bytes for each variable column.

If the rows are compressed, determine the average compressed row size and use this for the row length in the previous formulas.

To calculate SECQTY, you must estimate the growth statistics for the table space and the horizon over which this growth will occur.

For example, assume that you need to define the SECQTY for a table space that grows by 100 rows (growth statistics) over two months (growth horizon). If free space has been defined in the table space for 1,000 rows and you will reorganize this table space yearly (changing PRIQTY and SECQTY), you must provide for 200 rows in your SECQTY.

Divide the number of rows you want to provide for (in this case 200) by the number of rows per page. Round this number up to the next whole number divisible by 4 (to the track or cylinder boundary). Then specify this number as your SECQTY.

You might want to provide for secondary allocation in smaller chunks, not specifying the total number of rows in the initial SECQTY allocation. In the preceding example, you provided for 200 rows. By defining SECQTY large enough for 100 rows, you allocate three secondary extents before your yearly reorganization.

You may ask: why three? If each SECQTY can contain 100 rows and you must provide for 200 rows, shouldn't only two extents be allocated? No, there will be three. A secondary allocation is made when the amount of available space in the current extent reaches 50% of the next extent to be taken. So there are three allocations, but the third one is empty, or nearly empty.

As a general rule, avoid a large number of secondary extents. They decrease the efficiency of I/O, and I/O is the most critical bottleneck in most DB2 application systems.

Consider using DB2 Estimator to calculate space requirements for DB2 table space and index data sets. DB2 Estimator is a standalone tool provided by IBM at no cost with DB2 for OS/390. DB2 Estimator can be used to estimate the cost of running DB2 applications.

DB2 Estimator also provides a space calculation feature. To calculate space for a table, highlight the table and choose the Space Requirements option in the Tables menu, as shown in Figure 5.3. This will take you to the screen shown in Figure 5.4, which can be used to determine the space requirements for the selected table. This allows the DBA to save time by avoiding the manual space calculations we just covered.

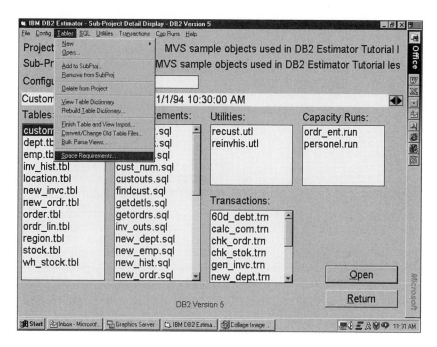

FIGURE 5.3   DB2 Estimator and space requirements.

Allocate Space on Cylinder Boundaries   Performance can be significantly affected based upon the choice of allocation unit. As an application inserts data into a table, DB2 will preformat space within the index and/or table space page set as necessary. This process will be more efficient if DB2 can preformat cylinders instead of tracks, because more space will be preformatted at once using cylinder allocation.

DB2 determines whether to use allocation units of tracks or cylinders based upon the value of PRIQTY and SECQTY. If either of these quantities is less than one cylinder, space for both primary and secondary will be allocated in tracks. For this reason, it is wise to specify both PRIQTY and SECQTY values of at least one cylinder for most table spaces and indexes.

Allocating space in tracks is a valid option, however, under any of the following conditions:

- For small table spaces and indexes that consume less than one cylinder of DASD

- For stable objects that are never updated SECQTY can be set to 0 causing DB2 to consider only PRIQTY when determining the allocation unit

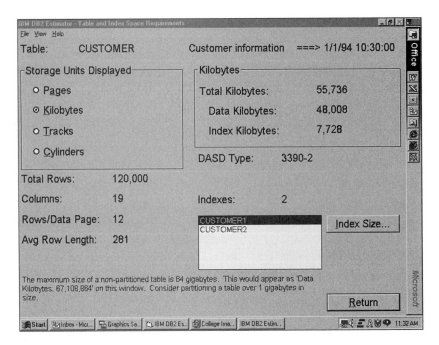

FIGURE 5.4   Using DB2 Estimator to calculate space.

Default Values for PRIQTY **and** SECQTY   If the PRIQTY parameter is not specified, and the data set is STOGROUP-defined, a default primary quantity value will be chosen by DB2. DB2 will base both the primary and secondary space allocation on the value of the TSQTY DSNZPARM parameter. If TSQTY is 0, then DB2 will default the size as follows, based on the page size of the data set:

- For 4KB page sizes: 12
- For 8KB page sizes: 24
- For 16KB page sizes: 48
- For 32KB page sizes: 96

If the SECQTY parameter is not specified, but the PRIQTY parameter is specified, the default value for SECQTY is 10% of the PRIQTY value or 3 times the page size of the table space, whichever value is greater.

If both the SECQTY and PRIQTY parameters are not specified, the default value for SECQTY follows the same pattern as for PRIQTY as indicated earlier.

Once again, avoid relying on default values. They are rarely, if ever, the correct choice. And even if the default happens to be the best choice, it is always better to explicitly specify the value to ensure that you are choosing the correct option.

SECQTY 0 **Versus No** SECQTY **Specified**   Specifying SECQTY 0 means that no secondary extents will be taken. This is not the same as failing to specify the SECQTY option (which causes DB2 to use the default value). Be sure you understand the difference and only specify SECQTY 0 if you want to avoid extents. If you try to INSERT data and no room is found in the table space and the table space is defined with SECQTY 0, the INSERT will fail. This is rarely desirable.

Free Space (PCTFREE and FREEPAGE)

The specification of free space in a table space or index can reduce the frequency of reorganization, reduce contention, and increase the efficiency of insertion. The PCTFREE parameter specifies what percentage of each page should remain available for future inserts. The FREEPAGE parameter indicates the specified number of pages after which a completely empty page is available.

> **CAUTION**
>
> Keep in mind that PCTFREE and FREEPAGE represent the accurate free space only immediately after the object is created or reorganized. As soon as data starts to be inserted or updated, the space set aside using these parameters will start to be used by DB2.

Increasing free space decreases the number of rows per page and therefore decreases the efficiency of the buffer pool because fewer rows are retrieved per I/O. Increasing free space can improve concurrent processing, however, by reducing the number of rows on the same page. For example, consider a table space that contains a table clustered on the DEPARTMENT column. Each department must access and modify its data independent of other departments. By increasing free space, you decrease the occurrences of departments coexisting on table space pages because fewer rows exist per page.

Space can be used to keep areas of the table space available for the rows to be inserted. This results in a more efficient insert process, as well as more efficient access—with less unclustered data—after the rows have been inserted.

Understanding how insert activity affects DB2 data pages will aid in understanding how optimal free space specification can aid performance. When a row is inserted, DB2 will perform a space search algorithm to determine the optimal placement of the new row in the table space. This algorithm is different for segmented and non-segmented (simple and partitioned) table spaces. For segmented table spaces DB2 will

- Identify the page in which the row should be inserted using the clustering index. (If no clustering index exists, DB2 will search all segments for available space to insert the row.)

- If space is available on that page, the row will be inserted; if space is not available, DB2 will search within the segment containing the target page for available space.

- If space is available in the segment, the row will be inserted; if space is not available, DB2 will search the last segment allocated in the table space for that specific table.

- If space is available, insert the row; otherwise DB2 will allocate a new segment.

For non-segmented table space DB2 searches for space as follows:

- Identify the page in which the row should be inserted using the clustering index.

- If space is available on that page, the row will be inserted; if space is not available, DB2 will search 16 contiguous pages before and after the target page.

- If space is available on any of those 32 pages, the row will be inserted; if space is not available, DB2 will scan from the beginning of the table space (or partition).

- If space is available, insert the row; otherwise DB2 will request a secondary extent.

For both segmented and non-segmented table spaces, DB2 will bypass locked pages even if they contain sufficient free space to hold the row to be inserted.

If insert activity is skewed, with inserts clustered at certain locations in the table space, you might want to increase the free space to offset the space used for the heavily updated portions of the table spaces. This increases the overall DASD usage but can provide better performance by decreasing the amount of unclustered data. Additionally, you could partition the table space such that the data area having the highest insert activity is isolated in its own partition. Free space could then be assigned by partition such that the insert "hot spot" has a higher PCTFREE and/or FREEPAGE specified. The other partitions could be assigned a lower free space.

If more than one table is assigned to a table space, calculate the free space for the table with the highest insert activity. This provides for more free space for tables with lower insert activity, but results in the best performance. Also, if the rows are compressed, calculate free space based on the average compressed row size.

When calculating free space, you must take into account that a certain amount of each page is wasted. DB2 uses 4K page sizes (of which 4,074 bytes are useable for data), and a maximum of 255 rows can be placed on one page. Consider a table space containing a single table with 122-byte rows. A single page can contain 33 rows. This leaves 48 bytes wasted per page, as follows:

    4074 / 122 = 33.39
    4074 − (122 * 33) = 48

Suppose that you want 10% free space in this table space. To specify that 10% of each page will be free space, you must factor the wasted space into the calculation. By specifying PCTFREE 10, 407 bytes are set aside as free space. However, 48 of those bytes can never be used, leaving 359 bytes free. Only two rows can fit in this space, whereas three would fit into 407 bytes. Factor the wasted space into your free-space calculations.

As a general rule, free space allocation depends on knowing the growth rate for the table, the frequency and impact of reorganization, and the concurrency needs of the application. Remember, PCTFREE is not the same as growth rate. Consider a table space that is allocated with a primary quantity of 7200K. If PCTFREE was set to 10, 720K is left free, with 6480K remaining for data storage. However, this provides a growth rate of 720/6480, or just over

11%, which is clearly a larger number than the PCTFREE specified. The general formula for converting growth rate to PCTFREE is:

PCTFREE = (growth rate) / (1 + growth rate)

To accommodate a 15% growth rate, only 13% (.15/1.15) of free space is necessary.

The other free space parameter is FREEPAGE. Specifying PCTFREE is sufficient for the free space needs of most table spaces. If the table space is heavily updated, however, consider specifying FREEPAGE in conjunction with PCTFREE. See Table 5.6 for free space suggestions based on update frequency. Modify these numbers to include wasted space, as described previously. These numbers should be used as rough guidelines only. You should always consider the growth rate for data used in your applications when specifying DB2 free space.

TABLE 5.6   Free Space Allocation Chart

Type of Table Processing	FREEPAGE	PCTFREE
Read only	0	0
Less than 20% of table volume inserted between REORGs	0	10 to 20
20 to 60% of table volumes inserted between REORGs	0	20 to 30
Greater than 60% of table volumes inserted between REORGs	0 or (SEGSIZE-1)	20 to 30
Most inserts done in sequence by the clustering index	0	0 to 10
Table space with variable length rows being updated	0	10 to 20

BUFFERPOOL
DB2 provides eighty buffer pool options for table space and index objects:

- 50 4KB buffer pools—BP0 through BP49

- 10 8KB buffer pools—BP8K0 through BP8K9

- 10 16KB buffer pools—BP16K0 through BP16K9

- 10 32KB buffer pools—BP32K through BP32K9

Data accessed from a DB2 table is first read from DASD, and then moved into a buffer pool, and then returned to the requester. Data in the buffer pool can remain resident in memory, avoiding the expense of I/O for future queries that access the same data. There are many strategies for specifying buffer pools, and each is discussed fully in Part V, "DB2 Performance Tuning." For now, it's sufficient to mention the following rules:

- Some small to medium DB2 shops use a single buffer pool, namely BP0. For these types of shops, DB2 does an adequate job of managing I/O using a single, large BP0 containing most (or all) of a shop's table spaces and indexes.

- As usage of DB2 grows, you should specify additional buffer pools tuned for specific applications, table spaces, indexes, or activities. The majority of mature DB2 shops fall into this category. Several buffer pool allocation and usage approaches are discussed in Part V.

- Avoid using BP32K for application table spaces. DB2 arranges a table space assigned to a 32K buffer pool as eight single 4K pages per 32K page. Therefore, every logical I/O to a 32K table space requires eight physical I/Os. To avoid using BP32K, consider denormalizing your tables, if necessary. (See the "Denormalization" section later in this chapter for more information.) With the addition of 8KB and 16KB buffer pools in DB2 V6, it is easier to manage DB2 table spaces having a page size greater than 4KB.

The number of buffer pools in use at your shop depends on the DB2 workload and the amount of real and extended memory that can be assigned to the DB2 buffer pools. These topics are covered in greater detail in Part V.

Always Specify a Buffer Pool   If you do not specify the BUFFERPOOL clause, the default buffer pools for the database are used (one for table spaces and one for indexes). Do not allow the BUFFERPOOL to default to the buffer pool of the database. It is better to explicitly specify the BUFFERPOOL clause on all table spaces and index CREATE statements.

BP32 and BP32K   Remember that BP32 and BP32K are two different sizes. BP32 is one of the fifty 4K buffer pools. BP32K is one of the ten 32K buffer pools. If you miss, or add, an erroneous "K" you may be using or allocating the wrong buffer pool.

> **TIP**
>
> Any buffer pool that contains a "K" in it is not a 4KB buffer pool; instead it is an 8KB, 16KB, or 32KB buffer pool. If the buffer pool does not contain a "K," it is a 4KB buffer pool.

CLOSE YES or NO
Prior to DB2 V2.3, the CLOSE option specified whether the underlying VSAM data sets for the table space (or index space) should be closed each time the table was used. CLOSE YES indicated that the underlying data set was to be closed after use; CLOSE NO indicated the opposite. A performance gain was usually realized when you specified CLOSE NO. For table spaces accessed infrequently (only once or twice daily), CLOSE YES might have been appropriate.

DB2 V2.3 introduced deferred close processing, sometimes referred to as *slow close*. Deferred close provided relief from the overhead associated with opening and closing data sets by closing the data sets only when the maximum number of open data sets was reached, regardless of whether CLOSE YES or CLOSE NO was specified. However, DB2 V2.3 will also update SYSLGRNX every time the data set is not in use. This speeds the recovery, because DB2 has a record of when updates could have occurred. However, the constant

SYSLGRNX updating can be a performance detriment during normal processing. Also, deferred close is a mixed blessing, because DB2 V2.3 table spaces that need to be closed after each access will remain open regardless of the CLOSE parameter specified.

DB2 V3 introduced a new open/close scenario referred to as *pseudo close*. Pseudo close offers the following features:

- A page set is not physically opened until it is first accessed, such as when an SQL statement or utility is executed against it.

- The VSAM open-for-update timestamp is not modified until data in the page set is updated. Previously, it was modified when the page set was first opened. This time-stamp can be used by some types of software to determine when an updated page set needs to be backed-up. If an updated page set has not been modified for a specified number of DB2 checkpoints (DSNZPARM PCLOSEN) or a specified amount of time (DSNZPARM PCLOSET), then it is switched to a read-only state.

- Page sets specified as CLOSE NO are candidates for physical close when either the DDLIMIT or DSMAX limit has been reached.

- SYSLGRNX records are updated for CLOSE YES data sets and are maintained by partition instead of at the data set level.

- The performance problems associated with updating SYSLGRNX are eliminated; SYSLGRNX entries will be written only when a data set (or partition) is converted to read-only state, not every time the data set is not in use.

> **TIP**
>
> Favor the use of CLOSE YES when operating with DB2 V3 and greater, because the SYSLGRNX modification performance problems have been eliminated.

V8 The maximum number of data sets that could be open in MVS at one time was 10,000. For V8, the number of open data sets can be up to 32,000 for z/OS V1.4 or 100,000 for z/OS V1.5.

ERASE YES or NO
The ERASE option specifies whether the physical DASD where the table space data set resides should be written over with binary zeroes when the table-space is dropped. Sensitive data that should never be accessed without proper authority should be set to ERASE YES. This ensures that the data in the table is erased when the table is dropped. Most table spaces, however, should be specified as ERASE NO.

NUMPARTS and SEGSIZE
See the "Use Proper Table space Definitions" section earlier in this chapter for NUMPARTS and SEGSIZE recommendations. The NUMPARTS option is used only for partitioned table spaces, SEGSIZE only for segmented table spaces.

Compression

Data compression can be specified directly in a DB2 table space. Compression is indicated in the DDL by specifying COMPRESS YES for the table space. Likewise, it can be turned off in the DDL by specifying COMPRESS NO. When compression is specified, DB2 builds a static dictionary to control compression. It saves from 2 to 17 dictionary pages in the table space. These pages are stored after the header and first space map page.

DB2 compression provides two very clear benefits:

- Hardware-assisted compression.

- It is provided free of charge with the base DB2 product.

Hardware-assisted compression is available only to those users owning IBM's high-end CPU models. This does not mean that DB2 compression features are only available to those with high-end CPUs. Hardware-assisted compression simply speeds up the compression and decompression of data—it is not a requirement for the inherent data compression features of DB2.

Of course, there are also potential disadvantages to using DB2 compression. Each compressed table space requires a compression dictionary that must be created, stored, and managed. It takes up DBM1 storage and can complicate recovery situations.

Overall, though, DB2 compression generally is efficient and effective. Users who never looked at compression before it was provided by DB2 because of the cost of third-party products should reevaluate their compression needs.

DDL Data Compression Versus Edit Procedures   DB2 data compression definitely should be used instead of the DSN8HUFF routine that is also supplied with DB2. But how does it compare to third-party tools? Most third-party vendors provide compression using EDITPROCs. However, these products are waning in popularity because of the excellent compression available to DB2 and the hardware-assist. Most users will find that DB2 can handle most of their compression requirements without needing a third-party compression tool.

However, before completely refusing to evaluate third-party solutions, consider the following:

- IBM compression supplies only a single compression routine (based on the Ziv-Lempel algorithm), whereas several third-party tools provide many different compression routines. This enables the user to better fit the algorithm to the composition of the data—using different compression algorithms for different types of data.

- The cost in time and effort to convert from prior compression methods to internal DB2 compression may not be cost-justifiable when compared to other tasks facing your enterprise.

- Third-party tool vendors are constantly enhancing their products to take better advantage of the operating system and the hardware environment. To ensure that you are getting the best "bang for your buck" in terms of data compression, it is wise to evaluate all of your options before settling on any given one. However, most of the third parties have fallen behind in updating their compression routines because of DB2's "out of the box" compression functionality.

CAUTION

For smaller table spaces, it is possible that the dictionary used by DB2 for compression could use more space than compression saves. For this reason, avoid compressing smaller table spaces.

General Data Compression Considerations   Why compress data? Consider an uncompressed table with a very large row size of 800 bytes. Therefore, five of this table's rows fit on a 4K page. If the compression routine achieves 30% compression, on average, the 800-byte row uses only 560 bytes, because $800 - (800 * .3) = 560$. Now seven rows fit on a 4K page. Because I/O occurs at the page level, the cost of I/O is reduced because fewer pages must be read for table space scans, and the data is more likely to be in the buffer pool because more rows fit on a physical page.

This can be a significant reduction. Consider the following scenarios. A 10,000-row table with 800-byte rows requires 2,000 pages. Using a compression routine as outlined previously, the table would require only 1,429 pages. Another table also with 800-byte rows but now having 1 million rows would require 200,000 pages without a compression routine. Using the compression routine, you would reduce the pages to 142,858—a reduction of more than 50,000 pages.

Of course, there is always a trade-off: DASD savings for CPU cost of compressing and decompressing data. However, the cost should be minimal with hardware-assisted compression. Indeed, overall elapsed time for certain I/O heavy processes may decrease when data is compressed. Furthermore, DB2 may require fewer buffer pages to process compressed data versus fully expanded data. Additionally, the compression dictionary is loaded into memory when the page set is opened. Loading lots of compression dictionaries into memory could eventually cause problems.

Encoding Scheme

The CCSID parameter is used to specify the data encoding scheme to use for the table space: ASCII or EBCDIC. All data stored within a table space must use the same encoding scheme.

NOTE

Do not specify an encoding scheme using CCSID for LOB table spaces or table spaces in a temporary database. The encoding scheme for a LOB table space will be inherited from its base table space. The LOB table space must have the same encoding scheme as its base table space—it cannot be different.

A table space in a TEMP database will not have an encoding scheme, because it can contain temporary tables having a variety of different encoding schemes.

The default encoding scheme for a table space is the encoding scheme of the database in which the table space is being created. So, obviously, the CCSID parameter can be coded for databases as well as table spaces. When `CCSID` is specified on a `CREATE DATABASE` statement, it specifies the default encoding scheme for data stored in the database. If no `CCSID` is specified for the database, the default will be the value specified to the `DEF ENCODING SCHEME` field on the `DSNTIPF` installation panel.

LOCKPART

Specifying `LOCKPART YES` enables selective partition locking (SPL). With SPL, individual partitions of a partitioned table space are locked only when accessed. SPL provides the following benefits:

- When SPL is enabled, applications accessing different partitions of a partitioned table space can enjoy greater concurrency.

- In a data sharing environment, DB2 and the IRLM can detect and optimize locking for situations in which no inter-subsystem activity exists by partition.

The default is `LOCKPART NO`, which indicates that locks are taken on the entire partitioned table space, not partition by partition.

MAXROWS

The `MAXROWS` parameter indicates the maximum number of rows that can be stored on a table space page. The default is 255. Specify `MAXROWS 255` unless there is a compelling reason to limit the number of rows per page, such as to limit contention for page locking.

> **CAUTION**
>
> Do not use `MAXROWS` for a LOB table space or a table space in a work file database.

Use `MAXROWS 1` Instead of Using Dummy Columns   A common design technique for older DB2 systems was to append dummy columns to DB2 tables to arbitrarily extend the row length. This was done to coerce DB2 into storing one row per page, effectively forcing a kludged type of row locking. However, this technique is invasive and undesirable because dummy columns will show up in `DCLGEN`s and might not always be recognized as "dummies." The same effect can be accomplished by specifying `MAXROWS 1`.

`MAXROWS 1` also can be a viable alternative to `LOCKSIZE ROW`.

MEMBER CLUSTER

The `MEMBER CLUSTER` parameter is used to indicate that inserted data is to ignore the clustering index (whether implicit or explicit). Instead, DB2 will choose where to put the data based on the space available in the table space.

Use this option with great care and only in certain specific situations. For example, if `INSERT`s are applied during batch processing and then the table space is always immediately reorganized, inserting the data by clustering index just slows down the `INSERT` processing. In this scenario, specifying `MEMBER CLUSTER` will speed up the batch jobstream and the subsequent `REORG` will recluster the data.

> **CAUTION**
>
> Do not use MEMBER CLUSTER for a LOB table space or a table space in a work file database.

TRACKMOD

The TRACKMOD parameter indicates whether DB2 should track modified pages in the space map pages of the table space or table space partition. If you specify TRACKMOD YES, DB2 tracks changed pages in the space map pages to improve the performance of incremental image copy. The default value is YES.

You can specify TRACKMOD NO to turn off the tracking of changed pages in the space map pages. Consider specifying TRACKMOD NO if you never take incremental image copies. Making an incremental copy can be significantly faster than making a full copy if the table space is defined with the TRACKMOD YES option.

Also, you cannot use the CHANGELIMIT option of the COPY utility for a table space or partition that is defined with TRACKMOD NO.

> **CAUTION**
>
> Do not use the TRACKMOD clause for a LOB table space.

Page Size

Each DB2 table space requires an underlying VSAM linear data set in which to store its data. The majority of DB2 table spaces will have 4KB page sizes. However, if the row size is so large that it will not fit onto a 4KB page, the table space can be created with a page size of 8KB, 16KB, or 32KB.

A VSAM CI, or control interval, is basically equivalent to DB2 page size. Prior to DB2 V8, the CI size of every underlying VSAM file was 4KB. DB2 would use multiple 4KB CIs to build up to 8KB, 16KB, or 32KB. For example, DB2 chains together eight separate 4KB CIs to build a 32KB page.

V8 However, as of DB2 V8 you can direct DB2 to use CI sizes of 8, 16, and 32KB to support table spaces with these large page sizes. To use this feature you need to set a new DSNZPARM. This parameter is set on the DSNTIP7 panel (VARY DS CONTROL INTERVAL).

> **NOTE**
>
> DB2 index spaces are still restricted to using 4KB page sizes.

After setting the DSNZPARM, all new 8KB, 16KB, and 32KB table spaces will use the same CI size instead of chaining 4KB CIs. Existing table spaces will be converted when they are reorganized or reloaded from scratch.

Consider using this new feature to synchronize CI size with table space page size to improve the performance of table space scans.

5

Multi-Table Table Spaces

Most DBAs follow a loose rule of placing only a single table in each table space. In general, this is a wise course of action for simple and segmented table spaces. Of course, it is mandatory for partitioned table spaces because only one table can be defined per partitioned table space. The one table per table space rule eases the administration process and helps to protect data integrity.

In a simple table space, data from more than one table can exist on the same page. Having multiple tables in a simple table space adversely affects concurrent data access, data availability, space management, and LOAD utility processing. For segmented table spaces, each page will contain data for only one table, so the concurrency issues are not relevant.

Another problem for multi-table table spaces is utility processing. DB2 utilities operate at the table space level, even when the code looks like it is for a single table. For example, consider the following LOAD statement:

```
LOAD DATA
REPLACE LOG NO
INDDN INPUT
INTO TABLE DSN8810.DEPT;
```

Most folks would read this statement to say that DB2 will read the data in the data set referenced by the INPUT DDNAME and use it to replace the data in the DEPT table only. That is mostly but not 100% accurate. DB2 will actually replace all of the data in the table space where the DEPT table resides. So, if the EMP table was defined in the same table space, then this LOAD statement would replace all of the DEPT data and completely eliminate all of the EMP data. That is probably not the intent of this LOAD operation. Obliterating data in this manner usually is unacceptable for most applications. This caveat applies to both segmented and simple table spaces.

Additionally, compression can be problematic for multi-table table spaces. The compression ratio can be adversely affected by storing multiple tables in a single table space.

Define One Table per Table Space   For the reasons outlined in the previous section, it is a good idea to follow the rule of placing only a single table into each table space. This is so regardless of the type of table space (simple, segmented, or partitioned). If you are going to put more than one table into the same table space, do so only for small, static tables that will not be loaded using the REPLACE option.

Defining Multiple Tables per Segmented Table Space

However, at times it is advisable to assign multiple tables to a single segmented table space. Although doing so in the wrong situation can be disastrous, there are advantages to multi-table table spaces, too, if they are implemented properly and with discretion. Consider the following advantages and disadvantages before proceeding with more than one table assigned to a segmented table space.

Advantages to defining multiple tables to a segmented table space are as follows:

- There are fewer open data sets, causing less system overhead.

- There are fewer executions of the COPY, REORG, and RECOVER utilities per application system because these utilities are executed at the table space level.

- It is easier to group like tables for administrative tasks because the tables reside in the same physical table space.

Disadvantages to defining multiple tables to a segmented table space are as follows:

- When only one table needs to be reorganized, all must be REORGed because they coexist in a single data set or group of data sets.

- If compression is used the compression ratio will be impacted by multiple tables instead of being optimized for the data patterns of a single table.

- The LOAD REPLACE utility will replace all data for all tables defined to the table space.

- There may be confusion about which tables are in which table spaces, making monitoring and administration difficult.

As a very rough general guideline, define small- to medium-size tables (less than 1 million pages) to a single, segmented table space. Create a partitioned table space for each large table (more than 1 million pages). If you decide to group tables in a segmented table space, group only small tables (less than 32 pages). Provide a series of segmented table spaces per application such that tables in the ranges defined in the following chart are grouped together. This will save space. Avoid grouping larger tables (more than 32 pages) with other tables.

Number of Pages	Table Space Segment Size
1 to 4	4
5 to 8	8
9 to 12	12
12 to 16	16
17 to 20	20
21 to 24	24
25 to 28	28
29 to 32	32

When the table space contains tables with the number of pages in the range on the left, assign the SEGSIZE indicated on the right to the table space.

When considering whether to place more than one table in a segmented table space, keep in mind that such a strategy is more preferable for static data than for rapidly changing data. This is so because there will be fewer requirements for running utilities against static data—and remember, DB2 utilities are run against table spaces.

Multi-Table Code and Reference Table Spaces   Consider placing your code and reference tables into multi-table segmented table spaces. Code and reference tables are likely to be static and frequently used by many programs. It is also plausible that a single application could have numerous code and reference tables. Placing multiple code and references tables into a single tablespace will reduce the number of open data sets required.

Multi-Table Table Spaces and RI   Consider grouping tables related by referential integrity into a single, segmented table space. This is not always feasible, because the size and access criteria of the tables might not lend themselves to multi-table segmented table spaces. Grouping referentially related tables, however, simplifies your QUIESCE processing.

Actually, RI can be a good reason to avoid multi-table table spaces entirely. If unrelated tables are assigned to the same table space you can wind up having to recover data unnecessarily because of a referential constraint.

Multi-Table Table Spaces and DBD Growth   Use caution when dropping and creating large numbers of tables in a single segmented table space, because over time, the DBD for the database containing the segmented table space will grow. There might be a high volume of tables being created and dropped in test environments, ad hoc environments, and any environment where end users have control over the creation and removal of DB2 tables.

Remember that a large DBD can affect storage and processing by consuming a large amount of EDM pool space.

General Table Space Guidelines

As you create DB2 table spaces, refer to the following list of guidelines for proper table space creation and usage.

Use Proper Table Space Definitions   Explicitly define table spaces. If a table space is not specified in the table creation statement, DB2 creates an implicit table space for new tables and sets all table space parameters to the default values. These values are unacceptable for most applications.

Favor Segmented Table Spaces   In general, use segmented table spaces except as follows:

- Use partitioned table spaces when you want to encourage parallelism. (Non-partitioned table spaces can be accessed in parallel, but partitioned table spaces are preferred for performance and data set placement reasons.)

- Use partitioned table spaces when the amount of data to be stored is very large (more than several million pages).

- Use partitioned table spaces to reduce utility processing time and decrease contention

- Use partitioned table spaces to isolate specific data areas in dedicated data sets.

- Use partitioned table spaces to improve data availability. If the data is partitioned by region, the partitions for the eastern, southern, and northern regions can be made available while the western region partition is being reorganized.

- Use partitioned table spaces to improve recoverability. If the data is partitioned by region and an error impacts data for the eastern region only, only the eastern partition needs to be recovered.

- Use a simple table space *only* when you need to mix data from different tables on one page.

Consider More Frequent Partitioning   To optimize query parallelism, it is wise to reevaluate your basic notions regarding partitioning. The common "rule of thumb" regarding whether to create a partitioned table space instead of a segmented table space was to use partitioning only for larger table spaces. This strategy is outdated.

Consider partitioning table spaces that are accessed in a read-only manner by long-running batch programs. Of course, very small table spaces are rarely viable candidates for partitioning, even with DB2's advanced I/O, CPU, and Sysplex parallelism features. This is true because the smaller the amount of data to access, the more difficult it is to break it into pieces large enough such that concurrent, parallel processing will be helpful.

Place Partitions on Separate DASD Devices   Move each partition of the same partitioned table space to separate DASD volumes. Failure to do so will negatively affect the performance of query parallelism performed against those partitions. Disk drive head contention will occur because concurrent access is being performed on separate partitions that coexist on the same device.

Consider Single Table Space Databases   For larger table spaces (100K pages and more) that are very active, consider defining a single table space per database. This can reduce contention. To increase efficiency, assign very active table spaces to volumes with low activity.

DB2 Storage and STOGROUPs

A DB2 storage group, also known as a STOGROUP, is an object used to identify a set of DASD volumes associated with an ICF catalog, or VCAT. Storage groups and user-defined VSAM are the two storage allocation options for DB2 data set definition. A STOGROUP can be assigned to a database, a table space, or an index. DB2 uses the volumes of the STOGROUP to assign table space and index space data sets to a device.

Define Useful Storage Groups

Define more than one volume per storage group to allow for growth and to minimize out-of-space abend situations. A data set extend failure causes DB2 to check the STOGROUP volume entries and issue a VSAM ALTER ADDVOLUMES for the data set.

When defining multiple volumes to a storage group, DB2 keeps track of which volume was specified first in the list and tries to use that volume first. DB2 does not attempt to balance the load on the DASD volumes. Data set allocation is performed by IBM's Data Facility Product (DFP). The order in which the volumes are coded in the CREATE STOGROUP statement determines the order in which the volumes are used by DB2. When the first volume is full, or if for any reason DFP determines that it cannot allocate a data set on that volume, DB2 (through DFP) moves to the next volume.

> **CAUTION**
>
> You cannot retrieve the ordering information for volumes in a STOGROUP from the DB2 Catalog, so make sure you have documentation detailing the order in which the volumes were defined to the storage group. This requires the DBA to explicitly document the order of the volumes in the CREATE STOGROUP statements by saving the DDL or by creating a word processing document or spreadsheet with the details. Without this information, it is impossible to determine the ordering of volumes in the STOGROUP.

If you would rather not administer multiple volume STOGROUPs, specifying only a single volume to a STOGROUP instead, you must be prepared to handle abends resulting from a volume being out of space. Handling out-of-space conditions usually involves one of the following:

- Moving the data set to a volume with more space by altering the STOGROUP and then recovering or reorganizing the table space

- Adding a volume to the STOGROUP to accommodate additional data set extents

Of course, you can also choose to use SMS to manage DB2 data sets. This option is discussed in the next section.

A good method of maintaining DB2 objects on multiple volumes is to define multiple STOGROUPs, each with a different volume as the first listed volume. For example, consider a new application assigned two volumes, called VOL1 and VOL2. Create two STOGROUPs as follows:

```
CREATE STOGROUP TESTSG1
   VOLUMES('VOL1', 'VOL2') VCAT appl ;
CREATE STOGROUP TESTSG2
   VOLUMES('VOL2', 'VOL1') VCAT appl ;
```

After creating these STOGROUPs, you can balance the load on the volumes by assigning some of the table spaces to TESTSG1 and some to TESTSG2. If one volume runs out of space, the other can serve as the backup.

The maximum number of volumes used by a storage group is 133 (even though DB2 allows more than 133 volumes to be defined to a storage group). It usually is difficult to monitor more than 3 or 4 volumes to a STOGROUP, however. All volumes in a storage group must be of the same type (for example, 3380, 3390, and so on).

> **CAUTION**
>
> Be sure to assign only DASD volumes of the same type to a single STOGROUP. When you mix multiple types of disks together in a single storage group, problems can ensue. For example, if DB2 must extend a STOGROUP-managed data set and the volumes are of different types, an extend failure will occur.

Using DFSMS with DB2

Another solution for avoiding multi-volume storage groups is to use DFSMS, or SMS for short. SMS stands for System Managed Storage. With SMS, the system determines where data sets are to be placed, easing the burden of data set creation and management on database administration.

You can define a DB2 STOGROUP with VOLUMES("*") to indicate SMS managed storage. When the "*" is specified in the VOLUMES clause, SMS will be used to assign a volume to the table space and index space data sets in that STOGROUP.

Using SMS, you can define storage and management classes to identify differing data set requirements. Storage and management classes are grouped into SMS storage groups.

ACS routines are used to assign DB2 table space and index data sets to SMS classes and Storage Groups. **ACS** stands for **Automatic Class Selection**. ACS is used to define policies for data set naming, volume naming, restrictions on usage, and other policies for data set creation and management.

ACS uses the data set name to decide where to place the data set. Many methods can be devised with specific naming standards to assign SMS classes based on the names of the DB2 data sets.

> **CAUTION**
>
> Do not confuse DB2 STOGROUPs with SMS Storage Groups. An SMS Storage Group refers to a set of volumes in an installation; a DB2 STOGROUP refers to a set of volumes containing a set of data. Different STOGROUPs can share the same disk volume or volumes. One disk volume can only belong to one SMS Storage Group.

With the new efficient DASD that is available, SMS is a more viable option than it was for past releases of DB2. However, if you want to ensure specific data set placement for all DB2 data sets, avoid SMS.

When using SMS, use ACS to differentiate between table spaces and index data sets and place them on different devices. This requires more setup work, but is required for achieving acceptable performance.

One possible scenario is to let SMS handle the majority of your DB2 data set placement, but use non-SMS data set placement techniques for high volume data sets to separate data from indexes on separate volumes or to ensure parallelism. In this way, SMS can be used to minimize the effort for the bulk of your data set placement tasks, while allowing you to target your "high need" data sets to specific devices.

SMS and Partitioned Table Spaces

One of the benefits of partitioning a table space is to spread the data across multiple physical devices. If you turn over data set placement to SMS, this benefit might be lost. There are three options for using SMS with partitioned table spaces:

- *SMS manages everything*—If the number of volumes in the Storage Group is much larger than the number of partitions in the table space, SMS might place each partition on a separate volume. However, this is by no means assured. To be certain that each partition is placed on a different volume, use another option.

If each partition is more than half a volume in size, however, you can be sure that SMS will place each partition on a separate volume, because two partitions will not fit on one volume. In this scenario, allowing SMS to manage everything might be an acceptable choice.

CAUTION

Be aware that space fragmentation on the volumes might result in a lack of volumes with suffi-cient free space, possibly resulting in REORGs failing due to lack of space.

- *One SMS storage group assigned per partition*—An SMS storage group consisting of only one volume can be defined for each table space partition. The ACS routine then assigns an SMS storage group to each partition. This method is similar to creating a DB2-defined partitioned table space using one STOGROUP for each partition.

  The advantage of this method is strict data set placement. The disadvantage is the complexity of the ACS routines required and the need for many SMS storage groups to be defined.

- *One SMS storage group assigned per partitioned table space*—The third and final alterna-tive to be discussed here is to define one SMS storage group for each partitioned table space. Be sure to assign sufficient volumes to the SMS storage group for all partitions in the table space. SMS will distribute the partitions onto those volumes. Be sure to assign no other table spaces or indexes to this SMS storage group. That way, no other data sets will ever be allocated on these volumes, practically reserving the space for this table space.

This discussion of SMS and DB2 has been brief. A comprehensive study of SMS is beyond the scope of this book. However, if you are implementing SMS with DB2, I recommend that you acquire a good understanding of SMS before proceeding. To do so, obtain and read (at a minimum) the following IBM manuals:

- SG24-5462: Storage Management with DB2 for OS/390
- SG24-4892: DFSMS/MVS Technical Overview
- SG24-5272: DFSMShsm Primer
- SC26-3123: DFSMS/MVS Implementing System-Managed Storage

Storage Guidelines

When creating DB2 objects, an efficient environment can be created by heeding the following storage guidelines.

Avoid Using SYSDEFLT   The default DB2 storage group is SYSDEFLT. SYSDEFLT is created when DB2 is installed and is used when a storage group is not explicitly stated (and VCAT is not used) in a database, a table space, or an index CREATE statement. I recommend that you avoid using SYSDEFLT. Objects created using SYSDEFLT are hard to maintain and track. Additionally, creating many different DB2 objects from diverse applications on the same DASD volumes degrades performance and, eventually, no more space will remain on the volumes assigned to SYSDEFLT. If you grant the use of SYSDEFLT only to SYSADMs, you can limit its use.

Favor STOGROUP-Defined Data Sets Over User-Defined VSAM   The need for specific VSAM data set definition has diminished as DB2 and disk devices have become more efficient. In general, unless you have very specific data set placement needs, favor using STOGROUPs (with or without SMS) over user-defined VSAM data set definition.

User-Defined VSAM Data Set Definitions   When creating DB2 objects with the VCAT option instead of the STOGROUP option, you must create user-defined VSAM data sets explicitly using the VSAM Access Method Services utility, IDCAMS. You can use two types of VSAM data sets for representing DB2 table spaces and index spaces: VSAM ESDS and VSAM LDS.

VSAM ESDS is an entry-sequenced data set, and VSAM LDS is a linear data set. A linear data set has a 4K CI size and does not contain the control information that entry-sequenced data sets normally contain. VSAM LDS and ESDS data sets are not used as plain VSAM data sets. DB2 uses the VSAM Media Manager to access these data sets. DB2 performs additional formatting of the VSAM data sets, causing them to operate differently than standard VSAM. Therefore, a direct VSAM read and write to a DB2 VSAM data set will fail.

Create DB2 data sets as VSAM linear data sets instead of as VSAM entry-sequenced data sets, because DB2 can use LDS more efficiently.

An example of the IDCAMS data set definition specification follows:

```
DEFINE CLUSTER --
    (NAME (vcat.DSNDBC.dddddddd.ssssssss.I0001.Annn) --
    LINEAR --
    REUSE --
    VOLUMES (volume list) --
    CYLINDER (primary   secondary) --
    SHAREOPTIONS (3  3) --
    ) --
DATA --
    (NAME (vcat.DSNDBD.dddddddd.ssssssss.I0001.Annn)) --
```

where:

vcat	High-level qualifier, indicating an ICF catalog
dddddddd	Database name
ssssssss	Table space name or index name
nnn	Partition number or data set number
volume list	Listing of physical DASD devices
primary	Primary space allocation quantity
secondary	Secondary space allocation quantity

5

Verify Disk Volumes Assigned to Your STOGROUPs   When you create a STOGROUP, DB2 does not verify that the volumes specified in the VOLUMES clause are valid, existing disk devices. Use care when creating your DB2 storage groups to ensure that only valid disk volumes are specified to the storage group in the CREATE STOGROUP.

Table Guidelines

The table is the basic unit of data that is accessible when using SQL. Data is inserted to, deleted from, and updated within DB2 tables. Once populated, data can be selected from a DB2 table. Basically, the table is the means by which end users gain access to DB2 data.

In general, you will define one table for each entity for which you will be storing data. A table can be thought of as a grouping of attributes that identify a physical entity. The table name should conform to the entity name. For example, consider the sample table for employees, DSN8810.EMP. EMP is the name of the table that represents an entity known as "employee." An employee has many attributes, some of which are EMPNO, FIRSTNME, and LASTNME. These attributes are columns of the table.

When you create one table for each entity, the tables are easy to identify and use because they represent real-world "things."

Of course, at times, the simple rule of one "physical" table per "logical" entity will need to be broken. This usually occurs when you need to denormalize for performance reasons. More details on are provided later in this chapter in the section "Denormalization."

DB2 Table Parameters

The preceding section concentrated on the rows and columns of a DB2 table. Other parameters also must be considered when creating DB2 tables. This section provides guidelines to assist you in your table creation endeavors.

Encoding Scheme

The CCSID parameter can be used to specify ASCII, EBCDIC, or UNICODE encoding at the table level as well as at the table space level. All data stored within a table space must use the same encoding scheme. Any indexes defined for tables in the table space will have the same encoding scheme as the table space.

V7 Support for Unicode is new as of DB2 Version 7.

DROP **Restriction**

To prohibit inadvertent table drops, use the WITH RESTRICT ON DROP clause of the CREATE TABLE statement. When WITH RESTRICT ON DROP is specified, drops cannot be issued for the table, its table space, and its database. To subsequently drop the table, it must first be altered to remove the RESTRICT ON DROP specification.

DB2-Enforced Table Auditing

If you must audit user access to DB2 tables, you can specify an audit rule for your tables. Although the auditing features of DB2 are rudimentary, sometimes they are useful. DB2 has three table audit options: NONE, CHANGES, and ALL.

DB2 table auditing is done on a unit-of-work basis only. DB2 audits only the first table access of any particular type for each unit of work, not every table access. AUDIT CHANGES writes an audit trace record for the first insert, update, and delete made by each unit of work. AUDIT ALL writes an audit trace record for the first select, insert, update, and delete made by each unit of work. By specifying AUDIT NONE or by failing to code an audit parameter, table auditing is inactivated.

Before deciding to audit DB2 table access, consider that table auditing incurs overhead—each time a table is accessed in a new unit of work, an audit trace record is written. Additionally, even if auditing has been specified for a given table, no audit trace records are written unless the appropriate DB2 audit trace classes are activated. For AUDIT CHANGES, activate audit trace classes 1, 2, 3, 4, 7, and 8. For AUDIT ALL, activate audit trace classes 1 through 8.

> **NOTE**
>
> Keep in mind that the ALTER TABLE statement itself is audited only if AUDIT CHANGES or AUDIT ALL is specified and the appropriate audit trace class has been activated.

In general, to alleviate overhead, do not audit table access unless your application absolutely requires it.

Specifying Your Own OBID

You can use the OBID parameter to explicitly specify a particular OBID (object identifier) for DB2 to use for the table being created. An OBID is an identifier assigned by DB2 for its own internal use and identification purposes.

You might choose to specify an OBID if you are re-creating a table that used to exist and you wish to keep the previous OBID that was assigned to the table. For example, if you are dropping a table but will be re-creating it with changes you may wish to keep the previous OBID for that table.

To obtain the current OBID of any table you can query the DB2 Catalog as follows (supplying the CREATOR and NAME of the table for the question marks in the query):

```
SELECT   OBID
FROM     SYSIBM.SYSTABLES
WHERE    CREATOR = ?
AND      NAME = ?;
```

You cannot use the OBID parameter to assign an OBID to a table that is already assigned to an existing DB2 table.

Augmenting the Log with Changed Information

If you are using a data propagation technology such as IBM's DataPropagator product, you may have to use the DATA CAPTURE parameter to augment the information captured on the DB2 log.

There are two options for DATA CAPTURE, NONE, and CHANGES. DATA CAPTURE NONE, which is the default, specifies that no additional information is to be recorded on the DB2 log. DATA

CAPTURE CHANGES, however, will cause DB2 to write additional information about inserted, updated, and deleted data. When a data propagation tool uses the DB2 log to capture changed information this additional data may be required to ensure the validity of the propagated data.

> **NOTE**
>
> DATA CAPTURE CHANGES will not capture additional information for LOB columns.

Temporary Tables

Most DB2 tables are permanent, meaning that once created, they exist until an authorized user drops them. At times, though, you may need to create DB2 tables that exist only for the duration of a program run. Such a table is known as a temporary table.

DB2 has provided the capability to create temporary tables since Version 5. But the initial functionality was practical only in certain circumstances due to some inherent limitations. This first type of temporary table is known as a created (or global) temporary table.

V7 IBM's support of temporary tables was expanded as of Version 7. Now DB2 offers two different types of temporary tables: created and declared.

Why Use Temporary Tables?

Before we investigate these two types of temporary tables, let's first address why anyone would want or need to use a temporary table in the first place.

One potential use of temporary tables is to store intermediate SQL results during a program run. Consider, for example, if the results of a first query need to be used in a subsequent query. Instead of rerunning the first query (or combining it with the subsequent query), the results of the first query can be stored in a temporary table. Then the temporary table can be joined into the second query without incurring the overhead of rerunning the first query. This is particularly useful if the first query is particularly complex or inefficient.

Or what about result sets that need to be returned more than once by the same program? Consider this scenario: A complex multi-table join is coded that consumes a lot of resources to run. Furthermore, that join statement needs to be run three times during the course of the program. Instead of running the join three times you can run it once and populate a temporary table with the results. The next two times you can simply read the temporary table which might be more efficient than re-executing the complex, resource-consuming multi-table join.

Temporary tables also are useful for enabling non-relational data to be processed using SQL. For example, you can create a global temporary table that is populated with IMS data (or any other non-relational data source) by a program. Then during the course of that program, the temporary table containing the IMS data can be accessed by SQL statements and even joined to other DB2 tables. The same could be done for data from a flat file, VSAM, IDMS, or any other non-relational data.

Another reason for IBM's inclusion of temporary table support in DB2 is to make conversion from other relational products easier. Microsoft SQL Server and Oracle both have supported temporary tables for quite some time now. Without such support in DB2 it was very difficult for developers to convert or port their Oracle or SQL Server applications to DB2. IBM alleviated this problem by enabling temporary table support in DB2.

Now let's examine the two types of temporary tables supported by DB2.

Created Temporary Tables

A created temporary table exists only as long as the process that uses it. Temporary tables are created using the CREATE GLOBAL TEMPORARY TABLE statement. When created, the schema for the table is stored in the DB2 system catalog (SYSIBM.SYSTABLES) just like any other table, but the TYPE column is set to 'G' to indicate a global temporary table. Created temporary tables are sometimes referred to as global temporary tables, but this is confusing since declared temporary tables are also referred to as global when they are created.

It is important to remember that a created global temporary table must be created using a DDL CREATE statement before it can be used in any program.

A created temporary table is instantiated when it is referenced in an OPEN, SELECT INTO, INSERT, or DELETE statement, not when it is created. Each application process that uses the temporary table creates a new instance of the table for its use. When using a temporary table, keep the following in mind:

- Because they are not persistent, locking, logging, and recovery do not apply to temporary tables.

- Indexes cannot be created on temporary tables, so all access is by a complete table scan.

- Constraints cannot be created on temporary tables.

- A null is the only default value permitted for columns of a temporary table.

- Temporary tables cannot be referenced by DB2 utilities.

- Temporary tables cannot be specified as the object of an UPDATE statement.

- When deleting from a temporary table, all rows must be deleted.

- Although views can be created on temporary tables, the WITH CHECK OPTION cannot be specified.

Work file data sets are used to manage the data of created temporary tables. The work database (DSNDB07) is used as storage for processing SQL statements that require working storage—not just for created temporary tables. If you are using created temporary tables, be sure to examine the DB2 Installation Guide for tactics to estimate the disk storage required for temporary work files.

When a temporary work file result table is populated using an INSERT statement, it uses work file space. No other process can use the same work file space as that temporary work file table until the table goes away. The space is reclaimed when the application process commits or rolls back, or when it is deallocated, depending on which RELEASE option was used when the plan or package was bound. It is a good idea to keep the work files in a separate buffer pool to make it easier to monitor. IFCID 0311 in performance trace class 8 can be used to distinguish these tables from other uses of the work file.

Declared Temporary Tables

V7 DB2 Version 7 introduces declared temporary tables. Actually, to be more accurate, declared temporary tables were made available in the intermediate DB2 Version 6 refresh.

This new type of temporary table is different from a created temporary table and overcomes many of their limitations. The first significant difference between declared and created temporary tables is that declared temporary tables are specified using a DECLARE statement in an application program—and not using a DDL CREATE statement. Because they are not persistent they do not have descriptions in the DB2 Catalog.

Additionally, declared temporary tables offer significant features and functionality not provided by created temporary tables. Consider

- Declared temporary tables can have indexes and CHECK constraints defined on them.

- You can issue UPDATE statements and positioned DELETE statements against a declared temporary table.

- You can implicitly define the columns of a declared temporary table and use the result table from a SELECT.

So, declared temporary tables offer much more flexibility and functionality than created temporary tables. To "create" an instance of a declared temporary table, you must issue the DECLARE GLOBAL TEMPORARY TABLE statement inside of an application program. That instance of the declared temporary table is known only to the process that issues the DECLARE statement. Multiple concurrent programs can be executed using the same declared temporary table name because each program will have its own copy of the temporary table.

But there is more work required to use a declared temporary table than there is to use a created temporary table. Before you can declare temporary tables you must create a temporary database and table spaces for them to use. This is accomplished by specifying the AS TEMP clause on a CREATE DATABASE statement. Then, you must create segmented table spaces in the temporary database. Only one temporary database for declared temporary tables is permitted per DB2 subsystem.

> **CAUTION**
>
> Everyone has the CREATETAB privilege in the temporary database by default—and you cannot REVOKE this privilege. It is implicitly granted when the temporary database is created.

When a DECLARE GLOBAL TEMPORARY TABLE statement is issued, DB2 will create an empty instance of the temporary table in the temporary table space. INSERT statements are used to populate the temporary table. Once inserted, the data can be accessed, modified, or deleted. When the program completes, DB2 will drop the instance of the temporary table. Also, be aware that users of temporary tables must have been granted USE authority on the temporary table space.

The following example shows a DECLARE statement that can be issued from an application program (assuming the temporary database and table spaces already have been defined):

```
DECLARE GLOBAL TEMPORARY TABLE TEMP_EMP
  (EMPNO      CHAR(6)      NOT NULL,
   FIRSTNME   VARCHAR(12)  NOT NULL,
   MIDINIT    CHAR(1)      NOT NULL,
   LASTNAME   VARCHAR(15)  NOT NULL,
   WORKDEPT   CHAR(3),
   PHONENO    CHAR(4)
  );
```

This creates a declared temporary table named TEMP_EMP. Additionally, you can use the LIKE clause to DECLARE a temporary table that uses the same schema definition as another currently existing table. You can use the INCLUDING IDENTITY COLUMN ATTRIBUTES clause to copy the IDENTITY columns as well. For example:

```
DECLARE GLOBAL TEMPORARY TABLE TEMP_PROJ
  LIKE DSN8810.PROJ
  INCLUDING IDENTITY
  ON COMMIT PRESERVE ROWS;
```

This example shows how to use the INCLUDING IDENTITY clause. However, the sample table DSN8810.PROJ does not use an IDENTITY column, so this statement would not work—it is shown as an example only. Identity columns are covered later in this chapter in the section titled "Sequence Objects and Identity Columns."

Notice also the ON COMMIT PRESERVE ROWS clause in the previous example. The ON COMMIT clause specifies what action DB2 is to take with the data in the declared temporary table when the program issues a COMMIT statement. There are two options: PRESERVE or DELETE rows. Specifying PRESERVE ROWS indicates that the rows of the table are to be kept. Beware, though, that the PRESERVE ROWS option impacts thread reuse. You will not be able to reuse threads for any application process that contains, at its most recent COMMIT, an active declared temporary table defined using the PRESERVE ROWS option of the ON COMMIT clause. The other option, which is the default, is ON COMMIT DELETE ROWS. In that case all of the rows of the table are deleted as long as there are no cursors defined using WITH HOLD.

V7

> **NOTE**
>
> Scrollable cursors, another new feature of DB2 V7, require declared temporary tables. A scrollable cursor provides the ability to scroll forward and backward through the data once the cursor is open.
>
> The data from a scrollable cursor is maintained in a declared temporary table. DB2 uses this mechanism to facilitate scrolling through data in multiple ways—forward, backward, or to a specific position.
>
> So, keep in mind, even if you do not choose to use temporary tables in your application programs, you may need to implement them to support scrollable cursors.

Declared Temporary Table Storage   Before using declared temporary tables, the temporary database and temporary table spaces must be defined to store the temporary data. For example,

```
CREATE DATABASE TEMPDB AS TEMP;

CREATE TABLESPACE TEMPTS
 IN TEMPDB
 SEGSIZE 4
 BUFFERPOOL BP7;
```

The table space is created as a temporary table space by virtue of it being in the temporary database.

The page size of the temporary table space must be large enough to hold the longest row in the declared temporary table. The size of a row in the declared temporary table might be considerably larger than the size of the row in the table for which the scrollable cursor is used. As with a regular table, the size of the row depends on the number of columns that are stored in the declared temporary table and the size of each column.

Consider creating a temporary table space for every page size. The buffer pool assignment determines the page size.

An in-depth discussion of calculating the storage requirements for a temporary table space for a declared temporary table is provided in the *DB2 Installation Guide*. Be sure to refer to that manual before implementing declared temporary tables or any features that rely on declared temporary tables (for example, scrollable cursors).

> **NOTE**
>
> Keep in mind that when there is more than one temporary table space defined to the DB2 subsystem, DB2 will select which temporary table spaces it will use for scrollable cursor processing. More information on scrollable cursors is provided in Chapter 11, "Using DB2 in an Application Program."

Temporary Table Guidelines
The following guidelines are provided for your assistance as you implement temporary tables for your DB2 applications.

Favor Declared Temporary Tables   For applications that require temporary tables, favor declared temporary tables over created temporary tables. Declared temporary tables are more flexible and functional than created temporary tables.

When using declared temporary tables you can index them, define CHECK constraints for them, and issue UPDATE statements and positioned DELETE statements against them, none of which can be done using created temporary tables.

When to Consider Created Temporary Tables   With all of the limitations of created temporary tables why would anyone still want to use them instead of declared temporary tables?

Well, there are a few potential problems with declared temporary tables, too. First of all, the DB2 Catalog (SYSIBM.SYSPACKDEP) will not show dependencies for declared temporary tables, but it will for created temporary tables. Second, some DBAs are leery of allowing database structures to be created by application programmers inside of an application programmer. With limited DDL and database design knowledge it may not be wise to trust programmers to get the table structure correct. Furthermore, the additional management of the temporary database and table spaces can become an administrative burden.

So, created temporary tables are still useful—in the right situations. They should be considered primarily when no updating of temporary data is needed and access to the temporary data is purely sequential.

Use Temporary Tables with Stored Procedures   Temporary tables are most useful when a large result set must be returned from a stored procedure. Refer to Chapter 15, "Using DB2 Stored Procedures," for in-depth guidelines on using stored procedures.

Use SQL to Access Non-Relational Data   Temporary tables are useful for enabling non-relational data to be processed using SQL. For example, you can create a temporary table (global or created) and then populate it with IMS data in your application program. Then, during the course of that program, the temporary table containing the IMS data can be accessed by SQL statements and even joined to other DB2 tables.

General Table Guidelines

The following guidelines provide helpful hints for you to follow as you implement and manage tables within your DB2 applications and systems.

Use LIKE to Duplicate a Table's Schema   Use the LIKE clause to create a table with the same columns as another table. The following SQL creates a new table OLD_PROJ using the PROJ table as a template:

```
CREATE TABLE DSN8810.OLD_PROJ
LIKE DSN8810.PROJ
IN db.ts;
```

The LIKE clause is particularly useful in the following instances:

- When creating exception tables required by the CHECK utility

- When multiple instances of a similar table must be created

- When creating a PLAN_TABLE

- When creating the same table for multiple users

Consider Using Comments   Consider using the COMMENT ON statement to document the entities you create. For V7 and previous releases, as many as 254 characters of descriptive text can be applied to each column, table, alias, index, distinct type, procedure, sequence, trigger, and UDF known to DB2. The maximum size of a comment is increased to 762 characters as of DB2 V8. The comment text is stored in a column named REMARKS in the appropriate DB2 Catalog table as follows:

- SYSIBM.SYSTABLES for aliases and tables

- SYSIBM.SYSCOLUMNS for columns

- SYSIBM.SYSINDEXES for indexes

- SYSIBM.SYSSEQUENCES for sequences

- SYSIBM.SYSTRIGGERS for triggers

- SYSIBM.SYSDATATYPES for distinct types

- SYSIBM.SYSROUTINES for stored procedures and UDFs

If useful descriptions are maintained for all columns and tables, the DB2 Catalog can function as a crude data dictionary for DB2 objects. However, be aware that comments are stored in a VARCHAR column in each of the preceding catalog tables.

> **CAUTION**
>
> When comments are specified, the overall size of the DB2 Catalog will expand and might grow to be larger than expected. Weigh the benefits of added documentation against the impact on the DB2 Catalog before adding comments on all columns and tables.

V7 **Avoid Specifying Labels for Columns**   DB2 provides the capability to label columns of DB2 tables using the LABEL ON statement. This was useful at times prior to DB2 Version 8 because the maximum length for a column name was 18 characters; the maximum length of a column label was 30 characters.

The label is stored in the DB2 Catalog in the SYSIBM.SYSCOLUMNS tables. QMF users can specify that they want to use labels rather than column names, thereby providing better report headings.

However, as of DB2 V8 the maximum length of a column name is 128 characters and the maximum length of the label is 90 characters, negating the benefit of a "descriptive" column label.

> **CAUTION**
>
> Be aware that specifying column labels will add to the overall size of the DB2 Catalog, specifically to the SYSIBM.SYSCOLUMNS table. However, labels will not cause the same amount of growth as comments because labels have a maximum size of 30 characters as opposed to 254 for comments; or, as of DB2 V8, 90 characters as opposed to 762 for comments.

Changing the Name of a Table   The RENAME statement enables DBAs to change the name of a DB2 table without dropping and re-creating the table. All table characteristics, data, and authorization is maintained. This feature is not available prior to DB2 Version 5.

Avoid Using the IN DATABASE Clause   When creating tables do not use the IN DATABASE clause. When IN DATABASE is used, a simple table space is implicitly created in the specified database. This simple table space will use all of the default parameters—which, as we have already learned, are usually not optimal. Additionally, no other tables can be assigned to this table space.

Instead, explicitly create a table space (of the proper type for the data), and then create the table in that table space.

Rows and Columns

When defining DB2 columns to a table you will need to choose a data type and perhaps a length for each column. Recall from Chapter 1, "The Magic Words," that DB2 supports the following data types:

CHAR	fixed length alphanumeric data
VARCHAR	variable length alphanumeric data
GRAPHIC	fixed length graphical data
VARGRAPHIC	variable length graphical data
SMALLINT	small integer numbers
INTEGER	larger integer numbers
DECIMAL(p,s)	numeric data
FLOAT(n) or FLOAT	single precision floating point (if n>21)
FLOAT(n) or REAL	double precision floating point (if n<21)
DATE	calendar date data
TIME	time data
TIMESTAMP	combination date and time data
ROWID	unique row identifier (internally generated by DB2)
BLOB	binary large object
CLOB	character large object
DBCLOB	double byte character large object

As you define your DB2 tables you also will have to worry about other factors and assign other characteristics to each column. For example,

- When creating a table you will need to define each column and therefore will be required to specify the columns in an effective sequence.

- Each column must be named.

- Each column must be defined as nullable or unable to be assigned null.

- Each column may be assigned a default value to use when data is inserted to a row but no value is provided for that particular column.

As you create DB2 tables, you should be mindful of their composition (rows and columns) and how this affects performance. This section outlines several guidelines that ensure efficient row and column specification.

ROWID

The ROWID data type is used to generate a unique value for every row in a table. The value is internally generated by DB2. A table can have only one ROWID column. The values in a ROWID column cannot be null.

An additional parameter, GENERATED, must be specified for a column defined as a ROWID. The GENERATED parameter is reserved for ROWID columns only (as of DB2 Version 6). It indicates that the values for the column are to be generated by DB2. There are two options for GENERATED, one of which must be supplied:

- The ALWAYS parameter indicates that DB2 will always generate a value for the column when a row is inserted into the table. Most ROWID columns should be defined with this option.

- The BY DEFAULT parameter indicates that DB2 will generate a value for the column when a row is inserted into the table unless a value is specified. The BY DEFAULT option can be useful if you are using data propagation to move ROWID values from one table to another. If you specify BY DEFAULT, the ROWID column must have a unique, single-column index. Until this index is created, you cannot add rows to the table regardless of whether you are using INSERT or LOAD.

> **CAUTION**
>
> DB2 will use an explicitly specified value for a ROWID only if it is a valid ROWID value that was previously generated by DB2.

Sequence Objects and Identity Columns

When designing database a frequent request is for a column to contain sequentially generated numbers. For example, each row has a counter associated with it. When a new row is inserted, the counter should be incremented by one for the new row. Until recently such a design was difficult to deliver.

Without sequence objects or identity columns an application program can implement similar functionality, but usually not in a manner that will perform adequately as a usage scale. One common technique is to maintain a one-row table that contains the sequence number. Each transaction locks that table, increments the number, and then commits to unlock the table. In this scenario only one transaction at a time can increment the sequence number. A variation uses something like this:

```
SELECT MAX()+ 1
FROM   ONEROW_TABLE
WITH RR;
```

The result is the next highest number to be used. This value is used by the application and ONEROW_TABLE must be updated with the incremented value. Performance bottlenecks will occur with this method when a lot of concurrent usage is required.

But now DB2 offers two methods of automatically generating sequential numbers for a column:

 • Identity columns.

• SEQUENCE objects.

Identity Columns   Identity columns were formally added to DB2 as of Version 7, but were also made available to DB2 Version 6 as a refresh. An identity column is defined to a DB2 column using the IDENTITY parameter. A column thusly defined will cause DB2 to automatically generate a unique, sequential value for that column when a row is added to the table. For example, identity columns might be used to generate unique primary key values or a value that somewhat mimics Oracle's row number capability. Using identity columns helps to avoid some of the concurrency and performance problems that can occur when application programs are used to populate sequential values for a "counter" column.

When inserting data into a table that uses an identity column, the program or user will not provide a value for the identity column. Instead, DB2 automatically generates the appropriate value to be inserted.

Only one identity column can be defined per DB2 table. Additionally, the data type of the column must be SMALLINT, INTEGER, or DECIMAL with a zero scale, that is DECIMAL(n,0). The data type also can be a user-defined DISTINCT type based on one of these numeric data types. The designer has control over the starting point for the generated sequential values, and the number by which the count is incremented.

An example of creating a table with an identity column follows:

```
CREATE TABLE EXAMPLE
   (ID_COL INTEGER NOT NULL
          GENERATED ALWAYS AS IDENTITY
          START WITH 100
          INCREMENT BY 10
    ...);
```

In this example, the identity column is named ID_COL. The first value stored in the column will be 100 and subsequent INSERTs will add 10 to the last value. So the identity column values generated will be 100, 110, 120, 130, and so on.

Note, too, that each identity column has a property associated with it assigned using the GENERATED parameter. This parameter indicates how DB2 generates values for the column. You must specify GENERATED if the column is to be considered an identity column or the data type of the column is a ROWID. This means that DB2 must be permitted to generate values for all identity columns. There are two options for the GENERATED parameter, ALWAYS and BY DEFAULT:

- GENERATED ALWAYS indicates that DB2 will always generate a value for the column when a row is inserted into the table. You will usually specify ALWAYS for your identity columns unless you are using data propagation.

- GENERATED BY DEFAULT indicates that DB2 will generate a value for the column when a row is inserted into the table unless a value is specified. So, if you want to be able to insert an explicit value into an identity column you must specify GENERATED BY DEFAULT.

Additionally, you can specify what to do when the maximum value is hit. Specifying the CYCLE keyword will cause DB2 to begin generating values from the minimum value all over again. Of course, this can cause duplicate values to be generated and should only be used when uniqueness is not a requirement.

Sometimes it is necessary to retrieve the value of an identity column immediately after it is inserted. For example, if you are using identity columns for primary key generation you may need to retrieve the value to provide the foreign key of a child table row that is to be inserted after the primary key is generated. The IDENTITY_VAL_LOCAL() function can be used to retrieve the value of an identity column after insertion. For example, run the following statement immediately after the INSERT statement that sets the identity value:

```
VALUES IDENTITY_VAL_LOCAL() INTO :IVAR;
```

The host variable IVAR will contain the value of the identity column.

Problems with Identity Columns   Identity columns can be useful, depending on your specific needs, but the problems that accompany identity column are numerous. Some of these problems include

- Handling the loading of data into a table with an identity column defined as GENERATED BY DEFAULT. The next identity value stored by DB2 to be assigned may not be the correct value that should be generated. This can be especially troublesome in a testing environment.

- LOAD INTO PART x is not allowed if an identity column is part of the partitioning index.

- What about environments that require regular loading and reloading (REPLACE) for testing? The identity column will not necessarily hold the same values for the same rows from test to test.

V8
- Prior to V8, it was not possible to change the GENERATED parameter (such as from GENERATED BY DEFAULT to GENERATED ALWAYS).

- The IDENTITY_VAL_LOCAL() function returns the value used for the last insert to the identity column. But it only works after a singleton INSERT. This means you cannot use INSERT INTO SELECT FROM or LOAD, if you need to rely on this function.

- When the maximum value is reached for the identity column, DB2 will cycle back to the beginning to begin reassigning values—which might not be the desired approach.

If you can live with these caveats, then identity columns might be useful to your applications. However, in general, these "problems" make identity columns a very niche solution. IBM has intentions to rectify some of these problems over time in upcoming versions of DB2.

SEQUENCE **Objects**   Recall that DB2 has two methods of automatically generating sequential numbers. The first method is to define an identity column for the table; the second is to create a SEQUENCE object. A SEQUENCE object is a separate structure that generates sequential numbers.

V8 New to DB2 V8, a SEQUENCE is a database object specifically created to generate sequential values. So, using a SEQUENCE object requires the creation of a database object; using an identity column does not.

A SEQUENCE objects is created using the CREATE SEQUENCE statement.

When the SEQUENCE object is created it can be used by applications to "grab" a next sequential value for use in a table. SEQUENCE objects are ideal for generating sequential, unique numeric key values. A sequence can be accessed and incremented by many applications concurrently without the hot spots and performance degradation associated with other methods of generating sequential values. SEQUENCE objects also can be used by more than one column in the same table.

Sequences are efficient and can be used by many users at the same time without causing performance problems. Multiple users can concurrently and efficiently access SEQUENCE objects because DB2 does not wait for a transaction to COMMIT before allowing the sequence to be incremented again by another transaction.

An example of creating a SEQUENCE object follows:

```
CREATE SEQUENCE ACTNO_SEQ
    AS SMALLINT
    START WITH 1
    INCREMENT BY 1
    NOMAXVALUE
    NOCYCLE
    CACHE 10;
```

This creates the SEQUENCE object named ACTNO_SEQ. Now it can be used to generate a new sequential value, for example

```
INSERT INTO DSN8810.ACT
    (ACTNO, ACTKWD, ACTDESC)
    VALUES
    (NEXT VALUE FOR ACTNO_SEQ, 'TEST', 'Test activity');
```

The NEXT VALUE FOR clause is known as a sequence expression. Coding the sequence expression causes DB2 to use the named SEQUENCE object to automatically generate the next value. You can use a sequence expression to request the previous value that was generated. For example,

```
SELECT PREVIOUS VALUE FOR ACTNO_SEQ
INTO   :IVAR
FROM   DSN8810.ACT;
```

As you can see, sequence expressions are not limited to INSERT statements, but can be used in UPDATE and SELECT statements, too.

CAUTION

If you specify the NEXT VALUE FOR clause more than once in the same SQL statement, DB2 will return the same value for each NEXT VALUE FOR specification.

SEQUENCE **Object Parameters**   Similar to identity columns, a SEQUENCE object has parameters to control the starting point for the generated sequential values, and the number by which the count is incremented. You can also specify the data type to be generated (the default is INTEGER). You can also specify a minimum value (MINVALUE) and a maximum value (MAXVALUE) if you wish to have further control over the values than is provided by the data type chosen.

Again, as with identity columns, you can specify how the SEQUENCE should handle running out of values when the maximum value is hit. Specifying the CYCLE keyword will cause the SEQUENCE object to wrap around and begin generating values from the minimum value all over again.

A final consideration for SEQUENCE objects is caching. Sequence values can be cached in memory to facilitate better performance. The size of the cache specifies the number of sequence values that DB2 will pre-allocate in memory. In the previous example CACHE 10 indicates that ten sequence values will be generated and stored in memory for subsequent use. Of course, you can turn off caching by specifying NO CACHE. With caching turned off each new request for a sequence number will cause I/O to the DB2 Catalog (SYSIBM.SYSSEQUENCES) to generate the next sequential value.

SEQUENCE **Object Guidelines**   DB2 does not wait for an application that has incremented a sequence to commit before allowing the sequence to be incremented again by another application. Applications can use one sequence for many tables, or create multiple sequences for use of each table requiring generated key values. In either case, the applications control the relationship between the sequences and the tables.

The name of the SEQUENCE object indicates that we are going to use it to generate activity numbers (ACTNO), but its usage is not limited to that. Of course, failure to control the use of a SEQUENCE object can result in gaps in the sequential values. For example, if we use the ACTNO_SEQ object to generate a number for a different column, the next time we use it for ACTNO there will be a gap where we generated that number.

Other scenarios can cause gaps in a SEQUENCE, too. For example, issuing a ROLLBACK after acquiring a sequence number will not roll back the value of the sequence generator—so that value is lost. A DB2 failure can also cause gaps because cached sequence values will be lost.

> **NOTE**
>
> When sequences were introduced in non-mainframe DB2, syntax was supported that did not conform to the SQL standard. This non-standard syntax is supported on the mainframe as well:
>
> - NEXTVAL can be used in place of NEXT VALUE
> - PREVVAL can be used in place of PREVIOUS VALUE

Choosing Between IDENTITY **and** SEQUENCE   Although both IDENTITY columns and SEQUENCE objects are useful for generating incremental numeric values, you will need to choose between the two. Consider the following criteria when choosing one over the other. IDENTITY columns are useful when

- Only one column in a table requires automatically generated values.
- Each row requires a separate value.
- An automatic generator is desired for a primary key of a table.
- The process of generating a new value is tied closely to inserting into a table, regardless of how the insert happens.

SEQUENCE objects are useful when

- Values generated from one sequence are to be stored in more than one table.
- More than one column per table requires automatically generated values (multiple values may be generated for each row using the same sequence or more than one sequence).
- The process of generating a new value is independent of any reference to a table.

Unlike SEQUENCE objects, which are more flexible, IDENTITY columns must adhere to several rigid requirements. For example, an IDENTITY column is always defined on a single table, and each table can have at most one IDENTITY column. Furthermore, when you create an IDENTITY column, the data type for that column must be numeric—not so for sequences. If you used a SEQUENCE object to generate a value, you could put that generated value into a CHAR column, for example. Finally, when defining an IDENTITY column you cannot specify the DEFAULT clause, and the column is implicitly defined as NOT NULL. Remember, DB2 automatically generates the IDENTITY column's value, so default values and nulls are not useful concepts.

Consult Table 5.7 for a summary comparison of SEQUENCE objects and IDENTITY column characteristics.

TABLE 5.7   IDENTITY Columns Versus SEQUENCE Objects

IDENTITY **Columns**	SEQUENCE **Objects**
Internal objects generated and maintained by DB2	Standalone database objects created by a DBA
Associated with a single table	Not associated with a specific table; useable across tables

TABLE 5.7   Continued

IDENTITY **Columns**	SEQUENCE **Objects**
Use IDENTITY_VAL_LOCAL() to get last value assigned	Use PREVIOUS VALUE FOR *seq-expr* to get last value assigned
N/A	Use NEXT VALUE FOR *seq-expr* to get next value to be assigned
Add/change using ALTER TABLE ...ALTER COLUMN (*DB2 V8 only*)	Administer using ALTER SEQUENCE, DROP, COMMENT, GRANT, and REVOKE
Version 6 refresh; Version 7	Version 8

Row and Column Guidelines

The following guidelines can be used to assist you as you design the row and column specifications of your DB2 tables.

Avoid Wasted Space   If you do not use very large and very small row sizes, you can reduce the amount of space wasted by unuseable bytes on the pages of a table space. Keep these rules in mind:

- A maximum of 255 rows can be stored on one table space page.

- A row length larger than 4,056 will not fit on a 4KB page. You will need to choose one of the other allowable page sizes. Page sizes supported by DB2 include 4KB, 8KB, 16KB, and 32KB.

- A row length less than 15 wastes space because no more than 255 rows can be stored on a DB2 page, regardless of the size of the row. For pre-V3 subsystems, a row length less than 31 bytes wastes space because the limit at that time was 127 rows per page.

- A row length of 2,029 results in only one row per (4K) page because the second row will be too large to exist on the same page.

Determine row size carefully to avoid wasting space. If you can combine small tables or split large tables to avoid wasting a large amount of space, do so. It usually is impossible to avoid wasting some space, however.

Define All Appropriate Columns   Be sure to apply normalization to your database design to arrive at the appropriate columns for each DB2 table. An introduction to normalization is forthcoming in a later section of this chapter.

Keep in mind, however, that the maximum number of columns that can be defined for a DB2 table is 750. If the table participates as a dependent to another table (referential integrity), then the maximum number of columns is reduced to 749.

For a table with more than 749 or 750 columns, you might need to break it into two tables, each with the same primary key, but with a different subset of the total number of columns.

Choose Meaningful Column Names   In many data processing shops, common names for data elements have been used for years. Sometimes these names seem arcane because they comply with physical constraints that have long since been overcome.

V8 With DB2 V8 a column name can comprise up to 128 bytes. For V7 and prior releases the maximum size of a column name is 18 bytes. You can enhance the useability of your applications if you use as many characters as necessary to achieve easy-to-understand column names. For example, use CUSTOMER_NAME instead of CNA0 for a customer name column. Do not use column names simply because people are accustomed to them.

This might be a tough sell in your organization, but it's well worth the effort. If you must support the older, non-descriptive names, consider creating tables with the fully descriptive names and then creating views of these tables with the old names. Eventually, people will convert to use the tables instead of the views.

Standardize Abbreviations   Every shop uses abbreviated data names. This isn't a bad practice—unless the specification of abbreviations is random, uncontrolled, or unplanned. Document and enforce strict abbreviation standards for data names in conjunction with your data-naming standards. For example, the CUSTOMER_NAME column mentioned in the previous guideline can be abbreviated in many ways (CST_NME, CUST_NM, CUST_NAME, and so on). Choose one standard abbreviation and stick to it.

Many shops use a list of tokens to create data abbreviation standards. This is fine as long as each token represents only one entity and each entity has only one abbreviation. For example:

Entity	Standard Abbreviation
CUSTOMER	CUST
NAME	NME

Sequence Columns to Achieve Optimal Performance   The sequencing of columns in a table is not important from a functionality perspective because the relational model states that columns must be non-positional. Columns and rows do not need to be sequenced for the retrieval commands to work on tables.

When you create a table, however, you must supply the columns in a particular order, and that becomes the order in which they physically are stored. The columns then can be retrieved in any order using the appropriate SQL SELECT statement.

When creating your tables, you will get better performance if you sequence the columns with an understanding of how DB2 logs. When data is modified in your database, DB2 will log every change made (in most circumstances). At a high level, this is how DB2 logs:

- For fixed-length rows, DB2 logs from the first byte changed to the last byte changed.

- For variable-length rows in which the size of the row changes due to the modification, DB2 logs from the first byte changed to the end of the row.

- For variable-length rows in which the size of the row does not change, DB2 logs from the first byte changed to the last byte changed.

"So what?" you may be asking. Logging can cause a significant performance bottleneck. You can optimize performance by sequencing your columns such that you minimize the amount of data logged. The less data DB2 needs to log, the better the performance of your data modification operations will be. So, follow these rules for column sequencing:

- Place the primary key columns first to ease identification.

- Place infrequently updated non-variable columns next.

- Place infrequently updated variable columns after the infrequently updated non-variable columns.

- Consider placing columns that are frequently modified at the same time next to one another in sequence in the table. This can help to reduce the amount of data that is logged. Do so even if it does not "appear" to be an elegant design; for example, if the MIDDLE_INITIAL column is often updated at the same time as the PHONE_NUMBER column, place the two columns contiguously next to each other. Even though it might "look nicer" to put the LAST_NAME column after MIDDLE_INITIAL, performance can be improved in this scenario by putting PHONE_NUMBER after MIDDLE_INITIAL.

- Only then, and given the preceding constraints, try to sequence the columns in an order that makes sense to the users of the table.

> **NOTE**
>
> A varying length row is any row that contains a VARCHAR or VARGRAPHIC column or any row that is compressed. Using ALTER TABLE to add a column to an existing table also makes the rows varying length (until the table space for the table is reorganized).

Avoid Special Sequencing for Nullable Columns   Treat nullable columns the same as you would any other column. Some DBAs advise you to place nullable columns of the same data type after non-nullable columns. This is supposed to assist in administering the null columns, but in my opinion it does not. Sequencing nullable columns in this manner provides no clear benefit and should be avoided.

See the "DB2 Table Parameters" section in this chapter for additional advice on nullable columns and Chapter 2, "Data Manipulation Guidelines," for advice on accessing nullable columns.

Use Nulls with Care   A null is DB2's attempt to record missing or unknown information. When you assign a null to a column instance, it means that a value currently does not exist for the column. It's important to understand that a column assigned to null logically means one of two things: The column does not apply to this row, or the column applies to this row, but the information is not known at present.

For example, suppose that a table contains information on the hair color of employees. The HAIR_COLOR column is defined in the table as being capable of accepting nulls. Three new employees are added today: a man with black hair, a woman with unknown hair color, and a bald man. The woman with the unknown hair color and the bald man both could be assigned null HAIR_COLOR, but for different reasons. The hair column color for the woman would be null because she has hair but the color presently is unknown. The hair color column for the bald man would be null also, but this is because he has no hair and so hair color does not apply.

DB2 does not differentiate between nulls that signify unknown data and those that signify inapplicable data. This distinction must be made by the program logic of each application.

DB2 represents null in a special hidden column known as an *indicator variable*. An indicator variable is defined to DB2 for each column that can accept nulls. The indicator variable is transparent to an end user, but must be provided for when programming in a host language (such as COBOL or PL/I). Every column defined to a DB2 table must be designated as either allowing or disallowing nulls.

The default definition for columns in a DB2 table is to allow nulls. Nulls can be prohibited for a column by specifying the NOT NULL or NOT NULL WITH DEFAULT option in the CREATE TABLE statement.

Avoid nulls in columns that must participate in arithmetic logic (for example, DECIMAL money values). The AVG, COUNT DISTINCT, SUM, MAX, and MIN functions omit column occurrences set to null. The COUNT(*) function, however, does not omit columns set to null because it operates on rows. Thus, AVG is not equal to SUM/COUNT(*) when the average is being computed for a column that can contain nulls. If the COMM column is nullable, the result of the following queries are not the same

```
SELECT   AVG(COMM)                      SELECT   SUM(COMM)/COUNT(*)
FROM     DSN8810.EMP;                   FROM     DSN8810.EMP;
```

For this reason, avoid nulls in columns involved in math functions.

When DATE, TIME, and TIMESTAMP columns can be unknown, assign them as nullable. DB2 checks to ensure that only valid dates, times, and timestamps are placed in columns defined as such. If the column can be unknown, it must be defined to be nullable because the default for these columns is the current date, current time, and current timestamp (unless explicitly defined otherwise using the DEFAULT clause). Null, therefore, is the only available option for the recording of missing dates, times, and timestamps.

For every other column, determine whether nullability can be of benefit before allowing nulls. Consider these rules:

- When a nullable column participates in an ORDER BY or GROUP BY clause, the returned nulls are grouped at the high end of the sort order.

- Nulls are considered to be equal when duplicates are eliminated by SELECT DISTINCT or COUNT (DISTINCT *column*).

- A unique index considers nulls to be equivalent and disallows duplicate entries because of the existence of nulls, unless the WHERE NOT NULL clause is specified in the index.

- For comparison in a SELECT statement, two null columns are not considered equal. When a nullable column participates in a predicate in the WHERE or HAVING clause, the nulls encountered cause the comparison to evaluate to UNKNOWN.

- When a nullable column participates in a calculation, the result is null.

- Columns that participate in a primary key cannot be null.

- To test for the existence of nulls, use the special predicate IS NULL in the WHERE clause of the SELECT statement.

- You cannot simply state WHERE *column* = NULL. You must state WHERE *column* IS NULL.

- It is invalid to test if a column is < NULL, <= NULL, > NULL, or >= NULL. These are all meaningless because null is the absence of a value.

- You can assign a column to null using the = predicate in the SET clause of the UPDATE statement.

Examine these rules closely. ORDER BY, GROUP BY, DISTINCT, and unique indexes consider nulls to be equal and handle them accordingly. The SELECT statement, however, deems that the comparison of null columns is not equivalence, but unknown. This inconsistent handling of nulls is an anomaly that you must remember when using nulls. The following are several sample SQL queries and the effect nulls have on them.

```
SELECT   JOB, SUM(SALARY)
FROM     DSN8810.EMP
GROUP BY JOB;
```

This query returns the average salary for each type of job. All instances in which JOB is null will group at the bottom of the output.

```
SELECT  EMPNO, PROJNO, ACTNO, EMPTIME,
        EMSTDATE, EMENDATE
FROM    DSN8810.EMPPROJACT
WHERE   EMSTDATE = EMENDATE;
```

This query retrieves all occurrences in which the project start date is equal to the project end date. This information is clearly erroneous, as anyone who has ever worked on a software development project can attest. The query does not return any rows in which either date or both dates are null for two reasons:

- Two null columns are never equal for purposes of comparison.

- When either column of a comparison operator is null, the result is unknown.

```
UPDATE DSN8810.DEPT
   SET MGRNO = NULL
 WHERE MGRNO = '000010';
```

This query sets the MGRNO column to null wherever MGRNO is currently equal to '000010' in the DEPT table.

> **NOTE**
>
> Nulls sometimes are inappropriately referred to as null values. Using the term *value* to describe a null column is incorrect because the term *null* implies the lack of a value. The relational model has abandoned the idea of nulls in favor of a similar concept called *marks*. The two types of marks are an *A-mark* and an *I-mark*. An A-mark refers to information that is applicable but presently unknown, whereas an I-mark refers to inapplicable information (information that does not apply). If DB2 would implement marks rather than nulls, the problem of differentiating between inapplicable and unknown data would disappear.
>
> No commercial DBMS products support A-marks and I-marks.

Define Columns Across Tables in the Same Way   When a column that defines the same attribute as another column is given a different column name, data administrators refer it to as a *column synonym*. In general, column synonyms should be avoided except in the situations detailed in this guideline.

Every attribute should be defined in one way, that is, with one distinct name and one distinct data type and length. The name should be different only if the same attribute needs to be represented as a column in one table more than once, or if the practical meaning of the attribute differs as a column from table to table. For example, suppose that a database contains a table that holds the colors of items. This column is called Color. The same database has a table with a Preferred Color column for customers. This is the same logical attribute, but its meaning changes based on the context. It is not wise to simply call the column Color in the Customer table, because it would imply that the customer is that color!

An attribute must be defined twice in self-referencing tables and in tables requiring multiple foreign key references to a single table. In these situations, create a standard prefixing or suffixing mechanism for the multiple columns. After you define the mechanism, stick to it. For example, the DSN8810.DEPT table in Appendix A, "DB2 Sample Tables," is a self-referencing table that does not follow these recommendations. The ADMRDEPT column represents the same attribute as the DEPTNO column, but the name is not consistent. A better name for the column would have been ADMR_DEPTNO. This adds the ADMR prefix to the attribute name, DEPTNO.

The practical meaning of columns that represent the same attribute can differ from table to table as well. In the sample tables, for example, the MGRNO column in the DSN8810.DEPT table represents the same attribute as the EMPNO column in the DSN8810.EMP table. The two columns can be named differently in this situation because the employee number in the DEPT table represents a manager, whereas the employee number in the EMP table represents any employee. (Perhaps the MGRNO column should have been named MGR_EMPNO.)

The sample tables provide another example of when this guideline should have been followed, but wasn't. Consider the same two tables: DSN8810.DEPT and DSN8810.EMP. Both contain the department number attribute. In the DEPT table, the column representing this attribute is DEPTNO, but in the EMP table, the column is WORKDEPT. This is confusing and should be avoided. In this instance, both should have been named DEPTNO.

5

Never use homonyms. A *homonym*, in DB2-column terminology, is a column that is spelled and pronounced the same as another column, but represents a different attribute.

Avoid Duplicate Rows   To conform to the relational model, every DB2 table should prohibit duplicate rows. Duplicate rows cause ambiguity and add no value.

If duplicates exist for an entity, either the entity has not been rigorously defined and normalized or a simple counter column can be added to the table. The counter column would contain a number indicating the number of duplicates for the given row.

Define a Primary Key   To assist in the unique identification of rows, define a primary (or unique) key for every DB2 table. The preferred way to define a primary key is with the PRIMARY KEY clause of the CREATE TABLE statement.

Consider Using a Surrogate Key   When the primary key for a table is very large it can be unwieldy to implement. For example, an eight-column key of 250 bytes could pose problems if there are numerous foreign keys that refer to it. If the primary key is defined using eight columns and 250 bytes, then every foreign key also will consume 250 bytes and use eight columns.

If the length of the primary key is impractical to implement, consider defining a surrogate key. You might be able to use a DB2 TIMESTAMP or a SEQUENCE object to generate unique surrogate key values.

Use Appropriate DB2 Data Types   Use the appropriate DB2 data type when defining table columns. Recall the list of valid DB2 data types presented earlier in this section. Some people may advise you to avoid certain DB2 data types—this is unwise. Follow these rules:

- Use the DB2 DATE data type to represent all dates. Do not use a character or numeric representation of the date.

- Use the DB2 TIME data type to represent all times. Do not use a character or numeric representation of the time.

- Favor the use of the DB2 TIMESTAMP data type when the date and time are always needed together, but rarely needed alone. Do not use a character or numeric representation of the timestamp. For additional insight, see the tradeoffs listed in the upcoming "Analyze DATE and TIME Columns Versus TIMESTAMP Columns" section.

- Using INTEGER and SMALLINT data types is interchangeable with using the DECIMAL data type without scale. Specifying DECIMAL without scale sometimes is preferable to INTEGER and SMALLINT because it provides more control over the domain of the column. However, DECIMAL without scale might use additional DASD. For additional insight, see the tradeoffs listed in the upcoming "Consider All Options When Defining Columns As INTEGER" section.

- When the data item is always numeric (and numeric only), use a numeric data type. Even if leading zeroes must be stored or reported, using the character data type is rarely acceptable. You can use program logic and reporting software to display any numeric data with leading blanks. Storing the data as a numeric data type has the benefit of providing automatic DB2 data integrity checking (non-numeric data can never be stored in a column defined with a numeric data type).

- Remember, DB2 uses the cardinality of a column to determine its filter factors used during access path selection. The specification of column data types can influence this access path selection.

There are more possible character (alphanumeric) values than there are numeric values for columns of equal length. For example, consider the following two columns:

```
COLUMN1    SMALLINT   NOT NULL
COLUMN2    CHAR(5)    NOT NULL
```

COLUMN1 can contain values only in the range –32,768 to 32,767, for a total of 65,536 possible values. COLUMN2, however, can contain all the permutations and combinations of legal alphabetic characters, special characters, and numerals. So you can see how defining numeric data as a numeric data type usually results in a more accurate access path selection by the DB2 optimizer; the specified domain is more accurate for filter factor calculations.

Analyze DATE and TIME Columns Versus TIMESTAMP Columns   When defining tables that require a date and time stamp, two solutions are available:

- Coding two columns, one as a DATE data type and the other as a TIME data type
- Coding one column specifying the TIMESTAMP data type

Each option has its benefits and drawbacks. Before choosing an approach, consider the following issues:

- With DATE and TIME you must use two columns. TIMESTAMP uses one column, thereby simplifying data access and modification.

- The combination of DATE and TIME columns requires 7 bytes of storage, while a TIMESTAMP column always requires 10 bytes of storage. Using the combination of DATE and TIME columns can save space.

- TIMESTAMP provides greater time accuracy, down to the microsecond level. TIME provides accuracy only to the second level. If precision is important, use TIMESTAMP; otherwise consider the combination of DATE and TIME.

- Date and time arithmetic can be easier to implement using TIMESTAMP data instead of a combination of DATE and TIME. Subtracting one TIMESTAMP from another results in a TIMESTAMP duration. To calculate a duration using DATE and TIME columns, two subtraction operations must occur: one for the DATE column and one for the TIME column.

- DB2 provides for the formatting of DATE and TIME columns via local DATE and TIME exits, the CHAR function, and the DATE and TIME precompiler options. These facilities are not available for TIMESTAMP columns. If the date and time information is to be extracted and displayed on a report or by an online application, the availability of these DB2-provided facilities for DATE and TIME columns should be considered when making your decision.

Consider the Display Format for DATE and TIME Data   DB2 provides four options for displaying DATE and TIME data, as shown in Table 5.8. Each format conforms to a standard means of displaying date and time data: EUR is European Standard, ISO is the International Standards Organization format, JIS is Japanese Industrial Standard, and USA is IBM United States of America Standard.

TABLE 5.8   DB2 Date and Time Formats

Format	Date	Time
EUR	DD.MM.YYYY	HH.MM.SS
ISO	YYYY-MM-DD	HH.MM.SS
JIS	YYYY-MM-DD	HH:MM:SS
USA	MM/DD/YYYY	HH:MM AM or PM

DB2 also allows for the creation of an installation-defined date format. One of these formats is chosen as the default standard for your DB2 subsystem at installation time. The default is ISO. Any format can be displayed using the CHAR() function (previously described in Chapter 3, "Using DB2 Functions").

CAUTION

Avoid choosing the USA format as the default. The USA format causes TIME data to be displayed without the seconds component, instead appending an AM or PM. EUR, ISO, and JIS all display TIME in military format, specifying 1 through 24 for the hour. The USA format does not, instead specifying 1 through 12 for the hour, and using AM and PM to designate morning and evening times.

If the default format is USA, TIME columns will be displayed without seconds and with the AM or PM extension. When data is unloaded using DSNTIAUL, the seconds information is lost. This can result in data integrity problems if the unloaded data is subsequently loaded to another table or used as input for other processes.

Consider Optimization When Choosing Data Type   The impact on optimization is another consideration when deciding whether to use a character or a numeric data type for a numeric column.

Consider, for example, a column that must store four byte integers. This can be supported using a CHAR(4) data type or a SMALLINT data type. Often times, the desire to use CHAR(4) is driven by the need to display leading zeroes on reports.

Data integrity will not be an issue assuming that all data is edit checked prior to insertion to the column (a big assumption). But even if edit checks are coded, DB2 is not aware of these and assumes that all combinations of characters are permitted. For access path determination on character columns, DB2 uses base 37 math. This assumes that usually one of the 26 alphabetic letters or the 10 numeric digits or a space will be used. This adds up to

37 possible characters. For a four-byte character column there are 37^4 or 1,874,161 possible values.

A SMALLINT column can range from –32,768 to 32,767 producing 65,536 possible small integer values. The drawback here is that negative or 5 digit product codes could be entered. However, if we adhere to our proper edit check assumption, the data integrity problems will be avoided here, as well.

DB2 will use the HIGH2KEY and LOW2KEY values to calculate filter factors. For character columns, the range between HIGH2KEY and LOW2KEY is larger than numeric columns because there are more total values. The filter factor will be larger for the numeric data type than for the character data type, which might influence DB2 to choose a different access path. For this reason, favor the SMALLINT over the CHAR(4) definition.

Choose a Data Type Closest to the Desired Domain   It is always best to choose the data type for each column to be the one that is closest to its domain. By doing so, DB2 will perform data integrity checking that otherwise would need to be coded into application programs or CHECK constraints. For example, if you are storing numeric data in the column, do not choose a character data type. In general, adhere to the following rules:

- If the data is numeric, favor SMALLINT, INTEGER, or DECIMAL data types. FLOAT is also an option.

- If the data is character, use CHAR or VARCHAR data types.

- If the data is date and time, use DATE, TIME, and TIMESTAMP data types.

- If the data is multimedia, use GRAPHIC, VARGRAPHIC, BLOB, CLOB, or DBCLOB data types.

Specify Appropriate Defaults   When a row is inserted or loaded into a table and no value is specified for a column but the column has a default specified, the column will be set to the value that has been identified in the column default specification. Two types of defaults are available: system-defined and user-defined.

Each column can have a default value specifically tailored to it. These are known as user-defined defaults. DB2 also provides specific system-defined defaults for each data type, which are used if an explicit default value is not specified. The system-defined defaults are outlined in Table 5.9.

TABLE 5.9   System-Defined Column Default Values

Data Type	Default Value
Numeric	Zero
Fixed-length String	Blanks
Varying-length String	String of length zero
Row identifier	Actual ROWID for the row
Date	Current date
Time	Current time
Timestamp	Current timestamp

For existing rows, when a non-nullable column is added to a table, DATE, TIME, and TIMESTAMP data types default to the lowest possible value instead of the current value. DATE types will default to January 1, 0001; TIME types will default to 0:00:00; and timestamp types will default to a date of January 1, 0001 and a time of 0:00:00.00.

Four options are available for user-defined defaults: a constant value, USER, CURRENT SQLID, and NULL. When specifying a constant, the value must conform to the column on which it is defined. Specifying USER causes the column to default to the contents of the USER special register. When CURRENT SQLID is specified, the default value will be the SQL authid of the process performing the INSERT. NULL is self-explanatory.

In general, it is best to explicitly define the default value to be used for each column. If the system-defined default values are adequate for your application, it is fine to use them by not providing a value following the DEFAULT clause. Consider the following column definitions:

```
BONUS       DECIMAL(9,2)   DEFAULT 500.00,
COMM        DECIMAL(9,2)   NOT NULL WITH DEFAULT,
```

If a row is inserted without specifying BONUS and COMM, BONUS will default to 500.00 and COMM will default to zero.

Choose VARCHAR Columns Carefully   You can save DASD storage space by using variable columns instead of placing small amounts of data in a large fixed space. Each variable column carries a 2-byte overhead, however, for storing the length of the data. Additionally, variable columns tend to increase CPU usage and can cause the update process to become inefficient. When a variable column is updated with a larger value, the row becomes larger; if not enough space is available to store the row, it must be moved to another page. This makes the update and any subsequent retrieval slower.

Follow these rules when defining variable character columns:

- Avoid variable columns if a sufficient amount of DASD is available to store the data using fixed columns.

- Do not define a variable column if its maximum length is less than 30 bytes. Instead, simply define the column as a fixed length CHAR (or GRAPHIC) column.

- Do not define a variable column if its maximum length is within 10 bytes of the average length of the column.

- Do not define a variable column when the data does not vary from row to row.

- Place variable columns at the end of the row, but before columns that are frequently updated. Refer back to the "Sequence Columns to Achieve Optimal Performance" section for more details.

- Consider redefining variable columns by placing multiple rows of fixed-length columns in another table or by shortening the columns and placing the overflow in another table.

Compression Versus VARCHAR **Columns**   Using DB2 compression, you can achieve similar results as with VARCHAR columns. However, DB2 compression avoids the two bytes of overhead and requires no programmatic intervention for handling the two-byte column length information.

On the other hand, VARCHAR columns affect data for the column only. With compression, the entire row is affected. Therefore, there is a greater chance that an UPDATE of a compressed row will need to be relocated to another page if its size has increased.

Altering VARCHAR **Columns**   As of DB2 V6, you can ALTER the length of a VARCHAR column to a greater length. However, you cannot ALTER the length of a VARCHAR column to a smaller length.

Monitor the Effectiveness of Variable Columns   Using views and SQL, it is possible to query the DB2 Catalog to determine the effectiveness of using VARCHAR for a column instead of CHAR. Consider, for example, the PROJNAME column of the DSN8810.PROJ table. It is defined as VARCHAR(24).

To gauge whether VARCHAR is appropriate follow these steps:

1. Create a view that returns the length of the NAME column for every row, for example:

   ```
   CREATE VIEW PROJNAME_LENGTH
        (COL_LGTH)
   AS    SELECT LENGTH(PROJNAME)
        FROM    DSN8810.PROJ;
   ```

2. Issue the following query using SPUFI to produce a report detailing the LENGTH and number of occurrences for that length:

   ```
   SELECT   COL_LGTH, COUNT(*)
   FROM     PROJNAME_LENGTH
   GROUP BY COL_LGTH
   ORDER BY COL_LGTH;
   ```

This query will produce a report listing the lengths (in this case, from 1 to 24, excluding those lengths which do not occur) and the number of times that each length occurs in the table. These results can be analyzed to determine the range of lengths stored within the variable column.

If you are not concerned about this level of detail, the following query can be used instead to summarize the space characteristics of the variable column in question:

```
SELECT   24*COUNT(*),
         24,
         SUM(2+LENGTH(PROJNAME)),
         AVG(2+LENGTH(PROJNAME)),
         24*COUNT(*)-SUM(2+LENGTH(PROJNAME)),
         24-AVG(2+LENGTH(PROJNAME))
FROM     DSN8810.PROJ;
```

The constant 24 will need to be changed in the query to indicate the maximum length of the variable column as defined in the DDL. The individual columns returned by this report are defined in the following list:

Definition	Calculation
Space used as CHAR(24)	24*COUNT(*)
Average space used as CHAR(24)	24
Space used as VARCHAR(24)	SUM(2+LENGTH(PROJNAME))
Average space used as VARCHAR(24)	AVG(2+LENGTH(PROJNAME))
Total space saved	24*COUNT(*)-SUM(2+LENGTH(PROJNAME))
Average space saved	24-AVG(2+LENGTH(PROJNAME))

Consider Using Odd DECIMAL Precision   Think about making the precision of all DECIMAL columns odd. This can provide an extra digit for the column being defined without using additional storage. For example, consider a column that must have a precision of 6 with a scale of 2. This would be defined as DECIMAL(6,2). By defining the column as DECIMAL(7,2) instead, numbers up to 99999.99 can be stored instead of numbers up to 9999.99. This can save future expansion efforts.

However, if you must ensure that the data in the column conforms to the specified domain (that is, even precision), specify even precision.

Consider All Options When Defining Columns As INTEGER   Use SMALLINT instead of INTEGER when the –32,768 to 32,767 range of values is appropriate. This data type usually is a good choice for sequencing type columns. The range of allowable values for the INTEGER data type is –2,147,483,648 to 2,147,483,647. These ranges might seem arbitrary, but are designed to store the maximum amount of information in the minimum amount of space. A SMALLINT column occupies 2 bytes, and an INTEGER column occupies only 4 bytes.

The alternative to SMALLINT and INTEGER data types is DECIMAL with a 0 scale. DECIMAL(5,0) supports the same range as SMALLINT, and DECIMAL(10,0) supports the same range as INTEGER. The DECIMAL equivalent of SMALLINT occupies 3 bytes of storage but permits values as large as 99,999 instead of only 32,767. The DECIMAL equivalent of INTEGER occupies 6 bytes but permits values as large as 9,999,999,999 instead of 2,147,483,647.

When deciding whether to use DECIMAL without scale to represent integer columns, another factor is control over the domain of acceptable values. The domain of SMALLINT and INTEGER columns is indicated by the range of allowable values for their respective data types. If you must ensure conformance to a domain, DECIMAL without scale provides the better control.

Suppose that you code a column called DAYS_ABSENT that indicates the number of days absent for employees in the DSN8810.EMP table. Suppose too that an employee cannot miss more than five days per year without being disciplined and that no one misses ten or more days. In this case, a single digit integer column could support the requirements for DAYS_ABSENT. A DECIMAL(1,0) column would occupy 2 bytes of physical storage and provide for values ranging from –9 to 9. By contrast, a SMALLINT column would occupy two bytes of physical storage and provide for values ranging from –32768 to 32,767. The DECIMAL(1,0) column, however, more closely matches the domain for the DAYS_ABSENT columns.

One final consideration: A decimal point is required with DECIMAL data, even when the data has no scale. For example, the integer 5 is 5, when expressed as a decimal. This can be confusing to programmers and users who are accustomed to dealing with integer data without a decimal point.

Consider all these factors when deciding whether to implement SMALLINT, INTEGER, or DECIMAL data types for integer columns.

Use LOBs for Large Multimedia Objects   As of V6, DB2 provides support for large multimedia data types. Using BLOB, CLOB, and DBCLOB data types, DB2 can be used to store complex, unstructured data, such as images, audio, text, and video. Such data types can be used to store much larger multimedia data than can be stored in VARGRAPHIC or VARCHAR columns. Of course, these data types need to be treated differently by application programs and there are management considerations (the larger they become the more difficult it is to administer the data). For more details on the object/relational capabilities of DB2, consult Chapter 9, "Large Objects and Object/Relational Databases."

Normalization and Denormalization

One of the biggest challenges of DB2 database design and implementation can be handling normalization. This section will help you by defining normalization and denormalization and providing tips and guidelines on when and how to denormalize.

Normalization

Normalization is a database design approach that minimizes data redundancy and optimizes data structures by systematically and properly placing data elements into appropriate groupings. A normalized data model can be translated into a physical database that is organized correctly.

Another way of putting it is that normalization is the process of putting one fact in one appropriate place. E.F. Codd, the father of the relational model, also created normalization. Like the relational model, normalization is based on the mathematical principles of set theory.

It is important to remember that normalization is a logical process and does not necessarily dictate physical database design. A normalized data model will ensure that each entity is well-formed and that each attribute is assigned to the proper entity.

Of course, the best situation is when a normalized logical data model can be physically implemented without major modifications. But keep in mind that normalization optimizes updates at the expense of retrievals. When a fact is stored in only one place, retrieving many different but related facts usually requires going to many different places. This tends to slow the retrieval process. Updating is quicker, however, because the fact you're updating exists in only one place.

Your DB2 tables should be based on a normalized logical data model. With a normalized data model, one fact is stored in one place, related facts about a single entity are stored together, and every column of each entity refers non-transitively to only the unique identifier for that entity.

Although an in-depth discussion of normalization is beyond the scope of this book, brief definitions of the first three normal forms follow.

- In *first normal form*, all entities must have a unique identifier, or key, that can be composed of one or more attributes. In addition, all attributes must be atomic and non-repeating. (*Atomic* means that the attribute must not be composed of multiple attributes. For example, EMPNO should not be composed of SSN and FIRSTNAME because these are separate attributes.)

- In *second normal form*, all attributes that are not part of the key must depend on the entire key for that entity.

- In *third normal form*, all attributes that are not part of the key must not depend on any other non-key attributes.

So, normalization can be summed up as "every attribute must depend upon the key, the whole key, and nothing but the key, so help me Codd."

Denormalization

Speeding the retrieval of data from DB2 tables is a frequent requirement for DBAs and performance analysts. One way to accomplish this is to denormalize DB2 tables for physical implementation. The opposite of normalization, *denormalization* is the process of putting one fact in many places. This speeds data retrieval at the expense of data modification. This is not necessarily a bad decision, but should be undertaken only when a completely normalized design will not perform optimally.

All that is really required to physically implement a DB2 database is first normal form—that is, the data must be in rows and columns. But that is the bare minimum and anything less than fully normalized can cause data integrity problems and needlessly complex INSERT, UPDATE, and DELETE operations.

Denormalization should be done based on the processing needs of applications accessing the data. Any denormalization decision must be based on how much the resulting design will optimize the most important queries. On the other hand, you must consider how difficult it will become to modify the data once it is implemented as a denormalized design. Consider these issues before denormalizing:

- Can the system achieve acceptable performance without denormalization?

- Will denormalization render the database design unuseable for ad hoc queries? (Is specialized expertise required to code queries against the denormalized design?)

- Will the performance of the system still be unacceptable after denormalization?

- Will the system be less reliable due to denormalization?

If the answer to any of these questions is "yes," you should not denormalize your tables because the benefit will not exceed the cost. If, after considering these issues, you decide to denormalize, there are rules you should follow.

- If enough DASD is available, create the fully normalized tables and populate denormalized versions using the normalized tables. Access the denormalized tables in a read-only fashion. Create a controlled and scheduled population function to keep denormalized and normalized tables synchronized.

- If sufficient DASD does not exist, maintain denormalized tables programmatically. Be sure to update each denormalized table representing the same entity at the same time; alternatively, provide a rigorous schedule whereby table updates are synchronized. If you cannot avoid inconsistent data, inform all users of the implications.

- When updating any column that is replicated in many tables, update all copies simultaneously, or as close to simultaneously as possible given the physical constraints of your environment.

- If denormalized tables are ever out of sync with the normalized tables, be sure to inform users that batch reports and online queries may not show up-to-date information.

- Design the application so that it can be easily converted from denormalized tables to normalized tables.

There is only one reason to denormalize a relational design: performance. Several indicators help identify systems and tables that are candidates for denormalization. These indicators follow:

- Many critical queries and reports rely on data from more than one table. Often these requests must be processed in an online environment.

- Repeating groups must be processed in a group instead of individually.

- Many calculations must be applied to one or many columns before queries can be answered successfully.

- Tables must be accessed in different ways by different users during the same timeframe.

- Many large primary keys are clumsy to query and use a large amount of DASD when carried as foreign key columns in related tables.

- Certain columns are queried a large percentage of the time. (Consider 60% or greater as a cautionary number flagging denormalization as an option.)

Many types of denormalized tables work around the problems caused by these indicators. Table 5.10 summarizes the types of denormalization, with a short description of when each type is useful. The sections that follow describe these denormalization types in greater detail.

TABLE 5.10   Types of Denormalization

Denormalization	Use
Pre-joined Tables	When the cost of joining is prohibitive
Report Tables	When specialized critical reports are needed
Mirror Tables	When tables are required concurrently by two types of environments
Split Tables	When distinct groups use different parts of a table
Combined Tables	When one-to-one relationships exist
Redundant Data	To reduce the number of table joins required
Repeating Groups	To reduce I/O and (possibly) DASD
Derivable Data	To eliminate calculations and algorithms
Speed Tables	To support hierarchies

Denormalization: Pre-joined Tables

If two or more tables need to be joined on a regular basis by an application, but the cost of the join is too prohibitive to support, consider creating tables of pre-joined data. The pre-joined tables should

- Contain no redundant columns.

- Contain only the columns necessary for the application to meet its processing needs.

- Be created periodically using SQL to join the normalized tables.

The cost of the join is incurred only once, when the pre-joined tables are created. A pre-joined table can be queried efficiently because every new query does not incur the overhead of the table join process.

Denormalization: Report Tables

Reports requiring special formatting or manipulation often are impossible to develop using SQL or QMF alone. If critical or highly visible reports of this nature must be viewed in an online environment, consider creating a table that represents the report. The table then can be queried using SQL or QMF.

Create the report using the appropriate mechanism in a batch environment. The report data then can be loaded into the report table in the appropriate sequence. The report table should

- Contain one column for every column of the report.

- Have a clustering index on the columns that provide the reporting sequence.

- Not subvert relational tenets (for example, atomic data elements).

Report tables are ideal for storing the results of outer joins or other complex SQL statements. If an outer join is coded and then loaded into a table, you can retrieve the results of the outer join using a simple SELECT statement instead of using the UNION technique discussed in Chapter 1.

Denormalization: Mirror Tables

If an application system is very active, you might need to split processing into two (or more) distinct components. This requires the creation of duplicate, or *mirror*, tables.

Consider an application system that has heavy online traffic during the morning and early afternoon. The traffic consists of querying and updating data. Decision-support processing also is performed on the same application tables during the afternoon. The production work in the afternoon disrupts the decision-support processing, resulting in frequent time-outs and deadlocks.

These disruptions could be corrected by creating mirror tables: a foreground set of tables for the production traffic and a background set of tables for the decision-support reporting. To keep the application data-synchronized, you must establish a mechanism to migrate the foreground data periodically to the background tables. (One such mechanism is a batch job executing the UNLOAD utility on the data followed by running the LOAD utility to the target.) Migrate the information as often as necessary to ensure efficient and accurate decision-support processing.

Because the access needs of decision support and the production environment often are considerably different, different data definition decisions such as indexing and clustering may be chosen.

Denormalization: Split Tables

If separate pieces of one normalized table are accessed by different and distinct groups of users or applications, consider splitting the table into one denormalized table for each distinct processing group. Retain the original table if other applications access the entire table; in this scenario, the split tables should be handled as a special case of mirror table.

Tables can be split in two ways: vertically or horizontally. Refer to Figure 5.5. A vertical split cuts a table column-wise, such that one group of columns is placed into a new table and the remaining columns are placed in another new table. Both of the split tables should retain the primary key columns. A horizontally split table is a row-wise split. To split a table horizontally, rows are classified into groups by key ranges. The rows from one key range are placed in one table, those from another key range are placed in a different table, and so on.

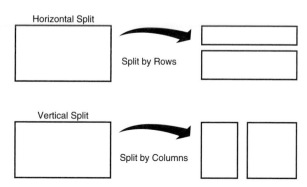

FIGURE 5.5   Two methods of splitting tables.

When splitting tables, designate one of the two tables as the parent table for referential integrity. If the original table still exists, it should be the parent table in all referential constraints. In this case, do not set up referential integrity for the split tables; they are derived from a referentially intact source.

When you split a table vertically, include one row per primary key in both tables to ease retrieval across tables. Do not eliminate rows from either of the two tables. Otherwise, updating and retrieving data from both tables is unnecessarily complicated.

When you split a table horizontally, try to split the rows between the new tables to avoid duplicating any one row in each new table. Simply stated, the operation of UNION ALL, when applied to the horizontally split tables, should not add more rows than those in the original, unsplit tables.

Denormalization: Combined Tables

If tables have a one-to-one relationship, consider combining them into a single table. Sometimes, one-to-many relationships can be combined into a single table, but the data update process is significantly complicated because of the increase in redundant data.

For example, consider combining the sample tables DSN8810.DEPT and DSN8810.EMP into a large table called DSN8810.EMP_WITH_DEPT. (Refer to Appendix A for a definition of the sample tables.) This new table would contain all the columns of both tables, except the DEPTNO column of DSN8810.DEPT. This column is excluded because it contains the same data as the ADMRDEPT column.

Each employee row therefore contains all the employee information, in addition to all the department information, for each employee. The department data is duplicated through-out the combined table because a department can employ many people. Tables of this sort should be considered pre-joined tables, not combined tables, and treated accordingly. Only tables with one-to-one relationships should be considered combined tables.

Denormalization: Redundant Data

Sometimes one or more columns from one table are accessed whenever data from another table is accessed. If these columns are accessed frequently with tables other than those in which they were initially defined, consider carrying them in the other tables as redundant data. By carrying the additional columns, you can eliminate joins and increase the speed of data retrieval. Because this technique violates a tenet of database design, it should be attempted only if the normal access cannot efficiently support your business.

Consider, once again, the DSN8810.DEPT and DSN8810.EMP tables. If most employee queries require the name of the employee's department, this column could be carried as redun-dant data in the DSN8810.EMP table. (Do not remove the column from the DSN8810.DEPT table, though.)

Columns you want to carry as redundant data should have the following attributes:

- Only a few columns are necessary to support the redundancy.

- The columns are stable, that is, updated infrequently.

- The columns are used by many users or a few important users.

Denormalization: Repeating Groups

When repeating groups are normalized, they are implemented as distinct rows instead of distinct columns. This usually results in higher disk storage requirements and less efficient retrieval, because there are more rows in the table and more rows must be read to satisfy queries that access the entire repeating group (or a subset of the repeating group).

Sometimes you can achieve significant performance gains when you denormalize the data by storing it in distinct columns. These gains, however, come at the expense of flexibility.

For example, consider an application that stores repeating group information in the following normalized table:

```
CREATE TABLE user.PERIODIC_BALANCES
   (CUSTOMER_NO        CHAR(11)        NOT NULL,
    BALANCE_PERIOD     SMALLINT        NOT NULL,
    BALANCE            DECIMAL(15,2),
    PRIMARY KEY (CUSTOMER_NO, BALANCE_PERIOD)
   )
```

Available storage and DB2 requirements are the only limits to the number of balances per customer that you can store in this table. If you decide to string out the repeating group, BALANCE, into columns instead of rows, you must limit the number of balances to be carried in each row. The following is an example of stringing out repeating groups into columns after denormalization:

```
CREATE TABLE user.PERIODIC_BALANCES
   (CUSTOMER_NO        CHAR(11)        NOT NULL,
    PERIOD1_BALANCE    DECIMAL(15,2),
    PERIOD2_BALANCE    DECIMAL(15,2),
    PERIOD3_BALANCE    DECIMAL(15,2),
    PERIOD4_BALANCE    DECIMAL(15,2),
    PERIOD5_BALANCE    DECIMAL(15,2),
    PERIOD6_BALANCE    DECIMAL(15,2),
    PRIMARY KEY (CUSTOMER_NO)
   )
IN SAMPLE.BALANCE;
```

In this example, only six balances can be stored for each customer. The number six is not important, but the limit on the number of values is important; it reduces the flexibility of data storage and should be avoided unless performance needs dictate otherwise.

Before you decide to implement repeating groups as columns instead of rows, be sure that the data:

- Rarely—preferably never—is aggregated, averaged, or compared in the row

- Occurs in a statistically well-behaved pattern

- Has a stable number of occurrences

- Usually is accessed collectively

- Has a predictable pattern of insertion and deletion

If any of the preceding criteria is not met, some SQL statements could be difficult to code—making the data less available due to inherently unsound data-modeling practices. This should be avoided, because you usually denormalize data to make it more readily available.

Denormalization: Derivable Data

If the cost of deriving data with complicated formulas is prohibitive, consider storing the derived data instead of calculating it. When the underlying values that compose the calculated value change, the stored derived data must be changed also; otherwise, inconsistent information could be reported.

Sometimes you cannot immediately update derived data elements when the columns on which they rely change. This can occur when the tables containing the derived elements are offline or are being operated on by a utility. In this situation, time the update of the derived data so that it occurs immediately after the table is available for update. Outdated derived data should never be made available for reporting and queries.

Denormalization: Hierarchies

A hierarchy is easy to support using a relational database such as DB2, but difficult to retrieve information from efficiently. For this reason, applications that rely on hierarchies often contain denormalized tables to speed data retrieval. Two examples of these types of systems are a Bill of Materials application and a Departmental Reporting system. A Bill of Materials application typically records information about parts assemblies, in which one part is composed of other parts. A Department Reporting system typically records the departmental structure of an organization, indicating which departments report to which other departments.

An effective way to denormalize a hierarchy is to create *speed tables*. Figure 5.6 depicts a department hierarchy for a given organization. The hierarchic tree is built so that the top node is the entire corporation. The other nodes represent departments at various levels in the corporation.

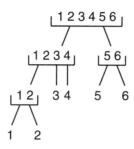

FIGURE 5.6   A department hierarchy.

Department 123456 is the entire corporation. Departments 1234 and 56 report directly to 123456. Departments 12, 3, and 4 report directly to 1234 and indirectly to department 123456, and so on. This can be represented in a DB2 table as follows:

DEPTNO	*PARENT_DEPTNO*	...other columns
	Department Table	
123456	------	
1234	123456	
56	123456	
12	1234	
3	1234	
4	1234	
1	12	
2	12	
5	56	
6	56	

This DB2 table is a classic relational implementation of a hierarchy. There are two department columns: one for the parent and one for the child. The table's data is an accurately normalized version of this hierarchy, containing everything represented in Figure 5.6. The complete hierarchy can be rebuilt with the proper data retrieval instructions.

Even though the implementation effectively records the entire hierarchy, a query to report all the departments under any other department is time consuming to code and inefficient to process. A sample query that returns all the departments reporting to the corporate node, 123456, is illustrated by this rather complex SQL statement:

```
SELECT  DEPTNO
FROM    DEPARTMENT
WHERE   PARENT_DEPTNO = '123456'
UNION
SELECT  DEPTNO
FROM    DEPARTMENT
```

```
WHERE    PARENT_DEPTNO IN
         (SELECT  DEPTNO
          FROM    DEPARTMENT
          WHERE   PARENT_DEPTNO = '123456')
UNION
SELECT  DEPTNO
FROM    DEPARTMENT
WHERE   PARENT_DEPTNO IN
        (SELECT  DEPTNO
         FROM    DEPARTMENT
         WHERE   PARENT_DEPTNO IN
                 (SELECT  DEPTNO
                  FROM    DEPARTMENT
                  WHERE   PARENT_DEPTNO = '123456'));
```

This query can be built only if you know in advance the total number of possible levels the hierarchy can achieve. If there are *n* levels in the hierarchy, you need *n-1* UNIONs. The previous SQL statement assumes that only three levels are between the top and bottom of the department hierarchy. For every possible level of the hierarchy, you must add a more complex SELECT statement to the query in the form of a UNION. This implementation works, but is difficult to use and inefficient.

A faster way to query a hierarchy is to use a speed table. A speed table contains a row for every combination of the parent department and all its dependent departments, regardless of the level. Data is replicated in a speed table to increase the speed of data retrieval. The speed table for the hierarchy presented in Figure 5.6 is:

PARENT DEPTNO	CHILD DEPTNO	LEVEL	DETAIL	...other columns
123456	1234	1	N	
123456	56	1	N	
123456	12	2	N	
123456	1	3	Y	
123456	2	3	Y	
123456	3	2	Y	
123456	4	2	Y	
123456	5	2	Y	
123456	6	2	Y	
1234	12	1	N	
1234	1	2	Y	
1234	2	2	Y	
1234	3	1	Y	
1234	4	1	Y	
3	3	1	Y	

PARENT DEPTNO	CHILD DEPTNO	LEVEL	DETAIL	...other columns
4	4	1	Y	
12	1	1	Y	
12	2	1	Y	
1	1	1	Y	
2	2	1	Y	
56	5	1	Y	
56	6	1	Y	
5	5	1	Y	
6	6	1	Y	

Contrast this to the previous table, which recorded only the immediate children for each parent. The PARENT_DEPTNO column is the top of the hierarchy. The CHILD_DEPTNO column represents all the dependent nodes of the parent. The LEVEL column records the level in the hierarchy. The DETAIL column contains Y if the row represents a node at the bottom of the hierarchy, or N if the row represents a node that is not at the bottom. A speed table commonly contains other information needed by the application. Typical information includes the level in the hierarchy for the given node and, if the order within a level is important, the sequence of the nodes at the given level.

After the speed table has been built, you can write speed queries. The following are several informative queries. They would be inefficient if executed against the classical relational hierarchy, but are efficient when run against a speed table.

To retrieve all dependent departments for department 123456,

```
SELECT   CHILD_DEPTNO
FROM     DEPARTMENT_SPEED
WHERE    PARENT_DEPTNO = '123456';
```

To retrieve only the bottom-most, detail departments that report to department 123456,

```
SELECT   CHILD_DEPTNO
FROM     DEPARTMENT_SPEED
WHERE    PARENT_DEPTNO = '123456'
AND      DETAIL = 'Y';
```

To return the complete department hierarchy for department 123456,

```
SELECT   PARENT_DEPTNO, CHILD_DEPTNO, LEVEL
FROM     DEPARTMENT_SPEED
WHERE    PARENT_DEPTNO = '123456'
ORDER BY LEVEL;
```

A speed table commonly is built using a program written in COBOL or another high-level language. SQL alone usually is too inefficient to handle the creation of a speed table.

V8

> **NOTE**
>
> With the advent of recursive SQL support in DB2 V8, the need to denormalize for hierarchies is greatly diminished. The nature of recursive SQL makes it ideal for traversing hierarchical data stored in normalized, DB2 tables. Refer back to Chapter 2 for more information on recursion.

Denormalization to Avoid Large Page Sizes

You can denormalize your tables to avoid using page sizes greater than 4KB. If a table space is so large as to have pages that require more than 4KB, DB2 will force the use of a larger page size (and buffer pool). DB2 supports 8KB, 16KB, and 32KB pages in addition to the standard 4KB page size.

A larger page size can increase overhead. For example, DB2 arranges a table space assigned to the BP32K buffer pool as 8 single 4KB pages per 32KB page. Every logical I/O to a 32KB table space requires 8 physical I/Os. You can use the vertical split technique to denormalize tables that would otherwise require pages greater than 4KB.

V8 With DB2 V8 you have the ability to specify the actual CI size of the VSAM file to synchronize it with the DB2 page size. Using this approach is generally preferable, and easier, than vertically splitting the table.

Denormalization Guidelines

Be sure to follow these tips and techniques when making your denormalization decision—and afterward to manage your databases effectively.

Look for Ways to Avoid Denormalization   Whenever possible, you should avoid denormalizing your DB2 databases. Look for DB2 features and functionality that can be used in place of a denormalized implementation.

V8 For example, DB2 V8 introduces recursive SQL. Therefore, as of DB2 V8, you should try to implement fully normalized hierarchies and query them using recursive queries instead of using a denormalization technique like speed tables. More information on recursion is provided in Chapter 2.

Periodically Test the Validity of Denormalization   The decision to denormalize *never* should be made lightly: Denormalization involves a lot of administrative dedication. This dedication takes the form of documenting denormalization decisions, ensuring valid data, scheduling migration, and keeping end users informed about the state of the tables. An additional category of administrative overhead is periodic analysis.

When an application has denormalized data, you should review the data and the environment periodically. Changes in hardware, software, and application requirements can alter the need for denormalization. To verify whether denormalization still is a valid decision, ask the following questions:

- Have the application-processing requirements changed such that the join criteria, the timing of reports, or the transaction throughput no longer require denormalized data?

- Did a new software release change performance considerations? For example, does the introduction of 8KB and 16KB page sizes in DB2 Version 6 alleviate the need for denormalization to avoid 32K page sizes? Or, did the introduction of a new join method or faster join processing undo the need for pre-joined tables?

- Did a new hardware release change performance considerations? For example, does a CPU upgrade reduce the amount of CPU consumption such that denormalization no longer is necessary?

In general, periodically test whether the extra cost related to processing with normalized tables justifies the benefit of denormalization. Monitor and reevaluate all denormalized applications by measuring the following criteria:

- I/O saved

- CPU saved

- Complexity of update programming

- Cost of returning to a normalized design

> **NOTE**
>
> To summarize, remember these basic rules:
>
> - All things being equal, always favor a normalized design over a denormalized design.
> - Normalization optimizes data modification at the expense of data access.
> - Denormalization optimizes data access at the expense of data modification.

Assuring Data Integrity in DB2

DB2 provides mechanisms to automatically enforce and maintain the integrity of data as it is added to, and modified within DB2 tables. The simplest form of data integrity enforcement available to DB2 is with data typing. By choosing the appropriate data types DB2 will force columns to contain only the proper form of data (for example, character, numeric, date, and so on). Of course, DB2 offers more sophisticated forms of ensuring data integrity, too. Features such as referential integrity, check constraints, triggers, validation routines, and edit procedures all can be used to ensure the integrity of DB2 data.

Automatically enforcing DB2 data integrity is usually a wise choice of action because it offloads such work from application programs. Additionally, DB2-enforced data integrity will be applied for both planned and ad hoc modifications.

Referential Integrity

When translating a logical model to a physical DB2 database the relationships are implemented as referential constraints. To define a referential constraint you must create a primary key in the parent table and a foreign key in the dependent table. The referential constraint ties the primary key to the foreign key. The table with the primary key is called the *parent* table and the table with the foreign key is called the *dependent* table (or *child* table). Foreign keys can refer to both primary keys and unique keys that are not explicitly defined as primary keys.

Referential integrity (RI), therefore, can be defined as a method of ensuring data integrity between tables related by primary and foreign keys. When RI is implemented between tables DB2 will guarantee that an acceptable value is always in each foreign key column based on the data values of the primary key columns.

RI defines the integrity and useability of a relationship by establishing rules that govern that relationship. The combination of the relationship and the rules attached to that relationship is referred to as a *referential constraint*. The rules that accompany the RI definition are just as important as the relationship to ensure correct and useful DB2 databases.

The RI rules defined for each referential constraint are specified to determine how DB2 will handle dependent rows when a primary key row is deleted or updated. For example, when a primary key is deleted that refers to existing foreign key values, the rule specifies whether DB2 should void the primary key deletion, delete the foreign key values too, or set the foreign key values to null.

The concept of RI can be summarized by the following "quick and dirty" definition: *RI is a guarantee that an acceptable value is always in each foreign key column.* Acceptable is defined in terms of an appropriate value as recorded in the corresponding primary key, or a null.

Two other important RI terms are parent and child tables. For any given referential constraint, the parent table is the table that contains the primary key and the child table is the table that contains the foreign key. Refer to Figure 5.7. The parent table in the employs relationship is the DEPT table. The child table is the EMP table. So the primary key (say DEPTNO) resides in the DEPT table and a corresponding foreign key of the same data type and length, but not necessarily the with same column name (say WORKDEPT), exists in the EMP table.

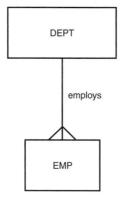

FIGURE 5.7   A relationship between two tables.

As a general rule of thumb it is a good physical design practice to implement referential integrity using database constraints instead of trying to program integrity into application programs. Using database RI will ensure that integrity is maintained whether data is changed in a planned manner through an application program or in an ad hoc manner through SQL statements or query tools. Of course, there are exceptions to every rule.

Defining DB2 Referential Constraints

Referential constraints are defined using the FOREIGN KEY clause. A referential constraint consists of three components: a constraint name, the columns comprising the foreign key and a references clause. The same constraint name cannot be specified more than once for the same table. If a constraint name is not explicitly coded, DB2 will automatically create a unique name for the constraint derived from the name of the first column in the foreign key.

For example, consider the relationship between the DSN8810.DEPT and DSN8810.EMP tables. The data model diagram in Figure A.1 of Appendix A graphically depicts this relationship:

```
CREATE TABLE DSN8810.EMP
  (EMPNO            CHAR(6)        NOT NULL,
   FIRSTNME         VARCHAR(12)    NOT NULL,
   MIDINIT          CHAR(1)        NOT NULL,
   LASTNAME         VARCHAR(15)    NOT NULL,
   WORKDEPT         CHAR(3),
   PHONENO          CHAR(4) CONSTRAINT NUMBER CHECK
                    (PHONENO >= '0000' AND
                     PHONENO <= '9999'),
   HIREDATE         DATE,
   JOB              CHAR(8),
   EDLEVEL          SMALLINT,
   SEX              CHAR(1),
   BIRTHDATE        DATE,
   SALARY           DECIMAL(9,2),
   BONUS            DECIMAL(9,2),
   COMM             DECIMAL(9,2),
   PRIMARY KEY (EMPNO)
   FOREIGN KEY RED (WORKDEPT)
     REFERENCES DSN8810.DEPT ON DELETE SET NULL
  )
EDITPROC DSN8EAE1
IN DSN8D81A.DSN8S81E;

CREATE TABLE DSN8810.DEPT
  (DEPTNO           CHAR(3)        NOT NULL,
   DEPTNAME         VARCHAR(36)    NOT NULL,
   MGRNO            CHAR(6),
   ADMRDEPT         CHAR(3)        NOT NULL,
   LOCATION         CHAR(16),
   PRIMARY KEY (DEPTNO)
  )
IN DSN8D81A.DSN8S81D;
ALTER TABLE DSN8810.DEPT
  FOREIGN KEY RDD (ADMRDEPT)
    REFERENCES DSN8810.DEPT ON DELETE CASCADE;
ALTER TABLE DSN8810.DEPT
  FOREIGN KEY RDE (MGRNO)
    REFERENCES DSN8810.EMP ON DELETE SET NULL;
```

5

The primary key of EMP is EMPNO; the primary key of DEPT is DEPTNO. Several foreign keys exist, but let's examine the foreign key that relates EMP to DEPT. The foreign key, named RDE, in the DEPT table relates the MGRNO column to a specific EMPNO in the EMP table. This referential constraint ensures that no MGRNO can exist in the DEPT table before the employee exists in the EMP table. The MGRNO must take on a value of EMPNO. Additionally, the foreign key value in DEPT cannot subsequently be updated to a value that is not a valid employee value in EMP, and the primary key of EMP cannot be deleted without the appropriate check for corresponding values in the DEPT foreign key column or columns.

To ensure that this integrity remains intact, DB2 has a series of rules for inserting, deleting, and updating:

- When inserting a row with a foreign key, DB2 checks the values of the foreign key columns against the values of the primary key columns in the parent table. If no matching primary key columns are found, the insert is disallowed.

- A new primary key row can be inserted as long as the primary key is unique for the table.

- When updating foreign key values, DB2 performs the same checks as when it is inserting a row with a foreign key.

- If a primary key value is updated, DB2 does not allow any existing foreign keys that refer back to the primary key that is changing. All foreign key rows first must be either deleted or be set to NULL before the value of the primary key can be changed.

- Deleting a row with a foreign key is always permitted.

- When deleting a row with a primary key, DB2 takes action as indicated in the DDL; it either restricts deletion, cascades deletes to foreign key rows, or sets all referenced foreign keys to null.

Each referential constraint must define the action that will be taken on foreign key rows when a primary key is deleted. There are four options that can be specified:

- RESTRICT—Disallows the deletion of the primary key row if any foreign keys relate to the row.

- CASCADE—Allows the deletion of the primary key row and also deletes the foreign key rows that relate to it.

- SET NULL—Allows the deletion of the primary key row and, instead of deleting all related foreign key rows, sets the foreign key columns to NULL.

- NO ACTION—The behavior of NO ACTION is similar to RESTRICT. The only difference between RESTRICT and NO ACTION is when the referential constraint is enforced. RESTRICT enforces the delete rule immediately; NO ACTION enforces the delete rule at the end of the statement.

The processing needs of the application dictate which delete option should be specified in the table create statements. All of these options are valid depending on the business rules that apply to the data.

If efficiency is your primary goal, the RESTRICT option usually uses fewer resources because data modification of dependent tables is not performed. If data modification is necessary, however, allowing DB2 to perform it is usually preferable to writing cascade or set null logic in a high-level language.

Referential Sets

A *referential set* is a group of tables that are connected together by referential constraints. It is a wise course of action to avoid very large referential sets. Try not to tie together all tables in a large system; otherwise, recovery, quiesce, and other utility processing will be difficult to develop and administer.

You should follow some general rules when deciding how to limit the scope of DB2-defined referential integrity:

- Consider removing code and reference tables from your referential structures. These tables are usually static and easy to control within your programs. Adding them to your referential sets can complicate administrative tasks.

- Reduce the size of very large referential sets by breaking them apart into smaller structures. Referential sets of more than a dozen (or so) tables can become unwieldy to manage. Consider breaking up referential sets into groups having a dozen or so related tables. Doing so makes it easier to keep track of the RI defined to DB2 and the rules that are in effect. However, it also opens the door to data integrity problems caused by updates outside the scope of the application programs that enforce the integrity. Weigh the performance impact against the possible loss of integrity before deciding to bypass DB2-enforced RI.

- Try to control the number of cycles in a referential set. A cycle is a referential path that connects a table to itself. In the cycle shown in Figure 5.8, Table A is connected to itself.

  Furthermore, a table cannot be delete-connected to itself in a cycle. A table is delete-connected to another table if it is a dependent of a table specified with a CASCADE delete rule.

- Whether RI is checked by DB2 or by an application program, overhead is incurred. Efficiency cannot be increased simply by moving RI from DB2 to the program. Be sure that the application program can achieve better performance than DB2 (by taking advantage of innate knowledge of the data that DB2 does not have) before eliminating DB2-enforced RI.

- If updates to tables are permitted in an uncontrolled environment (for example, QMF, SPUFI, or third-party table editors such as File-Aid for DB2), implement DB2-enforced RI if data integrity is important. Otherwise, you cannot ensure that data is correct from a referential integrity standpoint.

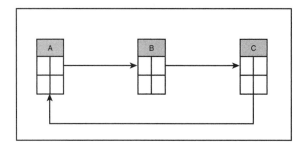

FIGURE 5.8   A cycle.

Referential Integrity Guidelines

The general rule for implementing referential integrity is to use DB2's inherent features instead of coding RI with application code. DB2 usually has a more efficient means of implementing RI than the application. Also, why should a programmer code what already is available in the DBMS? Exceptions to this rule are the subject of the subsequent guidelines in this section.

Consider Programmatic RI for Efficiency   DB2 does a referential integrity check for every row insertion. You can increase efficiency if your application does a single check of a row from the parent table and then makes multiple inserts to the child table. Of course, you should not allow any data modifications to be made outside the control of your programs if DB2 RI is not used.

Sometimes the flow of an application can dictate whether RI is more or less efficient than programmatic RI. If the application processing needs are such that the parent table is always (or usually) read before even one child is inserted, consider implementing programmatic RI instead of DB2 RI. DB2 RI would repeat the read process that the application must do anyway to satisfy its processing needs.

Of course, DB2 RI might still be preferable in both of these situations because it enforces data integrity for both planned and ad hoc updates, something that programmatic RI cannot do.

Consider Avoiding RI for Intact, Stable Data   When tables are built from an existing source system and are populated using existing data, and that source system is referentially intact, you might want to avoid using DB2 RI on those tables. This is especially so if data is propagated from the existing system and the new tables will not be modified in any other manner.

However, if the new tables will be modified, DB2 RI is the best way to ensure the on-going consistency and integrity of the data.

Avoid RI for Read-Only Systems   Do not use DB2 RI if tables are read-only. Tables containing static data that is loaded and then never (or even rarely) modified are not good candidates for RI. The data should be analyzed and scrubbed prior to loading so that it is referentially intact. Because of the stability of the data there is no need for on-going referential constraints to be applied to the data. For data that is updated, but rarely, using application programs to enforce integrity is usually preferable to DB2 RI.

Sometimes, to scrub the data when loading, you may want to use DB2 RI. Specifying ENFORCE CONSTRAINTS for the LOAD utility can save a lot of application coding to enforce RI.

If application code is used to load the tables, base your decision for implementing RI with DB2 DDL according to the other guidelines in this chapter.

Avoid RI for Read-Only Systems   Define a primary (or unique) key to prohibit duplicate table rows. This should be done to ensure entity integrity regardless of whether dependent tables are related to the table being defined. Entity integrity ensures that each row in a table represents a single, real-world entity.

Beware of Self-Referencing Constraints   A *self-referencing constraint* is one in which the parent table is also the dependent table. The sample table, DSN8810.PROJ, contains a self-referencing constraint specifying that the MAJPROJ column must be a valid PROJNO.

Self-referencing constraints must be defined using the DELETE CASCADE rule. Exercise caution when deleting rows from these types of tables because a single delete could cause all of the table data to be completely wiped out!

Beware of RI Implementation Restrictions   Take the following restrictions into consideration when implementing RI on your DB2 tables:

- A self-referencing constraint must specify DELETE CASCADE.

- A table cannot be delete-connected to itself.

- Tables that are delete-connected to another table through multiple referential paths must employ the same DELETE rule and it must be either CASCADE or RESTRICT.

Consider DELETE NO ACTION for Self-Referencing Constraints   When deleting multiple rows from a table with a self-referencing constraint, a DELETE rule of RESTRICT will prohibit the DELETE. If you use a DELETE rule of NO ACTION instead, DB2 can allow the DELETE to complete.

To specify ON DELETE NO ACTION in a referential constraint, the CURRENT RULES special register must be set to 'STD', not 'DB2'.

Check Constraints

Check constraints can be used to place specific data value restrictions on the contents of a column through the specification of an expression. The expression is explicitly defined in the table DDL and is formulated in much the same way that SQL WHERE clauses are formulated. Any attempt to modify the column data (for example, during INSERT or UPDATE processing) will cause the expression to be evaluated. If the modification conforms to the Boolean expression, the modification is permitted to continue. If not, the statement will fail with a constraint violation.

Check constraints consist of two components: a constraint name and a check condition. The same constraint name cannot be specified more than once for the same table. If a constraint name is not explicitly coded, DB2 will automatically create a unique name for the constraint derived from the name of the first column in the check condition.

The check condition defines the actual constraint logic. The check condition can be defined using any of the basic predicates (>, <, =, <>, <=, >=), as well as BETWEEN, IN, LIKE, and NULL. Furthermore, AND and OR can be used to string conditions together. However, please note the following restrictions:

- The entire length of the check condition can be no greater than 3800 total bytes.

- The constraint can only refer to columns in the table in which it is created. Other tables cannot be referenced in the constraint.

- Subselects, column functions, host variables, parameter markers, special registers, and columns defined with field procedures cannot be specified in a check constraint.

- The NOT logical operator cannot be used.

- The first operand *must be* the name of a column contained in the table. The second operand must be either another column name or a constant.

- If the second operand is a constant, it must be compatible with the data type of the first operand. If the second operand is a column, it must be the same data type as the first column specified.

The EMP table contains the following check constraint:

```
PHONENO  CHAR(4) CONSTRAINT NUMBER CHECK
                (PHONENO >= '0000' AND
                 PHONENO <= '9999'),
```

This constraint defines the valid range of values for the PHONENO column. The following are examples of check constraints that could be added to the EMP table:

```
CONSTRAINT CHECK_SALARY
CHECK (SALARY < 50000.00)

CONSTRAINT COMM_VS_SALARY
CHECK (SALARY > COMM)

CONSTRAINT COMM_BONUS
CHECK (COMM > 0 OR BONUS > 0)
```

The first check constraint ensures that no employee can earn a salary greater than $50,000; the second constraint ensures that an employee's salary will always be greater than his or her commission; and the third constraint ensures that each employee will have either a commission or a bonus set up.

The primary benefit of check constraints is the ability to enforce business rules directly in each database without requiring additional application logic. Once defined, the business rule is physically implemented and cannot be bypassed. Check constraints also provide the following benefits:

- Because there is no additional programming required, DBAs can implement check constraints without involving the application programming staff. However, the application programming staff should be consulted on what type of check constraints are required because they might have more knowledge of the data. Additionally, the application programming staff must be informed whenever check constraints have been implemented to avoid duplication of effort in the programs being developed.

- Check constraints provide better data integrity because a check constraint is always executed whenever the data is modified. Without a check constraint, critical business rules could be bypassed during ad hoc data modification.

- Check constraints promote consistency. Because they are implemented once, in the table DDL, each constraint is always enforced. Constraints written in application logic, on the other hand, must be executed by each program that modifies the data to which the constraint applies. This can cause code duplication and inconsistent maintenance, resulting in inaccurate business rule support.

- Typically check constraints coded in DDL will outperform the corresponding application code.

> **NOTE**
>
> The ALTER TABLE statement can be used to add CHECK constraints to existing tables. When adding a CHECK constraint to a table that is already populated with data, the data values are checked against the constraint depending on the value of the CURRENT RULES special register.
>
> - If CURRENT RULES is set to 'STD' (for SQL standard), the constraint is checked immediately and, if the data does not conform to the constraint, the ALTER fails and the table definition is unchanged.
>
> - If CURRENT RULES is set to 'DB2', however, the constraint is not immediately checked. Instead, the table is placed into check pending status and the CHECK utility must be run to ascertain if the data conforms to the newly added CHECK constraint.

Check Constraint Guidelines

When using check constraints the following tips and techniques can be helpful to assure effective constraint implementation.

Beware of Semantics with Check Constraints   DB2 performs no semantic checking on constraints and defaults. It will allow the DBA to define defaults that contradict check constraints. Furthermore, DB2 will allow the DBA to define check constraints that contradict one another. Care must be taken to avoid creating this type of problem. The following are examples of contradictory constraints:

```
CHECK (EMPNO > 10 AND EMPNO <9)
```

In this case, no value is both greater than 10 and less than 9, so nothing could ever be inserted. However, DB2 will allow this constraint to be defined.

```
EMP_TYPE    CHAR(8) DEFAULT 'NEW'
CHECK (EMP_TYPE IN ('TEMP', 'FULLTIME', 'CONTRACT'))
```

In this case, the default value is not one of the permitted EMP_TYPE values according to the defined constraint. No defaults would ever be inserted.

```
CHECK (EMPNO > 10)
CHECK (EMPNO >= 11)
```

In this case, the constraints are redundant. No logical harm is done, but both constraints will be checked, thereby impacting the performance of applications that modify the table in which the constraints exist.

Other potential semantic problems could occur:

- When the parent table indicates ON DELETE SET NULL but a rule is defined on the child table stating CHECK (COL1 IS NOT NULL)

- When two constraints are defined on the same column with contradictory conditions

- When the constraint requires that the column be NULL, but the column is defined as NOT NULL

Code Constraints at the Table-Level   Although single constraints (primary keys, unique keys, foreign keys, and check constraints) can be specified at the column-level, avoid doing so. In terms of functionality, there is no difference between an integrity constraint defined at the table-level and the same constraint defined at the column-level. All constraints can be coded at the table-level; only single column constraints can be coded at the column-level. By coding all constraints at the table-level maintenance will be easier and clarity will be improved.

Code this (table-level):

```
CREATE TABLE ORDER_ITEM
  (ORDERNO          CHAR(3)        NOT NULL,
   ITEMNO           CHAR(3)        NOT NULL,
   AMOUNT_ORD       DECIMAL(7,2)   NOT NULL,
   PRIMARY KEY (ORDERNO, ITEMNO)
   FOREIGN KEY ORD_ITM (ORDERNO)
     REFERENCES ORDER ON DELETE CASCADE
)
```

Instead of this (column-level):

```
CREATE TABLE ORDER_ITEM
  (ORDERNO          CHAR(3)        NOT NULL
     REFERENCES ORDER ON DELETE CASCADE,
   ITEMNO           CHAR(3)        NOT NULL,
   AMOUNT_ORD       DECIMAL(7,2)   NOT NULL,
   PRIMARY KEY (ORDERNO, ITEMNO)
)
```

Favor Check Constraints Over Triggers   If the same data integrity results can be achieved using a check constraint or a trigger, favor using the check constraint. Check constraints are easier to maintain and are more efficient than triggers.

Using DB2 Triggers for Data Integrity

DB2 triggers can be useful for enforcing complex integrity rules, maintaining redundant data across multiple tables, and ensuring proper data derivation. There are many considerations that must be addressed to properly implement triggers. For complete coverage of how and why to use DB2 triggers, consult Chapter 8, "Using DB2 Triggers for Integrity."

Using Field Procedures for Data Integrity

Field procedures are programs that transform data on insertion and convert the data to its original format on subsequent retrieval. You can use a FIELDPROC to transform character columns, as long as the columns are 254 bytes or less in length.

No FIELDPROCs are delivered with DB2, so they must be developed by the DB2 user. They are ideal for altering the sort sequence of values.

Using Edit Procedures for Data Integrity

An EDITPROC is functionally equivalent to a FIELDPROC, but it acts on an entire row instead of a column. Edit procedures are simply programs that transform data on insertion and convert the data to its original format on subsequent retrieval. Edit procedures are not supplied with DB2, so they must be developed by the user of DB2. They are ideal for implementing data compression routines.

Using Validation Routines for Data Integrity

A VALIDPROC receives a row and returns a value indicating whether LOAD, INSERT, UPDATE, or DELETE processing should proceed. A validation procedure is similar to an edit procedure but it cannot perform data transformation; it simply assesses the validity of the data.

A typical use for a VALIDPROC is to ensure valid domain values. For example, to enforce a Boolean domain, you could write a validation procedure to ensure that a certain portion of a row contains only T or F.

Views, Aliases, and Synonyms

DB2 provides several table-like database objects that can be used to assist in the development of queries and applications. These objects include views, aliases, and synonyms. Each of the objects can be accessed by SQL statements in much the same way as a DB2 table. However, there are significant differences among these objects that you must understand in order to use them effectively.

Views

DB2 enables you to create a virtual table known as a *view*. A view is a representation of data stored in one or more tables. Recall from Chapter 1 that all operations on a DB2 table result in another table. This is a requirement of the relational model. So a view is defined as a SELECT statement on other tables (or views).

A view is represented internally to DB2 by SQL statements, not by stored data. You therefore can define views using the same SQL statements that access data in base tables. The SQL comprising the view is executed only when the view is accessed. This allows the creation of logical tables that consist of a subset of columns from a base table or tables. When the data in the underlying base tables changes, the changes are reflected in any view that contains a base table. You also can create views based on multiple tables by using joins.

One of the most fertile grounds for disagreement between DB2 professionals is the appropriate use of views. Some analysts promote the liberal creation and use of views, whereas others preach a more conservative approach. Usually, their recommendations are based on notions of reducing a program's dependency on a DB2 object's data structure.

This section delineates the best philosophy for the creation and use of views based on my experience. By following each of the guidelines in this section, you can establish a sound framework for view creation and use in your organization.

The View Usage Rule

Create a view only when a specific, stated, and rational goal can be achieved by the view.

Each view must have a specific and logical use before it is created. (Do not simply create a view for each base table.) Views excel for the following six basic uses:

- To provide row and column level security

- To ensure proper data derivation

- To ensure efficient access paths

- To mask complexity from the user

- To provide limited domain support

- To rename columns

If you're creating a view that does not apply to one of these categories, you should reexamine your view requirements. Chances are, the use is not a good one.

Using Views to Implement Security

Views created to provide security on tables effectively create a logical table that is a subset of rows, columns, or both from the base table. By eliminating restricted columns from the column list and providing the proper predicates in the WHERE clause, you can create views to limit a user's access to portions of a table.

For additional details on using views to implement security consult Chapter 10, "DB2 Security and Authorization."

Using Views for Data Derivation

Data derivation formulas can be coded into the SELECT list of a view, thereby ensuring that everyone is using the same calculation. Creating a view that contains a column named TOTAL_COMP that is defined by selecting SALARY + COMM + BONUS is a good example of derived data in a view. Instead of trying to ensure that all queries requiring total compensation add the three component columns, the queries can use the view containing the TOTAL_COMP column instead and not worry about how it is calculated.

Using Views to Ensure Optimal Access

When you create a view for access, you can guarantee efficient access to the underlying base table by specifying indexed columns and proper join criteria. For efficient access, you can code views so that they specify columns indexed in the WHERE clause. Coding join logic into a view also increases the efficiency of access because the join is always performed properly. To code a proper join, use the WHERE clause to compare the columns from like domains.

Using Views to Mask Complexity

Somewhat akin to coding appropriate access into views, coding complex SQL into views can mask the complexity from the user. Coding this way can be extremely useful when your shop employs novice DB2 users (whether they are programmers, analysts, managers, or typical end users).

Consider the following rather complex SQL that implements relational division:

```
SELECT DISTINCT PROJNO
FROM    DSN8810.PROJACT P1
WHERE   NOT EXISTS
        (SELECT  ACTNO
         FROM    DSN8810.ACT A
         WHERE   NOT EXISTS
                 (SELECT PROJNO
                  FROM DSN8810.PROJACT P2
                  WHERE P1.PROJNO = P2.PROJNO
                  AND A.ACTNO = P2.ACTNO));
```

This query uses correlated subselects to return a list of all projects in the PROJACT table that require every activity listed in the ACT table. If you code this SQL into a view called ALL_ACTIVITY_PROJ, for example, the end user need only issue the following simple SELECT statement instead of the more complicated query:

```
SELECT  PROJNO
FROM    ALL_ACTIVTY_PROJ;
```

> **CAUTION**
>
> Using views to mask complexity can cause problems when used in DB2 application programs. It can be difficult to support and maintain programs, especially when they fail during the night. Think about it. Would you rather have the entire SQL statement coded in the program—even if it is complex—or would you rather have to hunt down the view definition in the DB2 Catalog (where it is stored in SYSIBM.SYSVIEWS without any formatting)?

Using Views to Mimic Domain Support

Most relational database management systems do not support *domains*, and DB2 is no exception. Domains are instrumental components of the relational model and, in fact, were in the original relational model published by Ted Codd in 1970—over three decades ago! A domain basically identifies the valid range of values that a column can contain.

> **NOTE**
>
> Domains are more complex than this simple definition, of course. For example, the relational model states that only columns pooled from the same domain should be able to be compared within a predicate (unless explicitly overridden).

Views and table check constraints can be used to create crude domains. In general, table check constraints should be preferred over views for creating domain-like functionality, because check constraints are easier to implement and maintain. However, using views with the WITH CHECK OPTION can provide domain-like functionality combined with other view features (such as securing data by eliminating columns).

You can implement some of the functionality of domains by using views and the WITH CHECK OPTION clause. The WITH CHECK OPTION clause ensures the update integrity of DB2 views. It guarantees that all data inserted or updated using the view adheres to the view specification. For example, consider the following view:

```
CREATE VIEW EMPLOYEE
  (EMP_NO, EMP_FIRST_NAME, EMP_MID_INIT,
   EMP_LAST_NAME, DEPT, JOB, SEX, SALARY)
AS
  SELECT  EMPNO, FIRSTNME, MIDINIT, LASTNAME,
          WORKDEPT, JOB, SEX, SALARY
  FROM    DSN8810.EMP
  WHERE   SEX IN ('M', 'F')
WITH CHECK OPTION;
```

The WITH CHECK OPTION clause, in this case, ensures that all updates made to this view can specify only the values 'M' or 'F' in the SEX column. Although this example is simplistic, you can easily extrapolate from this example where your organization can create views with predicates that specify code ranges using BETWEEN, patterns using LIKE, or a subselect against another table to identify the domain of a column.

Although you can create similar functionality by using check constraints, views can limit the columns and rows while providing data value checking. Consider the following example:

```
CREATE VIEW HIGH_PAID_EMP
    (EMP_NO, EMP_FIRST_NAME, EMP_MID_INIT,
     EMP_LAST_NAME, DEPT, JOB, SALARY)
  AS SELECT  EMPNO, FIRSTNME, MIDINIT, LASTNAME,
             WORKDEPT, JOB, SALARY
     FROM    DSN8810.EMP
     WHERE   SALARY > 75000.00
  WITH CASCADED CHECK OPTION;
```

This view eliminates several columns (for example, PHONENO, HIREDATE, SEX, and so on) and multiple rows (where SALARY is less than or equal to $75,000). The view is updateable because all the columns not included in the view are nullable. However, only rows in which the salary conforms to the predicate can be modified. This combined functionality cannot be provided by check constraints alone.

Let me add these words of caution, however: When inserts or updates are performed using these types of views, DB2 evaluates the predicates to ensure that the data modification conforms to the predicates in the view. Be sure to perform adequate testing prior to implementing domains in this manner to safeguard against possible performance degradation.

You can specify the WITH CHECK OPTION clause for updateable views. This way, you can ensure that all data inserted or updated using the view adheres to the view specification. Consider the following view:

```
CREATE VIEW HIGH_PAID_EMP
  (EMPLOYEE_NO, FIRST_NAME, MIDDLE_INITIAL,
   LAST_NAME, DEPARTMENT, JOB, SEX, SALARY)
AS SELECT EMPNO, FIRSTNME, MIDINIT, LASTNAME,
          WORKDEPT, JOB, SEX, SALARY
   FROM   DSN8810.EMP
   WHERE  SALARY > 75000.00;
```

Without the WITH CHECK clause, you can use this view to add data about employees who make less than $75,000. Because this approach is probably not desirable, add WITH CHECK OPTION to the view to ensure that all added data is appropriate given the view definition.

There are two forms of the WITH CHECK OPTION:

- WITH CASCADED CHECK OPTION specifies that all search conditions are checked for the view in which the clause exists and any views it accesses regardless of the check options specified.

- WITH LOCAL CHECK OPTION specifies that search conditions on underlying views are checked conditionally. If a check option exists in underlying views, it is checked; otherwise, it is not.

Views created specifying WITH CHECK OPTION only will provide WITH CASCADED CHECK OPTION functionality. The general rule of thumb, as always, is to explicitly specify the options you want. In other words, never specify WITH CHECK OPTION only; instead, you should specify either WITH CASCADED CHECK OPTION or WITH LOCAL CHECK OPTION.

Using Views to Rename Columns

You can rename columns in views. This capability is particularly useful if a table contains arcane or complicated column names. Sometimes, particularly for application packages purchased from third-party vendors, renaming columns using a view is useful to make the names more user-friendly. Good examples of such tables are the DB2 Catalog tables.

Consider the following view:

```
CREATE VIEW PLAN_DEPENDENCY
    (OBJECT_NAME, OBJECT_CREATOR, OBJECT_TYPE,
     PLAN_NAME, IBM_REQD)
AS SELECT BNAME, BCREATOR, BTYPE, DNAME, IBMREQD
    FROM   SYSIBM.SYSPLANDEP;
```

Not only does this view rename the entity from SYSPLANDEP to the more easily understood name PLAN_DEPENDENCY, but it also renames each of the columns. Understanding PLAN_NAME as the name of the plan is easier than understanding DNAME. You can create views on each of the DB2 Catalog tables in this manner so that your programmers can better determine which columns contain the information that they require. Additionally, if you have other tables with clumsy table and/or column names, views can provide an elegant solution to renaming without your having to drop and re-create anything.

You can rename columns in queries by using the AS clause. However, the AS clause does not provide the same function as column renaming using views because you must still specify the original name of the column in the query.

Reasons Not to Create One View Per Base Table

Often, the dubious recommendation is made to create one view for each base table in a DB2 application system. The reason behind such a suggestion usually involves the desire to insulate application programs from database changes. This insulation is purported to be achieved by mandating that all programs access views instead of base tables. Although this idea might sound good on the surface, upon further examination you will see that it is a bad idea.

The following is an example of a base table and the view that would be created for it. Here is the base table:

```
CREATE TABLE userid.BASE_TABLE
  (COLUMN1  CHAR(10)  NOT NULL,
   COLUMN2  DATE      NOT NULL WITH DEFAULT,
   COLUMN3  SMALLINT,
   COLUMN4  VARCHAR(50)
  ) IN DATABASE db_name;
```

Here is the base view:

```
CREATE VIEW userid.BASE_VIEW
  (COL1, COL2, COL3, COL4)
AS SELECT COLUMN1, COLUMN2, COLUMN3, COLUMN4
    FROM   userid.BASE_TABLE;
```

Because a base table view does not break any of the rules for view updateability, all SQL statements can be executed against it. The basic reasoning behind creating base table views is the erroneous belief that it provides increased data independence.

For every reason that can be given to create one view per base table, a better reason can be given to avoid doing so. This section details all the arguments for creating one view per base table and explains why the reasoning is not sound.

Adding Columns and the Impact on DB2 Programs   The first argument in favor of base table views is typically, "If I add a column to a table, I will not have to change any programs accessing that table." The reasoning behind this assertion is that you can write programs that are independent of the table columns. If a program retrieves data using SELECT * or INSERTs rows, no knowledge of new columns would be required if the column is added correctly.

The SELECT * statement returns all the columns in the table. If a column is added to a table after the program is coded, the program does not execute because the variable needed to store the newly retrieved column is not coded in the program. If the program uses a view, however, the program executes because the view has only the old columns, not including the new column just added.

If the program is coded to update views instead of base tables, the INSERT statement continues to work as well. However, the column added to the base table must allow default values. The default value can be either the null value or the DB2 default when a column is defined as NOT NULL WITH DEFAULT. The INSERT to the view continues to work even though the view does not contain the new column. The row is inserted, and the new column is assigned the appropriate default value.

It is not a good idea to use base table views to insulate programs from the impact of new columns. If you code your application programs properly, you do not have to make changes when a column is added. Proper program coding refers to coding all SQL statements with column names. If column names can be supplied in an SQL statement, the columns should always be explicitly specified in the SQL statement. This rule applies in particular to the INSERT and SELECT statements and is true whether you are using views or base tables.

The SELECT * statement should never be permitted in an application program. Every DB2 manual and text issues this warning—and with good reason. All DB2 objects can be dropped and re-created and/or altered. If a DB2 object upon which a program relies is modified, a SELECT * in that program ceases to function.

This caveat does not change because you're using views. Even views can be dropped and re-created. If the program uses SELECT * on a view and the view has changed, the program does not work until it is modified to reflect the changes made to the view.

Do not think that you will never modify a view. Some companies establish a policy of keeping views inline with their base tables. Doing so causes the view to change when the table changes. Others use views for security. As security changes, so do the views.

If you eliminate the SELECT * statement, you eliminate this reason for using views. An INSERT statement works against a base table the same as a base table view if the column names are provided in the INSERT statement. As long as you add the new column allowing a default value, the program continues to work.

Removing Columns and the Impact on DB2 Programs   When you remove a column from a DB2 table, you must drop and re-create the table without the column. You can re-create views that access the table being modified, substituting a constant value in place of the removed column. Application programs that access the views then return the constant rather than the column that was dropped.

It is not a good idea to use base table views to insulate programs from the impact of removing columns from a table. The thinking that, if you remove a column from a table, you do not have to change the application program is untrue. If you remove the column from the base table, you must remove it from the view. If you do not remove it from the view and instead add a constant, the view can no longer be updated. Also, all queries and reports return a constant instead of the old column value, and the integrity of the system is jeopardized.

Users must be able to rely on the data in the database. If constants are returned on screens and reports, confusion will arise. Also, if the data (that is now a constant) is used in any calculations, these values are also unreliable. These unreliable calculation results could be generated and then inserted into the database, propagating bad data.

The removal of data from a database must be analyzed in the same manner as any change. Simply returning constants is not a solution and will cause more problems than it solves.

Splitting Tables and the Impact on DB2 Programs   Another popular argument in favor of using base table views centers on anticipating the need to split a DB2 table into two tables. The argument is that if you split a table into two tables, you can change the base table view and thereby avoid changing any program accessing the table. Sometimes one DB2 table must be split into two tables. This is usually done based on access requirements to increase the efficiency of retrieval. For example, consider a table with 10 columns. Fifty percent of the queries against the table access the first 6 columns. The remaining 50% of the queries access the other 4 columns and the key column. This table could be a candidate for splitting into two tables to improve access: one new table containing the first 6 columns and the second new table containing the remaining 4 columns and the key column.

If the programs use a view, you can recode the view to be a join of the two new tables. You do not have to change the programs to reflect the modification; only the view changes.

It is not a good idea to use base table views to insulate programs from the impact of splitting tables. If you must split a table into two tables, you must have a very good reason for doing so. As I indicated, this action is usually driven by performance considerations. To increase efficiency, you must change the underlying SQL to take advantage of the tables that have been split. Queries accessing columns in only one of the new tables must be modified to access only that table.

Using the logic given by the view supporters, no changes are made to programs. If no changes are made, performance suffers because of the view changes, though. The views are now joins instead of straight SELECTs. No SQL code changes. Every straight SELECT now creates a join, which is less efficient than a straight SELECT.

A change of this magnitude requires a thorough analysis of your application code. When table column definitions change, SQL changes and programs change; these changes cannot be avoided. A trained analyst or DBA must analyze the application's SQL, including SQL in application plans, QMF queries, and dynamic SQL. Queries that access columns from both of the new tables must be made into a join. You do not want to create indiscriminate joins, however. Queries that access columns from only one of the two tables must be recoded as a straight SELECT against that table to increase performance. Also, any programs that update the view must be changed. Remember, views that join tables cannot be updated.

If, after investigating, you determine that some queries require joining the two new tables, you can create a view to accommodate these queries. The view can even have the same name as the old table so that you can minimize program changes. The two new tables can be given new names. The view is created only when it is needed—a more reasonable approach to change management.

A change of this magnitude is rarely attempted after an application has been moved to production. This fact is usually not considered when the recommendation is made to use views.

Combining Tables and the Impact on DB2 Programs   Base table view proponents also advocate using views to insulate programs from the effects of combining two tables into a single table. This situation is the inverse of the preceding situation. If two tables are almost always joined, you can increase efficiency by creating a "pre-joined" table. The overhead incurred by joining the two tables is avoided. Instead of a join, a straight SELECT can now be issued against the new table.

If the application programs use views in this instance, you can modify the views to subsets of the new combination table. In this way, you can avoid program changes.

Once again, base table views do not provide the level of insulation desired. The two tables are combined because most queries must access both of the tables. If you simply combine the two tables into one table and change the views to subsets of the new pre-joined table without changing the SQL, you degrade performance. The queries that were joins are still joins, but now they join the new views. Remember that the views are just subsets of one table now, so these queries join this one table to itself. This approach is usually less efficient than joining the two tables as they were previously defined.

Again, you must perform a great deal of analysis for a change of this magnitude. You must investigate all application SQL. If you determine that some queries access only one of the two old tables, you can define views with the same name as the old tables. You can give the new pre-joined table a new name. This way, you can minimize program modification.

Additional Base Table View Reasoning   One final reason some DBAs have for creating base table views is that some folks believe base table views give them a "feeling" of safety over using just the base tables. I can think of no valid reasoning to support this "feeling." Base table views do not provide a layer of protection between the application and the data. If one view is created for each base table, all types of SQL can be performed on the views. You can perform update and retrieval SQL in the same manner on the views as you can on the base tables.

The advice to create one view per base table is rooted in the fallacious assertion that applications can be ignorant of underlying changes to the database. Change impact analysis must be performed when tables are modified. Failure to do so results in a poorly performing application.

The bottom line is that you should avoid indiscriminate view creation.

Miscellaneous View Guidelines

To ensure appropriate view usage, implement the following tips, techniques, and guidelines.

Follow the Synchronization Rule   Keep all views logically pure by synchronizing them with their underlying base tables.

When you make a change to a base table, you should analyze all views dependent on the base table to determine whether the change affects them. The view was created for a reason (see "The View Usage Rule" section earlier in this chapter) and should remain useful for that reason. You can accomplish this goal only by ensuring that subsequent changes pertinent to a specified use are made to all views that satisfy that use.

Consider a view that is based on the sample tables `DSN8810.EMP` and `DSN8810.DEPT`. The view is created to satisfy an access use; it provides information about departments, including the name of the department's manager. If you add a column specifying the employee's middle initial to the `EMP` table, you should add the column also to the `EMP_DEPT` view because it is pertinent to that view's use: to provide information about each department and each department's manager. You must drop and re-create the view.

The synchronization rule requires you to have strict procedures for change impact analysis. Every change to a base table should trigger the use of these procedures. You can create simple SQL queries to assist in the change impact analysis. These queries should pinpoint `QMF` queries, application plans, and dynamic SQL users that could be affected by specific changes. The following queries should assist your change impact analysis process.

To find all views dependent on the table to be changed, use the following:

```
SELECT   DCREATOR, DNAME
FROM     SYSIBM.SYSVIEWDEP
WHERE    BCREATOR = 'Table Creator'
AND      BNAME = 'Table Name';
```

To find all `QMF` queries that access the view, use the following:

```
SELECT   DISTINCT OWNER, NAME, TYPE
FROM     Q.OBJECT_DATA
WHERE    APPLDATA LIKE '%View Name%';
```

To find all plans dependent on the view, use the following:

```
SELECT   DNAME
FROM     SYSIBM.SYSPLANDEP
WHERE    BCREATOR = 'View Creator'
AND      BNAME = 'View Name';
```

To find all potential dynamic SQL users, use the following:

```
SELECT  GRANTEE
FROM    SYSIBM.SYSTABAUTH
WHERE   TCREATOR = 'View Creator'
AND     TTNAME = 'View Name';
```

Always execute these queries to determine what views might be affected by changes to base tables.

Be Aware of Non-Updateable Views   If you adhere to the preceding guidelines, most of your views will not be updateable. Views that join tables, use functions, use DISTINCT, or use GROUP BY and HAVING cannot be updated, deleted from, or inserted to. Views that contain derived data using arithmetic expressions, contain constants, or eliminate columns without default values cannot be inserted to. Keep this information in mind when you're creating and using views.

Specify Column Names   When you're creating views, DB2 provides the option of specifying new column names for the view or defaulting to the same column names as the underlying base table or tables. Explicitly specify view column names rather than allow them to default, even when you plan to use the same names as the underlying base tables. This approach provides more accurate documentation and minimizes confusion when using views.

Be Aware of View Restrictions   Almost any SQL that can be issued natively can be coded into a view, except SQL that contains the FOR UPDATE OF clause, an ORDER BY specification, or the UNION operation.

Views can be accessed by SQL in the same way that tables are accessed by SQL. However, you must consider the rules about the types of views that can be updated. Table 5.11 lists the restrictions on view updating.

TABLE 5.11   Non-Updateable View Types

View Type	Restriction
Views that join tables	Cannot delete, update, or insert
Views that use functions	Cannot delete, update, or insert
Views that use DISTINCT	Cannot delete, update, or insert
Views that use GROUP BY and HAVING	Cannot delete, update, or insert
Views that contain derived data using arithmetic expression	Cannot insert
Views that contain constants	Cannot insert
Views that eliminate columns without a default value	Cannot insert

Consider Materialized Query Tables   A view is not materialized until it is accessed in a SQL statement. Depending on the context of the SQL, materialization can cause performance problems.

5

V8 As of DB2 V8 it is possible to create materialized query tables that are essentially materialized views. For some types of complex queries, MQTs can significantly outperform views. Of course, this comes at a cost. An MQT requires disk storage that a view does not need.

Details on how DB2 optimizes view access are provided in Chapter 21, "The Optimizer." In-depth coverage of materialized query tables is provided in Chapter 45, "Data Warehousing with DB2," because MQTs are most frequently used in data warehouse and analytical implementations.

Aliases

A DB2 ALIAS is an alternate name defined for a table. It was introduced to simplify distributed processing, but aliases can be used in any context, not just for easing data distribution. Remote tables add a location prefix to the table name. However, you can create an ALIAS for a remote table, thereby giving it a shorter, local name because it no longer requires the location prefix.

Synonyms

A DB2 SYNONYM is also an alternate name for a table. Aliases can be accessed by users other than their creator, but synonyms can be accessed only by their creator. When a table is dropped, its synonyms are dropped but its aliases are retained.

As a general rule of thumb, consider using synonyms for individuals during program development, aliases for distributed applications, and views for security, performance, and ease of use.

Index Guidelines

An *index* is a balanced B-tree structure that orders the values of columns in a table. When you index a table by one or more of its columns, you can access data directly and more efficiently because the index is ordered by the columns to be retrieved. Consult Chapter 6, "DB2 Indexes," for additional guidance on proper index creation, usage, and maintenance.

Naming Conventions

Before issuing any DDL, standard names must be identified for all objects that will be created. There are rules that DB2 will enforce for database object naming. For example:

- Object names must start with an alphabetic character or one of the national characters (@, #, $).

- Numeric characters are permissible in the object name, just not in the initial character of the name.

- The underscore (_) is used as a separator character.

- Special characters and blanks can be used in a DB2 object name, but the name must then be enclosed in double quotes (" ").

- STOGROUP, DATABASE, and TABLESPACE names must not contain any special characters.

Qualification of object names is required whenever two objects share the same name. When coding DDL, a fully qualified table space name is required for the IN *database-name.tablespace-name* clause when creating a table. Otherwise, the default database (DSNDB04) is used if a simple table space name is coded.

The next section offers DB2 naming conventions that conform to these rules.

Develop and Enforce DB2 Naming Conventions

The first step in creating an optimal DB2 environment is the development of rigorous naming standards for all DB2 objects. This standard should be used with all other IT naming standards in your shop. Where possible, the DB2 naming conventions should be developed to peacefully coexist with your other standards, but not at the expense of impairing the DB2 environment. In all cases, naming standards should be approved by the corporate data administration (DA) department, or the corporate database administration department if a DA group does not exist.

Do not impose unnecessary restrictions on the names of objects accessed by end users. DB2 is supposed to be a user-friendly database management system. Strict, limiting naming conventions, if not developed logically, can be the antithesis of what you are striving to achieve with DB2.

For example, many shops impose an eight-character encoded table-naming convention on their environment. DB2 provides for 18-character table names, and there is no reason to restrict your table names to eight characters. There is even less reason for these names to be encoded. A reasonable table-naming convention is a two- or three-character application identifier prefix, followed by an underscore, and then a clear, user-friendly name.

For example, consider the customer name and address table in a customer maintenance system. The name of this table could be

```
CMS_CUST_NAME_ADDR
```

The application identifier is CMS (for Customer Maintenance System), followed by an underscore and a clear table name, CUST_NAME_ADDR. If this table were named following an eight-character encoded name convention, it might appear as TCMSNMAD. This clearly is not a user-friendly name, and should be avoided.

In general, a standard naming convention should allow the use of all characters provided by DB2. (See Appendix D, "DB2 Limits," for a listing of DB2 size limitations for each type of object.) By using all available characters, the DB2 environment is easier to use and understand. All information pertaining to which indexes are defined for which tables, which tables are in which table spaces, which table spaces are in which databases, and so on can be found by querying the DB2 Catalog.

The only valid exception to using all available characters is when naming indexes. An index name can be 18 characters, but there are advantages to limiting it to eight charac-ters. Indexes are unknown to most end users, so a limiting index name is not as great a blow to user friendliness as a limiting table name.

The problem with 18-character index names is the result of the strict data set naming convention required by DB2. This convention is

```
vcat.DSNDBx.dddddddd.ssssssss.t0001.Annn
```

where:

vcat	High-level qualifier, indicating an ICF catalog
x	C if VSAM cluster component
	D if VSAM data component
dddddddd	Database name
ssssssss	Table space name or index name
t	I or J, depending on last fast switch
nnn	Partition number or the data set number

> **NOTE**
>
> A non-partitioned index can cover 32 2GB data sets. The first data set ends with 001, the second data set ends with 002, and so on.

If you use more than eight characters to name an index defined using a STOGROUP, or storage group, DB2 creates a unique, eight-character string to be used when defining the underlying data set for the index. If the index is created using native VSAM, the first eight characters of the name must be unique and must be used when defining the underlying VSAM data set. These two constraints can make the task of correlating indexes to data set names an administrative nightmare when indexes have names greater than 8 bytes.

Be sure to create and publish naming standards for all DB2 objects. A comprehensive list of objects follows:

STOGROUP	PLAN and PACKAGE
DATABASE	STORED PROCEDURE
TABLESPACE	PROGRAM
LOB TABLESPACE	TRIGGER
STORED PROCEDURE	USER-DEFINED FUNCTION
TABLE	DBRM
AUXILIARY TABLE	GLOBAL TEMPORARY TABLE
REFERENTIAL CONSTRAINT	CHECK CONSTRAINT
VIEW	UTILITY ID
ALIAS	INDEX

```
SYNONYM                        COLUMN

COLLECTION                     VERSION

USER-DEFINED DISTINCT TYPE
```

You might also consider creating naming standards for other related objects such as FIELDPROCs, EDITPROCs, image copy data set names, PDS library names, and so on. Creating a naming standard for cursors inside of DB2 programs is also recommended.

Sample DB2 Naming Conventions

Sample DB2 naming standards follow. These standards are only suggestions. Your shop standards are likely to vary from these standards. However, if you have yet to adopt a naming standard at your shop, consider using these. Valid characters are all alphabetic characters, the underscore, and numbers.

DB2 Database Names

Format:	*Daaadddd*
aaa	Application identifier
dddd	Unique description

DB2 Table Space Names

Format:	*Saaadddd*
aaa	Application identifier
dddd	Unique description

DB2 LOB Table Space Names

Format:	*Laaadddd*
aaa	Application identifier
dddd	Unique description

Table, View, and Alias Names

Format:	*aaa_d...d*
Limit:	128 total bytes (18 for V7 and previous)
aaa	Application identifier
d...d	Unique description up to 124 characters long

Synonym Names

Format:	*aaa_dddddddddddddd*
Limit:	18 total bytes

aaa	Application identifier
dddddddddddddd	Unique description up to 14 characters long

Auxiliary Table Names

Format:	*Xaaa_d...d*
Limit:	128 total bytes (18 for V7 and previous)
aaa	Application identifier
d...d	Unique description up to 123 characters long

V8

Temporary Table Names

Format:	*TMP_d...d*
Limit:	128 total bytes (18 for V7 and previous)
TMP	Constant temporary indicator (consider an alternate shop standard if you already use TMP as an application identifier)
d...d	Unique description up to 124 characters long

DB2 Index Names

Format:	*Xaaadddd*
aaa	Application identifier
dddd	Unique description

Index names should be limited to 8 characters even though DB2 allows up to 18 character index names. This is important because you can explicitly name DB2 indexes, but you cannot explicitly name DB2 index spaces. Yet, every DB2 index requires an index space name. The index space name is implicitly generated by DB2 from the index name. If the index name is 8 characters or less in length, then the "index space" name will be named the same as the index itself. If the index name is greater than 8 characters long, DB2 will use an internal, proprietary algorithm to generate a unique, 8-byte index space name. It is difficult to match indexes to index spaces when the names do not match, so it is wise to limit the length of index names to 8 characters.

STOGROUP **Names**

Format:	*Gaaadddd*
aaa	Application identifier
dddd	Unique description

Referential Constraint Names (Foreign Keys)

Format:	*Raaadddd*
aaa	Application identifier
dddd	Unique description

Check Constraint Names

Format:	*Caaadddd*
aaa	Application identifier
dddd	Unique description (for example, first four characters of column name)

DB2 Trigger Names

Format:	*Gaaadddd*
aaa	Application identifier
dddd	Unique description (for example, characters that tie back to the table on which the triggers are defined, if possible)

DB2 Stored Procedure Names

Format:	Up to 18 characters

DB2 stored procedure names should be as descriptive as possible to define the purpose of the stored procedure. Use as many of the 18 characters as needed to help identify the functionality of the stored procedure. For example, RETURN_ALL CUSTS is a better name for a stored procedure than is RTALLCST.

DB2 User-Defined Function Names

Format:	Up to 8 characters; should be as descriptive as possible to define the purpose of the function

DB2 Column Names

Format:	Up to 128 characters

DB2 column names should be as descriptive as possible to provide documentation. Version 8 changes the limit for column size from 18 bytes to 128. In general, use as many characters as necessary to make the column name understandable. When you use abbreviations to limit the size of a column, use the standard Data Management abbreviations. This ensures a consistent and effective database environment.

Even though DB2 supports column names of up to 128 bytes, use caution before taking advantage of all available characters. Be sure to consider issues such as storage space and interface display limits used by your applications before naming columns.

Columns that define the same attribute should be named the same. Additionally, the same name should never be used for different attributes. In other words, a column used as a primary key in one table should be named identically when used as a foreign key in other tables. The only valid exception is when the same attribute exists in one table multiple times. In this case, specify a substitute column name; you usually can use the attribute name with a descriptive suffix or prefix. For code supplied by vendors, you might have to make exceptions to this guideline of singular column names per attribute.

DB2 Distinct Type Names

Format: Up to 18 characters

DB2 distinct types should be defined with a similar mindset as defining DB2 columns. The distinct type name should be as descriptive as possible within the 18-character limitation.

DB2 Plan Names

Format: Up to eight characters

The convention is that the name of the plan should be the same as the name of the application program to which it applies. If multiple program DBRMs (Data Base Request Modules) are bound to a single large plan, or if one plan is composed of many packages, the name should be assigned by the database administration department such that the name successfully identifies the application, is not an actual program name, and is unique in the DB2 subsystem.

DB2 Package Names

Format: Up to eight characters

Packages are named the same as the DBRM.

DBRM Names

Format: Up to eight characters

DBRMs generally are named the same as the program. If a single program is used to create multiple DBRMs, consult with the database administration department for an acceptable name.

Collection Names

Format:	aaa_dddddddd_eeeee
aaa	Application identifier
dddddddd	Unique description
eeeee	Environment (BATCH, CAF, CICS, DLI, IMSDC, BMP, TSO, and so on)

Explicit Version Names

Format:	uuuuuuuu_date_tttt_s
uuuuuuuu	authid (of person performing precompile)
date	Date of precompile (ISO format)
tttt	Type of program (TEST, TEMP, PROD, QUAL, and so on)
s	Sequence number (if required)

The explicit version name should be used when the programmer is to specify the version instead of having DB2 supply the version automatically at precompile time. An example of an explicit version name would be DBAPCSM_2004-01-01_TEMP_3, indicating that on New Year's Day user DBAPCSM precompiled this version as a temporary fix (at least) three times.

Automatic Version Names   The automatic version name must be permitted when DB2 is to assign the version name automatically at precompile time. In this case, the version name is a 26-byte ISO timestamp. For example, 2004-07-21-15.04.26.546405.

Utility ID   DB2 utility IDs should be unique for each utility to be executed. No two utilities can be run concurrently with the same ID.

The utility ID for all regularly scheduled DB2 utilities should be allowed to default to the name of the job. Because MVS does not permit two identically named jobs to execute at the same time, DB2 utility IDs will be forced to be unique.

DCLGEN Declare Members

Format:	oaaadddd
o	Object identifier:

	T	table
	V	view
	A	alias
	S	synonym

aaa	Application identifier
dddd	Unique description

The unique description, *dddd*, should be the same as the table space to which the table has been defined. If more than one of any object type exists per table space, the database administration department should assign a unique name and provide that name to the appropriate application development staff.

Compliance

The database administration department should assign all DB2 object names. It is also the database administration department's responsibility to enforce DB2 naming conventions.

Database administration should work in conjunction with the corporate data administration group to ensure that naming conventions are consistent throughout the organization.

Miscellaneous DDL Guidelines

This section contains guidelines that are not easily categorized. They provide SQL guidance from an overall perspective of DB2 development.

Avoid Using DDL in an Application Program   Do not issue DDL from an application program. DDL statements should be planned by a database administrator and issued when they cause the least disruption to the production system.

When DROP, ALTER, and CREATE statements are used, DB2 must update its system catalog tables. These statements also place a lock on the database DBD being affected by the DDL. This can affect the overall performance of the DB2 system. When DDL is issued from an application program, DB2 object creation is difficult to control and schedule potentially causing lockout conditions in production systems.

It is okay to use declared temporary tables in your programs, because executing a DECLARE for a temporary table does not require DB2 to access the system catalog.

Plan the Execution of DDL   Because of the potential impact on the application system (such as locking, new functionality, or new access paths), schedule the execution of DDL statements during off-peak hours.

Strive for Relational Purity   Learn and understand the relational model and let your design decisions be influenced by it. Assume that DB2 eventually will support all features of the relational model and plan accordingly. For example, if a procedural method can be used to implement outer joins, favor this method over the implementation of physical tables containing outer join data. This provides for an orderly migration to the features of the relational model as they become available in DB2.

Favor Normalized Tables   Taking all the previous suggestions into account, avoid denormalization unless performance reasons dictate otherwise. Normalized tables, if they perform well, provide the optimal environment and should be favored over tables that are not normalized.

Maintain Standard Libraries   Create standard libraries for BIND parameters, utility JCL, utility parameters, VSAM IDCAMS delete and define parameters for user-defined VSAM table spaces, GRANT and REVOKE DCL, and DDL for all DB2 objects.

To maintain these libraries, ensure that all subsequent alterations to DDL are reflected in the DDL stored in the standard library. For example, if a table is altered to add a new column, be sure that the CREATE DDL table in the standard library is modified to also contain the new column. Because this task is time-consuming and error-prone, you should consider purchasing an add-on product that can generate DDL from the DB2 Catalog. Having such a product negates the need to store and maintain DDL in a standard library. For information on these (and other) types of add-on tools for DB2, consult Part VII.

Adhere to the Proliferation Avoidance Rule   Do not needlessly proliferate DB2 objects. Every DB2 object creation requires additional entries in the DB2 Catalog. Creating needless tables, views, and so on, causes catalog clutter—extraneous entries strewn about the DB2 Catalog tables. The larger the DB2 Catalog tables become, the less efficient your entire DB2 system will be.

The proliferation avoidance rule is based on common sense. Why create something that is not needed? It just takes up space that could be used for something that you do need.

CHAPTER **6**

DB2 Indexes

You can create indexes on DB2 table columns to speed up query processing. An index uses pointers to actual data to more efficiently access specific pieces of data. Once created, DB2 automatically maintains each index as data is added, modified, and deleted from the table. As data is selected from the table DB2 can choose to use the index to access the data more efficiently. It is important to remember that index modification and usage is automatic—you do not need to tell DB2 to modify indexes as data changes nor can you tell DB2 to use a particular index to access data. This automation and separation makes it easy to deploy DB2 indexes.

To illustrate how an index works think about the index in this book. If you are trying to find a reference to a particular term in this large book, you can look up the word in the index—which is arranged alphabetically. When you find the word in the index, one or more page numbers will be listed after the word. These numbers point to the actual pages in the book where information on the term can be found.

Just like using a book's index can be much faster than sequentially flipping through each page of a book, using a DB2 index can be much faster than sequentially accessing every page in a table. And, just like the book index, an index is only useful if the term you seek has been indexed.

An *index* is a balanced B-tree structure that orders the values of columns in a table. When you index a table by one or more of its columns, you can access data directly and more efficiently because the index is ordered by the columns to be retrieved.

Figure 6.1 depicts a simple b-tree index structure. By following the index tree structure data can be more rapidly accessed than by sequentially scanning all of the rows of the table. For example, a four level index (such as the one shown in the figure) can locate indexed data with 5 I/Os—one for each of the four levels and an additional read to the data page. This is much more efficient than a table scan which would have to access each table space page, of which there may be hundreds, thousands, or even millions depending on the size of the table.

There are 3 types of index data pages needed to form the internal index structure used by DB2: root, nonleaf, and leaf pages. The *root page* is the starting point of the search through an index. It is always at the top of the index structure and physically it is stored as the third page in the index space (after the header page and the space map page). Entries are made up of the key and RID of the highest key value contained in each page on the level below it. A RID is an internal pointer that uniquely identifies each row to DB2. The RID is made up of:

- Page number (3 or 4 bytes)—The page in the table space where the row is stored. The page number will be 4 bytes for LARGE table spaces; otherwise it will be 3 bytes.

- Identifier (1 byte)—The ID map entry number on the associated page that contains the page offset for the row.

So, DB2 index entries are made up of a key and a RID. But when multiple rows exist with the same key value, the index entry will contain a single key followed by chain of RIDs.

Nonleaf pages are index pages that point to other index pages. When the number of levels in an index reaches 3, the middle level will be this type of page. Prior to the index reaching 3 levels, there are no nonleaf pages in the internal index structure (just a root page that points to leaf pages). Entries in nonleaf pages are made up of the key and RID of the highest key value contained in each page on the level below it. *Leaf pages* contain key/RID combinations that point to actual user data rows.

Let's clarify these points by examining the simplified index structure in Figure 6.1 a little more closely. Suppose we wanted to find a row containing the value 59 using this index. Starting at the top we follow the left path because 59 is less than 98. Then we go right because 59 falls between 53 and 98. Then we follow the link to the leaf page containing 59. Leaf pages are at the bottom-most level of an index (level four in this case). Each leaf page contains indexed values followed by one or more RIDs.

More details on the structure and makeup of DB2 indexes, including index page layouts, is provided in Chapter 20, "DB2 Behind the Scenes."

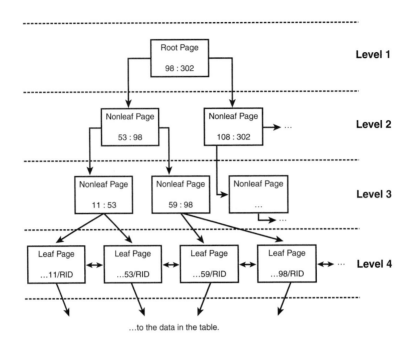

FIGURE 6.1   Conceptual diagram of a B-tree index structure.

Creating Indexes

A proper indexing strategy can be the most important factor to ensure optimal performance of DB2 applications. However, indexing is most likely improperly implemented at most DB2 sites. This is due to the nature of database development. Database objects typically are created near the beginning of a project—after the logical data model has been transformed into a physical database design, but before any application code or SQL has been written. So the DBA takes an initial best guess at creating some indexes on each table. Of course, indexes are best designed based on how the data will be accessed. Without the SQL, proper indexes cannot be created. Therefore, as the development process progresses an iterative approach is taken to index creation. New indexes are created to support new queries; old indexes are removed if they are not being used. Such an approach is fraught with potential problems, but such is life.

Indexes should be created to match the predicates of your most important and frequently executed SQL statements. When DB2 accesses data using an index, it can be much more efficient than scanning an entire table for the row(s) that apply. For example, consider the following SQL statement:

```
SELECT FIRSTNME, MIDINIT, LASTNAME, WORKDEPT,
       PHONENO, SALARY
FROM   DSN8810.EMP
WHERE  EDLEVEL = 2
AND    BONUS > 100.00;
```

If there are no indexes defined on the EMP table, DB2 will have to search every row of the table, looking for employees with an education level of 2 and a bonus greater than $100.00. But if we define an index on the table—on either or both of the two columns in the predicates—then DB2 can use the index to find the qualifying rows. This should reduce I/O and improve performance.

An index on EDLEVEL, BONUS would be the most beneficial for this query. DB2 can match on the equality predicate and scan on the range (>) predicate. So, DB2 can use the index to match the value of EDLEVEL and scan for BONUS values.

An index is created using the CREATE INDEX statement, which is similar in several ways to the CREATE TABLESPACE statement. Both require the user to specify storage (USING, PRIQTY, and SECQTY), free space (PCTFREE and FREEPAGE), a buffer pool (BUFFERPOOL), and how to close the underlying data sets (CLOSE). However, there are also many differences.

One big difference is that separate CREATE statements are not used to create an index and an index space. An index space is the underlying storage structure for index data and it is automatically created by DB2 whenever an index is created. There can only be one index in an index space.

Of course, there are many other differences because indexes are different from table spaces, and serve different data processing needs.

In DB2, uniqueness is enforced using an index. You can create a unique index that forces the columns specified for the index to be unique within the table. If you try to INSERT or UPDATE these columns with non-unique values, an error code is returned and the request fails. Creating a unique index is the only way to ensure uniqueness for a column (or columns) in DB2.

You can use an index to guide DB2 to control how table space data is physically stored on disk. This is called *clustering*. A DB2 index is a clustering index if the CLUSTER keyword is specified when the index is created. Clustering causes inserted rows to be stored contiguously in sequence whenever possible. Additionally, when the table space is reorganized the data will be sequenced according to the clustering index. Since there can only be one physical sequence for data on disk, there can only be one clustering index per table. If you do not specify a clustering index DB2 will choose to cluster the data using the oldest existing index. It is wise to explicitly specify a clustering index instead of letting DB2 decide because you will almost always choose better than the (basically random) choice DB2 makes.

V8 Indexes also can be used to control partitioning. Prior to DB2 V8, a partitioning index was the only way to partition data. As of V8, though, partitioning can be specified and controlled in the table DDL. Notwithstanding this separation of partitioning from indexing, an index can be partitioned itself into separate data sets.

Indexed columns can be specified as ascending or descending. This is accomplished by specifying either ASC or DESC after each column in the index. Specifying ASC causes index entries to be in ascending order by the column (this is the default). DESC puts the index entries in descending order by the column.

Finally, through the use of the DEFINE and DEFER parameters DB2 can delay the creation of the index and its data sets until a later time.

Index Considerations

Before creating any indexes, you should analyze your data and consider the following factors:

- Percentage of table access versus table update
- Data access patterns, both ad hoc and planned
- Amount of data accessed by each query against the table
- Impact on recovery
- Performance requirements of accessing the table
- Performance requirements of modifying the table
- Frequency of INSERT, UPDATE, and DELETE operations
- Storage requirements
- Impact of reorganization
- Impact on the LOAD utility

Remember that indexes are created to enhance performance. Although an index may speed up the performance of a query, each new index will degrade data modification. Keep the following in mind as you create indexes:

- Consider indexing on columns used in WHERE, GROUP BY, ORDER BY, and UNION ALL clauses.
- Limit the indexing of frequently updated columns.
- If indexing a table, explicitly create a clustering index. Failure to do so will result in DB2 clustering data by the first index created. If indexes are subsequently dropped and re-created, this can change the clustering sequence if the indexes are created in a different order.
- Consider clustering on columns in GROUP BY and ORDER BY specifications to improve sequential access.
- If no sorting or grouping is required, analyze your WHERE clauses and cluster on the columns most frequently referenced, or better yet, most frequently run.

---

[1] *Actually, if no clustering index is explicitly defined, DB2 uses the index with the lowest OBID to cluster the data. This usually results in the oldest index being used for clustering, but not necessarily because OBIDs can be reused.*

- Choose the first column of multi-column indexes wisely, based on the following hierarchy. First, choose columns that will be specified most frequently in SQL WHERE clauses (unless cardinality is very low). Second, choose columns that will be referenced most often in ORDER BY and GROUP BY clauses (once again, unless cardinality is very low). Third, choose columns with the highest cardinality.

> **NOTE**
>
> Low cardinality of the first column is not an issue if a filtering value will always be provided in each query using equality, for example, a predicate like WHERE COL = :HOSTVAR or WHERE COL IN (list).

- The biggest payback from an index comes from DB2's capability to locate and retrieve referenced data quickly. DB2's capability to do this is reduced when cardinality is low because multiple RIDs satisfy a given reference. Balance the cardinality of a column against the amount of time it is accessed, giving preference to data access over cardinality.

- There are no hard and fast rules for index creation. Experiment with different index combinations and gauge the efficiency of the results.

- Keep the number of columns in an index to a minimum. If only three columns are needed, index only those three columns. As more columns are added to the index, data modification degrades.

- Sometimes, however, it can be advantageous to include additional columns in an index to increase the chances of index-only access. (Index-only access is discussed further in Chapter 21, "The Optimizer.") For example, suppose that there is an index on the DEPTNO column of the DSN8810.DEPT table. The following query may use this index:

```
SELECT   DEPTNAME
FROM     DSN8810.DEPT
WHERE    DEPTNO > 'D00';
```

DB2 could use the index to access only those columns with a DEPTNO greater than D00, and then access the data to return the DEPT.

> **NOTE**
>
> A good rule of thumb for index creation is to keep creating indexes to enhance the performance of your queries until the performance of data modification becomes unacceptable. Then, delete the last index you created. This general approach is best described as creating indexes until it hurts.

Indexing Variable Columns

V8 Prior to Version 8, when indexing on a variable column, DB2 automatically pads the variable column out to its maximum size. So, for example, creating an index on a column defined as VARCHAR(50) will cause the index key to be padded out to the full 50 bytes. Padding poses several problems. You cannot get index-only access with a padded index because DB2 will always have to access the table space data to retrieve the actual size of each column. Remember, the size of a variable-length column is stored in a two-byte prefix and this information is not in a padded index. Also, padding very large variable columns can create a very large index with a lot of wasted space.

DB2 V8 offers the capability to direct DB2 as to whether variable columns in an index should be padded. Appropriately enough, a new option, PADDED (or NOT PADDED) can be specified when creating indexes. The specification is made at the index level, so every variable column in the index will be either padded or not padded.

When PADDED is specified, DB2 will create the index just as it did prior to V8—by padding all variable columns to their maximum size. When NOT PADDED is specified, DB2 will treat the columns as variable and you will be able to obtain index-only access. The length information will be stored in the index key.

> **NOTE**
>
> Keep in mind that DB2 cannot perform index-only access using a padded index—even if every required column exists in the index. This is so because the actual length of the VARCHAR column(s) is not stored in a padded index. So, DB2 will have to access the table to retrieve the length from the two-byte column prefix.

V8 A new DSNZPARM, named PADIX, is provided to control whether the default is PADDED or NOT PADDED when an index is created and neither is specified. By default, DB2 will create PADDED indexes if you migrate from V7 to V8 but will create NOT PADDED indexes if you install V8 from scratch.

> **CAUTION**
>
> Remember the precaution from Chapter 5, "Data Definition Guidelines," to avoid defaults. Set up the PADIX parameter to create the type of indexes you prefer by default, but when creating indexes be sure to explicitly specify either PADDED or NOT PADDED so that you are assured of creating the type of index you want to create every time. Relying on defaults is lazy and potentially fraught with problems.

Indexing and Partitioning

V8 The indexing requirements for partitioning change significantly in DB2 Version 8. For all releases of DB2 up through and including Version 7, a partitioning index is required to specify the limit keys for each partition; this means that a partitioning index was required and was used to determine which data goes into which partition.

This all changes with DB2 Version 8. To understand partitioning in DB2 V8, first we need to define some terminology: namely, partitioned versus partitioning.

> **Partitioned and non-partitioned**—A partitioned index means that the index itself is physically partitioned into separate data sets; a non-partitioned index, though, might still be a partitioning index.
>
> **Partitioning and secondary index**—A partitioning index means that the index keys correlate to the columns used to partition the data. The index might or might not also be partitioned.

Control of partitioning changes from index-controlled to table-controlled as of DB2 V8. Actually, DB2 V8 supports both types of partitioning, but table-controlled partitioning enables new features not supported under index-controlled partitioning. For example, the ability to easily add or rotate partitions is only supported with table-controlled partitioning.

> **CAUTION**
>
> DB2 will automatically switch from index-based to table-based partitioning if any of the following operations are performed:
>
> - Dropping the partitioning index
> - Altering the partitioning index to be not clustered
> - Adding a partition using ALTER TABLE ADD PART
> - Rotating partitions using ALTER TABLE ALTER PART ROTATE
> - Altering a partition using ALTER TABLE ALTER PART *n*
> - Creating a data-partitioned secondary index (DPSI)
> - Creating an index with the VALUES clause, but without the CLUSTER keyword

V8 When creating partitioned table spaces using DB2 Version 8 or greater, use table-controlled partitioning instead of index-controlled partitioning. Also, you should seriously consider switching your current index-controlled partitioning structures to be table-controlled because of the additional flexibility and functionality it provides.

Clustering and Partitioning

V8 Prior to DB2 V8, the partitioning index for a partitioned table space had to be a clustering index. This means that the data in the table space had to be clustered by the partitioning columns. As of DB2 V8, though, data in a partitioned table space no longer needs to be clustered by the partitioning key. That is, clustering and partitioning are completely independent from each other as of V8.

Data Partitioned Secondary Indexes

V8 One of the biggest problems DBAs face when they are managing large partitioned DB2 table spaces is contending with non-partitioned indexes. DB2 Version 8 helps to remedy these problems with a new type of index—the data partitioned secondary index, or DPSI (pronounced dipsy). However, before we examine the solution, let's first investigate the problem in a little more detail.

Problems With Non-Partitioning Indexes   Prior to V8, a partitioning index was required to define a partitioned table space. The CREATE INDEX statement specifies the range of values that DB2 will store in each specific partition. The partitioning index will have individual PART clauses, each of which specifies the highest value that can be stored in the partition. To illustrate, consider the following SQL to create a partitioning index:

```
CREATE INDEX XEMP2
  ON DSN8710.EMP (EMPNO ASC)
    USING STOGROUP DSN8G710
    PRIQTY 36 ERASE NO CLUSTER
      (PART 1 VALUES('H99'),
```

```
      PART 2 VALUES('P99'),
      PART 3 VALUES('Z99'),
      PART 4 VALUES('999'))
 BUFFERPOOL BP1
 CLOSE YES
 COPY YES;
```

This creates four partitions. Behind the scenes, DB2 will create four separate data sets—both for the table space data and for the index data. However, all other indexes defined on the table will be regular, non-clustering DB2 indexes—that is, non-partitioning indexes (NPIs). An NPI resides in a single data set unless the PIECESIZE clause is used to break it apart—and even then the data will not be broken apart by partition. (The PIECESIZE clause is covered in more detail later in this chapter.)

> **NOTE**
>
> **V8**   As of DB2 V8, NPIs are also referred to as NPSIs (where the S stands for secondary). In this book, the terms NPI and NPSI are used synonymously.

NPIs can cause contention, particularly with DB2 utilities. You can run a utility against a single table space or index partition, but you do not have that luxury with NPIs because they are not partitioned. You can minimize and manage downtime by running utilities a partition at a time. However, running utilities against NPIs can impact the availability of an entire table space. Because an NPI contains data for an entire table space, not just for a single partition, utility operations on an NPI can cause downtime across an entire table space. Additionally, contention on NPIs can cause performance bottlenecks during parallel update, insert, and delete operations.

V8 **Solving Problems with DPSIs?**   DB2 V8 introduces the Data Partitioned Secondary Index, or DPSI. DPSIs are significant because they help to resolve the problems involved with NPIs discussed in the preceding section. A DPSI is basically a partitioned NPI.

Consult Figure 6.2 for a graphical depiction of the difference between a DPSI and an NPI. This diagram shows a table space partitioned by month. We need to build an index on the CUSTNO for access requirements, but we have a choice as to whether we create an NPI or a DPSI. You can see the different results in the diagram: The DPSI will be partitioned by the same key ranges as the table, but the NPI will not be partitioned at all.

So, with a DPSI the index will be partitioned based on the data rows. The number of parts in the index will be equal to the number of parts in the table space—even though the DPSI is created based on columns that are different from those used to define the partitioning scheme for the table space. Therefore, partition 1 of the DPSI will be for the same rows as partition 1 of the table space, and so on. These changes provide many benefits, including

- The ability to cluster by a secondary index

- The ability to drop and rotate partitions easily

- Potentially less overhead in data sharing

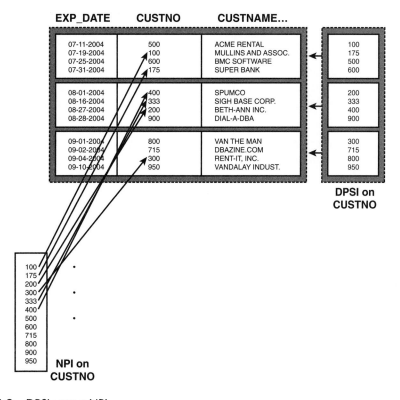

EXP_DATE   CUSTNO   CUSTNAME...

EXP_DATE	CUSTNO	CUSTNAME...	
07-11-2004	500	ACME RENTAL	100
07-19-2004	100	MULLINS AND ASSOC.	175
07-25-2004	600	BMC SOFTWARE	500
07-31-2004	175	SUPER BANK	600
08-01-2004	400	SPUMCO	200
08-16-2004	333	SIGH BASE CORP.	333
08-27-2004	200	BETH-ANN INC.	400
08-28-2004	900	DIAL-A-DBA	900
09-01-2004	800	VAN THE MAN	300
09-02-2004	715	DBAZINE.COM	715
09-04-2004	300	RENT-IT, INC.	800
09-10-2004	950	VANDALAY INDUST.	950

DPSI on CUSTNO

100
175
200
300
333
400
500
600
715
800
900
950

NPI on CUSTNO

FIGURE 6.2   DPSI versus NPI.

NPIs historically have caused DB2 performance and availability problems, especially with utilities. DPSIs solve many of these problems. With DPSIs there is an independent index tree structure for every partition. This means that utilities do not have to share pages or index structures. In addition, logical drains on indexes are now physically at the partition level. This helps utility processing in several useful ways. For example, you can run a LOAD by partition with no contention because the DPSI is partitioned the same way as the data and the partitioning index. Additionally, when reorganizing with DPSIs, the BUILD2 phase is not needed. Even your recovery procedures might be aided because you can copy and recover a single partition of a DPSI.

However, DPSIs are not magical objects that solve all problems. Indeed, changing an NPI to a DPSI will likely cause some queries to perform worse than before. Some queries will need to examine multiple partitions of the DPSI as opposed to the single NPI it previously used. On the other hand, if the query has predicates that reference columns in a single partition only, then performance might improve because only one DPSI partition needs to be probed.

Keep in mind that each DPSI partition has its own index structure. So, a query could potentially have to probe each of these individual index structures to use the DPSI. This type of operation, obviously, will not perform as well as a single probe that would be required against the NPI. So, of course, not every index on a partitioned table should be a DPSI. An additional drawback is that a DPSI cannot be defined as a unique index.

The bottom line on whether to create DPSIs or NPIs is that you will need to analyze your data access and utility processing requirements. DPSIs are easier to manage and can be processed more efficiently by utilities, but can require special query formulation to be efficient. NPIs are typically most efficient for general-purpose queries but come with a lot of administration baggage.

Before using DPSIs, you will have to examine your queries to determine predicate usage and the potential performance impact.

Indexes and Column Cardinality

Column cardinality (that is, the number of distinct values for a column) is an important consideration when building composite indexes. You should analyze column cardinality for columns in a multi-column index.

DB2 records and stores column cardinality in the DB2 Catalog and then uses this information when optimizing SQL to determine access paths. The following cardinality columns are used by the DB2 optimizer:

> COLCARDF—Contains the number of distinct values for this column. The optimizer uses this column to calculate the filter factor for a composite index when equals predicates are not specified for each column. Found in SYSIBM.SYSCOLUMNS for non-partitioned indexes or SYSIBM.SYSCOLSTATS for partitioned indexes.

> FIRSTKEYCARDF—Contains the number of distinct values of the first column in an index. This information is captured only for the first column in a multi-column index. It will be used by the DB2 optimizer when calculating the filter factor for a predicate on a single-column index. Found in SYSIBM.SYSINDEXES for non-partitioned indexes or SYSIBM.SYSINDEXSTATS for partitioned indexes.

> FULLKEYCARDF (SYSIBM.SYSINDEXES)—Contains the number of distinct values for the combined, entire key (all columns) of an index. The optimizer uses this column to calculate the filter factor for a composite index when an equality predicate is specified for each column of a multi-column index. Found in SYSIBM.SYSINDEXES for non-partitioned indexes or SYSIBM.SYSINDEXSTATS for partitioned indexes.

Modifying Indexes

As data is added to the table, it is also added to every index defined on the table. For INSERT operations, new keys are placed in the proper sequence in the index. Existing keys are moved to the right to make room for the new entry. If there is not enough room on the page for the new entry, DB2 will try to find space on *neighboring* pages or on the next free page. When a neighboring page is used, DB2 attempts to redistribute entries in the pages to accommodate the INSERT operation.

As data is deleted from the table, it must also be removed from every index defined on the table. The more indexes defined to a table, the more time it will take for DB2 to perform DELETE operations.

For UPDATE operations, indexes are impacted only if the columns being modified participate in an index. The more indexes containing the columns being modified, the longer the UPDATE will take.

Forming Index Levels

As data is added to the index it will grow and change. For very small indexes, the root page can also act as a leaf page. As data is added, the root page will fill up. When the index becomes too large to accommodate both root and leaf page data, DB2 creates two new leaf pages. Each of these leaf pages will contain half the entries that were in the original root page. The root page will contain pointers to the leaf pages. You have just witnessed the birth of a new index.

Over time, as more data is added, more index entries are added. Eventually, the root page grows too large, causing DB2 to create two more new pages. These will be nonleaf pages, each containing half of the entries that were in the root page. The root page now contains pointers to nonleaf pages—and thus, another new level is born.

The greater the number of levels in an index, the less efficient it becomes. This is so because DB2 needs to perform an additional I/O operation for an index lookup for each new level in the index.

Index Guidelines

Consider the following guidelines when planning the index strategy for your DB2 databases and applications.

Use Workload As a Basis for Indexing   The basic trick to creating the appropriate indexes is to analyze your workload and build indexes to match. Indexing one table at a time is unlikely to produce a batch of indexes that will match your actual workload. The trick is to choose a workload to optimize. Choose an important workload, such as month-end processing or another peak processing time. You might also choose a workload for a specific application or group of applications.

After you choose the workload, you will need to examine the queries in the workload, documenting each table that is accessed and the frequency of each query run during the workload. Favor building indexes to optimize the queries that run the most often. For example, it is more beneficial to create an index to optimize a query that runs 1,000 times a day, than for a query that runs 3 times a day.

Then, factor in the relative priority of each query. You might favor building indexes to optimize very important queries over other queries that might run more frequently. For example, a query (Q1) that is only run 10 times a day might be more important than another query (Q2) that runs 120 times a day. Why? Reasons might include the following:

- Q1 is more important to the business than Q2 because it brings in more revenue, satisfies more customers, or reduces spending.

- Q1 is used by an important business user, such as the CEO or perhaps your most important customers.

- Q1 is required for regulatory or legal reasons.

- The users of Q1 are willing to spend more to optimize their query than the users of Q2; of course, approach this scenario with caution, because financial clout should not be the only consideration for DB2 query optimization.

When you have sufficiently ranked each query in a particular workload you can begin to build indexes for the most important queries in the workload. At least the top 30% most critical processes should have optimal indexes built for them, taking into consideration the predicate filtering and sequencing required.

Be sure to consider each workload profile and its performance requirements as you embark on an index creation strategy.

Be Aware of Data Modification   Remember, indexing optimizes the performance of data access but degrades the performance of data modification. Every INSERT or DELETE performed on a table will also insert or delete the data from every index defined on the table. Additionally, an UPDATE to a column in a table will cause DB2 to update any index that references that column.

In general, keep adding indexes until the impact on data modification causes your applications to be able to meet the necessary performance and service levels. When modification performance becomes unacceptable, remove the last index (or indexes) created until the performance of modification becomes tolerable.

Uniqueness Recommendations   You can enforce the uniqueness of a column or a group of columns by creating a unique index on those columns. You can have more than one unique index per table.

It usually is preferable to enforce the uniqueness of columns by creating unique indexes, thereby allowing the DBMS to do the work. The alternative is to code uniqueness logic in an application program to do the same work that DB2 does automatically.

CAUTION

Remember: If security is liberal for application tables, ad hoc SQL users can modify table data without the application program, and thereby insert or update columns that should be unique to non-unique values. However, this cannot happen if a unique index is defined on the columns.

Create a Unique Index for Each Primary Key   Every primary key explicitly defined for a table must be associated with a corresponding unique index. If you do not create a unique index for a primary key, an incomplete key is defined for the table, making the table inaccessible.

Use WHERE NOT NULL to Allow Multiple Nulls in a UNIQUE Index   Specify the UNIQUE WHERE NOT NULL clause to enable multiple nulls to exist in a unique index. This is useful when an index contains at least one nullable column, but all non-null entries must be unique.

Create Indexes for Foreign Keys   Unless an index already exists for access reasons or the table is too small to be indexed, create an index for each foreign key defined for a table. Because DB2's referential integrity feature accesses data defined as a foreign key behind the scenes, it's a good idea to enhance the efficiency of this access by creating indexes.

When to Avoid Indexing   There are only a few situations when you should consider not defining indexes for a table. Consider avoiding indexing when the table is very small, that is, less than 100 or so pages. However, there are scenarios where even a small table can benefit from being indexed (for example, for uniqueness or for specific, high-performance access requirements).

Another scenario where indexing might not be advantageous is when the table has heavy insert and delete activity but is relatively small, that is, less than 200 or so pages.

A table also should not be indexed if it *always* is accessed with a scan—in other words, if there is no conditional predicate access to the table.

When to Avoid Placing Columns in an Index   Sometimes you should not define indexes for columns. If the column is updated frequently and the table is less than 200 or so pages, consider avoiding placing the column in an index.

Avoid defining an index for a column if an index on the column exists that would make the new index redundant. For example, if an index exists on COL1, COL2 in TABLE1, a second index on COL1 only is redundant. An index on COL2 alone is not redundant because it is not the first column in the index.

When to Specify Extra Index Columns   When the column or columns to be indexed contain non-unique data, consider adding an extra column to increase the cardinality of the index. This reduces the index RID list and avoids chaining—an inefficient method of processing index entries. Uniqueness can be gauged by determining the cardinality for the columns in the index. The cardinality for the columns is nothing more than the number of distinct values stored in the columns. If this number is small (for example, less than 10% of the total number of rows for the table), consider adding extra columns to the index. (A column's cardinality can be found in the DB2 Catalog using queries presented in Part IV, "DB2 Performance Monitoring.")

V8   **Control the Length of Index Keys**   DB2 V8 permits indexes to be defined with keys of up to 2,000 bytes. The previous limit for index key length was 255.

> **CAUTION**
>
> The maximum size of a partitioning key is still 255 whether partitioning is index-controlled or table-controlled.

Of course, just because DB2 permits greater key lengths does not mean that you should pad more columns into your indexes. For example, just blindly adding every column to every index to support more index-only access is generally not a wise idea. Be sure that there is a reasoned, practical need for each column defined to an index.

CAUTION

To calculate the actual physical limit for index key length you must take nullable columns into account. Subtract 1 from the maximum length for every column that is nullable. So, if an index contains 5 columns, 3 of which can be set to null, the total length of the 5 columns can be no greater than 1997 (2000–3 = 1997).

Indexing Large and Small Tables   For tables over 100 (or so) pages, it is best to define at least one index. If the table is very large (over 10,000 pages), try to limit the indexes to those that are absolutely necessary for adequate performance. When a large table has multiple indexes, data modification performance can suffer. When large tables lack indexes, however, access efficiency will suffer. This fragile balance must be monitored closely. In most situations, more indexes are better than fewer indexes because most applications are query-intensive rather than update-intensive.

For tables containing a small number of pages (up to 100 or so pages) consider limiting indexes to those required for uniqueness and perhaps to support common join criterion. Add indexes also when the performance of queries that access the table suffers. Test the performance of the query after the index is created, though, to ensure that the index helps. When you index a small table, increased I/O (due to index accesses) may cause performance to suffer when compared to a complete scan of all the data in the table.

Promote Index-Only Access   When an index contains all of the columns being selected in a query, DB2 can choose to use index-only access. With index-only access, DB2 will read all of the data required from the index without having to access the table space. Index-only access can reduce the number of I/Os required to satisfy a query. For example, consider the following query:

```
SELECT   DEPTNAME, MGRNO
FROM     DSN8810.DEPT
WHERE    DEPTNO > 'D00';
```

Now, also consider that there is only one index on this table—a two-column index on DEPTNO and MGRNO. DB2 will most likely choose to use this index to satisfy the DEPTNO > 'D00' predicate. But, if we add the DEPTNAME column to this index, DB2 can conceivably use this index for index-only access because all of the required columns are stored in the index.

So, it can be worthwhile to extend an index with an additional column or two to encourage index-only access. However, this practice should be deployed with care; you do not want to overload every index, because it will become unwieldy to manage.

When deciding whether to extend an index to encourage index-only access, be sure to consider the following factors:

- Adding extra columns to an index will increase the size of the index requiring additional storage.

- Adding extra columns to an index might increase the number of levels in the index, especially if the table is very large. Additional levels can degrade performance.

- The sequencing of columns in a multi-column index is important and can significantly impact performance if chosen improperly.

- Use caution when choosing the indexes to be overloaded; consider overloading indexes for index-only access only for the most important or performance-critical queries in your applications.

Multi-column Indexes   If a table has only multi-column indexes, try to specify the high-level column in the WHERE clause of your query. This action results in an index scan with at least one matching column.

A multi-column index *can* be used to scan data to satisfy a query in which the high-level column is not specified (but another column in the index is specified). However, a non-matching index scan of this sort is not as efficient as a matching index scan.

Consider Several Indexes Instead of a Multi-column Index   Because DB2 can utilize multiple indexes in an access path for a single SQL statement, multiple indexes might be more efficient (from a global perspective) than a single multi-column index. If access to the columns varies from query to query, multiple indexes might provide better overall performance for all your queries, at the expense of an individual query.

If you feel that multiple indexes might be of benefit for your specific situation, test their effectiveness first in a test environment by

- Dropping the multi-column index

- Creating a single index for each of the columns in the multi-column index

- Updating DB2 Catalog statistics to indicate production volume

- Running EXPLAIN on all the affected queries and analyzing the results

> **CAUTION**
>
> It is not common for the DB2 optimizer to choose multiple-index access in practice. Use caution before dropping a multi-column index in favor of multiple indexes because, after optimization, DB2 might choose to use only one of the indexes instead of a multiple index strategy.

Multi-Index Access   DB2 can use more than one index to satisfy a data retrieval request. For example, consider two indexes on the DSN8810.DEPT table: one index for DEPTNO and another index for ADMRDEPT. If you executed the following query, DB2 could use both of these indexes to satisfy the request:

```
SELECT    DEPTNO, DEPTNAME, MGRNO
FROM      DSN8810.DEPT
WHERE     DEPTNO > 'D00'
AND       ADMRDEPT = 'D01';
```

If multi-index access is used, the index on DEPTNO is used to retrieve all departments with a DEPTNO greater than 'D00', and the index on ADMRDEPT is used to retrieve only rows containing 'D01'. Then these rows are intersected and the correct result is returned.

An alternative to the multi-index access just described is a single multi-column index. If you create one index for the combination of columns ADMRDEPT and DEPTNO, DB2 could use this index, as well. When deciding whether to use multiple indexes or multi-column indexes, consider the following guidelines:

- Multi-index access is usually less efficient than access by a single multi-column index.

- Many multi-column indexes require more DASD than multiple single-column indexes.

- Consider the access criteria for all applications that will be querying the table that must be indexed. If the indexing needs are light, a series of multi-column indexes is usually the best solution. If the indexing needs are heavy and many combinations and permutations of columns are necessary to support the access criteria, multiple single-column indexes could be a better solution.

- Sometimes one multi-column index can fit the needs of many different access criteria. For example, suppose that the DSN8810.EMP table (see Appendix A, "DB2 Sample Tables") has three access needs, as follows:

LASTNAME only
LASTNAME and FIRSTNME
LASTNAME, FIRSTNME, and BONUS

One index on the concatenation of the LASTNAME, FIRSTNME, and BONUS columns would efficiently handle the access needs for this table. When only LASTNAME is required, only the first column of the index is used. When both LASTNAME and FIRSTNME are specified in a query, only the first two columns are used. Finally, if all three columns are specified in a query, the index uses all three columns.

With index screening, DB2 also could use the same three column index to satisfy a query specifying only LASTNAME and BONUS. A matching index scan would be performed on LASTNAME, and then DB2 could screen the index for the BONUS values.

Of course, you might need to create indexes for one (or both) of the other two indexes if they are needed to maintain uniqueness.

- Consider the tradeoff of DASD versus performance, and weigh the access criteria to determine the best indexing scenario for your implementation.

Specify Appropriate Index Parameters   The first design decision to be made when defining an indexing strategy for a table is to choose a useful clustering strategy. Clustering reduces I/O. The DB2 optimizer usually tries to use an index on a clustered column before using other indexes. Choose your clustering index wisely; in general, use the index accessed for scanning most often, because clustering improves sequential access more than random access.

Specify index-free space the same as the table space free space. The same reason for the free space in the table space applies to the free space in the index. Remember that index row sizes are smaller than table row sizes, so plan accordingly when calculating free space. Also, as PCTFREE increases, the frequency of page splitting decreases and the efficiency of index updates increases.

When an index page is completely filled and a new entry must be inserted, DB2 splits the index leaf page involved in two, moving half the data to a new page. Splits can cause DB2 to lock at many levels of the index, possibly causing splits all the way back to the root page. This splitting activity is inefficient and should be avoided by prudent use of free space and frequent index reorganizations. DB2 also uses a free page for splits if one is available within 64 pages of the original page being split. Use the suggestions in Table 6.1 as a rough guideline for specifying PCTFREE and FREEPAGE based on insert and update frequency. Of course, these are very rough guidelines and your free space allocations will vary according to the volatility of your data and the frequency of reorganization.

TABLE 6.1   Index Free Space Allocation Chart

Type of Index Processing	FREEPAGE	PCTFREE
Read only	0	0
Less than 20% of volume inserted or updated between REORGs	0	10 to 20
Twenty to 60% of volume inserted or updated between REORGs	63	20 to 30
Greater than 60% of volume inserted or updated between REORGs	15	20 to 30

Additionally, refer to the VCAT versus STOGROUP considerations presented in Chapter 5. The same considerations that apply to table space allocation also apply to index allocation.

Create Indexes Before Loading Tables   The LOAD utility updates indexes efficiently. Usually, the LOAD utility is more efficient than building indexes for tables that already contain data. The data being loaded should be sorted into the order of the clustering index before execution.

Consider Deferring Index Creation   The DEFER option on the CREATE INDEX statement allows the index to be created but not populated. The RECOVER INDEX utility can then be executed to populate the index. This will speed the index creation process because REBUILD INDEX usually populates index entries faster than CREATE INDEX.

Creating a STOGROUP-defined index with DEFER YES causes the underlying VSAM data set for the index to be allocated.

Additionally, the DB2 catalog is updated to record that the index exists. But, if the table being indexed currently contains data, DB2 will turn on the recover pending flag for the index space and issue a +610 SQLCODE. Subsequent execution of RECOVER INDEX will turn off the recover pending flag and populate the index.

Consider Deferring Index Data Set Definition   The DEFINE parameter can be used to control when the underlying data set(s) for the index space are created. DEFINE YES, which is the default, indicates that the data sets are created when the index is created. DEFINE NO indicates that data set creation will not occur until data is inserted in to the index. The DEFINE parameter should be used only with STORGROUP-defined indexes; it will be ignored if specified for VCAT-defined indexes.

Specifying DEFINE NO can be useful to minimize the number of data sets where indexes are being created on empty tables that will remain empty for some time.

Let DB2 Tell You What Indexes to Create   Consider using CREATE INDEX with the DEFER YES option to create many different indexes for new applications. The indexes will be recorded in the DB2 catalog, but will not be populated. Then, update the statistics in the DB2 catalog to indicate anticipated production volumes and run EXPLAIN on your performance-sensitive queries.

Use REBUILD INDEX to populate the indexes that were used and drop the indexes that were not used. In this way DB2 can help you choose which indexes will be useful.

Store Index and Table Space Data Sets Separately   You should assign indexes to different STOGROUPs or different volumes than the table spaces containing the tables to which the indexes apply. This reduces head contention and increases I/O efficiency. This is especially important for tables and indexes involved in parallel queries.

Consider Separate Index Buffer Pools   Consider placing critical indexes in a different buffer pool from your table spaces. For more in-depth buffer pool consideration, see Chapter 28, "Tuning DB2's Components."

PRIQTY **and** SECQTY   If you are defining indexes using the STOGROUP method, you must specify primary and secondary space allocations. The primary allocation is the amount of physical storage allocated when the index is created. As the amount of data in the index grows, secondary allocations of storage are taken. Use the guidelines specified for table space space allocations to guide your index space allocation efforts.

The default values for index PRIQTY and SECQTY are the same as the 4KB page size defaults for table space PRIQTY and SECQTY.

Use PIECESIZE **to Explicitly Define Index Data Set Size**   Consider using the PIECESIZE clause to specify the largest data set size for a non-partitioned index.

The creation of non-partitioning indexes (NPIs) on tables in a partitioned table space has been one of the most vexing problems facing DBAs. Partitioned table spaces tend to be large and by their very design will span multiple underlying data sets. The partitioning index that defines the partitioning key and key ranges also spans multiple data sets. There can be only one partitioning index per partitioned table space. What happens when you need to define more than one index on a table in a partitioned table space?

Well, in the old days (pre-V5), the DBA could not control the creation of the underlying data set(s) used for NPIs. As of V5, the PIECESIZE clause of the CREATE INDEX statement can be used during index creation to break an NPI into several data sets (or *pieces*). More accurately, the PIECESIZE clause specifies the largest data set size for a non-partitioned index. PIECESIZE can be specified in kilobytes, megabytes, or gigabytes. For example, the following statement will limit the size of individual data sets for the XACT2 index to 256 megabytes:

```
CREATE TYPE 2 UNIQUE INDEX DSN8710.XACT2
   ON DSN8710.ACT (ACTKWD ASC)
   USING STOGROUP DSN8G710
       PRIQTY 65536K
       SECQTY 8192K
       ERASE NO
   BUFFERPOOL BP0
   CLOSE NO
   PIECESIZE 256M;
```

Basically, PIECESIZE is used to enable NPIs to be created on very large partitioned table spaces. It breaks apart the NPI into separate pieces that can be somewhat managed individually. Without PIECESIZE, NPIs would be quite difficult to manage and administer. Keep in mind, though, that PIECESIZE does not magically partition an NPI based on the partitioning scheme of the table space. This is a common misperception of the PIECESIZE clause. So, if you have a partitioned table space with four partitions and then create an NPI with four pieces, the data in the NPI pieces will not match up with the data in the four partitions.

When using PIECESIZE, more data sets will be created, and therefore you can obtain greater control over data set placement. Placing the pieces on separate disk devices can help to reduce I/O contention for SQL operations that access NPIs during read or update processing. The elapsed time improvement might be even greater when multiple tasks are accessing the NPI.

Separating the NPI into pieces allows for better performance of INSERT, UPDATE, and DELETE processes by eliminating bottlenecks that can be caused by using only one data set for the index. The use of pieces also improves concurrency and performance of heavy INSERT, UPDATE, and DELETE processing against any size partitioned table space with NPIs.

Keep in mind that PIECESIZE is only a specification of the maximum amount of data that a piece (that is, a data set) can hold and not the actual allocation of storage, so PIECESIZE has no effect on primary and secondary space allocation. Each data set will max out at the PIECESIZE value, so specifying PRIQTY greater than PIECESIZE will waste space.

> **CAUTION**
>
> Avoid setting the PIECESIZE too small. A new data set is allocated each time the PIECESIZE threshold is reached. DB2 increments the A001 component of the data set name each time. This makes the *physical* limit 999 data sets (A001 through A999). If PIECESIZE is set too small, the data set name can limit the overall size of the table space. Ideally, the value of your primary quantity and secondary quantities should be evenly divisible into PIECESIZE to avoid wasting space.

To choose a PIECESIZE value, divide the overall size of the entire NPI by the number of data sets that you want to have. For example, for an NPI that is 8 megabytes, you can arrive at four data sets for the NPI by specifying PIECESIZE 2M. Of course, if your NPI grows over eight megabytes in total you will get additional data sets. Keep in mind that 32 pieces is the limit if the underlying table space is not defined with DSSIZE 4G or greater. The limit is 254 pieces if the table space is defined as DSSIZE 4G or greater.

Index Image Copies   As of DB2 V6 and later, it is possible to use the COPY utility to make backup image copies of index data sets. You also can use the RECOVER utility on index image copies to recover indexes. To use COPY on indexes, the COPY parameter must be set to YES. The default value for the COPY parameter is NO.

> **NOTE**
>
> The REBUILD utility can be used to rebuild indexes from the underlying data in the table. REBUILD can be executed on any index regardless of the value of the COPY parameter.

Indexing Auxiliary Tables   Only one index can be specified on an auxiliary table. The index cannot specify any columns. The default key for an index on an auxiliary table is implicitly defined as a ROWID, which is a unique 19-byte, DB2-generated value. For more information on auxiliary tables consult Chapter 9, "Large Objects and Object/Relational Databases."

Type 2 Indexes Are Required   Prior to DB2 V6, there were two types of indexes available to DB2: Type 1 and Type 2. Type 2 indexes were introduced with DB2 Version 4; Type 1 indexes had been available since Version 1 of DB2. However, as of DB2 V6, Type 1 indexes are obsolete and no longer supported. Type 2 indexes are the only type of index that can be defined. Type 2 indexes provide the following benefits over Type 1 indexes:

- Eliminate index locking (the predominant cause of contention in most pre-V4 DB2 applications).

- Do not use index subpages.

- Are the only type supported for ASCII encoded tables.

- Many newer DB2 features cannot be used unless Type 2 indexes are used; these features include row level locking, data sharing, full partition independence, uncommitted reads, UNIQUE WHERE NOT NULL, and CPU and Sysplex parallelism.

NOTE

The TYPE 2 clause can be explicitly specified in the CREATE INDEX statement. However, if it is not specified, DB2 will create a Type 2 index anyway. As of DB2 V6, it does not matter whether TYPE 2 is explicitly specified in the CREATE INDEX statement; Type 2 indexes are the only indexes that will be created by DB2. Furthermore, as of DB2 V8, DB2 will not work with Type 1 indexes, only Type 2 indexes.

9

CHAPTER **7**

Database Change Management and Schema Evolution

In Chapters 5 and 6 we examined how to create useful and efficient DB2 database objects. After we create databases, table spaces, tables, indexes, and so on, we build application programs to access the DB2 data and move everything into production. Eventually, we will need to change the database to meet changing business needs.

One of the bigger causes of database downtime is when changes are made to DB2 database structures. This is so because many of the most common changes required of DB2 objects cannot be supported with simple ALTERs. Instead, DBAs are required to DROP the object and then re-CREATE it with the desired changes.

Such changes can be tedious and error-prone. Suppose you need to extend the length of a column in a table, perhaps because business conditions have changed, necessitating longer values. For example, (for V7 and all previous releases) to change a CHAR(10) column to CHAR(15), the following steps need to occur:

1. Unload the data, and then extract the DDL and authorizations for the table you are about to change and all its dependent objects (indexes, views, synonyms, triggers, and so on).

2. Drop the table.

3. Modify the DDL for the table to change the length of the particular column from 10 to 15.

4. Run the CREATE statement to re-create the table.

V8

5. Run the CREATE statements for the dependent objects (indexes, views, synonyms, triggers, and so on).

6. Rebuild the authorizations for the table by running the appropriate GRANT statements.

7. Re-create all dependent objects and rebuild their authorizations.

8. Reload the data, taking care to build the LOAD statement properly, because there is a new column right in the middle of the other columns.

9. Don't forget to run RUNSTATS to gather statistics for optimization and run COPY to back up the data in its new format after it is loaded.

10. REBIND all affected plans and packages.

11. Test everything to make sure your changes were implemented correctly.

You can see how this intensive manual process can be very time-consuming, and the data is unavailable for the duration of this procedure. Furthermore, if you miss any single item or step, the resulting database structures will not be accurate and problems will arise.

Of course, not all database changes require such drastic steps. Many changes can be made using a simple ALTER to change specific aspects of a DB2 object. Sometimes the object will need to be stopped and started for the change to take effect, sometimes not. DB2 V8 features online schema evolution to begin the process of making more types of database changes possible without requiring objects to be dropped and re-created.

> **NOTE**
>
> Third-party ISV tools are available that make the process of modifying DB2 database structures easier and safer. These products provide a simple menu-driven interface that allows the user to indicate the changes to be made. The tool then automates the DROP and re-CREATE process. Examples of such products include BMC Software's Change Manager and Computer Associates' RC/Migrator. More information on products such as these is offered in Chapter 39, "Components of a Total DB2 Solution."

V8 DB2 V8 begins the process of making it easier to implement database changes with fewer steps and less downtime. IBM calls the changes being made to DB2 to facilitate simpler and quicker database changes *online schema evolution*. For example, as of V8 you can change a CHAR column to a larger size simply by using ALTER. The remainder of this chapter will focus on the improved schema changes supported by DB2 Version 8.

Online Schema Changes

DB2 database changes are more flexible with DB2 V8 due to online schema evolution. IBM also refers to this feature as simple schema evolution, online schema changes, or just schema changes.

V8

IBM introduced online schema evolution with DB2 V8 with the intention of allowing DB2 databases to be altered over time without causing an outage. Of course, this is the long-term goal of online schema evolution. We are in the first phases of this evolution with DB2 V8—and remember, evolution is a very lengthy process. It took many millions of years for life to evolve on Earth. The point is, it will take a long time for online schema evolution to enable every type of database change to be carried out without downtime.

> **CAUTION**
>
> For literal-minded readers, it most likely will not take millions of years for online schema evolution to support most types of database changes. I am simply using biological evolution as a metaphor for schema evolution.

Online Change Management Prior to V8

Of course, DB2 has offered some degree of online change management even prior to V8. For example, DB2 has provided the following capabilities for quite some time now:

- You can add a column to the end of a table without having to STOP access to the table or perhaps even modify any programs that access that table.

- A table can be renamed without dropping and re-creating the table.

- You can use ALTER to extend the length of a VARCHAR column to a greater size (but not to a smaller length).

- Application changes can be introduced and managed using package versioning.

- For DB2 data sharing, complex changes can be made to the DB2 engine code of a single member via PTFs while other members remain active.

- The REORG and LOAD RESUME utilities can be run online while concurrent workloads are being run against the data being reorganized or loaded.

These are just a few of the capabilities of DB2 change management, but some changes are not quite so easy.

Online Schema Changes for V8

Online schema evolution for DB2 V8 introduces some nice, new capabilities for managing database changes. What exactly can be changed today, as of DB2 Version 8?

You can extend the length of a CHAR column to a greater size (but not to a smaller length).

You can switch the data type of a column within character data types (CHAR, VARCHAR); within numeric data types (SMALLINT, INTEGER, FLOAT, REAL, FLOAT, DOUBLE, DECIMAL); and within graphic data types (GRAPHIC, VARGRAPHIC).

You cannot change character to numeric or graphic, numeric to character or graphic, or graphic to numeric or character.

The previous data type changes are permitted even for columns that are part of an index or referenced within a view.

You can alter identity columns.

You can add a column to an index.

You can change the clustering index for a table.

You can make many changes to partitioned and partitioning table spaces and indexes that were previously not allowed. For example, you can drop the partitioning index, create a table without a partitioning index, add a partition to the end of a table to extend the limit key value, rotate partitions, and re-balance partitions during a REORG.

You can better create and support indexes on variable length columns. Prior to V8 all indexes on variable columns were padded to their maximum size in the index. Now you can CREATE or ALTER an index to specify non-padded variable keys.

You can better support utility processing for database objects in utility-pending states (REORG pending, RECOVER pending, REBUILD pending).

Changing the Data Type of a Column

Sometimes it becomes necessary to change the data type of a column for an existing DB2 table. Prior to V8 this required dropping and re-creating the table, but as of V8 a column data type may be changed if the data can be converted from the old type to the new without losing significance. Essentially, this means that the new column definition has to allow for "larger" values than the current column definition.

The ALTER TABLE statement can be used to change the data type of a column as indicated in Table 7.1. If the combination is not shown in this table, it is not supported—that is, you cannot use ALTER to make such a change.

TABLE 7.1   Data Type Changes Supported By ALTER

Current Date Type	Supported New Data Type(s)
SMALLINT	INTEGER
	REAL
	DOUBLE,
	>=DECIMAL(5,0)
INTEGER	DOUBLE,
	>=DECIMAL(10,0)
REAL [or FLOAT(4)]	DOUBLE [or FLOAT(8)]
<=DECIMAL(15,m)	DOUBLE
DECIMAL(n,m)	DECIMAL(n+x,m+y)
CHAR(n)	CHAR(n+x)
	VARCHAR(n+x)
VARCHAR(n)	CHAR(n+x)
	VARCHAR(n+x)
GRAPHIC(n)	GRAPHIC(n+x)
	VARGRAPHIC(n+x)
VARGRAPHIC(n)	GRAPHIC(n+x)
	VARGRAPHIC(n+x)

V8

To change a data type under DB2 V8 you will use the SET DATATYPE clause of the ALTER TABLE statement. For example

```
ALTER TABLE DSN8810.EMP
  ALTER COLUMN EDLEVEL
  SET DATATYPE DECIMAL(7,0);
```

This is possible because the current data type of EDLEVEL was SMALLINT, so it can be changed to a DECIMAL with a scale of 5 or greater.

After the ALTER runs successfully, DB2 creates a new "version" of the table space. The definition of the data type is stored in the DB2 Catalog and immediately applies to the data. Up to 256 concurrent versions of a table space and up to 16 concurrent versions of an index can be maintained by DB2. See the section "Versioning for Online Schema Changes" later in this chapter for more details on versioning.

Keep in mind, though, that the existing data is not changed or reformatted on disk. Instead, when data is retrieved, the changed column(s) will be materialized in the new format.

Updating or inserting data will cause the row to be saved using the format of the new data type. When the object is reorganized or rebuilt, the data is converted to the format of the latest version specified in the DB2 Catalog. This technique allows DB2 to offer the greatest availability to users with minimal performance degradation.

Limitations on Changing a Data Type

Keep in mind that the data type can be changed only for character and numeric data types. You cannot change the data type of ROWID, DATE, TIME, TIMESTAMP, or FOR BIT DATA columns, nor can you change the length of an LOB column.

Additionally, you cannot change the data type or length of a column under the following circumstances:

- The column is part of a materialized query table.

- The column is part of a referential constraint.

- The column is defined as an IDENTITY column.

- The column has a FIELDPROC defined on it.

- There is an EDITPROC or VALIDPROC defined on the table in which the column resides.

For each of these items you will need to DROP and re-CREATE the table to modify the data type or change its length.

Impact of Changing a Data Type

When changing the data type for a column you need to be aware of the effect the change will have on other DB2 facilities and database objects. For example, when any column in a table has its data type changed, the *plans, packages, and cached dynamic statements* that reference the changed table are invalidated.

After changing a data type or length using ALTER, be sure to analyze all of the application programs that reference the column—using either static or dynamic SQL. You can query SYSIBM.SYSPLANDEP and SYSIBM.SYSPACKDEP to find which plans and packages reference the changed column's table using static SQL, but you will have to use other means such as your data dictionary or a SQL performance monitor to find dynamic SQL dependencies. As you examine the programs that are potentially impacted, pay particular attention to the *host variables* that are used in conjunction with the column. You will probably have to change the definition of the host variable to conform to the new definition of the column. Failure to do so can cause data to be truncated. For example, if a column is changed from CHAR(x) to CHAR(x+y), the processing application truncates the last y bytes unless the application is changed to accommodate the longer column.

Statistics in the DB2 Catalog are also an issue. Any distribution statistics for the column in SYSIBM.SYSCOLDIST and SYSIBM.SYSCOLDISTSTATS will be invalidated when its data type changes. Additionally, the STATSTIME column in SYSIBM.SYSCOLUMNS will be set to January 1, 0001. This tells the optimizer to ignore the distribution frequency statistics. Be sure to run the RUNSTATS utility to repopulate the catalog with accurate column and index statistics as soon as possible after changing a column data type or length.

Table spaces, indexes, and views are the obvious database objects that will need to be modified when a data type is changed. Check constraints are affected, as well.

Every data type change requires the column's table space to be modified. Upon completion of a data type change, the *table space* will be placed in an AREO* exception state, which stands for Advisory REORG Pending. Users can continue to access the data while the table space is in the AREO* state, but performance will suffer because the columns will need to be converted from the old format to the format of the new data type. Additionally, when the data is modified, the entire row will be logged. Performance will continue to suffer until the table space is reorganized.

Indexes need to be changed if the column whose data type has changed participates in an index. The availability of the index depends upon the data type of the column being changed.

The index will be immediately available for use if a CHAR, VARCHAR, GRAPHIC, or VARGRAPHIC column is altered to increase its length. Altering a numeric data type to increase its length will result in delayed availability for the index. This includes columns defined as SMALLINT, INTEGER, DECIMAL, NUMERIC, FLOAT, REAL, or DOUBLE. The index is not immediately available because changes to numeric data would create severe performance problems. Instead, the index is placed into RBPD exception state, which stands for REBUILD Pending. If an entire index is rebuilt from the data, all the keys are converted to the latest format. The utilities that can be used to rebuild an index include REBUILD INDEX, REORG TABLESPACE, and LOAD REPLACE.

CAUTION

DB2 will not choose any index in an RBDP exception state for an access path. To resolve this problem run the REBUILD INDEX utility to remove the RBDP exception.

V8

If the data type changes (for example, from SMALLINT to DECIMAL), reorganizing the index will reformat the index keys to the latest version unless the index is in ARBDP (Advisory Rebuild Pending). An index in the ARBDP exception state requires access to the data to determine the length of the index key.

Views that reference an impacted column will be immediately regenerated. DB2 will examine the DB2 Catalog to perform this regeneration. Affected views are retrieved from the SYSIBM.SYSVIEWDEP table and then SYSIBM.SYSVTREE and SYSIBM.SYSVLTREE are used to review and modify the parse tree for the views. Keep in mind that a view can be created on another view, so this process might be recursive. Also, as with tables, a change to any column within a view invalidates all plans, packages, and dynamic cached statements that are dependent on that view.

> **CAUTION**
>
> The regeneration of a view can fail if the precision for decimal arithmetic does not work with the application. In this case, you must DROP and re-CREATE the view in order to correct the problem.

Finally, when *check constraints* exist on a column whose data type or length has changed, the constraints will bea regenerated.

> **CAUTION**
>
> The regeneration of a check constraint can fail if the decimal point indicator or quote delimiter has changed since the check constraint was first defined.

Changing an Index

Prior to DB2 V8, the aspects of an index that could be altered were limited to mostly storage characteristics. With V8 and online schema evolution, additional index attributes can be changed; you can use ALTER to add columns to an index, change the clustering specification, and modify the manner in which varying length index keys are treated.

Adding Columns to an Index

To add a column to an index under DB2 V8 you will use the ADD COLUMN clause of the ALTER INDEX statement. For example, to add a column to the XDEPT2 index (currently defined on the MGRNO column only)

```
ALTER INDEX DSN8810.XDEPT2
  ADD COLUMN (ADMRDEPT);
```

Running this ALTER statement adds the ADMRDEPT column to the existing XDEPT2 index on the DSN8810.DEPT table. The new column will be appended to the end of the existing index key; you cannot change the existing order of a key or append a column to the beginning of the index key.

What is the impact of adding a column to an index? Well, if the column is added to both the table and the index in the same unit of work, then the index is immediately available for use and it is put in the AREO* exception state. If the column was not added to the table in the same unit of work, the index is put into the RBDP exception state. This would be the state of the example we just reviewed. Finally, if the index was created specifying DEFINE NO, then no exception state is set and a new version of the index is not created; the index is simply changed in the DB2 Catalog awaiting eventual definition.

Changing Clustering

Sometimes it becomes necessary to adjust the manner in which DB2 attempts to store data physically on disk. Recall from Chapter 5, "Data Definition Guidelines," that this is referred to as clustering. You might wish to change how data is clustered for several different reasons, such as

- Data that used to be accessed mostly randomly is now being accessed mostly sequentially.

- The initial clustering specification was chosen improperly.

- The sort order changed for large batch reporting jobs.

- The order in which data is being requested by applications has changed.

Prior to V8, changing clustering required dropping the clustering index and re-creating it without the CLUSTER keyword. To change clustering in DB2 V8, you can use the ALTER INDEX statement to specify either CLUSTER or NO CLUSTER. For example

```
ALTER INDEX DSN8810.XPROJAC1
  NO CLUSTER;
```

Running this ALTER statement will change the XPROJAC1 index such that it no longer controls clustering. Keep in mind, though, that simply removing explicit clustering might not change the clustering specification for the table space. Until another clustering index is specified for the table, DB2 will continue to use the index that was just changed as the implicit clustering index.

> **CAUTION**
>
> If no explicit clustering index is specified for a table, the first index created on each table will be used as the implicit clustering index.

When the clustering index is changed, new INSERT statements will cause data to be placed using the new clustering order. However, existing data is not immediately reclustered. Existing data will not be affected until the next time the table space is reorganized.

Of course, you are still restricted to having only one clustering index at any one point in time. So, you will need to order and time the execution of your ALTER INDEX statements so that there is never a state when two clustering indexes exist at the same time. For example, to change the clustering index from IX2 to IX5, you would issue the following sequence of ALTER statements:

```
ALTER INDEX IX2
  NO CLUSTER;

COMMIT;
```

```
ALTER INDEX IX5
  CLUSTER;

COMMIT;
```

> **NOTE**
>
> You can use the ALTER statement to respecify the clustering of your existing partitioned table spaces if you so desire. Prior to DB2 V8, the partitioning index for partitioned tables also had to be the clustering index. This is no longer the case. You can now specify a partitioning key that is not also the clustering key for a table.

Changing the Treatment of Variable Index Keys

Prior to DB2 V8, specifying a variable length column in an index caused DB2 to pad the data to its maximum length in the index key. This is no longer a requirement, because DB2 V8 allows you to specify PADDED or NOT PADDED to control whether the index key should be padded to its maximum length. This specification can be made when the index is defined using CREATE INDEX or changed using ALTER INDEX.

> **NOTE**
>
> The default is PADDED when you migrate from V7 to V8 in order to maintain compatibility with past implementations. However, for new V8 installations the default is NOT PADDED.
>
> A new DB2 V8 DSNZPARM named PADIX can be used to change the default.

When changing an index from PADDED to NOT PADDED, the index is placed in the ARBDP exception state and a value of 'N' is placed in the PADDED column of SYSIBM.SYSINDEXES. The index must be rebuilt, because DB2 cannot determine the accurate length of the index key without accessing the table space. The index is not available for use until it has been rebuilt, thereby setting all of the keys to varying lengths and resetting the pending state.

> **CAUTION**
>
> Be aware that recovery to a point in time may cause the ARBDP exception state to be set (if that point in time was before the index was rebuilt).

You can also change an index from NOT PADDED to PADDED using ALTER INDEX. If the index has varying length columns, it is placed in the AREO* exception state and a value of 'Y' is placed in the PADDED column of SYSIBM.SYSINDEXES. The index is available for use but performance will suffer. The index can be rebuilt or reorganized to pad the keys to the maximum length and reset the pending state.

Whenever the padding attribute of the index is changed, DB2 creates a new version of the index in the DB2 Catalog.

Changing Table Space Partitioning Specifications

Historically, one of the biggest impediments to managing DB2 database systems has been administering partitioned table spaces. Prior to DB2 V8, it was either difficult or impossible to modify the structure and many of the parameters of a partitioned table space.

Exacerbating this problem is the fact that most partitioned table spaces are the largest, most critical table spaces in the system with the highest availability requirements. Fortunately, DB2 V8 removes many of the barriers to managing partitioned table spaces.

With DB2 V8 you gain the ability to immediately add partitions, rotate partitions, and change the partitioning key values. In order to gain this flexibility, though, you will need to change from index-controlled partitioning to table-controlled partitioned tables. Then, you can use the ALTER TABLE statement to modify most of the partitioning specifications.

Adding Partitions

To add a partition to an existing table space the ALTER TABLE statement has been augmented with the ADD PART parameter. For example, consider a table space that is partitioned having one fiscal quarter worth of data per partition. Eventually, you might run out of partitions and need to add one. Assume that the last partition holds data up to the third quarter of 2004, but now you need to add data past this date. The following SQL shows how to use ALTER to add a new partition to a table:

```
ALTER TABLE CREATOR.TBNAME
  ADD PART VALUES('12-31-2004');
```

Of course, this assumes that your fourth quarter ends in December.

NOTE

You do not specify a partition number when you add a partition. DB2 will determine the next partition number to be used by examining information in the DB2 Catalog.

Along with adding a new data partition, a new partition is added for each partitioning index. This can include both the partitioning index and data-partitioned secondary indexes (DPSIs), as well.

You can add partitions up to the maximum limit; the maximum number of partitions depends on the DSSIZE parameter and page size of the table space (as defined in Chapter 5).

You cannot specify attributes such as PRIQTY and SECQTY; instead, DB2 uses the values in use for the previous logical partition. Before you begin to use the new partition, you should execute an ALTER TABLESPACE statement to provide accurate space parameters for the new partition.

If you are using STOGROUPs the next data set is automatically allocated for the table space and each partitioned index. When your DB2 objects are user managed (VCAT), you must pre-define the data sets using VSAM IDCAMS.

Each newly added partition will be immediately available for use, but you must stop the table space and partitioned index before adding the partition. When adding a partition, the table will be quiesced and all related plans, packages, and cached statements will be invalidated. This is required because certain access paths might be optimized to read only certain partitions. Automatic rebinds will occur if AUTO REBIND is enabled, but rebinding manually is usually a better approach to avoid performance problems, as applications wait to rebind before execution.

Rotating Partitions

If the requirement to add a partition can be satisfied by allowing an existing partition to be reused, you might be able to rotate the partition. Rotating partitions allows old data to "roll off," but the partition is kept for new data. This is a good option in the following situations:

- A year of data is kept in 13 partitions.

- Data is stored with a quarter in each partition but only the last 20 quarters (5 years) are needed online; *this might be any number of quarter or years.*

- Any time old data is periodically archived and only a limited number of partitions need to be active.

Partition rotation is implemented using the `ALTER TABLE ALTER PART ROTATE FIRST TO LAST` statement. When rotating, if you specify the `RESET` parameter, the data rows in the oldest (or logically first) partition are deleted, and a new table space high boundary is set so that partition becomes the last logical partition in sequence. This partition will then be ready to hold the new data as it is added. The partition that was rolled off is immediately available after the `ALTER` succeeds; a `REORG` is not required.

CAUTION

When specifying `RESET`, the existing data in the oldest partition is deleted and `SYSIBM.SYSCOPY` and `SYSLGRNX` rows associated with the partition being reset are deleted, too.

The aftermath of rotating a partition can be confusing. This is especially the case if you are trying to match partitions to physical data sets. The `.A001` data set is now the last logical partition, not the first. You will need to use the new `LOGICAL_PART` column in the `SYSIBM.SYSTABLEPART` table to match partitions to data sets. The `DISPLAY` command will list the status of table space partitions by logical partition.

Also, steps need to be taken if you need to keep the rolled off data for archival purposes. Be sure to unload the data immediately before rotating the partition using either the `UNLOAD` utility or a user-written program.

If this `REUSE` option is specified, a logical reset of the partition is done instead of deleting and redefining data sets. Existing extents for the partition will be kept.

Changing Partition Boundaries

DB2 V6 introduced the ability to modify limit keys for partitions. DB2 V8 adds the same capability for table-based partitioning with the `ALTER TABLE ALTER PART VALUES` statement. The affected data partitions are placed into the `REORG` pending state until they have been reorganized.

V8

Rebalancing Partitions

You can rebalance partitions when running DB2 V8, too. Unlike the schema changes previously discussed in this chapter, partition rebalancing is accomplished using the REORG utility instead of the ALTER statement. When reorganizing a table space you can specify a new parameter, REBALANCE, indicating that new partition boundaries should be set for the range of partitions being reorganized. DB2 will rebalance the data such that it is evenly distributed across the partitions. Rebalancing is most practical when the data is not skewed greatly.

> **CAUTION**
>
> When many duplicate values occur in the columns that define the partition boundaries, DB2 might not be able to evenly balance the data effectively.

Yes, you are reading this right. Running a REORG with the REBALANCE option can change the limit key for partition boundaries. The REORG will set new partition boundaries so that all the rows participating in the reorganization are evenly distributed across the partitions being reorganized. DB2 will update the SYSIBM.SYSTABLEPART and SYSIBM.SYSINDEXPART tables to record the new limit key values.

Using REORG to rebalance partitions has its advantages. Using this approach, your partitions will not be placed in the REORG exception state, as would be the case if you changed the partition boundaries using ALTER TABLE.

Keep the following restrictions in mind when considering whether to rebalance your partitions using REORG:

- You cannot specify the REBALANCE keyword if you are reorganizing a table space using the SHRLEVEL CHANGE option.

- You cannot specify the REBALANCE keyword with any of the following keywords: SCOPE PENDING, OFFPOSLIMIT, INDREFLIMIT, REPORTONLY, UNLOAD ONLY, and UNLOAD EXTERNAL.

- You cannot rebalance a partitioned table space that also has LOB columns.

- When the clustering sequence does not match the partitioning sequence, REORG must be run twice. The first REORG moves the rows to the right partition; the second REORG sorts the data into clustering sequence. After the first REORG, DB2 places the table space in the AREO* exception state—meaning that DB2 recommends running another REORG (to cluster the data).

> **CAUTION**
>
> After rebalancing is complete, plans, packages, and the dynamic statement cache records that reference the reorganized object are invalidated.

V8

Versioning for Online Schema Changes

To support online schema changes, DB2 has been enhanced to support multiple versions of DB2 objects. As certain schema changes are made, DB2 creates a new version to refer to the new structure. Multiple versions can exist at one time, each version referring to the object at a different stage of its life.

Issuing an ALTER for an existing DB2 object or column can cause a new format to be needed for tables, table spaces, and/or indexes. DB2 needs to know about the old format and the new format because all of the underlying data for an object (as well as its image copies) cannot be changed immediately to match the format of the latest version. By supporting multiple versions with different formats over time for tables and indexes, maximum data availability is achieved.

DB2 references the version information to appropriately store and use the data in its correct format. Versioning is tracked and recorded in the OLDEST_VERSION and CURRENT_VERSION columns in the following DB2 Catalog tables:

> SYSIBM.SYSTABLESPACE
>
> SYSIBM.SYSTABLEPART
>
> SYSIBM.SYSTABLES
>
> SYSIBM.SYSINDEXES
>
> SYSIBM.SYSINDEXPART
>
> SYSIBM.SYSOBDS
>
> SYSIBM.SYSCOPY

SYSIBM.SYSOBDS is a new V8 DB2 Catalog table that contains one row for each table space and index that can be recovered to an image copy that was made before the first version was generated.

However, the version information relevant to the data also is stored in system pages embedded in the table space or index page set. The system pages are stored along with the data so that the data can be properly interpreted. Doing so makes table spaces and indexes self-defining. Additionally, with the version information embedded in the page set, data can be accessed or unloaded from an image copy without DB2 being up.

> **NOTE**
>
> DB2 supported versioning prior to V8. When an indexed VARCHAR column in a table is enlarged, a new index version is created and tracked using the IOFACTOR column of SYSIBM.SYSINDEXES.
>
> In DB2 V8, the first ALTER that creates a new index version switches to DB2 V8 versioning by setting the OLDEST_VERSION and CURRENT_VERSION columns to the existing versions in the index.

The OLDEST_VERSION is the oldest format of the data in the object itself or any image copy still registered in SYSIBM.SYSCOPY. There is an upper bound for version numbers. A table space can have up to 256 different active versions; an index can have up to 16 different active versions. A version is active if it is used on any page within a page set (table space or index) or is in use in an existing image copy still registered in the DB2 Catalog.

> **CAUTION**
>
> When the upper bound is hit for a version and a new version must be created, the version number will wrap back to the beginning—starting again at version 1 (not zero). So, it is possible that the CURRENT_VERSION is a lower number than the OLDEST_VERSION.
>
> Of course, DB2 will not wrap if version number 1 is still an active version. If the maximum number of active versions is reached, a -4702 SQLCODE will be returned and the ALTER will fail.

An object that is never altered remains at version zero.

When Is a New Version Generated?

A new version is created for the table or index that is affected whenever the following types of changes are made:

- ALTER TABLE table-name ALTER COLUMN column-name
  SET DATA TYPE altered-data-type.

- ALTER INDEX index-name NOT PADDED.

- ALTER INDEX index-name PADDED.

- ALTER INDEX index-name ADD COLUMN column-name.

- Multiple ALTER COLUMN SET DATA TYPE statements in the same unit of work are included in one new schema version.

Deactivating Versions

For table spaces, and indexes defined as COPY YES, the MODIFY utility needs to be run to update the LOW_VERSION in the DB2 Catalog and reclaim the version by making it inactive. If there are entries for COPY, REORG, or REPAIR VERSIONS remaining in SYSIBM.SYSCOPY for the table space, MODIFY updates LOW_VERSION to be the lowest value of LOW_VERSION found from matching SYSCOPY rows. If no SYSCOPY rows remain for the object, MODIFY sets LOW_VERSION to the lowest version data row or key that exists in the active page set.

For indexes defined as COPY NO, running a REORG, REBUILD, or LOAD utility that resets the entire index updates the LOW_VERSION in SYSIBM.SYSINDEXES to be the same as HIGH_VERSION.

Database Exception States for Online Schema Changes

Exception states are used by DB2 to alert administrators and users to a database condition that needs to be managed or improved. Exception states have been used in all past releases of DB2, but two new states have been created to support online schema changes. Throughout this chapter, we have discussed these new database exception states, but we will review them here for easy reference:

Advisory Reorg (AREO*)—Indicates that the specified table space, index, or partition needs to be reorganized for performance to improve.

Advisory Rebuild Pending (ARBDP)—Indicates that the specified index needs to be rebuilt to improve performance and to allow DB2 to choose the index for index-only access.

As with any DB2 database exception state, these states will appear when you issue the DISPLAY command to monitor the status of your database objects. Consult Chapter 37, "DB2 Utility and Command Guidelines," for a complete discussion of the database exception states.

Online Schema Change Implementation Considerations

Keep in mind that existing access paths can become inefficient when a new version of an object is created. Therefore, making an online schema change might cause performance to degrade. Just because IBM has made it easier to implement changes to database objects does not mean that changes can be made indiscriminately and without planning.

Be sure to treat every database change as a potential impact to performance and availability. Whenever possible, schedule schema changes as close to a scheduled reorganization as possible. This will minimize the potential performance impact.

Certain types of online schema changes are more invasive than others. For example, rotating partitions can be very time-consuming. When rotating partitions of a partitioned table, the reset operation requires that the keys for deleted rows also be deleted from all NPIs. Because each NPI must be scanned to delete the keys this activity can consume an inordinate amount of elapsed time to complete.

Individual delete row processing is required for referential integrity relationships when DATA CAPTURE is enabled, or when there are delete triggers. In such scenarios, be sure to factor in additional time to delete data a row at a time.

CHAPTER 8

Using DB2 Triggers for Integrity

Triggers can be created on DB2 tables to extend the functionality of DB2 databases. By creating triggers, you can create active databases that take action based on naturally occurring database activities. Most of the other major relational database management systems have provided trigger support for a number of years. DB2 was late to the game with triggers (introducing them in V6), but IBM's offering is a very rich, functional implementation of triggers.

If you have not had the opportunity to use triggers, their power may elude you at first. However, once you have used them, living without triggers can be unthinkable.

What Is a Trigger?

Simply stated, a *trigger* is a piece of code that is executed in response to an SQL data modification statement; that is, an INSERT, UPDATE, or DELETE. To be a bit more precise: Triggers are event-driven specialized procedures that are stored in and managed by the RDBMS. Each trigger is attached to a single, specified table. A trigger can be thought of as an advanced form of "rule" or "constraint" written using an extended form of SQL. A trigger cannot be directly called or executed; it is automatically executed (or "fired") by DB2 as the result of an action—a data modification to the associated table.

After a trigger is created, it is always executed when its "firing" event occurs (INSERT, UPDATE, or DELETE). Therefore, triggers are automatic, implicit, and non-bypassable.

The Schema

Recall from Chapter 4, "Using DB2 User-Defined Functions and Data Types," that user-defined functions, user-defined distinct types, stored procedures, and triggers are all associated with a schema. By default, the schema name is the authid of the process that issues the CREATE FUNCTION, CREATE DISTINCT TYPE, CREATE PROCEDURE, or CREATE TRIGGER statement.

A schema, therefore, is simply a logical grouping of procedural database objects (user-defined functions, user-defined distinct types, stored procedures, and triggers).

You can specify a schema name when you create a user-defined function, type, or trigger. If the schema name is not the same as the SQL authorization ID, the issuer of the statement must have either SYSADM or SYSCTRL authority, or the authid of the issuing process has the CREATEIN privilege on the schema.

> **NOTE**
>
> A DB2 schema is not really a DB2 object. You cannot explicitly CREATE or DROP a schema. The schema is implicitly *created* when the first DB2 object is created using that schema name.

Triggers Are Hybrid DB2 Objects

Triggers are like other database objects, such as tables and indexes, in that they are created using DDL, stored in the database, and documented as entries in the DB2 Catalog.

Triggers also are like stored procedures and check constraints in that they contain code, or logic, and can be used to control data integrity.

Triggers Versus Stored Procedures

Triggers are similar in functionality to stored procedures. Both consist of procedural logic that is stored at the database level. However, stored procedures are not event-driven and are not attached to a specific table. A stored procedure is explicitly executed by invoking a CALL to the procedure (instead of implicitly being executed like triggers). Additionally, a stored procedure can access many tables without being specifically associated to any of them.

Triggers Versus Check Constraints

Triggers are similar to table check constraints because triggers can be used to control integrity when data is changed in a DB2 table. However, triggers are much more powerful than simple check constraints because they can be coded to accomplish more types of actions. A check constraint is used to specify what data is allowable in a column, but a trigger can do that, plus make changes to data. Furthermore, a trigger can act on data in other tables, whereas a check constraint cannot.

Furthermore, triggers have more knowledge of the database change. A trigger can view both the old value and the new value of a changed column and take action based on that information.

> **NOTE**
>
> When deciding whether to use a constraint or a trigger, keep in mind that triggers are more expensive than an equivalent constraint. You should always consider the relative cost of executing each. If the task at hand can be completed with either a trigger or a constraint, favor constraints because they are cheaper than triggers and it is always better to use the cheaper alternative.

Why Use Triggers?

Triggers are useful for implementing code that must be executed on a regular basis due to a predefined event. By utilizing triggers, scheduling and data integrity problems can be eliminated because the trigger will be fired whenever the triggering event occurs. You need not remember to schedule or code an activity to perform the logic in the trigger. It happens automatically by virtue of it being in the trigger. This is true of both static and dynamic SQL; planned and ad hoc. Simply stated: Whenever the triggering event occurs, the trigger is fired.

Triggers can be implemented for many practical uses. Quite often, it is impossible to code business rules into the database using only DDL. For example, DB2 does not support complex constraints (only value-based CHECK constraints) or various types of referential constraints (such as pendant DELETE processing or ON UPDATE CASCADE). Using triggers, a very flexible environment is established for implementing business rules and constraints in the DBMS. This is important because having the business rules in the database ensures that everyone uses the same logic to accomplish the same process.

Triggers can be coded to access and/or modify other tables, print informational messages, and specify complex restrictions. For example, consider the standard suppliers and parts application used in most introductory database texts. A part can be supplied by many suppliers and a supplier can supply many parts. Triggers can be used to support the following scenarios:

- What if a business rule exists specifying that no more than three suppliers are permitted to supply any single part? A trigger can be coded to check that rows cannot be inserted if the data violates this requirement.

- A trigger can be created to allow only orders for parts that are already in stock, or maybe for parts that are already in stock or are on order and planned for availability within the next week.

- Triggers can be used to perform calculations, such as ensuring that the order amount for the parts is calculated appropriately, given the suppliers chosen to provide the parts. This is especially useful if the order purchase amount is stored in the database as redundant data.

- Triggers can be used to automatically generate values for newly inserted rows. For example, you could generate customer profile information whenever a new row is inserted into a customer table.

- To curb costs, a business decision may be made that the low cost supplier will always be used. A trigger can be implemented to disallow any order that is not the current "low cost" order.

The number of business rules that can be implemented using triggers is truly limited only by your imagination (or, more appropriately, your business needs).

After you define a trigger on a table, it is stored in the database, and any application or ad hoc SQL that modifies that table uses it. Triggers can help ease application development and maintenance tasks. For example, if a business rule changes, you only have to update the trigger, not the application code. Furthermore, if ad hoc updates are allowed, triggers will enforce integrity rules that otherwise would have been bypassed because the update was ad hoc. Therefore, you should code business rules into triggers instead of application program logic whenever possible.

Additionally, triggers can access non-DB2 resources. This can be accomplished by invoking a stored procedure or a user-defined function that takes advantage of the OS/390 resource recovery services (RRS). Data stored in the non-DB2 resource can be accessed or modified in the stored procedure or user-defined function that is called from the trigger.

When Does a Trigger Fire?

At the basic level, we have already discussed when a trigger fires: that is, whenever its triggering activity occurs. For example, an UPDATE trigger will fire whenever an UPDATE is issued on the table on which the trigger is defined. But there is another, more subtle, question. Does the logic in the trigger get executed before the firing UPDATE or after?

Two options exist for when a trigger can fire: before the firing activity occurs or after the firing activity occurs. DB2 supports both "before" and "after" triggers. A "before" trigger executes before the firing activity occurs; an "after" trigger executes after the firing activity occurs. In DB2, "before" triggers are restricted because they cannot perform updates.

Knowing how the triggers in your databases function is imperative. Without this knowledge, properly functioning triggers cannot be coded, supported, or maintained effectively. Why is this?

Consider, for example, if the firing activity occurs before the trigger is fired. In other words, the INSERT, UPDATE, or DELETE occurs first; then, as a result of this action, the trigger logic is executed. If necessary, the trigger code can change transition variables. What if the trigger is fired before the actual firing event occurs? In this situation, DB2 disallows modification of transition variables.

Another interesting feature of DB2 triggers is the order in which they are fired. If multiple triggers are coded on the same table, which trigger is fired first? It can make a difference as to how the triggers should be coded, tested, and maintained. The rule for order of execution is basically simple to understand, but can be difficult to maintain. For triggers of the same type, they are executed in the order in which they were created. For example, if two DELETE triggers are coded on the same table, the one that physically was created first is executed first. Keep this in mind as you make changes to your database objects and triggers. If you need to DROP the table and re-create it to implement a database change, make sure you create the triggers in the same order as they originally were created to keep the functionality the same.

To understand why this is important, consider this simple example. Two INSERT triggers are created on TABLE1, as follows:

- TRIGGER1 adds +5 to COL1 of TABLE2

- TRIGGER2 multiplies COL1 of TABLE2 by 2

The triggers are of the same type, so because TRIGGER1 was created first, it will fire first whenever an INSERT occurs to TABLE1. If COL1 of TABLE2 is initially set to 1, after the triggers fire, the value will be

```
(1 + 5) * 2 = 12
```

However, if you later make changes requiring the triggers to be dropped and re-created, but inadvertently created them in reverse order, TRIGGER2 then TRIGGER1, the actions would change causing the following to occur:

```
(1 * 2) + 5 = 7
```

You can see that this can cause drastically different results. Determining the procedural activity that is required when triggers are present can be a complicated task. It is of paramount importance that all developers are schooled in the firing methods utilized for triggers in DB2.

To determine the order in which the triggers were created for a table, issue the following query substituting the table owner and table name in place of the question marks

```
SELECT    DISTINCT SCHEMA, NAME, CREATEDTS
FROM      SYSIBM.SYSTRIGGERS
WHERE     TBOWNER = ?
AND       TBNAME = ?
ORDER BY CREATEDTS;
```

The results will be returned in the order the triggers were created, earliest to latest. The DISTINCT is required because trigger definitions may require multiple rows in SYSIBM.SYSTRIGGERS.

Creating Triggers

Triggers are created using the CREATE TRIGGER DDL statement. Before creating any triggers, be sure you know

- The business rule you are trying to enforce with the trigger

- Whether or not the trigger will modify data in other tables

- What other triggers exist on the table

- What actions those triggers perform

- The order in which those triggers were created

- The referential integrity implemented on any impacted tables

- The RI rules for those referential constraints

- The firing activity (UPDATE, DELETE, or INSERT) for the new trigger

- Whether the trigger fires "before" or "after" the firing event

The DDL statement issued to CREATE a trigger requires the following details:

Trigger Name—The name of the trigger

Triggering Table—The table for which the trigger exists

Activation—Whether the trigger fires BEFORE or AFTER the data modification

Triggering Event—The statement that causes the trigger to fire, that is INSERT, UPDATE, or DELETE

Granularity—Whether the trigger fires FOR EACH ROW or FOR EACH STATEMENT

Transition Variables or Table—The names to be used to reference the information prior to, and after the data modification.

Trigger Condition—An optional condition can be specified whereby the triggered action that follows is only executed when the condition evaluates to true.

Triggered Action—The actual code that runs when the trigger is fired.

Furthermore, like any program you write, you should have the basic logic and flow of the trigger code mapped out before you sit down to write it.

So, let's examine the basic things that you must know before coding a trigger. The first consideration, of course, is for which table the trigger should be defined. The trigger must be defined for the table that you want to monitor for inserts, updates, or deletes. Next, you must decide what the triggering event should be: INSERT, UPDATE, or DELETE.

The next decision is to determine when the trigger is to be activated—before or after the triggering activity occurs. Keep in mind that BEFORE triggers are activated before DB2 makes any changes to the triggering table and cannot activate other triggers. AFTER triggers are activated after DB2 makes changes to the triggering table and can potentially activate other triggers.

The granularity of the trigger must be determined. Because SQL is a set-level language, any single SQL statement can impact multiple rows of data. For example, one DELETE statement can actually cause zero, one, or many rows to be removed. You must take this into account as you build triggers.

Therefore, there are two levels of granularity that a trigger can have: statement-level or row-level. A statement-level trigger is executed once on firing, regardless of the actual number of rows inserted, deleted, or updated. A statement-level trigger is coded by specifying the FOR EACH STATEMENT clause. A row-level trigger, once fired, is executed once for each and every row that is inserted, deleted, or updated. A row-level trigger is coded by specifying the FOR EACH ROW clause. Different business requirements will drive what type of trigger granularity should be chosen.

> **CAUTION**
>
> Only AFTER triggers can be defined with the FOR EACH STATEMENT clause; both BEFORE and AFTER triggers can be defined with the FOR EACH ROW clause.

> **CAUTION**
>
> Performance problems can ensue when triggers are defined with the FOR EACH ROW clause. Consider the impact of issuing a mass delete against a table with a FOR EACH ROW trigger defined on it. A delete trigger would fire once for every row that is deleted.

For row-level triggers, you might need to refer to the values of columns in each updated row of the triggering table. To do this, you can use specialized transition variables that provide, in essence, before and after views of the changed data. Each trigger can have one NEW view of the table and one OLD view of the table available. These "views" are accessible only from triggers. They provide access to the modified data by viewing information in the transaction log.

The OLD transition variables contain the values of columns before the triggering SQL statement updates them. This information is particularly useful if you need to access the prior value of a column before a triggering UPDATE or DELETE statement. The NEW transition variables contain the values of columns after the triggering SQL statement updates them. You can define NEW transition variables for UPDATE and INSERT triggers.

Refer to Figure 8.1 for a graphic representation of the OLD and NEW transition variables. When an INSERT occurs, the NEW table contains the rows that were just inserted into the table to which the trigger is attached. When a DELETE occurs, the OLD table contains the rows that were just deleted from the table to which the trigger is attached. An UPDATE statement logically functions as a DELETE followed by an INSERT. Therefore, after an UPDATE, the NEW table contains the new values for the rows that were just updated in the table to which the trigger is attached; the OLD table contains the old values for the updated rows.

You can also use transition tables to refer to the entire set of rows that a triggering SQL statement modifies, rather than individual rows.

Transition variables and transition tables are specified in the REFERENCING clause of the CREATE TRIGGER statement. Transition variables are defined using the OLD AS and NEW AS clauses; transition tables are defined using the OLD_TABLE AS and NEW_TABLE AS clauses.

Each trigger can include two correlation names, one for OLD and one for NEW, and two table names, one for the OLD_TABLE and one for the NEW_TABLE. Each of the correlation names must be unique from the others. Table 8.1 outlines the transition variables that are permitted for each type of trigger. In the table N/A indicates not allowed.

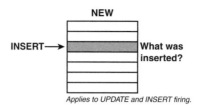

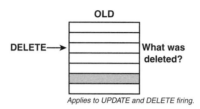

FIGURE 8.1   Trigger transition variables: NEW and OLD.

TABLE 8.1   Permitted Trigger Transition Variables

Activation Time	Triggering SQL	Granularity	Transition Variables	Transition Tables
BEFORE	INSERT	Row	NEW	N/A
	UPDATE	Row	OLD, NEW	N/A
	DELETE	Row	OLD	N/A
AFTER	INSERT	Row	NEW	NEW_TABLE
		Statement	N/A	NEW_TABLE
	UPDATE	Row	OLD, NEW	OLD_TABLE, NEW_TABLE
		Statement	N/A	OLD_TABLE, NEW_TABLE
	DELETE	Row	OLD	OLD_TABLE
		Statement	N/A	OLD_TABLE, NEW_TABLE

So, transition tables can be specified only for AFTER triggers. Similarly, transition variables are allowable only for triggers with row granularity (that is, triggers specifying FOR EACH ROW).

> **NOTE**
>
> Keep in mind that the scope of the transition variables and transition tables is the triggered action. Do not refer to transition variables or transition tables outside of the trigger.

The final consideration is how to code the actual logic that is to be performed when the trigger fires. This logic is placed inside of a BEGIN and END grouping as follows:

```
BEGIN ATOMIC
    triggered-SQL-statements
END
```

Like any "program," the SQL statements are executed in the order they are specified. You must code the keywords BEGIN ATOMIC and END only if you code more than one SQL statement. Each SQL statement must end with a semicolon (;).

Only certain types of SQL can be issued from certain types of triggers. Table 8.2 outlines the types of SQL statements that can be coded inside DB2 triggers.

TABLE 8.2   Allowable SQL Statements by Trigger Type

Trigger Type SQL Statement	BEFORE	AFTER
fullselect	Yes	Yes
CALL *stored procedure*	Yes	Yes
SIGNAL SQLSTATE	Yes	Yes
VALUES	Yes	Yes
SET *transition variable*	Yes	No
INSERT	No	Yes
DELETE *(searched)*	No	Yes
UPDATE *(searched)*	No	Yes

> **NOTE**
>
> SQL statements in triggers cannot refer to host variables, parameter markers, or undefined transition variables. The statements can refer only to tables and views at the current server.

The WHEN Clause

The WHEN clause is used to control the conditions under which the trigger will fire. A search condition consists of one or more predicates. Search conditions for the WHEN clause are formulated just like search conditions in an SQL WHERE clause. A search condition always evaluates to true, false, or unknown. If a condition is coded into the WHEN clause the triggered SQL statements are executed only if the search condition evaluates to true.

The WHEN clause is optional. If the WHEN clause is omitted, the triggered action always is executed. However, if a trigger search condition is coded, the trigger will stop executing and return control to the INSERT, UPDATE, or DELETE that triggered it as soon as the condition is determined to be false. Of course, when the condition is true, the trigger body is executed. Consider specifying a trigger condition when the trigger must fire only for a subset of rows that apply. The more specific the condition, the higher the chances of improving trigger performance.

Now let's take a look at some sample triggers to see how these clauses can be used in CREATE TRIGGER statements.

Trigger Examples

The following is an example of using the CREATE TRIGGER statement to create a very simple trigger:

```
CREATE TRIGGER SALARY_UPDATE
   BEFORE UPDATE OF SALARY
```

8

```
  ON DSN8810.EMP
  FOR EACH ROW MODE DB2SQL
WHEN (NEW.SALARY > (OLD.SALARY * 1.5))
BEGIN ATOMIC
  SIGNAL SQLSTATE '75001' ('Raise exceeds 50%');
END;
```

This statement creates an UPDATE trigger named SALARY_UPDATE. The trigger will fire before the actual UPDATE that fires it occurs. The trigger will execute for every row impacted by the UPDATE. If the new value for the SALARY column exceeds 50% of the old value, an error is raised giving an SQLSTATE code and message.

> **NOTE**
>
> This is a very simple trigger to impose a business rule on the database. It does not impact data in any other tables.

After the trigger has been created, it will automatically be fired any time the firing event (an UPDATE to the SALARY column in the EMP table) occurs.

When creating triggers, you can call stored procedures to deliver more trigger functionality. Consider the following trigger, for example:

```
CREATE TRIGGER ORDER_STOCK
   AFTER UPDATE OF PRENDATE ON DSN8810.PROJ
   REFERENCING NEW AS NEW
   FOR EACH ROW MODE DB2SQL
WHEN (NEW.PRENDATE < CURRENT DATE + 14 DAYS)
BEGIN ATOMIC
   CALL PROJCRIT(NEW.PROJNO);
END
```

In this case, if the date the project is to end is modified to be within the next two weeks (14 days), call the PROJCRIT stored procedure to perform functionality required for critical projects. This can be as simple as creating a report for management, or as complex as modifying project status information in multiple tables (or, really, whatever you can do within a stored procedure).

The following is another example of creating a trigger, this time an INSERT trigger:

```
CREATE TRIGGER TOT_COMP
   AFTER UPDATE OF SALARY, BONUS, COMM ON DSN8810.EMP
   REFERENCING NEW AS INSERTED, OLD AS DELETED
   FOR EACH ROW MODE DB2SQL
WHEN (INSERTED.SALARY <> DELETED.SALARY OR
      INSERTED.BONUS <> DELETED.BONUS OR
      INSERTED.COMM <> DELETED.COMM)
  BEGIN ATOMIC
   UPDATE EMP_SALARY
     SET TOT_COMP = INSERTED.SALARY + INSERTED.BONUS + INSERTED.COMM
   WHERE EMP_SALARY.EMPNO = INSERTED.EMPNO;
  END
```

This trigger is used to check for changes to the components of an employee's total compensation. The trigger keeps derived data in synch with its components. In this case, whenever SALARY, BONUS, or COMM are changed in the EMP table, a table named EMP_SALARY has its TOT_COMP column modified to be the new sum of salary, bonus, and commission information. Triggers can be used in this manner to maintain data integrity across tables when derived data is stored physically. Whenever any value in the three components of total compensation changes, the trigger automatically calculates a new TOT_COMP and updates it in the table.

Trigger Packages

When a trigger is created, DB2 creates a trigger package for the statements in the triggered action. The trigger package is recorded in SYSIBM.SYSPACKAGE and has the same name as the trigger. The trigger package is always accessible and can be executed only when a trigger is activated by a triggering operation.

Trigger packages do not follow the same rules as regular DB2 packages. For example, it is not possible to maintain multiple versions of a trigger package. Additionally, the user executing the triggering SQL operation does not need to have the authority to execute the trigger package. Furthermore, the trigger package does not need to be in the package list for the plan that is associated with the program that contains the SQL statement.

The only way to delete the trigger package is to use the DROP TRIGGER statement. Of course, if you issue a DROP TABLE and the table has a trigger, the trigger will be dropped, too.

The trigger package is implicitly bound when the trigger is created. When the trigger package is implicitly bound by DB2, it will use the following BIND attributes:

```
ACTION(ADD)

CURRENTDATA(YES)

DBPROTOCOL(DRDA)

DEGREE(1)

DYNAMICRULES(BIND)

ENABLE(*)

EXPLAIN(NO)

FLAG(I)

ISOLATION(CS)

NOREOPT(VARS)

NODEFER(PREPARE)

OWNER(authid)

QUERYOPT(1)

PATH(path)
```

```
RELEASE(COMMIT)

SQLERROR(NOPACKAGE)

QUALIFIER(authid)

VALIDATE(BIND)
```

Of course, you can REBIND the trigger package once it is created. In many instances you will want to do this to change the default options. By rebinding the trigger package right after it is created you can specify EXPLAIN(YES) or CURRENTDATA(NO), for example. Be sure to use REBIND to ensure you are using the BIND options that you choose—instead of the default options foisted on you by DB2.

Triggers Can Fire Other Triggers

As we've already learned, a trigger is fired by an INSERT, UPDATE, or DELETE statement. However, a trigger can also contain INSERT, UPDATE, or DELETE logic within itself. Therefore, a trigger is fired by a data modification, but can also cause another data modification, thereby firing yet another trigger. When a trigger contains INSERT, UPDATE, and/or DELETE logic, the trigger is said to be a *nested trigger*.

DB2 places a limit on the number of nested triggers that can be executed within a single firing event. If this were not done, it could be quite possible to have triggers firing triggers ad infinitum until all of the data was removed from an entire database.

If referential integrity is combined with triggers, additional cascading updates and/or deletes can occur. If a DELETE or UPDATE results in a series of additional UPDATEs or DELETEs that need to be propagated to other tables, the UPDATE or DELETE triggers for the second table also will be activated.

This combination of multiple triggers and referential integrity constraints are capable of setting a cascading effect into motion, which can result in multiple data changes. DB2 limits this cascading effect to 16 levels to prevent endless looping. If more than 16 levels of nesting occur, the transaction is aborted.

The ability to nest triggers provides an efficient method for implementing automatic data integrity. Because triggers generally cannot be bypassed, they provide an elegant solution to the enforced application of business rules and data integrity.

CAUTION

Use caution to ensure that the maximum trigger nesting level is not reached. Failure to heed this advice can cause an environment where certain types of data modification cannot occur because the number of nested calls will always be exceeded.

Trigger Guidelines

Triggers are a powerful feature of DB2 for z/OS and OS/390. They enable non-bypassable, event-driven logic to be intrinsically intermingled with data. The following guidelines can be used to help you implement effective and efficient triggers for your DB2 databases and applications.

Naming Triggers   A trigger name, along with its schema, must be unique within the DB2 subsystem. The schema name that qualifies the trigger is the owner of the trigger. The schema name for the trigger cannot begin with the letters 'SYS', unless the schema name is 'SYSADM'.

Because the trigger name is also used for the trigger package name, the trigger name cannot be the name of a package that already exists. For trigger packages, the schema of the trigger is used as the collection of the trigger package. The combination of schema.trigger must not be the same as an independently existing collection.package combination.

Keep It Simple   Each trigger should be coded to perform one and only one task. The trigger should be as simple as possible while still performing the desired task. Do not create overly complex triggers that perform multiple, complex tasks. It is far better to have multiple triggers, each performing one simple task, than to have a single, very complex trigger that performs multiple tasks. A simple trigger will be easier to code, debug, understand, and maintain when it needs to be modified.

Implement Triggers with Care   After a trigger is created, it impacts change processing for every user and program that modifies data in the table on which the trigger is defined. Because of this global nature of triggers, take great care to implement only thoroughly tested and debugged triggers.

Test Trigger Logic Outside the Trigger First   Whenever possible, test the SQL to be included in the trigger outside the trigger first. After the bugs and syntax errors have been eliminated, create the trigger using the debugged SQL.

This technique is not always possible, for example, if the SQL requires the NEW and OLD transition values or a transition table.

Try to Create Only One Trigger Per Type Per Table   Avoid creating multiple triggers of the same type for the same table—for example, two INSERT triggers both having an AFTER activation time defined on the same table.

This guideline is necessary because you cannot specify the order in which the triggers will fire. Instead, DB2 will execute multiple triggers of the same type on the same table in the order in which the triggers were created. This order can be difficult to maintain if changes are required that cause the triggers to be dropped and re-created.

However, this guideline can go against the "Keep It Simple" guideline. You need to determine, on a case-by-case basis, whether having multiple triggers of the same type on the same table is easier to understand and maintain than a single, more complex trigger.

Trigger Limitations   There are limits on how triggers can be used. For example, you cannot define triggers on:

- A DB2 system catalog table
- A view

- An alias

- A synonym

- Any table with a three-part name

You can create triggers on your PLAN_TABLE, DSN_STATEMNT_TABLE, or DSN_FUNCTION_TABLE. But you should not define INSERT triggers on these tables because the triggers will not be fired when DB2 adds rows to the tables.

BEFORE **Versus** AFTER **Triggers**   Assign the trigger activation specification carefully. Remember that a BEFORE trigger cannot cascade and fire other triggers because it cannot UPDATE data.

FOR EACH ROW **Versus** FOR EACH STATEMENT   Understand the implication of the granularity of the trigger. A statement-level trigger, one specifying FOR EACH STATEMENT, will only fire once. If you need to examine the contents of impacted columns, you will need a row-level trigger, one specifying FOR EACH ROW.

Also, remember that you cannot specify FOR EACH STATEMENT for a BEFORE trigger.

Using Triggers to Implement Referential Integrity   One of the primary uses for triggers is to support referential integrity (RI). Although DB2 supports a very robust form of declarative RI, no current DBMS fully supports all possible referential constraints. This is true of DB2, as well. Refer to Table 8.3 for a listing of the possible types of referential integrity.

Triggers can be coded, in lieu of declarative RI, to support **all** of the RI rules in Table 8.3. Of course, when you use triggers, it necessitates writing procedural code for each rule for each constraint, whereas declarative RI constraints are coded in the DDL that is used to create relational tables.

TABLE 8.3   Types of Referential Integrity

RI	Description
DELETE RESTRICT	If any rows exist in the dependent table, the primary key row in the parent table cannot be deleted.
DELETE CASCADE	If any rows exist in the dependent table, the primary key row in the parent table is deleted, and all dependent rows are also deleted.
DELETE NEUTRALIZE	If any rows exist in the dependent table, the primary key row in the parent table is deleted, and the foreign key column(s) for all dependent rows are set to NULL as well.
UPDATE RESTRICT	If any rows exist in the dependent table, the primary key column(s) in the parent table cannot be updated.
UPDATE CASCADE	If any rows exist in the dependent table, the primary key column(s) in the parent table are updated, and all foreign key values in the dependent rows are updated to the same value.

TABLE 8.3   Continued

RI	Description
UPDATE NEUTRALIZE	If any rows exist in the dependent table, the primary key row in the parent table is deleted, and all foreign key values in the dependent rows are updated to NULL as well.
INSERT RESTRICT	A foreign key value cannot be inserted into the dependent table unless a primary key value already exists in the parent table.
FK UPDATE RESTRICTION	A foreign key cannot be updated to a value that does not already exist as a primary key value in the parent table.
PENDANT DELETE	When the last foreign key value in the dependent table is deleted, the primary key row in the parent table is also deleted.

> **NOTE**
>
> DB2 does not provide native declarative RI support for pendant delete or update cascade referential constraint processing.

To use triggers to support RI rules, it is sometimes necessary to know the values impacted by the action that fired the trigger. For example, consider the case where a trigger is fired because a row was deleted. The row, and all of its values, has already been deleted because the trigger is executed after its firing action occurs. The solution is to use transition variables to view the NEW and OLD data values.

Using the VALUES Statement with Triggers   The VALUES statement can be used to introduce expressions to be evaluated, but without assigning the results to output variables. The VALUES statement can be used to invoke a user-defined function from a trigger. For example,

```
CREATE TRIGGER NEWPROJ
    AFTER INSERT ON DSN8810.PROJ
    REFERENCING NEW AS P
    FOR EACH ROW
  MODE DB2SQL
BEGIN ATOMIC
    VALUES(NEWPROJ(P.PROJNO));
END
```

This trigger invokes the UDF named NEWPROJ whenever a new project is inserted into the PROJ table.

Using the VALUES statement eliminates the need to use a SELECT statement to invoke the UDF. This can deliver a performance gain.

> **NOTE**
>
> If a negative SQLCODE is returned when the function is invoked, DB2 stops executing the trigger and rolls back any triggered actions that were performed.

Use Declarative RI   In general, if DB2 supports the declarative referential integrity processing that you require, use declarative RI DDL instead of triggers. It will be easier to develop and support. Use triggers to implement RI only when DB2 does not support the type of RI you require (for example, to implement pendant delete RI processing).

Name Transition Variables Appropriately   The transition variables for accessing OLD and NEW data values can be changed to any value you so desire. For example, you might use INSERTED for NEW and DELETED for OLD, to mimic the way Microsoft SQL Server and SYBASE use transition variables. This is especially useful if you have staff members who understand triggers on a DBMS other than DB2.

CHAPTER 9

Large Objects and Object/Relational Databases

Traditionally, database management systems were designed to manage simple, structured data types. Most any database can be used to store numbers, alphabetic characters, and basic date and time constructs. But modern database management systems must be able to store and manipulate complex, unstructured data including multimedia data such as images, video, sound, and long documents.

As of Version 6, it is possible to use DB2 to manage complex data types using large objects.

Defining the Term "Object/Relational"

Object/relational is one term that is used to describe database management systems that provide extensible data types to manage non-traditional data. IBM describes the term object/relational to encompass not just large objects, but also support for triggers, user-defined distinct types, and user-defined functions. These three topics are covered in Chapters 4, "Using DB2 User-Defined Functions and Data Types" and 8, "Using DB2 Triggers for Integrity." This chapter covers DB2's implementation of large objects.

Do not be confused by the use of the term "object" in the phrase "object/relational." An object/relational database management system has little to do with object-oriented technology or object-oriented programming and development.

> **NOTE**
>
> OO technology is fundamentally based upon the concept of, what else, but an object. Objects are defined based on object classes that determine the structure (variables) and behavior (methods) for the object. True objects, in traditional OO parlance, cannot be easily represented using a relational database. In the RDBMS, a logical entity is transformed into a physical representation of that entity solely in terms of its data characteristics. In DB2, you create a table that can store the data elements (in an underlying VSAM data file represented by a table space). The table contains rows that represent the current state of that entity. The table does not store all of the encapsulated logic necessary to act upon that data. By contrast, an object would define an entity in terms of both its state and its behavior. In other words, an object encapsulates both the data (state) and the valid procedures that can be performed upon the object's data (behavior). With stored procedures, triggers, and UDFs relational databases are "getting closer" to supporting OO techniques, but the implementation is significantly different.

Another term used in the industry when referring to extensible data type support is "universal." IBM went so far as to rename and brand DB2 as DB2 Universal Database for OS/390 as of Version 6—and it is still named DB2 Universal Database (or UDB) as of V8. Large object support is the primary factor governing the applicability of the term "universal" to DB2.

What Is a Large Object?

A large object is a data type used by DB2 to manage unstructured data. DB2 provides three built-in data types for storing large objects:

- BLOBs (Binary Large OBjects)—Up to 2GB of binary data. Typical uses for BLOB data include photographs and pictures, audio and sound clips, and video clips.

- CLOBs (Character Large OBjects)—Up to 2GB of single byte character data. CLOBs are ideal for storing large documents in a DB2 database.

- DBCLOBs (Double Byte Character Large OBjects)—Up to 1GB of double byte character data (total of 2GB). DBCLOBs are useful for storing documents in languages that require double byte characters, such as Kanji.

> **CAUTION**
>
> Actually, the three LOB data types can be used to store 1 byte less than 2 gigabytes of data.

BLOBs, CLOBs, and DBCLOBs are collectively referred to as LOBs. The three LOB data types are designed to efficiently store and access large amounts of unstructured data. DB2 understands that it is expensive to move and manipulate large objects. Therefore, LOBs are treated differently than the other standard built-in data types.

LOBs are not stored in the same structure as the rest of the data in the DB2 table. Instead, the table contains a descriptor that points to the actual LOB value. The LOB value itself is stored in separate LOB table space in an auxiliary table.

Application programs are written using LOB locators. A LOB locator represents the value of a LOB but does not actually contain the LOB data. This method is used because LOBs are typically very large and therefore expensive in terms of the resources required to move and store the LOB value. By using LOB locators, programs can avoid the expense associated with materializing LOBs.

When LOBs are created, the DBA can specify whether LOBs are to be logged or not. Once again, because LOBs are very large, logging them can be quite expensive and consume a large amount of log storage.

LOB Columns Versus VARCHAR and VARGRAPHIC Columns

It has been possible to store multimedia data in DB2 databases since Version 1 using VARCHAR and VARGAPHIC columns. But these data types provide limited functionality and usefulness when compared to LOBs.

The maximum size of a VARCHAR or VARGRAPHIC column is 32KB. This limitation may not pose a problem for smaller databases, but modern (often Web-enabled) applications usually require larger multimedia data. A 32KB text document is not a very large document at all. And 32KB is miniscule when it comes to storing multimedia data types such as audio, video, graphics, and images.

> **NOTE**
>
> One of the biggest considerations when using LOBs is their size. DBAs and developers who decide to use LOBs will need to understand that even small or simple graphics and text files can consume a large amount of space.
>
> For comparative purposes, consider that the document used to produce this chapter is approximately 95KB in size. In practice, many business documents are much larger.
>
> Once again, for comparative purposes, the file used to produce Figure 2.3 (in Chapter 2) is approximately 39KB in size. And the graphic contained in that file is quite simple compared to many other types of business graphics.

When you are sure that the text or graphic you wish to store will always consume less than 32KB of storage, then you can use a VARCHAR or VARGRAPHIC data type instead of one of the LOB data types. However, LOB data types might still be preferable because of the efficient manner in which they are handled by DB2. Remember, VARCHAR and VARGRAPHIC data is stored with the rest of the data in the table space, as opposed to LOB data, which is stored in an auxiliary LOB table space.

Creating Tables That Contain LOB Columns

There are four basic steps required to create and populate a table that uses LOB data types.

The first step is to define the appropriate columns in the DB2 table. Define one ROWID column and as many LOB columns as needed. Only one ROWID column is required regardless of the number of LOB columns you specify. The ROWID and LOB columns are defined using the CREATE TABLE or ALTER TABLE statement. The definition of the LOB column must specify whether the column is a BLOB, CLOB, or DBCLOB. Furthermore, you must specify a size for the LOB. Failure to specify a size causes DB2 to use the following default:

- For BLOBs—1 MB (or 1,048,576 bytes)

- For CLOBs—1,048,576 single byte characters

- For DBCLOBs—524,288 double-byte characters

> **NOTE**
>
> Regardless of the length you specify, a BLOB column is stored as a long string column of varying length.

The LOB column in the DB2 table will contain only information about the LOB, not the actual data value. The table containing the LOB definition is referred to as the base table.

The ROWID column is used by DB2 to locate the LOB data. A ROWID is a unique 19-byte system generated value. If you are adding a LOB column and a ROWID column to an existing table, you must use two ALTER TABLE statements. Add the ROWID with the first ALTER TABLE statement and the LOB column with the second ALTER TABLE statement.

In the second step you will need to create a table and a table space to store the LOB data. The table is referred to as an auxiliary table; the table space is called a LOB table space. The base table can be in a partitioned table space but the LOB table space cannot be partitioned.

> **NOTE**
>
> The LOB table space must be created in the same database as the base table.

If the base table is not partitioned, you must create one LOB table space and one auxiliary table for each LOB column. If the table space containing the base table is partitioned, you must create one LOB table space and one auxiliary table for each partition, for each LOB. For example, if your base table has six partitions, you must create six LOB table spaces and six auxiliary tables for each LOB column. To further illustrate the base table to auxiliary table relationship, refer to Figure 9.1.

Use the CREATE LOB TABLESPACE statement to create LOB table spaces and the CREATE AUXILIARY TABLE statement to create auxiliary tables.

The third step is to create a unique index on the auxiliary table. Each auxiliary table must have exactly one index. The CREATE INDEX statement is used to create the auxiliary table index. Do not specify any columns for the index key. When a CREATE INDEX is issued against an auxiliary table DB2 will implicitly define the index key on the ROWID column.

The final step is to populate the LOB data into the table. Though we know that the actual LOB data is stored in an auxiliary table in a LOB table space and not in the base table, when you populate the LOB data you must reference the base table. If the total length of the LOB column and the base table row is less than 32KB, you can use the LOAD utility to populate the data into DB2. If the LOB column is greater in size you must use INSERT or

UPDATE statements. When using `INSERT` to populate the LOB data you must ensure that your application has access to adequate storage to hold the entire LOB value that is to be inserted.

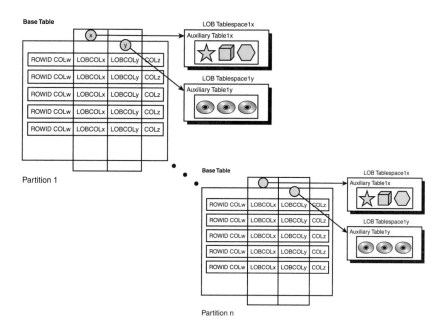

FIGURE 9.1   Base table to auxiliary table relationship for storing LOBs.

A Sample Table Using LOB Columns   Consider the steps you would need to take to add an org chart to the DSN8810.DEPT sample table. The org chart is a BLOB of no more than 5 megabytes in size. The first step would be to alter the table to add two columns: a `ROWID` column and a BLOB column. For example:

```
ALTER TABLE DSN8810.DEPT
  ADD ROW_ID ROWID GENERATED ALWAYS;
COMMIT;

ALTER TABLE DSN8810.DEPT
  ADD DEPT_ORG_CHART BLOB(5M);
COMMIT;
```

The next step would be to create the LOB table space and auxiliary table for the LOB column. For example:

```
CREATE LOB TABLESPACE TDORGCHT
  IN DSN8D81A
  LOG NO;
COMMIT;
CREATE AUXILIARY TABLE DEPT_ORGCHART_TAB
  IN DSN8D81A. TDORGCHT
```

```
     STORES DSN8810.DEPT
     COLUMN DEPT_ORG_CHART;
COMMIT;
```

Following this you must create the index on the auxiliary table. Remember, you do not need to specify columns for the index key when an index is defined on an auxiliary table. The following SQL CREATE statement defines the auxiliary table index:

```
CREATE UNIQUE INDEX XDEPTORG
   ON DEPT_ORGCHART_TAB;
COMMIT;
```

> **NOTE**
>
> If BIND parameter SQLRULES is set to STD, or if special register CURRENT RULES has been set to STD, DB2 will automatically create the LOB table space, auxiliary table, and auxiliary index when you issue the ALTER TABLE statement to add the LOB column.

Accessing LOB Data

LOB columns can be accessed using SQL just like other columns, in most cases. For example, you can code an SQL SELECT statement to retrieve the resume information stored in the EMP_RESUME column of the DSN8810.EMP table as follows

```
SELECT EMPNO, EMP_RESUME
FROM    DSN8810.EMP;
```

When embedding SQL in application programs you need to take the size of LOBs into consideration. By using a LOB locator you can manipulate LOB data without actually moving the data into a host variable. A LOB locator is a reference to the large object, and not the LOB data itself. Figure 9.2 illustrates this principle.

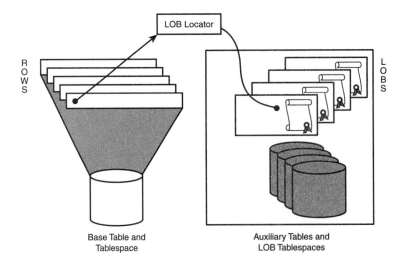

FIGURE 9.2   Using LOB locators.

A LOB locator is associated with a LOB data value or LOB expression, not with a row in a DB2 table or an actual physical storage location in a DB2 table space. So, once you SELECT the LOB value using a LOB locator the value of the locator should not change, but the actual value of the LOB might change.

DB2 provides two statements to work with LOB locators:

FREE LOCATOR   Removes the association between the LOB locator and its LOB value before a unit of work ends.

HOLD LOCATOR   Maintains the association between a LOB locator and its LOB value after the unit of work ends. After issuing the HOLD LOCATOR statement, the LOB locator will keep its association with the LOB data value until the program ends or FREE LOCATOR is issued.

> **NOTE**
>
> You cannot use EXECUTE IMMEDIATE with the HOLD LOCATOR or FREE LOCATOR statements when issuing dynamic SQL.

By using LOB locators your application programs will require significantly less memory than would be required if entire LOB values were returned to the program. The LOB locator can be returned from queries, inserted into new tables, and used by the application code like any other host variable. LOB locators enable the application to defer actually accessing the large object itself until the application needs the contents of that object.

You will need to DECLARE host variables to hold the LOB data or LOB locators. The host variables must be declared of SQL type BLOB, CLOB, or DBCLOB. DB2 will generate an appropriate declaration for the host language. For example, review Tables 9.1 and 9.2 for COBOL host variable declarations for LOB variables and LOB locators. In SQL statements you must refer to the LOB host variable or locator variable specified in the SQL type declaration. In host language statements (such as COBOL) you must use the variable generated by DB2.

TABLE 9.1   LOB Variable Declarations

Declared in the Program	Generated by DB2

01 BLOB-VAR USAGE IS
   SQL TYPE IS BLOB(1M).
	01 BLOB-VAR.
	   02 BLOB-VAR-LENGTH PIC 9(9) COMP.
	   02 BLOB-VAR-DATA.
	      49 FILLER PIC X(32767).
	            Repeat above line 31 times.
	      49 FILLER PIC X(32).

01 CLOB-VAR USAGE IS
   SQL TYPE IS CLOB(40000K).
	01 CLOB-VAR.
	   02 CLOB-VAR-LENGTH PIC 9(9) COMP.
	   02 CLOB-VAR-DATA.
	      49 FILLER PIC X(32767).
	            Repeat above line 1249 times.
	      49 FILLER PIC X(1250).

TABLE 9.1   Continued

Declared in the Program	Generated by DB2

01 DBCLOB-VAR USAGE IS
   SQL TYPE IS CLOB(40000K).
	01 DBCLOB-VAR.
	   02 DBCLOB-VAR-LENGTH PIC 9(9) COMP.
	   02 DBCLOB-VAR-DATA.
	      49 FILLER PIC G(32767)
	      USAGE DISPLAY-1.
	         Repeat above 2 lines 1249 times.
	      49 FILLER PIC G(1250).

The size limitation for COBOL variables is 32,767 bytes. This is a limit of the COBOL compiler. That is why DB2 generates multiple declarations of 32,767 bytes until it reaches the 1M specification.

TABLE 9.2   LOB Locator Variable Declarations

Declared in the Program	Generated by DB2
01 BLOB-LOC USAGE IS SQL TYPE IS BLOB-LOCATOR.	01 BLOB-LOC PIC S9(9) USAGE IS BINARY.
01 CLOB-LOC USAGE IS SQL TYPE IS CLOB-LOCATOR.	01 CLOB-LOC PIC S9(9) USAGE IS BINARY.
01 DBCLOB-LOC USAGE IS SQL TYPE IS DBCLOB-LOCATOR.	01 DBBLOB-LOC PIC S9(9) USAGE IS BINARY.

> **NOTE**
>
> The sizes of the LOBs you can declare and manipulate depend on the limits of the host language and the amount of storage available to your program. LOB host variables can be defined for the C, C++, COBOL, Assembler, PL/I, and Fortran programming languages.

LOB Materialization

When DB2 materializes a LOB it places the LOB value into contiguous storage in a data space. The amount of storage that is used in data spaces for LOB materialization depends on the size of the LOB data and the number of LOBs being materialized.

Because LOBs are usually quite large, LOB materialization should be avoided until it is absolutely required. DB2 will perform LOB materialization under the following circumstances:

- When a LOB host variable is assigned to a LOB locator host variable in an application program

- When a program calls a UDF that specifies a LOB as at least one of the arguments

- When a LOB is moved into or out of a stored procedure

- When a LOB is converted from one CCSID to another

By reducing the number of times you take these actions in your programs you can minimize LOB materialization and enhance the performance of applications that access LOB data. You cannot completely eliminate LOB materialization. However, using LOB locators you can minimize its impact on your applications.

LOBs and Locking

A lock that is held on a LOB value is referred to as a LOB lock.

When a row is read or modified in a table containing LOB columns the application will obtain a normal transaction lock on the base table. The locks on the base table also control concurrency for the LOB table space. When locks are not acquired on the base table, because of ISOLATION(UR) for example, DB2 maintains data consistency by using locks on the LOB table space.

Regardless of the isolation level, for other reasons DB2 also obtains locks on the LOB table space and the LOB values stored in that LOB table space. For more details on LOB locking refer to Chapter 23, "Locking DB2 Data."

LOB Guidelines

The following guidelines can be used to help you implement multimedia object/relational databases using LOBs with DB2.

Do Not Edit the ROWID   The ROWID columns required for implementing LOBs should be generated by DB2. The ROWID column cannot be modified. When supplying a value to a ROWID column in a LOAD, the value should have been previously generated by DB2 and then unloaded at some point. Do not attempt to create a ROWID value; they should always be generated by DB2 to ensure accuracy.

> **NOTE**
>
> You cannot use LOAD to load ROWID values if the ROWID column was created with the GENERATED ALWAYS clause.

Define the ROWID **Columns As** NOT NULL   A ROWID column cannot be null. You should explicitly indicate NOT NULL when defining the column. If you do not DB2 will implicitly create the column as NOT NULL. This is the exact opposite of what DB2 will do for other columns that do not specify NOT NULL. That is, when NOT NULL is specified, DB2 will make the column nullable (except for a ROWID column). This is another good reason for never relying upon defaults—because defaults can be confusing.

Implement LOBs with Care   When LOB columns are implemented and populated, they can consume a large amount of space. Be absolutely certain that the large objects are required by your applications before storing them using DB2.

Using LOBs Versus VARCHAR **and** VARGRAPHIC **Data Types**   A column defined as a VARCHAR data type holds alphanumeric data. The size of a VARCHAR column can range from 1 byte to a maximum of 8 bytes less than the record size. The record size depends upon the size of the table space page and whether or not an `EDITPROC` is being used. Table 9.3 outlines the maximum size of a `VARCHAR` column based on the page size of the table space.

TABLE 9.3   Maximum size of a `VARCHAR` column

EDITPROC Used?	Page 4K	Page 8K	Page 16K	Page 32K
YES	4046	8128	16320	32704
NO	4056	8138	16330	32714

If the `VARCHAR` specifies a size greater than 255, it is considered a `LONG VARCHAR` column.

Similar to `VARCHAR` columns, `VARGRAPHIC` columns are variable in size, but are used to store binary data. The size of a `VARGRAPHIC` column can range from 1 byte to a maximum of 2 bytes less than one half the record size. If the `VARGRAPHIC` specifies a size greater than 127, it is considered a `LONG VARGRAPHIC` column.

In general, BLOBs are preferable to `VARGRAPHIC` data types, and CLOBs or DBCLOBs are preferable to large `VARCHAR` data types. The LOB data types can be used to store larger amounts of data and have less impact on the other data elements of the table because LOBs are not stored in the same physical table space.

However, for smaller amounts of data `VARCHAR` and `VARGRAPHIC` data types can be easier to implement, administer, and manage. When dealing with character data less than 255 bytes or graphic data less than 127 bytes, consider using `VARCHAR` and `VARGRAPHIC` data types.

Use LOBs with User-Defined Distinct Types   Usually, you should not create tables with the LOB data types. Instead, for each LOB you wish to store, create a user-defined distinct type to use. Failure to do so can make it difficult to understand the type of data being stored in the table. For example, if you wish to store audio sound bites, consider creating a UDT such as

```
CREATE DISTINCT TYPE SOUND_BITE AS BLOB(1M)
```

Then, when you create the table, you can use the UDT. Instead of specifying `BLOB(1M)` as the data type you can specify `SOUND_BITE`, such as

```
CREATE TABLE CAMPAIGN_DETAILS
(CANDIDATE_LNAME     CHAR(40) NOT NULL,
 CANDIDATE_FNAME     CHAR(25) NOT NULL,
 ELECTION_YR         INTEGER,
 SPEECH_SAMPLE       SOUND_BITE)
```

Isn't it easier to determine that the `SPEECH_SAMPLE` column is actually audio because you used the `SOUND_BITE` data type? If you specified the underlying type, `BLOB(1M)` instead, it might be a photo or a movie of the candidate delivering the speech or some other binary object.

Use LOB Locators to Save Program Storage   By using LOB locators instead of directly accessing the actual LOB data, you can manipulate LOB data in your programs without retrieving the data from the DB2 table. This is a good technique because it reduces the amount of storage required by your program.

Defer Evaluation of LOB Expressions   LOB data is not moved until the program assigns a LOB expression to a target destination. So, when you use a LOB locator with string functions and operators, you can create an expression that DB2 does not evaluate until the time of assignment. This is called deferring evaluation of a LOB expression. Deferring evaluation can improve LOB I/O performance.

Use the Sample LOB Applications Shipped with DB2   DB2 ships with several sample applications that use LOB columns. Use these samples as templates to assist you when writing applications that use LOB columns. The sample applications include

DSN8DLPL	A C program that uses LOB locators and UPDATE statements to move binary data into a column of type BLOB.
DSN8DLRV	A C program that uses a LOB locator to manipulate CLOB data.
DSNTEP2	The dynamic SQL sample program written in PL/I allocates an SQLDA for rows that include LOB data and uses that SQLDA to describe a SQL statement and fetch data from LOB columns.

Consider Using UDFs to Limit LOB Overhead   You can create and use UDFs designed to return only a portion of a LOB, thereby limiting the transfer of LOB data to only the portion that the application requires. This can greatly reduce the amount of traffic required between a client application and the database server.

For example, consider a query designed to return a CLOB column, for example the EMP_RESUME column in DSN8810.EMP. The CLOB column contains character text. You can select the CLOB_LOCATOR into a host variable and then use the POSSTR() function to find the offset of a specific string within the CLOB. The CLOB_LOCATOR in the host variable is passed as the argument to POSSTR(). Finally, the SUBSTR() function can be used to select a portion of the CLOB.

Use Indicator Variables with LOB Locators for Nullable LOBs   DB2 uses indicator variables differently for LOB locators. When you SELECT a column that is null into a host variable (other than a LOB locator) an associated indicator variable is assigned a negative value to indicate that this column is set to null. But DB2 uses indicator variables a little differently for LOB locators because a LOB locator can never be null.

When you SELECT a LOB column using a LOB locator, and the LOB column is set to null, DB2 will assign a negative value to the associated indicator variable. But the LOB locator value does not change.

So, when using use LOB locators to retrieve data from columns that can contain nulls, always define indicator variables for the LOB locators. After fetching data into the LOB locators check the indicator variables. If the indicator variable indicates that the LOB column is null, do not use the value in the LOB locator. It is not valid because the LOB column is null.

Avoid Logging Large LOBs   Because LOBs are typically very large, logging changes to LOBs can become quite inefficient. Avoid logging by specifying `LOG NO` when creating the LOB table space. The default is `LOG YES`. If the size of the LOB is greater than 1MB, favor specifying `LOG NO`. For smaller LOBs, specifying `LOG NO` still can be beneficial, though.

When `LOG NO` is specified for the LOB table space, changes to the LOB column are not written to the log. `LOG NO` has no effect on a commit or rollback operation; the consistency of the database is maintained regardless of whether the LOB value is logged. When `LOG NO` is specified, changes to system pages and to the auxiliary index are still logged.

Another consideration when deciding whether or not to log LOBs is how frequently the LOB column is updated. For LOBs that are rarely or never changed, logging does not provide any advantage. Many LOB columns, such as graphics, are just replaced entirely when changes need to be made.

Keep in mind, though, that whenever logging is turned off, some form of recoverability still needs to be established. This can be as simple as retaining the input documents somewhere so they can be re-inserted to the LOB column in case of a database problem.

Isolate LOBs in Their Own Buffer Pool   Take special care when assigning LOBs to a buffer pool. Use a bufferpool that is not shared with other, non-LOB data. Additionally, assign the deferred write threshold (`DWQT`) to `0` for the LOB bufferpool(s).

For LOBs that are not logged, changed pages are written at `COMMIT`. With `DWQT` set to `0`, the writes will be processed in the background, continually, instead of all at once when committed. For LOBs that are logged, setting `DWQT` to `0` avoids huge amounts of data being written at DB2 checkpoints.

For more information on buffer pools and `DWQT`, refer to Chapter 28, "Tuning DB2's Components."

DB2 Extenders

LOB data types (`BLOB`, `CLOB`, and `DBCLOB`) provide an easy way to store large, unstructured data in DB2 databases. But LOBs are nondescript. The only thing you know about them is a general idea of the type of data:

- A `BLOB` is binary data

- A `CLOB` is character data

- A `DBCLOB` is double-byte character data

But DB2 comes equipped with extenders that can be used to provide additional meaning and functionality to LOBs. DB2 Extenders are available for image, audio, video, and text data. A DB2 Extender provides a distinct type for the LOB, and a set of user-defined functions for use with objects of its distinct type. Additionally, the DB2 Extenders automatically capture and maintain attribute information about the objects being stored. They also provide APIs for your applications to use.

Basically, the DB2 Extenders provide the functionality to make LOBs useful for your applications. With the DB2 Extenders, you could store LOBs, but doing anything very useful with them would be difficult and require a lot of work.

The DB2 Extenders use the MMDBSYS schema for all objects, including UDTs and UDFs. The following UDTs are created by the DB2 Extenders to support image, audio, and video data:

DB2AUDIO	A variable-length string containing information needed to access an audio object, also called an audio handle.
DB2IMAGE	A variable-length string containing information needed to access an image object, also called an image handle.
DB2TEXTH	A variable-length string containing information needed to access a text document, also called a text handle.
DB2TEXTFH	A variable length string containing information required for indexing an external text file, also referred to as a file handle.
DB2VIDEO	A variable-length string containing information needed to access a video object, also known as a video handle.

The DB2AUDIO, DB2IMAGE, and DB2VIDEO UDTs are based on a VARCHAR(250) data type. The DB2TEXTH UDT is based on a VARCHAR(60) data type with FOR BIT DATA.

The information in a text handle includes a document ID, the name of the server where the text is to be indexed, the name of the index, information about the text file, and information about the location of the file. File handles are stored in columns that Text Extender creates and associates with each group of external files. The audio, image, and video handles are stored in columns created by each specific extender for handling that type of data—audio, image, or video.

When enabled, each of the DB2 Extenders—audio, image, text, and video—also creates user-defined functions for use on columns defined as the UDT. The UDFs created by each of the DB2 Extenders are outlined in Tables 9.4, 9.5, 9.6, and 9.7.

TABLE 9.4   UDFs Created By the Audio Extender

UDF Name	Purpose of the UDF
AlignValue	Gets the bytes per sample value of the audio
BitsPerSample	Returns the number of bits used to represent the audio
BytesPerSec	Returns the average number of bytes per second of audio
Comment	Retrieves or modifies user comments
Content	Retrieves or modifies the audio content
ContentA	Updates the audio content with user-supplied attributes
DB2Audio	Stores the audio content
DB2AudioA	Stores the audio content with user-supplied attributes
Duration	Retrieves the audio playing time
Filename	Retrieves the name of the file that contains the audio

9

TABLE 9.4   Continued

UDF Name	Purpose of the UDF
FindInstrument	Retrieves the number of the audio track that records a specific instrument in an audio
FindTrackName	Retrieves the track number of a named track in an audio recording
Format	Retrieves the audio format
GetInstruments	Retrieves the names of the instruments in the audio recording
GetTrackNames	Retrieves the track names in an audio recording
Importer	Retrieves the user ID of the importer of an audio
ImportTime	Retrieves the timestamp when an audio was imported
NumAudioTracks	Retrieves the number of recorded tracks in an audio
NumChannels	Retrieves the number of audio channels
Replace	Modifies the content and user comments for an audio recording
ReplaceA	Modifies the content and user comments for an audio recording with user-supplied attributes
SamplingRate	Retrieves the sampling rate of the audio
Size	Retrieves the size of an audio in bytes
TicksPerQNote	Retrieves the number of clock ticks per quarter note used in recording an audio
TicksPerSec	Retrieves the number of clock ticks per second used in recording an audio
Updater	Retrieves the user ID of the updater of an audio
UpdateTime	Retrieves the timestamp when an audio was updated

TABLE 9.5   UDFs Created By the Image Extender

UDF Name	Purpose of the UDF
Comment	Retrieves or modifies user comments
Content	Retrieves or modifies the image content
ContentA	Updates the image content with user-supplied attributes
DB2Image	Stores the image content
DB2ImageA	Stores the image content with user-supplied attributes
Filename	Retrieves the name of the file that contains an image
Format	Retrieves the image format (for example, GIF)
Height	Retrieves the height of an image in pixels
Importer	Retrieves the user ID of the importer of an image
ImportTime	Retrieves the timestamp when an image was imported
NumColors	Retrieves the number of colors used in an image
Replace	Updates the content and user comments for an image
ReplaceA	Updates the content and user comments for an image with user-supplied attributes
Size	Retrieves the size of an image in bytes
Thumbnail	Retrieves a thumbnail-sized version of an image
Updater	Retrieves the user ID of the updater of an image
UpdateTime	Retrieves the timestamp when an image was updated
Width	Retrieves the width of an image in pixels

TABLE 9.6 UDFs Created By the Text Extender

UDF Name	Purpose of the UDF
CCSID	Returns the CCSID from a handle
Contains	Searches for text in a particular document
File	Retrieves or modifies the path and name of a file in an existing handle
Format	Retrieves or modifies the document format setting in a handle
Init_Text_Handle	Retrieves a partially initialized handle containing information such as format and language settings
Language	Retrieves or modifies the language setting in a handle
NO_of_Matches	Searches for matches and returns the number of matches found
Rank	Retrieves the rank value of a found text document
Refine	Returns a combined search argument from a specified search argument and refining search argument
Search_Result	Returns an intermediate table with the search result of the specified search string

TABLE 9.7 UDFs Created By the Video Extender

UDF Name	Purpose of the UDF
AlignValue	Gets the bytes per sample value of the audio track of the video
AspectRatio	Returns the aspect ratio of the first track of an MPEG1 and MPEG2 video
BitsPerSample	Returns the number of bits used to represent the audio
BytesPerSec	Returns the average number of bytes per second of the audio track of the video
Comment	Retrieves or modifies user comments
CompressType	Returns the compression format of a video (for example, MPEG-2)
Content	Retrieves or modifies the video content
ContentA	Updates the video content with user-supplied attributes
DB2Video	Stores the video content
DB2VideoA	Stores the video content with user-supplied attributes
Duration	Retrieves the video playing time
Filename	Retrieves the name of the file that contains the video
Format	Retrieves the video format
Importer	Retrieves the user ID of the importer of the video
ImportTime	Retrieves the timestamp when the video was imported
MaxBytesPerSec	Retrieves the maximum throughput of a video in bytes per second
NumAudioTracks	Retrieves the number of audio tracks in the video
NumChannels	Retrieves the number of audio channels in the audio track of the video
NumFrames	Retrieves the number of frames in the video
NumVideoTracks	Retrieves the number of video tracks in a video
Replace	Modifies the content and user comments for the video
ReplaceA	Modifies the content and user comments for the video with user-supplied attributes
SamplingRate	Retrieves the sampling rate for an audio track of the video
Size	Retrieves the size of the video audio in bytes

TABLE 9.7 Continued

UDF Name	Purpose of the UDF
Updater	Retrieves the user ID of the updater of an audio
UpdateTime	Retrieves the timestamp when an audio was updated
Width	Retrieves the width in pixels of a video frame

XML Extender

 DB2 V7 supports XML using a new data type extender for XML documents: the XML Extender. The XML Extender is similar to the other extenders for video, image, audio, and text that were added to DB2 V6. Like those previous extenders, the XML Extender combines user-defined distinct types, user-defined functions, and triggers to provide extended data type functionality for DB2 databases.

The XML Extender enables XML documents to be integrated with DB2 databases. By integrating XML into DB2 databases, you can more directly and quickly access the XML documents. You can search and store entire XML documents using SQL. You also have the option of combining XML documents with traditional data stored in relational tables.

When you store or compose a document, you can invoke DBMS functions to trigger an event to automate the interchange of data between applications. An XML document can be stored complete in a single text column. Alternatively, XML documents can be broken into component pieces and stored as multiple columns across multiple tables.

The XML Extender provides user-defined data types (UDTs) and user-defined functions (UDFs) to store and manipulate XML in the DB2 database. The XML Extender defines UDTs for XMLVARCHAR, XMLCLOB, and XMLFILE. After the XML is stored in the database, the UDFs can be used to search and retrieve the XML data as a complete document or in pieces. The UDFs supplied by the XML Extender include

- Storage functions to insert XML documents into a DB2 database

- Retrieval functions to access XML documents from XML columns

- Extraction functions to extract and convert the element content or attribute values from an XML document to the data type that is specified by the function name

- Update functions to modify element contents or attribute values (and to return a copy of an XML document with an updated value)

The UDFs created by the XML Extender are outlined in Table 9.8.

TABLE 9.8 UDFs Created By the XML Extender

UDF Name	Purpose of the UDF
XMLVarcharFromFile	Reads an XML document from a file and returns the document as an XMLVARCHAR type.
XMLCLOBFromFile	Reads an XML document from a file and returns the document as an XMLCLOB type.

TABLE 9.8   Continued

UDF Name	Purpose of the UDF
XMLFileFromVarchar	Reads an XML document from memory as VARCHAR, writes it to an external file, and returns the file name and path as an XMLFILE type.
XMLFileFromCLOB	Reads an XML document as a CLOB locator, writes it to an external file, and returns the file name and path as an XMLFILE type.
Content	Depending on parameters, will retrieve from XMLFILE to a CLOB; or, retrieve from XMLVARCHAR to an external file; or, retrieve from XMLCLOB to an external file.
extractInteger	Extracts the element content or attribute value from an XML document and returns the data as an INTEGER data type.
extractSmallint	Extracts the element content or attribute value from an XML document and returns the data as a SMALLINT data type.
extractDouble	Extracts the element content or attribute value from an XML document and returns the data as a DOUBLE precision data type.
extractReal	Extracts the element content or attribute value from an XML document and returns the data as a REAL data type.
extractChar	Extracts the element content or attribute value from an XML document and returns the data as a CHAR data type.
extractVarchar	Extracts the element content or attribute value from an XML document and returns the data as a VARCHAR data type.
extractCLOB	Extracts a portion of an XML document, including its element and attribute markup, as well as the content of elements and attributes (including sub-elements). This function differs from the other extract functions; they return only the content of elements and attributes. Use extractClob to extract document fragments; use extractVarchar or extractChar to extract simple values.
extractDate	Extracts the element content or attribute value from an XML document and returns the data as a DATE data type.
extractTime	Extracts the element content or attribute value from an XML document and returns the data as a TIME data type.
extractTimestamp	Extracts the element content or attribute value from an XML document and returns the data as a TIMESTAMP data type.
Update	Updates a specified element or attribute value in one or more XML documents stored in the XML column.
generate_unique()	Returns a character string that is unique compared to any other execution of the same function. No arguments should be specified for this function, but the empty parentheses are required. The result of the function is a unique value and cannot be null.

NOTE

You can add an "s" to the extract functions if you so desire. The functionality is the same as the function without the "s" on the end. For example, extractInteger will function the same as extractIntegers; the terms are synonymous.

For additional information on DB2's support for XML please consult Chapter 17, "DB2 and the Internet."

V8 XML Support

V8 DB2 V8 provides even further support for XML within DB2 databases.

A new XML data type is introduced in DB2 V8. This new data type is not like any other existing data type. It is a transient data type in that it exists only during query processing. There is no persistent data of this type and it is not an external data type that can be declared in application programs. In other words, the XML data type cannot be stored in a database or returned to an application.

A DB2 XML data type can be an element, a forest of elements, the textual content of an element, or an empty XML value. Furthermore, there are restrictions for the use of the XML data type. An XML data type is not compatible with any other DB2 data type. Query results cannot contain an XML data type; nor can columns in a view contain an XML data type. Furthermore, XML data cannot be used in a sort.

DB2 V8 also introduces the XML publishing functions. The XML publishing functions are built-in DB2 functions that run inside the DB2 address spaces. Contrast that with normal external User Defined Functions that run in a WLM managed address space outside of DB2. This operational aspect of the XML publishing functions provides better performance. For more details on the XML publishing functions consult Chapter 3, "Using DB2 Functions."

Net Search Extender

V7 Additionally, DB2 V7 added another new extender, the Net Search Extender. The Net Search Extender complements the Text Extender to provide an efficient, full-text retrieval engine for DB2 Web applications. The Net Search Extender works with Net.Data, Java, and DB2 CLI application programs.

The primary benefits and features of the Net Search Extender include very fast indexing, sophisticated search capabilities including fuzzy searching and document tagging for limiting searches, and advanced formatting of search results.

The Net Search Extender provides four DB2 stored procedures to provide search functionality:

- `textsearch`—Performs a standard search with no ranking
- `textsearch_t`—Performs a standard search with tracing but no ranking
- `textsearch_r`—Performs a standard search with ranking
- `textsearch_rt`—Performs a standard search with ranking and tracing

DB2 Extender Guidelines

The following guidelines cover the additional issues you may encounter as you implement and plan for DB2 Extender usage.

Be Aware of WLM Requirements for DB2 Extenders   The system administrator must enable the DB2 Extenders you wish to use at your site. When the extender is enabled it creates the UDTs, UDFs, administrative tables, and supporting APIs for the extender. The extenders require the use of WLM (Work Load Manager) application environments for the UDFs and stored procedures that are created. The extenders use stored procedures to process API requests. After the DB2 extenders are installed, you need to establish WLM environments for the extender UDFs and stored procedures.

Be Aware of Security Implications   Before you use the DB2 Extenders, you need to consider the security and authorization issues your will encounter. First, you must decide how to secure access to the actual content of the audio, image, text, and video data. Additionally, the DB2 Extenders create administrative support tables to store additional information about the extenders. Some administrative support tables identify user tables and columns that are enabled for an extender. Other administrative support tables contain attribute information about objects in enabled columns. One example is the QBIC tables created by the Image Extender (QBIC stands for Query By Image Content). You must decide who should have access to the metadata in the administrative support tables.

Secondly, you need to determine how to manage the privileges that are automatically granted when the DB2 Extender is enabled. For example, when a DB2 Extender is enabled, USE privilege is granted to PUBLIC for the UDT, its related CAST functions, and all the UDFs for the extender. This may, or may not, be acceptable in your shop. If you REVOKE the privileges and GRANT them to specific authids, be prepared for the potential headache of administering the list of authorized users of the extender's functionality.

Your audio, image, and video data can be stored in files external to DB2. In that case you can also control access to the content in external files. This can be achieved using operating system security commands, which are usually performed by a separate security group. By limiting access to the external files you limit the ability to retrieve the objects for the extender's data type.

> **CAUTION**
>
> The files must be in a file system that is compatible with Unix System Services (USS); for example, a hierarchical file system. USS was previously known as MVS Open Edition.

Another consideration is MMDBSYS. All of the DB2 Extenders use the MMDBSYS SQLID. The UDT and all of the UDFs created by the DB2 Extender will be created in the MMDBSYS schema. You should consider creating the MMDBSYS userid to manage the administrative support tables. Use an appropriate external security package (such as ACF2 or RACF) to create an MMDBSYS userid.

The DB2 Extenders also create administrative APIs, many of which require special authority. For example, SYSADM or the SELECT privilege on audio columns in all searched tables is required for the DBaAdminGetInaccessibleFiles API. This API returns the names of inaccessible files that are referenced in audio columns of user tables.

Finally, you must consider who can issue administration commands to the db2ext command line processor for DB2 Extenders.

The administrative APIs and administration commands are documented in the DB2 Extenders manuals:

Image, Audio, and Video Extenders Administration and Programming Guide

Net Search Extender Administration and Programming Guide

Text Extender Administration and Programming Guide

XML Extender Administration and Programming Guide

CHAPTER 10

DB2 Security and Authorization

This chapter provides tips and techniques for DB2 security and authorization, including (but not limited to) SQL DCL—data control language. The proper application of DB2 security can have a significant impact on the useability and performance of DB2 programs.

Granting and Revoking Privileges

The capability to access and modify DB2 objects and resources is authorized with SQL GRANT statements and removed with SQL REVOKE statements. The complete security picture, however, is not this simple.

Many features of DB2 security can complicate security administration, such as

• The cascading effect of the DB2 REVOKE statement

• Secondary authorization IDs

• PUBLIC access

• Use of dynamic SQL

To enable authorization, the GRANT statement is used to bestow privileges on authids. There are ten different classes of privileges that can be granted:

• COLLECTION—To GRANT the ability to BIND packages into specified collections or to GRANT PACKADM authority for specified collections

• DATABASE—To GRANT database-related privileges such as DBADM, DBCTRL, DBMAINT, or the ability to CREATE or DROP objects, display, start and stop objects, or execute utilities for specified databases

- DISTINCT TYPE or JAR—To GRANT the ability to use user-defined distinct types (UDTs) or a Java Archive File (JAR)

- FUNCTION or STORED PROCEDURE—To GRANT the ability to execute specified functions and stored procedures

- PACKAGE—To GRANT the ability to BIND and REBIND specified packages, to use the COPY option of BIND for specified packages, or to run application programs that use specified packages

- PLAN—To GRANT the ability to BIND, REBIND, FREE, or EXECUTE specified plans

- SCHEMA—To GRANT the ability to ALTER, CREATE, or DROP user-defined distinct types, user-defined functions, stored procedures, and triggers in the specified schema or schemata

- SYSTEM—To GRANT system management-related abilities including ARCHIVE, BINDADD, BINDAGENT, BSDS, CREATEALIAS, CREATEDBA, CREATEDBC, CREATESG, CREATETMTAB, DISPLAY, MONITOR1, MONITOR2, RECOVER, STOPALL, STOSPACE, SYSADM, SYSCTRL, SYSOPR, and TRACE

- TABLE or VIEW—To GRANT the ability to ALTER, CREATE or DROP triggers, indexes, and referential constraints, or to SELECT, INSERT, UPDATE, and DELETE data from the specified views or tables

- USE—To GRANT the ability to use and create objects in specific bufferpools, storage groups, table spaces, and sequences

Likewise, there are ten different classes of REVOKE statements that can be issued—one for each class of GRANT that can be issued. As might be expected, the REVOKE statement removes authority from authids.

Authorization Guidelines

Guidelines for using GRANT and REVOKE to properly implement DB2 security are addressed in this section on authorization guidelines.

Use Care When Granting PUBLIC **Access**   Administering security can be a complex duty. Simply allowing blanket access to certain DB2 objects and resources often appears easier. The PUBLIC authority of DB2 gives the security administrator this option, but it is usually an unwise choice.

For example, when many shops install DB2, they grant PUBLIC access to the default database, DSNDB04. Inevitably, users assign table spaces to this database. Because the table spaces are in a default area, they are difficult to monitor and control. The area quickly becomes overused. The DBA unit is unaware of some tables that exist. If an error occurs, recovery might be impossible. Additionally, the only way to move a table space to a different database is by dropping the table space and redefining it, specifying another database name.

The only valid uses for PUBLIC access are for objects and resources that should be available to everyone who has access to the DB2 subsystem or if another security mechanism is in place. An example of the first use is granting the BINDADD privilege to PUBLIC in a test environment to allow all DB2 programmers to create DB2 application plans and packages. An example of the second use is granting EXECUTE authority for CICS transactions to PUBLIC and using CICS transaction security to control access. Other exceptions to avoiding PUBLIC access follow.

In some installations, the security is thought to be adequately provided by application programs, so PUBLIC access is implemented for objects. Implementing this access is unwise unless ad hoc access to these objects is forbidden. If ad hoc use is allowed, users have access to the data through SPUFI or QMF, and could corrupt the data. In general, you should grant PUBLIC access only as a last resort. Even when ad hoc access is forbidden, objects granted PUBLIC access can be accessed by hackers or other folks who "bend the rules."

Grant SELECT Authority on SYSIBM.SYSDUMMY1 to PUBLIC   Be sure to grant SELECT authority to PUBLIC for the SYSIBM.SYSDUMMY1 table. SYSIBM.SYSDUMMY1 contains a single row. It is designed to be used with SQL statements in which a table reference is needed but the table contents are unimportant.

Grant DISPLAY Authority to PUBLIC   Consider granting DISPLAY authority for each DB2 subsystem to PUBLIC. PUBLIC DISPLAY authority will not pose a security threat, but can improve productivity. Application developers can use DISPLAY to identify active programs and utilities affecting performance without requiring DBA assistance.

Do Not Repeat Security Grants   DB2 allows authorization to be granted multiple times to the same grantee for the same object or resource. As of DB2 V3, duplicate grants from the same grantor are not recorded in the DB2 Catalog. However, if the grants are from different grantors, duplicate authorizations still can occur. You should avoid duplicate authorizations because they cause confusion and clutter the DB2 Catalog with useless entries.

Duplicate authority is recorded in the DB2 Catalog most commonly when SQL GRANT statements have been coded in a common CLIST, REXX EXEC, or standard job. An example is a CLIST used by application programmers to BIND a plan and then GRANT EXECUTE authority to a list of users automatically. You should not use this method because it can lead to duplicate authorization entries in the DB2 Catalog.

Consolidate Security Grants   SELECT, INSERT, UPDATE, and DELETE authority should be granted using a single GRANT statement, instead of two to four separate statements. If one statement is used, one catalog row is created, instead of multiple rows (one for each GRANT statement that is issued).

Do Not GRANT More Security Than Necessary   Secure your DB2 application environment. Using group-level authority (for example, SYSADM or SYSOPR) is tempting because coding and maintaining it is easier. Group authorities, however, often provide more security than is required. SYSADM authority is the most powerful level of authorization provided by DB2 and should be reserved only for those DBAs and system programmers who need the authority and know how to use it wisely.

10

If system-development staff members are allowed to access and modify table data but are not allowed to create indexes and tables, do not grant them DBADM authority. Simply grant them the appropriate authority for the appropriate tables—in this case, SELECT, UPDATE, INSERT, and DELETE.

Plan DCL When Issuing DDL   Remember that when DB2 objects are dropped, the security for the objects is dropped as well. If you plan to drop and re-create a database, for example, be prepared to re-create the security for the database and all subordinate objects (such as table spaces, tables, views, and indexes).

Remember also that when plans are freed, all security is removed for the freed plans. Take this fact into account before freeing plans that you might need later.

Be Aware of DB2's Built-in Security Groupings   DB2 provides several built-in groupings of authorization that can be assigned to users. When a user is granted one of the group-level authorities, all of the security that applies to the group will then apply to the user. Figure 1.5 in Chapter 1, "The Magic Words," outlines the DB2 security levels; refer to it now if you need to refresh your memory.

In general, these group-level authorizations should be used for system users, such as DBAs, systems programmers, and operators. The authorization contained within these groups is useful for administrative users, but not for end users and developers.

Use Group-Level Security and Secondary Authids   When possible, use group-level security (for example, DBADM and DBCTRL) and secondary authids to reduce administrative tasks. Do not use group-level security, however, if the group will provide unwanted authority to users.

An alternative authorization ID is provided when you use the secondary authid extension, a useful timesaving feature of DB2 security. Each primary authid can have secondary authids associated with it. You can create these associations by using an external security package such as RACF or a hard-coded table of IDs. You can then grant security to a secondary authid assigned to a functional group of users.

For example, if all users in the finance department have been assigned a secondary authid of FINANCE, you can provide them with blanket query access by granting the SELECT authority to FINANCE for all financial tables. No additional security at the primary authid level is necessary when personnel leave or are hired. This feature eases the administrative burden of security allocation.

Additionally, secondary authids can reduce the workload of the DBA staff by offloading authorization tasks to the corporate security group. Security administration groups typically can support adding and deleting authids from a RACF group, but are not usually capable of issuing appropriate DB2 DCL statements.

Create DB2 Objects Using a Secondary Authid   When objects are created, implicit authority is automatically granted to the object owner. By using secondary authids when creating DB2 objects, administrative burden can be reduced. This is important when DBAs do not have SYSADM authority or when the DBA staff changes. If a secondary authid is not used as the object owner, it might be necessary to drop and re-create entire object structures to revoke implicit authorization.

Use External Security with Caution   DB2 provides the ability to replace its internal security mechanism with an external security package, such as RACF. When doing this, all security to DB2 objects is handled outside of DB2 instead of inside of DB2. The advantage of this approach is the ability to offload DB2 security administration from the DBA staff to in-house security experts.

To determine who has the ability to access DB2 objects, DBAs will need to access the external security package instead of querying DB2 Catalog tables. Before replacing DB2 security with an external security package, be sure that your policies and procedures are changed to enable DB2 DBAs to, at least, review the authorizations as managed in the external security package.

Furthermore, be sure that any third-party DB2 products and applications used by your shop can operate without requiring DB2 authority to be stored in the DB2 Catalog.

V8   Of course, if you need to setup multilevel security (MLS) then you will need to use RACF with DB2. More information on MLS follows later in this chapter.

Restrict SYSADM Authority   SYSADM is a powerful group authority that you should use sparingly. You should restrict its use to the corporate DBA function and the appropriate system programming support staff. End users, managers, and application development personnel should never need SYSADM authority. In general, no more than a half dozen technical support personnel should have SYSADM authority.

Use SYSCTRL for Additional Control   You can limit SYSADM authority even further by granting SYSCTRL instead of SYSADM to database administration and technical support personnel who play a backup role. SYSCTRL gives the same authority as SYSADM without access to data in application tables that were not created by the SYSCTRL user. End users, managers, and application development personnel should never be granted SYSCTRL authority.

SYSCTRL authority is one of the most misunderstood security features of DB2. It cannot be used to completely ensure that the SYSCTRL user will never have access to end-user data. A primary objective of the SYSCTRL authority is to enable a user—who has no general requirement to manipulate table data—to administer a DB2 environment. In essence, you can think of SYSCTRL as SYSADM without explicit DB2 data authority.

Basically, SYSCTRL authority implies that the user can exercise DBCTRL authority over tables in any database. However, CREATEDBA authority is also implicit under SYSCTRL. Therefore, the SYSCTRL user can create databases and obtain DBADM authority over them, which enables the SYSCTRL user to access and modify the data in any table within that database.

To get around this problem, you should implement procedures or standards to ensure that the SYSCTRL user never creates databases. You must do so manually because there is no systematic way of prohibiting SYSCTRL from creating databases. Assign the database creation function to a SYSADM user. After the database is created by another user, the SYSCTRL user can administer the database without accessing the data. As long as the

SYSCTRL user has not created the database in question and has not been granted any other authority (that is, SELECT, DBADM, and so on), he or she cannot access the data in user tables.

Use BINDAGENT for Package and Plan Administration   Use the BINDAGENT authority to permit the binding of plans and packages without the ability to execute them. BINDAGENT authority is sometimes called "assigning" authority. BINDAGENT authority enables one user to assign another user the capability of performing tasks (in this case, plan and package binding) on his or her behalf.

A centralized area in your organization should be responsible for binding production plans and packages. This area can be granted the BINDAGENT authority from all production plan and package owners. This approach is preferable to granting SYSADM or SYSCTRL because only bind operations are enabled when you grant BINDAGENT. BINDAGENT provides all the authority necessary to administer the bind function effectively.

Bind Plans from a Restricted Userid   You can acquire a greater level of control over the bind function by using a restricted userid for all production binding. This userid should have no logon capability so that the only access to the userid is through a batch job, not online access. You can provide external security with RACF (or any other security tool) to prohibit the unauthorized use of this userid.

Batch jobs that bind the application plans and packages as necessary should be created. The restricted userid should have BINDAGENT authority to allow successful binding with the OWNER parameter. The batch jobs are then submitted with the restricted userid by the group in your organization responsible for binding. This solution permits multiple authorized individuals to submit batch binds from the same userid. This solution also can ease the administrative burden associated with plan and package ownership, the attrition of binding agent personnel, and plan monitoring.

This scenario might not be feasible if your data security standards prohibit restricted userids. Some data security shops think that restricted userids have a propensity to fall into unauthorized hands. If this situation cannot be prevented, restricted userids for binding might not be appropriate for your shop.

Do Not Issue DCL from Application Programs   Avoid issuing GRANT and REVOKE statements from an application program. Security is granted ideally by an agent who understands the authorization needs of the organization.

Although you can set up a parameter-driven program to administer security, you generally cannot automate the task completely. Also, your program must avoid granting duplicate privileges, which is allowed by DB2. Otherwise, many duplicate privileges could be granted for your system, impeding overall system performance.

Additionally, an application program that grants security must be executed by a user who has the appropriate security to issue the grants and revokes coded in the application program. This could be a loophole in the security structure.

Finally, a program that issues REVOKE and GRANT statements can have a great impact on the overall scheme of your operating environment. Consider the following problems that can be caused by a program issuing DCL:

- The program tries to REVOKE a privilege from a user who is currently executing a transaction that would no longer be valid after the REVOKE.

- The program REVOKEs a privilege, causing numerous cascading REVOKEs that are difficult to trace after invocation. After the program is finished, the potential for many missing authorizations exists. This situation can wreak havoc on a production DB2 subsystem.

- What should the COMMIT and ROLLBACK structure of the program be? If the program abends, should all security be committed or rolled back and reapplied? The answer to these questions may not be immediately obvious in the absence of in-depth system documentation. It is better to avoid these types of questions by mandating that all DCL be issued by skilled technicians that understand the ramifications of each GRANT and REVOKE statement.

Be Careful When Granting Access to a Synonym Avoid granting others access to a synonym. A synonym, by definition, can be used only by its creator. Granting access to a synonym grants access to the underlying base table for which the synonym was created.

For example, consider a synonym called USER1.DEPARTMENT for the DSN8810.DEPT table. If USER1 wants to grant USER2 the authority to query this synonym, USER1 could code the following:

```
GRANT SELECT
    ON TABLE USER1.DEPARTMENT
    TO USER2;
```

In this case, USER2 now has SELECT authority on the DSN8810.DEPT table, not on the synonym created by USER1. Because this situation can be confusing, you should avoid granting access to synonyms.

Be Aware of Automatic Security When you create a DB2 object, DB2 automatically grants you full security to

- Use the object in any way.

- Grant others the use of the object.

If users need access to an object they did not create, they must get the creator, a SYSADM, a SYSCTRL, or someone else with the proper authority to grant them access. Additionally, the only way to change implicit authority is to drop the object and re-create it (and all dependent objects).

Be Aware of Package and Plan Authorization Differences A user with the BIND privilege on a plan can free that plan, but a user with the BIND privilege on a package cannot free that package. To free a package, the user must meet one of the following conditions:

10

- Be the owner of the package.

- Have SYSADM or SYSCTRL authority.

- Have BINDAGENT privilege granted by the package owner.

Avoid WITH GRANT OPTION   Be careful with the multilevel security of DB2. When a privilege is granted to a user using WITH GRANT OPTION, the user can also grant that privilege. This capability can create an administrative nightmare for DB2 security agents. Consider the following scenario:

1. SYSADM grants a privilege to USER1 with the grant option.

2. USER1 grants this privilege to USER2 without the grant option.

3. USER1 grants this privilege to USER3 with the grant option.

4. SYSADM grants this privilege to USER5 with the grant option.

5. USER5 grants this privilege to PUBLIC.

6. USER3 grants this privilege to USER9.

7. SYSADM revokes the privilege from USER1.

Who has this privilege now? When SYSADM revokes the privilege from USER1, DB2 cascades the revokes to all the users who were granted this privilege directly or indirectly by USER1. This effectively revokes the privilege from everybody except USER5. However, USER5 granted this privilege to PUBLIC, so everybody—including USER1—still has this privilege. WITH GRANT OPTION is the only privilege removed by the SYSADM revoke.

As a general rule, never allow the WITH GRANT OPTION in a production environment, and control and limit the availability of the WITH GRANT OPTION in a test environment. Consider purchasing an add-on security maintenance tool to monitor and minimize the effects of DB2's cascading revoke. Security tools are described further in Part VII, "The Ideal DB2 Environment."

Revoking a SYSADM   Use caution when revoking a SYSADM from the system. Simply revoking the SYSADM authority from a user can cause cascading revokes. To revoke a SYSADM without causing cascading revokes, follow this procedure:

1. Create a DSNZPARM member specifying the SYSADM userid to be revoked as an Install SYSADM. If both Install SYSADM parameters are currently being used, simply remove one of them and place the SYSADM userid to be revoked in its place. Removing an Install SYSADM does not cause cascading revokes.

2. Revoke the SYSADM authority from the user.

3. Modify the DSNZPARM member to remove the userid as an Install SYSADM. Replace the old Install SYSADM userid (if one was removed).

> **CAUTION**
>
> If, after you revoke SYSADM, the userid is still valid in the system, its associated user can revoke privileges that were previously granted when the user was a SYSADM. This user has this capability because the userid remains as the GRANTOR of the authority in the DB2 Catalog.

Avoid Explicit DELETE, UPDATE, and INSERT Authority   Consider not permitting users to have DELETE, UPDATE, and INSERT authority on production tables. You can enable users to modify data through application programs by granting them execute authority on an application plan that performs the desired type of updates. This way, you can effectively limit data modification to a controlled environment.

You should strictly control data modification because DB2 set-level processing can cause entire tables to be destroyed with a single SQL statement. Consider this example:

```
UPDATE DSN8810.DEPT
    SET DEPT = 'YYY';
```

This statement sets every department in the DEPT table to 'YYY', which is probably not required. If uncontrolled deletion, insertion, and modification are permitted, data almost certainly will be lost because of careless SQL modification statements.

Limit Alter Authority with the REFERENCES Privilege   The REFERENCES privilege grants a user authority to CREATE or DROP referential constraints in which the named table is the parent table. Grant the REFERENCES privilege to administrators needing to maintain RI but not needing general ALTER authority on DB2 objects.

Consider Dynamic Authority   As of DB2 V4, authorization for dynamic SQL in application programs can be treated the same as static SQL. For more details, refer to Chapter 12, "Dynamic SQL Programming."

Follow the Proliferation Avoidance Rule   Do not needlessly proliferate DB2 security. Every DB2 authorization grant requires additional entries in the DB2 Catalog. Granting unneeded authority causes catalog clutter—extraneous entries strewn about the DB2 Catalog tables. The larger the DB2 Catalog tables become, the less efficient your entire DB2 system will be.

The proliferation avoidance rule is based on common sense. Why proliferate unneeded authorization?

Multilevel Security

V8 With *multilevel security (MLS)* in DB2 V8 it becomes possible to support applications that need a more granular security scheme. For example, you might want to set up an authorization scenario such that employees can see their own data but no one else's. Or your authorization needs might dictate that each employee's immediate manager is able to see his payroll information as well as all of his employee's data, and so on up through the org chart. Setting up such a security scheme is virtually impossible prior to DB2 V8.

10

MLS with Row Level Granularity

As database systems and applications become more sophisticated, the need for low-level access control to the business data becomes more critical. With the events of the past few years, issues such as security, privacy, and auditing are now more important than ever before. The need to ensure that each piece of data is secured such that only authorized users can perform authorized functions is growing. DB2 V8 adds support for row level granularity of access control with multilevel security.

DB2 V8 supports row-level security in conjunction with a security management product (like RACF). To activate this authorization mechanism, you will need to add a specially named column to act as the security label. The security label column is matched with the multilevel security hierarchy in the security manager. For example, you might want to set up a hierarchy representing the animal kingdom, as shown in Figure 10.1. Of course, the hierarchy need not be so complex—you might simply choose to use something simpler, such as TOP SECRET, SECRET, and UNCLASSIFIED.

> **CAUTION**
>
> To support MLS hierarchies, DB2 V8 requires several new RACF access control functions that are not available prior to V1R5 of z/OS.
>
> For other security server products, consult the vendor for guidance before attempting to use it with DB2 for multilevel security.

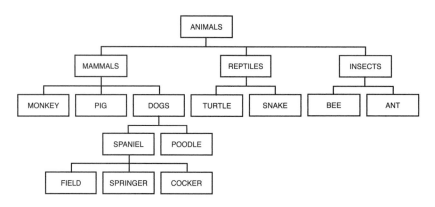

FIGURE 10.1   A sample MLS hierarchy.

In the example shown in Figure 10.1, an MLS hierarchy representing the animal kingdom is to be used. This hierarchy is established in RACF. At the top of the hierarchy, ANIMALS, is a security label that includes everything—for example, all mammals, reptiles, and insects. Middle levels of the hierarchy that represent additional security groupings can be created. In this case we have a second level of MAMMALS, REPTILES, and INSECTS. And under MAMMALS we have other levels/security labels: DOGS (SPANIEL, POODLE) and even SPANIEL breaks down to FIELD, SPRINGER, and COCKER. And so on throughout the hierarchy. Such a hierarchy provides great flexibility for assigning various levels of security to data in DB2 tables—and thereby appropriately securing the data from unauthorized user access.

Again, referring to the MLS hierarchy, let's discuss a few of the levels and what they imply. First of all, users designated with the ANIMALS authority can access anything. Users with authority to access MAMMALS data can access any row associated with MAMMALS, or any subordinate mammal (MONKEYS, PIGS, and DOGS), and so on down through the hierarchy (including SPANIELS and POODLES, as well as types of spaniels—FIELD, SPRINGER, and COCKER spaniels). This offers more powerful security than simple matching. To use this feature in DB2, you must define a special column for each table that is to have row-level security. This column, referred to as the SECLABEL, must be defined with the specification AS SECURITY LABEL. The SECLABEL column must be defined as CHAR(8) NOT NULL WITH DEFAULT. Furthermore, the SECLABEL column cannot have any field procedures, edit procedures or check constraints defined upon it. After a table has a SECLABEL defined, it cannot be disabled. Only one security label per table is permitted.

When row-level security is implemented, every user must be identified to RACF (or another security server with equivalent functionality) with a valid SECLABEL. If the user is not identified with a SECLABEL, an authorization error will occur. At a high level, then, row-level security works by matching the SECLABEL of the data to the SECLABEL of the user. One of the important features of multilevel security is that the person retrieving the row has no idea other rows even exist—and not that they simply cannot see them.

Of course, there are additional details that are needed to implement user row-level authorization properly in DB2. First of all, there is some new terminology that you will need to assimilate in order to understand how DB2 row-level security works. Controls put in place to prevent unauthorized users from accessing information at a higher classifications that their authorization level enforce *read up* security. But controls also must be put in place to prevent users from declassifying information—and this is known as *write down* security.

Additionally, you will need to understand the terms used when comparing SECLABELs. To enforce read up and write down security, comparison is not just a simple equivalency match. There are four possible outcomes when a user's SECLABEL is compared to the data's SECLABEL:

- **Dominate**—A SECLABEL dominates another if it is greater than or equal to it in the hierarchy.

- **Reverse Dominate**—A SECLABEL reverse dominates another if it is less than or equal to it in the hierarchy.

- **Equivalence**—Equivalence means that the SECLABELs are the same or have the same level and set of categories. Two SECLABELs are equivalent if both dominance and reverse dominance apply.

- **Null**—If none of the above are true, the null condition applies.

The following bulleted items describe the manner in which row-level security authorization operates:

- **SELECT**—The value of the user's SECLABEL is compared to the SECLABEL of the row to be selected. If the user's SECLABEL dominates the data's SECLABEL, the row is

10

returned. If the user's SECLABEL does not dominate the data's SECLABEL, then the row is not returned, and no error is reported.

- INSERT—If the user has a valid SECLABEL, then the user's SECLABEL value is used for the data's SECLABEL column for the row that is being inserted. If the user does not have the write-down privilege, then the SECLABEL of inserted rows will be exactly the current SECLABEL. Users with the write-down privilege can set the value of the SECLABEL column to any value.

- UPDATE—The user's SECLABEL is compared with the data's SECLABEL (for the row being updated), but only for users with a valid SECLABEL. If the SECLABELs match, then the row is updated. If the SECLABELs do not match, then both dominance and reverse dominance are checked. The UPDATE is allowed only if both are true. Also, the data's SECLABEL is set to the user's SECLABEL value.

- DELETE—The user's SECLABEL is compared with the data's SECLABEL (for the row being deleted), but only for users with a valid SECLABEL. If the SECLABELs match, then the row is deleted. If the SECLABELs do not match, then both dominance and reverse dominance are checked. The DELETE is allowed only if both are true. A user who has write down authority can access and delete down-level (dominance) rows, but not up-level (reverse dominance) rows.

Similar to normal data processing in DB2 tables, utility processing must be checked for authorization. As with normal processing, the user running the utility must be identified to RACF. The following outlines how the IBM DB2 utilities work with row-level MLS:

LOAD RESUME—Loading with the RESUME option functions similarly to INSERT processing. Without write down permission, the SECLABEL is set to the current SECLABEL. With write down permission, the user is permitted to specify the SECLABEL.

LOAD REPLACE—Because loading with the REPLACE option will DELETE all existing rows, write down authority is required.

UNLOAD—Unloading data functions similarly to SELECT processing. The only rows that can be unloaded are those where the user's SECLABEL dominates the data's SECLABEL. If this is not the case, the row is not returned (and no error is returned).

REORG UNLOAD EXTERNAL—Functions the same as the UNLOAD utility (just discussed).

REORG DISCARD—Reorganizing data with the DISCARD option functions similarly to DELETE processing. For each row that is unloaded during the REORG, if the row qualifies to be discarded, the user's SECLABEL is compared to the data's SECLABEL. If both dominance and reverse dominance is true, then the row is discarded, otherwise it is kept.

Be Aware of Row-Level MLS Restrictions   Although row-level MLS provides great control over data access and modifications, there are several restrictions that apply. These restrictions are as follows:

- Referential constraints cannot be defined on a security label column.

- Sysplex parallelism will not be used for any query that accesses a table with a security label column.

- Edit procedures and field procedures are not allowed on a security label column.

- Trigger transition tables cannot have security labels.

Additionally, the access control authorization exit, which used to ship with RACF, now ships with DB2. So, the exit is no longer in the RACF `SYS1.SAMPLIB` library, but in the DB2 `SDSNSAMP` library.

> **CAUTION**
>
> Your old authorization exits will no longer work with DB2 Version 8. Migration to the new authorization exit is required in order to support new object types and certain new features, such as long names. Be sure to plan the conversion as part of your V8 migration effort.

MLS for Access Control

Multilevel security access controls can be used in conjunction with native DB2 access controls (`GRANT/REVOKE`) or with RACF access controls. If you use RACF, then you can use security labels to define the access controls on most DB2 objects.

Access requires both the discretionary access control (`PERMIT`) and the mandatory access control (`SECLABEL` comparison). When implementing MLS on database objects be sure to define the `SECLABEL` of each object such that the higher object dominates all objects lower than it in the hierarchy. Figure 10.2 shows the DB2 object hierarchy for MLS security. This hierarchy is for security purposes, as opposed to the simple database object hierarchy shown in Chapter 1 (Figure 1.4), which is to be used to guide the order in which database objects should be created.

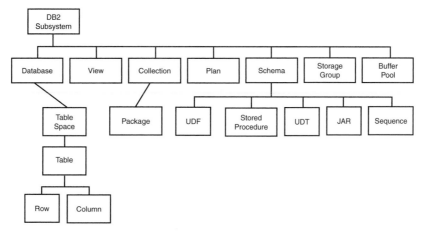

FIGURE 10.2   The DB2 database object hierarchy.

Session Variables

V8 Session variables, set by DB2 or by the user, provide another way to provide additional information to applications. The following session variables are set by DB2 (as of V8), and are therefore accessible to application programs and end users:

- PLAN_NAME—Name of the plan that is currently being run

- PACKAGE_NAME—Name of the package currently in use

- PACKAGE_SCHEMA—Schema name of the current package

- PACKAGE_VERSION—Version of the current package

- SECLABEL—The user's security label

- SYSTEM_NAME—Name of the system

- VERSION—Version of the DB2 subsystem

- DATA_SHARING_GROUP_NAME—Name of the data sharing group

- SYSTEM_ASCII_CCSID—CCSID information in ASCII

- SYSTEM_EBCDIC_CCSID—CCSID information in EBCDIC

- SYSTEM_UNICODE_CCSID—CCSID information in Unicode

Each of these session variables is qualified by SYSIBM. A new (V8) built-in function named GETVARIABLE is used to retrieve session variable values. So, you could create a view based on a security label, for example:

```
CREAT VIEW VSECLBL AS
  SELECT column-list
  FROM   table-name
  WHERE  SECLABEL_COL = GETVARIABLE(SYSIBM.SECLABEL);
```

The built-in function can be used in views, triggers, stored procedures, and constraints to enforce a security policy.

Users can add up to ten session variables by setting the name and value in their connection or signon exits. User-created session variables are qualified by SESSION. For example, the customer might have a connection or signon exit that examines the SQL user's IP address, and maps the IP address to the user's site within the company. This is recorded in a session variable, named say, USER_SITE. This session variable is then accessible using the built-in function, for example:

```
GETVARIABLE(SESSION.USER_SITE)
```

Using session variables much more information is available to application programs as they execute, and more control and security is provided, as well. Additionally, session variables can be trusted. They are set by DB2 and an application cannot modify them.

Additional DB2 Security Guidelines

As you adopt your security and authorization policies, consider the following guidelines and suggestions.

Consider DCE Security   DB2 V5 and later releases can use the Distributed Computing Environment (DCE) security services to authenticate remote users. Users can access any DCE-based server (including DB2 on OS/390) using a single DCE userid and password. DCE and DCE security are complex systems management topics for distributed, interconnected networks, and in-depth coverage is beyond the scope of this book.

V7 **Consider Kerberos Security**   DB2 V7 and later releases can use Kerberos as a replacement standard for DCE. Kerberos is a standard industry authentication technique. Many vendors have implemented Kerberos solutions on a variety of different platforms. For example, Kerberos provides for better integration with Windows 2000 security as well as offering a single sign-on solution for your applications. One advantage of using Kerberos security is that when you sign on to a Windows 2000 workstation you will not need to provide a host userid and password to use applications that access DB2 for z/OS database servers.

In-depth coverage of Kerberos security, however, is beyond the scope of this book.

V7 **Consider Encrypting Userids and Passwords**   DB2 V7 (and DB2 V5 and V6 with APAR PQ21252) supports password encryption. You can direct DB2 Connect to encrypt the password when it is sent to DB2 for z/OS for authentication. Any compliant DRDA Version 2 requester can use password encryption.

> **CAUTION**
>
> DB2 Connect V5.2 (Fixpack 7) and higher is required in order to support DRDA Version 2 password encryption.

To enable DB2 Connect to flow encrypted passwords, DCS authentication must be set to `DCS_ENCRYPT` in the DCS directory entry.

Userids, as well as passwords, can be encrypted with DB2 V7, but encrypted userids and passwords are supported when DB2 for z/OS (and OS/390) is acting as a server. DB2 for z/OS (and OS/390) cannot act as a requester and send encrypted userids and passwords to a DRDA server.

V8 **Consider Encrypting DB2 Data**   DB2 Version 8 adds several new built-in functions to facilitate the encryption and decryption of DB2 data. The functionality of these functions is described in Chapter 3, "Using DB2 Functions." Basically, there are functions for encrypting and decrypting the data, as well as for generating unique values, and getting a hint for your encryption password.

The encryption password is set using the `SET ENCRYPTION PASSWORD` statement. The encryption password can be a `CHAR` or `VARCHAR` variable or constant. Its length must be between 6 and 127 bytes and cannot be null.

Consider encrypting data if the data is sensitive and there is a good chance of unauthorized access to the data. Be aware that encrypting and decrypting data consumes CPU cycles, so performance will be impacted by data encryption.

Whenever data is encrypted, be sure to set a hint to facilitate decryption in case you forget the encryption password; for example:

```
SET ENCRYPTION PASSWORD = :hv1 WITH HINT :hv2;
```

The WITH HINT clause allows you to set a value as a password hint to help you to remember a data encryption password. For example, you might set the hint to "Dog" as a hint to remember the password "Jerry" (my dog's name). If a password hint is specified, the hint is used for the encryption function. If a password hint is not specified, no hint is embedded in data that is encrypted with the encryption function. The hint can be a CHAR or VARCHAR variable or constant up to 32 bytes.

The GETHINT function is used to retrieve the hint for an encrypted value.

Consider Using Views to Implement Security   Sometimes views can be used to implement row- and column-level security for DB2 applications. One approach is to create a view on a base table containing only those columns that you want a user to be able to access. Then you can GRANT the user the authority to use the view, not the base table. For example, suppose you want to allow users to access the DSN8810.EMP table, but not the sensitive salary-related columns SALARY, COMM, and BONUS. First you would create the following view:

```
CREATE VIEW EMP_DETAILS
AS
   SELECT EMPNO, FIRSTNME, MIDINIT, LASTNAME, WORKDEPT,
          PHONENO, HIREDATE, JOB, EDLEVEL, SEX, BIRTHDATE
   FROM   DSN8810.EMP;
```

This creates a view named EMP_DETAILS that can now be accessed using SQL statements. Then you would GRANT the appropriate authority to your users for this view, but not the EMP table. By granting users only the authority to use the view, access is given to only that data within the view, thereby securing the non-included data from unauthorized access. This effectively blocks access to the sensitive data.

But what about row-level security? You can implement crude row-level security using views, too. Of course, with DB2 V8, MLS security provides a much more efficient and effective means of securing data at the row-level. To use views for row-level security, simply code the appropriate WHERE clauses on the views to remove the rows you do not want your users to be able to access. For example, if we only wanted to allow access to male employees, we could code the view as follows:

```
CREAT VIEW MALE_EMP
AS
   SELECT EMPNO, FIRSTNME, MIDINIT, LASTNAME, WORKDEPT,
          PHONENO, HIREDATE, JOB, EDLEVEL, BIRTHDATE
   FROM   DSN8810.EMP
   WHERE  SEX = 'M'
WITH CHECK OPTION;
```

Notice that we chose to omit the SEX column because we know that all of these employees are MALE—this is optional, but probably a good idea. Be sure to specify the WITH CHECK OPTION clause on the view to assure that rows outside the scope of the WHERE clause cannot be modified.

Consider Using Stored Procedures to Implement Security   You can create stored procedures to provide specific, tailored security. You can do so by coding specific SQL statements within a stored procedure and granting specific access to that procedure. The users need not have authorization to the underlying tables accessed by the stored procedure. This approach allows you to hide complex authorization rules in the details of a stored procedure.

V7 **Userid and Password**   As of V7, it is possible specify a userid and password when connecting to a server from an application running on z/OS. You can CONNECT to a remote server or a local server. The password is used to verify that you are authorized to connect to the DB2 subsystem.

This is important because DB2 for Linux, Unix, and Windows supports the USER parameter as an option of the CONNECT statement. So, you can now port applications to z/OS (or OS/390). Additionally, you can develop applications on workstation DB2 platforms, and then move the application to production on the mainframe without having to reprogram.

Take Advantage of Special Registers   DB2 provides many special registers that store information for DB2 processes. When referencing a special register DB2 replaces the register name with its value at execution time. Several of these special registers are helpful for security and authorization purposes:

V8   CLIENT ACCTNG contains the value of the accounting string from the client information that is specified for the connection. The data type is VARCHAR(255).

V8   CLIENT APPLNAME contains the value of the application name from the client information specified for the connection. The data type is VARCHAR(255).

CURRENT SQLID specifies the current SQL authid of the process. The data type is VARCHAR(8).

V8   CLIENT USERID contains the value of the client userid from the client information that is specified for the connection. The data type is VARCHAR(255).

V8   CLIENT WORKSTNNAME contains the value of the workstation name from the client information that is specified for the connection. The data type is VARCHAR(255).

USER contains the primary authid of the process. The data type is VARCHAR(8). If USER is referred to in an SQL statement that is executed at a remote DB2 and the primary authid has been translated to a different authid, USER returns the translated authid.

10

IN THIS CHAPTER

- Embedded SQL Basics
- Embedded SQL Guidelines
- Host Variables
- Programming with Cursors
- Embedded SELECT and Cursor Coding Guidelines
- Modifying Data with Embedded SQL
- Application Development Guidelines
- Batch Programming Guidelines
- Online Programming Guidelines
- General SQL Coding Guidelines

CHAPTER **11**

Using DB2 in an Application Program

D̲B2 application development consists of the construction of DB2 application programs. This statement begs the question: What is a DB2 application program? Let me begin to answer this question by reviewing standard application program development.

The development of an application system usually requires the use of a high-level language to encode the processing requirements of the application. A high-level language is any language that you can use to operate on data. You can break down high-level languages into the following categories:

- Database sublanguages, such as SQL

- 3GLs (third-generation languages), such as COBOL and FORTRAN, which are procedural

- 4GLs (fourth-generation languages), such as RAMIS and FOCUS, which are procedural but raise the level of abstraction a notch, often enabling non-MIS personnel to develop applications

- GUI-based programming languages, such as Visual Basic and PowerBuilder, which are used to build distributed, client/server applications

- Internet and Web-based programming languages, using CGI scripts or Java applets, servlets, and programs

- CASE (computer-aided software engineering) tools, which enable analysts to analyze and specify application models and parameters (upper CASE) and automatically generate application programs (lower CASE)

- Productivity tools, such as report writers and QMF, which are useful for developing portions of an application but usually not robust enough to be used for the development of a complete application

Sometimes you can develop a complete application system entirely with SQL, 4GLs, code generators, or productivity tools. However, these systems are rare (although code generation is gaining approval and support in many DP shops). Even though an application system can be coded without the use of a true programming language (3GL or GUI programming language), often a 3GL is still used because it generally outperforms the other application development tools just mentioned. This case is particularly true with code generators because the SQL that is generated is basic and not optimized for performance.

Back to the initial question: What is a DB2 application program? I consider a DB2 application program to be any program—developed using any of the preceding methods—that accesses data stored in DB2.

Most of the information in Part II of this book covers developing DB2 programs using third-generation languages, which constitute the bulk of DB2 applications. This is true for many reasons. Third-generation languages have been around longer than other application development tools and therefore have a larger installed base and a wider selection of professional programmers who understand them. Batch interfaces abound, but few online interfaces (CICS and IMS/TM) exist for most 4GLs and report writer tools.

Of course, GUI-based programming is on the rise, and many client/server applications are being developed to access DB2 data using these tools. The issues surrounding GUI-based DB2 programming are covered in Chapter 14, "Alternative DB2 Application Development Methods."

3GLs have proliferated for several other reasons. Their procedural nature eases the coding of complex logic structures (for example, IF-THEN-ELSE logic and looping). Other methods cannot usually meet complex reporting needs, such as the explosion of a hierarchy or side-by-side reporting of multiple, joined repeating groups. In addition, the performance of applications developed using alternative methods usually does not compare to the superb performance that you can achieve using 3GLs.

Embedded SQL Basics

To develop application programs that access DB2 tables, you must embed SQL statements in the program statements of the high-level language being used. Embedded DB2 SQL statements are supported in the following high-level languages: ADA, APL2, Assembler, BASIC, C, COBOL, FORTRAIN, Java, PL/I, Prolog, and REXX. Refer to the IBM manuals for the specific release and version numbers for the compiler or runtime environment supported for each language.

These programs can be run in the following execution environments:

MVS batch using CAF

TSO batch

DL/I batch

CICS

WebSphere MQ

IMS/TM (previously known as IMS/DC)

IMS BMP

TSO (interactive)

RRSAF (Recovery Resource Manager Services Attachment Facility)

In this chapter, I focus on the rules for embedding SQL in COBOL application programs because COBOL is the most widely used language in the business data processing community. Much of the information is similar for the other languages. For language-specific information and syntax, consult the appropriate IBM manuals.

Additionally, this chapter will focus on embedded static SQL because this is the predominant method used to develop DB2 application programs. Other methods include embedded dynamic SQL, ODBC, and JDBC. Chapter 12, "Dynamic SQL Programming," focuses on dynamic SQL, and Chapter 14 discusses ODBC and JDBC.

To embed SQL statements in an application program, you must follow strict rules. These rules have been established for a few reasons. One, they enable parsing programs (a DB2 precompiler) to identify embedded SQL statements easily in application code. Two, they ensure that the impedance mismatch between the non-procedural, set-level processing of SQL and the procedural, record-level processing of the high-level language has been taken into account. Three, these rules provide programs with the capability to change variables in the predicates of the embedded SQL at processing time. And four, they enable communication between the DB2 DBMS and the application program (for example, the reception of error and warning messages).

The capability to embed SQL statements in an application program allows high-level programming languages to access DB2 data. This capability provides the mechanism for the development of just about any type of DB2 application system.

All DB2 statements can be embedded in an application program. The list of SQL statements supported for embedding in an application program is presented in Table 11.1.

TABLE 11.1   Types of Embedded SQL Statements

SQL Type	SQL Statements
DCL	GRANT and REVOKE
DDL	ALTER, CREATE, DROP, COMMENT ON, and LABEL ON
DML	DELETE, INSERT, SELECT, and UPDATE
Dynamic SQL	DESCRIBE, EXECUTE, EXECUTE IMMEDIATE, and PREPARE
Distributed control	CONNECT, RELEASE, SET CONNECTION, RELEASE
Stored Procedures/LOBs	CALL, ALLOCATE CURSOR, ASSOCIATE LOCATORS, FREE LOCATOR, HOLD LOCATOR
Triggers	VALUES, SQL/PSM features
Definition control	BEGIN DECLARE SECTION, INCLUDE
Embedding control	CLOSE, DECLARE, FETCH, and OPEN
Transaction control	COMMIT, ROLLBACK, SAVEPOINT, RELEASE SAVEPOINT

TABLE 11.1   Continued

SQL Type	SQL Statements
Assignment	SET, VALUES INTO
General	EXPLAIN*, LOCK TABLE
Error handling	WHENEVER, SIGNAL SQLSTATE, GET DIAGNOSTICS

You can embed EXPLAIN only in TSO programs.

A DB2 program with embedded SQL statements is somewhat similar to an application program issuing reads and writes against a flat file or VSAM data set. The SQL statements are similar in function to file I/O. With a little basic understanding of embedded SQL rules and constructs, you, as an application programmer, can learn the methods necessary to embed SQL in a third-generation language, such as COBOL.

In the following sections, I discuss the techniques used to embed SQL statements in DB2 application programs.

Embedded SQL Guidelines

Table 11.2 outlines the differences between a DB2 program with embedded SQL statements and an application program accessing flat files. Flat files and DB2 tables, however, are not synonymous. The functionality of the two types of data storage objects are quite dissimilar.

TABLE 11.2   DB2 Programming Versus Flat File Programming

DB2 Programming Considerations	Flat File Programming Considerations
No FD required for DB2 tables; DB2 tables must be declared	FD is required for each flat file to be processed by the program
No DD card needed in execution JCL for programs accessing DB2 tables	DD card required (unless the flat file is allocated dynamically)
DB2 tables need not be opened; instead, cursors are opened for each SQL statement*	Flat files must be opened before being processed
DB2 tables need not be closed; instead, cursors are closed for each SQL statement*	Flat files must be closed (if opened)
Set-level processing	Record-level processing
Access to tables can be specified at the column (field element) level	Access to files based on reading a full record; all fields are always read or written
Success or failure of data is indicated by SQL	VSAM return code indicates success or failure return code
No more data indicated by +100 SQL return code	End of file is reported to the program
Cursors used to mimic record-level processing (see the section on cursors)	READ and WRITE statements are used to implement record-level processing

DB2 opens and closes the VSAM data sets that house DB2 table spaces "behind the scenes."

Delimit All SQL Statements   You must enclose all embedded SQL statements in an EXEC SQL block. This way, you can delimit the SQL statements so that the DB2 precompiler can efficiently parse the embedded SQL. The format of this block is

```
EXEC SQL
    put text of SQL statement here
END-EXEC.
```

For COBOL programs, you must code the EXEC SQL and END-EXEC delimiter clauses in your application program starting in column 12.

Explicitly DECLARE All DB2 Tables   Although you are not required to declare DB2 tables in your application program, doing so is good programming practice. Therefore, explicitly DECLARE all tables to be used by your application program. You should place the DECLARE TABLE statements in the WORKING-STORAGE section of your program, and they should be the first DB2-related variables defined in WORKING-STORAGE. This way, you can reduce the precompiler's work and make the table definitions easier to find in the program source code.

Additionally, standard DECLARE TABLE statements should be generated for every DB2 table. Create them with the DCLGEN command (covered in Chapter 13, "Program Preparation"), and then include them in your application program.

Comment Each SQL Statement   Make liberal use of comments to document the nature and purpose of each SQL statement embedded in your program. You should code all comments pertaining to embedded SQL in the comment syntax of the program's host language. Code COBOL comments as shown in the following example:

```
Column Numbers
        111
123456789012
    **
    **  Retrieve department name and manager from the
    **  DEPT table for a particular department number.
    **
        EXEC SQL
            SELECT    DEPTNAME, MGRNO
            INTO      :HOSTVAR-DEPTNAME,
                      :HOSTVAR-MGRNO
            FROM      DEPT
            WHERE     DEPTNO = :HOSTVAR-DEPTNO
        END-EXEC.
```

Include the SQLCA   You must include a structure called the SQLCA (SQL Communication Area) in each DB2 application program. You do so by coding the following statement in your WORKING-STORAGE section:

```
EXEC SQL
    INCLUDE SQLCA
END-EXEC.
```

The COBOL layout of the expanded SQLCA follows:

```
01  SQLCA.
    05  SQLCAID             PIC X(8).
    05  SQLCABC             PIC S9(9) COMPUTATIONAL.
    05  SQLCODE             PIC S9(9) COMPUTATIONAL.
    05  SQLERRM.
        49  SQLERRML        PIC S9(4) COMPUTATIONAL.
        49  SQLERRMC        PIC X(70).
    05  SQLERRP             PIC X(8).
    05  SQLERRD             OCCURS 6 TIMES
                            PIC S9(9) COMPUTATIONAL.
    05  SQLWARN.
        10  SQLWARN0        PIC X(1).
        10  SQLWARN1        PIC X(1).
        10  SQLWARN2        PIC X(1).
        10  SQLWARN3        PIC X(1).
        10  SQLWARN4        PIC X(1).
        10  SQLWARN5        PIC X(1).
        10  SQLWARN6        PIC X(1).
        10  SQLWARN7        PIC X(1).
    05  SQLEXT.
        10  SQLWARN8        PIC X(1).
        10  SQLWARN9        PIC X(1).
        10  SQLWARNA        PIC X(1).
        10  SQLSTATE        PIC X(5).
```

The SQLCA is used to communicate information describing the success or failure of the execution of an embedded SQL statement. The following list defines each SQLCA field:

SQLCAID	Set to the constant value SQLCA to enable easy location of the SQLCA in a dump.
SQLCABC	Contains the value 136, the length of the SQLCA.
SQLCODE	Contains the return code passed by DB2 to the application program. The return code provides information about the execution of the last SQL statement. A value of zero indicates successful execution, a positive value indicates successful execution but with an exception, and a negative value indicates that the statement failed.
SQLERRM	This group-level field consists of a length and a message. SQLERRML contains the length of the message in SQLERRMC. The message contains additional information about any encountered error condition. Usually, only technical support personnel use this field for complex debugging situations, when the value of SQLCODE is not sufficient. Note that if SQLERRML is set to 70 the message may have been truncated.
SQLERRP	Contains the name of the CSECT that detected the error reported by the SQLCODE. This information is not typically required by application programmers.
SQLERRD	This array contains six values used to diagnose error conditions. Only SQLERRD(3) and SQLERRD(5) are of use to most application programmers:
	SQLERRD(1) is the relational data system error code.
	SQLERRD(2) is the Data Manager error code.

V7

SQLERRD(1) and SQLERRD(2) can contain the number of rows in a result table when the cursor position is after the last row for a sensitive static cursor when the SQLCODE is +100.

SQLERRD(3) is the number of rows inserted, deleted, or updated by the SQL statement.

V8

SQLERRD(3) also will contain the number of rows in a rowset for a multirow FETCH and the number of rows inserted by a REFRESH TABLE.

SQLERRD(4) is the estimate of resources required for the SQL statement (timerons).

SQLERRD(5) is the column (position) of the syntax error for a dynamic SQL statement.

SQLERRD(6) is the Buffer Manager error code.

SQLWARN0	Contains W if any other SQLWARN field is set to W.
SQLWARN1	Contains W if a character column is truncated when it is assigned to a host variable by the SQL statement.
SQLWARN2	Contains W when a null-valued column is eliminated by built-in function processing.
SQLWARN3	Contains W when the number of columns retrieved does not match the number of fields in the host variable structure into which they are being selected.
SQLWARN4	Contains W when the SQL statement is an UPDATE or DELETE without a WHERE clause.

V7

For a scrollable cursor, SQLWARN4 contains a D for sensitive dynamic cursors, I for insensitive cursors, and S for sensitive static cursors after the OPEN CURSOR, ALLOCATE CURSOR, or DESCRIBE CURSOR statement; blank if cursor is not scrollable.

SQLWARN5	Contains W when an SQL statement that applies only to SQL/DS is issued.
SQLWARN6	Contains W when a DATE or TIMESTAMP conversion is performed during date arithmetic. For example, if 4 months are added to 2003-01-31, the result is 2003-04-31. Because April does not have 31 days, the results are converted to 2003-04-30.
SQLWARN7	Contains W when non-zero digits are dropped from the fractional part of a number used as the operand of a divide or multiply operation.
SQLWARN8	Contains W if a substitute character is used when a conversion routine cannot convert the character.
SQLWARN9	Contains W when COUNT DISTINCT processing ignores an arithmetic exception.
SQLWARNA	Contains W when any form of character conversion error is encountered.
SQLSTATE	Contains a return code indicating the status of the most recent SQL statement.

Check SQLCODE **or** SQLSTATE   SQLCODE contains the SQL return code, which indicates the success or failure of the last SQL statement executed. SQLSTATE is similar to SQLCODE but is consistent across DB2 (and ANSI-compliant SQL) platforms.

Code a COBOL IF statement immediately after every SQL statement to check the value of the SQLCODE. In general, gearing your application programs to check for SQLCODEs is easier because a simple condition can be employed to check for negative values.

If the SQLCODE returned by the SQLCA is less than zero, an SQL "error" was encountered. The term *error*, in this context, is confusing. A value less than zero could indicate a condition that is an error using SQL's terminology but is fine given the nature of your application. Thus, certain negative SQL codes are acceptable depending on their context.

For example, suppose that you try to insert a row into a table and receive an SQL code of -803, indicating a duplicate key value. (The row cannot be inserted because it violates the constraints of a unique index.) In this case, you might want to report the fact (and some details) and continue processing. You can design your application programs to check SQLCODE values like this instead of first checking to make sure that the insert does not violate a unique constraint, and only then inserting the row.

Check the SQLSTATE value, however, when you must check for a group of SQLCODEs associated with a single SQLSTATE or when your program runs on multiple platforms. SQLSTATE values consist of five characters: a two-character class code and a three-character subclass code. The class code indicates the type of error, and the subclass code details the explicit error within that error type.

You can find a complete listing of SQLCODEs, SQLSTATEs, and SQLSTATE class codes in the IBM DB2 Messages and Codes manual. Some of the most common DB2 SQLCODE values are listed on the inside back cover of this book.

V8 **Consider Using** GET DIAGNOSTICS   DB2 Version 8 augments DB2 error handling with the new GET DIAGNOSTICS statement. GET DIAGNOSTICS complements and extends the diagnostics available in the SQLCA. This is necessary because some error messages will not fit into the 70-byte SQLERRRC field.

GET DIAGNOSTICS provides additional information than is provided in the SQLCA. The information it provides can be broken down into several areas: statement information, condition information, connection information, and combined information. Combined information contains a text representation of all the information gathered about the execution of the SQL statement. Table 11.3 delineates the many different types of diagnostic information that can be returned with GET DIAGNOSTICS.

You use GET DIAGNOSTICS similarly to how you check the SQLCODE: You issue it after executing an SQL statement, and it returns information about the execution of the last statement, along with at least one instance of condition information.

GET DIAGNOSTICS is particularly useful for checking each condition when multiple conditions can occur—such as with multiple row processing. GET DIAGNOSTICS also supports SQL error message tokens larger than the 70-byte limit of the SQLDA.

A quick example using GET DIAGNOSTICS follows:

```
GET DIAGNOSTICS :RC = ROW_COUNT;
```

After executing this statement the :RC host variable will be set to the number of rows that were affected by the last SQL statement that was executed.

TABLE 11.3   GET DIAGNOSTICS Details

Type	Specific Name	Description
Statement	DB2_GET_DIAGNOSTICS_DIAGNOSTICS	Textual information about errors or warnings in the execution of the GET DIAGNOSTICS statement.
	DB2_LAST_ROW	For a multiple-row FETCH statement, contains a value of +100 if the last row currently in the table is in the set of rows that have been fetched.
	DB2_NUMBER_PARAMETER_MARKERS	For a PREPARE statement, contains the number of parameter markers in the prepared statement.
	DB2_NUMBER_RESULT_SETS	For a CALL statement, contains the actual number of result sets returned by the procedure.
	DB2_RETURN_STATUS	Identifies the status value returned from the previous CALL statement (for SQL procdures).
	DB2_SQL_ATTR_CURSOR _HOLD	For an ALLOCATE or OPEN statement, indicates whether a cursor can be held open across multiple units of work.
	DB2_SQL_ATTR_CURSOR_ROWSET	For an ALLOCATE or OPEN statement, indicates whether a cursor can be accessed using rowset positioning.
	DB2_SQL_ATTR_CURSOR_SCROLLABLE	For an ALLOCATE or OPEN statement, indicates whether a cursor can be scrolled forward and backward.
	DB2_SQL_ATTR_CURSOR_SENSITIVITY	For an ALLOCATE or OPEN statement, indicates whether a cursor does or does not show updates to cursor rows made by other connections.
	DB2_SQL_ATTR_CURSOR_TYPE	For an ALLOCATE or OPEN statement, indicates the type of cursor: normal, scrollable static, or scrollable dynamic.
	MORE	Indicates whether there are more warning and errors than could be stored (or whether all the warnings and errors are stored).
	NUMBER	Returns the number of errors and warnings detected by the execution of the previous SQL statement.
	ROW_COUNT	Identifies the number of rows associated with the previous SQL statement.

TABLE 11.3   Continued

Type	Specific Name	Description
Condition	CATALOG_NAME	Returns the name of the constraint or table that caused the error.
	CONDITION_NUMBER	Returns the number of the diagnostic returned.
	CURSOR_NAME	Returns the name of the cursor.
	DB2_ERROR_CODE1	Returns an internal error code.
	DB2_ERROR_CODE2	Returns an internal error code.
	DB2_ERROR_CODE3	Returns an internal error code.
	DB2_ERROR_CODE4	Returns an internal error code.
	DB2_INTERNAL_ERROR_POINTER	For some errors, this is a negative value that is an internal error pointer.
	DB2_LINE_NUMBER	For a CREATE PROCEDURE (for SQL procedures), contains the line number where an error possibly occurred in the procedure code.
	DB2_MODULE_DETECTING_ERROR	Returns an identifier indicating which module detected the error.
	DB2_ORDINAL_TOKEN_*n*	Returns the *n*th token, where *n* is a value between 1 and 100.
	DB2_REASON_CODE	Contains the reason code for errors that have a reason code token in their message text.
	DB2_RETURNED_SQLCODE	Returns the SQLCODE for the specified diagnostic.
	DB2_ROW_NUMBER	For a statement involving multiple rows, the row number where DB2 detected the exception.
	DB2_TOKEN_COUNT	Returns the number of tokens available for the specified diagnostic ID.
	MESSAGE_OCTET_LENGTH	The length of the message text (in bytes).
	MESSAGE_TEXT	The message text associated with the SQLCODE (including substituted tokens).
	RETURNED_SQLSTATE	Returns the SQLSTATE for the specified diagnostic.
	SERVER_NAME	For CONNECT, DISCONNECT, or SET CONNECTION statements, the name of the server; otherwise, the name of the server where the statement executes is returned.
Connection	DB2_AUTHENTICATION_TYPE	Contains the authentication type: server, client, DB2 Connect, DCE security services, or blank.
	DB2_AUTHORIZATION_ID	Authorization ID used by connected server.
	DB2_CONNECTION_STATE	Whether the connection is unconnected, local, or remote.

TABLE 11.3   Continued

Type	Specific Name	Description
	DB2_CONNECTION_STATUS	Whether committable updates can be performed on the connection for this unit of work.
	DB2_SERVER_CLASS_NAME	Contains a value specifying the platform of the server.
	DB2_ENCRYPTION_TYPE	The level of encryption.
	DB2_PRODUCT_ID	Returns a product signature.
Combined	ALL	All of the diagnostic items combined into a single string.
	STATEMENT	All statement diagnostic items combined into a single string.
	CONNECTION	All connection diagnostic items combined into a single string.

Standardize Your Shop's Error Routine   Consider using a standardized error-handling paragraph, one that can be used by all DB2 programs in your shop. The programs should load values to an error record that can be interpreted by the error-handling paragraph. When a severe error is encountered, the programs invoke the error-handling paragraph.

The error-handling paragraph should do the following:

1. Call the DSNTIAR module, a program provided with DB2 that returns standard, textual error messages for SQLCODEs.

2. Display, print, or record the following information: the error record identifying the involved table, the paragraph, and pertinent host variables; the error text returned by DSNTIAR; and the current values in the SQLCA.

3. Issue a ROLLBACK. (This action is not absolutely required because an implicit rollback occurs if one is not requested.)

4. Call an ABEND module to generate a dump.

Your error-handling paragraph can be as complex and precise as you want. Depending on the SQL code, different processing can occur; for example, you might not want to abend the program for every SQLCODE.

Listing 11.1 shows sample COBOL code with an error-handling paragraph as just described. You can tailor this code to meet your needs.

LISTING 11.1   Sample COBOL Error-Handling Paragraph

```
          .
          .
          .
WORKING-STORAGE SECTION.
```

LISTING 11.1   Continued

```
               .
               .
               .
77  ERROR-TEXT-LENGTH          PIC S9(9)    COMP VALUE +960.
01  ERROR-RECORD.
    05  FILLER                 PIC X(11)    VALUE 'SQLCODE IS '.
    05  SQLCODE-DISP           PIC -999.
    05  FILLER                 PIC X(05)    VALUE SPACES.
    05  ERROR-TABLE            PIC X(18).
    05  ERROR-PARA             PIC X(30).
    05  ERROR-INFO             PIC X(40).
01  ERROR-MESSAGE.
    05  ERROR-MSG-LENGTH       PIC S9(9)    COMP VALUE +960.
    05  ERROR-MSG-TEXT         PIC X(120)   OCCURS 8 TIMES
                                            INDEXED BY ERROR-INDEX.
01  ERROR-ROLLBACK.
    05  FILLER        PIC X(20)    VALUE 'ROLLBACK SQLCODE IS '.
    05  SQLCODE-ROLLBACK       PIC -999.
               .
               .
PROCEDURE DIVISION.
               .
               .
1000-SAMPLE-PARAGRAPH.
    EXEC SQL
        SQL statement here
    END-EXEC.
    IF SQLCODE IS LESS THAN ZERO
        MOVE SQLCODE                   TO SQLCODE-DISP
        MOVE 'Table_Name'              TO ERR-TABLE
        MOVE '1000-SAMPLE-PARAGRAPH' TO ERR-PARA
        MOVE 'Misc info, host variables, etc.'     TO ERR-INFO
        PERFORM 9999-SQL-ERROR
    ELSE
        Resume normal processing.
               .
               .
9990-SQL-ERROR.
    DISPLAY ERR-RECORD.
    CALL 'DSNTIAR' USING SQLCA,
                         ERROR-MESSAGE,
                         ERROR-TEXT-LENGTH.
    IF RETURN-CODE IS EQUAL TO ZERO
        PERFORM 9999-DISP-DSNTIAR-MSG
            VARYING ERROR-INDEX FROM 1 BY 1
            UNTIL ERROR-INDEX > 8
    ELSE
        DISPLAY 'DSNTIAR ERROR'
        CALL 'abend module'.
    DISPLAY 'SQLERRMC   ', SQLERRMC.
    DISPLAY 'SQLERRD1   ', SQLERRD(1).
    DISPLAY 'SQLERRD2   ', SQLERRD(2).
    DISPLAY 'SQLERRD3   ', SQLERRD(3).
```

LISTING 11.1   Continued

```
    DISPLAY 'SQLERRD4   ', SQLERRD(4).
    DISPLAY 'SQLERRD5   ', SQLERRD(5).
    DISPLAY 'SQLERRD6   ', SQLERRD(6).
    DISPLAY 'SQLWARN0   ', SQLWARN0.
    DISPLAY 'SQLWARN1   ', SQLWARN1.
    DISPLAY 'SQLWARN2   ', SQLWARN2.
    DISPLAY 'SQLWARN3   ', SQLWARN3.
    DISPLAY 'SQLWARN4   ', SQLWARN4.
    DISPLAY 'SQLWARN5   ', SQLWARN5.
    DISPLAY 'SQLWARN6   ', SQLWARN6.
    DISPLAY 'SQLWARN7   ', SQLWARN7.
    DISPLAY 'SQLWARN8   ', SQLWARN8.
    DISPLAY 'SQLWARN9   ', SQLWARN9.
    DISPLAY 'SQLWARNA   ', SQLWARNA.
    EXEC SQL
        ROLLBACK
    END-EXEC.
    IF SQLCODE IS NOT EQUAL TO ZERO
        DISPLAY 'INVALID ROLLBACK'
        MOVE SQLCODE      TO SQLCODE-ROLLBACK
        DISPLAY ERROR-ROLLBACK.
    CALL 'abend module'.

9990-EXIT.
    EXIT.
9999-DISP-DSNTIAR-MSG.
    DISPLAY ERROR-MSG-TEXT(ERROR-INDEX).
9999-EXIT.
    EXIT.
```

When a negative `SQLCODE` is encountered—in paragraph 1000, for example—an error message is formatted and an error paragraph is performed. The error paragraph displays the error message returned by `DSNTIAR`, dumps the contents of the `SQLCA`, and rolls back all updates, deletes, and inserts since the last `COMMIT` point.

> **NOTE**
>
> Use a formatted `WORKING-STORAGE` field to display the `SQLCODE`; otherwise, the value will be unreadable.

You can code the error-handling paragraph in Listing 11.1 in a copy book that can then be included in each DB2 program. This way, you can standardize your shop's error processing and reduce the amount of code that each DB2 programmer must write.

Handle Errors and Move On When Possible   Certain `SQLCODE` and/or `SQLSTATE` error conditions are not disastrous, and sometimes your program can continue to process after receiving an error code. Of course, it depends on the type of error and the type of work your program is performing. Consider coding your program to handle the "problem" codes, such as the common errors that are outlined in Table 11.4.

TABLE 11.4 Handling SQL Errors

SQLCODE	SQLSTATE	Meaning	Response
-904	57011	Resource unavailable	Try again (once), then attempt alternate processing; inform user and write out error message.
-911	40000	Timeout or deadlock	Retry several times and try to continue processing; if multiple failures, inform user and write out error message.
-53x	235xx	RI problem	Inform user, write out error message, and reverify data.
-551	42501	Authorization	Inform user of lack of authority to perform the function and write a log to record the attempted access.

Avoid Using WHENEVER   SQL has an error trapping statement called WHENEVER that you can embed in an application program. When the WHENEVER statement is processed, it applies to all subsequent SQL statements issued by the application program in which it is embedded. WHENEVER directs processing to continue or to branch to an error handling routine based on the SQLCODE returned for the statement. Several examples follow.

The following example indicates that processing will continue when an SQLCODE of +100 is encountered:

```
EXEC SQL
    WHENEVER NOT FOUND
        CONTINUE
END-EXEC.
```

When a warning is encountered, the second example of the WHENEVER statement causes the program to branch to a paragraph (in this case, ERROR-PARAGRAPH) to handle the warning:

```
EXEC SQL
    WHENEVER SQLWARNING
        GO TO ERROR-PARAGRAPH
END-EXEC.
```

When any negative SQLCODE is encountered, the next WHENEVER statement branches to a paragraph (once again, ERROR-PARAGRAPH) to handle errors:

```
EXEC SQL
    WHENEVER SQLERROR
        GO TO ERROR-PARAGRAPH
END-EXEC.
```

Each of the three types of the WHENEVER statement can use the GO TO or CONTINUE option, at the discretion of the programmer. These types of the WHENEVER statements trap three "error" conditions:

NOT FOUND	The SQLCODE is equal to +100
SQLWARNING	The SQLCODE is positive but not +100 or SQLWARN0 equal to W
SQLERROR	The SQLCODE is negative

Avoid using the WHENEVER statement. It is almost always safer to code specific SQLCODE checks after each SQL statement and process accordingly. Additionally, you should avoid coding the GO TO verb as used by the WHENEVER statement. The GO TO construct is generally avoided in structured application programming methodologies.

Name DB2 Programs, Plans, Packages, and Variables Cautiously   Use caution when naming DB2 programs, plans, packages, and variables used in SQL statements. Do not use the following:

- The characters *DB2*, *SQL*, *DSN*, and *DSQ*

- SQL reserved words

You should avoid the listed character combinations for the following reasons. *DB2* is too generic and could be confused with a DB2 system component. Because SQLCA fields are prefixed with *SQL*, using these letters with another variable name can cause confusion with SQLCA fields. IBM uses the three-character prefix *DSN* to name DB2 system programs and *DSQ* to name QMF system programs.

If SQL reserved words are used for host variables (covered in the next section) and are not preceded by a colon, an error is returned. However, you should not use these words even if all host variables are preceded by a colon. Avoiding these words in your program, plan, and variable names reduces confusion and ambiguity. Table 11.5 lists all DB2 SQL reserved words.

TABLE 11.5   SQL Reserved Words

ADD	AFTER	ALL	ALLOCATE
ALLOW	ALTER	AND	ANY
AS	ASSOCIATE	ASUTIME	AUDIT
AUX	AUXILIARY	BEFORE	BEGIN
BETWEEN	BUFFERPOOL	BY	CALL
CAPTURE	CASCADED	CASE	CAST
CCSID	CHAR	CHARACTER	CHECK
CLOSE	CLUSTER	COLLECTION	COLLID
COLUMN	COMMENT	COMMIT	CONCAT
CONDITION	CONNECT	CONNECTION	CONSTRAINT
CONTAINS	CONTINUE	CREATE	CURRENT
CURRENT_DATE	CURRENT_LC_CTYPE	CURRENT_PATH	CURRENT_TIME
CURRENT_TIMESTAMP	CURSOR	DATA	DATABASE
DAY	DAYS	DBINFO	DB2SQL
DECLARE	DEFAULT	DELETE	DESCRIPTOR
DETERMINISTIC	DISALLOW	DISTINCT	DO
DOUBLE	DROP	DSNHATTR	DSSIZE
DYNAMIC	EDITPROC	ELSE	ELSEIF
ENCODING	END	END-EXEC	ERASE
ESCAPE	EXCEPT	EXECUTE	EXISTS
EXIT	EXTERNAL	FENCED	FETCH

TABLE 11.5   Continued

FIELDPROC	FINAL	FOR	FROM
FULL	FUNCTION	GENERAL	GENERATED
GET	GLOBAL	GO	GOTO
GRANT	GROUP	HANDLER	HAVING
HOUR	HOURS	IF	IMMEDIATE
IN	INDEX	INHERIT	INNER
INOUT	INSENSITIVE	INSERT	INTO
IS	ISOBID	JAR	JAVA
JOIN	KEY	LABEL	LANGUAGE
LC_CTYPE	LEAVE	LEFT	LIKE
LOCAL	LOCALE	LOCATOR	LOCATORS
LOCK	LOCKMAX	LOCKSIZE	LONG
LOOP	MICROSECOND	MICROSECONDS	MINUTE
MINUTES	MODIFIES	MONTH	MONTHS
NO	NOT	NULL	NULLS
NUMPARTS	OBID	OF	ON
OPEN	OPTIMIZATION	OPTIMIZE	OR
ORDER	OUT	OUTER	PACKAGE
PARAMETER	PART	PATH	PIECESIZE
PLAN	PRECISION	PREPARE	PRIQTY
PRIVILEGES	PROCEDURE	PROGRAM	PSID
QUERYNO	READS	REFERENCES	RELEASE
RENAME	REPEAT	RESTRICT	RESULT
RESULT_SET_LOCATOR	RETURN	RETURNS	REVOKE
RIGHT	ROLLBACK	RUN	SAVEPOINT
SCHEMA	SCRATCHPAD	SECOND	SECONDS
SECQTY	SECURITY	SELECT	SENSITIVE
SET	SIMPLE	SOME	SOURCE
SPECIFIC	STANDARD	STATIC	STAY
STOGROUP	STORES	STYLE	SUBPAGES
SYNONYM	SYSFUN	SYSIBM	SYSPROC
SYSTEM	TABLE	TABLESPACE	THEN
TO	TRIGGER	UNDO	UNION
UNIQUE	UNTIL	UPDATE	USER
USING	VALIDPROC	VALUE	VALUES
VARIANT	VCAT	VIEW	VOLUMES
WHEN	WHERE	WHILE	WITH
WLM	YEAR	YEARS	

NOTE

As of DB2 V7, APPLICATION, NAME, and TYPE are no longer reserved words.

Additionally, IBM SQL reserves additional words. Using these words will not result in an error, but you should avoid their use to eliminate confusion. Additionally, these words are good candidates for future status as DB2 SQL reserved words when functionality is added to DB2. Table 11.6 lists all IBM SQL reserved words that are not also SQL reserved words. Therefore, Tables 11.5 and 11.6 collectively list all the IBM and DB2 SQL database reserved words.

TABLE 11.6   IBM SQL Reserved Words

ACQUIRE	ASC	AUTHORIZATION
AVG	CASCADE	COUNT
CROSS	DATE	DBA
DBSPACE	DECIMAL	DESC
EXCEPTION	EXCLUSIVE	EXPLAIN
FOREIGN	GRAPHIC	IDENTIFIED
INDICATOR	INTERSECT	MAX
MIN	MODE	NAMED
NHEADER	ONLY	OPTION
PAGE	PAGES	PCTFREE
PCTINDEX	PRIMARY	PRIVATE
PUBLIC	RESET	RESOURCE
ROW	ROWS	RRN
SCHEDULE	SHARE	STATISTICS
STORPOOL	SUBSTRING	SUM
TRANSACTION	TRIM	VARIABLE
WORK		

> **NOTE**
>
> You also should avoid using any ANSI SQL reserved words (that are not already included in the previous two lists) in your program, plan, and variable names. Refer to the ANSI SQL standard for a list of the ANSI reserved words.
>
> You can search for and order documentation on the ANSI SQL standard (and any other ANSI standard) at http://web.ansi.org/default.htm.

The guidelines in this section are applicable to every type of DB2 application program. Chapters 12 through 14 present guidelines for programming techniques used by specific types of DB2 application programs. Additionally, Chapter 15, "Using DB2 Stored Procedures," contains programming guidelines to follow when writing stored procedures.

Host Variables

When embedding SQL in an application program, you, as the programmer, rarely know every value that needs to be accessed by SQL predicates. Often you need to use variables to specify the values of predicates. For example, when a program reads a flat file for data or accepts user input from a terminal, a mechanism is needed to hold these values in an SQL statement. This is the function of host variables.

A *host variable* is an area of storage allocated by the host language and referenced in an SQL statement. You define and name host variables using the syntax of the host language. For COBOL, you must define host variables in the DATA DIVISION of your program in the WORKING-STORAGE section or the LINKAGE section. Additionally, when you're using INCLUDE, you must delimit the host variable specifications by using EXEC SQL and END-EXEC (as previously discussed).

When you use host variables in SQL statements, prefix them with a colon (:). For example, a COBOL variable defined in the DATA DIVISION as

```
EXAMPLE-VARIABLE    PIC X(5)
```

should be referenced as follows when used in an embedded SQL statement:

```
:EXAMPLE-VARIABLE
```

When the same variable is referenced by the COBOL program outside the context of SQL, however, do not prefix the variable with a colon. If you do so, a compilation error results.

> **CAUTION**
>
> Prior to DB2 Version 6, DB2 allowed users to "forget" prefixing host variables with a colon. If a colon was not specified, an informational warning was generated, but the SQL statement was still processed. For DB2 V6 and later releases, this is no longer the case. If the colon is missing, an error message will be generated and the SQL will not execute.

Host variables are the means of moving data from the program to DB2 and from DB2 to the program. Data can be read from a file, placed into host variables, and used to modify a DB2 table (through embedded SQL). For data retrieval, host variables are used to house the selected DB2 data. You also can use host variables to change predicate values in WHERE clauses. You can use host variables in the following ways:

- As output data areas in the INTO clause of the SELECT and FETCH statements

- As input data areas for the SET clause of the UPDATE statement

- As input data areas for the VALUES clause of the INSERT statement

- As search fields in the WHERE clause for SELECT, INSERT, UPDATE, and DELETE statements

- As literals in the SELECT list of a SELECT statement

Several examples of host variables used in SQL statements follow. In the first example, host variables are used in the SQL SELECT statement as literals in the SELECT list and as output data areas in the INTO clause:

```
EXEC SQL
    SELECT  EMPNO, :INCREASE-PCT,
            SALARY * :INCREASE-PCT
    INTO    :HOSTVAR-EMPNO,
            :HOSTVAR-INCRPCT,
            :HOSTVAR-SALARY
```

```
        FROM    EMP
        WHERE   EMPNO = '000110'
    END-EXEC.
```

In the second example, host variables are used in the SET clause of the UPDATE statement and as a search field in the WHERE clause:

```
EXEC SQL
    UPDATE EMP
        SET SALARY = :HOSTVAR-SALARY
    WHERE   EMPNO = :HOSTVAR-EMPNO
END-EXEC.
```

A third example shows a host variable used in the WHERE clause of an SQL DELETE statement. In this statement every row that refers to a WORKDEPT equal to the host variable value will be deleted from the table:

```
EXEC SQL
    DELETE FROM  EMP
    WHERE  WORKDEPT = :HOSTVAR-WORKDEPT
END-EXEC.
```

The final example depicts host variables used in the VALUES clause of an SQL INSERT statement:

```
EXEC SQL
    INSERT INTO DEPT
    VALUES (:HOSTVAR-DEPTNO,
            :HOSTVAR-DEPTNAME,
            :HOSTVAR-MGRNO,
            :HOSTVAR-ADMRDEPT)
END-EXEC.
```

Host Structures

In addition to host variables, SQL statements can use host structures. Host structures enable SQL statements to specify a single structure for storing all retrieved columns. A host structure, then, is a COBOL group-level data area composed of host variables for all columns to be returned by a given SELECT statement.

The following is a host structure for the DSN8810.DEPT table:

```
01  DCLDEPT.
    10  DEPTNO              PIC X(3).
    10  DEPTNAME.
        49  DEPTNAME-LEN    PIC S9(4) USAGE COMP.
        49  DEPTNAME-TEXT   PIC X(36).
    10  MGRNO               PIC X(6).
    10  ADMRDEPT            PIC X(3).
    10  LOCATION            PIC X(16).
```

DCLDEPT is the host structure name in this example. You could write the following statement using this host structure:

```
EXEC SQL
    SELECT  DEPTNO, DEPTNAME, MGRNO, ADMRDEPT, LOCATION
    FROM    DEPT
    INTO    :DCLDEPT
    WHERE   DEPTNO = 'A00'
END-EXEC.
```

This statement populates the host variables for all columns defined under the DCLDEPT group-level data area.

Null Indicator Variables and Structures

Before you select or insert a column that can be set to null, it must have an indicator variable defined for it. You can use indicator variables also with the UPDATE statement to set columns to null. A third use for null indicators occurs when any column (defined as either nullable or not nullable) is retrieved using the built-in column functions AVG, MAX, MIN, and SUM. Finally, null indicators should be used in outer join statements for each column that can return a null result (even if the column is defined as not null).

If you fail to use an indicator variable, a -305 SQLCODE is returned when no rows meet the requirements of the predicates for the SQL statement containing the column function. For example, consider the following statement:

```
SELECT  MAX(SALARY)
FROM    DSN8810.EMP
WHERE   WORKDEPT = 'ZZZ';
```

Because no ZZZ department exists, the value of the maximum salary that is returned is null—not zero or blank. So be sure to include a null indicator variable whenever you use a built-in column function.

You should define null indicators in the WORKING-STORAGE section of your COBOL program as computational variables, with a picture clause specification of PIC S9(4). The null indicator variables for the DSN8810.EMP table look like this:

```
01  EMP-INDICATORS.
    10  WORKDEPT-IND    PIC S9(4) USAGE COMP.
    10  PHONENO-IND     PIC S9(4) USAGE COMP.
    10  HIREDATE-IND    PIC S9(4) USAGE COMP.
    10  JOB-IND         PIC S9(4) USAGE COMP.
    10  EDLEVEL-IND     PIC S9(4) USAGE COMP.
    10  SEX-IND         PIC S9(4) USAGE COMP.
    10  BIRTHDATE-IND   PIC S9(4) USAGE COMP.
    10  SALARY-IND      PIC S9(4) USAGE COMP.
    10  BONUS-IND       PIC S9(4) USAGE COMP.
    10  COMM-IND        PIC S9(4) USAGE COMP.
```

This structure contains the null indicators for all the nullable columns of the DSN8810.EMP table.

To associate null indicator variables with a particular host variable for a column, code the indicator variable immediately after the host variable, preceded by a colon. For example, to retrieve information regarding SALARY (a nullable column) from the DSN8810.EMP table, you can code the following embedded SQL statement:

```
EXEC SQL
    SELECT  EMPNO, SALARY
    INTO    :EMPNO,
            :SALARY:SALARY-IND
    FROM    EMP
    WHERE   EMPNO = '000100'
END-EXEC.
```

The null indicator variable is separate from both the column to which it pertains and the host variable for that column. To determine the value of any nullable column, a host variable and an indicator variable are required. The host variable contains the value of the column when it is not null. The indicator variable contains one of the following values to indicate a column's null status:

- A negative number indicates that the column has been set to null.

- The value -2 indicates that the column has been set to null as a result of a data conversion error.

- A positive or zero value indicates that the column is not null.

- If a column defined as a CHARACTER data type is truncated on retrieval because the host variable is not large enough, the indicator variable contains the original length of the truncated column.

You can use null indicator variables with corresponding host variables in the following situations:

- SET clause of the UPDATE statement

- VALUES clause of the INSERT statement

- INTO clause of the SELECT or FETCH statement

You can code null indicator structures in much the same way you code the host structures discussed previously. Null indicator structures enable host structures to be used when nullable columns are selected. A null indicator structure is defined as a null indicator variable with an OCCURS clause. The variable should occur once for each column in the corresponding host structure, as shown in the following section of code:

```
01  IDEPT PIC S9(4) USAGE COMP OCCURS 5 TIMES.
```

This null indicator structure defines the null indicators needed for retrieving rows from the DSN8810.DEPT table using a host structure. The DCLDEPT host structure has five columns, so the IDEPT null indicator structure occurs five times. When you're using a host structure for a table in which any column is nullable, one null indicator per column in the host structure is required.

You can use the host structure and null indicator structure together as follows:

```
EXEC SQL
    SELECT  DEPTNO, DEPTNAME, MGRNO, ADMRDEPT, LOCATION
    FROM    DEPT
    INTO    :DCLDEPT:DEPT-IND
    WHERE   DEPTNO = 'A00'
END-EXEC.
```

Based on the position in the null indicator structure, you can determine the null status of each column in the retrieved row. If the *n*th null indicator contains a negative value, the *n*th column is null. So, in this example, if DEPT-IND(3) is negative, MGRNO is null.

CAUTION

Always use a null indicator variable when referencing a nullable column. Failure to do so results in a -305 SQLCODE. If you fail to check the null status of the column being retrieved, your program may continue to execute, but the results will be questionable.

NOTE

You can avoid using null indicator variables by using the VALUE or COALESCE function. Both of these functions can be used to supply a value whenever DB2 would return a null. For example, VALUE(MANAGER_NAME,'*** No Manager Name ***') will return the actual value of MANAGER_NAME when the column is not null and the literal '*** No Manager Name ***' when the MANAGER_NAME column is null.

COALESCE works the same as VALUES and uses the same syntax—COALESCE(MANAGER_NAME,'*** No Manager Name ***').

Host Variable Guidelines

Practice the following tips and techniques to ensure proper host variable usage.

Use Syntactically Valid Variable Names   Host variables can use any naming scheme that is valid for the definition of variables in the host language being used. For host variables defined using COBOL, underscores are not permitted. As a general rule, use hyphens instead of underscores.

Avoid Certain COBOL Clauses   COBOL host variable definitions cannot specify the JUSTIFIED or BLANK WHEN ZERO clauses.

You can specify the OCCURS clause only when you're defining a null indicator structure. Otherwise, you cannot use OCCURS for host variables.

Using Host Structures   In general, favor individual host variables over host structures. Individual host variables are easier to understand, easier to support, and less likely to cause errors as a result of changes to tables. Additionally, using individual host variables promotes proper SQL usage. When using host structures, too often developers try to fit every SQL SELECT to the host structure. Instead of limiting each SQL SELECT statement to retrieve only the columns required, developers sometimes will force every SELECT statement in a program to fit a single host structure. To optimize performance, this must be avoided.

However, when it is necessary to squeeze every last bit of performance out of an application, consider using host structures. When a host structure is used, some minimal number of instructions are saved because DB2 does not have to move each column separately to an individual host variable. Instead, one move is required to move the columns into the host structure.

> **CAUTION**
>
> When host structures are used, be sure not to fall into the trap of making every SELECT statement use a single host structure, or performance will suffer.

Avoid Null Indicator Structures   Favor individual null indicator variables over null indicator structures. Individual null indicator variables can be named appropriately for each column to which they apply. Null indicator structures have a single common name and a subscript. Tying a subscripted variable name to a specific column can be tedious and error-prone.

For example, consider the host structure and its corresponding null indicator structure shown previously. The fact that IDEPT(2) is the null indicator variable for the DEPTNAME host variable is not obvious. If you had used separate null indicators for each nullable column, the null indicator for DEPTNAME could be called DEPTNAME-IND. With this naming convention, you can easily see that DEPTNAME-IND is the null indicator variable for DEPTNAME.

Be forewarned that null indicator structures can be generated by DCLGEN (as of DB2 V4), whereas individual indicator variables must be explicitly coded by hand. Even so, individual null indicator variables are easier to use and therefore recommended over null indicator structures.

Define Host Variables Precisely   Define all your host variables correctly. Consult Appendix C, "Valid DB2 Data Types," for a complete list of valid DB2 data types and their corresponding COBOL definitions. Failure to define host variables correctly can result in precompiler errors or poor performance due to access path selection based on non-equivalent data types, data conversions, and data truncation.

Use DCLGEN for Host Variable Generation   Use DCLGEN to generate host variables automatically for each column of each table to be accessed. DCLGEN ensures that the host variables are defined correctly.

Avoid DCLGEN for Null Indicator Generation   As I mentioned earlier, DCLGEN can optionally generate null indicator host structures. However, host structures are more difficult to use than individual null indicator variables and generally should be avoided.

Embedded SELECT Statements   The two types of embedded SQL SELECT statements are singleton SELECTs and cursor SELECTs. So far, all examples in the book have been singleton SELECTs.

Remember, SQL statements operate on a set of data and return a set of data. Host language programs, however, operate on data a row at a time. A singleton SELECT is simply an SQL SELECT statement that returns only one row. As such, it can be coded and embedded in a host language program with little effort: The singleton SELECT returns one row and the application program processes one row.

You code a singleton SELECT as follows:

```
EXEC SQL
    SELECT  DEPTNAME, MGRNO
    INTO    :HOSTVAR-DEPTNAME,
            :HOSTVAR-MGRNO
    FROM    DEPT
    WHERE   DEPTNO = 'A11'
END-EXEC.
```

The singleton SELECT statement differs from a normal SQL SELECT statement in that it must contain the INTO clause. In the INTO clause, you code the host variables that accept the data returned from the DB2 table by the SELECT statement.

Singleton SELECTs are usually quite efficient. Be sure, however, that the singleton SELECT returns only one row. If more than one row is retrieved, the first one is placed in the host variables defined by the INTO clause, and the SQLCODE is set to -811.

V7 Of course, as of DB2 V7, you can append the FETCH FIRST 1 ROW ONLY clause to any SQL statement and DB2 will only return one row—regardless of how many may actually qualify. This is one way of avoiding -811 problems.

If your application program must process a SELECT statement that returns multiple rows, you must use a cursor, which is an object designed to handle multiple row results tables. As of DB2 V8, though, rowset positioning cursors can be coded to FETCH multiple rows at a time.

Programming with Cursors

Recall from Chapter 1, "The Magic Words," that an impedance mismatch occurs between SQL and the host language, such as COBOL. COBOL operates on data a row at a time; SQL operates on data a set at time. Without a proper vehicle for handling this impedance mismatch (such as arrays), using embedded SELECT statements would be impossible. IBM's solution is the structure known as a *symbolic cursor*, or simply *cursor*.

DB2 application programs use cursors to navigate through a set of rows returned by an embedded SQL SELECT statement. A cursor can be likened to a pointer. As the programmer, you declare a cursor and define an SQL statement for that cursor. After that, you can use the cursor in much the same manner as a sequential file. The cursor is opened, rows are fetched from the cursor one row at a time, and then the cursor is closed.

You can perform four distinct operations on cursors:

DECLARE	Defines the cursor, gives it a name unique to the program in which it is embedded, and assigns an SQL statement to the cursor name. The DECLARE statement does not execute the SQL statement; it merely defines the SQL statement.
OPEN	Readies the cursor for row retrieval. OPEN is an executable statement. It reads the SQL search fields, executes the SQL statement, and sometimes builds the results table. It does not assign values to host variables, though.
FETCH	Returns data from the results table one row at a time and assigns the values to specified host variables. If the results table is not built at cursor OPEN time, it is built FETCH by FETCH.
CLOSE	Releases all resources used by the cursor.

Whether the results table for the SQL statement is built at cursor OPEN time or as rows are fetched depends on the type of SQL statement and the access path. You will learn about access paths in Chapter 21, "The Optimizer."

When you're processing with cursors, an SQL statement can return zero, one, or many rows. The following list describes the cursor processing that occurs for the different number of retrieved rows:

One row	Use of the cursor is optional. A result set of one row occurs either because the SQL predicates provided specific qualifications to make the answer set distinct or because a unique index exists for a column or columns specified in the predicates of the WHERE clause.
Many rows	Cursor processing is mandatory. When multiple rows are returned by an SQL statement, a cursor must be coded. If multiple rows are returned by a SELECT statement not coded using a cursor, DB2 returns a -811 SQLCODE (the SQLSTATE value is 21000).
Zero rows	No rows exist for the specified conditions, or the specified conditions are improperly coded. When no rows are returned, the SQL return code is set to +100.

When cursors are used to process multiple rows, a FETCH statement is typically coded in a loop that reads and processes each row in succession. When no more rows are available to be fetched, the FETCH statement returns an SQLCODE of +100, indicating no more rows. For an example of cursor processing, consult Listing 11.2.

LISTING 11.2   Cursor Processing

```
WORKING-STORAGE SECTION.
    .
    .
    .
    EXEC SQL
```

LISTING 11.2   Continued

```
        DECLARE C1 CURSOR FOR
            SELECT  DEPTNO, DEPTNAME, MGRNO
            FROM    DEPT
            WHERE   ADMRDEPT = :ADMRDEPT
    END-EXEC.
        .
        .
        .
PROCEDURE DIVISION.
        .
        .
        .
    MOVE  'A00'      TO ADMRDEPT.
    EXEC SQL
        OPEN C1
    END-EXEC.

IF SQLCODE < 0
        PERFORM 9999-ERROR-PARAGRAPH.
    MOVE  'YES'     TO MORE-ROWS.
    PERFORM 200-PROCESS-DEPTS
        UNTIL MORE-ROWS = 'NO'.

    EXEC SQL
        CLOSE C1
    END-EXEC.
    GOBACK.
200-PROCESS-DEPTS.
        .
        .
        .
    EXEC SQL
        FETCH C1
        INTO :DEPTNO,
            :DEPTNAME,
            :MGRNO
    END-EXEC.
    IF SQLCODE < 0
        PERFORM 9999-ERROR-PARAGRAPH.

    IF SQLCODE = +100
        MOVE  'NO'     TO MORE-ROWS
    ELSE
        perform required processing.
```

In Listing 11.2, a cursor is declared for an SQL SELECT statement in WORKING-STORAGE.
Values are moved to the host variables, and the cursor is opened. A loop fetches and
processes information until no more rows are available; then the cursor is closed.

Using a Cursor for Data Modification

Often an application program must read data and then, based on its values, either update or delete the data. You use the UPDATE and DELETE SQL statements to modify and delete rows from DB2 tables. These statements, like the SELECT statement, operate on data a set at a time. How can you then first read the data before modifying it?

You do so by using a cursor and a special clause of the UPDATE and DELETE statements that can be used only by embedded SQL: WHERE CURRENT OF. You declare the cursor with a special FOR UPDATE OF clause.

Refer to Listing 11.3, which declares a cursor named C1 specifying the FOR UPDATE OF clause. The cursor is opened and a row is fetched. After examining the contents of the retrieved data, the program updates or deletes the row using the WHERE CURRENT OF C1 clause.

LISTING 11.3   Updating with a Cursor

```
WORKING-STORAGE SECTION.
    EXEC SQL
        DECLARE C1 CURSOR FOR
            SELECT  DEPTNO, DEPTNAME, MGRNO
            FROM    DEPT
            WHERE   ADMRDEPT = :ADMRDEPT
            FOR UPDATE OF MGRNO
    END-EXEC.
PROCEDURE DIVISION.
            .
            .
            .
        MOVE   'A00'     TO ADMRDEPT.

        EXEC SQL
            OPEN C1
        END-EXEC.

        MOVE   'YES'     TO MORE-ROWS.

        PERFORM 200-MODIFY-DEPT-INFO
            UNTIL MORE-ROWS = 'NO'.

        EXEC SQL
            CLOSE C1
        END-EXEC.
        GOBACK.
    200-MODIFY-DEPT-INFO.
            .
            .
            .
        EXEC SQL
            FETCH C1
            INTO  :DEPTNO,
                  :DEPTNAME,
                  :MGRNO
```

LISTING 11.3   Continued

```
        END-EXEC.
        IF SQLCODE < 0
            PERFORM 9999-ERROR-PARAGRAPH.
        IF SQLCODE = +100
            MOVE  'NO'      TO MORE-ROWS
        ELSE
            EXEC SQL
                UPDATE DEPT
                SET MGRNO = '000060'
                WHERE CURRENT OF C1
            END-EXEC.
```

These features enable you to perform row-by-row operations on DB2 tables, effectively mimicking sequential file processing.

Scrollable Cursors

One of the more significant new application development features of DB2 V7 is the scrollable cursor. Scrollable cursors provide the ability to scroll forward and backward through data in an application program. Contrast this with a "normal" cursor, in which data can only be accessed one row at a time in a forward direction using the FETCH statement.

With scrollable cursors, no additional host language code (COBOL, C, etc.) is required to move forward and backward through the results set of a SELECT statement. A scrollable cursor makes navigating through SQL result sets much easier. The SCROLL keyword is used to specify a cursor as a scrollable cursor.

DB2 V7 introduced two types of scrollable cursors:

- SENSITIVE:—The results are updateable; the program can access data that is changed by the user or other users.

- INSENSITIVE:—Not updateable; the cursor results will not show any changes that are subsequently made to the data.

More details on cursor sensitivity are provided later in this section. Scrollable cursors allow developers to move through the results of a query in multiple ways. The FETCH statement is still used, but it is combined with keywords to move the fetching in a specific direction. The following keywords are supported when fetching data from a scrollable cursor:

- NEXT—Will FETCH the next row, the same way that the pre-V7 FETCH statement functioned.

- PRIOR—Will FETCH the previous row.

- FIRST—Will FETCH the first row in the results set.

- LAST—Will FETCH the last row in the results set.

- CURRENT—Will re-FETCH the current row from the result set.

- BEFORE—Positions the cursor before the first row of the results set.

- AFTER—Positions the cursor after the last row of the results set.

- ABSOLUTE *n*—Will FETCH the row that is *n* rows away from the first row in the results set.

- RELATIVE *n*—Will FETCH the row that is *n* rows away from the last row fetched.

For both ABSOLUTE and RELATIVE, the number *n* must be an integer. It can be either a positive or a negative number, and it can be represented as a numeric constant or as a host variable.

All of the FETCH options for scrollable cursors also reposition the cursor before fetching the data. For example, consider the following cursor logic:

```
DECLARE csr1 SENSITIVE STATIC SCROLL CURSOR
FOR SELECT   FIRSTNAME, LASTNME
    FROM     DSN8710.EMP
    ORDER BY LASTNME;

OPEN csr1;

FETCH LAST csr1 INTO :FN, :LN;
```

Issuing these SQL statements will declare a scrollable cursor named *csr1*, open that cursor, and then FETCH the last row from the cursor's results set. The FETCH LAST statement will reposition the cursor to the last row of the results set, and then FETCH the results into the host variables as specified. Scrollable cursors reduce the amount of time and effort required to move backward and forward through the results of SQL queries.

Sensitive Versus Insensitive

An INSENSITIVE cursor causes the results to be materialized and changes to the underlying data will never be reflected in the results set.

A SENSITIVE cursor, on the other hand, causes updates and deletes to be reflected in the answer set. Whether or not you can actually see the modifications depends on whether the cursor is defined as STATIC or DYNAMIC (which is covered in the next section).

Any UPDATE or DELETE that is processed will cause a SENSITIVE STATIC cursor to show the change as an update or delete hole; any INSERTs, however, will not be reflected in the answer set. A SENSTIVE DYNAMIC cursor will show the actual changed data—including all data affected by UPDATE, DELETE, and INSERT operations.

Update and delete holes pose a coding challenge for programmers. You will need to write additional code in your program to test the SQLCODE returned. Pay attention to the following SQLCODEs:

-222	An UPDATE or DELETE operation was attempted against a hole using the following cursor name (SQLSTATE: 24510)
-223	An UPDATE or DELETE operation was attempted against an update hole using the following cursor name (SQLSTATE: 24511)

V8 ASENSITIVE **Scrollable Cursors**   Flexibility is offered for declaring cursor sensitivity with the ASENSITIVE option for scrollable cursors. An ASENSITIVE cursor that is read-only behaves as an INSENSITIVE cursor. If the ASENSITIVE cursor is not read-only, it will behave as a SENSITIVE DYNAMIC cursor.

The default for cursor sensitivity is ASENSITIVE. Such a cursor is helpful for distributed applications where you do not know for sure whether the server supports sensitivity or scrollability.

Dynamic Versus Static

V8 When using a SENSITIVE scrollable cursor, an additional parameter is required to specify whether the cursor is to be DYNAMIC or STATIC. For DB2 V7, STATIC is the only option, but as of DB2 V8, scrollable cursors can be DYNAMIC.

To use scrollable cursors in DB2 V7 you must use declared temporary tables, another new feature of DB2 Version 7. Declared temporary tables are discussed in-depth in Chapter 5, "Data Definition Guidelines." DB2 uses a declared temporary table to hold and maintain the data returned by the scrollable cursor. When a static scrollable cursor is opened, qualifying rows are copied to a declared temporary table that is created automatically by DB2. DB2 drops the result table when the cursor is closed. So, before you begin to use scrollable cursors in V7, be sure to define a temporary database.

CAUTION

Be careful when using scrollable cursors with DB2 V7. Every new scrollable cursor creates a physical table in the temporary database.

With DB2 V8 IBM now supports dynamic scrollable cursors. So, as of V8, a SENSITIVE cursor can now be specified as DYNAMIC, too. A dynamic scrollable cursor does not use a temporary table to store the results set. Instead, it simply accesses the data right out of the base table. Some SQL statements cannot be used in a dynamic scrollable cursor; for example, a read-only cursor cannot be DYNAMIC.

Dynamic scrolling is possible because DB2 V8 allows us to backward scan through an index for the first time. This allows DB2 to move backward and forward through the scrollable cursor using an index.

Use a dynamic scrollable cursor when your application must be able to see all modified rows.

CAUTION

If a result table has to be materialized at the time cursor is opened, dynamic scrolling is not possible.

Scrollable Cursor Guidelines
The following guidelines are offered to help you implement effective scrollable cursors in your DB2 application programs.

Use Scrollable Cursors with Caution   As helpful as scrollable cursors are, do not make every cursor a scrollable cursor. Scrollable cursors require substantially more overhead than a traditional, non-scrollable cursor. Analyze the requirements of your applications and deploy scrollable cursors only where it makes sense to do so.

No Scrollable Cursors in Pseudo-Conversational CICS   Pseudo-conversational CICS programs cannot use scrollable cursors. Do not attempt to code a scrollable cursor in a pseudo-conversational CICS program.

Use Dynamic Cursors to See Changes   If you need to see the changes made to data by concurrent processes, be sure to use a dynamic scrollable cursor. This is the only type of scrollable cursor that has visibility to underlying changes.

CAUTION

Concurrent INSERT activity will not be visible to any scrollable cursor—only concurrent UPDATE and DELETE activity can be made visible to the cursor.

Know Your Scrollable Cursor Types   The resources required and the flexibility of processing are greatly affected by the proper sensitivity and dynamism settings for your scrollable cursors. Consult Table 11.7 for a short synopsis of the features and requirements for each type of scrollable cursor at your disposal. The visibility column refers to whether the cursor has visibility to changes made to the data; the updatability column refers to whether data can be updated using the cursor.

TABLE 11.7   Types of Scrollable Cursors

Dynamism	Sensitivity	Visibility	Updatability
N/A	INSENSITIVE	No	No
STATIC	SENSITIVE	1	Yes
DYNAMIC	SENSITIVE	Yes	Yes

¹ Inserts are not visible; updates and deletes are visible as holes.

Be sure to choose the appropriate cursor for the type of processing you require. Consider the following precautions as you decide on your cursor type:

- If you do not need to move forward and backward through your results set, do not use a scrollable cursor.

- If the query will cause DB2 to materialize a results set, do not use a DYNAMIC scrollable cursor—it will not work.

- Use common sense; if no concurrent modifications are possible, do not choose a DYNAMIC scrollable cursor.

- If you want to see updates and deletes but do not want to see newly inserted data, choose a STATIC SENSITIVE scrollable cursor.

- If you do not want to see any modifications, choose an INSENSITIVE scrollable cursor.

Rowset Positioning Cursors (Multiple Row FETCH)

V8 When you need to retrieve multiple rows, consider using a cursor defined with rowset positioning. A *rowset* is a group of rows that are operated on as a set. Such a cursor enables your program to retrieve more than one row using a single FETCH statement. This capability is new as of DB2 Version 8. By fetching multiple rows at once, your request might become more efficient, especially for distributed requests.

To use this feature, you must DECLARE your cursor as using the WITH ROWSET POSITIONING parameter. For example

```
EXEC SQL
   DECLARE CURSOR SAMPCURS
   WITH ROWSET POSITIONING
   FOR
   SELECT DEPTNO
   FROM   DSN8810.DEPT
END-EXEC.
```

Furthermore, to use a multi-row fetch you must have defined the appropriate structures to receive multi-row data. This means you must have defined an array of host variables into which the fetched rows can be placed. Each column fetched requires its own host variable array into which its values will be placed. Be sure to match the array size to the rowset size. With the appropriate setup coded, FETCH statements can be written to retrieve more than a single row from the result set. For example

```
FETCH ROWSET FROM SAMPCURS
   FOR 5 ROWS
   INTO HOSTVAR-ARRAY;
```

As you can see, the multiple-row fetch block is identical to the existing single-row-fetch block in DB2 V7, except that there are two additional clauses—ROWSET and FOR *n* ROWS. The ROWSET clause specifies that the orientation of this cursor is rowset positioning (instead of single row). The FOR *n* ROWS clause specifies the size of the rowset to be returned. The maximum rowset size is 32,767.

Rowset cursors are very useful when you need to retrieve many rows or large amounts of data in distributed systems. By retrieving multiple rows with a single FETCH, multiple trips between the application and the database can be eliminated, thereby improving network performance.

Rowset positioning can be combined with scrollable cursors to deliver very flexible and efficient data access. To FETCH from a scrollable cursor with rowset positioning, you will need to deploy similar keywords as are used with simple scrollable cursors, namely

- NEXT ROWSET

- PRIOR ROWSET

- FIRST ROWSET

- LAST ROWSET

- CURRENT ROWSET

- ROWSET STARTING AT ABSOLUTE *n*

- ROWSET STARTING AT RELATIVE *n*

Each of these provides similar functionality as described in the previous section on scrollable cursors, but with a rowset orientation—that is, they operate on multiple rows.

> **CAUTION**
>
> Multiple-row fetch is not supported in FORTRAN, Java, REXX, or SQL procedures.

An application program can combine single-row and multiple-row fetches from a rowset positioning cursor. This is done simply by specifying the ROWSET orientation clause for multiple-row fetches and removing it for single-row fetches. If FOR *n* ROWS is not specified for a rowset positioning cursor, then the size of the rowset will be the same as the previous multiple row FETCH.

Modifying Data Using Rowset Positioning Cursors

V8 Data that has been fetched using a rowset positioning cursor can be subsequently modified (using positioned UPDATEs and DELETEs). You can either modify all of the rows in the rowset or just one specific row in the rowset. If you specify WHERE CURRENT OF *cursor*, all of the rows in the rowset will be affected (that is, either deleted of updated). For example, the following SQL statements will impact the entire rowset (assuming, of course, that *csr1* and *csr2* in the following statements are rowset positioning cursors):

```
UPDATE EMP
SET SALARY = 50000.00
WHERE CURRENT OF CSR1;

DELETE DEPT
WHERE CURRENT OF CSR2;
```

New syntax is offered to modify just a single row within the rowset. A new clause, FOR CURSOR *csr* FOR ROW *n* OF ROWSET, allows you to direct DB2 to UPDATE or DELETE just a single row. For example

```
UPDATE EMP
SET SALARY = 50000.00
FOR CURSOR CSR1 FOR ROW :HV OF ROWSET;

DELETE DEPT
FOR CURSOR CSR2 FOR ROW 3 OF ROWSET;
```

Inserting Multiple Rows

V8 Similar to FETCH processing, INSERT processing can be used in conjunction with the FOR *n* ROWS clause as of DB2 Version 8. Consider using this feature to INSERT multiple rows with a single statement when your application program needs to do bulk data insertion.

By coding your program to fill up an array with data to be inserted and then using
INSERT...FOR *n* ROWS, the INSERT process can be made more efficient. For example

```
INSERT INTO SAMPLE_TABLE
FOR :N ROWS
VALUES(:HOSTVAR-ARRAY1, : HOSTVAR-ARRAY2, ...)
ATOMIC;
```

The [NOT] ATOMIC clause is used to specify whether the INSERT should fail or succeed as a
complete unit. By specifying ATOMIC, if one row fails, every row fails. On the other hand,
specifying NOT ATOMIC allows each row to fail or succeed on its own accord. Before deciding to use specify ATOMIC, take into consideration the number of rows and row size. If one
row out of thousands fails, performance can suffer as DB2 rolls back previous changes and
logs information.

> **NOTE**
>
> To handle nulls, you will need to supply a null indicator array. This array is required for nullable
> columns and must be specified following the host variable array.

Embedded SELECT and Cursor Coding Guidelines

Ensure efficient and accurate embedded SQL by following the subsequent guidelines.

Use Singleton SELECTs to Reduce Overhead   Whenever possible, try to use singleton
SELECTs rather than cursors because the definition and processing of cursors adds overhead
to a DB2 application program. However, be sure that the singleton SELECT returns only
one row. You can ensure that only a single row is to be returned in several ways:

- Selecting data only by the primary key column(s)

- Selecting data only by columns defined in a unique index

- Using the FETCH FIRST 1 ROW ONLY clause on the singleton SELECT statement

If the program requires a SELECT statement that returns more than one row, you must use
cursors. In other words, a singleton SELECT cannot be used to return more than one row.

Code SQL for Efficient Existence Checking   There are times when a program just needs to
know that some given data exists and does not need to actually retrieve and use that data.
For these situations, you will need to develop the most efficient SQL possible that just
checks whether the specific data exists. But what is the best way to accomplish an existence check?

Prior to DB2 V7, the best way to check for existence is to use a correlated query against
the SYSIBM.SYSDUMMY1 table. For example, to check for the existence of an employee with
the last name of Jones in the EMP table, the SQL would look like this:

```
SELECT  1
FROM    SYSIBM.SYSDUMMY1 A
WHERE   EXISTS (SELECT 1
```

```
FROM    EMP B
WHERE   LASTNAME = 'JONES'
AND A.IBMREQD = A.IBMREQD);
```

First, notice that we just SELECT the constant 1. Because the data does not need to be returned to the program, the SQL statement need not specify any columns in the SELECT-list. We simply check the SQLCODE. If the SQLCODE is zero, data exists; if not, the data does not exist.

Next, notice that we use the EXISTS predicate in the correlated subquery. This is an efficient formulation because EXISTS causes DB2 to stop processing as soon as one row is found that matches the WHERE clause in the subquery. This is fine, because all we want to know is that at least one row exists that matches the predicate(s). If you do not use a correlated query with EXISTS, but instead simply issued the SELECT statement, performance can suffer as DB2 scans to find subsequent occurrences of the data—which might be many, especially for a common name such as Jones.

V7   Which brings us to DB2 V7. In this version, there is a new clause called FETCH FIRST *n* ROWS ONLY. This solves our problem for existence checking and can become a new standard once you move to DB2 V7. Recoding the previous example using this new clause becomes

```
SELECT 1
FROM    EMP B
WHERE   LASTNAME = 'JONES'
FETCH FIRST 1 ROW ONLY;
```

We still do not need to specify columns in the SELECT-list, but we no longer need the correlated query. DB2 will stop after one row has been checked, which is the desired result.

> **NOTE**
>
> You might still choose to use the correlated subquery approach even after DB2 V7. This is particularly so when the next operation requires you to request data from DB2. If you can combine this next work into the subquery formulation, then it can be more efficient because you will not be going back and forth between the program and the DB2 engine in between existence checks.

Consider Cursor-Free Browsing   When a program needs to browse through the rows of a table based on a single column where a unique index exists, consider avoiding a cursor in favor of the following two SQL statements:

```
SELECT VALUE(MIN(SALARY),0)
INTO   :NEW-SAL-HVAR
FROM   EMP
WHERE  SALARY > :OLD-SAL-HVAR

SELECT EMPNO, LASTNAME, SALARY, BONUS
INTO   :HV-EMPNO, :HV-LASTNAME, :HV-SALARY, :HV-BONUS
FROM   EMP
WHERE  SALARY = :NEW-SAL-HVAR
```

The first time through the program, the host variable OLD-SAL-HVAR should be set to a value just lower than the lowest value that needs to be retrieved. By looping through the preceding two SQL statements, the program can avoid a cursor and browse the table rows until no more rows exist or the highest value is obtained. This technique can outperform a cursor in some situations.

Declare As Many Cursors As Needed   You can declare and open more than one cursor in any given program at any time. No limit is placed on the number of cursors permitted per application program.

Avoid Using Certain Cursors for Data Modification   You cannot use a cursor for updates or deletes if the DECLARE CURSOR statement includes any of the following:

UNION clause

DISTINCT clause

GROUP BY clause

ORDER BY clause

Joins

Subqueries

Correlated subqueries

Tables in read-only mode, ACCESS(RO)

Tables in utility mode, ACCESS(UT)

Read-only views

Place the DECLARE CURSOR Statement First   The DECLARE CURSOR statement must precede any other commands (such as OPEN, CLOSE, and FETCH) relating to the cursor because of the way the DB2 precompiler parses and extracts the SQL statements from the program.

The DECLARE CURSOR statement is not an executable statement and should not be coded in the PROCEDURE DIVISION of an application program. Although doing so does not cause a problem, it makes your program difficult to understand and could cause others to think that DECLARE is an executable statement.

You should place all cursor declarations in the WORKING-STORAGE section of the application program, immediately before PROCEDURE DIVISION. All host variable declarations must precede the DECLARE CURSOR statement in the application program.

Include Only the Columns Being Updated   When you're coding the FOR UPDATE OF clause of the DECLARE CURSOR statement, you should specify only the columns that will be updated. Coding more columns than is necessary can degrade performance.

In the FOR UPDATE OF clause of the DECLARE CURSOR statement, you must include all columns to be modified. Otherwise, subsequent UPDATE...WHERE CURRENT OF statements will not be allowed for those columns.

Use FOR UPDATE OF **When Updating with a Cursor**   Although doing so is not mandatory, you should code the FOR UPDATE OF clause of a DECLARE CURSOR statement used for deleting rows. This technique effectively locks the row before it is deleted so that no other process can access it. If rows earmarked for deletion are accessible by other programs and ad hoc users, the integrity of the data could be compromised.

Use WHERE CURRENT OF **to Delete Single Rows Using a Cursor**   Use the WHERE CURRENT OF clause on UPDATE and DELETE statements that are meant to modify only a single row. Failure to code the WHERE CURRENT OF clause results in the modification or deletion of every row in the table being processed.

Avoid the FOR UPDATE OF **Clause on Non-Updateable Cursors**   You cannot code the FOR UPDATE OF clause on cursors that access read-only data. These cursors contain SELECT statements that

- Access read-only views
- Join any tables
- Issue subqueries for two or more tables
- Access two or more tables using UNION
- Use built-in functions
- Use ORDER BY, GROUP BY, or HAVING
- Specify DISTINCT
- Specify literals or arithmetic expressions in the SELECT list

Open Cursors Before Fetching   Similar to a sequential file, a cursor must be opened before it can be fetched from or closed. You also cannot open a cursor twice without first closing it.

Initialize Host Variables   Initialize all host variables used by the cursor before opening the cursor. All host variables used in a cursor SELECT are evaluated when the cursor is opened, not when the cursor is declared or fetched from.

Use Care When Specifying Host Variables Used with FETCH   The FETCH statement retrieves data one row at a time only in a forward motion. In other words, rows that have already been retrieved cannot be retrieved again.

Synchronize the host variables fetched (or selected) with the SELECT list specified in the cursor declaration (or singleton SELECT). If the data type of the columns does not match the host variable, and the data cannot be converted, a compilation error results. This error can occur if host variables are transposed as follows:

```
EXEC SQL
    DECLARE C1 CURSOR
    SELECT  DEPTNO, ADMRDEPT
    FROM    DEPT
END-EXEC.
```

```
EXEC SQL
    FETCH C1
    INTO  :ADMRDEPT, :DEPTNO
END-EXEC.
```

The DEPTNO host variable is switched with the ADMRDEPT host variable in the FETCH statement. This switch does not cause a compilation error because both columns are the same data type and length, but it does cause data integrity problems.

Explicitly Close Cursors   When a DB2 program is finished, DB2 implicitly closes all cursors opened by the program. To increase performance, however, you should explicitly code the CLOSE statement for each cursor when the cursor is no longer required. The CLOSE statement can be executed only against previously OPENed cursors.

Use the WITH HOLD Clause to Retain Cursor Position   When a COMMIT is issued by the program, open cursors are closed unless the WITH HOLD option is coded for the cursor.

You can add the WITH HOLD parameter to a cursor as shown in the following example:

```
EXEC SQL
    DECLARE CSR1 CURSOR WITH HOLD FOR
        SELECT  EMPNO, LASTNAME
        FROM    EMP
        WHERE   SALARY > 30000
END-EXEC.
```

WITH HOLD prevents subsequent COMMITs from destroying the intermediate results table for the SELECT statement, thereby saving positioning within the cursor. This technique will not hold the cursor position over separate tasks in pseudo-conversational programs.

> **NOTE**
>
> Be aware that the manner in which DB2 handles locks for held cursors is influenced by the value of the RELCURHL DSNZPARM parameter. The default value is YES, which causes DB2 to release the row or page lock at COMMIT for the row where the cursor is positioned. Prior to V7, the default was NO, causing DB2 to hold the lock at COMMIT. The lock is not necessary for maintaining cursor position, so specify YES to improve concurrency.

Open Cursors Only When Needed   Do not open a cursor until just before you need it. Close the cursor immediately after your program receives an SQLCODE of +100, which means that the program has finished processing the cursor. This way, you can reduce the consumption of system resources.

Modifying Data with Embedded SQL

Previously, I discussed the capability to update and delete single rows based on cursor positioning. You can also embed pure set-level processing UPDATE, DELETE, and INSERT SQL statements into a host language program.

Simply code the appropriate SQL statement, and delimit it with EXEC SQL and END-EXEC. The statement can contain host variables. When issued in the program, the statement is processed as though it were issued interactively. Consider the following example:

```
EXEC SQL
    UPDATE EMP
        SET SALARY = SALARY * 1.05
        WHERE EMPNO = :EMPNO
END-EXEC.

EXEC SQL
    DELETE FROM PROJACT
    WHERE ACENDATE < CURRENT DATE
END-EXEC.

EXEC SQL
    INSERT INTO DEPT
        (DEPTNO,
         DEPTNAME,
         MGRNO,
         ADMRDEPT)
    VALUES
        (:DEPTNO,
         :DEPTNAME,
         :MGRNO,
         :ADMRDEPT)
END-EXEC.
```

These three SQL statements are examples of coding embedded data modification statements (UPDATE, DELETE, and INSERT) using host variables.

Embedded Modification SQL Guidelines

The following guidelines should be followed to ensure that optimal SQL data modification techniques are being deployed in your DB2 applications.

Favor Cursor-Controlled UPDATE **and** DELETE   Favor UPDATE and DELETE with a cursor specifying the FOR UPDATE OF clause over individual UPDATE and DELETE statements that use the set-level processing capabilities of SQL.

Set-level processing is preferable, however, when an OPEN, a FETCH, and a CLOSE are performed for each UPDATE or DELETE. Sometimes, performing these three actions cannot be avoided (for example, when applying transactions from a sequential input file).

Use FOR UPDATE OF **to Ensure Data Integrity**   If a program is coded to SELECT or FETCH a row and then, based on the row's contents, issue an UPDATE or DELETE, use a cursor with FOR UPDATE OF to ensure data integrity. The FOR UPDATE OF clause causes a lock to be taken on the data page when it is fetched, ensuring that no other process can modify the data before your program processes it. If the program simply SELECTs or FETCHs without the FOR UPDATE OF specification and then issues an SQL statement to modify the data, another process can modify the data in between, thereby invalidating your program's modification, overwriting your program's modification, or both.

> **CAUTION**
>
> When programming pseudo-conversational CICS transactions, FOR UPDATE OF is not sufficient to ensure integrity. A save and compare must be done prior to any update activity.

Specify a Primary Key in the WHERE Clause of UPDATE and DELETE Statements   Never issue independent, embedded, non-cursor controlled UPDATE and DELETE statements without specifying a primary key value or unique index column values in the WHERE clause unless you want to affect multiple rows. Without the unique WHERE clause specification, you might be unable to determine whether you have specified the correct row for modification. In addition, you could mistakenly update or delete multiple rows.

Of course, if your desired intent is to delete multiple rows, by all means, issue the embedded, non-cursor controlled UPDATE and DELETE statement. Just be sure to test the statement thoroughly to ensure that the results you desire are actually achieved.

Use Set-at-a-Time INSERTs   When you need to issue INSERT statements in your program, try to use the set-level processing capabilities. Using the set-level processing of INSERT is usually possible only when rows are being inserted into one table based on a SELECT from another table. For example

```
INSERT INTO user.EMP_SMITH
    SELECT *
    FROM DSN8810.EMP
    WHERE LASTNAME = 'SMITH';
```

This SQL statement causes every row in the EMP table, for employees whose last name is "Smith", to be inserted into the EMP_SMITH table.

V8 **Consider Multi-Row INSERTs Using Host Variable Arrays**   As discussed previously in this chapter, as of DB2 V8 it is possible to insert multiple rows with a single INSERT using host-variable arrays. Consider using this approach when your application program logic requires many rows to be inserted during a single program invocation.

Use LOAD Rather Than Multiple INSERTs   Favor the LOAD utility over an application program performing many insertions in a table. If the inserts are not dependent on coding constraints, format the input records to be loaded and use the LOAD utility. If the inserts are dependent on application code, consider writing an application program that writes a flat file that can subsequently be loaded using the LOAD utility. In general, LOAD outperforms a program issuing INSERTs.

One reason LOAD outperforms INSERTs is logging overhead. You can LOAD data without logging by specifying LOG NO, but INSERTs are always logged. By removing the overhead of logging, LOAD performance improves significantly. Of course, you will need to take an image copy backup of the data after the LOAD to preserve recoverability.

Application Development Guidelines

The guidelines in this section aid you in coding more efficient DB2 application programs by

- Coding efficient embedded SQL

- Coding efficient host language constructs to process the embedded SQL

- Increasing concurrency

- Promoting the development of easily maintainable code

When you're designing a DB2 program, you can easily get caught up in programming for efficiency, thereby compromising the effectiveness of the program. Efficiency can be defined as "doing things right," whereas effectiveness can be defined as "doing the right thing."

Design embedded SQL programs to be as efficient as possible (following the guidelines in this book) without compromising the effectiveness of the program. Gauge program efficiency by the following criteria:

- CPU time

- Elapsed time

- Number and type of I/Os

- Lock wait time

- Transaction throughput

For a thorough discussion of DB2 performance monitoring and tuning, consult Parts IV and V. Gauge program effectiveness by the following criteria:

- User satisfaction

- Expected results versus actual results

- Integrity of the processed data

- Capability to meet prearranged service-level requirements

Avoid "Black Boxes"   Often, DB2 professionals are confronted with the "black box" approach to database access. The basic idea behind a "black box" is that instead of having programs issue direct requests to the database, they will make requests of a "black box" data engine. This "black box" program is designed to accept parameter-driven requests and then issue common SQL statements to return results to the program.

So, a black box is a database access program that sits in between your application programs and DB2. It is designed so that *all* application programs call the black box for data instead of containing their own embedded SQL statements. The general idea behind such a contraption is that it will simplify DB2 development, because programmers will not need to know how to write SQL. Instead, the programmer just calls the black box program to request whatever data is required. SQL statements become calls—and every programmer knows how to code a call, right?

Basically, proponents of the "black box" solution believe that access to data by calling a program with parameters is easier than learning SQL. But the "black box" approach is complete rubbish and should be avoided at all costs. The proper way to formulate requests for DB2 data is by coding well-designed, efficient SQL statements. A "black box" will never be able to completely mimic the functionality of SQL. Furthermore, the "black box" approach is sure to cause performance problems because it will have been coded for multiple users and will forgo the efficient SQL design techniques discussed in Chapter 2, "Data Manipulation Guidelines."

For example, what if the data access requirements of the programs calling the "black box" call for the following:

- One program requires three columns from TABLE1

- A second program requires two columns from TABLE1

- Two additional programs require four columns from TABLE1

- A fifth program requires all of the columns from TABLE1

In this case, the "black box" is almost sure to be designed with a single SQL SELECT that returns all of the columns from TABLE1. But, based on which program calls the "black box," only the required rows would be returned. We know this is bad SQL design because we should always return the absolute minimum number of columns and rows per SQL SELECT statement to optimize performance. But even if four different SELECT statements were used by the "black box," if requirements change, so must the "black box." The additional maintenance required for the "black box" program adds unneeded administrative overhead. Furthermore, the "black box" program is a single-point-of-failure for any application that uses it.

Perhaps more importantly, using a "black box" always consumes more CPU than simply using embedded SQL statements in your program. The black box application requires additional lines of code to be executed than would be without the black box. It is elementary when you think about it. The CALL statement in the calling program is extra, and the code surrounding the statements in the black box that ties them together is extra. None of this is required if you just plug your SQL statements right into your application programs.

This extra code must be compiled and executed. When extra code is required (no matter how little or efficient it may be) extra CPU will be expended to run the application. More code means more work, and that means degraded performance.

All in all, "black boxes" provide no benefit but at significant cost. Application programs should be designed using SQL to access DB2 data. No "black boxes" should be allowed.

Code Modular DB2 Programs   You should design DB2 programs to be modular. One program should accomplish a single, well-defined task. If you need to execute multiple tasks, structure the programs so that tasks can be strung together by having the programs call one another. This approach is preferable to a single, large program that accomplishes many tasks for two reasons. First, single tasks in separate programs make the programs easier to understand and maintain. Second, if each task can be executed either alone or with other tasks, isolating the tasks in a program enables easier execution of any single task or list of tasks.

Minimize the Size of DB2 Programs   Code DB2 programs to be as small as possible. Streamlining your application code to remove unnecessary statements results in better performance. This recommendation goes hand-in-hand with the preceding one.

Consider Stored Procedures for Reuseability   When you're modularizing a DB2 application, do so with an eye toward reuseability. Whenever a particular task must be performed across many programs, applications, or systems, consider developing a stored procedure. A stored procedure, after it is created, can be called from multiple applications. However, when you modify the code, you need to modify only the stored procedure code, not each individual program.

For more information on stored procedures, refer to Chapter 15.

Consider User-Defined Functions for Reuseability   If your organization relies on business rules that transform data, consider implementing user-defined functions. Data transformation tasks that are performed by many programs, applications, or systems, can benefit from the reuseability aspects of user-defined functions. Consider developing user-defined functions for the business rule and then using it in subsequent SQL statements. This reuse is preferable to coding the business rule into multiple applications because

- You can be sure the same code is being used in all programs.

- You can optimize the performance of the UDF and impact multiple programs at once, instead of requiring massive logic changes in many programs.

- When the rule changes, you need to modify the UDF once, not in each individual program.

For more information on user-defined functions, refer to Chapter 4, "Using DB2 User-Defined Functions and Data Types."

Be Aware of Active Database Constructs   You can create active DB2 databases using features such as referential integrity and triggers. An active database takes action based on changes to the state of the data stored in it. For example, if a row is deleted, subsequent activity automatically occurs (such as enforcing a DELETE CASCADE referential constraint or an INSERT trigger firing that causes other data to be modified).

You need to be aware of the active database features that have been implemented to appropriately code DB2 application programs. This awareness is required because you need to know the processes that the database itself will automatically perform so your application programs do not repeat the process.

Use Unqualified SQL   Use unqualified table, view, synonym, and alias names in application programs. This way, you can ease the process of moving programs, plans, and packages from the test environment to the production environment. If tables are explicitly qualified in an application program, and tables are qualified differently in test DB2 than they are in production DB2, programs must be modified before they are turned over to an operational production application.

When the program is bound, the tables are qualified by one of the following:

- If neither the OWNER nor QUALIFIER parameter is specified, tables are qualified by the userid of the binding agent.

- If only the OWNER is specified, tables are qualified by the token specified in the OWNER parameter.

- If a QUALIFIER is specified, all tables are qualified by the token specified to that parameter.

Avoid SELECT *   Never use SELECT * in an embedded SQL program. Request each column that needs to be accessed. Also, follow the SQL coding recommendations in Chapter 2.

Filter Data Using the SQL WHERE Clause   Favor the specification of DB2 predicates to filter rows from a desired results table instead of the selection of all rows and the use of program logic to filter those not needed. For example, coding the embedded SELECT

```
SELECT   EMPNO, LASTNAME, SALARY
FROM     EMP
WHERE    SALARY > 10000
```

is preferred to coding the same SELECT statement without the WHERE clause and following the SELECT statement with an IF statement:

```
IF SALARY < 10000
    NEXT SENTENCE
ELSE
    Process data.
```

The WHERE clause usually outperforms the host language IF statement because I/O is reduced.

Use SQL to Join Tables   To join tables, favor SQL over application logic, except when the data retrieved by the join must be updated. In this situation, consider coding multiple cursors to mimic the join process. Base the predicates of one cursor on the data retrieved from a fetch to the previous cursor.

Listing 11.4 presents pseudo-code for retrieving data from a cursor declared with an SQL join statement.

LISTING 11.4   Pseudo-code for Retrieving Data from an SQL Join

```
EXEC SQL
    DECLARE JOINCSR CURSOR FOR
    SELECT   D.DEPTNO, D.DEPTNAME, E.EMPNO, E.SALARY
    FROM     DEPT    D,
             EMP     E
    WHERE    D.DEPTNO = E.WORKDEPT
END-EXEC.
```

LISTING 11.4   Continued

```
EXEC SQL
    OPEN JOINCSR
END-EXEC.
Loop until no more rows returned or error
EXEC SQL
      FETCH JOINCSR
        INTO :DEPTNO, :DEPTNAME, :EMPNO, :SALARY
    END-EXEC
    Process retrieved data
end of loop
```

The criteria for joining tables are in the predicates of the SQL statement. Compare this method to the application join example in Listing 11.5. The pseudo-code in this listing employs two cursors, each accessing a different table, to join the EMP table with the DEPT table using application logic.

LISTING 11.5   Pseudo-code for Retrieving Data from an Application Join

```
EXEC SQL
    DECLARE DEPTCSR CURSOR FOR
    SELECT  DEPTNO, DEPTNAME
    FROM    DEPT
END-EXEC.

EXEC SQL
    DECLARE EMPCSR CURSOR FOR
    SELECT  EMPNO, SALARY
    FROM    EMP
    WHERE   WORKDEPT = :HV-WORKDEPT
END-EXEC.

EXEC SQL
    OPEN DEPTCSR
END-EXEC.

Loop until no more department rows or error

    EXEC SQL
        FETCH DEPTCSR
        INTO :DEPTNO, :DEPTNAME
    END-EXEC.

    MOVE DEPTNO TO HV-WORKDEPT.

    EXEC SQL
        OPEN EMPCSR
    END-EXEC.

    Loop until no more employee rows or error

        EXEC SQL
            FETCH EMPCSR
```

LISTING 11.5   Continued

```
        INTO :EMPNO, :SALARY
    END-EXEC.

    Process retrieved data

  end of loop

end of loop
```

Joining tables by application logic requires additional code and is usually less efficient than an SQL join. When data will be updated in a cursor-controlled fashion, favor application joining over SQL joining because the results of an SQL join are not always updated directly. When you're updating the result rows of an application join, remember to code FOR UPDATE OF on each cursor, specifying every column that can be updated. When you're only reading the data without subsequent modification, remember to code FOR READ ONLY (or FOR FETCH ONLY) on the cursor.

Avoid Host Structures   Avoid selecting or fetching INTO a group-level host variable structure. Your program is more independent of table changes if you select or fetch into individual data elements. For example, code

```
EXEC SQL
    FETCH C1
    INTO :DEPTNO,
         :DEPTNAME:DEPTNAME-IND,
         :MGRNO:MGRNO-IND,
         :ADMDEPT:ADMRDEPT-IND
END-EXEC.
```

instead of

```
EXEC SQL
    FETCH C1
    INTO  :DCLDEPT:DEPT-IND
END-EXEC.
```

Although the second example appears easier to code, the first example is preferred. Using individual host variables instead of host structures makes programs easier to understand, easier to debug, and easier to maintain.

Use ORDER BY to Ensure Sequencing   Always use ORDER BY when your program must ensure the sequencing of returned rows. Otherwise, the rows are returned to your program in an unpredictable sequence. The *only* way to guarantee a specific sequence for your results set is to use the ORDER BY clause on your SELECT statement.

Use FOR READ ONLY for Read-Only Access   Code all read-only SELECT cursors with the FOR READ ONLY (or FOR FETCH ONLY) cursor clause. Doing so tells DB2 that you will not be modifying data using the cursor. This makes the cursor non-ambiguous and provides DB2 with better options to optimize query performance.

Explicitly Code Literals   When possible, code literals explicitly in the SQL statement rather than move the literals to host variables and then process the SQL statement using the host variables. This technique gives the DB2 optimization process the best opportunity for arriving at an optimal access path.

Although DB2 offers an option to reoptimize SQL statements on the fly (that is, REOPT(VARS)), explicit literal coding still should be considered when feasible. It should not, however, be a forced standard. As a general rule of thumb, if the value will not change for more than a year, consider coding it as a literal instead of using a host variable.

Use Temporary Tables to Simulate a Host Variable List   Sometimes the need arises to check a column for equality against a list of values. This can be difficult to do efficiently without using temporary tables. For example, suppose you have a list of twelve employee numbers for which you want names. You could code a loop that feeds the twelve values, one-by-one, into a host variable, say HVEMPNO, and execute the following SQL

```
SELECT EMPNO, LASTNAME, FIRSTNME
FROM    EMP
WHERE   EMPNO = :HVEMPNO;
```

Of course, this requires twelve executions of the SQL statement. Wouldn't it be easier if you could supply the twelve values in a single SQL statement, as shown in the following?

```
SELECT EMPNO, LASTNAME, FIRSTNME
FROM    EMP
WHERE   EMPNO IN (:HV1, :HV2, :HV3, :HV4, :HV5, :HV6,
                  :HV7, :HV8, :HV9, :HV10, :HV11, :HV12);
```

Well, that SQL is valid, but it requires twelve host variables. What if the number of values is not constant? If fewer than twelve values are supplied, you can put a non-existent value (low values, for example) in the remaining host variables and still be able to execute the SQL. But if more than twelve values are supplied, the statement has to be run multiple times—exactly the situation we were trying to avoid.

Instead, declare and use a temporary table. For example

```
EXEC SQL DECLARE userid.GTT
  (COL_LIST  INTEGER NOT NULL);
```

Insert all the values for the list into the COL_LIST column of the temporary table (GTT) and issue the following SQL:

```
SELECT EMPNO, LASTNAME, FIRSTNME
FROM    EMP
WHERE   EMPNO IN (SELECT COL_LIST FROM GTT);
```

Of course, each of the previous SELECT statements should be embedded in a cursor because multiple rows can be retrieved.

V7 Remember, there are two types of temporary tables: declared and created. Refer to Chapter 5 in the section titled "Temporary Tables" for the pros and cons of both types of temporary tables before deciding which to use.

Joining Non-Relational Data Using SQL   Consider using temporary tables when you need to join non-relational data to DB2 data. Recall from Chapter 5 that there are two types of temporary tables supported by DB2: declared and created.

Temporary tables are quite useful for storing non-relational data in a relational, or tabular, format. For example, consider an application that needs to join employee information stored in an IMS database to employee information in the a DB2 table, such as the EMP table. One approach, of course, would be to retrieve the required data from the IMS database and join it using program logic to the DB2 data. However, you could also create a temporary table and INSERT the IMS data as it is retrieved into the temporary table. After the temporary table is populated, it can be joined to the EMP table using a standard SQL join.

This technique is not limited to IMS data. Any non-relational data source can be read and inserted into a temporary table, which can then be accessed using SQL for the duration of the unit of work.

Avoid Cursors If Possible   Whenever doing so is practical, avoid the use of a cursor. Cursors add overhead to an application program. You can avoid cursors, however, only when the program retrieves a single row from an application table or tables.

Code Cursors to Retrieve Multiple Rows   If you do not check for -811 SQLCODEs, always code a cursor for each SELECT statement that does not access tables either by the primary key or by columns specified in a unique index.

V7 | **Use Scrollable Cursors to Move Within a Result Set**   When writing a program that needs to move forward and backward through the SQL results set, use a scrollable cursor. In terms of both ease of development and performance, scrollable cursors are preferable to coding a scrolling capability using host language code.

Specify Isolation Level by SQL Statement   Individual SQL statements can specify a different, appropriate isolation level. Although each DB2 plan and package has an isolation level, you can override it for individual SQL statements by using the WITH clause. You can specify the WITH clause for the following types of SQL statements:

- SELECT INTO
- DECLARE CURSOR
- INSERT
- Searched DELETE
- Searched UPDATE

Valid options are as follow:

- RR and RR KEEP UPDATE LOCKS (Repeatable Read)
- RS and RS KEEP UPDATE LOCKS (Read Stability)

- CS (Cursor Stability)

- UR (Uncommitted Read)

The KEEP UPDATE LOCKS clause was added as of DB2 V5. It indicates that DB2 is to acquire X locks instead of U or S locks on all qualifying rows or pages. Use KEEP UPDATE LOCKS sparingly. Although it can better serialize updates, it can reduce concurrency.

In Chapter 13, "Program Preparation," you can find additional guidance for each of the isolation levels.

Use the Sample Programs for Inspiration   IBM provides source code in several host languages for various sample application programs. This source code is in a PDS library named SYS1.DB2V8R1.DSNSAMP (or something similar) supplied with the DB2 system software. Samples of COBOL, PL/I, FORTRAN, Assembler, and C programs for TSO, CICS, and IMS are available in the aforementioned library.

Favor Complex SQL for Performance   When embedding SQL in application programs, developers are sometimes tempted to break up complex SQL statements into smaller, easier-to-understand SQL statements and combine them together using program logic. Avoid this approach. When SQL is properly coded, DB2 is almost always more efficient than equivalent application code when it comes to accessing and updating DB2 data.

Batch Programming Guidelines

When coding batch DB2 programs the following tips and tricks can be used to create effective and useful applications.

Favor Clustered Access   Whenever sequential access to table data is needed, process the table rows in clustered sequence. This reduces I/O cost because pages need not be re-read if the data is processed by the clustering sequence.

Increase Parallel Processing   The architecture of IBM mainframes is such that multiple engines are available for processing. A batch program executing in a single, standard batch job can be processed by only a single engine. To maximize performance of CPU-bound programs, increase the parallelism of the program in one of two ways:

- *Program Cloning*—Clone the program and stratify the data access. Stratifying data access refers to dividing data access into logical subsets that can be processed independently.

- *Query Parallelism*—Utilize partitioned table spaces and bind the application program specifying DEGREE(ANY) to indicate that DB2 should try to use query I/O, CPU, and Sysplex parallelism.

Using the first method, you, as the application developer, must physically create multiple clone programs. Each program clone must be functionally identical but will process a different subset of the data. For example, you could split a program that reads DSN8810.EMP to process employees into a series of programs that perform the same function, but each processes only a single department. The data can be stratified based on any consistent grouping of data that is comprehensive (all data to be processed is included) and non-overlapping (data in one subset does not occur in a different subset). For example, you can accomplish data stratification based on the following:

- Unique key ranges

- Table space partitions

- Functional groupings (for example, departments or companies)

Ensure that the data is stratified both programmatically and in the structure of the database. For example, if you're stratifying using partitioned table spaces, ensure that each job operates only on data from a single partition. If data from multiple partitions can be accessed in concurrent jobs, timeout and deadlock problems might occur. Refer to Chapter 5 for DDL recommendations for increasing concurrency.

Also note that concurrency problems can still occur. When data from one subset physically coexists with data from another subset, lockout and timeout can take place. DB2 locks at the page level (*usually*). If data is stratified at any level other than the table space partition level, data from one subset can coexist on the same table space page as data from another subset.

Using the second method, DB2's inherent query parallelism feature, you can develop a single program. DB2 determines whether parallelism is of benefit. If you specify DEGREE(ANY), DB2 formulates the appropriate degree of parallelism for each query in the program. The primary benefits accrued from allowing DB2 to specify parallelism are as follow:

- The avoidance of code duplication. Only one program is required. DB2 itself handles the parallel query execution.

- The ability of DB2 to determine the appropriate number of parallel engines per query (not per program).

- The ability of DB2 to change the degree of parallelism on the fly. If the resources are not available to process parallel queries, DB2 can automatically "turn off" parallelism at runtime.

- The ability of DB2 to enable Sysplex parallelism. With data sharing, when capacity requirements increase you can add extra engines. The cost to add additional engines is minimal and DB2 will automatically take advantage of additional engines.

- Finally, if the nature of the data changes such that a change to the degree of parallelism is warranted, all that is required is a new bind. DB2 automatically formulates the degree of parallelism at bind time.

However, potential problems arise when you're using query parallelism instead of program cloning:

- DB2 controls the number of parallel engines. The developer can exert no control. When program cloning is used, the number of parallel jobs is fixed and unchanging.

- One program can contain multiple queries, each with a different degree. Although this can be considered a benefit, it can also be confusing to novice programmers.

- DB2 I/O, CPU, and Sysplex parallelism are for read-only SQL. Updates, inserts, and deletes cannot be performed in parallel yet.

- DB2 can "turn off" parallelism at runtime. Once again, though, this can be considered a benefit because DB2 is smart enough to disengage parallelism because of an overexerted system.

Both methods of achieving parallelism are viable for DB2 V6 and later releases (for CPU parallelism, V4 is required; for Sysplex parallelism V5 is required). Whenever possible, favor DB2 parallelism over program cloning, because it is simpler to implement and modify.

Use LOCK TABLE with Caution   As a general rule, use the LOCK TABLE command with caution. Discuss the implications of this command with your DBA staff before deciding to use it.

Issuing a LOCK TABLE statement locks all tables in the table space containing the table specified. It holds all locks until COMMIT or DEALLOCATION. This statement reduces concurrent access to all tables in the table space affected by the command.

The preceding rule notwithstanding, LOCK TABLE can significantly improve an application program's processing time. If a significant number of page locks are taken during program execution, the addition of LOCK TABLE eliminates page locks, replacing them with table (or table space) locks. It thereby enhances performance by eliminating the overhead associated with page locks.

Balance the issuing of the LOCK TABLE command with the need for concurrent data access, the locking strategies in the DDL of the table spaces, and the plans being run.

> **NOTE**
>
> You can use LOCK TABLE to explicitly limit concurrent access. For example, issuing a LOCK TABLE statement in a batch program can prevent online transactions from entering data before the batch cycle has completed.

Parameterize Lock Strategies   If a batch window exists wherein concurrent access is not required, but a high degree of concurrency is required after the batch window, consider coding batch programs with dynamic lock-switching capabilities. For example, if the batch window extends from 2:00 a.m. to 6:00 a.m., and a batch DB2 update program must run during that time, make the locking parameter-driven or system-clock-driven.

The program can read the system clock and determine whether it can complete before online processing begins at 6:00 a.m. This decision should be based on the average elapsed time required for the program to execute. If possible, the program should issue the LOCK TABLE statement. If this is not possible, the program should use the normal locking strategy as assigned by the table space DDL. A flexible locking strategy increases performance and reduces the program's impact on the online world.

An alternative method is to let the program accept a parameter to control locking granularity. For example, the value TABLE or NORMAL can be passed as a parameter. If TABLE is specified as a parameter, the program issues LOCK TABLE statements. Otherwise, normal locking ensues. If NORMAL is specified, normal locking requires manual intervention and is not as easily implemented as the system time method.

Periodically COMMIT Work in Batch Modification Programs   Favor issuing COMMITs in all DB2 programs where data is modified (INSERT, UPDATE, and DELETE). A COMMIT externalizes all modifications that occurred in the program since the beginning of the program or the last COMMIT. Failing to code COMMITs in a DB2 data modification program is sometimes referred to as "Bachelor Programming Syndrome"—that is, fear of committing.

> **NOTE**
>
> COMMIT does not flush data from the DB2 buffer pool and physically apply the data to the table. It does, however, ensure that all modifications have been physically applied to the DB2 log, thereby ensuring data integrity and recoverability.

One important factor affecting the need for a COMMIT strategy is the amount of elapsed time required for the program to complete. The greater the amount of time needed, the more you should consider using COMMITs (to reduce rollback time and reprocessing time in the event of program failure). You can safely assume, however, that the elapsed time increases as the number of modifications increases.

Issuing COMMITs in an application program is important for three reasons. First, if the program fails, all the modifications are backed out to the last COMMIT point. This process could take twice the time it took to perform the modifications in the first place—especially if you are near the end of a program with no COMMITs that performed hundreds or thousands of modification operations.

Second, if you resubmit a failing program that issues no COMMITs, the program redoes work unnecessarily.

Third, programs bound using the repeatable read page locking strategy or the RELEASE(COMMIT) table space locking strategy hold their respective page and table space locks until a COMMIT is issued. If no COMMITs are issued during the program, locks are not released until the auto-COMMIT when the program completes, thereby negatively affecting concurrent access. This can cause lock timeouts and lock escalation.

Given these considerations for COMMIT processing, the following situations should compel you to code COMMIT logic in your batch programs:

- The modification program must run in a small batch processing window

- Concurrent batch or online access must occur during the time the batch program is running

> **NOTE**
>
> If the concurrent batch or online access uses ISOLATION(UR), COMMIT processing is irrelevant. However, most processing requires accurate data and as such does not use ISOLATION(UR).

In some rare circumstances, you might be able to avoid issuing COMMITs in your batch DB2 programs. When modification programs without COMMITs fail, you can generally restart them from the beginning because database changes have not been committed. Additionally, COMMITs require resources. By reducing or eliminating COMMITs, you might conceivably be able to enhance performance (albeit at the expense of concurrency due to additional locks being held for a greater duration).

Before you decide to avoid COMMIT processing, remember that all cataloged sequential files must be deleted, any updated VSAM files must be restored, and any IMS modifications must be backed out before restarting the failing program. If the outlined situations change, you might need to retrofit your batch programs with COMMIT processing—a potentially painful process.

I recommend that you plan to issue COMMITs in every batch program. You can structure the logic so that the COMMIT processing is contingent on a parameter passed to the program. This approach enables an analyst to turn off COMMIT processing but ensures that all batch programs are prepared if COMMIT processing is required in the future.

Use Elapsed Time to Schedule COMMITs Base the frequency of COMMITs on the information in Table 11.8 or on the elapsed time since the last COMMIT. Doing so provides a more consistent COMMIT frequency. If you insist on basing COMMIT processing on the number of rows processed instead of the elapsed time, consider estimating the elapsed time required to process a given number of rows and then correlate this time to Table 11.8 to determine the optimal COMMIT frequency.

TABLE 11.8 Recommendations for COMMIT Frequency

Application Requirement	COMMIT Recommendations
No concurrent access required and unlimited time for reprocessing in the event of an abend	Code program for COMMITs, but consider processing without COMMITs (using a parameter)
No concurrency required but limited reprocessing time available	COMMIT in batch approximately every 15 minutes
Limited batch concurrency required; no concurrent online activity	COMMIT in batch every 1 to 5 minutes (more frequently to increase concurrency)
Online concurrency required	COMMIT in batch every 5 to 15 seconds

Modify As Close As Possible to the COMMIT You can reduce the amount of time that locks are held and thereby minimize lock timeouts by issuing INSERT, UPDATE, and DELETE statements as close as possible to your COMMIT statements. By limiting the lines of code that must be executed in between your data modification statements and your COMMIT statements, you can optimize DB2 locking. The quicker modified data is committed to the database (or rolled back), the shorter the amount of time that data will need to be locked out from other users.

Of course, programmers might balk at implementing this suggestion. Moving data modification code might not fall in line with the aesthetics of programming. However, from a data integrity perspective, all that matters is that the appropriate INSERT, UPDATE, and DELETE statements fall within the appropriate units of work. So, keep in mind that moving your data modification statements closer to the COMMIT statement can improve application performance.

Sequence Modification Statements Within the Unit of Work   You can minimize the number of deadlocks that occur by coding all data modification statements (issuing INSERT, UPDATE, and DELETE statements) within each unit of work in a prespecified sequence. For example, code modifications in alphabetical order by table name. Doing so reduces the chance of deadlocks, because the order of the modification statements will be the same from program to program.

Choose Meaningful Units of Work   A *unit of work* is a portion of processing that achieves data integrity, is logically complete, and creates a point of recovery. Units of work are defined by the scope of the COMMITs issued by your program. (All data modification that occurs between COMMITs is considered to be in a unit of work.) Use care in choosing units of work for programs that issue INSERT, UPDATE, or DELETE statements.

Choosing a unit of work that provides data integrity is of paramount importance for programs that issue COMMITs. For example, consider an application program that modifies the project start and end dates in tables DSN8810.PROJACT and DSN8810.EMPPROJACT. The start and end DSN8810.PROJACT columns are

ACSTDATE	Estimated start date for the activity recorded in this row of the project activity table
ACENDATE	Estimated end date for the activity recorded in this row of the project activity table

The columns for DSN8810.EMPPROJACT are

EMSTDATE	Estimated start date when the employee will begin work on the activity recorded in this row of the employee project
EMENDATE	Estimated end date when the employee will have completed the activity recorded in this row of the employee project activity

The start and end dates in these two tables are logically related. A given activity for a project begins on a specified date and ends on a specified date. A given employee is assigned to work on each activity and is assigned also a start date and an end date for the activity.

Many employees can work on a single activity, but each employee can start and end his or her involvement with that activity at different times. The only stipulation is that the employees must begin and end their involvement within the start and end dates for that activity. Therein lies the relationship that ties these four columns together.

The unit of work for the program should be composed of the modifications to both tables. In other words, the program should not commit the changes to one table without committing the changes to the other table at the same time. If it does commit the changes to one but not the other, the implicit relationship between the dates in the two tables can be destroyed.

Consider the following situation. A project has a start date of 2002-12-01 and an end date of 2004-03-31. This information is recorded in the DSN8810.PROJACT table. Employees are assigned to work on activities in this project with start and end dates in the stated range. These dates are recorded in the DSN8810.EMPPROJACT table.

Later, you must modify the end date of the project to 2004-01-31. This new end date is earlier than the previous end date. Consider the status of the data if the program updates the end date in the DSN8810.PROJACT table, commits the changes, and then abends. The data in the DSN8810.EMPPROJACT table has not been updated, so the end dates are not synchronized. An employee can still be assigned an activity with the old end date. For this reason, you should be sure to group related updates in the same unit of work.

V7 **Consider Using External** SAVEPOINTs   As of DB2 V7, you can set a SAVEPOINT within a transaction—without committing your work. You can think of a SAVEPOINT as a sub-UOW (unit of work) "stability" point. After the SAVEPOINT is set, you can use application logic to undo any data modifications and database schema changes that were made since the application set the SAVEPOINT. Using a SAVEPOINT can be more efficient, because you will not need to include contingency and what-if logic in your application code.

Remember, issuing a SAVEPOINT does not COMMIT work to DB2. It is simply a mechanism for registering milestones within a transaction or program. Let's learn by example. Consider the following pseudo-code:

```
SAVEPOINT POINTX ON ROLLBACK RETAIN CURSORS;
...
Subsequent processing
...
ROLLBACK TO SAVEPOINT POINTX;
```

The ROLLBACK will cause any data or schema changes made in the "subsequent processing" to be undone.

You can code multiple SAVEPOINTs within a UOW, and you can ROLLBACK to any SAVEPOINT (as long as you do not reuse the SAVEPOINT name). The UNIQUE keyword can be specified to ensure that the SAVEPOINT name is not reused within the unit of recovery.

There are two clauses that can be specified to further define the nature of the SAVEPOINT when a ROLLBACK is issued:

RETAIN CURSORS   Any cursors opened after the SAVEPOINT is set are not tracked and will not be closed when rolling back to that SAVEPOINT.

RETAIN LOCKS   Any locks acquired after the SAVEPOINT is set are not tracked and will not be released when rolling back to the SAVEPOINT.

Even if RETAIN CURSORS is specified, some of the cursors might not be useable. For example, if the ROLLBACK removes a row (that is, rolls back an INSERT) upon which the cursor was positioned, DB2 will raise an error.

> **NOTE**
>
> SAVEPOINTs can be very useful for stored procedures that need to maintain sub-UOW stability points.

Make Programs Restartable   In time-critical applications, DB2 batch programs that modify table data should be restartable if a system error occurs. To make a batch program restartable, you first create a DB2 table to control the checkpoint and restart processing for all DB2 update programs. A checkpoint is data written by an application program during its execution that identifies the status and extent of processing. This checkpoint is usually accomplished by storing the primary key of the table row being processed. The program must update the primary key as it processes before each COMMIT point. During restart processing, the primary key information is read, enabling the program to continue from where it left off.

The following DDL illustrates a DB2 table (and an associated index) that can be used to support checkpoint and restart processing:

```
CREATE TABLE CHKPT_RSTRT
    (PROGRAM_NAME       CHAR(8)      NOT NULL,
     ITERATION          CHAR(4)      NOT NULL,
     COMMIT_FREQUENCY   SMALLINT     NOT NULL,
     NO_OF_COMMITS      SMALLINT     NOT NULL WITH DEFAULT,
     CHECKPOINT_TIME    TIMESTAMP    NOT NULL WITH DEFAULT,
     CHECKPOINT_AREA    CHAR(254)    NOT NULL WITH DEFAULT.

     PRIMARY KEY (PROGRAM_NAME, ITERATION)
     )
IN DATABASE.TBSPACE
;
CREATE UNIQUE INDEX XCHKPRST
    (PROGRAM_NAME, ITERATION)
    CLUSTER
    other parameters
;
```

When a batch program is restarted after an abend, it can continue where it left off if it follows certain steps. This is true because a checkpoint row was written indicating the last committed update, the time that the employee was processed, and the key of the processed employee table (ACTNO).

The following steps show you the coding necessary to make a program restartable:

1. Declare two cursors to SELECT rows to be updated in the PROJACT table. Code an ORDER BY for the columns of the unique index (PROJNO, ACTNO, and ACSTDATE). The first cursor should select the rows you want. It is used the first time the request is processed. For example,

```
EXEC SQL DECLARE CSR1
      SELECT   PROJNO, ACTNO, ACSTDATE,
               ACSTAFF, ACENDATE
```

```
    FROM      PROJACT
    ORDER BY PROJNO, ACTNO, ACSTDATE
END-EXEC.
```

This statement reflects the needs of your application. The second cursor is for use after issuing COMMITs and for restart processing. It must reposition the cursor at the row following the last row processed. You can reposition the cursor by using WHERE clauses that reflect the ORDER BY on the primary key (or the unique column combination). For example,

```
EXEC SQL DECLARE CSR2
    SELECT    PROJNO, ACTNO, ACSTDATE,
              ACSTAFF, ACENDATE
    FROM      PROJACT
    WHERE     ((PROJNO = :CHKPT-PROJNO
    AND         ACTNO = :CHKPT-ACTNO
    AND         ACSTDATE > :CHKPT-ACSTDATE)
    OR         (PROJNO = :CHKPT-PROJNO
    AND         ACTNO > :CHKPT-ACTNO)
    OR         (PROJNO > :CHKPT-PROJNO))
    AND        PROJNO >= :CHKPT-PROJNO
    ORDER BY PROJNO, ACTNO, ACSTDATE
END-EXEC.
```

This cursor begins processing at a point other than the beginning of the ORDER BY list. Although, technically you can use only the second cursor by coding low values for the host variables the first time through, doing so is not recommended. The first cursor usually provides better performance than the second, especially when the second cursor is artificially constrained by bogus host variable values. However, if you can determine (using EXPLAIN or other performance monitoring techniques) that the first cursor provides no appreciable performance gain over the second, use only one cursor.

2. SELECT the row from the CHKPT-RESTRT table for the program and iteration being processed. You can hard-code the program name into the program. Or, if the program can run parallel with itself, it should be able to accept as parameter-driven input an iteration token, used for identifying a particular batch run of the program.

3. If it is the first time through and CHECKPOINT_AREA contains data, the program is restarted. Move the appropriate values from the CHECKPOINT_AREA to the host variables used in the second cursor and OPEN it. If it is the first time through and the program is not restarted, OPEN the first PROJACT cursor.

4. FETCH a row from the opened cursor.

5. If the FETCH is successful, increment a WORKING-STORAGE variable that counts successful fetches.

6. Perform the UPDATE for the PROJACT row that was fetched.

7. If the fetch counter is equal to COMMIT_FREQUENCY, perform a commit paragraph. This paragraph should increment and update NO_OF_COMMITS and the CHECKPOINT_AREA column with the PROJNO, ACTNO, and ACSTDATE of the PROJACT row retrieved, and set CHECKPOINT_TIME to the current timestamp. It should then issue a COMMIT and reset the fetch counter to zero.

8. After a COMMIT, cursors are closed unless you specified the WITH HOLD option. If the WITH HOLD option is not used, the cursor must change after the first COMMIT is executed (unless only the second cursor shown previously is used). Remember, the first time through, the program can use the C1 cursor above; subsequently, it should always use C2.

9. When update processing is complete, reset the values of the columns in the CHKPT_RSTRT table to their original default values.

   If the CHKPT_RSTRT row for the program is reread after each COMMIT, you can modify the COMMIT_FREQUENCY column on the fly. If you determine that too few or too many checkpoints have been taken, based on the state of the data and the time elapsed and remaining, he or she can update the COMMIT_FREQUENCY (using QMF, SPUFI, or some other means) for that program only. Doing so dynamically changes the frequency at which the program COMMITs.

   Incurring the extra read usually causes little performance degradation because the page containing the row usually remains in the bufferpool because of its frequent access rate.

Following these nine steps enables you to restart your programs after a program failure. During processing, the CHKPT_RSTRT table is continually updated with current processing information. If the program abends, all updates—including updates to the CHKPT_RSTRT table—are rolled back to the last successful checkpoint. This way, the CHKPT_RSTRT table is synchronized with the updates made to the table. You can then restart the update program after you determine and correct the cause of the abend.

On restart, the CHKPT_RSTRT table is read, and the CHECKPOINT_AREA information is placed into a cursor that repositions the program to the data where the last update occurred.

Additional Notes on Restartability   If a restartable program uses the WITH HOLD option to prohibit cursor closing at COMMIT time, it can avoid the need to reposition the cursor constantly, thereby enabling more efficient processing. To be restartable, however, the program still requires a repositioning cursor so that it can bypass the work already completed.

When you specify the WITH HOLD option, the repositioning cursor is used only when the program is restarted, not during normal processing. Additional code and parameters are required to signal the program when to use the repositioning cursors.

Restartable programs using sequential input files can reposition the input files using one of two methods. The first way is to count the records read and place the counter in the CHKPT_RSTRT table. On restart, the table is read and multiple reads are issued (number of reads equals READ_COUNTER). Alternatively, for input files sorted by the checkpoint key, the program can use the information in the CHECKPOINT_AREA to read to the appropriate record.

Restartable programs writing sequential output files must handle each output file separately. Most sequential output files can have their disposition modified to MOD in the JCL, allowing the restarted program to continue writing to them. For the following types of output files, however, you must delete or modify output file records before restarting:

- Headers for report files with control break processing

- Output files with different record types

- Any output file requiring specialized application processing

> **NOTE**
>
> If you have a budget for ISV tools, one of the best investments is a checkpoint/restart tool. Such tools provide the ability to resume the processing of failed or interrupted batch applications from the most recent checkpoint rather than from the beginning of the job step. Many also enable you to control the checkpoint frequency outside the application. They save a lot of coding and are not typically very expensive. Examples of such tools include BMC Software's Application Restart Control and Softbase Systems' Database Rely.

Hold Cursors Rather Than Reposition   You also can use the concept of cursor repositioning for programs not coded to be restartable. If COMMITs are coded in a program that updates data using cursors, you have two options for repositioning cursors. You can use the WITH HOLD option of the cursor, or you can code two cursors, an initial cursor and a repositioning cursor, as shown in the previous example.

The best solution is to code the WITH HOLD clause for each cursor that needs to be accessed after a COMMIT. WITH HOLD prohibits the closing of the cursor by the COMMIT statement and maintains the position of the cursor.

Online Programming Guidelines

Utilize the following techniques to create efficient online DB2 applications.

Limit the Number of Pages Retrieved   To achieve subsecond transaction response time, try to limit the number of pages retrieved or modified. When subsecond response time is not required, the number of pages to be accessed can be increased until the service level agreement is not met. In general, try to avoid having an impact on more than 100 pages in online transactions.

Limit Online Joins   When you're joining rows, try to limit the number of rows returned by the transaction. There is a practical limit to the amount of data that a user can assimilate while sitting in front of a computer screen. Whenever possible, set a low limit on the number of rows returned (for example, approximately 125 rows, or 5 screens of data). For data intensive applications, adjust this total, as required, with the understanding that performance may degrade as additional data is accessed and returned to the screen.

V8 As of Version 8, DB2 enables up to 225 tables to be referenced in a single SQL statement. This limit was driven by ERP vendors who developed their applications on other DBMS platforms. Just because DB2 supports up to 225 tables in a SQL statement does not mean you should code such SQL statements, particularly online. As indicated previously, limit online joins to retrieve only the amount of data that actually can be consumed by an online user.

> **NOTE**
>
> DB2 allowed up to 225 tables to be referenced in a single SQL statement as of DB2 V6, but you had to jump through hoops in order to make it happen. In reality, DB2 allowed up to 15 query blocks per SQL statement, and each query block could reference up to 15 tables—thus, 15 × 15 = 225. As of DB2 V8, you can reference 225 tables in each SQL statement without worrying about the number of query blocks.

Limit Online Sorts   To reduce online data sorting, try to avoid using GROUP BY, ORDER BY, DISTINCT, and UNION unless appropriate indexes are available. Of course, if your transaction absolutely requires sorting (to return data in a particular sequence, to group columns, or to remove duplicates), then perform the sort in DB2. Doing so will almost always outperform returning the data and sorting it in the program logic (or using an external sort package, such as DFSORT or Syncsort).

Issue COMMITs Before Displaying   Always issue commits (CICS SYNCPOINT, TSO COMMIT, or IMS CHKP) before sending information to a terminal.

Modularize Transactions   When possible, design separate transactions for selecting, updating, inserting, and deleting rows. This way, you can minimize page locking and maximize modular program design.

Minimize Cascading DELETEs   Avoid online deletion of parent table rows involved in referential constraints specifying the CASCADE delete rule. When a row in the parent table is deleted, multiple deletes in dependent tables can occur. This result degrades online performance.

Keep in mind that as of V6, triggers also can cause cascading data modification. Be sure to include the impact of triggers when analyzing the overall impact referential integrity-invoked cascading deletes can cause.

Be Aware of Overactive Data Areas   An *overactive* data area is a portion of a table or index that is accessed and updated considerably more than other tables (or portions thereof) in the online application. Be aware of overactive data areas.

Overactive data areas are characterized by the following features: a relatively small number of pages (usually 10 pages or fewer, and sometimes only 1 row), and a large volume of retrievals and updates (usually busy more than half the time that the online application is active).

Overactive data areas can be caused, for example, by using a table with one row (or a small number of rows) to assign sequential numbers for columns in other tables or files; or by using a table to store counters, totals, or averages of values stored in other tables or files. You also can cause overactive data areas when you use tables to implement domains that are volatile or heavily accessed by the online system. These situations cause many different programs to access and modify a small amount of data over and over. An inordinate number of resource unavailable and timeout abends can be caused by overactive data areas unless they are monitored and maintained.

Reduce the impact of overactive data areas by designing transactions with the following characteristics:

- Issue OPEN, FETCH, UPDATE, and CLOSE cursor statements (hereafter referred to as *update sequences*) as close to each other as possible.

- Invoke update sequences as rapidly as possible in the transaction; in other words, do not place unrelated operations in the series of instructions that update the overactive data area.

- Code as few intervening instructions as possible between the OPEN, FETCH, and CLOSE statements.

- Place the update sequence as close to the transaction commit point as possible (that is, near the end of the transaction code).

- Isolate the active range to a single partition (or several partitions). Assign the partitions to a dedicated buffer pool (perhaps with a related hiperspace) and to a device and controller that has excess capacity during peak periods.

- Try to use DDL options to reduce the impact of overactive data areas and increase concurrent access. You can do so by increasing free space on the table space and indexes for the tables or by increasing the MAXROWS table space parameter (or adding a large column to the end of the row for each table thus reducing the number of rows per page).

Consider Using TIMESTAMP **for Sequencing**   Sometimes you will need to automatically set the value for a column. Consider using TIMESTAMP data types instead of sequentially assigned numbers. You can generate timestamps automatically using the CURRENT TIMESTAMP special register (or the NOT NULL WITH DEFAULT option). A timestamp column has the same basic functionality as a sequentially assigned number, without the requirement of designing a table to assign sequential numbers. Remember, a table with a sequencing column can cause an overactive data area.

A column defined with the TIMESTAMP data type is marked by the date and time (down to the microsecond) that the row was inserted or updated. These numbers are serial unless updates occur across multiple time zones. Although duplicate timestamps can be generated if two transactions are entered at the same microsecond, this circumstance is rare. You can eliminate this possibility by coding a unique index on the column and checking for a -803 SQLCODE (duplicate index entry).

The only other drawback is the size of the timestamp data type. Although physically stored as only 10 bytes, the timestamp data is presented to the user as a 26-byte field. If users must remember the key, a timestamp usually does not suffice.

A common workaround for numbers that must be random is to use the microsecond portion of the timestamp as a random number generator to create keys automatically, without the need for a table to assign them. Note, though, that these numbers will not be sequenced by order of input.

V7 **Consider Using** IDENTITY **Columns or** SEQUENCE **Objects**   At times it is necessary for an application to have a column that stores sequential values. For every new row that is inserted, the previous value needs to be incremented and then stored in the new row. DB2 provides two mechanisms for automatically generating these sequential values: IDENTITY columns and SEQUENCE objects.

V8 IDENTITY columns were added to DB2 V7 (actually, they were made available during the V6 refresh); SEQUENCE objects were added to DB2 V8. Both provide a means of creating a column that is automatically incremented by DB2. In general, SEQUENCE objects are more flexible and manageable than IDENTITY columns. However, be sure to consult Chapter 5, where the details of each are discussed in-depth.

Consider Using ROWID **for Direct Row Access**   When the table you need to access contains a ROWID column, you can use that column to directly access a row without using an index or a table space scan. DB2 can directly access the row because the ROWID column contains the location of the row. Direct row access is very efficient.

To use direct row access, you must first SELECT the row using traditional methods. DB2 will either use an index or a scan to retrieve the row the first time. Be sure to retrieve the ROWID column and store it in a host variable. After the row has been accessed once, the ROWID column can be used to directly access the row again. Simply include a predicate in the WHERE clause for the ROWID column, such as the following:

```
WHERE ROWID_COL = :HVROWID
```

Of course, DB2 may revert to an access type other than direct row access if it determines that the row location has changed. You must plan for the possibility that DB2 will not choose to use direct row access, even if it indicates its intent to do so during EXPLAIN. If the predicate you are using to do direct row access is not indexable, and if DB2 is unable to use direct row access, a table space scan will be used instead. This can negatively impact performance.

For a query to qualify for direct row access, the search condition must be a stage 1 predicate of one of the following forms:

- A simple Boolean predicate formulated as

  ```
  COLUMN = non-column expression
  ```

  where COLUMN is a ROWID data type and non-column expression contains a ROWID value

- A simple Boolean predicate formulated as

  ```
  COLUMN IN 'list'
  ```

where COLUMN is a ROWID data type and the values in the list are ROWID values and an index is defined on the COLUMN

- A compound predicate using AND where one of the component predicates fits one of the two previous descriptions

> **CAUTION**
>
> Do not attempt to "remember" ROWID values between executions of an application program because the ROWID value can change, due to a REORG, for example.
>
> Additionally, do not attempt to use ROWID values across tables, even if those tables are exact shadow copies. The ROWID values will not be the same across tables.

Do Not INSERT into Empty Tables   Avoid inserting rows into empty tables in an online environment. Doing so causes multiple I/Os when you're updating indexes and causes index page splits. If you must insert rows into an empty table, consider one of the following options. You can format the table by prefilling it with index keys that can be updated online instead of inserted. This way, you can reduce I/O and eliminate index page splitting because the index is not updated.

Another option is to partition the table so that inserts are grouped into separate partitions. This method does not reduce I/O, but it can limit page splitting because the index updates are spread across multiple index data sets instead of confined to just one.

Increase Concurrent Online Access   Limit deadlock and timeout situations by coding applications to increase their concurrency. One option is to code all transactions to access tables in the same order. For example, do not sequentially access departments in alphabetical order by DEPTNAME in one transaction, from highest to lowest DEPTNO in another, and from lowest to highest DEPTNO in yet another. Try to limit the sequential access to a table to a single method.

Another option is to update and delete using the WHERE CURRENT OF cursor option instead of using independent UPDATE and DELETE statements. A third option for increasing online throughput is to plan batch activity in online tables during inactive or off-peak periods.

Consider Saving Modifications Until the End of the UOW   You can write an application program so that all modifications occur at the end of each unit of work instead of spreading them throughout the program. Because modifications do not actually occur until the end of the unit of work, the placement of the actual SQL modification statements is of no consequence to the eventual results of the program. If you place inserts, updates, and deletes at the end of the unit of work, the duration of locks held decreases. This technique can have a significant positive impact on concurrency and application performance.

Use OPTIMIZE FOR 1 ROW to Disable List Prefetch   Turning off list prefetch for online applications that display data on a page-by-page basis is often desirable. When you use list prefetch, DB2 acquires a list of RIDs from matching index entries, sorts the RIDs, and then accesses data pages using the RID list. The overhead associated with list prefetch usually causes performance degradation in an online, paging environment. OPTIMIZE FOR 1 ROW disables list prefetch and enhances performance.

Implement a Repositioning Cursor for Online Browsing   Use repositioning techniques, similar to those discussed for repositioning batch cursors, to permit online browsing and scrolling of retrieved rows by a primary key. Implement this cursor to reposition using a single column key:

```
EXEC SQL
    DECLARE SCROLL0 FOR
        SELECT   PROJNO, PROJNAME, MAJPROJ
        FROM     PROJ
        WHERE    PROJNO > :LAST-PROJNO
        ORDER BY PROJNO
END-EXEC.
```

You have two options for repositioning cursors when browsing data online. Both are efficient if indexes appear on columns in the predicates. Test both in your critical online applications to determine which performs better.

The first uses predicates tied together with AND:

```
EXEC SQL
    DECLARE SCROLL1 FOR
        SELECT   PROJNO, ACTNO, ACSTDATE,
                 ACSTAFF, ACENDATE
        FROM     PROJACT
        WHERE    (PROJNO = :LAST-PROJNO
        AND       ACTNO = :LAST-ACTNO
        AND       ACSTDATE > :LAST-ACSTDATE)
        OR       (PROJNO = :LAST-PROJNO
        AND       ACTNO > :LAST-ACTNO)
        OR       (PROJNO > :LAST-PROJNO)
        ORDER BY PROJNO, ACTNO, ACSTDATE
END-EXEC.
```

The second uses predicates tied together with OR:

```
EXEC SQL
    DECLARE SCROLL2 FOR
        SELECT   PROJNO, ACTNO, ACSTDATE,
                 ACSTAFF, ACENDATE
        FROM     PROJACT
        WHERE    (PROJNO >= :LAST-PROJNO)
        AND NOT  (PROJNO = :LAST-PROJNO AND ACTNO < :LAST-ACTNO)
        AND NOT  (PROJNO = :LAST-PROJNO AND ACTNO = :LAST-ACTNO
        AND       ACSTDATE <= :LAST-ACSTDATE)
        ORDER BY PROJNO, ACTNO, ACSTDATE
END-EXEC.
```

The rows being browsed must have a primary key or unique index that can be used to control the scrolling and repositioning of the cursors. Otherwise, rows might be eliminated because the cursors cannot identify the last row accessed and displayed. If all occurrences of a set of columns are not displayed on a single screen, and more than one row has the same values, rows are lost when the cursor is repositioned after the last value (a duplicate) on the previous screen.

General SQL Coding Guidelines

This final section on SQL guidelines contains advice for creating understandable and easily maintained SQL. When developing an application, you might be tempted to "let it be if it works." This advice is not good. You should strive for well-documented, structured code. The following miscellaneous guidelines will help you achieve that goal with your SQL statements.

Code SQL Statements in Block Style   You should code all SQL in block style. This standard should apply to all SQL code, whether embedded in a COBOL program, coded as a QMF query, or implemented using another tool. Use the following examples as standard templates for the SELECT, INSERT, UPDATE, and DELETE statements.

The following is the SELECT statement:

```
EXEC SQL
    SELECT   EMPNO, FIRSTNME, MIDINIT, LASTNAME
             WORKDEPT, PHONENO, EDLEVEL
    FROM     EMP
    WHERE    BONUS = 0
    OR       SALARY < 10000
    OR       (BONUS < 500
    AND       SALARY > 20000)
    OR       EMPNO IN ('000340', '000300', '000010')
    ORDER BY EMPNO, LASTNAME
END-EXEC.
```

The following is the INSERT statement:

```
EXEC SQL
    INSERT
    INTO DEPT
        (DEPTNO,
         DEPTNAME,
         MGRNO,
         ADMRDEPT
        )
    VALUES
        (:HOSTVAR-DEPTNO,
         :HOSTVAR-DEPTNAME,
         :HOSTVAR-MGRNO:NULLVAR-MGRNO,
         :HOSTVAR-ADMRDEPT
        )
END-EXEC.
```

The following is the DELETE statement:

```
EXEC SQL
    DELETE
    FROM    DEPT
    WHERE   DEPTNO = 'E21'
END-EXEC.
```

The following is the UPDATE statement:

```
EXEC SQL
    UPDATE EMP
    SET    JOB = 'MANAGER',
           EDLEVEL = :HOSTVAR-EDLEVEL,
           COMM = NULL,
           SALARY = :HOSTVAR-SALARY:NULLVAR-SALARY,
           BONUS = 1000
    WHERE  EMPNO = '000220'
END-EXEC.
```

These examples demonstrate the following rules:

- Code keywords such as SELECT, WHERE, FROM, and ORDER BY so that they are easily recognizable and begin at the far left of a new line.

- For SQL embedded in a host program, code the EXEC SQL and END-EXEC clauses on separate lines.

- Use parentheses where appropriate to clarify the intent of the SQL statement.

- Use indentation to show the levels in the WHERE clause.

These examples are embedded SQL syntax, because this shows more detail for coding in the block style. You can easily convert these examples to interactive SQL by removing the EXEC SQL, END_EXEC, and host variable references.

Comment All SQL Liberally   Comment ad hoc SQL statements using SQL comment syntax. Comment all embedded SQL statements using the syntax of the host language. Code all comments above the SQL statement. Specify the reason for the SQL and the predicted results.

V7 **Consider Using SQL Assist**   DB2 V7 introduced SQL Assist, a new feature that can aid application developers in coding SQL statements. Consider using SQL Assist to ensure that your SQL statements are syntactically correct. SQL Assist does not provide SQL performance advice, but it is useful for promoting a standard SQL format within your organization—such as just discussed in the previous guideline.

CHAPTER **12**

Dynamic SQL Programming

In Chapter 11, "Using DB2 in an Application Program," you learned about embedding static SQL into application programs to access DB2 tables. As you may recall from Chapter 1, "The Magic Words," though, you can embed another type of SQL in an application program: dynamic SQL.

Static SQL is hard-coded, and only the values of host variables in predicates can change. Dynamic SQL is characterized by its capability to change columns, tables, and predicates during a program's execution. This flexibility requires different techniques for embedding dynamic SQL in application programs.

Before you delve into the details of these techniques, you should know up front that the flexibility of dynamic SQL does not come without a price. In general, dynamic SQL is less efficient than static SQL. Read on to find out why.

Dynamic SQL Performance

The performance of dynamic SQL is one of the most widely debated DB2 issues. Some shops avoid it, and many of the ones that allow it place strict controls on its use. Completely avoiding dynamic SQL is unwise, but placing controls on its use is prudent. As new and faster versions of DB2 are released, many of the restrictions on dynamic SQL use will be eliminated.

You can find some good reasons for prohibiting dynamic SQL. You should avoid dynamic SQL when the dynamic SQL statements are just a series of static SQL statements in disguise. Consider an application that needs two or three predicates for one SELECT statement that is otherwise unchanged. Coding three static SELECT statements is more efficient than coding one dynamic SELECT with a changeable predicate. The static SQL takes more time to code but less time to execute.

Another reason for avoiding dynamic SQL is that it almost always requires more overhead to process than equivalent static SQL. Dynamic SQL incurs overhead because the cost of the dynamic bind, or PREPARE, must be added to the processing time of all dynamic SQL programs. However, this overhead is not quite as costly as many people think it is. To determine the cost of a dynamic bind, consider running some queries using SPUFI with the DB2 Performance trace turned on. Then examine the performance reports or performance monitor output to determine the elapsed and TCB time required to perform the PREPARE. The results should show elapsed times less than 1 second and subsecond TCB times. The actual time required to perform the dynamic prepare will vary with the complexity of the SQL statement. In general, the more complex the statement, the longer DB2 will take to optimize it. So be sure to test SQL statements of varying complexity.

Of course, the times you get will vary based on your environment, the type of dynamic SQL you use, and the complexity of the statement being prepared. Complex SQL statements with many joins, table expressions, unions, and subqueries take longer to PREPARE than simple queries. However, factors such as the number of columns returned or the size of the table being accessed have little or no effect on the performance of the dynamic bind.

Performance is not the only factor when deciding whether or not to use dynamic SQL. For example, if a dynamic SQL statement runs a little longer than a static SQL statement but saves days of programming cost, then perhaps dynamic SQL is the better choice. It all depends on what is more important—the cost of development and maintenance or squeezing out every last bit of performance.

Overhead issues notwithstanding, there are valid performance reasons for favoring dynamic SQL, too. For example, dynamic SQL can enable better use of indexes, choosing different indexes for different SQL formulations. Properly coded, dynamic SQL can use the column distribution statistics stored in the DB2 catalog, whereas static SQL is limited in how it can use these statistics. Use of the distribution statistics can cause DB2 to choose different access paths for the same query when different values are supplied to its predicates.

The REOPT(VARS) bind parameter can be used to allow static SQL to make better use of non-uniform distribution statistics. When dynamic reoptimization is activated, a dynamic bind similar to what is performed for dynamic SQL is performed. For more information on reoptimization of static SQL, refer to Chapter 13, "Program Preparation."

Additionally, consider that the KEEPDYNAMIC bind option can enhance the performance of dynamic SQL. When a plan or package is bound specifying KEEPDYNAMIC(YES), the prepared statement is maintained across COMMIT points. Contrast that with KEEPDYNAMIC(NO), where only cursors using the WITH HOLD option keep the prepared statement after a COMMIT.

Dynamic SQL usually provides the most efficient development techniques for applications with changeable requirements (for example, numerous screen-driven queries). In addition, dynamic SQL generally reduces the number of SQL statements coded in your application program, thereby reducing the size of the plan and increasing the efficient use of system memory. If you have a compelling reason to use dynamic SQL, ensure that the reason is sound and complies with the considerations listed in the following section.

Dynamic SQL Guidelines

The following tips, tricks, and guidelines should be followed to ensure that dynamic SQL is used in an optimal manner in your shop.

Favor Static SQL   Static SQL might be more efficient than dynamic SQL because dynamic SQL requires the execution of the PREPARE statement during program execution. Static SQL is prepared (bound) before execution.

Static SQL should be sufficient for the programming needs of as much as 90% of the applications you develop. If static SQL does not provide enough flexibility for the design of changeable SQL statements, consider using dynamic SQL. But keep in mind that in many cases the perceived need for dynamic SQL is merely the need for a series of static SQL statements in disguise.

> **NOTE**
>
> Many newer applications use dynamic SQL. ODBC and JDBC require dynamic SQL. Most third-party applications, such as Peoplesoft and SAP R/3, use dynamic SQL. Usage of dynamic SQL is increasing and the days of being able to ignore dynamic SQL are long gone.

Use the Appropriate Class of Dynamic SQL   After you decide to use dynamic SQL rather than static SQL, be sure to code the correct class of dynamic SQL. Do not favor one class of dynamic SQL over another based solely on the difficulty of coding. Consider both the efficiency of the program and the difficulty of maintenance, as well as the difficulty of coding a dynamic SQL program. Performance is often the most important criterion. If a dynamic SQL program does not perform adequately, you should convert it to either static SQL or another class of dynamic SQL.

Favor non-select dynamic SQL over EXECUTE IMMEDIATE because the former gives the programmer additional flexibility in preparing SQL statements, which usually results in a more efficient program. Also, favor varying-list dynamic SQL over fixed-list dynamic SQL because the first gives the programmer greater control over which columns are accessed. Additionally, varying-list dynamic SQL gives the DB2 optimizer the greatest amount of freedom in selecting an efficient access path (for example, a greater opportunity for index-only access).

When you use varying-list dynamic SQL, overhead is incurred as the program determines the type of SQL statement and uses the SQLDA to identify the columns and their data types. Weigh the cost of this overhead against the opportunities for a better access path when you decide between fixed-list and varying-list dynamic SQL.

Do Not Fear Dynamic SQL   Dynamic SQL provides the DB2 programmer with a rich and useful set of features. The belief that dynamic SQL always should be avoided in favor of static SQL is slowly but surely evaporating. Dynamic SQL becomes more efficient with each successive release of DB2, thereby enticing users who have been frustrated in their attempts to mold dynamic SQL into the sometimes-rigid confines of static SQL.

If you design dynamic SQL programs with care and do not abuse SQL's inherent functionality, you can achieve great results. Follow all the guidelines in this chapter closely. See Part V, "DB2 Performance Tuning," for a discussion of tuning and resource governing for dynamic SQL applications.

By this guideline, I do not mean to imply that you should use dynamic SQL where it is not merited. Simply apply common sense when deciding between static and dynamic SQL for your DB2 applications. Remember, any rule with a "never" in it (such as "*never* use dynamic SQL") is *usually* unwise!

Avoid Dynamic SQL for Specific Statements   Not every SQL statement can be executed as dynamic SQL. Most of these types of SQL statements provide for the execution of dynamic SQL or row-at-a-time processing. The following SQL statements cannot be executed dynamically:

```
BEGIN DECLARE SECTION

CLOSE

CONNECT

DECLARE

DESCRIBE

END DECLARE SECTION

EXECUTE

EXECUTE IMMEDIATE

FETCH

INCLUDE

OPEN

PREPARE

RELEASE connection

SIGNAL SQLSTATE

VALUES

VALUES INTO

WHENEVER
```

> **CAUTION**
>
> Be aware of the following additional restrictions on dynamic SQL:
>
> - Although the CALL statement can be dynamically prepared, it cannot be issued dynamically.

- You can DECLARE a global temporary table using dynamic SQL, but you cannot DECLARE a cursor, a table, or a statement.
- Usage of the SET statement is limited. You can use SET to set CURRENT DEGREE, CURRENT LC_TYPE, CURRENT OPTIMIZATION HINT, CURRENT PRECISION, CURRENT RULES, CURRENT SQLID, PATH, or a host variable to CURRENT APPLICATION ENCODING SCHEME. You **cannot** use SET to set CURRENT APPLICATION ENCODING SCHEME, CONNECTION, CURRENT PACKAGE PATH, CURRENT PACKAGESET, or a host variable to anything other than CURRENT APPLICATION ENCODING SCHEME.

Use Parameter Markers Instead of Host Variables   Dynamic SQL statements cannot contain host variables. They must use instead a device called a *parameter marker*. A parameter marker can be thought of as a dynamic host variable.

Use parameter markers instead of simply changing the dynamic SQL to code a new, specific literal in the predicate each time. Doing so allows DB2 to make use of the dynamic statement cache and avoid rebinding the mini-plan for the statement. To take advantage of the dynamic SQL cache the dynamic SQL statement must be exactly the same for each execution, and changing a literal changes the statement invalidating the mini-plan for use. For example, favor this dynamic statement:

```
SELECT  LASTNAME
FROM    DSN8810.EMP
WHERE   EMPNO = ?;
```

over this one:

```
SELECT  LASTNAME
FROM    DSN8810.EMP
WHERE   EMPNO = '000010';
```

In the first case you can supply multiple different values for the parameter marker. In the second case, each time the EMPNO value changes you will have to change the SQL statement (and thereby forgo use of the dynamic statement cache).

Consider Dynamic SQL When Accessing Non-Uniform Data   If you're accessing a table in which the data is not evenly distributed, dynamic SQL may perform better than static SQL. Distribution statistics are stored in the DB2 Catalog in two tables: SYSIBM.SYSCOLDISTSTAT and SYSIBM.SYSCOLDIST.

By default, RUNSTATS stores the 10 values that appear most frequently in the first column of an index along with the percentage that each value occurs in the column. As of DB2 V5, the RUNSTATS utility provides options for which distribution statistics can be collected for any number of values (and for any number of columns).

In some cases, the optimizer uses this information only for dynamic SQL. Static SQL still assumes even distribution unless the pertinent predicates use hard-coded values instead of host variables or dynamic reoptimization was specified at bind time using the REOPT(VARS) parameter.

Use Bind-Time Authorization Checking   Prior to DB2 V4, users of dynamic SQL programs required explicit authorization to the underlying tables accessed by the program being executed. For complex programs, the task of granting authority multiple types (INSERT, UPDATE, DELETE, INSERT) of security for multiple tables to multiple users is time consuming, error prone, and difficult to administer.

The DYNAMICRULES parameter of the BIND command provides flexibility of authorization checking for dynamic SQL programs. Specifying DYNAMICRULES(BIND) causes DB2 to check for authorization at BIND time using the authority of the binding agent. Just like static SQL programs, no additional runtime authorization checking is required.

Specifying DYNAMICRULES(RUN) causes dynamic SQL programs to check for authorization at runtime (just like pre-V4 dynamic programs).

Consider Caching Prepared Statements   Prepared dynamic SQL statements can be cached in memory so that they can be reused. This feature enables programs to avoid redundant optimization and its associated overhead. Dynamic SQL caching must be enabled by the system administrator, and is either on or off at the DB2 subsystem level.

When dynamic SQL caching is enabled, dynamic SELECT, INSERT, UPDATE, and DELETE statements are eligible to be cached. The first PREPARE statement creates the dynamic plan and stores it in the EDM pool. If a PREPARE is requested for the same SQL statement, DB2 can reuse the cached statement. DB2 performs a character-by-character comparison of the SQL statement, rejecting reuse if any differences are found between what is cached and what is being requested for execution. A good rule of thumb is to assume that the second execution of a dynamic SQL statement costs approximately .01 more than the same static SQL statement. For example, if the static SQL executes in 1 second, the second execution of an equivalent, already optimized dynamic SQL statement should take about 1.01 seconds.

To ensure that dynamic statements are cached, the following two conditions must be met:

- Dynamic SQL cache is turned on by the system administrator. Dynamic SQL caching is not the default; it must be explicitly specified to be turned on.

- Do not use the NOREOPT(VARS) BIND option for the plan or package. The purpose of caching is to avoid having to reoptimize, so NOREOPT(VARS) is the compatible option for dynamic SQL caching.

Cached statements can be shared among threads, plans, and packages. However, cached statements cannot be shared across data sharing groups because each member has its own EDM pool.

> **NOTE**
>
> To share a cached dynamic SQL statement, the following must be the same for both executions of the statement:
>
> - BIND authority
> - DYNAMICRULES value
> - CURRENTDATA value
> - ISOLATION level

- `SQLRULES` value
- `QUALIFIER` value
- `CURRENT DEGREE` special register
- `CURRENT RULES` special register

In general, for systems with heavy dynamic SQL use, especially where dynamic SQL programs issue the same statement multiple times, dynamic SQL caching can improve performance by reducing the overhead of multiple PREPAREs. However, dynamic SQL caching requires additional memory to increase the size of the EDM pool and can cause performance degradation for dynamic SQL that does not meet the preceding requirements because of the following:

- A cost is associated with caching an SQL statement. (DB2 must spend time moving the dynamic plan to the EDM pool.)

- If the SQL statements do not match, a cost is associated with the comparison that DB2 performs.

- EDM pool contention can occur when caching is enabled for environments in which dynamic SQL is used heavily.

The bottom line is that each shop must determine whether dynamic SQL caching will be beneficial given its current and planned mix of static and dynamic SQL. At any rate, the DBA group must communicate whether dynamic SQL caching is enabled to assist application developers in their decisions to use dynamic or static SQL.

> **CAUTION**
>
> Caching dynamically prepared statements can have a dramatic impact on your EDM pool usage. Be sure to plan accordingly and ensure that you have sized your EDM pool appropriately to accommodate the additional usage for dynamic statement caching. Even better, set up your dynamic statement cache in a data space to avoid thrashing in the EDM pool.

Reduce Prepares with `KEEPDYNAMIC(YES)`   Use the `KEEPDYANMIC(YES)` BIND option to save dynamic plans across COMMIT points. With `KEEPDYNAMIC(NO)`, dynamic SQL statements must be re-prepared after a COMMIT is issued. By specifying `KEEPDYNAMIC(YES)`, dynamic SQL programming is easier and more resulting programs can be efficient because fewer PREPAREs are required to be issued.

Encourage Parallelism   Use the `SET CURRENT DEGREE = "ANY"` statement within dynamic SQL programs to encourage the use of query I/O, CPU, and Sysplex parallelism. When DB2 uses multiple, parallel engines to access data, the result can be enhanced performance.

Before you blindly place this statement in all dynamic SQL programs, however, be sure to analyze your environment to ensure that adequate resources are available to support parallelism. For example, ensure that adequate buffer space is available for multiple concurrent read engines.

Use Dynamic SQL to Access Dynamic Data   Dynamic SQL can prove beneficial for access to very active tables that fluctuate between many rows and few rows between plan rebinding. If you cannot increase the frequency of plan rebinding, you can use dynamic SQL to optimize queries based on current RUNSTATS.

Consider the QMFCI   QMF customers have another reason to use dynamic SQL—to take advantage of the capabilities of the QMF Command Interface (QMFCI). Dynamic SQL is invoked when you use QMF to access DB2 data. The functionality provided by the QMFCI includes left and right scrolling and data formatting. The addition of these capabilities can offset any performance degradation that dynamic SQL might cause.

Be Wary of Poorly Designed Dynamic SQL   Online transaction-based systems require well-designed SQL to execute with subsecond response time. If you use dynamic SQL, the system is less likely to have well-designed SQL. If a program can change the SQL "on the fly," the control required for online systems is relinquished and performance can suffer.

Do Not Avoid Varying-List SELECT   Often, application developers do not take the time to design a dynamic SQL application properly if it requires variable SELECTs. Usually, a varying-list SELECT is needed for proper performance, but a fixed-list SELECT is used to avoid using the SQLDA and pointer variables. This use limits the access path possibilities available to the optimizer and can degrade performance.

Be Aware of Dynamic SQL Tuning Difficulties   Dynamic SQL is more difficult to tune because it changes with each program execution. Dynamic SQL cannot be traced using the DB2 Catalog tables (SYSDBRM, SYSSTMT, SYSPLANREF, and SYSPLAN) because the SQL statements are not hard-coded into the program and therefore are not in the application plan.

If your shop is using dynamic SQL, you should consider purchasing a SQL performance monitor that can track and analyze dynamic SQL—for example, Apptune from BMC Software or Detector from Computer Associates.

Use DB2's Performance Governing Facilities   DB2 provides two types of resource governing: reactive and predictive. Both types of governing can be used to control the amount of resources consumed by dynamic SQL.

Proper administration of the Resource Limit Facility (RLF) is needed to control DB2 resources when dynamic SQL is executed. Thresholds for CPU use are coded in the RLF on an application-by-application basis.

When the RLF threshold is reached, the application program does not ABEND with reactive governing. An SQL error code is issued when any statement exceeds the predetermined CPU usage. This environment requires additional support from a DBA standpoint for RLF administration and maintenance, as well as additional work from an application development standpoint for enhancing error-handling procedures.

With predictive governing, you can code the RLF to stop a statement from even starting to execute. This is not possible with reactive governing where the statement must execute until the threshold is reached, at which point the RLF stops the query. By stopping a resource-hogging query before it begins to execute, you can avoid wasting precious resources on a statement that will never finish anyway.

For details on using the RLF to set up reactive and predictive governing, refer to Chapter 29, "DB2 Resource Governing."

Use Dynamic SQL for Tailoring Access   If you need to tailor access to DB2 tables based on user input from a screen or pick list, using dynamic SQL is the most efficient way to build your system. If you use static SQL, all possible rows must be returned, and the program must skip those not requested. This method incurs additional I/O and usually is less efficient than the corresponding dynamic SQL programs.

Consider the following: What if, for a certain query, 20 predicates are possible. The user of the program is permitted to choose up to 6 of these predicates for any given request. How many different static SQL statements do you need to code to satisfy these specifications?

First, determine the number of different ways that you can choose 6 predicates out of 20. To do so, you need to use combinatorial coefficients. So, if n is the number of different ways, then

```
n = (20 x 19 x 18 x 17 x 16 x 15) / (6 x 5 x 4 x 3 x 2 x 1)
n = (27,907,200) / (720)
n = 38,760
```

You get 38,760 separate static SELECTs, which is quite a large number, but it is still not sufficient to satisfy the request! The total number of different ways to choose 6 predicates out of 20 is 38,760 if the ordering of the predicates does not matter (which, for all intents and purposes, it does not). However, because the specifications clearly state that the user can choose *up to* six, you have to modify the number. You therefore have to add in the following:

- The number of different ways of choosing 5 predicates out of 20

- The number of different ways of choosing 4 predicates out of 20

- The number of different ways of choosing 3 predicates out of 20

- The number of different ways of choosing 2 predicates out of 20

- The number of different ways of choosing 1 predicate out of 20

You can calculate this number as follows:

Ways to Choose 6 Predicates Out of 20

```
(20 x 19 x 18 x 17 x 16 x 15) / (6 x 5 x 4 x 3 x 2 x 1) = 38,760
```

Ways to Choose 5 Predicates Out of 20

```
(20 x 19 x 18 x 17 x 16) / (5 x 4 x 3 x 2 x 1) = 15,504
```

Ways to Choose 4 Predicates Out of 20

```
(20 x 19 x 18 x 17) / (4 x 3 x 2 x 1) = 4,845
```

Ways to Choose 3 Predicates Out of 20

```
(20 x 19 x 18) / (3 x 2 x 1) = 1,140
```

Ways to Choose 2 Predicates Out of 20

```
(20 x 19) / (2 x 1) = 190
```

Ways to Choose 1 Predicate Out of 20

```
20 / 1 = 20
```

Total Ways to Choose Up To 6 Predicates Out of 20

```
38,760 + 15,504 + 4,845 + 1,140 + 190 + 20 = 60,459
```

The grand total number of static SQL statements that must be coded actually comes to 60,459. In such a situation, in which over 60,000 SQL statements must be coded if static SQL must be used, you have one of two options:

- You can code for 40 days and 40 nights hoping to write 60,459 SQL statements successfully.

- You can compromise on the design and limit the users' flexibility.

Of course, the appropriate solution is to abandon static SQL and use dynamic SQL in this situation.

Use Dynamic SQL for Flexibility   Dynamic SQL programs sometimes respond more rapidly to business rules that change frequently. Because dynamic SQL is formulated as the program runs, the flexibility is greater than with static SQL programs. Users can react more quickly to changing business conditions by changing their selection criteria.

Using Dynamic SQL or Static SQL with Reoptimization   Both dynamic SQL and static SQL using the REOPT(VARS) BIND option can be used to reoptimize SQL when host variables or parameter marker values change. The ability to reoptimize enables DB2 to choose an appropriate access path for the SQL statement. When the values to be used in SQL statements vary considerably and impact the access path, be sure to enable one of the reoptimization strategies to optimize performance. But which is the better choice? It depends on the following factors:

- Dynamic SQL is more flexible but more complex.

- Dynamic SQL is implemented at the statement level. A program can contain both dynamic and static SQL statements.

- Static SQL with REOPT(VARS) is easy to specify because it is a simple BIND parameter. The program does not need to be changed.

- The REOPT(VARS) parameter is specified at the plan or package level. It cannot be specified at the statement level.

In general, favor dynamic SQL with the dynamic statement cache when the cost of the bind is high compared to the cost of running the SQL. Use static SQL with reoptimization when the cost of the bind is low compared to the cost of running the SQL.

Reexamine Database Design for Systems with High Dynamic SQL Usage   For systems with a lot of dynamic SQL, consider designing your database objects with maintenance in mind. For example, you might choose to create one table space per database (as well as one table per table space) to improve the availability window for making structural changes.

To understand why such an approach can be helpful, consider the following scenario. TABLE_A and TABLE_B are defined within the same database. Now then, suppose a column must be added to TABLE_A. You must perform such an operation when no concurrent dynamic SQL is accessing any table in the database—that is, both TABLE_A and TABLE_B. However, if the tables are assigned to separate databases, the problem is limited to just the table being changed.

Reasons You Should Know Dynamic SQL

You should understand what dynamic SQL is and what it can do for you for many reasons. As IBM improves the efficiency and functionality of dynamic SQL, more applications will use dynamic SQL. A working knowledge of dynamic SQL is necessary if you want to use DB2 fully and understand all its applications and utility programs. This section should make abundantly clear the fact that dynamic SQL is here to stay.

Dynamic SQL makes optimal use of the distribution statistics accumulated by RUNSTATS. Because the values are available when the optimizer determines the access path, it can arrive at a better solution for accessing the data. Static SQL, on the other hand, cannot use these statistics unless all predicate values are hard-coded or REOPT(VARS) is specified.

Distributed queries executed at the remote site using DB2 DUW private protocol use dynamic SQL. Some current distributed application systems are based on this requirement.

QMF, SPUFI, and many other DB2 add-on tools for table editing and querying use dynamic SQL. Also, many fourth-generation language interfaces to DB2 support only dynamic SQL. Although the users of these tools are not required to know dynamic SQL, understanding its capabilities and drawbacks can help users develop efficient data access requests. Also, the JDBC and ODBC call-level interfaces deploy dynamic SQL, not static.

Using dynamic SQL is the only way to change SQL criteria such as complete predicates, columns in the SELECT list, and table names during the execution of a program. As long as application systems require these capabilities, dynamic SQL will be needed.

Dynamic SQL is optimized at runtime, and static SQL is optimized before execution. As a result, dynamic SQL may perform slower than static SQL. Sometimes, however, the additional overhead of runtime optimization is offset by the capability of dynamic SQL to change access path criteria based on current statistics during a program's execution.

The four classes of dynamic SQL are EXECUTE IMMEDIATE, non-SELECT dynamic SQL, fixed-list SELECT, and varying-list SELECT. The following sections cover each of these classes in depth.

EXECUTE IMMEDIATE

EXECUTE IMMEDIATE implicitly prepares and executes complete SQL statements coded in host variables.

Only a subset of SQL statements is available when you use the EXECUTE IMMEDIATE class of dynamic SQL. The most important SQL statement that is missing is the SELECT statement. Therefore, EXECUTE IMMEDIATE dynamic SQL cannot retrieve data from tables.

If you don't need to issue queries, you can write the SQL portion of your program in two steps. First, move the complete text for the statement to be executed into a host variable. Second, issue the EXECUTE IMMEDIATE statement specifying the host variable as an argument. The statement is prepared and executed automatically.

Listing 12.1 shows a simple use of EXECUTE IMMEDIATE that DELETEs rows from a table. The SQL statement is moved to a string variable and then executed.

LISTING 12.1   A COBOL Program Using EXECUTE IMMEDIATE

```
WORKING-STORAGE SECTION.
        .
        .
        .
    EXEC SQL
        INCLUDE SQLCA
    END-EXEC.
        .
        .
        .
    01  STRING-VARIABLE.
        49  STRING-VAR-LEN    PIC S9(4)   USAGE COMP.
        49  STRING-VAR-TXT    PIC X(100).
        .
        .
        .
PROCEDURE DIVISION.
        .
        .
        .
    MOVE +45 TO STRING-VAR-LEN.
    MOVE "DELETE FROM DSN8810.PROJ WHERE DEPTNO = 'A00'"
        TO STRING-VARIABLE.
    EXEC SQL
        EXECUTE IMMEDIATE :STRING-VARIABLE
    END-EXEC.
        .
        .
        .
```

You can replace the DELETE statement in Listing 12.1 with any of the following supported statements:

    ALTER

    COMMENT ON

    COMMIT

    CREATE

    DELETE

    DROP

    EXPLAIN

    GRANT

    INSERT

    LABEL ON

    LOCK TABLE

    REVOKE

    ROLLBACK

    SET

    UPDATE

Despite the simplicity of the EXECUTE IMMEDIATE statement, it usually is not the best choice for application programs that issue dynamic SQL for two reasons. One, as I mentioned, EXECUTE IMMEDIATE does not support the SELECT statement. Two, performance can suffer when you use EXECUTE IMMEDIATE in a program that executes the same SQL statement many times.

After an EXECUTE IMMEDIATE is performed, the executable form of the SQL statement is destroyed. Thus, each time an EXECUTE IMMEDIATE statement is issued, it must be prepared again. This preparation is automatic and can involve a significant amount of overhead. A better choice is to code non-SELECT dynamic SQL using PREPARE and EXECUTE statements.

EXECUTE IMMEDIATE Guidelines

When developing dynamic SQL programs that use EXECUTE IMMEDIATE, observe the following guidelines.

Verify Dynamic SQL Syntax   Verify that the SQL statement to be executed with dynamic SQL uses the proper SQL syntax. This way, you can reduce the overhead incurred when improperly formatted SQL statements are rejected at execution time.

Use EXECUTE IMMEDIATE for Quick, One-Time Tasks   The EXECUTE IMMEDIATE class of dynamic SQL is useful for coding quick-and-dirty one-time processing or DBA utility-type programs. Consider using EXECUTE IMMEDIATE in the following types of programs:

- A DBA utility program that issues changeable GRANT and REVOKE statements

- A program that periodically generates DDL based on input parameters

- A parameter-driven modification program that corrects common data errors

Declare EXECUTE IMMEDIATE **Host Variables Properly**   The definition of the host variable used with EXECUTE IMMEDIATE must be in the correct format. Assembler, COBOL, and C programs must declare a varying-length string variable. FORTRAN programs must declare a fixed-list string variable. PL/I programs can declare either type of variable.

Non-SELECT **Dynamic SQL**

Non-SELECT dynamic SQL is the second of the four classes of dynamic SQL. You use it to explicitly prepare and execute SQL statements in an application program.

This class of dynamic SQL uses PREPARE and EXECUTE to issue SQL statements. As its name implies, non-SELECT dynamic SQL cannot issue the SELECT statement. Therefore, this class of dynamic SQL cannot query tables.

Listing 12.2 shows a simple use of non-SELECT dynamic SQL that DELETEs rows from a table.

LISTING 12.2   A COBOL Program Using Non-SELECT Dynamic SQL

```
WORKING-STORAGE SECTION.
     .
     .
     .
   EXEC SQL
       INCLUDE SQLCA
   END-EXEC.
     .
     .
     .
   01  STRING-VARIABLE.
       49  STRING-VAR-LEN     PIC S9(4)    USAGE COMP.
       49  STRING-VAR-TXT     PIC X(100).
     .
     .
     .
PROCEDURE DIVISION.
     .
     .
     .
   MOVE +45 TO STRING-VAR-LEN.
   MOVE "DELETE FROM DSN8810.PROJ WHERE DEPTNO = 'A00'"
       TO STRING-VARIABLE.
   EXEC SQL
       PREPARE STMT1 FROM :STRING-VARIABLE;
   END-EXEC.
```

LISTING 12.2   Continued

```
EXEC SQL
    EXECUTE STMT1;
END-EXEC.
        .
        .
        .
```

As I noted before, you can replace the DELETE statement in this listing with any of the following supported statements:

    ALTER

    COMMENT ON

    COMMIT

    CREATE

    DELETE

    DROP

    EXPLAIN

    GRANT

    INSERT

    LABEL ON

    LOCK TABLE

    REVOKE

    ROLLBACK

    SET

    UPDATE

Non-SELECT dynamic SQL can use a powerful feature of dynamic SQL called a *parameter marker*, which is a placeholder for host variables in a dynamic SQL statement. In Listing 12.3, a question mark is used as a parameter marker, replacing the 'A00' in the predicate. When the statement is executed, a value is moved to the host variable (:TVAL) and is coded as a parameter to the CURSOR with the USING clause. When this example is executed, the host variable value replaces the parameter marker.

LISTING 12.3   Non-SELECT Dynamic SQL Using Parameter Markers

```
WORKING-STORAGE SECTION.
        .
        .
        .
    EXEC SQL INCLUDE SQLCA END-EXEC.
        .
        .
        .
    01   STRING-VARIABLE.
```

LISTING 12.3   Continued

```
        49  STRING-VAR-LEN     PIC S9(4)    USAGE COMP.
        49  STRING-VAR-TXT     PIC X(100).
         .
         .
         .
PROCEDURE DIVISION.
         .
         .
         .
     MOVE +40 TO STRING-VAR-LEN.
     MOVE "DELETE FROM DSN8810.PROJ WHERE DEPTNO = ?"
         TO STRING-VARIABLE.
     EXEC SQL
         PREPARE STMT1 FROM :STRING-VARIABLE;
     END-EXEC.
     MOVE 'A00' TO TVAL.
     EXEC SQL
         EXECUTE STMT1 USING :TVAL;
     END-EXEC.
```

Non-SELECT dynamic SQL can provide huge performance benefits over EXECUTE IMMEDIATE. Consider a program that executes SQL statements based on an input file. A loop in the program reads a key value from the input file and issues a DELETE, INSERT, or UPDATE for the specified key. The EXECUTE IMMEDIATE class would incur the overhead of a PREPARE for each execution of each SQL statement inside the loop.

Using non-SELECT dynamic SQL, however, you can separate PREPARE and EXECUTE, isolating PREPARE outside the loop. The key value that provides the condition for the execution of the SQL statements can be substituted using a host variable and a parameter marker. If thousands of SQL statements must be executed, you can avoid having thousands of PREPAREs by using this technique. This method greatly reduces overhead and runtime and increases the efficient use of system resources.

Non-SELECT Dynamic SQL Guidelines

When developing non-SELECT dynamic SQL programs, heed the following guidelines.

Verify Dynamic SQL Syntax   Verify that the SQL statement to be executed with dynamic SQL uses the proper SQL syntax. This way, you can reduce the overhead incurred when improperly formatted SQL statements are rejected at execution time.

Use As Many Parameter Markers As Necessary   A prepared statement can contain more than one parameter marker. Use as many as necessary to ease development.

Execute Prepared Statements Multiple Times in a Unit of Work   After a statement is prepared, you can execute it many times in one unit of work without issuing another PREPARE. When you're using non-SELECT dynamic SQL, keep this guideline in mind and avoid the PREPARE verb as much as possible because of its significant overhead.

Know the Difference Between EXECUTE IMMEDIATE and Non-SELECT Dynamic SQL   You must understand the difference between EXECUTE IMMEDIATE and non-SELECT dynamic

SQL before development. `EXECUTE IMMEDIATE` prepares the SQL statement each time it is executed, whereas non-`SELECT` dynamic SQL is prepared only when the program explicitly requests it. Using non-`SELECT` dynamic SQL can result in dramatic decreases in program execution time. For this reason, favor non-`SELECT` dynamic SQL over `EXECUTE IMMEDIATE` when issuing an SQL statement multiple times in a program loop.

Fixed-List `SELECT`

Until now, you have been unable to retrieve rows from DB2 tables using dynamic SQL. The next two classes of dynamic SQL provide this capability. The first and simplest is fixed-list `SELECT`.

You can use a fixed-list `SELECT` statement to explicitly prepare and execute SQL `SELECT` statements when the columns to be retrieved by the application program are known and unchanging. You need to do so to create the proper working-storage declaration for host variables in your program. If you do not know in advance the columns that will be accessed, you must use a varying-list `SELECT` statement.

Listing 12.4 shows a fixed-list `SELECT` statement. This example formulates a `SELECT` statement in the application program and moves it to a host variable. Next, a cursor is declared and the `SELECT` statement is prepared. The cursor then is opened and a loop to `FETCH` rows is invoked. When the program is finished, the cursor is closed.

LISTING 12.4   Fixed-List `SELECT` Dynamic SQL

```
SQL to execute:
   SELECT  PROJNO, PROJNAME, RESPEMP
   FROM    DSN8810.PROJ
   WHERE   PROJNO   = ?
   AND     PRSTDATE = ?
   Move the "SQL to execute" to STRING-VARIABLE
   EXEC SQL DECLARE CSR2 CURSOR FOR FLSQL;
   EXEC SQL PREPARE FLSQL FROM :STRING-VARIABLE;
   EXEC SQL OPEN CSR2 USING :TVAL1, :TVAL2;
   Loop until no more rows to FETCH
   EXEC SQL
       FETCH CSR2 INTO :PROJNO, :PROJNAME, :RESPEMP;
   EXEC SQL CLOSE CSR2;
```

This example is simple because the SQL statement does not change. The benefit of dynamic SQL is its capability to modify the SQL statement. For example, you could move the SQL statement

```
   SELECT  PROJNO, PROJNAME, RESPEMP
   FROM    DSN8810.PROJ
   WHERE   RESPEMP  = ?
   AND     PRENDATE = ?
```

to the `STRING-VARIABLE` as shown in Listing 12.4 without modifying the `OPEN` or `FETCH` logic. Note that the second column of the predicate is different from the SQL statement as presented in Listing 12.4 (`PRENDATE` instead of `PRSTDATE`). Because both are the same data type (DATE), however, you can use TVAL2 for both if necessary. The host variables passed as parameters in the OPEN statement must have the same data type and length as the columns in the WHERE clause. If the data type and length of the columns in the WHERE clause change, the OPEN statement must be recoded with new USING parameters.

If parameter markers are not used in the SELECT statements, the markers could be eliminated and values could be substituted in the SQL statement to be executed. No parameters would be passed in the OPEN statement.

You can recode the OPEN statement also to pass parameters using an SQLDA (SQL Descriptor Area). The SQLDA would contain value descriptors and pointers to these values. You can recode the OPEN statement as follows:

```
EXEC-SQL
    OPEN CSR2 USING DESCRIPTOR :TVAL3;
END_EXEC.
```

DB2 uses the SQLDA to communicate information about dynamic SQL to an application program. The SQLDA sends information such as the type of SQL statement being executed and the number and data type of columns being returned by a SELECT statement. It can be used by fixed-list SELECT and varying-list SELECT dynamic SQL. The following code illustrates the fields of the SQLDA:

```
*********************************************************
***    SQLDA: SQL DESCRIPTOR AREA FOR COBOL II      ***
*********************************************************
01  SQLDA.
    05 SQLDAID              PIC X(8)   VALUE 'SQLDA'.
    05 SQLDABC         COMP PIC S9(8)  VALUE 13216.
    05 SQLN            COMP PIC S9(4)  VALUE 750.
    05 SQLD            COMP PIC S9(4)  VALUE 0.
    05 SQLVAR OCCURS 1 TO 750 TIMES DEPENDING ON SQLN.
        10 SQLTYPE       COMP PIC S9(4).
            88 SQLTYPE-BLOB              VALUE 404 405.
            88 SQLTYPE-CLOB              VALUE 408 409.
            88 SQLTYPE-DBCLOB            VALUE 412 413.
            88 SQLTYPE-FLOAT             VALUE 480 481.
            88 SQLTYPE-DECIMAL           VALUE 484 485.
            88 SQLTYPE-SMALLINT          VALUE 500 501.
            88 SQLTYPE-INTEGER           VALUE 496 497.
            88 SQLTYPE-DATE              VALUE 384 385.
            88 SQLTYPE-TIME              VALUE 388 389.
            88 SQLTYPE-TIMESTAMP         VALUE 392 393.
            88 SQLTYPE-CHAR              VALUE 452 453.
            88 SQLTYPE-VARCHAR           VALUE 448 449.
            88 SQLTYPE-LONG-VARCHAR      VALUE 456 457.
            88 SQLTYPE-VAR-ONUL-CHAR     VALUE 460 461.
            88 SQLTYPE-GRAPHIC           VALUE 468 469.
            88 SQLTYPE-VARGRAPH          VALUE 464 465.
            88 SQLTYPE-LONG-VARGRAPH     VALUE 472 473.
            88 SQLTYPE-ROWID             VALUE 904 905.
            88 SQLTYPE-BLOB-LOC          VALUE 961 962.
            88 SQLTYPE-CLOB-LOC          VALUE 964 965.
            88 SQLTYPE-DBCLOB-LOC        VALUE 968 969.
```

```
10 SQLLEN      COMP PIC S9(4).
10 SQLDATA          POINTER.
10 SQLIND           POINTER.
10 SQLNAME.
   15 SQLNAMEL COMP PIC S9(4).
   15 SQLNAMEC COMP PIC X(30).
```

A description of the contents of the SQLDA fields is in the discussion of the next class of dynamic SQL, which relies heavily on the SQLDA.

Quite a bit of flexibility is offered by fixed-list SELECT dynamic SQL. Fixed-list dynamic SQL provides many of the same benefits for the SELECT statement as non-SELECT dynamic SQL provides for other SQL verbs. An SQL SELECT statement can be prepared once and then fetched from a loop. The columns to be retrieved must be static, however. If you need the additional flexibility of changing the columns to be accessed while executing, use a varying-list SELECT.

> **CAUTION**
>
> For fixed-list SELECT dynamic SQL, you cannot code the SQLDA in a VS/COBOL program. You will need to use LE COBOL.

Fixed-List SELECT **Guidelines**

Follow the guidelines provided in this section when developing fixed-list SELECT dynamic SQL programs.

Use As Many Parameter Markers As Necessary   A prepared statement can contain more than one parameter marker. Use as many as necessary to ease development.

Issue Prepared Statements Multiple Times in a Unit of Work   After a statement is prepared, you can execute it many times in one unit of work without issuing another PREPARE.

Varying-List SELECT

Varying-list SELECT is the last class of dynamic SQL. You use it to explicitly prepare and execute SQL SELECT statements when you do not know in advance which columns will be retrieved by an application program.

Varying-list SELECT provides the most flexibility for dynamic SELECT statements. You can change tables, columns, and predicates "on-the-fly."

> **WARNING**
>
> Because everything about the query can change during one invocation of the program, the number and type of host variables needed to store the retrieved rows cannot be known before-hand. The lack of knowledge regarding what is being retrieved adds considerable complexity to your application programs. (Note that FORTRAN and VS/COBOL programs cannot perform varying-list SELECT dynamic SQL statements.)

The SQLDA, as I mentioned, is the vehicle for communicating information about dynamic SQL between DB2 and the application program. It contains information about the type of

SQL statement to be executed, the data type of each column accessed, and the address of each host variable needed to retrieve the columns. The `SQLDA` must be hard-coded into the COBOL II program's `WORKING-STORAGE` area, as shown here:

```
EXEC-SQL
    INCLUDE SQLDA
END_EXEC.
```

Table 12.1 defines each item in the `SQLDA` when it is used with varying-list `SELECT`.

TABLE 12.1   SQLDA Data Element Definitions

SQLDA **Field Name**	**Use in** DESCRIBE **or** PREPARE **Statement**
SQLDAID	Descriptive only; usually set to the literal "SQLDA" to aid in program debugging
SQLDABC	Length of the SQLDA
SQLN	Number of occurrences of SQLVAR available
SQLD	Number of occurrences of SQLVAR used
SQLTYPE	Data type and indicator of whether NULLs are allowed for the column; for UDTs, SQLTYPE is set based on the base data type
SQLLEN	External length of the column value; 0 for LOBs
SQLDATA	Address of a host variable for a specific column
SQLIND	Address of NULL indicator variable for the preceding host variable
SQLNAME	Name or label of the column

The steps needed to code varying-list `SELECT` dynamic SQL to your application program vary according to the amount of information known about the SQL beforehand. Listing 12.5 details the steps necessary when you know that the statement to be executed is a `SELECT` statement. The code differs from fixed-list `SELECT` in three ways: The `PREPARE` statement uses the `SQLDA`, the `FETCH` statement uses the `SQLDA`, and a step is added to store host variable addresses in the `SQLDA`.

LISTING 12.5   Varying-List SELECT Dynamic SQL

```
SQL to execute: SELECT PROJNO, PROJNAME, RESPEMP
                FROM DSN8810.PROJ
                WHERE PROJNO = 'A00'
                AND PRSTDATE = '1988-10-10';
Move the "SQL to execute" to STRING-VARIABLE
EXEC SQL DECLARE CSR3 CURSOR FOR VLSQL;
EXEC SQL
    PREPARE VLSQL INTO SQLDA FROM :STRING-VARIABLE;
EXEC SQL OPEN CSR3;
Load storage addresses into the SQLDA
Loop until no more rows to FETCH
    EXEC SQL FETCH CSR3 USING DESCRIPTOR SQLDA;
EXEC SQL CLOSE CSR3;
```

When `PREPARE` is executed, DB2 returns information about the columns being returned by the `SELECT` statement. This information is in the `SQLVAR` group item of the `SQLDA`. Of particular interest is the SQLTYPE field. For each column to be returned, this field indicates the data type and whether NULLs are permitted. Note that in the SQLDA layout presented previously, all possible values for SQLTYPE are coded as 88-level COBOL structures. They can be used in the logic of your application program to test for specific data types. The valid values for SQLTYPE are shown in Table 12.2.

TABLE 12.2   Valid Values for SQLTYPE

SQLTYPE **Value**		
NULL **Allowed**	NULL **Not Allowed**	**Data Type**
384	385	DATE
388	389	TIME
392	393	TIMESTAMP
400	401	null-terminated graphic string
404	405	BLOB
408	409	CLOB
412	413	DBCLOB
448	449	Small VARCHAR
452	453	Fixed CHAR
456	457	Long VARCHAR
460	461	VARCHAR optionally null-terminated
464	465	Small VARGRAPHIC
468	469	Fixed GRAPHIC
472	473	Long VARGRAPHIC
480	481	FLOAT
484	485	DECIMAL
496	497	INTEGER
500	501	SMALLINT
904	905	ROWID
961	962	BLOB locator
964	965	CLOB locator
968	969	DBCLOB locator
972	973	result set locator
976	977	table locator

The first value listed is returned when NULLs are permitted; the second is returned when NULLs are not permitted. These two codes aid in the detection of the data type for each column. The application program issuing the dynamic SQL must interrogate the SQLDA, analyzing each occurrence of SQLVAR. This information is used to determine the address of a storage area of the proper size to accommodate each column returned. The address is stored in the SQLDATA field of the SQLDA. If the column can be NULL, the address of the NULL indicator is stored in the SQLIND field of the SQLDA. When this analysis is complete, data can be fetched using varying-list SELECT and the SQLDA information.

Note that the group item, SQLVAR, occurs 750 times. This number is the limit for the number of columns that can be returned by one SQL SELECT. You can modify the column limit number by changing the value of the SQLN field to a smaller number but not to a larger one. Coding a smaller number reduces the amount of storage required. If a greater number of columns is returned by the dynamic SELECT, the SQLVAR fields are not populated.

You can also code dynamic SQL without knowing anything about the statement to be executed. An example is a program that must read SQL statements from a terminal and execute them regardless of statement type. You can create this type of program by coding two SQLDAs: one full SQLDA and one minimal SQLDA (containing only the first 16 bytes of the full SQLDA) that PREPAREs the statement and determines whether it is a SELECT. If the statement is not a SELECT, you can simply EXECUTE the non-SELECT statement. If it is a SELECT, PREPARE it a second time with a full SQLDA and follow the steps in Listing 12.6.

LISTING 12.6   Varying-List SELECT Dynamic SQL with Minimum SQLDA

```
EXEC SQL INCLUDE SQLDA
EXEC SQL INCLUDE MINSQLDA
Read "SQL to execute" from external source
Move the "SQL to execute" to STRING-VARIABLE
EXEC SQL DECLARE CSR3 CURSOR FOR VLSQL;
EXEC SQL
    PREPARE VLSQL INTO MINSQLDA FROM :STRING-VARIABLE;
IF SQLD IN MINSQLDA = 0
    EXECUTE IMMEDIATE (SQL statement was not a SELECT)
    FINISHED.
EXEC SQL
    PREPARE VLSQL INTO SQLDA FROM :STRING-VARIABLE;
EXEC SQL OPEN CSR3;
Load storage addresses into the SQLDA
Loop until no more rows to FETCH
    EXEC SQL FETCH CSR3 USING DESCRIPTOR SQLDA;
EXEC SQL CLOSE CSR3;
```

In this section, I've provided a quick introduction to varying-list SELECT dynamic SQL. If you want to code parameter markers or need further information on acquiring storage or pointer variables, consult the appropriate compiler manuals and the following DB2 manuals:

> *DB2 Application Programming and SQL Guide*
>
> *DB2 SQL Reference*

Varying-List SELECT Guidelines

The following guidelines should be adhered to when developing varying-list SELECT dynamic SQL programs.

Use Varying-List SELECT with Care   Be sure that you understand the fundamental capabilities of varying-list SELECT dynamic SQL before trying to use it. You should understand completely the SQLDA, pointer variables, and how the language you're using implements pointers before proceeding.

CHAPTER 13

Program Preparation

A DB2 application program must go through a process known as *program preparation* before it can run successfully. This chapter describes this procedure and its components. Accompanying guidelines for program preparation are provided, including the following:

- Choosing program preparation options to achieve optimum performance

- Plan and package management

- Preparing programs with minimum down time

Program Preparation Steps

Your first question might be "Just what is DB2 program preparation?" Quite simply, it is a series of code preprocessors that—when enacted in the proper sequence—create an executable load module and a DB2 application plan. The combination of the executable load module and the application plan is required before any DB2 program can be run, whether batch or online. CICS programs require an additional preprocessing step. This step is covered in Chapter 18, "The Doors to DB2."

Figure 13.1 shows DB2 program preparation graphically. This section outlines each program preparation step and its function.

Issue the DCLGEN Command

Issue the DCLGEN command for a single table. On a table-by-table basis, DCLGEN produces a module that can be included in DB2 application programs. It reads the DB2 Catalog to determine the structure of the table and builds a COBOL copybook. The copybook contains a SQL DECLARE TABLE statement along with WORKING-STORAGE host variable definitions for each column in the table.

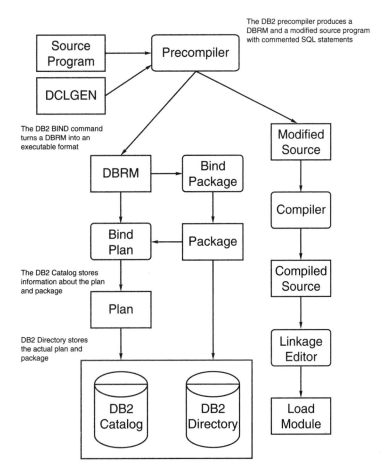

FIGURE 13.1   DB2 program preparation.

DCLGEN can be used to create table declarations for PL/I, C, and C++ programs, too.

DCLGEN is not a required step because the DECLARE TABLE statement and corresponding host variables could be hard-coded in the application program. Skipping this step, however, is not recommended. Run the DCLGEN command for every table that will be embedded in a COBOL program. Then every program that accesses that table should be required to INCLUDE the generated copybook as the only means of declaring that table for embedded use. For the DEPTTABL copybook, use the following INCLUDE statement:

```
EXEC SQL
    INCLUDE DEPTTABL
END-EXEC.
```

DB2 must be running to invoke the DCLGEN command. See "Program Preparation Using DB2I" (in this chapter) and Chapter 36, "DB2 Commands," for more information on DCLGEN. A sample DCLGEN for the DSN8810.DEPT table follows:

```
****************************************************************
* DCLGEN TABLE(DSN8810.DEPT)                                   *
*        LIBRARY(DBAPCSM.DB2.CNTL(DCLDEPT))                    *
*        ACTION(REPLACE)                                       *
*        QUOTE                                                 *
* ... IS THE DCLGEN COMMAND THAT MADE THE                     *
*     FOLLOWING STATEMENTS                                     *
****************************************************************
EXEC SQL DECLARE DSN8810.DEPT TABLE
     ( DEPTNO        CHAR(3) NOT NULL,
       DEPTNAME      VARCHAR(36) NOT NULL,
       MGRNO         CHAR(6),
       ADMRDEPT      CHAR(3) NOT NULL,
       LOCATION      CHAR(16)
     ) END-EXEC.
**************************************************************
* COBOL DECLARATION FOR TABLE DSN8810.DEPT        *
**************************************************************
01  DCLDEPT.
    10  DEPTNO              PIC X(3).
    10  DEPTNAME.
        49  DEPTNAME-LEN    PIC S9(4) USAGE COMP.
        49  DEPTNAME-TEXT   PIC X(36).
    10  MGRNO               PIC X(6).
    10  ADMRDEPT            PIC X(3).
    10  LOCATION            PIC X(16).
**************************************************************
* THE NUMBER OF COLUMNS DESCRIBED BY THIS          *
* DECLARATION IS 5                                 *
**************************************************************
```

As the example shows, the DCLGEN command produces a DECLARE TABLE statement and a COBOL field layout for DB2 host variables that can be used with the table.

> **NOTE**
>
> The DCLGEN command produces qualified table names in the DECLARE TABLE statement. You might need to edit these before embedding the DCLGEN output in an application program. Alternatively, setting the current SQLID to the table owner will generate unqualified table names.

Column Prefixing   Column prefixing, awkwardly enough, is specified using the COLSUFFIX(YES) parameter and the NAMES parameter. When these two options are specified, DCLGEN produces field names by appending the column name to the literal prefix specified by the NAMES parameter. If the previous DCLGEN is created specifying COLSUFFIX(YES) and NAMES(DPT), for example, the results would be as follows:

```
****************************************************************
* DCLGEN TABLE(DEPT)                                           *
*        LIBRARY(DBAPCSM.DB2.CNTL(DCLDEPT))                    *
*        ACTION(REPLACE)                                       *
*        QUOTE                                                 *
*        COLSUFFIX(YES) NAMES(DPT)                             *
* ... IS THE DCLGEN COMMAND THAT MADE THE                     *
*     FOLLOWING STATEMENTS                                     *
```

```
**************************************************************
EXEC SQL DECLARE DEPT TABLE
     ( DEPTNO          CHAR(3) NOT NULL,
       DEPTNAME        VARCHAR(36) NOT NULL,
       MGRNO           CHAR(6),
       ADMRDEPT        CHAR(3) NOT NULL,
       LOCATION        CHAR(16)
     ) END-EXEC.
**************************************************************
* COBOL DECLARATION FOR TABLE DEPT                          *
**************************************************************
01  DCLDEPT.
    10  DPT-DEPTNO              PIC X(3).
    10  DPT-DEPTNAME.
        49  CPT-DEPTNAME-LEN    PIC S9(4) USAGE COMP.
        49  DPT-DEPTNAME-TEXT   PIC X(36).
    10  DPT-MGRNO               PIC X(6).
    10  DPT-ADMRDEPT            PIC X(3).
    10  DPT-LOCATION            PIC X(16).
**************************************************************
* THE NUMBER OF COLUMNS DESCRIBED BY THIS                   *
* DECLARATION IS 5                                          *
**************************************************************
```

Note that each field defined in the COBOL declaration is prefixed with the value DPT, which is specified in the NAMES parameter.

Null Indicator Variables   You can use DCLGEN to create an array of null indicator variables by specifying INDVAR(YES). However, use this feature with caution as null indicator arrays are more difficult to use than individual null indicator variables (for more details, refer to Chapter 11, "Using DB2 in an Application Program").

Precompile the Program

DB2 programs must be parsed and modified before normal compilation. The DB2 precompiler performs this task. When invoked, the precompiler performs the following functions:

- Searches for and expands DB2-related INCLUDE members

- Searches for SQL statements in the body of the program's source code

- Creates a modified version of the source program in which every SQL statement in the program is commented out and a CALL to the DB2 runtime interface module, along with applicable parameters, replaces each original SQL statement

- Extracts all SQL statements from the program and places them in a database request module (DBRM)

- Places a timestamp token in the modified source and the DBRM to ensure that these two items are inextricably tied

- Reports on the success or failure of the precompile process

The precompiler searches for SQL statements embedded in EXEC SQL and END-EXEC keywords. For this reason, every SQL statement, table declaration, or host variable in an INCLUDE copybook must be in an EXEC SQL block. DB2 does not need to be operational to precompile a DB2 program.

Precompiler Services Can Reduce Compilation Steps

V7 DB2 V7 introduced a new component called *precompiler services*. A compiler that supports this feature can invoke precompiler services to produce an SQL statement coprocessor that performs the same function as the DB2 precompiler—except it is done at compile time. So, if you are using a compiler with an SQL statement coprocessor, you can eliminate the precompile step in your batch program preparation jobs for C, COBOL, and PL/I programs.

Issue the BIND Command

The BIND command is a type of compiler for SQL statements. In general, BIND reads SQL statements from DBRMs and produces a mechanism to access data as directed by the SQL statements being bound.

You can use two types of BINDs: BIND PLAN and BIND PACKAGE. BIND PLAN accepts as input one or more DBRMs produced from previous DB2 program precompilations, one or more packages produced from previous BIND PACKAGE commands, or a combination of DBRMs and package lists.

The output of the BIND PLAN command is an application plan containing executable logic representing optimized access paths to DB2 data. An application plan is executable only with a corresponding load module. Before you can run a DB2 program, regardless of environment, an application plan name must be specified.

The BIND PACKAGE command accepts as input a DBRM and produces a single package containing optimized access path logic. You then can bind packages into an application plan using the BIND PLAN command. A package is not executable and cannot be specified when a DB2 program is being run. You must bind a package into a plan before using it.

BIND performs many functions to create packages and plans that access the requested DB2 data, including the following:

- Reads the SQL statements in the DBRM and checks the syntax of those statements
- Checks that the DB2 tables and columns being accessed conform to the corresponding DB2 Catalog information
- Performs authorization validation (this task is optional)
- Optimizes the SQL statements into efficient access paths

The application packages and plans contain the access path specifications developed by the BIND command. The BIND command invokes the DB2 optimizer (discussed in depth in Chapter 21, "The Optimizer") to determine efficient access paths based on DB2 Catalog statistics (such as the availability of indexes, the organization of data, and the table size) and other pertinent information (such as number of processors, processor speed, and bufferpool specifications). The `BIND` command is performed in the Relational Data Services component of DB2.

A package can be bound for only a single DBRM. A package, therefore, is nothing more than optimized SQL from a single program. Although packages are discrete entities in the DB2 Catalog and Directory, they cannot be executed until they are bound into a plan. Plans are composed of either one or more DBRMs or one or more packages. A plan can contain both DBRMs and packages. Further discussion of plans and packages is deferred until later in this chapter.

> **NOTE**
>
> User-defined functions and triggers are an exception to the rule of packages requiring a plan to execute. The `CREATE FUNCTION` and `CREATE TRIGGER` statements also `BIND` a package, which is used by DB2 whenever the UDF or trigger is executed. No plan need be bound by the user before the UDF or trigger can be used. For more information, refer to Chapter 4, "Using DB2 User-Defined Functions and Data Types," and Chapter 8, "Using DB2 Triggers for Integrity."

The DB2 subsystem must be operational so that you can issue the `BIND` command. See "Program Preparation Using DB2I" and Chapter 36 for more information on the `BIND` command.

Compile the Program

The modified COBOL source data set produced by the DB2 precompiler must then be compiled. Use the standard LE/370 COBOL compiler (or the compiler for whichever version of COBOL you are using). DB2 does not need to be operational for you to compile your program.

If you are using a language other than COBOL, you will need to follow the same basic steps as you would for COBOL. Of course, you would use the compiler for your language of choice. For an overview of Java program preparation, consult Chapter 14.

Link the Program

The compiled source then is link-edited to an executable load module. The appropriate DB2 host language interface module also must be included by the link edit step. This interface module is based on the environment (TSO, CICS, or IMS/TM) in which the program will execute.

If you have a call attach product or use an environment other than TSO, CICS, or IMS/TM, consult your shop standards to determine the appropriate language interface routine to include with your link edited program. The output of the link edit step is an executable load module, which then can be run with a plan containing the program's DBRM or package.

The link edit procedure does not require the services of DB2; therefore, the DB2 subsystem can be inactive when your program is being link edited.

Running a DB2 Program

After a program has been prepared as outlined in Figure 13.1, two separate, physical components have been produced: a DB2 plan and a link edited load module. Neither is executable without the other. The plan contains the access path specifications for the SQL statements in the program. The load module contains the executable machine instructions for the COBOL statements in the program.

If you attempt to run a load module for a DB2 program outside the control of DB2, the program will abend when it encounters the first SQL statement. Furthermore, a load module is forever tied to a specific DBRM—the DBRM produced by the same precompile that produced the modified source used in the link-edit process that produced the load module in question.

When you run an application program containing SQL statements, you must specify the name of the plan that will be used. The plan name must include the DBRM that was produced by the precompile process in the program preparation that created the load module being run. This is enforced by a timestamp token placed into both the DBRM and the modified source by the DB2 precompiler. At execution time, DB2 checks that the tokens indicate the compatibility of the plan and the load module. If they do not match, DB2 will not allow the SQL statements in the program to be run. A -818 SQL code is returned for each SQL call attempted by the program.

DB2 programs can be executed in one of following four ways:

- Batch TSO
- Call attach
- CICS
- IMS

Listing 13.1 provides the JCL to execute the program using TSO batch. For information about other methods, see Chapter 18.

LISTING 13.1   Running a DB2 Program in TSO Batch

```
//DB2JOBB  JOB (BATCH),'DB2 BATCH',MSGCLASS=X,CLASS=X,
//         NOTIFY=USER
//*
//**************************************************************
//*
//*        JCL TO RUN A DB2 PROGRAM IN BATCH
//*        USING THE TSO TERMINAL MONITOR PROGRAM
//*
//**************************************************************
//*
//JOBLIB    DD DSN=SYS1.DB2V810.DSNEXIT,DISP=SHR
//          DD DSN=SYS1.DB2V810.DSNLOAD,DISP=SHR
//BATCHPRG  EXEC PGM=IKJEFT1B,DYNAMNBR=20
//SYSTSPRT  DD  SYSOUT=*
```

LISTING 13.1   Continued

```
//SYSPRINT   DD   SYSOUT=*
//SYSUDUMP   DD   SYSOUT=*
//SYSTSIN    DD   *
  DSN SYSTEM(DSN)
  RUN PROGRAM(Place program name here)  -
  PLAN(Place plan name here)  -
  LIB('SYS1.DB2V810.RUNLIB.LOAD')
  END
/*
//
```

Preparing a DB2 Program

You can prepare a DB2 program in many ways. Following are the most common methods:

- Using the DB2I panels

- Using a standard DB2 program preparation procedure

- Using a DB2 program preparation CLIST or REXX EXEC

- Any combination of the preceding methods

Each shop has its own standards. Consult your shop standards for the supported method or methods of DB2 program preparation. This section discusses each of the preceding methods.

Program Preparation Using DB2I

DB2I, or DB2 Interactive, is an online, TSO/ISPF based interface to DB2 commands, DB2 administrative functions, and CLISTs provided with DB2. It is a panel-driven application that enables a user to prepare a DB2 program, among other things.

You can use eight DB2I panels to assist with DB2 program preparation. The DB2I main menu, shown in Figure 13.2, appears when you select the DB2I option from the main menu.

> **NOTE**
>
> Some installations require the user to execute a preallocation CLIST before invoking DB2I. Consult your shop standards.

Before proceeding to the main task of program preparation using DB2I, you first must ensure that the DB2I defaults have been properly set. Option D from the main menu displays the DB2I Defaults panel, which is shown in Figure 13.3. The default values usually are adequate. When you first enter DB2I, however, ensure that the correct DB2 subsystem name, application language, and delimiters are set.

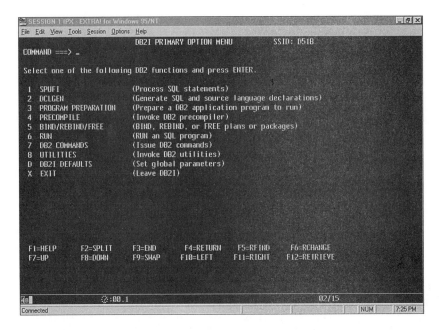

FIGURE 13.2   The DB2I main menu.

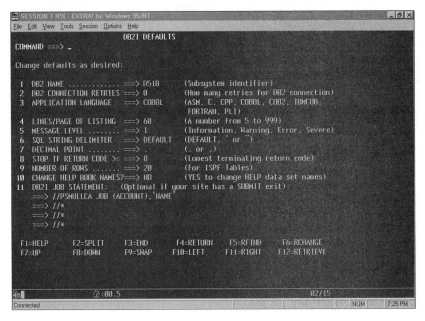

FIGURE 13.3   The DB2I Defaults panel.

After checking the DB2I Defaults panel, you need to create DCLGEN members for all tables that will be accessed in application programs. You should do this before writing any application code.

Choosing option 2 from the DB2I main menu displays the DCLGEN panel (see Figure 13.4). Specify the name of the table in option 1 and the name of the data set in which the DBRM will be placed in option 2. DB2 automatically creates the DCLGEN member, including WORKING-STORAGE fields and the DECLARE TABLE statement. DCLGEN will not allocate a new data set, so you must preallocate the data set specified in option 2 as a sequential data set with an LRECL of 80. Refer to the DCLGEN member (presented earlier in this chapter) for the DSN8810.DEPT table.

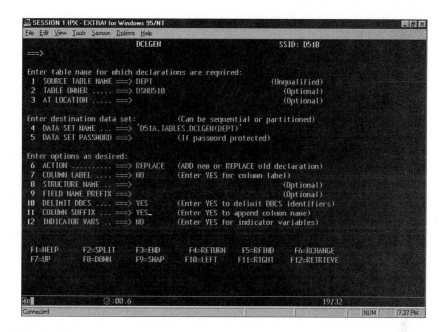

FIGURE 13.4   The DB2I DCLGEN panel.

You use option 3 of DB2I to precompile DB2 application programs. Figure 13.5 shows the Precompile panel. To precompile a program, provide the following information in the specified locations on the Precompile panel:

- The name of the input data set containing the source code for the program you want to precompile

- The name of the DCLGEN library that contains the table declarations to be used by this program

- A DSNAME qualifier to be used by DB2I to build data set names for temporary work files required by the precompiler

- The name of the DBRM library that the precompiler will write to (this must be a partitioned data set with 80-byte records)

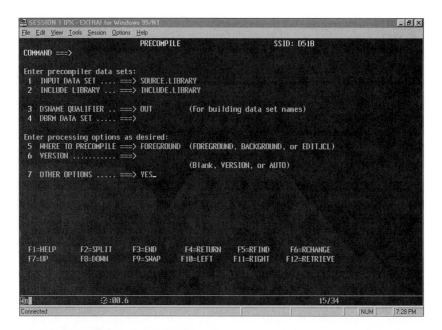

FIGURE 13.5   The DB2I Precompile panel.

> **NOTE**
>
> You can run the precompiler in the foreground or the background.

You can bind, rebind, and free DB2 plans and packages using DB2I option 5. In this section, I discuss the BIND option because it is the only one needed for program preparation. Two bind panels are available: one for binding plans, as shown in Figure 13.6, and one for binding packages, as shown in Figure 13.7. The BIND process creates plans or packages or both from one or more DBRMs. You should not attempt binding until the precompile is completed successfully.

You may have noticed that the compile and link edit steps are missing from the previous discussions of program preparation. DB2I option 3 takes you step-by-step through the entire DB2 program preparation procedure, displaying the previous panels (and an additional one). By entering the appropriate selections in the Program Preparation panel, shown in Figure 13.8, you can completely prepare and then run a source program.

After you enter the necessary information in the Program Preparation panel, you are navigated through the Precompile panel (refer to Figure 13.5); a new panel for the specification of compilation, link edit, and run parameters (see Figure 13.9), and the Bind panels (refer to Figures 13.6 and 13.7).

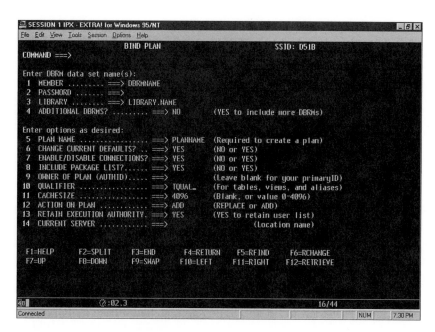

FIGURE 13.6   The DB2I Bind Plan panel.

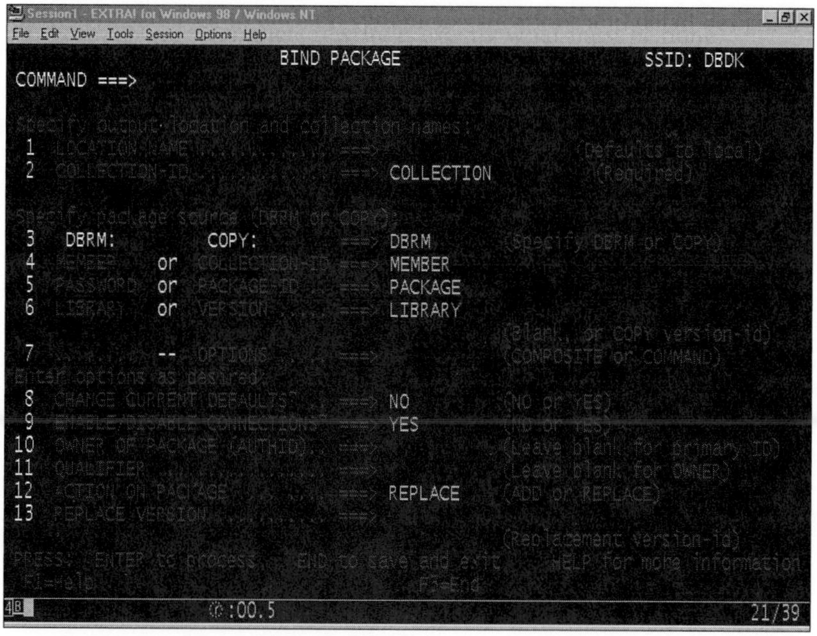

FIGURE 13.7   The DB2I Bind Package panel.

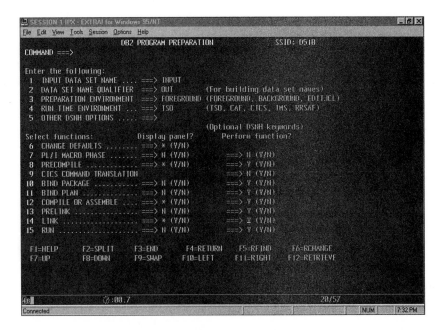

FIGURE 13.8   The DB2I Program Preparation panel.

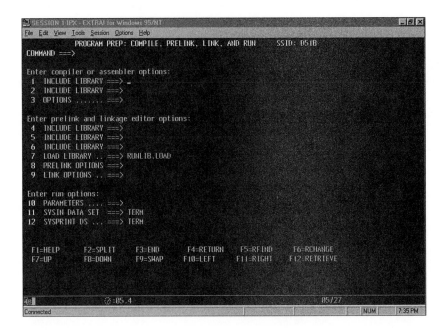

FIGURE 13.9   The DB2I Compile, Prelink, Link, and Run panels.

The panels are prefilled with the information provided in the Program Preparation panel. This probably is the easiest method of preparing a DB2 program. Following is a sample of the output generated by DB2I program preparation:

```
%DSNH  parameters
  SOURCE STATISTICS
      SOURCE LINES READ: 459
      NUMBER OF SYMBOLS: 77
      SYMBOL TABLE BYTES EXCLUDING ATTRIBUTES: 4928
THERE WERE 0 MESSAGES FOR THIS PROGRAM.
THERE WERE 0 MESSAGES SUPPRESSED BY THE FLAG OPTION.
101944 BYTES OF STORAGE WERE USED BY THE PRECOMPILER.
RETURN CODE IS 0
  DSNH740I ======= PRECOMPILER FINISHED, RC = 0 ======
          LISTING IN TEMP.PCLIST ===================
  DSNT252I - BIND OPTIONS FOR PLAN planname
        ACTION     ADD
        OWNER      authid
        VALIDATE   BIND
        ISOLATION  CS
        ACQUIRE    USE
        RELEASE    COMMIT
        EXPLAIN    YES
  DSNT253I - BIND OPTIONS FOR PLAN planname
        NODEFER    PREPARE
  DSNH740I ======= BIND FINISHED, RC = 0 ============
  DSNH740I ======= COB2 FINISHED, RC = 0 ======
          LISTING IN TEMP.LIST ===================
  DSNH740I ======= LINK FINISHED, RC = 0 ======
          LISTING IN TEMP.LINKLIST ===================
***
```

When you're using the DB2I Program Preparation option, the status of the program preparation appears onscreen. The italicized sections in the listing are replaced by the options you select when preparing your programs. Additionally, if you set any return codes to a non-zero number, you will encounter program preparation warnings or errors.

You can run DB2 programs using DB2I only if they are TSO programs. You also can simply run a DB2 program from DB2I option 6 (see Figure 13.10). Before you can run the program, however, you must first prepare it.

Program Preparation Using Batch Procedures

Some shops prefer to handle all DB2 program preparation with a batch job. The batch procedure handles all the steps required for DB2 program preparation, which results in an executable load module and plan.

Programmers often choose batch procedures to automate and standardize the specification of work data set names; compile, link, and bind parameters; and source, DBRM, and DCLGEN library names. A batch procedure invoked by common JCL with an override for the program name limits an application programmer's exposure to these miscellaneous program preparation factors. Listing 13.2 shows a common batch procedure. Note that the data set names and libraries for your shop may be different, as may the COBOL compile step.

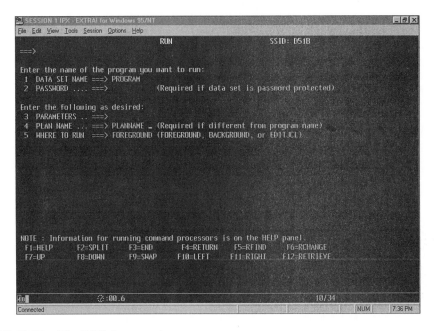

FIGURE 13.10   The DB2I Run panel.

LISTING 13.2   Sample Program Preparation Procedure

```
//COMPBAT PROC MBR='XXXXXXXX',    ** MEMBER NAME        **
//        FLEVEL='APPL.ID'        ** LIBRARY PREFIX     **
//        DB2='SYS1.DB2V810',     ** DB2 SYSTEM PREFIX  **
//        WORK='SYSDA',           ** WORK FILES UNIT    **
//        SOURCE='APPL.ID.SOURCE',** SOURCE DATASET     **
//        SYSOUT='*'
//*************************************************************
//*       DB2 PRECOMPILE STEP FOR COBOL—BATCH
//*************************************************************
//DB2PC    EXEC  PGM=DSNHPC,
//         PARM='DATE(ISO),TIME(ISO),HOST(IBMCOB),APOST'
//STEPLIB  DD DSN=&DB2..DSNEXIT,DISP=SHR
//         DD DSN=&DB2..DSNLOAD,DISP=SHR
//SYSLIB   DD DSN=&FLEVEL..INCLUDE,DISP=SHR
//         DD DSN=&FLEVEL..DCLGENLB,DISP=SHR
//SYSCIN   DD DSN=&&SRCOUT,DISP=(NEW,PASS,DELETE),
//         UNIT=&WORK,
//         DCB=BLKSIZE=800,SPACE=(800,(800,500))
//SYSIN    DD DSN=&SOURCE(&MBR),DISP=SHR
//DBRMLIB  DD DSN=&FLEVEL..DBRMLIB(&MBR),DISP=SHR
//SYSPRINT DD SYSOUT=&SYSOUT
//SYSTERM  DD SYSOUT=&SYSOUT
//SYSUT1   DD SPACE=(800,(500,500)),UNIT=&WORK
```

LISTING 13.2   Continued

```
//SYSUT2    DD SPACE=(800,(500,500)),UNIT=&WORK
//****************************************************************
//*      COBOL COMPILE
//****************************************************************
//COB       EXEC PGM=IGYCRCTL,
//           COND=(5,LT,DB2PC),
//           PARM=('NODYNAM,LIB,OBJECT,RENT,RES,APOST',
//           'DATA(24),XREF')
//STEPLIB   DD DSN=SYS1.COBLIB,DISP=SHR
//SYSPRINT DD DSN=&&SPRNT,DISP=(MOD,PASS),UNIT=SYSDA,
//           SPACE=(TRK,(175,20)),DCB=BLKSIZE=16093
//SYSTERM   DD SYSOUT=&SYSOUT
//SYSUT1    DD UNIT=&WORK,SPACE=(CYL,(5,1))
//SYSUT2    DD UNIT=&WORK,SPACE=(CYL,(5,1))
//SYSUT3    DD UNIT=&WORK,SPACE=(CYL,(5,1))
//SYSUT4    DD UNIT=&WORK,SPACE=(CYL,(5,1))
//SYSUT5    DD UNIT=&WORK,SPACE=(CYL,(5,1))
//SYSUT6    DD UNIT=&WORK,SPACE=(CYL,(5,1))
//SYSUT7    DD UNIT=&WORK,SPACE=(CYL,(5,1))
//SYSLIN    DD DSN=&&OBJECT,DISP=(NEW,PASS,DELETE),
//           UNIT=&WORK,SPACE=(TRK,(25,10),RLSE),
//           DCB=(RECFM=FB,LRECL=80,BLKSIZE=2960)
//SYSLIB    DD DSN=&FLEVEL..COPYLIB,DISP=SHR
//SYSIN     DD DSN=&&SRCOUT,DISP=(OLD,DELETE,DELETE)
//****************************************************************
//*   PRINT THE SYSPRINT DATA SET IF THE RETURN CODE IS > 4
//****************************************************************
//GEN1      EXEC PGM=IEBGENER,COND=(5,GT,COB)
//SYSPRINT DD SYSOUT=*
//SYSUT3    DD UNIT=SYSDA,SPACE=(TRK,(10)),DISP=NEW
//SYSUT4    DD UNIT=SYSDA,SPACE=(TRK,(10)),DISP=NEW
//SYSIN     DD DUMMY
//SYSUT1    DD DSN=&&SPRNT,DISP=(OLD,PASS)
//SYSUT2    DD SYSOUT=*
//****************************************************************
//*      LINK EDIT THE BATCH PROGRAM FOR DB2
//****************************************************************
//LINKIT    EXEC PGM=HEWL,
//           COND=((5,LT,DB2PC),(5,LT,COB)),
//           PARM='LIST,XREF'
//SYSLIB    DD DSN=SYS1.COBLIB,DISP=SHR
//           DD DSN=SYS1.COBCOMP,DISP=SHR
//           DD DSN=&DB2..DSNEXIT,DISP=SHR
//           DD DSN=&DB2..DSNLOAD,DISP=SHR
//           DD DSN=&FLEVEL..BATCH.LOADLIB,DISP=SHR
//DB2LOAD   DD DSN=&DB2..DSNLOAD,DISP=SHR
//SYSLIN    DD DSN=&&OBJECT,DISP=(OLD,PASS)
//           DD DSN=&FLEVEL..LINKLIB(&MBR),DISP=SHR
//SYSLMOD  DD DSN=&FLEVEL..BATCH.LOADLIB(&MBR),DISP=SHR
//SYSPRINT DD SYSOUT=&SYSOUT
//SYSUT1    DD UNIT=&WORK,SPACE=(CYL,(1,2))
//****************************************************************
```

13

LISTING 13.2   Continued

```
//*      BIND PLAN FOR THE MODULE
//**********************************************************
//BIND1    EXEC PGM=IKJEFT1B,DYNAMNBR=20,
//         COND=((5,LT,DB2PC),(5,LT,COB),(5,LT,LINKIT))
//STEPLIB  DD DSN=&DB2..DSNEXIT,DISP=SHR
//         DD DSN=&DB2..DSNLOAD,DISP=SHR
//SYSTSPRT DD SYSOUT=*
//SYSPRINT DD SYSOUT=*
//SYSUDUMP DD SYSOUT=*
//DBRMLIB  DD DSN=&FLEVEL..DBRMLIB,DISP=SHR
//SYSTSIN  DD *
  DSN SYSTEM(DSN)
  BIND  PLAN(&MEMBER.)   MEMBER(&MEMBER.) -
        ACTION(REPLACE)  RETAIN           -
        VALIDATE(BIND)   ACQUIRE(USE)     -
        RELEASE(COMMIT)  ISOLATION(CS)    -
        DEGREE(1)        EXPLAIN(YES)
  END
//
```

Program Preparation Using `CLIST` or `REXX` `EXEC`

Another common practice for some shops is to create a `CLIST` or `REXX` `EXEC` that can be invoked to prompt the user to enter program preparation options. The `CLIST` or `EXEC` reads the options as specified by the programmer and builds JCL to invoke program preparation using those parameters.

This method enables programmers to make quick changes to precompile, compile, and link edit parameters without requiring them to explicitly change parameters in JCL that they do not always fully understand. This method also can force specific options to be used, such as all binds must use `ISOLATION(CS)` or all links must use `RMODE=31`, by not allowing users to change them.

> **CAUTION**
>
> Be aware that "forcing" the use of specific `BIND` parameters can result in subpar performance. The best approach for specifying `BIND` parameters is to determine the type of program including the work to be done, its environment, the number of times it will be executed, and the performance required. Only after obtaining and analyzing all of these issues can you appropriately determine the best parameters to use.

The `CLIST` or `EXEC` can use a standard procedure, as discussed in the preceding section, and automatically submit the job.

Program Preparation Using Multiple Methods

When you develop program preparation standards, the following goals should be paramount:

- Increase the understanding and usability of program preparation procedures

- Disable dangerous and undesired program preparation parameters

- Standardize the program preparation procedure

- Enable fast turnaround for programmers using the procedures

To accomplish the preceding goals, using a combination of the techniques described in this chapter is probably best. The only DB2 program preparation steps that require DB2 to be operational, for example, are DCLGEN and BIND. DCLGEN is not a factor because it normally is invoked outside the program preparation loop. The BIND command, however, usually is embedded in the procedure, CLIST, or REXX EXEC. If this is true, as shown in Listing 13.2, you could be inhibiting your program preparation process.

If DB2 is not operational, all program preparation jobs will fail in the bind step. Additionally, if your shop is configured with multiple CPUs, a job with a bind step must be run on the CPU containing the DB2 subsystem that will perform the bind. Without the bind step, the job is free to execute in any available machine because DB2 resources are not required.

I recommend the establishment of a common procedure to run all program preparation, except the bind step. You then should code CLIST or REXX EXEC to prompt only for the parameters your shop allows to be changed. It then will build JCL using the common procedure (without the bind step). CLIST or EXEC can ask whether a bind step should be added. This way, application programmers can precompile, compile, and link edit programs when DB2 is not operational, but they have the option of binding when DB2 is operational. This can reduce the amount of downtime because a single machine running a test DB2 subsystem will not become a bottleneck due to a vast number of compiles being submitted to a single machine.

You can code a separate CLIST that enables programmers to bind after a successful execution of the precompile, compile, and link—or whenever a bind is required. It should accept only certain bind parameters as input, thereby enforcing your shop's bind standards. Ideally, the CLIST should be able to bind the program in the foreground or the background using batch JCL.

Listings 13.3 and 13.4 are sample CLISTs to accomplish DB2 program preparation. You can use these samples as templates for creating your own program preparation CLISTs that follow your organization's standards and procedures.

LISTING 13.3   Precompile, Compile, and Link CLIST

```
PROC 1 PLANNAME  JOB(BB)
/*    THIS CLIST ACCEPTS A PROGRAM NAME AS INPUT, PROMPTS
/*    FOR THE REQUIRED PROGRAM PREPARATION PARAMETERS,
/*    AND SUBMITS A BATCH JOB TO PREPARE THE PROGRAM
/*    FOR EXECUTION.
CONTROL PROMPT NOFLUSH END(DONE)
   K
   WRITE
```

LISTING 13.3   Continued

```
ASKMSG: -
    WRITE
    WRITE     ENTER OUTPUT MESSAGE CLASS:
    WRITENR    =====>
    READ &MSG
    IF &MSG NE X AND &MSG NE A THEN DO-
        WRITE
        WRITE             INVALID MESSAGE CLASS ENTERED
        GOTO ASKMSG
    DONE
ASKSORC: -
    WRITE
    WRITE     ENTER NAME OF PROGRAM SOURCE LIBRARY TO USE:
    WRITE     (PRESS ENTER TO ACCEPT DEFAULT SOURCE LIBRARY)
    WRITENR    =====>
    READ &SORC
    IF &SORC =    THEN SET &SORCLB=&STR(DEFAULT.SORCLIB)
    ELSE              SET &SORCLB=&SORC
ASKPREFX: -
    WRITE
    WRITE     ENTER THE PREFIX FOR YOUR APPLICATION LINK
    WRITE     AND DBRM LIBRARIES:
    WRITE     (PRESS ENTER TO ACCEPT DEFAULT PREFIX)
    WRITENR    =====>
    READ &PREF
    IF &PREF =    THEN SET &PREFX=&STR(DEFAULT.PREFIX)
    ELSE              SET &PREFX=&PREF
BUILDJCL: -
    K
    WRITE             BUILDING PROGRAM PREPARATION JCL, PLEASE WAIT...
EDIT COMPLINK.CNTL NEW EMODE
10 //&SYSUID.&JOB JOB(job information),'PROG PREP &PROGNAME',
11 //     MSGLEVEL=(1,1),NOTIFY=&SYSUID.,MSGCLASS=&MSG,CLASS=X
15 //JOBLIB DD DSN=SYS1.DB2V2R3.LINKLIB,DISP=SHR
20 //PROGPREP    EXEC     COMPBAT,MBR=&PROGNAME.,FLEVEL=&PREFIX.,
22 //        SOURCE=&SORCLB.
24 /*
26 //
SUBM: -
    WRITE             PROGRAM, &PROGNAME WILL BE
    WRITE                 PRECOMPILED, COMPILED, AND LINKED
    WRITE                 FROM &SORCLB
    SUBMIT
    END NO
EXIT
```

LISTING 13.4   Bind CLIST

```
PROC 1 PLANNAME  JOB(BB)
/*    THIS CLIST ACCEPTS A PLANNAME AS INPUT, PROMPTS FOR  */
/*    THE REQUIRED BIND PARAMETERS, AND SUBMITS A BATCH    */
/*    JOB TO BIND THE PLAN                                 */
```

LISTING 13.4   Continued

```
CONTROL PROMPT NOFLUSH END(DONE)
    K
    WRITE
ASKMSG:-
    WRITE
    WRITE     ENTER OUTPUT MESSAGE CLASS:
    WRITENR   =====>
    READ &MSG
    IF &MSG NE X AND &MSG NE A THEN DO-
        WRITE
        WRITE     INVALID MESSAGE CLASS ENTERED
        GOTO ASKMSG
    DONE
ASKLIB:-
    WRITE
    WRITE     ENTER NAME OF DBRM LIBRARY TO USE:
    WRITE     (PRESS ENTER TO ACCEPT DEFAULT DBRMLIB)
    WRITENR   =====>
    READ &LIB
    IF &LIB =     THEN SET &DLIB=&STR(DEFAULT.DBRMLIB)
    ELSE              SET &DLIB=&LIB
ASKEXPL:-
    WRITE
    WRITE     DO YOU WANT TO DO AN EXPLAIN OF THIS PLAN (Y/N) ?
    WRITENR   =====>
    READ &EXP
    IF &EXP NE Y AND &EXP NE N THEN DO-
        WRITE
        WRITE      INVALID RESPONSE PLEASE ENTER ONLY Y OR N
        GOTO ASKEXPL
    DONE
    IF &EXP = N THEN SET &EXPL=&STR(NO)
    ELSE              SET &EXPL=&STR(YES)
ASKDBRM:-
    K
    WRITE
    WRITE     ENTER THE NAME OF ALL DBRMS TO BE BOUND INTO THIS
    WRITE     PLAN. BE SURE TO PLACE A COMMA BETWEEN EACH DBRM &
    WRITE     INCLUDE QUOTATION MARKS IF THERE IS MORE THAN ONE
    WRITE     DBRM. ( FOR EXAMPLE:: &STR(')DBRM1,DBRM2&STR(')  )
    WRITE     OR PRESS ENTER TO DEFAULT DBRM TO &PLANNAME
    WRITENR   =====>
    READ &DLIST
    IF &DLIST =     THEN SET &DBRM=&PLANNAME
    ELSE              SET &DBRM=&LIST
BUILDJCL:-
    K
    WRITE     BUILDING BIND JCL, PLEASE WAIT...
EDIT BIND.CNTL NEW EMODE
10 //&SYSUID.&JOB JOB(job information),'BIND &PLANNAME',
11 //     MSGLEVEL=(1,1),NOTIFY=&SYSUID.,MSGCLASS=&MSG,CLASS=X
15 //JOBLIB DD DSN=SYS1.DB2V5R1.LINKLIB,DISP=SHR
20 //BIND     EXEC     PGM=IKJEFT1B,DYNAMBR=20
```

LISTING 13.4 Continued

```
22 //SYSTSPRT    DD     SYSOUT=*
24 //SYSPRINT    DD     SYSOUT=*
26 //SYSABOUT  DD      SYSOUT=*
28 //SYSTSIN     DD      *
30 DSN SYSTEM(DSN)
32    BIND PLAN (&PLANNAME)    &STR(-)
34        MEMBER (&DBRM)       &STR(-)
36        LIBRARY (&DLIB)      &STR(-)
38        ACTION (REPLACE)     &STR(-)
40        VALIDATE (BIND)      &STR(-)
42        ISOLATION (CS)       &STR(-)
44        FLAG (I)             &STR(-)
46        ACQUIRE (USE)        &STR(-)
48        RELEASE (COMMIT)     &STR(-)
50        DEGREE (1)           &STR(-)
52        EXPLAIN (&EXPL)
54 END
56 /*
58 //
SUBM:-
    WRITE           &PLANNAME WILL BE BOUND
    WRITE               USING &DBRM
    WRITE               FROM &DLIB
    SUBMIT
    END NO
EXIT
```

What Is a DBRM?

Confusion often arises about the definition of a DBRM and its relationship to programs, plans, and packages. A *DBRM* is nothing more than a module containing SQL statements extracted from a source program by the DB2 precompiler. It is stored as a member of a partitioned data set. It is not stored in the DB2 Catalog or DB2 Directory.

Although a DB2 Catalog table named SYSIBM.SYSDBRM exists, it does not contain the DBRM. It also does not contain every DBRM created by the precompiler. It consists of information about DBRMs that have been bound into application plans and packages. If a DBRM is created and never bound, it is not referenced in this table.

When a DBRM is bound into a plan, all its SQL statements are placed into the SYSIBM.SYSSTMT DB2 Catalog table. When a DBRM is bound into a package, all its SQL statements are placed into the SYSIBM.SYSPACKSTMT table.

What Is a Plan?

A *plan* is an executable module containing the access path logic produced by the DB2 optimizer. It can be composed of one or more DBRMs and packages.

Plans are created by the BIND command. When a plan is bound, DB2 reads the following DB2 Catalog tables:

SYSIBM.SYSCOLDIST	SYSIBM.SYSCOLDISTSTATS
SYSIBM.SYSCOLSTATS	SYSIBM.SYSCOLUMNS
SYSIBM.SYSINDEXES	SYSIBM.SYSINDEXSTATS
SYSIBM.SYSPLAN	SYSIBM.SYSPLANAUTH
SYSIBM.SYSTABLES	SYSIBM.SYSTABLESPACE
SYSIBM.SYSTABSTATS	SYSIBM.SYSUSERAUTH

> **NOTE**
>
> The SYSIBM.SYSUSERAUTH table (the last one in the list) is read-only for BIND ADD.

Information about the plan is then stored in the following DB2 Catalog tables:

SYSIBM.SYSDBRM	SYSIBM.SYSPACKAUTH
SYSIBM.SYSPACKLIST	SYSIBM.SYSPLAN
SYSIBM.SYSPLANAUTH	SYSIBM.SYSPLANDEP
SYSIBM.SYSPLSYSTEM	SYSIBM.SYSSTMT
SYSIBM.SYSTABAUTH	

Note that the DB2 Catalog stores only information about the plans. The executable form of the plan, called a *skeleton cursor table*, or SKCT, is stored in the DB2 Directory in the SYSIBM.SCT02 table. To learn more about the way that DB2 handles SKCTs at execution time, see Chapter 22, "The Table-Based Infrastructure of DB2."

What Is a Package?

A *package* is a single, bound DBRM with optimized access paths. By using packages, the table access logic is "packaged" at a lower level of granularity, at the package (or program) level.

To execute a package, you first must include it in the package list of a plan. Packages are not directly executed—they are only indirectly executed when the plan in which they are contained executes (as discussed previously, UDFs and triggers are exceptions to this rule). A plan can consist of one or more DBRMs, one or more packages, or a combination of packages and DBRMs.

To help differentiate between plans and packages, consider a grocery store analogy. Before going to the grocery store, you should prepare a shopping list. As you go through the aisles, when you find an item on your list, you place the item in your shopping cart. After your paying for the items at the check-out register, the clerk places your grocery items in a bag. You can think of the purchased items as DBRMs. The bag is the plan. You have multiple DBRMs (grocery items) in your plan (shopping bag).

In a package environment, rather than actually removing the items from the shelf, you would mark on your shopping list the location of each item in the store. Upon checking out, you would give the list to the clerk at the counter. The clerk then would place the list in the bag—not the actual items. The plan (bag) contains a list pointing to the physical location of the packages (grocery items) that are still on the shelf. This approach is a good way to compare and contrast the two different environments.

Package information is stored in its own DB2 Catalog tables. When a package is bound, DB2 reads the following DB2 Catalog tables:

SYSIBM.SYSCOLDIST	SYSIBM.SYSCOLDISTSTATS
SYSIBM.SYSCOLSTATS	SYSIBM.SYSCOLUMNS
SYSIBM.SYSINDEXES	SYSIBM.SYSINDEXSTATS
SYSIBM.SYSPACKAGE	SYSIBM.SYSPACKAUTH
SYSIBM.SYSTABLES	SYSIBM.SYSTABLESPACE
SYSIBM.SYSTABSTATS	SYSIBM.SYSUSERAUTH

> **NOTE**
>
> The SYSIBM.SYSUSERAUTH table (the last one in the list) is read only for BIND ADD.

Information about the package then is stored in the following DB2 Catalog tables:

SYSIBM.SYSPACKAGE	SYSIBM.SYSPACKAUTH
SYSIBM.SYSPACKDEP	SYSIBM.SYSPACKSTMT
SYSIBM.SYSPKSYSTEM	SYSIBM.SYSTABAUTH

The DB2 Catalog stores only information about the packages. The executable form of the package is stored as a skeleton package table in the DB2 Directory in the SYSIBM.SPT01 table.

A package also contains a location identifier, a collection identifier, and a package identifier. The location identifier specifies the site at which the package was bound. If your processing is local, you can forgo the specification of the location ID for packages.

The collection identifier represents a logical grouping of packages, and is covered in more detail in the next section of this chapter. The package identifier is the DBRM name bound into the package. This ties the package to the program to which it applies. A package is uniquely identified as follows when used in a statement to bind packages into a plan:

```
LOCATION.COLLECTION.PACKAGE
```

One final consideration when using packages is versioning. A package can have multiple versions, each with its own version identifier. The version identifier is carried as text in the DBRM, and is covered in more depth in the "Package Version Maintenance" section.

Package Benefits

Reduced bind time is the package benefit most often cited. When you are utilizing packages and the SQL within a program changes, only the package for that particular program needs to be rebound. If packages are not used when multiple DBRMs are bound into a plan and the SQL within one of those programs changes, the entire plan must be rebound. This wastes time because you must still rebind all the other DBRMs in that plan that did not change.

Another benefit of packages involves the granularity of bind parameters. With packages, you can specify your bind options at the program level because many of the bind parameters are now available to the BIND PACKAGE command, such as the ISOLATION level and RELEASE parameters. By specifying different parameters for specific packages and including these packages in a plan, many combinations of isolation level and release are possible. You can, for example, create a single plan that provides an isolation level of cursor stability (CS) for one of its packages and an isolation level of repeatable read (RR) for another package. This combination of strategies is not possible in a plan-only environment.

The third benefit, versioning, probably is the biggest benefit of all. Packages can be versioned, thus enabling you to have multiple versions of the same package existing at the same time in the DB2 Catalog. Simply by running the appropriate load module, DB2 chooses the correct package to execute. DB2 uses a package selection algorithm to execute the correct access path.

Packages also provide improved support for mirror tables. Because a package has a high level qualifier of collection, you can specify a collection for each of your mirror table environments. Suppose that you have an environment in which you have current and history data in separate tables. Using only plans, the following two options were available:

- You could write a program that specifically selected the appropriate high-level qualifier for each appropriate table, such as CURRENT or HISTORY, and hard-code that qualifier into your program.

- You could BIND the program's DBRM into different plans, specifying a different owner for each.

In a package environment, you can use separate collections for each of these environments. This technique is discussed in detail in the "What Is a Collection?" and "Bind Guidelines" sections later in this chapter.

Additionally, packages provide for remote data access. If you are using a DB2 remote unit of work, you can specify the location in which you want to bind the package. The DBRM will exist at the site from which you are issuing the BIND, but the package is created at the remote site indicated by the high-level qualifier of the package.

Package Administration Issues

Before deciding to implement packages, you will need to consider the potential administrative costs of packages. This section covers several areas of administrative concern surrounding package implementation.

Systematic Rebinding

A concern that might not be obvious immediately is the approach to systematic rebinding. At some shops, a production job is set up to rebind plans after executing a REORG and RUNSTATS. This setup ensures that access paths are optimal given the current state of the DB2 table spaces and indexes. In an environment in which plans consist of multiple DBRMs, you can rebind a plan in a single job step. However, after migrating to an environment in which multiple packages exist per plan (rather than multiple DBRMs) you need to rebind each package individually. Remember that access paths exist at the package level, not at the plan level, so packages must be rebound. This results in multiple job steps: one per package. The administration of this environment will be more difficult because you will need to create and maintain additional job steps.

Package Version Maintenance

Another potential administrative headache is *package version maintenance*. Every time a DBRM with a different version identifier is bound to a package, a new version is created. This can cause many unused package versions to be retained. Additionally, when packages are freed, you must specify the location, collection, package, and version of each package you want to free.

If your shop allows many versions of packages to be created, a method is required to remove versions from the DB2 Catalog when their corresponding load modules no longer exist. Your shop, for example, may institute a policy that specifies the 5 most recent package versions are maintained in a production environment. The number 5 is not important; your shop may support 2, 12, or whatever is deemed appropriate. What *is* important is the notion that the number of versions be limited. Failure to do so causes your DB2 environment to be inundated with a very large DB2 Catalog. To administer versions, consider using a third party tool to manage package versions as required.

Whenever the need arises to drop an old package from the system, you must know the version name associated with it. Consider the situation in which 100 versions exist and only 5 must be kept. To accomplish this, you must know the 95 version names you want to drop. If you created these versions using the VERSION(AUTO) option, you will need to remember versions named using a 26-byte timestamp. Without a tool to automate package maintenance, remembering automatic version names is a difficult task.

Consider using DB2 Catalog queries to generate statements you can use to remove package versions. By using the information in the DB2 Catalog and the power of SQL, you can eliminate many of the tedious tasks associated with freeing old package versions. The following SQL will generate the commands required to free all but the most recently created package version, as in the following:

```
SELECT   'FREE PACKAGE(' || COLLID || '.' ||
         NAME || '.(' || VERSION || '))'
FROM     SYSIBM.SYSPACKAGE A
WHERE    TIMESTAMP < (SELECT   MAX(TIMESTAMP)
                      FROM     SYSIBM.SYSPACKAGE B
                      WHERE    A.COLLID = B.COLLID
                      AND      A.NAME = B.NAME)
```

The result of this query is a series of FREE commands that can be submitted to DB2. Alternatively, you can modify the query to generate DROP statements that can be submitted to DB2 via SPUFI. You can add additional predicates to generate FREE commands for specific collections or packages.

Before executing the FREE commands, be sure that you really want to eliminate all package versions except for the most recent one. Additionally, inspect the generated FREE commands to ensure that they are syntactically correct. These statements may need to be modified prior to being executed. And, of course, after the package versions have been freed, you cannot use them again.

Production and Test in the Same Subsystem

There may be some easing of the overall administrative burden by moving to packages. Consider shops that support both test and production applications within the same DB2 subsystem. Although these types of shops are becoming increasingly rare, some still do exist and they may have valid reasons for the continuing coexistence of production and test with the same DB2 subsystem. In this case, converting to packages eases the administrative burden by enabling the application developer to specify production and test collections. An indicator, for example, can be embedded within the collection name specifying PROD or TEST. By binding packages into the appropriate collection, the production environment is effectively separated from the test environment.

Package Performance

Probably the biggest question that most shops have as they implement packages is "How will the packages perform in comparison to my current environment?" By following the advice in this section you will understand how to make packages perform every bit as well, if not better than, your current environment.

Usually, DB2 can retrieve the package quite easily because indexes exist on the DB2 Catalog tables that contain package information. Indexes on the LOCATION, COLLID (collection), NAME (package), and CONTOKEN columns make efficient package retrieval quite common.

Improper package list specification, however, *can* impact performance. Specifying the appropriate package list can shave critical sub-seconds from performance-critical applications. Follow these general rules of thumb when specifying your PKLIST:

- Keep the plan package list as short as possible. Do not go to excessive lengths, however, to make the list contain only one or two packages. Make the PKLIST as short as possible, given the considerations and needs of your application.

- Place the most frequently used packages first in the package list.

- Consider specifying collection.* to minimize plan binding. If you bind multiple packages into a collection, you can include all those packages in the plan simply by binding the plan with collection.*. Any package that is added to that collection at a future point in time automatically is available to the plan.

- Avoid *.* because of the runtime authorization checking associated with that.

> **NOTE**
>
> Specifying `collection.*` should perform best because only a single search is performed for everything in that collection.

What Is a Collection?

A *collection* is a user-defined name from 1 to 128 characters that the programmer must specify for every package. A collection is not an actual, *physical* database object.

V8

> **NOTE**
>
> Prior to DB2 V8, the maximum length of a collection name was 18 characters; this was increased to a maximum of 128 characters as of DB2 V8.

You can compare collections to databases. A DB2 database is not actually a *physical* object (ignoring, for the moment, the DBD). In much the same way that a database is a grouping of DB2 objects, a collection is a grouping of DB2 packages.

By specifying a different collection identifier for a package, the same DBRM can be bound into different packages. This capability permits program developers to use the same program DBRM for different packages, enabling easy access to tables that have the same structure (DDL) but different owners.

Assume, for example, that you have created copies of the DB2 sample tables and given them an authid of DSNCLONE. You now have a DSN8810.DEPT table and a DSNCLONE.DEPT table with the same physical construction (such as the same columns and keys). Likewise, assume that you have duplicated all the other sample tables. You then could write a single program, using unqualified embedded SQL, to access either the original or the cloned tables.

The trick is to use unqualified SQL. You could simply bind a program into one package with a collection identifier of ORIG and into another package with a collection identifier of CLONE. The bind for the package with the ORIG collection identifier specifies the DSN8810 qualifier, and the bind for the CLONE collection package specifies the DSNCLONE qualifier. You would store both of these in the DB2 Catalog.

But how do you access these packages? Assume that both packages were generated from a DBRM named SAMPPROG. This would give you packages named ORIG.SAMPPROG and CLONE.SAMPPROG. You can bind both these packages into a plan called SAMPPLAN, for example, as in the following:

```
BIND  PLAN (SAMPPLAN)
      PKLIST(ORIG.SAMPPROG, CLONE.SAMPPROG)
```

The program then specifies which collection to use with the SET CURRENT PACKAGESET statement. By issuing the following statement, the plan is instructed to use the package identified by the value of the host variable (in this example, either ORIG or CLONE).

```
EXEC SQL
    SET CURRENT PACKAGESET = :HOST-VAR
END-EXEC.
```

Another use of packages is to identify and relate a series of programs to a given plan. You can bind a plan and specify a wildcard for the package identifier. This effectively ties to the plan all valid packages for the specified collection. Consider the following BIND statement, for example:

```
BIND  PLAN(SAMPLE)    PKLIST(ORIG.*)
```

All valid packages in the ORIG collection are bound to the SAMPLE plan. If new packages are bound specifying the ORIG collection identifier, they are included automatically in the SAMPLE plan; no bind or rebind is necessary.

CURRENT PACKAGE PATH Special Register

V8 DB2 V8 adds the CURRENT PACKAGE PATH special register to ease distributed development, because not every environment supports package list specification using PKLIST. You can use CURRENT PACKAGE PATH to specify the collections to use for package resolution. CURRENT PACKAGE PATH differs from CURRENT PACKAGESET, because the package path contains a list of collection names, whereas the PACKAGESET is a single collection. Whichever was set last is used to determine the package that is to be invoked.

Consider setting CURRENT PACKAGE PATH for DB2 for z/OS Application Requestors connected via DRDA and requesting the execution of a package on a remote DB2 for z/OS. Doing so can reduce network traffic and improve performance.

Another useful purpose for CURRENT PACKAGE PATH is to set the list of collections in programs that run from a workstation to access DB2 for z/OS. Such programs do not have a plan, and therefore have no PKLIST. Such programs had to issue a new SET CURRENT PACKAGESET statement each time the program needed to switch to a different collection. With CURRENT PACKAGE PATH multiple collections may be specified once.

Finally, stored procedure and user-defined functions may benefit from using CURRENT PACKAGE PATH to specify multiple collections.

Collection Size

Do not concern yourself with collection size. Bind as many packages into a single collection as you want. Remember, a collection is not a physical entity. It is merely a method of referencing packages.

Quite often people confuse collections with package lists. The size of a collection is irrelevant. The size of a package list can be relevant—the smaller the better.

Package List Size

You do not need to go to extraordinary means to limit the size of the package list as the performance gain realized due to smaller package lists usually is not significant. A recently conducted test shows that the difference between accessing the first entry in a package list is only milliseconds faster than accessing the one hundredth entry in the package list. Of course, milliseconds can sometimes make a difference.

The length of the PKLIST starts to become a performance issue only when the list contains thousands of packages. A better reason to limit the size of the package list is to enhance maintainability. The fewer entries in the package list, the easier maintenance will be.

Consider using wildcarding to limit the size of the package list, thereby simplifying maintenance.

Versions

When using packages, you can keep multiple versions of a single package that refer to different versions of the corresponding application program. This way, the programmer can use a previous incarnation of a program without rebinding. Before the availability of packages, when programmers wanted to use an old version of a program, they were forced to rebind the program's plan using the correct DBRM. If the DBRM was unavailable, they had to repeat the entire program preparation process.

You can specify a version as a parameter to the DB2 precompiler identifier up to 64 characters long. If so instructed, the precompiler can automatically generate a version identifier (which will be a timestamp). The version identifier is stored, much like the consistency token, in the DBRM and the link is generated from the precompile.

Other than the specification of the version at precompilation time, versioning is automatic and requires no programmer or operator intervention. Consider the following:

- When a package is bound into a plan, all versions of that package are bound into the plan.

- When a program is executed specifying that plan, DB2 checks the version identifier of the link that is running and finds the appropriate package version in the plan.

- If that version does not exist in the plan, the program will not run.

- To use a previous version of the program, simply restore and run the load module.

Versioning is a powerful feature of DB2 packages. You must take care, however, to administer the versions properly. Whenever a package is bound from a DBRM with a new version identifier, a new version of the package is created. As old versions of a package accumulate, you must periodically clean them up using the FREE command. Monitoring this accumulation is particularly important when the version identifier defaults to a timestamp because every new bind creates a new version.

Program Preparation Objects

The program preparation process is composed of many objects. Each of these objects is described as follows:

Source	Every program starts as a series of host language statements, known as the *application source*. The source gets run through the DB2 precompiler to have its SQL statements removed and placed in a DBRM.
Modified source	The DB2 precompiler creates the modified source module by stripping the source module of all its SQL statements. The modified source is passed to the host language compiler.
Load module	The linkage editor creates a load module using the output of the host language compiler. The load module contains the executable form of the host language statements and is executable in conjunction with an application plan.
DBRM	The DBRM is created by the DB2 precompiler from the SQL statements stripped from the program source code.
Plan	A plan is created by the BIND statement. It consists of the access paths required to execute the SQL statements for all DBRMs bound into the plan (either explicitly or as packages). The plan is executable in conjunction with the corresponding program load module.
Package	A package also is created by the BIND statement. It contains the access paths for a single DBRM.
Collection	A collection is an identifier used to control the creation of multiple packages from the same DBRM. (Technically, a collection is not an object at all, but it is included in this list for completeness.)
Version	A version is a token specified to the DB2 precompiler that enables multiple versions of the same collection and package to exist.

13

Program Preparation Guidelines

Although the chapter has discussed DB2 program preparation, few guidelines have been provided for its adequate implementation and administration. This section provides standard program preparation guidelines. The sections that follow provide guidelines for each program preparation component.

Be Aware of Default Names   If DB2 program preparation options are allowed to default, the following data set names are created:

`USERID.TEMP.PCLIST`	Precompiler listing
`USERID.TEMP.COBOL`	Modified COBOL source from the precompiler
`USERID.TEMP.LIST`	COBOL compiler listing
`USERID.TEMP.LINKLIST`	Linkage editor listing

Prepare DB2 Programs in the Background   Avoid running DB2 program preparation in the foreground. Background submission prevents your terminal from being tied up during program preparation. Additionally, if an error occurs during program preparation, a background job can be printed to document the error and assist in debugging.

Use the CICS Preprocessor   When preparing online DB2 application programs for the CICS environment, an additional program preparation step is required to preprocess CICS calls. Refer to Chapter 18 for additional information on CICS program preparation.

DCLGEN **Guidelines**

Follow these guidelines when issuing DCLGEN statements at your shop.

Use the Appropriate DCLGEN **Library**   Most shops allocate DCLGEN libraries. They are commonly either a partitioned data set or in the format specified by your shop's change management tool.

Control Who Creates DCLGEN **Members**   The DBA usually is responsible for creating DCLGEN members for each table. This establishes a point of control for managing change.

Avoid Modifying DCLGEN **Members**   Avoid modifying the code produced by the DCLGEN command. When the DECLARE TABLE code or WORKING-STORAGE variables are manually changed after DCLGEN creates them, the risk of syntax errors and incompatibilities increases.

Consider Prefixing DCLGEN **Host Variables**   The DCLGEN command produces WORKING-STORAGE fields with the same names as the DB2 column names, except that underscores are converted to hyphens. It should be standard practice for shops to use DCLGEN with COLSUFFIX and NAMES to produce prefixed field names. When COLSUFFIX is not utilized, two tables having identical column names would have identical field names for each table.

Use Unqualified Table References   When you're using the DCLGEN command, set the current SQLID to the creator of the table to ensure that DCLGEN does not generate a quali-fied table name. Then, when specifying the DCLGEN options, provide an unqualified table name. This produces an unqualified DECLARE TABLE statement.

An alternative method can be used whereby a SYNONYM for every table is created for the DBA issuing the DCLGEN. The SYNONYM must be named the same as the table for which it has been created. The DBA should then specify the unqualified SYNONYM to DCLGEN. This produces an unqualified DECLARE TABLE statement.

Unfortunately, because DCLGEN does not provide the option of producing a qualified or unqualified DECLARE TABLE statement, DBAs must perform gyrations to unqualify their DECLARE TABLE statements.

Avoid Breaking DCLGEN **Host Variables into Components**   Although doing so is not gener-ally recommended, you can modify the WORKING-STORAGE variables generated by DCLGEN to "break apart" columns into discrete components. Consider, for example, the following DCLGEN-created WORKING-STORAGE variables for the DSN8810.PROJACT table:

```
01  DCLPROJACT.
    10  PROJNO     PIC X(6).
    10  ACTNO      PIC S9(4)      USAGE COMP.
    10  ACSTAFF    PIC S999V99    USAGE COMP-3.
    10  ACSTDATE   PIC X(10).
    10  ACENDATE   PIC X(10).
```

The two date columns, ACSTDATE and ACENDATE, are composed of the year, the month, and the day. By changing the structure to "break apart" these columns, you could reference each component separately, as in the following example:

```
01  DCLPROJACT.
    10   PROJNO                PIC X(6).
    10   ACTNO                 PIC S9(4)    USAGE COMP.
    10   ACSTAFF               PIC S999V99 USAGE COMP-3.
    10   ACSTDATE.
         15   ACSTDATE-YEAR.
              20   ACSTDATE-CC  PIC X(2).
              20   ACSTDATE-YY  PIC X(2).
         15   ACSTDATE-FILLER1 PIC X.
         15   ACSTDATE-MONTH   PIC X(2).
         15   ACSTDATE-FILLER2 PIC X.
         15   ACSTDATE-DAY     PIC X(2).
    10   ACENDATE.
         15   ACENDATE-YEAR    PIC X(4).
         15   ACENDATE-FILLER1 PIC X.
         15   ACENDATE-MONTH   PIC X(2).
         15   ACENDATE-FILLER2 PIC X.
         15   ACENDATE-DAY     PIC X(2).
```

This approach is not favored because it is invasive to the generated DCLGEN code, which can result in errors, as mentioned previously. Instead, you should code structures that can be used to "break apart" these columns outside the DCLGEN, and then move the necessary columns to the structures outside the DCLGEN variables.

Avoid the Field Name PREFIX   Avoid the field name PREFIX option of DCLGEN. This option generates WORKING-STORAGE variables with a numeric suffix added to the PREFIX text. For example, if you ran DCLGEN for the DSN8510.PROJACT table and specified a PREFIX of COL, the following WORKING-STORAGE variable names would be generated:

```
01  DCLPROJACT.
    10   COL01      PIC X(6).
    10   COL02      PIC S9(4)     USAGE COMP.
    10   COL03      PIC S999V99   USAGE COMP-3.
    10   COL04      PIC X(10).
    10   COL05      PIC X(10).
```

Note how each column begins with the supplied prefix and ends with a number that steadily increases by 1. The COL01 column is used for the PROJNO column, COL02 for ACTNO, and so on. This type of DCLGEN should be avoided because the generated column names are difficult to trace to the appropriate WORKING-STORAGE variables.

Precompiler Guidelines

Follow these guidelines when precompiling DB2 programs.

Use the Appropriate DBRM Library   Most shops allocate DBRM libraries. These libraries must be set up as partitioned data sets with 80-byte records.

Retain DBRMs Only When Absolutely Necessary   Although the DBRM produced by the precompiler must be placed in a partitioned data set, DBRMs sometimes do not need to be retained. If the DBRM will be temporary due to the replication of program preparation during the testing process, it can be written to a temporary PDS. When the program is out of the testing phase, the DBRM can be written to a permanent PDS before it is migrated to production status.

Name the DBRM the Same As the Program   Ensure that the DBRM is named the same as the program from which it was created. This eases the administration of objects created and modified by the program preparation process.

Precompile Only When Required   Precompilation is not required by BASIC and APL2 programs that contain SQL statements. Refer to the appropriate BASIC and APL2 programming guides for additional information about these environments.

Use DEC31 to Impact Decimal Precision   DB2 supports decimal precision of either 15 or 31, depending upon the precompiler option. If decimal numbers with a precision greater than 15 are to be utilized, you must specify the DEC31 precompiler option.

When you're using this option, examine the application program to verify that the host variables can accommodate 31-digit decimal precision.

Using LEVEL to Avoid Binding   LEVEL is a precompiler option that can be used when a program is modified but the SQL in the program has not changed. LEVEL is specified as a character string to be used by DB2 for consistency checking in place of the timestamp token. By precompiling a DBRM with the same level as before, a BIND can be avoided. You do not need to bind because SQL has not changed allowing DB2 to use the same access paths and the program to use the same package or plan as before.

Using LEVEL, a programmer can change his program without modifying the embedded SQL, and avoid worrying about having to bind. But care must be taken to ensure that the SQL is not changed. If the SQL is changed but a bind does not occur, unpredictable results can occur.

If LEVEL is used, DB2 will use the level as the consistency token and the default for version (if no version is specified).

> **CAUTION**
>
> Avoid using LEVEL as much as possible. Unpredictable and undesirable results can occur when using the LEVEL option improperly.

Specify the Version with Care   Remember, you basically have two options for specifying the version name. Versions can be automatically defined by DB2 specifying VERSION(AUTO) or explicitly named using the VERSION(name) precompile parameter. When versions are automatically assigned by DB2, a timestamp will be used.

If you explicitly name your versions, they will be more difficult to implement but easier to administer. The difficult part is providing a mechanism to ensure that programmers always specify an appropriate version when precompiling a program.

On the other hand, if you use automatic versioning, packages are easier to implement because DB2 is automatically naming the version for you, but much more difficult to administer. The administration difficulty occurs because the auto timestamp version is unwieldy to manually enter when package administration is necessary. Consider this when deciding how to name versions at your shop.

If your shop does not have an automated means of administering versions, consider explicitly specifying the version when precompiling a program.

BIND **Guidelines**

Using the following tips and techniques will ensure effective execution of the BIND statement and the creation of efficiently bound DB2 application programs.

Administer Initial Binds Centrally   A centralized administration group (DBA, bind agent, and so on) should be responsible for all initial binds of applications plans (BIND ADD). This provides a point of control for administering plan and package use and freeing old or unused plans and packages when they are no longer required. Centralized control also makes it easier to enforce your shop's DB2 naming standards.

Keep Statistics Current for Binding   Before binding, ensure that the RUNSTATS utility has been executed recently for every table accessed by the plan or package to be bound. This allows the bind process to base access path selections on the most recent statistical information. Without up-to-date statistics, DB2 will create access paths based on inaccurate information—which can cause poor performance due to sub-optimal access paths.

Avoid Default Parameters   Specify every bind parameter. Defaults are used for certain bind parameters when the BIND command is issued without specifying them. This could be dangerous because the default options are not always the best for performance and concurrency.

Group Like Programs into Collections   You should group like programs by binding them to packages and specifying the same collection identifier. If a customer application is composed of 12 DB2 programs, for example, bind each into a separate package with a collection identifier of CUSTOMER. This makes the administration of packages belonging to the same application easy.

Use Wildcard Package Lists   When multiple packages must exist in the same plan, favor using the wildcard capability of the PKLIST parameter of the BIND PLAN statement. To bind the 12-customer application packages (mentioned in the last guideline) to a single plan, for example, you could specify PKLIST(CUSTOMER.*). Additionally, all new packages bound in the CUSTOMER collection are automatically added to that plan.

Specify Collections and Packages Carefully in the PKLIST   Avoiding the following scenario will eliminate confusing which package is actually being used during program execution:

- Binding the same DBRM into different collections (such as C1 and C2)

13

- Binding a plan with a package list specifying both collections (C1.*,C2.*), both packages (C1.PACKAGE, C2.PACKAGE), or a combination (C1.*,C2.PACKAGE or C1.PACKAGE,C2.*)

- Failing to specify SET CURRENT PACKAGESET in the application program

If the current package set is blank, the package is in any collection in the EDM pool, and the consistency tokens match, DB2 will return the package. It does not matter whether the package is from C1 or C2. For this reason, specifying SET CURRENT PACKAGESET is imperative if you have a package bound into more than one collection in the PKLIST of the same plan. Although many think that DB2 uses packages in the order specified in the package list, this is only true if none of the packages are in the EDM Pool when the plan executes. If a matching package is in the EDM pool and can be used, DB2 will use it and the program might execute an improper package.

Specify Explicit Consistency Tokens   Favor the specification of an explicit consistency token for package versioning over allowing it to default to a timestamp. If a new version with a new timestamp is created every time a package is bound, the DB2 Catalog quickly becomes cluttered with unused versions. Explicitly specifying a consistency token to control versions that must be saved is better. You could, for example, specify a release number such as REL100, and then increment the number to REL101, REL102, REL200, and so on, to indicate different versions of the software. In this manner, only one version, rather than many versions of each release will exist.

Use the QUALIFIER Parameter   When binding packages, use the QUALIFIER parameter to specify an identifier to be used by the bind process to qualify all tables referenced by SQL statements in the DBRM being bound. The DSN8510.DEPT table, for example, is accessed if the following statement is embedded in a program bound to a package specifying a QUALIFIER of DSN8510:

```
EXEC SQL
    SELECT  DEPTNO, DEPTNAME
    INTO    :DEPTNO, :DEPTNAME
    FROM    DEPT
END-EXEC.
```

Users can specify a qualifier different from their userid if they have the necessary authority to issue the BIND command for the plan or package. The users do not need to be SYSADM or have a secondary authid, as is required with the OWNER parameter.

Optionally, the OWNER parameter can be used to qualify tables at BIND time. When specifying an OWNER, however, the binding agent must be either a SYSADM or set up with a secondary authid equal to the owner being specified.

Strategically Implement Multiple Qualified Tables   If a single plan needs to access tables with different qualifiers, consider one of the following two strategies. The first strategy is to create aliases or synonyms such that every table or view being accessed has the same qualifier. The second method is to separate the tables being accessed into logical processing groups by qualifier. Code a separate program to access each processing group. Then bind each program to a separate package, specifying the qualifier of the tables in that program. Finally, bind all the packages into a single plan.

Use One Program and Multiple Packages for Mirror Tables   When you use mirror tables, one program can access different tables. Suppose that you need an employee table for every month of the year. Each employee table is modeled after DSN8810.EMP but contains only the active employees for the month it supports. The following tables, for example, are differentiated by their qualifier:

```
JANUARY.EMP

FEBRUARY.EMP

MARCH.EMP

    .

    .

    .

NOVEMBER.EMP

DECEMBER.EMP
```

Assume that you need 12 reports, each one providing a list of employees for a different month. One program can be coded to access a generic, unqualified EMP table. You then could bind the program to 12 separate packages (or plans), each specifying a different qualifier (JANUARY through DECEMBER). For more information on mirror tables, refer to Chapter 5, "Data Definition Guidelines."

> **CAUTION**
>
> This approach will likely increase EDM pool usage. This is so because the package will be allocated once for every collection.

Use the Correct ACTION Parameter   Specify the proper ACTION parameter for your bind. You can specify two types of actions: ADD or REPLACE. ADD indicates that the plan is new. REPLACE indicates that an old plan by the same name will be replaced. Specifying ACTION (REPLACE) for a new plan does not cause the bind to fail—it merely causes confusion.

Establish BIND PLAN Parameter Guidelines   Favor the use of the following parameters when binding application plans:

```
ISOLATION (CS)

VALIDATE (BIND)

ACTION (REPLACE)

NODEFER (PREPARE)

FLAG (I)

ACQUIRE (USE)

RELEASE (COMMIT)
```

```
DEGREE (1)

CURRENTDATA (NO)

EXPLAIN (YES)
```

These `BIND PLAN` parameters usually produce the most efficient and effective DB2 plan. However, one set of `BIND` parameters will **not** be applicable for every DB2 application program. Reasons for choosing different options are discussed in other guidelines in this chapter.

Establish `BIND PACKAGE` **Parameter Guidelines**   Favor the use of the following parameters when binding packages:

```
ISOLATION (CS)

VALIDATE (BIND)

ACTION (REPLACE)

SQLERROR (NOPACKAGE)

FLAG (I)

RELEASE (COMMIT)

DEGREE (1)

CURRENTDATA (NO)

EXPLAIN (YES)
```

These `BIND PACKAGE` parameters usually produce the most efficient and effective DB2 package. Once again, one set of `BIND` parameters will **not** be applicable for every DB2 application program. Other guidelines in this chapter cover the occasions when you should choose different options.

Take Care When Specifying Isolation Level   The `ISOLATION` parameter of the `BIND` command specifies the isolation level of the package or plan. The isolation level determines the mode of page locking implemented by the program as it runs.

DB2 implements page and row locking at the program execution level, which means that all page or row locks are acquired as needed during the program run. Page or row locks are released when the program issues a `COMMIT` or `ROLLBACK`.

You can specify the following four isolation levels:

- Cursor stability (`CS`)
- Repeatable read (`RR`)
- Read stability (`RS`)
- Uncommitted read (`UR`)

They significantly affect how the program processes page locks.

Use Uncommitted Read with Caution   Anyone accustomed to application programming when access to a database is required understands the potential for concurrency problems. To ensure data integrity when one application program attempts to read data that is in the process of being changed by another, the DBMS must forbid access until the modification is complete. Most DBMS products, DB2 included, use a locking mechanism for all data items being changed. Therefore, when one task is updating data on a page, another task cannot access data (read or update) on that same page until the data modification is complete and committed.

Programs that read DB2 data typically access numerous rows during their execution and are thus quite susceptible to concurrency problems. DB2 provides read-through locks, also know as a *dirty read* or *uncommitted read*, to help overcome concurrency problems. When you're using an uncommitted read, an application program can read data that has been changed but is not yet committed.

Dirty read capability is implemented at BIND time by specifying ISOLATION(UR). Application programs bound using the UR isolation level will read data without taking locks. This way, the application program can read data contained in the table as it is being manipulated. Consider the following sequence of events:

1. To change a specific value, at 9:00 a.m. a transaction containing the following SQL is executed:

```
UPDATE     DSN8810.EMP
   SET FIRSTNME = '"MICHELLE'"
WHERE      EMPNO = '10020';
```

   The transaction is a long-running one and continues to execute without issuing a COMMIT.

2. At 9:01 a.m., a second transaction attempts to SELECT the data that was changed, but not committed.

If the UR isolation level was specified for the second transaction, it would read the changed data even though it had yet to be committed. Obviously, if the program doesn't need to wait to take a lock and merely reads the data in whatever state it happens to be at that moment, the program will execute faster than if it had to wait for locks to be taken and resources to be freed before processing.

The implications of reading uncommitted data, however, must be carefully examined before being implemented. Several types of problems can occur. Using the previous example, if the long-running transaction rolled back the UPDATE to EMPNO '10020', the program using dirty reads may have picked up the wrong name ("'MICHELLE'") because it was never committed to the database.

Inaccurate column values are not the only problems that can be caused by using ISOLATION(UR). A dirty read can cause duplicate rows to be returned where none exist. Alternatively, a dirty read can cause no rows to be returned when one (or more) actually exists. Additionally, an ORDER BY clause does not guarantee that rows will be returned in order if the UR isolation level is used. Obviously, these problems must be taken into

consideration before using the UR isolation level. The following rules apply to
ISOLATION(UR):

- The UR isolation level applies to read-only operations: SELECT, SELECT INTO, and
  FETCH from a read-only result table.

- Any application plan or package bound with an isolation level of UR will use uncommitted read functionality for any read-only SQL. Operations contained in the same plan or package that are not read-only will use an isolation level of CS.

- The isolation level defined at the plan or package level during BIND or REBIND can be overridden as desired for each SQL statement in the program. You can use the WITH clause to specify the isolation level for any individual SQL statement, as in the following example:

```
SELECT EMPNO, LASTNAME
FROM    DSN8810.EMP
WITH UR;
```

  The WITH clause is used to allow an isolation level of RR, RS, CS, or UR to be used on a statement-by-statement basis. The UR isolation level can be used only with read-only SQL statements. This includes read-only cursors and SELECT INTO statements. The CS, RR, and RS isolation levels can be specified for SELECT, INSERT, UPDATE, and DELETE statements. The WITH clause, however, cannot be used with subselects.

- DB2 will not choose UR isolation with an access path that uses a Type-1 index. If the plan or package is rebound to change to UR isolation, DB2 will not consider any access paths that use a Type-1 index. If an acceptable Type-2 index cannot be found, DB2 will choose a table scan. This applies only to DB2 V5 and older subsystems because Type 2 indexes are the only type of indexes supported as of DB2 V6.

When is it appropriate to use UR isolation? The general rule of thumb is to avoid UR whenever the results must be 100% accurate. Following are examples of when this would be true:

- Calculations that must balance are being performed on the selected data

- Data is being retrieved from one source to insert into or update another

- Production, mission-critical work is being performed that cannot contain or cause data integrity problems

In general, most current DB2 applications will not be candidates for dirty reads. In a few specific situations, however, the dirty read capability will be of major benefit. Consider the following cases in which the UR isolation level could prove to be useful:

- Access is required to a reference, code, or look-up table that basically is static in nature. Due to the non-volatile nature of the data, a dirty read would be no different from a normal read the majority of the time. In those cases when the code data is being modified, any application reading the data would incur minimum, if any, problems.

- Statistical processing must be performed on a large amount of data. Your company, for example, might want to determine the average age of female employees within a certain pay range. The impact of an uncommitted read on an average of multiple rows will be minimal because a single value changed will not greatly impact the result.

- Dirty reads can prove invaluable in a data warehousing environment that uses DB2 as the DBMS. A data warehouse is a time-sensitive, subject-oriented, store of business data that is used for online analytical processing. Other than periodic data propagation and/or replication, access to the data warehouse is read-only. Because the data is generally not changing, an uncommitted read is perfect in a read-only environment due to the fact that it can cause little damage. More data warehouse projects are being implemented in corporations worldwide and DB2 with dirty read capability is a very wise choice for data warehouse implementation.

- In those rare cases when a table, or set of tables, is used by a single user only, UR can make a lot of sense. If only one individual can be modifying the data, the application programs can be coded such that all (or most) reads are done using UR isolation level, and the data will still be accurate.

- Finally, if the data being accessed already is inconsistent, little harm can be done using a dirty read to access the information.

> **CAUTION**
>
> Although the dirty read capability can provide relief of concurrency problems and deliver faster performance in specific situations, it also can cause data integrity problems and inaccurate results. Be sure to understand the implications of the UR isolation level and the problems it can cause before diving headlong into implementing it in your production applications.

Sometimes, just ensuring that you are using lock avoidance can deliver better performance and can be a good alternative to dirty read processing. More information on lock avoidance follows later in this chapter.

Use Caution Before Binding with Repeatable Read ISOLATION   With repeatable read, or RR, all page locks are held until they are released by a COMMIT. Cursor stability, or CS, releases read-only page locks as soon as another page is accessed.

In most cases, you should specify CS to enable the greatest amount of application program concurrency. RR, however, is the default isolation level.

Use the RR page locking strategy only when an application program requires consistency in rows that may be accessed twice in one execution of the program, or when an application program requires data integrity that cannot be achieved with CS. Programs of this nature are rare.

For an example of the first reason to use RR page locking, consider a reporting program that scans table to produce a detail report, and then scans it again to produce a summarized managerial report. If the program is bound using CS, the results of the first report might not match the results of the second.

Suppose that you are reporting the estimated completion dates for project activities. The first report lists every project and the estimated completion date. The second, managerial report lists only the projects with a completion date greater than one year.

The first report indicates that two activities are scheduled for more than one year. After the first report but before the second, however, an update occurs. A manager realizes that she underestimated the resources required for a project. She invokes a transaction (or uses QMF) to change the estimated completion date of one of her project's activities from 8 months to 14 months. The second report is produced by the same program, but reports 3 activities.

If the program has used an isolation level of RR rather than CS, an update between the production of the two reports would not have been allowed because the program would have maintained the locks it held from the generation of the first report.

For an example of the second reason to use RR page locking, consider a program that is looking for pertinent information about employees in the information center and software support departments who make more than $30,000 in base salary. The program opens a cursor based on the following SELECT statement:

```
SELECT  EMPNO, FIRSTNME, LASTNAME,
        WORKDEPT, SALARY
FROM    DSN8810.EMP
WHERE   WORKDEPT IN ('C01', 'E21')
AND     SALARY > 30000;
```

The program then begins to fetch employee rows. Department 'C01' is the information center and department 'E21' is software support. Assume further, as would probably be the case, that the statement uses the DSN8810.XEMP2 index on the WORKDEPT column. An update program that implements employee modifications is running concurrently. The program, for example, handles transfers by moving employees from one department to another, and implements raises by increasing the salary.

Assume that Sally Kwan, one of your employees, has just been transferred from the information center to software support. Assume further that another information center employee, Heather Nicholls, received a 10% raise. Both of these modifications will be implemented by the update program running concurrently with the report program.

If the report program were bound with an isolation level of CS, the second program could move Sally from C01 to E21 after she was reported to be in department C01 but before the entire report was finished. Thus, she could be reported twice: once as an information center employee and again as a software support employee. Although this circumstance is rare, it can happen with programs that use cursor stability. If the program were bound instead with RR, this problem could not happen. The update program probably would not be allowed to run concurrently with a reporting program, however, because it would experience too many locking problems.

Now consider Heather's dilemma. The raise increases her salary 10%, from $28,420 to $31,262. Her salary now fits the parameters specified in the WHERE condition of the SQL statement. Will she be reported? It depends on whether the update occurs before or after the row has been retrieved by the index scan, which is clearly a tenuous situation. Once again, RR avoids this problem.

You might be wondering, "If CS has the potential to cause so many problems, why are you recommending its use? Why not trade the performance and concurrency gain of CS for the integrity of RR?" The answer is simple: The types of problems outlined are rare. The expense of using RR, however, is so great in terms of concurrency that the tradeoff between the concurrency expense of RR and the efficiency of CS usually is not a sound one.

Consider Read Stability (RS) Over Repeatable Read (RR)   The RS isolation level is similar in functionality to the RR isolation level. It indicates that a retrieved row or page is locked until the end of the unit of work. No other program can modify the data until the unit of work is complete, but other processes can insert values that might be read by your application if it accesses the row a second time.

Use read stability only when your program can handle retrieving a different set of rows each time a cursor or singleton SELECT is issued. If using read stability, be sure your application is not dependent on having the same number of rows returned each time.

Favor Acquiring Table Space Locks When the Table Space Is Used   In addition to a page locking strategy, every plan also has a table space locking strategy. This strategy is implemented by two bind parameters: ACQUIRE and RELEASE.

Remember that a page lock is acquired when the page is requested, and is released after a COMMIT or a ROLLBACK. Table space locking is different. DB2 uses a mixed table space locking strategy—the programmer specifies when to acquire and release table space locks by means of the ACQUIRE and RELEASE parameters. Table space locking is implemented only at the plan level; it is not implemented at the package level.

The options for the ACQUIRE parameter are USE and ALLOCATE. When you specify USE, table space locks are taken when the table space is accessed. With ALLOCATE, table space locks are taken when the plan is first allocated.

The options for RELEASE are COMMIT and DEALLOCATE. When you specify the COMMIT option, locks are released at commit or rollback time. When you specify DEALLOCATE all locks are held until the plan finishes and is deallocated.

In general, use the following table space locking allocation strategy:

```
ACQUIRE(USE)
RELEASE(COMMIT)
```

This provides your program with the highest degree of concurrency.

When you have conditional table access in your program, consider using the following lock and resource allocation strategy:

```
ACQUIRE(USE)
RELEASE(DEALLOCATE)
```

With conditional table access, every invocation of the program does not cause that section of code to be executed. By specifying that locks will be acquired only when used, and released only when deallocated, you can increase the efficiency of a program because locks, once acquired, are held during the entire course of the program. This does reduce concurrency, however.

For a batch update program in which you know that you will access every table coded in your program, use the following lock and resource allocation strategy:

```
ACQUIRE(ALLOCATE)
RELEASE(DEALLOCATE)
```

All locks are acquired as soon as possible and are not released until they are absolutely not needed. This strategy, too, will reduce concurrency.

For high-volume transactions (one or more transactions per second throughput), use a CICS protected entry thread (RCT TYPE=ENTRY) with the following strategy:

```
ACQUIRE(ALLOCATE)
RELEASE(DEALLOCATE)
```

A high-volume transaction generally executes much faster if it is not bogged down with the accumulation of table space locks.

In all cases, you should obtain database administration approval before binding with parameters other than ACQUIRE(USE) and RELEASE(COMMIT).

Specify Validation at BIND Time   A validation strategy refers to the method of checking for the existence and validity of DB2 tables and DB2 access authorization. You can use two types of validation strategies: VALIDATE(BIND) or VALIDATE(RUN).

VALIDATE(BIND), the preferred option, validates at bind time. If a table is invalid or proper access authority has not been granted, the bind fails.

VALIDATE(RUN) validates DB2 table and security each time the plan is executed. This capability is useful if a table is changed or authority is granted after the bind is issued. It does, however, impose a potentially severe performance degradation because each SQL statement is validated each time it is executed.

Always specify VALIDATE(BIND) for production plans. Use VALIDATE(RUN) only in a testing environment.

Request All Error Information   Always specify FLAG(I), which causes the BIND command to return all information, warning, error, and completion messages. This option provides the greatest amount of information pertaining to the success or failure of the bind.

Specify an Appropriate CACHESIZE   The CACHESIZE parameter specifies the size of the authorization cache for a plan. The authorization cache is a portion of memory set aside for a plan to store valid authids that can execute the plan. By storing the authids in memory, the cost of I/O can be saved.

The cache can vary in size from 0 to 4096 bytes in 256 byte increments. For a plan with a small number of users, specify the minimum size, 256. If the plan will have large number of users, calculate the appropriate size as follows:

```
CACHESIZE = ( [number of concurrent users] * 8 ) + 32
```

Take the number returned by the formula and round up to the next 256 byte increment making sure not to exceed 4096.

> **NOTE**
>
> The number 32 is added because the authid cache always uses 32 control bytes.

One final suggestion—if the plan is executed only infrequently, or has been granted to PUBLIC, do not cache authids. Specify a CACHESIZE of zero.

As of DB2 V5, authorization can be cached for packages as well as plans. However, no CACHESIZE BIND parameter is available for packages. Instead, package caching must be enabled by the system administrator at the subsystem level.

Consider Using CURRENTDATA(NO) for Lock Avoidance   DB2 uses the lock avoidance technique to reduce the number of locks that need to be taken for read only processes. To enable lock avoidance for read only and ambiguous cursors, NO must be specified for the CURRENTDATA option. Unfortunately, YES is the default. By specifying CURRENTDATA(NO) you indicate that currency is not required for cursors that are read only or ambiguous.

Do not use CURRENTDATA(NO) if your program dynamically prepares and executes a DELETE WHERE CURRENT OF statement against an ambiguous cursor after that cursor is opened. DB2 returns a negative SQLCODE to the program if it attempts a DELETE WHERE CURRENT OF statement for any of the following cursors:

- Cursor uses block fetching
- Cursor uses query parallelism
- Cursor that is positioned on a row that is modified by this or another application process

> **NOTE**
>
> For local access, CURRENTDATA(YES) means that the data cannot change while the cursor is positioned on it. CURRENTDATA(NO) is similar to CURRENTDATA(YES) except when a cursor is accessing a base table rather than a result table in a work file. With CURRENTDATA(YES), DB2 can guarantee that the cursor and the base table are current, whereas CURRENTDATA(NO) does not.
>
> For remote access, CURRENTDATA(YES) turns off block fetching for ambiguous cursors. The data returned with the cursor is current with the contents of the remote table or index for ambiguous cursors.

Consider Using DEGREE(ANY) for Parallelism   When DEGREE(ANY) is specified, DB2 will attempt to execute queries using parallel engines whenever possible. Parallel queries are typically deployed against partitioned table spaces, and can be used to access non-partitioned table spaces when specified in a join with at least one partitioned table space.

At optimization time, DB2 can be directed to consider parallelism by specifying DEGREE(ANY) at BIND time for packages and plan. Following are the three types of parallelism:

- I/O—multiple read engines

- CPU—multiple processor and multiple read engines

- Sysplex—multiple data sharing subsystems

Parallelism can significantly enhance the performance of queries against partitioned table spaces. By executing in parallel, elapsed time usually will decrease, even if CPU time does not. This results in an overall perceived performance gain because the same amount of work will be accomplished in less clock time.

Following are the types of queries that will benefit most from I/O parallelism:

- Access large amount of data, but return only a few rows

- Use column functions (AVG, COUNT, COUNT_BIG, MIN, MAX, STDDEV, SUM, VARIANCE)

- Access long rows

CPU parallelism extends the capabilities of I/O parallelism. When CPU parallelism is invoked, it is always used in conjunction with I/O parallelism. The reverse of this is not necessarily true. Most of the queries that benefit from I/O parallelism also will benefit from CPU parallelism because as the I/O bottlenecks are reduced, the CPU bottlenecks become more apparent.

Sysplex parallelism extends the parallel capabilities of DB2 even further. When Sysplex parallelism is employed, DB2 can spread a single query across multiple central processor complexes within a data sharing group. For more information on data sharing and Sysplex parallelism, refer to Chapter 19, "Data Sharing."

CAUTION

Before attempting to achieve parallel query operations using DEGREE(ANY), be sure that your environment is suitable for parallelism. Do you have enough memory and the proper buffer pool configurations to take advantage of parallelism? Is the machine on which you are running your queries capable of parallelism? For example, a machine without multiple CPUs will not be able to run CPU parallelism.

You can use the PARAMDEG DSNZPARM to specify the maximum degree of parallelism for a parallel group. By specifying a maximum value DB2 is limited to the PARAMDEG value as the maximum degree of parallelism. This parameter can be used to throttle DB2 so that it does not create too many parallel tasks and therefore use too much virtual storage.

Specify NODEFER(PREPARE)   Specify NODEFER(PREPARE) rather than DEFER(PREPARE) unless your program contains SQL statements that access DB2 tables at a remote location and are executed more than once during the program's invocation. In this case, specifying DEFER(PREPARE) can reduce the amount of message traffic by preparing each SQL statement only once at the remote location, when it is first accessed. Subsequent execution of the same statement in the same unit of recovery does not require an additional PREPARE.

Use SQLERROR to Control Package Creation   Two options for the SQLERROR parameter exist: NOPACKAGE and CONTINUE. NOPACKAGE is the recommended option when not operating in a distributed environment. By specifying NOPACKAGE, a package will not be created when an SQL error is encountered.

The other option is CONTINUE, which will create a package even if an error is encountered. Because SQL syntax varies from environment to environment, CONTINUE is a viable option when operating in a distributed environment. The package can be created, regardless of the error with the understanding that the SQL will function properly at the remote location.

Specify EXPLAIN(YES) for Production BINDs   At a minimum, all production BINDs should be performed with the EXPLAIN(YES) option. This allows the proper monitoring of the production access path selection made by DB2. Binding without producing EXPLAIN output will hamper your performance tuning abilities, because you will not be able to determine the access paths chosen by DB2 without the EXPLAIN data.

Of course, in a testing environment you will not need to specify EXPLAIN(YES) for every single BIND. This is especially the case at the beginning of the development process. However, you should consider specifying EXPLAIN(YES) even in a test environment once your development efforts are significantly underway. By binding your test programs using EXPLAIN(YES), you will have access path information at your disposal for your tuning efforts.

> **CAUTION**
>
> You will not necessarily assure efficient production access paths just because you achieve desirable access paths in your test environment. The only way to assure that access paths are the same in both test and production is to be sure that **everything** about the two environments are the same: statistics, system parameters, memory, and so on.

Use the ENABLE and DISABLE Parameters Effectively   You can use the ENABLE and DISABLE bind options to control the environment in which the plan or package being bound can be executed. ENABLE ensures that the plan or package operates in only the enabled environments. DISABLE permits execution of the plan or package by all subsystems except those explicitly disabled. ENABLE and DISABLE are mutually exclusive parameters (only one can be used per package or plan).

If a plan is bound specifying ENABLE(IMS), for example, only the IMS subsystem is permitted to execute the plan. If a plan is bound with the DISABLE(CICS) option, the CICS subsystem is not permitted to execute this plan.

Be careful when using ENABLE and DISABLE because they may function differently than one might originally think. ENABLE explicitly enables an environment for execution. The enabled environment, however, is the only environment that can execute the plan or package. So ENABLE limits the environments in which a package or plan can execute. By contrast, specifying DISABLE actually is more open because only one specific area is disabled, thereby implicitly enabling everything else. The bottom line is that ENABLE is more limiting than DISABLE.

Table 13.1 shows valid ENABLE and DISABLE specifications.

TABLE 13.1   Environments that Can Be Enabled or Disabled

Specification	Package or plan is executed only
BATCH	As a batch job
DLIBATCH	As an IMS batch job
DB2CALL	With the Call Attach Facility
CICS	Online through CICS
IMS	Under the control of IMS
IMSBMP	As an IMS BMP (batch message processor)
IMSMPP	As an online IMS message processing program (that is, a transaction)
RRSAF	With the RRS Attachment Facility
REMOTE	As a remote program

ENABLE and DISABLE are great keywords to consider for plans granted to PUBLIC that rely on an external security mechanism (such as RACF) to control unauthorized access.

Retain Security When BINDing Existing Plans   Be sure to specify the RETAIN parameter for existing plans. RETAIN indicates that all BIND and EXECUTE authority granted for this plan will be retained. If you fail to specify the RETAIN parameter, all authority for the plan is revoked.

Retain DBRMs Bound in Plans   Develop a consistent scheme for the maintenance and retention of DBRMs bound to application plans and packages. Ensure that DBRMs are copied to the appropriate library (test, education, production, and so on) before the binding of plans in the new environment. This applies to both new and modified programs.

Consider Dynamic Reoptimization   When host variables or parameter markers are used in SQL statements in an application program, DB2 does not know the values that will be supplied at execution time. This lack of information causes DB2 to guess at the best access path using the information available at BIND time.

By specifying the BIND parameter REOPT(VARS), DB2 will reevaluate the access path at runtime when the host variable and parameter marker values are known. This should result in a better-formulated access path. Reoptimization, however, is not a panacea. Because DB2 must reevaluate access paths at execution time, additional overhead will be consumed. This overhead can negate any performance gains achieved by the new access paths. Enabling reoptimization does not guarantee a different access path; it only allows DB2 to formulate the access path based on the runtime values used.

In general, reoptimization can be an easy-to-implement alternative to dynamic SQL. The overhead of reoptimization will be less than that associated with dynamic SQL because reoptimization does not require statement parsing, authorization checking, dependency checking, or table decomposition.

Do Not Blindly Enable Reoptimization for All Programs   In general, consider specifying REOPT(VARS) in the following situations:

- Application programs in which multiple SQL statements utilize host variables (or parameter markers)

- SQL statements in which host variables (or parameter markers) are deployed against columns with very skewed distribution statistics

- Application programs in which dynamic SQL was considered, but avoided because of its complexity or overhead

Before implementing reoptimization, conduct performance tests to determine its impact on transaction performance.

Consider Isolating Reoptimized Statements   The REOPT and NOREOPT parameters must be specified for an entire program when it is bound into a plan or package. Most programs commonly contain multiple SQL statements, not all of which will benefit from reoptimization.

Consider isolating specific SQL statements into a separate program, and binding it into a package. In this manner, individual SQL statements can be set for reoptimization without impacting the rest of the SQL in a program.

Consider Keeping Prepared Statements Past COMMIT   By specifying KEEPDYNAMIC(YES), dynamic SQL statements can be held past a COMMIT point. Specify KEEPDYNAMIC(YES) for dynamic SQL programs in DB2 subsystems in which the dynamic SQL prepare cache is enabled. This causes fewer dynamic binds and optimizes the performance of dynamic SQL programs.

Note that when KEEPDYNAMIC(YES) is specified, you also must use NOREOPT(VARS).

Specify the PATH **Parameter**   If UDTs, UDFs, or stored procedures are used in your program, be sure to specify the appropriate PATH parameter. The PATH identifies the schema names in the SQL path to be used for function resolution. Refer to Chapter 4 for more information on UDFs and UDTs and Chapter 15, "Using DB2 Stored Procedures," for more information on stored procedures.

You can specify a SQL PATH of up to 254 bytes in length. To determine the length of the SQL path, use the following calculation:

```
  length of each schema name
+ (2 * total number of names) (for delimiters)
+ (total number of names - 1) (for commas)
```

For example, consider the following SQL path definition

```
SQLPATH('SCHEMA21', 'SCHZ', 'SYSPROC')
```

The length of this SQL path would be calculated as follows:

The length of each schema name added together: (8 + 4 + 7) = 19

Total number of schema names times two: (3 * 2) = 6

Total number of schema names minus one: (3 − 1) = 2

Added together is 19 + 6 + 2 = 27

CAUTION

Be sure to specify the schema names in uppercase in the PATH definition.

Specify the Appropriate DYNAMICRULES **Option for Dynamic SQL**   The DYNAMICRULES parameter determines the characteristics of dynamic SQL. There are four types of behavior that dynamic SQL can exhibit:

- BIND behavior
- DEFINE behavior
- INVOKE behavior
- RUN behavior

The following are the six options for the DYNAMICRULES parameter:

DYNAMICRULES(RUN)	Dynamic SQL statements are processed using run behavior. Run behavior means that DB2 uses the authid of the running application and the SQL authid of the CURRENT SQLID special register for authorization checking for dynamic SQL statements. Furthermore, the CURRENT SQLID is used as the qualifier for unqualified table, view, and alias names. When bound with this option, the program can issue dynamic DCL (GRANT and REVOKE) or dynamic DDL (ALTER, CREATE, DROP, and RENAME). Run behavior is the only behavior that permits dynamic DCL and DDL.
DYNAMICRULES(BIND)	Dynamic SQL statements are processed using bind behavior. Bind behavior means that DB2 uses the authid of the plan or package for dynamic SQL authorization checking. The QUALIFIER value of the BIND is used as the qualifier for unqualified table, view, and alias names. If QUALIFIER is not specified, the authid of the plan or package owner is used to qualify table objects.

DYNAMICRULES(DEFINEBIND)	Dynamic SQL statements are processed using define or bind behavior. When the package is run as a standalone DB2 program, it uses bind behavior as described previously for DYNAMICRULES(BIND). When the package is run as a stored procedure or UDF, DB2 processes dynamic SQL statements using define behavior. Define behavior means that DB2 uses the authid of the UDF or stored procedure owner for dynamic SQL authorization checking. The owner of the UDF or stored procedure is used as the qualifier for unqualified table, view, and alias names.
DYNAMICRULES(DEFINERUN)	Dynamic SQL statements are processed using define or run behavior. When the package is run as a standalone DB2 program, it uses run behavior as described previously for DYNAMICRULES(RUN). When the package is run as a stored procedure or UDF, DB2 processes dynamic SQL statements using define behavior, as described under DYNAMICRULES(DEFINEBIND).
DYNAMICRULES(INVOKEBIND)	Dynamic SQL statements are processed using invoke or bind behavior. When the package is run as a standalone DB2 program, it uses bind behavior as described previously for DYNAMICRULES(BIND). When the package is run as a stored procedure or UDF, DB2 processes dynamic SQL statements using invoke behavior. Invoke behavior means that DB2 uses the authid of the UDF or stored procedure invoker for dynamic SQL authorization checking. The invoker of the UDF or stored procedure is to qualify any unqualified table, view, and alias names.
DYNAMICRULES(INVOKERUN)	Dynamic SQL statements are processed using invoke or run behavior. When the package is run as a standalone DB2 program, it uses run behavior as described previously for DYNAMICRULES(RUN). When the package is run as a stored procedure or UDF, DB2 processes dynamic SQL statements using invoke behavior, as described under DYNAMICRULES(INVOKEBIND).

Use OPTHINT to Change Access Paths   The OPTHINT parameter can be used "tell" DB2 what access paths to use for the plan or package. This information is conveyed to DB2 using rows in a PLAN_TABLE. For more information on optimizer hints, refer to Chapter 21.

Consider the IMMEDWRITE Parameter for Data Sharing   The IMMEDWRITE parameter indicates whether immediate writes will be done for updates made to group buffer pool dependent page sets or partitions. This option applies to data sharing environments only.

An immediate write means that the page is written to the group buffer pool (or to DASD for GBPCACHE NO group buffer pools or GBPCACHE NONE or SYSTEM page sets) as soon as the buffer update completes. To enable immediate write, specify IMMEDWRITE(YES).

Consider specifying IMMEDWRITE(YES) when one transaction can spawn another transaction that can run on another DB2 member, and the spawned transaction depends on uncommitted updates made by the original transaction. With immediate writes, the original transaction can write the updated data immediately to the group bufferpool-dependent buffers to ensure that the spawned transaction retrieves the correct, updated data.

Linkage Editor Guidelines

The following guideline is useful to know when link-editing DB2 programs.

Link the Appropriate Language Interface Module   You must link the proper language interface module with the program's compiled module. The modules to use depend on the execution environment of the program being link edited. Table 13.2 shows a list of modules required for different DB2 environments.

TABLE 13.2   Link-Edit Modules for DB2 Programs

Environment	Language Interface
TSO	DSNELI(for online ISPF and TSO batch)
CICS	DSNCLI
IMS/TM	DFSLI000
Call Attach	DSNALI
RRSAF	DSNRLI

CHAPTER **14**

Alternative DB2 Application Development Methods

Part II has dealt primarily with DB2 application development using embedded SQL in a third-generation language such as COBOL. However, as I mentioned at the outset of Part II, you can use other methods to develop DB2 applications. With the growing popularity of client/server computing, these methods are gaining acceptance in the IT community.

In this chapter, I discuss the ramifications of using six alternative but perhaps complementary development methods to build DB2 applications: using stand-alone SQL, client/server programming languages, ODBC (Call Level Interface), fourth-generation languages, CASE tools, and report writers.

Developing Applications Using Only SQL

Although it is uncommon for an entire application to be developed with SQL alone, it is quite common for components of an application to be coded using only SQL. Pure SQL is a good choice for the quick development of code to satisfy simple application requirements. Examples include the following:

- Using the UPDATE statement to reset indicators in tables after batch processing

- Deleting every row from a table using a mass DELETE or deleting a predefined set of rows from a table after batch processing

- Any type of application that is composed entirely of data modification statements (that is, just a bunch of INSERT, UPDATE, and DELETE statements)

- Creating simple, unformatted table listings
- Performing simple data entry controlled by a CLIST or REXX EXEC

Additionally, now that DB2 supports code-based objects that enhance the functionality of SQL, more processing can be accomplished using SQL alone. With triggers, stored procedures, and user-defined functions, very powerful SQL-based "applications" can be developed.

> **NOTE**
>
> You still need to write application code when you develop stored procedures and user-defined functions. Once the code is written, it is possible to write SQL-only applications that call the stored procedures and utilize the user-defined functions.

SQL Application Guidelines

The following guidelines are helpful when developing an application using only SQL.

Use Native SQL Applications Sparingly   Although using native SQL (without embedding it into a program) in some circumstances is technically possible, avoid doing so unless the application truly can be developed without advanced formatting features or procedural logic. Achieving the level of professionalism required for most applications is difficult if you use SQL alone. For example, you cannot use SQL alone to format reports, loop through data a row at a time, or display a screen of data.

DB2 stored procedures can be coded using IBM's version of SQL/PSM, the procedural dialect of SQL. However, standalone SQL statements cannot use SQL/PSM functionality.

Enforce Integrity Using DB2 Features   If you develop a complete application or major portions of an application using only SQL, be sure to use the native features of DB2 to enforce the integrity of the application. For example, if data will be entered or modified using SQL alone, enforce user-defined integrity rules using triggers, check constraints or VALIDPROCs coded for each column and specified in the CREATE TABLE DDL.

Additionally, specify referential constraints for all relationships between tables and create unique indexes to enforce uniqueness requirements. This approach is the only way to provide integrity when a host language is not used.

> **NOTE**
>
> It is a wise course of action to enforce data integrity using DB2 features regardless of the type of application. DB2-based integrity is non-bypassable, and therefore, generally preferable. For stand-alone SQL applications, though, DB2-based integrity is a requirement because there is no other code in which you can code integrity constraints.

Simulate Domains Using Check Constraints or Tables   Mimic the use of domains when possible using domain tables or check constraints. Domain tables are two-column tables that contain all valid values (along with a description) for columns in other tables. For standalone SQL applications, be sure to use referential integrity to tie these "domain" tables to the main tables. For example, you can create a "domain" table for the SEX column of the DSN8810.EMP table consisting of the following data:

SEX	DESCRIPTION
M	MALE
F	FEMALE

The primary key of this "domain" table is SEX. You specify the SEX column in the DSN8810.EMP as a foreign key referencing the domain table, thereby enforcing that only the values M or F can be placed in the foreign key column. This way, you can reduce the number of data entry errors.

> **CAUTION**
>
> The advice in the previous two paragraphs is not intended to be a general purpose rule of thumb, but a guideline to be followed when SQL-only applications are being developed. In more typical DB2 application systems referential constraints on "domain"-like tables are not generally recommended. Large applications with many domain tables can create large, unruly table space sets which are difficult to manage, backup, and recover. Instead, programming constructs can be used to manipulate and use "domain"-like tables (for example, in-memory table structures).

Check constraints provide an alternative approach to enforcing domain values. Instead of creating a new table coupled with referential constraints, you can add a single check constraint to the column to enforce the data content. Consider this example:

```
SEX              CHAR(1)
CONSTRAINT GENDER CHECK (SEX IN ("M", "F"))
```

Whether to choose domain tables or check constraints depends on the circumstances. Each is useful in different situations. Weigh the following benefits and drawbacks before choosing one method over the other:

- Check constraints are simply SQL predicates and cannot carry description columns (or any other columns), whereas domain tables can. Therefore, a domain table can be more self-documenting.

- Check constraints should outperform referential integrity because DB2 does not need to read data from multiple user tables to determine the validity of the data.

- Domain tables are easier to use when the domain is not static. Adding values to a check constraint requires DDL changes; adding values to a domain table requires a simple SQL INSERT.

- As the number of valid values increases, domain tables are easier to implement and maintain. The full text of a check constraint can contain no more than 3,800 bytes.

- For smaller domains, check constraints are preferable not only for performance reasons, but because no additional table space or index administration is required.

- When you're tying together domain tables using referential integrity, sometimes large referential sets are created. They can be difficult to administer and control.

14

Large referential sets, however, may be preferable to program-enforced RI or, worse yet, allowing inaccurate data. When you're deciding whether to enforce RI for domain tables, balance performance and recoverability issues against possible data integrity violations. When large referential sets are created, consider breaking them up using check constraints for some of the simpler domains.

Follow SQL Coding Guidelines   When you're developing native SQL applications, follow the SQL coding guidelines presented in Chapter 2, "Data Manipulation Guidelines," to achieve optimal performance.

Using Client/Server Programming Languages

Distributed processing and client/server processing are quite widespread in the data processing community. Distributed processing describes the interaction of multiple computers working together to solve a business problem. Client/server processing is a specific type of distributed processing in which a client computer requests services from a server. The client is typically a personal computer with a graphical user interface (GUI). DB2 is a popular candidate as a database server.

The popularity of client/server development has an impact on the DB2 application development environment. Often, DB2 developers access DB2 using a client/server application development product that communicates to DB2 using a gateway product. Popular client/server programming languages include PowerBuilder, Visual Basic, Visual C++, VisualAge, Kylix, and Delphi.

Connecting to DB2

Applications that run on a non-S/390 platform require DB2 Connect and CAE to access DB2 for OS/390 data. IBM's DB2 Connect is available to enable applications written for Windows, OS/2, and Unix. You can use this gateway product to connect client applications directly to DB2 for z/OS and OS/390. The Client Application Enabler (CAE) is also required and available on Windows, OS/2, and multiple Unix variants.

The application (or ODBC driver) calls CAE, which in turn sends the request to the DB2 Connect gateway. DB2 Connect passes the call to DB2 for OS/390 in the form of a DRDA request, as illustrated in Figure 14.1. CAE and DB2 Connect enable your applications or third-party products such as Microsoft Access and Lotus Approach running on the Windows platform to access DB2 for z/OS directly.

Actually, there are two options for client applications:

- Use CAE and DB2 Connect Personal Edition on the client machine.

- Use a server machine where DB2 Connect Enterprise Edition is installed. Then the client machine requires only CAE. CAE is connected to the server machine through NetBIOS, IPX, or TCP/IP.

Regardless of which of the above option is deployed, the DB2 for z/OS location name must be defined in CAE. For additional information and guidelines on using DB2 Connect please refer to Chapter 43, "DB2 Connect."

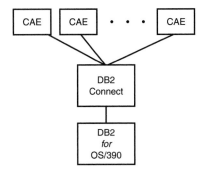

FIGURE 14.1.   Using DB2 Connect and CAE to Connect to DB2 for z/OS.

Of course, DB2 Connect is not the only gateway product on the market. Other popular gateway products exist for connecting DB2 for z/OS to client/server applications, such as Neon Systems' Shadow Direct gateway product.

Client/Server Guidelines

Building client/server applications requires knowledge of multiple platforms and the network used to connect them. The following tips and tricks can be useful when building applications that span platforms.

Be Aware of SQL Anomalies   GUI-based client/server development tools may not offer SQL that is completely compatible with DB2 for z/OS. As such, certain features discussed in the DB2 manuals (and this book) may not be available when you're using a client/server language.

Likewise, some client/server languages require a call level interface to SQL (such as ODBC). This requirement causes the application to use dynamic SQL with all the performance implications as discussed in Chapter 12, "Dynamic SQL Programming."

Consult the Documentation for the Tools Being Used   Some of the rules and advice laid out in the preceding three chapters of Part II may not hold true for client/server programming with DB2. For example, the client/server development tool might build SQL statements for you and submit them to DB2 through the gateway. Sometimes, odd constructs, such as allowing SELECT ... INTO for multiple rows can be permitted because the gateway provides buffering services and automatically handles building cursors. It is imperative that you understand not only how your client/server development tools work to create applications, but how they interface to the database management system, which in this case is DB2 for z/OS.

Be Aware of the Complex Nature of Client/Server Computing   Additionally, the client/server environment relies upon a complex network of computing resources.

Mainframes, midranges, PCs, and workstations are commonly networked together, as illustrated in Figure 14.2.

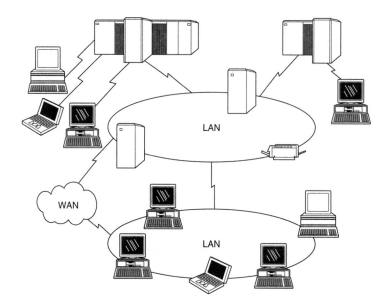

FIGURE 14.2.   A complex client/server environment.

In a client/server environment, rely on the documentation that came with your application development tool and middleware product(s).

Use Stored Procedures   Minimize network traffic by implementing stored procedures for frequently executed pieces of code. If you concentrate multiple SQL statements within a stored procedure, less data needs to be sent across the network. Network traffic is usually the single most important determinant of client/server application performance.

Use Triggers   By using triggers to maintain database integrity you can further minimize SQL requests over the network. When data integrity routines exist within the database, application programs do not need to check for invalid data because the database will ensure only valid data is entered. By doing more work within the DB2 database and requiring fewer program requests the performance of a client/server application can be improved.

Consolidate SQL Requests When Possible   Consolidate related SQL statements into a single request to reduce the number of requests and responses transmitted across the network. For example, change

```
SELECT EMPNO, LASTNAME FROM EMP WHERE EMPNO < '001000';
SELECT EMPNO, LASTNAME FROM EMP WHERE EMPNO > '009000';
```

into

```
SELECT  EMPNO, LASTNAME
FROM    EMP
WHERE   EMPNO < '001000'
OR      EMPNO > '009000';
```

One SQL statement sends fewer requests across the network. You can use this technique on all SQL statements, not just SELECT statements.

Ensure FOR READ ONLY for Distributed Cursors   Be sure that the FOR READ ONLY (or FOR FETCH ONLY) is used on each DECLARE CURSOR statement. Failure to do so has a negative impact on performance by disabling efficient block fetching. The FOR READ ONLY clause is ODBC-compliant and therefore more appropriate in a complex client/server environment.

Consult Chapter 41, "DRDA," Chapter 42, "Distributed DB2," Chapter 43, "DB2 Connect," and Chapter 44, "Distribution Guidelines," for more information on the following topics:

- DB2 distributed database support

- The use of DB2 as a database server

- Techniques for deploying DB2 Connect

- General distribution techniques and guidelines

14

Using Fourth-Generation Languages

Several fourth-generation languages (4GLs) are available at most IT shops. FOCUS, RAMIS, and NOMAD are examples of popular 4GLs. 4GLs, which operate at a higher level of abstraction than the standard 3GLs, can usually read, modify, process, and update data a set or a row at a time. For example, a 4GL can often issue a single command to list and display the contents of data stores. A 3GL program, in contrast, must read the data, test for the end of the file, move the data to an output format, and issue commands to control the display of a screen of data (for example, backward and forward scrolling, or counting the items per screen).

Consider using 4GLs for two reasons. First, a single 4GL statement usually corresponds to many 3GL statements. Because this capability provides a quicker programming cycle, production applications are online faster than traditional 3GL-developed applications. Second, 4GLs have a greatly reduced instruction set, which makes them easier to learn and master than 3GLs.

Be careful, though, because applications based on 4GLs rarely deliver the same level of performance as applications based on traditional languages. As with using pure SQL, writing entire applications using 4GL is uncommon but possible. More often, you will use 4GL to develop only certain components, such as

- Quick, one-time requests that are not run repeatedly in production.

- Specialized reports.

- Important portions of an application. (When critical components of an application are not delivered with the first release of the application, you can use a 4GL to deliver the most important portions of those components, thereby satisfying the users until you can fully develop the components using a traditional language.)

4GL Application Guidelines

Apply the following guidelines to optimize your DB2-based 4GL development efforts.

Avoid 4GLs When Performance Is Crucial　Avoid coding performance-oriented DB2 systems using fourth-generation languages. You can usually achieve a greater level of performance using traditional, third-generation languages.

Provide In-Depth 4GL Training　If you decide to use a 4GL, be sure that proper training is available. Although 4GLs can achieve results similar to 3GLs, they do not use the same techniques or methods. Developers unfamiliar with 4GLs usually do not produce the most efficient applications because of their tendency to use 3GL techniques or poorly developed 4GL techniques.

Avoid Proprietary Storage Formats　When you're using 4GLs, try to query data directly from DB2 tables instead of extracts. Extracting the data into the (sometimes proprietary) format of the 4GL can cause data consistency problems. By avoiding extracts, you ensure that the data queried using the 4GL is consistent with the data queried using conventional DB2 and SQL methods.

Extract Data As a Last Resort　Consider moving the data from DB2 tables to the 4GL format only if the performance of the 4GL program is unacceptable. (You should consider this approach only as a last resort.) If data will be extracted from DB2, you must run a regularly scheduled extraction procedure to keep the 4GL data current.

Use Embedded SQL If Possible　To retrieve DB2 data, try to use SQL embedded in the 4GL rather than use the language of the 4GL. The reasons for doing so follow:

- SQL is a universally accepted standard. Many 4GL products are on the market, and none are standard.

- Hiring SQL programmers who understand the SQL embedded in the 4GL is easier than hiring programmers who understand the syntax of the 4GL.

- Embedding SQL in a host language is a common and well-understood practice. Therefore, embedding SQL in a 4GL should, for the most part, correlate to embedding SQL in COBOL or another traditional language.

Join Tables Using SQL Instead of 4GL　If the 4GL provides a technique of relating or joining data from two physical data sources, avoid using it when accessing data from DB2 tables. Instead, create a DB2 view that joins the required tables, and query that view using the 4GL. This approach almost always provides better performance. For example, I converted one application using a 4GL "join" into a 4GL query of a view that joined tables. The application reduced elapsed time by more than 250 percent after the conversion.

Understand the Weaknesses of Your Particular 4GL   Some 4GL products interface to DB2 in unusual ways. Be sure that you understand the interface between the 4GL and DB2, as well as any potential "features" that could cause performance problems or management difficulties. For example, one 4GL I have worked with creates a DB2 view for every query issued via the 4GL. The management of these views can become troublesome as the number of queries issued using the 4GL grows.

Understand the Strengths of 4GL   Use the strong points of the 4GL and DB2. You should use DB2 to control the integrity of the data, the modification of the data, and the access to the data. You should use the 4GL to generate reports, perform complex processes on the data after it has been retrieved, and mix non-DB2 data with DB2 data.

Using CASE

Computer-aided software engineering (CASE) is the name given to software that automates the software development process. CASE tools provide an integrated platform (or, more commonly, a series of non-integrated platforms) that can be used to drive the application development process from specification to the delivery of source code and an executable application system. The term *CASE*, however, has no universally accepted definition and can comprise anything from a diagramming tool to a data dictionary to a code generator. CASE tools usually are separated into two categories: upper CASE tools and lower CASE tools.

You use an upper CASE tool to develop system specifications and detail design. It generally provides a front-end diagramming tool as well as a back-end dictionary to control the components of the application design. CASE tools can also provide support for enforcing a system methodology, documenting the development process, and capturing design elements from current application systems.

Lower CASE tools support the physical coding of the application. Tools in this category include system and program testing tools, project management tools, and code generators. This section concentrates on the code generation portion of CASE. An application code generator usually reads application specifications input into the CASE tool in one or more of the following formats:

- A macro-level or English-like language that details the components of the application system at a pseudo-code level

- Data flow diagrams generated by another component of the CASE tool (or sometimes by a different CASE tool)

- Reverse-engineered program specifications or flowcharts

Based on the input, the code generator develops a program or series of programs to accomplish the specification of the application. IBM's VisualAge Generator (which replaced Cross System Product, or CSP) is an example of a code generator. The application programmer codes instructions, which can be executed in 4GL fashion, or host language code (such as COBOL) can be generated. Code-generating CASE tools try to provide the

14

best portions of both the 3GL and 4GL worlds. They provide a quick application development environment because they raise the level of programming abstraction by accepting high-level designs or macro languages as input. They generally provide better performance than 4GLs because they can generate true, traditional 3GL source code.

Be careful when developing applications with this new method. Automatic code generation does not always produce the most efficient code. To produce efficient CASE-generated applications, follow the guidelines in the next section.

CASE Application Guidelines

The following guidelines are useful when using CASE tools to deploy DB2 applications.

Analyze Generated SQL Carefully   Code generators that develop embedded SQL programs usually produce functional SQL but do not always produce the most efficient SQL. Analyze the embedded SQL to verify that it conforms to the standards for efficient SQL outlined in Chapter 2.

Avoid Generalized I/O Routines   Sometimes a code generator produces source code that can be executed in multiple environments. This code often requires the use of an I/O routine to transform application requests for data into VSAM reads and writes, sequential file reads and writes, or database calls. When you use an I/O module, determining what SQL is accessing the DB2 tables is difficult. In addition, I/O routines usually use dynamic SQL instead of static SQL.

Favor code generators that produce true embedded SQL programs over products that use I/O routines. The programs are easier to debug, easier to maintain, and easier to tune.

Avoid Runtime Modules   Some code generators require the presence of a runtime module when the programs it generates are executed. Avoid these types of products because a runtime module adds overhead and decreases the efficiency of the generated application.

Favor Integrated CASE Tools   Choose a CASE tool that provides an integrated development platform instead of a wide array of disparate products to automate the system development life cycle. When a CASE tool provides integration of the system development life cycle, you can save a lot of time because the tool automatically carries the application forward from stage to stage until it is finished. If the CASE tools are not integrated, time is wasted performing the following tasks:

- Converting the data from one phase to a format that can be read by the tool that supports the next phase.

- Verifying that the data in the tool that accepts data from another tool is accurate and conforms to the expected results based on the status of the data in the sending tool.

- Moving data from one tool to another. (Time is wasted installing and learning these tools, as well as debugging any problems that result from the migration process.)

To avoid these types of problems, choose a CASE tool that provides as many of the features listed in Table 14.1 as possible. Use this chart to evaluate and rank CASE tools to support the complete DB2 program development life cycle.

TABLE 14.1   CASE Tool Features Checklist

Features	Supported (Y/N)?	Ranking
Supports the Business Strategy		
Enterprise data model capabilities		
Business data modeling		
Business decision matrices		
Integrates with any ERP packages in use at your site		
Supports Prototyping		
Screen formatting		
Report formatting		
Rapidly developing executable modules		
Supports Process Modeling		
Methodologies		
Supports UML		
Linked to the data model		
Linked to the code generator		
Documentation		
Supports Data Modeling		
Entity relationship diagramming		
Normalization		
Conceptual data model		
Supports subject areas		
Logical data model		
Physical data model		
Provides physical design recommendations		
Generates physical objects (such as tables or indexes)		
Linked to process model		
Documentation		
Supports Diagramming		
Graphical interface		
Linked to process model		
Linked to data model		
Multiple diagramming techniques		
Documentation		

14

TABLE 14.1   Continued

Features	Supported (Y/N)?	Ranking
Supports System Testing		
Administers test plan		
Creates test data		
User simulation		
Performance testing		
Stress testing		
Supports System Testing		
Acceptance testing		
Documentation		
Supports EXPLAIN		
Supports Quality Assurance		
System failure administration		
Quality acceptance testing		
Documentation		
Supports Development		
Automatically generates SQL		
Supports override of automatic SQL		
Automates precompile and bind		
Supports plans		
Supports collections		
Supports packages		
Supports versioning		
Generates code in your language of choice		
Supports the Technical Environment		
Supports current hardware platforms		
Supports current software platforms (such as DBMS or languages)		
Supports distributed data		
Supports client/server processing		
Supports required printer(s)		
Interfaces with mainframes		
Interfaces with midranges		
Interfaces with PCs		
LAN capability		
Web capability		

TABLE 14.1   Continued

Features	Supported (Y/N)?	Ranking
Supports Metadata Management		
Captures metadata from applications		
Captures metadata from database structures		
Integrated with data modeling components		
User-extensible to support non-standard applications and structures		
Supports Input from Multiple Platforms		
Word processors		
Spreadsheets		
Databases		
HTML and XML		
Other CASE tools		

Using Report Writers

Report writers are development tools you can use to generate professional reports from multiple data sources. You can consider a report writer as a specialized type of 4GL. Like 4GLs, they raise the level of abstraction by using fewer statements to produce reports than 3GLs do. They differ from true 4GLs in that they commonly are designed for one purpose: the generation of formatted reports.

For example, a report writer can often generate a report with a single command, whereas a 3GL must read data, format the data, program control breaks, format headers and footers, and then write the report record. IBM's Query Management Facility (QMF) and Computer Associates' Report Facility are examples of mainframe-based report writers for DB2.

PC-based report writers also are quite popular. They require a gateway setup as discussed earlier. Examples of this type of tool include Seagate's Crystal Reports, Business Objects, and Cognos Powerplay; IBM also offers a version of QMF for Windows.

Report Writer Application Guidelines

When using report writers to build DB2 applications be sure to consider the following guidelines.

Follow Previous Guidelines   The rules for fourth-generation languages also apply to report writers. Refer to the "4GL Application Guidelines" presented previously in this chapter.

Likewise, many popular report writers work in a client/server environment instead of completely on the mainframe. For example, the user interface runs on a workstation but accesses data from DB2 tables on the mainframe. When you're using a report writer in a client/server environment, refer to the "Client/Server Guidelines" presented previously in this chapter for guidance.

Learn the Report Writer Capabilities   Use the capabilities of the report writer to format your output. Most report writers have formatting codes to guide how each column is to be displayed on the final report. For example, if you are using a report writer that supports displaying numeric data with leading zeroes, use that capability instead of storing the numeric data in a character column and forcing the leading zeroes to be stored.

Using ODBC (*Call Level Interface*)

ODBC is another alternative development option. ODBC provides a Call Level Interface, or CLI, for accessing DB2 data. ODBC provides an alternative to embedded dynamic SQL. It is an application programming interface (API) that uses function calls to pass dynamic SQL statements as function arguments. IBM's ODBC support in DB2 is based on the Microsoft Open Database Connectivity (ODBC) specification and the X/Open Call Level Interface specification.

> **NOTE**
>
> X/Open is an independent, worldwide open systems organization whose goal is to increase the portability of applications by combining existing and emerging standards.
>
> Microsoft's ODBC is based on the X/Open CLI specification and is the most popular CLI for relational database access.

ODBC for DB2 is designed to be used by C and C++ programs. ODBC can be used to make API calls to DB2 instead of using embedded SQL.

> **NOTE**
>
> DB2 Version 5 introduced the DB2 Call Level Interface (CLI). In Version 6, the DB2 CLI was renamed to DB2 ODBC (Open Database Connectivity). The rename was cosmetic only; the functionality of the interface was not impacted, so your CLI applications will continue to function using ODBC.
>
> Over time IBM continues to augment and improve the capabilities and functionality of ODBC for DB2.

ODBC applications differ from traditional DB2 programs using embedded, static SQL. When ODBC is used, a specific set of function calls is used at runtime to execute SQL statements and access database services. No precompilation is required. Contrast this system with a traditional, embedded SQL program that requires a precompiler to convert the SQL statements into executable code. The program is compiled, the SQL executables are bound to the data source, and only then can the program be executed.

Any statement that can be executed using dynamic SQL can be executed using DB2 ODBC. Because DB2 ODBC is based on open specifications, DB2 applications using ODBC are more portable than embedded SQL applications. Further, because a precompiler is not required, the code is not bound to the data source (in this case, DB2). This capability gives the application a degree of independence, allowing the code to connect directly to the appropriate data source at runtime without changing or preparing (precompiling/ compiling/binding) the program.

A DB2 ODBC application consists of three main tasks as shown in Figure 14.3. The initialization task allocates and initializes resources in preparation for the transaction processing task. The bulk of the program is performed during the transaction processing task. It is here where SQL statements are passed to ODBC to access and modify DB2 data. The final step is the termination phase where allocated resources are freed.

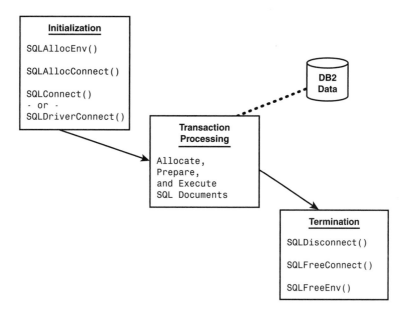

FIGURE 14.3.   An ODBC application.

Listing 14.1 shows a brief code example using ODBC to access DB2 data. Note the use of functions such as `SQLAllocStmt()` and `SQLExecDirect()` to issue SQL instead of explicitly embedded SQL statements.

LISTING 14.1   Sample DB2 ODBC Code

```
int
process_stmt(SQLHENV henv,
             SQLHDBC hdbc,
             SQLCHAR * sqlstr)
{
    SQLHSTMT        hsql;
    SQLRETURN       rc;
    /* allocate a statement handle */
    SQLAllocStmt(hdbc, &hsql);
    /* execute the SQL statement in "sqlstr"    */
    rc = SQLExecDirect(hsql, sqlstr, SQL_NTS);
    if (rc != SQL_SUCCESS)
        if (rc == SQL_NO_DATA_FOUND)
           {
           printf("\nThe SQL statement finished without an\n");
           printf("error but no data was found or modified\n");
```

LISTING 14.1   Continued

```
                return (SQL_SUCCESS);
                } else
        /*  perform error checking routine */
```

DB2 ODBC Guidelines

When building application programs using DB2 ODBC, keep the following tips and techniques in mind.

Be Aware of DB2 ODBC Differences   DB2's support of ODBC is not 100% functionally equivalent to standard ODBC. The CLI contains all ODBC level 1 functionality, most of ODBC 2.0, most ODBC 3.0 functionality, as well as IBM extensions for DB2-specific features.

V7 As of V7, DB2 supports many ODBC 3.0 APIs which allows your application code to be more compatible with industry standards, as well as more portable across platforms. Although using DB2's ODBC implementation eases the portability of applications from DB2 to other ODBC-compliant DBMSs, you might need to make some modifications for the port to operate properly.

Be Aware of DB2 ODBC Restrictions   When using ODBC to access DB2 data, be aware that some traditional DB2 features cannot be used by ODBC applications. For example, the following are not supported by ODBC:

- Large objects (LOBs) and LOB locators

- Scrollable cursors

- Using the SQLCA to obtain detailed diagnostic information

- Control over null termination of output strings

Use ODBC to Reduce the Application Administration Burden   Using DB2 ODBC can reduce the amount of application management and administration. Each DB2 ODBC program does not need to be bound to each data source. Bind files provided with DB2 ODBC need to be bound only once for all ODBC applications.

However, use of ODBC with DB2 requires dynamic SQL and C or C++ programming skills. Ensure that this trade-off is effective before switching to ODBC programming for administrative reasons.

Understand That DRDA and ODBC Are Complementary Techniques   Developers sometimes confuse ODBC with DRDA. DRDA is a remote connectivity architecture; ODBC is an API for data manipulation in relational databases. You should view DRDA and ODBC as complementary to one another—not competitive.

Consider Using Both Embedded SQL and ODBC   An application can use both embedded SQL and ODBC to its advantage. You can create a stored procedure using embedded, static SQL. The stored procedure can then be called from within a DB2 ODBC application. After the stored procedure is created, any DB2 ODBC application can call it.

You also can write a mixed program that uses both DB2 ODBC and embedded SQL. For example, you could write the bulk of the application using ODBC calls, but you could write critical components using embedded static SQL for performance or security reasons. Deploy your applications using this scenario only if static SQL stored procedures do not meet your application's needs. For more information on stored procedures, consult Chapter 15, "Using DB2 Stored Procedures."

Do Not Code Cursors with ODBC   When you're using ODBC with DB2, explicit cursor declaration is not required. ODBC automatically creates cursors as needed, and the application can use the generated cursor in using fetches for multiple row SELECT statements as well as positioned UPDATE and DELETE statements.

Likewise, the OPEN statement is not required when you're using ODBC. When SELECT is executed, ODBC automatically opens the cursor.

Increase Portability Using ASCII-Encoded Tables   When an application has a high probability of being ported to another environment, use ODBC and ASCII-encoded tables to improve open data access. As support for Unicode becomes more pervasive, you might choose to specify Unicode table encoding instead of ASCII.

Use Parameter Markers with ODBC   Unlike embedded SQL, ODBC allows the use of parameter markers when issuing the SQLExecDirect() function. The SQLExecDirect() function is the ODBC equivalent of the EXECUTE IMMEDIATE statement.

Code COMMIT and ROLLBACK Using SQLTransact()   A COMMIT or ROLLBACK in ODBC is issued via the SQLTransact() function call rather than by passing it as an SQL statement.

Check the Basic ODBC Function Return Code   Each ODBC function returns one of the following basic return codes:

- SQL_SUCCESS: The function completed successfully.

- SQL_SUCCESS_WITH_INFO: The function completed successfully, with a warning or other information.

- SQL_NO_DATA_FOUND: The function returned successfully, but no relevant data was found.

- SQL_NEED_DATA: The application tried to execute an SQL statement, but required parameter data is missing.

- SQL_ERROR: The function failed.

- SQL_INVALID_HANDLE: The function failed because of an invalid input handle.

These return codes provide only rudimentary success or failure information. For detailed information, use the SQLError() function.

Use SQLError() to Check SQLSTATE   You can use the SQLError() function to obtain additional details that are not supplied by the basic ODBC function return codes. Use SQLError() to check the success or failure of each call using the CLI when error diagnostic checking must be performed by the program.

The `SQLError()` function returns the following information:

- `SQLSTATE` code.

- The native DB2 error code. If the error or warning was detected by DB2 for z/OS, this code is the `SQLCODE`; otherwise, it is set to `-99999`.

- The message text associated with the `SQLSTATE`.

The format and specification of most of the `SQLSTATE` values specified by ODBC are consistent with the values used by DB2 for OS/390, but some differences do exist. Refer to Table A.3 in Appendix A, "DB2 Sample Tables," for a listing of the DB2 ODBC-specific `SQLSTATE` values.

Using Java and DB2

Java is another alternative programming technique. It is an increasingly popular choice for DB2 application development. Just about everybody has at least heard of Java. But just because you've heard about it doesn't mean you understand it. Even if you know a bit about it, there is always more to discover. Let's face it, there's a lot of hype out there regarding anything that concerns the Internet. Now that DB2 for z/OS fully supports Java, Java usage will continue to increase. So, let's learn a bit about Java.

What Is Java?

First and foremost, Java is an object-oriented programming language. Developed by Sun Microsystems in 1991, Java was modeled after, and most closely resembles C++. But Java requires a smaller footprint and eliminates some of the more complex and error-prone features of C and C++ (such as pointer management and the go to construct). Additionally, many tasks have been moved from the language itself to the JVM (Java Virtual Machine).

Java enables animation for and interaction with the World Wide Web. Although Web interaction is Java's most touted feature, it is a fully functional programming language that can be used for developing general-purpose programs independent from the Web.

Using HTML, developers can run Java programs, called applets, over the Web. But Java is a completely different language from HTML, and it does not replace HTML. Java applets are automatically downloaded and executed by users as they surf the Web. The Java applet is run by the Web browser.

What makes Java special is that it was designed to be multi-platform. In theory, regardless of the machine and operating system you are running, any Java program should be able to run. Many possible benefits accrue because Java enables developers to write an application once and then distribute it to be run on any platform. Benefits can include reduced development and maintenance costs, lower systems management costs, and more flexible hardware and software configurations.

So, to summarize, the major qualities of Java are

- It is similar to other popular languages.

- It can enable Web interaction.

- It can enable executable Web content.

- It can run on multiple platforms.

Now that DB2 for z/OS supports application development using Java, all of these qualities are available to DB2 applications.

Java Bytecodes and the Java Virtual Machine

After a Java program is written, the source code is compiled into machine-independent constructs called *bytecodes* using the Java compiler. Bytecodes are the manner in which Java achieves its platform independence. Because the Java bytecode is in a machine-independent, architecture-neutral format, it can run on any system with a standard Java implementation.

The Java bytecodes are then processed by the Java Virtual Machine (JVM). The JVM interprets the bytecodes for the platform on which the Java program is to be run. The JVM loads and verifies the Java bytecode. It is then passed to the Java interpreter to be executed. Alternatively, the bytecodes can be passed to a just-in-time (JIT) compiler to be compiled into machine code to be executed.

> **CAUTION**
>
> Java has a reputation as a "slow" language. That is, the performance of Java is questionable. The major disadvantage is that Java is an interpretive language. Both the Java interpreter and the JIT compiler consume resources and take time to process the Java bytecodes before execution.
>
> The performance of a Java program will pale in comparison to a program compiled and link-edited into object code (such as a COBOL program). As a developer, you must decide whether the platform independence and Web development capabilities offset the potential for performance degradation.

Java Applications, Applets, and Servlets

There are three types of Java implementation methods that you can implement when accessing DB2 data from Java—Java applications, applets, and servlets.

A *Java application* program is basically the same as a program written in any other programming language. It can perform all of the tasks normally associated with programs, including many tasks that Java applets cannot perform. Furthermore, a Java application does not need a browser to be executed. It can be executed in a client or server machine.

A *Java applet* is a small application program that must be downloaded before it is run within a Java-enabled Web browser. Java applets reside on a Web server. When the Web server returns an HTML page that points to a Java applet, the Java-enabled Web browser requests the applet to be downloaded from the Web server. After the applet is received at the browser, either the browser starts the applet internally, or an external JVM executes it.

14

Applets typically perform simple operations, such as editing input data, control screen interaction, and other client functionality. Of course, Java applets can be written to perform more complex functionality, but to load and run non-Java code in the client requires signed applets, which have the authority needed to run code in the client machine.

> **NOTE**
>
> You should be aware of the performance implications of the requirement for Java applets to be downloaded before they can be run. In general, Java applets are small, so the performance impact should be negligible. Additionally, Java applets can be cached by the Web browser, further diminishing the performance impact.

A *Java servlet* is basically server-side Java. A Java servlet runs on the Web server, just like an applet runs in the Web browser. Java servlets can be used to extend the functionality of the Web server. The Web server hands requests to the servlet, which replies to them. Servlets can be used instead of CGI applications.

> **NOTE**
>
> To run Java servlets, your Web server must support the Java servlet API, developed by JavaSoft. This API defines how the servlet communicates with the server.

Java servlets have security advantages over client-side Java applets. A servlet that runs on a Web server inside a firewall can control access to sensitive data and business logic. Java applets do not inherently provide these security capabilities.

Before choosing which Java development style to use, you must know the basics of the environment in which the program must run. Ask the following questions when deciding what type of Java program is required for your development needs:

- How will the program be executed? Must it run over the Internet, as an intranet or extranet application, or merely as a standalone application?

- What is the business logic that this program must perform?

- How complicated is the program?

- How large (or small) is the program, and can it be downloaded quickly?

- What are the security requirements?

- Who are the target users and at what speed will they be connected to the Web?

Java applications, Java applets, and Java servlets are similar in nature. However, a different method is used to invoke each of them. Java applets and servlets are started from an HTML page. Java applications do not require a Web component but can be used as part of an intranet solution.

To implement any Java programs, you need to use the Java Developers Kit, or JDK for short. The JDK is a development environment for writing Java. The JDK includes the Java

Virtual Machine (JVM), Java classes, source files to create the classes in the JVM, documentation, and the JDK tools required for building and testing Java bytecode. These tools include the Java compiler and interpreter, the Java applet viewer, and the Java debugger.

Enterprise Java Beans

Enterprise Java Beans, or EJBs for short, are part of Java 2 Enterprise Edition (J2EE). EJBs are Java programs written as components that reside on the server. They are used to simplify the delivery of distributed applications and Web services by assembling components to achieve business functionality. Such an approach can greatly reduce the amount of time required to develop and deploy scalable enterprise Java applications.

A typical Java development environment for DB2 includes J2EE and WebSphere for building enterprise applications.

JDBC Versus SQLJ

There are two options for accessing DB2 for z/OS data in Java application programs: JDBC and SQLJ. It is imperative that you understand the differences between these two methods in order to develop proper database access for your Java programs.

Java Database Connectivity, or *JDBC*, is an API that enables Java to access relational databases. Similar to ODBC, JDBC consists of a set of classes and interfaces that can be used to access relational data. Anyone familiar with application programming and ODBC (or any call-level interface) can get up and running with JDBC quickly. JDBC uses dynamic SQL to access DB2 data. The primary benefits of JDBC include the following:

- Develop an application once and execute it anywhere.

- Enable the user to change between drivers and access a variety of databases without recoding your Java program.

- JDBC applications do not require precompiles or binds.

Potential drawbacks of JDBC include in the following:

- JDBC uses dynamic SQL, which can add overhead when the SQL is bound.

- Programs using JDBC can become quite large.

SQLJ enables developers to embed SQL statements in Java programs. SQLJ provides static SQL support to Java. Developers can embed SQL statements into Java, and a precompiler is used to translate SQL into Java code. Then the Java program can be compiled into byte-codes, and a bind can be run to create a package for the SQL. Simply stated, SQLJ enables Java programs to be developed the way most DB2 programs have been developed for years.

Of course, SQLJ does not allow dynamic SQL. But you can mix SQLJ and JDBC in a single Java program, which effectively enables you to choose static or dynamic SQL for your Java programs. The primary benefits of SQLJ include the following:

- The ability to code static, embedded SQL in Java programs.

- SQLJ source programs usually are smaller than equivalent JDBC programs.

- SQLJ does data type checking during the program preparation process and enforces strong typing between table columns and Java host expressions. JDBC passes values without compile-time data type checking.

Potential drawbacks of the SQLJ approach include the following:

- SQLJ programs must be precompiled and bound.

- SQLJ is not yet a standard, but it has been proposed to ANSI for inclusion and has the widespread support of the major DBMS vendors.

To get a quick understanding of the differences between JDBC and SQLJ, review the code fragments in Listings 14.2 and 14.3. These listings do not show complete programs, but you can use them to understand the different means by which a SQL statement is issued with JDBC versus with SQLJ.

LISTING 14.2   JDBC Code Fragment

```
// Create the connection
// change the following URL to match the location name
// of your local DB2 for OS/390.
// The URL format is: "jdbc:db2os390:location_name"
String url = "jdbc:db2os390:st11db2g";
Connection con = DriverManager.getConnection (url);

// Create the Statement
Statement stmt = con.createStatement();
System.out.println("**** JDBC Statement Created");

// Execute the query and generate a ResultSet instance
ResultSet rs = stmt.executeQuery("SELECT LASTNAME, HIREDATE FROM EMP");
System.out.println("**** JDBC Result Set Created");

// Close the statement
stmt.close();

// Close the connection
con.close();
```

LISTING 14.3   SQLJ Code Fragment

```
{
#sql public iterator ByPos(String,Date);
                        // Declare positioned iterator class ByPos
ByPos positer; // Declare object of ByPos class
String name = null;
Date hrdate;
#sql positer = { SELECT LASTNAME, HIREDATE FROM EMP };
#sql { FETCH :positer INTO :name, :hrdate };
```

LISTING 14.3   Continued

```
// Retrieve the first row from the result table
 while ( !positer.endFetch() )
 { System.out.println(name + " was hired in " + hrdate);
   #sql { FETCH :positer INTO :name, :hrdate };
// Retrieve the rest of the rows
  }
}
```

So, in general, JDBC programs are more portable and manage their own connections to DB2, but require dynamic SQL. SQLJ programs are easier to code because they require fewer lines of code and can be more efficient because they use static SQL, but require program preparation and are less portable.

> **NOTE**
>
> Be sure to check out the Java sections of IBM's Web site for additional information regarding Java support and sample Java code. Two good URLs to bookmark are
>
> http://www.ibm.com/developer/java/
> http://www-4.ibm.com/software/data/db2/java/

Java Program Preparation

Both JDBC and SQLJ programs need to be prepared before they can be run. But a SQLJ program requires precompilation and binding, whereas a JDBC program does not.

To prepare a JDBC-only Java program is the same as preparing any Java program with no database access. The only required step is to compile the program using the javac command.

To prepare a Java program that contains SQLJ calls, you will need to follow the program preparation steps as depicted in Figure 14.4. In general, you will follow similar steps to what you would for preparing a COBOL program, but with some differences. The first step is to run the source code through the SQLJ Translator (sqlj). This produces a modified source file and a SQLJ "serialized profile." The modified source is compiled into a Java class to produce Java bytecodes. The SQLJ "serialized profile" is customized into standard DB2 DBRMs using db2profc. At this point you can BIND the DBRMs into packages and then the packages in to a plan; or you can simply BIND the DBRMs directly into a single plan.

Using Result Set Iterators to Retrieve Multiple Rows

Traditional DB2 application programs written in host languages use a DB2 cursor to retrieve individual rows from a multi-row result set. The SQLJ equivalent of a cursor is a *result set iterator*. A result set iterator can be passed as a parameter to a method.

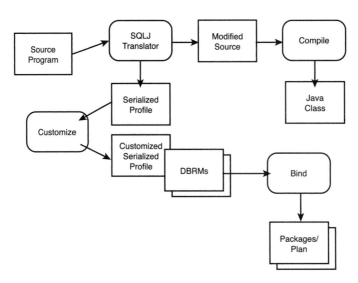

FIGURE 14.4.   SQLJ program preparation.

The result set iterator is defined using an iterator declaration clause specifying a list of Java data types. The Java data types represent columns of the table in the result set. The information in Table 14.2 shows the SQL data types and their equivalent SQLJ data types that can be specified in result set iterator declarations. The SQLJ data type in the left column can be used for data retrieved that is of any of the SQL data types listed in the right column.

TABLE 14.2   SQLJ and SQL Data Type Equivalents

SQLJ Data Type	SQL Data Type
java.lang.String	CHAR
	VARCHAR
	LONG VARCHAR
	GRAPHIC
	VARGRAPHIC
	LONG VARGRAPHIC
java.math.BigDecimal	NUMERIC
	INTEGER
	DECIMAL
	SMALLINT
	FLOAT
	REAL
	DOUBLE
Boolean	INTEGER
	SMALLINT

TABLE 14.2   Continued

SQLJ Data Type	SQL Data Type
Integer	INTEGER
	SMALLINT
	DECIMAL
	NUMERIC
	FLOAT
	DOUBLE
Float	INTEGER
	SMALLINT
	DECIMAL
	NUMERIC
	FLOAT
	DOUBLE
Double	INTEGER
	SMALLINT
	DECIMAL
	NUMERIC
	FLOAT
	DOUBLE
byte[]	CHARACTER
	VARCHAR
	LONG VARCHAR
	GRAPHIC
	VARGRAPHIC
	LONG VARGRAPHIC
java.sql.Date	DATE
java.sql.Time	TIME
java.sql.Timestamp	TIMESTAMP

14

> **NOTE**
>
> The byte[] SQLJ data type is equivalent to the SQL data type with a subtype of FOR BIT DATA.
>
> The java.sql.Date, java.sql.Time, and java.sql.Timestamp data types are part of the JDBC API.

Java Guidelines

The following guidelines apply to Java application development against DB2 for z/OS data.

Beware of Java Performance   As already noted, Java has a reputation for sluggish performance due to being interpreted instead of compiled. Java applications will tend to consume more CPU than COBOL applications. A good rule of thumb is to assume that Java will consume about 3 times more than COBOL in a DB2 V6 environment or about 2 times more in a DB2 V7 or V8 environment.

Beware of Character Data   Java does not have a native fixed-length text data type. For this reason, many Java shops favor defining VARCHAR columns in their tables instead of CHAR columns—even for very small character columns. This allows the Java variables to match up with the DB2 columns without degrading from Stage 1 to Stage 2.

V8 Of course, DB2 V8 helps to remedy this problem by allowing mismatched data types to be compared at Stage 1 within data type families. So, for V8, a Java variable length variable can be compared to a DB2 CHAR column at Stage 1.

V8
> **NOTE**
>
> Prior to DB2 V8, it was a somewhat common practice for designers to specify VARCHAR as the data type for *every* column in DB2 tables that were predominantly accessed by Java programs. This is no longer necessary and should be avoided once you have migrated to DB2 Version 8.

Beware of SMALLINT Data   There is no Java host variable equivalent for a SMALLINT data type. For this reason, it is a good idea to specify INTEGER columns in tables that are predominantly accessed by Java instead of SMALLINT—even for very small integers. This allows the Java program to match up Integer host variables with the DB2 INTEGER columns.

V8
> **NOTE**
>
> Once again, DB2 V8 provides relief for this situation because a Java Integer variable can be used with a DB2 SMALLINT column and still be processed at Stage 1 because the conversion is within the data type "family."

Use Dynamic SQL Caching for JDBC   If you are using JDBC programs then you are issuing dynamic SQL statements. Be sure to turn on dynamic SQL caching so that dynamic access paths can be reused when the same SQL statement is executed multiple times. This can greatly enhance the performance of all your dynamic SQL statements, because DB2 can reuse an access path instead of preparing a new one each time the statement is executed.

Of course, for dynamic SQL caching to work the SQL statement must be 100% the same—meaning that the statement must be exactly the same length and there can be no stray or trailing blanks.

Release Your Java Resources   Be sure to release your Java resources as soon as your program no longer requires them. This means you should intelligently close result sets, prepared statements, and callable statements in your code.

Access Only the Columns Required   Although this guideline applies to any DB2 program, it is even more important to follow in your Java programs. This is so because a Java object is created for each column that is retrieved. Therefore, be sure to SELECT only the columns you absolutely require—and never any extras. Each column accessed by your Java program adds overhead and therefore degrades the performance of your application.

Use Procedural Objects to Reduce SQL in Your Java Programs   Consider using triggers, functions, and stored procedures to reduce the amount of SQL in your Java program. Triggers can be used to validate data, functions to transform data, and stored procedures to reduce network traffic.

Use the Appropriate JDBC Driver Type   There are four types of JDBC drivers:

- Type 1—Provided by Sun, this was the first JDBC driver type that was available. It is the slowest and should only be used if no other driver is available for the DBMS (this is not the case for DB2).

- Type 2—Usually provided by the DBMS vendor, this type of driver is vendor-specific and sits on top of the database API.

- Type 3—Similar to Type 2, but no database software is required on the local machine. Useful for Java applets.

- Type 4—A native-protocol Java driver type that talks directly to the database server.

For applets, favor a Type 4 driver as it will give better performance than a Type 3 driver.

For most DB2 applications, favor a Type 2 driver.

Setting the Isolation Level in a Java Program   You can use the SET TRANSACTION ISOLATION LEVEL clause to set the isolation level for a unit of work within an SQLJ program. For Java programs that contain both SQLJ and JDBC connections, setting the isolation level in this way will affect both the SQLJ connection and the JDBC connection. You can change the isolation level only at the beginning of a transaction. Refer to Table 14.3 for a summary of the valid values that you can specify in the SET TRANSACTION ISOLATION LEVEL clause and their equivalent DB2 for z/OS ISOLATION parameter values.

Table 14.3 shows the SQLJ isolation levels and their DB2 for OS/390 and z/OS equivalents.

TABLE 14.3   SQLJ and DB2 Isolation Levels

SET TRANSACTION ISOLATION LEVEL	DB2 ISOLATION Parameter
READ COMMITTED	CS (Cursor Stability)
READ UNCOMMITTED	UR (Uncommitted Read)
REPEATABLE READ	RS (Read Stability)
SERIALIZABLE	RR (Repeatable Read)

Using REXX and DB2

You can also create applications using REXX that access and manipulate DB2 data. REXX is a procedural programming language developed at IBM and used by most mainframe organizations. REXX was designed to make easy the manipulation of the kinds of symbolic objects that people normally deal with such as words and numbers.

> **NOTE**
>
> Although REXX began as an IBM-only language, there is now an ANSI standard for the language. The American National Standard for REXX is called "Programming Language—REXX," and its number is X3.274-1996.

In general, you can code SQL statements in a REXX procedure wherever you can use REXX commands. The only SQL statements that are not supported are

- BEGIN DECLARE SECTION

- DECLARE STATEMENT

- END DECLARE SECTION

- INCLUDE

- SELECT INTO

- WHENEVER

Furthermore, you cannot execute a SELECT, INSERT, UPDATE, or DELETE statement that contains host variables. Instead, you must use parameter markers and then PREPARE the statement as with typical dynamic SQL statements.

Each SQL statement in a REXX procedure must begin with EXECSQL. Following the EXECSQL you must code either an SQL statement enclosed in single or double quotation marks or a REXX variable that contains the SQL statement. If the SQL statement spans multiple lines, follow the REXX rules for statement continuation. For example, you can code

```
EXECSQL ,
"UPDATE DSN8810.EMP" ,
"SET BONUS = 1000" ,
"WHERE EMPNO = '000340'"
```

> **NOTE**
>
> You cannot include REXX comments (/* ... */) or SQL comments (- -) within SQL statements. However, you can include REXX comments anywhere else in the REXX procedure.

When DB2 prepares a REXX procedure that contains SQL statements, DB2 automatically includes an SQL communication area (SQLCA) in the procedure. Do not attempt to use the INCLUDE SQLCA statement to include an SQLCA in a REXX procedure. Remember, INCLUDE is not allowed when using REXX.

If you will be using any of the following SQL statements you will need to code an SQLDA in your REXX procedure:

```
CALL...USING DESCRIPTOR descriptor-name

DESCRIBE statement INTO descriptor-name

DESCRIBE CURSOR host-variable INTO descriptor-name

DESCRIBE INPUT statement INTO descriptor-name

DESCRIBE PROCEDURE host-variable INTO descriptor-name

DESCRIBE TABLE host-variable INTO descriptor-name

EXECUTE...USING DESCRIPTOR descriptor-name

FETCH...USING DESCRIPTOR descriptor-name
```

```
OPEN...USING DESCRIPTOR descriptor-name

PREPARE...INTO descriptor-name
```

A REXX procedure can contain multiple SQLDAs. Once again, though, you cannot use INCLUDE to bring the SQLDA into a REXX procedure.

Before attempting to code a REXX procedure to access DB2, be sure to refer to the IBM documentation for assistance.

REXX Guidelines

Consider these guidelines when building REXX procedures that access DB2.

A REXX Null Is Not a DB2 NULL   As you build REXX procedures that access DB2 data, keep in mind that a REXX null and an SQL NULL are not the same thing. The REXX language has a null string that is a string of length 0 and a null clause that is a clause that contains only blanks and comments.

Recall from Chapter 5 that the SQL NULL is a special value that denotes the absence of a value. Assigning a REXX null to a DB2 column does not make the column a DB2 NULL.

REXX Host Variables   Host variables are not declared in REXX procedures. Instead, when a new variable is needed, you simply use it in a REXX command. As with COBOL host variables, when you use a REXX variable as a host variable in an SQL statement, be sure to precede the variable name with a colon.

REXX and Data Types   All REXX data is string data. Therefore, when a REXX procedure assigns input data to a table column, DB2 converts the data from a string type to the table column type. When a REXX procedure assigns column data to an output variable, DB2 converts the data from the column type to a string type.

When you assign input data to a DB2 table column, you can either let DB2 determine the type that your input data represents, or you can use an SQLDA to tell DB2 the intended type of the input data.

To use the SQLDA to convert the string to an INTEGER, DECIMAL, FLOAT, VARCHAR, or VARGRAPHIC data type, refer to the chart of valid SQLTYPE (SQLDA field) values as shown in Chapter 12 (Table 12.2).

14

CHAPTER **15**

Using DB2 Stored Procedures

In the distant past, DBMS products were designed only to manage and store *data* in an optimal manner. Although this core capability is still required of modern DBMS products, the purview of the DBMS is no longer limited just to data. With the advent of client/server computing and active databases, procedural business logic also is being stored and managed by the DBMS. DB2 is maturing and gaining more functionality. The clear trend is that more and more procedural logic is being stored in the DBMS. DB2 stored procedures enable you to write in-depth application programs and use them to extend the functionality of DB2.

In Chapter 8, "Using DB2 Triggers for Integrity," we examined triggers, one example of business logic that is stored in DB2 databases. Another example of business logic stored in the database is user-defined functions, which we explored in Chapter 4, "Using DB2 User-Defined Functions and Data Types." In this chapter, we will learn about stored procedures including what they are, when to use them, and guidelines for proper implementation.

> **NOTE**
>
> One example of logic being stored in the DBMS is the exit routine. DB2 has supported exit routines for many years, whereas stored procedure (V4), trigger (V6), and UDF (V6) support is more recent.
>
> An exit routine, such as an EDITPROC or VALIDPROC, is coded in Assembler language. This code is then attached to a specific database object and is executed at a specified time, such as when data is inserted or modified. Exit routines have been available in DB2 for a long time; typically, the DBA is responsible for coding and maintaining them. Exit routines, however, are primitive when compared with the procedural logic support provided by a modern RDBMS.

The most popular RDBMS products support additional forms of database-administered procedural logic. Triggers, UDFs, and stored procedures are examples of this phenomenon.

What Is a Stored Procedure?

Stored procedures are specialized programs that are executed under the control of the relational database management system. You can think of stored procedures as similar to other database objects such as tables, views, and indexes because they are managed and controlled by the RDBMS. But you can think of stored procedures as similar to application programs, too, because they are coded using a procedural programming language. Depending on the particular implementation, stored procedures can also physically reside in the DBMS. However, a stored procedure is not "physically" associated with any other object in the database. It can access and/or modify data in one or more tables. Basically, you can think of stored procedures as "programs" that "live" in the RDBMS.

A stored procedure must be directly and explicitly invoked before it can be executed. In other words, stored procedures are not event-driven. Contrast this concept with the concept of triggers, which are event-driven and never explicitly called. Instead, triggers are automatically executed (sometimes referred to as "fired") by the RDBMS as the result of an action. Stored procedures are never automatically invoked.

DB2 has provided stored procedure support since V4, and IBM continues to enhance the functionality of stored procedures with each successive DB2 release. The major motivating reason for stored procedure support is to move SQL code off the client and on the database server. Implementing stored procedures can result in less overhead than alternative development methods because one client request can invoke multiple SQL statements.

DB2's Stored Procedure Implementation

DB2's implementation of stored procedures is a bit different from the stored procedure support available using other DBMS products. For example, both Microsoft SQL Server and Oracle require you to code stored procedures using procedural extensions to SQL: Microsoft provides Transact-SQL, and Oracle provides PL/SQL. DB2, on the other hand, enables you to write stored procedures using traditional programming languages. You can use any LE/370-supported language to code stored procedures. The supported languages are Assembler, C, C++, COBOL, OO COBOL, and PL/I. Additionally, IBM provides support for REXX and Java stored procedures, as well as their own extended SQL Procedure Language (procedural SQL) for developing stored procedures. A description of the procedural SQL option is provided in the "Procedural SQL" section later in this chapter.

> **NOTE**
>
> The language of the calling program can be different from the language used to write the stored procedure. For example, a COBOL program can CALL a C stored procedure.

V7 DB2 stored procedures can issue both static and dynamic SQL statements with the exception SET CURRENT SQLID. As of V7, stored procedures can issue COMMIT and ROLLBACK statements. But keep in mind that these statements apply to the entire unit of work, not just the stored procedure code. A COMMIT in a stored procedure will commit all of the work done in the stored procedure, as well as all of the work done in the calling program since the last COMMIT. The same goes for ROLLBACK. However, COMMIT and ROLLBACK cannot be issued in a stored procedure under the following conditions:

- When the stored procedure is called by a trigger or user-defined function

- When the stored procedure is called by a client that uses two-phase COMMIT processing

- When the client program uses a type-2 connection to connect to the remote server that houses the stored procedure

---

CAUTION

Because it will become difficult to manage and control what exactly is being committed (or rolled back), it is best not to issue COMMIT and ROLLBACK statements in your stored procedures if you can avoid it.

Additionally, a stored procedure can issue DB2 commands and IFI (Instrumentation Facility Interface) calls. Stored procedures can access flat files, VSAM files, and other files, as well as DB2 tables. Additionally, stored procedures can access resources in CICS, IMS, and other MVS address spaces, but no commit coordination exists between DB2 and the other resources.

NOTE

DB2 stored procedures can connect to an IMS DBCTL or IMS DB/DC system using IMS Open Database Access (ODBA) support. The stored procedure can issue DL/I calls to access IMS databases. IMS ODBA supports the use of OS/390 RRSAF for syncpoint control of DB2 and IMS resources. Stored procedures that use ODBA can run only in WLM-established stored procedures address spaces, not a DB2-established address space.

DB2 stored procedures run under the control of the Work Load Manager (WLM). WLM effectively fences off user-developed code from running in DB2 address spaces with IBM-developed code. This layer of protection is useful to prohibit a stored procedure from causing an entire DB2 subsystem to fail.

NOTE

When stored procedures were first introduced, a DB2-managed address space known as the *stored procedure address space*, or SPAS for short, was used to fence stored procedures from DB2. Although the SPAS is still supported as of V8, IBM is phasing it out and it will be eliminated completely in a future version of DB2. Start migrating your DB2-managed stored procedures from the SPAS to WLM as soon as possible.

To further clarify, you cannot create a DB2-managed stored procedure in V8. V8 only tolerates existing DB2 managed stored procedures. Even altering an existing SP will force it to be WLM managed.

Why Use Stored Procedures?

DB2 stored procedures have many potentially time-saving and useful applications. The major uses can be broken down into six categories: reuseability, consistency, data integrity, maintenance, performance, and security, as described here.

- *Reuseability*—The predominant reason for using stored procedures is to promote code reuseability. Instead of replicating code on multiple servers and in multiple programs, stored procedures allow code to reside in a single place—the database server. Stored procedures then can be called from client programs to access DB2 data. This approach is preferable to cannibalizing sections of program code for each new application system being developed. By developing a stored procedure, you can invoke the logic from multiple processes as needed, instead of rewriting it directly into each new process every time the code is required. When they are implemented wisely, stored procedures are useful for reducing the overall code maintenance effort. Because the stored procedure exists in one place, you can make changes quickly without propagating the change to multiple applications or workstations.

- *Consistency*—An additional benefit of stored procedures is increased consistency. If every user with the same requirements calls the same stored procedures, the DBA can be assured that everyone is running the same code. If each user uses his or her own individual, separate code, no assurance can be given that the same logic is being used by everyone. In fact, you can be almost certain that inconsistencies will occur.

- *Maintenance*—Stored procedures are particularly useful for reducing the overall code maintenance effort. Because the stored procedure exists in one place, you can make changes quickly without propagating the change to multiple workstations.

- *Data Integrity*—Additionally, you can code stored procedures to support database integrity constraints. You can code column validation routines into stored procedures, which are called every time an attempt is made to modify the column data. Of course, these routines catch only planned changes that are issued through applications that use the stored procedure. Ad hoc changes are not checked. Triggers provide better capabilities for enforcing data integrity constraints, but a trigger can be coded to CALL a stored procedure.

- *Performance*—Another common reason to employ stored procedures is to enhance performance. In a client/server environment, stored procedures can reduce network traffic because multiple SQL statements can be invoked with a single execution of a procedure instead of sending multiple requests across the communication lines. The diagram in Figure 15.1 depicts a call to a DB2 stored procedure. The passing of SQL and results occurs within the SPAS, instead of over the network as would be necessary without the stored procedure. Only two network requests are required: one to request that the stored procedure be run and one to pass the results back to the calling agent.

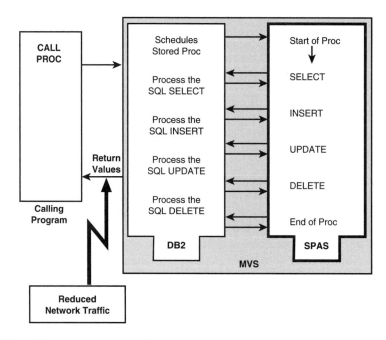

FIGURE 15.1   Calling a stored procedure.

- *Security*—You can use stored procedures to implement and simplify data security requirements. If a given group of users requires access to specific data items, you can develop a stored procedure that returns only those specific data items. You can then grant access to call the stored procedure to those users without giving them any additional authorization to the underlying objects accessed within the body of the stored procedure. Furthermore, it is more difficult to tamper with a DB2 package on the mainframe than it would be to modify DLL code on a workstation.

Stored procedures provide a myriad of other useful benefits including:

- *Flexibility*—Stored procedures can issue both static and dynamic SQL statements and access DB2 and non-DB2 data.

- *Ease of Training*—DB2 stored procedures can be written in traditional programming languages that application programmers already know, or in procedural SQL that is easier for DBAs to learn and utilize.

- *DBMS Protection*—Stored procedures run in a separate address space from the database engine, thereby eliminating the possibility of users corrupting the DBMS installation.

Implementing DB2 Stored Procedures

Now that you understand what stored procedures are and why you would want to use them, you're ready to investigate how to implement stored procedures in DB2.

Developing a Stored Procedure

You can design and develop stored procedures in a similar manner to the way you develop any other application program. However, stored procedures have some special design requirements that you need to understand prior to developing them: using LE/370, coding parameters, returning result sets, and changing the program preparation procedure.

Using LE/370

You must develop stored procedures using an LE/370 language. LE/370 is mandatory for the use of stored procedures. LE/370 provides a common runtime environment for multiple, disparate programming languages. The runtime services available to LE/370 include error handling, storage management, and debugging. The benefit to DB2 is that the runtime services are the same for every programming language used to deploy stored procedures.

Coding Parameters

Parameters are essential to the effective use of stored procedures. Parameters allow data to be sent to and received from a stored procedure.

Each stored procedure has a parameter list associated with it. This list must be static and predefined. The parameter list defines the data type, size, and disposition (output, input, or both) of each parameter. The complete process of registering stored procedures, including parameter lists, is outlined in the upcoming section "Registering Stored Procedures."

You must define the parameters to the stored procedure using the appropriate technique for the language you're using. For COBOL programs, you must define parameters in the LINKAGE SECTION. Refer to Listing 15.1 for a sample stored procedure shell using COBOL.

LISTING 15.1   COBOL Stored Procedure Shell

```
Must set up IDENTIFICATION and
    ENVIRONMENT DIVISIONS.

DATA DIVISION.
LINKAGE SECTION.
***********************************************************
**        PARAMETERS DEFINED IN LINKAGE SECTION        **
***********************************************************
01  IN-PARM        PIC X(20).
01  OUT-PARM       PIC X(30).


***********************************************************
** INDICATOR VARIABLES USED ONLY IF PARMS CAN BE NULL **
***********************************************************
01  NULL-INDVARS.
    05  INDVAR-1   PIC S9(4) COMP.
    05  INDVAR-2   PIC S9(4) COMP.

WORKING-STORAGE SECTION.

    Must declare all necessary variables.
```

15

LISTING 15.1   Continued

```
**********************************************************
**   PARAMETERS SPECIFIED TO THE PROCEDURE DIVISION   **
**********************************************************
PROCEDURE DIVISION USING PARM-A, PARM-B, NULL-INDVARS.

MAIN-PARAGRAPH.
      .
      .
      .
    IF INDVAR-1 < 0
        if input parameter is null perform an error-routine
      .
      .
      .
    MOVE "SOME VALUE" TO OUT-PARM.
    MOVE ZERO TO INDVAR-2.
PROGRAM-END.
    GOBACK.
```

Be sure to test all input parameters that can be null. If the input parameter is null, you must code the program to handle that situation. Likewise, for output parameters that can be null, be sure to set the null indicator variable to zero if not null or -1 if null.

Additionally, be sure to set all input parameters to an appropriate value in the calling program prior to issuing the CALL to the stored procedure. The value of the stored procedure parameters is set at the time of the procedure CALL.

Nesting Stored Procedure Calls

Prior to DB2 V6, a stored procedure could not issue the CALL statement, thereby forbidding one stored procedure to call another stored procedure. This limitation is removed for DB2 V6 and above.

When one stored procedure calls another stored procedure, it is referred to as a *nested procedure call*. DB2 supports 16 levels of nesting. When more than 16 levels of nesting are attempted a –746 SQLCODE is returned (SQLSTATE 57053).

The nesting level includes calls to stored procedure, as well as trigger and user-defined function invocations. Nesting can occur within a single DB2 subsystem or when a stored procedure or user-defined function is invoked at a remote server. If a stored procedure returns any query result sets, the result sets are returned to the caller of the stored procedure.

CAUTION

DB2 restricts certain procedures from being called from another stored procedure, trigger, or UDF. A stored procedure, UDF, or trigger cannot call a stored procedure that is defined with the COMMIT ON RETURN attribute. Additionally, a stored procedure can CALL another stored procedure only if both stored procedures execute in the same type of address space. In other words, they must both execute in a DB2-established address space (SPAS) or both execute in a WLM-established address space.

If the CALL statement is nested, the result sets generated by the stored procedure are visible only to the program that is at the previous nesting level. Figure 15.2 depicts three levels of nested procedure calls. The results set returned from PROCZ is only available to PROCY. The calling program and PROCX have no access to the result sets returned from PROCX.

Furthermore, the result sets from PROCY would be available only to PROCX, and the result sets from PROCX would be available to the calling program.

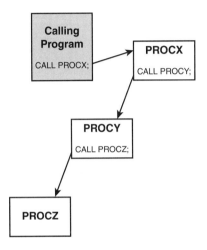

FIGURE 15.2   Stored procedure nesting.

Returning Result Sets

A stored procedure can return multiple row result sets back to the calling program. If you enable result sets to be returned, stored procedures become more efficient and effective. Benefits include the following:

- Reduced network traffic, because an entire result set requires only a single network request

- Better application design, because stored procedures do not need to loop artificially through cursors to return data one row at a time

- Better flexibility, because more work can be done using stored procedures

Figure 15.3 shows the impact of result sets on stored procedure processing.

CAUTION

Stored procedure result sets can only be returned to the program that called the stored procedure. For example, if PRG1 calls SP1 and SP1 calls SP2, SP2 cannot return a result set to PRG1.

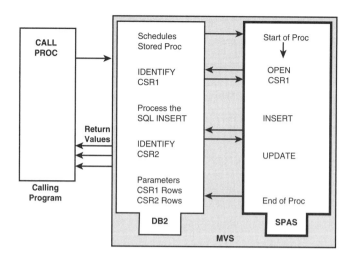

FIGURE 15.3 A stored procedure returning result sets.

To implement stored procedures that return result sets, you must perform several steps. The first step is to ensure that the RESULT_SETS parameter is specified correctly for the stored procedure. The RESULT_SETS parameter is specified on the CREATE or ALTER PROCEDURE statement and indicates the maximum number of result sets that can be returned by the stored procedure. To enable the stored procedure to return result sets, you must set the RESULTS SETs parameter to a value greater than 0.

The second step is to specify the WITH RETURN clause on each OPEN cursor statement for which result sets are to be returned. The cursors must not be closed by the stored procedure. When the stored procedure ends, the result sets are returned to the calling program. This can cause trouble if you try to issue a COMMIT in the stored procedure and you are not using WITH HOLD or you try to issue a ROLLBACK.

The last step is coding the calling program to accept result sets from the stored procedure. Refer to Figure 15.4 to view the interaction of a stored procedure with a calling program that accepts result sets. The first step is to declare a result set locator variable. Next, the calling program issues the CALL to execute the stored procedure. The stored procedure executes, opening a cursor that specifies the WITH RETURN clause. The stored procedure ends without closing the cursor, causing DB2 to return the result set automatically to the calling program. The calling program issues the ASSOCIATE LOCATOR statement to assign a value to the result set locator that was previously defined. The calling program then issues the ALLOCATE CURSOR statement to associate the query with the result set. Finally, the program can execute a loop to FETCH the rows of the result set.

The preceding outlines the tasks necessary when the calling program knows what result sets can be returned by the stored procedure it is calling. However, special SQL statements—DESCRIBE PROCEDURE and DESCRIBE CURSOR—are available when the calling program does not know in advance the number of result sets that a stored procedure can return.

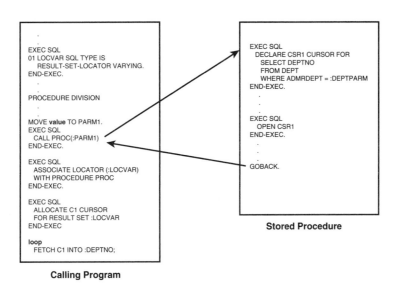

```
EXEC SQL
01 LOCVAR SQL TYPE IS
      RESULT-SET-LOCATOR VARYING.
END-EXEC.
      .
      .
PROCEDURE DIVISION
      .
      .
MOVE value TO PARM1.
EXEC SQL
      CALL PROC(:PARM1)
END-EXEC.

EXEC SQL
      ASSOCIATE LOCATOR (:LOCVAR)
      WITH PROCEDURE PROC
END-EXEC.

EXEC SQL
      ALLOCATE C1 CURSOR
      FOR RESULT SET :LOCVAR
END-EXEC

loop
      FETCH C1 INTO :DEPTNO;
```

Calling Program

```
EXEC SQL
      DECLARE CSR1 CURSOR FOR
      SELECT DEPTNO
      FROM DEPT
      WHERE ADMRDEPT = :DEPTPARM
END-EXEC.
      .
      .
EXEC SQL
      OPEN CSR1
END-EXEC.
      .
      .
GOBACK.
```

Stored Procedure

FIGURE 15.4   Coding to return a result set.

The DESCRIBE PROCEDURE statement returns the following information for a stored procedure that has already been called. The information, which is returned to the SQLDA, includes

- The number of result sets to be returned

- The result set locator value for each result set

- The name of the SQL cursor used by the stored procedure for each result set

The DESCRIBE CURSOR statement also returns information to the SQLDA, but it describes the columns accessed by the cursor.

Preparing Stored Procedure Programs

The program preparation process for stored procedures is essentially the same as for any program that accesses DB2. The program code must be precompiled, compiled, and then link-edited into an executable form. The DBRM must be bound into a package; no plan is required for the stored procedure.

When the program is link-edited, the LE/370 program library must be included. Likewise, the program for the stored procedure must link-edit either DSNALI (for CAF) or DSNRLI (for RRSAF), depending on which attachment facility is to be used. Of course, you also can link-edit the stored procedure program to run in multiple environments if you choose.

No impact to the program preparation process is required for the calling program; you should use normal DB2 program preparation steps.

15

> **NOTE**
>
> A plan is still required for the calling program. Only the stored procedure (*the called program*) does not require a plan.
>
> The package for the stored procedure does not have to be bound in the package list of the calling program.

Creating Stored Procedures

As of DB2 V6, stored procedures are registered and managed within DB2 like other DB2 objects, using standard DDL statements—ALTER, CREATE, and DROP. After a stored procedure has been developed and is ready to be tested, the stored procedure must be created in the DB2 subsystem.

```
CREATE PROCEDURE SYSPROC.PROCNAME(INOUT CHAR(20))
    LANGUAGE COBOL
    EXTERNAL NAME LOADNAME
    PARAMETER STYLE GENERAL
    NOT DETERMINISTIC
    MODIFIES SQL DATA
    WLM ENVIRONMENT WLMNAME
    STAY RESIDENT YES
    RESULT SETS 1;
```

This statement creates a stored procedure named PROCNAME in the SYSPROC schema using an external load module name of LOADNAME. The stored procedure is written in COBOL and runs under the control of WLM. It returns one result set.

The ALTER statement can be used to change most characteristics of the stored procedure (except the stored procedure name, its schema, and parameters). The stored procedure can be removed from the DB2 subsystem using the DROP statement.

Information about the stored procedures defined to DB2 is stored in the SYSIBM.SYSROUTINES table in the DB2 Catalog. This table is used to store information about stored procedures and user-defined functions. When ALTER, CREATE, and DROP statements are issued for those objects the structural definition of those objects is stored in SYSIBM.SYSROUTINES. When parameters are used, the parm lists are stored in SYSIBM.SYSPARMS.

> **NOTE**
>
> Prior to DB2 V6, you had to manually register stored procedures in the DB2 Catalog using SQL. Because in past releases of DB2 stored procedures were not created within DB2, nor were they created using DDL, the DBA had to use SQL INSERT statements to populate a DB2 Catalog table, SYSIBM.SYSPROCEDURES, that contained the metadata for the stored procedure.
>
> The following SQL provides an example of an INSERT to register a stored procedure named PROCNAME:
>
> ```
> INSERT INTO SYSIBM.SYSPROCEDURES
>     (PROCEDURE, AUTHID, LUNAME, LOADMOD, LINKAGE,
>      COLLID, LANGUAGE, ASUTIME, STAYRESIDENT,
>      IBMREQD, RUNOPTS, PARMLIST, RESULT_SETS,
> ```

```
    WLM_ENV, PGM_TYPE, EXTERNAL_SECURITY,
    COMMIT_ON_RETURN)
VALUES
    ('PROCNAME', ' ', ' ', 'LOADNAME', ' ',
    'COLL0001', 'COBOL', 0, 'Y',
    'N', ' ', 'NAME CHAR(20) INOUT', 1,
    ' ', 'M', 'N', 'N');
```

Configuring Parameter Lists

The parameters to be used by DB2 stored procedures must be specified in parentheses after the procedure name in the CREATE PROCEDURE statement. You can define three types of parameters:

- IN—An input parameter

- OUT—An output parameter

- INOUT—A parameter that is used for both input and output

The type of parameter must be predetermined and cannot be changed without dropping and re-creating the stored procedure.

Consider, for example, a stored procedure with three parameters: an employee number, bonus, and total compensation. The stored procedure calculates the total compensation for a specified employee and returns it to the calling program. The bonus parameter is either set to 0 (in which case, no additional processing is performed) or to a percentage that the employee bonus is to be increased. If total compensation is greater than $100,000, the bonus percentage is cut in half. In this case, you could code the PARMLIST as follows:

CREATE PROCEDURE PROCNAME(IN EMPNO CHAR(6), INOUT BONUS DEC(5,2), OUT COMPNSTN DEC(9,2)...

This way, the stored procedure receives the employee number; receives, modifies, and then returns the bonus; and returns the total compensation.

Providing names for the parameters is optional.

An additional consideration when you're coding parameters for stored procedures is whether the parameters can be null. You use the PARAMETER STYLE parameter to specify nullability. You have three choices:

- DB2SQL—In addition to the parameters on the CALL statement, the following are also passed to the stored procedure: a null indicator for each parameter, the SQLSTATE to be returned to DB2, the qualified name of the stored procedure, the specific name of the stored procedure, and a SQL diagnostic string to be returned to DB2.

- GENERAL—Only the parameters on the CALL statement are passed to the stored procedure, and the parameters are not allowed to be null.

- GENERAL WITH NULLS—In addition to the parameters on the CALL statement, an array of null indicators is passed to the stored procedure for each of the parameters on the CALL statement that enables the stored procedure to accept or return null parameter values.

15

Refer to Listing 15.1 for an example of the indicator variables being passed to the stored procedure as an array.

Managing Stored Procedures

Whether or not programs can call a stored procedure is controlled using commands to start and stop the stored procedure. Of course, the program must have been granted the appropriate privileges to run the stored procedure even if it has been started.

The -START PROCEDURE command activates a stored procedure that is stopped or refreshes one that is cached. When a stored procedure is first created, you will not need to start the procedure before it can be called. DB2 will automatically activate the new procedure the first time it is referenced by a CALL statement. To issue -START PROCEDURE simply reference the procedure name to be started as follows:

```
-START PROCEDURE(procedure name)
```

Similarly, the -STOP PROCEDURE command prevents DB2 from accepting SQL CALL statements for stored procedures:

```
-STOP PROCEDURE(procedure name) ACTION(REJECT | QUEUE)
```

When stopping stored procedures you can specify how CALL statements that are issued while the procedure is stopped are to be treated. This is accomplished with the ACTION parameter of the -STOP PROCEDURE command. There are two options:

- QUEUE—Queues the requested stored procedure CALL until either the stored procedure is started again, or you exceed your installation timeout value

- REJECT—Rejects the requested stored procedure CALL

To execute the -START and -STOP PROCEDURE commands, you must be authorized as either the owner of the stored procedure, or as SYSOPR, SYSCTRL, or SYSADM.

Another part of management is monitoring. You can use the DISPLAY command to monitor the status of stored procedures:

```
-DISPLAY PROCEDURE(procedure name)
```

This command shows

- Whether the named procedure is currently started or stopped

- How many requests are currently executing

- The high water mark for concurrently running requests

- How many requests are currently queued

- How many times a request has timed out

Controlling Failures

V7 Stored procedures can be difficult to manage when problems occur in production systems. It can be particularly problematic to manage stored procedure availability when problems cause stored procedures to abend. Do you really want a single program failure to make the stored procedure unavailable? As of DB2 V7, controlling stored procedure failures becomes somewhat easier.

The DSNZPARM value STORMXAB (on installation panel DSNTIPX) can be set to specify a value for the maximum abend. You can use this value to indicate the number of times a stored procedure (or UDF) is allowed to terminate abnormally before it is stopped. This parameter is subsystem-wide—it applies to all stored procedures and UDFs the same across the entire DB2 subsystem.

V8 As of DB2 V8, you gain further control. The parameter allows you to specify a maximum number of failures value for each stored procedure or UDF. This brings the control to each individual object, instead of at the DB2 subsystem level.

The options available include

STOP AFTER *n* FAILURES—The stored procedure (or UDF) will be stopped only after *n* failures have occurred. The value *n* can range from 1 to 32,767.

STOP AFTER SYSTEM DEFAULT FAILURES—The stored procedure (or UDF) will be stopped when it reaches the number of abnormal terminations specified in the STORMXAB DSNZPARM. This is the default.

CONTINUE AFTER FAILURE—The stored procedure (or UDF) is never placed in a stopped state, unless you explicitly use the -STOP PROCEDURE command.

> **CAUTION**
>
> The preceding parameters cannot be used for sourced functions or SQL scalar functions.
>
> Furthermore, after altering the stored procedure (or UDF) to specify one of these parameters, you must first STOP and then START the corresponding stored procedure or UDF to activate the new settings.

Executing a Stored Procedure

To run a stored procedure, you must explicitly issue a CALL statement. For example, the following statement calls a stored procedure named SAMPLE, sending a literal string as a parameter:

```
EXEC SQL
    CALL SAMPLE('ABC')
END-EXEC.
```

15

To issue a CALL statement for a stored procedure requires the EXECUTE privilege on the stored procedure, as well as on the stored procedure package and packages (other than for UDFs and triggers) that run under the stored procedure.

DB2 runs stored procedure code isolated from the core DB2 code. This is done to ensure that a rogue or buggy stored procedure does not crash DB2. There are two ways that DB2 isolates stored procedures:

- In a DB2-managed stored procedure address space (SPAS)
- Using Work Load Manager (WLM)

Using a SPAS to run stored procedures was the first method used by DB2 and it continues to be completely supported through V7. However, there is only one SPAS and your management options are limited when choosing this method. Furthermore, the SPAS is destined for the scrap heap—as we will discuss in a moment.

As of DB2 V5 and subsequent releases, you can use multiple stored procedure address spaces. Doing so requires the use of the z/OS Workload Manager (WLM). Running stored procedures in the WLM allows you to isolate code in separate address spaces based on the type of processing being performed. For example, OLTP stored procedures can be separated from data warehousing stored procedures. In this manner you can create an environment with multiple physical address spaces for stored procedures executing at the same dispatching priority as the calling program.

What Is Workload Manager?

The z/OS Workload Manager, or WLM, is used to implement workload management for your mainframe system. The purpose of workload management is to match the available system resources with the demands of z/OS components (such as CICS, batch, TSO, and so on). WLM will balance the work across available processors so as to most effectively utilize the resources of the machine.

The goal is for z/OS to distribute workload automatically to achieve the desired response time, such as described in Service Level Agreements (SLAs). WLM works to distribute work without over-committing resources while at the same time attempting to maximize system throughput.

WLM was introduced as a component of MVS/ESA V5. From this release onward, MVS can run in either "compatibility mode" or "goal mode," at the discretion of the installation. When in goal mode, WLM allows more effective use of a single system, because resource adjustment is automatic. WLM in goal mode is required for DB2 V8.

Using WLM to control stored procedures has the following benefits:

- It allows the creation of multiple environments to segregate stored procedures by processing type.
- It isolates stored procedures by address space. (If a stored procedure bug brings down one address space, others are still available.)
- It provides two-phase commit for non-SQL resources using RRSAF.

- It allows individual MVS dispatching priorities.

- It enables RACF control over access to non-SQL resources.

V8 Furthermore, as of DB2 V8, managing WLM-managed stored procedures is made easier because DB2 can exploit proactive WLM administration functionality. Work Load Manager and System Resource Manager can analyze resource utilization and recommend changes in the number of tasks operating inside a WLM-managed stored procedure address space. This helps to make the environment more self-managing.

For DB2 V7 and before, whenever the number of TCBs running in a WLM-managed stored procedure address space exceeded the value of NUMTCB a new WLM address space will be started. But as of V8, the value specified in NUMTCB is regarded as a maximum limit. WLM will determine the actual number of TCBs to run inside the WLM-managed address space based on resource usage.

> **NOTE**
>
> Consider specifying a higher number for NUMTCB after you move to V8 to allow WLM some flexibility in choosing the number of tasks.

> **CAUTION**
>
> Certain stored procedures require NUMTCB to be set to 1. The utility stored procedure provided with DB2, DSNUTILS, is an example of such a stored procedure. REXX stored procedures have to have a NUMTCB of 1.

V8 With DB2 Version 8, IBM has begun to remove support for DB2-managed stored procedures. All new stored procedures must be WLM-managed. This means that once you move to V8, each SPAS must be established using the z/OS Workload Manager. No new stored procedures can be created without specifying a WLM environment.

Stored procedures created prior to V8 without a WLM environment will still run correctly and they can be altered using ALTER PROCEDURE. However, if the stored procedure is dropped you cannot re-CREATE it without changing it to a WLM-managed stored procedure.

What Happens When a Stored Procedure Is Called?

To execute a stored procedure, a program must issue the SQL CALL statement. When the CALL is issued, the name of the stored procedure, its schema name, and its list of parameters are sent to DB2. DB2 searches SYSIBM.SYSROUTINES for the appropriate row that defines the stored procedure to be executed. If the row is not found, the stored procedure does not run.

If the row is found, DB2 retrieves the pertinent information to allow the stored procedure to execute, including the actual load module. DB2 then finds a TCB to use for the stored procedure in the appropriate SPAS (either WLM- or DB2-managed) and indicates to the SPAS that the stored procedure is to be executed. The SPAS reuses the thread of the calling program to run the stored procedure. The stored procedure runs, assigns values to input/output and output parameters, and returns control to the calling program.

The calling program receives the input/output and output parameters and continues processing. The entire processing within the stored procedure is within the same unit of work as the CALL in the calling program. Locks acquired within the stored procedure continue to be held until released by the calling program (with a COMMIT or ROLLBACK).

Built-In Stored Procedures

V7 DB2 V7 ships three built-in stored procedures to support Java. DB2 V7 also ships a new built-in schema, SQLJ, which contains these built-in procedures.

The three built-in procs are used to install JAR files into DB2. They are:

- SQLJ.INSTALL_JAR—Installs a JAR file into DB2.

- SQLJ.REPLACE_JAR—Replaces a JAR file in DB2 with a new file.

- SQLJ.REMOVE_JAR—Removes a previously installed JAR file from DB2.

Stored Procedure Guidelines

On the surface, stored procedures appear to be simple and highly effective new devices for enabling better application performance, enhancing database administration, and promoting code reuseability. However, as with every DB2 feature, you can find good and bad ways to proceed with implementing stored procedures. Keep the following guidelines in mind as you develop stored procedures at your shop.

V8 **Exercise Control Over Stored Procedure Stopping**   Use the FAILURE parameters when creating stored procedures to explicitly control how DB2 should treat each stored procedure when failures occur. By specifying the most appropriate value for an individual routine, you can let some routines continue to be invoked for development and debugging, and stop other routines for maintenance before they cause problems in a production environment.

Recall that the available options that can be specified using CREATE or ALTER PROCEDURE are: STOP AFTER FAILURE, STOP AFTER n FAILURES, and CONTINUE AFTER FAILURE.

Minimize Nested Procedure Calls   When a procedure calls another procedure, the ensuing structure is called a *nested procedure*. Nested procedures are difficult to test and modify. Furthermore, when one procedure calls another, the likelihood of reuse decreases because the complexity increases.

However, in some cases, the benefits of nesting procedures can outweigh the problems. If you decide to nest procedure calls, be sure to analyze the number of nested stored procedures, triggers, and user-defined functions that can be executed for any given SQL statement and ensure that the limit of 16 levels of nesting is not exceeded.

Consider Using Subprograms   A stored procedure can call another program using the facilities of the programming language. The program being called cannot be a stored procedure, though. The use of subprograms enables better program reuse.

If you use subprograms, be sure to document their use within the stored procedure that calls the subprogram. The call statements used to execute the subprogram might be confused with the SQL CALL statement used to execute a stored procedure unless the program makes liberal use of comments.

Plan Stored Procedure Implementation   Design and implement only useful stored procedures. By *useful*, I mean only those stored procedures that support a business rule and are robust enough to perform a complete task without being too small to be trivial (a two-line procedure) or too large to be understood (a thousand-line procedure that performs every customer function known to the organization). To be useful, a stored procedure must

- Perform one task and perform it very well

- Correspond to a useful business function

- Be documented (including a description of the input, output, and the process)

Specify Atomic Parameters   Always specify parameters at an atomic level. In other words, every stored procedure parameter must be complete and non-divisible. For example, use

```
(IN FNAME CHAR(20), IN LNAME CHAR(30))
```

instead of

```
(IN FULLNAME CHAR(50))
```

When you code parameters as non-atomic variable blocks, the stored procedure logic must parse the block. If changes occur to the data causing lengths or data type to change, procedures using atomic parameters are easier to modify and test.

Learn LE/370   You must write DB2 stored procedures using an LE/370 language. You therefore cannot use VS COBOL II to code stored procedures.

However, stored procedures can be called from any DB2-compatible programming language (even non-LE/370 languages).

Consider Using CODE/370   IBM offers CODE/370, an integrated toolset consisting of editing, compilation, and debugging tools. Without a tool such as CODE/370, testing and debugging DB2 stored procedures can be difficult. Both mainframe and workstation interfaces are available for CODE/370.

Use Stored Procedures for Internal DBA Tools   If your shop has technical DBAs who like to code their own administration tools performance monitoring applications, consider using stored procedures to issue DB2 commands and access trace records using IFI (Instrumentation Facility Interface). You can develop generalized procedures that are maintained by the DBA and accessed by multiple programs to start, stop, and display database objects or analyze IFCIDs and display performance details.

Use Appropriate Data Types for Parameters   Make sure that the calling program and the stored procedure use the same data type and length for each parameter. DB2 converts compatible data types, but by using the same data types and lengths, you can ensure efficient and effective execution.

You can use user-defined distinct types for stored procedure parameters.

Do Not Use LONG VARCHAR **and** LONG VARGRAPHIC **Parameters**   When defining parameters to be used in your stored procedures, you can use the same built-in and user-defined data types as for the CREATE TABLE statement, except for LONG VARCHAR and LONG VARGRAPHIC data types. Instead, specify the parameter as a VARCHAR or VARGRAPHIC with an explicit length.

Consider Using Output Parameters for the SQLCA   The SQLCA information for SQL statements executed in stored procedures is not returned to the calling program. Consider using output parameters to send SQLCA information to the calling program. This way, you can enable the calling program to determine the success or failure of SQL, as well as possibly provide error resolution information.

A separate output parameter is required for each SQL statement in the stored procedure (because the SQLCA of the stored procedure changes for each SQL statement execution).

Use the Appropriate PARAMETER STYLE   When coding a stored procedure with parameters, use the PARAMETER STYLE option to identify the convention to be used to pass parameters to the stored procedure. The following options are available:

- DB2SQL—Indicates that the following arguments are passed to the stored procedure in addition to the parameters: a null indicator for each parameter, the SQLSTATE, the qualified and specific name of the stored procedure, and the SQL diagnostic string.

- GENERAL—Indicates that only the parameters are passed to the stored procedure, and the parameters cannot be null.

- GENERAL WITH NULLS—Indicates that in addition to the parameters being passed, an additional argument is passed that contains a vector of null indicators for each parameter.

- JAVA—Indicates that the stored procedure is a Java procedure and should follow Java conventions for parameter passing.

> **CAUTION**
>
> You cannot specify PARAMETER STYLE DB2SQL with a REXX stored procedure.

Consider Using Temporary Tables   Stored procedures can make excellent use of temporary tables to store intermediate results. Consider the following uses:

- The stored procedure can INSERT data into a temporary table. A cursor can then be opened for the table with the results sent back to the calling program.

- Because stored procedures can access non-DB2 resources, data from IMS or IDMS can be accessed and stored in a temporary table. That data can then be accessed by the stored procedure using SQL, effectively enabling DB2 to perform joins with non-DB2 data sources such as IMS or IDMS.

Promote Reuseability   As I mentioned earlier, the predominant reason for using stored procedures is to increase reuseability. By reusing components—in this case, stored procedures—you can write applications more quickly using code that is already developed, tested, and working.

However noble the goal of reuseable components, though, simply mandating the use of stored procedures does not ensure that goal. Documentation and management support (perhaps coercion) are necessary to ensure successful reuse. The basic maxim applies: "How can I reuse it if I don't know it exists or don't know what it does?"

Make Stored Procedures Reentrant   Stored procedures perform better if they are prepared to be reentrant. When a stored procedure is reentrant, a single copy of the stored procedure is used by many clients. A reentrant stored procedure does not have to be loaded into storage every time it is called. Compiling and link-editing your programs as reentrant reduces the amount of virtual storage required for the stored procedure address space. You can use the RENT compiler option to make a COBOL stored procedure reentrant. Link-edit the program as reentrant and reuseable.

Furthermore, to make a reentrant stored procedure remain resident in storage, specify the STAY RESIDENT YES option in your CREATE or ALTER PROCEDURE statement.

> **NOTE**
>
> For details on compiling programs coded in languages other than COBOL to be reentrant, refer to the appropriate manual for the programming language you are using.

Make Stored Procedures Resident   Better use of system resources occurs if stored procedures are made reuseable and remain resident in the SPAS. Specify the STAY RESIDENT parameter when creating stored procedures, and avoid the NOREUS link-edit option. A program must be reentrant before it can be specified to stay resident. Therefore, the general recommendation is to make all stored procedures reentrant, reuseable, and resident.

Accurately Specify DETERMINISTIC or NOT DETERMINISTIC   Be sure to specify accurately whether the stored procedure will always return the same result for identical input arguments. If the stored procedure always returns the same result for identical input arguments, it is DETERMINISTIC. If not, the stored procedure should be identified as NOT DETERMINISTIC. Any stored procedure that relies on external data sources that can change should be specified as NOT DETERMINISTIC. Other examples of stored procedures that are NOT DETERMINISTIC include stored procedures that contain SQL SELECT, INSERT, UPDATE, or DELETE statements or a random number generator.

DB2 will not check to ensure that the [NOT] DETERMINISTIC parameter is specified appropriately. You must specify it accurately when you CREATE (or ALTER) the stored procedure.

Specifying Collection IDs   A specific collection ID can be assigned to a stored procedure using the COLLID parameter of the CREATE PROCEDURE statement. If NO COLLID is specified, the collection ID defaults to that of the package of the calling program. This result can be confusing. Explicitly specifying the collection ID is usually the better alternative. The default is NO COLLID.

Returning Column Names from Stored Procedure Results Sets   If the SELECT statements in your stored procedure are static, the DESCSTAT subsystem parameter must be turned on to retrieve column names from your stored procedure result sets. Set the subsystem parameter on the host DB2 where the procedure was compiled. After setting this parameter, you will have to REBIND your stored procedure packages.

If the SELECT statements inside of the stored procedure are dynamic, the result-set column names should be returned automatically.

The Procedural DBA

To implement and manage DB2 stored procedures effectively, a new type of DBA—a Procedural DBA—must be created. The reasoning behind the Procedural DBA and the roles and responsibilities required of Procedural DBAs can be found in Chapter 16, "The Procedural DBA."

Procedural SQL

The major difference between DB2's stored procedure support and the other RDBMS vendors is the manner in which the stored procedure is coded. As I mentioned at the beginning of this chapter, other popular RDBMS products require procedural dialects of SQL for stored procedure creation. Oracle uses PL/SQL and Sybase, and Microsoft SQL Server uses Transact SQL. Each of these languages is proprietary, and they cannot interoperate with one another.

As of DB2 V6, IBM supports a procedural dialect of SQL based on the ANSI standard. The IBM DB2 version of procedural SQL is called *SQL procedures language*, or SPL for short.

> **NOTE**
>
> SQL/PSM is the ANSI standard specification for developing stored procedures and routines using SQL. PSM is an acronym for Persistent Stored Modules. IBM's implementation of its SQL Stored Procedure Language is based on SQL/PSM, but is not a complete implementation of the ANSI SQL/PSM standard.

But what is procedural SQL? One of the biggest benefits derived from SQL (and relational technology in general) is the capability to operate on sets of data with a single line of code. By using a single SQL statement, you can retrieve, modify, or remove multiple rows. However, this capability also limits SQL's functionality. A procedural dialect of SQL eliminates this drawback through the addition of looping, branching, and flow of control statements. Procedural SQL has major implications on database design.

Procedural SQL will look familiar to anyone who has ever written any type of SQL or coded using any type of programming language. Typically, procedural SQL dialects contain constructs to support looping (WHILE or REPEAT), exiting (LEAVE), conditional processing (IF...THEN...ELSE), blocking (BEGIN...END), and variable definition and use.

IBM's SQL Procedure Language

Stored procedure language for creating SQL stored procedures was added after the general availability of DB2 V6.

SQL stored procedures are like other stored procedures in that the SQL stored procedure must have a name and a schema, as well as the definition of the stored procedure characteristics and the actual code for the stored procedure. The code, however, is written in SQL alone—no 3GL program is required.

SQL stored procedures differ from external stored procedures in the way that the code is defined. SQL stored procedures include the actual SQL procedural source code in the CREATE PROCEDURE statement, whereas external stored procedures specify only the definition of the stored procedure in the CREATE PROCEDURE statement. The actual code of an external stored procedure is developed independently and is not included in the CREATE statement.

SQL stored procedures are developed entirely in IBM's SQL procedures language but must be converted to C before they can be executed. This process is described later in this chapter in the section titled "Creating SQL Stored Procedures."

The actual SQL code in the SQL stored procedure is referred to as the *body* of the SQL stored procedure. The body of an SQL stored procedure can include most valid SQL statements, but also extended, procedural SQL statements. The procedure body consists of a single simple or compound statement. The following statements can be included in an SQL stored procedure body.

- Most regular SQL statements can be coded in an SQL stored procedure. Some SQL statements are valid in a compound statement, but they are not valid if the SQL is the only statement in the procedure body.

- Assignment statements can be used to assign a value (or null) to an output parameter or an SQL variable. An SQL variable is defined and used only within the body of an SQL stored procedure.

- CASE statements are used to select an execution path based on the evaluation of one or more conditions. The SQL procedures language CASE statement is similar to the SQL CASE expression previously described in Chapter 1, "The Magic Words."

- IF statements can be coded to select an execution path based on conditional logic.

- The LEAVE statement transfers program control out of a loop or a block of code.

- A LOOP statement is provided to execute a single statement or grouping of statements multiple times.

- The REPEAT statement executes a single statement or group of statements until a specified condition evaluates to true.

- The WHILE statement is similar to the REPEAT statement, but it executes a single statement or group of statements while a specified condition is true.

V8
- The RETURN statement can be used to return a status in the form of an integer value to the invoking application.

V8
- The SIGNAL statement works in conjunction with the RETURN statement. The SIGNAL statement can be used to set the SQLSTATE to a specific value. You can also use it to

15

specify an optional MESSAGE_TEXT, the first 70 bytes of which will be stored in the SQLERRMC field of the SQLCA. The full message text can be obtained from the MESSAGE_TEXT and MESSAGE_LENGTH fields of GET DIAGNOSTICS.

V8

- The RESIGNAL statement enables a condition handler within an SQL procedure to raise a condition with a specific SQLSTATE and message text, or to return the same condition that activated the handler.

- Compound statements can be coded that contain one or more of any of the other SQL procedures language statements. In addition, a compound statement can contain SQL variable declarations, condition handlers, and cursor declarations. Compound statements cannot be nested.

> **NOTE**
>
> When coding a compound statement, you must code the component statements in the following specific order:
>
> 1. SQL variable and condition declarations
>
> 2. Cursor declarations
>
> 3. Handler declarations
>
> 4. Procedure body statements (CASE, IF, LOOP, REPEAT, WHILE, and other SQL statements)

Sample SQL Stored Procedures

The following SQL code implements an SQL stored procedure that accepts an employee number and a rate as input. The stored procedure raises the salary of the specified employee by the specified rate. However, using an IF statement, the stored procedure also checks to make sure that no raise exceeds 50%.

```
CREATE PROCEDURE UPDATE_SALARY
  (IN EMPLOYEE_NUMBER CHAR(10),
   IN RATE DECIMAL(6,2))
LANGUAGE SQL
WLM ENVIRONMENT SAMP1
COMMIT ON RETURN YES
IF RATE <= 0.50
THEN UPDATE EMP
     SET SALARY = SALARY * RATE
     WHERE EMPNO = EMPLOYEE_NUMBER;
ELSE UPDATE EMP
     SET SALARY = SALARY * 0.50
     WHERE EMPNO = EMPLOYEE_NUMBER;
END IF
```

Another sample stored procedure follows:

```
CREATE PROCEDURE PROC1(OUT NOROWS INT)
LANGUAGE SQL
BEGIN
  DECLARE var_firstnme VARCHAR(12);
  DECLARE var_midinit CHAR(1);
```

```
   DECLARE var_lastname VARCHAR(15);
   DECLARE at_end INT DEFAULT 0;
   DECLARE not_found CONDITION FOR '02000'
   DECLARE cempname CURSOR FOR
     SELECT   FIRSTNME, MIDINIT, LASTNAME
     FROM     EMP
     ORDER BY LASTNAME;
   DECLARE CONTINUE HANDLER FOR not_found SET NOROWS=1;
   OPEN cempname;
   FETCH cempname INTO var_firstnme, var_midinit, var_lastname;
   CLOSE cempname;
END
```

This SQL stored procedure declares a cursor on the EMP table and fetches a row from the cursor. The condition handler is used to handle the row-not-found condition. You could code a loop construct to fetch all rows from a cursor until no more rows are found. For example,

```
   .
   .
   .
fetch_loop:
REPEAT
  FETCH cempname INTO
        var_firstnme, var_midinit, var_lastname;
UNTIL SQLCODE <> 0
END REPEAT fetch_loop
   .
   .
   .
```

Of course, a similar effect could be achieved using the LOOP construct with a LEAVE statement.

Creating SQL Stored Procedures

There are three steps to creating SQL stored procedures:

1. Write the procedural SQL source statements.

2. Create the executable form of the SQL procedure.

3. Define the SQL procedure to DB2.

There are two different ways for you to accomplish these three steps to create an SQL procedure:

- Use the IBM DB2 Stored Procedure Builder to guide you through the steps of specifying the source statements for the SQL procedure, defining the SQL procedure to DB2, and preparing the SQL procedure for execution.

- Code a CREATE PROCEDURE statement for the SQL procedure. Then use JCL or DSNTPSMP to define the SQL procedure to DB2 and create an executable procedure.

V8

> **NOTE**
>
> As of DB2 V8, Stored Procedure Builder is renamed to DB2 Development Center.

Using JCL to Create SQL Stored Procedures   Use the following steps to prepare an SQL procedure using JCL. This JCL is similar to the JCL used for program preparation presented in Chapter 13, "Program Preparation," with an additional step to generate C source code.

First, preprocess the CREATE PROCEDURE statement using the DSNHPSM program. The output from this step is

- A C language source program

- A CREATE PROCEDURE statement (or for V5, an INSERT statement for defining the stored procedure in SYSIBM.SYSPROCEDURES for V5)

Next, precompile the generated C language program. This produces a DBRM and modified C language source statements. Ensure that the DBRM name is the same as the name of the load module for the SQL procedure.

The third step is to compile and link-edit the modified C source statements, producing an executable C language program. The default name for the C language program is the first eight bytes of the SQL procedure name. Finally, BIND the DBRM into a package and define the stored procedure to DB2.

Using DSNTPSMP to Create SQL Stored Procedures   DSNTPSMP, also known as the SQL procedure processor, is a REXX stored procedure that you can use to prepare an SQL procedure for execution. You can also use DSNTPSMP to perform selected steps in the preparation process or delete an existing SQL procedure. The following sections contain information on invoking DSNTPSMP.

DSNTPSMP can be executed only by issuing a CALL statement inside an application program or through DB2 Stored Procedure Builder or DB2 Development Center. Before you can run DSNTPSMP, you need to ensure that the appropriate PTFs and APARs have been applied to DB2, install the REXX language support feature, and code a program that issues a CALL statement for DSNTPSMP.

Use the Sample Programs Provided by IBM   IBM provides quite a few sample programs and jobs to assist you in developing SQL stored procedures. The samples can be found in the SDSNSAMP data set. Examine these for examples of how to implement effective DB2 SQL stored procedures. The SQL stored procedure samples that ship with DB2 are listed in Table 15.1.

TABLE 15.1   SQL Stored Procedure Samples

Name	Description
DSNHSQL	Sample JCL to preprocess, precompile, compile, prelink-edit, and link-edit SQL stored procedures.
DSNTEJ63	Sample JCL to prepare the DSN8ES1 SQL stored procedure for execution.

TABLE 15.1   Continued

Name	Description
DSN8ES1	An example of an SQL stored procedure that uses the DB2 sample tables. It accepts a department number as input and returns a result set that contains salary information for each employee in that department.
DSNTEJ64	Sample JCL to prepare DSN8ED3 for execution.
DSN8ED3	A sample C program that calls the DSN8ES1 SQL stored procedure

The SQL Procedures Language "Catalog"   SQL procedures language requires two additional supportive tables, similar to DB2 Catalog tables. These tables contain information such as the source code of the SQL stored procedure code and the options used to develop the SQL stored procedure. The two tables are SYSIBM.SYSPSM and SYSIBM.SYSPSMOPTS.

SYSIBM.SYSPSM holds the source code for SQL stored procedures. The table contains one or more rows for each SQL stored procedure prepared by DSNTPSMP, Stored Procedure Builder, or DB2 Development Center. If the SQL stored procedure consists of more than 3,800 bytes, more than one row is required to hold the source code for the SQL procedure. Refer to Table 15.2 for a definition of SYSIBM.SYSPSM.

TABLE 15.2   SYSIBM.SYSPSM (SQL Procedure Source Table)

Column Name	Column Definition
SCHEMA	Schema of the SQL procedure. Blank if the SQL procedure was created prior to DB2 V6.
PROCEDURENAME	Name of the SQL stored procedure.
SEQNO	Sequence number between 1 and CEILING(x/3800), where x is the number of bytes in the SQL procedure source statement.
PSMDATE	The date on which the SQL procedure was created.
PSMTIME	The time at which the SQL procedure was created.
PROCCREATESTMT	A VARCHAR(3800) column containing all or part of an SQL procedure source. If the SQL procedure statement is more than 3,800 bytes, this column contains the portion of the source statement indicated by SEQNO.

The SYSIBM.SYSPSM table has two indexes defined on it: DSNPSMX1 (nonunique) and DSNPSMX2 (unique).

SYSIBM.SYSPSMOPTS holds the program preparation options for SQL stored procedures. The table contains one row for each SQL stored procedure prepared by DSNTPSMP, Stored Procedure Builder, or DB2 Development Center. Refer to Table 15.3 for a definition of SYSIBM.SYSPSMOPTS.

The SYSIBM.SYSPSMOPTS table has one unique index, DSNPSMOX1 defined on it. This index must be defined before DSNTPSMP is executed.

TABLE 15.3   `SYSIBM.SYSPSMOPTS` (SQL Procedure Options Table)

Column Name	Column Definition
SCHEMA	Schema of the SQL procedure. Blank if the SQL procedure was created prior to DB2 V6.
PROCEDURENAME	Name of the SQL stored procedure.
BUILDSCHEMA	The schema name that qualifies the procedure name specified in the `BUILDNAME` column.
BUILDNAME	A procedure name associated with stored procedure `DSNTPSMP`. You can create multiple definitions for the `DSNTPSMP` stored procedure to run `DSNTPSMP` in different WLM environments.
BUILDOWNER	The authorization ID used to create the SQL stored procedure.
PRECOMPILE_OPTS	The options that were specified in the precompiler-options parameter for the most recent invocation of `DSNTPSMP` for this SQL stored procedure.
COMPILE_OPTS	The options that were specified in the compiler-options parameter for the most recent invocation of `DSNTPSMP` for this SQL stored procedure.
PRELINK_OPTS	The options that were specified in the prelink-edit-options parameter for the most recent invocation of `DSNTPSMP` for this SQL stored procedure.
LINK_OPTS	The options that were specified in the link-edit-options parameter for the most recent invocation of `DSNTPSMP` for this SQL stored procedure.
BIND_OPTS	The options that were specified in the bind-options parameter in the most recent invocation of `DSNTPSMP` for this SQL stored procedure.
SOURCEDSN	The name of the data set that contains the source code for the SQL stored procedure (if the SQL procedure source code was input to `DSNTPSMP` stored in an external data set).

The Benefits of Procedural SQL

The most useful procedural extension to SQL is the addition of procedural flow control statements. Flow control within procedural SQL is handled by typical programming constructs that you can mix with standard SQL statements. These typical constructs enable programmers to

- Embed SQL statements within a loop

- Group SQL statements together into executable blocks

- Test for specific conditions and perform one set of SQL statements when the condition is true, another set when the condition is false (IF...ELSE)

- Perform branches to other areas of the procedural code

The addition of procedural commands to SQL provides a more flexible environment for application developers. Often, major components of an application can be delivered using nothing but SQL. You can code stored procedures and complex triggers using procedural SQL, thereby reducing the amount of host language (COBOL, C, Visual Basic, and so on) programming required.

Additionally, when stored procedures can be written using just SQL, more users will be inclined to use these features. DB2 requires stored procedures to be written in a host language. This requirement may scare off many potential developers. Most DBAs I know avoid programming (especially in COBOL) like the plague.

In addition to SQL stored procedures, procedural SQL extensions also enable more complicated business requirements to be coded using nothing but SQL. For example, an independent SQL statement cannot examine each row of a result set during processing. Procedural SQL can accomplish this task quite handily using cursors and looping.

The Drawbacks of Procedural SQL

The biggest drawback to procedural SQL is that it is late getting into the ANSI standard. Although DB2's stored procedure support is based on the ANSI SQL3 standard, other DBMS vendors support different flavors of procedural SQL because they were developed before the ANSI standard. If your shop has standardized on one particular DBMS or does not need to scale applications across multiple platforms, you may not have this problem. But, then again, how many shops does this description actually describe? Probably not very many!

The bottom line is that scalability will suffer when applications are coded using non-standard extensions—such as procedural SQL. Recoding applications that were designed to use stored procedures and triggers written using procedural SQL constructs is a non-trivial task. If an application needs to be scaled to a platform which uses a DBMS that does not support procedural SQL, a complete rewrite is exactly what must be done.

Performance drawbacks can be realized when using procedural SQL if the developer is not careful. For example, improper cursor specification can cause severe performance problems. Of course, this problem can happen just as easily when cursors are used inside a host language. The problem is more inherent to application design than it is to procedural SQL.

One final drawback is that even procedural SQL dialects are not computationally complete. Most dialects of procedural SQL lack programming constructs to control the users' screens and mechanisms for data input/output (other than to relational tables).

DB2 Development Center

IBM also provides DB2 Development Center (previously known as Stored Procedure Builder), a free product for developing SQL and Java stored procedures. The product is GUI-based and provides an easy-to-use interface for quickly developing and testing DB2 stored procedures written in Java or IBM's SQL Procedures Language.

DB2 Development Center provides a development environment for creating, installing, and testing stored procedures, that enables developers to focus on creating stored procedure logic instead of the mundane details of registering, building, and installing DB2 stored procedures. Additionally, with DB2 Development Center, you can develop stored procedures on one operating system and build them on other server operating systems.

Refer to Figures 15.5 for an example of using the DB2 Development Center to build a stored procedure.

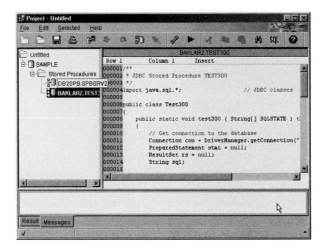

FIGURE 15.5   Using DB2 Development Center to create a stored procedure.

You can launch the DB2 Development Center as a separate application, or from any of the following application development applications:

- Microsoft Visual Studio

- Microsoft Visual Basic

- IBM VisualAge for Java

The DB2 Development Center can be downloaded from the IBM Web site.

CHAPTER 16

The Procedural DBA

In the past, DBMS products were designed only to manage and store data in an optimal manner. Although these core capabilities are still required of modern DBMS products, the purview of the DBMS is no longer limited just to data. With the advent of client/server computing and active databases, procedural logic also is being stored and managed by the DBMS.

DB2 is maturing and gaining more functionality. The clear trend is that more and more procedural logic is being stored in the DBMS. Triggers, user-defined functions, and stored procedures enable developers to use the DBMS to accomplish programming tasks that used to be outside the domain of DB2.

> **NOTE**
>
> But DB2 has been able to store logic in its databases for years using exit routines. How do the more modern procedural database techniques differ from exit routines?
>
> An exit routine, such as an EDITPROC, FIELDPROC, or VALIDPROC, is usually coded in Assembler language. This code is then attached to a specific database object and is executed at a specified time, such as when data is inserted or modified. Exit routines have been available in DB2 for many years; typically, the DBA or systems programmer is responsible for coding and maintaining them. Exit routines, however, are primitive when compared with the procedural logic support provided by a modern DBMS. Exit routines are structured to accomplish only one type of task.
>
> - A FIELDPROC transforms data on insertion and converts the data to its original format on subsequent retrieval.
> - An EDITPROC is functionally equivalent to a FIELDPROC, but it acts on an entire row instead of a column.
> - A VALIDPROC receives a row and returns a value indicating whether a data modification is valid, and therefore should proceed. It simply assesses the validity of the data.

Triggers, user-defined functions, and stored procedures, all examples of modern database-administered procedural logic, can be programmed to accomplish many different types of tasks. They are not limited in scope like exit routines.

This chapter discusses the management and administrative challenges of implementing and controlling procedural logic in the database. For details on DB2's support and implementation for procedural database objects, refer to Chapter 4, "Using DB2 User-Defined Functions and Data Types," for user-defined functions, Chapter 8, "Using DB2 Triggers for Integrity," for triggers, and Chapter 15, "Using DB2 Stored Procedures," for stored procedures. In this chapter, you will learn the reasoning and requirements for the Procedural DBA.

The Classic Role of the DBA

Just about every database developer has his or her favorite curmudgeon DBA story. You know, those famous anecdotes that begin with "I have a problem..." and end with "...and then he told me to stop bothering him and read the (expletive-deleted) manual." DBAs do not have a "warm and fuzzy" image. This image has more to do with the nature and scope of the job than anything else. The DBMS spans the enterprise, effectively placing the DBA on call for the applications of the entire organization.

To make matters worse, the role of the DBA has expanded over the years. In the prerelational days, both database design and data access were complex. Programmers were required to explicitly code program logic to navigate through the database and access data. Typically, the prerelational DBA was assigned the task of designing the hierarchic or network database design. This process usually consisted of both logical and physical database design, although it was not always recognized as such at the time. After the database was planned, designed, and implemented, and the DBA created backup and recovery jobs, little more than space management and reorganization were required. Keep in mind that I don't want to belittle these tasks. The prerelational DBMS products such as IMS and IDMS required the DBA to run a complex series of utility programs to perform backup, recovery, and reorganization. These tasks consumed a large amount of time, energy, and effort.

As relational products displaced older DBMS products, the role of the DBA expanded. Of course, DBAs still designed databases, but increasingly these databases were generated from logical data models created by data administration staffs. The up-front effort in designing the physical database was reduced but not eliminated. Relational design still required physical implementation decisions such as indexing, denormalization, and partitioning schemes. Instead of merely concerning themselves with physical implementation and administration issues, however, DBAs found that they were becoming more intimately involved with procedural data access.

The nature of the relational model requires additional involvement during the design of data access routines. No longer are programmers navigating through the data; the DBMS is. Optimizer technology embedded into the DBMS is responsible for creating the access paths to the data. The optimization choices must be reviewed by the DBA. Program and SQL design reviews are now a vital component of the DBA's job. Furthermore, the DBA must take on additional monitoring and tuning responsibilities. Backup, recovery, and reorganization are just a starting point. Now, DBAs use EXPLAIN, performance monitors, and SQL analysis tools to administer applications proactively.

Often, DBAs are not adequately trained in these areas, though. Programming is a distinctly different skill than creating well-designed relational databases. DBAs, more often than not, need to be able to understand application logic and programming techniques to succeed as a DBA in a relational world.

The Role of the Procedural DBA

Administering and managing data structures is the traditional duty of the DBA, and is well-defined in the industry. But most DBAs are experts in database design, DDL implementation, and database utilities. It is unreasonable to expect them to be able to code and debug procedures and functions written in C, COBOL, Java, or even procedural SQL (SQL/PSM). To implement and manage DB2 triggers, user-defined functions, and stored procedures effectively, a new type of DBA—a Procedural DBA—should be created.

The infrastructure required to manage procedural objects is different from that required to manage data alone. These new, procedural objects are a mixture of application program and traditional database objects (such as tables and indexes). Procedural objects, therefore, need to be managed like *both* database objects *and* application programs.

The creation of the new Procedural DBA role will have an impact on the roles and responsibilities of the DBA and programming staff. But effective implementation of the Procedural DBA function will result in an optimal environment for supporting procedural logic in the database.

The role of the DBA is expanding to encompass too many responsibilities for a single job function to perform the job capably in most shops. The Procedural DBA can be used to offload some of the duties of the traditional DBA. Start by splitting the DBA's job into two separate parts based on the database object to be supported: data objects and procedural objects (like triggers, UDFs, and stored procedures).

The traditional scope of the DBA role does not involve issues like debugging and testing. When triggers, UDFs, and stored procedures are implemented, you must treat them like any other program and make sure that they have been coded properly and then thoroughly tested and debugged. DBAs do not normally perform these tasks when they create database objects. The DBA may need to tweak some parameters or change syntax, but no testing and debugging is required of DDL CREATE statements for databases, tables, table spaces, and indexes.

The role of supporting procedural objects should fall to a group of professionals skilled in program development and procedural logic, as well as SQL and database administration.

The manner in which your shop implements Procedural DBA functionality will depend on the size of your organization and the degree to which you implement triggers, UDFs, and stored procedures. For smaller shops, or those not heavily implementing procedural code in the database, you may be able to get by with current staff if you train them accordingly.

Procedural DBA Tasks   The Procedural DBA should be defined to support and manage stored procedures, triggers, and UDFs, as well as other code-related DBA tasks, such as the following:

- *DBMS Logic Support*—Reviewing, supporting, debugging, tuning, and possibly even coding stored procedures, triggers, and user-defined functions. This task must include "on call" support.

- *Application Program Design Reviews*—Reviewing every application program completely before migrating the code to a production environment. This must include both traditional application programs and program logic required to implement stored procedures and user-defined functions.

- *Access Path Review and Analysis*—Using EXPLAIN and other tools to determine, review, and tune the access paths chosen by DB2. Additionally, the procedural DBA needs to understand how to tweak SQL for optimal performance and how to specify optimization hints using PLAN_TABLE to direct DB2 to use different access paths.

- *SQL Debugging*—Assisting developers with difficult SQL syntax and structures.

- *View Analysis and Design*—Assisting DBAs in creating optimal SQL for view definitions.

- *Complex SQL Analysis and Rewrite*—The Procedural DBA should be skilled in coding and developing complex SQL statements.

The role of the Procedural DBA is depicted graphically in Figure 16.1. Preferable, the Procedural DBA should report through the same management unit as the traditional DBA and not through the application programming staff. Reporting this way enables better skills sharing between the two distinct DBA types. Of course, your shop's needs may differ causing you to place the Procedural DBA functionality elsewhere in the organization. At any rate, synergy is required between the Procedural DBA and the application programmer/analyst. In fact, the typical job path for the Procedural DBA is most likely from the application programming ranks because the coding skill-base exists there.

When the procedural tasks are off-loaded from the traditional, data-oriented DBAs, the DBAs will be free to concentrate on the actual physical design and implementation of databases. The result should be much better database design and enhanced performance.

The Political Issues   After stored procedures and UDFs are coded and made available to DB2, applications and developers will begin to rely on them. Now that procedural logic is being managed by DB2, DBAs must grapple with the issues of quality, maintainability, and availability. How and when will these objects be tested? The impact of a failure is enterprise-wide, not relegated to a single application. This increases the visibility and criticality of these objects. Who is responsible if objects fail? The answer must be "a DBA"—preferably a Procedural DBA who understands the implementation and operation of procedural database objects.

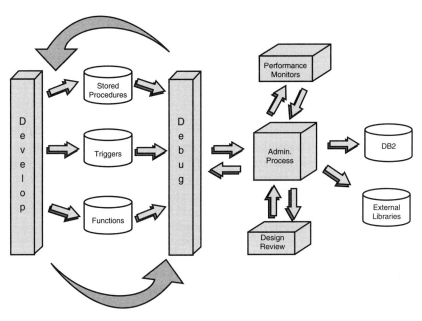

FIGURE 16.1   Procedural DBA tasks.

Establishing a Procedural DBA function ensures that the political aspects of trigger, stored procedure, and UDF creation, use, and support have been adequately determined and documented prior to implementation. Failure to do so will cause a multitude of questions that are not easy to answer without a centralized support group.

For example, who will code stored procedures and UDFs, DBAs or application programmers? This decision can vary from shop to shop based on the size of the organization, the number of DBAs, and the commitment of the organization to stored procedures. A credible case can be made that the task should be a centralized function in order to promote reuseability and documentation.

After the decision is made as to who develops the stored procedures and UDFs, the next decision that needs to be made is who supports them. Stored procedure support must encompass design and code review, QA testing, documentation review, reuseability testing, and "on call" support.

If a centralized group is not "on call" for stored procedure failures, organizational infighting can occur. Consider, for example, a stored procedure developed by a Marketing application staff that modifies customer information. The stored procedure is developed, tested, documented, and migrated to production. Because proper reuseability guidelines were followed, the Sales application staff calls the same stored procedure in their code. Once it is in production, the Sales application fails at 2:00 a.m. Who gets called in to fix the problem? The Sales staff argues that the stored procedure was created by Marketing and no one on the Sales staff understands how the stored procedure works. The Marketing staff argues that their application did not bomb, the Sales application did. Without a centralized support function, the argument could go on all night. These issues need to be addressed before reuseable, procedural logic is implemented in the database.

Procedural DBAs must be technically astute and aware of the intricate details of implementing triggers, UDFs, and stored procedures. For example, the Procedural DBA must understand the firing order for triggers.

The Technical Issues   The Procedural DBA is not just a political role. Technical acumen is required to do the role justice. A thorough knowledge of DB2's implementation of procedural objects is required. Consider, for example, managing schemas.

DB2 triggers, UDFs, and stored procedures are created within a schema. A schema is a logical grouping of procedural database objects. By default, the schema name is the authid of the process that issues the CREATE statement for the procedural object.

> **NOTE**
>
> In addition to triggers, stored procedures, and UDFs, user-defined data types (UDTs) also are created within a schema. For this reason, consider also assigning the creation and management of UDTs to the Procedural DBA.

The Procedural DBA needs to understand schemas including:

- How procedural objects are created in a schema
- How the schema factors into execution of the procedural objects
- How to set the SQL path and how the SQL path influences execution
- How functions are resolved at run time

But schemas are not the only technical issue complicating the Procedural DBA role. Recall from Chapter 6, "DB2 Indexes," that when multiple triggers are coded on the same table, the order in which the triggers were created can impact their operation and subsequently data integrity. The rule for order of execution is: Triggers of the same type are executed in the order in which they were created. So, when triggers are dropped and re-created, the order of creation is important. This level of detail most likely will elude programmers that do not specialize in procedural objects—another reason to implement Procedural DBAs.

As DB2 matures, more and more procedural logic will be managed by, stored in, and administered by the DBMS, causing database administration to become more complex. The role of the DBA is rapidly expanding to the point at which no single professional can be reasonably expected to be an expert in all facets of the job. Without a Procedural DBA function, supporting the DBMS-coupled logic used by DB2 applications will be difficult.

Procedural SQL   Procedural objects in DB2 are written using 3GL programming languages or a procedural dialect of SQL. Most of the other major DBMS vendors only support procedural SQL—Oracle uses PL/SQL, Sybase and Microsoft use Transact-SQL, and Informix uses SPL. Each of these languages is proprietary, and they cannot interoperate with one another.

But what is procedural SQL? One of the biggest benefits derived from SQL (and relational technology in general) is the capability to operate on sets of data with a single line of code. By using a single SQL statement, you can retrieve, modify, or remove multiple rows. However, this capability also limits SQL's functionality. A procedural dialect of SQL eliminates this drawback through the addition of looping, branching, and flow of control statements. Procedural SQL has major implications on database design. For more details on SQL procedures language, DB2's version of procedural SQL, refer to Chapter 15.

The Procedural DBA needs to understand the various methods of creating procedural objects in DB2. Furthermore, the Procedural DBA must be ready to support all of these development methods. Therefore, the Procedural DBA should understand the traditional programming languages in use at their shop (such as COBOL, C, and Java), as well as procedural SQL.

In a heterogeneous environment, where more than one DBMS is used, the Procedural DBA needs to understand the methods for creating procedural objects in each of the DBMSs being used. There are many similarities between DB2 and Oracle triggers, for example, but there are also stark differences. The Procedural DBA group needs to be knowledgeable about these differences in order to support heterogeneous procedural database objects.

16

CHAPTER **17**

DB2 and the Internet

The data processing world is increasingly becoming an online world. This phenomenon is being driven by the Internet. By providing a vehicle for interconnecting computer systems across national and international boundaries, the Internet has brought computing power to the masses and established a sense of community where none previously existed. Such is the case for the DB2 community—the Internet allows us to stay connected to one another, share information, and send DB2 data anywhere we might please.

How to Access the Internet

All of the large, commercial online service providers such as America Online and the Microsoft Network offer access to the Internet. If you are accessing the Internet from home, you will probably access it from one of these servers. Or, you may have broadband access through a provider such as Roadrunner.

Most corporations provide broadband Internet access directly via an ISP (Internet Service Provider) and a T1 connection. If this is the case, you will not have to set yourself up with an online service. The best way to find out whether your corporation has an ISP is to do some snooping. Ask your Help Desk, DBA, or manager whether your company is hooked up to the Internet. If so, all you will need is a TCP/IP connection and some basic software to begin surfing the Net for DB2 nuggets!

The Internet Phenomenon

When discussing the Internet, most folks limit themselves to the World Wide Web. However, there are many components that make up the Internet. For purposes of this book, I will discuss the three primary components most useful to DB2 professionals: the World Wide Web, Usenet Newsgroups, and mailing lists.

The World Wide Web

The World Wide Web (WWW) uses a graphical interface and hypertext protocol to display information in a point and click environment. Using a Web browser (such as Netscape Navigator or Microsoft Internet Explorer), you can navigate through the Internet, accessing Web pages and FTP and gopher sites. A vast array of multimedia information (text, audio, video, and more) can be accessed using the WWW.

Having secured access to a Web browser, the first thing to do is to access a Web page. Web sites on the Internet provide a simple address that lets users access their site. That address, known as a URL (or Uniform Resource Locator), can be fed into a Web browser, thereby providing access to the site. The address is always preceded by the following:

```
http://
```

HTTP stands for HyperText Transfer Protocol, a communication protocol that understands that any document it retrieves contains information about future links referenced by the user. Of course, other Internet resources, such as gopher or ftp, can be accessed using a Web browser. For example, instead of typing `http`, the user can also specify the following:

`ftp://`	To access an FTP site
`file://`	To access a local (or networked) data file
`gopher://`	To access a gopher site
`mailto://`	To send mail
`news://`	To access Usenet Newsgroups

A Web page is a combination of text and graphics that provides hypertext links to other documents and services. The hypertext links are coded in the standard language known as HTML. An example showing my home page is depicted in Figure 17.1. The URL for this Web site is `http://www.craigsmullins.com`.

If you look closely, you can see the URL depicted in the address box in Figure 17.1.

A page is the basic unit of every Web site. A Web page contains text, links, and images, but can also contain forms, frames, and tables.

Text on most Web pages is formatted into multiple, layered headers and accompanying body text to help organize the information on the page. A link, sometimes referred to as a hyperlink, takes you to another page or to a graphic or other related file. Links can be textual or graphical. Textual links are underlined and in color. When you roll the cursor over a link it will change from an arrow to a pointing finger.

Forms are Web pages that have been organized using input boxes, pull-down lists, and radio buttons to enable easy data entry by users. Typically, forms are used to accept a user's demographic information or to enter credit card information when buying products over the Web. Frames allow several windows to be shown on a single Web page. The most common use is to display a Table of Contents in one frame while the user navigates through the Web site in another frame. Tables display information in formatted rows and columns.

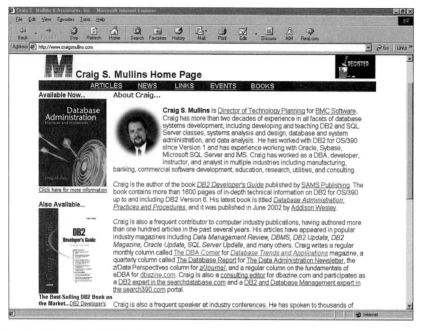

FIGURE 17.1   The Craig S. Mullins home page. (`http://www.craigsmullins.com`)

After a Web page is accessed, hypertext links can be pointed to and clicked on leading the user through layers of information. The Web browser allows the user to navigate through pages and pages of useful information. The information can be printed, saved to disk, or simply browsed.

Usenet Newsgroups

A very fertile source of information on the Internet is found in various Usenet Newsgroups. Usenet, an abbreviation for User Network, is a large collection of discussion groups called newsgroups. Each newsgroup is a collection of articles pertaining to a single, predetermined topic. Newsgroup names usually reflect their focus. For example, `comp.databases.ibm-db2` contains discussions about the DB2 family of products.

Using News Reader software, any Internet user can access a newsgroup and read the information contained therein. There are more than 30,000 different newsgroups available—more than enough to satisfy anyone's curiosity. Refer to Figure 17.2 for an example using the Forte Agent newsgroup reader to view messages posted to `comp.databases.ibm-db2`.

Mailing Lists

Mailing Lists are a sort of community bulletin board. You can think of mailing lists as equivalent to a mass mailing. There are thousands of mailing lists available on the Internet, and they operate using a list server. A list server is a program that automates the mailing list subscription requests and messages. The two most common list servers are Listserv and Majordomo. Listserv is also a common synonym for mailing list, but it is actually the name of a particular list server program.

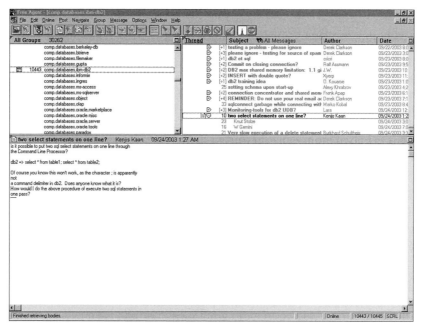

FIGURE 17.2   A Newsgroup reader.

Simply by subscribing to a mailing list, information is sent directly to your email in-box. After subscribing to a mailing list, articles will begin to arrive in your email box from a remote computer called a list server. The information that you will receive varies—from news releases, to announcements, to questions, to answers. this information is very similar to the information contained in a CompuServe forum, except that it comes directly to you via email. Users can also respond to LISTSERV messages. Responses are sent back to the list server as email, and the list server sends the response out to all other members of the mailing list.

To subscribe to a mailing list, simply send an email to the appropriate subscription address requesting a subscription.

Using the Internet with DB2

There are two main reasons for DB2 professionals to use the Internet:

- To develop applications that allow for Web-based access to DB2 data

- To search for DB2 product, technical, and training information

Now take a look at ways of doing both of these.

Accessing DB2 Over the Internet

Allowing for Web-based access to valuable corporate data stored in relational databases makes this data more readily accessible to more people. Companies can obtain a competitive advantage by making their data available to employees over an intranet, or to customers and partners over an extranet.

> **NOTE**
>
> An intranet is a special Internet adaptation that can only be accessed by internal employees. Likewise, an extranet extends the accessibility in a secure manner only to authorized individuals.

One option IBM provides for accessing DB2 data over the Web is called Net.Data.

Using Net.Data to Connect to the Internet

Net.Data is an IBM product that provides developers the ability to build Web applications using data from DB2 and other enterprise databases. Using Net.Data, you can build interactive Web sites with data included dynamically from a variety of data sources, including relational and non-relational data and flat file data.

Net.Data is a macro processor that executes as middleware on a Web server. Using a Web browser and Net.Data, it is possible to rapidly develop applications that use the Internet as a front-end to DB2 databases.

Net.Data applications are macro files containing named sections specifying Web page text, HTML, the SQL statement to be executed, programs and scripts to be called, and application control logic.

Using Net.Data macros, you can develop programs that access and manipulate variables, call functions, and use report-generating tools. Net.Data processes the macro and produces output that can be displayed by a Web browser. Macros provide the developer with the simplicity of HTML coupled with the advanced functionality of Web server programs.

Simply stated, developers can use Net.Data to present data stored in DB2 tables to users in the style of a Web page. This lets savvy Internet users quickly come up to speed at accessing DB2 data.

Figure 17.3 outlines the flow of a Net.Data process. The entire flow can be broken down into a simple eight-step process:

1. A user issues a request by specifying a URL in his Web browser. The URL points to a Net.Data macro.

2. The Web server receives the request for the URL and invokes Net.Data, passing the name of the macro to be invoked.

3. Net.Data creates the HTML for the input form and sends it to the browser via the Web server.

4. The person using the Web browser fills in the input form and submits it to the Web server.

5. Net.Data receives the input form and interprets it to access the requested data.

6. Net.Data invokes the appropriate language environment. The language environment, in turn, processes the information by accessing DB2. It then returns the results to Net.Data.

7. Net.Data creates the HTML for the output report form and sends it with the data retrieved from the database through the Web server to the Web browser.

8. The results are formatted by the Web browser and the requesting user has retrieved DB2 data over the Web.

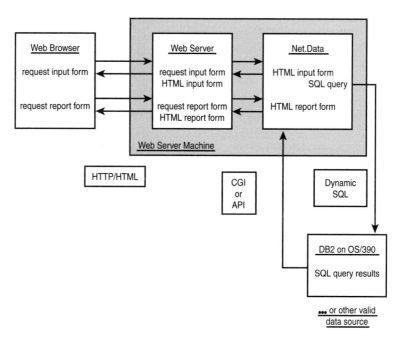

FIGURE 17.3 How Net.Data works.

Because Net.Data applications use native HTML and SQL, developers do not need to learn complex new languages and syntax to connect DB2 databases to the Web. Furthermore, SQL SELECT, INSERT, UPDATE, and DELETE statements are supported for both data query and modification.

You can use Net.Data to support two-tier and three-tier client/server environments. In a two-tier environment, the database resides on the Internet server and client Web browsers access the data. For DB2 running on OS/390, this is applicable only if you use the mainframe as your Internet server. In a two-tier z/OS environment, Net.Data communicates with DB2 for z/OS through RRS or the Call Attach Facility (CAF).

In a three-tier environment, the data can reside on both the local Internet server and a remote platform. This requires DB2 Connect, CAE (Client Application Enabler), or DataJoiner. The three-tier setup is useful when your Internet server is a Unix or Windows NT machine, and you need to access DB2 data from the mainframe.

In a three-tier environment, Net.Data macros can access a variety of data sources such as DB2, Oracle, Sybase, and ODBC. In a two-tier environment, Net.Data for z/OS can access DB2 for z/OS and IMS.

Net.Data Guidelines

The following guidelines can help you to implement Net.Data effectively in your organization.

Consider Using Stored Procedures   In addition to regular SQL SELECT, INSERT, UPDATE, and DELETE statements, Net.Data can invoke stored procedures. Consider calling stored procedures to quickly extend the functionality of Net.Data applications. Furthermore, stored procedures use static SQL, which, at times, can provide enhanced performance. Stored procedures also can be used to minimize network traffic.

Finally, remember that DB2 stored procedures can return result sets, if necessary.

Provide Net.Data Macro Language Training   Net.Data programs are written in Net.Data's macro language. A Net.Data macro is a mixture of HTML and Net.Data-specific keywords. Although macros can be easy to develop, it is wise to provide an appropriate level of Net.Data macro language training for your Net.Data developers before they develop any Net.Data applications.

Net.Data macros can invoke programs written in other languages, such as Perl, REXX, and C. Net.Data also can be used to invoke DB2 stored procedures. Keep in mind that these features can complicate relatively simple Net.Data macros.

Enhance Net.Data Using Java Applets and JavaScripts   Net.Data provides Java applet and JavaScript interfaces to enhance the Web client's ability to perform client-side processing. You can use a Java applet to enhance the results of a Net.Data application with graphical elements such as charts and graphs.

IBM provides sample Java applets and JavaScripts on the Net.Data Web site at the following link:

`http://www.ibm.com/software/data/net.data/`

Use Direct Requests When Possible   Direct requests improve performance because Net.Data does not have to read and process a macro file. The SQL, ODBC, System, Perl, and REXX Net.Data-supplied language environments support direct requests.

Consider Net.Data Live Connections   Before a query can be executed, the process must identify itself and connect to DB2. This can cause performance problems.

Net.Data can be used to establish a live connection by continuously running processes to perform the startup tasks. Once started, the process waits to execute subsequent requests.

NOTE

Live connections are required for API connections, but can be used for CGI connections, too.

Use Good Programming Techniques Be sure to use your standard application development and programming techniques when developing Net.Data macros. Make sure to include comments in the macro file indicating the purpose of the program, as well as a log of changes.

Additionally, follow the SQL formulation guidelines covered in Chapters 1, "The Magic Words," and 2, "Data Manipulation Guidelines," and the application programming techniques outlined in Chapter 11, "Using DB2 in an Application Program."

Design Web Applications with the User in Mind Be aware that the equipment on which you are developing your Web-based applications is probably more state-of-the-art than the equipment on which the application will be used. It is common for developers to have access to high-resolution monitors and a lot of memory. Be sure to test the application on PC setups with less memory and on monitors of varying dot pitch and resolution.

Plan Your Security Requirements When developing DB2 applications that are accessible using the Internet, be sure to plan adequate security into the application. Net.Data provides authorization features that should be utilized to ensure that only authorized users are permitted access.

Using Java and DB2

Java is an increasingly popular language for DB2 application development. Part of its popularity is its ability to make Web applications dynamic. For Java usage guidelines, please refer back to Chapter 14, "Alternative DB2 Application Development Methods."

General DB2-Internet Guidelines

The following guidelines can be applied to DB2 applications that are written to exploit the Internet.

Minimize Network Traffic The biggest potential for degrading the performance of DB2 Internet applications is network traffic. In general, the fewer network calls required to perform the same amount of work, the better performance will be.

Consider the following ideas for minimizing network traffic in your DB2-Internet applications:

- Use stored procedures to process SQL and consolidate results. Stored procedures are especially helpful for pieces of code that can be executed many times from many different places. Putting the logic into a stored procedure can reduce network calls.

- Consider using BEFORE triggers to validate data. Doing so removes the need to code intensive data validation logic running on the client.

- Consider using user-defined functions (UDFs) to offload work from the client to the server. A good use of UDFs is to reformat data. Perhaps you have data that is stored differently than it needs to be displayed (onscreen or in a report). A UDF can be written to perform the formatting—and that removes the need to write repetitive client code.

17

Keep Up-to-Date   Make sure that you are using the most up-to-date versions of software, including JDKs, drivers, and compilers. Running with outdated software likely means that you are forgoing performance upgrades that can be accrued by using the latest versions.

Using XML and DB2

Another newer technology vexing DBAs these days is XML. XML is getting a lot of publicity and, if you believe everything you read, then XML is going to solve all of our interoperability problems, completely replace SQL, and possibly even deliver world peace. Realistically, XML won't do any of those things. But XML does allow designers to create their own customized tags, thereby enabling the definition, transmission, validation, and interpretation of data between applications and organizations.

XML stands for Extensible Markup Language. Like HTML, XML is based upon SGML (Standard Generalized Markup Language). HTML uses tags to describe how data appears on a Web page. But XML uses tags to describe the data itself. XML retains the key SGML advantage of self-description, while avoiding the complexity of full-blown SGML. XML allows tags to be defined by users that describe the data in the document. This capability gives users a means for describing the structure and nature of the data in the document. In essence, the document becomes self-describing.

The simple syntax of XML makes it easy to process by machine while remaining understandable to people. Once again, let's use HTML as a metaphor to help us understand XML. HTML uses tags to describe the appearance of data on a page. For example the tag, "text", would specify that the "text" data should appear in bold face. XML uses tags to describe the data itself, instead of its appearance. For example, consider the following XML describing a customer address:

```
<CUSTOMER>
    <first_name>Craig</first_name>
    <middle_initial>S.</middle_initial>
    <last_name>Mullins</last_name>
    <company_name>BMC Software, Inc.</company_name>
    <street_address>2101 CityWest Blvd.</street_address>
    <city>Houston</city>
    <state>TX</state>
    <zip_code>77042</zip_code>
    <country>USA</country>
</CUSTOMER>
```

XML is actually a meta-language—that is, a language for defining other markup languages. These languages are collected in dictionaries called Document Type Definitions (DTDs). The DTD stores definitions of tags for specific industries or fields of knowledge. So, the meaning of a tag must be defined in a "document type declaration" (DTD), such as:

```
<!DOCTYPE CUSTOMER [
<!ELEMENT CUSTOMER (first_name, middle_initial, last_name,
          company_name, street_address, city, state,
          zip_code, country)>
<!ELEMENT first_name (#PCDATA)>
<!ELEMENT middle_initial (#PCDATA)>
```

```
<!ELEMENT last_name (#PCDATA)>
<!ELEMENT company_name (#PCDATA)>
<!ELEMENT street_address (#PCDATA)>
<!ELEMENT city (#PCDATA)>
<!ELEMENT state (#PCDATA)>
<!ELEMENT zip_code (#PCDATA)>
<!ELEMENT country (#PCDATA)>
]
```

The DTD for an XML document can either be part of the document or stored in an external file. The XML code samples shown are meant to be examples only. By examining them, you can quickly see how the document itself describes its contents.

For data management professionals, this is a plus because it eliminates the trouble of tracking down the meaning of data elements. One of the biggest problems associated with database management and processing is finding and maintaining the meaning of stored data. If the data can be stored in documents using XML, the documents themselves will describe their data content. Of course, the DTD is a rudimentary vehicle for defining data semantics. Standards committees are working on the definition of the XML Schema to replace the DTD for defining XML tags. The XML Schema will allow for more precise definition of data, such as data types, lengths, and scale.

The important thing to remember about XML is that it solves a different problem than HTML. HTML is a markup language, but XML is a meta-language. In other words, XML is a language that generates other kinds of languages. The idea is to use XML to generate a language specifically tailored to each requirement you encounter. It is essential to understand this paradigm shift in order to understand the power of XML.

> **NOTE**
>
> XSL, or Extensible Stylesheet Language, can be used with XML to format XML data for display.

In short, XML allows designers to create their own customized tags, thereby enabling the definition, transmission, validation, and interpretation of data between applications and between organizations. So, the most important reason to learn XML is that it is quickly becoming the de facto standard for application interfaces.

There are, however, some problems with XML. The biggest problem with XML lies largely in market hype. Throughout the industry, there is plenty of confusion surrounding XML. Some believe that XML will provide metadata where none currently exists, or that XML will replace SQL as a data access method for relational data. Neither of these assertions is true.

There is no way that any technology, XML included, can conjure up information that does not exist. People must create the metadata tags in XML for the data to be described. XML enables self-describing documents; it doesn't describe your data for you.

Moreover, XML doesn't perform the same functions as SQL. As a result, XML can't replace it. As the standard access method for relational data, SQL is used to "tell" a relational DBMS what data is to be retrieved. XML, on the other hand, is a document description language that describes the contents of data. XML might be useful for defining databases, but not for accessing them.

DB2, as well as most of the other popular DBMS products, now provides built-in support for XML. By integrating XML into DB2 databases, you can more directly and quickly access the XML documents, as well as search and store entire XML documents using SQL. Integration can involve simply storing XML in a large VARCHAR or CLOB column or breaking down the XML into multiple columns in one or more DB2 tables.

When you store or compose a document, you can use the capabilities of the DB2 XML extender, which provides functions and tools to help integrate XML with DB2. The user-defined distinct types XMLVARCHAR, XMLCLOB, and XMLFILE are delivered to help store XML data in DB2 tables.

V8 DB2 also provides several functions to facilitate XML storage, retrieval, extraction, and updating. These functions are documented in Chapter 3, "Using DB2 Functions."

XML Access Methods

When storing XML documents in DB2, you will have to decide on either the *column* or *collection* access method. Once you choose a method you will need to tell DB2 how you plan on storing and retrieving the documents. This is done through a Data Access Definition (DAD) file. The DAD is a file used by DB2 to define the access method needed to process an XML document as either a column or a collection.

XML Column Access Method

The column access method stores and retrieves XML documents as DB2 column data. This means the entire XML document is stored in a single DB2 column.

Consider choosing this method in the following situations:

- The XML document already exists and you just want to store it in DB2 for integrity, archival, or auditing purposes.

- The XML document is usually read, but not modified.

- The document has large text paragraphs and you want to use DB2 Text Extender capabilities to search the document.

- You want to store the XML document in the native file system and use DB2 to manage and search the documents.

XML Collection Access Method

The column access method composes XML documents from a collection of DB2 tables and columns, or decomposes XML documents into a collection of DB2 tables and columns. This means that the XML document is broken apart and stored in various tables and columns.

Consider choosing this method in the following situations:

- You have an existing database that you would like to compose XML documents from based on a given document type definition (DTD).

- The data will need to be accessed using SQL and treated like relational data more than it will need to be treated like XML data.

- The XML document needs to be updated often and performance is critical.

The Data Access Definition File

The DAD file is an XML document that is used to map the structure of an XML document to how it is stored in DB2. The DAD file is used when storing XML documents in a column and when composing or decomposing XML data.

This is where DB2 stores the information pertaining to the method of XML storage (column versus collection).

XML-DB2 Administration

DB2 also provides some administration tools. But remember, the XML Extender requires IBM USS (Unix System Services). But, you can use either an administration wizard from a Windows or Unix client, or from z/OS using the USS command line and HFS, or TSO. You can avoid using a non-mainframe platform for XML administration tasks by using either the USS command line and odb2, or TSO and batch to perform administration tasks.

The XML Extender installation creates sample files and executable files in partitioned data sets. After these partitioned data sets are installed, it is recommended that you create HFS files in your USS environment by running the DXXGPREP batch job. The DXXGPREP JCL executes the needed BINDs, creates sample DB2 tables, and copies sample files to HFS.

Keep in mind that all the XML Extender facilities supplied for application programs run in the z/OS MVS environment as stored procedures or user-defined functions (UDFs). Some of the UDFs that refer to the XMLFILE data type require access to an HFS system.

When you use the odb2 command line to enter DB2 commands from USS, DB2 uses the Call Attach Facility to execute dynamic SQL and commands from the z/OS Unix shell.

To start the odb2 command line, simply type the following from the USS command shell:

```
odb2
```

A command prompt will be displayed and you will be able to enter DB2 commands.

XML Administration Support Tables

The XML Extender creates two administration support tables to manage your XML-DB2 environment.

The first table is the DTD repository table, or DB2XML.DTD_REF. This table is used to validate XML data in an XML column or XML collection.

Each DTD in the `DTD_REF` table has a unique ID. The XML Extender creates the `DTD_REF` table when you enable a database for XML. The columns of the DTD repository table are as follows:

DTDID—Used to identify the DTD. This primary key is defined as `VARCHAR(128)`, must be unique, and is not nullable. It must be the same as the `SYSTEM ID` on the `DOCTYPE` line in each XML document, when validation is used.

CONTENT—Contains the content of the DTD in an `XMLCLOB` column.

USAGE_COUNT—Contains the number (`INTEGER`) of XML columns and XML collections in the database that are using this DTD to define a `DAD`.

AUTHOR—Specifies the author of the DTD. The column is defined as `VARCHAR(128)` and is optional.

CREATOR—Specifies the user ID that does the first insertion (`VARCHAR(128)`).

UPDATOR—Specifies the user ID that does the last update (`VARCHAR(128)`).

The second XML administration support table is the XML usage table, or `DB2XML.XML_USAGE`. This table stores common information for each XML-enabled column.

The XML Extender maintains the `XML_USAGE` table as XML is stored in your DB2 tables. The columns of the `XML-USAGE` table are as follows:

TABLE_SCHEMA—Contains the schema name of the user table that contains an XML column (for XML column) or a value of `DXX_COLL` as the default schema name (for XML collection).

TABLE_NAME—Contains the name of the user table that contains an XML column (for XML column) or a value `DXX_COLLECTION`, which identifies the entity as a collection (for XML collection).

COL_NAME—Contains the name of the XML column or XML collection. It is part of the composite key along with the `TABLE_NAME`.

DTDID—Contains a string associating a DTD inserted into `DTD_REF` with a DTD specified in a `DAD` file. The value of this column must match the value of the `DTDID` element in the `DAD`.

DAD—The content of the `DAD` file that is associated with the column or collection.

ROW_ID—An identifier of the row.

ACCESS_MODE—Specifies which access mode is used: 1 indicates XML collection; 0 indicates XML column.

DEFAULT_VIEW—Stores the default view name if there is one.

TRIGGER_SUFFIX—Used for unique trigger names.

VALIDATION—Will be 1 for yes, or 0 for no.

XML-DB2 Guidelines

Consider the following guidelines as you embark on using XML with your DB2 databases.

Use the Sample Scripts to Get Started　IBM supplies a set of sample scripts you can use as a guideline for setting up your DB2-XML environment. You can find these files in the following directory:

`dxx_install/samples/cmd`

For *dxx_install*, substitute the USS directory name where the sample DTD, DAD, and XML files were copied by your DXXGPREP job.

Validate Your XML　You can use a DTD to validate XML data in an XML column. The XML Extender creates a table in the XML-enabled database, called `DTD_REF`. The table is known as the DTD reference and is available for you to store DTDs. When you validate XML documents, you must store the DTD in this repository.

Backup the XML Administration Support Tables　The XML administration support tables, `XML_USAGE` and `DTD_REF`, are required for many XML Extender activities. Be sure that you consistently backup these tables to. ensure recoverability of your XML-DB2 environment.

Learn All You Can About XML　Before you begin to mix XML and DB2, be sure that you have a solid grasp of XML. The short introduction in this section is merely the tip of the iceberg. You will need to understand that XML is truly hierarchical and, as such, will not match up well with your relational, DB2 way of thinking and processing data.

Additional information on XML and the DB2 XML Extender can be found at the following Web sites:

`http://www.ibm.com/software/data/db2/extenders/xmlext/index.html`

`http://www.ibm.com/developer/`

`http://www.sswug.org/centerxml/`

`http://www.oasis-open.org`

`http://www.xml.org`

Finding DB2 Information Using the Internet

The Internet provides a wealth of easily accessible information for the DB2 professional. The days of IBM-Link being the only place to turn for DB2 information are most decidedly over. Immediate access to volumes of information is readily available for the asking. Now examine some of the best places to look for DB2 information in cyberspace!

Internet Resources

A wealth of information is available through the Internet. However, it is rather difficult to learn what is available. The most useful Internet resources for DB2 professionals are Usenet Newsgroups, mailing lists, and access to the World Wide Web (WWW).

DB2-Related Usenet Newsgroups

There are newgroups available to satisfy just about every interest, and DB2 usage is no foreigner to Usenet. There are three primary newsgroups that DB2 users can access for DB2 news and information:

```
comp.databases.ibm-db2

bit.listserv.db2-l

comp.databases
```

Generic database information can be found on the `comp.databases` newsgroup. Some DB2 users post questions, comments, and information to this newsgroup, but DB2-specific traffic is very light.

The `bit.listserv.db2-l` newsgroup is relatively active with DB2 discussions and information. At one point in time this newsgroup was a mirror copy of the DB2 mailing list. But no longer. Some messages are duplicates of the mailing list, others are not.

The third newsgroup is `comp.databases.ibm-db2`. It was instituted in early 1995 to provide a dedicated newsgroup for DB2 users. However, the postings to this newsgroup predominantly pertain to non-z/OS DB2 platforms (primarily for Linux, Unix, and Windows platforms). For a listing of other Usenet Newsgroups that may be of interest to DB2 and DBMS users, see Table 17.1.

TABLE 17.1   Interesting Usenet Newsgroups

Newsgroup Name	Description
`comp.client-server`	Information on client/server technology
`comp.data.administration`	Issues regarding data administration, data modeling, and repositories
`comp.databases`	Issues regarding databases and data management
`comp.databases.adabas`	Information on Software AG's Adabas product line
`comp.databases.ibm-db2`	Information on IBM's DB2 Family of products
`comp.databases.informix`	Information on IBM's Informix DBMS products
`comp.databases.ingres`	Information on the CA-Ingres DBMS
`comp.databases.object`	Information on object-oriented database systems
`comp.databases.oracle.server`	Information on the Oracle database server
`comp.databses.sybase`	Information on the Sybase Adaptive Server RDBMS
`comp.databases.theory`	Discussions on database technology and theory
`comp.edu`	Computer science education
`comp.infosystems`	General discussion of information systems
`comp.languages.java.databases`	Information about accessing databases using Java
`comp.misc`	General computer-related topics not covered elsewhere
`comp.unix.admin`	Unix administration discussions
`comp.unix.aix`	Information pertaining to IBM's version of Unix—AIX
`bit.listserv.cics-l`	Information pertaining to CICS
`bit.listserv.db2-l`	Information pertaining to DB2

TABLE 17.1   Continued

Newsgroup Name	Description
bit.listserv.idms-l	Information pertaining to CA's IDMS DBMS
bit.listserv.ibm-main	IBM mainframe newsgroup
bit.listserv.sqlinfo	Information pertaining to SQL

The DB2 Mailing List

The DB2 mailing list is hosted by IDUG—the International DB2 Users Group. It can be subscribed to by sending a message to the subscription address, LISTSERV@WWW.IDUG.ORG. The message should read as follows:

```
SUBSCRIBE DB2-L
```

> **NOTE**
>
> Because the subscription address begins with LISTSERV, the DB2 mailing list is sometimes referred to as the DB2 LISTSERV, or list server. LISTSERV is also the name of the software that manages the mailing list on the server machine.

After issuing the preceding command, the list server will send you a message asking you to confirm the subscription. Upon doing so, information will quickly begin flowing into your email box (perhaps at a much quicker rate than you can reasonably digest). Literally, hundreds of messages may be sent to you every week.

To sign off of the newsgroup, send the following message to the same subscription address:

```
SIGNOFF DB2-L
```

All of these commands, that is, subscribing and signing off, as well as many others, can be performed on the Web, too. Simply access the DB2-L page at the following link:

```
http://www.idugdb2-l.org/adminscripts/wa.exe?REPORT&z=3
```

In addition to a subscription address, mailing lists also have a posting address. This is the address to which mailing list posts must be sent. Never send subscription requests to the list's posting address. Correspondingly, never send a post to the subscription address.

The posting address for the DB2-L mailing list is DB2-L@WWW.IDUG.ORG. When a message is sent to this address, it will automatically be forwarded to everyone currently subscribed to the list.

Postings to the DB2 mailing list are archived so that you can find old messages of interest you might not have saved. Use this link to access the archive of past DB2-L postings:

```
http://www.idugdb2-l.org/archives/db2-l.html
```

If you have a problem or question with the list, or just need some help, you can send an email to DB2-L-REQUEST@WWW.IDUG.ORG for assistance.

17

> **NOTE**
>
> Another mailing list that contains useful DB2 and z/OS information is the IBM mainframe mailing list, known as IBM-MAIN. The email address to subscribe to the mainframe list is LISTSERV@BAMA.UA.EDU. To post messages, use the following email address: IBM-MAIN@BAMA.UA.EDU.
>
> Additional information about the mainframe mailing list can be found at
>
> http://www.mainframes.com/ibm-main.htm

DB2 Information on the Web

There are many Web pages providing useful DB2 information. Foremost, of course, is IBM's Web site. The DB2 for OS/390 and z/OS Web page contains a plethora of useful information, and you should most definitely bookmark this page for future reference (see Figure 17.4). From this page, you will be able to access release information, technical information, DB2 manuals online, and additional DB2 product information.

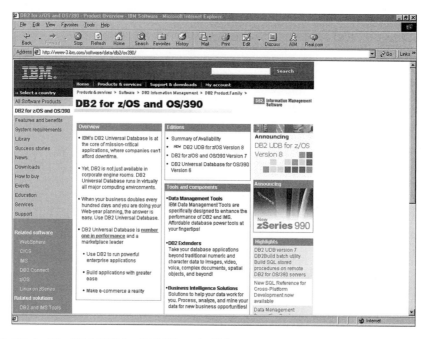

FIGURE 17.4 The IBM DB2 for OS/390 and z/OS page.
(http://www.software.ibm.com/data/db2/os390)

Another useful IBM site is the Redbook site. IBM's International Technical Support Organization (ITSO) publishes many books on technical topics. The IBM ITSO Redbook site can be accessed at

http://www.redbooks.ibm.com/

The Redbook site provides a searchable online catalog, the ability to order redbooks directly from IBM over the Web, and, in many cases, to download redbooks for free in Adobe Acrobat format.

Four other Web sites worth checking out and bookmarking are the DB2 USA site, Eric Loriaux's MVS site, DB2 Times, and the DBAzine.com site. Refer to Figures 17.5 through 17.8. These sites are very useful as they contain pages of links to other DB2-related sites and stories, as well as original content in some cases.

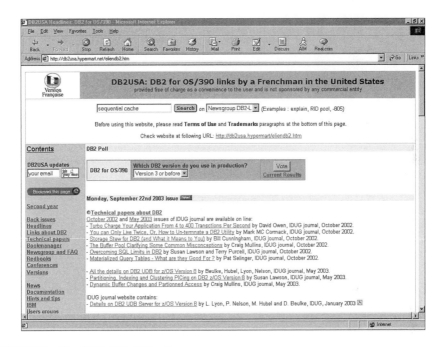

FIGURE 17.5   The DB2 USA Web site.
(http://db2usa.hypermart.net/eliendb2.htm)

Many DB2 experts and consultants have their own Web sites that contain useful tips, tricks, and techniques, as well as their speaking schedules and copies of their presentations. Two of the best of these sites are the Sheryl Larsen Inc. site and Yevich, Lawson, and Associates' site (see Figures 17.9 and 17.10).

Several of the many DB2 user groups also have Web sites. These sites contain many useful DB2 resources, such as meeting schedules, newsletters, DB2 tips, and presentations. The IDUG Web site (see Figure 17.11) is one that every DB2 professional should visit regularly. It contains information on upcoming conferences, as well as an online version of its DB2-related magazine, *IDUG Solutions Journal*.

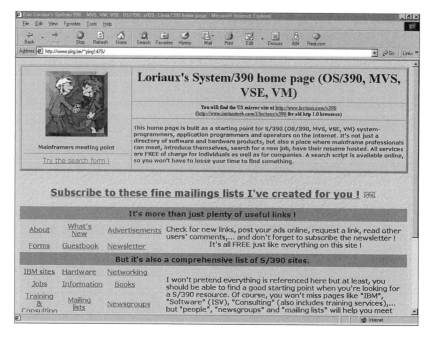

FIGURE 17.6   Eric Loriaux's MVS site.
(http://www.loriaux.com/s390/)

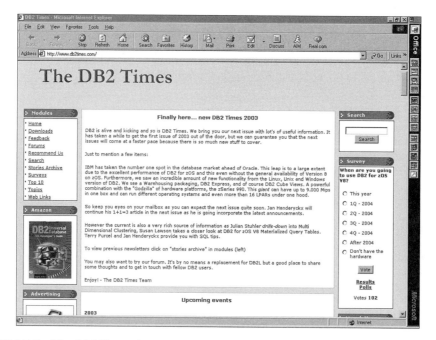

FIGURE 17.7   The DB2 Times site.
(http://www.DB2Times.com)

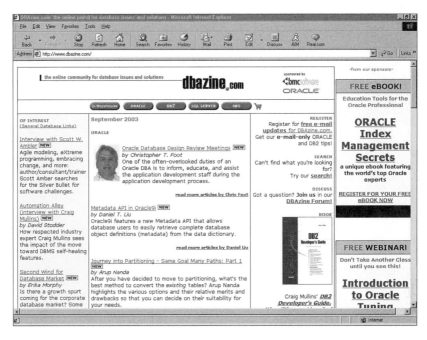

FIGURE 17.8   The DBAzine.com Web Portal.
(http://www.dbazine.com)

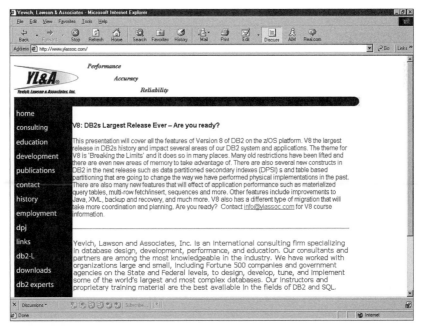

FIGURE 17.9   The Yevich, Lawson, and Associates site.
(http://www.ylassoc.com)

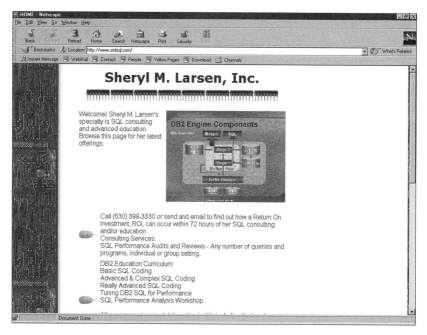

FIGURE 17.10   The Sheryl M. Larsen, Inc. site.
(http://www.smlsql.com)

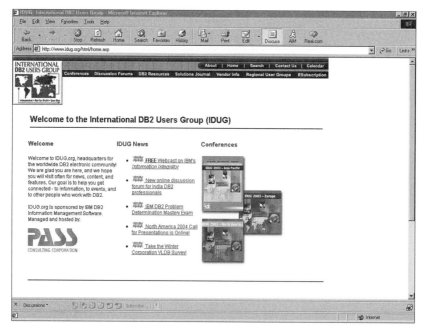

FIGURE 17.11   The International DB2 User Group site.
(http://www.idug.org)

Another interesting site is provided by the U.K. DB2 Working Group (see Figure 17.12). This site contains some useful DB2 shareware and informative hints and tips from DB2 experts.

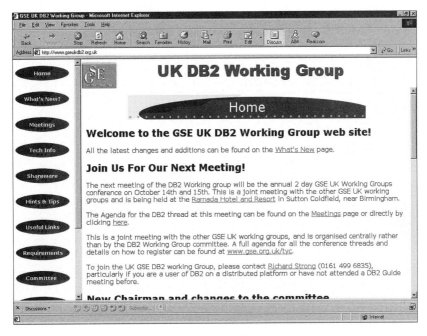

FIGURE 17.12   The GSE U.K. DB2 Working Group site.
(http://www.gseukdb2.org.uk)

Another Web site worth reviewing on a regular basis is the DB2 Magazine site (see Figure 17.13). DB2 Magazine is published quarterly and the publisher makes the contents of each issue available online. Articles from past issues are available as well. IBM is a sponsor of DB2 Magazine, but it is independently published by Miller Freeman, so the content is usually up-to-date, technically accurate, and mostly non-biased.

Finally, most of the third-party DB2 tool vendors also have Web sites. For an example, see Figure 17.14. In addition to information about their products, vendor sites often provide useful DB2 information such as tips, white papers, and newsletters. Refer to Chapter 39, "Components of a Total DB2 Solution" and Appendix B "DB2 Tool Vendors," for information on DB2 third-party tools and vendors.

17

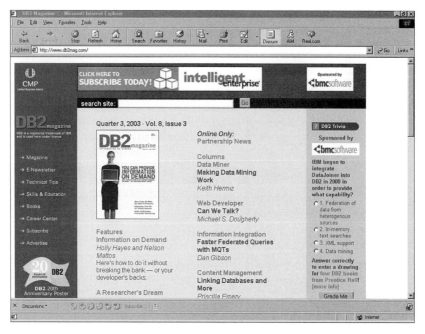

FIGURE 17.13   DB2 Magazine Online site.
(http://www.db2mag.com)

FIGURE 17.14   The BMC Software site.
(http://www.bmc.com)

Internet Guidelines

The following helpful guidelines can make your search for DB2 information on the Internet easier and more rewarding.

Newsgroups Versus Mailing Lists   A newsgroup can only be viewed using News Reader software. You only need to point and click with most News Readers to view the contents of a newsgroup. A mailing list is an email server. Notes are automatically forwarded to everyone on the distribution list. All you have to do is read your email to access the information.

When a mailing list is mirrored to a newsgroup, use the newsgroup instead of the mailing list. Managing hundreds of emails from multiple mailing lists can be difficult. When the email is mixed in with other email messages in your in-box, it is difficult to keep up-to-date with the mailings. However, you can use a News Reader to read the newsgroup at your convenience. Interesting posts can be saved as text files.

Consider Digesting Mailing Lists   Many mailing lists offer the capability to accumulate messages and send them as one big email. This is known as a digest. The benefit is that instead of receiving multiple daily messages from a mailing list, only one daily digest is sent.

To request digesting, simply send an email to the subscription address requesting a digest. The digest request must be made after you have successfully subscribed to the mailing list.

For the DB2 mailing list, send the following message to the subscription address, LISTSERV@IDUG.ORG:

```
SET DB2-L DIGEST
```

The drawbacks to digests are that threads can be hard to follow, it is difficult to respond to messages, and they can become quite large.

Read the Archives   Contributions sent to the DB2 mailing list are automatically archived. You can get a list of the available archive files by sending the following command to LISTSERV@IDUG.ORG:

```
INDEX DB2-L
```

The files returned can be ordered using the following command:

```
GET DB2-L LOGxxxx
```

If Privacy Is an Issue, Conceal Your Identity   It is possible for others to determine that you are signed up to the DB2 mailing list by using the review command. This command sends the email address and name of all subscribers to the requester. To block your name and address from appearing in this list, issue the following command:

```
SET DB2-L CONCEAL
```

Be Skeptical of Information Found on the Internet   Because the Internet provides access to anyone with a computer and a modem, the information received can be less than reliable. It is quite common to post a question and receive multiple, conflicting answers (usually, the answers range from "yes," to "no," to "maybe, if...," to "that question is not appropriate for this newsgroup").

17

Always use common sense before trying any posted tip, trick, or technique that seems dangerous. It probably is.

Avoid Cross-Posting   Cross-posting is the act of posting a single message to multiple newsgroups. Cross-posting is considered impolite and should be avoided. When a post is sent to multiple newsgroups, the cross-posted threads are difficult to read, usually off-topic, increase network traffic, and reduce the quality of the newsgroup discussions.

Know and Use Emoticons   Emoticons are drawings composed of text characters that are meant to look like a face expressing an emotion (hence the name emoticon). They are used on the Internet because it is difficult to convey emotions using text-based media such as email and newsgroups. The following are a few of the most popularly used emoticons:

> :)   a smile
>
> ;)   a wink

Read the FAQs   FAQs (Frequently Asked Questions) are documents defining the focus of a newsgroup and answering the basic questions that most new users always ask. Be sure to read the FAQ for any newsgroup before posting to it. Unfortunately, the DB2 newsgroups do not have FAQs.

Use the Internet FAQ Consortium Web page (shown in Figure 17.15) to find Usenet FAQs.

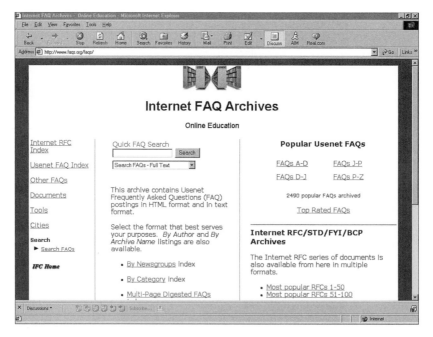

FIGURE 17.15   Internet FAQ Consortium.
(http://www.faqs.org)

Avoid Flames   Flames are posts that are hostile, rude, or otherwise confrontational. Just as these things are not proper to do in person, they are improper on the Internet, as well. It is usually best to ignore flame messages.

Do Not Respond to Spams   The term spam is used to describe junk emails and postings that are off-topic, commercial, or otherwise violate good taste. When you receive a spam, just ignore it. Posting a long, nasty response to the spam back to the newsgroup or mailing list is just as inconsiderate as the original spam.

Basic Newsgroup Tips   Before reading and responding to Internet Newsgroups, you should familiarize yourself with the Internet in general, and each Newsgroup specifically. The following tips will ensure that you effectively utilize Internet Newsgroups:

- Read the messages in the newsgroup for a period before posting. This will enable you to understand the dynamics of the newsgroup helping you to conform to its structure.

- Never post an off-topic message; be sure that it contains information pertinent to the newsgroup readers. Postings that are not relevant to the readers of the newsgroup are a waste of effort, time, and money.

- Always quote appropriate portions of messages to which you are responding. Do not quote the entire message if you are only responding to a portion of it.

- Even readers who might otherwise appreciate your message will be upset if it appears in the wrong group. Also, make sure that the subject of the message is accurate, descriptive, and specific to help readers decide whether to view it.

- Consider replying with an email message if the response is not useful to the entire population of newsgroup readers.

- Keep messages as short and concise as possible. Do not post large files, graphics, or otherwise annoying messages.

Use the List of Lists   There are over 30,000 public mailing lists available on the Internet. Of course, there are many more private mailing lists that are not open for public enrollment. Finding the appropriate list can be a daunting task. Fortunately, Tile.Net can help. Simply point your web browser to `http://Tile.Net/` and you will have access to a nice interface for finding information about discussion and information lists, Usenet newsgroups, and useful FTP sites.

Additionally, you can subscribe to a mailing list for information about new and updated mailing lists. This is called the `new-list` and can be subscribed to by sending the following to `listserv@vm1.nodak.edu`:

```
subscribe new-list Craig Mullins
```

Substitute your name where I specified Craig Mullins.

Develop a List of Bookmarks   When you find a Web page that has useful information, use the bookmarking feature of your Web browser to record the URL for later use.

17

Use Search Engines on the Web   There is a wealth of information available on the WWW that will make the job of a database developer, database analyst, system programmer, or DBA much easier. However, finding all of it can be quite a task. Developing a list of bookmarks, while useful, can be difficult to create and even more difficult to maintain. Web sites are constantly moving, dying, and coming online. It is impossible for a bookmark file (which is a static file containing links to other sites) to remain accurate for any length of time.

Instead of hunting and guessing for information resources, you can use a Web search engine, instead. There are quite a few search sites available, including Yahoo!, Excite, and Google. These sites are designed to accept search keywords as input and return links to Web sites that contain information related to the keywords. With a search engine, the user types in a word or phrase (such as **database** or **DB2**). The response will be a listing of links to sites that match the search. The most popular search engine is undoubtedly Google—shown in Figure 17.16.

FIGURE 17.16   The Google Search Engine site.
(`http://www.google.com`)

CHAPTER **18**

The Doors to DB2

You have learned how to embed SQL in application programs to access DB2 data, but you have yet to explore the possibilities when executing these programs. When accessing DB2 data, an application program is not limited to a specific technological platform. You can choose from the following environments when developing DB2 application systems (depending on their availability at your shop): TSO, CICS, IMS/VS, CAF, and RRSAF. You can think of each of these environments as a door that provides access to DB2 data. This chapter covers the advantages and disadvantages of each of these environments. First, I will discuss the basics of DB2 program execution that apply to all operating environments.

Each DB2 program must be connected to DB2 by an attachment facility, which is the mechanism by which an environment is connected to a DB2 subsystem. Additionally, a thread is established for each embedded SQL program that is executing. A *thread* is a control structure used by DB2 to communicate with an application program. The thread is used to send requests to DB2, to send data from DB2 to the program, and to communicate (through the SQLCA) the status of each SQL statement after it is executed. Every program communicates with DB2 by means of a thread (see Figure 18.1).

Now you can explore the process of invoking a DB2 application program. First, the program is initiated and the attachment facility appropriate for the environment in which the program is running is called. Next, security is checked (external z/OS security, internal environment security, and DB2 security). Finally, upon execution of the first SQL statement in the program, a thread is created.

After the thread is established, DB2 loads the executable form of the appropriate plan from the DB2 Directory, where it is physically stored as a skeleton cursor table (SKCT). If the plan is composed of packages, DB2 loads the package table for the

IN THIS CHAPTER

- TSO (Time-Sharing Option)
- CICS (Customer Information Control System)
- IMS (Information Management System)
- CAF (Call Attach Facility)
- RRSAF (Recoverable Resource Manager Services Attach Facility)
- Comparison of the Environments
- The Critical Mass

required packages into an area of memory reserved for DB2 program execution; this area is called the *Environmental Descriptor Management Pool*, or the EDM Pool. All DBDs required by the plan are also loaded into the EDM Pool from the DB2 Directory when the thread is established. Simply put, when a thread is created, DB2 performs the necessary housekeeping to ensure that the application program operates successfully.

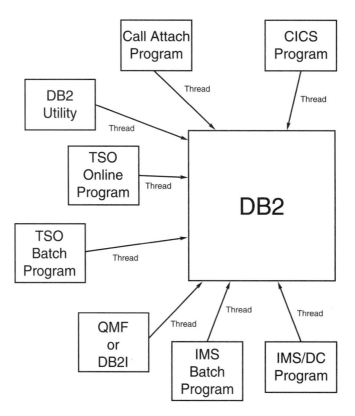

FIGURE 18.1   Programs access DB2 using threads.

Now that you have an overall picture of the way that an application program communicates with DB2, you can explore the processing environments. DB2 programs can be run in the foreground (also called *online*) or in the background (also called *batch*).

Online applications are characterized by interaction with an end user through a terminal. Most online applications display a screen that prompts the user for input, accept data from that screen, process the data, and display another screen until the user decides to end the session. Online programs are generally used to provide real-time update and query capabilities or to enter transactions for future batch processing.

Batch applications are characterized by their lack of user interactions. A batch program is typically submitted using JCL. It can accept parameters as input, but it does not rely on an end user being present during its execution. Batch programs are generally used to perform mass updates, to create reports, and to perform complex non-interactive processes.

Each environment provides different modes of operation, depending on whether the application is online or batch. For an overview of which environment supports which mode, consult Table 18.1.

TABLE 18.1 DB2 Processing Environments

Environment	Batch	Online
TSO	Yes	Yes
CICS	No	Yes
IMS	Yes	Yes
CAF	Yes	Yes*
RRSAF	Yes	Yes
*Only when used with TSO		

TSO (Time-Sharing Option)

TSO, or Time-Sharing Option, is one of the five basic environments from which DB2 data can be accessed. TSO enables users to interact with the system using an online interface that is either screen- or panel-driven. The Interactive System Productivity Facility, or ISPF, provides the mechanism for communicating by panels, which is the common method for interaction between TSO applications and users. The TSO Attachment Facility provides access to DB2 resources in two ways:

- Online, in the TSO foreground, driven by application programs, CLISTs, or REXX EXECs coded to communicate with DB2 and TSO, possibly using ISPF panels

- In batch mode using the TSO Terminal Monitor Program, IKJEFT01 (or IKJEFT1B), to invoke the DSN command and run a DB2 application program

TSO is one of the three online environments supported by DB2, but unlike the other two, TSO is not transaction-driven. The TSO Attachment Facility operates by means of a communication channel that uses a single thread to direct DB2 calls. Each user can be logged on, in the foreground, to a single TSO address space at any time.

Each batch TSO job, however, initiates a different invocation of the TMP, enabling numerous batch TSO jobs submitted by the same user to run simultaneously. The batch jobs are independent of any foreground TSO activity. Thus, a single user, at any given time, can have one online TSO session communicating with DB2 and multiple batch TSO jobs communicating with DB2.

The TSO Attachment Facility is available for use by simply installing DB2. Communication between DB2 and TSO is accomplished with the DSN command processor, which is bundled with DB2. The DSN command processor enables users to issue DB2 commands in the TSO environment. One of these commands, the RUN command, executes DB2 application programs. (IBM bundles an online TSO application that can be used to access DB2 data: DB2 Interactive, or DB2I. DB2I is discussed in greater depth later in this section.)

18

As you can see in Figure 18.2, the DSN command processor establishes the thread that enables TSO to communicate with DB2. An alternative method is to use the Call Attach Facility in TSO to communicate with DB2. The Call Attach Facility is discussed later in the "CAF (Call Attach Facility)" section of this chapter.

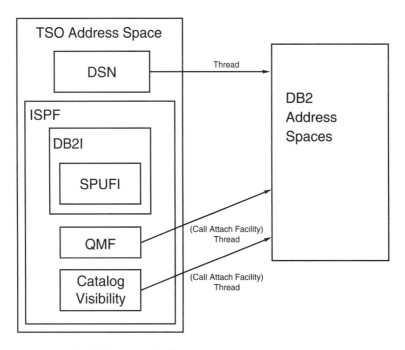

FIGURE 18.2   Using the TSO Attach Facility.

TSO/DB2 Parameters

DB2 is a parameter-driven subsystem. A series of parameters known as DSNZPARMs, or simply ZPARMs, is passed to DB2 when it is started. A complete discussion of the DSNZPARMs is supplied in Chapter 28, "Tuning DB2's Components." Because two of these parameters—IDFORE and IDBACK—apply directly to TSO, however, I will discuss them here.

IDFORE controls the number of users that can access DB2 simultaneously from the TSO foreground. The types of TSO foreground users include the following:

- DB2I

- QMF

- Users running the DSN command (through ISPF, CLISTs, REXX, and so on)

- Users running TSO/DB2 programs through the Call Attach Facility

- Users running any DB2 tool online in foreground TSO

DB2 limits the number of TSO foreground tasks to the number specified in the IDFORE parameter. When the limit is reached, any subsequent request for additional foreground TSO tasks is rejected.

IDBACK controls the number of concurrent DB2 batch connections. These connections, however, are not limited to TSO batch connections. They include the following:

- Batch DB2 jobs using the DSN command
- Batch DB2 jobs using the Call Attach Facility
- QMF batch jobs
- DB2 utilities

DB2 Access Using Batch TSO

DB2 batch programs are executed in the background under the control of the TSO terminal monitor program. A TSO session is thereby created in batch. The DSN command is invoked by this session through input specified in the SYSTSIN data set. See Listing 18.1 for JCL to run a batch TSO/DB2 program.

LISTING 18.1   Batch JCL for a TSO/DB2 Program

```
//DB2JOBB JOB (BATCH),'DB2 BATCH',MSGCLASS=X,CLASS=X,
//         NOTIFY=USER
//*
//****************************************************************
//*
//*       JCL TO RUN A DB2 PROGRAM IN BATCH
//*       USING THE TSO TERMINAL MONITOR PROGRAM
//*
//****************************************************************
//*
//JOBLIB     DD DSN=SYS1.DB2V810.DSNLOAD,DISP=SHR
//BATCHPRG   EXEC PGM=IKJEFT01,DYNAMNBR=20
//SYSTSPRT   DD  SYSOUT=*
//SYSPRINT   DD  SYSOUT=*
//SYSUDUMP   DD  SYSOUT=*
//SYSTSIN    DD  *
  DSN SYSTEM(DB2P)
  RUN PROGRAM(PROG0001)   -
  PLAN(PLAN0001)  -
  LIB('APPL.LOAD.LIBRARY')
  END
/*
//
```

This JCL invokes TSO in batch, reads the SYSTSIN input, and invokes the DSN command processor for the DB2P subsystem. Next, it runs the program named PROG0001 using the plan PLAN0001. When the program is complete, the DSN session ends.

DB2 Access Using Foreground TSO

Another way to access DB2 data is through online, or foreground, TSO using the DSN command processor. You simply issue the following command from either ISPF option 6 or the TSO READY prompt:

```
DSN SYSTEM(xxxx)
```

Here, *xxxx* represents the DB2 subsystem name. This command places you under the control of DSN. A prompt labeled DSN appears, indicating that you are in the middle of a DSN session. You can issue any DSN subcommand, including the RUN subcommand. The DSN command processor and its associated subcommands are discussed more fully in Chapter 36, "DB2 Commands."

Suppose that you want to run a DB2 program called SAMPLE2 using the plan SAM2PLAN in foreground TSO. To do so, you can issue the following commands:

```
READY
   DSN SYSTEM(DB2T)
DSN
   RUN PROGRAM(SAMPLE2) PLAN(SAM2PLAN)
DSN
     END
READY
```

The boldface words are entered by the user. The other words are system prompts returned by TSO or the DSN command processor.

Rather than using the DSN command directly from a terminal, as just discussed, embedding the execution of a DB2 program in a CLIST or REXX EXEC is more common. A TSO user can invoke the CLIST or EXEC either directly by entering its name from ISPF option 6 or the TSO READY prompt, or as a selection from an ISPF panel. Figure 18.3 shows a common configuration for an online, TSO, ISPF-driven DB2 application.

Online TSO/DB2 Design Techniques

Programmers can follow two basic scenarios for developing online TSO programs that access DB2 data. Each scenario provides a different level of runtime efficiency and support for application development. These two scenarios provide either fast application development or efficient performance.

Using the fast application development scenario enables programmers to make full use of the development tools provided by TSO and ISPF. The normal processing flow for this scenario is a seven-step process

1. An ISPF menu appears, containing options for one or more TSO/DB2 application programs.

2. The user selects an option for the DB2 application he or she wants to execute.

3. The option invokes a CLIST that issues the DSN command and the RUN subcommand for the selected option.

4. The program displays a panel, engaging in a dialog with the user whereby data can be entered, validated, and processed. The user selects an option or function key on the panel to signal when he or she has finished.

5. The user can process multiple panels but only for the selected program.

6. When the user indicates that he or she has finished, the program ends and control is returned to the CLIST. The CLIST immediately issues the DSN END subcommand, which ends the connection to DB2.

7. The original menu is then displayed so that the user can select another option.

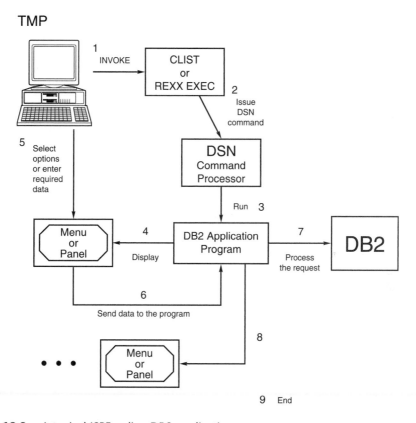

FIGURE 18.3 A typical ISPF online DB2 application.

This scenario provides maximum programming flexibility using minimum system resources. It has two drawbacks, however. Each time the user selects a menu option, a large amount of overhead is involved to load and run the CLIST, invoke DSN, issue the RUN command, load the program module, and create the thread. Also, each menu option consists of a single load module and plan. This scenario effectively eliminates the capability to switch from program to program using ISPLINK because one program and its associated plan accomplish one task.

The scenario to process a TSO application achieving efficient performance is a nine-step process:

1. An ISPF menu appears, containing an option for one or more TSO/DB2 application programs.

2. The user selects an option for the DB2 application he or she wants to execute.

3. The option invokes a CLIST that issues the DSN command and the RUN subcommand for the selected option.

4. The program displays a menu from which the user can select the programs that make up the TSO/DB2 application.

5. When a menu option is chosen, the program calls another program. (All programs are linked into a single load module.)

6. The called program displays a panel, engaging in a dialog with the users whereby data can be entered, validated, and processed. The user selects an option or function key on the panel to signal when he or she has finished.

7. The user can process multiple panels in the program. You also can provide options to run other programs in the application based on user input or function keys.

8. When the user indicates that he or she has finished, the control program redisplays the menu. The user can then back out of the menu that causes the CLIST to issue the DSN END subcommand, ending the connection to DB2.

9. The original ISPF menu is then displayed so that the user can select another option.

When you develop applications using this scenario, overhead is reduced significantly. The CLIST is loaded and executed only once, DSN is invoked only once, the program modules are loaded only once, and a single thread is established once and used for the duration of the user's stay in the application.

This scenario has some drawbacks, however. The application can contain one potentially very large program load module. Each time a program is modified, the entire module must be link-edited again. This process uses a lot of CPU time. Also, application downtime is required because the application must wait for the link-edit process to complete. In addition, more virtual storage is required to store the program load module as it executes.

Additionally, you must take extra care when determining how to bind the application. For applications developed on older releases of DB2 (prior to V2.3), a single large plan may exist that consists of every DBRM in the application. This used to be required by DB2. This scenario causes the same types of problems as a large program load module:

- Extra CPU time is used for a bind.

- Application downtime is increased while waiting for the bind.

- More virtual storage is required to hold the plan in the EDM Pool as the program runs.

The better application design option is for each program DBRM to be bound to a single package. All the packages are then included in the package list of a plan (either explicitly or using wildcards). This scenario reduces bind time, thereby decreasing CPU time and application downtime waiting for the bind to complete.

A final drawback to this scenario is that when the DSN command is used to run online TSO programs, the thread is created when the first SQL call is made. When the program is composed of many programs that call one another, a thread can be tied up for an inordinate amount of time.

When the application is invoked, the DSN command is issued, specifying the online application's load module and the composite plan. The thread created for this program's execution remains active until the program ends. One thread is used for each user of the TSO/DB2 application for the duration of its execution.

TSO is not a transaction-driven system. Users can enter a TSO application and leave a terminal inactive in the middle of the application, thus tying up a DB2 thread. That thread is not necessary when the user is thinking about what to do next or has walked away from the terminal.

An alternative solution is to use the Call Attach Facility to control the activation and deactivation of threads. This technique is addressed in the upcoming section on CAF.

DB2I and SPUFI

DB2I is a TSO-based DB2 application. It consists of a series of ISPF panels, programs, and CLISTs enabling rapid access to DB2 services and data. Using DB2I can increase the TSO DB2 developer's productivity. DB2I provides many features that can be exploited by the TSO user to query and administer DB2 data. To access DB2I, follow this sequence:

1. Log on to TSO as you normally would.

2. If the logon procedure does not automatically place you into ISPF, enter ISPF. The ISPF main menu appears.

3. Choose the DB2I option. This option most often is available directly from the main ISPF menu. However, DB2I could be on a different ISPF menu (for example, a System Services, Database Options, or User menu), or it could be accessible only through a CLIST. (Consult your shop standards, if necessary, to determine the correct method of accessing DB2I.)

After you select the DB2I option, the main menu appears, as shown in Figure 18.4. This figure shows all DB2I features, including those used for program preparation and execution, as discussed in Chapter 13, "Program Preparation." Each DB2I option is discussed in the following sections.

SPUFI Option

The first option in the DB2I main menu is SPUFI, or SQL Processor Using File Input. It reads SQL statements contained as text in a sequential file, processes those statements, and places you in an ISPF browse session to view the results. Figure 18.5 shows the SPUFI panel.

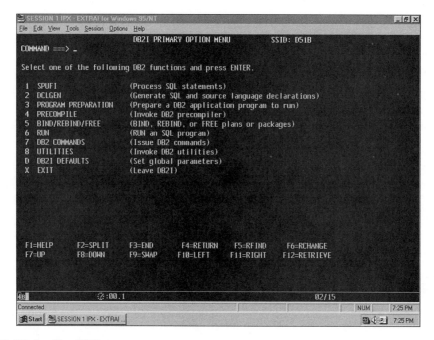

FIGURE 18.4   The DB2I menu.

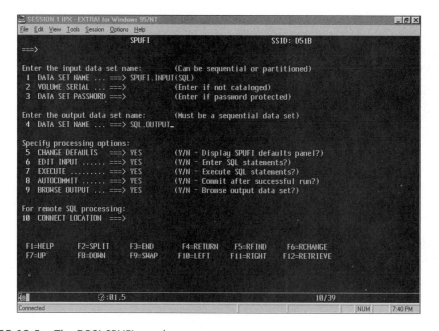

FIGURE 18.5   The DB2I SPUFI panel.

By specifying an input and output data set and selecting the appropriate options, you can execute SQL statements in an online mode. The SPUFI options follow:

Change Defaults	When Y is specified , the SPUFI defaults panel appears, as shown in Figure 18.6.
Edit Input	When Y is specified, SPUFI places you in an ISPF edit session for the input data set. This way, you can change the input SQL before its execution. Never specify N in this field. When you want to bypass editing your input file, place an asterisk (*) in this field; DB2I bypasses the edit step but resets the field to its previous value the next time SPUFI is invoked. If you use N and you forget to change the field back to Y, your next invocation of SPUFI executes SQL without allowing you to edit your SQL.
Execute	When Y is specified, the SQL in the input file is read and executed.
Autocommit	When Y is specified, a COMMIT is issued automatically after the successful execution of the SQL in the input file. When you specify N, SPUFI prompts you about whether a COMMIT should be issued. If the COMMIT is not issued, all changes are rolled back.
Browse Output	When Y is specified, SPUFI places you in an ISPF browse session for the output data set. You can view the results of the SQL that was executed.

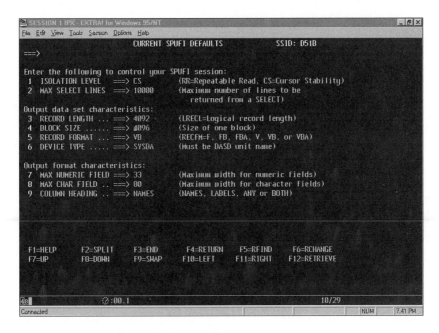

FIGURE 18.6 The DB2I SPUFI Defaults panel.

Specifying Y for all these options except Change Defaults is common. Typically, defaults are changed only once—the first time someone uses SPUFI. ISPF saves the defaults entered

18

from session to session. Use these options—as you see fit—to control your SPUFI executions. The defaults panel is shown in Figure 18.6.

The SPUFI input data set can contain multiple SQL statements, as long as they are separated by semicolons. For example, you could successfully code the following statements in a SPUFI input data set:

```
--
-- THIS SQL STATEMENT WILL SELECT ALL ROWS OF THE
-- SAMPLE TABLE, DSN8810.DEPT
  SELECT * FROM DSN8810.DEPT;
--
-- THIS SQL STATEMENT WILL SET THE SALARY FOR ALL EMPLOYEES
-- WITH THE LAST NAME OF 'KWAN' TO ZERO
  UPDATE DSN8810.EMP
  SET SALARY = 0
  WHERE LASTNAME = 'KWAN';
--
-- THIS SQL STATEMENT WILL ROLL BACK THE CHANGES MADE BY
-- THE PREVIOUS SQL STATEMENT
  ROLLBACK;
```

This sample input for the SPUFI processor contains three SQL statements. Each SQL statement is separated from the others by the semicolon that terminates each statement. Comments are preceded by two hyphens. When the SQL is executed and browsed, an output data set like the following appears:

```
--------+--------+--------+--------+--------+--------+-
-- THIS SQL STATEMENT WILL SELECT ALL ROWS OF THE
-- SAMPLE TABLE, DSN8810.DEPT
  SELECT * FROM DSN8810.DEPT;
--------+--------+--------+--------+--------+--------+-
DEPTNO  DEPTNAME                   MGRNO     ADMRDEPT
--------+--------+--------+--------+--------+--------+-
A00     SPIFFY COMPUTER SERVICE DIV.  000010    A00
B01     PLANNING                   000020    A00
C01     INFORMATION CENTER         000030    A00
D01     DEVELOPMENT CENTER         -------   A00
E01     SUPPORT SERVICES           000050    A00
D11     MANUFACTURING SYSTEMS      000060    D01
D21     ADMINISTRATION SYSTEMS     000070    D01
E11     OPERATIONS                 000090    E01
E21     SOFTWARE SUPPORT           000010    E01
DSNE610I NUMBER OF ROWS DISPLAYED IS 9
DSNE616I STATEMENT EXECUTION WAS SUCCESSFUL, SQLCODE IS 100
--------+--------+--------+--------+--------+--------+-
--
--THIS SQL STATEMENT WILL SET THE SALARY FOR ALL EMPLOYEES
--WITH THE LAST NAME OF 'KWAN' TO ZERO
  UPDATE DSN8810.EMP
  SET SALARY = 0
  WHERE LASTNAME = 'KWAN';
```

```
........+........+........+........+........+........+-
DSNE615I NUMBER OF ROWS AFFECTED IS 1
DSNE616I STATEMENT EXECUTION WAS SUCCESSFUL, SQLCODE IS 0
........+........+........+........+........+........+-
--
-- THIS SQL STATEMENT WILL ROLL BACK THE CHANGES MADE BY
-- THE PREVIOUS SQL STATEMENT
   ROLLBACK;
........+........+........+........+........+........+-
DSNE616I STATEMENT EXECUTION WAS SUCCESSFUL, SQLCODE IS 0
........+........+........+........+........+........+-
DSNE617I COMMIT PERFORMED, SQLCODE IS 0
DSNE616I STATEMENT EXECUTION WAS SUCCESSFUL, SQLCODE IS 0
........+........+........+........+........+........+-
DSNE601I SQL STATEMENTS ASSUMED TO BE BETWEEN COLUMNS 1 AND 72
DSNE620I NUMBER OF SQL STATEMENTS PROCESSED IS 3
DSNE621I NUMBER OF INPUT RECORDS READ IS 17
DSNE622I NUMBER OF OUTPUT RECORDS WRITTEN IS 48
```

The data set used for input of SQL must be allocated before invoking SPUFI. The data set can be empty and can be edited as part of the SPUFI session. It is recommended that each SPUFI user maintain a partitioned data set containing his or her SPUFI input. This way, users can keep and reference frequently used SQL statements. The SPUFI input data set should be defined as a fixed, blocked data set with an LRECL of 80. You can write SQL statements in all but the last 8 bytes of each input record; this area is reserved for sequence numbers.

You do not need to allocate the output data set before using SPUFI. If the output data set does not exist, SPUFI creates a virtual, blocked sequential data set with an LRECL of 4092.

Set the proper SPUFI defaults (see Figure 18.6). You can set these defaults the first time you use SPUFI and then bypass them on subsequent SPUFI runs. Be sure to specify the following defaults:

Isolation Level	Favor setting this option to CS. You might choose UR to improve performance, but at the expense of possible data integrity problems. If you require an Isolation Level of RR, you probably should be accessing the data programmatically rather than with SPUFI.
Max Select Lines	Set to an appropriate number. If you will be selecting from large tables that return more than 250 rows, the installation default value of 250 is insufficient. SPUFI stops returning rows after reaching the specified limit, and it issues a message indicating so.

The other default values are appropriate for most situations.

DCLGEN Option

The DCLGEN option in the DB2I main menu automatically produces a data set containing a DECLARE TABLE statement and valid WORKING-STORAGE host variables for a given DB2 table.

18

You can include the data set in a COBOL program to enable embedded SQL access. See Chapter 13 for more details on DCLGEN.

Program Preparation Option
The Program Preparation option in the DB2I main menu prepares a program containing embedded SQL for execution. See Chapter 13 for more details on DB2 program preparation.

Precompile Option
Precompile is the fourth option on the DB2I main menu. In precompilation, a program containing embedded SQL is parsed to retrieve all SQL and replace it with calls to a runtime interface to DB2. See Chapter 13 for more details on precompiling a DB2 program.

Bind/Rebind/Free Option
When you select Option 5 of the DB2I menu, the Bind/Rebind/Free menu shown in Figure 18.7 appears.

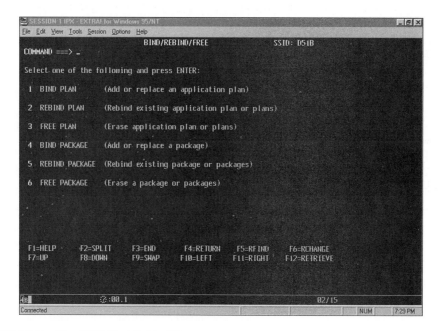

FIGURE 18.7   The DB2I Bind/Rebind/Free menu.

Option 1 on this menu provides the capability to bind a DB2 plan, and option 4 binds a package. These options are discussed fully in Chapter 13.

The second option is Rebind Plan. When you choose this option, the panel in Figure 18.8 appears. A plan can be rebound, thereby rechecking syntax, reestablishing access paths, and in general, redoing the bind. However, rebind does not enable you to add a DBRM to the plan. In addition, if any of the rebind parameters are not specified, they default to the options specified at bind time, not to the traditional bind defaults. Rebind is particularly useful for determining new access paths after running the RUNSTATS utility.

Option 5 provides the capability to rebind a package. You rebind packages in much the same way you rebind plans. Figure 18.9 shows the Rebind Package panel.

FIGURE 18.8   The DB2I Rebind Plan panel.

There is a significant amount of confusion about the difference between the REBIND command and the BIND REPLACE command. A REBIND simply *reevaluates access paths* for the DBRMs currently in a plan (or the single DBRM in a package). BIND REPLACE, on the other hand, *replaces* all the DBRMs in the plan. So, if you must use a different DBRM, BIND REPLACE is your only option. If you must simply change access path selections based on current statistics, REBIND will do the trick.

On the Bind/Rebind/Free menu, Option 3, Free Plan, and Option 6, Free Package, enable you to remove plans and packages from the system. Figure 18.10 shows the Free Plan panel, and Figure 18.11 shows the Free Package panel. You simply specify the names of the plans or packages to remove from the system, and they are *freed*.

Packages and plans you no longer use should be freed from the DB2 subsystem. Doing so frees DB2 Directory and DB2 Catalog pages for use by other packages and plans.

CAUTION

Avoid issuing the FREE (*) command. This command drops every plan in the DB2 subsystem, which is probably not your intention. Additionally, a large amount of resources is used to execute this command.

18

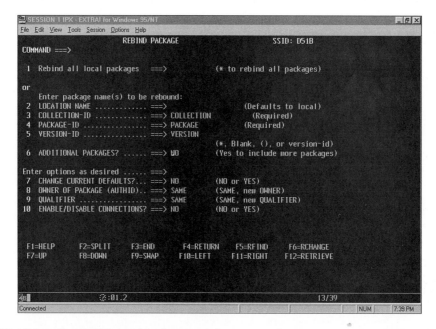

FIGURE 18.9   The DB2I Rebind Package panel.

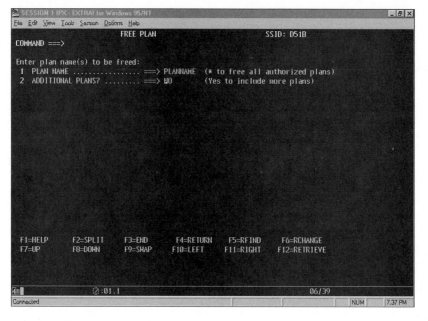

FIGURE 18.10   The DB2I Free Plan panel.

FIGURE 18.11 The DB2I Free Package panel.

Run Option

The sixth DB2I option enables you to run a DB2 application program. The Run option is rarely used. More often, foreground DB2 programs are invoked by CLISTs, REXX EXECs, or ISPF panels, and background DB2 programs are invoked through preexisting batch JCL. When you select this option, the Run panel appears, as shown in Figure 18.12. You simply specify the load library data set (including the member name) for the program to be run, along with any necessary parameters, the appropriate plan name, and a WHERE TO RUN option. The three WHERE TO RUN options follow:

FOREGROUND	The program is run to completion, tying up the terminal from which the run was submitted for the duration of the program's run.
BACKGROUND	JCL is automatically built to run the program and is submitted in batch for processing.
EDITJCL	JCL is automatically built and displayed for you. You have the option of editing the JCL. You then can submit the JCL.

DB2 Commands Option

When you select DB2I option 7, DB2 Commands, the panel in Figure 18.13 appears, enabling you to submit DB2 commands using TSO. For example, the command shown in Figure 18.12 displays the status of adatabase. In-depth coverage of DB2 commands is included in Part VI.

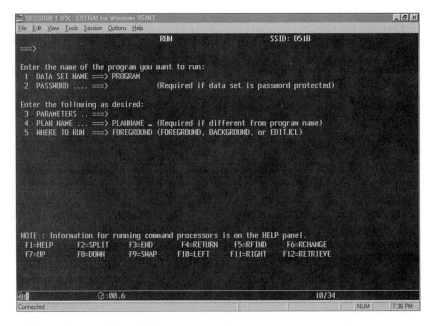

FIGURE 18.12   The DB2I Run panel.

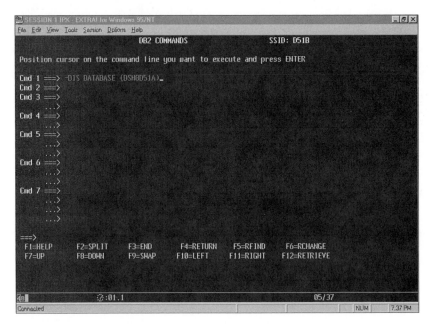

FIGURE 18.13   The DB2I Commands panel.

Utilities Option

DB2I also provides panels that ease the administrative burdens of DB2 utility processing. Using option 8 of DB2I, the Utilities option, you can generate utility JCL, submit the utility JCL, display the status of utilities, and terminate utilities using a panel-driven interface. For a complete discussion of the DB2 utilities and the use of DB2I to control DB2 utility processing, consult Part VI.

DB2I Defaults Option

The defaults panel, DB2I option D, lets you modify parameters that control the operation of DB2I (see Figure 18.14). Be sure that the proper DB2 subsystem is specified in the DB2 Name parameter. If your production DB2 subsystem runs on the same central electronic complex as your test DB2 subsystem, disaster can result if the name is not coded properly. Be sure also that you supply the proper language to be used for preparing DB2 programs in the Application Language parameter and a valid job card for your shop in the DB2I Job Statement parameter. A second default panel (such as the one shown in Figure 18.15) can be displayed for language defaults based on the Application Language chosen.

FIGURE 18.14   The DB2I Defaults panel.

QMF

IBM's Query Management Facility, or QMF, is an interactive query tool used to produce formatted query output. QMF enables you to submit SQL queries dynamically, much like DB2I's SPUFI facility. QMF goes much further, however. Using a mechanism called a *QMF form*, you can format the results of your SQL queries into professional-looking reports.

18

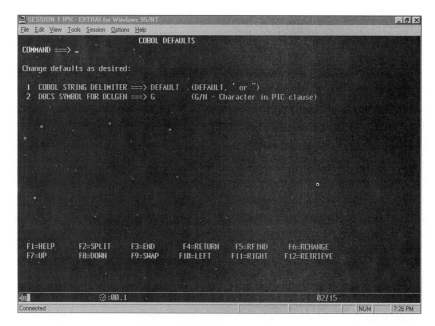

FIGURE 18.15   The DB2I Defaults panel #2: COBOL Defaults.

To depict the basics of QMF, assume that you must produce a formatted report of all employees in the company. You invoke QMF, generally by choosing an option from the ISPF main menu. The QMF Home panel then appears, as shown in Figure 18.16. Notice the numbered options along the bottom portion of the screen. These numbers correspond to QMF functions that you can invoke by pressing the function key for the number indicated. For example, press F1 to request the first function, Help.

You can use three basic QMF objects to produce formatted reports of DB2 data: queries, forms, and procs. You begin by creating a query. Press F6 to navigate to the QMF Query panel, which is initially blank.

You will produce an employee report, so type the following statement at the COMMAND prompt:

```
COMMAND ===> DRAW SYSIBM.SYSPLAN
```

The panel shown in Figure 18.17 then appears.

To run this query, press F2. Doing so produces the report shown in Figure 18.18. You can print this report using F4 or format it using F9. When you press F9, the report form appears, as shown in Figure 18.19. A default form is generated for each query when it is run.

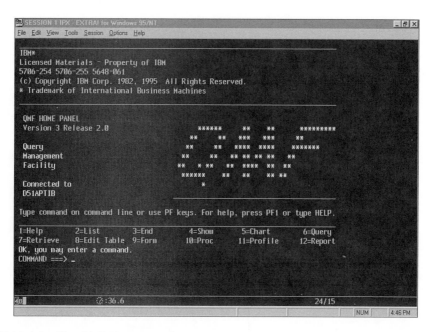

FIGURE 18.16   The QMF Home panel.

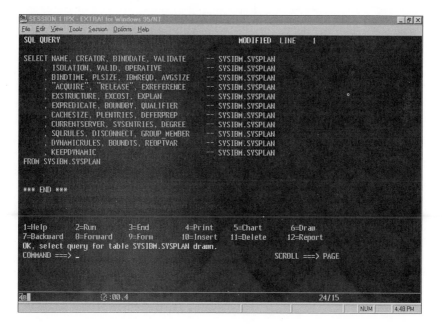

FIGURE 18.17   The QMF Query panel.

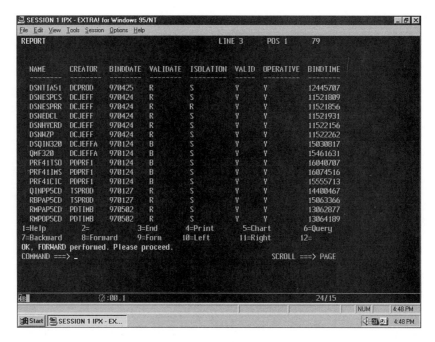

FIGURE 18.18   The QMF Report panel.

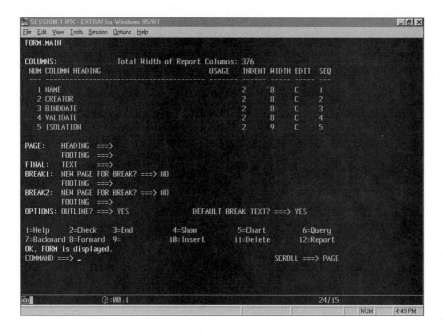

FIGURE 18.19   The QMF Form panel.

You can use a QMF Form to produce a formatted report for the query output. QMF Forms enable you to perform the following:

- Code a different column heading

- Specify control breaks

- Code control-break heading and footing text

- Specify edit codes to transform column data (for example, suppress leading zeroes or display a currency symbol)

- Compute averages, percentages, standard deviations, and totals for specific columns

- Display summary results across a row, suppressing the supporting detail rows

- Omit columns in the query from the report

You can see how QMF gives you a great deal of power for creating quick, formatted reports from simple SQL queries.

The third QMF object, the QMF Proc, is another important feature of QMF. A QMF query can contain only one SQL statement. Contrast this capability with SPUFI, which can contain multiple SQL statements as long as they are separated by a semicolon.

To execute multiple SQL statements at one time, you use a QMF Proc. QMF Procs contain QMF commands that are tied together and executed serially. For an example, see Figure 18.20. This QMF Proc runs one query, prints the results, and then runs another query and prints its results. You can string together as many run statements as necessary and store them as a QMF Proc.

Using QMF is a quick way to produce high-quality professional reports. Following is a typical QMF user's session, shown also in Figure 18.21. If you type a single SQL statement and press a few function keys, an end-user report is generated.

1. Enter QMF, and the QMF Home panel appears.

2. Press F6 to display the QMF Query panel. Code the SQL SELECT statement.

3. Press F2 to display the QMF Report panel. Execute the SQL statement to produce the report.

4. Press F9 to display the QMF Form panel. Modify the report parameters and headings as necessary.

5. Press F12 to display the QMF Report panel. Print the final formatted report.

Other TSO-Based DB2 Tools

A host of vendor-supplied tools use TSO as their execution environment. In addition to QMF, IBM provides other tools with a TSO interface such as DB2-PM. Additionally, most of the third-party tools for DB2 database administration, analysis, and development are TSO-based. A comprehensive list of DB2 tool vendors is provided in Appendix B, "DB2 Tool

Vendors," and coverage of the types of tools available is provided in Chapter 39, "Components of a Total DB2 Solution."

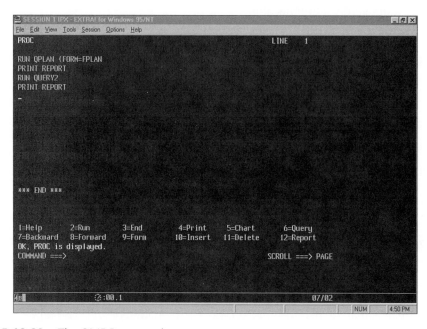

FIGURE 18.20   The QMF Proc panel.

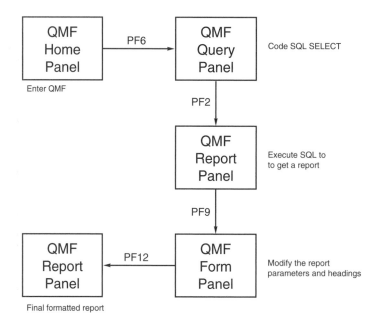

FIGURE 18.21   A typical QMF session.

TSO Guidelines

When utilizing DB2 in conjunction with TSO, the following guidelines should be used to ensure effective usage of DB2 and TSO.

Create MVS Performance Groups for DB2 Users   To ensure fast TSO response time, create separate MVS performance groups for TSO users who will access DB2 applications. TSO is generally associated with three periods, designated here as period1, period2, and period3. These periods dictate the amount of MVS resources assigned to a TSO user. Period1 provides more resources than period2, which in turn provides more resources than period3. As TSO users run DB2 applications, their address space is moved from an initial period to lower periods as resources are used. As the address space is moved lower, the TSO response time becomes slower.

For DB2 and QMF users, you can create TSO performance groups with higher levels of resources in period1 and period2. Also, you can prevent the lowering of their TSO sessions to period3. This way, you can provide an optimal environment for high-priority TSO/DB2 applications.

Integrate All Resources into the DB2 Unit of Work When Using TSO   When COMMIT processing is performed in online, TSO-based applications, DB2 controls the committing of its resources. The commit and recovery of any other resources, such as sequential input and output files, must be controlled through a program. This is in contrast to the other online environments, which control commit processing by commands native to the environment.

COMMIT processing in batch TSO/DB2 programs should follow the guidelines presented in Part II.

COMMIT Frequently in TSO/DB2 Applications   Online TSO/DB2 applications are subject to more frequent deadlocks and timeouts than DB2 applications using other transaction-oriented online environments. For this reason, you should commit more frequently in an online TSO/DB2 application than in DB2 applications running in other environments. Consider committing updates every row or two, rather than after a full screen. Committing might affect the efficiency of the application and should be handled on a program-by-program basis. Failure to commit frequently, however, can result in an unusable application because of lock contention.

Use ISPF Panels to Validate Screen Input   To perform validation checking, use the native functionality of ISPF rather than code validation routines. When ISPF performs the checking, the data is validated before it is processed by the application. This approach can reduce the overhead of loading the program and allocating the thread and other overhead related to program execution.

In addition, error checking is handled by the ISPF routines rather than by the application code. Code provided by the system is generally more error free than functionally equivalent application code. Finally, if you use the validation facilities of ISPF, you can greatly reduce the time it takes to develop TSO/DB2 applications.

Avoid TSO in Performance-Critical Applications   As a development platform for DB2-based applications, TSO is limited in its functionality and efficiency. You should follow these basic rules when deciding whether to use TSO as your online monitor. Do not choose TSO as the development platform for an online DB2-based application if you need subsecond response time or if more than 10 users will be accessing the application concurrently. However, you should choose TSO if you need an environment that speeds up the application development cycle. TSO provides a rich set of tools for developing and testing programs and ISPF screens.

Use ISPF Tables   Consider copying a DB2 table that must be browsed to an ISPF table at the beginning of the program and processing from the ISPF table instead of the DB2 table. This way, you can dramatically increase performance when an online TSO/DB2 program must continually reopen a cursor with an ORDER BY due to COMMIT processing. Instead, the ISPF table can be created from a cursor, sorted appropriately, and COMMIT processing will not cause the program to lose cursor positioning on the ISPF table.

However, you must consider the update implications of using an ISPF table when programming and executing programs using this technique. Updates made to the DB2 table by other users are not made to the ISPF table because it is a copy of the DB2 table for your program's use only. These updates can cause two problems.

One, updates made by other programs might be bypassed rather than processed by the program using the ISPF table. For example, if another program updates data and an ISPF table-driven program generates reports, the report might not contain the most current data.

Another potential problem is that the program using the ISPF table might make incorrect updates. For example, if the program reads the ISPF table and then updates the DB2 table, the following scenario could result:

Program 1	Time	Program 2
Copy EMP table	1	
to ISPF table	2	
	3	Update Emp 000010
	4	Commit
Read ISPF table	5	Update Emp 000020
Update Emp 000010	6	Commit
Read ISPF table	7	
Update Emp 000020	8	And so on

At time 1, Program 1 begins executing. It copies the EMP table to the ISPF table before Program 2 begins. At time 3, Program 2 begins executing, serially processing employees and adding 100 to each employee's bonus. After Program 1 copies the entire EMP table, it begins giving all employees in department B01 a 10-percent raise in their bonus.

You can see how the employees in department B01 will be disappointed when their bonus paycheck arrives. Program 2 adds 100, but Program 1, unaware of the additional 100, adds 10 percent to the old bonus amount. Consider employee 000020, who works in department B01. He starts with a bonus of $800. Program 2 adds 100, making his bonus $900. Then Program 1 processes employee 000020, setting his bonus to 800×1.10, or $880. Instead of a $990 bonus, he receives only $880.

Avoid Running Batch Programs in TSO Foreground   A DB2 program developed to run as a batch program (that is, with no user interaction while the program is running) can be run in the TSO foreground using the DSN command processor, but doing so is not recommended. Running a DB2 batch program in this manner needlessly ties up a user's TSO session and, more important, consumes a valuable foreground thread that could be used for true online processing. (Remember that the IDFORE DSNZPARM value limits the number of foreground threads available for use.)

Use IKJEFT1B   You must use the TSO Terminal Monitor Program (TMP) to invoke the DSN command and run a DB2 application program in batch mode. The generic program name is IKJEFT01. However, system errors and user abends are not honored by IKJEFT01, making it difficult to perform error checking in subsequent JCL steps. To rectify this problem, you can use IKJEFT1B instead of IKJEFT01. IKJEFT1B is an alternate entry point to the TSO TMP.

If an ABEND occurs and you are using IKJEFT01, the result will be a dump of TSO and the ABEND code will not be passed to the next step of your job. This is probably not the results you are looking for. The use of IKJEFT1B will give the same results as a standard MVS batch job because IKJEFT1B passes non-zero return codes through to JES where they can be checked in the JCL job stream.

CICS (Customer Information Control System)

The second of the four "doors to DB2" is CICS (Customer Information Control System). CICS is a teleprocessing monitor that enables programmers to develop online, transaction-based programs. By means of BMS (Basic Mapping Support) and the data communications facilities of CICS, programs can display formatted data on screens and receive formatted data from users for further processing. A typical scenario for the execution of a CICS transaction follows:

1. The operator enters data on a terminal, including a transaction ID, and presses Enter. The data can simply be a transaction ID entered by the operator or a formatted BMS screen with the transaction ID.

2. CICS reads the data into the terminal I/O area, and a task is created.

3. CICS checks that the transaction ID is valid.

4. If the program for this transaction is not in main storage, the program is loaded.

5. The task is placed into the queue, waiting to be dispatched.

6. When the task is dispatched, the appropriate application program is run.

18

7. The program requests BMS to read data from the terminal.

8. BMS reads the data, and the program processes it.

9. The program requests BMS to display the data to a terminal.

10. BMS displays the data.

11. The task is terminated.

When DB2 data is accessed using CICS, multiple threads can be active simultaneously, giving multiple users concurrent access to a DB2 subsystem of a single CICS region. Contrast this functionality with the TSO environment, in which only one thread can be active for any given TSO address space.

A mechanism named the CICS Attach Facility connects CICS with DB2. Using the CICS Attach Facility, you can connect each CICS region to only one DB2 subsystem at a time. You can connect each DB2 subsystem, however, to more than one CICS region at one time, as you can see in Figure 18.22.

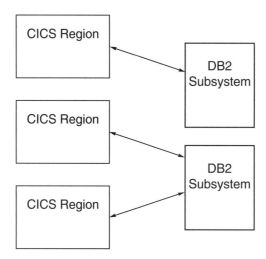

FIGURE 18.22   CICS region to DB2 subsystem relationship.

DB2 provides services to CICS via MVS TCBs. All of these TCBs reside in the CICS address space and perform cross-memory instructions to execute the SQL code in the DB2 database services address space (DSNDBM1). Before you delve too deeply into the specifics of the CICS Attach Facility, you should explore the basics of CICS further.

CICS Terminology and Operation

To fully understand the manner in which CICS controls the execution of an application program, you must first understand the relationships among tasks, transactions, and programs. These three terms define separate entities that function together, under the control of CICS, to create an online processing environment.

A *task* is simply a unit of work scheduled by the operating system. CICS, a batch job, DB2, and TSO are examples of tasks. CICS, however, can schedule tasks under its control, much like the way an operating system schedules tasks. A *CICS task*, therefore, is a unit of work, composed of one or more programs, scheduled by CICS.

The purpose of a *transaction* is to initiate a task. A transaction is initiated by a 1- to 4-byte identifier that is defined to CICS through a control table. Generally, a one-to-one correspondence exists between CICS transactions and CICS tasks, but one transaction can initiate more than one task.

Finally, a *program* is an organized set of instructions that accomplishes an objective in a given unit of work. A CICS program can perform one or many CICS tasks.

CICS Tables

Older versions of CICS use tables, maintained by a systems programmer, to administer its online environment. These tables control the availability of CICS resources and direct CICS to operate in specific ways. Based on the values registered in these tables, CICS can be customized for each user site. The major tables that affect CICS-DB2 application programs are outlined in the subsections that follow.

PPT (Processing Program Table)

CICS programs and BMS maps must be registered in the PPT (Processing Program Table). If the program or map has not been recorded in the PPT, CICS cannot execute the program or use the map. This is true for all CICS programs, including those with embedded SQL. For programs, the name recorded in the PPT must be the name of the program load module as it appears in the load library.

PCT (Program Control Table)

The PCT (Program Control Table) is used to register CICS transactions. CICS reads this table to identify and initialize transactions. Therefore, all transactions must be registered in the PCT before they can be initiated in CICS.

FCT (File Control Table)

Every file that will be read from or written to using CICS operations must be registered in the FCT (File Control Table). This requirement does not apply to DB2 tables, however. The underlying VSAM data sets for DB2 table spaces and indexes do not need to be registered in the FCT before CICS-DB2 programs read from them. DB2 data access is accomplished through SQL, and the DB2 subsystem performs the I/O necessary to access the data in DB2 data sets. A CICS-DB2 program that reads any file using conventional methods (that is, non-SQL), however, must ensure that the file has been registered in the FCT before accessing its data.

RCT (Resource Control Table)

When a DB2 program will be run under CICS, an additional table called the RCT (Resource Control Table) is used to control the interface. The RCT applies only to CICS transactions that access DB2 data; it defines the manner in which DB2 resources will be used by CICS transactions. In particular, the RCT defines a plan for each transaction that can access DB2. Additionally, it defines parameters detailing the number and type of threads available for application plans and the DB2 command processor.

Other Tables

Other tables used by CICS control resource security, terminal definitions, logging and journaling, and the automatic invocation of program at CICS startup. A discussion of these tables is beyond the scope of this book.

RDO (Resource Definition Online)

As of CICS V4, the manner in which the interface between CICS and a DB2 subsystem is defined began to change. Instead of populating tables and updating the configuration using macros, a new method of changing parameters online is available. This new method is known as *Resource Definition Online*, or *RDO*. Whether you use the RCT or the RDO depends on the version of CICS that you are using:

- For CICS/ESA Version 4 (and prior releases) and CICS/TS Version 1 Release 1, the CICS-DB2 interface is defined using the RCT.

- For CICS/TS Version 1 Release 2, the CICS-DB2 interface can be defined using the RCT or using RDO.

- For CICS/TS Version 1 Release 3 and subsequent releases, the CICS-DB2 interface must be defined using RDO.

> **NOTE**
>
> Most shops using CICS will have already converted to using the RDO, or will need to convert soon. The most current release of CICS (circa early 2004) is CICS Transaction Server for z/OS V2.3.

The RDO is simply a new mechanism for defining the interface. It offers several benefits and it is relatively easy to migrate from using the RCT to using RDO. IBM provides a utility named DFHCSDUP that can be used to migrate RCT parameters to RDO names.

The benefits RDO provides over the RCT are:

- You can add, delete, or change RDO definitions without stopping the CCIS-DB2 connection.

- You can use wildcarding to specify groups of transactions and thereby simplify the setup of your CICS-DB2 transactions.

- The CICS-DB2 control blocks are moved above the 16MB line.

Additionally, conversion is not difficult because the RCT parameters and RDO names are similar. You can find more details about the RCT and RDO in the section "CICS-DB2 Connection Guidelines" later in this chapter.

CICS-DB2 Program Preparation

Another consideration when you're using CICS is the program preparation process. When CICS programs are prepared for execution, a step is added to the process to prepare the embedded CICS commands: the execution of the CICS command language translator (see Figure 18.23). You can think of the CICS command language translator as a precompiler for CICS commands. The CICS command language translator comments out the code embedded between EXEC CICS and END-EXEC and replaces it with standard COBOL CALL statements.

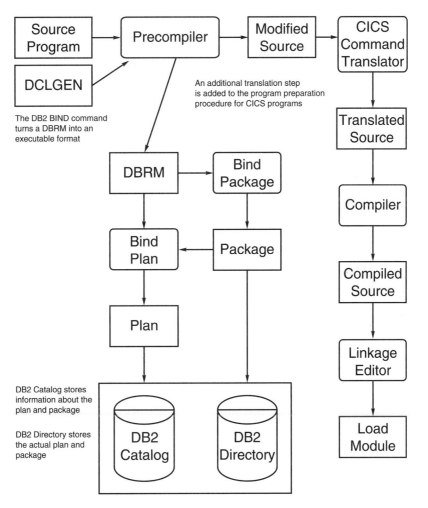

FIGURE 18.23   CICS/DB2 program preparation.

The rest of the program preparation procedure is essentially unchanged. One notable exception is that you must link the CICS language interface (DSNCLI), rather than the TSO language interface (DSNELI), to the load module.

When embedded CICS commands are encountered, the DB2 precompiler bypasses them, but the CICS command language translator returns warning messages. Thus, you might want to run the DB2 precompiler before running the CICS command language translator. Functionally, which precompiler is run first does not matter. Running the DB2 precompiler first, however, eliminates a host of unwanted messages and speeds up program preparation somewhat because the CICS command language translator needs to perform less work.

CICS Attach Facility

As mentioned, CICS must be attached to DB2 before any transaction can access DB2 data. This is accomplished with the CICS Attach Facility. Figure 18.24 depicts the basic operation of the CICS Attach Facility.

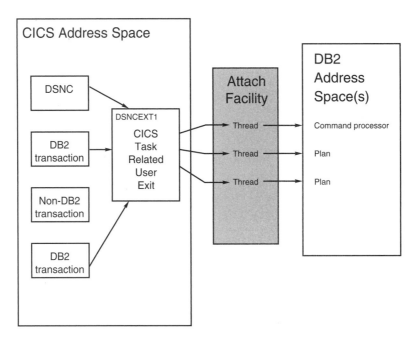

FIGURE 18.24   The CICS Attach Facility.

The CICS Attach Facility provides support for multiple transactions using multiple threads to access data in a single DB2 subsystem. CICS transactions requiring DB2 resources are routed to DB2 by DSNCLI each time an SQL statement is encountered. The routing is accomplished using the functionality of the CICS Task Related User Exit (TRUE). The TRUE formats the request for DB2 data and passes it to the CICS Attach Facility, which creates a new thread or reuses an existing one.

The following activities occur when a thread is created:

1. A DB2 sign-on is initiated, whereby the authorization ID identifying the user of the thread is established based on a parameter specified in the RCT.

2. A DB2 accounting record is written.

3. Authorization is checked for the user.

4. The executable form of the plan is loaded into memory as follows. The header portion of the SKCT is loaded into the EDM Pool, if it is not already there. This SKCT header is then copied to an executable form called a *cursor table*, which is also placed in the EDM Pool. (These terms are fully defined in Chapter 22, "The Table-Based Infrastructure of DB2.")

5. If VALIDATE(RUN) was specified at bind time for the plan, an incremental bind is performed. Avoid incremental binds by specifying VALIDATE(BIND).

6. If ACQUIRE(ALLOCATE) was specified at bind time for the plan, the following occurs. Locks are acquired for all table spaces used by the plan, all DBDs are loaded into memory (EDM Pool) referenced by the plan, and all data sets to be used by the plan are opened, if they are not already open.

After the thread is created, the plan corresponding to the transaction being executed is allocated, and the SQL statement is processed. When the request for DB2 resources is satisfied, the data is passed back to the requesting CICS program through the TRUE. The thread is placed in an MVS-wait state until it is needed again. When the next SQL statement is encountered, the CICS program repeats the entire process except the thread creation because the thread has already been allocated and is waiting to be used.

When the CICS task is terminated or a CICS SYNCPOINT is issued, the thread is terminated and the following actions occur:

1. The CICS Attach Facility performs a two-phase commit, which synchronizes the updates and commits made to all defined CICS resources (for example, IMS databases, VSAM files, and sequential files) and DB2 tables. This process is described in more detail in the "Two-Phase Commit" section, later in this chapter.

2. A DB2 accounting record is written.

3. Table space locks are released.

4. The executable form of the plan is freed from the EDM Pool.

5. Memory used for working storage is freed.

6. If CLOSE(YES) was specified for table spaces or indexes used by the thread, the underlying VSAM data sets are closed (provided no other resources are accessing them).

The CICS Attach Facility is started using the DSNC STRT command, indicating the RCT to use.

The CICS attachment facility is provided on the CICS product tape starting with CICS V4. The CICS attachment that shipped on the DB2 product tape is for versions of CICS prior to V4.

The CICS attachment facility programs are named like DSN2xxxx for CICS V4 and subsequent releases; for prior versions of CICS the programs were named like DSNCxxxx.

> **CAUTION**
>
> If you switch CICS attachment facilities due to moving to CICS V4, be sure to check your CSD definitions, Program List Tables (PLTs), and CICS application programs for references to all old attachment facility programs named like DSNCxxxx, and change them to the new DSN2xxxx name.

Types of Threads

You will use the RCT or RDO to define the attachment of CICS to DB2 and to assign threads to each CICS-DB2 transaction. CICS transactions can use three types of threads to access DB2: command threads, entry threads, and pool threads.

Command threads can be used only by the DSNC command processor. If no command threads are available, pool threads are used.

Entry threads, also called dedicated threads, are associated with a single application plan. Multiple transactions can be assigned to an entry thread grouping, but each transaction must use the same application plan. Subsequent CICS transactions that use the same application plan can reuse entry threads. This can result in decreased runtime because you avoid the cost of establishing the thread.

You can define entry threads to be either protected or unprotected. A protected thread remains available for a preset time, waiting for transactions that can reuse the thread to be run. An unprotected thread is terminated upon completion unless another transaction is already waiting to use it.

Finally, if an entry thread is not available for a transaction's use, it may be diverted to the pool, where it will utilize a pool thread. Any transaction specifically defined to the pool can use the *pool threads*. In addition, you can define any transaction to be divertable. A divertable transaction is one defined to an entry or command thread that, when no appropriate threads are available, will be diverted to use a pool thread. A pool thread is not reusable and is always terminated when the transaction using it is finished.

You define command, entry, and pool threads by specifying the appropriate parameters in the RCT or RDO. The following list summarizes the capabilities of the thread types:

COMD	Used solely for DSNC commands.
ENTRY	Used primarily for high-volume or high-priority transactions. Entry threads can be protected, reused, or diverted to the pool.
POOL	Used primarily for low-priority and low-volume transactions. Pool threads cannot be protected and cannot be diverted. Very limited thread reuse is available with pool threads (only when the first transaction in the queue requests the same plan as the one used by the thread being released—a rare occurrence indeed).

The next several sections discuss the specific parameters used by the two methods of configuring a DB2-CICS connection: the RCT and RDO.

The RCT Parameters

The RCT is one method to define the relationship environment between CICS transactions and DB2 plans. In essence, it defines the working environment for CICS/DB2 applications. Keep in mind, though, that it will soon be obsolete and replaced by the RDO as you move to later versions of CICS.

Each CICS region can have only one RCT active at any time. Typically, the CICS or DB2 systems programmer handles RCT changes, but application programmers, systems analysts, and DBAs should understand what is contained in the RCT. A sample RCT is shown in Listing 18.2.

LISTING 18.2 A Sample Resource Control Table (RCT)

```
*
*     DEFINE DEFAULTS IN INIT, A COMMAND MACRO, AND A POOL MACRO
*
      DSNCRCT TYPE=INIT,SUBID=DB2T,SUFFIX=1,SIGNID=XXXXXX,            X
            THRDMAX=22,TOKENI=YES

      DSNCRCT TYPE=COMD,THRDM=2,THRDA=1,THRDS=1,TWAIT=POOL

      DSNCRCT TYPE=POOL,THRDM=4,THRDA=4,PLAN=POOLPLAN
*
*     DEFINE AN ENTRY MACRO FOR PROTECTED THREADS
*
      DSNCRCT TYPE=ENTRY,TXID=TXN1,THRDM=4,THRDA=2,                   X
            THRDS=2,PLAN=TXN1PLAN,TWAIT=YES,AUTH=(TXID,*,*)


*
*     DEFINE AN ENTRY MACRO FOR HIGH-PRIORITY UNPROTECTED THREADS
*
      DSNCRCT TYPE=ENTRY,TXID=(TXN2,TXN3),THRDM=2,THRDA=2,           X
            THRDS=0,PLAN=MULTPLAN,TWAIT=POOL,AUTH=(TXID,*,*)
*
*     DEFINE AN ENTRY MACRO FOR LOW-PRIORITY UNPROTECTED THREADS
*
      DSNCRCT TYPE=ENTRY,TXID=TXN4,THRDM=1,THRDA=0,                   X
            THRDS=0,PLAN=TXN4PLAN,TWAIT=POOL,AUTH=(TXID,*,*)
*
*     DEFINE AN ENTRY MACRO FOR A MENUING SYSTEM BOUND TO A
*           SINGLE, LARGE PLAN
*
      DSNCRCT TYPE=ENTRY,TXID=(MENU,OPT1,OPT2,OPT3,OPT4),            X
            THRDM=4,THRDA=4,THRDS=3,PLAN=APPLPLAN,                   X
            TWAIT=POOL,AUTH=(SIGNID,*,*)
*
*     DEFINE AN ENTRY MACRO THAT WILL ABEND IF NO THREADS
*           ARE AVAILABLE (TWAIT=NO)
*
      DSNCRCT TYPE=ENTRY,TXID=SAMP,THRDM=1,THRDA=1,THRDS=1,          X
            PLAN=SAMPPLAN,TWAIT=NO,AUTH=(TXID,*,*)
*
```

18

LISTING 18.2 Continued

```
*    DEFINE AN ENTRY THREAD FOR DYNAMIC PLAN SELECTION
*
     DSNCRCT TYPE=ENTRY,TXID=TXNS,THRDM=1,THRDA=1,                    X
            PLNEXIT=YES,PLNPGME=DSNCUEXT,AUTH=(CONSTANT,*,*)

     DSNCRCT TYPE=FINAL

     END
```

You can code five types of entries, known as macros, in the RCT. Each macro defines a portion of the CICS-DB2 attachment. The valid RCT TYPE entries follow:

INIT   Defines the basic parameters affecting the attachment of DB2 to CICS and the setup of defaults for threads

COMD   Defines the setup parameters for DSNC commands

ENTRY   Defines the dedicated threads

POOL   Defines the parameters for defining pool threads

FINAL   Specifies that no more RCT entries follow

Consult Tables 18.2 through 18.6 for the parameters that you can code for the RCT INIT, COMD, POOL, and ENTRY types of macros. No parameters are specified for the RCT FINAL macro.

TABLE 18.2 RCT INIT Macro Parameters

RCT INIT Macro Parameters

Parameter	Default	Valid Values	Description
DPMODI	HIGH	HIGH, EQ, LOW	Specifies the default for the DPMODE parameter if it is not coded on subsequent ENTRY and POOL macros.
ERRDEST	(CSMT,*,*)	Valid transient	Specifies destinations data destinations for unsolicited messages.
PCTEROP	AEY9	AEY9, N906, N906D	Specifies the type of processing to occur following a create thread error.
PLANI	Entry PLAN or TXID	plan name	Specifies the default name of any plan not using dynamic plan selection. If not specified, the plan name must be specified in each subsequent RCT ENTRY macro; otherwise, it will default to the transaction ID.
PLNPGMI	DSNCUEXT	- - -	Specifies the default value for the PLNPGME parameter if it is not coded on subsequent ENTRY and POOL macros for transactions using the dynamic plan selection.

TABLE 18.2 Continued

RCT INIT Macro Parameters

Parameter	Default	Valid Values	Description
PLNXTR1	193	1 to 200	Specifies the trace ID for the dynamic plan entry.
PLNXTR2	194	1 to 200	Specifies the trace ID for the dynamic plan exit.
PURGEC	(0,30)	(0,30) thru (59,59)	Specifies the purge cycle for a protected thread. The first value indicates minutes; the second indicates seconds.
ROLBI	YES	YES, NO	Specifies the default value for the ROLBE parameter if it is not coded on subsequent ENTRY and POOL macros.
SHDDEST	CSSL	*Valid transient* destination *data*	Specifies a *destinations* for the statistical report during CICS shutdown.
SIGNID	*application name of CICS subsystem*	8-character string	Specifies the authorization ID used by the CICS Attach Facility when signing on to DB2.
SNAP	A	*Valid* SYSOUT *classes*	Specifies the SYSOUT class to be used by the CICS Attach Facility for snap dumps.
STANDBY	ABEND	ABEND, SQLCODE	Indicates how the CICS Attach Facility will respond to SQL requests when it is not connected to DB2. ABEND causes the attachment to disable the TRUE when in stand by mode (usually results in AEY9 abends); SQLCODE causes a -923 or -924 SQLCODE to be issued instead of an ABEND.
STRTWT	YES	YES, NO, AUTO	Specifies action to be taken by the CICS Attach Facility during startup if DB2 is not operational. YES directs the CICS Attach Facility to wait for DB2 to come up and then attach. NO indicates that the CICS Attach Facility startup will fail. AUTO indicates that the CICS Attach Facility will be automatically restarted when DB2 is stopped and started.
SUBID	DSN	*4-character DB2 ID*	Specifies the DB2 subsystem to which this RCT will be attached.

18

TABLE 18.2   Continued

RCT INIT Macro Parameters

Parameter	Default	Valid Values	Description
SUFFIX	0	*1 byte*	Specifies an identifier for the RCT. It is the identifier *x*, as supplied in the DSNC STRT *x* command.
THRDMAX	12	*Any integer*	Specifies the *greater than 4* absolute maximum number of threads that can be created by this Attach Facility.
TRACEID	192	*Any valid CICS trace ID*	Specifies a userid to be used by the CICS Attach Facility to be used for tracing.
TWAITI	YES	YES, NO, POOL	Specifies the default for the TWAIT parameter if it is not coded on subsequent ENTRY and POOL macros.
TOKENI	NO	YES, NO	Specifies the default for the TOKENE parameter if it is not coded on a subsequent ENTRY macro.
TXIDSO	YES	YES, NO	Specifies whether sign-ons are to be suppressed during thread reuse for pool threads and threads with multiple TXIDs.

> **NOTE**
>
> The STANDBY option and the AUTO parameter of the STARTWT option are available as of CICS Transaction Server V1.1. You must specify STARTWT=AUTO to specify STANDBY=SQLCODE.

TABLE 18.3   RCT COMD Macro Parameters

RCT COMD Macro Parameters

Parameter	Default Value	Valid Values	Description
AUTH	(USER, TERM,TXID)	*Character string*, GROUP, SIGNID, TERM, TXID, USER, USERID, * AUTH	Defines the authorization scheme to be used for the given transaction. As many as three values can be specified. The attachment facility tries to use them in the order specified from left to right. For the default values, it first tries to use the CICS sign-on ID, and then the CICS transaction ID. For a description of each AUTH value, see Table 18.6.

TABLE 18.3   Continued

RCT COMD Macro Parameters

Parameter	Default Value	Valid Values	Description
ROLBE	NO	YES, NO	Defines the action to be taken if this transaction will be the victim in the resolution of a deadlock. If YES is coded, a CICS SYNCPOINT ROLLBACK is issued and a -911 SQLCODE is returned to the program. If NO is coded, a CICS SYNCPOINT ROLLBACK is not issued and the SQLCODE is set to -913.
THRDA	1	*Positive integer or zero*	Defines the maximum number of threads that can be connected for the transaction, group of transactions, or pool. When the limit is reached, action is taken according to the values coded in the TWAIT parameter.
THRDM	1	*Positive integer or zero*	Defines the absolute maximum number of threads that can ever be connected for the transaction, group of transactions, or the pool. This number must be equal to or greater than the value of THRDA. If it is greater than THRDA, you can issue the DSNC MODIFY TRANSACTION command to change the value of THRDA to a greater value but not a value greater than THRDM.
THRDS	1	*Positive integer or zero*	Specifies the number of protected threads. The value cannot exceed THRDA or 99, whichever is greater.
TWAIT	YES	YES, NO, POOL*	Specifies the action to be taken when a thread is required but the limit (THRDA) has been reached. YES indicates that the transaction should wait until a thread is available. NO causes the transaction to abend. POOL diverts the transaction to the pool, causing a pool thread to be used.
TXID	DSNC	DSNC	Specifies the transaction ID for DB2 command threads. It should always be set to DSNC.

18

TABLE 18.4   RCT ENTRY Macro Parameters

RCT ENTRY Macro Parameters

Parameter	Default Value	Valid Values	Description
AUTH	(USER, TERM,TXID)	*Character string,* SIGNID, TERM, USERID, *	Defines the GROUP authorization scheme to be used for the given transaction. You can specify as many as three values. The attachment facility tries to use them in the order specified from left to right. For the default values, it tries to use first the CICS sign-on ID, and then the CICS terminal ID, and then the CICS transaction ID. For a description of each AUTH value, see Table 18.6.
DPMODE	HIGH	HIGH, EQ, LOW	Defines the dispatching priority limit that can be assigned to the task. This limit overrides the DPMODI parameter if it was coded on the INIT macro.
PLAN	TXID	*Plan name*	Defines the name of the plan to use for the transaction or transactions being defined. If it is not specified, the plan name defaults to the transaction ID.
PLNEXIT	NO	YES, NO	Indicates whether the dynamic plan selection will be used.
PLNPGME	DSNCUEXT	*Program name*	Specifies the name of the exit program used to assign a plan name when the dynamic plan selection is used. This name overrides the PLNPGMI parameter if it was coded on the INIT macro.
ROLBE	YES	YES, NO	Defines the action to be taken if this transaction will be the victim in the resolution of a deadlock. If YES is coded, a CICS SYNCPOINT ROLLBACK is issued and a -911 SQLCODE is returned to the program. If NO is coded, a CICS SYNCPOINT ROLLBACK is not issued and the SQLCODE is set to -913.
TASKREQ	- - -	PA1-PA3,	This parameter is PF1-PF24, used when a OPID, LPA, transaction will be MSRE started by a 3270 function key.

TABLE 18.4   Continued

RCT ENTRY Macro Parameters

Parameter	Default Value	Valid Values	Description
THRDA	0	*Positive integer or zero*	Defines the maximum number of threads that can be connected for the transaction, group of transactions, or pool. When the limit is reached, action is taken according to the values coded in the TWAIT parameter.
THRDM	0	*Positive integer or zero*	Defines the absolute maximum number of threads that can ever be connected for the transaction, group of transactions, or the pool. This number must be equal to or greater than the value of THRDA. If it is greater than THRDA, you can issue the DSNC MODIFY TRANSACTION command to change the value of THRDA to a greater value but not a value greater than THRDM.
THRDS	0	*Positive integer or zero*	Specifies the number of protected threads. The value cannot exceed THRDA or 99, whichever is greater.
TWAIT	YES	YES, NO, POOL	Specifies the action to be taken when a thread is required but the limit (THRDA) has been reached. YES indicates that the transaction should wait until a thread is available. NO causes the transaction to abend. POOL diverts the transaction to the pool, causing a pool thread to be used.
TOKENE	NO	NO, YES	Specifies whether the CICS attachment facility will produce an accounting trace record for every transaction.
TXID	- - -	*Transaction ID or list of transaction IDs*	Specifies the transaction for this entry.

18

TABLE 18.5   RCT POOL Macro Parameters

RCT POOL Macro Parameters

Parameter	Default Value	Valid Values	Description
AUTH	(USER, TERM,TXID)	*Character string,* GROUP, SIGNID, TERM, TXID, USER, USERID, * AUTH	Defines the authorization scheme to be used for the given transaction. You can specify as many as three values. The attachment facility tries to use them in the order specified from left to right. For the default values, it tries to use first the CICS sign-on ID, the CICS terminal ID, and then the CICS transaction ID. For a description of each value, see Table 18.6.
DPMODE	HIGH	HIGH, EQ, LOW	Defines the dispatching priority limit that can be assigned to the task. This limit overrides the DPMODI parameter if it was coded on the INIT macro.
PLAN	DEFAULT	*Plan name*	Defines the name of the plan to use for the transaction or transactions being defined. If it is not specified, the plan name defaults to the character string DEFAULT.
PLNEXIT	NO	YES, NO	Indicates whether the dynamic plan selection will be used.
PLNPGME	DSNCUEXT	*Program name*	Specifies the name of the exit program used to assign a plan name when the dynamic plan selection is used. This name overrides the PLNPGMI parameter if it was coded on the INIT macro.
ROLBE	YES	YES, NO	Defines the action to be taken if this transaction will be the victim in the resolution of a deadlock. If YES is coded, a CICS SYNCPOINT ROLLBACK is issued and a -911 SQLCODE is returned to the program. If NO is coded, a CICS SYNCPOINT ROLLBACK is not issued and the SQLCODE is set to -913.

TABLE 18.5   Continued

RCT POOL Macro Parameters

Parameter	Default Value	Valid Values	Description
TASKREQ	- - -	PA1-PA3, PF1-PF24, OPID, LPA, MSRE	This parameter is used when a transaction will be started by a 3270 function key.
THRDA	3	Positive integer or zero	Defines the maximum number of threads that can be connected for the transaction, group of transactions, or pool. When the limit is reached, action is taken according to the values coded in the TWAIT parameter.
THRDM	3	Positive integer or zero	Defines the absolute maximum number of threads that can ever be connected for the transaction, group of transactions, or the pool. This number must be the value of THRDA. If it is greater than THRDA, you can issue the DSNC MODIFY TRANSACTION command to change the value of THRDA to a greater value but not a value greater than THRDM.
THRDS	0	Positive integer or zero	Specifies the number of protected threads. The value cannot exceed THRDA or 99, whichever is greater.
TWAIT	YES	YES, NO	Specifies the action to be taken when a thread is required but the limit (THRDA) has been reached. YES indicates that the transaction should wait until a thread is available. NO causes the transaction to abend.
TXID	POOL	Transaction ID or list of transaction IDs	Specifies the transaction for this entry.

TABLE 18.6   RCT AUTH Values

AUTH Value	Description
Character string	The character string specified is used for the authorization ID.
GROUP	The RACF group ID is used for the authorization ID.
SIGNID	The SIGNID specified in the INIT RCT macro is used for the authorization ID.
TERM	The CICS terminal ID is used for the authorization ID.

TABLE 18.6   Continued

AUTH **Value**	**Description**
TXID	The CICS transaction ID is used for the authorization ID.
USER	The CICS sign-on ID is used for the authorization ID.
USERID	This value is similar to the USER option but can be extended using DSN3@SGN to work with RACF to send a secondary authid.
*	Null. You can specify this value only for the second and third values. It Indicates that no additional authorization scheme will be used.

RDO Parameters

When using RDO there are similar parameters for defining transactions as in the RCT. However, as the name implies, RDO (or Resource Definition Online) parameters are set using an online interface.

RDO uses three sets of parameters to define the DB2-CICS connection. These parameters are grouped into the following definitions:

- DB2CONN
- DB2ENTRY
- DB2TRAN

DB2CONN

The first set of parameters to understand is used to define the global attributes of the DB2-CICS connection, as well as the attributes of pool threads and command threads. These parameters are referred to as the DB2CONN definitions.

Only one DB2CONN can be installed in a CICS system at any one time. If you attempt to install a second DB2CONN, the existing DB2CONN will be discarded along with its associated DB2ENTRY and DB2TRAN definitions. The DB2CONN must be installed before any DB2ENTRY or DB2TRAN definitions can be set up.

A definition of each of the DB2CONN parameters follows. The definitions are broken up into three sections because DB2CONN is used to defined connection attributes, pool thread attributes, and command thread attributes.

Connection Attributes   The following DB2CONN parameters are used to define basic DB2-CICS connection attributes:

DB2CONN—Specifies a name of up to eight characters used to identify this DB2CONN definition.

CONNECTERROR(SQLCODE | ABEND)—Indicates how the CICS Attach Facility responds to SQL requests when it is not connected to DB2. ABEND causes the attachment to return an AEY9 abend; SQLCODE causes a -923 SQLCODE to be issued instead of an abend.

DB2ID—The name of the DB2 subsystem to which the CICS-DB2 attachment facility is to connect.

DESCRIPTION—Up to 58 characters describing the resource that is being defined.

MSGQUEUE1—Specifies the first transient data destination to which unsolicited messages from the CICS-DB2 attachment facility are sent. The first destination cannot be blank.

MSGQUEUE2—Specifies a second transient data destination.

MSGQUEUE3—Specifies a third transient data destination.

NONTERMREL(YES | NO)—Specifies whether or not a non-terminal transaction releases threads for reuse at intermediate syncpoints.

PURGECYCLE(*x,y*)S—Specifies the duration of the purge cycle for protected threads in minutes and seconds. The default is 0, 30; that is, 0 minutes and 30 seconds.

SIGNID—Specifies the authorization ID to be used by the CICS-DB2 attachment facility when signing on to DB2 for pool and DB2ENTRY threads specified using AUTHTYPE(SIGN).

STANDBYMODE(RECONNECT | CONNECT | NOCONNECT)—Indicates that action the CICS-DB2 attachment facility will take if DB2 is not active CICS attempts to connect to DB2.

Specifying CONNECT causes the CICS-DB2 attachment facility to wait in standby mode for DB2 to become active. If the connection is made and then DB2 fails, the CICS-DB2 attachment facility terminates.

Specifying NOCONNECT causes the CICS DB2 attachment facility to terminate.

Specifying RECONNECT causes the CICS DB2 attachment facility to wait in standby mode for DB2 to become active. If DB2 subsequently fails after the connection is made, the CICS DB2 attachment facility reverts to standby mode again.

STATSQUEUE(CDB2 | name)—Specifies the transient data destination for CICS-DB2 attachment statistics that are produced when the attachment facility is shut down.

THREADERROR(N906D | N906 | ABEND)—Specifies the processing that is to occur following a create thread error.

Specifying ABEND causes CICS to take a transaction dump for AD2S, AD2T, and AD2U errors. For the first error, no abend occurs; but an abend will occur for subsequent errors. The transaction must be terminated and reinitialized before another SQL request can succeed.

Specifying N906D indicates that CICS will take a transaction dump. The transaction receives a -906 SQLCODE if another SQL is issued, unless the transaction issues SYNCPOINT ROLLBACK.

Specifying N906 indicates that CICS will not take a transaction dump. The transaction receives a -906 SQLCODE if another SQL is issued, unless the transaction issues SYNCPOINT ROLLBACK.

TCBLIMIT—Specifies the maximum number of subtask TCBs that can be attached by the CICS-DB2 attachment facility to process DB2 requests. The default is 12. The minimum number is 4 and the maximum is 2000.

Pool Thread Attributes   The following DB2CONN parameters are used to define pool thread attributes:

ACCOUNTREC(NONE | TASK | TXID | UOW)—Specifies the minimum amount of DB2 accounting required for transactions using pool threads.

Specifying NONE indicates that no accounting records are required for transactions using pool threads. DB2 will produce at least one accounting record for each thread when the thread is terminated.

Specifying TASK indicates that a minimum of one accounting record for each CICS task will be produced. A transaction with multiple units-of-work (UOWs) may use a different thread for each of its UOWs. This can result in an accounting record being produced for each UOW.

Specifying TXID causes an accounting record to be produced when the transid using the thread changes. Once again, there is a chance that a transaction containing multiple UOWs will use a different thread for each UOW causing an accounting record to be produced per UOW.

Specifying UOW causes an accounting record to be produced for each UOW, assuming that the thread is released at the end of the UOW.

AUTHID—Specifies the ID that should be used for security checking when using pool threads.

AUTHTYPE(USERID | OPID | GROUP | SIGN | TERM | TX)—Specifies the type of ID that can be used for pool threads.

Specifying USERID indicates that the 1 to 8-character USERID associated with the CICS transaction is used as the authorization ID.

Specifying OPID indicates that the operator identification associated with the user of the CICS transaction is used as the authorization ID.

Specifying GROUP indicates that the 1 to 8-character USERID and the connected group name is used as the authorization ID. To use the GROUP option, the CICS system must have SEC=YES specified in the CICS system initialization table (SIT).

Specifying SIGN indicates that the SIGNID parameter of the DB2CONN is used as the resource authorization ID.

Specifying TERM indicates that the terminal identification is used as the authorization ID.

Specifying TX indicates that the transaction identification is used as the authorization ID.

DROLLBACK(YES | NO)—Specifies whether or not the CICS DB2 attachment facility should initiate a SYNCPOINT ROLLBACK if a transaction is selected as the victim of a deadlock resolution.

Specifying YES indicates that the attachment facility will issue a SYNCPOINT ROLLBACK before returning control to the application. This causes a -911 to be returned to the program.

Specifying NO indicates that the attachment facility will not issue a rollback for the transaction. This causes a -911 to be returned to the program.

PLAN—Specifies the name of the plan to be used for pool threads.

PLANEXITNAME—Specifies the name of the dynamic plan exit to be used for pool threads. If PLANEXITNAME is specified, PLAN may not be specified (and vice versa). The default plan exit name is DSNCUEXT.

PRIORITY(HIGH | EQUAL | LOW)—Specifies the priority of the pool thread subtasks relative to the CICS main task.

Specifying HIGH indicates that subtasks will have a higher priority than the CICS main task.

Specifying EQUAL indicates that subtasks and the CICS main task will have equal priority.

Specifying LOW indicates that subtasks will have a lower priority than the CICS main task.

THREADLIMIT—Specifies the maximum number of pool threads that can be active before requests are forced to wait or are rejected (depending on the value of the THREADWAIT parameter). The default thread limit is 3, which is also the minimum; the maximum cannot exceed the value of TCBLIMIT.

THREADWAIT(YES | NO)—Specifies whether or not transactions will wait for a pool thread or fail if the number of active pool threads reaches the THREADLIMIT.

Specifying YES causes a transaction to wait until a thread becomes available when all threads are busy.

Specifying NO causes the transaction to terminate with an error code of AD2T or AD3T.

Command Thread Attributes

The following DB2CONN parameters are used to define command thread attributes:

COMAUTHID—Specifies the ID for the CICS-DB2 attachment facility to use for security checking when using command threads. If COMAUTHID is specified, COMAUTHTYPE may not be specified, and vice versa.

COMAUTHTYPE(USERID | OPID | GROUP | SIGN | TERM | TX)—Specifies the type of ID to be used for security checking when using command threads.

Specifying USERID indicates that the 1 to 8-character USERID associated with the CICS transaction is used as the authorization ID.

Specifying OPID indicates that the operator identification associated with the user of the CICS transaction is used as the authorization ID.

Specifying GROUP indicates that the 1 to 8-character USERID and the connected group name is used as the authorization ID. To use the GROUP option, the CICS system must have SEC=YES specified in the CICS system initialization table (SIT).

Specifying SIGN indicates that the SIGNID parameter of the DB2CONN is used as the resource authorization ID.

Specifying TERM indicates that the terminal identification is used as the authorization ID.

Specifying TX indicates that the transaction identification is used as the authorization ID.

COMTHREADLIMIT—Specifies the maximum number of command threads that can be attached before requests overflow to the pool. The default is 1, but the value can range from 0 to 2000.

DB2ENTRY

After defining a DB2CONN, you can then define DB2ENTRY definitions. A DB2ENTRY specification can apply to one specific transaction or a group of transactions using wildcard characters. And, as we will learn in the next section, additional transactions can be associated with a DB2ENTRY by defining DBTRAN specifications.

18

You can install a DB2ENTRY only if you have previously installed a DB2CONN.

A definition of each of the DB2ENTRY parameters follows. The definitions are broken up into two sections because DB2ENTRY is used to select threads and control thread operations.

Thread Selection Attributes   The following DB2ENTRY parameters are used to define thread selection attributes:

DB2ENTRY—Specifies a name of up to eight characters used to identify this DB2ENTRY definition.

TRANSID—Specifies the transaction ID associated with the entry. Wildcards can be used to make this specification apply to multiple transactions. Additionally, more transactions can be defined for this entry by defining a DB2TRAN that refers to this DB2ENTRY. TRANSID is optional; if it is not specified all transactions are associated with a DB2ENTRY using DB2TRAN definitions instead.

Thread Operation Attributes   The following DB2ENTRY parameters are used to define thread operation attributes:

ACCOUNTREC(NONE | TASK | TXID | UOW)—Specifies the minimum amount of DB2 accounting required for transactions using this DB2ENTRY.

Specifying NONE indicates that no accounting records are required for transactions using threads from this DB2ENTRY.

Specifying TASK indicates that a minimum of one accounting record for each CICS task is to be produced. A transaction containing multiple UOWs can use a different thread for each UOW, resulting in an accounting record being produced for each UOW.

Specifying TXID indicates that an accounting record is to be produced when the transaction ID using the thread changes. This option applies to DB2ENTRYs that are used by more than one transaction ID. A transaction with multiple UOWs can use a different thread for each UOW, resulting in an accounting record being produced for each UOW.

Specifying UOW indicates that an accounting is to be produced for each UOW (if the thread is released at the end of the UOW).

AUTHID—Specifies the ID to be used for security checking when using this DB2ENTRY. If AUTHID is specified, AUTHTYPE may not be specified, and vice versa.

AUTHTYPE(USERID | OPID | GROUP | SIGN | TERM | TX)—Specifies the type of ID that can be used for threads on this DB2ENTRY. The options mean the same as those specified for AUTHTYPE on a DB2CONN specification as discussed in the previous section.

DROLLBACK(YES | NO)—Specifies whether the CICS DB2 attachment should initiate a SYNCPOINT rollback in the event of a transaction being selected as victim of a deadlock resolution. The options mean the same as those specified for DROLLBACK on a DB2CONN specification as discussed in the previous section.

PLAN—Specifies the name of the plan to be used for this entry. If PLAN is specified, PLANEXITNAME cannot be specified.

PLANEXITNAME—Specifies the name of the dynamic plan exit to be used for this DB2ENTRY.

PRIORITY(HIGH | MEDIUM | LOW)—Specifies the priority of the thread subtasks in this DB2ENTRY relative to the CICS main task.

Specifying HIGH indicates that subtasks will have a higher priority than the CICS main task.

Specifying EQUAL indicates that subtasks and the CICS main task will have equal priority.

Specifying LOW indicates that subtasks will have a lower priority than the CICS main task.

PROTECTNUM—Specifies the maximum number of protected threads allowed for this DB2ENTRY.

THREADLIMIT—Specifies the maximum number of threads for this DB2ENTRY that can be active before requests are forced to overflow to the pool, wait, or be rejected (depending on the value of the THREADWAIT parameter).

THREADWAIT(POOL | YES | NO)—Specifies whether or not transactions should wait for a DB2ENTRY thread, terminate, or overflow to the pool when the number of active DB2ENTRY threads reach the THREADLIMIT.

Specifying POOL causes a transaction to use a thread from the pool if the maximum number of threads is reached and they are all busy. If the pool is also busy, and NO has been specified for the THREADWAIT parameter on the DB2CONN, the transaction is terminated with an AD3T error code.

Specifying YES causes a transaction to wait until a thread becomes available when all threads are busy.

Specifying NO causes the transaction to terminate with an error code of AD2P when all threads are busy.

DB2TRAN

The final RDO category for defining DB2-CICS transactions is the DB2TRAN. A DB2TRAN resource definition defines additional transactions to be associated with a particular DB2ENTRY definition. You can use DB2TRAN to enable a DB2ENTRY to have an unrestricted number of transactions associated with it, including names using wildcard characters. Multiple DB2TRAN definitions can be associated with a single DB2ENTRY definition.

You can install a DB2TRAN only if you have previously installed a DB2ENTRY. A definition of each of the DB2TRAN parameters follows:

DB2TRAN—Specifies a one to eight character name to identify this DB2TRAN.

ENTRY—Specifies the name of the DB2ENTRY to which this DB2TRAN definition applies.

TRANSID—Specifies the transaction ID to be associated with the entry. If the TRANSID is not specified, it defaults to the first four characters of the DB2TRAN name. The following wildcard characters can be used:

The asterisk (*) character can be used to indicate one or more characters.

The plus sign (+) can be used in any position to indicate any single character.

18

Comparing the RCT and RDO

There are many similarities between the older RCT parameters and the newer RDO parameters. Before embarking on a mission to move from the RCT to RDO, take some time to examine the parameters in each method and note the differences and similarities. A quick comparison chart of the major parameters is provided in Table 18.7.

TABLE 18.7   RCT versus RDO: The Major Parameters

RCT Parameter	RDO Option	Description
TYPE=INIT	DB2CONN	To define connection limits and default values
TYPE=COMD	DB2CONN	To define DB2 command threads
TYPE=POOL	DB2CONN	To define threads that are not associated with a specific transaction
TYPE=ENTRY	DB2ENTRY	To define threads that are associated with specific transaction(s)
TXID	TRANSID or DB2TRAN	Transaction(s) associated with entry threads
PLAN	PLAN	DB2 plan associated with transaction(s)
AUTH	AUTHID or AUTHTYPE	Primary authid for a thread
DPMODE	PRIORITY	Relative dispatching priority for the thread TCB
THRDA	THREADLIMIT	Maximum number of threads for entry or pool
THRDS	PROTECTNUM	Number of protected threads for entry
TWAIT	THREADWAIT	Action to take when all threads for an entry are busy
TOKENE	ACCOUNTREC	Specifies when a DB2 accounting record is to be cut
ROLBE	DROLLBACK	Controls whether a SYNCPOINT ROLLBACK is issued and whether −911 or −913 is issued.
SIGNID	SIGNID	Authid used by the CICS attached for DB2 signon
STANDBY	CONNECTERROR	Specifies error to return when DB2-CICS connection is down.
THRDMAX	TCBLIMIT	Maximum number of thread TCBs for the CICS region

CICS-DB2 Connection Guidelines

The following guidelines provide helpful advice for generating an efficient CICS-DB2 connection using the RCT or RDO. This section also offers guidance on using CICS commands and features with DB2.

Migrate RCTs to RDO   If you are currently using the RCT to define your DB2-CICS connection, you will eventually have to migrate to using RDO. The RCT is being phased out and is no longer supported as of CICS/TS Version 1 Release 3. Fortunately, existing RCTs can be migrated easily to RDO resource definitions using the DFHCSDUP utility.

Use Caution Before Grouping Transactions   Grouping a set of transaction identifiers together using wildcard characters can reduce the number of DB2ENTRY and DB2TRAN definitions you will need, but this diminishes your ability to collect statistics by transaction. CICS-DB2 resource statistics are collected for each DB2ENTRY. If you want separate

CICS-DB2 statistics for a specific transaction, you need to give that transaction its own definition.

Specify DB2 Subsystem ID   Which DB2 subsystem CICS connects to is controlled using the DB2ID parameter when using RDO. But this DB2ID can be overridden by specifying a DB2 subsystem on the DSNC STRT command, by a DB2ID specified on a SET DB2CONN command, or by a subsystem ID specified using INITPARM.

If you do not override the subsystem in any of these manners, the DB2ID value is used. If DB2ID is not specified the default value is blanks. This causes the connection to be attempted to the default DB2 subsystem identifier, which is DSN.

Allow for an Appropriate Number of CICS TCBs   The THRDMAX (RCT) or TCBLIMIT (RDO) parameters are used to control the maximum number of subtask TCBs that can be attached by the CICS-DB2 attachment facility to process DB2 requests. Specify this value with care. A good rule of thumb is to set the parameter to the sum of all the thread limit values, up to a limit of 2,000. For the RCT, add up all the THRDA values and for the RDO add up all the THREADLIMIT values and the COMTHREADLIMIT value.

CAUTION

If the sum of your thread limit values exceed the number of TCBs, it is possible that a task could acquire a thread and then find that there is no available TCB. This will cause the task to be suspended.

Also, when specifying a value for the maximum number of TCBs, be sure to take into account the value specified for the CTHREAD DSNZPARM system parameter. The maximum number of TCBs for the CICS-DB2 attach should not exceed the CTHREAD value.

Avoid AUTHID with RACF Authorization   Do not use AUTHID if you are using RACF (or another external security product) for some or all of your DB2 security. This is because threads using an AUTHID do not pass the required RACF access control environment element to DB2.

Instead, use AUTHTYPE with the USERID or GROUP options.

Implement Security Without Sacrificing Performance   While you're planning your security needs, keep performance in mind. If all security can be implemented with CICS transaction security, for each transaction specify AUTH=(TXID,*,*) in the RCT or use AUTHID for the RDO. In DB2, grant EXECUTE authority on the plan to the transaction name. This way, you can reduce the amount of authorization checking overhead.

Simplify Administration Using RDO Parameter Wildcarding   Consider using the wildcarding capabilities of RDO when setting up your CICS-DB2 transactions. For example, examine the following RDO specification:

```
TRANSID(TX*)
```

This is equivalent to the following RCT specification:

```
TXID=(TX01,TX02,TX03,TX04,TX05,TX06,TX07,TX08,TX09)
```

18

Which one is easier to code? Of course, this approach is workable only if all of the transactions can be defined the same.

Consider Protected Threads for High Volume Transactions   Protected threads can improve the performance of high-volume CICS-DB2 transactions because a new instance of a transaction might not have to wait for a thread to be created. Instead, it can reuse a previously allocated thread.

A protected thread is not terminated immediately when it is released. It is terminated only after two completed purge cycles, if it has not been reused in the meantime. Therefore, if the purge cycle is set to 30 seconds, a protected thread is purged 30 to 60 seconds after it is released. The first purge cycle after the attachment facility starts is always 5 minutes. After that the purge cycle values are applied as specified in the RDO parameters. The parameters for setting the purge cycle are PURGECYCLE (RDO) and PURGEC (RCT).

An unprotected thread is terminated when it is released (at a SYNCPOINT or at the end of the task) if there are no other transactions waiting for a thread on that DB2ENTRY. Only entry threads can be protected; pool and command threads cannot be protected.

You can control the number of protected threads using the PROTECTNUM parameter (RDS) or THRDS (RCT).

Explicitly Code a COMD Entry   When using the RCT, be sure to explicitly code a COMD entry. A command thread is generated regardless of whether it is specified in the RCT. Coding a COMD macro for command threads rather than using defaults, however, is a good idea. This way, you can track and change the parameters for command threads more easily.

Ensure a Sufficient Number of Pool Threads   Be sure to plan for an appropriate number of pool threads on the POOL entry (RCT) or using DB2CONN (RDO). The pool is used not only for threads defined as TYPE=POOL, but also for entry threads defined as TWAIT=POOL. Protected threads can also use the pool if no protected threads are available.

Use your knowledge of your transaction workflow to arrive at a reasonable number for the thread limit for pool threads. Attempt to determine the number of each of the following types of threads that will be running at one time, and use that number (plus a little buffer) for pool threads:

- Explicitly defined pool threads (TYPE=POOL)
- Overflow threads

Favor Overflowing Entry Threads to the Pool   When you're coding the ENTRY macro (RCT), favor the use of TWAIT=POOL to avoid an excessive wait time or abends. For the RDO the same specification is accomplished by setting THREADWAIT to POOL.

Avoid specifying TWAIT=NO (RCT) or THREADWAIT(NO) (RDO) because it increases the number of abends.

Code THRDM Greater Than THRDA   When setting up the DB2-CICS attach using the RCT, code the THRDM parameter to be at least one greater than the THRDA parameter. This provides a buffer of at least one additional thread for tuning if additional entry threads are required.

Favor Rolling Back Automatically   Use ROLBE=YES (RCT) or DROLLBACK(YES) (RDO) to roll back changes automatically in the event of a deadlock or timeout. Specifying NO to ROLBE or DROLLBACK places the onus on the application program to decide whether to back out changes. Specifying YES can reduce the amount of coding needed in CICS programs.

Favor Dispatching Priorities that are Equal or High   Use DPMODE=HIGH (RCT) or PRIORITY(HIGH) (RDO) for only a few very high-priority transactions. Use DPMODE=EQ (RCT) or PRIORITY(EQUAL) (RDO) for most transactions.

Avoid DPMODE=LOW (RCT) and PRIORITY(LOW) (RDO) unless someone you hate will be using transactions assigned to those threads. You *might* also choose to specify a low DPMODE or PRIORITY for new transactions if your mainframe is very heavily utilized.

Matching CICS and DB2 Accounting Records   To make it easier to manage the performance of CICS-DB2 applications, it is beneficial to match DB2 accounting records with CICS accounting records. To help match CICS and DB2 accounting records, specify ACCOUNTREC(UOW) or ACCOUNTREC(TASK) in the DB2ENTRY definition when using RDO. By specifying UOW or TASK for ACCOUNTREC, the CICS LU 6.2 token is included in the DB2 trace records (in field QWHCTOKN of the correlation header).

When using the RCT, accounting records are not cut when threads are reused, unless the TOKENE=YES parameter is coded on an ENTRY macro (or TOKENI=YES is coded on the INIT macro). Failure to specify TOKENE=YES might cause your performance monitor to report multiple transactions as a single transaction. DB2 checks the token and, when the token changes, DB2 creates a new trace record.

Specifying TOKENE=YES also causes the CICS attachment facility to pass the CICS LU6.2 token to the DB2 accounting trace record. This capability is important because CICS produces accounting records at the transaction level, whereas DB2 produces accounting records at the thread level. If you include the token in the accounting records, DB2 and CICS accounting records can be easily correlated. This token is contained in the DB2 trace correlation header field (IFCID 148).

Consider Coding Threads to Avoid AEY9 Abends   When using the RCT, code STARTWT=AUTO and STANDBY=SQLCODE to avoid the AEY9 abend when the CICS attachment is not available. You must be using CICS Transaction Server V1.1 or later to specify these options.

Be sure to check for -923 and -924 SQLCODEs in your application programs that use threads defined with STARTWT=AUTO and STANDBY=SQLCODE. A -923 indicates that the CICS Attachment Facility is not up; a -924 indicates that the DB2 error translator is not at a late enough level.

When using RDO, the CONNECTERROR parameter is used to control how the DB2-CICS attachment responds to SQL requests when it is not connected to DB2. Specifying CONNECTERROR(SQLCODE) causes a -923 SQLCODE to be issued instead of an AEY9 abend.

18

Use the Appropriate Thread Type   Table 18.8 suggests the types of threads to use for different transaction requirements. These are general rule of thumb guidelines only; define your transactions to achieve optimal performance in your environment. In general, transactions requiring high availability or throughput should have dedicated and protected threads. Low-volume or low-priority threads can be diverted to the pool.

TABLE 18.8   Thread Specification by the Type of Transaction

Transaction	Thread Type to Use	Other Recommendations
Very high volume		
High priority	Entry	THRDM > THRDA
		THRDA > 3
		THRDS > 1
		TWAIT = POOL (or YES)
		DPMODE = HIGH
Moderate to high volume		
High priority	Entry	THRDM > THRDA
		THRDA > 0
		THRDS > 0
		TWAIT = POOL
Low volume		
High priority	Entry	THRDM = 2
		THRDA = 1
		THRDS = 0
		TWAIT = POOL
		DPMODE = HIGH
Low volume		
Moderate priority	Entry	THRDM = THRDA = 1
		THRDS = 0
		TWAIT = POOL
Low volume		
Low priority	Entry	THRDM = THRDA = THRDS = 0
		TWAIT = POOL
Very low volume	Pool	THRDM > 3
		THRDA > 2
		TWAIT = YES

Consider specifying transactions explicitly to the pool if you cannot accurately gauge their volume and priority. You can usually get better performance by explicitly defining entry threads and specifying the appropriate parameters for the performance and importance of the transactions. Even if all of your transactions are defined as entry threads, always define the pool to allow for overflow.

Use DSNC   Use the DSNC DISPLAY STATISTICS command to monitor the CICS environment. You can find details on this command in Chapter 36.

Plan Management and Dynamic Plan Selection   In the CICS environment, multiple programs can be executed in a single task. For CICS, the task defines the unit of work. For DB2, the application plan defines the unit of work. The scope of the unit of work for these two environments must be synchronized for them to operate in harmony. DB2 provides this synchronization in two ways:

- You can bind all programs that can be initiated in a single CICS task to a single plan specified in the RCT for each transaction that can invoke any of the programs. An example was shown in Listing 18.2 for the menuing application.

- You can specify that dynamic plan selection is to be used. Listing 18.2 shows an example of this synchronization also.

Dynamic plan selection uses an exit routine, specified in the RCT by coding PLNEXIT=YES and PLNPGME=exit-routine. If using the RDO, you will code the exit routine name using the PLANEXITNAME parameter. The exit routine determines the plan that should be used for the program being run. IBM supplies a sample exit routine called DSNCUEXT with DB2. This exit routine assigns the plan name to be the same as the program name. This approach is usually adequate, but you can code exit routines to assign plan names as your installation sees fit. Exit routines cannot contain SQL statements.

The first SQL statement executed after a CICS SYNCPOINT signals to DB2 that a new plan name must be selected. When you're using dynamic plan selection, your CICS programs must heed the following rules:

- Use the CICS LINK or XCTL command to call one program from another.

- Issue a CICS SYNCPOINT before the LINK or XCTL. Otherwise, the first SQL statement in the new program receives an SQLCODE of -805.

- Design your programs so that a complete application unit of work is completed in a single program. Failure to do so results in logical units of work that span physical units of work. Data integrity problems can result.

The second option for the synchronization of DB2 plans to CICS tasks is to create large plans consisting of the DBRMs or packages of all programs that can be called in a single CICS task. Prior to DB2 V2.3, this could not be achieved with packages, so all DBRMs had to be bound into a single plan. This approach had the following negative effects.

When a program changed, a new DBRM was created, which caused the large plan to be bound again. You could not use the REBIND command, and you had no way of simply adding or replacing a single DBRM. As the number of DBRMs added to a plan increased, the time to bind that plan increased. As the plan was being bound, execution of the CICS transactions using that plan was not permitted. Therefore, program changes effectively took the entire application offline. When dynamic plan selection or packages were used, however, only the programs being changed were unavailable.

A second negative effect was that as the plan's size increased, it used more virtual storage. Even though DB2 uses techniques to load only those portions of the plan needed to execute the SQL at hand, performance suffers somewhat as plans increase in size. When

18

you use dynamic plan selection, however, plans are generally much smaller. When packages are used, the plan is broken into smaller pieces that the system can manage more easily.

The recommendation is to create plans using packages, not DBRMs. This technique should be easier to manage and more efficient than either large plans composed of DBRMs or dynamic plan selection. Packages, instead of DBRMs bound directly into plans, should be the standard for all DB2 shops. Yet, many shops still avoid packages because they avoid (or fear) change or simply have not had the time to convert older applications. So, if your installation has stubbornly shunned packages (or, heaven forbid, is running a version of DB2 prior to V2.3), the recommendations change. Use dynamic plan selection for very large applications. Doing so decreases downtime due to program changes. For small applications (four or fewer programs), use a large plan composed of the DBRMs of each program.

Two-Phase Commit

As I already mentioned, changes made in a CICS program are committed by the CICS SYNCPOINT command. Likewise, you can invoke the SYNCPOINT ROLLBACK command to back out unwanted changes. You code these commands as follows:

```
EXEC CICS
    SYNCPOINT
END-EXEC.

EXEC CICS
    SYNCPOINT
    ROLLBACK
END-EXEC.
```

The SQL COMMIT and ROLLBACK verbs are not valid in CICS programs. An implicit commit is performed when a CICS transaction ends with the EXEC CICS RETURN command.

When a CICS SYNCPOINT is requested in a CICS-DB2 program, a two-phase commit is performed. The commit is done in two phases because CICS must commit changes made to resources under its jurisdiction (such as changes made to VSAM files), and DB2 must control the commit for changes made with SQL UPDATE, INSERT, and DELETE statements.

Figure 18.25 shows the two-phase commit process for CICS. CICS acts as the coordinator of the process, and DB2 acts as a participant. The first phase consists of CICS informing DB2 that a SYNCPOINT was requested. DB2 updates its log but retains all locks because the commit is not complete. When the log update is finished, DB2 informs CICS that it has completed phase 1. CICS then updates its log, retaining all locks.

CICS signals DB2 to begin phase 2, in which DB2 logs the commit and releases its locks. If successful, DB2 sends control back to CICS so that CICS can release its locks and record the success of the SYNCPOINT.

The two-phase commit process virtually ensures the integrity of DB2 data modified by CICS transactions. If changes cannot be committed in either environment for any reason, they are rolled back in both. In a connection failure or a system crash, however, the commit status of some transactions may be in doubt. These transactions are referred to as *in-doubt threads*. After a system failure, when DB2 and CICS are started and the connection is reestablished, most in-doubt threads are resolved automatically. If any in-doubt threads exist, you can use the RECOVER INDOUBT command to commit or roll back the changes pending for these threads.

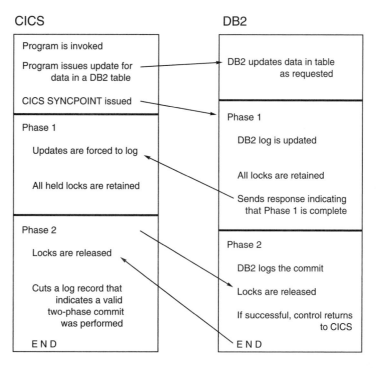

FIGURE 18.25   The CICS two-phase commit process.

CICS Design Guidelines

When designing CICS transactions that access DB2 data, keep the following tips, tricks, and techniques in mind.

Bind CICS Plans for Performance   When you're binding plans for CICS transactions, follow these BIND guidelines:

High volume	ACQUIRE(ALLOCATE), RELEASE(DEALLOCATE)
All others	ACQUIRE(USE), RELEASE(COMMIT)

Binding high-volume transactions in this manner reduces overhead by ensuring that all resources are acquired before they are accessed. Why is this so? Consider the ramifications of binding a plan for high-volume CICS transaction with RELEASE(COMMIT). Say the transaction uses a protected thread and that thread is reused 200 times by the same transaction. Each time the transaction ends (causing a COMMIT), DB2 would release the table space locks acquired during the course of the program, and then reacquire them again when the transaction runs again and the thread is reused—200 times. With `RELEASE(DEALLOCATE)`, resources are not released until the thread is deallocated. So, the table space locks would not need to be released and reacquired 200 times as long as the purge cycle is not met and the thread keeps getting reused. This can save a significant amount of CPU—perhaps up to 10%.

> **CAUTION**
>
> Be aware that using protected threads and binding with `RELEASE(DEALLOCATE)` can cause administrative issues. You will probably need to increase the size of your EDM pool, because utilization will increase as more pages become non-stealable due to reuse.
>
> Additionally, rebinding plans may become difficult. You cannot rebind while the plan is in use. But the plan will be in use as long as the thread used to execute the program is allocated. So, binding your CICS-DB2 plans will likely become something that is done only during off hours.

Avoid Conditional Table Access   Additionally, high-volume transactions should eliminate (or minimize) built-in conditional table access and should be as small as possible.

Decrease the Size of Your CICS Programs   The smaller the executable load module for a CICS program, the more efficient it will be. Therefore, CICS programmers should strive to reduce the size of their code. One way to do so is to increase the amount of reuseable code. For example, modularize your program and use common modules rather than recode modules everywhere they are needed.

A second way to increase your reuseable code is to use the COBOL `REDEFINES` clause to reduce the number of `WORKING-STORAGE` variables defined by the program. For example, consider a program requiring three text variables all used by different portions of the code. The first variable is 3 bytes long, the second is 8 bytes long, and another is 15 bytes long. Consider defining them as follows:

```
01   COMMON-VARS-1.
     05  THREE-BYTE-VAR    PIC X(3).
     05  FILLER            PIC X(12).

01   COMMON-VARS-2 REDEFINES COMMON-VARS-1.
     05  EIGHT-BYTE-VAR    PIC X(8).
     05  FILLER            PIC X(7).

01   COMMON-VARS-3 REDEFINES COMMON-VARS-1.
     05  FIFTEEN-BYTE-VAR  PIC X(15).
```

This way, you can save space. Before deciding to use this approach, however, you should consider the following factors:

- The readability of the code is reduced when you use `REDEFINES`.

- The program cannot use redefined variables concurrently. Ensure that any variable redefined as another variable can never be used by the program at the same time as another variable assigned for the same redefined group.

Another way to increase reuseable code is to use explicit constants in the program code to reduce the number of WORKING-STORAGE variables required. This approach can enhance performance, but it usually makes maintaining the program more difficult.

Avoid COBOL File Processing   Do not use the COBOL file processing verbs READ, WRITE, OPEN, and CLOSE to access non-DB2 data sets required by your CICS/DB2 programs. If you use these functions in a CICS program, an MVS wait results, causing severe performance degradation. Instead, use the corresponding CICS file processing services (see Table 18.9).

TABLE 18.9   CICS File Processing Commands

Random Access Commands	
READ	Reads a specific record
WRITE	Writes a specific record
REWRITE	Updates a specific record
DELETE	Deletes a specific record
Sequential Access Commands	
STARTBR	Establishes sequential positioning in the file
READNEXT	Reads the next record sequentially
Sequential Access Commands	
READPREV	Reads the previous record sequentially
RESETBR	Resets positioning in the file
ENDBR	Ends sequential file access

Avoid Resource-Intensive COBOL Verbs   Avoid the following COBOL verbs and features in CICS programs because they use a large amount of system resources:

    ACCEPT

    DISPLAY

    EXAMINE

    EXHIBIT

    SORT

    TRACE

    UNSTRING

    VARIABLE MOVE

Use WORKING-STORAGE to Initialize Variables   To initialize variables, use the VALUES clause in WORKING-STORAGE rather than the MOVE and INITIALIZE statements.

Avoid Excessive PERFORMs and GOTOs   Design your programs to execute paragraphs sequentially as much as possible. The fewer PERFORMs and GOTOs you use, the better the program performance will be in CICS.

Avoid Conversational Programs   A conversational program receives data from a terminal, acts on the data, sends a response to the terminal, and waits for the terminal operator to respond. This process ties up a thread for the duration of the conversation.

Instead, use pseudo-conversational techniques for your CICS-DB2 programs. *Pseudo-conversational* programs appear to the operator as a continuous "conversation" consisting of requests and responses, but they are actually a series of separate tasks.

Favor Transfer Control Over Linking   Favor the use of the XCTL command over the LINK command to pass control from one program to another. LINK acquires extra storage, and XCTL does not.

Reduce the Overhead of Sequential Number Assignment   Consider using counters in main storage to assign sequential numbers. This way, you can reduce the overhead associated with other forms of assigning sequential numbers, such as reading a table containing the highest number. Remember that a rollback does not affect main storage. Therefore, rolling back a transaction can cause gaps in the numbering sequence.

V8   AS of DB2 V8, consider using sequence objects to assign sequential numbers. Sequence objects are covered in Chapter 5.

Plan for Locking Problems   Plan for deadlocks and timeouts, and handle them accordingly in your program. If the RCT specifies ROLBE=YES or RDO specifies DROLLBACK(YES) all changes are backed out automatically and a -911 SQLCODE is returned to your program. For ROLBE=NO (RCT) or DROLLBACK(NO) (RDO), -913 is passed to the SQLCODE and automatic backout does not occur. In this case, the application program must decide whether to issue a CICS SYNCPOINT ROLLBACK to back out the changes.

Synchronize Programs and RCT/RDO Entries   You must know the RCT or RDO parameters for your transaction before coding your program. Specifically, coding NO for ROLBE (RCT) or DROLLBACK (RDO) parameters affects the program design significantly by adding a great deal of code to handle rollbacks. Also, coding NO for TWAIT (RCT) or THREADWAIT (RDO) requires additional programming to handle abends.

Place SQL As Deep in the Program As Possible   Minimize thread use by placing all SQL statements as far as possible into the transaction. A thread is initiated when the first SQL call is encountered. The later in the execution that the SQL statement is encountered, the shorter the time during which the thread is used.

Avoid DDL   Avoid issuing DDL from a CICS program. DDL execution is time intensive and acquires locks on the DB2 Catalog and DB2 Directory. Because CICS programs should be quick, they should avoid DDL.

Check the Availability of the Attach Facility   You must start the CICS Attach Facility for the appropriate DB2 subsystem before you execute CICS transactions that will run programs requiring access to DB2 data. If the CICS-to-DB2 connection is unavailable, the task abends with a CICS abend code of AEY9.

To avoid this type of abend, consider using the CICS HANDLE CONDITION command to check whether DB2 is available, as shown in Listing 18.3. This COBOL routine tests whether the CICS-to-DB2 connection has been started before issuing any SQL.

LISTING 18.3   Checking for DB2 Availability

```
WORKING-STORAGE.
      .
      .
      .
   77  WS-LGTH     PIC 9(8)  COMP.
   77  WS-PTR      PIC 9(4)  COMP.
      .
      .
      .
PROCEDURE DIVISION.
0000-MAINLINE.
      .
      .
      .
   EXEC CICS
       HANDLE CONDITION
       INVEXITREQ(9900-DB2-UNAVAILABLE)
   END-EXEC.

   EXEC CICS
       EXTRACT EXIT
       PROGRAM('DSNCEXT1')
       ENTRYNAME('DSNCSQL')
       GASET(WS-PTR)
       GALENGTH(WS-LGTH)
   END-EXEC.
      .
      .
      .
9900-DB2-UNAVAILABLE.

   Inform the user that DB2 is unavailable

   Perform exception processing
```

Use Debugging Tools   Use CICS debugging facilities such as EDF to view CICS commands before and after their execution.

IMS (Information Management System)

IMS is IBM's pre-relational database management system offering. It is based on the structuring of related data items in inverted trees or hierarchies. Although usually perceived as only a DBMS, IMS is a combination of two components:

- IMS/DB, the database management system

- IMS/TM, the transaction management environment or data communications component (previously known as IMS/DC, and still called by that name by many DBAs and systems programmers)

You can use these IMS components separately or together. Online access to IMS databases is achieved through IMS/TM or CICS. Access to IMS databases is provided also in a batch environment. When an IMS database is accessed through IMS/TM, it is said to be *online*; when it is accessed in batch, it is said to be *offline*. IMS/TM provides an online environment in which you can run application programs that communicate with a terminal, much like CICS. Like CICS, IMS/TM can be used by programs that access not only IMS databases but also DB2 tables.

IMS and CICS are alike in many respects, but they also have significant differences, outlined in the following paragraphs. For example, IMS uses a facility called MFS (Message Format Services) to format messages to terminals and printers; CICS uses BMS (Basic Mapping Support). IMS/TM controls its environment not through tables, but through a series of macros known as a SYSGEN. The SYSGEN defines the terminals, programs, transactions, and the general online environment for IMS/TM. Another difference is that all IMS programs require a program specification block (PSB), which defines the access to IMS/DB databases and IMS/TM resources. Along with IMS DBDs that define the structure of the IMS databases to be accessed, the PSBs are defined to control a program's scope of operation. An additional control block, the ACB (application control block), is used in the online world (and optionally in the batch environment) to combine the PSBs and DBDs into a single control block defining the control structure and scope of all IMS programs.

All IMS/TM activity is processed through a region. There are two types of regions. One control region manages IMS activity and processes commands. Application programs execute from dependent regions. As many as 255 dependent regions can exist for each IMS/TM subsystem. See Figure 18.26 for clarification.

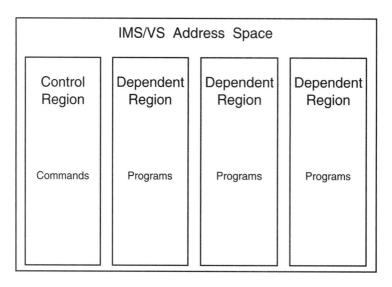

FIGURE 18.26   IMS/TM regions.

Types of IMS Programs

IMS programs are categorized, based on the environment in which they run and the types of databases they can access. The four types of IMS programs are batch programs, batch message processors, message processing programs, and fast path programs.

An *IMS batch program* is invoked by JCL and runs as an MVS batch job. IMS batch programs can access only offline IMS databases, unless IMS Data Base Recovery Control (DBRC) is used. When DB2 tables are accessed by IMS batch programs, they are commonly referred to as DL/I batch. DL/I (Data Language/I) is the language used to access data in IMS databases, just as SQL is the language used to access data in DB2 tables. Batch DL/I programs run independently of the IMS/TM environment.

The second type of IMS program is called a *batch message processor*, or BMP. BMPs are hybrid programs combining elements of both batch and online programs. A BMP runs under the jurisdiction of IMS/TM but is invoked by JES and operates as a batch program. All databases accessed by a BMP must be online to IMS/TM. The following are the two types of BMPs:

- Terminal-oriented BMPs can access the IMS message queue to send or receive messages from IMS/TM terminals.

- Batch-oriented BMPs do not access the message queue and cannot communicate with terminals.

True online IMS programs are called *message processing programs*, or MPPs. They are initiated by a transaction code, access online databases, and communicate with terminals through the message queue.

The final type of IMS program is a *fast path program*. Fast path programs are very high performance MPPs that access a special type of IMS database known as a fast path database.

The IMS Attach Facility

As with the other environments, a specialized attachment facility is provided with DB2 to enable IMS to access DB2 resources. The IMS Attach Facility, due to the nature of IMS, provides more flexibility in connecting to DB2 than the Attach Facilities for TSO or CICS.

In Figure 18.27, you can see that the following connections are supported using the IMS Attach Facility:

- One DB2 subsystem can connect to multiple IMS subsystems.

- One IMS subsystem can connect to multiple DB2 subsystems.

- One IMS region can connect to multiple DB2 subsystems.

- One IMS application program can access only one DB2 subsystem.

18

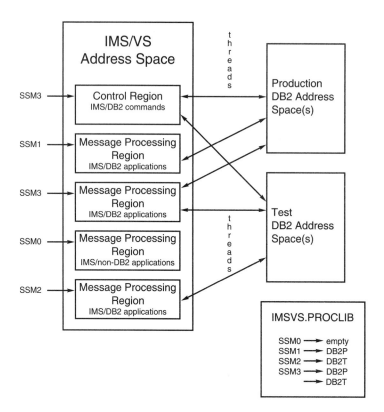

FIGURE 18.27   The IMS Attach Facility.

DB2 is connected to IMS by a subsystem member (SSM). The SSM defines the parameters of the IMS Attach Facility for both online and batch connections. The following list outlines the SSM parameters:

SSN   The DB2 subsystem identifier (for example, DSN).

LIT   The language interface token used to route SQL calls to the appropriate DB2 subsystem. Usually equal to SYS1.

ESMT   The name of the DB2 initialization module, which must be set to DSNMIN10.

RTT   The optional Resource Translation Table to be used. The RTT can be used to override IMS region options, such as the capability to specify a plan name different from the program name.

ERR   The action IMS takes if the plan is not found or the DB2 subsystem is unavailable. The ERR options follow:

R   IMS returns control to the application program and sets the SQLCODE in the SQLCA to -923. R is the default.

Q   IMS causes an abend when operating in DL/1 batch. In an online environ-
        ment, IMS PSTOPs the program and issues a U3051 user abend code, backs
        out this transaction's activity to the last checkpoint, and requeues the input
        message.

A   IMS forces an abend with a U3047 abend code. If executing in the online
        environment, the input message is deleted.

CRC   The command recognition character to be used to identify a DB2 command in the
             IMS/TM environment using /SSR. CRC is not used in the DL/1 batch environment.

CONNECTION   The connection name for a DL/1 batch program. This name must be unique for
             each concurrent batch IMS program that will access DB2. If a program is running
             with a given connection name, and another program with the same name tries to
             execute at the same time, the second program will fail. This parameter is invalid for
             the online attach.

PLAN   The name of the plan to be used by the batch IMS/DB2 application program. This
             parameter is required only if the plan name is different from the program name.
             This parameter is invalid for the online attach.

PROGRAM   The name of the program to be run. This parameter is invalid for the online attach.

Online Attach Considerations

Enabling the IMS Attach Facility for the online environment is the responsibility of a
system programmer. IMS-to-DB2 connections are defined by changing the JCL used to
invoke the IMS subsystem. The SSM is assigned to the JCL by a parameter on the EXEC
card. The IMS SYSGEN procedure is unaffected by the addition of an IMS-to-DB2 connection.

To establish the connection between IMS/TM and DB2, you must perform the following
steps:

1. Code an SSM line for each DB2 subsystem that must be connected to this IMS/TM
   region.

2. Place the SSM in the IMSVS.PROCLIB PDS defined to the IMS control region and
   specify the name in the SSM parameter of the EXEC statement, for example

```
//IMS        EXEC      IMS . . . ,SSM=SSM1 . . .
//STEPLIB    DD        DSN=IMSVS.RESLIB,DISP=SHR
//           DD        DSN=SYS1.DB2V510.DSNLOAD,DISP=SHR
//           DD        DSN=SYS1.DB2V510.DSNEXIT,DISP=SHR
//PROCLIB    DD        DSN=IMSVS.PROCLIB,DISP=SHR
```

The SSM defined to the control region is the default for all dependent regions. If you do
not want this default, code a separate SSM for each dependent region that has different
IMS-to-DB2 connection needs, and follow the preceding steps for each of the dependent
regions.

If more than one DB2 subsystem will be connected to a single region (control or dependent), the SSM for that region must contain a line for each of the DB2 subsystems. Then a second language interface module must be generated. The standard language interface module is DFSLI000; it uses SYS1 as its language interface token (LIT) in the SSM. You can create a second language interface module, DFSLI002, for example, by using SYS2 for its LIT.

You can generate the second language interface module using the DFSLI macro provided with IMS/VS. Consider this example:

```
DFSLI002   DFSLI    TYPE=DB2,LIT=SYS2
```

A program executing in any region connected to more than one DB2 subsystem accesses the appropriate DB2 subsystem based on which language interface module the program was link-edited with at program preparation time. In this example, the module would be either DFSLI000 or DFSLI002.

CONNECTION, PLAN, and PROGRAM are batch parameters and, as such, are invalid when defining the SSM for IMS/TM. Sample online SSM definitions follow. The first is a simple SSM connecting the DB2P subsystem to IMS/TM:

```
DB2P,SYS1,DSNMIN10,,R,-
```

You use the second to connect two DB2 subsystems, DB2A and DB2B, to a single IMS/TM:

```
DB2A,SYS1,DSNMIN10,,R,-
DB2B,SYS2,DSNMIN10,,R,+
```

To access DB2A, INCLUDE the DFSLI000 module (because it is associated with LIT SYS1) in the link-edit step for your programs. DFSLI002, on the other hand, is associated with LIT SYS2, so it is link-edited into programs that must access DB2B resources.

An online IMS/TM program (BMP, MPP, or fast path) must follow standard DB2 program preparation procedures (precompile, compile, link edit, and BIND). However, a few special considerations apply:

- The appropriate language interface module (DFSLI000, DFSLI002, and so on) for the DB2 subsystem to be accessed must be link-edited into the load module.

- A PSB must be generated for the program to define the IMS databases and online resources that will be accessed by the program.

- The PSB (and all DBDs accessed by the program) must be included in the ACB for the online IMS/TM subsystem.

- The appropriate IMS SYSGEN macros must be coded for the transaction and program before it can be executed online.

The Resource Translation Table

You can define a resource translation table (RTT) using the DSNMAPN assembler macro. An RTT is necessary only when the plan name is not the same as the program name. Consider this example:

```
DSNMAPN    APN=PROGRAMX,PLAN=PLANX, . . .
```

This statement assigns the plan name, PLANX, to the program PROGRAMX. This macro must be linked to the DB2 load library with the name specified in the RTT parameter of the SSM being used.

IMS/TM Thread Use

Two types of threads are used by IMS/TM: command threads and transaction threads. The type of thread is contingent on the type of region it has been created for. Each region can have only one thread at any given time.

Threads emanating from IMS/TM are not created until they are needed, even though the IMS-to-DB2 connection has been established. The following process is for a command thread emanating from the control region:

1. After IMS/TM is brought up, the first DB2 command is issued from a terminal connected to IMS/TM using the /SSR IMS command.

2. IMS verifies that the user is permitted to issue the /SSR command.

3. IMS issues a SIGNON request using that user's userid, if available. If SIGNON security is not used, the LTERM is used (or, for a non-message-driven BMP, the PSB name is used).

4. IMS requests that DB2 create a thread.

5. When the thread has been created, the command is processed. Subsequent DB2 commands issued from IMS can reuse the thread. SIGNON is performed for these subsequent commands.

Additional processing is required for transaction threads. Transaction threads are created from a dependent region that was scheduled by the control region. The procedure for transaction thread creation and its use is shown in Figure 18.28.

Two-Phase Commit

Recall that CICS programs commit changes by means of CICS commands and not the normal DB2 COMMIT statement. Likewise, changes made in IMS/TM programs are committed and rolled back by means of IMS commands. You code the IMS checkpoint command, which implements a COMMIT, as follows:

```
CALL    'CBLTDLI' USING NUM-OPS,
                        'CHKP',
                        IO-PCB,
                        CHKP-LENGTH,
                        CHKP-AREA.
```

18

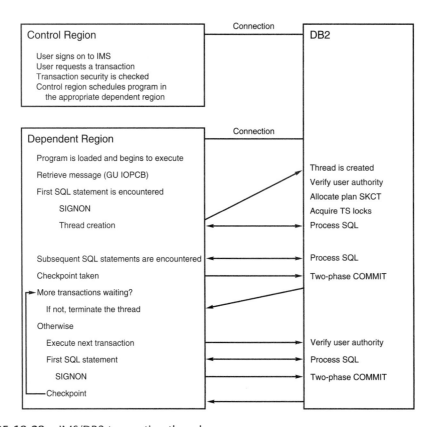

FIGURE 18.28   IMS/DB2 transaction threads.

You code the IMS rollback command as follows:

```
CALL    'CBLTDLI' USING NUM-OPS,
                        'ROLB',
                        IO-PCB,
                        CHKP-LENGTH,
                        CHKP-AREA.
```

The SQL verbs COMMIT and ROLLBACK are not valid in IMS/TM programs. An implicit commit is performed when a GET UNIQUE is issued to the message queue.

When a checkpoint is requested in an IMS/TM program, a two-phase commit is performed much like the two-phase commit discussed in the previous section on CICS. The commit is done in two phases to synchronize the updates made to IMS databases with those made to DB2 tables.

The two-phase commit process for IMS/TM programs is outlined in Figure 18.29. A component of IMS/TM called the *syncpoint coordinator* handles the coordination of commits.

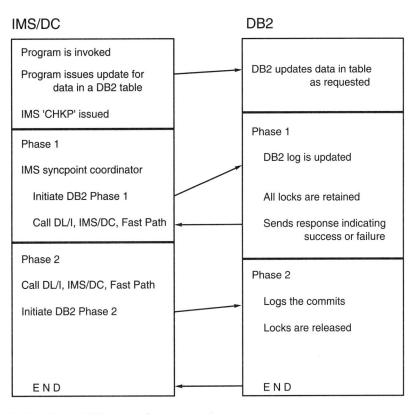

FIGURE 18.29   The IMS/TM two-phase commit process.

Phase 1 of the commit process consists of IMS/TM informing each participant that a syncpoint has been reached and that each participant should prepare to commit. The participants can include DB2, DL/I, IMS/TM, and IMS Fast Path. Each participant performs the needed tasks to ensure that a commit is possible for that environment. DB2 updates its log, retains all locks, and informs the IMS syncpoint coordinator that phase 1 has been completed successfully.

If all other participants signal that the commit can proceed, phase 2 is initiated, whereby each participant is responsible for completing the commit. If any participant signals that phase 1 cannot be completed successfully, the entire unit of work is aborted and the updates are backed out. In phase 2, DB2 logs the commit and releases all locks.

The two-phase commit process virtually ensures the integrity of DB2 data modified by IMS/TM. If changes cannot be committed in either DB2 or IMS for any reason, they are rolled back in both. In a connection failure of a system crash, however, the commit status of some transactions may be in doubt. They are referred to as *in-doubt threads*. When DB2 and IMS/TM are started after a system failure, and the IMS-to-DB2 connection is reestablished, most in-doubt threads are resolved automatically. If any in-doubt threads remain, you can use the RECOVER INDOUBT command to commit or roll back the changes pending for these threads.

18

Restart

The restart capabilities of IMS/TM can be used by online programs. You code the IMS restart command, XRST, as follows:

```
CALL 'CBLTDLI' USING 'XRST',
                     IO-PCB,
                     IO-LENGTH,
                     IO-AREA,
                     CHKP-LENGTH,
                     CHKP-AREA.
```

XRST reads the last checkpoint from the IMS log and passes the data stored in the checkpoint area to the program issuing the command. The program can use that information to reposition DB2 cursors and reestablish IMS database positioning.

It is imperative, though, that each checkpoint call passes all requisite information for repositioning each time it is issued. For DB2 cursors, this information should include the name of the cursor, the tables being accessed, and the last key or keys retrieved. For IMS databases, this information includes the name of the database, the segment being accessed, and the complete concatenated key. This information should be saved for every DB2 cursor and IMS database PCB that must be repositioned.

IMS/DB2 Deadlocks

DB2 locks and IMS locks are managed independently. DB2 uses a lock manager called the IRLM. IMS can use the IRLM to control locks, but it can also use a technique known as program isolation. Even if both subsystems use an IRLM to control locks, IMS locks are issued independently from DB2 locks. As a result, a deadlock can occur. A complete description of deadlocks is included in Chapter 23, "Locking DB2 Data." An example of an IMS and DB2 deadlock is presented in the following processing sequence for two concurrently executing application programs:

Program 1		Program 2
Update IMS DBD1		Update DB2 Table A
Lock established		Lock established
Intermediate processing		Intermediate processing
Update DB2 Table A		Update IMS DBD1
Lock (wait)	*Deadlock*	Lock (wait)

Program 1 requests a lock for DB2 resources that Program 2 holds, and Program 2 requests a lock for IMS resources that Program 1 holds. This deadlock must be resolved before either program can perform subsequent processing. One of the two programs must be targeted as the victim of the deadlock; in other words, it either abends or is timed out.

The deadlock situation is resolved differently depending on the program and the resource. When an MPP is the victim in a deadlock, it abends with a U777 abend. When a batch-oriented BMP is the victim in a deadlock, the abend received depends on the type of resource that could not be locked:

- If only DL/I databases are affected, a U777 abend results.

- If DL/I databases are affected in conjunction with fast path databases or DB2 tables, the PCB status field is set to FD.

- If fast path databases are involved, the PCB status field is set to FD.

- If DB2 tables are involved, the SQLCODE is set to -911.

IMS SYSGEN Guidelines

The following guidelines are useful when performing an IMS SYSGEN for DB2.

Promote Thread Use with PROCLIM   Specify the PROCLIM parameter of the TRANSACT macro to be greater than 1 to encourage thread reuse for IMS transactions that access DB2 tables. When multiple transactions are processed during the same PSB schedule, DB2 can reuse the thread, thereby reducing overhead by avoiding thread creation.

Use WFI and Fast Path Only for Critical Transactions   Threads are always reused by WFI (Wait For Input) transactions and Fast Path regions. The thread is not terminated unless the WFI or Fast Path region is stopped, so these regions tie up a thread indefinitely. For this reason, use WFI transactions and Fast Path regions for only high-volume, critical transactions. For low-volume transactions, use the PROCLIM parameter to control thread reuse.

Define the Transaction Mode Carefully   You can define a transaction to operate in one of two modes: MODE=SNGL or MODE=MULTI. MODE=SNGL transactions define a unit of work at the transaction level, whereas MODE=MULTI transactions string multiple transactions together into a unit of work. Single mode transactions cause a syncpoint when the transaction is completed. Multiple mode transactions do not reach a syncpoint until the program is terminated.

As the programmer, you must know the mode of the transaction before coding to implement CHKP processing effectively and to reestablish cursor and database positioning properly.

Use INQUIRY=YES for Read-Only Transactions   You can define read-only transactions by coding INQUIRY=YES for the TRANSACT macro. Transactions defined to be read-only cannot update IMS databases. When the transaction accesses DB2, it cannot modify data in DB2 tables. An attempt to issue the following SQL statements in a read-only transaction results in a -817 SQLCODE:

```
ALTER

CREATE

DELETE

DROP

GRANT
```

18

      INSERT

      REVOKE

      UPDATE

DL/I Batch Interface

The DL/I batch interface enables batch IMS programs to access DB2 data. DL/I batch programs access DB2 data under the auspices of the IMS attach facility, which is defined by an SSM. When you're establishing an IMS-to-DB2 connection for a batch program, the JCL used to execute the batch program must contain the SSM parameters. It is assigned to the DDITV02 DD name, as shown in the following example:

```
//DDITV02   DD  *
DB2T,SYS1,DSNMIN10,,R,-,APPL01,,PGM01
/*
```

This SSM connects the PGM01 program to DB2T using a plan with the same name as the program. The program does not abend if DB2 is unavailable. Another SSM example follows:

```
//DDITV02   DD  *
DSN,SYS1,DSNMIN10,,A,-,APPL02,PLANNAME,PGM02
/*
```

This SSM uses plan PLANNAME to connect the PGM02 program to the DB2 subsystem named DSN. An abend is forced if DB2 is unavailable. If the DDITV02 DD name is missing or specified incorrectly, a connection is not made and the job abends.

Additionally, you can specify an output data set containing status and processing information by using the DDOTV02 DD name. If you do not specify the DDOTV02 DD name, processing continues without sending the status and processing information.

Sample JCL to run a DL/I batch program that accesses DB2 tables is shown in Listing 18.4. This JCL runs the BTCHPROG program using the BTCHPLAN plan. Notice that the JCL contains two steps. The first step runs the DL/I batch program, and the second step prints the contents of the DDOTV02 data set. Printing the DDOTV02 data set is a good idea because it can contain pertinent information for resolving any processing errors.

LISTING 18.4   JCL to Run a DL/I Batch DB2 Program

```
//DB2JOBB  JOB (BATCH),'DL/I BATCH',MSGCLASS=X,CLASS=X,
//      NOTIFY=USER,REGION=4096K
//*
//******************************************************************
//*
//*      JCL TO RUN AN IMS/DB2 PROGRAM IN BATCH
//*
//*      PROGRAM NAME    :: BTCHPROG
//*      PLAN NAME       :: BTCHPLAN
//*      CONNECTION NAME :: DB2B0001
//*
```

LISTING 18.4   Continued

```
//******************************************************************
//*
//JOBLIB      DD DSN=SYS1.DB2V810.DSNLOAD,DISP=SHR
//BATCHPRG    EXEC DLIBATCH,DBRC=Y,LOGT=SYSDA,COND=EVEN,
//            MSGCLASS='X',CLASS='X'
//G.STEPLIB   DD
//            DD
//            DD Add a DD for each DB2, COBOL, and program
//               load library
//G.IEFRDER   DD DSN=IMSLOG,DISP=(NEW,CATLG,CATLG),. . .
//G.STEPCAT   DD DSN=IMSCAT,DISP=SHR
//G.DDOTV02   DD DSN=&DDOTV02,DISP=(NEW,PASS,DELETE),
//            UNIT=SYSDA,DCB=(RECFM=VB,BLKSIZE=4096,LRECL=4092),
//            SPACE=(TRK,(1,1),RLSE)
//G.DDITV02   DD *
  DB2P,SYS1,DSNMIN10,,A,-,DB2B0001,BTCHPLAN,BTCHPROG
/*
//*
//******************************************************************
//*
//*          PRINT THE DDOTV02 DATASET IF THERE ARE PROBLEMS
//*
//******************************************************************
//*
//PRINTOUT   EXEC PGM=DFSERA10,COND=EVEN
//STEPLIB    DD DSN=IMS.RESLIB,DISP=SHR
//SYSPRINT   DD SYSOUT=X
//SYSUT1     DD DSN=&DDOTV02,DISP=(OLD,DELETE)
//SYSIN      DD *
CONTROL     CNTL   K=000,H=8000
OPTION      PRINT
/*
//
```

A DL/I batch program must follow standard DB2 program preparation procedures (precompile, compile, link-edit, and bind). However, a few special considerations apply:

- All DL/I batch programs must be link-edited using the RMODE=24 and AMODE=24 parameters.

- The DFSLI000 language interface module must be link-edited to the load module.

- A PSB must be generated for the program to define the IMS databases to be accessed.

IMS/TM Design Guidelines

The following techniques should be applied when designing IMS transactions that access DB2 data.

Avoid DDL   Avoid issuing DDL in an IMS/TM program. DDL execution is time intensive and acquires locks on the DB2 Catalog and the DB2 Directory. Because IMS/TM programs should be quick, they should avoid DDL.

Copy PCBs Before Each Checkpoint   Application programs should save the PCBs for all IMS databases before invoking an IMS CHKP. After the CHKP, copy the saved PCB back to the original to reestablish positioning in the IMS databases. Otherwise, the IMS database positioning is lost, much like DB2 cursor positioning is lost when a COMMIT is performed.

Be Aware of Cursor Closing Points   IMS closes all DB2 cursors in WFI and MODE=SINGL transactions when the program does a get unique (GU) to the message queue (IOPCB). Cursors also are closed when the program issues a CHKP call or when the program terminates.

Use a Scratch Pad Area   Use the SPA (Scratch Pad Area) to store temporary work and to implement pseudoconversational programs.

Use Fast Path for Sequential Number Assignment   Consider using IMS Fast Path database storage to assign sequential numbers. Accessing sequential numbers for assignment using Fast Path databases is more efficient than other conventional means (for example, reading a table containing the highest number).

Use Testing Tools   Use testing tools such as the Batch Terminal Simulator (BTS). The requirements for using BTS follow:

- The user must have MONITOR2 and TRACE authority.

- MONITOR Trace Class 1 must be activated for the plan being tested.

- The plan must be specified on the ./T control card.

- A new control card must be added as follows:

  ```
  ./P MBR=BTSCOM00 PA 000C14 PC=DB2T
  ```

Note that any valid DB2 subsystem ID can be substituted for DB2T.

Do Not Share IRLMs   The DBRC facility of IMS uses an IRLM to control locking when multiple jobs access shared databases. Never share a single IRLM between DB2 and IMS because doing so results in inefficient locking for both IMS and DB2. Also, a shared IRLM is difficult to monitor and tune. Specify a single IRLM for each DB2 subsystem and an IRLM for the IMS subsystem.

Consider IMS/ESA Quick Reschedule   For very active, critical transactions, use the quick reschedule feature of IMS/ESA. Quick reschedule creates a "hot region" for the execution of MPPs. When quick reschedule is implemented, the MPP region does not terminate when the PROCLIM count is reached if the message queue holds a qualifying transaction waiting to execute.

CAF (Call Attach Facility)

The next "door to DB2" is provided by the CAF, or Call Attach Facility. CAF differs from the previous attach mechanisms in that it does not provide teleprocessing services. CAF is used to manage connections between DB2 and batch and online TSO application programs, without the overhead of the TSO terminal monitor program.

CAF programs can be executed as one of the following:

- An MVS batch job

- A started task

- A TSO batch job

- An online TSO application

CAF is used to control a program's connection to DB2, as shown in Figure 18.30. The DB2 program communicates to DB2 through the CAF language interface, DSNALI. The primary benefit of using CAF is that the application can control the connection with CAF calls. Five CAF calls are used to control the connection:

CONNECT	Establishes a connection between the program's MVS address space and DB2
DISCONNECT	Eliminates the connection between the MVS address space and DB2
OPEN	Establishes a thread for the program to communicate with DB2
CLOSE	Terminates the thread
TRANSLATE	Provides the program with DB2 error message information, placing it in the SQLCA

Typically, a control program is created to handle the establishment and termination of the DB2 connection. It is the CAF module shown in Figure 18.30. Although this module is not required, it is recommended so that you can eliminate the repetitious coding of the tedious tasks associated with connecting, disconnecting, opening, and closing.

CAF programs must be link-edited with the CAF language interface module, DSNALI.

Thread Creation and Use

Two distinct methods for the creation of a CAF thread can be followed. In the first, shown in Figure 18.31, the application program explicitly requests a thread by using the CAF OPEN call. The application uses the CLOSE call to explicitly terminate the thread. Explicit creation of CAF threads is particularly useful for online TSO CAF programs.

As I mentioned in the TSO section, an online TSO/DB2 program can tie up a thread for a long time when the DSN command is used to attach to DB2. When users of this type of application spend time thinking about their next action, or leave their terminal in the middle of the application, a program using the TSO attach consumes an active thread.

If the program instead uses CAF to create a thread, each time the user presses Enter, the thread is terminated before the next screen appears. Although this use of DB2 resources is more effective because a thread is not consumed when no activity occurs, it is also less efficient because the overhead of thread termination and creation is added to each user action. Online TSO applications are not known for their speed, though, so fewer dormant threads in return for a slower response time might not be a bad trade-off.

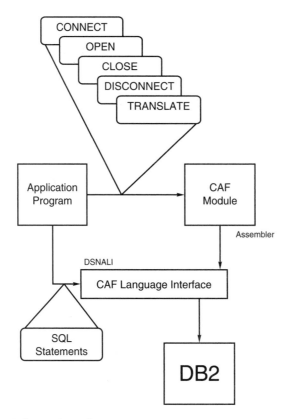

FIGURE 18.30   The Call Attach Facility.

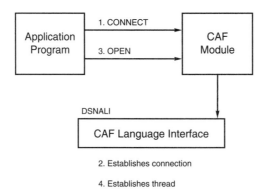

FIGURE 18.31   Explicit CAF thread creation.

The second method of thread creation is shown in Figure 18.32. This figure shows the implicit creation and termination of CAF threads. If the OPEN and CLOSE calls are not used, a thread is created when the first SQL statement is issued.

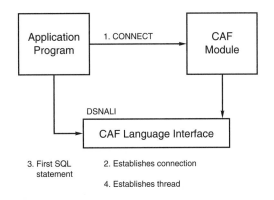

FIGURE 18.32   Implicit CAF thread creation.

Benefits and Drawbacks of CAF

Before deciding to use CAF, you should consider all the ramifications of this decision. If used properly, CAF can enhance the performance and resource utilization of a DB2 application. If used improperly, CAF can cause problems.

One benefit of using CAF is that it provides explicit control of thread creation. In addition, CAF is more efficient than DSN because of the elimination of overhead required by the TSO TMP, IKJEFT01 (or IKJEFT1B). Another benefit is that a program designed to use CAF can run when DB2 is down. It cannot access DB2 resources, but it can perform other tasks. This capability can be useful when the DB2 processing is optional, parameter driven, or contingent on other parts of the program.

CAF has its drawbacks too, though. For example, CAF requires more complex error handling procedures. DSN automatically formats error messages for connection failures, but CAF returns only a return code and a reason code. Another drawback is that DSN handles the connection automatically, but CAF requires the program to handle the connection. These drawbacks can be eliminated, however, if you modify the CAF interface module used at your site. Note that by modifying the CAF module your shop must support logic that otherwise is provided with DB2 (and supported by IBM).

Vendor Tools

Some vendor tools provide an interface to the Call Attach Facility. They are generally used to enable DB2 batch programs to run without the TSO TMP. By simply link-editing your DB2 program with the vendor-supplied language interface module, you can run DB2 batch programs as MVS batch programs instead of TSO batch programs. Although these tools do not usually provide the same level of flexibility as true CAF (for example, control over thread creation and termination), they are useful for eliminating the need for TSO in batch, thereby reducing overhead.

Sample CAF Code

You can use several sample CAF programs provided with DB2 as models for the development of your own CAF applications. These programs follow:

DSN8CA	Assembler interface to CAF
DSN8SPM	CAF connection manager for ISPF
DSN8SP3	PL/I program that interfaces with CAF
DSN8SC2	COBOL program that interfaces with CAF

RRSAF (Recoverable Resource Manager Services Attach Facility)

RRSAF, or the Recoverable Resource Manager Services Attach Facility, is the final "door to DB2." RRSAF is available as of DB2 V5. RRSAF is similar in functionality to CAF but without the implicit connection capabilities. However, RRSAF provides the following additional capabilities and benefits:

- Applications can reuse DB2 threads for different userids (with SIGNON and AUTH SIGNON; this requires RACF or a similar system authorization product).

- Applications (and stored procedures) can coordinate MVS-wide commitment of recoverable resources through OS/390. To qualify for participation in the MVS-wide commit, stored procedures must be executed in an MVS WLM-managed SPAS.

- DB2 threads can run under different TCBs.

As with CAF, RRSAF controls program connections to DB2. Seven functions are used to control the DB2 connections:

SIGNON	Specifies a userid (and optionally a secondary authid) for the connection
AUTH SIGNON	Specifies a userid (and optionally a secondary authid) for the connection and invokes the signon exit. The program must be APF authorized to execute this function.
IDENTIFY	Specifies that the program is a user of DB2 services.
CREATE THREAD	Establishes a connection between the program's MVS address space and DB2.
TERMINATE THREAD	Deallocates DB2 resources from the program.
TERMINATE IDENTIFY	Deallocates DB2 resources.
TRANSLATE	Provides the program with DB2 error message information, placing it in the SQLCA.

Consider using RRSAF as an alternative to CAF when the performance benefits of thread reuse are deemed necessary.

When you're preparing a program for RRSAF, you must link DSNRLI (the RRSAF interface) to the load module.

V8 DB2 V8 makes it easier to migrate CAF applications to RRSAF. This is useful when a current CAF application needs two-phase commit (because CAF does not support 2PC and RRSAF does).

Explicit DB2 connections are coded similarly in CAF and RRSAF. For CAF applications, you issue a CONNECT and OPEN. To accomplish the same thing in RRSAF you issue an IDENTIFY and CREATE THREAD. SQL statements can then be issued in your program. To disconnect, CAF uses a CLOSE and DISCONNECT, whereas RRSAF uses a TERMINATE THREAD and TERMINATE IDENTIFY.

But, CAF applications also can connect implicitly to a DB2 subsystem just by issuing SQL statements or IFI calls (without first issuing CONNECT and OPEN). For DB2 V7 and prior releases this was not possible with RRSAF, but DB2 V8 allows implicit connections to DB2 using RRSAF by just issuing SQL statements or IFI calls.

Comparison of the Environments

Now that you have learned about each environment in which DB2 programs can execute, you can begin to compare their features and capabilities. When choosing an operating environment for a DB2 application, you should ensure that it can support the data needs of the application. Typically, a corporation's data is spread across disparate processing platforms and data storage devices. Additionally, the data is stored in many different physical manifestations.

When you're choosing an environment for your application, consider the following:

- Do you have access to the environment that you want to use for a development platform? If not, can you obtain access?

- Can you access data key to your enterprise in the format in which it exists today, or will your choice of environment require that the data be duplicated and placed in a readable format?

- Are the programmers who will be working on the project knowledgeable in the chosen environment, or will extensive training be required?

Resource Availability

Table 18.10 presents resource availability categorized by each processing environment that has been discussed. You can use this table as a reference when deciding on a processing environment for your DB2 applications.

18

TABLE 18.10   A Comparison of Resource Availability

Resource	CICS	TSO Online	TSO Batch	CAF	RRSAF	IMS MPP	IMS Fast Path	IMS BMP	DL/I Batch
Flat file access	Yes	Yes	Yes	Yes	Yes	No	No	No[*]	Yes[*]
VSAM access	Yes	Yes	Yes	Yes	Yes	No	No[**]	No[**]	Yes[**]
Online IMS database	Yes	No	No	No	No	Yes	Yes	Yes	No
Offline IMS database	Yes	No	No	No	Yes	No	No	No	Yes
Invoked by JCL	No	No	Yes	Yes	Yes	No	No	Yes	Yes
Invoked by transaction	Yes	No	No	No	No	Yes	Yes	No	No
Invoked by CLIST or REXX EXEC	No	Yes	No	Yes	Yes	No	No	No	No
Invoked by ISPF	No	Yes	No	No	Yes	No	No	No	No

[*]IMS GSAM database
[**]IMS SHISAM database

You might find some of the entries in Table 18.10 confusing. The following explains these entries in more detail:

- *Yes* indicates that the processing environment listed across the top can access the resource defined along the left. Simply because the resource is accessible (as IBM delivers the products that support the environment), however, does not mean that you can use it in your shop. Some shops restrict and limit access, so consult your shop standards before proceeding with development plans based on Table 18.10.

- Flat file access is available using IMS calls when a GSAM (Generalized Sequential Access Method) database is defined for the flat file. IMS BMPs and batch programs can access flat files as GSAM databases. Access to flat files using pure OS/VS reads and writes is available only to IMS batch programs.

- All IMS programs can access VSAM KSDS data sets as a SHISAM (Simple Hierarchic Indexed Sequential Access Method) database. Again, IMS batch programs are the only type of IMS program that can access a VSAM file using VSAM data set commands.

- IMS online databases are those defined to the IMS control region and started for online access in IMS/TM. Conversely, an offline IMS database either is not defined under the IMS control region and is thus not accessible by IMS/TM, or it is stopped (sometimes referred to as DBRed) to IMS/TM.

Feasibility

After ensuring that what you want is possible, your next step is to ascertain whether it is feasible. An application is feasible in a specified environment if the response time and availability requirements of the application can be met satisfactorily by the environment. Typically, you should draw up a service-level agreement for each new application, developing a price-to-performance matrix. Consider this example:

> The online portion of the system must provide an average response time of x seconds, y percent of the time, for an average of z users. The cost per transaction is approximately a.

Use the information in Table 18.11 to determine which online environment is feasible for your project.

TABLE 18.11 Comparison of Online Development Capabilities

Characteristic	TSO	CICS	IMS/TM
Response time	Slow	Fast	Fast
Flexibility	High	Low	Low
Number of concurrent users	Fewer than 10	Many	Many
Overhead per user	Very high	Very low	Low
Program linking	Not easy	XCTL/LINK	Message switching
Online screen language	ISPF Dialog	BMS	MFS Manager
Screen development	Fast	Cumbersome	Cumbersome
Program development	Fast	Medium	Slow
Prototyping and testing tools	Many	Some	Few

As you ponder the choices of development environments for your DB2 applications, ask the following questions:

- What is the deadline for system development? What programming resources are available to meet this deadline? Do you have the requisite talent to develop the system in the optimal environment? If not, should you hire programmers or settle for a less than optimal solution?

- What are the performance requirements of the system? How many concurrent users will be using the system during peak processing time, and can the given environment support the workload?

Sometimes you have little or no choice. If a shop has only one environment, the decision is easy. If your shop has more than one environment, the right decision is never to confine yourself to only one environment. Each environment has its own strengths and weaknesses, and you should consider them in your application development solution.

When multiple environments are used to access DB2 data, they become inextricably wound in a critical mass. This situation can be difficult to administer and warrants consideration.

Batch Considerations

Although this chapter is primarily concerned with coverage of the online processing opportunities available to DB2, a quick discussion of the various batch processing options is in order. DB2 batch processing can be implemented using the following:

- DSN under TSO

- CAF or RRSAF

- Batch DL/I

- BMP under IMS/TM

In terms of performance, no significant differences exist among DSN, CAF, batch DL/I, and BMPs. However, if you need to squeeze every last bit of performance out of a batch application, consider these points:

- Because DSN uses TSO, you will have some additional overhead for TSO resources when compared to an equivalent CAF program.

- Because BMPs execute in an IMS control region, initialization will take longer than an equivalent DSN or CAF program.

- Commit processing tends to take longer for BMPs because they check for DB2 and IMS update activity.

Although performance differences are minimal, you will discover several coding implications:

- CAF and RRSAF programs require connection logic and error handling not required by DSN.

- IMS SYNCPOINT must be used in lieu of COMMMIT for BMPs.

- DL/I batch programs require coding for the DDITV02 data set.

The Critical Mass

Prior to DB2 V4, when an application required DB2 access, the teleprocessing monitor (TSO, CICS, or IMS/TM) had to reside on the same MVS system as DB2. This situation created a critical mass, which is the set of subsystems tied by a single common attribute; they must access DB2 resources. For example, if a data-processing shop uses both CICS and IMS/TM to develop DB2 applications, the shop's critical mass would consist of the following:

- IMS/TM subsystem

- All CICS subsystems requiring DB2 access

- DB2 subsystem

- TSO subsystem if DB2I access is required

All of them had to operate on the same CPU. Additionally, when an error occurred, they could not be moved independently without losing DB2 access. A large shop could quickly use up the resources of its machine if all DB2 applications were developed on a single DB2 subsystem.

However, data sharing enables multiple DB2 subsystems to access the same data, which frees up resources, enables flexible configuration and management, expands capacity, and improves availability. Prior to data sharing, organizations had to slice applications into disparate, independently operating units in one of the following ways:

- You could develop IMS/TM applications on one DB2 subsystem, develop CICS applications on another, and develop TSO applications on yet another. This approach reduces the critical mass so that IMS/TM and CICS are not married together.

- Another method is to provide the separate DB2 subsystems with distributed access to DB2 data that must be shared.

- Yet another method is to choose a single teleprocessing environment for all DB2 applications.

- Last, by avoiding DB2I and QMF access, you can eliminate TSO from the critical mass. Instead, you submit SQL and DSN commands as batch invocations of TSO. Because this hampers ease of use and detracts from the overall user-friendliness of DB2, however, doing so is not recommended.

However, today the preferred method of avoiding the critical mass is to implement data sharing, which is covered in the next chapter.

18

CHAPTER **19**

Data Sharing

D B2 data sharing allows applications running on multiple DB2 subsystems to concurrently read and write to the same data sets. Simply stated, data sharing enables multiple DB2 subsystems to behave as one.

DB2 data sharing is optional; it need not be implemented. Check with your DBA or system administrator if you are not sure if data sharing is used in your organization.

Prior to DB2 V4, the only methods available for sharing DB2 data across subsystems were through distributed DB2 connections or using shared read only databases (using the ROSHARE option when creating databases). However, both of these options have drawbacks. The distributed option requires coding changes and the ROSHARE option supported read only access (and is no longer available as of DB2 V6).

Data Sharing Benefits

DB2 data sharing, though somewhat complex to implement and administer, provides many benefits. In the long run, most organizations will move to DB2 data sharing because of the many benefits outlined in this section.

The primary benefit of data sharing is to provide increased availability to data. DB2 data sharing provides a powerful technology for solving complex business problems in an optimal manner. Data is available for direct access across multiple DB2 subsystems. Furthermore applications can be run on multiple smaller, more competitively priced microprocessor-based machines, thereby enhancing data availability and the price/performance ratio.

An additional benefit is expanded capacity. Capacity is increased because more processors are available to execute the DB2 application programs. Instead of a single DB2 subsystem on a single logical partition, multiple CPCs can be used to execute a program (or even a single query).

Each data sharing group may consist of multiple members; application programs are provided with enhanced data availability. There is no primary or "owner" DB2 subsystem. All DB2 subsystems in a data sharing group are peers. One or more members of a group may fail without impacting application programs because the workload will be spread across the remaining DB2 members. Therefore, failure of one DB2 subsystem cannot cause the other subsystems to become unavailable.

Data sharing increases the flexibility of configuring DB2. New members can be added to a data sharing group when it is necessary to increase the processing capacity of the group (for example, at month end or year end to handle additional processing). The individual members that were added to increase the processing capacity of the data sharing group are easily removed when it is determined that the additional capacity is no longer required. Finally, prior to data sharing, larger organizations with multiple MVS machines often devoted individual processors to groups of users. When a DB2 application needed to span the organization, it was usually necessary to create a duplicate copy of the application for each DB2 on each system image used by the organization. With data sharing, a single data sharing group can be created for the entire organization (within the limit of 32 subsystems per group). This can alleviate the need to create multiple copies of an application.

What Are Sysplex and Parallel Sysplex?

A Sysplex is a set of OS/390 images that are connected and coupled by sharing one or more Sysplex timers. A Parallel Sysplex is a basic Sysplex that additionally shares a Coupling Facility whose responsibility is to provide external shared memory and a set of hardware protocols that allow enabled applications and subsystems to share data with integrity by using external shared memory. Parallel Sysplex enhances scalability by extending the ability to increase the number of processors within a single OS/390 image with the ability to have multiple OS/390 images capable of cooperatively processing a shared workload.

Additionally, Parallel Sysplex enhances availability by providing customers with the ability to non-disruptively remove one or more OS/390 images and/or CECs from a configuration to accommodate hardware and software maintenance.

Consider obtaining and reviewing the following IBM manuals and redbooks before learning more about the Parallel Sysplex:

- Getting the Most Out of a Parallel Sysplex (SG24-2073)

- Parallel Sysplex Configuration Overview (SG24-5637)

- Parallel Sysplex Test Report (GC28-1236)

- Parallel Sysplex Performance Report (SG24-4356)

- Parallel Sysplex Operational Scenarios (SG24-2079)

19

Data Sharing Requirements

Data sharing consists of a complex combination of hardware and software. To share data, DB2 subsystems must belong to a predefined data sharing group. Each DB2 subsystem contained in the data sharing group is a member of that group. All members of the data sharing group access a common DB2 catalog and directory.

Each data sharing group is an OS/390 Cross-system Coupling Facility (XCF) group. The group services provided by XCF enable DB2 data sharing groups to be defined. In addition, XCF enables the data sharing environment to track all members contained in the data sharing group. A site may have multiple OS/390 Sysplexes, each consisting of one or more OS/390 systems. Each individual Sysplex can consist of multiple data sharing groups.

> **NOTE**
>
> XCF was introduced in MVS/SP 4.1 with the MVS Sysplex.

DB2 data sharing requires a Sysplex environment that consists of the following:

- One or more central processor complexes (CPCs) that can attach to a coupling facility. A CPC is a collection of hardware consisting of main storage, one or more central processors, timers, and channels.

- At least one coupling facility. The coupling facility is the component that manages the shared resources of the connected CPCs. DB2 uses the coupling facility to provide data sharing groups with coordinated locking, buffer pools and communication. MVS V5 is required to install a DB2 coupling facility.

- At least one Sysplex timer. The Sysplex timer keeps the processor timestamps synchronized for all DB2s in the data sharing group.

- Connection to shared DASD. The user data, system catalog and directory data, and MVS catalog data must all reside on shared DASD.

> **NOTE**
>
> The DB2 logs and boot strap data sets (BSDS) belong to each DB2 member individually. However, they too must reside on shared DASD.

Your shop also should have a security facility that supports security in a Parallel Sysplex environment before implementing DB2 data sharing.

> **NOTE**
>
> For IBM's RACF, Version 2 Release 1 functions in a Parallel Sysplex environment.

Refer to Figure 19.1 for an overview of a DB2 data sharing environment consisting of two DB2 subsystems connected using a coupling facility.

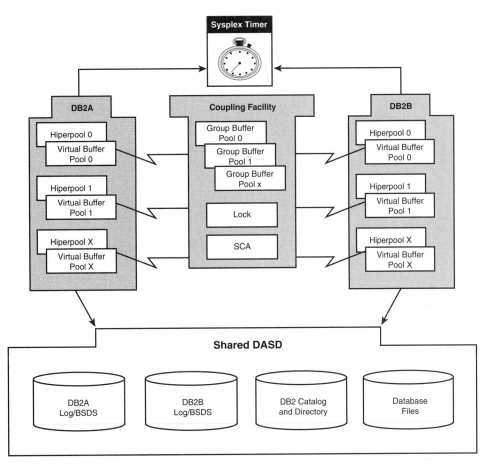

FIGURE 19.1   A DB2 data sharing environment.

DB2 Data Sharing Groups

Data sharing groups may span multiple MVS systems. A data sharing group consists of individual DB2 subsystems, called members. Data sharing group members must belong to the same MVS Sysplex. Data sharing group members can only belong to one data sharing group.

Up to 32 DB2 subsystems can be members of a DB2 data sharing group. Each DB2 subsystem of the data sharing group can access all of the data in each of the subsystems as if it were local. Any DB2 object (table space, index, table, and so on), in any of the DB2 subsystems in the data sharing group, is available to all members of the group. This includes the shared DB2 catalog and directory.

Data sharing is done within the members of the data sharing group; a request cannot span multiple groups.

Certain DB2 objects must be shared between members, whereas other objects are owned by members. Refer to Table 19.1 for a breakdown of the shared versus non-shared objects.

TABLE 19.1   Shared and Non-Shared Objects

Shared Objects	Non-Shared Objects
DB2 Catalog	BSDS
DB2 Directory	Archive and Active Logs
Coupling Facility Structures	DSNDB07
Lock Structures	Sort, RID, and EDM Pools
Group Buffer Pools	Local Buffer Pools
Shared Communication Area	Trace Data

Application Impact

No special programming is required for applications to access data in a DB2 data sharing environment. Each individual subsystem in the data sharing group uses the coupling facility to communicate with the other subsystems. The intersystem communication provided by DB2 data sharing provides a system image that resembles a single, standalone DB2 subsystem to the application.

No application programming changes are required. The only modifications that may need to be made to current application programs to run in a data sharing environment are to provide additional error checking for "data sharing" return codes.

There is a one-to-one relationship between OS/390 and data sharing transactions. The DB2 member where the transaction was initiated keeps all of the information related to that transaction that is needed to successfully execute it. Once a unit of work begins processing on a member, it is executed in its entirety on that member.

Impact on Attachment Interfaces

Likewise, DB2 data sharing has no impact on existing attachment interfaces. The DB2 subsystem name may still be used to attach to a particular DB2 subsystem. Application programs using the subsystem name will only be able to attach to those DB2 subsystems that reside on the same OS/390 system as they do.

TSO and CALL ATTACH support a GROUP ATTACH name. This generic name is created during the group's originating member installation. The GROUP ATTACH name allows TSO and batch jobs to connect to any DB2 in the group. This eliminates the need to know the DB2 subsystem name on local OS/390 systems.

IMS and CICS transaction managers are unable to take advantage of the group attach name. They must remain sensitive to a specific DB2 subsystem to be able to resolve any in-doubt units of recovery.

Impact on DCL and DDL

Because all members of the data sharing group share a common catalog, security grants, table definitions and program definitions only need to be executed once. DDL and DCL do not need to be rerun for each data sharing member.

Sysplex and Distributed Access

Distributed access requests, using both public and private DB2 protocols, can be made to a data sharing group. All members of the group have the same location name. This enables distributed requests to be made in a data sharing environment transparent to the application program.

Application Support

Even though the impact of data sharing on applications is minimal, the impact on application support is substantial. When DB2 subsystems are grouped together using data sharing, any application can access any database in any of the data sharing member subsystems. This can make debugging, supporting, and testing difficult.

Additionally, the software licensing impact of data sharing can also be quite problematic. Do not implement data sharing without first considering what supporting software is necessary. In a data sharing environment, software licenses that previously applied to a single machine only may have to be renegotiated for multiple machines (those in the Sysplex).

The DB2 Coupling Facility

DB2 uses the coupling facility to provide intermember communications. The primary function of the coupling facility is to ensure data availability while maintaining data integrity across systems. This requires the coupling facility to provide core services to the data sharing group such as locking and caching of data. To do so, the CF requires three structures to synchronize the activities of the data sharing group members:

- *Lock structures* are required to control global locking across the data sharing group members. Global locks are required because multiple members can access the same data. As such, each member needs to know the state of the data before it can be modified. The lock structure propagates locks to all members of the data sharing group.

- The *list structure* enables communication across the sysplex environment.

- *Cache structures* provide common buffering for the systems in the sysplex. When a data page is updated by an individual data sharing member, a copy of that page is written to one of the global buffer pools. If other members need to refresh their copy of the data page in question, the copy is obtained from the coupling facility's global buffer pool instead of from DASD. This requires the members to check the appropriate coupling facility global buffer pool first, to determine if the desired page needs to be read from DASD or not.

These structures ensure that data is synchronized between the members of the DB2 data sharing group.

Defining the Coupling Facility

A coupling facility is defined using Coupling Facility Resource Management (CFRM). CFRM is created by the IXCMIAPU utility. The CFRM is used to identify

- Each individual coupling facility

- Each structure within the individual coupling facilities

- Space allocated to these structures

- Ordered preferences and which coupling facility is used to store this ordered preference structure

- Unordered exclusion list, which defines the structures to keep separate from this structure

Global Lock Management

Because data sharing group members can access any object from any member in the group, a global locking mechanism is required. This is done by the lock structure defined in the coupling facility. The lock structure is charged with managing intermember locking. Without a global lock management process data integrity problems could occur when one member attempts to read (or change) data that is in the process of being changed by another member.

Data sharing groups utilize a global locking mechanism to preserve the integrity of the shared data. The global locking mechanism enables locks to be recognized between members.

For more details on the lock management process for data sharing environments, refer to Chapter 23, "Locking DB2 Data."

CF Lock Propagation Reduction

 DB2 V8 reduces the propagation of locks to the coupling facility. This enhancement helps to reduce the cost of global contention processing and improve availability due to a reduction in retained locks in the event of a subsystem failure.

Global Inter-System Communication

The list structure component of the coupling facility contains status information used for inter-system communications. The list structure is also referred to as the Shared Communication Area, or SCA. The SCA maintains information about the state of databases, log files, and other details needed for DB2 recovery.

Global Data Buffering

Similar to the need for a global lock management technique, data sharing also requires global data buffering. Once again, this is so because a data sharing environment consists of multiple member DB2 subsystems. Each of those members has its own separate local buffer pools and each member can access and change data in any database on any subsystem within the data sharing group.

In a data sharing environment, data pages may be found in

- Local buffer pools

- Hiperpools

- Group buffer pools

- DASD (disk)

Updating and Reading Data

When data is modified, the changed data is stored in the buffer pool of the DB2 subsystem executing the transaction. The change is not immediately available to transactions that are executing in other members of the data sharing group. The coupling facility is used to provide all members of a data sharing group with a set of global buffer pools.

When modifications occur in a data sharing environment, DB2 must use force-at-commit processing. Force-at-commit writes pages changed by the transaction to the appropriate global buffer pools when a commit point is reached. Force-at-commit processing is used solely in a data sharing environment.

> **CAUTION**
>
> The changed page may be written prior to commit if local buffer pool write thresholds are reached.

> **NOTE**
>
> In a non-data sharing environment, DB2 does not write changed pages at a commit point. Instead, the buffer manager uses a deferred write algorithm, which moves the expensive buffer write operations outside of the transaction path length.

During the write to the global buffer pool, the coupling facility notifies DB2 members that currently have the page cached in their local buffer pool to invalidate it so that the next access will cause the page to be read from the global buffer pool (or disk).

The read transaction tests the validity of all pages it finds in its local buffer pool. If the page is still valid, the read transaction accesses the page from its local buffer pool. If the page is marked invalid (due to a previous update by another member), the read transaction will refresh the changed page from the global buffer pool (or disk).

Defining Data Sharing Buffer Pools

Data sharing members must use the same name for the global buffer pool as is used for the local buffer pool. For example, if BP5 is defined at the local subsystem level, BP5 must also be defined at the group buffer pool level. A group buffer pool must be defined for each associated local buffer pool. If a local buffer pool does not have a corresponding global buffer pool, resources utilizing the pool can only be used locally and cannot be shared.

For more information on group buffer pool specification and tuning, refer to Chapter 28, "Tuning DB2's Components."

Group Buffer Pool Duplexing

Prior to DB2 V6, if a group buffer pool failed, the only options for recovery were

- Recovering group buffer pools, whereby DB2 recovers data from its logs in case the group buffer pool structure is damaged, or if all members lose connectivity to the group buffer pool.

- Rebuilding group buffer pools, whereby DB2 copies pages from the group buffer pool to a new allocation of the structure in an alternative coupling facility (or to DASD, if DB2 cannot get enough storage in the alternate coupling facility).

However, as of DB2 V6 (or DB2 V5 with an APAR), when you have more than one coupling facility, you can duplex the group buffer pools. With group buffer pool duplexing, a secondary group buffer pool is waiting on standby in another coupling facility. In the event of a connection failure or if the primary group buffer pool fails, the secondary group buffer pool can take over (see Figure 19.2).

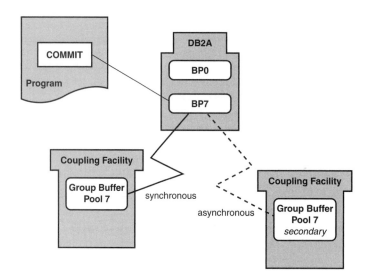

FIGURE 19.2   Group buffer pool duplexing.

With group buffer pool duplexing, you have two allocations of the same group buffer pool that use one logical connection. Each group buffer pool structure must be allocated in a different coupling facility.

With group buffer pool, duplexing pages that need to be written are written to the secondary group buffer pool structure asynchronously and to the primary group buffer pool structure synchronously. After all the required pages are written to the primary group buffer pool structure, DB2 double-checks on the writes to the secondary group buffer pool structure to ensure they have successfully completed. If any writes were not completed, DB2 forces them to completion.

Data Sharing Naming Conventions

It is imperative that appropriate naming conventions are developed for data sharing constructs. This is important to enable effective management of the data sharing environment. Data sharing naming conventions fall into two categories:

- Group-level names for structures owned by the data sharing group. These names are shared by all members of the data sharing group. Group-level names that must be created include the following:

  DB2 group name—The name that is used to define the DB2 data sharing group to MVS. The group name can be no longer than characters and can be comprised of the characters A-Z, 0-9, $, #, and @. The group name must begin with an alphabetic character.

  Catalog alias—The name of the MVS catalog alias. This catalog alias can be up to 8 characters long. The DB2 group name should be used for the catalog alias name.

  IRLM group name—The name used to define the IRLM to the data sharing group.

  Location name—Each data sharing group has one DDF location name. This location is used by remote requests to indicate the data sharing group. This name can be up to 16 characters long.

  Generic LU name—This name allows remote requesters to configure their systems to treat the data sharing group as a single LU. The generic LU name can be up to 8 characters in length.

  Group attach name—A generic four character name that is used by applications using TSO or CALL ATTACH. This enables the application to attach to any DB2 member that is contained in the data sharing group.

  Coupling facility structure names—Names are required for the lock structure, SCA, and group buffer pools. These names are predefined by DB2 as shown in Table 19.2. In place of the groupname, substitute the actual DB2 group name. For group buffer pools, the only difference is the prefix "G" added to the buffer pool name.

- Member-level names for structures owned by each DB2 data sharing member. Member-level names that must be created include:

  DB2 member name—The name that is used to identify the individual DB2 subsystem to OS/390 for inclusion into the data sharing group. Like the data sharing group name, this name can be no longer than 8 characters and can be comprised of the characters A-Z, 0-9, $, #, and @. The DB2 member name is used by DB2 to form its OS/390 cross-system coupling facility (XCF) member name.

  Subsystem name—The name can be up to four characters long and is used by all attachment interfaces.

  LU name—Must be unique within the data sharing group and the network.

19

Work file database name—Each data sharing member must have its own work file database. The work file database in the non-data sharing environment is known as DSNDB07. The work file database name can be up to eight characters long.

Command prefix—Up to eight-character prefix used for DB2 command execution.

IRLM subsystem name—Defines the IRLM subsystem.

IRLM procedure name—Defines the IRLM startup procedure.

ZPARM name—Each member of a data sharing group has its own DSNZPARM load module.

TABLE 19.2   Coupling Facility Structure Naming Conventions

Structure Type	Naming Standard
Lock Structure	*groupname*_LOCK1
SCA	*groupname*_SCA
Group Buffer Pools	*groupname*_Gbufferpool

Data Sharing Administration

One of the benefits of data sharing is that the entire environment can be administered from a single MVS console. The DB2 command prefix, which can be up to eight characters long, is used to differentiate between the different members of a data sharing group.

> **NOTE**
>
> Individual data sharing group member names can be used as command prefixes.

In a sysplex environment administrative DB2 commands can be routed to any DB2 member from a single console. This eliminates the need to know the MVS system name to send DB2 commands. In addition, there is no need to use ROUTE DB2 commands in this environment (see Figure 19.3).

Data Sharing Group Creation

To enable data sharing, a common DB2 catalog is required. IBM does not provide an automated mechanism for merging data from multiple existing DB2 subsystems. The process of merging systems is complex and should not be undertaken lightly. Merging subsystems is not solely a physical data movement problem but includes other administrative issues including the creation and enforcement of naming standards, DB2 security and authorization, backup and recovery, utility execution, data distribution, and on and on. Indeed, the decision to merge subsystems into a data sharing group will impact almost every aspect of database administration for the subsystems involved.

If you are still interested in merging pre-existing DB2 subsystems into a data sharing, an exhaustive 16 step process for merging data from individual DB2 subsystems is available in the IBM manual *Data Sharing: Planning and Administration* (SC26-9935).

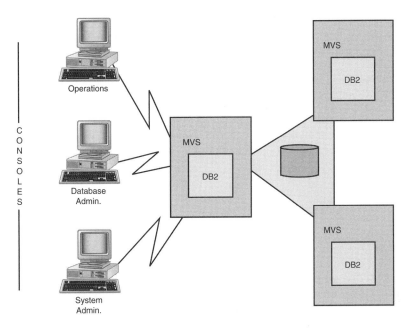

FIGURE 19.3   Administering the DB2 data sharing environment.

CAUTION

Watch for duplicate object names when merging multiple DB2 catalogs into the shared DB2 catalog for the data sharing group. Because the objects were originally created in isolation from one another, it is likely that duplicate object names (for example, databases, tablespaces, indexes, and so on) may be encountered when catalogs are merged.

Backup and Recovery

Each DB2 member still maintains its own recovery logs and BSDS data sets. Each DB2 member must be able to read the logs of every other data sharing group member. This is required because logs from multiple members may be required to do media recovery for a single member. If logs are required from multiple members, the multiple logs are merged together during the recovery process.

Log Record Sequence Numbers (LRSN) are used to provide common log record sequencing across members. The LRSNs are used to control "redo"/"undo" for data sharing environments and are identified by a 6 byte value derived from the DB2 timestamp. The RBA is still used during non-data sharing recoveries.

Data Sharing Database Statuses

In a data sharing environment, there are two new page set statuses that can occur—GRECP and LPL. These statuses can appear on the output of the -DISPLAY DATABASE command.

The GRECP status stands for "Group buffer pool recovery pending." It indicates that the group buffer pool was lost. This means that there are changes recorded in the log that need to be applied to the page set.

DB2 will automatically recover GRECP page sets when the group buffer pool is defined with AUTOREC(YES) and at least one member was connected when the failure occurred.

The LPL status stands for "Logical page list." It indicates that some pages were not read from or written to the group buffer pool. An LPL status can be caused by a disk failure, a channel failure (between the group buffer pool and the processor), or some other transient disk problem.

Improved LPL Recovery

V8 Through DB2 V7, you had to manually recover pages that DB2 put into the LPL. DB2 V8 adds automatic recovery of LPL pages. When pages are added to the LPL, DB2 issues error message DSNB250E, which includes the reason the pages were added to the LPL. Then, DB2 will attempt automatic recovery, except for disk I/O error, during DB2 restart or end restart, group buffer pool structure failures, or a complete loss of connection to the group buffer pool.

Subsystem Availability

DB2 data sharing improves data availability by providing redundant failover capabilities. In the event of a DB2 data sharing group member failure, the remaining members are used to process the data requests. The workload is spread across the remaining DB2 members.

Uncommitted locks held by the failed member are retained. No member is permitted to obtain a lock that is not compatible with the retained locks. All other (non-locked) data is still accessible to the remaining DB2 members. Retained locks are purged during the restart process for the failed member.

The failed DB2 member can restart on the same or different z/OS system.

Restart Light

V7 DB2 Version 7 introduced a new feature of the START DB2 command allowing a DB2 member to be restarted specifying *restart light*. The LIGHT(YES) parameter of the START command is used to select this feature. The restart light basically allows a DB2 data sharing member to be restarted simply to free retained locks. With the restart light the data sharing member is brought up with a minimal storage footprint, and then terminates normally after DB2 frees all retained locks.

The restart light simplifies data sharing administration. Because the storage required is significantly reduced, the restart light can potentially start up a system with minimal resources that would not be able to be started and stopped in normal mode.

If you experience a system failure in a Parallel Sysplex, the automated restart in light mode removes retained locks with minimum disruption.

V8 DB2 V8 further improves restart light capability by allowing indoubt units of recovery (UR) to be handled. If indoubt URs exist after a restart recovery, DB2 will continue running so that the indoubt URs can be resolved. After all the indoubt URs have been resolved, the DB2 member that is running in light mode will shut down and can be restarted normally.

Monitoring Data Sharing Groups

The DISPLAY GROUP command can be issued from any active member of a group to determine information about all members of a data sharing group. An example of issuing a DISPLAY GROUP command follows:

```
-DB1G DISPLAY GROUP
```

The results of this command will be a listing of the group members, the status of all members in the group, SCA and lock structure sizes and percentages in use. The maximum number of lock and list entries possible with the number of entries in use are shown. An example of the information returned by DISPLAY GROUP is depicted in Listing 19.1.

LISTING 19.1   Results of the DISPLAY GROUP Command

```
DSN7100I -DB1G DSN7GCMD
*** BEGIN DISPLAY OF GROUP(DSNDB0G)
------------------------------------------------------------
DB2                              SYSTEM   IRLM
MEMBER   ID  SUBSYS CMDPREF   STATUS  NAME     SUBSYS IRLMPROC
--------  ---  ----  --------  -------  --------  ----  --------
DB1G     1 DB1G   -DB1G     ACTIVE  MVS1     DJ1G   DB1GIRLM
DB2G     2 DB2G   -DB2G     ACTIVE  MVS2     DJ2G   DB2GIRLM
DB3G     3 DB3G   -DB3G     ACTIVE  MVS3     DJ3G   DB3GIRLM
DB4G     4 DB4G   -DB4G     ACTIVE  MVS4     DJ4G   DB4GIRLM

------------------------------------------------------------
SCA   STRUCTURE SIZE:  2560 KB, STATUS= AC,  SCA IN USE:     48 %
LOCK1 STRUCTURE SIZE: 16384 KB,           LOCK1 IN USE:      1 %
NUMBER LOCK ENTRIES:    4194304, LOCK ENTRIES IN USE:      981
NUMBER LIST ENTRIES:      59770, LIST ENTRIES IN USE:      719
*** END DISPLAY OF GROUP(DSNDB0G )
DSN9022I -DB1G DSN7GCMD 'DISPLAY GROUP ' NORMAL COMPLETION
```

Coupling Facility Recovery

Although unlikely, it is possible for the coupling facility to fail causing its structures to be lost. A dynamic rebuild of the coupling facility structures (lock, SCA) is executed during coupling facility recovery. However, if the dynamic rebuild fails, and the structures cannot be rebuilt on another coupling facility, all DB2 members contained in the data sharing group are brought down.

To recover from this scenario, a group restart is required. Group restart rebuilds the information that was lost from the SCA and/or lock structure using the logs of the DB2 group members. All of the logs for every data sharing group member must be available during the group restart process.

19

> **NOTE**
>
> Group restart does not necessarily mean that all DB2s in the group start up again, but information from all DB2s must be used to rebuild the lock structure or SCA.

Data Sharing Application Development Guidelines

When preparing applications to utilize data sharing in your shop, be sure to abide by the following guidelines.

Favor Binding IMMEDWRITE(NO)   The IMMEDWRITE parameter of the BIND command controls whether immediate writes are to be done for updates that are made to group buffer pool dependent page sets or partitions. This BIND parameter only applies for data sharing environments.

When binding plans and packages with IMMEDWRITE(YES), the originating transaction will immediately write its updated GBP-dependent buffers instead of waiting until a COMMIT or ROLLBACK. Doing so ensures that the transaction will always obtain the same results regardless of whether or not it runs on the same member as the originating transaction.

But IMMEDWRITE(YES) can negatively impact performance. The more buffer updates to GBP-dependent pages performed by the program, the less efficient it will be.

If consistency is an issue, consider other options, such as always running the dependent transaction on the same DB2 member as the originating transaction or possibly binding with ISOLATION(RR) instead of using IMMEDWRITE(YES).

V8 Prior to V8, changed pages in a data sharing environment were written during phase 2 of the commit process. As of DB2 V8, default processing will be to write changed pages during phase 1 of commit processing.

> **NOTE**
>
> The IMMEDWRI DSNZPARM can also be used to specify the immediate write characteristics for data sharing operations. If either the BIND parameter or the DSNZPARM is set to YES, the YES will override a NO.

Bind to Minimize Locks with Data Sharing   Favor binding with ISOLATION(CS) and CURRENTDATA(NO) for programs to be run in a data sharing environment. By doing so DB2 will avoid taking locks for read only cursors whenever possible.

If your application can live with "dirty reads," consider binding with ISOLATION(UR) to eliminate even more locks. Beware, though, that reading uncommitted data can cause data integrity problems and should not be used if your application can tolerate such possibilities.

In general, avoid ISOLATION(RR) in a data sharing environment if you can.

Furthermore, encourage thread reuse by binding with the ACQUIRE(USE) and RELEASE(DEALLOCATE) parameters. This, too, can reduce global lock contention.

Ensure Proper COMMIT Scope   Ensure that your batch application programs take frequent COMMITs to reduce the duration of restart and recovery processes.

Encourage Lock Avoidance   DB2 can use the lock avoidance technique to reduce the number of locks that need to be taken for read-only processes. Recall from Chapter 13, "Program Preparation," that lock avoidance can be enabled for read only cursors by binding plans and packages using CURRENTDATA(NO).

Lock avoidance reduces the number of locks taken and thereby reduces overhead for data sharing applications.

Be Aware of Sysplex Parallelism   With sysplex parallelism, DB2 provides the ability to utilize the power of multiple DB2 subsystems on multiple CPCs to execute a single query. As with any type of DB2 parallel querying, you will need to BIND your plan or package specifying DEGREE(ANY) to take advantage of sysplex parallelism. Use caution before doing so because you will need to appropriately configure your environment to support parallelism first, before you will gain anything from query parallelism.

Refer to Chapter 21, "The Optimizer," for more information on all forms of query parallelism available with DB2.

Data Sharing Administration Guidelines

When implementing and managing data sharing in your shop, be sure to abide by the following guidelines.

Consider Multiple Coupling Facilities   To reduce the risk of downtime, deploy multiple coupling facilities. If one coupling facility fails, you can always switch to another "backup" coupling facility.

A recommended implementation is to have one coupling facility to house the group buffer pools and a second coupling facility for the SCA and lock structures.

Implement Group Buffer Pool Duplexing   Duplex your group buffer pool structures to provide failover capability for buffering in your data sharing environment. With group buffer pool duplexing a secondary group buffer pool is waiting on standby to take over buffering activity if the primary group buffer pool fails.

To start group buffer pool duplexing, at least one DB2 member must be actively connected to the group buffer pool. When group buffer pool duplexing is started, all activity to the group buffer pools is quiesced until duplexing is established. This usually lasts only a few seconds.

> **CAUTION**
>
> Initiate group buffer pool duplexing during a period of low system activity to avoid resource unavailable conditions while duplexing is being established.

You must use CFRM policies to activate group buffer pool duplexing. There are two ways to start duplexing a group buffer pool:

19

- Activate a new CFRM policy specifying `DUPLEX(ENABLED)` for the structure. If the group buffer pool is currently allocated, OS/390 can automatically initiate the process to establish duplexing as soon as you activate the policy. If the group buffer pool is not currently allocated, the duplexing process can be initiated when the group buffer pool is allocated.

- Activate a new CFRM policy specifying `DUPLEX(ALLOWED)` for the structure. If the group buffer pool is currently allocated, you must rebuild duplexing using the following command:

  ```
  SETXCF START,REBUILD,DUPLEX,STRNAME=strname
  ```

  If the group buffer pool is not currently allocated, you need to wait until it is allocated before using the `SETXCF` command to start the duplexing rebuild.

Take Action to Help Prevent Coupling Facility Failures To limit down time due to coupling facility failure consider taking the following actions:

- Configure multiple coupling facilities.

- Reserve space in an alternate coupling facility in case the lock and SCA structures must be rebuilt.

- Use dedicated coupling facilities so that the MVS image is not lost during processor failure.

- Use uninterruptible power supplies for all dedicated coupling facilities.

- Implement group buffer pool duplexing.

- Configure more than one Sysplex timer.

Consider Archiving Logs to Disk Consider archiving the primary DB2 log files to DASD. Doing so can significantly speed up the amount of time it takes to recover.

Of course, you should favor writing the second archive copy to tape for disaster recovery purposes.

Avoid Confusing Names for Data Sharing Groups Avoid names that IBM uses for its XCF groups by avoiding the letters A-I as the first character of the group name (unless the first three characters are "DSN"). Additionally, avoid using "SYS" as the first three characters, and do not use the string "UNDESIG" as your group name.

Avoid Using DSNDB07 As a Work File Database Name Each data sharing group member must have a work file database defined for it. Although one of the members of the data sharing group can use DSNDB07, this is not advisable. Instead, create a descriptive name, for each work file database, for example the string "WK" concatenated to the member name.

> **CAUTION**
>
> You cannot specify a name that begins with DSNDB unless the name is DSNDB07.

V7 **Consider** CASTOUT(NO) **to Speed Member Shutdown**   As of DB2 V7, you can achieve a faster shutdown of DB2 data sharing members by specifying CASTOUT(NO) when stopping a member. By specifying CASTOUT(NO) when you STOP a member for maintenance, the window of unavailability decreases because it take less time to shutdown.

Be aware, though, that when you shutdown multiple members of a data sharing group with CASTOUT(NO), some changed data might remain in the group buffer pools after the members have been stopped. If you need to ensure consistent data on disk (for example, to make a copy), then specify CASTOUT(YES) instead of CASTOUT(NO).

You can check on the status of castout by displaying the DB2 member. The status will appear as QC on the display output if the member quiesced with some castout processing not completed.

Allocate Buffer Pools for Data Sharing   Specify separate buffer pools for shared data and non-shared data. Doing so makes it easier to manage and tune the group buffer pools in the coupling facility.

Keep an Eye on the EDM Pool   After implementing data sharing applications be sure to closely monitor EDM Pool storage. Because data sharing applications should be bound using RELEASE(DEALLOCATE), storage used by the EDM Pool tends to increase when data sharing is in use.

Avoid Row-Level Locking   Row-level locking will increase data sharing overhead. The resources required to acquire, maintain, and release a row lock are about the same as required for a page lock. Use LOCKSIZE(ROW) sparingly, if at all, in a data sharing environment.

Specify Lock Structure Size with Care   The size of the coupling facility's locking structure directly affects the number of false contentions (collisions) that occur. If the hash table is too small, the propensity for false collisions increases. Any contention, including false contention, requires additional asynchronous processing which negatively impacts performance.

CHAPTER **20**

DB2 Behind the Scenes

After reading the first nineteen chapters of this book, you should have a sound understanding of the fundamental concepts of the DB2 database management system. You are familiar with the functionality and nature of SQL, and you understand the process of embedding SQL in an application program and preparing it for execution. Additionally, you've learned many tips and techniques for achieving proper performance.

But what is actually going on behind the scenes in DB2? When you create a table, how does DB2 create and store it? When you issue an SQL statement, what happens to it so that it returns your answer? Where are these application plans kept? What is going on "under the covers"? The remainder of Part III helps you answer these questions.

The Physical Storage of Data

The first segment of your journey behind the scenes of DB2 consists of learning the manner in which DB2 data is physically stored. Before you proceed, however, recall the types of DB2 objects: storage groups (or STOGROUPs), databases, table spaces, tables, and indexes. Refer to Figure 20.1. A database can be composed of many table spaces, which in turn can contain one or more tables, which in turn can have indexes defined for them.

V8 Prior to DB2 V8, a partitioned table space required a partitioning index to set up the partition boundaries. As of DB2 V8, though, partition boundaries are set up in the table parameters, not the index. If an index exists on the partition keys, though, it is referred to as a partitioning index. Furthermore, DB2 V8 introduced DPSIs, or data partitioned secondary indexes. A DPSI is partitioned such that its data matches up with the table space partitions, even though the key of the index is not the partitioning key. Finally, a partitioned table space might have non-partitioned indexes, or NPIs. An NPI is neither partitioned, nor does its key match the partitioning key of the table space.

When LOB data types are used, LOB table spaces are required. In addition, databases, table spaces, and indexes can all be assigned STOGROUPs.

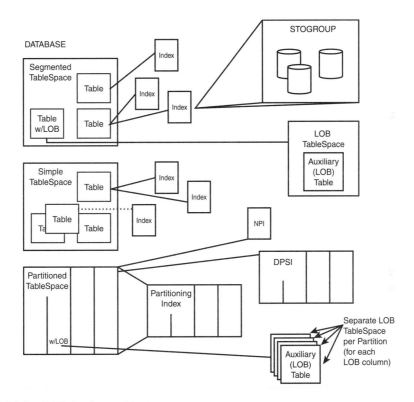

FIGURE 20.1 DB2 database objects.

Of these five objects, only three represent actual physical entities. STOGROUPs represent one or more physical DASD devices. Table spaces and indexes relate to physical data sets. But tables and databases have no actual physical representation. A table is assigned to a table space, and one table space can have one or multiple tables assigned to it. Table spaces are created within a database; one database can have multiple table spaces. Any tables created in a table space in the database, and the indexes on that table, are said to be in the database. But the mere act of creating a database or creating a table does not create a physical manifestation in the form of a data set or disk usage.

20

> **NOTE**
>
> A DBD is created by DB2 for databases. The DBD is a component that is managed in the EDM
> pool and contains the structure of the database objects in that database. It is used by DB2 to
> help access the objects assigned to the database.

DB2 Physical Characteristics

There are a myriad of things that go on behind the scenes in DB2 as you create and access
database structures. The following sections contain descriptions and guidelines regarding
the physical implementation and control of DB2 objects.

The Identifiers: OBIDs, PSIDs, and DBIDs   When an object is created, DB2 assigns it an
identifier that is stored in the DB2 Catalog. These identifiers are known as OBIDs.
Furthermore, table spaces and index spaces are assigned PSIDs, otherwise known as page
set IDs, because these objects require a physical data set. Databases are assigned DBIDs.

DB2 uses these identifiers behind the scenes to distinguish one DB2 object from another.

Storage Groups   You can assign up to 133 DASD volumes to a single STOGROUP. The practical limit, though, is far fewer. To ease administration and management, keep the number
of volumes assigned to a STOGROUP to a dozen or so.

You can use a DB2 STOGROUP to turn over control to SMS. This is accomplished by specifying an asterisk as the volume when creating the DB2 storage group.

VSAM Data Sets

Data sets used by DB2 can be either VSAM entry-sequenced data sets (ESDS) or VSAM
linear data sets (LDS). Linear data sets are more efficient because they do not contain the
VSAM control interval information that an ESDS does. Additionally, an LDS has control
intervals with a fixed length of 4,096 bytes.

Data Sets for Non-Partitioned Objects   Usually only one VSAM data set is used for each
non-partitioning index, simple table space, and segmented table space defined to DB2.
But, each data set can be no larger than 2 gigabytes. When the 2-gigabyte limit is reached,
a new VSAM data set is allocated. DB2 can use as many as 32 VSAM data sets per object.

Recall from Chapter 5, "Data Definition Guidelines," the data set naming standard that is
used by DB2 for table space and index data sets:

```
vcat.DSNDBx.dddddddd.ssssssss.y0001.znnn
```

where:

vcat	High-level qualifier, indicating an ICF catalog
x	C if VSAM cluster component
	D if VSAM data component
dddddddd	Database name

sssssss	Table space name or index space name
y0001	Instance qualifier
znnn	Partition number or the data set number

The instance qualifier normally will be I0001. However, if you run REORG with the FASTSWITCH YES option, the instance qualifier will switch back and forth between I0001 and J0001 after reorganizing.

V8 The data set number is controlled by the last component of the data set name.

For simple and segmented table spaces, the data set number is always preceded by A. The data set number for the first data set is always A001. When the size of the data set for a simple or a segmented table space approaches the maximum, another data set will be defined (for STOGROUP-controlled objects) with the data set number set to A002. For user-defined VSAM data sets, the DBA will have to allocate the data set using A002 as the data set number. The next data set will be A003, and so on.

Data Sets for Partitioned Objects   Multiple VSAM data sets are used for partitioned table spaces, partitioning indexes, and DPSIs. One data set is used per partition. For partitioned table spaces, the data set number is used to indicate the partition number.

V8 The first character of the data set number, represented by the *z*, will contain a letter from A through E. This letter corresponds to the value 0, 1, 2, 3, or 4 as the first digit of the partition number. Prior to DB2 V8, this character was the letter A. But now that Version 8 allows up to 4096 partitions, the letters A, B, C, D, and E must be used.

If the partition number is less than 1000, the data set number is A*nnn*. For example, the data set number for partition 750 would be A750. For partitions 1000 to 1999, the data set number is B*nnn*. For example, the data set number for partition 1025 would be B025, and so on. The same rules apply to the naming of data sets for partitioned indexes.

The maximum size of each data set is based on the number of defined partitions. If the partitioned table space is not defined with the LARGE parameter, and the DSSIZE is not greater than 2GB, the maximum number of partitions is 64 and the maximum size per partition is as follows:

Partitions	Maximum Size of VSAM Data Set
1 through 16	4GB
17 through 32	2GB
33 through 64	1GB

> **NOTE**
>
> Recall from Chapter 5 that the DSSIZE parameter is used to specify the maximum size for each partition of partitioned and LOB table spaces. Valid DSSIZE values are 1GB, 2GB, 4GB, 8GB, 16GB, 32GB, or 64GB.

> To specify a DSSIZE greater than 4GB, you must be running DB2 with DFSMS V1.5, and the data sets for the table space must be associated with a DFSMS data class defined with extended format and extended addressability. DFSMS's extended addressability function is necessary to create data sets larger than 4GB in size.

If the partitioned table space is defined with the LARGE parameter, the maximum number of partitions is 4096 and the maximum size per partition is 4GB.

If the partitioned table space is defined with a DSSIZE greater than 2GB, the maximum size per partition is 64GB, but it depends on the page size, too. With a DSSIZE of 4GB and a page size of 4K, you can define up to 4096 partitions, but with a DSSIZE of 64GB the maximum number of partitions using 4K pages is 256.

Data Sets for LOB Table Spaces   For LOB data, up to 127TB of data per LOB column can be stored (using 254 partitions). If DSSIZE is not specified for a LOB table space, the default for the maximum size of each data set is 4GB. The maximum number of data sets is 254.

V8   If 4096 partitions need to be supported, no more than 5 LOBs can be put in the table. This is so because each individual LOB would require 12,288 objects to support it, and DB2 has a limit of 65,535 objects allowed per database.

For more information on LOBs, refer to Chapter 9, "Large Objects and Object/Relational Databases."

The Structure of a Page

Now that you know how data sets are used by DB2, the next question is likely to be "How are these data sets structured?"

Every VSAM data set used to represent a DB2 table space or index is composed of pages. Up through V7, DB2 is limited to using pages that consist of 4,096 bytes, or 4KB. Actually, even for DB2 V8, the vast majority of all DB2 table spaces and indexes will use 4K pages. You therefore can think of a data set used by DB2 table spaces or indexes as shown in Figure 20.2.

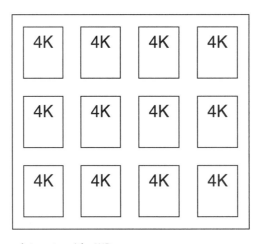

FIGURE 20.2   DB2 uses data sets with 4KB pages.

But what about table spaces with larger page sizes? As you might recall, DB2 table spaces can have page sizes of 4KB, 8KB, 16KB, or 32KB. Up through V7, DB2 groups 4KB pages together to create virtual page sizes greater than 4KB. For example, a table space defined with 32KB pages uses a logical 32KB page composed of eight physical 4KB pages, as represented in Figure 20.3. A table space with 32KB pages is physically structured like a table space with 4KB pages. It differs only in that rows of a 32KB page table space can span 4K pages, thereby creating a logical 32KB page.

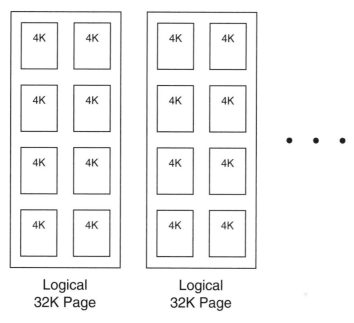

FIGURE 20.3   32KB pages are composed of eight 4KB pages.

V8   As of DB2 V8, though, you can specify that DB2 use the correct CI size for DB2 page sizes greater than 4K. This is controlled system-wide using a parameter in the DSNZPARMs. Consult your DBA or system programmer to determine whether your organization uses grouped 4K pages for page sizes larger than 4K, or matches the page size to the VSAM CI size.

DB2 Page Types

DB2 uses different types of pages to manage data in data sets. Each type of page has its own purpose and format. The type of page used is based on the type of table space or index for which it exists and the location of the page in the data set defined for that object.

Before proceeding any further, I must introduce a new term, *page set,* which is a physical grouping of pages. Page sets come in two types: linear and partitioned. DB2 uses *linear page sets* for simple table spaces, segmented table spaces, and indexes. DB2 uses *partitioned page sets* when it implements partitioned table spaces.

Each page set is composed of several types of pages, as follows.

- Header page
- Space Map pages
- Dictionary pages
- System pages
- Data pages

V8

Figure 20.4 shows the basic layout of a DB2 table space.

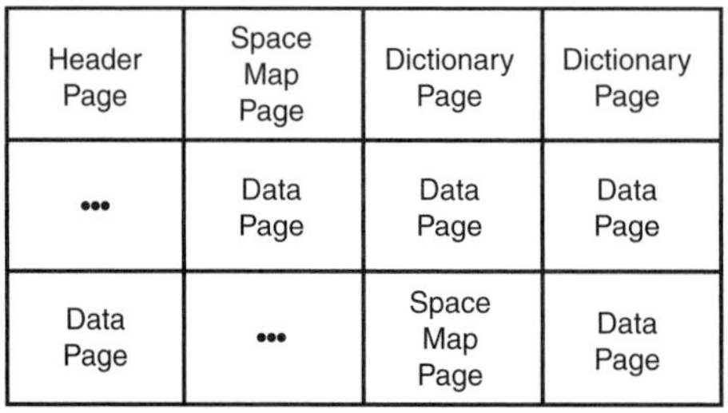

Header Page	Space Map Page	Dictionary Page	Dictionary Page
•••	Data Page	Data Page	Data Page
Data Page	•••	Space Map Page	Data Page

FIGURE 20.4   DB2 table space layout.

The *header page* contains control information used by DB2 to manage and maintain the table space. For example, the `OBID` and `DBID` (internal object and database identifiers used by DB2) of the table space and database are maintained here, as well as information on logging. Each linear page set has one header page; every partition of a partitioned page set has its own header page. The header page is the first page of a VSAM data set and can occur only once per page set.

Space map pages contain information pertaining to the amount of free space available on pages in a page set. A space map page outlines the space available for a range of pages. Refer to Figure 20.5 for the number of pages covered by a space map page based on the type of table space. More than one space map can exist per page set.

Dictionary pages are used for table spaces that specify `COMPRESS YES`. Information is stored in the dictionary pages to help DB2 control compression and decompression. The dictionary pages are stored after the header page and first space map page, but before any data pages.

> **NOTE**
>
> Each table space or table space partition that contains compressed data has a compression dictionary that is used to control compression and decompression. The dictionary contains a fixed number of entries, up to a maximum of 4096. The dictionary content is based on the data at the time it was built, and it does not change unless the dictionary is rebuilt or recovered, or compression is disabled using `ALTER` with `COMPRESS NO`.

4K Pages

Segmented Tablespace

SEGSIZE	4	8	12	18	20	24	28	32	36	40	44	48	52	56	60	64
# Pages	1712	2704	3360	3824	4160	4416	4616	4800	4932	5080	5148	5232	5304	5376	5460	5504

Simple Table Space		Partitioned Table Space

Pages
10764

Pages
10764

32K Pages

Segmented Tablespace

SEGSIZE	4	8	12	18	20	24	28	32	36	40	44	48	52	56	60	64
# Pages	13784	21824	27084	30800	33560	35712	37408	38784	39924	40920	41712	42432	43056	43624	44100	44544

Simple Table Space		Partitioned Table Space

Pages
87216

Pages
87216

FIGURE 20.5 Number of pages per space map page.

System pages are new as of DB2 V8 and contain information about the version of the object and hence the structure of its rows, as well as other system-related details.

Data pages contain the user data for the table space or index page set. The layout of a data page depends on whether it is an index data page or a table space data page.

Table Space Data Pages

Each table space data page is formatted as shown in Figure 20.6. Each page begins with a 20-byte header that records control information about the rest of the page. For example, the header contains the page set page number, pointers to free space in the page, and information pertaining to the validity and recoverability of the page.

20

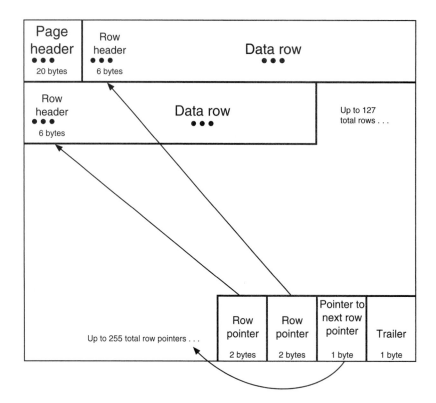

FIGURE 20.6 Table space data page layout.

At the very end of the page is a 1-byte trailer used as a consistency check token. DB2 checks the value in the trailer byte against a single bit in the page header to ensure that the data page is sound. DB2 ensures that these two bits are the same when the page is read.

The next-to-last byte of each page contains a pointer to the next available ID map entry. The ID map is a series of contiguous 2-byte row pointers. One row pointer exists for every data row in the table. A maximum of 255 of these pointers can be defined per data page. The maximum number of rows per page can be specified for each table space using the MAXROWS clause. Each row pointer identifies the location of a data row in the data page.

Each data page can contain one or more data rows. One data row exists for each row pointer, thereby enforcing a maximum of 255 data rows per data page. Each data row contains a 6-byte row header used to administer the status of the data row.

LOB Pages

LOB columns are stored in auxiliary tables, not with the primary data. An auxiliary table is stored in a LOB table space. For complete details on large object support, refer to Chapter 9.

The layout of data pages in a LOB table space differs from a regular DB2 table space. There are two types of LOB pages:

- LOB map pages
- LOB data pages

LOB map pages contain information describing the LOB data. A LOB map page always precedes the LOB data. Figure 20.7 describes the LOB map page. There are potentially five components of the LOB map page.

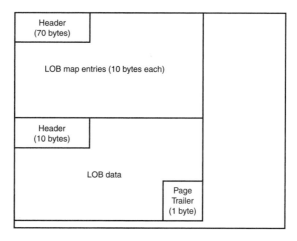

FIGURE 20.7   LOB map page layout.

The LOB map page header connects the LOB page with the base table. The LOB map entries point to the page number where LOB data exists, as well as containing information about the length of the LOB data.

The final two components of the LOB map page exist only when the LOB map page also contains LOB data. The LOB map page data header, LOB data, and page trailer exist when the last LOB map page contains LOB data.

The LOB data page contains the actual LOB data. The layout of a LOB data page is depicted in Figure 20.8.

Index Pages

The data pages for a DB2 index are somewhat more complex than those for a DB2 table space. Before you delve into the specifics of the layout of index data pages, you should examine the basic structure of DB2 indexes.

A DB2 index is a modified *b-tree* (balanced tree) structure that orders data values for rapid retrieval. The values being indexed are stored in an inverted tree structure, as shown in Figure 20.9.

20

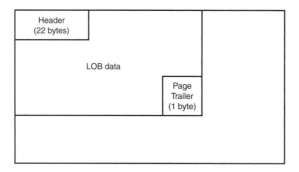

FIGURE 20.8   LOB data page layout.

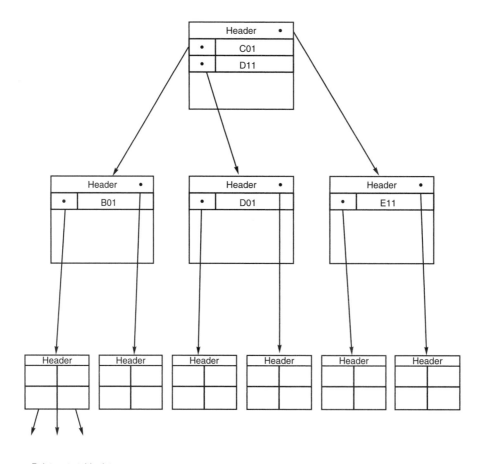

FIGURE 20.9   DB2 index structure.

As values are inserted and deleted from the index, the tree structure is automatically balanced, realigning the hierarchy so that the path from top to bottom is uniform. This realignment minimizes the time required to access any given value by keeping the search paths as short as possible.

Every DB2 index resides in an index space. When an index is created, the physical space to hold the index data is automatically created if STOGROUPs are used. This physical structure is called the index space. Refer to Figure 20.10 for a depiction of the layout of an index space.

Header Page	Space Map Page	Index Data Page (Root Page)	Index Data Page
Index Data Page	Index Data Page	Index Data Page	Index Data Page
Index Data Page	•••	Space Map Page	Index Data Page

FIGURE 20.10   DB2 index space layout.

Index data pages are always 4KB in size. To implement indexes, DB2 uses the following types of index data pages:

Space map pages   Space map pages determine what space is available in the index for DB2 to utilize. An index space map page is required every 32,632 index pages. Figure 20.11 shows the layout of an index space map page.

Root page   Only one root page is available per index. The third page in the index space, after the header page and (first) space map page, is the root page. The root page must exist at the highest level of the hierarchy for every index structure. It is always structured as a non-leaf page.

Non-leaf pages   Non-leaf pages are intermediate-level index pages in the b-tree hierarchy. Non-leaf pages need not exist. If they do exist, they contain pointers to other non-leaf pages or leaf pages. They never point to data rows.

Leaf pages   Leaf pages contain the most important information within the index. Leaf pages contain pointers to the data rows of a table.

The pointers in the leaf pages of an index are called a *record ID*, or *RID*. Each RID is a combination of the table space page number and the row pointer for the data value, which together indicate the location of the data value.

20

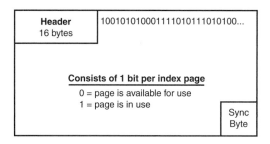

FIGURE 20.11   Index space map page layout.

> **NOTE**
>
> A RID is a **record** ID, not a **row** ID as is commonly assumed. A DB2 record is the combination of the record prefix and the row. Each record prefix is 6 bytes long. RIDs point to the record, not the row; therefore, a RID is a record ID. But don't let this information change the way you think. The data returned by your SELECT statements are still rows!

The level of a DB2 index indicates whether it contains non-leaf pages. The smallest DB2 index is a two-level index. A two-level index does not contain non-leaf pages. The root page points directly to leaf pages, which in turn point to the rows containing the indexed data values.

A three-level index, such as the one shown in Figure 20.9, contains one level for the root page, another level for non-leaf pages, and a final level for leaf pages. The larger the number of levels for an index, the less efficient it will be. You can have any number of intermediate non-leaf page levels. The more levels that exist for the index, the less efficient the index becomes, because additional levels must be traversed to find the index key data on the leaf page. Try to minimize the number of levels in your DB2 indexes; when more than three levels exist, indexes generally start to become inefficient.

Type 1 Index Data Pages

Type 1 indexes are DB2's legacy index type. These are the indexes that were available with DB2 since V1. They started to be called Type 1 indexes with the introduction of DB2 V4, which added a new type of index (Type 2 indexes).

As of V6, DB2 uses only Type 2 indexes. Type 1 indexes are no longer supported.

V8
> **CAUTION**
>
> You will not be able to migrate to DB2 V8 if any Type 1 indexes still exist.

However, if you are using a past release of DB2 and want to read more about Type 1 indexes, refer to the CD accompanying this book, where you can find a file containing a section from a previous edition of this book covering Type 1 indexes.

Type 2 Index Data Pages

Non-leaf pages are physically formatted as shown in Figure 20.12. Each non-leaf page contains the following:

- A 12-byte index page header that houses consistency and recoverability information for the index.

- A 16-byte physical header that stores control information for the index page. For example, the physical header controls administrative housekeeping, such as the type of page (leaf or non-leaf), the location of the page in the index structure, and the ordering and size of the indexed values.

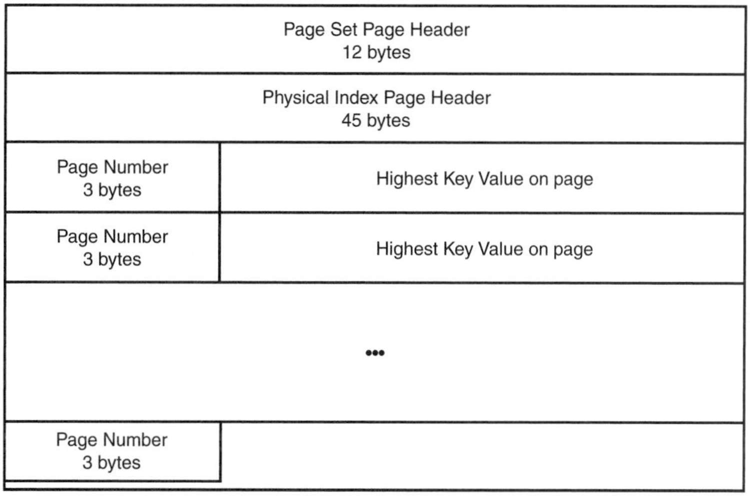

Page Set Page Header 12 bytes	
Physical Index Page Header 45 bytes	
Page Number 3 bytes	Highest Key Value on page
Page Number 3 bytes	Highest Key Value on page
•••	
Page Number 3 bytes	

FIGURE 20.12   *Type 2 index non-leaf page layout.*

Each non-leaf page contains high keys with child page pointers. The last page pointer has no high key because it points to a child page that has entries greater than the highest high key in the parent.

Additionally, Type 2 index non-leaf pages deploy suffix truncation to reduce data storage needs and increase efficiency. Suffix truncation allows the non-leaf page to store only the most significant bytes of the key. For example, consider an index in which a new value is being inserted. The value, `ABCE0481`, is to be placed on a new index page. The last key value on the previous page was `ABCD0398`. Only the significant bytes needed to determine that this key is new need to be stored—in this case, `ABCE`.

> **NOTE**
>
> In the older, Type 1 indexes, the entire length of each key was stored. Truncation helps to reduce index size, thereby possibly reducing the number of index levels and incurring less I/O.

Entries on a Type 2 leaf page are not stored contiguously in order on the page. A collated key map exists at the end of the Type 2 leaf page to order the entries. Type 2 index leaf pages are formatted as shown in Figure 20.13. When an entry is added to the index, the collated key map grows backward from the end of the page into the page. By traversing the key map within the page, DB2 can read entries in order by the index key. Additionally, Type 2 indexes have no subpages.

20

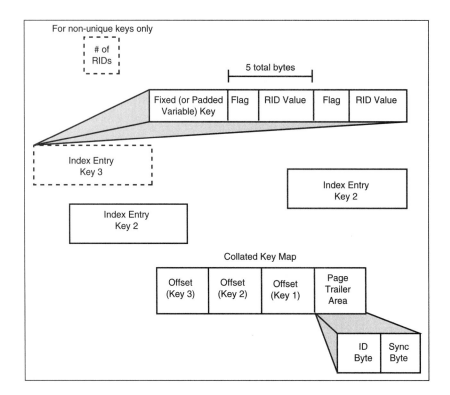

FIGURE 20.13   Type 2 Index leaf page layout.

Type 2 leaf page entries add a flag byte. The *flag byte* indicates the status of the RID. The first bit indicates whether the RID is pseudo-deleted. A *pseudo-delete* occurs when a RID has been marked for deletion. The second bit indicates that the RID is possibly uncommitted, and the third bit indicates that a RID hole follows. An array of RIDs is stored contiguously in ascending order to allow binary searching. For non-unique indexes, each index entry is preceded by a count of the number of RIDs.

> **NOTE**
>
> Type 2 indexes will need to be reorganized periodically to physically delete the pseudo-deleted RIDS. Information about pseudo-deleted RIDs can be found in the DB2 Catalog in SYSIBM.SYSINDEXPART and in the Real Time Statistics tables. Consider tracking the historical size of indexes for those that are larger than normal and thus, candidates for reorganization.

The final physical index structure to explore is the index entry. You can create both unique and non-unique indexes for each DB2 table. When the index key is of varying length, DB2 pads the columns to their maximum length, making the index keys a fixed length. A unique index contains entries, and each entry has a single RID. In a unique index, no two index entries can have the same value because the values being indexed are unique (see Figure 20.14).

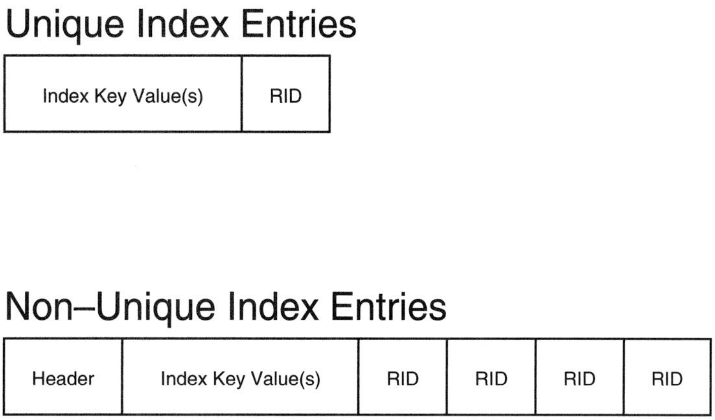

Unique Index Entries

Index Key Value(s)	RID

Non–Unique Index Entries

Header	Index Key Value(s)	RID	RID	RID	RID

FIGURE 20.14   Index entries.

You can add the `WHERE NOT NULL` clause to a unique index causing multiple nulls to be stored. Therefore, an index specified as unique `WHERE NOT NULL` has multiple unique entries and possibly one non-unique entry for the nulls.

If the index can point to multiple table rows containing the same values, however, the index entry must support a RID list. In addition, a header is necessary to maintain the length of the RID list. This type of index entry is shown in Figure 20.9.

The Storage Impact of Type 2 Indexes   Type 2 indexes provide numerous benefits to a DB2 subsystem. The primary benefit is the elimination of index locking. However, many newer DB2 features, such as row level locking and uncommitted reads, require Type 2 indexes. Type 1 indexes were no longer supported as of DB2 V6, but DB2 would continue to operate if Type 1 indexes still exist. You cannot migrate to DB2 V8 without dropping or converting all of your Type 1 indexes. So, you are now forced to move to Type 2 indexes.

If you have already migrated your Type 1 indexes to Type 2, you can ignore the rest of this short section. Otherwise, be sure you understand all of the storage ramifications of converting to Type 2 indexes.

What will the impact of Type 2 indexes be with regard to storage requirements? The answer, not surprisingly, is "it depends!" There are quite a few differences between Type 1 and Type 2 indexes that impact storage. The first difference is in the amount of useable space on an index page. A Type 2 leaf page has 4038 bytes of useable space; a Type 2 non-leaf page has 4046 bytes. Type 1 leaf and non-leaf pages have 4050 useable bytes per page. So, Type 2 indexes have less useable space per page.

Additionally, Type 2 indexes require an additional one-byte RID prefix in addition to the four-byte RID found in both Type 1 and Type 2 indexes. The new one-byte RID prefix found in a Type 2 index contains three flags: pseudo-deleted, possibly uncommitted, and RID hole follows.

Because Type 2 indexes have a different internal structure, two pieces of header information needed on Type 1 indexes are no longer required: the subpage header and the non-unique key header. Because Type 2 indexes do not use subpages, the 17-byte logical subpage header required of a Type 1 index is not in Type 2 indexes.

Non-unique Type 1 indexes have a six-byte header and will repeat an entry (header and key) if a key has more than 255 RIDs. Type 2 indexes have a two-byte header and can have more than 255 RIDs in each entry. The entry is only repeated if there is not enough room in a leaf page to hold all of the RIDs; the same is true for a Type 1 index. Type 2 indexes also have a two-byte MAPID for each key at the end of the page, so total savings per key is two bytes (six bytes for the Type 1 header, minus two bytes for the Type 2 header and two bytes for the MAPID).

Type 2 indexes store truncated keys instead of the complete key. Only the portion of the key required to make it uniquely identifiable is stored on non-leaf pages. However, if there are many duplicate keys so that the same key is on more than one leaf page, a Type 2 index will have RIDs stored in the non-leaf pages, causing more space to be used instead of less. This is due to Type 2 indexes keeping the RIDs in sequence.

Finally, Type 2 indexes are required for LARGE table spaces (that is, DSSIZE greater than 2GB). In this case, the RID is five bytes (plus the one-byte RID prefix, which is still required).

As you can see, there is no clear-cut answer as to whether a Type 1 or Type 2 index will utilize more storage.

Taking all these points into consideration, here are some general rules of thumb on index storage requirements that you can apply when developing DB2 databases:

- A Type 1 index with a subpage count of 16 usually wastes a lot of space. A Type 2 index will almost always use less space than a Type 1 with 16 subpages (but so will a Type 1 index with a subpage of 1).

- A Type 1 with a subpage of 1 usually will use slightly less space than a Type 2 index for both unique and non-unique keys. For the average user, the space difference is relatively small and usually should not be a factor.

- Beware of Type 2 space usage if numerous row deletes occur. Type 1 indexes clean up after a delete, while DB2 pseudo-deletes index RID entries. A pseudo-delete is when DB2 marks the index entry for deletion, but does not physically delete it. When high levels of activity occur, you could encounter numerous pages of nothing but pseudo-deleted RIDs. DB2 should periodically cleanup the pseudo-deleted entries, but in some cases, users report seeing them staying around for weeks at a time wasting space. A reorganization or rebuild will clean up the pseudo-deleted RIDs and free the wasted space.

- Beware of space usage when numerous inserts occur. Type 1 index entries move around in the page and finally, when a split occurs, one half of the index entries are moved to another page, usually causing the one half page to be wasted. This is known as the "half full" problem. Type 2 index pages will also split, but provision has been made at the end of a data set to avoid the "half full" problem. Also, Type 2 indexes with non-unique keys will chain RIDs within a page. Each chain entry requires a chain pointer and the normal RID. The additional overhead is two bytes plus the Type 2 RID. Reorganizing or rebuilding the index can solve all of these problems.

- The DBA should monitor the disk space usage of indexes and reorganize the indexes when they grow too large or when performance problems arise.

Be sure to factor all of these issues into your index storage requirement exercises.

Record Identifiers

A RID is a 4-byte record identifier that contains record location information. RIDs are used to locate any piece of DB2 data. For large partitioned table spaces, the RID is a 5-byte record identifier.

The RID stores the page number and offset within the page where the data can be found. For pages in a partitioned table space, the high-order bits are used to identify the partition number.

Now that you know the physical structure of DB2 objects, you can explore the layout of DB2 itself.

What Makes DB2 Tick

Conceptually, DB2 is a relational database management system. Physically, DB2 is an amalgamation of address spaces and intersystem communication links that, when adequately tied together, provide the services of a relational database management system.

"What does all this information have to do with me?" you might wonder. Understanding the components of a piece of software helps you use that software more effectively. By understanding the physical layout of DB2, you can arrive at system solutions more quickly and develop SQL that performs better.

The information in this section is not very technical and does not delve into the bits and bytes of DB2. Instead, it presents the basic architecture of a DB2 subsystem and information about each subcomponent of that architecture.

Each DB2 subcomponent is comprised of smaller units called CSECTs. A CSECT performs a single logical function. Working together, a bunch of CSECTs provide general, high-level functionality for a subcomponent of DB2.

> **NOTE**
> DB2 CSECT names begin with the characters DSN.

There are three major subcomponents of DB2: system services (SSAS), database services (DBAS), and distributed data facility services (DDFS).

The SSAS, or System Services Address Space, coordinates the attachment of DB2 to other subsystems (CICS, IMS/TM, or TSO). SSAS is also responsible for all logging activities (physical logging, log archival, and BSDS). DSNMSTR is the default name for this address

20

space. (The address spaces might have been renamed at your shop.) DSNMSTR is the started task that contains the DB2 log. The log should be monitored regularly for messages indicating the errors or problems with DB2. Products are available that monitor the log for problems and trigger an event to contact the DBA or systems programmer when a problem is found.

The DBAS, or Database Services Address Space, provides the facility for the manipulation of DB2 data structures. The default name for this address space is DSNDBM1. This component of DB2 is responsible for the execution of SQL and the management of buffers, and it contains the core logic of the DBMS. Database services use system services and z/OS to handle the actual databases (tables, indexes, and so on) under the control of DB2. Although DBAS and SSAS operate in different address spaces, they are interdependent and work together as a formal subsystem of z/OS.

The DBAS can be further broken down into three components, each of which performs specific data-related tasks: the Relational Data System (RDS), the Data Manager (DM), and the Buffer Manager (BM) (see Figure 20.15). The Buffer Manager handles the movement of data from disk to memory; the Data Manager handles the application of Stage 1 predicates and row-level operations on DB2 data; and the Relational Data System, or Relational Data Services, handles the application of Stage 2 predicates and set-level operations on DB2 data.

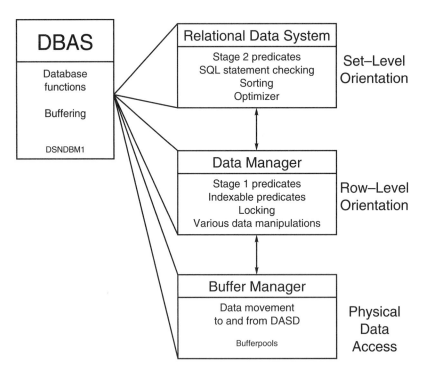

FIGURE 20.15   The components of the Database Services Address Space.

The next DB2 address space, DDFS, or Distributed Data Facility Services, is optional. DDFS, often simplified to DDF, is required only when you want distributed database functionality. If your shop must enable remote DB2 subsystems to query data between one another, the DDF address space must be activated. DDF services use VTAM or TCP/IP to establish connections and communicate with other DB2 subsystems using either DRDA or private protocols. Details about DB2's distributed database capabilities are covered later, in Part VIII of this book.

DB2 also requires an additional address space to handle locking. The IRLM, or Intersystem Resource Lock Manager, is responsible for the management of all DB2 locks (including deadlock detection). The default name of this address space is IRLMPROC.

Finally, DB2 uses additional address spaces to manage the execution of stored procedures and user-defined functions. These address spaces are known as the Stored Procedure Address Spaces, or SPAS.

V8 If you're running DB2 V4, only one SPAS is available. For DB2 V5 and later releases, however, if you're using the z/OS Workload Manager (WLM), you can define multiple address spaces for stored procedures. Indeed, as of DB2 V8, WLM-defined is the only approved method for new stored procedures. Pre-existing stored procedures will continue to run in a non-WLM-defined SPAS under DB2 V8. Of course, if the stored procedure is dropped and re-created, it must use the WLM. The non-WLM-defined SPAS is being phased out and will be completely removed in a future version of DB2.

So, at a high level, DB2 uses five address spaces to handle all DB2 functionality. DB2 also communicates with allied agents, such as CICS, IMS/TM, and TSO. And database services use the VSAM Media Manager to actually read data. A summary of the DB2 address spaces and the functionality they perform is provided in Figure 20.16.

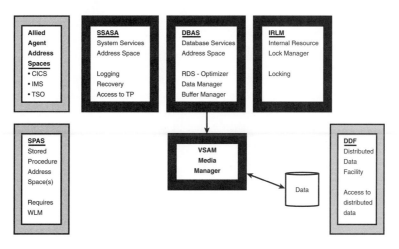

FIGURE 20.16   The DB2 address spaces.

Database Services

Recall that the DBAS is composed of three distinct elements. Each component passes the SQL statement to the next component, and when results are returned, each component passes the results back (see Figure 20.17). The operations performed by the components of the DBAS as an SQL statement progresses on its way toward execution are discussed next.

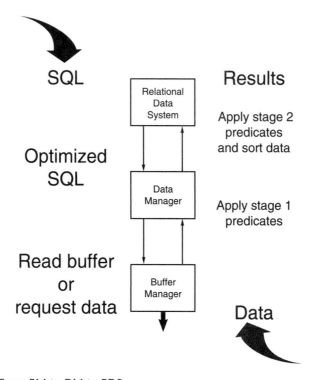

FIGURE 20.17   From BM to DM to RDS.

The RDS is the component that gives DB2 its set orientation. When an SQL statement requesting a set of columns and rows is passed to the RDS, the RDS determines the best mechanism for satisfying the request. Note that the RDS can parse an SQL statement and determine its needs. These needs, basically, can be any of the features supported by a relational database (such as selection, projection, or join).

When the RDS receives a SQL statement, it performs the following procedures:

- Checks authorization
- Resolves data element names into internal identifiers
- Checks the syntax of the SQL statement
- Optimizes the SQL statement and generates an access path

The RDS then passes the optimized SQL statement to the Data Manager (DM) for further processing. The function of the DM is to lower the level of data that is being operated on. In other words, the DM is the DB2 component that analyzes rows (either table rows or index rows) of data. The DM analyzes the request for data and then calls the Buffer Manager (BM) to satisfy the request.

The Buffer Manager accesses data for other DB2 components. It uses pools of memory set aside for the storage of frequently accessed data to create an efficient data access environment.

When a request is passed to the BM, it must determine whether the data is in the bufferpool. If the data is present, the BM accesses the data and sends it to the DM. If the data is not in the bufferpool, it calls the VSAM Media Manager, which reads the data and sends it back to the BM, which in turn sends the data back to the DM.

The DM receives the data passed to it by the BM and applies as many predicates as possible to reduce the answer set. Only Stage 1 predicates are applied in the DM. (These predicates are listed in Chapter 2, "Data Manipulation Guidelines.")

Finally, the RDS receives the data from the DM. All Stage 2 predicates are applied, the necessary sorting is performed, and the results are returned to the requester.

Now that you have learned about these components of DB2, you should be able to understand how this information can be helpful in developing a DB2 application. For example, consider Stage 1 and Stage 2 predicates. Now you can understand more easily that Stage 1 predicates are more efficient than Stage 2 predicates because you know that they are evaluated earlier in the process (in the DM instead of the RDS) and thereby avoid the overhead associated with the passing of additional data from one component to another.

20

CHAPTER **21**

The Optimizer

The optimizer is the heart and soul of DB2. Before any SQL statement is run, the optimizer analyzes the SQL and determines the most efficient access path available for satisfying the statement. It accomplishes this by parsing the SQL statement to determine which tables and columns must be accessed. It then queries statistics stored in the DB2 Catalog to determine the best method of accomplishing the tasks necessary to satisfy the SQL request.

Statistics used by the optimizer include information about the current status of the tables, indexes, columns, and tablespaces (including partitioning information) that need to be accessed. The optimizer plugs this information into a series of complex formulas that it uses as it builds optimized access paths, as shown in Figure 21.1. In addition to the DB2 Catalog statistics, the optimizer will take into account other system information, such as the CPU being used and the size of your buffer pools. This approach allows the optimizer to estimate the number of rows that qualify for each predicate, and then use the proper algorithm to access the required data.

The optimizer basically works like an expert system. An expert system is a set of standard rules that when combined with situational data can return an expert opinion. For example, a medical expert system takes the set of rules determining which medication is useful for which illness, combines it with data describing the symptoms of ailments, and applies that knowledge base to a list of input symptoms. The DB2 optimizer renders expert opinions on data retrieval methods for SQL queries based on the situational data housed in the DB2 Catalog. In this chapter, you discover the methods and strategies used by the optimizer as it creates optimized access paths for SQL statements.

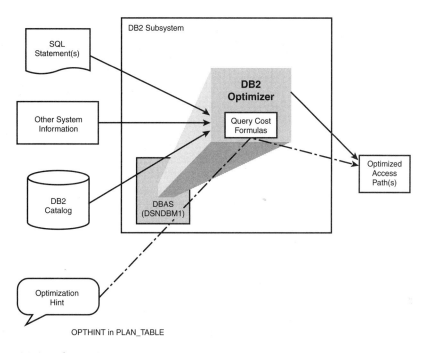

FIGURE 21.1   The DB2 optimizer.

Physical Data Independence

The notion of optimizing data access in the DBMS, a piece of system software, is one of the most powerful capabilities of DB2. Access to DB2 data is achieved by telling DB2 what to retrieve, not how to retrieve it. Regardless of how the data is physically stored and manipulated, DB2 and SQL can still access that data. This separation of access criteria from physical storage characteristics is called *physical data independence*. DB2's optimizer is the component that accomplishes this physical data independence.

If indexes are removed, DB2 can still access the data (albeit less efficiently). If a column is added to the table being accessed, the data can still be manipulated by DB2 without changing the program code. This is all possible because the physical access paths to DB2 data are not coded by programmers in application programs, but are generated by DB2.

Compare this with older, legacy data manipulation mechanisms (such as VSAM, IMS, and flat files), in which the programmer must know the physical structure of the data. If there is an index, the programmer must write appropriate code so that the index is used. If the index is removed, the program will not work unless changes are made. Not so with DB2 and SQL. All this flexibility is attributable to DB2's capability to optimize data manipulation requests automatically.

> **NOTE**
>
> Physical data independence is the primary reason that it is a best practice to put as much work as possible into SQL statements, instead of into host program logic. When data statistics and characteristics change, DB2 can formulate another access path for the SQL; programmers are required to rewrite host language code to change access requirements. Heed this advice or suffer the peril of poor performance and extra programming.

How the Optimizer Works

The optimizer performs complex calculations based on a host of information. To simplify the functionality of the optimizer, you can picture it as performing a four-step process:

1. Receive and verify the SQL statement.

2. Analyze the environment and optimize the method of satisfying the SQL statement.

3. Create machine-readable instructions to execute the optimized SQL.

4. Execute the instructions or store them for future execution.

The second step of this process is the most intriguing. How does the optimizer decide how to execute the vast array of SQL statements that can be sent its way?

The optimizer has many types of strategies for optimizing SQL. How does it choose which of these strategies to use in the optimized access paths? IBM does not publish the exact details and logic used by the optimizer, but the optimizer is cost-based. This means that the optimizer will always attempt to formulate an access path for each query that reduces overall cost. To accomplish this, the DB2 optimizer evaluates and weighs four factors for each potential access path: the CPU cost, the I/O cost, the DB2 Catalog statistics, and the SQL statement itself.

CPU Cost

The optimizer tries to determine the cost of execution of each access path strategy for the query being optimized. Based on the serial number of the CPU, the optimizer estimates the CPU time required to accomplish the tasks associated with the access path it is analyzing. As it calculates this cost, it determines the costs involved in applying predicates, traversing pages (index and tablespace), and sorting.

I/O Cost

The optimizer estimates the cost of physically retrieving and writing the data. In so doing, the optimizer estimates the cost of I/O by using a series of formulas based on the following data: DB2 Catalog statistics, the size of the buffer pools, and the cost of work files used (sorting, intermediate results, and so on). These formulas result in a *filter factor,* which determines the relative I/O cost of the query. Filter factors are covered in more detail in the "Filter Factors" section, later in this chapter.

DB2 Catalog Statistics

Without the statistics stored in the DB2 Catalog, the optimizer would have a difficult time optimizing anything. These statistics provide the optimizer with information pertinent to the state of the tables that will be accessed by the SQL statement that is being optimized. A complete listing of the DB2 Catalog statistics and values used by the optimizer is in Table 21.1. Partition-level statistics are used when determining the degree of parallelism for queries using I/O, CP, and Sysplex parallelism.

TABLE 21.1   DB2 Catalog Columns Analyzed by the Optimizer

Catalog Table	Column	Description
SYSIBM.SYSTABLES	CARDF	Number of rows for the table
	NPAGES	Number of pages used by the table
	EDPROC	Name of the EDITPROC exit routine, if any
	PCTROWCOMP	Percentage of active rows compressed for this table
SYSIBM.SYSTABSTATS	CARDF	Number of rows for the partition
	NPAGES	Number of pages on which rows of the partition appear
SYSIBM.SYSTABLESPACE	NACTIVEF	Number of allocated, active tablespace pages
SYSIBM.SYSCOLUMNS	LOW2KEY	Second lowest value for the column (first 2,000 bytes only)
	HIGH2KEY	Second highest value for the column (first 2,000 bytes only)
	COLCARDF	Estimated number of distinct values for the column
SYSIBM.SYSINDEXES	CLUSTERRATIOF	Percentage (multiplied by 100) of rows in clustering order
	CLUSTERING	Whether CLUSTER YES was specified when the index was created
	FIRSTKEYCARDF	Number of distinct values for the first column of the index key
	FULLKEYCARDF	Number of distinct values for the full index key
	NLEAF	Number of active leaf pages
	NLEVELS	Number of index b-tree levels
SYSIBM.SYSINDEXPART	LIMITKEY	The limit key of the partition
SYSIBM.SYSCOLDIST	TYPE	Type of RUNSTATS gathered; frequent value (F) or cardinality (C)
	COLVALUE	Non-uniform distribution column value
	FREQUENCYF	Percentage (multiplied by 100) of rows that contain the value indicated in the COLVALUE column
	CARDF	Number of distinct values for the column
	COLGROUPCOLNO	Set of columns for the statistics gathered
	NUMCOLUMNS	The number of columns associated with the statistics

TABLE 21.1   Continued

Catalog Table	Column	Description
SYSIBM.SYSROUTINES	IOS_PER_INVOC	Estimated number of I/Os per invocation of this routine
	INSTS_PER_INVOC	Estimated number of instructions per invocation of this routine
	INITIAL_IOS	Estimated number of I/Os for the first and last time the routine is invoked
	INITIAL_INSTS	Estimated number of instructions for the first and last time the routine is invoked
	CARDINALITY	Predicted cardinality for a table function

The columns that have an **F** at the end of their names were changed from INTEGER columns to FLOAT columns (as of DB2 V5). This enabled DB2 to store larger values in these columns. The largest value that can be stored in an INTEGER column is 2,147,483,647; a floating point column can store values up to 7.2×10^{75}—a very large number indeed.

RUNSTATS can also keep track of correlated columns. *Correlated columns* have values that are related to one another. An example of a set of correlated columns is CITY, STATE, and ZIP_CODE. For example, the combination of CHICAGO for CITY and IL for STATE is much more likely to occur than CHICAGO and AK. Such correlations are useful for the optimizer to analyze when formulating access paths.

The RUNSTATS utility also generates information about the frequency of data values. This information is useful to the optimizer because a different access path may be chosen for a predicate when retrieving a value that occurs 40% of the time than for the same predicate when retrieving a value that occurs only 2% of the time.

The SQL Statement

The formulation of the SQL statement also enters into the access path decisions made by the optimizer. The complexity of the query, the number and type of predicates used (Stage 1 versus Stage 2), the usage of column and scalar functions, and the presence of ordering clauses (ORDER BY, GROUP BY, and DISTINCT) enter into the estimated cost that is calculated by the optimizer.

Additionally, certain SQL formulations are recognized as optimizer tweaks—for example, adding OR 0=1 to a predicate to affect indexing.

Filter Factors

Do you recall the discussion of filter factors from Chapter 1, "The Magic Words"? The optimizer calculates the filter factor for a query's predicates based on the number of rows that will be filtered out by the predicates.

The filter factor is a ratio (a number between 0 and 1) that estimates I/O costs. It is an estimate of the proportion of table rows for which a predicate is true. The formulas used by the optimizer to calculate the filter factor are proprietary IBM information, but Table 21.2

provides rough estimates for the formulas based on the type of predicate. These formulas assume uniform data distribution, so they should be used only when determining the filter factor for static SQL queries or queries on tables having no distribution statistics stored in the DB2 Catalog. The filter factor for dynamic SQL queries is calculated using the distribution statistics, in SYSCOLDIST, if available.

TABLE 21.2   Filter Factor Formulas

Predicate Type	Formula	Default FF
COL = value	1/FIRSTKEYCARDF [COL]	.04
COL = :host-var	1/FIRSTKEYCARDF [COL]	.04
COL <> value	1-(1/FIRSTKEYCARDF [COL])	.96
COL <> :host-var	1-(1/FIRSTKEYCARDF [COL])	.96
COL IN (list of values)	(list size)?(1/FIRSTKEYCARDF [COL])	.04?(list size)
COL NOT IN (list of values)	1-[(list size)?(1/FIRSTKEYCARDF [COL])]	1-[.04?(list size)]
COL IS NULL	1/FIRSTKEYCARDF [COL]	.04
COL IS NOT NULL	1-(1/FIRSTKEYCARDF [COL])	.96
COLA = COLB	smaller of 1/FIRSTKEYCARDF [COLA] 1/FIRSTKEYCARDF [COLB]	.04
COLA <> COLB	smaller of 1/FIRSTKEYCARDF [COLA] 1/FIRSTKEYCARDF [COLB]	.96
COL < value	(LOW2KEY-value)/ (HIGH2KEY-LOW2KEY)	.33
COL <= value	(LOW2KEY-value)/ (HIGH2KEY-LOW2KEY)	.33
COL ¬> value	(LOW2KEY-value)/ (HIGH2KEY-LOW2KEY)	.33
COL > value	(HIGH2KEY-value)/ (HIGH2KEY-LOW2KEY)	.33
COL >= value	(HIGH2KEY-value)/ (HIGH2KEY-LOW2KEY)	.33
COL ¬< value	(HIGH2KEY-value)/ (HIGH2KEY-LOW2KEY)	.33
COL BETWEEN val1 AND val2	(val2-val1)/ (HIGH2KEY-LOW2KEY)	.01
COL LIKE 'char%'	(val2-val1)/ (HIGH2KEY-LOW2KEY)	.01
COL LIKE '%char'	1	1
COL LIKE '_char'	1	1
COL op ANY (non-corr. sub)	- - -	.83

TABLE 21.2 Continued

Predicate Type	Formula	Default FF
COL op ALL (non-corr. sub)	- - -	.16
COL IN (non-corr. sub)	FF(noncor. subquery)	.90
COL NOT IN (non-corr. sub)	1-FF(noncor. subquery)	.10
predicate1 AND predicate2	Multiply the filter factors of the two predicates, FF1?FF2	
predicate1 OR predicate2	Add filter factors and subtract the product, FF1+FF2-(FF1?FF2)	

For example, consider the following query:

```
SELECT   EMPNO, LASTNAME, SEX
FROM     DSN8810.EMP
WHERE    WORKDEPT = 'A00';
```

The column has an index called DSN8810.XEMP2. If this query were being optimized by DB2, the filter factor for the WORKDEPT predicate would be calculated to estimate the number of I/Os needed to satisfy this request.

Using the information in Table 21.2, you can see that the filter factor for this predicate is 1/FIRSTKEYCARDF. So, if the value of the FIRSTKEYCARDF column in the SYSIBM.SYSINDEXES DB2 Catalog table is 9, the filter factor for this query is 1/9, or .1111. In other words, DB2 assumes that approximately 11% of the rows from this table will satisfy this request.

You might be wondering how this information helps you. Well, with a bit of practical knowledge, you can begin to determine how your SQL statements will perform before executing them. If you remember nothing else about filter factors, remember this: *The lower the filter factor, the lower the cost and, in general, the more efficient your query will be.*

Therefore, you can easily see that as you further qualify a query with additional predicates, you make it more efficient because more data is filtered out and I/O requirements diminish.

Access Path Strategies

The optimizer can choose from a wealth of solutions when selecting the optimal access path for each SQL statement. These solutions, called *strategies,* range from the simple method of using a series of sequential reads to the complex strategy of using multiple indexes to combine multiple tables. This section describes the features and functionality of these strategies.

Scans

Of the many decisions that must be made by the optimizer, perhaps the most important decision is whether an index will be used to satisfy the query. To determine this, the optimizer must first discover whether an index exists. Remember that you can query any column of any table known to DB2. An index does not have to be defined before SQL can be written to access that column. Therefore, it is important that the optimizer provide the capability to access non-indexed data as efficiently as possible.

Basically, an index will be used unless no indexes exist for the table and columns being accessed, or the optimizer determines that the query can be executed more efficiently without using an index.* When an index is not used, the query is satisfied by sequentially reading the tablespace pages for the table being accessed.

Why would the optimizer determine that an index should not be used? Aren't indexes designed to make querying tables more efficient? The optimizer decides that an index should not be used for one of two reasons. The first reason is when the table being accessed has only a small number of rows. Using an index to query a small table can degrade performance because additional I/O is required. For example, consider a tablespace consisting of one page. Accessing this page without the index would require a single I/O. But if you use an index, at least one additional I/O is required to read the index page. Even more I/O may be required if index root pages, index non-leaf pages, and additional index leaf pages must be accessed.

The second reason for not using an index is that, for larger tables, the organization of the index could require additional I/O to satisfy the query. Factors affecting this are the full and first key cardinality of the index and the cluster ratio of the index.

When an index is not used to satisfy a query, the resulting access path is called a tablespace scan (see Figure 21.2). A tablespace scan performs page-by-page processing, reading every page of a tablespace (or table).

Following are the steps involved in a tablespace scan:

1. The RDS passes the request for a tablespace scan to the DM.

2. The DM asks the BM to read all the data pages of the accessed table, one by one. Tablespace scans usually invoke a fast type of bulk read known as *sequential prefetch*.

3. The BM determines whether the requested page is in the buffer and takes the appropriate action to retrieve the requested page and return it to the DM.

4. The DM scans the page and returns the selected columns to the RDS row by row. Predicates are applied by either the DM or the RDS, depending on whether the predicate is a Stage 1 or Stage 2 predicate.

5. The results are returned to the requesting agent.

The actual type of tablespace scan used by DB2 depends on the type of tablespace being scanned. A simple tablespace uses a tablespace scan as shown in Figure 21.2. Every page of the tablespace being scanned is read. This is true even if multiple tables are defined to the simple tablespace (which is one of the reasons to avoid multi-table simple tablespaces).

---

*Additionally, DB2 may forgo indexed access when type 2 indexes are required for a specific feature (such as uncommitted read isolation) but only type 1 indexes exist. This is true only for pre-V6 subsystems because type 1 indexes are no longer supported as of DB2 V6.

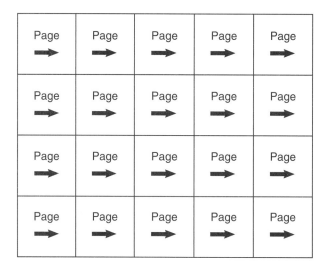

FIGURE 21.2   A tablespace scan.

When a segmented tablespace is scanned, a tablespace scan such as the one in Figure 21.3 is invoked. A segmented tablespace scan reads pages from only those segments used for the table being accessed. This could more appropriately be termed a *table scan*.

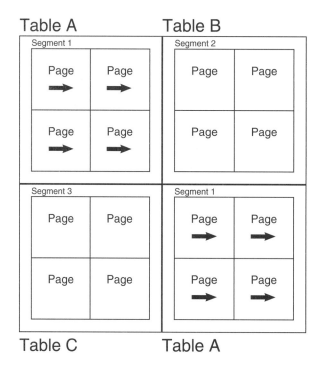

FIGURE 21.3   A segmented tablespace scan.

Partitioned tablespace scans differ from simple and segmented tablespace scans because whole partitions can be skipped. DB2 can limit the partitions scanned to only those partitions that contain data relevant to the query. To do so, however, the query must specify a predicate that matches columns in the partitioning index.

To understand how limited partition scans function, consider the following query in conjunction with Figure 21.4:

```
SELECT  COL1, COLx
FROM    T1
WHERE   PART_KEY BETWEEN "H" AND "J"
AND     PART_KEY = "T";
```

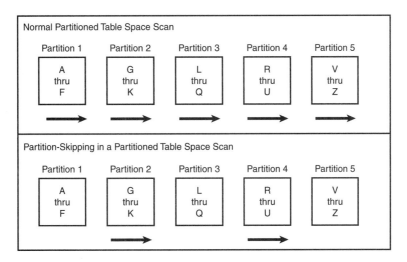

FIGURE 21.4   Partitioned tablespace scans.

Table T1 is partitioned on the PART_KEY column. Note that there are five partitions in this tablespace as depicted in Figure 21.4, but DB2 understands that only partitions 2 through 4 contain data that will satisfy this request. (Data values containing H through J are in partition 2; T is in partition 4.) Therefore, DB2 can avoid scanning the data contained in partitions 1 and 5. But DB2 can also avoid scanning partition 3 because it does not contain any data needed to satisfy the query. This is called partition skipping within a tablespace scan. If DB2 determines that partitions can be skipped during a scan, it will do so. Otherwise it will revert back to scanning all of the tablespace partitions.

Limited partition scans can be combined with matching index scans when appropriate. A limited partition scan can also be used for each table accessed in a join, as long as the access is sequential.

> **NOTE**
>
> When host variables or parameter markers are used in the first column of a multi-column partitioning key, DB2 will not limit the partitions scanned. In these circumstances, DB2 doesn't know the qualified partition range at bind time. By binding with the REOPT(VARS) parameter though, you can direct DB2 to redetermine the access path at run time each time the statement is run.
>
> **V8**   As of DB2 V8, REOPT(ALWAYS) can be used as a synonym for REOPT(VARS).

Sequential Prefetch

Before discussing the various types of indexed data access, a discussion of sequential prefetch is in order. *Sequential prefetch* is a read-ahead mechanism invoked to prefill DB2's buffers so that data is already in memory before it is requested. When sequential prefetch is requested, DB2 can be thought of as playing the role of a psychic, predicting that the extra pages being read will need to be accessed, because of the nature of the request.

The optimizer requests sequential prefetch when it determines that sequential processing is required. The sequential page processing of a tablespace scan is a good example of a process that can benefit from sequential prefetch. The optimizer requests sequential prefetch in one of three ways.

The first way is static. A static request is made when the optimizer deems the request to be sequential and causes the optimizer to choose sequential prefetch at bind time. The second way is when a dynamic request invokes sequential prefetch at execution time.

The third way in which sequential prefetch is requested is called sequential detection. *Sequential detection* dynamically invokes sequential prefetch during the middle of running a query. Sequential detection "turns on" sequential prefetch for static requests that were not thought to be sequential at bind time but resulted in sequential data access during execution.

Sequential detection uses groupings of pages based on the size of the buffer pool to determine whether sequential prefetch should be requested. The size of the buffer pool is called the sequential detection indicator and is determined using the Normal Processing column of Table 21.3. The values in Table 21.3 apply to buffer pools with a 4KB page size (BP0 through BP49). Call the sequential detection indicator D. Sequential detection will request prefetch when $((D/4)+1)$ out of $(D/2)$ pages are accessed sequentially within a grouping of D pages.

TABLE 21.3   Sequential Prefetch and Detection Values for 4KB Page Bufferpools

Bufferpool Size	Number of Pages Read (Normal Processing)	Number of Pages Read (Utility Processing)
0-223	8	16
224-999	16	32
1000+	32	64

For example, in an environment having 800 buffers, the sequential detection indicator would be 16. If 4 out of 8 pages accessed are sequential within a 16-page grouping, sequential detection invokes prefetch.

The sequential prefetch numbers are different for larger page sizes. DB2 will prefetch fewer pages because the buffer pools are larger (a 32KB pages is 8 times larger than a 4K page). Tables 21.5 through 21.7 shows the number of pages read by sequential prefetch for 8KB, 16KB, and 32KB page buffer pools. For utility processing, the number of pages read are double the amount specified in Tables 21.4, 21.5, and 21.6.

TABLE 21.4   Sequential Prefetch Values for 8KB Page Bufferpools

Bufferpool Size	Number of Pages Read
0-112	4
112-499	8
500+	16

TABLE 21.5   Sequential Prefetch Values for 16KB Page Bufferpools

Bufferpool Size	Number of Pages Read
0-56	2
57-249	4
250+	8

TABLE 21.6   Sequential Prefetch Values for 32KB Page Bufferpools

Bufferpool Size	Number of Pages Read
0-16	0 (prefetch disabled)
17-99	2
100+	4

Figure 21.5 shows the potential effect of sequential prefetch on a request. A normal DB2 I/O reads one page of data at a time. By contrast, a sequential prefetch I/O can read up to 32 pages at a time, which can have a dramatic effect on performance because you skip the seek and rotational delay time. Everything else being constant, sequential prefetch I/O can enhance efficiency significantly over standard I/O.

The number of pages that can be requested in a single I/O by sequential prefetch depends on the number of pages allocated to the DB2 buffer pool, as shown in Tables 21.4 through 21.7.

As you plan your environment for the optimal use of sequential prefetch, keep these final notes in mind. When sequential prefetch is requested by the optimizer, it is invoked immediately after the first single page I/O is performed. After this first I/O, DB2 kicks off two sequential prefetch I/Os—one for the pages that must be processed almost immediately and another for the second set of prefetched pages. This is done to reduce I/O wait time. Thereafter, each successive prefetch I/O is requested before all the currently prefetched pages have been processed. This scenario is shown in Figure 21.6.

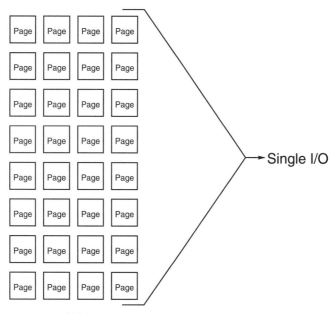

Normal I/O occurs one page at a time.

With sequential prefetch, up to 32 pages
can be retrieved with a single I/O.

FIGURE 21.5   Sequential prefetch.

Sequential prefetch is not the sole dominion of tablespace scans. Any process that relies on the sequential access of data pages (either index pages or tablespace pages) can benefit from sequential prefetch. Sequential prefetch can be requested by DB2 under any of the following circumstances:

- A tablespace scan of more than one page

- An index scan in which the data is clustered and DB2 determines that eight or more pages must be accessed

- An index-only scan in which DB2 estimates that eight or more leaf pages must be accessed

Indexed Access

Generally, the fastest way to access DB2 data is with an index. Indexes are structured in such a way as to increase the efficiency of finding a particular piece of data. However, the manner in which DB2 uses an index varies from statement to statement. DB2 uses many different internal algorithms to traverse an index structure. These algorithms are designed to elicit optimum performance in a wide variety of data access scenarios.

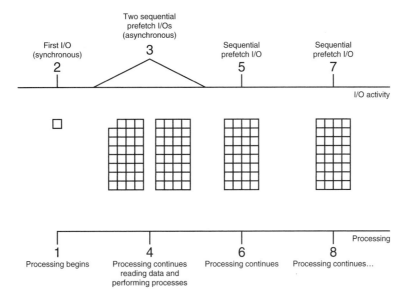

FIGURE 21.6   Sequential prefetch processing.

Before DB2 will use an index to satisfy a data access request, the following criteria must be met:

- At least one of the predicates for the SQL statement must be indexable. Refer to Chapter 2, "Data Manipulation Guidelines," for a list of indexable predicates.

- One of the columns (in any indexable predicate) must exist as a column in an available index.

This is all that is required for DB2 to consider indexed access as a possible solution for a given access path. As you progress further into the types of indexed access, you will see that more specific criteria might be required before certain types of indexed access are permitted.

The first, and most simple, type of indexed access is the *direct index lookup,* shown in Figure 21.7. The arrows on this diagram outline the processing flow through the highlighted pages. The following sequence of steps is performed during a direct index lookup:

1. The value requested in the predicate is compared to the values in the root page of the index.

2. If intermediate non-leaf pages exist, the appropriate non-leaf page is read, and the value is compared to determine which leaf page to access.

3. The appropriate leaf page is read, and the RIDs of the qualifying rows are determined.

4. Based on the index entries, DB2 reads the appropriate data pages.

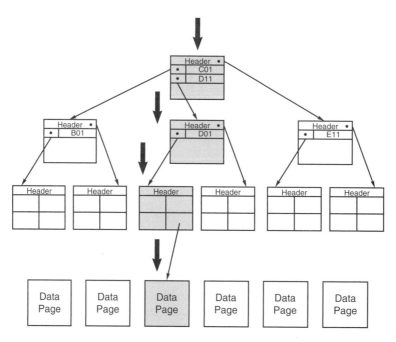

FIGURE 21.7   Direct index lookup.

For DB2 to perform a direct index lookup, values must be provided for each column in the
index. For example, consider an index on one of the sample tables, DSN8810.XPROJAC1 on
DSN8810.PROJACT. This index consists of three columns: PROJNO, ACTNO, and ACSTDATE. All
three columns must appear in the SQL statement for a direct index lookup to occur. For
example, consider the following:

```
SELECT   ACSTAFF, ACENDATE
FROM     DSN8810.PROJACT
WHERE    PROJNO = '000100'
AND      ACTNO = 1
AND      ACSTDATE = '2001-12-31';
```

If only one or two of these columns were specified as predicates, a direct index lookup
could not occur because DB2 would not have a value for each column and could not
match the full index key. Instead, an index scan could be chosen. There are two basic
types of index scans: *matching index scans* and *non-matching index scans*. A matching index
scan is sometimes called *absolute positioning*; a non-matching index scan is sometimes
called *relative positioning*.

Remember the previous discussion of tablespace scans? Index scans are similar. When you invoke an index scan, the leaf pages of the index being used to facilitate access are read sequentially. Let's examine these two types of index scans more closely.

A matching index scan begins at the root page of an index and works down to a leaf page in much the same manner as a direct index lookup does. However, because the complete key of the index is unavailable, DB2 must scan the leaf pages using the values that it does have, until all matching values have been retrieved. This is shown in Figure 21.8.

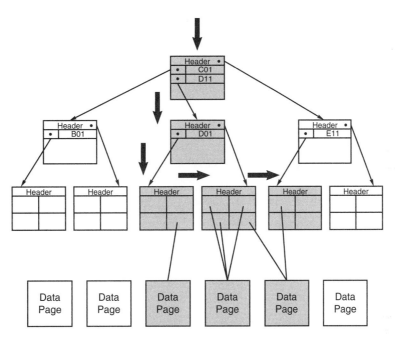

FIGURE 21.8   A matching index scan.

To clarify, consider again a query of the DSN8810.PROJACT table. This time, the query is recoded without the predicate for the ACSTDATE column:

```
SELECT    ACSTAFF, ACENDATE
FROM      DSN8810.PROJACT
WHERE     PROJNO = '000100'
AND       ACTNO = 1;
```

The matching index scan locates the first leaf page with the appropriate value for PROJNO and ACTNO by traversing the index starting at the root. However, there can be multiple index entries with this combination of values and different ACSTDATE values. Therefore, leaf pages are sequentially scanned until no more valid PROJNO, ACTNO, and varying ACSTDATE combinations are encountered.

For a matching index scan to be requested, you must specify the high order column in the index key, which is PROJNO in the preceding example. This provides a starting point for DB2 to traverse the index structure from the root page to the appropriate leaf page. What would happen, though, if you did not specify this high order column? Suppose that you alter the sample query such that a predicate for PROJNO is not specified:

```
SELECT   ACSTAFF, ACENDATE
FROM     DSN8810.PROJACT
WHERE    ACTNO = 1
AND      ACSTDATE = '2001-12-31';
```

In this instance, a non-matching index scan can be chosen. When a starting point cannot be determined because the first column in the key is unavailable, DB2 cannot use the index tree structure, but it can use the index leaf pages, as shown in Figure 21.9. A non-matching index scan begins with the first leaf page in the index and sequentially scans subsequent leaf pages, applying the available predicates.

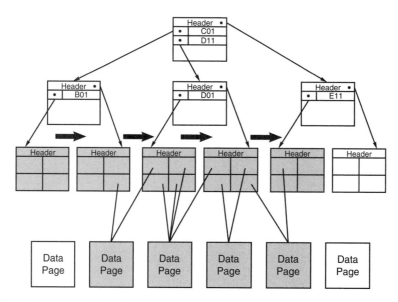

FIGURE 21.9   A non-matching index scan.

DB2 uses a non-matching index scan instead of a tablespace scan for many reasons. A non-matching index scan can be more efficient than a tablespace scan, especially if the data pages that must be accessed are in clustered order. As discussed in Chapter 2, you can create clustering indexes that dictate the order in which DB2 should attempt to store data. When data is clustered by key columns, I/O can be reduced. Of course, a non-matching index scan be done on a non-clustered index, also.

Compare the clustered index access shown in Figure 21.10 with the non-clustered index access in Figure 21.11. Clustered index access, as it proceeds from leaf page to leaf page, never requests a read for the same data page twice. It is evident from the figure that the same cannot be said for non-clustered index access.

Furthermore, scanning an index can be more efficient than scanning the table because index rows usually are smaller than table rows so more data can be stored on an index page than a data page.

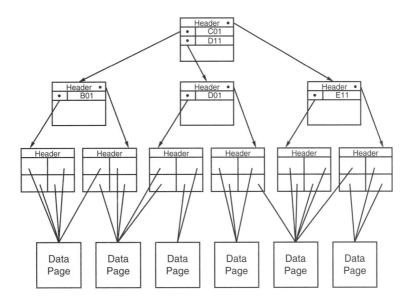

FIGURE 21.10 Clustered index access.

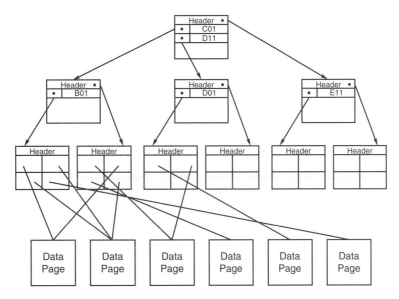

FIGURE 21.11 Non-clustered index access.

Another time when a non-matching index might be chosen is to maintain data in a particular order to satisfy an ORDER BY or GROUP BY.

Another indexed access technique that DB2 can deploy is *index screening*. With index screening, a matching index scan is done on the leading columns of a composite index and then additional predicates are applied to the composite index. This technique is useful if columns of a multi-column index are not specified in the query. Consider our sample query revised once more

```
SELECT   ACSTAFF, ACENDATE
FROM     DSN8810.PROJACT
WHERE    ACTNO = 1
AND      ACSTDATE > '2001-12-31';
```

Now, assume a composite index exists on the following—ACTNO, one or more other columns, and then ACSTDATE. The index can be screened by applying a matching index scan on ACTNO, and then a nonmatching scan for the specified ACSTDATE values greater than '2001-12-31'—but only for those rows that matched the ACTNO = 1 predicate.

DB2 can avoid reading data pages completely if all the required data exists in the index. This feature is known as *index-only access* and is pictured in Figure 21.12.

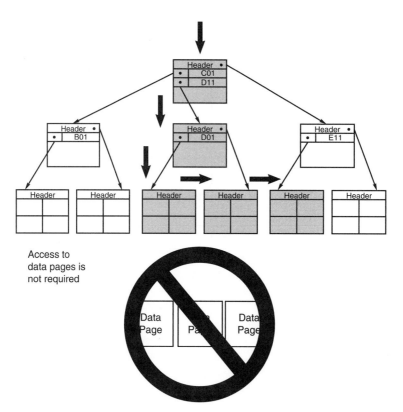

FIGURE 21.12   Index-only access.

Consider again the sample query. This time, it is recoded so that the only columns that must be accessed are ACTNO and ACSTDATE for predicate evaluation and PROJNO, which is returned in the select list:

```
SELECT    PROJNO
FROM      DSN8810.PROJACT
WHERE     ACTNO = 1
AND       ACSTDATE = '2001-12-31';
```

DB2 can satisfy this query by simply scanning the leaf pages of the index. It never accesses the tablespace data pages. A non-matching index-only scan is usually much faster than a tablespace scan because index entries are generally smaller than the table rows that they point to.

> **CAUTION**
>
> **V8**
>
> Be careful with indexes having VARCHAR columns in the key. Prior to DB2 V8 there was no such thing as a non-padded index, so the data was expanded to its maximum length in the index. This eliminated the possibility of index-only access for such indexes because DB2 had to access the table data to get the length of the variable length data. Of course, DB2 V8 supports variable length keys in non-padded indexes, so this problem is not as troublesome any longer.

DB2 can use three other methods to provide indexed access for optimized SQL. The first is *list prefetch*. As mentioned, accessing non-clustered data with an index can be inefficient. However, if DB2 determines beforehand that the degree of clustering is such that a high number of additional page I/Os might be requested, list prefetch can be requested to sort the access requests before requesting the data page I/Os (see Figure 21.13).

List prefetch performs the following tasks:

1. The first leaf page is located using a matching index scan.

2. A list of RIDs for the matching index entries is acquired from the leaf pages as they are scanned.

3. These RIDs can be sorted into sequence by data page number to reduce the number of I/O requests. If the index is at least 80% clustered, the sort is bypassed.

4. Using the ordered RID list, data pages are accessed to satisfy the request.

When the RIDs are sorted by list prefetch, the order in which they were retrieved from the index is changed. Therefore, an additional sort of the results might be required if an ORDER BY clause was specified. If an ORDER BY clause was not specified, the use of list prefetch will probably cause the results to be unordered, even though an index was used.

The term *skip sequential prefetch* is used to categorize the type of access that list prefetch performs on data pages. When the sorted RID list is used to retrieve data pages, list prefetch effectively performs a type of sequential prefetch, whereby only the needed data pages are accessed. Those that are not needed are skipped.

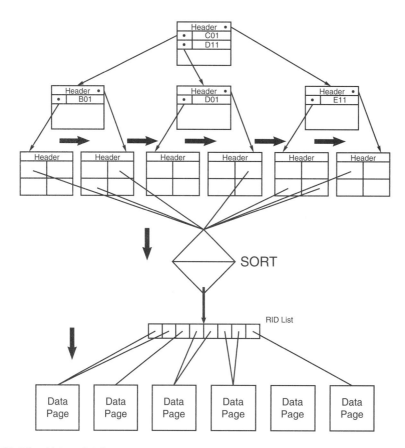

FIGURE 21.13   List prefetch.

Multi-index access is another type of indexed access used by DB2. The idea behind multi-index access is to use more than one index for a single access path. For example, consider the DSN8810.EMP table, which has two indexes: DSN8810.XEMP1 on column EMPNO and DSN8810.XEMP2 on column WORKDEPT.

Here is a query of three employees who work in a specific department:

```
SELECT   LASTNAME, FIRSTNME, MIDINIT
FROM     DSN8810.EMP
WHERE    EMPNO IN ('000100', '000110', '000120')
AND      WORKDEPT = 'A00';
```

This query specifies predicates for two columns that appear in two separate indexes. Doesn't it stand to reason that it might be more efficient to use both indexes than to estimate which of the two indexes will provide more efficient access? This is the essence of multi-index access.

There are two types of multi-index access, depending on whether the predicates are tied together using AND or OR. DB2 invokes the following sequence of tasks when multi-index access is requested:

1. The first leaf page for the first indexed access is located using a matching index scan.

2. A list of RIDs for the matching index entries is acquired from the leaf pages as they are scanned.

3. These RIDs are sorted into sequence by data page number to reduce the number of I/O requests.

4. Steps 1, 2, and 3 are repeated for each index used.

5. If the SQL statement being processed concatenated its predicates using the AND connector (such as in the sample query), the RID lists are intersected as shown in Figure 21.14. RID intersection is the process of combining multiple RID lists by keeping only the RIDs that exist in both RID lists.

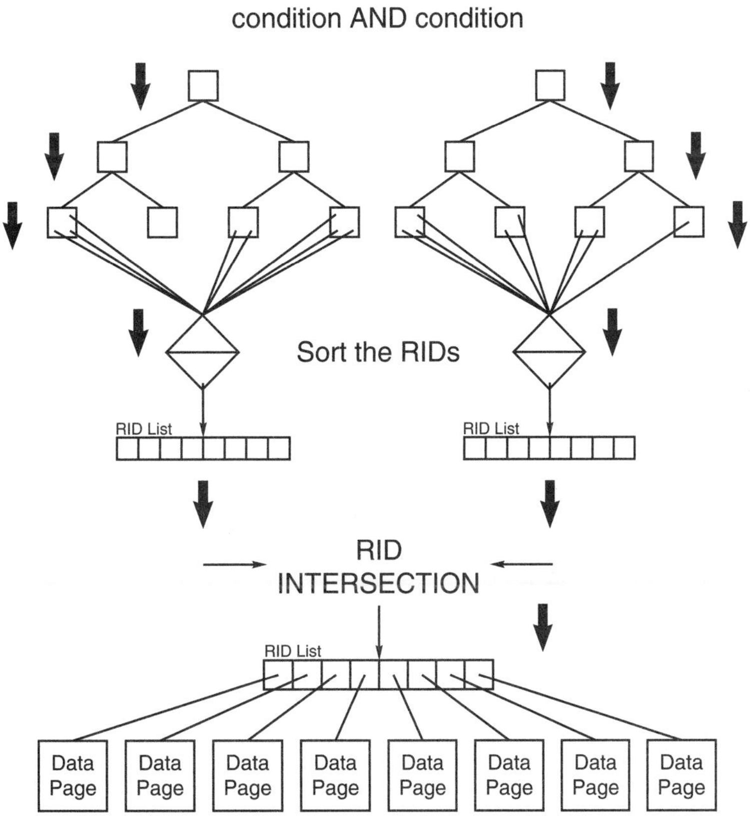

FIGURE 21.14   Multi-index access (AND).

6. If the SQL statement being processed concatenated its predicates using the OR connector (such as the following query), the RID lists are combined using a UNION, as shown in Figure 21.15.

```
SELECT   LASTNAME, FIRSTNME, MIDINIT
FROM     DSN8810.EMP
WHERE    EMPNO IN ('000100', '000110', '000120')
OR       WORKDEPT = 'A00';
```

RID UNION is the process of combining multiple RID lists by appending all the RIDs into a single list and eliminating duplicates.

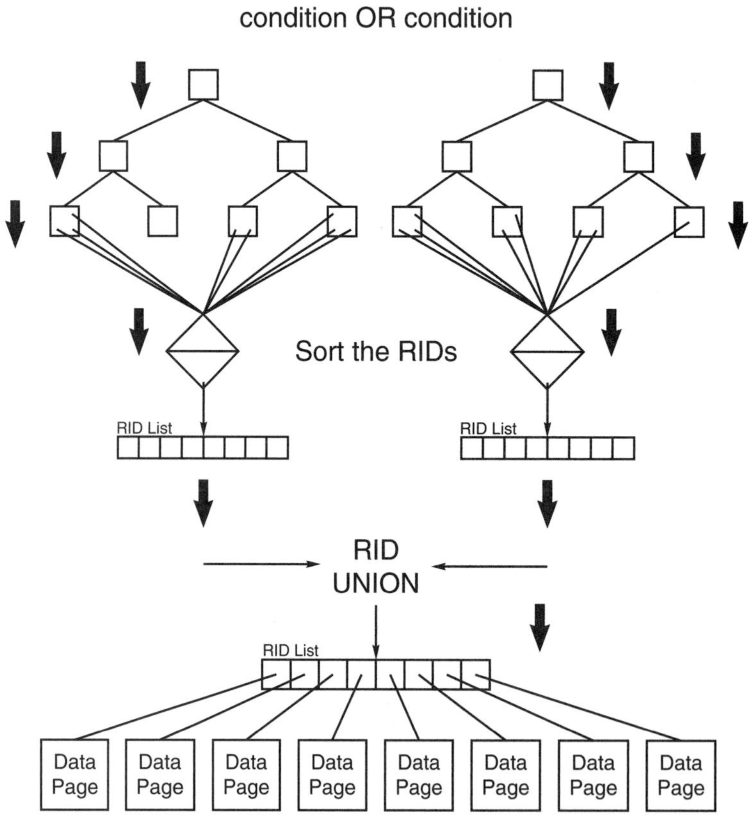

FIGURE 21.15   Multi-index access (OR).

7. Using the final, combined RID list, data pages are accessed to satisfy the request. As with list prefetch, skip sequential prefetch is used to access these pages.

A final indexed access technique is *index lookaside*. Although index lookaside is technically not an access path but a technique employed by DB2, it is still appropriate to discuss it in the context of indexed access. Index lookaside optimizes the manner in which index pages can be accessed (see Figure 21.16). Of course, you have no control over whether DB2 uses index lookaside or not—it is a technique used by DB2 at the sole discretion of DB2.

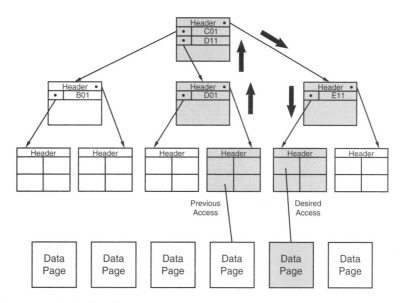

FIGURE 21.16   Index lookaside.

Normally, DB2 traverses the b-tree structure of the index to locate an index entry. This can involve significant overhead as DB2 checks the root and intermediate non-leaf index pages. When using index lookaside, the path length required to find a particular leaf page can be reduced. The index lookaside technique begins only after an initial index access has taken place. Using index lookaside, DB2 checks for the RID of the desired row first on the current leaf page and next on the immediately higher non-leaf page. If unsuccessful, DB2 then reverts to a standard index lookup.

By checking the current leaf page and the immediately higher non-leaf page, DB2 increases its chances of locating the desired RID sooner and adds only a minimal amount of overhead (because the ranges of values covered by the leaf and non-leaf pages are stored in cache memory upon first execution of the SELECT).

Join Methods

When more than one DB2 table is referenced in the FROM clause of a single SQL SELECT statement, a request is being made to join tables. Based on the join criteria, a series of instructions must be carried out to combine the data from the tables. The optimizer has a series of methods to enable DB2 to join tables.

Multi-table queries are broken down into several access paths. The DB2 optimizer selects two of the tables and creates an optimized access path for accomplishing that join. When that join is satisfied, the results are joined to another table. This process continues until all specified tables have been joined.

When joining tables, the access path defines how each single table will be accessed and also how it will be joined with the next table. Thus, each access path chooses not only an access path strategy (for example, a tablespace scan versus indexed access) but also a join algorithm. The join algorithm, or *join method*, defines the basic procedure for combining the tables. DB2 has three basic methods for joining tables:

- Nested loop join

- Merge scan join

- Hybrid join

Each method operates differently from the others but achieves the same basic results—accessing data from multiple tables. However, the choice of join method has an important effect on the performance of the join. Each join method used by DB2 is engineered such that, given a set of statistics, optimum performance can be achieved. Therefore, you should understand the different join methods and the factors that cause them to be chosen.

How do these join methods operate? A basic series of steps is common to each join method. In general, the first decision to be made is which table should be processed first. This table is referred to as the *outer table*. After this decision is made, a series of operations are performed on the outer table to prepare it for joining. Rows from that table are then combined to the second table, called the *inner table*. A series of operations are also performed on the inner table either before the join occurs, as the join occurs, or both. This general join procedure is depicted in Figure 21.17.

Although all joins are composed of similar steps, each of DB2's three join methods is strikingly dissimilar when you get beyond the generalities. The optimizer understands the advantages and disadvantages of each method and how the use of that method can affect performance. Based on the current statistics in the DB2 Catalog, the optimizer understands also which tables are best accessed as the inner table versus the outer table.

Nested Loop Join

The most common type of join method is the *nested loop join*, which is shown in Figure 21.18. A qualifying row is identified in the outer table, and then the inner table is scanned searching for a match. (A *qualifying row* is one in which the local predicates for columns in the table match.) When the inner table scan is complete, another qualifying row in the outer table is identified. The inner table is scanned for a match again, and so on. The repeated scanning of the inner table is usually accomplished with an index so as not to incur undue I/O costs. Filtering the outer table for qualifying rows also is likely to be accomplished using an index.

Nested loop join is a viable access path when the whole answer set is not required.

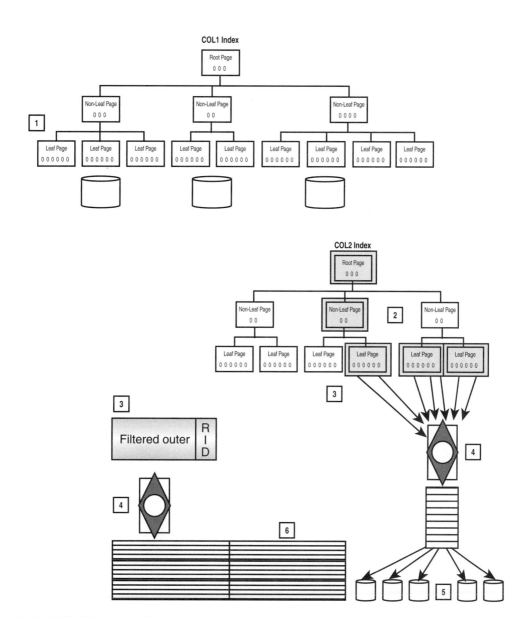

FIGURE 21.17 Generalized join process.

Merge Scan Join

The second type of join method that can be used by DB2 is the *merge scan join*. In a merge scan join, the tables to be joined are ordered by the keys. This ordering can be the result of either a sort or indexed access (see Figure 21.19). After ensuring that both the outer and inner tables are properly sequenced, each table is read sequentially, and the join columns are matched. Neither table is read more than once during a merge scan join.

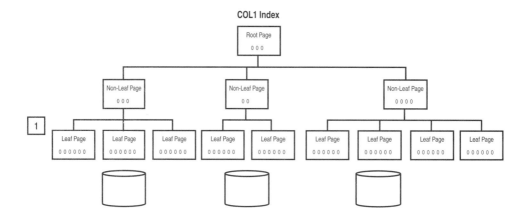

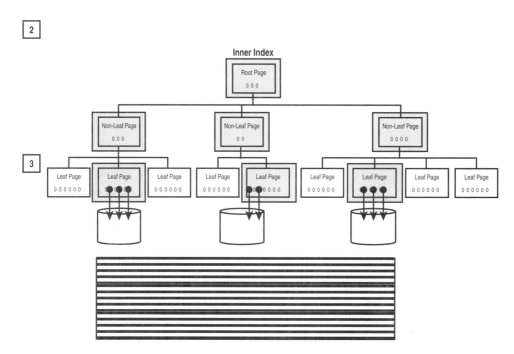

FIGURE 21.18 Nested loop join.
(Diagram provided courtesy of Sheryl M. Larsen, Inc.)

Hybrid Join

The third type of join is the hybrid join. In practice, relatively few joins turn out to be optimal as hybrid joins. The *hybrid join* can be thought of as a mixture of the other join methods coupled with list prefetch.

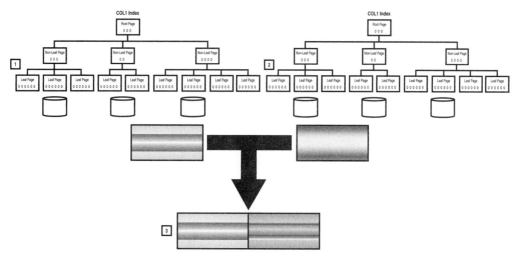

1. Filter outer table (sort if needed)
2. Filter inner table (sort if needed)
3 Join
•   If sorts are not needed, no work files are required

FIGURE 21.19   Merge scan join.
(Diagram provided courtesy of Sheryl M. Larsen, Inc.)

Figure 21.20 shows the processing flow used by the hybrid join.

The hybrid join works as follows:

1. Using either indexed access or a sort, qualifying outer table rows are accessed in order by the join columns.

2. As the outer table rows are accessed in sequence, they are compared to an appropriate index on the inner table. In a hybrid join, there must be an index on the join columns of the inner table.

3. The index RIDs from the qualifying inner table are combined with the required columns of the outer table, forming an intermediate table. This intermediate table consists of the selected outer table columns and the RIDs of the matching rows from the index on the inner table. The RIDs are also placed in the RID pool, forming a RID list.

4. Both the RID list and the intermediate table are sorted. If the index on the inner table is a clustering index, DB2 can skip this sort.

5. The RID list in the intermediate table is resolved into a results table using list prefetch. The appropriate inner table rows are returned by following the RIDs.

6. Finally, if an ORDER BY is specified in the join SQL, a sort is usually required to order the final results table.

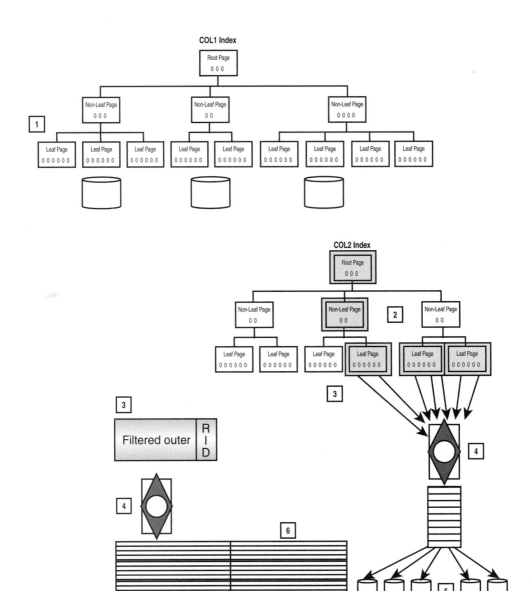

FIGURE 21.20   Hybrid join.
(Diagram provided courtesy of Sheryl M. Larsen, Inc.)

The hybrid join method can provide modest performance gains for some applications that process medium-sized table joins. However, most shops have few access paths that use this type of join.

> **NOTE**
>
> Hybrid joins apply to inner joins only. Either of the other two join methods can be used for both inner and outer joins.

Star Join

A final type of join provided by DB2 is the *star join*. The star join is a special join technique used most often by analytical and data warehousing queries where the tables being joined use a star schema. A star schema is when one large fact table is related to many separate and smaller dimension tables. This is referred to as a star schema because a data model diagram of the tables resembles a star. More details on star schema are provided in Chapter 45, "Data Warehousing with DB2."

Unlike the other DB2 join methods where only two tables are joined in each step, the star join can involve three or more tables per step. The fact table is always the last table in the star join step. For a star join to operate effectively there must be a well-defined, multi-column index on the fact table for each of the dimension table keys involved in the join.

Figure 21.21 depicts the basic flow of a star join. The steps involved in the star join are as follows:

1. Filter and sort (if needed) data from the dimension tables participating in the star join.

2. Create a sparse index consisting of just the required data from each of the dimension tables.

3. Emulate building a Cartesian product using entries from the smaller dimension tables pointed to by the sparse index.

4. Probe the fact table index once for every calculated combination of dimension table join values.

5. Join the qualify fact table values with the qualifying dimension table values and place the result.

6. Use sophisticated feedback loop technology to omit unnecessary fact table index probes.

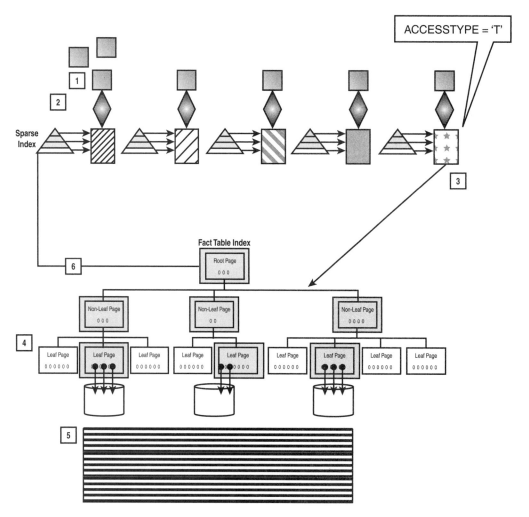

FIGURE 21.21 Merge scan join.
(Diagram provided courtesy of Sheryl M. Larsen, Inc.)

The following conditions must be met before DB2 can use the star join technique:

- The subsystem must have been enabled for star join processing. This means that the value of the STARJOIN DSNZPARM must not be set to DISABLE (which is the default).

- The number of tables in the query block must be at least 10. However, this value can be changed using the SJTABLES DSNZPARM parameter.

- All join predicates must be between the fact table and the dimension tables, or within tables of the same dimension.

- All join predicates between the fact and dimension tables must be equijoins.

- The join predicates between the fact and dimension tables cannot use OR.

21

- A local predicate on a dimension table cannot be combined using OR with a local predicate of another dimension table.

- A single fact table column cannot be joined to columns of different dimension tables.

- No correlated subqueries can be coded across dimensions.

- The data type and length of both sides of a join predicate must be the same between the fact and dimension tables.

- A dimension table cannot be a table function.

- No outer join operations can exist between the fact and dimension tables.

If all of the criteria are met, the query qualifies for star join.

Join Method Comparison

You might be wondering which join method DB2 uses in a given circumstance. Although there is no foolproof method to determine which method will be used for every circumstance, there are some general guidelines:

- Merge scan joins are usually chosen when an appropriate index is unavailable on one of the tables. This involves sorting and can use a high amount of overhead.

- Nested loop joins are very effective when an index exists on the inner table, thereby reducing the overhead of the repeated table scan.

- The smaller of the two tables being joined is usually chosen as the outer table in a nested loop join. Actually, the size of the table is not as relevant as the amount of data that needs to be accessed. The fewer rows accessed from the outer table the more efficient the repeated inner table scan will be.

- The hybrid join can be chosen only if an index exists on the inner table.

- A star join is a viable solution when a very large table is joined to many other smaller tables.

- Query parallelism can be combined with any of the join methods, enabling joins to be processed in parallel. More information on parallelism follows in the next section of this chapter.

Many shops are biased toward the nested loop join, feeling that nested loop joins almost always outperform merge scan joins. However, the performance of the merge scan join has been significantly enhanced over the life of DB2. Merge scan joins are a viable, production-quality join method.

See Figure 21.22 for an estimate of the performance of the join methods as a function of the number of qualifying rows being joined.

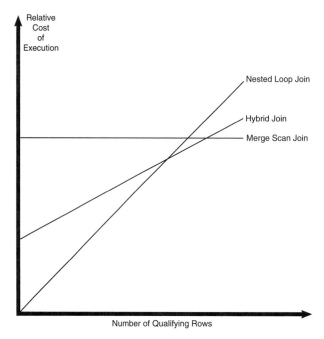

FIGURE 21.22   Relative join performance.

In general, the guidelines are as follows:

- The nested loop join is preferred in terms of execution cost when a small number of rows qualify for the join.

- The nested loop join is preferred whenever the OPTIMIZE FOR *n* ROWS clause is used, regardless of the number of qualifying rows.

- As the number of qualifying rows increases, the merge scan join becomes the preferred method.

- Finally, for a small number of cases with a medium number of rows, the hybrid join is the best performer.

These generalizations are purposefully vague. The exact number of qualifying rows for these cut-offs depends on many influencing factors. These factors include, but are not limited to, the following:

- Database design

- Type of CPU

- Type of DASD device

- Use of DASD cache

- Version of DB2

- Data Sharing environment

- Amount of memory and size of the buffer pools

- Buffer pool tuning specifications

- Availability of hardware (microcode) sorting

- Compression settings and hardware-assisted compression availability

- Uniqueness of the join columns

- Cluster ratio

Query Parallelism

Another technique that can be applied by the optimizer is *query parallelism*. When query parallelism is invoked, DB2 activates multiple parallel tasks to access the data. A separate subtask MVS SRB is initiated for each parallel task. Both partitioned and non-partitioned tablespaces can take advantage of query parallelism.

After determining the initial access path, the optimizer can be directed to perform an additional step to determine whether parallelism is appropriate. This access path formulated during this step is referred to as a *parallel plan*. The initial access path (pre-parallelism) is referred to as the *sequential plan*.

When processing in parallel, the elapsed time required to access the data can decrease because more activity occurs at the same time (see Figure 21.23). Although the serial task takes fewer resources, it requires more elapsed, sequential time to complete than breaking the request up into multiple components that can be processed in parallel.

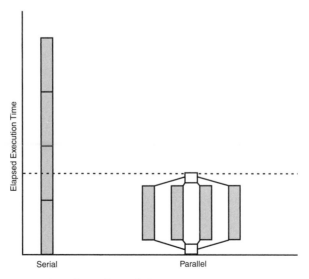

FIGURE 21.23   Parallel tasks reduce elapsed time.

The optimizer will consider parallelism when you set the DEGREE parameter to ANY. This is done at BIND time for static SQL with the DEGREE(ANY) specification and at execution time for dynamic SQL with the CURRENT DEGREE special register. The default for degree is set using the CDSSRDEF DSNZPARM parameter. Of course, as always, it is best not to rely on defaults.

There are three types of query parallelism that DB2 can perform:

- Query I/O parallelism
- Query CP parallelism
- Query Sysplex parallelism

Query I/O parallelism enables concurrent I/O streams to be initiated for a single query, as shown in Figure 21.24. This can significantly enhance the performance of I/O bound queries. Breaking the data access for the query into concurrent I/O streams executed in parallel should reduce the overall elapsed time for the query. With query I/O parallelism, DB2 is limited to operating on a single processor for each query.

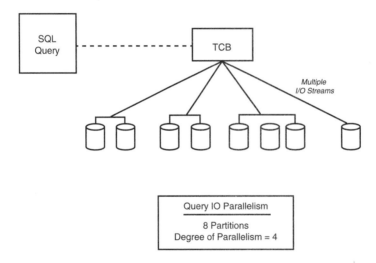

FIGURE 21.24   Query I/O parallelism.

Query CP parallelism enables multitasking of I/O streams and CPU processing within a query (see Figure 21.25). CP parallelism always uses I/O parallelism; it cannot be invoked separately. In query CP parallelism, a large query is decomposed into multiple smaller queries that can be executed concurrently with one another on multiple processors. Query CP parallelism should further reduce the elapsed time for a query.

Query Sysplex parallelism further enhances parallel operations by enabling a single query to be broken up and run across multiple DB2 members of a data-sharing group (see Figure 21.26). By allowing a single query to take advantage of the processing power of multiple DB2 subsystems, the overall elapsed time for a complex query can be significantly decreased.

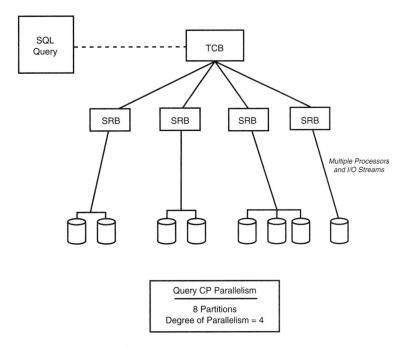

FIGURE 21.25   Query CP parallelism.

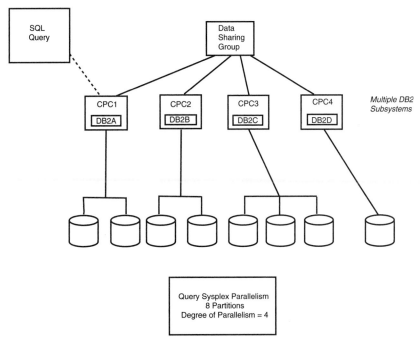

FIGURE 21.26   Query Sysplex parallelism.

Although not specifically depicted in the figure, multiple DB2 subsystems in a data-sharing group can access the same physical partition when participating in a query Sysplex parallelism operation.

When parallelism is invoked, an access path can be broken up into parallel groups. Each parallel group represents a series of concurrent operations with the same degree of parallelism. *Degree of parallelism* refers to the number of concurrent tasks used to satisfy the query.

Figures 21.24 thru 21.26 show a tablespace scan accessing a tablespace with a degree of parallelism of 4. The degree of parallelism is determined by the optimizer based upon the estimated CPU and I/O cost using partition-level statistics stored in the SYSIBM.SYSCOLSTATS table.

DB2 can downgrade the degree of parallelism at runtime if host variables indicate that only a portion of the data is to be accessed or if sufficient buffer pool space is not available.

It is particularly important to note that DB2 might choose not to issue one parallel task per partition for partitioned tablespace access. Determination of the degree of parallelism is based upon the information in the DB2 Catalog, the number of partitions for the accessed tablespaces, system resources, and the nature of the query. Each parallel task can access the following:

- An entire partition
- A portion of a single partition
- Multiple partitions
- Portions of multiple partitions

Likewise, DB2 can horizontally partition data in a non-partitioned tablespace to benefit from query parallelism. Horizontal data partitioning is the process of creating range predicates for non-partitioned tablespaces to mimic partitioning. For example, horizontal data partitioning is performed to enable query parallelism to be maintained when data in a partitioned tablespace is being joined to data in a non-partitioned tablespace. DB2 will not horizontally partition a non-partitioned tablespace for single table access.

By processing queries in parallel, overall elapsed time should decrease significantly, even if CPU time increases. This is usually a satisfactory trade-off, resulting in an overall performance gain because the same amount of work is accomplished using less clock time. Additionally, the CPU usage can be spread out across multiple CPUs within the same central processor complex (CPC) or even across CPCs with data sharing and query Sysplex parallelism.

The best types of queries for parallel processing are I/O bound queries. The types of queries that stand to benefit most from query I/O parallelism are those that perform the following functions:

- Access large amounts of data but return only a few rows.
- Use column functions (AVG, COUNT, MIN, MAX, SUM).
- Access long rows.

Query CP parallelism is most beneficial for scans of large partitioned tablespaces, and query Sysplex parallelism is most beneficial for complex queries that require a lot of processing power.

Query Sysplex Parallelism Terms and Issues

The DB2 subsystem that originates the SQL query is referred to as the *parallelism coordinator*. A member that assists in the processing of a parallel query is called a *parallelism assistant*. Data must be returned to the parallelism coordinator from each parallelism assistant. This is accomplished in one of two ways. When work files are required (for example, for sorting), the parallelism coordinator can access the data directly from the work files. Otherwise, the cross-system coupling facility is used to return the data to the parallelism coordinator.

Restrictions on Query Parallelism Usage

Note the following query parallelism restrictions:

- For all types of query parallelism, a limited partition scan can be invoked for queries against a single table only.

- Query Sysplex parallelism cannot be used with multiple index access, list prefetch, or queries using RR and RS isolation levels.

- For cursors defined using the WITH HOLD clause, the only type of parallelism that can be deployed is query I/O parallelism.

- Parallelism is for queries only; as such, only SELECT statements can benefit from parallelism. Furthermore, the SELECT statement must not be in an updateable or ambiguous cursor.

- The CURRENTDATA(NO) bind parameter must be specified for parallelism to be invoked.

- Parallelism cannot be used with multicolumn merge scan joins, type-N hybrid joins, materialized views, or materialized nested table expressions, and it cannot be used across UNION query blocks, when accessing a temporary table, or when EXISTS is specified.

> **NOTE**
>
> A type-N hybrid join retrieves the inner table RIDs using a clustered index (when SORTN_JOIN="N" in the PLAN_TABLE).

Parallel Joins

Parallel I/O processing during a join can occur for both the outer and the inner table of a join, for only the outer table, or for only the inner table.

For any join method, the outer table can be separated into logical partitions. As is true with any query executed in parallel, the optimizer determines the degree of parallelism, which can be adjusted at runtime. The logical partitions are processed using multiple parallel I/O streams applying the outer table predicates.

Subsequent inner table processing is based on the type of join being performed.

Nested Loop Join and Parallelism   To perform a nested loop join in parallel, the key ranges for the inner table logical partitions might need to be adjusted to match the logical partitioning of the outer table. This ensures that the number of logical partitions is equivalent for the outer and inner tables. Likewise, if the outer table was not processed using parallelism, the filtered outer table rows will need to be logically partitioned to match the inner table partitioning. In both cases, the logical partitioning is accomplished using the ESA sort assist. It is possible, however, that the outer table rows need not be sorted. In this case, the ESA sort assist will simply adjust the outer table key range to match the partitioning key range of the inner table.

Additionally, if the inner table is not partitioned, it can be horizontally partitioned to enable parallelism to continue. Alternatively, the inner table can be passed to the ESA sort assist, causing sort output to be partitioned to match outer table sort output.

Multiple parallel I/O streams are then used to join the filtered outer table rows to the inner table using the nested loop procedure described previously. The rows are returned in random order unless an additional sort is required for ORDER BY, GROUP BY, or DISTINCT.

Merge Scan Join and Parallelism   To enable parallel merge scan joining, outer table rows are passed into the ESA sort assist, causing the sort output to be repartitioned to match the logical partitioning of the inner table. The outer table access could have been either parallel or non-parallel. A single column merge scan join is then executed using multiple parallel I/O streams. (Query I/O parallelism cannot sort all of the join columns for merge scan join.)

If the inner table is not partitioned, it can be horizontally partitioned to enable parallelism to continue.

The rows are returned in random order unless an additional sort is required for ORDER BY, GROUP BY, or DISTINCT.

Hybrid Join and Parallelism   Hybrid join processing with query I/O parallelism also passes outer table rows to the ESA sort assist to logically repartition the output to match the logical partitioning of the inner table.

After the outer table results are repartitioned to match the logical partitioning of the inner table, hybrid join processing is executed using parallel I/O streams. The rows are returned in page number order unless an additional sort is required for ORDER BY, GROUP BY, or DISTINCT.

For parallelism to be invoked on the inner table, a highly clustered index must exist on the join columns. If such an index does not exist, the sort of the RID list and intermediate table will prevent parallel access to the inner table.

Parallel Join Notes
In any case, remember that during join processing, parallel access can occur as follows:

- On just the inner table
- On just the outer table

- On both the inner and outer tables

- On neither the inner nor outer tables

Other Operations Performed by the Optimizer

So far, you have learned about sequential access methods, indexed access methods, and join methods. The optimizer can perform other operations as well. For example, using a feature known as *predicate transitive closure,* the optimizer can make a performance decision to satisfy a query using a predicate that isn't even coded in the SQL statement being optimized. Consider the following SQL statements:

```
SELECT   D.DEPTNAME, E.LASTNAME
FROM     DSN8810.DEPT    D,
         DSN8810.EMP     E
WHERE    D.DEPTNO = E.WORKDEPT
AND      D.DEPTNO = 'A00'
```

and

```
SELECT   D.DEPTNAME, E.LASTNAME
FROM     DSN8810.DEPT    D,
         DSN8810.EMP     E
WHERE    D.DEPTNO = E.WORKDEPT
AND      E.WORKDEPT = 'A00'
```

These two statements are functionally equivalent. Because DEPTNO and WORKDEPT are always equal, you could specify either column in the second predicate. The query is usually more efficient, however, if the predicate is applied to the larger of the two tables (in this case, DSN8810.DEPT), thereby reducing the number of qualifying rows.

With predicate transitive closure, the programmer doesn't have to worry about this factor. DB2 considers the access path for both columns regardless of which is coded in the predicate. Therefore, DB2 can optimize a query based on predicates that are not even coded by the programmer.

Predicate transitive closure is not performed on every type of predicate. The IN and LIKE predicates are excluded from predicate transitive closure. The DB2 optimizer is currently not capable of determining when predicate transitive closure could be useful for the IN and LIKE predicates.

Subqueries

The DB2 optimizer also is responsible for generating optimized access paths for subqueries. Remember from Chapter 1 that there are two types of subqueries: non-correlated and correlated. The type of subquery determines the type of access path that DB2 chooses.

The access path for a non-correlated subquery always processes the subselect first. This type of processing is called *inside-out subquery access.* The table in the subselect is the inner table and is processed first. The table in the outer SELECT is the outer table and is processed last, hence the name inside-out processing. Consider the following subquery:

```
SELECT    LASTNAME
FROM      DSN8810.EMP
WHERE     WORKDEPT IN
          (SELECT  DEPTNO
            FROM    DSN8810.DEPT
            WHERE   DEPTNAME = 'OPERATIONS');
```

The access path formulated by the optimizer for a non-correlated subquery is shown in Figure 21.27.

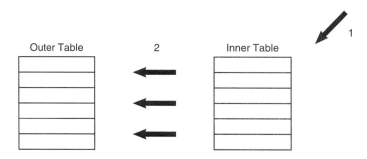

FIGURE 21.27   A non-correlated subquery.

The access path for a non-correlated subquery consists of the following steps:

1. Access the inner table, the one in the subselect (DSN8810.DEPT), using either a table-space scan or an index.

2. Sort the results and remove all duplicates.

3. Place the results in an intermediate table.

4. Access the outer table, comparing all qualifying rows to those in the intermediate results table for a match.

A correlated subquery, on the other hand, is performed using *outside-in-outside subquery access*. Consider the following correlated subquery:

```
SELECT    LASTNAME, SALARY
FROM      DSN8810.EMP  E
WHERE     EXISTS
          (SELECT  1
            FROM    DSN8810.EMPPROJACT  P
            WHERE   P.EMPNO = E.EMPNO);
```

The access path formulated by the optimizer for this correlated subquery consists of the following steps:

1. Access the outer table, which is the DSN8810.EMP table, using either a tablespace scan or indexed access.

2. For each qualifying outer table row, evaluate the subquery for the inner table.

3. Pass the results of the inner table subquery to the outer SELECT one row at a time. (In this case, the row is not returned because of the EXISTS predicate; instead, a flag is set to true or false.)

4. Evaluate the outer query predicate using the inner query results (row by row). This causes a round-robin type of access such as that shown in Figure 21.28.

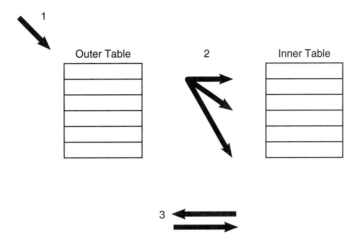

FIGURE 21.28   A correlated subquery.

Some further notes on subqueries follow. In general, the subselect portion of a correlated subquery is reevaluated for each qualifying outer row. However, if the subquery returns a single value, it can be saved in an intermediate work area such that it need not be reevaluated for every qualifying outer table row. An example of a correlated subquery where this is possible follows:

```
SELECT    LASTNAME
FROM      DSN8810.EMP   E1
WHERE     SALARY <
          (SELECT   AVG(SALARY)
           FROM      DSN8810.EMP   E2
           WHERE    E1.WORKDEPT = E2.WORKDEPT)
```

One average salary value is returned for each department. Thus, only a single inner table evaluation is required for each department, instead of a continual reevaluation for each qualifying outer table row.

Although subqueries are often the most obvious way to access data from multiple tables, they might not be the most efficient. A good rule of thumb is to recode subqueries as joins and perform tests to determine which formulation provides better performance results. The DB2 optimizer may choose more efficient access paths for joins than for subqueries. For example, the following query

```
SELECT    LASTNAME, SALARY
FROM      DSN8810.EMP
WHERE     WORKDEPT IN
```

```
(SELECT  DEPTNO
  FROM    DSN8810.DEPT
  WHERE   ADMRDEPT = 'A00')
```

can be recoded as a join:

```
SELECT   E.LASTNAME, E.SALARY
FROM     DSN8810.EMP      E,
         DSN8810.DEPT     D
WHERE    E.WORKDEPT = D.DEPTNO
AND      D.ADMRDEPT = 'A00'
```

One final type of operation that can be performed by the optimizer is the optimization of queries based on views. DB2 employs one of two methods when accessing data in views: view merge or view materialization.

View merge is the more efficient of the two methods. Using this technique, DB2 will merge the SQL in the view DDL with the SQL accessing the view. The merged SQL is then used to formulate an access path against the base tables in the views. This process is depicted in Figure 21.29.

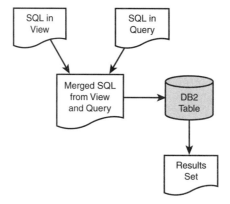

FIGURE 21.29   View merge.

View materialization is chosen when DB2 determines that it is not possible to merge the SQL in the view DDL with the SQL accessing the view. Instead of combining the two SQL statements into a single statement, view materialization creates an intermediate work table using the view SQL and then executes the SELECT from the view against the temporary table. Figure 21.30 outlines the view materialization process.

Consult Table 21.7 to determine the circumstances under which view materialization is used instead of view merge. If the SELECT from the view contains any of the components listed in the left column, combined with the view DDL containing any of the components listed along the top, analyze the column entry in the table. MAT represents view material-ization; MER represents view merge. If the view SELECT/view DDL combination does not appear in the table, view merge will be used. This table applies to table expressions as well as views.

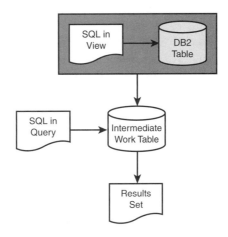

FIGURE 21.30   View materialization.

TABLE 21.7   When Does View Materialization Occur

SELECT **in View Definition**

SELECT from View	DISTINCT	GROUP BY	Column Function	Col. Func. w/DISTINCT	UNION	UNION ALL
Join	MAT	MAT	MAT	MAT	MAT	MER
DISTINCT	MAT	MER	MER	MAT	MAT	MER
GROUP BY	MAT	MAT	MAT	MAT	MAT	MER
Column Function	MAT	MAT	MAT	MAT	MAT	MAT
Column Function w/DISTINCT	MAT	MAT	MAT	MAT	MAT	MER
SELECT subset of View Cols	MAT	MER	MER	MER	MAT	MER

V7

> **NOTE**
>
> As of DB2 V7, UNION is permitted in views.

Access Path Strategy Compatibility

The optimizer combines access path strategies to form an efficient access path. However, not all the strategies are compatible, as shown in Table 21.8. As you can plainly see, the optimizer must follow a mountain of rules as it performs its optimization.

Here are some further notes on Table 21.8:

- Each access path is composed of at least one strategy and possibly many. A *Yes* in any block in the matrix indicates that the two strategies can be used together in a single access path; a *No* indicates incompatibility.

- For the join methods, the matrix entries apply to any one portion of the join (that is, the access path for either the inner table or the outer table).

- Sequential detection is always invoked in conjunction with sequential prefetch.

- Index-only access must be used in conjunction with one of the index access path strategies.

- For the hybrid join method, the inner table is always accessed with an index using a form of list prefetch; the outer table can be accessed using any access method deemed by the optimizer to be most efficient.

You have covered a large number of topics under the heading of the DB2 optimizer. This should drive home the point that the optimizer is a complex piece of software. Although we know quite a bit about what the optimizer can do, we know little about how exactly it decides what to do. This is not surprising. IBM has invested a great amount of time, money, and effort in DB2 and has also staked a large portion of its future on DB2's success. IBM wouldn't want to publish the internals of the optimizer, thus enabling competitors to copy its functionality.

The optimizer and the access paths it chooses are the most complex parts of DB2. Even though the subject is complex, an understanding of the optimizer is crucial for every user. This chapter fulfills this requirement. But where does the DB2 optimizer get the information to formulate efficient access paths? Where else—from the DB2 Catalog, the subject of the next chapter.

TABLE 21.8 Access Path Strategy Compatibility Matrix

	Simple Tablespace Scan	Partitioned Tablespace Scan	Segmented Tablespace Scan	Sequential Prefetch/ Detection	Query Parallelism	Direct Index Lookup	Matching Index Scan
Simple Tablespace Scan	--	No	No	Yes	Yes	No	No
Partitioned Tablespace Scan	No	--	Yes	Yes	Yes	No	No
Segmented Tablespace Scan	No	No	--	Yes	Yes	No	No
Sequential Prefetch/ Detection	Yes	Yes	Yes	--	Yes	No	Yes
Query Parallelism	No	Yes	No	Yes	--	No	Yes
Direct Index Lookup	No	No	No	No	No	--	Yes
Matching Index Scan	No	No	No	Yes	Yes	Yes	--
Nonmatching Index Scan	No	No	No	Yes	Yes	No	No
Index Lookaside	No	No	No	No	No	No	Yes
Multi-Index Access	No	No	No	Yes	No	No	Yes
Index-Only Access	No	No	No	Yes	Yes	Yes	Yes
List Prefetch	No	No	No	No	No	No	Yes
Nested Loop Join	Yes	Yes	Yes	Yes	Yes	Yes	Yes
Merge Scan Join	Yes	Yes	Yes	Yes	Yes	Yes	Yes
Hybrid Join	Yes	Yes	Yes	Yes	Yes	Yes	Yes

TABLE 21.8   Continued

	Non-Matching Index Scan	Index Lookaside	Multi-Index Access	Index-Only Access	List Prefetch	Nested Loop Join	Merge Scan	Hybrid Join
Simple Tablespace Scan	No	No	No	No	No	Yes	Yes	Yes
Partitioned Tablespace Scan	No	No	No	No	No	Yes	Yes	Yes
Segmented Tablespace Scan	No	No	No	No	No	Yes	Yes	Yes
Sequential Prefetch/Detection	Yes	No	No	Yes	No	Yes	Yes	Yes
Query Parallelism	Yes	No	No	Yes	No	Yes	Yes	Yes
Direct Index Lookup	No	No	No	Yes	No	Yes	Yes	Yes
Matching Index Scan	No	Yes	Yes	Yes	Yes	Yes	Yes	Yes
Nonmatching Index Scan	- -	Yes	No	Yes	No	Yes	Yes	Yes
Index Lookaside	Yes	- -	No	Yes	No	Yes	Yes	Yes
Multi-Index Access	No	No	- -	No	Yes	Yes	Yes	Yes
Index-Only Access	Yes	Yes	No	- -	No	Yes	Yes	Yes
List Prefetch	No	No	Yes	No	- -	Yes	Yes	Yes
Nested Loop Join	Yes	Yes	Yes	Yes	Yes	- -	- -	- -
Merge Scan Join	Yes	Yes	Yes	Yes	Yes	- -	- -	- -
Hybrid Join	Yes	Yes	Yes	Yes	Yes	- -	- -	- -

CHAPTER 22

The Table-Based Infrastructure of DB2

Appropriately enough for a relational database, DB2 has a set of tables that functions as a repository for all DB2 objects. These tables define the infrastructure of DB2, enabling simple detection of and access to DB2 objects. Two sets of tables store all the data related to DB2 objects: the DB2 Catalog and the DB2 Directory.

The DB2 Catalog

The entire DBMS relies on the system catalog, or the DB2 Catalog. If the DB2 optimizer is the heart and soul of DB2, the DB2 Catalog is its brain, or memory. The knowledge base of every object known to DB2 is stored in the DB2 Catalog.

What Is the DB2 Catalog?

The tables in the DB2 Catalog collectively describe the objects and resources available to DB2. You can think of the DB2 Catalog as a metadata repository for your DB2 databases. The DB2 Catalog is contained in a single database named DSNDB06. Consult Table 22.1 for a short description of each table in the DB2 Catalog. Tables new to DB2 V7 and V8 are indicated with the version number in parentheses following the table name.

TABLE 22.1   Tables in the DB2 Catalog

Table	Contents
IPLIST (V8)	Associates multiple IP addresses to a given LOCATION
IPNAMES	Contains the LUs associated with other systems accessible to the local DB2 subsystem
LOCATIONS	Contains distributed location information for every accessible remote server
LULIST	Contains the list of LUNAMEs for a given distributed location (when multiple LUNAMEs are associated with a single location)
LUMODES	Information on distributed conversation limits
LUNAMES	Contains information for every SNA client or server that communicates with the DB2 subsystem
MODESELECT	Information assigning mode names to conversations supporting outgoing SQL requests
SYSAUXRELS	Information on the auxiliary tables required for LOB columns
SYSCHECKDEP	Column references for CHECK constraints
SYSCHECKS	CHECK constraint specifications
SYSCHECKS2 (V7)	Information about CHECK constraints on DB2 Catalog tables created for V7 or later
SYSCOLAUTH	The UPDATE privileges held by DB2 users on table or view columns
SYSCOLDIST	Cardinality, frequent value, and non-padded frequent value distribution statistics for the first key column of an index key
SYSCOLDIST_HIST (V7)	Column distribution statistics history
SYSCOLDISTSTATS	The non-uniform distribution statistics for the ten most frequently occurring values for the first key column in a partitioned index
SYSCOLSTATS	The partition statistics for selected columns
SYSCOLUMNS	Information about every column of every DB2 table and view
SYSCOLUMNS_HIST (V7)	Historical column statistics
SYSCONSTDEP	Information regarding columns that are dependent on CHECK constraints and user-defined defaults
SYSCOPY	Information on the execution of DB2 utilities required by DB2 recovery
SYSDATABASE	Information about every DB2 database
SYSDATATYPES	Information about the user-defined distinct types defined to the DB2 subsystem
SYSDBAUTH	Database privileges held by DB2 users
SYSDBRM	DBRM information only for DBRMs bound into DB2 plans
SYSDUMMY1	Contains no information; this table is for use in SQL statements requiring a table reference without regard to data content
SYSFIELDS	Information on field procedures implemented for DB2 tables
SYSFOREIGNKEYS	Information about all columns participating in foreign keys
SYSINDEXES	Information about every DB2 index
SYSINDEXES_HIST (V7)	Historical index statistics
SYSINDEXPART	Information about the physical structure and storage of every DB2 index
SYSINDEXPART_HIST (V7)	Historical index partition statistics
SYSINDEXSTATS	Partitioned index statistics by partition

TABLE 22.1   Continued

Table	Contents
SYSINDEXSTATS_HIST (V7)	Historical partitioned index statistics by partition
SYSJARCONTENTS (V7)	Java class source for installed JAR
SYSJARDATA (V7)	Auxiliary table for the BLOB data from SYSJAROBJECTS
SYSJAROBJECTS (V7)	The contents of the installed JAR
SYSJARCLASS_SOURCE (V7)	Auxiliary table for the CLOB data from SYSJARCONTENTS
SYSKEYCOLUSE (V7)	Columns that participate in unique constraints (primary key or unique key) from the SYSTABCONST table
SYSKEYS	Information about every column of every DB2 index
SYSLINKS	Information about the links between DB2 Catalog tables
SYSLOBSTATS	Statistical information for LOB table spaces
SYSLOBSTATS_HIST (V7)	Historical LOB statistics
SYSPACKAGE	Information about every package known to DB2
SYSPACKAUTH	Package privileges held by DB2 users
SYSPACKDEP	A cross-reference of DB2 objects required for DB2 packages
SYSPACKLIST	The package list for plans bound specifying packages
SYSPACKSTMT	All SQL statements contained in each DB2 package
SYSPARMS	Parameters for defined routines
SYSPKSYSTEM	The systems (such as CICS, IMS, or batch) enabled for DB2 packages
SYSPLAN	Information about every plan known to DB2SYSPLANSYSPLANAUTH Plan privileges held by DB2 users
SYSPLANDEP	A cross-reference of DB2 objects required by DB2 plans
SYSPLSYSTEM	The systems (such as CICS, IMS, or batch) enabled for DB2 plans
SYSPROCEDURES	The stored procedures available to the DB2 subsystem
SYSRELS	The referential integrity information for every relationship defined to DB2
SYSRESAUTH	Resource privileges held by DB2 users
SYSROUTINEAUTH	Privileges held by DB2 users on routines
SYSROUTINES	Information about every routine (that is, user-defined functions and stored procedures) defined to the DB2 subsystem
SYSROUTINES_OPTS (V7)	Information about the options used by DB2-generated routines
SYSROUTINES_SRC (V7)	The source code for routines generated by DB2
SYSSCHEMAAUTH	Schema privileges granted to users
SYSSEQUENCEAUTH (V8)	Privileges held by DB2 users on SEQUENCE objects
SYSSEQUENCES (V7)	Information about identity columns and SEQUENCE objects
SYSSEQUENCESDEP (V8)	Records the dependencies of identity columns on tables
SYSSTMT	All SQL statements contained in each DB2 plan bound from a DBRM
SYSSTOGROUP	Information about every DB2 storage group
SYSSTRINGS	Character conversion information
SYSSYNONYMS	Information about every DB2 synonym
SYSTABAUTH	Table privileges held by DB2 users
SYSTABCONST (V7)	Information about every unique constraint (primary key or unique key) created in DB2 V7 or later
SYSTABLEPART	Information about the physical structure and storage of every DB2 table space

22

TABLE 22.1   Tables in the DB2 Catalog

Table	Contents
SYSTABLEPART_HIST (V7)	Historical table space partition statistics
SYSTABLES	Information about every DB2 table
SYSTABLES_HIST (V7)	Table statistics history
SYSTABLESPACE	Information about every DB2 table space
SYSTABSTATS	Partitioned table space statistics by partition
SYSTABSTATS_HIST (V7)	Historical partitioned table space statistics by partition
SYSTRIGGERS	Information about every trigger defined to the DB2 subsystem
SYSUSERAUTH	System privileges held by DB2 users
SYSVIEWDEP	A cross-reference of DB2 objects required by DB2 views
SYSVIEWS	The SQL CREATE VIEW statement for every DB2 view
SYSVLTREE	A portion of the internal representation of complex or long views
SYSVOLUMES	A cross-reference of DASD volumes assigned to DB2 storage groups
SYSVTREE	The first 4000 bytes of the internal representation of the view; the remaining portion of longer or complex views is stored in SYSVLTREE
USERNAMES	Outbound and inbound ID translation information

> **NOTE**
>
> Prior to DB2 V5, the catalog tables controlling distributed DB2 were stored in a separate database named DSNDDF, known as the Communication Database (or CDB). The CDB was used to describe the connections of a local DB2 subsystem to other systems. The CDB tables are now part of the DB2 Catalog. The CDB tables that have been renamed and rolled into the DB2 Catalog are as follows:
>
> | Old CDB Table Name | New DB2 Catalog Table Name |
> |---|---|
> | SYSIBM.SYSLOCATIONS | SYSIBM.LOCATIONS |
> | SYSIBM.SYSLULIST | SYSIBM.LULIST |
> | SYSIBM.SYSLUMODES | SYSIBM.LUMODES |
> | SYSIBM.SYSLUNAMES | SYSIBM.LUNAMES |
> | SYSIBM.SYSMODESELECT | SYSIBM.MODESELECT |
> | SYSIBM.SYSUSERNAMES | SYSIBM.USERNAMES |

V8 The DB2 Catalog is composed of 20 table spaces and 85 tables all in a single database, DSNDB06. For DB2 V6, there were 63 tables; for DB2 V7, there were 82.

Each DB2 Catalog table maintains data about an aspect of the DB2 environment. In that respect, the DB2 Catalog functions as a data dictionary for DB2, supporting and maintaining data about the DB2 environment. (A *data dictionary* maintains metadata, or data about data.) The DB2 Catalog records all the information required by DB2 for the following functional areas:

Objects	STOGROUPS, databases, table spaces, partitions, tables, auxiliary tables, columns, user-defined distinct types, views, synonyms, aliases, sequences, indexes, index keys, foreign keys, relationships, schemas, user-defined functions, stored procedures, triggers, plans, packages, DBRMs, and Java JARs

Security	Database privileges, plan privileges, schema privileges, system privileges, table privileges, view privileges, and use privileges
Utility	Image copy data sets, REORG executions, LOAD executions, and object organization efficiency information
Distribution	How DB2 subsystems are connected for data distribution and DRDA usage
Environmental	Links and relationships between the DB2 Catalog tables and other control information

How does the DB2 Catalog support data about these areas? For the most part, the tables of the DB2 Catalog cannot be modified using standard SQL data manipulation language statements. You do not use INSERT statements, DELETE statements, or UPDATE statements (with a few exceptions) to modify these tables. Instead, the DB2 Catalog operates as a semiactive, integrated, and nonsubvertible data dictionary. The definitions of these three adjectives follow.

First, the DB2 Catalog is said to be *semiactive*. An active dictionary is built, maintained, and used as the result of the creation of the objects defined to the dictionary. In other words, as the user is utilizing the intrinsic functions of the DBMS, metadata is being accumulated and populated in the active data dictionary.

The DB2 Catalog, therefore, is active in the sense that when standard DB2 SQL is issued, the DB2 Catalog is either updated or accessed. All the information in the DB2 Catalog, however, is not completely up-to-date, and some of the tables must be proactively populated (such as SYSIBM.IPNAMES and SYSIBM.IPLIST). You can see where the DB2 Catalog operates as an active data dictionary. Remember that the three types of SQL are DDL, DCL, and DML. When DDL is issued to create DB2 objects such as databases, tablespaces, and tables, the pertinent descriptive information is stored in the DB2 Catalog.

Figure 22.1 shows the effects of DDL on the DB2 Catalog. When a CREATE, DROP, or ALTER statement is issued, information is recorded or updated in the DB2 Catalog. The same is true for security SQL data control language statements. The GRANT and REVOKE statements cause information to be added or removed from DB2 Catalog tables (see Figure 22.2). Data manipulation language SQL statements use the DB2 Catalog to ensure that the statements accurately reference the DB2 objects being manipulated (such as column names and data types).

Why then is the DB2 Catalog classified as only semiactive rather than completely active? The DB2 Catalog houses important information about the physical organization of DB2 objects. For example, the following information is maintained in the DB2 Catalog:

- The number of rows in a given DB2 table or a given DB2 tablespace

- The number of distinct values in a given DB2 index

- The physical order of the rows in the table for a set of keys

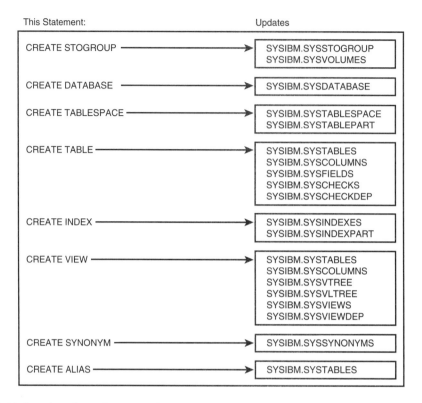

FIGURE 22.1   The effect of DDL on the DB2 Catalog.

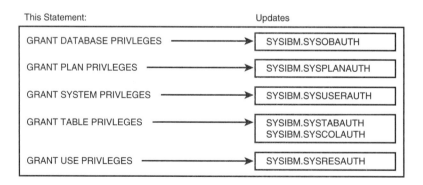

FIGURE 22.2   The effect of DCL on the DB2 Catalog.

This information is populated by means of the DB2 RUNSTATS utility. A truly active data dictionary would update this information as data is populated in the application table spaces, tables, and indexes. But this was deemed to be too costly. Therefore, the DB2 Catalog is only semiactive.

> **NOTE**
>
> **V7**
>
> As of DB2 V7, DB2 collects some statistics proactively without requiring a utility to be run. These statistics are known as *Real Time Stats*, or *RTS*. For information about RTS, consult Chapter 28, "Tuning DB2's Components."

The DB2 Catalog is also described as being *integrated*. The DB2 Catalog and the DB2 DBMS are inherently bound together, neither having purpose or function without the other. The DB2 Catalog without DB2 defines nothing; DB2 without the DB2 Catalog has nothing defined that it can operate on.

The final adjective used to classify the DB2 Catalog is *nonsubvertible*. This simply means that the DB2 Catalog is continually updated as DB2 is being used; the most important metadata in the DB2 Catalog cannot be updated behind DB2's back. Suppose that you created a table with 20 columns. You cannot subsequently update the DB2 Catalog to indicate that the table has 15 columns instead of 20 without using standard DB2 data definition language SQL statements to drop and re-create the table.

An Exception to the Rule

As with most things in life, there are exceptions to the basic rule that the SQL data manipulation language cannot be used to modify DB2 Catalog tables. You can modify columns (used by the DB2 optimizer) that pertain to the physical organization of table data. This topic is covered in depth in Chapter 28.

The Benefits of an Active Catalog

The presence of an active catalog is a boon to the DB2 developer. The DB2 Catalog is synchronized to each application database. You can be assured, therefore, that the metadata retrieved from the DB2 Catalog is 100% accurate. Because the DB2 Catalog is composed of DB2 tables (albeit modified for performance), you can query these tables using standard SQL. The hassle of documenting physical database structures is handled by the active DB2 Catalog and the power of SQL.

DB2 Catalog Structure

The DB2 Catalog is structured as DB2 tables, but they are not always standard DB2 tables. Many of the DB2 Catalog tables are tied together hierarchically—not unlike an IMS database—using a special type of relationship called a *link*. You can determine the nature of these links by querying the SYSIBM.SYSLINKS DB2 Catalog table. This DB2 Catalog table stores the pertinent information defining the relationships between other DB2 Catalog tables. To view this information, issue the following SQL statement:

```
SELECT    PARENTNAME, TBNAME, LINKNAME,
          CHILDSEQ, COLCOUNT, INSERTRULE
FROM      SYSIBM.SYSLINKS
ORDER BY  PARENTNAME, CHILDSEQ;
```

The following data is returned:

PARENTNAME	TBNAME	LINKNAME	CHILD SEQ	COL COUNT	INSERT RULE
SYSCOLUMNS	SYSFIELDS	DSNDF#FD	1	0	O
SYSDATABASE	SYSDBAUTH	DSNDD#AD	1	0	F
SYSDBRM	SYSSTMT	DSNPD#PS	1	0	L
SYSINDEXES	SYSINDEXPART	DSNDC#DR	1	1	U
SYSINDEXES	SYSKEYS	DSNDX#DK	2	1	U
SYSPLAN	SYSDBRM	DSNPP#PD	1	1	U
SYSPLAN	SYSPLANAUTH	DSNPP#AP	2	0	F
SYSPLAN	SYSPLANDEP	DSNPP#PU	3	0	F
SYSRELS	SYSLINKS	DSNDR#DL	1	0	O
SYSRELS	SYSFOREIGNKEYS	DSNDR#DF	2	1	U
SYSSTOGROUP	SYSVOLUMES	DSNSS#SV	1	0	L
SYSTABAUTH	SYSCOLAUTH	DSNAT#AF	1	0	F
SYSTABLES	SYSCOLUMNS	DSNDT#DF	1	1	U
SYSTABLES	SYSRELS	DSNDT#DR	2	1	U
SYSTABLES	SYSINDEXES	DSNDT#DX	3	0	F
SYSTABLES	SYSTABAUTH	DSNDT#AT	4	0	F
SYSTABLES	SYSSYNONYMS	DSNDT#DY	5	0	F
SYSTABLESPACE	SYSTABLEPART	DSNDS#DP	1	1	U
SYSTABLESPACE	SYSTABLES	DSNDS#DT	2	0	F
SYSVTREE	SYSVLTREE	DSNVT#VL	1	0	L
SYSVTREE	SYSVIEWS	DSNVT#VW	2	1	U
SYSVTREE	SYSVIEWDEP	DSNVT#VU	3	0	F

This information can be used to construct the physical composition of the DB2 Catalog links. To accomplish this, keep the following rules in mind:

- The PARENTNAME is the name of the superior table in the hierarchy. The TBNAME is the name of the subordinate table, or child table, in the hierarchy.

- The CHILDSEQ and COLCOUNT columns refer to the clustering and ordering of the data in the relationship.

- The INSERTRULE column determines the order in which data is inserted into the relationship. This concept is similar to the insert rule for IMS databases. Valid insert rules are shown in Table 22.2.

TABLE 22.2   DB2 Catalog Link Insert Rules

Insert Rule	Meaning	Description
F	FIRST	Inserts new values as the first data value in the relationship
L	LAST	Inserts new values as the last data value in the relationship
O	ONE	Permits only one data value for the relationship
U	UNIQUE	Does not allow duplicate data values for the relationship

The newer DB2 Catalog tables do not use links; they use proper referential constraints. Hierarchical diagrams of the DB2 Catalog depicting relationships between the tables are shown in Figures 22.3 through 22.6. These diagrams show the major relationships and do not show every DB2 Catalog table in order to remain legible and useful.

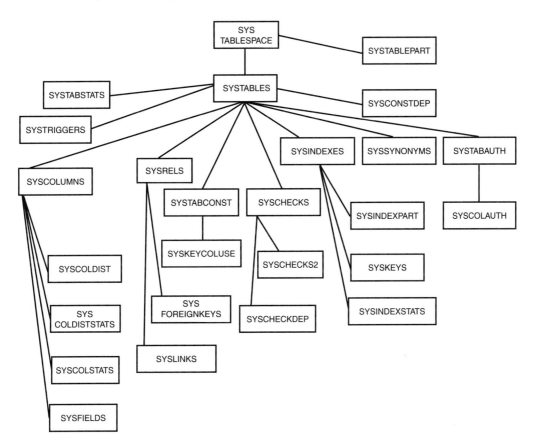

FIGURE 22.3   The DB2 Catalog: tablespaces, tables, and indexes.

As you query the DB2 Catalog, remember that DB2 indexes are used only by SQL queries against the DB2 Catalog, never by internal DB2 operations. For example, when the BIND command queries the DB2 Catalog for syntax checking and access path selection, only the internal DB2 Catalog links are used.

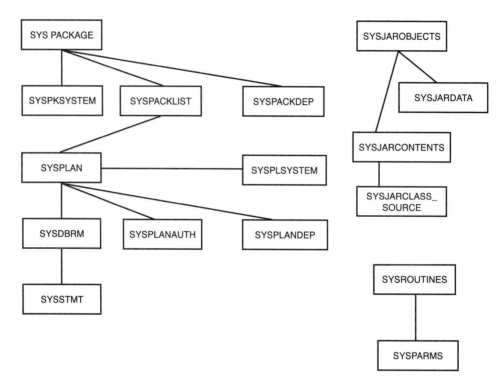

FIGURE 22.4   The DB2 Catalog: programs, plans, packages, and routines.

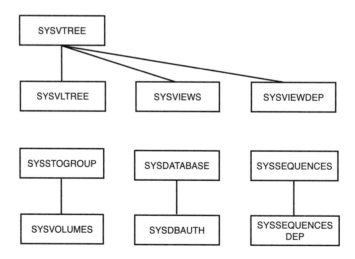

FIGURE 22.5   The DB2 Catalog: views, storage groups, sequences, and databases.

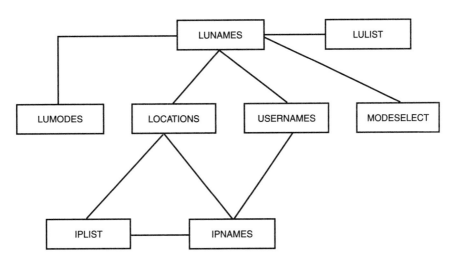

FIGURE 22.6   The DB2 Catalog: distributed information and the CDB.

The DB2 Directory

Many DB2 application developers are unaware that DB2 uses a second dictionary-like structure in addition to the DB2 Catalog. This is the DB2 Directory. Used for storing detailed, technical information about aspects of DB2's operation, the DB2 Directory is for DB2's internal use only.

The DB2 Directory is composed of five "tables." These tables, however, are not true DB2 tables because they are not addressable using SQL. From here on, they are referred to as structures instead of tables. These structures control DB2 housekeeping tasks and house complex control structures used by DB2. See Figure 22.7 for a summation of the relationships between the DB2 Catalog, the DB2 Directory, and DB2 operations. The objects in the DB2 Directory can be listed by issuing the following command:

```
-DIS DB(DSNDB01) SPACE(*) LIMIT(*)
```

A quick rundown of the information stored in the DB2 Directory is in the following sections.

SCT02

The SCT02 structure holds the skeleton cursor tables (SKCTs) for DB2 application plans. These skeleton cursor tables contain the instructions for implementing the access path logic determined by the DB2 optimizer.

The BIND PLAN command causes skeleton cursor tables to be created in the SCT02 structure. Executing the FREE PLAN command causes the appropriate skeleton cursor tables to be removed from SCT02. When a DB2 program is run, DB2 loads the skeleton cursor table into an area of memory called the EDM Pool to enable execution of the SQL embedded in the application program.

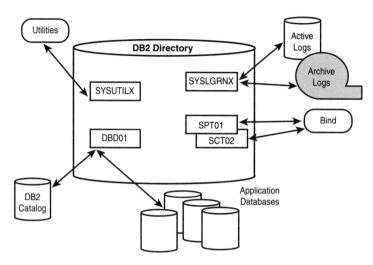

FIGURE 22.7   The DB2 Directory.

SPT01

Similar to the skeleton cursor tables are skeleton package tables which are housed in the SPT01 DB2 Directory structure. The skeleton package tables contain the access path information for DB2 packages.

The BIND PACKAGE command causes skeleton package tables to be created in the SPT01 structure. Executing the FREE PACKAGE command causes the appropriate skeleton package tables to be removed from the DB2 Directory. When running a DB2 program that is based on a plan with a package list, DB2 loads both the skeleton cursor table for the plan and the skeleton package tables for the packages into memory to enable execution of the SQL embedded in the application program.

DBD01

Database descriptors, or DBDs, are stored in the DBD01 DB2 Directory structure. A DBD is an internal description of all the DB2 objects defined within a database. DB2 uses the DBD as an efficient representation of the information stored in the DB2 Catalog for these objects. Instead of accessing the DB2 Catalog for DB2 object information, DB2 accesses the DBD housed in the DB2 Directory because it is more efficient to do so.

The DBD in the DB2 Directory can become out of sync with the physical DB2 objects that it represents, but this is unlikely. If this does happen, you will encounter many odd and unexplainable abends. The situation can be corrected using the REPAIR DBD utility, which is covered in Chapter 32, "Backup and Recovery Utilities." Furthermore, the REPAIR DBD TEST DATABASE utility can be run to detect when a DBD is out of sync with the actual physical objects.

SYSUTILX

DB2 monitors the execution of all online DB2 utilities. Information about the status of all started DB2 utilities is maintained in the SYSUTILX DB2 Directory structure. As each utility progresses, the step and its status are recorded. Utility restart is controlled through the information stored in SYSUTILX.

Note that this structure maintains information only for started DB2 utilities. There are two "tables" within the SYSUTILX tablespace: SYSUTIL and SYSUTILX. Each utility step consumes a separate row, or record, in SYSUTIL, and in SYSUTILX when the amount of information exceeds the capacity of SYSUTIL. When the utility finishes normally or is terminated, all information about that utility is purged from SYSUTIL and SYSUTILX.

SYSLGRNX

The RBA ranges from the DB2 logs are recorded on SYSLGRNX for tablespace updates. When recovery is requested, DB2 can efficiently locate the required logs and quickly identify the portion of those logs needed for recovery.

22

CHAPTER **23**

Locking DB2 Data

D<small>B2</small> automatically guarantees the integrity of data by enforcing several locking strategies. These strategies permit multiple users from multiple environments to access and modify data concurrently.

DB2 combines the following strategies to implement an overall locking strategy:

- Table and table space locking
- IRLM page and row locking
- Internal page and row latching
- Claims and drains to achieve partition independence
- Checking commit log sequence numbers (CLSN) and PUNC bits to achieve lock avoidance
- Global locking through the coupling facility in a data sharing environment

What exactly is locking? How does DB2 utilize these strategies to lock pages and guarantee data integrity? Why does DB2 have to lock data before it can process it? What is the difference between a lock and a latch? How can DB2 provide data integrity while operating on separate partitions concurrently? Finally, how can DB2 avoid locks and still guarantee data integrity?

These questions are answered in this chapter. In addition, this chapter provides practical information on lock compatibilities that can aid you in program development and scheduling.

How DB2 Manages Locking

Anyone accustomed to application programming when access to a database is required understands the potential for concurrency problems. When one application program tries to read data that is in the process of being changed by another, the DBMS must forbid access until the modification is complete to ensure data integrity. Most DBMS products, DB2 included, use a locking mechanism for all data items being changed. Therefore, when one task is updating data on a page, another task cannot access data (read or update) on that same page until the data modification is complete and committed.

When multiple users can access and update the same data at the same time, a locking mechanism is required. This mechanism must be capable of differentiating between stable data and uncertain data. *Stable data* has been successfully committed and is not involved in an update in a current unit of work. *Uncertain data* is currently involved in an operation that could modify its contents. Consider the example in Listing 23.1.

LISTING 23.1   A Typical Processing Scenario

```
Program #1                  Timeline  Program #2
.                           T1        .
.                                     .
.                                     .
.                                     .
SQL statement               T2        .
accessing EMPNO '000010'              .
.                                     .
.                                     .
SQL statement               T3        .
updating '000010'                     .
.                                     .
.                                     .
.                           T4        SQL statement
                                      accessing EMPNO '000010'
.                                     .
.                                     .
Commit                      T5        .
.                                     .
.                                     .
.                                     .
.                           T6        SQL statement updating '000010'
.                                     .
.                                     .
.                                     .
.                           T7        Commit
```

If program #1 updates a piece of data on page 1, you must ensure that program #2 cannot access the data until program #1 commits the unit of work. Otherwise, a loss of integrity could result. Without a locking mechanism, the following sequence of events would be possible:

1. Program #1 retrieves a row from DSN8810.EMP for EMPNO '000010'.

2. Program #1 issues an update statement to change that employee's salary to 55000.

3. Program #2 retrieves the DSN8810.EMP row for EMPNO '000010'. Because the change was not committed, the old value for the salary, 52750, is retrieved.

4. Program #1 commits the change, causing the salary to be `55000`.

5. Program #2 changes a value in a different column and commits the change.

6. The value for salary is now back to `52750`, negating the change made by program #1.

The DBMS avoids this situation by using a locking mechanism. DB2 supports locking at four levels, or *granularities*: table space-, table-, page-, and row-level locking. DB2 also provides LOB locking for large objects (BLOBs, CLOBs, and DBCLOBs). More precisely, DB2 locks are enacted on data as shown in Figure 23.1.

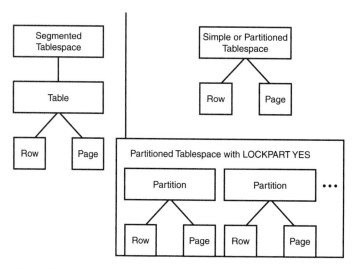

FIGURE 23.1   The DB2 locking hierarchy.

These two charts are hierarchical. Locks can be taken at any level in the locking hierarchy without taking a lock at the lower level. However, locks cannot be taken at the lower levels without a compatible higher-level lock also being taken. For example, you can take a table space lock without taking any other lock, but you cannot take a page lock without first securing a table space-level lock (and a table lock as well if the page is part of a table in a segmented table space).

Additionally, as illustrated in the diagrams in Figure 23.1, a page lock does not have to be taken before a row lock is taken. Your locking strategy requires an "either/or" type of choice by table space: either row locking or page locking. An in-depth discussion on the merits of both follows later in this chapter. Both page locks and row locks escalate to a table level and then to a table space level for segmented tables or straight to a table space level for simple or partitioned table spaces. A table or table space cannot have both page locks and row locks held against it at the same time.

Many modes of locking are supported by DB2, but they can be divided into two types:

- Locks to enable the reading of data
- Locks to enable the updating of data

But this overview is quite simplistic; DB2 uses varieties of these two types to indicate the type of locking required. They are covered in more depth later in this chapter.

Locks Versus Latches

A true lock is handled by DB2 using the IRLM. However, whenever doing so is practical, DB2 tries to lock pages without going to the IRLM. This type of lock is called a *latch*.

True locks are always set in the IRLM. Latches, by contrast, are set internally by DB2, without going to the IRLM.

When a latch is taken instead of a lock, it is handled in the Buffer Manager by internal DB2 code; so the cross-memory service calls to the IRLM are eliminated. Latches are usually held for a shorter duration than locks. Also, a latch requires about one-third the number of instructions as a lock. Therefore, latches are more efficient than locks because they avoid the overhead associated with calling an external address space. Latches are used when a resource serialization situation is required for a short time. Both latches and locks guarantee data integrity. In subsequent sections, when I use the term *lock* generically, I am referring to both locks and latches.

Lock Duration

Before you learn about the various types of locks that can be acquired by DB2, you should understand *lock duration*, which refers to the length of time that a lock is maintained.

The duration of a lock is based on the BIND options chosen for the program requesting locks. Locks can be acquired either immediately when the plan is requested to be run or iteratively as needed during the execution of the program. Locks can be released when the plan is terminated or when they are no longer required for a unit of work.

The BIND parameters affecting DB2 locking are covered in detail in Chapter 13, "Program Preparation." They are summarized in the following sections as a reminder.

BIND **Parameters Affecting Table Space Locks**

ACQUIRE(ALLOCATE) versus ACQUIRE(USE): The ALLOCATE option specifies that locks will be acquired when the plan is allocated, which normally occurs when the first SQL statement is issued. The USE option indicates that locks will be acquired only as they are required, SQL statement by SQL statement.

RELEASE(DEALLOCATE) versus RELEASE(COMMIT): When you specify DEALLOCATE for a plan, locks are not released until the plan is terminated. When you specify COMMIT, table space locks are released when a COMMIT is issued.

BIND **Parameters Affecting Page and Row Locks**

ISOLATION level (CS, RR, RS, UR): There are four choices for isolation level.

- ISOLATION(CS), or *Cursor Stability*, acquires and releases page locks as pages are read and processed. CS provides the greatest level of concurrency at the expense of potentially different data being returned by the same cursor if it is processed twice during the same unit of work.

- `ISOLATION(RR)`, or *Repeatable Read*, holds page and row locks until a `COMMIT` point; no other program can modify the data. If data is accessed twice during the unit of work, the same exact data will be returned.

- `ISOLATION(RS)`, or *Read Stability*, holds page and row locks until a `COMMIT` point, but other programs can `INSERT` new data. If data is accessed twice during the unit of work, new rows may be returned, but old rows will not have changed.

- `ISOLATION(UR)`, or *Uncommitted Read*, is also known as dirty read processing. `UR` avoids locking altogether, so data can be read that never actually exists in the database.

Regardless of the `ISOLATION` level chosen, all page locks are released when a `COMMIT` is encountered.

Implementing Dirty Reads Using `ISOLATION(UR)`

Programs that read DB2 data typically access numerous rows during their execution and are thus quite susceptible to concurrency problems. DB2 provides read-through locks, also known as "dirty reads" or "uncommitted reads," to help overcome concurrency problems. When using uncommitted reads, an application program can read data that has been changed but is not yet committed.

Dirty read capability is implemented using the `UR` isolation level (`UR` stands for uncommitted read). When an application program uses the `UR` isolation level, it reads data without taking locks. This way, the application program can read data contained in the table as it is being manipulated.

How does "dirty read" impact data availability and integrity? Consider the following sequence of events:

1. At 9:00 a.m., a transaction is executed containing the following SQL to change a specific value:

```
UPDATE DSN8810.EMP
   SET FIRSTNME = "MICHELLE"
WHERE EMPNO = '010020';
```

   The transaction, which is a long-running one, continues to execute without issuing a `COMMIT`.

2. At 9:01 a.m., a second transaction attempts to `SELECT` the data that was changed but not committed.

If the `UR` isolation level were specified for the second transaction, it would read the changed data even though it had yet to be committed. Obviously, if the program does not wait to take a lock and merely reads the data in whatever state it happens to be at that moment, the program will execute faster than if it has to wait for locks to be taken and resources to be freed before processing.

However, you must carefully examine the implications of reading uncommitted data before implementing such a plan. Several types of "problems" can occur. A dirty read can cause duplicate rows to be returned where none exist. Also, a dirty read can cause no rows to be returned when one (or more) actually exists. Dirty reads might even cause rows to be returned out of order even when using an ORDER BY. Obviously, you must take these "problems" into consideration before using the UR isolation level.

ISOLATION(UR) **Requirements**   The UR isolation level applies to read-only operations: SELECT, SELECT INTO, and FETCH from a read-only result table. Any application plan or package bound with an isolation level of UR uses uncommitted read functionality for read-only SQL. Operations that are contained in the same plan or package that are not read-only use an isolation level of CS.

You can override the isolation level that is defined at the plan or package level during BIND or REBIND as you want for each SQL statement in the program by using the WITH clause, as shown in the following SQL:

```
SELECT EMPNO, FIRSTNME, LASTNAME
FROM    DSN8810.EMP
WITH UR;
```

The WITH clause allows an isolation level to be specified at the statement level in an application program. However, the restriction that the UR isolation level can be used with read-only SQL statements only still applies.

CAUTION

If you are running on a pre-V6 DB2 subsystem, be aware that dirty read processing requires type-2 indexes. The UR isolation level is incompatible with type-1 indexes. If the plan or package is rebound to change to UR isolation, DB2 does not consider any access paths that use a type-1 index. If an acceptable type-2 index cannot be found, DB2 chooses a table space scan.

When to Use Dirty Reads   When is using UR isolation appropriate? The general rule of thumb is to avoid UR whenever the results must be 100% accurate. Examples would be when

- Calculations that must balance are performed on the selected data

- Data is retrieved from one source to insert to or update another

- Production, mission-critical work that cannot contain or cause data-integrity problems is performed

In general, most current DB2 applications are not candidates for dirty reads. However, in a few specific situations, the dirty read capability is of major benefit. Consider the following cases in which the UR isolation level could prove to be useful:

- Access is required to a reference, code, or lookup table that is basically static in nature. Due to the non-volatile nature of the data, a dirty read would be no different than a normal read the majority of the time. In the cases in which the code data is being modified, any application reading the data would incur minimum, if any, problems.

- Statistical processing must be performed on a large amount of data. For example, your company may want to determine the average age of female employees within a certain pay range. The impact of an uncommitted read on an average of multiple rows is minimal because a single value changed usually does not have a significant impact on the result.

- Dirty reads can prove invaluable in a DB2 data warehousing environment. A data warehouse is a time-sensitive, subject-oriented store of business data that is used for online analytical processing. Refer to Chapter 45, "Data Warehousing with DB2," for more information on DB2 data warehouses. Other than periodic data propagation and/or replication, access to a data warehouse is read only. An uncommitted read is perfect in a read-only environment because it can cause little damage because the data is generally not changing. More and more data warehouse projects are being implemented in corporations worldwide, and DB2 with dirty read capability can be a wise choice for data warehouse implementation.

- In the rare cases in which a table, or set of tables, is used by a single user only, UR can make a lot of sense. If only one individual can modify the data, the application programs can be coded so that all (or most) reads are done using UR isolation level, and the data will still be accurate.

- Dirty reads can be useful in pseudo-conversational transactions that use the save and compare technique. A program using the save and compare technique saves data for later comparison to ensure that the data was not changed by other concurrent trans-actions.

  Consider the following sequence of events: transaction 1 changes customer A on page 100. A page lock will be taken on all rows on page 100. Transaction 2 requests customer C, which is on page 100. Transaction 2 must wait for transaction 1 to finish. This wait is not necessary. Even if these transactions are trying to get the same row, the save then compare technique would catch this.

- Finally, if the data being accessed is already inconsistent, little harm can be done by using a dirty read to access the information.

Table Space Locks

A table space lock is acquired when a DB2 table or index is accessed. Note that I said *accessed*, not *updated*. The table space is locked even when simple read-only access is occur-ring.

Refer to Table 23.1 for a listing of the types of table space locks that can be acquired during the execution of an SQL statement. Every table space lock implies two types of access: the access acquired by the lock requester and the access allowed to other subse-quent, concurrent processes.

TABLE 23.1   Table Space Locks

Lock	Meaning	Access Acquired	Access Allowed to Others
S	SHARE	Read only	Read only
U	UPDATE	Read with intent to update	Read only
X	EXCLUSIVE	Update	No access
IS	INTENT SHARE	Read only	Update
IX	INTENT EXCLUSIVE	Update	Update
SIX	SHARE/INTENT EXCLUSIVE	Read or Update	Read only

When an SQL statement is issued and first accesses data, it takes an intent lock on the table space. Later in the process, actual S-, U-, or X-locks are taken. The intent locks (IS, IX, and SIX) enable programs to wait for the required S-, U-, or X-lock that needs to be taken until other processes have released competing locks.

The type of table space lock used by DB2 during processing is contingent on several factors, including the table space LOCKSIZE specified in the DDL, the bind parameters chosen for the plan being run, and the type of processing requested. Table 23.2 provides a synopsis of the initial table space locks acquired under certain conditions.

TABLE 23.2   How Table Space Locks Are Acquired

Type of Processing	LOCKSIZE	Isolation	Initial Lock Acquired
MODIFY	ANY	CS	IX
MODIFY	PAGE/ROW	CS	IX
MODIFY	TABLESPACE	CS	X
MODIFY	ANY	RR	X
MODIFY	PAGE/ROW	RR	X
MODIFY	TABLESPACE	RR	X
SELECT	ANY	CS	IS
SELECT	PAGE/ROW	CS	IS
SELECT	TABLESPACE	CS	S
SELECT	ANY	RR	S
SELECT	PAGE/ROW	RR	S
SELECT	TABLESPACE	RR	S

A table space U-lock indicates intent to update, but an update has not occurred. This is caused by using a cursor with the FOR UPDATE OF clause. A U-lock is non-exclusive because it can be taken while tasks have S-locks on the same table space. More information on table space lock compatibility follows in Table 23.3.

An additional consideration is that table space locks are usually taken in combination with table and page locks, but they can be used on their own. When you specify the LOCKSIZE TABLESPACE DDL parameter, table space locks alone are used as the locking mechanism for the data in that table space. This way, concurrent access is limited and concurrent update processing is eliminated.

Similar in function to the `LOCKSIZE` DDL parameter is the `LOCK TABLE` statement. The `LOCK TABLE` statement requests an immediate lock on the specified table. The `LOCK TABLE` statement has two forms—one to request a share lock and one to request an exclusive lock.

```
LOCK TABLE table_name IN SHARE MODE;
```

```
LOCK TABLE table_name IN EXCLUSIVE MODE;
```

> **CAUTION**
>
> The `LOCK TABLE` statement locks all tables in a simple table space even though only one table is specified.

A locking scheme is not effective unless multiple processes can secure different types of locks on the same resource concurrently. With DB2 locking, some types of table space locks can be acquired concurrently by discrete processes. Two locks that can be acquired concurrently on the same resource are said to be compatible with one another.

Refer to Table 23.3 for a breakdown of DB2 table space lock compatibility. A *Yes* in the matrix indicates that the two locks are compatible and can be acquired by distinct processes on the same table space concurrently. A *No* indicates that the two locks are incompatible. In general, two locks cannot be taken concurrently if they allow concurrent processes to negatively affect the integrity of data in the table space.

TABLE 23.3   Table Space Lock Compatibility Matrix

Locks for PGM2	Locks for PGM1					
	S	U	X	IS	IX	SIX
S	Yes	Yes	No	Yes	No	No
U	Yes	No	No	Yes	No	No
X	No	No	No	No	No	No
IS	Yes	Yes	No	Yes	Yes	Yes
IX	No	No	No	Yes	Yes	No
SIX	No	No	No	Yes	No	No

Table Locks

DB2 can use table locks only when segmented table spaces are involved in the process. Table locks are always associated with a corresponding table space lock.

The same types of locks are used for table locks as are used for table space locks. S, U, X, IS, IX, and SIX table locks can be acquired by DB2 processes when data in segmented table spaces is accessed. Table 23.1 describes the options available to DB2 for table locking. The compatibility chart in Table 23.3 applies to table locks as well as table space locks.

For a table lock to be acquired, an IS-lock must first be acquired on the segmented table space in which the table exists. The type of table lock to be taken depends on the

`LOCKSIZE` specified in the DDL, the bind parameters chosen for the plan being run, and the type of processing requested. Table 23.4 is a modified version of Table 23.2, showing the initial types of table spaces and table locks acquired given a certain set of conditions. Table locks are not acquired when the `LOCKSIZE TABLESPACE` parameter is used.

TABLE 23.4 How Table Locks Are Acquired

Type of Processing	LOCKSIZE	Isolation	Table Space Lock Acquired	Table Lock Acquired
MODIFY	ANY	CS	IS	IX
MODIFY	PAGE	CS	IS	IX
MODIFY	TABLE	CS	IS	X
MODIFY	ANY	RR	IS	X
MODIFY	PAGE	RR	IS	X
MODIFY	TABLE	RR	IS	X
SELECT	ANY	CS	IS	IS
SELECT	PAGE	CS	IS	IS
SELECT	TABLE	CS	IS	S
SELECT	ANY	RR	IS	S
SELECT	PAGE	RR	IS	S
SELECT	TABLE	RR	IS	S

Page Locks

The types of page locks that DB2 can take are outlined in Table 23.5. S-locks allow data to be read concurrently but not modified. With an X-lock, data on a page can be modified (with `INSERT`, `UPDATE`, or `DELETE`), but concurrent access is not allowed. U-locks enable X-locks to be queued, whereas S-locks exist on data that must be modified.

TABLE 23.5 Page Locks

Lock	Meaning	Access Acquired	Access Allowed to Others
S	SHARE	Read only	Read only
U	UPDATE	Read with intent to update	Read only
X	EXCLUSIVE	Update	No access

As with table space locks, concurrent page locks can be acquired but only with compatible page locks. The compatibility matrix for page locks is shown in Table 23.6.

TABLE 23.6 Page Lock Compatibility Matrix

Locks for PGM2	Locks for PGM1		
	S	U	X
S	Yes	Yes	No
U	Yes	No	No
X	No	No	No

When are these page locks taken? Page locks can be acquired only under the following conditions:

- The DDL for the object requesting a lock specifies LOCKSIZE PAGE or LOCKSIZE ANY.

- If LOCKSIZE ANY was specified, the NUMLKTS threshold or the table space LOCKMAX specification must not have been exceeded. You learn more about these topics later in this section.

- If ISOLATION(RR) was used when the plan was bound, the optimizer might decide not to use page locking.

If all these factors are met, page locking progresses as outlined in Table 23.7. The type of processing in the left column causes the indicated page lock to be acquired for the scope of pages identified in the right column. DB2 holds each page lock until it is released as specified in the ISOLATION level of the plan requesting the particular lock.

> **NOTE**
>
> Page locks can be promoted from one type of lock to another based on the type of processing that is occurring. A program can FETCH a row using a cursor with the FOR UPDATE OF clause, causing a U-lock to be acquired on that row's page. Later, the program can modify that row, causing the U-lock to be promoted to an X-lock.

TABLE 23.7   How Page Locks Are Acquired

Type of Processing	Page Lock Acquired	Pages Affected
SELECT/FETCH	S	Page by page as they are fetched
OPEN CURSOR for SELECT	S	All pages affected
SELECT/FETCH FOR UPDATE OF	U	Page by page as they are fetched
UPDATE	X	Page by page
INSERT	X	Page by page
DELETE	X	Page by page

Row Locks

The smallest piece of DB2 data that you can lock is the individual row. The types of row locks that DB2 can take are similar to the types of page locks that it can take. Refer to Table 23.8. S-locks allow data to be read concurrently but not modified. With an X-lock, you can modify data in that row (using INSERT, UPDATE, or DELETE), but concurrent access is not allowed. U-locks enable X-locks to be queued, whereas S-locks exist on data that must be modified.

TABLE 23.8   Row Locks

Lock	Meaning	Access Acquired	Access Allowed to Others
S	SHARE	Read only	Read only
U	UPDATE	Read with intent to update	Read only
X	EXCLUSIVE	Update	No access

Once again, concurrent row locks can be acquired but only with compatible row locks. Table 23.9 shows the compatibility matrix for row locks.

TABLE 23.9   Row Lock Compatibility Matrix

Locks for PGM2	Locks for PGM1		
	S	U	X
S	Yes	Yes	No
U	Yes	No	No
X	No	No	No

When are these row locks taken? Row locks can be acquired when the DDL for the object requesting a lock specifies LOCKSIZE ROW. (Although it is theoretically possible for LOCKSIZE ANY to choose row locks, in practice I have yet to see this happen.) Row locking progresses as outlined in Table 23.10. The type of processing in the left column causes the indicated row lock to be acquired for the scope of rows identified in the right column. A row lock is held until it is released as specified by the ISOLATION level of the plan requesting the particular lock.

> **NOTE**
>
> Row locks can be promoted from one type of lock to another based on the type of processing that is occurring. A program can FETCH a row using a cursor with the FOR UPDATE OF clause, causing a U-lock to be acquired on that row. Later, the program can modify that row, causing the U-lock to be promoted to an X-lock.

TABLE 23.10   How Row Locks Are Acquired

Type of Processing	Row Lock Acquired	Rows Affected
SELECT/FETCH	S	Row by row as they are fetched
OPEN CURSOR for SELECT	S	All rows affected
SELECT/FETCH FOR UPDATE OF	U	Row by row as they are fetched
UPDATE	X	Row by row
INSERT	X	Row by row
DELETE	X	Row by row

Page Locks Versus Row Locks

The answer to the question of whether to use page locks or row locks is, of course, "It depends!" The nature of your specific data and applications determines whether page or row locks are most applicable.

The resources required to acquire, maintain, and release a row lock are just about the same as the resources required for a page lock. Therefore, the number of rows per page must be factored into the row-versus-page locking decision. The more rows per page, the more resources row locking will consume. For example, a table space with a single table that houses 25 rows per page can consume as much as 25 times more resources for locking if row locks are chosen over page locks. Of course, this estimate is very rough, and other factors (such as lock avoidance) can reduce the number of locks acquired, and thereby reduce the overhead associated with row locking. However, locking a row-at-a-time instead of a page-at-a-time can reduce contention. Row locking almost always consumes more resources than page locking. Likewise, if two applications running concurrently access the same data in different orders, row locking might actually decrease concurrent data access.

You must therefore ask these questions:

- What is the nature of the applications that access the objects in question? Of course, the answer to this question differs not only from organization to organization, but also from application to application within the same organization.

- Which is more important, reducing the resources required to execute an application or increasing data availability? The answer to this question will depend upon the priorities set by your organization and any application teams accessing the data.

As a general rule of thumb, favor specifying LOCKSIZE PAGE, as page locking is generally the most practical locking strategy for most applications. If you're experiencing severe contention problems on a table space that is currently using LOCKSIZE PAGE, consider changing to LOCKSIZE ROW and gauging the impact on performance, resource consumption, and concurrent data access. Alternatively, you also might choose to specify LOCKSIZE ANY and let DB2 choose the type of locking to be performed.

> **NOTE**
>
> A possible alternative to row locking is to specify MAXROWS 1 for the table space and use LOCKSIZE PAGE (or LOCKSIZE ANY), instead of LOCKSIZE ROW.

Lock Suspensions, Timeouts, and Deadlocks

The longer a lock is held, the greater the potential impact to other applications. When an application requests a lock that is already held by another process, and the lock cannot be shared, that application is suspended. A suspended process temporarily stops running until the lock can be acquired. Lock suspensions can be a significant barrier to acceptable performance and application availability.

When an application has been suspended for a pre-determined period of time, it will be terminated. When a process is terminated because it exceeds this period of time, it is said to timeout. In other words, a *timeout* is caused by the unavailability of a given resource. For example, consider the following scenario:

Program 1	Program 2
Update Table A/Page 1	
Lock established	
Intermediate processing	Update Table A/Page 1
.	Lock (wait)
.	Lock suspension
. *Timeout*	-911 received

If Program 2, holding no other competitive locks, requests a lock currently held by Program 1, DB2 tries to obtain the lock for a period of time. Then it quits trying. This example illustrates a timeout. This timeout scenario is also applicable to row locks, not just page locks.

The length of time a user waits for an unavailable resource before being timed out is determined by the IRLMRWT DSNZPARM parameter. You also can set this period of time by using the RESOURCE TIMEOUT field on the DB2 installation panel DSNTIPI.

When a lock is requested, a series of operations is performed to ensure that the requested lock can be acquired (see Figure 23.2). Two conditions can cause the lock acquisition request to fail: a deadlock or a timeout.

A *deadlock* occurs when two separate processes compete for resources held by one another. DB2 performs deadlock detection for both locks and latches. For example, consider the following processing sequence for two concurrently executing application programs:

Program 1	Program 2
Update Table B/Page 1	Update Table A/Page 1
Lock established	Lock established
Intermediate processing	Intermediate processing
Update Table A/Page 1	Update Table B/Page 1
Lock (wait) *Deadlock*	Lock (wait)

A deadlock occurs when Program 1 requests a lock for a data page held by Program 2, and Program 2 requests a lock for a data page held by Program 1. A deadlock must be resolved before either program can perform subsequent processing. DB2's solution is to target one of the two programs as the victim of the deadlock and deny that program's lock request by setting the SQLCODE to -911. This deadlocking scenario is also applicable to row locks, not just page locks. A graphic depiction of a deadlock is shown in Figure 23.3.

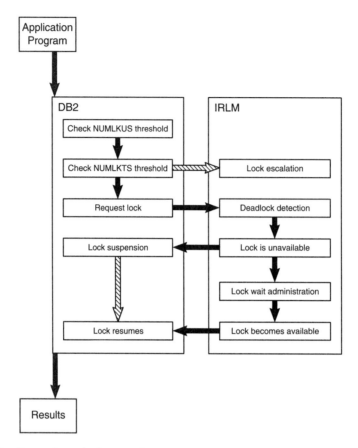

FIGURE 23.2   Processing a lock request.

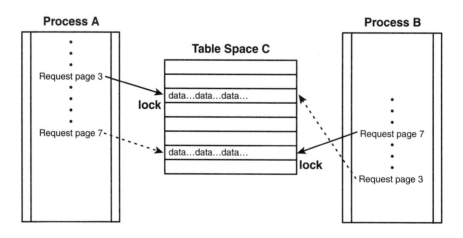

Process A is waiting on Process B   Process B is waiting on Process A

FIGURE 23.3   A deadlock.

The length of time DB2 waits before choosing a victim of a deadlock is determined by the DEADLOK IRLM parameter. You also can set this parameter using the RESOURCE TIMEOUT field on the DB2 installation panel DSNTIPJ.

Partition Independence

DB2 augments resource serialization using claims and drains in addition to transaction locking. The claim and drain process enables DB2 to perform concurrent operations on multiple partitions of the same table space.

Claims and drains provide another "locking" mechanism to control concurrency for resources between SQL statements, utilities, and commands. Do not confuse the issue: DB2 continues to use transaction locking, as well as claims and drains.

As with transaction locks, claims and drains can time out while waiting for a resource.

Claims

DB2 uses a *claim* to register that a resource is being accessed. The following resources can be claimed:

- Simple table spaces

- Segmented table spaces

- A single data partition of a partitioned table space

- A non-partitioned index space

V8   - A single index partition of a partitioned index (of either the partitioning index or a DPSI)

Think of claims as usage indicators. A process stakes a claim on a resource, telling DB2, in effect, "Hey, I'm using this!"

Claims prevent drains from acquiring a resource. A claim is acquired when a resource is first accessed. This is true regardless of the ACQUIRE parameter specified (USE or ALLOCATE). Claims are released at commit time, except for cursors declared using the WITH HOLD clause or when the claimer is a utility.

Multiple agents can claim a single resource. Claims on objects are acquired by the following:

- SQL statements (SELECT, INSERT, UPDATE, DELETE)

- DB2 restart on INDOUBT objects

- Some utilities (for example, COPY SHRLEVEL CHANGE, RUNSTATS SHRLEVEL CHANGE, and REPORT)

Every claim has a *claim class* associated with it. The claim class is based on the type of access being requested, as follows:

- A CS claim is acquired when data is read from a package or plan bound specifying ISOLATION(CS).

- An RR claim is acquired when data is read from a package or plan bound specifying ISOLATION(RR).

- A write claim is acquired when data is deleted, inserted, or updated.

Drains

Like claims, *drains* also are acquired when a resource is first accessed. A drain acquires a resource by quiescing claims against that resource. Drains can be requested by commands and utilities.

Multiple drainers can access a single resource. However, a process that drains all claim classes cannot drain an object concurrently with any other process.

To more fully understand the concept of draining, think back to the last time that you went to a movie theater. Before anyone is permitted into the movie, the prior attendees must first be cleared out. In essence, this example illustrates the concept of draining. DB2 drains make sure that all other users of a resource are cleared out before allowing any subsequent access.

The following resources can be drained:

- Simple table spaces

- Segmented table spaces

- A single data partition of a partitioned table space

- A non-partitioned index space

V8
- A single index partition of a partitioned index (of either the partitioning index or a DPSI)

A drain places drain locks on a resource. A drain lock is acquired for each claim class that must be released. Drain locks prohibit processes from attempting to drain the same object at the same time.

The process of quiescing a claim class and prohibiting new claims from being acquired for the resource is called *draining*. Draining allows DB2 utilities and commands to acquire partial or full control of a specific object with a minimal impact on concurrent access.

Three types of drain locks can be acquired:

- A cursor stability drain lock

- A repeatable read drain lock

- A write drain lock

A drain requires either partial control of a resource, in which case a write drain lock is taken, or complete control of a resource, accomplished by placing a CS drain lock, an RR drain lock, and a write drain lock on an object.

You can think of drains as the mechanism for telling new claimers, "Hey, you can't use this in that way!" The specific action being prevented by the drain is based on the claim class being drained. Draining write claims enables concurrent access to the resource, but the resource cannot be modified. Draining read (CS and/or RR) and write claims prevents any and all concurrent access.

Drain locks are released when the utility or command completes. When the resource has been drained of all appropriate claim classes, the drainer acquires sole access to the resource.

Claim and Drain Lock Compatibility

As with transaction locks, concurrent claims and drains can be taken, but only if they are compatible with one another. Table 23.11 shows which drains are compatible with existing claims.

TABLE 23.11   Claim/Drain Compatibility Matrix

Existing Claim for PGM2	Drain required by PGM1		
	Write	CS	RR
Write	No	No	No
RR	Yes	No	No
CS	Yes	No	No

Table 23.12 shows which drains are compatible with existing drains.

TABLE 23.12   Drain/Drain Compatibility Matrix

Existing Drain for PGM2	Drain required by PGM1		
	Write	CS	RR
Write	Yes	No	No
RR	No	No	No
CS	No	No	No

Transaction Locking Versus Claims and Drains   DB2 uses transaction locks to serialize access to a resource between multiple claimers, such as two SQL statements or an SQL statement and a utility that takes claims, such as RUNSTATS SHRLEVEL(CHANGE).

Claims and drains serialize access between a claimer and a drainer. For example, an INSERT statement is a claimer that must be dealt with by the LOAD utility, which is a drainer.

Drain locks are used to control concurrency when both a command and a utility try to access the same resource.

Lock Avoidance

Lock avoidance is a mechanism employed by DB2 to access data without locking while maintaining data integrity. It prohibits access to uncommitted data and serializes access to pages. Lock avoidance improves performance by reducing the overall volume of lock requests. Let's face it, the most efficient lock is the one never taken.

In general, DB2 avoids locking data pages if it can determine that the data to be accessed is committed and that no semantics are violated by not acquiring the lock. DB2 avoids locks by examining the log to verify the committed state of the data.

When determining if lock avoidance techniques will be practical, DB2 first scans the page to be accessed to determine whether any rows qualify. If none qualify, a lock is not required.

For each data page to be accessed, the RBA of the last page update (stored in the data page header) is compared with the log RBA for the oldest active unit of recovery. This RBA is called the Commit Log Sequence Number, or CLSN. If the CLSN is greater than the last page update RBA, the data on the page has been committed and the page lock can be avoided.

Additionally, a bit is stored in the record header for each row on the page. The bit is called the Possibly UNCommitted, or PUNC, bit (see Figure 23.4). The PUNC bit indicates whether update activity has been performed on the row. For each qualifying row on the page, the PUNC bit is checked to see whether it is off. This indicates that the row has not been updated since the last time the bit was turned off. Therefore, locking can be avoided.

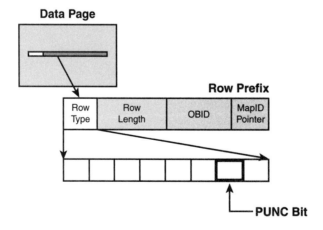

FIGURE 23.4   The PUNC bit.

> **NOTE**
>
> IBM provides no external method for you to determine whether the PUNC bit is on or off for each row. Therefore, you should ensure that any table that can be modified should be reorganized on a regularly scheduled basis.

If neither CLSN nor PUNC bit testing indicates that a lock can be avoided, DB2 acquires the requisite lock.

In addition to enhancing performance, lock avoidance increases data availability. Data that in previous releases would have been considered locked, and therefore unavailable, is now considered accessible.

When Lock Avoidance Can Occur

Lock avoidance *can be used only for data pages*. Further, DB2 Catalog and DB2 Directory access does not use lock avoidance techniques. You can avoid locks under the following circumstances:

- For any pages accessed by read-only or ambiguous queries bound with ISOLATION(CS) and CURRENTDATA NO

- For any unqualified rows accessed by queries bound with ISOLATION(CS) or ISOLATION(RS)

- When DB2 system-managed referential integrity checks for dependent rows caused by either the primary key being updated, or the parent row being deleted and the DELETE RESTRICT rule is in effect

- For both COPY and RUNSTATS when SHRLEVEL(CHANGE) is specified

An *ambiguous cursor* is one where DB2 cannot determine whether there is intent to modify data retrieved using that cursor. The cursor is ambiguous if it is in a plan or package containing either PREPARE or EXECUTE IMMEDIATE SQL statements, along with the following conditions: the cursor is not defined with the FOR READ ONLY clause or the FOR UPDATE OF clause; the cursor is not defined on a read-only result table; the cursor is not the target of a WHERE CURRENT clause on an UPDATE or DELETE statement.

Data Sharing Global Lock Management

Because data sharing group members can access any object from any member in the group, a global locking mechanism is required. It is handled by the lock structure defined in the coupling facility. The lock structure is charged with managing inter-member locking. Without a global lock management process, data integrity problems could occur when one member attempts to read (or change) data that is in the process of being changed by another member.

Data sharing groups utilize a global locking mechanism to preserve the integrity of the shared data. The global locking mechanism allows locks to be recognized between members.

Global Locking

All members of a data sharing group must be aware of locks that are held or requested by the other members. The DB2 data sharing group utilizes the coupling facility to establish and administer global locks.

The IRLM performs locking within each member DB2 subsystem. Additionally, the IRLM communicates with the coupling facility to establish global locks. Each member of the data sharing group communicates lock requests to the coupling facility's lock structure. The manner in which a transaction takes locks during execution does not change. The only difference is that, instead of being local locks, the locks being taken are global in nature.

DB2 data sharing does not use message passing to perform global locking. The members DB2 IRLMs use the coupling facility to do global locking. Contention can be identified quickly without having to suspend the tasks to send messages around to the other DB2 members contained in the data sharing group. The following list outlines the events that occur when transactions from different DB2 members try to access the same piece of data:

1. TXN1 requests a lock that is handled by the local IRLM.

2. The local IRLM passes the request to the coupling facility global lock structures to ensure that no other members have incompatible locks. No incompatible locks are found, so the lock is taken.

3. TXN2 requests a lock that is handled by its local IRLM. The lock is for the same data held by TXN1 executing in a different DB2 subsystem.

4. Once again, the local IRLM passes the request to the coupling facility global lock structures to check for lock compatibility. In this case, an incompatible lock is found, so the lock request cannot be granted. The task is suspended.

5. Eventually, TXN1 executes a COMMIT, which releases all local and global locks.

6. TXN2 now can successfully execute the lock and continue processing.

> **NOTE**
>
> Consider specifying TRACKMOD NO for objects used in a data sharing environment to avoid locking problems.

Lock Structures

The coupling facility contains several lock structures that are used for global locking purposes. The lock lists contain names of modified resources. This information is used to notify members of the data sharing group that the various resources have been changed.

Additionally, a hash table is used to identify compatible and incompatible lock modes. If the same hash value is used for the same resource name from different systems (with incompatible lock modes), lock contention will occur. If the same hash value is used for different resource names (called a *hashing collision*), false contention will occur. Any contention requires additional asynchronous processing to occur.

Hierarchical Locking

DB2 data sharing introduces the concept of explicit hierarchical locking to reduce global locking overhead (which increases global locking performance). Explicit hierarchical locking allows data sharing to differentiate between global and local locks. When no inter-DB2 interest occurs in a resource, the local IRLM can grant locks locally on the resources that are lower in the hierarchy. This feature allows the local DB2 to obtain local locks on pages or rows for that table space without notifying the coupling facility. In a data sharing environment, locks on the top parents are always propagated to the coupling facility lock structures. (These structures are detailed on the previous page.) In addition, the local DB2 propagates locks on children, depending on the compatibility of the maximum lock held on a table space that also has other members of the DB2 data sharing group requesting locks on it.

P-Locks Versus L-Locks

DB2 data sharing introduces two new lock identifiers: P-locks and L-locks.

P-Locks

P-locks preserve inter-DB2 coherency of buffered pages. P-locks are owned by the member DB2 subsystem and are used for physical resources such as page sets. These physical resources can be either data objects or index objects. P-locks are held for the length of time the pages are locally cached in the local buffer pool. As such, data can be cached beyond a transaction commit point.

P-locks are negotiable. If multiple DB2 members hold incompatible P-locks, the IRLMs try to downgrade lock compatibility. P-locks are never timed out. Because P-locks are not owned by transactions, they cannot be deadlocked. The sole job of a P-lock is to ensure inter-DB2 coherency. P-locks notify the data sharing group that a member of that group is performing work on that resource. This way, the coupling facility can become involved and begin treating the resources globally.

L-Locks

L-locks are used for both intra- and inter-DB2 concurrency between transactions. L-locks can either be local or global in scope. L-locks are owned by transactions and are held for COMMIT or allocation duration. L-locks are not negotiable and, as such, must wait for incompatible L-locks held by other DB2 members to be released before they can be taken. Suspended L-locks can be timed out by the IRLM.

LOBs and Locking

When a row is read or modified in a table containing LOB columns, the application will obtain a normal transaction lock on the base table. Recall from Chapter 9, "Large Objects and Object/Relational Databases," that the actual values for LOBs are stored in a separate table space from the rest of the table data. The locks on the base table also control concurrency for the LOB table space. But DB2 uses locking strategies for large objects, too. A lock that is held on a LOB value is referred to as a *LOB lock*. LOB locks are deployed to manage the space used by LOBs and to ensure that LOB readers do not read partially updated LOBs.

> **NOTE**
>
> For applications reading rows using ISOLATION(UR) or lock avoidance, page or row locks are not taken on the base table. However, DB2 takes S-locks on the LOB to ensure that a partial or inconsistent LOB is not accessed.

One reason LOB locks are used is to determine whether space from a deleted LOB can be reused by an inserted or updated LOB. DB2 will not reuse the storage for a deleted LOB until the DELETE has been committed and there are no more readers on the LOB.

Another purpose for locking LOBs is to prevent deallocating space for a LOB that is currently being read. All readers, including "dirty readers" acquire S-locks on LOBs to prevent the storage for the LOB they are reading from being deallocated.

Types of LOB Locks

There are only two types of LOB locks:

S-locks, or SHARE—The lock owner and any concurrent processes can SELECT, DELETE, or UPDATE the locked LOB. Concurrent processes can acquire an S-lock on the LOB.

X-locks, or EXCLUSIVE—The lock owner can read or change the locked LOB, but concurrent processes cannot access the LOB.

Just like regular transaction locking, though, DB2 also takes LOB table space locks. If the LOB table space has a gross lock, DB2 does not acquire LOB locks. The following lock modes can be taken for a the LOB table space:

S-lock, or SHARE—The lock owner and any concurrent processes can read and delete LOBs in the LOB table space. The lock owner does not need to take individual LOB locks.

IS-lock, or INTENT SHARE—The lock owner can UPDATE LOBs to null or zero-length, or SELECT or DELETE LOBs in the LOB table space. Concurrent processes can both read and modify LOBs in the same table space. The lock owner acquires a LOB lock on any data that it reads or deletes.

X-lock, or EXCLUSIVE—The lock owner can read or change LOBs in the LOB table space. The lock owner does not need to take individual LOB locks.

IX-lock, or INTENT EXCLUSIVE—The lock owner and any concurrent process can read and change data in the LOB table space. The lock owner acquires an individual LOB lock for any LOB it accesses.

SIX-lock, or SHARE WITH INTENT EXCLUSIVE—The lock owner can read and change data in the LOB table space. The lock owner obtains a LOB locks when inserting or updating. Concurrent processes can SELECT or DELETE data in the LOB table space (or UPDATE the LOB to a null or zero-length).

As with transaction locking, there is a hierarchical relationship between LOB locks and LOB table space locks (see Figure 23.5). If the LOB table space is locked with a gross lock, LOB locks are not acquired.

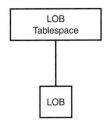

FIGURE 23.5 The DB2 LOB locking hierarchy.

The type of locking used is controlled using the `LOCKSIZE` clause for the LOB table space. `LOCKSIZE TABLESPACE` indicates that no LOB locks are to be acquired by processes that access the LOBs in the table space. Specifying `LOCKSIZE LOB` indicates that LOB locks and the associated LOB table space locks (`IS` or `IX`) are taken. The `LOCKSIZE ANY` specification allows DB2 to choose the size of the lock, which is usually to do LOB locking.

Duration of LOB Locks

The `ACQUIRE` option of `BIND` has no impact on LOB table space locking. DB2 will take locks on LOB table spaces as needed. However, the `RELEASE` option of `BIND` does control when LOB table space locks are releases. For `RELEASE(COMMIT)`, the LOB table space lock is released at `COMMIT` (unless `WITH HOLD` is specified or a LOB locator is held).

LOB locks are taken as needed and are usually released at `COMMIT`. If that LOB value is assigned to a LOB locator, the S-lock on the LOB remains until the application commits. If the application uses `HOLD LOCATOR`, the locator (and the LOB lock) is not freed until the first commit operation after a `FREE LOCATOR` statement is issued, or until the thread is deallocated. If a cursor is defined `WITH HOLD`, LOB locks are held through `COMMIT` operations.

LOB Table Space Locking Considerations

Under some circumstances, DB2 can avoid acquiring a lock on a LOB table space. For example, when deleting a row where the LOB column is null, DB2 need not lock the LOB table space.

DB2 does not access the LOB table space in the following instances:

- A `SELECT` of a LOB that is null or zero-length
- An `INSERT` of a LOB that is null or zero-length
- When a null or zero-length LOB is modified (by `UPDATE`) to a null or zero-length
- A `DELETE` for a row where the LOB is null or zero-length

DB2 Locking Guidelines

Locking is a complex subject, and it can take much time and effort to understand and master its intricacies. Do not be frustrated if these concepts escape you after an initial reading of this chapter. Instead, refer to the following guidelines to assist you in designing your application's locking needs. Let this information sink in for a while and then reread the chapter.

Be Aware of the Effect of Referential Integrity on Locking   When table space locks are acquired because of the processing of referential constraints, all locking specifications, except the ACQUIRE bind parameter, are obeyed. Locks acquired because of referential integrity always acquire locks when needed, acting as though ACQUIRE(USE) were specified, regardless of the ACQUIRE parameter.

Establish Acceptable BIND Plan Parameters   This information is covered in more detail in Chapter 13, "Program Preparation," but it is repeated here because it affects DB2 locking. Favor the use of the following parameters when binding application plans because they usually produce the most efficient and effective DB2 plan. In particular, the ISOLATION, ACQUIRE, and RELEASE parameters specified in the following list create an efficient plan in terms of enabling a large degree of concurrent processing.

Favor the use of the following parameters when binding application plans:

```
ISOLATION (CS)

VALIDATE (BIND)

ACTION (REPLACE)

NODEFER (PREPARE)

FLAG (I)

ACQUIRE (USE)

RELEASE (COMMIT)

DEGREE (1)

CURRENTDATA (NO)

EXPLAIN (YES)
```

These BIND PLAN parameters usually produce the most efficient and effective DB2 plan.

Establish Acceptable BIND Package Parameters   The ISOLATION parameter is the most important in terms of locking for DB2 packages. The following list of parameters should be favored when binding packages:

```
ISOLATION (CS)

VALIDATE (BIND)

ACTION (REPLACE)

SQLERROR (NOPACKAGE)

FLAG (I)

RELEASE (COMMIT)

DEGREE (1)

CURRENTDATA (NO)

EXPLAIN (YES)
```

Usually, these BIND PACKAGE parameters produce the most efficient and effective DB2 package. Other guidelines in this chapter cover the occasions when you should choose another option.

Be Aware of Lock Promotion   When binding a plan with an ISOLATION level of RR, the optimizer sometimes decides that table space locks will perform better than page locks. As such, the optimizer promotes the locking level to table space locking, regardless of the LOCKSIZE specified in the DDL. This process is called *lock promotion*.

Be Aware of Lock Escalation   When you set the LOCKSIZE bind parameter to ANY, DB2 processing begins with page-level locking. As processing continues and locks are acquired, however, DB2 might decide that too many page (or row) locks have been acquired, causing inefficient processing.

In this scenario, DB2 escalates the level of locking from page (or row) locks to table or tablespace locks—a procedure called *lock escalation*. The threshold governing when lock escalation occurs is set in one of two ways:

- The DSNZPARM start-up parameters for DB2

- The LOCKMAX parameter of the CREATE or ALTER TABLESPACE statement (which is stored in the MAXROWS column of SYSIBM.SYSTABLESPACE)

Lock escalation applies only to objects defined with LOCKSIZE ANY in the DDL. A table lock can never be escalated to a table space lock. Table space locks are the highest level of locking and, therefore, cannot be escalated.

User Lock Escalation   If a single user accumulates more page locks than are allowed by the DB2 subsystem (as set in DSNZPARMs), the program is informed via a -904 SQLCODE. The program can either issue a ROLLBACK and produce a message indicating that the program should be modified to COMMIT more frequently or, alternately, escalate the locking strategy itself by explicitly issuing a LOCK TABLE statement within the code.

Prior to implementing the second approach, refer to the upcoming guideline, "Use LOCK TABLE with Caution," for further clarification on the ramifications of using LOCK TABLE.

Use DSNZPARM Parameters to Control Lock Escalation   The two DSNZPARM parameters used to govern DB2 locking are NUMLKTS and NUMLKUS. NUMLKTS defines the threshold for the number of page locks that can be concurrently held for any one table space by any single DB2 application (thread). When the threshold is reached, DB2 escalates all page locks for objects defined as LOCKSIZE ANY according to the following rules:

- All page locks held for data in segmented table spaces are escalated to table locks.

- All page locks held for data in simple or partitioned table spaces are escalated to table space locks.

NUMLKUS defines the threshold for the total number of page locks across all table spaces that can be concurrently held by a single DB2 application. When any given application attempts to acquire a lock that would cause the application to surpass the NUMLKUS threshold, the application receives a resource unavailable message (SQLCODE of -904).

Consider LOCKSIZE ANY   In general, letting DB2 handle the level of locking required is a fine strategy. Turning over the determination for lock size to DB2 requires setting LOCKSIZE ANY.

Of course, you might have a compelling reason to use a specific LOCKSIZE. For example, you might choose to specify LOCKSIZE PAGE to explicitly direct DB2 to lock at the page level. Or, under certain conditions you might choose LOCKSIZE ROW to implement row-level locking. Chapter 5, "Data Definition Guidelines," provides more details on the LOCKSIZE parameter.

Use LOCKMAX **to Control Lock Escalation by Table Space**   The LOCKMAX parameter specifies the maximum number of page or row locks that any one process can hold at any one time for the table space. When the threshold is reached, the page or row locks are escalated to a table or table space lock. The LOCKMAX parameter is similar to the NUMLKTS parameter, but for a single table space only.

Set IRLM Parameters to Optimize Locking   When the IRLM is installed, you must code a series of parameters that affect the performance of DB2 locking. In particular, you should define the IRLM so that it effectively utilizes memory to avoid locking performance problems. The IRLM parameters are detailed in Table 23.13.

TABLE 23.13   Recommended IRLM Parameters

Parameter	Recommended Value	Reason
SCOPE	LOCAL	The IRLM should be local.
DEADLOK	(15,4)	Every 15 seconds, the IRLM goes into a deadlock detection cycle.
PC	NO	Cross-memory services are not used when requesting IRLM functions; instead, the locks are stored in ECSA and therefore are directly addressable.
ITRACE	NO	Never turn on the IRLM trace because it uses a vast amount of resources.

Use LOCK TABLE **with Caution**   Use the LOCK TABLE statement to control the efficiency of locking in programs that will issue many page lock requests. The LOCK TABLE statement is coded as a standard SQL statement and can be embedded in an application program.

There are two types of LOCK TABLE requests. The LOCK TABLE...IN SHARE MODE command acquires an S-lock on the table specified in the statement. This locking strategy effectively eliminates the possibility of concurrent modification programs running while the LOCK TABLE is in effect. *Note:* The S-lock is obtained on the table space for tables contained in non-segmented table spaces.

The LOCK TABLE...IN EXCLUSIVE MODE command acquires an X-lock on the table specified in the statement. All concurrent processing is suspended until the X-lock is released. *Note:* The X-lock is obtained on the table space for tables contained in non-segmented table spaces.

The table locks acquired as a result of the LOCK TABLE statement are held until the next COMMIT point unless ACQUIRE(DEALLOCATE) was specified for the plan issuing the LOCK TABLE statement. In that situation, the lock is held until the program terminates.

Encourage Lock Avoidance   To encourage DB2 to avoid locks, try the following:

- Whenever practical, specify ISOLATION(CS) and CURRENTDATA NO when binding packages and plans.

- Avoid ambiguous cursors by specifying FOR READ ONLY (or FOR FETCH ONLY) when a cursor is not to be used for updating.

Be Aware of Concurrent Access with Partition Independence   Partition independence allows more jobs to be run concurrently. This capability can strain system resources. You should monitor CPU usage and I/O when taking advantage of partition independence to submit concurrent jobs that would have needed to be serialized with previous versions.

Use Caution When Specifying WITH HOLD   Using the CURSOR WITH HOLD clause causes locks and claims to be held across commits. This capability can increase the number of timeouts and affect availability. Before coding the WITH HOLD clause on a cursor, be sure that the benefit gained by doing so is not negated by reduced availability.

Use the DSNZPARM RELCURHL to minimize these locks. Specify whether DB2 should, at COMMIT time, release a page or row lock on which a cursor defined WITH HOLD is positioned. This lock is *not* necessary for maintaining cursor position. YES is the default causing DB2 to release this lock after a COMMIT is issued. Specifying RELCURHL YES can improve concurrency. If you choose NO, DB2 holds the lock for WITH HOLD cursors after the COMMIT. This option is provided so that existing applications that rely on this lock can continue to work correctly.

Access Tables in the Same Order   Design all application programs to access tables in the same order. Doing so reduces the likelihood of deadlocks. Consider the following:

Program 1	Program 2
Lock on DEPT	Lock on EMP
Request Lock on EMP	Request Lock on DEPT

In this scenario, a deadlock occurs. However, if both programs accessed DEPT, followed by EMP, the deadlock situation could be avoided.

Design Application Programs with Locking in Mind   Minimize the effect of locking through proper application program design. Limit the number of rows that are accessed by coding predicates to filter unwanted rows. Doing so reduces the number of locks on pages containing rows that are accessed but not required, thereby reducing timeouts and deadlocks.

Also, you should design update programs so that the update is as close to the COMMIT point as possible. Doing so reduces the time that locks are held during a unit of work, which also reduces timeouts and deadlocks.

Keep Similar Things Together   Place tables for the same application into the same database. Although minimizing the number of databases used by an application can ease administration, it can negatively impact availability. For example, while dynamic SQL is accessing a table in a database, another table cannot be added to that database. When scheduled downtime is limited due to extreme availability requirements, such as is common in data warehousing and e-business environments, consider using one database for each large or active table.

Furthermore, each application process that creates private tables should have a dedicated private database in which to create the tables. Do not use a database that is in use for other, production database objects.

> **CAUTION**
>
> As with all advice, remember the cardinal rule of DB2: *It depends!* There are legitimate reasons for storing similar things separately. For example, as databases grow in size and activity increases, it might make sense to reduce the database size by storing fewer table spaces per database.

Use LOCKPART to Optimize Partition Independence   Enable selective partition locking by specifying LOCKPART YES when you create table spaces. With selective partition locking, DB2 will lock only those partitions that are accessed. If you specify LOCKPART NO, the table space is locked with a single lock on the last partition. This has the effect of locking all partitions in the table space.

> **CAUTION**
>
> You cannot specify LOCKPART YES if you also specify LOCKSIZE TABLESPACE.

Cluster Data   Use clustering to encourage DB2 to maintain data that is accessed together on the same page. If you use page locking, fewer locks are required to access multiple rows if the rows are clustered on the same page or pages.

Choose Segmented Over Simple Table Spaces for Locking Efficiency   Both simple and segmented table spaces can contain more than one table. A lock on a simple table space locks all the data in every table because rows from different tables can be intermingled on the same page. In a segmented table space, rows from different tables are contained in different pages. Locking a page does not lock data from more than one table. Additionally, for segmented table spaces only, DB2 can acquire a lock on a single table.

Consider Increasing Free Space   If you increase free space, fewer rows are stored on a single page. Therefore, fewer rows are locked by a single page lock. This approach can decrease contention. However, it consumes additional DASD, and it can also decrease the performance of table space scans.

Consider Decreasing Number of Rows Per Page   The MAXROWS option of the CREATE TABLESPACE statement can be used to decrease the number of rows stored on a table space page. The fewer rows per page, the less intrusive page locking will be because fewer rows will be impacted by a page lock.

Control LOB Locking for INSERT with Subselects   Because LOB locks are held until COMMIT, it is possible that a statement, such as an INSERT, with a subselect involving LOB columns can acquire and hold many more locks than if LOBs are not involved. To prevent system problems caused by too many locks, consider the following tactics:

- Enable lock escalation by specifying a non-zero LOCKMAX parameter for LOB table spaces impacted by the INSERT statement.

- Change the LOCKSIZE to LOCKSIZE TABLESPACE for the LOB table space prior to executing the INSERT statement.

- Use the LOCK TABLE statement to lock the LOB table space.

Other DB2 Components

You are near the end of your excursion behind the scenes of DB2. Before you finish, however, you should know about two other DB2 components that operate behind the scenes: the Boot Strap Data Set (BSDS) and DB2 logging.

The BSDS is a VSAM KSDS data set utilized by DB2 to control and administer the DB2 log data sets. It is an integral component of DB2, controlling the log data sets and managing an inventory of those logs. The BSDS is also used to record the image copy backups taken for the SYSIBM.SYSCOPY DB2 Catalog table. Because SYSIBM.SYSCOPY records all other DB2 image copies, another location must be used to record image copies of the SYSIBM.SYSCOPY table.

DB2 logs every modification made to every piece of DB2 data. Log records are written for every INSERT, UPDATE, and DELETE SQL statement that is successfully executed and committed. DB2 logs each updated row from the first byte updated to the end of the row. These log records are written to the active logs. DB2 usually has two active log data sets to safeguard against physical DASD errors. The active logs must reside on DASD. (They cannot reside on tape.) The active log data sets are managed by DB2 using the BSDS.

> **NOTE**
>
> For tables defined using the DATA CAPTURE CHANGES option, an UPDATE causes DB2 to log the entire updated row, even if only one column is changed.

As the active logs are filled, DB2 invokes a process called *log offloading* to move the log information offline to archive log data sets (see Figure 23.6). This process reduces the chances of the active logs filling up during DB2 processing, which would stifle the DB2 environment. DB2 can access archive logs to evoke table space recovery. The BSDS manages and administers the archive logs.

23

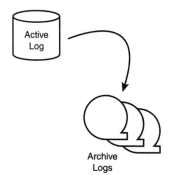

FIGURE 23.6   DB2 log offloading.

The Big Picture

Now that you have seen what is happening in DB2 "behind the scenes," I will tie all this information together with a single picture. Figure 23.7 depicts all the DB2 components that operate together to achieve an effective and useful relational database management system.

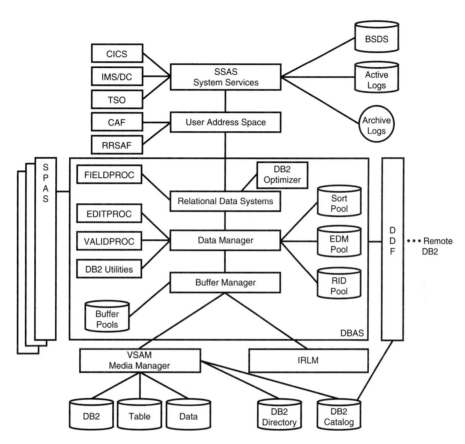

FIGURE 23.7   DB2: The big picture.

IN THIS CHAPTER

- DB2 Traces
- Trace Destinations
- Tracing Guidelines
- DB2 Performance Monitor (DB2 PM)
- Using DB2 PM
- Online DB2 Performance Monitors
- Viewing DB2 Console Messages
- Displaying the Status of DB2 Resources
- Monitoring z/OS and OS/390

CHAPTER 24

Traditional DB2 Performance Monitoring

The first part of any DB2 performance management strategy should be to provide a comprehensive approach to the monitoring of the DB2 subsystems operating at your shop. This approach involves monitoring not only the threads accessing DB2, but also the DB2 address spaces. You can accomplish this task in three ways:

- Batch reports run against DB2 trace records. While DB2 is running, you can activate traces that accumulate information, which can be used to monitor both the performance of the DB2 subsystem and the applications being run.

- Online access to DB2 trace information and DB2 control blocks. This type of monitoring also can provide information on DB2 and its subordinate applications.

- Sampling DB2 application programs as they run and analyzing which portions of the code use the most resources.

I will examine these monitoring methods later in this chapter, but first I will outline some performance monitoring basics. When you're implementing a performance monitoring methodology, keep these basic caveats in mind:

- Do not overdo monitoring and tracing. DB2 performance monitoring can consume a tremendous amount of resources. Sometimes the associated overhead is worthwhile because the monitoring (problem determination or exception notification) can help alleviate or avoid a problem. However, absorbing a large CPU overhead for monitoring a DB2 subsystem that is already performing within the desired scope of acceptance might not be worthwhile.

- Plan and implement two types of monitoring strategies at your shop: 1) ongoing performance monitoring to ferret out exceptions, and 2) procedures for monitoring exceptions after they have been observed.

- Do not try to drive a nail with a bulldozer. Use the correct tool for the job, based on the type of problem you're monitoring. You would be unwise to turn on a trace that causes 200% CPU overhead to solve a production problem that could be solved just as easily by other types of monitoring (using EXPLAIN or DB2 Catalog reports, for example).

- Tuning should not consume your every waking moment. Establish your DB2 performance tuning goals in advance, and stop when they have been achieved. Too often, tuning goes beyond the point at which reasonable gains can be realized for the amount of effort exerted. (For example, if your goal is to achieve a five-second response time for a TSO application, stop when you have achieved that goal.)

> **NOTE**
>
> Tuning goals should be set using the discipline of *service level management (SLM)*. A *service level* is a measure of operational behavior. SLM ensures applications behave accordingly by applying resources to those applications based on their importance to the organization. Depending on the needs of the organization, SLM can focus on availability, performance, or both. In terms of availability, the service level can be defined as "99.95% up time, during the hours of 9:00 AM to 10:00 PM on weekdays." Of course, a service level can be more specific, stating "average response time for transactions will be two seconds or less for workloads of 500 or fewer users."
>
> For a service level agreement (SLA) to be successful, all of the parties involved must agree upon stated objectives for availability and performance. The end users must be satisfied with the performance of their applications, and the DBAs and technicians must be content with their ability to manage the system to the objectives. Compromise is essential to reach a useful SLA.
>
> If you do not identify service levels for each transaction, then you will always be managing to an unidentified requirement. Without a predefined and agreed upon SLA, how will the DBA and the end users know whether an application is performing adequately? Without SLAs, business users and DBAs might have different expectations, resulting in unsatisfied business executives and frustrated DBAs. Not a good situation.

DB2 Traces

The first type of performance monitoring I discuss here is monitoring based on reading trace information. You can think of a DB2 trace as a window into the performance characteristics of aspects of the DB2 workload. DB2 traces record diagnostic information describing particular events. As DB2 operates, it writes trace information that can be read and analyzed to obtain performance information.

DB2 provides six types of traces, and each describes information about the DB2 environment. These six types of traces are outlined in Table 24.1.

TABLE 24.1   DB2 Trace Types

Trace	Started By	Description
Accounting	DSNZPARM or -START TRACE	Records performance information about the execution of DB2 application programs
Audit	DSNZPARM or -START TRACE	Provides information about DB2 DDL, security, utilities, and data modification
Global	DSNZPARM or -START TRACE	Provides information for the servicing of DB2
Monitor	DSNZPARM or -START TRACE	Records data useful for online monitoring of the DB2 subsystem and DB2 application programs
Performance	-START TRACE	Collects detailed data about DB2 events, enabling database and performance analysts to pinpoint the causes of performance problems
Statistics	DSNZPARM or -START TRACE	Records information regarding the DB2 subsystem's use of resources

Note that you start DB2 traces in two ways: by specifying the appropriate DSNZPARMs at DB2 startup or by using the -START TRACE command to initiate specific traces when DB2 is already running.

Each trace is broken down further into classes, each of which provides information about aspects of that trace. Classes are composed of IFCIDs. An IFCID (sometimes pronounced *if-kid*) is an Instrumentation Facility Component Identifier. An IFCID defines a record that represents a trace event. IFCIDs are the single smallest unit of tracing that can be invoked by DB2.

The six DB2 trace types are discussed in the following sections.

Accounting Trace

The accounting trace is probably the single most important trace for judging the performance of DB2 application programs. Using the accounting trace records, DB2 writes data pertaining to the following:

- CPU and elapsed time of the program

- EDM pool use

- Locks and GETPAGE page requests, by buffer pool, issued by the program

- Number of synchronous writes

- Thread wait times

- Type of SQL issued by the program

- Number of COMMITs and ABORTs issued by the program

- Program's use of sequential prefetch and other DB2 performance features (RLF, distributed processing, and so on)

There are ten groups of DB2 accounting trace classes:

Class 1—Standard accounting information

Class 2—Entry or exit from DB2 events

Class 3—Elapsed wait time in DB2

Class 4—Installation-defined accounting record

Class 5—Time spent processing IFI requests

Class 6—Reserved

Class 7—Entry or exit from event signaling package or DBRM accounting

Class 8—Wait time for a package

Class 10 thru 29—Reserved

Class 30 thru 32—Local use

Estimated overhead: DB2 accounting class 1 adds approximately 3% CPU overhead. DB2 accounting classes 1, 2, and 3 together add approximately 5% CPU overhead. You cannot run class 2 or 3 without also running class 1.

Accounting trace classes 7 and 8 provide performance trace information at the package level. Enabling this level of tracing can cause significant overhead.

Audit Trace

The audit trace is useful for installations that must meticulously track specific types of DB2 events. Not every shop needs the audit trace. However, those wanting to audit by AUTHID, specific table accesses, and other DB2 events will find the audit trace invaluable. Eight categories of audit information are provided:

- All instances in which an authorization failure occurs, for example, if USER1 attempts to SELECT information from a table for which he or she has not been granted the appropriate authority

- All executions of the DB2 data control language GRANT and REVOKE statements

- Every DDL statement issued for specific tables created by specifying AUDIT CHANGES or AUDIT ALL

- The first DELETE, INSERT, or UPDATE for an audited table

- The first SELECT for only the tables created specifying AUDIT ALL

- DML statements encountered by DB2 when binding

- All AUTHID changes resulting from execution of the SET CURRENT SQLID statement

- All execution of IBM DB2 utilities

This type of data is often required of critical DB2 applications housing sensitive data, such as payroll or billing applications.

There are eleven groups of DB2 audit trace classes:

Class 1—Attempted access denied due to lack of authority

Class 2—GRANT and REVOKE statements

Class 3—CREATE, ALTER, and DROP statements against audited tables

Class 4—First change made to an audited object

Class 5—First read made against an audited object

Class 6—BIND information for SQL statements on audited objects

Class 7—Assignment or change of an AUTHID

Class 8—Utility execution

Class 9—Installation-defined audit trace record

Class 10 thru 29—Reserved

Class 30 thru 32—Local use

Estimated overhead: Approximately 5% CPU overhead per transaction is added when all audit trace classes are started. See the "Tracing Guidelines" section later in this chapter for additional information on audit trace overhead.

Global Trace

Global trace information is used to service DB2. Global trace records information regarding entries and exits from internal DB2 modules as well as other information about DB2 internals. It is not accessible through tools that monitor DB2 performance. Most sites will never need to use the DB2 global trace. You should avoid it unless an IBM representative requests that your shop initiate it.

> **CAUTION**
>
> IBM states that the global trace can add up to 100% CPU overhead to your DB2 subsystem.

Monitor Trace

An amalgamation of useful performance monitoring information is recorded by the DB2 monitor trace. Most of the information in a monitor trace is also provided by other types of DB2 traces. The primary reason for the existence of the monitor trace type is to enable you to write application programs that provide online monitoring of DB2 performance.

Information provided by the monitor trace includes the following:

- DB2 statistics trace information

- DB2 accounting trace information

- Information about current SQL statements

There are ten groups of DB2 monitor trace classes:

Class 1—Activate the READS IFCIDs

Class 2—Entry or exit from DB2 events

Class 3—DB2 wait for I/O or locks

Class 4—Installation-defined monitor trace record

Class 5—Time spent processing IFI requests

Class 6—Changes to tables created with DATA CAPTURE CHANGES

Class 7—Entry or exit from event signaling package or DBRM accounting

Class 8—Wait time for a package

Class 9 thru 29—Reserved

Class 30 thru 32—Local use

Estimated overhead: The overhead that results from the monitor trace depends on how it is used at your site. If, as recommended, class 1 is always active, and classes 2 and 3 are started and stopped as required, the overhead is minimal (approximately 2 to 5%, depending on the activity of the DB2 system and the number of times that the other classes are started and stopped). However, if your installation makes use of the reserved classes (30 through 32) or additional classes (as some vendors do), your site will incur additional overhead.

> **NOTE**
>
> Some online performance monitoring tools do not use the monitor trace; instead, they read the information directly from the DB2 control blocks. Sampling DB2 control blocks requires less overhead than a monitor trace.

Performance Trace

The DB2 performance trace records an abundance of information about all types of DB2 events. You should use it only after you have exhausted all other avenues of monitoring and tuning because it consumes a great deal of system resources.

When a difficult problem persists, the performance trace can provide valuable information, including the following:

- Text of the SQL statement
- Complete trace of the execution of SQL statements, including details of all events (cursor creation and manipulation, actual reads and writes, fetches, and so on) associated with the execution of the SQL statement
- All index accesses
- All data access due to referential constraints

There are twenty groups of DB2 performance trace classes:

Class 1—Background events

Class 2—Subsystem events

Class 3—SQL events

Class 4—Reads to and writes from buffer pools and the EDM pool

Class 5—Writes to log or archive log

Class 6 and 7—Summary (6) and detailed (7) lock information

Class 8—Data scanning detail

Class 9—Sort detail

Class 10—Detail on BIND, commands, and utilities

Class 11—Execution

Class 12—Storage manager

Class 13—Edit and validation exits

Class 14—Entry from and exit to an application

Class 15—Installation-defined performance trace record

Class 16—Distributed processing

Class 17—Claim and drain information

Class 18 thru 19—Reserved

Class 20 and 21—Data sharing coherency summary (20) and detail (21)

Class 23 thru 29—Reserved

Class 30 thru 32—Local use

Estimated overhead: When all DB2 performance trace classes are active, as much as 100% CPU overhead can be incurred by each program being traced. The actual overhead might be greater if the system has a large amount of activity. Furthermore, due to the large number of trace records cut by the DB2 performance trace, systemwide (DB2 and non-DB2) performance might suffer because of possible SMF or GTF contention. The overhead when using only classes 1, 2, and 3, however, ranges from 20 to 30% rather than 100%

Statistics Trace

Information pertaining to the entire DB2 subsystem is recorded in statistics trace records. This information is particularly useful for measuring the activity and response of DB2 as a whole. Information on the utilization and status of the buffer pools, DB2 locking, DB2 logging, and DB2 storage is accumulated.

There are ten groups of DB2 statistics trace classes:

Class 1—Statistics data

Class 2—Installation-defined statistics record

Class 3—Data on deadlocks, lock escalation, group buffers, data set extension, long-running units of recovery, and active log shortage

Class 4—Exceptional conditions

Class 5—Data sharing statistics

Class 6—Storage usage

Class 7—Reserved

Class 8—Data set I/O

Class 9 thru 29—Reserved

Class 30 thru 32—Local use

Estimated overhead: An average of 2% CPU overhead per transaction.

Trace Destinations

When a trace is started, DB2 formats records containing the requested information. After the information is prepared, it must be externalized. DB2 traces can be written to six destinations:

GTF (Generalized Trace Facility) is a component of MVS and is used for storing large volumes of trace data.

RES   RES is a wraparound table residing in memory.

SMF   SMF (System Management Facility) is a source of data collection used by MVS to accumulate information and measurements. This destination is the most common for DB2 traces.

SRV   SRV is a routine used primarily by IBM support personnel for servicing DB2.

OP*n*   OP*n* (where *n* is a value from 1 to 8) is an output buffer area used by the Instrumentation Facility Interface (IFI).

OPX   OPX is a generic output buffer. When used as a destination, OPX signals DB2 to assign the next available OP*n* buffer (OP1 to OP8).

The Instrumentation Facility Interface, which is a DB2 trace interface, enables DB2 programs to read, write, and create DB2 trace records and issue DB2 commands. Many online DB2 performance monitors are based on the IFI.

Consult Table 24.2 for a synopsis of the available and recommended destinations for each DB2 trace type. Y indicates that the specified trace destination is valid for the given type of trace; N indicates that it is not.

TABLE 24.2   DB2 Trace Destinations

Type of Trace	GTF	RES	SMF	SRV	OPn	OPX	Recommended Destination
Statistics	Y	N	Default	Y	Y	Y	SMF
Accounting	Y	N	Default	Y	Y	Y	SMF
Audit	Y	N	Default	Y	Y	Y	SMF
Performance	Y	N	Default	Y	Y	Y	GTF
Monitor	Y	N	Y	Y	Y	D	OPn
Global	Y	Default	Y	Y	Y	Y	SRV

Tracing Guidelines

Consider abiding by the following guidelines to implement an effective DB2 tracing strategy at your shop.

Collect Basic Statistics   At a minimum, start the DB2 accounting classes 1 and 2 and statistics class 1 traces at DB2 start-up time. This way, you can ensure that basic statistics are accumulated for the DB2 subsystem and every DB2 plan executed. These traces require little overhead. If you do not start these traces, you cannot use traces to monitor DB2 performance (the method used by IBM DB2 PM).

Consider starting accounting class 3 at DB2 start-up time as well. It tracks DB2 wait time and is useful for tracking I/O and tracking problems external to DB2.

Note that accounting classes 2 and 3 cannot be activated unless accounting class 1 is active.

You might also consider starting statistics class 6 to accrue storage information, which can be useful for monitoring and tuning systems with heavy data growth expectations.

Use Accounting Trace Classes 7 and 8 with Caution   Accounting classes 7 and 8 cause DB2 to write trace records at the package level. Although monitoring DB2 applications at the package level may seem appropriate, do so with caution to avoid undue performance degradation.

If package level performance monitoring is absolutely essential for certain applications, consider starting these trace classes for only those plans. This way, you can produce the requisite information with as little overhead as possible.

Use the Audit Trace Wisely   If your shop has tables created with the AUDIT parameter, start all audit trace classes.

If your shop has no audited tables, use the DSNZPARMs at DB2 startup to start only audit classes 1, 2, and 7 to audit authorization failures, DCL, and utility execution. Except for these types of processing, audit classes 1, 2, and 7 add no additional overhead. Because most transactions do not result in authorization failures or issue GRANTs, REVOKEs, or utilities, running these trace classes is cost-effective.

Let Your Performance Monitor Start Traces   Do not start the monitor trace using DSNZPARMs unless online performance monitors in your shop explicitly require you to do so. It is best to start only monitor trace class 1 and to use a performance monitor that starts and stops the other monitor trace classes as required.

Avoid starting the monitor trace through the use of the -START TRACE command under DB2I. When this command is entered manually in this manner, a great degree of coordination is required to start and stop the monitor trace according to the requirements of your online monitor.

Use Caution When Running Performance Traces   In each instance where -START is written, the dash "-" cannot be separated from the START in the final production of the book (as it is in the next to last sentence of the following paragraph below).

Use the performance trace with great care. Performance traces must be explicitly started with the -START TRACE command. Starting the performance trace only for the plan (or plans) you want to monitor by using the PLAN parameter of the -START TRACE command is wise. Here's an example:

```
-START TRACE(PERFM) CLASS(1,2,3) PLAN(PLANNAME) DEST(GTF)
```

Failure to start the trace at the plan level can result in the trace being started for all plans, which causes undue overhead on all DB2 plans that execute while the trace is active.

Avoid Performance Trace Class 7   Never use performance trace class 7 unless directed by IBM. Lock detail trace records are written when performance trace class 7 is activated. They can cause as much as a 100% increase in CPU overhead per program being traced.

Avoid Global Trace   Avoid the global trace unless directed to use it by a member of your IBM support staff. This trace should be used only for servicing DB2.

Use IFCIDs   Consider avoiding the trace classes altogether, and start traces specifying only the IFCIDs needed. This way, you can reduce the overhead associated with tracing by recording only the trace events that are needed. You can do so by using the -START TRACE command, as follows:

```
-START TRACE(PERFM) CLASS(1) IFCID(1,2,42,43,107,153)
```

This command starts only IFCIDs 1, 2, 42, 43, 107, and 153.

Because this task can be tedious, if you decide to trace only at the IFCID level, use a performance monitor that starts these IFCID-level traces based on menu choices. For example, if you choose to trace the elapsed time of DB2 utility jobs, the monitor or tool would have a menu option for this, initiating the correct IFCID traces (for example, IFCIDs 023 through 025). For more information on the Instrumentation Facility Interface and IFCIDs, consult the *DB2 Administration Guide*.

DB2 Performance Monitor (DB2 PM)

IBM's DB2 PM is the most widely used batch performance monitor for DB2. Although DB2 PM also provides an online component, it is not as widely used (though it has been significantly improved since its initial release). I discuss the online portion of DB2 PM briefly in the next section. In this section, I concentrate solely on the batch performance monitoring characteristics of DB2 PM. Other DB2 performance monitoring solutions offer similar reports and information, so you should be able to translate this information for the particular product in use at your site.

DB2 PM permits performance analysts to review formatted trace records to assist in evaluating the performance of not only the DB2 subsystem, but also DB2 applications (see Figure 24.1). As the DB2 subsystem executes, trace records are written to either GTF or SMF. Which trace records are written depends on which DB2 traces are active. The trace information is then funneled to DB2 PM, which creates requested reports and graphs.

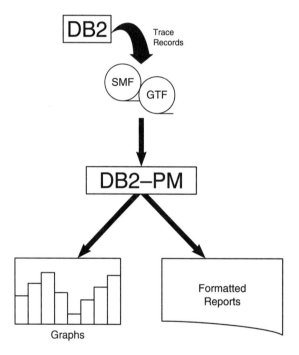

FIGURE 24.1   DB2 PM operation.

DB2 PM can generate many categories of performance reports, known as *report sets*. A brief description of each report set follows:

Accounting	Summarizes the utilization of DB2 resources such as CPU and elapsed time, SQL use, buffer use, and locking.
Audit	Tracks the access of DB2 resources. Provides information on authorization failures, GRANTs and REVOKEs, access to auditable tables, SET SQLID executions, and utility execution.
I/O Activity	Summarizes DB2 reads and writes to the bufferpool, EDM pool, active and archive logs, and the BSDS.

Locking	Reports the level of lock suspension and contention in the DB2 subsystem.
Record Trace	Displays DB2 trace records from the input source.
SQL Trace	Reports on detailed activity associated with each SQL statement.
Statistics	Summarizes the statistics for an entire DB2 subsystem. Useful for obtaining a synopsis of DB2 activity.
Summary	Reports on the activity performed by DB2 PM to produce the requested reports.
System Parameters	Creates a report detailing the values assigned by DSNZPARMs.
Transit time	Produces a report detailing the average elapsed time for DB2 units of work by component.

Many types and styles of reports can be generated within each set. The following sections describe each DB2 PM report set.

Accounting Report Set

The DB2 PM accounting report set provides information on the performance of DB2 applications. Two basic layouts are provided for accounting reports: short and long. The accounting reports provide the following type of information about the performance of DB2 applications:

- The start and stop time for each program

- The number of commits and aborts encountered

- The type of SQL statements used and how often each type was issued

- The number of buffer manager requests

- Use of locks

- Amount of CPU resources consumed

- Asynchronous and synchronous I/O wait time

- Lock and latch wait time

- RID pool processing

- Distributed processing

- Resource limit facility (RLF) statistics

For an example of the type of information provided on a short accounting report, refer to the accounting report excerpt shown in Listing 24.1. This report provides a host of summarized performance data for each plan, broken down by DBRM.

24

LISTING 24.1   DB2 PM Accounting Report—Short

PLANNAME	#OCCURS #DISTRS	#ROLLBK #COMMIT	SELECTS FETCHES	INSERTS OPENS	UPDATES CLOSES	DELETES PREPARE	CLASS1 EL.TIME CLASS1 TCBTIME	CLASS2 EL.TIME CLASS2 TCBTIME	GETPAGES BUF.UPDT	SYN.READ TOT.PREF	LOCK SUS #LOCKOUT
PRG00001	19	0	8.24	2.39	3.33	2.49	2.938984	2.879021	81.29	12.29	0.49
	0	27	2.35	2.35	2.35	0.00	0.019870	0.017809	30.42	0.59	0

PROGRAM NAME	TYPE	#OCCUR	SQLSTMT	CL7 ELAP.TIME	CL7 TCB.TIME	CL8 SUSP.TIME	CL8 SUSP
PRG00100	DBRM	10	12.00	3.298190	0.015465	3.198018	9.71
PRG00150	DBRM	2	8.00	1.981201	0.017810	1.980012	8.92
PRG00192	DBRM	7	7.00	2.010191	0.189153	1.702439	9.28

> **NOTE**
>
> Please note that the DB2 PM report excerpts shown in this chapter might not look exactly like the reports that you will generate using DB2 PM. The listings in this chapter are excerpts and are shown to highlight the performance information that can be gleaned from each type of report.

Each plan is reported in two rows. Refer to the first row of the report, the one for PRG00000. Two rows of numbers belong to this plan. The first row corresponds to the first row of the header. For example, this row shows 19 occurrences of this plan (#OCCUR), 0 rollback requests (#ROLLBK), 8.24 SELECTS, and 2.39 INSERTS. The second row corresponds to the second row of the report header. For example, it has no distributed requests, 27 COMMITS, and 2.35 FETCHES.

The second component of this report details each of the packages and/or DBRMs for the plan. For each package or DBRM, DB2 PM reports the number of occurrences and SQL statements, along with elapsed, TCB, and suspension times and total number of suspensions. This information is provided only if Accounting Trace Classes 7 and 8 are specified.

The report shown was generated by requesting DB2 PM to sort the output by PLANNAME only. The following sort options are available:

- CONNECT   Connection ID
- CONNTYPE   Connection type
- CORRNAME   Correlation name
- CORRNMBR   Correlation number
- ORIGAUTH   Original authorization ID
- PLANNAME   Plan name
- PRIMAUTH/AUTHID   Primary authorization ID/authorization ID
- REQLOC   Requesting location

Likewise, you can combine these options together, such as PRIMAUTH-PLANNAME-REQLOC. This combination would cause a report to be generated containing a row for each unique combination of primary authorization ID, plan name, and requesting location.

The short accounting report is useful for monitoring the overall performance of your DB2 applications. Using this report, you can perform the following functions:

- Determine how many times a plan was executed during a specific timeframe. The #OCCURS column specifies this information.

- With the appropriate request, determine how many times a given user executed a given plan.

- Investigate basic performance statistics, such as elapsed and CPU time, at the DBRM or package level.

- Spot-check plans for average SQL activity. If you know the basic operations performed by your plans, you can use the short accounting report to determine whether the SQL being issued by your plans corresponds to your expectations. For example, you can determine whether update plans are actually updating. Columns 3 through 6 of this report contain basic SQL information. Remember, however, that this information is averaged. For example, plan PRG00000 issued 2.39 inserts on average, but the plan was executed 19 times. Obviously, the same number of inserts does not occur each time the plan is executed.

- Determine dynamic SQL activity. By checking for PREPARE activity, you can determine which plans are issuing dynamic SQL.

- Obtain an overall reflection of response time. The Class 1 and Class 2 Elapsed and TCB Time columns report the overall average elapsed and CPU time for the given plan. Class 1 is the overall application time; Class 2 is the time spent in DB2. If these numbers are very large or outside the normal expected response time range, further investigation might be warranted.

- Review average I/O characteristics. The average number of GETPAGEs corresponds to requests for data from DB2. SYN.READ corresponds to a non-sequential prefetch direct read. You can skim these numbers quickly to obtain an overall idea of the efficiency of reading DB2 data.

- Monitor other information such as lock suspensions (LOCK SUS) and timeouts and deadlocks (#LOCKOUT) using this report to determine whether contention problems exist.

24

At the end of the short accounting report, a synopsis of the plans on the report is presented. The plans are sorted in order by TCB time spent in DB2 and wait time spent in DB2. This synopsis is useful when you're analyzing which plan takes the longest time to execute.

If the short accounting report signals that potential problems exist, a long accounting report can be requested. This report provides much more detail for each entry on the short accounting report. The long accounting report documents performance information in great depth and is one of the most useful tools for performance analysis. The long accounting report is composed of eight distinct sections:

Part 1	CPU and elapsed time information, broken down by class, at the plan level
Part 2	Overall highlights for the particular plan
Part 3	In-depth SQL activity for the plan
Part 4	Detailed locking statistics for the plan
Part 5	Program status information for the plan
Part 6	Miscellaneous plan information, including data sharing, query parallelism information, and data capture processing
Part 7	Database code usage statistics (stored procedures, user-defined functions, and triggers)
Part 8	In-depth buffer pool (virtual pool and hiperpool) usage statistics
Part 9	DBRM and Package detail information

You should use the long accounting report to further analyze the performance of particular plans. The detail on this report can appear intimidating at first, but reading it is simple after you get used to it.

The first step after producing this report is to scan it quickly for obvious problems. In the following sections, you will examine each of the individual components of this report in more detail.

Long Accounting Report: CPU and Elapsed Time

The CPU and Elapsed Time portion of the long accounting report contains a breakdown of the amount of time the plan took to execute. Elapsed time, CPU time, I/O time, and locking time are displayed in great detail (see Listing 24.2).

LISTING 24.2   Accounting Report—Long (Part 1)

PRIMAUTH: DBPCSM   PLANNAME: PROG0049

AVERAGE	APPL (CL.1)	DB2 (CL.2)	IFI (CL.5)	CLASS 3 SUSPENSIONS	AVERAGE TIME	AV.EVENT
ELAPSED TIME	1:01.092617	1:01.037903	N/P	LOCK/LATCH(DB2+IRLM)	4.143163	31.83
NONNESTED	1:01.092617	1.01.037903	N/A	SYNCHRON. I/O	0.865210	163.31
STORED PROC	0.000000	0.000000	N/A	DATABASE I/O	0.865210	163.31
UDF	0.000000	0.000000	N/A	LOG WRITE I/O	0.000000	0.00
TRIGGER	0.000000	0.000000	N/A	OTHER READ I/O	1.648050	96.83
				OTHER WRTE I/O	0.021439	0.64
CPU TIME	56.896970	56.883519	N/C	SER.TASK SWTCH	1.664584	20.66
AGENT	13.210102	13.179621	N/A	UPDATE COMMIT	0.000000	0.00
NONNESTED	13.210102	13.179621	N/C	OPEN/CLOSE	1.564075	10.31
STORED PROC	0.000000	0.000000	N/A	SYSLGRNG REC	0.005812	1.00
UDF	0.000000	0.000000	N/A	EXT/DEL/DEF	0.086883	3.23
TRIGGER	0.000000	0.000000	N/A	OTHER SERVICE	0.007851	6.00
PAR.TASKS	43.658789	43.658789	N/A	ARC.LOG(QUIES)	0.000000	0.00
				ARC.LOG READ	0.000000	0.00
SUSPEND TIME	N/A	8.359872	N/A	STOR.PRC SCHED	0.000000	0.00
AGENT	N/A	1.310241	N/A	UDF SCHEDULE	0.000000	0.00
PAR.TASKS	N/A	7.049512	N/A	DRAIN LOCK	0.000000	0.00
				CLAIM RELEASE	0.000000	0.00
NOT ACCOUNT.	N/A	46.499738	N/A	PAGE LATCH	0.000000	0.00
DB2 ENT/EXIT	N/A	19.00	N/A	NOTIFY MSGS	0.000000	0.00
EN/EX-STPROC	N/A	0.00	N/A	GLOBAL CONTENTION	0.000000	0.00
EN/EX-UDF	N/A	0.00	N/P	COMMIT PH1 WRITE I/O	0.000000	0.00
DCAPT.DESCR.	N/A	N/A	N/P	ASYNCH IXL REQUESTS	0.000000	0.00
LOG EXTRACT.	N/A	N/A	N/P	TOTAL CLASS 3	8.342446	0.00

When you're analyzing this section, first compare the application times (Class 1) to the DB2 times (Class 2). If a huge discrepancy exists between these numbers, the problem may be outside the realm of DB2 (for example, VSAM opens and closes, application loops, or waiting for synchronous I/O). Also, keep in mind that the DB2 times do not include:

- The time before the first SQL statement, which for a distributed application includes the inbound network delivery time

- The create and terminate time for the DB2 thread

- The time to deliver the response to a commit if database access thread pooling is used (for distributed applications)

For IMS, CICS, and WebSphere transactions, compare the not-in DB2 time (class 1 minus class 2) against the time reported on your IMS, CICS, or WebSphere monitor report. Sometimes a performance culprit reveals itself by comparing the results of two different monitors (that is, DB2 versus IMS/CICS/WebSphere). Class 3 information reports wait time. Read and write suspensions are shown in the SYNCHRON. I/O, OTHER READ I/O, and WRITE I/O entries of this report. Of particular interest is the amount of time spent waiting for I/O. If the average SYNCHRON. I/O wait time is high, investigate the application for reasons that would cause additional reads, such as the following:

- Was the program recently modified to perform more SELECT statements?

- Was the plan recently rebound, causing a different access path to be chosen?

- Was query I/O parallelism recently "turned on" for this plan using DEGREE(ANY)?

- Was additional data added to the tables accessed by this plan?

If no additional data is being read, investigate other reasons such as insufficient buffers, insufficient EDM pool storage, or disk contention.

As a general rule of thumb, an asynchronous read (sequential prefetch or sequential detection) requires from 0.4 to 2 milliseconds per page. List prefetch reads range from 1 to 4 milliseconds. A synchronous write requires about 1 to 4 milliseconds per page.

Turning your attention to locking, if LOCK/LATCH(DB2+IRLM) suspension time is higher than expected, review the lock detail shown in Part 4 of the long accounting report. Potential causes of such a problem include a new inefficient access path, unclustered data, or a system problem.

The Long Accounting Report also breaks out time spent processing stored procedures, user-defined functions, and triggers.

Long Accounting Report: Highlights

After you peruse the execution times, a quick analysis of the highlights portion of the report is useful. The highlights section is located just to the right of the section containing execution times. It contains some basic details about the nature of the application that will be useful for subsequent performance analysis (see Listing 24.3).

LISTING 24.3   Accounting Report—Long (Part 2)

```
HIGHLIGHTS
- - - - - - - - - - - - - - - - - - - - - - - - - -
#OCCURENCES      :        6
#ALLIEDS         :        6
#ALLIEDS DISTRIB:         0
#DBATS           :        0
#DBATS DISTRIB.  :        0
#NO PROGRAM DATA:         6
#NORMAL TERMINAT:         6
#ABNORMAL TERMIN:         0
#CP/X PARALLEL.  :        6
#IO PARALLELISM  :        0
#INCREMENT. BIND:         0
#COMMITS         :       12
#SVPT REQUESTS   :        0
#SVPT RELEASE    :        0
#SVPT ROLLBACKS  :        0
MAX SQL CASC LVL:         0
UPDATE/COMMIT    :      N/C
SYNCH I/O AVG    : 0.005408
```

You should review the following highlight fields:

- To determine the number of times a plan was executed during the reported time-frame, review the total number of occurrences (#OCCURENCES).

- If the number of commits is not higher than the number of normal terminations, the program did not perform more than one commit per execution. You might need to review the program to ensure that a proper commit strategy is in place. This situation is not necessarily bad, but it warrants further investigation.

- Analyze the number of normal and abnormal terminations for each plan. Further investigation may be warranted if a particular plan has an inordinate number of aborts.

- If the value for #INCREMENT. BIND is not 0, the plan is being automatically rebound before it is executed. This situation is referred to as an incremental bind. Either the plan is marked as invalid because an index was removed (or because of some other DDL change), causing an automatic rebind, or the plan was bound with VALIDATE(RUN). To optimize performance, avoid these situations when possible.

- Two fields can be examined to determine if the reported process is using parallelism. #CP/X PARALLEL shows CPU parallelism and #IO PARALLELISM shows I/O parallelism.

Long Accounting Report: SQL Activity
An understanding of the type of SQL being issued by the application is essential during performance analysis. The long accounting report provides a comprehensive summary of the SQL issued, grouped into DML, DCL, and DDL sections (see Listing 24.4).

LISTING 24.4   Accounting Report—Long (Part 3)

SQL DML	AVERAGE	TOTAL	SQL DCL	TOTAL	SQL DDL	CREATE	DROP	ALTER
SELECT	1.00	17	LOCK TABLE	0	TABLE	0	0	0
INSERT	0.00	0	GRANT	0	CRT TABLE	0	N/A	N/A
UPDATE	0.00	0	REVOKE	0	DCL TABLE	0	N/A	N/A
DELETE	0.00	0	SET CURR.SQLID	0	AUX TABLE	0	N/A	N/A
			SET HOST VAR	0	INDEX	0	0	0
DESCRIBE	0.00	0	SET CURR.DEGREE	0	TABLESPACE	0	0	0
DESC.TBL	0.00	0	SET RULES	0	DATABASE	0	0	0
PREPARE	0.00	0	SET CURR.PATH	0	STOGROUP	0	0	0
OPEN	3.00	51	SET CURR.PREC.	0	SYNONYM	0	0	0
FETCH	4553.00	77401	CONNECT TYPE 1	0	VIEW	0	0	N/A
CLOSE	3.00	51	CONNECT TYPE 2	0	ALIAS	0	0	N/A
			SET CONNECTION	0	PACKAGE	N/A	0	N/A
			RELEASE	0	PROCEDURE	0	0	0
DML-ALL	4559.00	77503	CALL	0	FUNCTION	0	0	0
			ASSOC LOCATORS	0	TRIGGER	0	0	0
			ALLOC CURSOR	0	DIST TYPE	0	0	N/A
			HOLD LOCATOR	0	SEQUENCE	0	0	N/A
			FREE LOCATOR	0				
			DCL-ALL	0	TOTAL	0	0	0
					RENAME TBL	0		
					COMMENT ON	0		
					LABEL ON	0		

Scan the DML section of the report to verify the type of processing that is occurring. You can quickly uncover a problem if the application is thought to be read-only but INSERT, UPDATE, and/or DELETE activity is not 0. Likewise, if DESCRIBE, DESC.TBL, and or PREPARE

are not 0, the application is performing dynamic SQL statements and should be analyzed accordingly.

V7 Additionally, DDL is not generally permitted in application programs. When you spot unplanned DDL activity within an application program, you should consider it a problem. The only exception to this "rule of thumb" is for declared temporary tables, as reported under DCL TTABLE, which must be created using a DECLARE statement in an application program.

I can say the same about DCL GRANT and REVOKE statements. They are not generally coded in application programs, either. However, LOCK TABLE, SET, and CONNECT are valid and useful statements that will show up from time to time. When they do, ensure that they have valid uses, as follows:

- LOCK TABLE should be used with caution because it takes a lock on the entire table (or tablespace) instead of page locking. It reduces concurrency but can improve performance.

- SET is used to control aspects of program execution. For example, SET CURR.DEGREE is specified for dynamic SQL query I/O parallelism.

- CONNECT activity indicates distributed processing.

Long Accounting Report: Locking Activity

The locking activity component of the long accounting report is useful for isolating the average and total number of locks, timeouts, deadlocks, lock escalations, and lock/latch suspensions (see Listing 24.5).

LISTING 24.5   Accounting Report—Long (Part 4)

```
LOCKING            AVERAGE    TOTAL
---------------    -------    -----
TIMEOUTS             0.06         1
DEADLOCKS            0.00         0
ESCAL.(SHARED)       0.00         0
ESCAL.(EXCLUS)       0.00         0
MAX LOCKS HELD       0.41         3
LOCK REQUEST         8.00       136
UNLOCK REQUEST       1.00        17
QUERY REQUEST        0.00         0
CHANGE REQUEST       0.00         0
OTHER REQUEST        0.00         0
LOCK SUSPENSIONS     0.00         0
IRLM LATCH SUSPENS   0.06         1
OTHER SUSPENSIONS    0.00         0
TOTAL SUSPENSIONS    0.06         1

DRAIN/CLAIM        AVERAGE    TOTAL
---------------    -------    -----
DRAIN REQUESTS       0.00         0
DRAIN FAILED         0.00         0
CLAIM REQUESTS       3.00        51
CLAIM FAILED         0.00         0
```

Additionally, average and total claims and drains are detailed in this section.

Consider the following general rules of thumb for locking analysis:

- If the value for MAX LOCKS HELD is very high, it may be beneficial to consider issuing LOCK TABLE.

- If the value for TIMEOUTS is very high, consider either reevaluating the type of access being performed by the application or changing the DSNZPARM value for the length of time to wait for a resource timeout. Factors that could increase the number of timeouts include different programs accessing the same tables in a different order, inappropriate locking strategies (RR versus CS), and heavy concurrent ad hoc access.

- If ESCAL.(SHARED) and ESCAL.(EXCLUS) are not 0, lock escalation is occurring. The plan therefore causes page locks to escalate to tablespace locks (for those tablespaces defined as LOCKSIZE ANY). This situation could cause lock contention for other plans requiring these tablespaces.

- If the value for TOTAL SUSPENS. is high (over 10,000), there is probably a great deal of contention for the data that your plan requires. This situation usually indicates that index subpages should be increased or page locking specified instead of ANY.

Long Accounting Report: Program Status

If a large number of abnormal terminations were reported in the long accounting report highlights section, analysis of the program status section may be appropriate (see Listing 24.6).

LISTING 24.6   Accounting Report—Long (Part 5)

NORMAL TERM.	AVERAGE	TOTAL	ABNORMAL TERM.	TOTAL	IN DOUBT	TOTAL
NEW USER	0.94	17	APPL.PROGR. ABEND	1	APPL.PGM ABEND	0
DEALLOCATION	0.00	0	END OF MEMORY	0	END OF MEMORY	0
APPL.PROGR. END	0.00	0	RESOL.IN DOUBT	0	END OF TASK	0
RESIGNON	0.00	0	CANCEL FORCE	0	CANCEL FORCE	0
DBAT INACTIVE	0.00	0				
RRS COMMIT	0.00	0				

Long Accounting Report: Miscellaneous Information

The miscellaneous information reported in this section of the long accounting report can be crucial in performance analysis (see Listing 24.7). Six independent components are reported in this section:

- Data capture

- Data Sharing

- Query parallelism

- Stored procedures

- User-defined functions

- Triggers

LISTING 24.7   Accounting Report—Long (Part 6)

DATA CAPTURE	AVERAGE	TOTAL	DATA SHARING	AVERAGE	TOTAL	QUERY PARALLELISM	AVERAGE	TOTAL
IFI CALLS MADE	N/C	0	GLOBAL CONT RATE(%)	N/C	N/A	MAXIMUM MEMBERS USED	N/A	0
RECORDS CAPTURED	N/C	0	FALSE CONT RATE(%)	N/C	N/A	MAXIMUM DEGREE	N/A	0
LOG RECORDS READ	N/C	0	LOCK REQ - PLOCKS	0.00	0	GROUPS EXECUTED	2.00	12
ROWS RETURNED	N/C	0	UNLOCK REQ - PLOCKS	0.00	0	RAN AS PLANNED	2.00	12
RECORDS RETURNED	N/C	0	CHANGE REQ - PLOCKS	0.00	0	RAN REDUCED	0.00	0
DATA DESC. RETURN	N/C	0	LOCK REQ - XES	0.00	0	ONE DB2-COORDINATOR = NO	0.00	0
TABLES RETURNED	N/C	0	UNLOCK REQ - XES	0.00	0	ONE DB2-ISOLATION LEVEL	0.00	0
DESCRIBES	N/C	0	CHANGE REQ - XES	0.00	0	SEQUENTIAL-CURSOR	0.00	0
			SUSPENDS - IRLM	0.00	0	SEQUENTIAL-NO ESA SORT	0.00	0
			SUSPENDS - XES	0.00	0	SEQUENTIAL-NO BUFFER	0.00	0
			SUSPENDS - FALSE	0.00	0	SEQUENTIAL-ENCLAVE SERVICES	0.00	0
			INCOMPATIBLE LOCKS	0.00	0	MEMBER SKIPPED (%)	N/C	N/A
			NOTIFY MSGS SENT	0.00	0	DISABLED BY RLF	0.00	0

Careful analysis of the query parallelism section is appropriate whenever you're analyzing performance statistics for a plan or package bound with DEGREE(ANY):

- When RAN REDUCED is not zero (0), insufficient resources were available to execute the application with the optimal number of read engines. You might need to evaluate the overall mix of applications in the system at the same time. Reducing concurrent activity may release resources that the program can use to run with the planned number of parallel read engines.

- When any of the SEQUENTIAL categories is not zero (0), DB2 reverted to a sequential plan. Therefore, I/O parallelism was "turned off." You might need to analyze the program and the environment to determine why query I/O parallelism was disabled.

Long Accounting Report: Database Code Usage Information

The database code usage section provides detailed statistics on the usage of stored procedures, UDFs, and triggers. This section can be particularly helpful to track down performance problems caused by triggers, UDFs, and stored procedures (see Listing 24.8).

LISTING 24.8   Accounting Report—Long (Part 7)

STORED PROCEDURES	AVERAGE	TOTAL	UDF	AVERAGE	TOTAL	TRIGGERS	AVERAGE	TOTAL
CALL STATEMENTS	0.00	0	EXECUTED	0.00	0	STATEMENT TRIGGER	0.00	0
ABENDED	0.00	0	ABENDED	0.00	0	ROW TRIGGER	0.00	0
TIMED OUT	0.00	0	TIMED OUT	0.00	0	SQL ERROR OCCUR	0.00	0
REJECTED	0.00	0	REJECTED	0.00	0			

Long Accounting Report: Buffer Pool Information

The buffer pool information is probably the most important portion of the long accounting report. A poorly tuned buffer pool environment can greatly affect the performance of a DB2 subsystem. Analysis of this section of the report (see Listing 24.9) provides a performance analyst with a better understanding of how the program utilizes available buffers.

LISTING 24.9 Accounting Report—Long (Part 8)

BP0	AVERAGE	TOTAL	BP10	AVERAGE	TOTAL
BPOOL HIT RATIO		N/A	BPOOL HIT RATIO		N/A
GETPAGES	85.47	1453	GETPAGES	219.00	3723
BUFFER UPDATES	86.00	1462	BUFFER UPDATES	0.00	0
SYNCHRONOUS WRITE	0.00	0	SYNCHRONOUS WRITE	0.00	0
SYNCHRONOUS READ	0.18	3	SYNCHRONOUS READ	0.00	0
SEQ. PREFETCH REQS	0.00	0	SEQ. PREFETCH REQS	0.00	0
LIST PREFETCH REQS	0.00	0	LIST PREFETCH REQS	0.00	0
DYN. PREFETCH REQS	1.00	17	DYN. PREFETCH REQS	0.00	0
PAGES READ ASYNCHR.	8.00	136	PAGES READ ASYNCHR.	0.00	0
HPOOL WRITES	0.00	0	HPOOL WRITES	0.00	0
HPOOL WRITES-FAILED	0.00	0	HPOOL WRITES-FAILED	0.00	0
PAGES READ ASYN-HPOOL	0.00	0	PAGES READ ASYN-HPOOL	0.00	0
HPOOL READS	0.00	0	HPOOL READS	0.00	0
HPOOL READS FAILED	0.00	0	HPOOL READS FAILED	0.00	0

TOT4K	AVERAGE	TOTAL
BPOOL HIT RATIO		N/A
GETPAGES	304.47	5176
BUFFER UPDATES	86.00	1462
SYNCHRONOUS WRITE	0.00	0
SYNCHRONOUS READ	0.18	3
SEQ. PREFETCH REQS	7.00	119
LIST PREFETCH REQS	0.00	0
DYN. PREFETCH REQS	1.00	17
PAGES READ ASYNCHR.	8.00	136
HPOOL WRITES	0.00	0
HPOOL WRITES-FAILED	0.00	0
PAGES READ ASYN-HPOOL	0.00	0
HPOOL READS	0.00	0
HPOOL READS FAILED	0.00	0

24

The first step is to get a feeling for the overall type of I/O requested for this plan. You should answer the following questions:

- How many buffer pools were accessed? Were more (or fewer) buffer pools used than expected?

- Were any 8K, 16K, or 32K buffer pools accessed? Should they have been? Use of buffer pools larger than 4K can greatly affect the performance by increasing I/O costs.

- Did the program read pages from an associated hiperpool?

- Was sequential prefetch used? Based on your knowledge of the program, should it have been? Was dynamic prefetch enabled (sequential detection)?

- Was list prefetch invoked? If so, be sure to analyze the RID List Processing in the Miscellaneous Information section of this report (discussed in the preceding section).

- How many pages were requested (GETPAGES)? The number of GETPAGES is a good indicator of the amount of work being done by the program.

- Were any synchronous writes performed? A synchronous write is sometimes called a non-deferred write. Synchronous writes occur immediately on request. Most DB2 writes are deferred, which means that they are made in the buffer pool and recorded in the log but not physically externalized to DASD until later. Synchronous writes usually indicate that the buffer pool is over-utilized.

All the aforementioned information is broken down by buffer pool.

The next task when analyzing this report is to review the buffer pool hit ratio. It is reported in the BPOOL HIT RATIO (%) field for each buffer pool accessed. The buffer pool hit ratio is calculated as follows:

```
BPOOL HIT RATIO = ((GETPAGES - PAGES READ FROM DASD) / GETPAGES ) * 100
```

PAGES READ FROM DASD is the sum of synchronous reads, and the number of pages read using prefetch (sequential prefetch, list prefetch, and dynamic prefetch). The buffer pool hit ratio gives you an idea of how well the SQL in this plan has used the available buffer pools.

In general, the higher the buffer pool hit ratio, the better. The highest possible value for the hit ratio percentage is 100. When every page requested is always in the buffer pool, the hit ratio percentage is 100. The lowest buffer pool hit ratio happens when all of the requested pages are not in the buffer pool. The buffer pool hit ratio will be 0 or less when that happens. A negative hit ratio can mean one of two things:

- Prefetch (sequential or dynamic) has read pages into the buffer pool that were not referenced, or;

- Thrashing in the buffer pool caused by a buffer pool that is too small or by a large batch job running during a busy time. One scenario has the batch job requesting prefetch and then getting suspended waiting for CPU. During the interim, pages requested by prefetch were over-written by another process—so they have to be read into the buffer pool all over again.

A low buffer pool hit ratio is not necessarily bad. The buffer pool hit ratio can vary greatly from program to program. A program that accesses a large amount of data using table space scans could have a very low hit ratio. But that does not mean the application is performing poorly. You should compare the buffer pool hit ratio for different executions of the same program. If the percentage lowers significantly over time, there may be a problem that needs correcting.

General guidelines for acceptable buffer pool hit ratios follow:

- For online transactions with significant random access, the buffer pool hit ratio can be low while still providing good I/O utilization.

- For transactions that open cursors and fetch numerous rows, the buffer pool hit ratio should be higher. However, it is not abnormal for online transactions to have a low hit ratio.

- For batch programs, shoot for a high buffer pool hit ratio. The actual buffer pool hit ratio each program can achieve is highly dependent on the functionality required for that program. Programs with a large amount of sequential access should have a much higher read efficiency than those processing randomly.

- When programs have very few SQL statements, or SQL statements returning a single row, the buffer pool hit ratio is generally low. Because few SQL statements are issued, the potential for using buffered input is reduced.

The buffer pool hit ratio also can be calculated by buffer pool for all processes. This hit ratio can be compared to the hit ratio for the plan in question to determine its effectiveness versus other processes. Remember, though, when the buffer pool hit ratio is calculated using the information from an accounting report, it is for a single plan only. You can ascertain the overall effectiveness of each buffer pool by calculating hit ratio based on information from a DB2 PM system statistics report or from the -DISPLAY BUFFERPOOL command.

Long Accounting Report: Package/DBRM Information

The final component of the long accounting report is detailed information for each package and DBRM in the plan (see Listing 24.10). To obtain this information, you must start the appropriate accounting traces (Class 7 and Class 8).

LISTING 24.10 Accounting Report—Long (Part 9)

PRG00100	VALUE	PRG00100	TIMES	PRG00100	AVERAGE TIME	AVG.EV	TIME/EVENT
TYPE	DBRM	ELAP-CL7 TIME-AVG	0.670800	LOCK/LATCH	0.009924	1.00	0.009924
		TCB	0.556637	SYNCHRONOUS I/O	0.000000	0.00	N/C
LOCATION	N/A	WAITING	0.114162	OTHER READ I/O	0.000000	0.00	N/C
COLLECTION ID	N/A	SUSPENSION-CL8	0.009924	OTHER WRITE I/O	0.000000	0.00	N/C
PROGRAM NAME	PRG00100	NOT ACCOUNTED	0.110076	SERV.TASK SWITCH	0.000000	0.00	N/C
				ARCH.LOG(QUIESCE)	0.000000	0.00	N/C
OCCURENCES	17	AVG.DB2 ENTRY/EXIT	9122.00	ARCHIVE LOG READ	0.000000	0.00	N/C
SQL STMT - AVERAGE	4559.0	DB2 ENTRY/EXIT	155074	DRAIN LOCK	0.000000	0.00	N/C
SQL STMT - TOTAL	77503			CLAIM RELEASE	0.000000	0.00	N/C
		NOT NULL (CL7)	17	PAGE LATCH	0.000000	0.00	N/C
				TOTAL CL8 SUSPENS.	0.009924	1.00	0.009924
				NOT NULL (CL8)	7		
PRG00101	VALUE	PRG00101	TIMES	PRG00101	AVERAGE TIME	AVG.EV	TIME/EVENT
TYPE	DBRM	ELAP-CL7 TIME-AVG	0.781030	LOCK/LATCH	0.006902	1.00	0.006902
		TCB	0.461371	SYNCHRONOUS I/O	0.000000	0.00	N/C
LOCATION	N/A	WAITING	0.101390	OTHER READ I/O	0.000000	0.00	N/C
COLLECTION ID	N/A	SUSPENSION-CL8	0.010430	OTHER WRITE I/O	0.000000	0.00	N/C
PROGRAM NAME	PRG00101	NOT ACCOUNTED	0.102061	SERV.TASK SWITCH	0.000000	0.00	N/C
				ARCH.LOG(QUIESCE)	0.000000	0.00	N/C
OCCURENCES	17	AVG.DB2 ENTRY/EXIT	4573.00	ARCHIVE LOG READ	0.000000	0.00	N/C
SQL STMT - AVERAGE	392.0	DB2 ENTRY/EXIT	77741	DRAIN LOCK	0.000000	0.00	N/C
SQL STMT - TOTAL	6664			CLAIM RELEASE	0.000000	0.00	N/C
		NOT NULL (CL7)	17	PAGE LATCH	0.000000	0.00	N/C
				TOTAL CL8 SUSPENS.	0.006902	1.00	0.006902
				NOT NULL (CL8)	7		

24

This level of detail might be necessary for plans composed of multiple DBRMs and/or packages. For example, if a locking problem is identified, determining which DBRM (or package) is experiencing the problem may be difficult if you don't have the appropriate level of detail.

Long Accounting Report: Other Information

There are other portions of the long accounting report that can prove useful. For example, information on RID list processing is provided before the bufferpool section (see Listing 24.11).

LISTING 24.11   Accounting Report—Long (Other)

```
RID LIST          AVERAGE
---------------   --------
USED                 0.00
FAIL-NO STORAGE      0.00
FAIL-LIMIT EXC.      0.00
```

If any access path in the application program requires either list prefetch or a hybrid join, analysis of the RID LIST performance statistics is essential. Of particular importance is the FAIL-NO STORAGE value. Whenever this value is not zero (0), you should take immediate action either to increase the size of the RID pool or tweak the access path to eliminate RID list processing.

Other useful information you can obtain from the long accounting report includes ROWID access, logging details, and reoptimization statistics.

Accounting Trace Reports

The accounting report set also contains two additional reports: the Short and Long Accounting Trace reports. These reports produce similar information, but for a single execution of a plan. By contrast, the short and long accounting reports provide performance information averaged for all executions of a plan by a given user. If you need to investigate a single, specific execution of a DB2 program, use the accounting trace reports.

Audit Report Set

The DB2 PM audit report set shows DB2 auditing information. Although this data is generally not performance-oriented, you can use it to monitor usage characteristics of a DB2 subsystem. The Audit Summary report, shown in Listing 24.12, is a synopsis of the eight audit trace categories (as outlined previously in this chapter).

LISTING 24.12   DB2 PM Audit Summary Report

```
        LOCATION: HOUSTON                      DB2 PERFORMANCE MONITOR                      PAGE: 1-1
           GROUP: DB2G1P                       AUDIT REPORT - SUMMARY           REQUESTED FROM: NOT SPECIFIED
          MEMBER: DB2P                                                                      TO: NOT SPECIFIED
       SUBSYSTEM: DB2P                         ORDER: PRIMAUTH-PLANNAME            ACTUAL FROM: 12/02/03 07:28:39.17
     DB2 VERSION: V7                           SCOPE: MEMBER                               TO: 12/02/03 11:31:12.25
```

PRIMAUTH PLANNAME	TOTAL	AUTH FAILURE	GRANT/ REVOKE	DDL ACCESS	DML READ ACCESS	DML WRITE ACCESS	DML AT BIND	AUTHID CHANGE	UTILITY ACCESS
AUTHID2									
DSNTEP2	4	0	0	0	0	0	4	0	0
DSNUTIL	4	0	0	0	0	0	0	0	4
TXN00001	12	1	0	1	2	2	0	0	0
TXN00012	10	0	0	0	2	5	0	10	0
TOTAL	30	1	0	1	4	7	4	10	4
AUTHID5									
DSNTEP2	4	0	0	0	0	0	4	0	0
TXN00030	16	2	1	8	2	2	0	2	0
TOTAL	20	2	1	8	2	2	4	2	4
GRAND TOTAL	50	3	1	9	6	9	8	12	8
END OF REPORT									

If you require further audit detail, DB2 PM also provides an Audit Detail report and an Audit Trace report. The Audit Detail report breaks each category into a separate report, showing the resource accessed, the date and the time of the access, and other pertinent information. The Audit Trace report displays each audit trace record in timestamp order.

The Explain Report Set

The explain report set describes the DB2 access path of selected SQL statements. DB2 uses the EXPLAIN command and information from the DB2 Catalog to produce a description of the access path chosen. Combining information from the PLAN_TABLE and the DB2 Catalog is the primary purpose of the DB2 PM explain report set. To execute reports in the explain report set, you must have access to DB2. This requirement differs from most of the other DB2 PM reports.

I/O Activity Report Set

The I/O activity report set is somewhat misnamed. It does not report on the I/O activity of DB2 applications. Instead, it offers details on the I/O activity of DB2 buffer pools, the EDM pool, and the log manager. An example of the information provided on the I/O Activity Summary report is shown in Listing 24.13.

24

LISTING 24.13   DB2 PM I/O Activity Summary Report

```
                                    AET
BUFFER POOL                TOTALS SSSS.THT
------------------------   ------ --------
TOTAL I/O REQUESTS            262  0.014
TOTAL READ I/O REQUESTS       247  0.012
  NON-PREFETCH READS          171
  PREFETCH REQUESTS
    UNSUCCESSFUL                1
    SUCCESSFUL                 75
    PAGES READ               N/C
    PAGES READ / SUCC READ   N/C
TOTAL WRITE REQUESTS           68  0.164
  SYNCH WRITES                  1  0.021
   PAGES WRITTEN PER WRITE    1.0
  ASYNCH WRITES               67  0.164
   PAGES WRITTEN PER WRITE    2.3
```

```
                         CT/PT/DBD   LOADS       AET     AVG LEN
EDM POOL                 REFERENCES  FROM DASD SSSS.THT (BYTES)
------------------------ ----------  --------- -------- -------
CURSOR TABLE - HEADER         1          1      0.000   2049.0
CURSOR TABLE - DIRECTORY      0          0       N/C       0.0
CURSOR TABLE - RDS SECTION    4          4      0.000    634.0
  -- TOTAL PLANS --           5          5      0.000   5474.0
  -- TOTAL PLANS --           5          5      0.000   5474.0
PACKAGE TABLE - HEADER        2          2      0.003   1208.0
PACKAGE TABLE - DIRECTORY     2          2      0.001    156.0
PACKAGE TABLE - RDS SECTION   6          6      0.001    747.7
  -- TOTAL PACKAGES --       10         10      0.002    719.6
  -- TOTAL PACKAGES --       10         10      0.002    719.6
DATABASE DESCRIPTORS          1          1      0.000   4012.0
```

```
                                 AET
ACTIVE LOG                TOTALS SSSS.THT
------------------------  ------ --------
TOTAL WAITS                  22   0.015
READ REQUESTS                 0    N/C
WRITE REQUESTS               22   0.015
CONT. CI / WRITE            1.6
OTHER WAITS                   0    N/C
  ALLOCATE                    0    N/C
  DEALLOCATE                  0    N/C
  ARCHIVE UNAVAILABLE         0    N/C
  BUFFERS UNAVAILABLE         0    N/C
  DATASET UNAVAILABLE         0    N/C
  OPEN                        0    N/C
  CLOSE                       0    N/C
```

```
                             AET
ARCHIVE LOG/BSDS   TOTALS SSSS.THT
-----------------  ------ --------
ARCHIVE WAITS         0    N/C
ARCHIVE READ REQ      0    N/C
  DASD READ           0
  TAPE READ           0
ARCHIVE WRITE REQ     0    N/C
BLOCK / WRITE       N/C
BSDS READ REQ         2   0.089
BSDS WRITE REQ        2   0.044
```

As with the other report sets, the I/O activity report set provides detail reports that show in greater detail the I/O activity for each of these resources.

Locking Report Set

The locking report set provides reports that disclose lock contention and suspensions in the DB2 subsystem. These reports can be helpful when you're analyzing locking-related problems.

For example, if a Long Accounting report indicated a high number of timeouts or deadlocks, a Lock Contention Summary report, such as the one shown in Listing 24.14, could be produced. This report provides information on who was involved in the contention and what resource was unavailable because of the lock.

LISTING 24.14   DB2 PM Lock Contention Summary Report

```
LOCK CONTENTION SUMMARY
LOCATION: CHICAGO                      BY PRIMAUTH/PLANNAME
------ TASK HOLDING RESOURCE ------ ---- TASK WAITING ON RESOURCE ----
PRIMAUTH   PLANNAME       PRIMAUTH   PLANNAME        DATABASE   OBJECT    TIMEOUTS   DEADLOCK
--------   --------       --------   --------        --------   --------  --------   --------
AUTHID01   DSNESPRR       AUTHID02   TXN00001        DSN8D23A   DSN8S23D         1          0
```

If more details on locking problems are needed, you can use the Lock Suspension Summary report. This report is useful when an accounting report indicates a high number of lock suspensions. The Lock Suspension Summary details the cause of each suspension and whether it was subsequently resumed or resulted in a timeout or deadlock.

Record Trace Report Set

The record trace report set provides not reports per se, but a dump of the trace records fed to it as input. The record trace reports are not molded into a report format as are the other DB2 PM reports. They simply display DB2 trace records in a readable format.

The three record trace reports are the Record Trace Summary report, the Sort Record Trace report, and the Long Record Trace report. The Record Trace Summary report lists an overview of the DB2 trace records, without all the supporting detail. The Sort Record Trace report provides a listing of most of the DB2 trace records you need to see, along with supporting detail. Several serviceability trace records are not displayed. The Long Record Trace report lists all DB2 trace records.

The record trace reports are useful for determining what type of trace data is available for an input source data set. If another DB2 PM execution (to produce, for example, an accounting detail report) is unsuccessful or does not produce the data you want, you can run a record trace to ensure that the input data set contains the needed trace records to produce the requested report.

Note that the record trace reports might produce a large amount of output. You can specify which types of DB2 trace records should be displayed. If you're looking for a particular type of trace record, be sure to reduce your output by specifying the data for which you're looking.

SQL Trace Report Set

To monitor the performance of data manipulation language statements, you can use the SQL trace report set. These reports are necessary only when a program has encountered a performance problem. The SQL trace breaks down each SQL statement into the events that must occur to satisfy the request. This information includes preparation, aborts, commits, the beginning and ending of each type of SQL statement, cursor opens and closes, accesses due to referential integrity, I/O events, thread creation and termination, and all types of indexed accesses.

You will find four types of SQL trace reports. The SQL Trace Summary report provides a synopsis of each type of SQL statement and the performance characteristics of that statement.

The second type of SQL trace report is the SQL Short Trace report. It lists the performance characteristics of each SQL statement, including the beginning and end of each statement and the work accomplished in between. It does not provide I/O activity, locking, and sorting information.

The SQL Long Trace report provides the same information as the SQL Short Trace report but includes I/O activity, locking, and sorting information.

Finally, the SQL DML report extends the SQL Trace Summary report, providing data for each SQL statement, not just for each SQL statement type.

The SQL Short and Long Trace reports can be extremely long reports that are cumbersome to read. Therefore, producing these reports only when a performance problem must be corrected is usually wise. In addition, the SQL trace reports require the DB2 performance trace to be active. This trace carries a large amount of overhead. Before you request this report, you would be wise to "eyeball" the offending program for glaring errors (such as looping or Cartesian products) and to tinker with the SQL to see whether you can improve performance.

Also, after you produce these reports, you should have more than one experienced analyst read them. I have seen SQL trace reports that were six feet long. Be prepared for a lot of work to ferret out the needed information from these reports.

Statistics Report Set

The second most popular DB2 PM report set (next to the accounting report set) is the statistics report set. Statistics reports provide performance information about the DB2 subsystem. The data on these reports can help you detect areas of concern when you're monitoring DB2 performance. Usually, these reports point you in the direction of a problem; additional DB2 PM reports are required to fully analyze the complete scope of the performance problem.

Listing 24.15, an example of the DB2 PM Statistics Short report, shows a summary of all DB2 activity for the DB2 subsystem during the specified time.

LISTING 24.15   DB2 PM Statistics Short Report

```
                          STATISTICS REPORT - SHORT
```

---- HIGHLIGHTS --

INTERVAL START: 07/10/03 12:32:09.73	INTERVAL ELAPSED: 24:32.77260	INCREMENTAL BINDS : 0.00	DBAT QUEUED: N/P
INTERVAL END : 07/10/03 12:56:42.51	OUTAGE ELAPSED : 0.000000	AUTH SUCC.W/OUT CATALOG: 2.00	DB2 COMMAND: 3.00
SAMPLING START: 07/10/03 12:32:09.73	TOTAL THREADS : 1.00	BUFF.UPDT/PAGES WRITTEN: 2.52	TOTAL API : 0.00
SAMPLING END : 07/10/03 12:56:42.51	TOTAL COMMITS : 4.00	PAGES WRITTEN/WRITE I/O: 1.17	MEMBER : N/A

CPU TIMES	TCB TIME	SRB TIME	TOTAL TIME	OPEN/CLOSE ACTIVITY	QUANTITY
SYSTEM SERVICES ADDRESS SPACE	0.213783	0.097449	0.311232	OPEN DATASETS - HWM	29.00
DATABASE SERVICES ADDRESS SPACE	0.292474	0.155593	0.448066	OPEN DATASETS	29.00
IRLM	0.002940	0.447174	0.450114	IN USE DATA SETS	19.00
DDF ADDRESS SPACE	N/P	N/P	N/P	SUCCESSFUL LOGICAL REOPEN	6.00
NON-CPU TIME		N/A	N/A	24:31.563191	

SQL DML	QUANTITY	SQL DCL	QUANTITY	SQL DDL	QUANTITY	LOCKING ACTIVITY	QUANTITY	DATA SHARING LOCKS	QUANTITY
SELECT	4.00	LOCK TABLE	0.00	CREATES	0.00	DEADLOCKS	0.00	LOCK REQ.(P-LOCK)	48.00
INSERT	16.00	GRANT	0.00	DROPS	0.00	TIMEOUTS	0.00	UNLOCK REQ.(P-LCK)	0.00
UPDATE	12.00	REVOKE	0.00	ALTERS	0.00	SUSPENSIONS-LOCK	2.00	CHANGE REQ.(P-LCK)	9.00
DELETE	0.00	SET HOST VAR.	0.00	COMMENT ON	0.00	SUSPENSIONS-OTHR	0.00	SYNC.XES - LOCK	186.00
PREPARE	0.00	SET SQLID	0.00	LABEL ON	0.00	LOCK REQUESTS	351.00	SYNC.XES - CHANGE	13.00
DESCRIBE	0.00	SET DEGREE	0.00	TOTAL	0.00	UNLOCK REQUEST	178.00	SYNC.XES - UNLOCK	154.00
DESC.TBL	0.00	SET RULES	0.00			LOCK ESCALAT(SH)	0.00	ASYN.XES-RESOURCES	0.00
OPEN	16.00	CONNECT TYPE 1	0.00			LOCK ESCALAT(EX)	0.00	TOTAL SUSPENDS	30.00
CLOSE	8.00	CONNECT TYPE 2	0.00			DRAIN REQUESTS	0.00	P-LCK/NFY ENG.UNAV	0.00
FETCH	20.00	RELEASE	0.00			CLAIM REQUESTS	96.00	INCOM.RETAINED LCK	0.00
TOTAL	76.00	SET CONNECTION	0.00					PSET/PART NEGOTIAT	16.00
		TOTAL	0.00					PAGE NEGOTIATION	0.00

RID LIST	QUANTITY	STORED PROCEDURES	QUANTITY	QUERY PARALLELISM	QUANTITY	PLAN/PACKAGE PROC.	QUANTITY
MAX BLOCKS ALLOCATED	0.00	CALL STATEMENTS	0.00	MAX DEGREE	0.00	PLAN ALLOC-ATTEMPTS	1.00
CURRENT BLKS ALLOC.	0.00	PROCEDURE ABENDS	0.00	GROUPS EXECUTED	0.00	PLAN ALLOC-SUCCESS	1.00
FAILED-NO STORAGE	0.00	CALL TIMEOUTS	0.00	PLANNED DEGREE	0.00	PACK ALLOC-ATTEMPTS	0.00
FAILED-RDS LIMIT	0.00	CALL REJECTED	0.00	REDUCED-NO BUFFER	0.00	PACK ALLOC-SUCCESS	0.00
FAILED-DM LIMIT	0.00			FALL TO SEQUENTIAL	0.00	AUTOBIND ATTEMPTS	0.00
FAILED-PROCESS LIMIT	0.00					AUTOBIND SUCCESSFUL	0.00

SUBSYSTEM SERVICES	QUANTITY	LOG ACTIVITY	QUANTITY	EDM POOL	QUANTITY
IDENTIFY	0.00	READS SATISFIED-OUTPUT BUFFER	0.00	PAGES IN EDM POOL	225.00
CREATE THREAD	1.00	READS SATISFIED-ACTIVE LOG	0.00	FREE PAGES IN FREE CHAIN	196.00
SIGNON	4.00	READS SATISFIED-ARCHIVE LOG	0.00	FAILS DUE TO POOL FULL	0.00
TERMINATE	0.00	READ DELAYED-UNAVAILABLE RESOURCE	0.00	PAGES USED FOR CT	8.00
ROLLBACK	0.00	READ DELAYED-ARCH.ALLOC. LIMIT	N/A	PAGES USED FOR PT	0.00
COMMIT PHASE 1	4.00	WRITE-NOWAIT	76.00	PAGES USED FOR DBD	12.00
COMMIT PHASE 2	4.00	WRITE OUTPUT LOG BUFFERS	8.00	PAGES USED FOR SKCT	9.00
READ ONLY COMMIT	0.00	BSDS ACCESS REQUESTS	2.00	PAGES USED FOR SKPT	0.00
UNITS OF RECOVERY GONE INDOUBT	0.00	UNAVAILABLE OUTPUT LOG BUFFER	0.00	REQUESTS FOR CT SECTIONS	10.00
UNITS OF RECOVERY INDOUBT RESOLV	0.00	CONTROL INTERVAL CREATED-ACTIVE	3.00	CT NOT IN EDM POOL	10.00
SYNCHS (SINGLE PHASE COMMIT)	0.00	ARCHIVE LOG READ ALLOCATION	0.00	REQUESTS FOR PT SECTIONS	0.00
QUEUED AT CREATE THREAD	0.00	ARCHIVE LOG WRITE ALLOCAT.	0.00	PT NOT IN EDM POOL	0.00
SYSTEM EVENT CHECKPOINT	0.00			REQUESTS FOR DBD SECTIONS	3.00
				DBD NOT IN EDM POOL	0.00

24

LISTING 24.15   Continued

BP0 GENERAL	QUANTITY	BP2 GENERAL	QUANTITY	TOT4K GENERAL	QUANTITY
EXPANSIONS	N/A	EXPANSIONS	N/A	EXPANSIONS	N/A
GETPAGES-SEQ&RANDOM	2302.00	GETPAGES-SEQ&RANDOM	72.00	GETPAGES-SEQ&RANDOM	2375.00
GETPAGES-SEQ.ONLY	0.00	GETPAGES-SEQ.ONLY	0.00	GETPAGES-SEQ.ONLY	0.00
SYNC.READ-SEQ&RANDOM	12.00	SYNC.READ-SEQ&RANDOM	27.00	SYNC.READ-SEQ&RANDOM	39.00
SYNC.READ-SEQ.ONLY	0.00	SYNC.READ-SEQ.ONLY	0.00	SYNC.READ-SEQ.ONLY	0.00
SEQ.PREFETCH REQ	10.00	SEQ.PREFETCH REQ	0.00	SEQ.PREFETCH REQ	10.00
SEQ.PREFETCH READS	10.00	SEQ.PREFETCH READS	0.00	SEQ.PREFETCH READS	10.00
PAGES READ-SEQ.PREF.	159.00	PAGES READ-SEQ.PREF.	0.00	PAGES READ-SEQ.PREF.	159.00
LST.PREFETCH REQUEST	0.00	LST.PREFETCH REQUEST	0.00	LST.PREFETCH REQUEST	0.00
LST.PREFETCH READS	0.00	LST.PREFETCH READS	0.00	LST.PREFETCH READS	0.00
PAGES READ-LST.PREF.	0.00	PAGES READ-LST.PREF.	0.00	PAGES READ-LST.PREF.	0.00
DYN.PREFETCH REQUEST	0.00	DYN.PREFETCH REQUEST	0.00	DYN.PREFETCH REQUEST	0.00
DYN.PREFETCH READS	0.00	DYN.PREFETCH READS	0.00	DYN.PREFETCH READS	0.00
PAGES READ-DYN.PREF.	0.00	PAGES READ-DYN.PREF.	0.00	PAGES READ-DYN.PREF.	0.00
BUFFER UPDATES	37.00	BUFFER UPDATES	16.00	BUFFER UPDATES	53.00
SYNCHRONOUS WRITES	0.00	SYNCHRONOUS WRITES	0.00	SYNCHRONOUS WRITES	0.00
ASYNCHRONOUS WRITES	15.00	ASYNCHRONOUS WRITES	3.00	ASYNCHRONOUS WRITES	18.00
DATA SET OPENS	10.00	DATA SET OPENS	8.00	DATA SET OPENS	18.00
HDW THRESHOLD	0.00	HDW THRESHOLD	0.00	HDW THRESHOLD	0.00
VDW THRESHOLD	0.00	VDW THRESHOLD	0.00	VDW THRESHOLD	0.00
DM THRESHOLD	0.00	DM THRESHOLD	0.00	DM THRESHOLD	0.00

GROUP BP0	QUANTITY	GROUP BP2	QUANTITY	GROUP TOT4K	QUANTITY
SYN.READ(XI)-RETURN	422.00	SYN.READ(XI)-RETURN	9.00	SYN.READ(XI)-RETURN	431.00
SYN.READ(XI)-R/W INT	0.00	SYN.READ(XI)-R/W INT	0.00	SYN.READ(XI)-R/W INT	0.00
SYN.READ(XI)-NO R/W	0.00	SYN.READ(XI)-NO R/W	0.00	SYN.READ(XI)-NO R/W	0.00
SYN.READ(NF)-RETURN	0.00	SYN.READ(NF)-RETURN	0.00	SYN.READ(NF)-RETURN	0.00
SYN.READ(NF)-R/W INT	1.00	SYN.READ(NF)-R/W INT	0.00	SYN.READ(NF)-R/W INT	1.00
SYN.READ(NF)-NO R/W	0.00	SYN.READ(NF)-NO R/W	0.00	SYN.READ(NF)-NO R/W	0.00
ASYN.READ-RETURNED	0.00	ASYN.READ-RETURNED	0.00	ASYN.READ-RETURNED	0.00
ASYN.READ-R/W INT.	0.00	ASYN.READ-R/W INT.	0.00	ASYN.READ-R/W INT.	0.00
ASYN.READ-NO R/W INT	0.00	ASYN.READ-NO R/W INT	0.00	ASYN.READ-NO R/W INT	0.00
CLEAN PAGES SYN.WRTN	0.00	CLEAN PAGES SYN.WRTN	0.00	CLEAN PAGES SYN.WRTN	0.00
CHANGED PGS SYN.WRTN	20.00	CHANGED PGS SYN.WRTN	9.00	CHANGED PGS SYN.WRTN	29.00
CLEAN PAGES ASYN.WRT	0.00	CLEAN PAGES ASYN.WRT	0.00	CLEAN PAGES ASYN.WRT	0.00
CHANGED PGS ASYN.WRT	12.00	CHANGED PGS ASYN.WRT	3.00	CHANGED PGS ASYN.WRT	15.00
REG.PG LIST (RPL) RQ	0.00	REG.PG LIST (RPL) RQ	0.00	REG.PG LIST (RPL) RQ	0.00
CLEAN PGS READ RPL	0.00	CLEAN PGS READ RPL	0.00	CLEAN PGS READ RPL	0.00
CHANGED PGS READ RPL	0.00	CHANGED PGS READ RPL	0.00	CHANGED PGS READ RPL	0.00
PAGES CASTOUT	18.00	PAGES CASTOUT	3.00	PAGES CASTOUT	21.00
CASTOUT CLASS THRESH	0.00	CASTOUT CLASS THRESH	0.00	CASTOUT CLASS THRESH	0.00
GROUP BP CAST.THRESH	0.00	GROUP BP CAST.THRESH	0.00	GROUP BP CAST.THRESH	0.00
CASTOUT ENG.UNAVAIL.	0.00	CASTOUT ENG.UNAVAIL.	0.00	CASTOUT ENG.UNAVAIL.	0.00
WRITE ENG.UNAVAIL.	0.00	WRITE ENG.UNAVAIL.	0.00	WRITE ENG.UNAVAIL.	0.00
READ FAILED-NO STOR.	0.00	READ FAILED-NO STOR.	0.00	READ FAILED-NO STOR.	0.00
WRITE FAILED-NO STOR	0.00	WRITE FAILED-NO STOR	0.00	WRITE FAILED-NO STOR	0.00
OTHER REQUESTS	43.00	OTHER REQUESTS	17.00	OTHER REQUESTS	60.00

You can use this report to monitor a DB2 subsystem at a glance. Pertinent systemwide statistics are provided for buffer pool management, log management, locking, and EDM pool utilization.

The Statistics Short report is useful for monitoring the DB2 buffer pools, specifically regarding I/O activity and buffer pool utilization. One statistic of interest is the DATA SET

OPENS number, which indicates the number of times a VSAM open was requested for a DB2 tablespace or index. In the example, the number for BP0 is 10; for BP2, it is 8. A large number of data set opens could indicate that an object was defined with CLOSE YES. This may not be a problem, however, because the number is relatively low (in this example) and objects are also opened when they are first requested.

You should analyze the other buffer pool report items to get an idea of the overall efficiency of the buffer pool. For example, you can calculate the overall efficiency of the buffer pool using this calculation:

GETPAGE REQUESTS / ((PREFETCH READ I/O OPERATIONS) + (TOTAL READ I/O OPERATIONS))

In the example, the buffer pool read efficiency for BP0 is

2302 / [12 + 10] = 104.63

This number is quite good. It is typically smaller for transaction-oriented environments and larger for batch-oriented environments. Also, this number is larger if you have large buffer pools. Other factors affecting read efficiency are the length of the sample, the amount of time since the last recycle of DB2, and the mix of concurrent applications.

In addition, the following buffer pool report numbers should be zero (0):

> Buffer Pool Expansions
>
> Synchronous Writes
>
> HDW Threshold
>
> VDW Threshold
>
> DM Threshold
>
> Work File Not Created—No Buffer

If these numbers are not zero, the buffer pools have not been specified adequately. Refer to Chapter 28, "Tuning DB2's Components," for advice on setting up your buffer pools.

Information on group buffer pools for data sharing environments follows the local buffer pool information.

The Statistics reports also can assist you in monitoring log management. You can determine the types of processing during this timeframe from viewing the *Log Activity* section. If *Reads Satisfied from Active Log* or *Reads Satisfied from Archive Log* is greater than zero, a recover utility was run during this timeframe. You can glean additional recovery information from the *Subsystem Service* portion of the report.

Also, ensure that the *Unavailable Output Log Buffers* is zero. If it is not, you should specify additional log buffers in your DSNZPARM start-up parameters.

Another aspect of DB2 system-wide performance that the DB2 Statistics report helps to monitor is locking. This report is particularly useful for monitoring the number of suspensions, deadlocks, and timeouts in proportion to the total number of locks requested. Use the following calculation:

```
LOCK REQUESTS / (SUSPENSIONS-LOCK + SUSPENSIONS-OTHER + DEADLOCKS + TIMEOUTS)
```

This calculation provides you with a ratio of troublesome locks to successful locks, as shown here:

```
351 / (2 + 0 + 0 + 0) = 175.5
```

The larger this number, the less lock contention your system is experiencing. Data sharing lock requests (P-locks) are also displayed on the DB2 Statistics report.

EDM pool utilization is the final system-wide performance indicator that you can monitor using the DB2 Statistics Short report. To calculate the efficiency of the EDM pool, use the following formula:

```
((REQ FOR CT SECTIONS) + (REQUESTS FOR DBD)) / ((LOAD CT SECT FROM DASD) + (LOAD DBD FROM DASD))
```

Using the example, here's the calculation:

```
(151 + 432) / (70 + 0) = 8.32
```

Therefore, on average, 8.32 cursor tables and DBDs were requested before DB2 had to read one from DASD. This number should be as high as possible to avoid delays due to reading objects from the DB2 Directory.

In addition to the Statistics Summary report, a Statistics Detail report provides multiple pages of detail supporting the summary information. Also, the Short and Long Statistics Trace reports are useful for analyzing DB2 resource use in-depth.

Summary Report Set

The summary report set is used to provide a summarization of DB2 PM events. Three summary reports are provided every time DB2 PM is run.

The Job Summary Log details the traces that were started and stopped during the time-frame that was reported. Additionally, a summary of the requested DB2 PM reports is provided. The Message Log contains any DB2 PM error messages. Finally, the Trace Record Distribution report provides a synopsis of the types of DB2 trace records and the number of times they were encountered in this job.

These reports are not useful for evaluating DB2 performance. They are used solely to support DB2 PM processing.

System Parameters Report Set

The DB2 PM System Parameters report provides a formatted listing of the DSNZPARM parameters specified when DB2 was started. This two-page report shows information such as the following:

- Install SYSADM IDs and Install SYSOPR IDs

- EDM Pool Size

- Bufferpool Sizes and Information

- IRLM Information (IRLM Name, IRLMRWT, Auto Start)

- User Information (CTHREAD, IDFORE, IDBACK)

- Automatic Trace Start Information

- Lock Escalation

- Log Information (Number of Archive Logs, Archive Copy Prefixes, Checkpoint Frequency)

- Data Definition Control Support

- Distributed Database Information (DDF)

- Stored Procedure Information (SPAS)

- DFHSM Usage

- Other System Parameters

The System Parameters report can be produced automatically in conjunction with any other DB2 PM reports. It is produced only if a -START TRACE command was issued during the timeframe for the requested report. This report is useful for determining the parameters in use for the DB2 subsystem.

Transit Time Report Set

The final report set is the transit time report set. A transit report differs from other types of reports in that it provides performance information for all events that occur between a create thread and a terminate thread. A transit can be several plan executions due to thread reuse.

The Transit Time Summary report, shown in Listing 24.16, breaks down transit information into its components. For example, the transit for the DSNUTIL plan is broken down into the time for each separate phase of the REORG.

LISTING 24.16   DB2 PM Transit Time Summary Report

```
INTERVAL FROM 7/25/03 12:24:35.63              DB2 PERFORMANCE MONITOR          DB2 ID:   DB2T          PAGE    1
         TO    7/25/03 00:05:43.02

                                               TRANSIT TIME SUMMARY            REQUESTED FROM      NOT SPECIFIED
                                                                                         TO        NOT SPECIFIED

                                               BY PRIMAUTH/PLANNAME
------------------------------ AVERAGE  ELAPSED TIMES -----           TOTAL          DETAIL
                                                                ---- WORKLOAD ----  ---- WORKLOAD ----
          TRANSITS, #CREATE CREATE  COMMIT,
            TOTAL     THREAD, THREAD, TERM.     DB2,    TRANSIT
PRIMAUTH PLANNAME TRANSIT AET #COMMIT SIGNON  THREAD  UNATTRIB.  TYPE  # OCCUR   AET    TYPE      #OCCUR AET
          MMM:SS.THT           SSS.THT SSS.THT MMM:SS.THT                MMM:SS.THT
-------- -------- ----------- ------- ------- ------- ---------- ------- ------- ----------  ----------- ------- ---

AUTHID02 DSNUTIL       1         1   0.001   0.091    8.702  UTILITY    1       8.702  PHASE  TYPE #ITEMS  PHS ET
                   9.552         4   0.000   0.019    0.809  REORG      1              UNLOAD   R    18   0.527
                                                                                      RELOAD   R     9   3.980
                                                                                      SORT     I    18   4.102
                                                                                      BUILD    I    18   0.893
```

Different levels of detail are provided by the three other types of transit time reports: Transit Time Detail report, Short Transit Time Trace report, and Long Transit Time Trace report.

Transit time reports are useful for determining the performance of DB2 utility phases and SQL activity. Like the SQL trace reports, they may contain a large amount of information and should be used only when specific performance problems are encountered.

Using DB2 PM

Before you can run DB2 PM, you must have trace records produced by DB2 to feed into DB2 PM. Each DB2 PM report set requires certain traces to be started. For a synopsis of which traces to start for which information, refer to Table 24.3. Note that DB2 PM will not fail if you request a report for which no information or insufficient information is available. The report that DB2 PM generates, however, will be empty or incomplete.

TABLE 24.3   Traces to Initiate for each DB2 PM Report Type

Report Type	Recommended Traces	Information Provided
Accounting (General)	Accounting Class 1	General accounting information
	Accounting Class 2	In DB2 times
	Accounting Class 3	Suspension times, out of DB2 times, system events
Accounting Long	Accounting Class 1	General accounting information
	Accounting Class 2	In DB2 times
	Accounting Class 3	Suspension times, out of DB2 times, system events
	Accounting Class 4	Installation-defined
	Accounting Class 5	Time spent processing IFI requests
	Accounting Class 7	Entry or exit from DB2 event signaling for package and DBRM accounting
	Accounting Class 8	Package wait time
Audit	Audit Class 1	Authorization failures
	Audit Class 2	DCL
	Audit Class 3	DDL
	Audit Class 4	DML: First SELECT of audited table
	Audit Class 5	DML: First UPDATE for audited tables
	Audit Class 6	Bind
	Audit Class 7	SET CURRENT SQLID
	Audit Class 8	Utility executions
	Audit Class 9	User-defined
I/O Activity	Performance Class 4	Buffer pool and EDM pool statistics
	Performance Class 5	Logging and BSDS statistics
Locking	Performance Class 6	Lock suspensions, lock resumes, and lock contention information
Record Trace	No traces specifically required	Formatted dump of all DB2 trace records in the given input data set

TABLE 24.3   Continued

Report Type	Recommended Traces	Information Provided
SQL Trace	Accounting Class 1	General accounting information
	Accounting Class 2	In DB2 times
	Performance Class 2	Aborts, commits, and thread-related data
	Performance Class 3	Sort, AMS, plan, cursor, static SQL, and dynamic SQL statistics
	Performance Class 4	Physical reads and writes
	Performance Class 6	Lock suspensions, lock resumes, and lock contention information
	Performance Class 8	Index access and sequential scan data
	Performance Class 13	EDITPROC and VALIDPROC access
Statistics	Statistics Class 1	System and database services statistics
	Statistics Class 2	Installation-defined
	Statistics Class 3	Deadlock information
	Statistics Class 4	DB2 exception condition
	Statistics Class 6	DB2 storage information
Summary	No traces specifically required	Basic summary of the steps taken by DB2 PM to produce other reports
System Parameters	At least one type of trace	Installation parameters (DSNZPARMs)
Transit Time	Performance Class 1	Background events
	Performance Class 2	Aborts, commits, and thread-related data
	Performance Class 3	Sort, AMS, plans, cursor, static SQL, and dynamic SQL statistics
	Performance Class 4	Physical reads and writes
	Performance Class 6	Lock suspensions, lock resumes, and lock contention information
	Performance Class 10	Optimizer and bind statistics
	Performance Class 13	EDITPROC and VALIDPROC access

Be sure to start the appropriate traces as outlined in Table 24.3 before running DB2 PM. To run a report indicated in the left column, you should start the recommended traces to get useful information from DB2 PM. If a particular trace is not started, the DB2 PM report still prints, but you do not get all the information the report can provide. Failure to start all these traces may result in some report values being left blank or listed as N/C.

You should develop standards for the production of DB2 PM reports to monitor the performance of DB2 and its applications at your shop. Use the chart in Table 24.4 as a guideline for establishing a regular DB2 PM reporting cycle. You can modify and augment this table based on your shop's DB2 performance monitoring requirements and standards.

TABLE 24.4   DB2 PM Monitoring Reference

Resource to Monitor	DB2 PM Report	Frequency
DB2 Subsystem	Statistics Summary	Weekly
	Statistics Detail	As needed
	I/O Activity Summary	Monthly
	I/O Buffer Pool Activity Detail	As needed
	I/O EDM Pool Activity Detail	As needed
	I/O Log Manager Activity Detail	As needed
	System Parameters	When DB2 is recycled
	Audit Summary	Weekly
DB2 Applications	Accounting Short	Daily
	Accounting Long	As needed
	Audited DML Access	Weekly
	Lock Contention	As needed
	Lock Suspension	As needed
Exception	Transit Time report solving	Problem Monitoring
	SQL Trace	Problem solving
	Record Trace	DB2 or DB2 PM problem solving
	Summary report	DB2 PM problem solving
	Lock Contention	Problem solving
	Lock Suspension	Problem solving
Security	Audit Authorization Failures	Weekly
	Audit Authorization Control	Weekly
	Audit Authorization Change	Weekly
	Audited DDL Access	Weekly
	Audited DML Access	Weekly
	Audit Utility Access	Weekly

Some performance monitoring software from other vendors can provide the same batch reporting functionality as DB2 PM. You might want to reconsider whether you need DB2 PM, because DB2 PM is not as mature an online performance monitor as other products, or maybe your company has standardized on a monitoring family of products (such as MainView or Omegamom) that monitor not just DB2, but also CICS, IMS, z/OS, and other resources. Before you decide to avoid DB2 PM in favor of the batch performance monitoring provided by another tool, consider the following:

- When performance problems that require IBM intervention persist, IBM often requests that you run a performance trace and generate DB2 PM reports for the trace. To be sure that IBM will accept reports generated by the third-party tool, compare the output from the vendor tool to the output from DB2 PM. If the reports are almost identical, you usually will not have a problem. To be absolutely sure, ask your IBM support center.

- DB2 PM is an industry standard for batch performance monitoring. Taking classes on performance monitoring is easier when the monitoring is based on DB2 PM reports.

Classes offered by IBM (and others) on DB2 performance usually use DB2 PM reports as examples. As such, having access to DB2 PM is helpful for students. Additionally, if you need to add staff, DB2 PM trained personnel can be easier to find.

- DB2 PM may be updated for new releases of DB2 more quickly than third-party monitoring tools because IBM is closer than anyone else to the code of DB2. If you need to migrate to new versions of DB2 rapidly, DB2 PM may be the only monitor positioned for the new release at the same time as your shop.

Online DB2 Performance Monitors

In addition to a batch performance monitor such as DB2 PM, DB2 shops must also have an online performance monitor, which is a tool that provides real-time reporting on DB2 performance statistics as DB2 operates. In contrast, a batch performance monitor reads previously generated trace records from an input data set. Sometimes, a single product can serve both purposes.

With online DB2 performance monitors, you can usually perform proactive performance management tasks. In other words, you can set up the monitor such that when it detects a problem it alerts a DBA and possibly takes actions on its own to resolve the problem. The leading DB2 online performance monitors are MainView from BMC Software (shown in Figure 24.2), Omegamon from Candle Corporation, and TMON from Allen Systems Group.

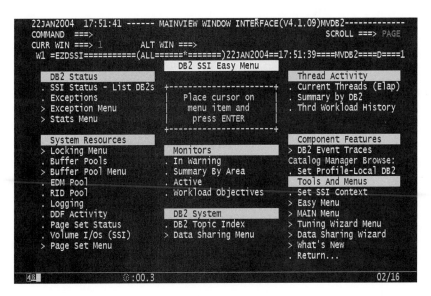

FIGURE 24.2   MainView for DB2 (BMC Software).

Traditional VTAM Performance Monitors

The most common way to provide online performance monitoring capabilities is by online access to DB2 trace information in the MONITOR trace class. These tools are accessed directly through VTAM in the same way that CICS or TSO are accessed through VTAM. You generally specify OPX or OP*n* for the destination of the MONITOR trace. This way, you can place the trace records into a buffer that can be read using the IFI.

Some online DB2 performance monitors also provide direct access to DB2 performance data by reading the control blocks of the DB2 and application address spaces. This type of monitoring provides a "window" to up-to-the-minute performance statistics while DB2 is running. This information is important if quick reaction to performance problems is required.

Most online DB2 performance monitors provide a menu-driven interface accessible from TSO or VTAM. It enables online performance monitors to start and stop traces as needed based on the menu options chosen by the user. Consequently, you can reduce overhead and diminish the learning curve involved in understanding DB2 traces and their correspondence to performance reports.

Following are some typical uses of online performance monitors. Many online performance monitors can establish effective exception-based monitoring. When specified performance thresholds are reached, triggers can offer notification and take action. For example, you could set a trigger when the number of lock suspensions for the TXN00002 plan is reached; when the trigger is activated, a message is sent to the console and a batch report is generated to provide accounting detail information for the plan. You can set any number of triggers for many thresholds. Following are suggestions for setting thresholds:

- When a buffer pool threshold is reached (PREFETCH DISABLED, DEFERRED WRITE THRESHOLD, or DM CRITICAL THRESHOLD).

- For critical transactions, when predefined performance objectives are not met. For example, if TXN00001 requires sub-second response time, set a trigger to notify a DBA when the transaction receives a class 1 accounting elapsed time exceeding 1 second by more than 25%.

- Many types of thresholds can be established. Most online monitors support this capability. As such, you can customize the thresholds for the needs of your DB2 environment.

Online performance monitors can produce real-time EXPLAINs for long-running SQL statements. If an SQL statement is taking a significant amount of time to process, an analyst can display the SQL statement as it executes and dynamically issue an EXPLAIN for the statement. Even as the statement executes, an understanding of why it is taking so long to run can be achieved.

> **NOTE**
>
> A complete discussion of the EXPLAIN statement is provided in the next chapter.

Online performance monitors can also reduce the burden of monitoring more than one DB2 subsystem. Multiple DB2 subsystems can be tied to a single online performance monitor to enable monitoring of distributed capabilities, multiple production DB2s, or test and production DB2 subsystems, all from a single session.

Some online performance monitors provide historical trending. These monitors track performance statistics and store them in DB2 tables or in VSAM files with a timestamp. They also provide the capability to query these stores of performance data to assist in the following:

- Analyzing recent history. Most SQL statements execute quickly, making difficult the job of capturing and displaying information about the SQL statement as it executes. However, you might not want to wait until the SMF data is available to run a batch report. Quick access to recent past-performance data in these external data stores provides a type of online monitoring that is as close to real time as is usually needed.

- Determining performance trends, such as a transaction steadily increasing in its CPU consumption or elapsed time.

- Performing capacity planning based on a snapshot of the recent performance of DB2 applications.

Some monitors also run when DB2 is down to provide access to the historical data accumulated by the monitor.

A final benefit of online DB2 performance monitors is their capability to interface with other MVS monitors for IMS/TM, CICS, MVS, or VTAM. This way, an analyst gets a view of the entire spectrum of system performance. Understanding and analyzing the data from each of these monitors, however, requires a different skill. Quite often, one person cannot master all these monitors.

GUI Workstation Performance Management

Many of the leading database tools vendors are offering GUI front-ends for their performance monitoring products. These products run on a workstation PC and connect to the mainframe to obtain performance trace information or to probe DB2 control blocks for performance statistics.

Usually these performance management tools require separate portions to be installed on the server and the client. The server component constantly monitors and polls for predefined events; the client component provides console operations that accept alerts triggered by the server. In a DB2 environment, the z/OS (or OS/390) machine is the server; the client is typically a PC running Windows.

In many cases, the tool vendors are basing their DB2 for z/OS GUI performance management tools on their popular management products for open systems DBMSs (such as Oracle and Microsoft SQL Server). A GUI product has advantages over a green-screen offering because more information can be presented on a single screen. The main screen acts as a dashboard (see Figure 24.3), delivering the high-level pertinent information to the DBA or performance analyst all on one console. Users can then drill down into more detailed information as desired, such as showing details about all active DB2 threads (see Figure 24.4).

FIGURE 24.3   SmartDBA System Performance Console (BMC Software).

Examples of popular GUI-based performance monitors include BMC Software's SmartDBA and Quest Software's Quest Central. The screens shown in Figures 24.3 and 24.4 are examples of BMC's SmartDBA System Performance for DB2 offering.

Online Performance Monitoring Summary

Some vendors sell monitors in all these areas, providing a sort of seamless interface that can simplify movement from one type of monitoring to another. For example, if a DB2 monitor reports that a CICS transaction is experiencing a performance problem, being able to switch to a CICS monitor to further explore the situation would be beneficial.

In Chapter 39, "Components of a Total DB2 Solution," I discuss online performance monitors for DB2 further and list several vendors that supply them. You also can write your own DB2 performance monitor using the Instrumentation Facility Interface (IFI) provided with DB2. However, you should not undertake this task unless you are a skilled system programmer willing to retool your home-grown monitor for every new release of DB2.

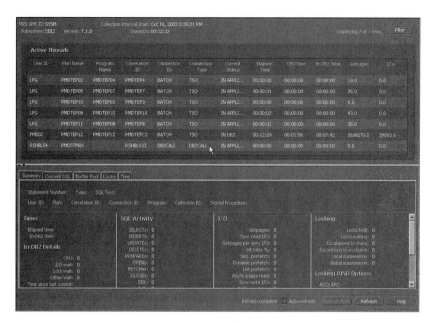

FIGURE 24.4   SmartDBA Active Thread Drill Down (BMC Software).

Viewing DB2 Console Messages

Another way to monitor DB2 performance is to view the DB2 console messages for the active DSNMSTR address space. You can obtain a wealth of statistics from this log.

To view DB2 console messages, you must be able to view the DSNMSTR region either as it executes or, for an inactive DB2 subsystem, from the spool. Most shops have a tool for displaying the outlist of jobs that are executing or have completed but remain on the queue. An example of such a tool is IBM's SDF.

Using your outlist display tool, select the DSNMSTR job. (This job may have been renamed at your shop to something such as DB2TMSTR or DB2MSTR.) View the JES message log, which contains DB2 messages that are helpful in determining problems.

Information in the DB2 message log can help you monitor many situations. Several examples follow.

When you first view the console messages, a screen similar to Figure 24.5 is displayed. In the DB2 start-up messages, look for the DSNZ002I message code. It shows you the DSNZPARM load module name that supplied DB2 with its start-up parameters. From this first part of the DB2 console log, you also can determine the following:

- The time DB2 was started (in the example, 18:01:52)
- The name of the Boot Strap Data Set (BSDS) and associated information
- The name of the active log data sets and associated log RBA information

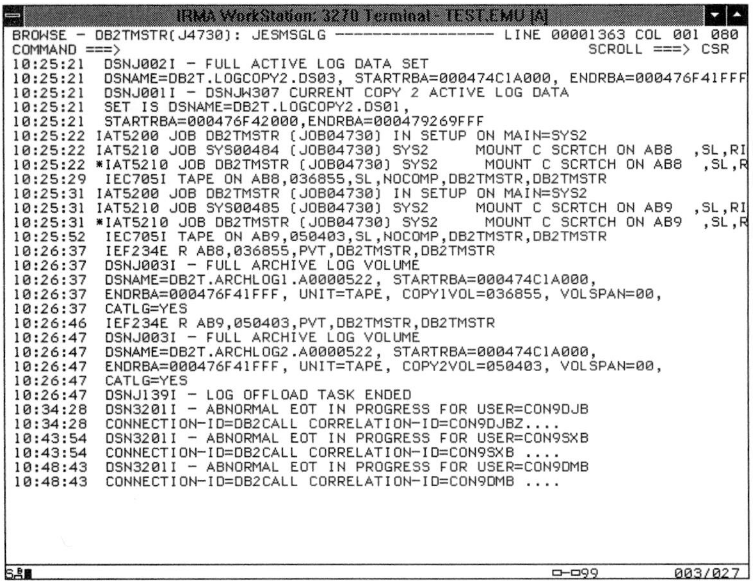

```
┌────────────────────IRMA WorkStation: 3270 Terminal - TEST.EMU [A]──────▼─▲─┐
│BROWSE - DB2TMSTR(J4730): JESMSGLG ---------------- LINE 00001363 COL 001 080│
│COMMAND ===>                                              SCROLL ===> CSR    │
│10:25:21   DSNJ002I - FULL ACTIVE LOG DATA SET                              │
│10:25:21   DSNAME=DB2T.LOGCOPY2.DS03, STARTRBA=000474C1A000, ENDRBA=000476F41FFF│
│10:25:21   DSNJ001I - DSNJW307 CURRENT COPY 2 ACTIVE LOG DATA               │
│10:25:21   SET IS DSNAME=DB2T.LOGCOPY2.DS01,                                │
│10:25:21   STARTRBA=000476F42000,ENDRBA=000479269FFF                        │
│10:25:22   IAT5200 JOB DB2TMSTR (JOB04730) IN SETUP ON MAIN=SYS2            │
│10:25:22   IAT5210 JOB SYS00484 (JOB04730) SYS2     MOUNT C SCRTCH ON AB8  ,SL,RI│
│10:25:22  *IAT5210 JOB DB2TMSTR (JOB04730) SYS2      MOUNT C SCRTCH ON AB8  ,SL,R│
│10:25:29   IEC705I TAPE ON AB8,036855,SL,NOCOMP,DB2TMSTR,DB2TMSTR           │
│10:25:31   IAT5200 JOB DB2TMSTR (JOB04730) IN SETUP ON MAIN=SYS2            │
│10:25:31   IAT5210 JOB SYS00485 (JOB04730) SYS2     MOUNT C SCRTCH ON AB9  ,SL,RI│
│10:25:31  *IAT5210 JOB DB2TMSTR (JOB04730) SYS2      MOUNT C SCRTCH ON AB9  ,SL,R│
│10:25:52   IEC705I TAPE ON AB9,050403,SL,NOCOMP,DB2TMSTR,DB2TMSTR           │
│10:26:37   IEF234E R AB8,036855,PVT,DB2TMSTR,DB2TMSTR                       │
│10:26:37   DSNJ003I - FULL ARCHIVE LOG VOLUME                               │
│10:26:37   DSNAME=DB2T.ARCHLOG1.A0000522, STARTRBA=000474C1A000,            │
│10:26:37   ENDRBA=000476F41FFF, UNIT=TAPE, COPY1VOL=036855, VOLSPAN=00,     │
│10:26:37   CATLG=YES                                                        │
│10:26:46   IEF234E R AB9,050403,PVT,DB2TMSTR,DB2TMSTR                       │
│10:26:47   DSNJ003I - FULL ARCHIVE LOG VOLUME                               │
│10:26:47   DSNAME=DB2T.ARCHLOG2.A0000522, STARTRBA=000474C1A000,            │
│10:26:47   ENDRBA=000476F41FFF, UNIT=TAPE, COPY2VOL=050403, VOLSPAN=00,     │
│10:26:47   CATLG=YES                                                        │
│10:26:47   DSNJ139I - LOG OFFLOAD TASK ENDED                               │
│10:34:28   DSN320I - ABNORMAL EOT IN PROGRESS FOR USER=CON9DJB              │
│10:34:28   CONNECTION-ID=DB2CALL CORRELATION-ID=CON9DJBZ....                │
│10:43:54   DSN320II - ABNORMAL EOT IN PROGRESS FOR USER=CON9SXB             │
│10:43:54   CONNECTION-ID=DB2CALL CORRELATION-ID=CON9SXB ....                │
│10:48:43   DSN320II - ABNORMAL EOT IN PROGRESS FOR USER=CON9DMB             │
│10:48:43   CONNECTION-ID=DB2CALL CORRELATION-ID=CON9DMB ....                │
│                                                                            │
│                                                                            │
│                                                                            │
│                                                                            │
├────────────────────────────────────────────────────┬─○99──────003/027─────┤
└────────────────────────────────────────────────────┴──────────────────────┘
```

FIGURE 24.5   DB2 console messages.

Sometimes, when DB2 performs a log offload, the overall performance of the DB2 subsystem suffers. This outcome can be the result of the physical placement of log data sets and DASD contention as DB2 copies data from the active logs to archive log tapes and switches active logs.

In Figure 24.6, find the DB2 message DSNJ002I, which indicates the time an active log data set is full (10:25:21 in the example). The DSNJ139I message is issued when the log offload has completed successfully (10:26:47 in the example). This efficient log offload required a little more than one minute to complete. If users complain about poor performance that can be tracked back to log offload periods, investigate the DASD placement of your active logs. Specify multiple active logs, and place each active log data set on a separate DASD device. As an additional consideration, think about caching the DASD devices used for DB2 active logs.

Resource unavailable messages are also in this message log. You can find them by searching for DSNT501I messages. For example, refer to the portion of the log displayed in Figure 24.7. It shows a resource unavailable message occurring at 10:17:26. From this message, you can determine who received the unavailable resource message (correlation-ID), what was unavailable, and why. In this case, a tablespace was unavailable for reason code 00C900A3, which is a check pending situation. (As you can see by scanning further messages in the log, the check pending situation is cleared up approximately four minutes later.)

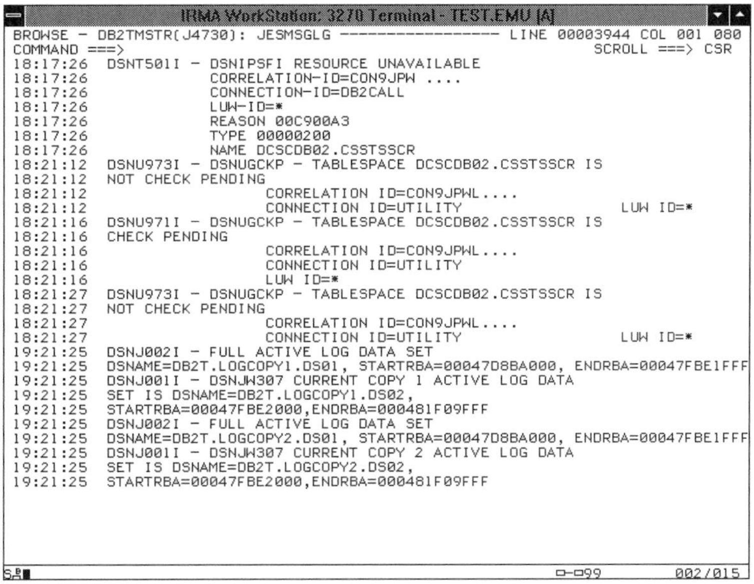

FIGURE 24.6   Log offloading.

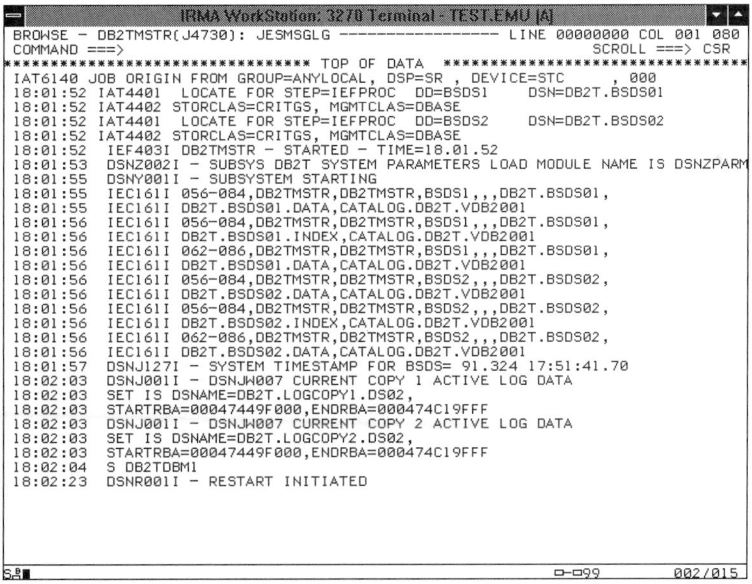

FIGURE 24.7   Resource unavailable.

Another area that requires monitoring is locking contention. When a high degree of lock contention occurs in a DB2 subsystem, you get many timeout and deadlock messages. Message code DSNT375I is issued when a deadlock occurs, and DSNT376I is issued for every timeout. Figure 24.8 shows two examples of timeouts due to lock contention. You can determine who is timing out, who holds the lock that causes the timeout, and what resource has been locked so that access is unavailable. In the example, the `DSNDB01.DBD01` DB2 Directory database is locked, probably due to the concurrent execution of DDL by the indicated correlation-ID.

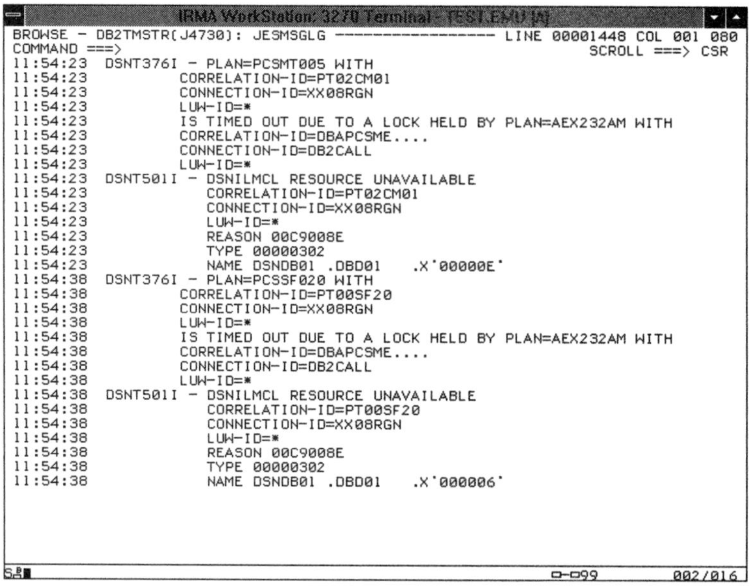

```
┌───────────────────── IRMA WorkStation: 3270 Terminal - TEST.EMU [A] ──────── ▼ ▲
│ BROWSE - DB2TMSTR(J4730): JESMSGLG ───────────────── LINE 00001448 COL 001 080
│ COMMAND ===>                                                    SCROLL ===> CSR
│ 11:54:23  DSNT376I - PLAN=PCSMT005 WITH
│ 11:54:23            CORRELATION-ID=PT02CM01
│ 11:54:23            CONNECTION-ID=XX08RGN
│ 11:54:23            LUW-ID=*
│ 11:54:23            IS TIMED OUT DUE TO A LOCK HELD BY PLAN=AEX232AM WITH
│ 11:54:23            CORRELATION-ID=DBAPCSME....
│ 11:54:23            CONNECTION-ID=DB2CALL
│ 11:54:23            LUW-ID=*
│ 11:54:23  DSNT501I - DSNILMCL RESOURCE UNAVAILABLE
│ 11:54:23            CORRELATION-ID=PT02CM01
│ 11:54:23            CONNECTION-ID=XX08RGN
│ 11:54:23            LUW-ID=*
│ 11:54:23            REASON 00C9008E
│ 11:54:23            TYPE 00000302
│ 11:54:23            NAME DSNDB01 .DBD01    .X'00000E'
│ 11:54:38  DSNT376I - PLAN=PCSSF020 WITH
│ 11:54:38            CORRELATION-ID=PT00SF20
│ 11:54:38            CONNECTION-ID=XX08RGN
│ 11:54:38            LUW-ID=*
│ 11:54:38            IS TIMED OUT DUE TO A LOCK HELD BY PLAN=AEX232AM WITH
│ 11:54:38            CORRELATION-ID=DBAPCSME....
│ 11:54:38            CONNECTION-ID=DB2CALL
│ 11:54:38            LUW-ID=*
│ 11:54:38  DSNT501I - DSNILMCL RESOURCE UNAVAILABLE
│ 11:54:38            CORRELATION-ID=PT00SF20
│ 11:54:38            CONNECTION-ID=XX08RGN
│ 11:54:38            LUW-ID=*
│ 11:54:38            REASON 00C9008E
│ 11:54:38            TYPE 00000302
│ 11:54:38            NAME DSNDB01 .DBD01    .X'000006'
│
│
│ S.8█                                              □─□99          002/016
└──────────────────────────────────────────────────────────────────────────────
```

FIGURE 24.8   Locking contention and timeouts.

The final monitoring advice in this section concentrates on two internal plans used by DB2: BCT (Basic Cursor Table) and `BINDCT`. DB2 uses the `BCT` plan to issue commands. For example, assume that you issue a `-STOP DATABASE` command, but the database cannot be stopped immediately because someone is holding a lock on the DBD. The database is placed in stop pending (`STOPP`) status, and DB2 continues issuing the command using the BCT plan until it is successful.

In Figure 24.9, the `BCT` plan is timed out at 14:58:26 and then again at 14:59:41. This timeout occurred because an attempt was made to issue `-STOP DATABASE` while another job was issuing DDL for objects in the database. The `BCT` plan tries to stop the database repeatedly until it succeeds.

DB2 uses the `BINDCT` plan to bind packages and plans. If users have problems binding, the cause of the problem can be determined by looking in the log for occurrences of `BINDCT`. In the example in Figure 24.10, the bind failed because someone was using a vendor tool that held a lock on the DB2 Catalog. Because the `BIND` command must update the DB2 Catalog with plan information, the concurrent lock on the catalog caused the `BIND` to fail.

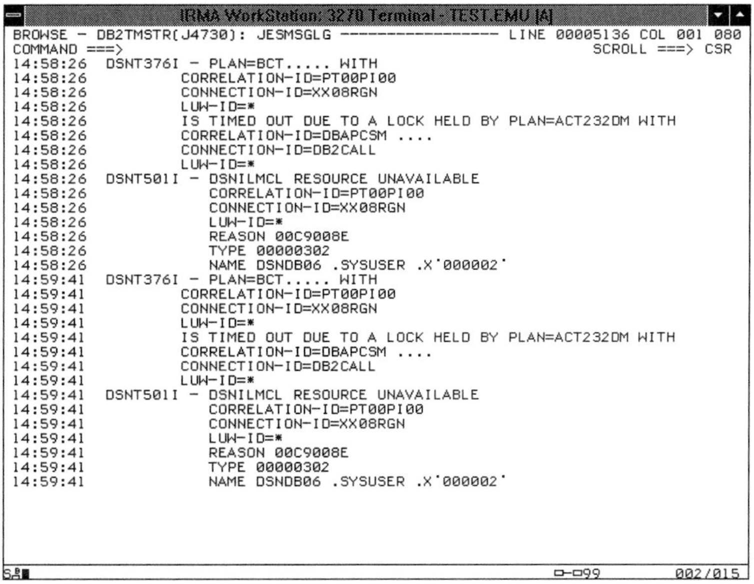

```
┌─────────────────────────────────────────────────────────────────────────┐
│ ▄                    IRMA WorkStation: 3270 Terminal - TEST.EMU [A]   ▼  ▲│
│ BROWSE - DB2TMSTR(J4730): JESMSGLG ---------------- LINE 00005136 COL 001 080│
│ COMMAND ===>                                            SCROLL ===> CSR   │
│ 14:58:26   DSNT376I - PLAN=BCT..... WITH                                  │
│ 14:58:26             CORRELATION-ID=PT00PI00                              │
│ 14:58:26             CONNECTION-ID=XX08RGN                                │
│ 14:58:26             LUW-ID=*                                             │
│ 14:58:26             IS TIMED OUT DUE TO A LOCK HELD BY PLAN=ACT232DM WITH │
│ 14:58:26             CORRELATION-ID=DBAPCSM ....                          │
│ 14:58:26             CONNECTION-ID=DB2CALL                                │
│ 14:58:26             LUW-ID=*                                             │
│ 14:58:26   DSNT501I - DSNILMCL RESOURCE UNAVAILABLE                       │
│ 14:58:26              CORRELATION-ID=PT00PI00                             │
│ 14:58:26              CONNECTION-ID=XX08RGN                               │
│ 14:58:26              LUW-ID=*                                            │
│ 14:58:26              REASON 00C9008E                                     │
│ 14:58:26              TYPE 00000302                                       │
│ 14:58:26              NAME DSNDB06 .SYSUSER .X`000002`                     │
│ 14:59:41   DSNT376I - PLAN=BCT..... WITH                                  │
│ 14:59:41             CORRELATION-ID=PT00PI00                              │
│ 14:59:41             CONNECTION-ID=XX08RGN                                │
│ 14:59:41             LUW-ID=*                                             │
│ 14:59:41             IS TIMED OUT DUE TO A LOCK HELD BY PLAN=ACT232DM WITH │
│ 14:59:41             CORRELATION-ID=DBAPCSM ....                          │
│ 14:59:41             CONNECTION-ID=DB2CALL                                │
│ 14:59:41             LUW-ID=*                                             │
│ 14:59:41   DSNT501I - DSNILMCL RESOURCE UNAVAILABLE                       │
│ 14:59:41              CORRELATION-ID=PT00PI00                             │
│ 14:59:41              CONNECTION-ID=XX08RGN                               │
│ 14:59:41              LUW-ID=*                                            │
│ 14:59:41              REASON 00C9008E                                     │
│ 14:59:41              TYPE 00000302                                       │
│ 14:59:41              NAME DSNDB06 .SYSUSER .X`000002`                     │
│                                                                           │
│                                                                           │
│                                                                           │
│ S.▐▀                                           ▫-▫99        002/015       │
└─────────────────────────────────────────────────────────────────────────┘
```

FIGURE 24.9   The BCT plan.

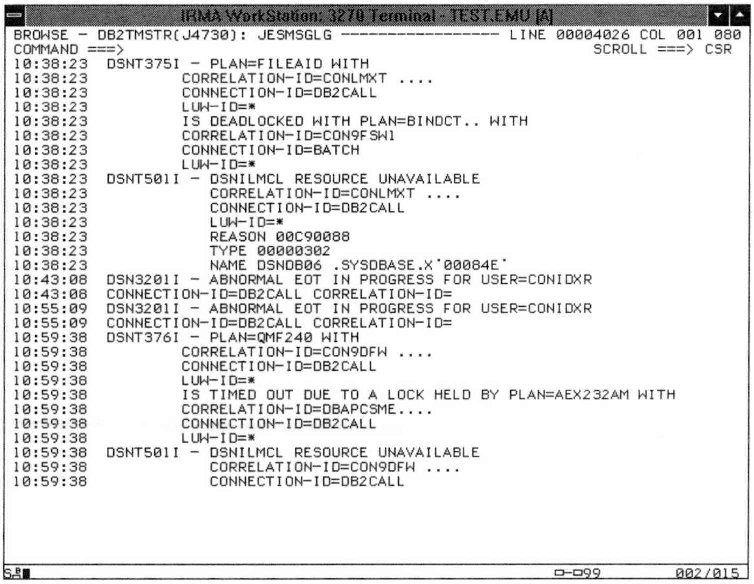

```
┌─────────────────────────────────────────────────────────────────────────┐
│ ▄                    IRMA WorkStation: 3270 Terminal - TEST.EMU [A]   ▼  ▲│
│ BROWSE - DB2TMSTR(J4730): JESMSGLG ---------------- LINE 00004026 COL 001 080│
│ COMMAND ===>                                            SCROLL ===> CSR   │
│ 10:38:23   DSNT375I - PLAN=FILEAID WITH                                   │
│ 10:38:23             CORRELATION-ID=CONLMXT ....                          │
│ 10:38:23             CONNECTION-ID=DB2CALL                                │
│ 10:38:23             LUW-ID=*                                             │
│ 10:38:23             IS DEADLOCKED WITH PLAN=BINDCT.. WITH                │
│ 10:38:23             CORRELATION-ID=CON9FSW1                              │
│ 10:38:23             CONNECTION-ID=BATCH                                  │
│ 10:38:23             LUW-ID=*                                             │
│ 10:38:23   DSNT501I - DSNILMCL RESOURCE UNAVAILABLE                       │
│ 10:38:23              CORRELATION-ID=CONLMXT ....                         │
│ 10:38:23              CONNECTION-ID=DB2CALL                               │
│ 10:38:23              LUW-ID=*                                            │
│ 10:38:23              REASON 00C90088                                     │
│ 10:38:23              TYPE 00000302                                       │
│ 10:38:23              NAME DSNDB06 .SYSDBASE.X`00084E`                     │
│ 10:43:08   DSN3201I - ABNORMAL EOT IN PROGRESS FOR USER=CONIDXR           │
│ 10:43:08   CONNECTION-ID=DB2CALL CORRELATION-ID=                          │
│ 10:55:09   DSN3201I - ABNORMAL EOT IN PROGRESS FOR USER=CONIDXR           │
│ 10:55:09   CONNECTION-ID=DB2CALL CORRELATION-ID=                          │
│ 10:59:38   DSNT376I - PLAN=QMF240 WITH                                    │
│ 10:59:38             CORRELATION-ID=CON9DFW ....                          │
│ 10:59:38             CONNECTION-ID=DB2CALL                                │
│ 10:59:38             LUW-ID=*                                             │
│ 10:59:38             IS TIMED OUT DUE TO A LOCK HELD BY PLAN=AEX232AM WITH │
│ 10:59:38             CORRELATION-ID=DBAPCSME....                          │
│ 10:59:38             CONNECTION-ID=DB2CALL                                │
│ 10:59:38             LUW-ID=*                                             │
│ 10:59:38   DSNT501I - DSNILMCL RESOURCE UNAVAILABLE                       │
│ 10:59:38              CORRELATION-ID=CON9DFW ....                         │
│ 10:59:38              CONNECTION-ID=DB2CALL                               │
│                                                                           │
│                                                                           │
│ S.▐▀                                           ▫-▫99        002/015       │
└─────────────────────────────────────────────────────────────────────────┘
```

FIGURE 24.10   The BINDCT plan.

The situations covered here are a few of the most common monitoring uses for the DB2 console message log. Look for corroborating evidence in this log when you're trying to resolve or track down the cause of a DB2 problem.

Displaying the Status of DB2 Resources

You can perform another method of performance monitoring by using the DB2 -DISPLAY command. DB2 commands are covered in-depth in Chapter 36, "DB2 Commands." At this point, mentioning that you can monitor the status and general condition of DB2 databases, threads, and utilities using the -DISPLAY command is sufficient.

Monitoring z/OS and OS/390

In addition to monitoring DB2, you must monitor the MVS system and its subsystems that communicate with DB2. Most MVS shops already support this type of monitoring. In this section, I outline the types of monitoring that should be established.

First, you should monitor memory use and paging system-wide for z/OS, for the DB2 address spaces, and for each DB2 allied agent address space (CICS, IMS/TM, and every TSO address space accessing DB2—both batch and online). A memory monitoring strategy should include guidelines for monitoring both CSA (common storage area) and ECSA (expanded common storage area). You can do so by using IBM's RMF (Resource Measurement Facility).

You should also monitor the CPU consumption for the DB2 address spaces. RMF can do this job.

You should also monitor the DASD space used by DB2 data. Underlying VSAM data sets used by DB2 for tablespaces and indexes must be properly placed on multiple data sets to avoid disk contention and increase the speed of I/O. They also must be monitored so that the number of data set extents is minimized, preferably with each data set having a single extent. This way, you can reduce seek time because multi-extent data sets rarely have their extents physically contiguous (thereby causing additional I/O overhead).

CICS and IMS/TM performance monitors should be available for shops that use these teleprocessing environments. IBM provides the CICS Monitoring Facility and CICSPARS for monitoring CICS performance, and the IMS/TM Monitor and IMSPARS for monitoring IMS/TM performance. The other leading vendors (BMC, Candle, and ASG) also supply monitors for CICS and IMS/TM.

Another monitoring task is to use a VTAM network monitor to analyze communication traffic. Finally, analysts can use other monitors to determine which statements in a single program are consuming which resources. This tool can be a valuable adjunct to RMF.

CHAPTER 25

Using EXPLAIN

You can use the EXPLAIN feature to detail the access paths chosen by the DB2 optimizer for SQL statements. EXPLAIN should be a key component of your performance monitoring strategy. The information provided by EXPLAIN is invaluable for determining the following:

- The work DB2 does "behind the scenes" to satisfy a single SQL statement

- Whether DB2 uses available indexes and, if indexes are used, how DB2 uses them

- The order in which DB2 tables are accessed to satisfy join criteria

- Whether a sort is required for the SQL statement

- Intentional table space locking requirements for a statement

- Whether DB2 uses query parallelism to satisfy an SQL statement

- The performance of an SQL statement based on the access paths chosen

- The estimated cost of executing an SQL statement

- The manner in which user-defined functions are resolved in SQL statements

How EXPLAIN Works

To see how EXPLAIN works, refer to Figure 25.1. A single SQL statement, or a series of SQL statements in a package or plan, can be the subject of an EXPLAIN. When EXPLAIN is requested, the SQL statements are passed through the DB2 optimizer, and the following three activities are performed:

- The access paths that DB2 chooses are externalized, in coded format, into a PLAN_TABLE.

- Cost estimates for the SQL statements are formulated and inserted into a DSN_STATEMNT_TABLE.

- The user-defined functions that will be used are placed into a DSN_FUNCTION_TABLE.

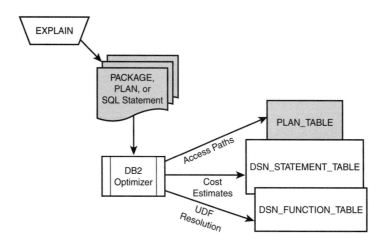

FIGURE 25.1   How EXPLAIN works.

The PLAN_TABLE, DSN_STATEMNT_TABLE, and DSN_FUNCTION_TABLE objects are nothing more than standard DB2 tables that must be defined with predetermined columns, data types, and lengths.

To EXPLAIN a single SQL statement, precede the SQL statement with the EXPLAIN command as follows:

```
EXPLAIN ALL SET QUERYNO = integer FOR
SQL statement ;
```

It can be executed in the same way as any other SQL statement. QUERYNO, which you can set to any integer, is used for identification in the PLAN_TABLE. For example, the following EXPLAIN statement populates the PLAN_TABLE with the access paths chosen for the indicated sample table query:

```
EXPLAIN ALL SET QUERYNO = 1 FOR
   SELECT   FIRSTNME, MIDINIT, LASTNAME
   FROM     DSN8610.EMP
   WHERE    EMPNO = '000240';
```

Another method of issuing an EXPLAIN is as a part of the BIND command. If you indicate EXPLAIN(YES) when binding a package or a plan, DB2 externalizes the access paths chosen for all SQL statements in that DBRM (or DBRMs) to the PLAN_TABLE.

The final method of issuing EXPLAIN is to use the Visual Explain tool to invoke EXPLAIN for dynamic SQL statements. Visual Explain also provides an easy to use interface for displaying access paths graphically and suggesting alternate SQL formulations.

Access Paths and the PLAN_TABLE

EXPLAIN populates the PLAN_TABLE with access path information. You can use the DDL in Listing 23.1 to create a PLAN_TABLE.

> **NOTE**
>
> The PLAN_TABLE will be created in the default database (DSNDB04) and STOGROUP (SYSDEFLT) in a DB2-generated table space, unless a database and a table space are created for the PLAN_TABLE and they are referenced in the IN clause of the CREATE TABLE statement. Avoid using the default database and table space.

DB2 supports many different formats for the PLAN_TABLE. The other formats exist to provide support for PLAN_TABLEs built under older versions of DB2 that did not support all the current columns. In general, though, you should use all of the columns available for the version of DB2 that you are using in order to obtain as much information from EXPLAIN as possible.

If a PLAN_TABLE already exists, you can use the LIKE clause of CREATE TABLE to create PLAN_TABLEs for individual users based on a master PLAN_TABLE. Having a PLAN_TABLE for the following users is a good idea:

- Every DB2 application programmer. This way, they can analyze and evaluate the access paths chosen for the SQL embedded in their application programs.

- Every individual owner of every production DB2 plan. This way, an EXPLAIN can be run on production DB2 packages and plans.

- Every DBA and system programmer. This way, they can analyze access paths for ad hoc and dynamic SQL statements.

Changes for DB2 Versions 7 and 8

V7 The PARENT_QBLOCK and TABLE_TYPE columns were added to the PLAN_TABLE as of DB2 Version 7.

25

LISTING 25.1   DDL to Create the PLAN_TABLE

```
CREATE TABLE userid.PLAN_TABLE
(
  QUERYNO             INTEGER       NOT NULL,
  QBLOCKNO            SMALLINT      NOT NULL,
  APPLNAME            CHAR(8)       NOT NULL,
  PROGNAME            VARCHAR(128)  NOT NULL,
  PLANNO              SMALLINT      NOT NULL,
  METHOD              SMALLINT      NOT NULL,
  CREATOR             VARCHAR(128)  NOT NULL,
  TNAME               VARCHAR(128)  NOT NULL,
  TABNO               SMALLINT      NOT NULL,
  ACCESSTYPE          CHAR(2)       NOT NULL,
  MATCHCOLS           SMALLINT      NOT NULL,
  ACCESSCREATOR       VARCHAR(128)  NOT NULL,
  ACCESSNAME          VARCHAR(128)  NOT NULL,
  INDEXONLY           CHAR(1)       NOT NULL,
  SORTN_UNIQ          CHAR(1)       NOT NULL,
  SORTN_JOIN          CHAR(1)       NOT NULL,
  SORTN_ORDERBY       CHAR(1)       NOT NULL,
  SORTN_GROUPBY       CHAR(1)       NOT NULL,
  SORTC_UNIQ          CHAR(1)       NOT NULL,
  SORTC_JOIN          CHAR(1)       NOT NULL,
  SORTC_ORDERBY       CHAR(1)       NOT NULL,
  SORTC_GROUPBY       CHAR(1)       NOT NULL,
  TSLOCKMODE          CHAR(3)       NOT NULL,
  TIMESTAMP           CHAR(16)      NOT NULL,
  REMARKS             VARCHAR(762)  NOT NULL,
  PREFETCH            CHAR(1)       NOT NULL WITH DEFAULT,
  COLUMN_FN_EVAL      CHAR(1)       NOT NULL WITH DEFAULT,
  MIXOPSEQ            SMALLINT      NOT NULL WITH DEFAULT,
  VERSION             VARCHAR(64)   NOT NULL WITH DEFAULT,
  COLLID              VARCHAR(128)  NOT NULL WITH DEFAULT,
  ACCESS_DEGREE       SMALLINT,
  ACCESS_PGROUP_ID    SMALLINT,
  JOIN_DEGREE         SMALLINT,
  JOIN_PGROUP_ID      SMALLINT,
  SORTC_PGROUP_ID     SMALLINT,
  SORTN_PGROUP_ID     SMALLINT,
  PARALLELISM_MODE    CHAR(1),
  MERGE_JOIN_COLS     SMALLINT,
  CORRELATION_NAME    VARCHAR(128),
  PAGE_RANGE          CHAR(1)       NOT NULL WITH DEFAULT,
  JOIN_TYPE           CHAR(1)       NOT NULL WITH DEFAULT,
  GROUP_MEMBER        CHAR(8)       NOT NULL WITH DEFAULT,
  IBM_SERVICE_DATA    VARCHAR(254)  NOT NULL WITH DEFAULT,
  WHEN_OPTIMIZE       CHAR(1)       NOT NULL WITH DEFAULT,
  QBLOCK_TYPE         CHAR(6)       NOT NULL WITH DEFAULT,
  BIND_TIME           TIMESTAMP     NOT NULL WITH DEFAULT,
  OPTHINT             VARCHAR(128)  NOT NULL WITH DEFAULT,
  HINT_USED           VARCHAR(128)  NOT NULL WITH DEFAULT,
  PRIMARY_ACCESSTYPE  CHAR(1)       NOT NULL WITH DEFAULT,
  PARENT_QBLOCK       SMALLINT      NOT NULL WITH DEFAULT,
  TABLE_TYPE          CHAR(1),
```

LISTING 25.1   Continued

```
TABLE_ENCODE        CHAR(1)      NOT NULL WITH DEFAULT,
TABLE_SCCSID        SMALLINT     NOT NULL WITH DEFAULT,
TABLE_MCCSID        SMALLINT     NOT NULL WITH DEFAULT,
TABLE_DCCSID        SMALLINT     NOT NULL WITH DEFAULT,
ROUTINE_ID          INTEGER      NOT NULL WITH DEFAULT
) IN database.tablespace;
```

V8 The TABLE_ENCODE, TABLE_SCCSID, TABLE_MCCSID, TABLE_DCCSID, and ROUTINE_ID columns were added to the PLAN_TABLE as of DB2 Version 8. Also, many columns were extended to support long names, as follows:

- PROGNAME was modified from CHAR(8) to VARCHAR(128).

- CREATOR was modified from CHAR(8) to VARCHAR(128).

- TNAME was modified from CHAR(18) to VARCHAR(128).

- ACCESSCREATOR was modified from CHAR(8) to VARCHAR(128).

- ACCESSNAME was modified from CHAR(18) to VARCHAR(128).

- COLLID was modified from CHAR(18) to VARCHAR(128).

- CORRELATION_NAME was modified from CHAR(18) to VARCHAR(128).

- OPTHINT was modified from CHAR(8) to VARCHAR(128).

- HINT_USED was modified from CHAR(8) to VARCHAR(128).

The final V8 modification is to the REMARKS column, which was extended from VARCHAR(254) to VARCHAR(762).

Querying the PLAN_TABLE

After you issue the EXPLAIN command on your SQL statements, the next logical step is to inspect the results. Because EXPLAIN places the access path information in a DB2 table, you can use an SQL query to retrieve this information, as follows:

```
SELECT   QUERYNO, QBLOCKNO, QBLOCK_TYPE, APPLNAME, PROGNAME, PLANNO,
         METHOD, CREATOR, TNAME, TABNO, ACCESSTYPE, JOIN_TYPE, MATCHCOLS,
         ACCESSNAME, INDEXONLY, SORTN_PGROUP_ID, SORTN_UNIQ, SORTN_JOIN,
         SORTN_ORDERBY, SORTN_GROUPBY, SORTC_PGROUP_ID, SORTC_UNIQ,
         SORTC_JOIN, SORTC_ORDERBY, SORTC_GROUPBY, TSLOCKMODE, TIMESTAMP,
         PREFETCH, COLUMN_FN_EVAL, MIXOPSEQ, COLLID, VERSION,
         ACCESS_DEGREE, ACCESS_PGROUP_ID, JOIN_DEGREE, JOIN_PGROUP_ID,
         PARALLELISM_MODE, MERGE_JOIN_COLS, CORRELATION_NAME,
         PAGE_RANGE, GROUP_MEMBER, WHEN_OPTIMIZE, BIND_TIME, HINT_USED,
         PRIMARY_ACCESSTYPE, PARENT_QBLOCK, TABLE_TYPE, TABLE_ENCODE,
         TABLE_SCCSID, TABLE_MCCSID, TABLE_DCCSID, ROUTINE_ID
FROM     ownerid.PLAN_TABLE
ORDER BY APPLNAME, COLLID, VERSION, PROGNAME, TIMESTAMP DESC,
         QUERYNO, QBLOCKNO, PLANNO, MIXOPSEQ;
```

A common method of retrieving access path data from the PLAN_TABLE is to use QMF or a GUI-based query tool to format the results of a simple SELECT statement. This way, you can organize and display the results of the query in a consistent and manageable fashion.

It is crucial that the TIMESTAMP column be in descending order. Because EXPLAINs are executed as a result of the BIND command, access path data is added to the PLAN_TABLE with a different timestamp. The old data is not purged from the PLAN_TABLE each time an EXPLAIN is performed. If you specify the descending sort option on the TIMESTAMP column, you can ensure that the EXPLAIN data in the report is sorted in order from the most recent to the oldest access path for each SQL statement in the PLAN_TABLE. Sorting this way is important if the PLAN_TABLEs you are working with are not purged.

If you want to retrieve information placed in the PLAN_TABLE for a single SQL statement, you can issue the following query:

```
SELECT    QUERYNO, QBLOCKNO, QBLOCK_TYPE, PLANNO, METHOD, TNAME,
          ACCESSTYPE, JOIN_TYPE, MATCHCOLS, ACCESSNAME, INDEXONLY,
          SORTN_PGROUP_ID, SORTN_UNIQ, SORTN_JOIN, SORTN_ORDERBY,
          SORTN_GROUPBY, SORTC_PGROUP_ID, SORTC_UNIQ, SORTC_JOIN,
          SORTC_ORDERBY, SORTC_GROUPBY, TSLOCKMODE, PREFETCH,
          COLUMN_FN_EVAL, MIXOPSEQ, ACCESS_DEGREE, ACCESS_PGROUP_ID,
          JOIN_DEGREE, JOIN_PGROUP_ID, PARALLELISM_MODE,
          MERGE_JOIN_COLS, CORRELATION_NAME, PAGE_RANGE, GROUP_MEMBER,
          WHEN_OPTIMIZE, BIND_TIME, HINT_USED, PRIMARY_ACCESSTYPE,
          PARENT_QBLOCK, TABLE_TYPE, TABLE_ENCODE, TABLE_SCCSID,
          TABLE_MCCSID, TABLE_DCCSID, ROUTINE_ID
FROM      ownerid.PLAN_TABLE
ORDER BY QUERYNO, QBLOCKNO, PLANNO, MIXOPSEQ;
```

The preceding eliminates from the query the package and plan information, as well as the name of the table creator. Throughout the remainder of this chapter, I present PLAN_TABLE information for several types of SQL statements. Variants of this query are used to show the PLAN_TABLE data for each EXPLAIN statement.

The PLAN_TABLE Columns

Now that you have some basic PLAN_TABLE queries to assist you with DB2 performance monitoring, you can begin to EXPLAIN your application's SQL statements and analyze their access paths. But remember, because the access path information in the PLAN_TABLE is encoded, you must have a type of decoder to understand this information. This information is provided in Table 25.1. A description of every column of the PLAN_TABLE is provided.

TABLE 25.1   PLAN_TABLE Columns

Column	Description
QUERYNO	Indicates an integer value assigned by the user issuing the EXPLAIN, or by DB2. Enables the user to differentiate between EXPLAIN statements.
QBLOCKNO	Indicates an integer value enabling the identification of blocks within a query (for example, subselects or SELECTs in a union).

TABLE 25.1   Continued

Column	Description
APPLNAME	Contains the plan name for rows inserted as a result of running BIND PLAN specifying EXPLAIN(YES). Contains the package name for rows inserted as a result of running BIND PACKAGE with EXPLAIN(YES). Otherwise, contains blanks for rows inserted as a result of dynamic EXPLAIN statements.
PROGNAME	Contains the name of the program in which the SQL statement is embedded. If a dynamic EXPLAIN is issued from QMF, this column contains DSQIESQL.
PLANNO	Contains an integer value indicating the step of the plan in which QBLOCKNO is processed (that is, the order in which plan steps are undertaken).
METHOD	Contains an integer value identifying the access method used for the given step: 0 First table accessed (can also indicate an outer table or a continuation of the previous table accessed) 1 Nested loop join 2 Merge scan join 3 Independent sort; Sort happens as a result of ORDER BY, GROUP BY, SELECT DISTINCT, a quantified predicate, or an IN predicate (the step does not access a new table) 4 Hybrid join
CREATOR	Indicates the creator of the table identified by TNAME or is blank when METHOD equals 3.
TNAME	Indicates the name of the table, MQT, temporary table (created or declared), materialized view, or materialized table expression being accessed; or blank when METHOD equals 3.
TABNO	IBM use only.
ACCESSTYPE	Indicates the method of accessing the table: I Indexed access I1 One-fetch index scan R Table space scan RW Work file scan T Sparse index access (star join) V Buffers for an INSERT within a SELECT N Index access with an IN predicate D Direct row access (by a ROWID column) M Multiple index scan MX Specification of the index name for multiple index access MI Multiple index access by RID intersection MU Multiple index access by RID union *blank* Not applicable to current row
MATCHCOLS	Contains an integer value with the number of index columns used in an index scan when ACCESSTYPE is I, I1, N, or MX. Otherwise, contains 0.
ACCESSCREATOR	Indicates the creator of the index when ACCESSTYPE is I, I1, N, or MX. Otherwise, it is blank.
ACCESSNAME	Indicates the name of the index used when ACCESSTYPE is I, I1, N, or MX. Otherwise, it is blank.

TABLE 25.1   Continued

Column	Description
INDEXONLY	A value of Y indicates that access to the index is sufficient to satisfy the query. N indicates that access to the table space is also required.
SORTN_UNIQ	A value of Y indicates that a sort must be performed on the new table to remove duplicates.
SORTN_JOIN	A value of Y indicates that a sort must be performed on the new table to accomplish a merge scan join. Or a sort is performed on the RID list and intermediate table of a hybrid join.
SORTN_ORDERBY	A value of Y indicates that a sort must be performed on the new table to order rows.
SORTN_GROUPBY	A value of Y indicates that a sort must be performed on the new table to group rows.
SORTC_UNIQ	A value of Y indicates that a sort must be performed on the composite table to remove duplicates.
SORTC_JOIN	A value of Y indicates that a sort must be performed on the composite table to accomplish a join (any type).
SORTC_ORDERBY	A value of Y indicates that a sort must be performed on the composite table to order rows.
SORTC_GROUP	A value of Y indicates that a sort must be performed on the composite table to group rows.
TSLOCKMODE	Contains the lock level applied to the new table, its table space, or partitions. If the isolation level can be determined at BIND time, the values can be as follow: IS Intent share lock IX Intent exclusive lock S Share lock U Update lock X Exclusive lock SIX Share with intent exclusive lock N No lock (UR isolation level) If the isolation level cannot be determined at BIND time, the lock mode values can be as follow: NS For UR, no lock; for CS, RS, or RR, an S-lock. NIS For UR, no lock; for CS, RS, or RR, an IS-lock. NSS For UR, no lock; for CS or RS, an IS-lock; for RR, an S-lock. SS For UR, CS, or RS, an IS-lock; for RR, an S-lock.
TIMESTAMP	Indicates the date and time the EXPLAIN for this row was issued. This internal representation of a date and time is not in DB2 timestamp format.
REMARKS	Contains a 254-byte character string for commenting EXPLAIN results.
PREFETCH	Contains an indicator of which type of prefetch will be used: S Sequential prefetch can be used. L List prefetch can be used. D Dynamic prefetch expected. *blank* Prefetch is not used, or prefetch use is unknown.

TABLE 25.1   Continued

Column	Description
COLUMN_FN_EVAL	Indicates when the column function is evaluated:
	R Data retrieval time
	S Sort time
	blank Unknown (runtime division)
MIXOPSEQ	Contains a small integer value indicating the sequence of the multiple index operation.
VERSION	Contains the version identifier for the package.
COLLID	Contains the collection ID for the package.
ACCESS_DEGREE	Indicates the number of parallel tasks utilized by the query. For statements containing host variables, this column is set to 0. (Although this column is set at bind time, it can be re-determined at execution time.)
ACCESS_PGROUP_ID	Contains a sequential number identifying the parallel group accessing the new table. (Although this column is set at bind time, it can be re-determined at execution time.)
JOIN_DEGREE	Indicates the number of parallel tasks used in joining the composite table with the new table. For statements containing host variables, this column is set to 0. (Although this column is set at bind time, it can be re-determined at execution time.)
JOIN_PGROUP_ID	A sequential number identifying the parallel group joining the composite table to the new table. (Although this column is set at bind time, it can be re-determined at execution time.)
SORTC_PGROUP_ID	Contains the parallel group identifier for the parallel sort of the composite table.
SORTN_PGROUP_ID	Contains the parallel group identifier for the parallel sort of the new table.
PARALLELISM_MODE	Indicates the type of parallelism used at bind time:
	I Query I/O parallelism
	C Query CPU parallelism
	X Query sysplex parallelism
	null No parallelism, or mode will be determined at runtime
MERGE_JOIN_COLS	Indicates the number of columns joined during a merge scan join (METHOD = 2).
CORRELATION_NAME	Indicates the correlation name for the table or view specified in the statement. Blank if no correlation name. A correlation name is an alternate name for a table, view, or inline view. It can be specified in the FROM clause of a query and in the first clause of an UPDATE or DELETE statement. For example, D is the correlation name in the following clause: FROM DSN8810.DEPT D
PAGE_RANGE	Indicates whether the table qualifies for page range table space scans in which only a subset of the available partitions are scanned:
	Y Yes
	blank No

25

TABLE 25.1 Continued

Column	Description
JOIN_TYPE	Indicates the type of join being implemented:
	F Full outer join
	L Left outer join (or a converted right outer join)
	S Star join
	blank Inner join (or no join)
GROUP_MEMBER	Indicates the member name of the DB2 that executed EXPLAIN. The column is blank if the DB2 subsystem was not in a data sharing environment when EXPLAIN was executed.
IBM_SERVICE_DATA	IBM use only.
WHEN_OPTIMIZE	Specifies when the access path was determined:
	blank At BIND time
	B At BIND time, but will be reoptimized at runtime (bound with REOPT(VARS))
	R At runtime (bound with REOPT(VARS))
QBLOCK_TYPE	Indicates the type of SQL operation performed for the query block:
	SELECT SELECT
	SELUPD SELECT with FOR UPDATE OF
	INSERT INSERT
	UPDATE UPDATE
	UPDCUR UPDATE WHERE CURRENT OF CURSOR
	DELETE DELETE
	DELCUR DELETE WHERE CURRENT OF CURSOR
	CORSUB Correlated subselect
	NCOSUB Non-correlated subselect
	TABLEX Table expression
	TRIGGER WHEN clause on a TRIGGER
	UNION UNION
	UNIONA UNION ALL
BIND_TIME	Indicates the time the plan or package for the statement or query block was bound.
OPTHINT	A string used to identify this row as an optimization hint for DB2. DB2 will use this row as input when choosing an access path.
HINT_USED	If an optimization hint is used, the hint identifier is put in this column (that is, the value of OPTHINT).
PRIMARY_ACCESSTYPE	Indicates if direct row access will be attempted:
	D DB2 will try to use direct row access. At runtime, if DB2 cannot use direct row access, it uses the access path described in ACCESSTYPE.
	blank DB2 will not try to use direct row access.
PARENT_QBLOCKNO	Indicates the QBLOCKNO of the parent query block.

TABLE 25.1   Continued

Column	Description
TABLE_TYPE	Indicates the type of table, as follows:
	B Buffers for an INSERT within a SELECT
	F Table function
	M Materialized query table (MQT)
	Q Temporary intermediate result table (not materialized)
	T Table
	W Work file
	null Query uses GROUP BY, ORDER BY, or DISTINCT, which requires an implicit sort
TABLE_ENCODE	Indicates the encoding scheme for the table, as follows:
	A ASCII
	E ENCDIC
	U Unicode
	M Multiple CCSID sets
TABLE_SCCSID	The SBCS CCSID value of the table; if TABLE_ENCODE is set to M, this value is 0.
TABLE_MCCSID	The mixed CCSID value of the table; if TABLE_ENCODE is set to M, this value is 0.
TABLE_DCCSID	The DBCS CCSID value of the table; if TABLE_ENCODE is set to M, this value is 0.
ROUTINE_ID	IBM use only.

Recall from Chapter 20, "DB2 Behind the Scenes," the access strategies that DB2 can choose in determining the access path for a query. Understanding how these access path strategies relate to the PLAN_TABLE columns is useful. The following sections provide a synopsis of the strategies and how to recognize them based on particular PLAN_TABLE columns.

The specific type of operation to which the PLAN_TABLE row applies is recorded in the QBLOCK_TYPE column. This column, in conjunction with the ACCESSTYPE column, can be used to identify the specific operations taken to satisfy each portion of the query. Table space scans are indicated by ACCESSTYPE being set to R. For a partitioned table space scan in which specific partitions can be skipped, ACCESSTYPE is set to R and PAGE_RANGE is set to Y. Index scans are indicated by ACCESSTYPE being set to any other value except a space.

When PREFETCH is set to S, sequential prefetch can be used; when it is set to L, list prefetch can be used. Even if the PREFETCH column is not set to L or S, however, prefetch can still be used at execution time. Whether sequential detection is used cannot be determined from the PLAN_TABLE because it is specified for use only at execution time.

If an index is used to access data, it is identified by creator and name in the ACCESSCREATOR and ACCESSNAME columns. A direct index lookup *cannot* be determined from the PLAN_TABLE *alone*. In general, a direct index lookup is indicated when the MATCHCOLS column equals the same number of columns in the index and the index is unique. For a non-unique index, this same PLAN_TABLE row can indicate a matching index scan. This additional information must be retrieved from the DB2 Catalog.

A non-matching index scan is indicated when the MATCHCOLS=0. The INDEXONLY column is set to Y for index-only access, or to N when the table space data pages must be accessed in addition to the index information. Index screening cannot be determined by looking at the PLAN_TABLE data, but if MATCHCOLS is less than the number of columns in the index key index screening is possible.

A one-fetch index access is used when ACCESSTYPE equals I1. This type of access is used when a single row can be used to resolve a MIN or MAX function. And, multiple-index access can be determined by the existence of M, MX, MI, or MU in the ACCESSTYPE column.

Clustered and non-clustered index access cannot be determined using the PLAN_TABLE. You will need to query the DB2 Catalog to determine whether each index is clustered. Also, index lookaside is generally available when DB2 indexes are used (but is not shown in the PLAN_TABLE).

A parallel query is indicated by values in ACCESS_DEGREE indicating the number of parallel streams to be invoked. It is the number of parallel tasks that BIND deems optimal. The degree can be decreased at runtime. The type of parallelism (I/O, CPU, or Sysplex) is recorded in the PARALLELISM_MODE column. Parallel tasks are grouped into parallel groups as indicated by the value(s) in ACCESS_PGROUP_ID. JOIN_DEGREE and JOIN_PGROUP_ID are populated when tables are joined in parallel.

For the different join methods, the METHOD column is set to 1 for a nested loop join, 2 for a merge scan join, or 4 for a hybrid join. If the METHOD column is 3, it indicates a sort operation on data from a previous step.

Now that you know what to look for, you can examine some sample access paths.

Sample Access Paths

The primary objective of EXPLAIN is to provide a means by which an analyst can "see" the access paths chosen by DB2. This section provides some EXPLAIN examples showing the SQL statement, rows from a PLAN_TABLE that were the result of an EXPLAIN being run for that SQL statement, and an analysis of the output. Based on the results of the EXPLAIN, you might decide that a better access path is available for that SQL statement. This process involves tuning, which is discussed in Part V, "DB2 Performance Tuning." This section concentrates solely on showing the EXPLAIN results for different types of accesses.

PLAN_TABLE rows for various types of accesses follow. You can use them as a guide to recognizing access path strategies in the PLAN_TABLE. Italicized column data is unique to the access path strategy being demonstrated. (For example, in the first row shown, the *R* in the TYP column is italicized, indicating that a table space scan is used.)

Tablespace Scan

QUERY NUMBER	QRY BLK	*PLANNO* QBLK STEP	METH	TABLE NAME	TYP	MCOL	INDEX	IXO	SORT NNNN UJOG	SORT CCCC UJOG	LOCK MODE	PF	COL FN EVAL	MULT IDX SEQ
1	1	1	0	PROJ	*R*	0		N	NNNN	NNNN	IS			0

Partitioned Tablespace Scan

QUERY NUMBER	QRY BLK	PLANNO QBLK STEP	METH	TABLE NAME	TYP	MCOL	INDEX	IXO	SORT NNNN UJOG	SORT CCCC UJOG	LOCK MODE	PF	COL FN EVAL	MULT IDX SEQ	PAGE RANGE
2	1	1	0	EMP	R	0		N	NNNN	NNNN	IS			0	Y

Sequential Prefetch

QUERY NUMBER	QRY BLK	PLANNO QBLK STEP	METH	TABLE NAME	TYP	MCOL	INDEX	IXO	SORT NNNN UJOG	SORT CCCC UJOG	LOCK MODE	PF	COL FN EVAL	MULT IDX SEQ
3	1	1	0	EMP	R	0		N	NNNN	NNNN	IS	S		0

Index Lookup

QUERY NUMBER	QRY BLK	PLANNO QBLK STEP	METH	TABLE NAME	TYP	MCOL	INDEX	IXO	SORT NNNN UJOG	SORT CCCC UJOG	LOCK MODE	PF	COL FN EVAL	MULT IDX SEQ
4	1	1	0	EMP	I	1	XEMP1	N	NNNN	NNNN	IS			0

Index Scan

QUERY NUMBER	QRY BLK	PLANNO QBLK STEP	METH	TABLE NAME	TYP	MCOL	INDEX	IXO	SORT NNNN UJOG	SORT CCCC UJOG	LOCK MODE	PF	COL FN EVAL	MULT IDX SEQ
5	1	1	0	EMP	I	0	XEMP1	N	NNNN	NNNN	IS			0

List Prefetch

QUERY NUMBER	QRY BLK	PLANNO QBLK STEP	METH	TABLE NAME	TYP	MCOL	INDEX	IXO	SORT NNNN UJOG	SORT CCCC UJOG	LOCK MODE	PF	COL FN EVAL	MULT IDX SEQ
6	1	1	0	EMP	I	0	XEMP1	N	NNNN	NNNN	IS	L		0

Multi-Index Access (RID Union)

QUERY NUMBER	QRY BLK	PLANNO QBLK STEP	METH	TABLE NAME	TYP	MCOL	INDEX	IXO	SORT NNNN UJOG	SORT CCCC UJOG	LOCK MODE	PF	COL FN EVAL	MULT IDX SEQ
7	1	1	0	DEPT	M	0		N	NNNN	NNNN	IS	L		0
7	1	1	0	DEPT	MX	0	XDEPT1	Y	NNNN	NNNN	IS	S		1
7	1	1	0	DEPT	MX	0	XDEPT2	Y	NNNN	NNNN	IS	S		2
7	1	1	0	DEPT	MU	0		N	NNNN	NNNN	IS			3

25

Multi-Index Access (RID Intersection)

QUERY NUMBER	QRY BLK	PLANNO QBLK STEP	METH	TABLE NAME	TYP	MCOL	INDEX	IXO	SORT NNNN UJOG	SORT CCCC UJOG	LOCK MODE	PF	COL FN EVAL	MULT IDX SEQ
8	1	1	0	DEPT	M	0		N	NNNN	NNNN	IS	L		0
8	1	1	0	DEPT	MX	0	XDEPT1	Y	NNNN	NNNN	IS	S		1
8	1	1	0	DEPT	MX	0	XDEPT2	Y	NNNN	NNNN	IS	S		2
8	1	1	0	DEPT	MI	0		N	NNNN	NNNN	IS			3

Index Only Access

QUERY NUMBER	QRY BLK	PLANNO QBLK STEP	METH	TABLE NAME	TYP	MCOL	INDEX	IXO	SORT NNNN UJOG	SORT CCCC UJOG	LOCK MODE	PF	COL FN EVAL	MULT IDX SEQ
9	1	1	0	PROJACT	I	0	XPROJAC1	Y	NNNN	NNNN	IS			0

Index Access (When IN Predicate is Used)

QUERY NUMBER	QRY BLK	PLANNO QBLK STEP	METH	TABLE NAME	TYP	MCOL	INDEX	IXO	SORT NNNN UJOG	SORT CCCC UJOG	LOCK MODE	PF	COL FN EVAL	MULT IDX SEQ
10	1	1	0	PROJACT	N	0	XPROJAC1	N	NNNN	NNNN	IS			0

Sorting: ORDER BY Specified in a Query (and sort is required)

QUERY NUMBER	QRY BLK	PLANNO QBLK STEP	METH	TABLE NAME	TYP	MCOL	INDEX	IXO	SORT NNNN UJOG	SORT CCCC UJOG	LOCK MODE	PF	COL FN EVAL	MULT IDX SEQ
11	1	1	0	DEPT	R	0		N	NNNN	NNNN	IS	S		0
11	1	2	3	DEPT		0		N	NNNN	NNNN				

Sorting: GROUP BY Specified in a Query (and sort is required)

QUERY NUMBER	QRY BLK	PLANNO QBLK STEP	METH	TABLE NAME	TYP	MCOL	INDEX	IXO	SORT NNNN UJOG	SORT CCCC UJOG	LOCK MODE	PF	COL FN EVAL	MULT IDX SEQ
12	1	1	0	DEPT	R	0		N	NNNN	NNNN	IS			0
12	1	2	3	DEPT		0		N	NNNN	NNNY				

Merge Scan Join

QUERY NUMBER	QRY BLK	PLANNO QBLK STEP	METH	TABLE NAME	TYP	MCOL	INDEX	IXO	SORT NNNN UJOG	SORT CCCC UJOG	LOCK MODE	PF	COL FN EVAL	MULT IDX SEQ
13	1	1	0	DEPT	R	0		N	NNNN	NNNN	IS	S		0
13	1	2	2	EMP	R	0		N	NYNN	NYNN	IS			

Nested Loop Join

QUERY NUMBER	QRY BLK	PLANNO QBLK STEP	M E T H	TABLE NAME	TYP	MCOL	INDEX	I X O	SORT NNNN UJOG	SORT CCCC UJOG	LOCK MODE	PF	COL FN EVAL	MULT IDX SEQ
14	1	1	0	DEPT	I	0	XDEPT1	N	NNNN	NNNN	IS			0
14	1	2	1	EMP	I	1	XEMP1	N	NNNN	NNNN	IS	L		

Hybrid Join (Access via Clustered Index)

QUERY NUMBER	QRY BLK	PLANNO QBLK STEP	M E T H	TABLE NAME	TYP	MCOL	INDEX	I X O	SORT NNNN UJOG	SORT CCCC UJOG	LOCK MODE	PF	COL FN EVAL	MULT IDX SEQ
15	1	1	0	DEPT	I	1	XDEPT1	N	NNNN	NNNN	IS			0
15	1	2	4	EMP	I	1	XEMP1	N	NNNN	NNNN	IS	L		

Hybrid Join (Access via Non-Clustered Index)

QUERY NUMBER	QRY BLK	PLANNO QBLK STEP	M E T H	TABLE NAME	TYP	MCOL	INDEX	I X O	SORT NNNN UJOG	SORT CCCC UJOG	LOCK MODE	PF	COL FN EVAL	MULT IDX SEQ
16	1	1	0	DEPT	I	1	XDEPT2	N	NYNN	NNNN	IS			0
16	1	2	4	EMP	I	1	XEMP1	N	NNNN	NNNN	IS	L		

Union

QUERY NUMBER	QRY BLK	PLANNO QBLK STEP	M E T H	TABLE NAME	TYP	MCOL	INDEX	I X O	SORT NNNN UJOG	SORT CCCC UJOG	LOCK MODE	PF	COL FN EVAL	MULT IDX SEQ
17	1	1	0	DEPT	I	1	XDEPT1	N	NNNN	NNNN	IS			0
17	2	1	0	DEPT	R	0		N	NNNN	NNNN	IS	S		
17	2	2	3			0		N	NNNN	YNNN				

SELECT With Column Function

QUERY NUMBER	QRY BLK	PLANNO QBLK STEP	M E T H	TABLE NAME	TYP	MCOL	INDEX	I X O	SORT NNNN UJOG	SORT CCCC UJOG	LOCK MODE	PF	COL FN EVAL	MULT IDX SEQ
18	1	1	0	EMP	R	0		N	NNNN	NNNN	IS	S	R	0

SELECT Using an Index With MAX/MIN

QUERY NUMBER	QRY BLK	PLANNO QBLK STEP	M E T H	TABLE NAME	TYP	MCOL	INDEX	I X O	SORT NNNN UJOG	SORT CCCC UJOG	LOCK MODE	PF	COL FN EVAL	MULT IDX SEQ
19	1	1	0	DEPT	11	1	XDEPT1	Y	NNNN	NNNN	IS		R	0

SELECT From Partitioned Tablespace Showing I/O Parallelism

QUERY NUMBER	QRY BLK	PLANNO QBLK STEP	M E T H	TABLE NAME	TYP	MCOL	IDX	I X O	SORT NNNN UJOG	SORT CCCC UJOG	LOCK MODE	PF	ACCESS DEGREE	ACCESS PGROUP ID	PAR MODE
20	1	1	0	DEPT_P	R	0		N	NNNN	NNNN	S	S	4	1	1

SELECT From Partitioned Tablespace Showing CPU Parallelism

QRY NBR	QRY BLK	PLANNO QBLK STEP	M E T H	TABLE NAME	TYP	MCOL	INDX	I X O	SORT NNNN UJOG	SORT CCCC UJOG	LOCK MODE	PF	ACCESS DEGREE	ACCESS PGROUP ID	PAR MODE
21	1	1	0	DEPT_P	R	0		N	NNNN	NNNN	S	S	4	1	C

Joining and I/O Parallelism

QRY NBR	QRY BLK	PLANNO QBLK STEP	M E T H	TABLE NAME	TYP	SORT NNNN UJOG	SORT CCCC UJOG	LOCK MODE	PF	ACCESS DEGREE	ACCESS PGROUP ID	JOIN DEGREE	JOIN GROUP ID	PAR MODE
22	1	1	0	TAB1	R	NNNN	NNNN	S	S	8	1			I
22	1	2	2	TAB2	R	NN YN	NN YN	S	S	4	2	2	3	I

Left Outer Join (or a converted Right Outer Join)

QRY NUMBER	QRY BLK	PLANNO QBLK STEP	M E T H	TABLE NAME	TYP	MCOL	INDEX	I X O	SORT NNNN UJOG	SORT CCCC UJOG	LOCK MODE	PF	COL FN EVAL	JOIN TYPE
23	1	1	0	DEPT	I	0	XDEPT1	N	NNNN	NNNN	IS			
23	1	2	1	EMP	I	1	XEMP1	N	NNNN	NNNN	IS			L

Full Outer Join

QRY NUMBER	QRY BLK	PLANNO QBLK STEP	M E T H	TABLE NAME	TYP	MCOL	INDEX	I X O	SORT NNNN UJOG	SORT CCCC UJOG	LOCK MODE	PF	COL FN EVAL	JOIN TYPE
24	1	1	0	DEPT	I	0	XDEPT1	N	NNNN	NNNN	IS			
24	1	2	1	EMP	I	1	XEMP1	N	NNNN	NNNN	IS			F

Relational Division

QUERY NUMBER	QRY BLK	PLANNO QBLK STEP	M E T H	TABLE NAME	TYP	MCOL	INDEX	I X O	SORT NNNN UJOG	SORT CCCC UJOG	LOCK MODE	P F	COL FN EVAL
25	1	1	0	PROJACT	R	0		N	NNNN	NNNN	IS	S	
25	2	1	0	ACT	R	0		N	NNNN	NNNN	IS	S	
25	3	1	0	PROJACT	I	2	XPROJACT1	Y	NNNN	NNNN	IS		

Star Join

QUERY NUMBER	QRY BLK	METH	TABLE NAME	TYP	MCOL	INDEX	JOIN TYPE	SORT NNNN UJOG	SORT CCCC UJOG	PF	COL FN EVAL
26	1	0	DIMENSION1	R	0		S	NYNN	NNNN		
26	1	1	DIMENSION2	R	0		S	NYNN	NNNN		
26	1	1	DIMENSION3	R	0		S	NYNN	NNNN		
26	1	1	FACT_TABLE	1	3	XFCT1	S	NNNN	NNNN		

View Materialization (VDEPT_DIS is a view with a SELECT DISTINCT in it)

QUERY NUMBER	QRY BLK	PLANNO QBLK STEP	METH	QBLK TYPE	TABLE NAME	TABLE NAME
27	1	1	0	SELECT	DEPT	T
27	2	1	0	NOCOSUB	VDEPT_DIS	W
27	2	2	3	NOCOSUB		
27	3	1	0	NOCOSUB	EMP	T
27	3	2	3	NOCOSUB		

Materialized Query Table Scan

QUERY NUMBER	QRY BLK	PLANNO QBLK STEP	METH	TABLE NAME	TYP	MCOL	INDEX	IXO	SORT NNNN UJOG	SORT CCCC UJOG	PF	TABLE TYPE
28	1	1	0	MOT_EMP	R	0		N	NNNN	NNNN		M

Cost Estimates and the DSN_STATEMNT_TABLE

At the same time EXPLAIN populates the PLAN_TABLE with access path information, it also can populate cost estimate information into another table, DSN_STATEMNT_TABLE. The DSN_STATEMNT_TABLE is also referred to simply as the *statement table*. You can use the DDL in Listing 25.2 to create a DSN_STATEMNT_TABLE.

LISTING 25.2   DDL to Create the DSN_STATEMNT_TABLE

```
CREATE TABLE creator.DSN_STATEMNT_TABLE
  (
  QUERYNO              INTEGER        NOT NULL WITH DEFAULT,
  APPLNAME             CHAR(128)      NOT NULL WITH DEFAULT,
  PROGNAME             CHAR(128)      NOT NULL WITH DEFAULT,
  COLLID               CHAR(128)      NOT NULL WITH DEFAULT,
  GROUP_MEMBER         CHAR(8)        NOT NULL WITH DEFAULT,
  EXPLAIN_TIME         TIMESTAMP      NOT NULL WITH DEFAULT,
  STMT_TYPE            CHAR(6)        NOT NULL WITH DEFAULT,
  COST_CATEGORY        CHAR(1)        NOT NULL WITH DEFAULT,
  PROCMS               INTEGER        NOT NULL WITH DEFAULT,
  PROCSU               INTEGER        NOT NULL WITH DEFAULT,
```

LISTING 25.2   Continued

```
REASON                  VARCHAR(254)    NOT NULL WITH DEFAULT,
STMT_ENCODE             CHAR(1)         NOT NULL WITH DEFAULT
) IN database.tablespace;
```

An EXPLAIN provides cost estimates, in service units and in milliseconds, for static and dynamic SELECT, INSERT, UPDATE, and DELETE statements. Keep in mind that the estimates are indeed just estimates. DB2 does not factor parallel processing, triggers, or user-defined functions into the cost estimation process.

The cost estimate information is useful in helping you to determine general performance characteristics of an application. You can use the cost estimates to determine roughly whether or not your programs can execute within planned service levels.

The cost estimates determined by DB2 will be tagged with a category. The category represents the confidence DB2 has in the estimate. There are two categories—category A and category B. Category A estimates were formulated based on sufficient information. Estimates in category A are more likely to be closer to reality than estimates in category B. A cost estimate is tagged as category B if DB2 must use default values when formulating the estimate. This can occur when RUNSTATS has not been run or when host variables are used in a query.

Changes for DB2 Version 8

V8   The STMT_ENCODE column was added to the DSN_STATEMNT_TABLE as of DB2 Version 8 (to support multiple encoding schemes).

The DSN_STATEMNT_TABLE Columns

When EXPLAIN is run and an appropriate statement table exists, DB2 populates that table with SQL cost estimates. To review these estimates, you need to understand the meaning of the DSN_STATEMNT_TABLE columns. A description of every column of the DSN_STATEMNT_TABLE is provided in Table 25.2.

TABLE 25.2   DSN_STATEMNT_TABLE Columns

Column	Description
QUERYNO	Indicates an integer value assigned by the user issuing the EXPLAIN, or by DB2. Enables the user to differentiate between EXPLAIN statements.
APPLNAME	Contains the plan name for rows inserted as a result of running BIND PLAN specifying EXPLAIN(YES). Contains the package name for rows inserted as a result of running BIND PACKAGE with EXPLAIN(YES). Otherwise, contains blanks for rows inserted as a result of dynamic EXPLAIN statements.
PROGNAME	Contains the name of the program in which the SQL statement is embedded. If a dynamic EXPLAIN is issued from QMF, this column contains DSQIESQL.
COLLID	Contains the collection ID for the package.

TABLE 25.2 Continued

Column	Description
GROUP_MEMBER	Indicates the member name of the DB2 that executed EXPLAIN. The column is blank if the DB2 subsystem was not in a data sharing environment when EXPLAIN was executed.
EXPLAIN_TIME	Indicates the time the plan or package for the statement or query block was explained. The time is the same as the BIND_TIME column in the PLAN_TABLE.
STMT_TYPE	The type of statement being explained. Possible values are as follow:

SELECT	SELECT
INSERT	INSERT
UPDATE	UPDATE
DELETE	DELETE
SELUPD	SELECT with FOR UPDATE OF
DELCUR	DELETE WHERE CURRENT OF CURSOR
UPDCUR	UPDATE WHERE CURRENT OF CURSOR

Column	Description
COST_CATEGORY	Indicates whether the estimate is in category A or B. Informs as to whether DB2 had to use default values when formulating cost estimates. Valid values are as follow:

A	DB2 had enough information to make a cost estimate without using default values.
B	At least one condition existed forcing DB2 to use default values. The REASON column outlines why DB2 was unable to put this estimate in cost category A.

Column	Description
PROCMS	The cost estimate in milliseconds, for the SQL statement (rounded up to the next whole integer). The maximum value is 2,147,483,647 milliseconds (the equivalent of about 24.8 days). If the estimated value exceeds this maximum, the maximum value is reported.
PROCSU	The cost estimate in service units, for the SQL statement (rounded up to the next whole integer). The maximum value for this cost is 2,147,483,647 service units. If the estimated value exceeds this maximum, the maximum value is reported.
REASON	A character string representing the reasons a cost estimate was tagged as category B.

HOST VARIABLES	The statement uses host variables, parameter markers, or special registers.
TABLE CARDINALITY	The cardinality statistics are missing for one or more of the tables that are used in the statement (or, the statement required materialization of views or nested table expressions).
UDF	The statement uses user-defined functions.
TRIGGERS	Triggers are defined on the target table of an INSERT, UPDATE, or DELETE statement.
REFERENTIAL CONSTRAINTS	CASCADE or SET NULL referential constraints exist on the target table of a DELETE statement

25

TABLE 25.2   Continued

Column	Description
STMT_ENCODE	Indicates the encoding scheme for the statement, as follows:
	A ASCII
	E ENCDIC
	U Unicode
	M Multiple CCSID sets

Function Resolution and the DSN_FUNCTION_TABLE

In addition to cost estimates and access paths, EXPLAIN also can populate function resolution information. Simply by defining an appropriate DSN_FUNCTION_TABLE, also known as the *function table*, EXPLAIN will populate that function table with information about the UDFs used during the plan, package, or SQL statement. Refer to Listing 25.3 for DSN_FUNCTION_TABLE DDL.

LISTING 25.3   DDL to Create the DSN_FUNCTION_TABLE

```
CREATE TABLE userid.DSN_FUNCTION_TABLE
    (QUERYNO        INTEGER      NOT NULL WITH DEFAULT,
     QBLOCKNO       INTEGER      NOT NULL WITH DEFAULT,
     APPLNAME       CHAR(8)      NOT NULL WITH DEFAULT,
     PROGNAME       CHAR(128)    NOT NULL WITH DEFAULT,
     COLLID         CHAR(128)    NOT NULL WITH DEFAULT,
     GROUP_MEMBER   CHAR(8)      NOT NULL WITH DEFAULT,
     EXPLAIN_TIME   TIMESTAMP    NOT NULL WITH DEFAULT,
     SCHEMA_NAME    CHAR(128)    NOT NULL WITH DEFAULT,
     FUNCTION_NAME  CHAR(128)    NOT NULL WITH DEFAULT,
     SPEC_FUNC_NAME CHAR(128)    NOT NULL WITH DEFAULT,
     FUNCTION_TYPE  CHAR(2)      NOT NULL WITH DEFAULT,
     VIEW_CREATOR   CHAR(128)    NOT NULL WITH DEFAULT,
     VIEW_NAME      CHAR(128)    NOT NULL WITH DEFAULT,
     PATH           VARCHAR(254) NOT NULL WITH DEFAULT,
     FUNCTION_TEXT  VARCHAR(254) NOT NULL WITH DEFAULT
    ) IN database.tablespace;
```

When a function is invoked in an SQL statement, DB2 must choose the correct function to run to satisfy the request. DB2 will check for candidate functions to satisfy the function request. The manner in which DB2 chooses which function to run is documented in Chapter 4, "Using DB2 User-Defined Functions and Data Types."

Changes for DB2 Version 8

V8   For DB2 V8, several columns were extended to support long names, as follows:

- PROGNAME was modified from CHAR(8) to VARCHAR(128).

- COLLID was modified from CHAR(18) to VARCHAR(128).

- SCHEMA_NAME was modified from CHAR(8) to VARCHAR(128).

- FUNCTION_NAME was modified from CHAR(18) to VARCHAR(128).

- SPEC_FUNC_NAME was modified from CHAR(18) to VARCHAR(128).

- VIEW_CREATOR was modified from CHAR(8) to VARCHAR(128).

- VIEW_NAME was modified from CHAR(18) to VARCHAR(128).

Additionally, two columns were extended in size for DB2 V8. The PATH column was extended from VARCHAR(254) to VARCHAR(2048), and the FUNCTION_TEXT column was extended from VARCHAR(254) to VARCHAR(1500).

The DSN_FUNCTION_TABLE Columns

A description and definition of the DSN_FUNCTION_TABLE columns is provided in Chapter 4. Please refer to that chapter for the detail.

EXPLAIN Guidelines

Implement the following guidelines to effectively EXPLAIN and optimize the SQL statements used in your DB2 applications.

Influence the Optimizer to Obtain Efficient Access Paths   You can influence the optimizer to choose different access paths in a variety of ways. Methods for accomplishing this task are outlined in Chapter 28, "Tuning DB2's Components." The best approach for influencing the Optimizer is to use optimization hints. This approach uses the PLAN_TABLE to define the access path you want DB2 to use.

Populate the EXPLAIN Tables in Production   Bind production packages and plans using EXPLAIN(YES). This way, you can create a trail of access paths, cost estimates, and function resolution information that can be examined in the event of a performance problem or UDF bug.

It is a good practice to use a managed, common PLAN_TABLE in production. You do not want to have to search through multiple PLAN_TABLEs to find explain output.

Understand How the PLAN_TABLE Is Populated   When EXPLAIN is issued a PLAN_TABLE is required to receive the EXPLAIN output. If the EXPLAIN statement is embedded in an application program, the authorization rules that apply are those defined for embedding the specified SQL statement in an application program. In addition, the authid of the owner of the plan or package must also either be the owner of the PLAN_TABLE or have an alias on another plan table (with SELECT and INSERT privileges).

Educate All DB2 Technicians in the Use of EXPLAIN   Train all technical DB2 users in the use of EXPLAIN. Although not everyone will be able to analyze the results in depth, all programmers, analysts, and systems programmers should understand, at a minimum, how to issue EXPLAIN for plans, packages, and single SQL statements, the meaning of each column in the PLAN_TABLE, and how to identify whether an index was used for a query.

25

Identify Modifications with Care   Use the QBLOCK_TYPE column in the PLAN_TABLE to identify INSERT, UPDATE, and DELETE statements. This column contains a description of the type of statement that was analyzed for each specific query block. Sometimes all performance tuning attention is focused on queries and not data modification statements. Be sure to review this column when you analyze PLAN_TABLE rows.

Consider Using REMARKS for Documentation   Use the REMARKS column in the PLAN_TABLE to record historical information in the PLAN_TABLE for specific access paths. One recommendation is to record in the REMARKS column the SQL statement that was EXPLAINed to produce the given PLAN_TABLE rows. Another recommendation is to record identifying comments. For example, if the rows represent the access path for a given query after an index was added, set the REMARKS column to something like ADDED INDEX *INDEXNAME*.

Keep RUNSTATS Accurate   The EXPLAIN results are only as good as the statistics in the DB2 Catalog. Ensure that RUNSTATS has been run before issuing any EXPLAIN commands. If RUNSTATS has not been run, verify that the DB2 Catalog statistics are still appropriate before running EXPLAIN.

Be Aware of Missing Pieces   Keep in mind that to analyze SQL performance properly, you will require more than just the EXPLAIN results in the PLAN_TABLE. Proper performance analysis requires the following:

- A listing of the actual SQL statement

- A listing of the actual DDL (or the DB2 Catalog information) for the objects being accessed and/or modified

- The actual filter factors used when creating the access path

- The high-level code (3GL/4GL) in which the SQL statement is embedded

- The actual DB2 Catalog statistics that were in place at the time the EXPLAIN was performed

- The DB2 release level and maintenance level at the time the EXPLAIN was run

- Knowledge of the bind parameters used for the plan(s) and/or package(s) in which the SQL statement is embedded

- Knowledge of the DB2 subsystem(s) in which the SQL statement will be executed (including settings for bufferpools, hiperpools, EDM Pool, locking parameters, and so on)

- Knowledge of the hardware environment where the SQL is being run (including type of mainframe, number and type of processors, amount of memory, and so on)

- Knowledge of concurrent activity in the system when the SQL statement was (or will be) executed

This additional information can be used, along with the PLAN_TABLE output, to estimate the performance of any given SQL statement.

Several other pieces of information are missing from the PLAN_TABLE, thus making the task of performance estimation significantly more difficult. The first missing EXPLAIN component is that the PLAN_TABLE does not show access paths for referentially accessed tables. For example, the following statement accesses not only the DEPT table but also the EMP table and the PROJ table because they are tied to DEPT by referential constraints:

```
DELETE
FROM    DSN8810.EMP
WHERE   EMPNO = '000100';
```

EXPLAIN should record the fact that these tables are accessed because of the RI defined on the EMP table, but it does not. (This information should also be recorded in the DB2 Catalog in the SYSIBM.SYSPLANDEP table, but it is not there either.) The only way to determine the extent of referentially accessed data is with a performance monitoring tool.

When indexes are accessed as the result of a DELETE or UPDATE statement, EXPLAIN fails to record this information. RID sorts invoked (or not invoked) by list prefetch also are not reported by EXPLAIN.

Runtime modifications to the access path determined at bind time are not recorded in the PLAN_TABLE. For example, simply by examining the PLAN_TABLE, you cannot determine whether sequential detection will be invoked or whether the degree of parallelism will be reduced at runtime.

Additionally, EXPLAIN cannot provide information about the high-level language in which it is embedded. An efficient access path could be chosen for an SQL statement that is embedded improperly in an application program. Examples of inefficient SQL embedding follow:

- The SQL statement is executed more than once unnecessarily.

- A singleton SELECT is embedded in a loop and executed repeatedly when fetching from a cursor is more efficient.

- Cursor OPENs and CLOSEs are not evaluated as to their efficiency; a program might perform many opens and closes on a single cursor unnecessarily, and EXPLAIN will not record this fact.

EXPLAIN does not provide information on the order in which predicates are applied. For example, consider the following statement:

```
SELECT  DEPTNO, DEPTNAME
FROM    DSN8610.DEPT
WHERE   MGRNO > '000030'
AND     ADMRDEPT = 'A00';
```

Which predicate does DB2 apply first?

```
MGRNO > '000030'
```

or

```
ADMRDEPT = 'A00'
```

EXPLAIN does not provide this data. Pieces of some of this data are available in the DSN_STATEMNT_TABLE in the REASONS column. Of course, the statement table only contains general indications to help you further analyze potential problems. It does not contain detailed information. But it can help to indicate if referential constraints, UDFs, triggers, or host variables are utilized for SQL statements.

Delete Unneeded PLAN_TABLE Rows   Periodically purge rows from your PLAN_TABLEs to remove obsolete access path information. However, you might want to retain more than the most recent EXPLAIN data to maintain a history of access path selection decisions made by DB2 for a given SQL statement. Move these "history" rows to another table defined the same as the PLAN_TABLE but not used by EXPLAIN. This way, you can ensure that the PLAN_TABLEs used by EXPLAIN are as small as possible, thus increasing the efficiency of EXPLAIN processing.

Consider PLAN_TABLE Indexes   Create indexes for very large PLAN_TABLEs. Consider indexing on columns frequently appearing in predicates or ORDER BY clauses. If you join the PLAN_TABLE to the DB2 Catalog consider creating indexes on the join columns.

Run RUNSTATS on All EXPLAIN Tables   Always run RUNSTATS on the table spaces for the PLAN_TABLE, DSN_STATEMNT_TABLE, and DSN_FUNCTION_TABLE. These tables are frequently updated and queried. As such, DB2 needs current statistics to create optimal access paths for these queries. Furthermore, the statistics accumulated by RUNSTATS can help to determine if a REORG of these table spaces is required.

Be aware, though, that indexes on these tables can slow down the BIND process when EXPLAIN(YES) is specified because DB2 must update the three EXPLAIN tables and their indexes.

Consider Compressing PLAN_TABLEs   For PLAN_TABLEs that will grow to be very large, consider enabling compression to reduce the amount of disk space required for EXPLAIN data.

Specify EXPLAIN(YES) in Production   Be sure to specify EXPLAIN(YES) when binding production plans and packages. Doing so will ensure that you have an accurate recording of the access paths and function resolution details for all production programs.

Strive for the Most Efficient Access Path   As you analyze PLAN_TABLE results, remember that some access paths are more efficient than others. Only three types of access paths can be chosen: direct index lookup, index scan, or table space scan. However, these three types of accesses can be combined with other DB2 performance features (refer to Chapter 21, "The Optimizer"). A basic hierarchy of efficient access paths from most efficient (those incurring the least I/O) to least efficient (those incurring the most I/O) follows:

> Index-only direct index lookup
>
> Direct index lookup with data access
>
> Index-only matching index scan
>
> Index-only non-matching index scan
>
> Matching clustered index access

Matching non-clustered index access

Non-matching clustered index access

Non-matching non-clustered index access

Partitioned table space scan skipping multiple partitions (partition scan)

Segmented table space scan (table scan)

Simple table space scan

This list represents only general cases in which a limited number of rows are to be retrieved. The hierarchy should be viewed in reverse order when most of the rows of a table are being accessed. For example, a table space scan can outperform indexed access if as little as 25% of the rows of the table are accessed to satisfy the query. Likewise, a table space scan almost always outperforms indexed access for small tables (fewer than ten pages), regardless of the number of rows to be accessed. Although keeping the preceding hierarchy in mind when evaluating EXPLAIN results is a good idea, each SQL statement should be analyzed independently to determine the optimal access paths.

When determining which path is most efficient, the answer always comes down to the number of rows required to be read and the number of rows that qualify.

In general, the optimizer does a great job for this complete task. The exceptional cases, however, will compel you to become an EXPLAIN/access path expert so that you can tune the troublesome queries.

Use Tools to Assist in EXPLAIN Analysis   Several products that augment the functionality of the EXPLAIN command are available. Examples include BMC Software's SQL-Explorer and Computer Associates' Plan Analyzer. Refer to Chapter 39, "Components of a Total DB2 Solution," for a discussion of SQL access path analysis products.

Use Cost Estimate Information with Caution   The cost estimates provided by EXPLAIN are rough estimates. Although they can be used to provide a general estimation of application performance, they are not 100% accurate. Additionally, other factors impact the performance of application programs. The cost estimates are for SQL statements only. DB2 and EXPLAIN do not provide cost estimates for work done by programs outside of DB2.

CHAPTER **26**

DB2 Object Monitoring Using the DB2 Catalog and RTS

To maintain efficient production DB2-based systems, you must periodically monitor the DB2 objects that make up those systems. This type of monitoring is an essential component of post-implementation duties because the production environment is dynamic. Fluctuations in business activity, errors in the logical or physical design, or lack of communication can cause a system to perform inadequately. An effective strategy for monitoring DB2 objects in the production environment will catch and forestall problems before they affect performance.

Additionally, if you have a DB2 database object monitoring strategy in place, reacting to performance problems becomes simpler. This chapter describes two types of DB2 database object statistics and how to query those statistics: DB2 Catalog queries and Real Time Statistics.

DB2 Catalog Queries

The first type of statistics for monitoring DB2 database objects is stored in the DB2 Catalog. These statistics are populated when you run the RUNSTATS utility and are only as up-to-date as the last time you ran RUNSTATS. Additionally, some information in the DB2 Catalog is accurate and useful even if RUNSTATS has never been run. Indeed, much useful information about the DB2 objects you are using can be found in the DB2 Catalog. This section documents in several categories to help you monitor DB2 object usage using the DB2 Catalog:

- Navigational queries, which help you to maneuver through the sea of DB2 objects in your DB2 subsystems

- Physical analysis queries, which depict the physical state of your application table-spaces and indexes

- Queries that aid programmers (and other analysts) in identifying the components of DB2 packages and plans

- Application efficiency queries, which combine DB2 Catalog statistics with the PLAN_TABLE output from EXPLAIN to identify problem queries quickly

- Authorization queries, which identify the authority implemented for each type of DB2 security

- Historical queries, which use the DB2 Catalog HIST tables to identify and monitor changing data patterns

- Partition statistics queries, which aid the analysis of partitioned tablespaces

You can implement these queries using SPUFI or QMF. You should set them up to run as a batch job; otherwise, your terminal will be needlessly tied up executing them. You also would be wise to schedule these queries regularly and then save the output on paper, on microfiche, or in a report storage facility with an online query facility.

Each category contains several DB2 Catalog queries you can use for performance monitoring. Each query is accompanied by an analysis that highlights problems that can be trapped by reviewing the output results of the query.

In implementing this DB2 Catalog monitoring strategy, I have made the following assumptions:

- All application plans are bound with the EXPLAIN(YES) option.

- Each application has its own PLAN_TABLE for the storage of the EXPLAIN results.

- Scheduled production STOSPACE and RUNSTATS jobs are executed on a regular basis to ensure that the statistical information in the DB2 Catalog is current; otherwise, the queries might provide inaccurate information.

- Plans are rebound when RUNSTATS has been executed so that all access paths are based on current statistical information. If you have not done so, you should have a valid, documented reason. When the access paths for your packages and plans are not based on current DB2 Catalog statistics, tuning SQL using the DB2 Catalog queries presented in this chapter is difficult.

Having a report of each PLAN_TABLE for each application is also useful. This way, you can check the DB2 Catalog information against the optimizer access path selection information. You can obtain these reports by using the queries shown in Chapter 25 "Using EXPLAIN."

Navigational Queries

To perform database and system administration functions for DB2, often you must quickly locate and identify objects and their dependencies. Suppose that a DBA must analyze a poorly performing query. The DBA has the query and a report of the EXPLAIN for the query, but no listing of available indexes and candidate columns for creating indexes. Or what if a query accessing a view is performing poorly? An analyst must find the composition of the view and the tables (or views) on which it is based. The navigational queries identified in this section provide object listing capabilities and more.

The first navigational query provides a listing of the tables in your DB2 subsystem by database, tablespace, and creator:

```
SELECT    T.DBNAME, T.TSNAME, T.CREATOR, T.NAME, T.CREATEDTS,
          T.ALTEREDTS, C.COLNO, C.NAME, C.COLTYPE, C.LENGTH,
          C.SCALE, C.NULLS, C.DEFAULT, C.COLCARDF,
          HEX(C.HIGH2KEY) AS HIGH2KEY, HEX(C.LOW2KEY) AS LOW2KEY, C.STATSTIME, C.FLDPROC
FROM      SYSIBM.SYSCOLUMNS   C,
          SYSIBM.SYSTABLES    T
WHERE     T.CREATOR = C.TBCREATOR
AND       T.NAME = C.TBNAME
AND       T.TYPE = 'T'
ORDER BY T.DBNAME, T.TSNAME, T.CREATOR, T.NAME, C.COLNO;
```

This query is good for identifying the composition of your DB2 tables, down to the data type and length of the columns. The STATSTIME column will show the last time RUNSTATS was run, thereby giving you a clue as to the accuracy of the HIGH2KEY and LOW2KEY values reports.

> **NOTE**
>
> **V8** For DB2 V8, you can add the T.SECURITY_LABEL column to this query to report on the multi-level security information for tables and MQTs.

If you want to also report on the number of rows in each table, you can use another short query that lists tables and their cardinality:

```
SELECT    CREATOR, NAME, CARDF, NPAGES, STATSTIME
FROM      SYSIBM.SYSTABLES
WHERE     TYPE IN ('T', 'X')
ORDER BY CREATOR, NAME;
```

This query will list all normal tables and auxiliary tables. The CARDF column shows the total number of rows in the table or the total number of LOBs in an auxiliary table. The NPAGES column shows the total number of pages that hold rows for this table.

> **NOTE**
>
> **V8** For DB2 Version 8, you can add the VERSION column to this query to report on the version of the rows in the table. Recall from Chapter 7, "Database Change Management and Schema Evolution," that when online schema changes are made, DB2 can create new versions of the database objects being changed.

V8 If you use materialized query tables, you will want to run the following query to monitor information about your MQTs:

```
SELECT    CREATOR, NAME, CARDF, NPAGESF,
          NUM_DEP_MQTS, STATSTIME
FROM      SYSIBM.SYSTABLES
WHERE     TYPE = 'M'
ORDER BY CREATOR, NAME;
```

Another useful navigational query presents an index listing:

```
SELECT    T.DBNAME, T.TSNAME, T.CREATOR, T.NAME, I.CREATOR,
          I.NAME, I.INDEXTYPE, I.UNIQUERULE, I.CLUSTERING,
          I.CLUSTERRATIOF*100, I.CREATEDTS, I.ALTEREDTS,
          I.PIECESIZE, K.COLSEQ, K.COLNAME, K.ORDERING
FROM      SYSIBM.SYSKEYS      K,
          SYSIBM.SYSTABLES    T,
          SYSIBM.SYSINDEXES   I
WHERE     (I.TBCREATOR = T.CREATOR   AND  I.TBNAME = T.NAME)
AND       (K.IXCREATOR = I.CREATOR   AND  K.IXNAME = I.NAME)
ORDER BY 1, 2, 3, 4, 5, 6, 14;
```

This query lists all indexes in your DB2 subsystem by database, tablespace, table creator, and table. It is similar to the table listing query and can be used to identify the columns that make up each index.

> **NOTE**
>
> **V8**
>
> For DB2 Version 8, you should add the following columns to this query: I.PADDED (for variable length keys, indicates whether the index is padded or not), I.AVGKEYLEN (average length of the keys in the index), I.VERSION, I.OLDEST_VERSION, and I.CURRENT_VERSION (for information on the data row format version for this index).

By viewing the output from these two queries, you can ascertain the hierarchy of DB2 objects (indexes in tables in tablespaces in databases). Additionally, these queries report the time the table or index was initially created and the time each was last altered. This information can be useful in an emergency situation when you need to determine what has been changed.

The output from these queries is superb for navigation. The DBA can easily get lost in a flood of production objects. By periodically running these queries and saving the output, a DBA can have a current profile of the environment in each DB2 subsystem that must be monitored.

Large installations might have thousands of tables and indexes, making the reports generated by these queries unwieldy. If these queries produce too much information to be easily digested for one report, consider adding a WHERE clause to query only the objects you're interested in at the time. For example, add the following clause to report on information contained in specific databases only:

```
WHERE T.DBNAME IN ('DATABAS1', 'DATABAS2', DATABAS9')
```

Eliminating the sample databases (DSN8D61A, DSN8D61P), the DB2 Catalog database (DSNDB06), the RTS database (DSNRTSDB), and any extraneous databases (such as QMF and databases for third-party products) is usually desirable. However, doing so is optional; you may want to monitor everything known to DB2.

Although the primary purpose of these two queries is navigation, they also can aid in problem determination and performance tuning. For example, note the following query:

```
SELECT   A.COL1, A.COL2, B.COL3
FROM     TABLE1 A,
         TABLE2 B
WHERE    A.COL1 = B.COL4;
```

If this query is not performing properly, you would want to know the column types and lengths for COL1 in TABLE1 and COL4 in TABLE2. The type and length for both columns should be the same. If they are not, you can deduce that DB2 is performing a data conversion to make the comparison, which affects performance. (Of course, DB2 V8 mitigates this type of performance problem somewhat by performing conversions within data type families in Stage 1; all previous DB2 versions performed such conversion in Stage 2.)

If the data type and length are the same, you would want to see what indexes (if any) are defined on these columns and then analyze the EXPLAIN output. Other significant data might be the uniqueness of each index, the cluster ratio for the index (these items influence the optimizer's choice of access path), data conversion due to online schema change versioning, and the number of tables in a tablespace (can cause performance degradation for non-segmented tablespaces). You can obtain all this information from these reports.

You also will need a list of user-defined distinct types (UDTs). UDTs can be used in tables and it will be helpful to know how each UDT is defined as you peruse the table and column listing. To obtain a list of UDTs defined to DB2 issue the following query:

```
SELECT   SCHEMA, NAME, METATYPE, SOURCESCHEMA, SOURCETYPEID, LENGTH,
         SCALE, SUBTYPE, ENCODING_SCHEME, CREATEDTS, CREATEDBY
FROM     SYSIBM.SYSDATATYPES
ORDER BY SCHEMA, NAME;
```

The output from this query shows all user-defined distinct types, along with the base data type from which the UDT was sourced. If you need to find all of the UDTs sourced from a base data type, you might want to change the ORDER BY clause as follows:

```
ORDER BY SOURCESCHEMA, SOURCETYPEID;
```

You might also need to examine a listing of the objects used to support your LOB columns. The following query can be used to report on the LOB columns, auxiliary tables, and LOB tablespaces used in your DB2 subsystem:

```
SELECT   T.DBNAME, T.TSNAME, T.CREATOR, T.NAME,
         A.AUXTBOWNER, A.AUXTBNAME, A.COLNAME, S.LOG
FROM     SYSIBM.SYSTABLESPACE  S,
         SYSIBM.SYSTABLES      T,
         SYSIBM.SYSAUXRELS     A
WHERE    T.DBNAME = S.DBNAME
AND      T.TSNAME = S.NAME
AND      S.TYPE = 'O'
AND      A.TBNAME = T.NAME
```

```
AND       A.TBOWNER = T.CREATOR
ORDER BY  T.DBNAME, T.TSNAME, T.CREATOR, T.NAME,
          A.AUXTBOWNER, A.AUXTBNAME;
```

The `LOG` column pertains specifically to LOB tablespaces. Examine this column to determine which LOB columns are logged and which are not.

Another useful navigational report is the view listing query:

```
SELECT   CREATOR, NAME, SEQNO, CHECK, TEXT
FROM     SYSIBM.SYSVIEWS
ORDER BY CREATOR, NAME, SEQNO;
```

The output from this query identifies all views known to DB2 along with the SQL text used to create the view. This information is useful when you're monitoring how SQL performs when it accesses DB2 views.

> **NOTE**
>
> This report may have multiple rows per view.

Monitoring the aliases and synonyms defined for DB2 tables also is desirable. The next query provides a listing of all aliases known to the DB2 subsystem:

```
SELECT   CREATOR, NAME, TBCREATOR, TBNAME, CREATEDBY
FROM     SYSIBM.SYSTABLES
WHERE    TYPE = 'A'
ORDER BY CREATOR, NAME;
```

This one provides a listing of all synonyms:

```
SELECT   CREATOR, NAME, TBCREATOR, TBNAME, CREATEDBY
FROM     SYSIBM.SYSSYNONYMS
ORDER BY CREATOR, NAME;
```

By scanning the names returned by the table, view, alias, and synonym listing queries, you can reference the complete repository of objects that can be specified in the `FROM` clause of SQL `SELECT` statements. One additional table-related query reports on the temporary tables defined to DB2:

```
SELECT   CREATOR, NAME, CREATEDBY
FROM     SYSIBM.SYSTABLES
WHERE    TYPE = 'G'
ORDER BY CREATOR, NAME;
```

Temporary tables are used to house temporary results in application programs that are required only for the life of the program but can benefit from being accessed using SQL.

When referential integrity is implemented for a DB2 application, DBAs, programmers, and analysts must have quick access to the referential constraints defined for the tables of the application. This information is usually in the form of a logical data model depicting the relationships between the tables. However, this information is not sufficient because physical design decisions could have overridden the logical model. Although these design

26

decisions should be documented, having ready access to the physical implementation of the referential integrity defined to your system is wise. This query provides a listing of referential constraints by dependent table:

```
SELECT    F.CREATOR, F.TBNAME, R.REFTBCREATOR, R.REFTBNAME,
          F.RELNAME, R.DELETERULE, F.COLSEQ, F.COLNAME
FROM      SYSIBM.SYSFOREIGNKEYS    F,
          SYSIBM.SYSRELS           R
WHERE     F.CREATOR = R.CREATOR
AND       F.TBNAME = R.TBNAME
AND       F.RELNAME = R.RELNAME
ORDER BY F.CREATOR, F.TBNAME, R.REFTBCREATOR, R.REFTBNAME;
```

This one provides a listing of all referential constraints by parent table:

```
SELECT    R.REFTBCREATOR, R.REFTBNAME, F.CREATOR, F.TBNAME,
          F.RELNAME, R.DELETERULE, F.COLSEQ, F.COLNAME
FROM      SYSIBM.SYSFOREIGNKEYS    F,
          SYSIBM.SYSRELS           R
WHERE     F.CREATOR = R.CREATOR
AND       F.TBNAME = R.TBNAME
AND       F.RELNAME = R.RELNAME
ORDER BY R.REFTBCREATOR, R.REFTBNAME, F.CREATOR, F.TBNAME;
```

These two queries provide the same information in two useful formats: the first by dependent (or child) table and the second by parent table. For a refresher on these referential integrity terms, refer to Figure 26.1.

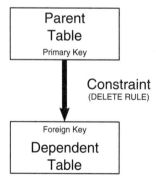

FIGURE 26.1   Referential integrity terms.

The output from both of these referential integrity queries is useful when you're searching for relationships between tables—both forward from the parent table and backward from the dependent table. This query returns all the information that defines each referential constraint, including the following:

- The creator and name of the parent and dependent tables that make up the referential constraint

- The constraint name

- The DELETE RULE for each referential constraint

- The columns that make up the foreign key

This information is useful for programmers and analysts writing data modification programs. The referential constraints affect both the functions that modify data in tables participating in referential constraints and the SQLCODEs returned to the program. DBAs need this information, with the index listing data described previously, to ensure that adequate indexes are defined for all foreign keys.

Knowing all the check constraints used in the DB2 subsystem is also useful. The following query displays all the check constraints and lists the columns to which each check constraint applies:

```
SELECT    TBOWNER, TBNAME, CHECKNAME, COLNAME
FROM      SYSIBM.SYSCHECKDEP
ORDER BY  TBOWNER, TBNAME, CHECKNAME;
```

To find the actual text of each check constraint, you can issue the following SQL:

```
SELECT    TBOWNER, TBNAME, CHECKNAME, TIMESTAMP,
          CHECKCONDITION
FROM      SYSIBM.SYSCHECKS
ORDER BY  TBOWNER, TBNAME, CHECKNAME;
```

You can also implement data integrity constraints using triggers. Triggers are assigned to specific tables such that when data changes in the table the trigger code is executed. The following query can help you to find the triggers on a table:

```
SELECT    TBOWNER, TBNAME, SCHEMA, NAME,
          TRIGTIME, TRIGEVENT, GRANULARITY, CREATEDTS
FROM      SYSIBM.SYSTRIGGERS
WHERE     SEQNO = 1
ORDER BY  TBOWNER, TBNAME, SCHEMA, NAME;
```

The following query can help you to find the table if you know the trigger:

```
SELECT    SCHEMA, NAME, TBOWNER, TBNAME,
          TRIGTIME, TRIGEVENT, GRANULARITY, CREATEDTS
FROM      SYSIBM.SYSTRIGGERS
WHERE     SEQNO = 1
ORDER BY  SCHEMA, NAME, TBOWNER, TBNAME;
```

The previous two queries do not return the actual text of the trigger because it can be very long. The column used to store the trigger code, TEXT, is defined as VARCHAR(6000) for V8 or VARCHAR(3460) for V7 and previous versions. Additionally, multiple rows can be required to store very long triggers. That is why the SEQNO column is used to retrieve only one row per trigger instance. If you want to retrieve the trigger text, use the following query:

```
SELECT    SCHEMA, NAME, SEQNO, TBOWNER, TBNAME
          TRIGTIME, TRIGEVENT, GRANULARITY, TEXT
FROM      SYSIBM.SYSTRIGGERS
ORDER BY  SCHEMA, NAME, SEQNO;
```

26

Queries to obtain stored procedure and UDF information are presented later in this chapter.

V8 If you use SEQUENCE objects (new to DB2 V8), the following query can be used to produce a list of available SEQUENCEs:

```
SELECT    SCHEMA, OWNER, NAME, SEQTYPE, CREATEDBY, START, INCREMENT,
          MINVALUE, MAXVALUE, CYCLE, DATATYPEID, SOURCETYPEID, PRECISION,
          CACHE, ORDER, MAXASSIGNEDVAL, CREATEDTS, ALTEREDTS
FROM      SYSIBM.SYSSEQUENCES
ORDER BY  NAME, SCHEMA;
```

> **NOTE**
>
> Sequences used by IDENTITY columns are listed in the results of this query, too. If the value of SEQTYPE is 'S' it applies to a SEQUENCE object, but if the value is 'I' it applies to an IDENTITY column. For more information on sequences and identity columns, refer to Chapter 5, "Data Definition Guidelines."

You also might find it useful to have a list of tables that use IDENTITY columns. The following query produces such a report in order by table name:

```
SELECT    DNAME, DCREATOR, DCOLUMN, DTYPE,
          BSCHEMA, BNAME
FROM      SYSIBM.SYSSEQUENCESDEP
WHERE     DTYPE = 'I'
ORDER BY DNAME, DCREATOR;
```

Finally, here is the STOGROUP listing query:

```
SELECT    A.NAME, A.VCATNAME,  A.SPACE,
          A.STATSTIME, A.CREATEDBY, B.VOLID
FROM      SYSIBM.SYSSTOGROUP  A,
          SYSIBM.SYSVOLUMES   B
WHERE     A.NAME = B.SGNAME
ORDER BY A.NAME;
```

This query shows each storage group defined to your DB2 subsystem, along with pertinent information about the STOGROUP, such as

- The associated VCAT, used as the high-level qualifier for all data sets created for objects assigned to this storage group

- The total space used by objects assigned to this STOGROUP

- The authorization ID of the storage group creator

- The IDs of the DASD volumes assigned to the STOGROUP or * if SMS is being used

Of course, the STOSPACE utility must have been run in order for this query to be useful. If STATSTIME is '0001-01-01-00.00.00.000000' then the STOSPACE utility has never been run.

Use caution in reviewing the output from this query because the volumes are not returned in the order in which they were specified when the storage group was created. DB2 does not provide the capability of retrieving the order of the volumes in the STOGROUP.

Navigational monitoring is only one level of DB2 performance monitoring using the DB2 Catalog. The next level delves deeper into the physical characteristics of DB2 objects.

Physical Analysis Queries

Sometimes you must trace a performance problem in a DB2 query to the physical level. Most physical characteristics are specified when DB2 objects are defined and can be modified by SQL ALTER statements. Statistics about other physical characteristics that reflect the state of the data in the physical objects are accumulated by RUNSTATS. This section concentrates on tablespaces and indexes because these objects require a physical data set.

You have many options for creating any DB2 object. If poor choices are made, performance can suffer. You will find an analysis of the proper DDL choices in Chapter 5. You can use the physical statistics queries that follow to monitor these options.

The physical tablespace statistics query provides a listing of all tablespaces in each database and lists the physical definitions and aggregate statistics detail for each tablespace:

```
SELECT   T.DBNAME, T.NAME, T.STATUS, T.IMPLICIT, T.LOCKMAX, T.LOCKRULE,
         T.BPOOL, T.ERASERULE, T.CLOSERULE, T.PARTITIONS, T.TYPE,
         T.SEGSIZE, T.DSSIZE, T.NTABLES, T.NACTIVEF, T.PGSIZE,
         T.MAXROWS, T.ENCODING_SCHEME, P.CARDF, P.FARINDREF,
         P.NEARINDREF, P.PERCACTIVE, P.PERCDROP, P.COMPRESS, P.PAGESAVE,
         P.FREEPAGE, P.PCTFREE, P.STORNAME, P.VCATNAME, P.STATSTIME,
         P.PARTITION, P.GBPCACHE, P.EXTENTS, P.DSNUM
FROM     SYSIBM.SYSTABLESPACE   T,
         SYSIBM.SYSTABLEPART    P
WHERE    T.NAME = P.TSNAME
AND      T.DBNAME = P.DBNAME
ORDER BY T.DBNAME, T.NAME, P.PARTITION;
```

> **NOTE**
>
> **V8**
>
> For DB2 Version 8, you should add the following columns to this query: T.SPACEF (DASD storage), T.AVGROWLEN (average length of the rows in the tablespace), P.CREATEDTS (time the partition was created), P.AVGROWLEN (average length of the rows in the partition), T.OLDEST_VERSION and T.CURRENT_VERSION (version information).
>
> You will also need to add information about the logical partitioning due to online schema changes (P.LOGICAL_PART and P.LIMITKEY_INTERNAL).

Having reported on physical tablespace statistics, the next step is to analyze physical index statistics. The physical index statistics query provides a report of all indexes grouped by owner, along with the physical definitions and aggregate statistics supporting each index:

```
SELECT   I.CREATOR, I.NAME, I.INDEXTYPE, I.UNIQUERULE, I.CLUSTERING,
         I.CLUSTERED, I.CLUSTERRATIOF*100, P.PQTY, P.SECQTYI,
         I.FIRSTKEYCARDF, I.FULLKEYCARDF, I.NLEAF, I.NLEVELS,
         I.PGSIZE, I.ERASERULE, I.CLOSERULE, I.SPACEF,
```

```
              P.CARDF, P.FAROFFPOSF, P.LEAFDIST, P.NEAROFFPOSF, P.FREEPAGE,
              P.PCTFREE, P.STORNAME, P.VCATNAME, P.STATSTIME, P.PARTITION,
              P.LEAFFAR, P.LEAFNEAR, P.PSEUDO_DEL_ENTRIES
FROM          SYSIBM.SYSINDEXES    I,
              SYSIBM.SYSINDEXPART  P
WHERE         I.NAME = P.IXNAME
AND           I.CREATOR = P.IXCREATOR
ORDER BY I.CREATOR, I.NAME, P.PARTITION;
```

V8 Keep in mind that `SYSIBM.SYSINDEXPART` contains one row for each non-partitioned index, and one row per partition for each partitioning index and data-partitioned secondary index (DPSI).

NOTE

V8 For DB2 Version 8, you should add the following columns to this query: `I.PADDED` (for variable-length keys, indicates whether the index is padded or not), `I.AVGKEYLEN` (average length of the keys in the index), `I.VERSION`, `I.OLDEST_VERSION`, and `I.CURRENT_VERSION` (for information on the data row format version for this index).

These reports are invaluable tools for diagnosing performance problems when they happen. Frequently, you also can use them to catch problems before they occur.

Review each tablespace and index to determine the `CLOSE RULE` for it. Objects accessed infrequently or only once per day do not need to remain open. Although pseudo-closing reduces the impact of implicit, behind-the-scenes data set opening and closing, choosing the proper `CLOSE RULE` is important. Most tablespaces and indexes should use `CLOSE YES` to take advantage of DB2's improved data set `OPEN` and `CLOSE` management techniques.

The physical analysis queries are also useful in determining the frequency of reorganization. Monitor the following information:

PERCDROP	PAGESAVE
NEAROFFPOSF	FAROFFPOSF
NEARINDREF	FARINDREF
LEAFDIST	CLUSTERRATIOF

NOTE

NEAROFFPOSF, FAROFFPOSF, and CLUSTERRATIOF apply to clustering indexes only.

The `PERCDROP` column for tablespaces indicates the percentage of space occupied by rows from dropped tables. Non-segmented tablespaces cannot reclaim this space until they are reorganized.

The `PAGESAVE` column for tablespaces indicates the percentage of pages saved (per partition) by using ESA compression.

Both the tablespace and index queries display the STATSTIME column. It is crucial because STATSTIME provides a timestamp indicating when RUNSTATS was run to produce the statistical information being reported.

Far-off and near-off pages indicate the degree of tablespace or index disorganization. For non-segmented tablespaces, a page is *near off* if the difference between the page and the next one is between 2 and 15 pages inclusive. For segmented tablespaces, a page is considered near off the present page if the difference between the two pages is between 2 and the SEGSIZE×2. A page is *far off* if the difference is 16 or greater. NEAROFFPOSF for an index indicates the number of times a different near-off page must be accessed when accessing all the tablespace rows in indexed order. The definition of FAROFFPOSF is the same except that far-off page is substituted for near-off page.

> **NOTE**
>
> For segmented tablespaces only: After a REORG, the NEAROFFPOSF can be greater than 0 if there are multiple space map pages.

NEAROFFPOSF and FAROFFPOSF are measures to gauge the organization of the data in the underlying table. It assumes that the index in question is the clustering index. Given that assumption, the values indicate how many of the rows in the table are ill-placed. If the index is not the clustering index, FAROFFPOSF and NEAROFFPOSF are not useful as indicators of data organization.

The NEARINDREF and FARINDREF columns for a tablespace indicate the number of rows that have been relocated either near (2 to 15 pages) or far away (16 or more pages) from their original location. This relocation can occur as the result of updates to variable length rows (that is, rows with VARCHAR columns, tables with EDITPROCs, or compressed rows).

LEAFDIST helps determine the relative efficiency of each index. LEAFDIST indicates the average number of pages between successive index leaf pages. The more intervening pages, the less efficient the index will be.

Finally, you can use CLUSTERRATIOF to determine the overall condition of the index as it corresponds to the physical order of the tablespace data. The more clustered an index is, the greater its conformance to the order of the rows as they are physically aligned in the tablespace. A cluster ratio of 100% indicates that the index and the tablespace ordering matches exactly. As the cluster ratio diminishes, access that uses the index becomes less efficient.

> **NOTE**
>
> CLUSTERRATIOF for partitioned indexes can be found in SYSIBM.SYSINDEXSTATS. This CLUSTERRATIOF is at the partition level and can help to determine if only a subset of the partitions needs to be reorganized.

Table 26.1 is a guide to using this information to determine how frequently tablespaces and indexes should be reorganized. A + indicates that you should REORG more frequently as the value in that column gets larger. A – indicates that you should REORG more frequently as the value gets smaller. As the number of + or – increases, the need to REORG becomes more urgent. For example, as PERCDROP gets larger, the need to REORG is very urgent, as indicated by five plus signs. For CLUSTERRATIOF, as the value gets smaller, the need to REORG increases.

TABLE 26.1   Reorganization Indicators

Column	Object	Impact
PERCDROP	Tablespace	+++++
NEAROFFPOSF	Tablespace	+
FAROFFPOSF	Tablespace	++++
NEARINDREF	Index	+
FARINDREF	Index	++++
LEAFDIST	Index	+++
CLUSTERRATIOF	Index	– – – – –

You also can use the physical analysis queries to learn at a glance the physical characteristics of your tablespaces and indexes. For example, these queries return the following:

- Tablespace and index information about partitioning, page size, erase rule, close rule, cardinality, and storage group or VCAT specification

- Information about tablespace lock rules, segment size, and whether the tablespace was created implicitly (without explicit DDL)

- Index-specific statistics such as uniqueness and clustering information

Analyzing the tablespace and index space usage also is useful. By monitoring PERCACTIVE, FREEPAGE, and PCTFREE and using a data set allocation report or a LISTCAT output, you can review and modify space utilization. Generally, when PERCACTIVE is low, you should redefine the tablespace or index with a smaller PRIQTY, a smaller SECQTY, or both. Free space can be changed as well. In any event, you must monitor these reports with the data set statistics. Also remember that changes to space characteristics do not take effect unless the tablespace being altered is reorganized and the index is reorganized or recovered.

Following are notes on using LISTCAT with DB2 data sets. LISTCAT reads the ICF catalog and displays pertinent values for data sets. The values returned by LISTCAT are generally useful for determining the overall status of a data set. However, when the data set is a VSAM data set used by DB2 for tablespaces or indexes, only some fields in the ICF catalog are accurate. They are as follows:

> High used RBA
>
> Number of extents
>
> High allocated RBA
>
> Size of each extent
>
> DFP indicators
>
> Volumes for each extent

> **CAUTION**
>
> If the `PREFORMAT` option is used, the high used RBA value can be misleading.

You can analyze DB2 tablespace and index DASD use further with the following queries. You can monitor tablespace DASD use by analyzing the results of this query:

```
SELECT   T.DBNAME, T.NAME, T.PARTITIONS, T.NTABLES, T.NACTIVEF, T.SPACE,
         P.PARTITION, P.PQTY, P.SECQTYI, P.STORTYPE, P.STORNAME, P.VCATNAME,
         (CASE NACTIVEF WHEN 0 THEN 0
          ELSE (100*T.NACTIVEF*T.PGSIZE)/T.SPACE END) AS SPACEUSED
FROM     SYSIBM.SYSTABLESPACE   T,
         SYSIBM.SYSTABLEPART    P
WHERE    T.DBNAME = P.DBNAME
AND      T.NAME = P.TSNAME
ORDER BY 1, 2, 3, 4, 5, 6, 7, 8;
```

> **NOTE**
>
> For partitioned tablespaces, consider joining to the `SYSIBM.SYSTABSTATS` table to get the statistics by partition.

> **NOTE**
>
> For DB2 Version 8, you should add `P.LOGICAL_PART` column to show the logical partition number (in addition to the `PARTITION` column, which shows the physical partition number).

V8

You can monitor index disk storage usage by analyzing the results of the following query:

```
SELECT   I.CREATOR, I.NAME, I.INDEXTYPE, I.INDEXSPACE, I.SPACE, I.PGSIZE,
         P.PARTITION, P.PQTY, P.SECQTYI, P.STORTYPE, P.STORNAME, P.VCATNAME
FROM     SYSIBM.SYSINDEXES    I,
         SYSIBM.SYSINDEXPART  P
WHERE    I.NAME = P.IXNAME
AND      I.CREATOR = P.IXCREATOR
ORDER BY 1, 2, 3, 4, 5, 6, 7;
```

These queries return information about only the particular object's DASD space use. The index DASD use query simply repeats the information from the previous physical index statistics query, presenting only DASD space use information. The tablespace DASD query adds a calculation column:

```
[(100*T.NACTIVEF*T.PGSIZE)/T.SPACE]
```

> **CAUTION**
>
> Several factors can cause the previous queries to be inaccurate. The `SPACE` values are only collected for `STOGROUP`-defined objects that have not been archived by SMS. Furthermore, if the `PREFORMAT` option is used, the space information might be misleading.
>
> The `CASE` expression is used to eliminate the possibility of dividing by zero. The `SPACE` column in `SYSIBM.SYSTABLESPACE` can be zero if the `STOSPACE` utility has not been run or if the tablespace was not defined using `STOGROUP`s.

26

This calculation shows the percentage of the tablespace being utilized. This number should be monitored to determine a tablespace's DASD requirements. If this number remains below 75% for an extended time, and little growth is expected, decrease the space and reorganize the tablespace, or use DSN1COPY to migrate rows to a smaller data set. If the number is 100% or close to it, and growth is expected, increase the space and reorganize.

The final physical statistics query presented here is the column value occurrence query:

```
SELECT   T.DBNAME, T.TSNAME, D.TBOWNER, D.TBNAME,
         D.NAME, D.FREQUENCYF, D.COLVALUE, D.STATSTIME
FROM     SYSIBM.SYSCOLDIST    D,
         SYSIBM.SYSTABLES     T
WHERE    D.TBOWNER = T.CREATOR
AND      D.TBNAME = T.NAME
AND      D.TYPE = 'F'
ORDER BY T.DBNAME, T.TSNAME, D.TBOWNER, D.TBNAME, D.NAME;
```

Because DB2 enables non-uniform distribution statistics (NUDS) to be collected for groups of multiple columns, the information in the NAME column is the first column in the grouping of columns in the "key." Also, FREQUENCY changed to FREQUENCYF (an integer column changed to a floating-point column).

> **CAUTION**
>
> Prior to DB2 V3, NUDS were stored in SYSFIELDS instead of SYSCOLDIST. If SYSIBM.SYSFIELDS was never purged after migrating to later versions of DB2, old NUDS still may be stored in SYSFIELDS, but not used. These artifacts can be misleading if misconstrued to be current.

These queries display the non-uniform distribution statistics stored in the DB2 Catalog for specific columns of each table. The output is arranged in order by database, tablespace, table creator, and table name. The output includes as many as 10 of the most frequently occurring values for table columns that are the first column of the index key.

The data shows the column value along with the percentage of times (multiplied by 100) it occurs for that column. This information is useful for tuning dynamic SQL queries. DB2 can choose a different access path for the same SQL statement when predicates contain literals for columns with distribution statistics. The optimizer uses this occurrence information to calculate filter factors. The higher the number of occurrences, the fewer rows the optimizer assumes it can filter out. Column values that appear in this report therefore could require SQL tuning.

After this level of performance analysis has been exhausted, you must broaden the scope of your tuning effort. Doing so involves analyzing SQL statements in application programs and possibly building new indexes or changing SQL in application queries.

Partition Statistics Queries

Partition-level statistics are accumulated by RUNSTATS to enable the optimizer to make query parallelism decisions. SYSIBM.SYSCOLDISTSTATS contains partition-level, non-uniform distribution statistics. RUNSTATS collects values for the key columns of each partitioned index. You can use the following query in conjunction with the column value occurrence query presented earlier:

```
SELECT   T.DBNAME, T.TSNAME, D.PARTITION, D.TBOWNER,
         D.TBNAME, D.NAME, D.FREQUENCYF, D.COLVALUE, D.STATSTIME
FROM     SYSIBM.SYSCOLDISTSTATS   D,
         SYSIBM.SYSTABLES         T
WHERE    D.TBOWNER = T.CREATOR
AND      D.TBNAME = T.NAME
AND      D.TYPE = 'F'
ORDER BY T.DBNAME, T.TSNAME, D.PARTITION,
         D.TBOWNER, D.TBNAME, D.NAME;
```

The information in the NAME column is the first column in the grouping of columns in the "key."

Be sure to label the results of the queries in this section as partition-level statistics so that they are not confused with the equivalent non-partitioned reports discussed in previous sections.

The results of the queries in the previous section depicted all tablespaces and indexes, whether partitioned or not. Additional statistics are maintained at the partition level for partitioned tablespaces and indexes. Partition-level physical statistics queries can be issued to retrieve these statistics.

The following query provides a report of partitioned tablespaces only, by database, listing the partition-level statistics for each tablespace partition:

```
SELECT   DBNAME, TSNAME, OWNER, NAME, PARTITION, NACTIVE,
         CARDF, PCTPAGES, PCTROWCOMP, STATSTIME
FROM     SYSIBM.SYSTABSTATS
ORDER BY DBNAME, TSNAME, NAME, PARTITION;
```

You can issue a partition-level physical index statistics query to retrieve partition statistics for partitioning indexes and DPSIs. The following query provides a report of partitioned indexes only, listing the partition-level statistics for each partition:

```
SELECT   OWNER, NAME, PARTITION, CLUSTERRATIOF, FIRSTKEYCARDF,
         FULLKEYCARDF, NLEAF, NLEVELS, KEYCOUNTF, STATSTIME
FROM     SYSIBM.SYSINDEXSTATS
ORDER BY OWNER, NAME, PARTITION;
```

You can analyze the results of the tablespace and index partition-level statistics reports to help you determine whether query parallelism could enhance performance of queries accessing these partitioned tablespaces.

Programmer's Aid Queries

Often, you must determine which plans and packages are in a DB2 subsystem. The following programmer's aid queries help you keep this information accurate. Plans can contain DBRMs, packages, or both. The following query lists the plans that contain DBRMs and the DBRMs they contain:

```
SELECT    P.NAME, P.CREATOR, P.BOUNDBY, P.BOUNDTS, P.ISOLATION,
          P.VALID, P.OPERATIVE, P.ACQUIRE, P.RELEASE, P.EXPLAN,
          P.GROUP_MEMBER, P.DYNAMICRULES, P.REOPTVAR, P.KEEPDYNAMIC,
          P.OPTHINT, D.NAME, D.PDSNAME, D.HOSTLANG, D.PRECOMPTS
FROM      SYSIBM.SYSPLAN P,
          SYSIBM.SYSDBRM D
WHERE     P.NAME = D.PLNAME
ORDER BY  P.NAME, D.NAME, D.PRECOMPTS;
```

The next programmer's aid query lists all plans that contain packages and the packages
they contain. Remember that packages are composed of a single DBRM.

```
SELECT    P.NAME, P.CREATOR, P.BOUNDBY, P.BOUNDTS, P.ISOLATION,
          P.VALID, P.OPERATIVE, P.ACQUIRE, P.RELEASE, P.EXPLAN,
          P.GROUP_MEMBER, P.DYNAMICRULES, P.REOPTVAR, P.KEEPDYNAMIC,
          P.OPTHINT, K.LOCATION, K.COLLID, K.NAME, K.TIMESTAMP
FROM      SYSIBM.SYSPLAN      P,
          SYSIBM.SYSPACKLIST  K
WHERE     P.NAME = K.PLANNAME
ORDER BY  P.NAME, K.LOCATION, K.COLLID, K.NAME, K.TIMESTAMP;
```

You can use the following query to track the DBRM libraries and packages. It details DBRM
information for all packages. Although the DBRM name and the package name are equivalent, and a one-to-one correlation exists between packages and DBRMs, monitoring the
DBRM information for each package is useful.

```
SELECT    COLLID, NAME, CREATOR, QUALIFIER, TIMESTAMP,
          BINDTIME, ISOLATION, VALID, OPERATIVE, RELEASE,
          EXPLAIN, PCTIMESTAMP, PDSNAME, VERSION,
          GROUP_MEMBER, DEFERPREPARE, DYNAMICRULES, REOPTVAR, KEEPDYNAMIC
FROM      SYSIBM.SYSPACKAGE
ORDER BY  COLLID, NAME, VERSION;
```

You can use the output from these three queries to track the composition and disposition
of all DB2 plans and packages. For example, you can determine whether a plan or package
is valid and operative. Invalid and inoperative plans require rebinding (and possible
program changes) before execution. You can check on the parameters used to bind the
plan or package, such as the isolation level specified (for example, CS versus RR versus UR)
or whether reoptimization is available for dynamic SQL (REOPTVARS). The OPTHINT column
identifies those plans using an optimization hint as input to the bind process. These
queries should be used to monitor your bind parameters to ensure that they are specified
as outlined in Chapter 13, "Program Preparation." Finally, you can trace -818 SQLCODEs by
checking PRECOMPTS against the date and time stored for the appropriate program load
module.

Another query that may be useful is to determine which plan and packages have SQL
statements that use explicit, statement-level dirty reads (isolation UR). You can use the
following queries to find these plans and packages. Use this query to find plans containing
SQL using the WITH 'UR' clause:

```
SELECT    DISTINCT S.PLNAME
FROM      SYSIBM.SYSPLAN    P,
          SYSIBM.SYSSTMT    S
WHERE     P.NAME = S.PLNAME
AND       S.ISOLATION = 'U'
ORDER BY S.PLNAME;
```

Use this query to find packages containing SQL using the WITH 'UR' clause:

```
SELECT    DISTINCT P.COLLID, P.NAME, P.VERSION
FROM      SYSIBM.SYSPACKAGE  P,
          SYSIBM.SYSPACKSTMT S
WHERE     P.LOCATION = S.LOCATION
AND       P.COLLID = S.COLLID
AND       P.NAME = S.NAME
AND       P.VERSION = S.VERSION
AND       S.ISOLATION = 'U'
ORDER BY P.COLLID, P.NAME, P.VERSION;
```

Three other queries are useful as programmer's aids. The plan dependency query follows:

```
SELECT    D.DNAME, P.CREATOR, P.QUALIFIER, P.VALID, P.ISOLATION,
          P.ACQUIRE, P.RELEASE, P.EXPLAN, P.PLSIZE, D.BCREATOR,
          D.BNAME, D.BTYPE
FROM      SYSIBM.SYSPLANDEP  D,
          SYSIBM.SYSPLAN     P
WHERE     P.NAME = D.DNAME
ORDER BY D.DNAME, D.BTYPE, D.BCREATOR, D.BNAME;
```

Likewise, the package dependency query can be quite useful:

```
SELECT    P.COLLID, D.DNAME, P.CONTOKEN, P.CREATOR,
          P.QUALIFIER, P.VALID, P.ISOLATION, P.RELEASE,
          P.EXPLAIN, P.PKSIZE, D.BQUALIFIER, D.BNAME, D.BTYPE
FROM      SYSIBM.SYSPACKDEP  D,
          SYSIBM.SYSPACKAGE  P
WHERE     P.NAME = D.DNAME
AND       P.COLLID = D.DCOLLID
AND       P.CONTOKEN = D.DCONTOKEN
ORDER BY P.COLLID, D.DNAME, P.CONTOKEN, D.BTYPE, D.BQUALIFIER,
          D.BNAME;
```

These queries detail the DB2 objects used by every DB2 plan and package. When database changes are needed, you can analyze the output from these queries to determine which packages and plans might be affected by structural changes.

Finally, programmers may need to know what stored procedures and user-defined functions are available and how they are defined. This query can be used to gather information about DB2 stored procedures:

```
SELECT    SCHEMA, NAME, LANGUAGE, PROGRAM_TYPE, SPECIFICNAME,
          COLLID, PARAMETER_STYLE, ASUTIME, SQL_DATA_ACCESS,
          DBINFO, COMMIT_ON_RETURN, STAYRESIDENT, RUNOPTS,
          PARM_COUNT, EXTERNAL_ACTION, RESULT_SETS, WLM_ENVIRONMENT,
          WLM_ENV_FOR_NESTED, EXTERNAL_SECURITY
```

26

```
FROM      SYSIBM.SYSROUTINES
WHERE     ROUTINETYPE = 'P'
ORDER BY SCHEMA, NAME;
```

For user-defined function information, execute the following query:

```
SELECT    SCHEMA, NAME, LANGUAGE, SPECIFICNAME, FUNCTION_TYPE, ORIGIN,
          SOURCESCHEMA, SOURCESPECIFIC, DETERMINISTIC, NULL_CALL,
          CAST_FUNCTION, SCRATCHPAD, SCRATCHPAD_LENGTH, FINAL_CALL,
          PARALLEL, PROGRAM_TYPE, COLLID, PARAMETER_STYLE, SQL_DATA_ACCESS,
          DBINFO, STAYRESIDENT, RUNOPTS, PARM_COUNT, EXTERNAL_ACTION,
          WLM_ENVIRONMENT, WLM_ENV_FOR_NESTED, EXTERNAL_SECURITY,
          ASUTIME, IOS_PER_INVOC, INSTS_PER_INVOC, INITIAL_IOS, INITIAL_INSTS,
          CARDINALITY, RESULT_COLS
FROM      SYSIBM.SYSROUTINES
WHERE     ROUTINETYPE = 'F'
ORDER BY SCHEMA, NAME;
```

The next section takes this form of DB2 performance monitoring to the next level, incorporating DB2 Catalog monitoring with EXPLAIN.

Application Efficiency Queries

The application efficiency queries combine the best of EXPLAIN monitoring with the best of DB2 Catalog monitoring. The reports produced by these queries show many potential performance problems. By combining the DB2 Catalog information with the output from EXPLAIN, you can identify a series of "problem queries."

These problem queries are grouped into two categories: tablespace scans and index scans. DB2 scans data sets to satisfy queries using tablespace scans and index scans. A tablespace scan reads every page in the tablespace and does not use an index. An index scan might or might not read every index subpage.

The tablespace scan query follows:

```
SELECT    E.APPLNAME, E.PROGNAME, E.QUERYNO, E.TNAME,
          T.NPAGES, E.TIMESTAMP, S.SEQNO, S.TEXT
FROM      ownerid.PLAN_TABLE  E,
          SYSIBM.SYSTABLES    T,
          SYSIBM.SYSSTMT      S
WHERE     ACCESSTYPE = 'R'
AND       (T.NPAGESF > 50 OR T.NPAGESF < 0)
AND       T.NAME = E.TNAME
AND       T.CREATOR = E.CREATOR
AND       S.NAME = E.PROGNAME
AND       S.PLNAME = E.APPLNAME
AND       S.STMTNO = E.QUERYNO
ORDER BY E.APPLNAME, E.PROGNAME, E.TIMESTAMP DESC,
          E.QUERYNO, S.SEQNO;
```

The following is the index scan query:

```
SELECT    E.APPLNAME, E.PROGNAME, E.QUERYNO, I.NAME, I.NLEAF,
          I.COLCOUNT, E.MATCHCOLS, E.INDEXONLY, E.TIMESTAMP,
          S.SEQNO, S.TEXT
```

```
FROM       ownerid.PLAN_TABLE  E,
           SYSIBM.SYSINDEXES   I,
           SYSIBM.SYSSTMT      S
WHERE      E.ACCESSTYPE = 'I'
AND        I.NLEAF > 100
AND        E.MATCHCOLS < I.COLCOUNT
AND        I.NAME = E.ACCESSNAME
AND        I.CREATOR = E.ACCESSCREATOR
AND        S.NAME = E.PROGNAME
AND        S.PLNAME = E.APPLNAME
AND        S.STMTNO = E.QUERYNO
ORDER BY E.APPLNAME, E.PROGNAME, E.TIMESTAMP DESC,
         E.QUERYNO, S.SEQNO;
```

Because these queries usually take a long time to run, they should not be executed in parallel with heavy production DB2 processing or during the online DB2 transaction window. To ensure that the scan queries operate efficiently, make sure that the PLAN_TABLE used in each query does not contain extraneous data. Strive to maintain only the most recent EXPLAIN data from production BIND jobs in the table. Also, keep EXPLAIN information only for plans that must be monitored. Executing RUNSTATS on your PLAN_TABLES also can increase the performance of these queries.

The tablespace scan report lists queries that scan more than 50 pages and queries that access tables without current RUNSTATS information. If NPAGES is -1 for any table, RUNSTATS has not been run. A RUNSTATS job should be executed as soon as possible, followed by a rebind of any plan that uses this table. Everything else on this report should be monitored closely. For tables just over the 50-page threshold, the effect on performance is uncertain. As the number of scanned pages increases, so does the potential for performance problems.

The 50-page cutoff is arbitrary; you might want to redefine it as you gauge the usefulness of the information returned. If you monitor only large tables, you might want to increase this number to 100 (or larger). This number varies according to your shop's definition of a "large table." If you have a small buffer pool (fewer than 1,000 buffers), you might want to reduce this number.

For tables with 20 or more pages, try to create indexes to satisfy the predicates of each query. Keep in mind, though, that creating an index for every predicate is not always possible. There is a trade-off between read efficiency and update efficiency as the number of indexes on a particular table increases.

The index scan query reports on all SQL statements that scan more than 100 index leaf pages on which a match on the columns in the query is not a complete match on all index columns. As the number of matching columns increases, performance problems decrease. The worst case is zero matching columns, but even this number might be acceptable for an index-only scan.

You might need to modify the 100-page cutoff value for the index scan query too. You might want to use the same number as the one chosen for the tablespace scan report (or some other value that works well in your environment).

26

Although every query listed in these reports is not necessarily a problem query, you should closely monitor each one. Corrective actions for poorly performing queries are outlined in Part V, "DB2 Performance Tuning."

Historical Queries

V7 DB2 V7 introduced nine new tables containing historical statistics to the DB2 Catalog. Historical statistics are accumulated by RUNSTATS when the HISTORY parameter is specified. The DB2 Catalog tables that contain historical statistics are as follows:

SYSIBM.SYSCOLDIST_HIST   SYSIBM.SYSCOLUMNS_HIST

SYSIBM.SYSINDEXES_HIST   SYSIBM.SYSINDEXPART_HIST

SYSIBM.SYSINDEXSTATS_HIST   SYSIBM.SYSLOBSTATS_HIST

SYSIBM.SYSTABLEPART_HIST   SYSIBM.SYSTABSTATS_HIST

SYSIBM.SYSTABLES_HIST

You can use these history tables to identify trends, patterns, and issues by comparing old statistics to current statistics. For example, run the following query to identify tablespace partitions that have grown in extents between RUNSTATS executions:

```
SELECT   P.DBNAME, P.TSNAME, P.PARTITION, P.PQTY, P.SECQTYI,
         P.NEARINDREF, P.FARINDREF, P.PERCACTIVE, P.PERCDROP,
         P.PAGESAVE, P.SPACEF, P.EXTENTS, P.STATSTIME
FROM     SYSIBM.SYSTABLEPART      P,
         SYSIBM.SYSTABLEPART_HIST H
WHERE    P.EXTENTS > H.EXTENTS
AND      P.DBNAME = H.DBNAME
AND      P.TSNAME = H.TSNAME
AND      P.PARTITION = H.PARTITION
AND      H.STATSTIME = (SELECT MAX(STATSTIME)
                        FROM SYSIBM.SYSTABLEPART_HIST H2
                        WHERE H2.DBNAME = P.DBNAME
                        AND   H2.TSNAME = P.TSNAME
                        AND   H2.PARTITION = P.PARTITION
                        )
ORDER BY P.DBNAME, P.TSNAME, P.PARTITION;
```

This query joins the history table to the current table for tablespace partition statistics. The subselect is to make sure that we retrieve only the last historical statistic. That is the maximum STATSTIME from SYSIBM.SYSTABLEPART_HIST, because there can be multiple historical rows in the history tables.

You can create similar queries for any of the historical tables, checking on changes to any of the statistics (not just EXTENTS).

Another interesting historical query you can use is a simple listing of the statistics over time. In this case we will look at index statistics using SYSIBM.SYSINDEXES_HIST:

```
SELECT   TBCREATOR, TBNAME, CREATOR, NAME, STATSTIME,
         CLUSTERING, CLUSTERRATIOF, NLEAF, NLEVELS,
         FIRSTKEYCARDF, FULLKEYCARDF, SPACEF, AVGKEYLEN
FROM     SYSIBM.SYSINDEXES_HIST
ORDER BY TBCREATOR, TBNAME, CREATOR, NAME, STATSTIME DESC;
```

This query will produce a report of historical statistics for each index in order by the table and index names, and in chronological order from oldest to most recent statistic row. You can examine this report to analyze the number of levels for the index over time, whether or not clustering has changed, and cardinality information over time. Similar reports can be generated for each of the historical statistics tables in the DB2 Catalog.

Authorization Queries

You can implement five types of security in DB2: database security, plan and package security, system-level authorization, security on tables and views, and resource privileges:

Database security	Controls database-level privileges. Anyone holding a database privilege can perform actions on all dependent database objects.
Plan and package	Dictates whether users can copy security packages and bind or execute plans and packages.
System-level	Indicates systemwide authority, *authorization* such as global authority to create new objects, authority to trace, and the capability to hold specific systemwide authorities, such as SYSADM, SYSCTRL, and SYSOPR.
Security on tables	Indicates whether the data in the tables and views can be accessed or updated. This authorization is granted at the table, view, or column level.
Resource privileges	Indicates whether users can use DB2 resources such as buffer pools, table-spaces, and storage groups.
Routine privileges	Indicates whether users can execute stored routines, such as stored procedures and user-defined functions.

You can execute the following queries to ascertain the authority granted for each of these types of security. Note that two forms of each query are provided; the authorization information can be returned either in DB2 object (or DB2 resource) order or by the user who possesses the authority.

Database authority query:

```
SELECT   NAME, GRANTEE, GRANTOR, GRANTEDTS, GRANTEETYPE,
         CREATETABAUTH, CREATETSAUTH, DBADMAUTH,
         DBCTRLAUTH, DBMAINTAUTH, DISPLAYDBAUTH,
         DROPAUTH, IMAGCOPYAUTH, LOADAUTH, REORGAUTH,
         RECOVERDBAUTH, REPAIRAUTH, STARTDBAUTH,
         STATSAUTH, STOPAUTH, AUTHHOWGOT
FROM     SYSIBM.SYSDBAUTH
ORDER BY NAME, GRANTEE, GRANTOR;
```

26

Table authority query:

```
SELECT   TCREATOR, TTNAME, SCREATOR, STNAME, GRANTEE, GRANTOR,
         GRANTEETYPE, UPDATECOLS, ALTERAUTH, DELETEAUTH, GRANTEDTS,
         INDEXAUTH, INSERTAUTH, SELECTAUTH, UPDATEAUTH,
         REFCOLS, REFERENCESAUTH, AUTHHOWGOT
FROM     SYSIBM.SYSTABAUTH
ORDER BY TCREATOR, TTNAME, GRANTEE, GRANTOR;
```

Column authority query:

```
SELECT   CREATOR, TNAME, COLNAME, PRIVILEGE, GRANTEE, GRANTOR,
         GRANTEETYPE, TIMESTAMP, GRANTEDTS
FROM     SYSIBM.SYSCOLAUTH
ORDER BY CREATOR, TNAME, COLNAME, GRANTEE;
```

Resource authority query:

```
SELECT   QUALIFIER, NAME, OBTYPE, GRANTEE, GRANTOR,
         GRANTEDTS, USEAUTH, AUTHHOWGOT
FROM     SYSIBM.SYSRESAUTH
ORDER BY GRANTEE, QUALIFIER, NAME, GRANTOR;
```

Routine authority query:

```
SELECT   SCHEMA, SPECIFICNAME, ROUTINETYPE,
         GRANTEE, GRANTEETYPE, EXECUTEAUTH,
         GRANTEDTS, AUTHHOWGOT
FROM     SYSIBM.SYSROUTINEAUTH
ORDER BY GRANTEE, SCHEMA, SPECIFICNAME, GRANTOR;
```

User authority query:

```
SELECT   GRANTEE, GRANTOR, GRANTEDTS, ALTERBPAUTH,
         BINDADDAUTH, BSDSAUTH, CREATETMTABAUTH,
         CREATEDBAAUTH, CREATEDBCAUTH, CREATESGAUTH,
         CREATEALIASAUTH, DISPLAYAUTH, RECOVERAUTH,
         STOPALLAUTH, STOSPACEAUTH, SYSADMAUTH, SYSCTRLAUTH,
         SYSOPRAUTH, BINDAGENTAUTH, ARCHIVEAUTH,
         TRACEAUTH, MON1AUTH, MON2AUTH, AUTHHOWGOT
FROM     SYSIBM.SYSUSERAUTH
ORDER BY GRANTEE, GRANTOR;
```

Plan authority query:

```
SELECT   NAME, GRANTEE, GRANTOR, GRANTEDTS,
         GRANTEETYPE,BINDAUTH, EXECUTEAUTH, AUTHHOWGOT
FROM     SYSIBM.SYSPLANAUTH
ORDER BY NAME, GRANTEE, GRANTOR;
```

Package authority query:

```
SELECT   COLLID, NAME, GRANTEE, GRANTOR, CONTOKEN,
         TIMESTAMP, GRANTEETYPE, AUTHHOWGOT,
         BINDAUTH, COPYAUTH, EXECUTEAUTH
FROM     SYSIBM.SYSPACKAUTH
ORDER BY COLLID, NAME, GRANTEE, GRANTOR;
```

V8 **Sequence authority query:**

```
SELECT   SCHEMA, NAME, GRANTEE, COLLID, CONTOKEN, GRANTOR,
         GRANTEDTS, GRANTEETYPE, AUTHHOWGOT,
         ALTERAUTH, USEAUTH, EXECUTEAUTH
FROM     SYSIBM.SYSSEQUENCEAUTH
ORDER BY SCHEMA, NAME, GRANTEE, GRANTOR;
```

Security is not often associated with performance monitoring, but it can help you determine the following items. If certain types of authority are granted to many users, and security checking becomes inefficient, you might want to grant the authority to PUBLIC. This way, you can reduce the number of entries in the DB2 Catalog, thereby reducing the strain on the DB2 subsystem. Don't grant PUBLIC access, however, if audit regulations or data sensitivity is an issue.

In addition, monitoring who can access data can help you determine the potential effect on workload. As the number of users who can access a piece of data increases, the potential for workload and capacity problems increases.

DB2 Catalog Query Guidelines

Heed the following advice when implementing DB2 Catalog queries to obtain information about your DB2 environment.

Use Queries As a Starting Point   The queries in this chapter are only suggestions. If you want to change the sort order or alter the columns being queried, you can use the queries in this chapter as templates. For example, to determine the table authority granted to users, you can modify the sort order of the table authority query, as shown in the following SQL statement:

```
SELECT   TCREATOR, TTNAME, SCREATOR, STNAME, GRANTEE, GRANTOR,
         GRANTEETYPE, UPDATECOLS, ALTERAUTH, DELETEAUTH, GRANTEDTS,
         INDEXAUTH, INSERTAUTH, SELECTAUTH, UPDATEAUTH,
         REFCOLS, REFERENCESAUTH, AUTHHOWGOT
FROM     SYSIBM.SYSTABAUTH
ORDER BY GRANTEE, TCREATOR, TTNAME, GRANTOR;
```

The reports in this chapter are suggestions that have worked well for me. Changing them to suit your needs is easy because of the ad hoc nature of SQL.

Use QMF to Create Formatted Reports   The queries in this chapter were developed using QMF. You can run them weekly using a batch QMF job. Using the batch job is easier than submitting the queries weekly from QMF or through SPUFI. Simply build batch QMF JCL, incorporate all these queries and forms into a proc, and then run the proc.

You can create QMF forms for each query to present the output in a pleasing format. You can change control breaks, different headings for columns, and the spacing between columns. A sample QMF form for the table listing query is presented in Listing 26.1. To create a form for any of the queries in this chapter in QMF, simply type and execute the query. Press F9 to display the form panel and then modify the form.

26

LISTING 26.1   Sample QMF Form for the Table Listing Query

```
FORM.COLUMNS
Total Width of Report Columns: 216
NUM  COLUMN HEADING USAGE    INDENT  WIDTH   EDIT    SEQ
1    _DATABASE      BREAK1   1       8       C       1
2    TABLE_SPACE    BREAK2   1       8       C       2
3    TABLE_CREATOR  BREAK3   1       8       C       3
4    _TABLE         BREAK3   1       18      C       4
5    CREATEDTS               1       26      TSI     5
6    ALTEREDTS               1       26      TSI     6
7    COL_NO                  1       3       L       7
8    COLUMN_NAME             1       18      C       8
9    COLUMN_TYPE             1       8       C       9
10   COLUMN_LENGTH           1       6       L       10
11   SCALE                   1       6       L       11
12   NU_LL                   1       2       C       12
13   DF_LT                   1       2       C       13
14   COL_CARD                1       8       L       14
15   HIGH2_KEY               1       8       C       15
16   LOW2_KEY                1       8       C       16
17   STATSTIME               1       26      TSI     17
18   FLD_PROC                1       4       C       18
```

The table listing query is presented again to help you visualize how the QMF form helps to display the query results:

```
SELECT   T.DBNAME, T.TSNAME, T.CREATOR, T.NAME, T.CREATEDTS, T.ALTEREDTS,
         C.COLNO, C.NAME, C.COLTYPE, C.LENGTH, C.SCALE, C.NULLS,
         C.DEFAULT, C.COLCARDF, HEX(C.HIGH2KEY) AS HIGH2KEY,
         HEX(C.LOW2KEY) AS LOW2KEY, C.STATSTIME, C.FLDPROC
FROM     SYSIBM.SYSCOLUMNS   C,
         SYSIBM.SYSTABLES    T
WHERE    T.CREATOR = C.TBCREATOR
AND      T.NAME = C.TBNAME
AND      T.TYPE = 'T'
ORDER BY T.DBNAME, T.TSNAME, T.CREATOR, T.NAME, C.COLNO;
```

Become Familiar with the Data in the DB2 Catalog   You can produce many reports from the DB2 Catalog to aid in performance monitoring. This chapter details some of them. As you become more familiar with the DB2 Catalog and the needs of your application, you can formulate additional queries geared to the needs of your organization.

A complete listing and description of the DB2 Catalog tables and columns can be found in the IBM SQL Reference manual (SC26-9944 for Version 7; SC18-7426 for Version 8).

Use the DECIMAL Function for Readability   When retrieving floating point data, such as the columns that end with the letter F, use the DECIMAL function to display the results as a decimal number. For example,

```
SELECT ... DECIMAL(NACTIVEF) ...
```

This will produce more readable query results. Without the DECIMAL function, the results will be displayed as an exponential expression, such as $2.013 * 10^{12}$.

Real Time Statistics

V7 Real Time Statistics (RTS) is the first step in IBM's grand plans to automate parts of DB2 database administration. Introduced after the general availability of Version 7, but before Version 8, RTS provides functionality that maintains statistics about DB2 databases "on the fly," without having to run a utility program.

Prior to the introduction of RTS, the only way to gather statistics about DB2 database structures was by running the RUNSTATS utility. As discussed in Chapter 34, "Catalog Manipulation Utilities," RUNSTATS collects statistical information about DB2 database objects and stores this data in the DB2 Catalog. RTS, on the other hand, runs in the background and automatically updates statistics in two special tables as the data in DB2 databases is modified. Where RUNSTATS is a hands-on administrative process, RTS is hands-off.

> **NOTE**
>
> Real Time Statistics was announced with APARs PQ48447, PQ48448, PQ46859, and PQ56256.

The RTS Tables

Although DB2 is always collecting RTS data, nothing is externalized until you set up the RTS database and tables to store the real time statistics. The RTS database is named DSNRTSDB and there is one table space (DSNRTSTS) with two tables:

SYSIBM.TABLESPACESTATS—Contains statistics on tablespaces and tablespace partitions

SYSIBM.INDEXSPACESTATS—Contains statistics on index spaces and index space partitions

Tables 26.2 and 26.3 describe the columns of these two tables. Each table has a unique index defined on it. Both are defined on the DBID, PSID, and PARTITION columns. The indexes' names are

SYSIBM.TABLESPACESTATS_IX

SYSIBM.INDEXSPACESTATS_IX

TABLE 26.2 SYSIBM.TABLESPACESTATS Columns

Column	Description
DBNAME	Database name.
NAME	Tablespace name.
PARTITION	The data set number within the tablespace. For partitioned tablespaces, contains the partition number for a single partition. For non-partitioned tablespaces, contains 0.
DBID	Internal database identifier.
PSID	Internal page set identifier (for the tablespace).
UPDATESTATSTIME	The timestamp when this statistics row was inserted or last updated.
TOTALROWS	The total number of rows or LOBs in the tablespace or partition. Indicates the number of rows in all tables for multi-table tablespaces.

TABLE 26.2   Continued

Column	Description
NACTIVE	The number of active pages in the tablespace or partition. Indicates the total number of preformatted pages in all data sets for multi-piece tablespaces.
SPACE	The amount of space (in kilobytes) that is allocated to the tablespace or partition. Indicates the amount of space in all data sets for multi-piece linear page sets.
EXTENTS	The number of extents used by the tablespace or partition. Indicates the number of extents for the last data set for multi-piece tablespaces. For a data set that is striped across multiple volumes, the value is the number of logical extents.
LOADRLASTTIME	The timestamp when the last LOAD REPLACE was run for the tablespace or partition.
REORGLASTTIME	The timestamp when the last REORG was run on the tablespace or partition.
REORGINSERTS	The number of records or LOBs that have been inserted since the last REORG or LOAD REPLACE was run on the tablespace or partition.
REORGDELETES	The number of records or LOBs that have been deleted since the last REORG or LOAD REPLACE on the tablespace or partition.
REORGUPDATES	The number of rows that have been updated since the last REORG or LOAD REPLACE was run on the tablespace or partition. Does not include LOB updates because they are implemented as deletions followed by insertions.
REORGDISORGLOB	The number of LOBs that were inserted since the last REORG or LOAD REPLACE that are not perfectly chunked. A LOB is perfectly chunked if the allocated pages are in the minimum number of chunks.
REORGUNCLUSTINS	The number of records that were inserted since the last REORG or LOAD REPLACE that are not *well-clustered* with respect to the clustering index. A record is well-clustered if the record is inserted into a page that is within 16 pages of the ideal candidate page.
REORGMASSDELETE	The number of mass deletes from a segmented or LOB tablespace, or the number of dropped tables from a segmented tablespace, since the last REORG or LOAD REPLACE was run.
REORGNEARINDREF	The number of overflow records created and relocated near the pointer record since the last REORG or LOAD REPLACE was run. For non-segmented tablespaces, a page is near the present page if the two page numbers differ by 16 or less. For segmented tablespaces, a page is near the present page if the two page numbers differ by SEGSIZE*2 or less.
REORGFARINDREF	The number of overflow records created and relocated far from the pointer record since the last REORG or LOAD REPLACE was run. For non-segmented tablespaces, a page is far the present page if the two page numbers differ by more than 16. For segmented tablespaces, a page is far from the present page if the two page numbers differ by more than SEGSIZE*2.
STATSLASTTIME	The timestamp when RUNSTATS was last run on this tablespace or partition.
STATSINSERTS	The number of records or LOBs that have been inserted since the last RUNSTATS was executed on this tablespace or partition.

TABLE 26.2   Continued

Column	Description
STATSDELETES	The number of records or LOBs that have been deleted since the last RUNSTATS was executed on this tablespace or partition.
STATSUPDATES	The number of records or LOBs that have been updated since the last RUNSTATS was executed on this tablespace or partition.
STATSMASSDELETE	The number of mass deletes from a segmented or LOB tablespace, or the number of dropped tables from a segmented tablespace, since the last RUNSTATS was run.
COPYLASTTIME	The timestamp of the last full or incremental image copy on the tablespace or partition.
COPYUPDATEDPAGES	The number of distinct pages that have been updated since the last COPY was run.
COPYCHANGES	The number of INSERT, UPDATE, and DELETE operations since the last COPY was run.
COPYUPDATELRSN	The LRSN or RBA of the first update after the last COPY was run.
COPYUPDATETIME	Specifies the timestamp of the first UPDATE made after the last COPY was run.

TABLE 26.3   SYSIBM.INDEXSPACESTATS Columns

Column	Description
DBNAME	Database name.
NAME	Index space name.
PARTITION	The data set number within the index space. For partitioned index spaces, contains the partition number for a single partition. For non-partitioned index spaces, contains 0.
DBID	Internal database identifier.
ISOBID	Internal identifier of the index space page set descriptor.
PSID	Internal page set identifier (for the tablespace holding the table on which this index was created).
UPDATESTATSTIME	The timestamp when this statistics row was inserted or last updated.
TOTALENTRIES	The number of entries, including duplicates, in the index space or partition.
NLEVELS	The number of levels in the index tree.
NACTIVE	The number of active pages in the index space or partition.
SPACE	The amount of space (in kilobytes) that is allocated to the index space or partition. Indicates the amount of space in all data sets for multi-piece linear page sets.
EXTENTS	The number of extents used by the index space or partition. Indicates the number of extents for the last data set for multi-piece tablespaces. For a data set that is striped across multiple volumes, the value is the number of logical extents.
LOADRLASTTIME	Timestamp of the last LOAD REPLACE on the index space or partition.
REBUILDLASTTIME	Timestamp of the last REBUILD INDEX on the index space or partition.
REORGLASTTIME	Timestamp of the last REORG INDEX on the index space or partition.

26

TABLE 26.3   Continued

Column	Description
REORGINSERTS	The number of index entries that have been inserted since the last REORG, REBUILD INDEX, or LOAD REPLACE on the index space or partition.
REORGDELETES	The number of index entries that have been deleted since the last REORG, REBUILD INDEX, or LOAD REPLACE on the index space or partition.
REORGAPPENDINSERT	The number of index entries that have been inserted since the last REORG, REBUILD INDEX, or LOAD REPLACE on the index space or partition that have a key value greater than the maximum key value in the index or partition.
REORGPSEUDODELETES	The number of index entries that have been pseudo-deleted since the last REORG, REBUILD INDEX, or LOAD REPLACE on the index space or partition.
REORGMASSDELETE	The number of times that an index or index space partition was mass deleted since the last REORG, REBUILD INDEX, or LOAD REPLACE.
REORGLEAFNEAR	The number of index page splits that occurred since the last REORG, REBUILD INDEX, or LOAD REPLACE in which the higher part of the split page was near the location of the original page. The higher part is near the original page if the two page numbers differ by 16 or less.
REORGLEAFFAR	The number of index page splits that occurred since the last REORG, REBUILD INDEX, or LOAD REPLACE in which the higher part of the split page was far from the location of the original page. The higher part is far from the original page if the two page numbers differ by more than 16.
REORGNUMLEVELS	The number of levels in the index tree that were added or removed since the last REORG, REBUILD INDEX, or LOAD REPLACE.
STATSLASTTIME	Timestamp of the last RUNSTATS on the index space or partition.
STATSINSERTS	The number of index entries that have been inserted since the last RUNSTATS on the index space or partition.
STATSDELETES	The number of index entries that have been deleted since the last RUNSTATS on the index space or partition.
STATSMASSDELETE	The number of times that the index or index space partition was mass deleted since the last RUNSTATS.
COPYLASTTIME	Timestamp of the last full image copy on the index space or partition.
COPYUPDATEDPAGES	The number of distinct pages that have been updated since the last COPY.
COPYCHANGES	The number of INSERT and DELETE operations since the last COPY.
COPYUPDATELRSN	The LRSN or RBA of the first update after the last COPY.
COPYUPDATETIME	Timestamp of the first update after the last COPY.

When Are Real Time Stats Externalized?

As soon as RTS is applied (by running the proper version or maintenance level of DB2), DB2 begins to gather real-time statistics. However, the RTS tables must exist in order for DB2 to externalize the real-time statistics that it gathers.

After the RTS tables have been created and started, DB2 externalizes real-time statistics to the tables at the following times:

- When the RTS database is stopped, DB2 first externalizes all RTS values from memory into the RTS tables before stopping the database.

- When an individual RTS tablespace is stopped, DB2 first externalizes all RTS values for that particular tablespace from memory into the RTS tables before stopping the database. Keep in mind, though, that the default installation uses only a single tablespace to store both RTS tables.

- When you issue -STOP DB2 MODE(QUIESCE), DB2 first externalizes all RTS values. Of course, if you stop using MODE(FORCE), no RTS values are externalized; instead, they are lost when DB2 comes down.

- As specified by the DSNZPARM STATSINT value. The default is every 30 minutes.

- During REORG, REBUILD INDEX, COPY, and LOAD REPLACE utility operations, DB2 externalizes the appropriate RTS values affected by running that utility.

RTS Accuracy   In certain situations, the RTS values might not be 100% accurate. Situations that can cause the real-time statistics to be off include

- Sometimes a restarted utility can cause the RTS values to be wrong.

- Utility operations that leave indexes in a restrictive state, such as RECOVER pending (RECP), will cause stats to be inaccurate.

- A DB2 subsystem failure.

- A notify failure in a data sharing environment.

To fix RTS statistics that are inaccurate, run a REORG, RUNSTATS, or COPY on the objects for which those stats are suspect.

> **CAUTION**
>
> If you are using DB2 utilities from a third-party vendor other than IBM, be sure that those utilities work with RTS. The third-party utilities should be able both to reset the RTS values and use the RTS stats for recommending when to run utilities.

DSNACCOR: **The RTS Stored Procedure**

IBM supplies a sample stored procedure called DSNACCOR that can be used to query the RTS tables and make recommendations based on the statistics. You can use DSNACCOR to recommend when to run a REORG, take an image copy, or run RUNSTATS. Additionally, DSNACCOR can report on the data set extents of tablespaces and index spaces as well as on objects in a restricted state.

You can specify parameters to indicate to DSNACCOR which tablespaces and indexes to analyze, or just run it without parameters to evaluate all tablespaces and index spaces in the subsystem.

26

> **CAUTION**
>
> If the RTS values are inaccurate, the recommendations made by DSNACCOR will not be correct.
>
> Also, DSNACCOR makes recommendations based on general formulas requiring user input about your maintenance policies. These recommendations might not be accurate for every installation or subsystem.

You should consider using DSNACCOR in conjunction with DB2 Control Center. Control Center provides a nice GUI interface to the parameters of DSNACCOR, making it easier to use than directly calling the procedure would be.

Using the Real Time Statistics

The following RTS guidelines and queries can be used to help you identify maintenance and administration that needs to be carried out for database objects in your DB2 subsystems.

Checking for Activity   Because real-time statistics are updated in an ongoing manner as DB2 operates, you can use them to see if any activity has occurred during a specific timeframe. To determine whether any activity has happened in the past several days for a particular tablespace or index, use the UPDATESTATSTIME column. Here is an example checking whether any activity has occurred in the past ten days for a tablespace (just supply the tablespace name):

```
SELECT   DBNAME, NAME, PARTITION, UPDATESTATSTIME
FROM     SYSIBM.TABLESPACESTATS
WHERE    UPDATESTATSTIME > CURRENT TIMESTAMP - 10 DAYS
AND      NAME = ?;
```

Basic Tablespace Information   The RTS tables contain some good basic information about tablespaces. The following query can be run to report on the number of rows, active pages, space used, number of extents, and when the COPY, REORG, LOAD REPLACE, and RUNSTATS were last run:

```
SELECT   DBNAME, NAME, PARTITION, TOTALROWS, NACTIVE,
         SPACE, EXTENTS, UPDATESTATSTIME, STATSLASTTIME,
         LOADRLASTTIME, REORGLASTTIME, COPYLASTTIME
FROM     SYSIBM.TABLESPACESTATS
ORDER BY DBNAME, NAME, PARTITION;
```

You can add a WHERE clause to this query to limit the output to only a certain database or for specific tablespaces.

Pay particular attention to the timestamps indicating the last time that COPY, REORG, and RUNSTATS were run. If the date is sufficiently old, consider further investigating whether you should take an image copy, reorganize the tablespace, or run RUNSTATS.

Keep in mind though, that the span of time between utility runs is not the only indicator for when to copy, reorganize, or capture statistics. For example, RUNSTATS might need to be run only once on static data; similar caveats apply to COPY and REORG when data does not change.

Reorganizing Tablespaces   Statistics that can help determine when to reorganize a tablespace include space allocated, extents, number of INSERTs, UPDATEs, and DELETEs since the last REORG or LOAD REPLACE, number of unclustered INSERTs, number of disorganized LOBs, and number of near and far indirect references created since the last REORG. The following query can be used to monitor reorganization RTS statistics:

```
SELECT   DBNAME, NAME, PARTITION, SPACE, EXTENTS,
         REORGLASTTIME, REORGINSERTS, REORGDELETES, REORGUPDATES,
         REORGINSERTS+REORGDELETES+REORGUPDATES AS TOTAL_CHANGES,
         REORGDISORGLOB, REORGUNCLUSTINS, REORGMASSDELETE,
         REORGNEARINDREF, REORGFARINDREF
FROM     SYSIBM.TABLESPACESTATS
ORDER BY DBNAME, NAME, PARTITION;
```

You might want to add a WHERE clause that limits the tablespaces returned to just those that exceed a particular limit. For example,

Specify	Description
WHERE EXTENTS > 20	Tablespaces having more than 20 extents
WHERE TOT_CHANGES > 100000	Tablespaces with more than 100K changes
WHERE REORGFARINDREF > 50	Tablespaces with more than 50 far indirect references

Another way to get more creative with your RTS queries is to build formulas into them to retrieve only those tablespaces that need to be reorganized. For example, the following query will return only those tablespaces having more than 10% of their rows as near or far indirect references:

```
SELECT   DBNAME, NAME, PARTITION, SPACE, EXTENTS
FROM     SYSIBM.TABLESPACESTATS
WHERE    TOTALROWS > 0
AND      (((REORGNEARINDREF + REORGFARINDREF)*100)/TOTALROWS) > 10
ORDER BY DBNAME, NAME, PARTITION;
```

Of course, you can change the percentage as you wish. After running the query, you have a list of tablespaces meeting your criteria for reorganization.

Examining the Impact of a Program   You can use the TOTALROWS column of SYSIBM.TABLESPACESTATS to determine how many rows were impacted by a particular program or process. Simply check TOTALROWS for the tablespace both before and after the process; the difference between the values is the number of rows impacted.

When to Run RUNSTATS for a Tablespace   There are also statistics to help in determining when RUNSTATS should be executed. Run the following query to show the number of INSERTs, UPDATEs, and DELETEs since the last RUNSTATS execution:

```
SELECT   DBNAME, NAME, PARTITION, STATSLASTTIME,
         STATSINSERTS, STATSDELETES, STATSUPDATES,
         STATSINSERTS+STATSDELETES+STATSUPDATES AS TOTAL_CHANGES,
         STATSMASSDELETE
FROM     SYSIBM.TABLESPACESTATS
ORDER BY DBNAME, NAME, PARTITION;
```

26

When to Take an Image Copy for a Tablespace   You can issue the following query to report on statistics that will help you to determine whether a COPY is required:

```
SELECT   DBNAME, NAME, PARTITION, COPYLASTTIME, COPYUPDATEDPAGES,
         COPYCHANGES, COPYUPDATELRSN, COPYUPDATETIME
FROM     SYSIBM.TABLESPACESTATS
ORDER BY DBNAME, NAME, PARTITION;
```

Basically, as the number of distinct updated pages and changes since the last COPY execution increases, the need to take an image copy increases. A good rule of thumb to follow is when the percentage of updated pages since the last COPY is more than 25% of the active pages, then it is time to COPY the tablespace. You can add the following WHERE clause to the previous query to limit the output to only these tablespaces:

```
WHERE ((COPYUPDATEDPAGES*100) / NACTIVE) > 25
```

Basic Index Space Information   Do not forget that there are also RTS statistics gathered on indexes. The following query can be run to report on the number of rows, active pages, space used, number of extents, and when the COPY, REORG, LOAD REPLACE, and RUNSTATS were last run:

```
SELECT   DBNAME, INDEXSPACE, PARTITION, TOTALENTRIES, NLEVELS, NACTIVE,
         SPACE, EXTENTS, UPDATESTATSTIME, LOADRLASTTIME, REBUILDLASTTIME,
         REORGLASTTIME, STATSLASTTIME, COPYLASTTIME
FROM     SYSIBM.INDEXSPACESTATS
ORDER BY DBNAME, INDEXSPACE, PARTITION;
```

Reorganizing Index Spaces   Just like the tablespace stats, there are index space statistics that can be used to determine when to reorganize indexes. These statistics include the last time REBUILD, REORG, or LOAD REPLACE occurred, as well as statistics showing the number of INSERTs and DELETEs since the last REORG or REBUILD. RTS does not skimp in the details. You get both real and pseudo DELETEs, as well as both singleton and mass DELETE information. RTS also tracks both the number of index levels and index page split information resulting in near and far indirect references since the last REORG, REBUILD INDEX, or LOAD REPLACE. The following query can be used to return this information:

```
SELECT   DBNAME, INDEXSPACE, PARTITION,
         REORGLASTTIME, LOADRLASTTIME, REBUILDLASTTIME,
         TOTALENTRIES, NACTIVE, SPACE, EXTENTS,
         NLEVELS, REORGNUMLEVELS,
         REORGINSERTS, REORGAPPENDINSERT,
         REORGDELETES, REORGPSEUDODELETES, REORGMASSDELETE,
         REORGLEAFNEAR, REORGLEAFFAR
FROM     SYSIBM.INDEXSPACESTATS
ORDER BY DBNAME, INDEXSPACE, PARTITION;
```

These statistics can be examined after running jobs or processes that cause heavy data modification.

> **NOTE**
>
> Pay particular attention to the REORGAPPENDINSERT column. It contains the number of inserts into an index since the last REORG for which the index key was higher than any existing key value. If this column consistently grows, you have identified an object where data is inserted using an ascending key sequence. Think about lowering the free space for such objects, because the free space is wasted space if inserts are always done in ascending key sequence.

When to Run RUNSTATS for an Index Space   RTS provides index space statistics to help determine when to run RUNSTATS similar to the tablespace statistics. Run the following query to show the number of INSERTs, UPDATEs, and DELETEs since the last RUNSTATS execution:

```
SELECT   DBNAME, NAME, PARTITION, STATSLASTTIME,
         STATSINSERTS, STATSDELETES, STATSMASSDELETE
FROM     SYSIBM.TABLESPACESTATS
ORDER BY DBNAME, NAME, PARTITION;
```

Reviewing the Rules for an Effective Monitoring Strategy

DB2 has a reputation of being easy for users to understand; they specify *what* data to retrieve, not *how* to retrieve it. The layer of complexity removed for the users, however, had to be relegated elsewhere: to the code of DB2.

DB2 also has a reputation as a large resource consumer. This reputation is largely because of DB2's complexity. Because DB2 performance analysts must understand and monitor this complexity, they require an array of performance monitoring tools and techniques. Part IV outlines the majority of these tools. (Refer to Chapter 39, "Components of a Total DB2 Solution," for information on third-party performance monitoring tools and Appendix B for a listing of third-party tool vendors.)

To review, an effective monitoring strategy includes the following:

- Scheduled batch performance monitor jobs to report on the recent performance of DB2 applications and the DB2 subsystem

- An online monitor that executes when DB2 executes to enable quick monitoring of performance problems as they occur

- Online monitors for all teleprocessing environments in which DB2 transactions execute (for example, CICS, IMS/TM, or TSO)

- Regular monitoring of z/OS for memory use and VTAM for network use

- Scheduled reports from the DB2 Catalog and queries run against the RTS tables

- Access to the DB2 DSNMSTR address space to review console messages

- Use of the DB2 -DISPLAY command to view databases, threads, and utility execution

Part V delves into tuning the performance of DB2.

IN THIS CHAPTER

- Tuning the z/OS and OS/390 Environment
- Tuning the Teleprocessing Environment

CHAPTER 27

Tuning DB2's Environment

System tuning for DB2 performance can be applied outside DB2—to the environment in which DB2 operates—or inside DB2—to the components of DB2 or under DB2's control. This chapter concentrates on the tuning of DB2's environment.

Tuning the z/OS and OS/390 Environment

Operating system tuning is a complex task best accomplished by extensively trained technicians. All DB2 users, however, should understand the basics of z/OS resource exploitation and the avenues for tuning it. Operating system tuning, as it affects DB2 performance, can be broken down into four areas:

- Memory use
- CPU use
- I/O use
- Operating system environment parameters

Now turn your attention to each of these four areas. The sections that follow offer various tuning guidelines and strategies along the way.

Tuning Memory Use

How does DB2 utilize available memory? Before answering this question, you need a basic understanding of what memory is and how it is used by z/OS. *Memory* is the working storage available for programs and the data the programs use as they operate.

Storage is often used as a synonym for memory. MVS stands for Multiple Virtual Storage, which refers to MVS's capability to manage virtual memory. To manage virtual memory, the operating system uses a large pool of memory, known as *virtual storage*, to "back up" *real storage*. (Real storage is also called central storage. Virtual storage is also called expanded storage.)

Real storage is addressable. Programs and their data must be placed in real storage before they can run. Virtual memory management is the reason that multiple address spaces can execute concurrently, regardless of the physical memory they eventually use. This way, the system can process more jobs than can be held in real storage; information is swapped back and forth between virtual storage and real storage, a process known as *paging*.

You'll discover two types of paging. The first, moving data between virtual and real storage, is inexpensive in terms of resource consumption and occurs regularly. As more real storage is requested, a second type of paging can result. This type of paging consists of moving portions of memory to disk temporarily. This type is expensive and should be avoided.

> **TUNING STRATEGY**
>
> Consider using storage isolation to fence the DB2 address spaces. Doing so prevents DB2 from paging to disk. Storage isolation must be implemented by systems programmers.

Virtual storage can be broken down further in two ways:

- Common area versus private area

- Above the line versus below the line

The *common area* is the portion of virtual storage addressable from any address space. The *private area* stores data that is addressable by only an individual address space. A common area and private area exist both above and below the line. But what does that mean?

Above and below the line refers to an imaginary line in virtual storage at the 16-megabyte level. Memory above the line is often called *extended storage*. In earlier versions of MVS, 16 megabytes was the upper limit for virtual and real storage addressability. New releases of MVS add addressability above the 16-megabyte line. And z/OS provides addressability up to 16-exabytes. The constraints imposed by the addressing schemes of older systems, however, can cause dense packing of applications into memory below the line. Systems that use memory above the line provide more efficient memory management, as well as relief for systems requiring memory use below the line.

How does DB2 fit into this memory structure? The answer differs quite a bit depending on whether you are running DB2 V8 or a previous release. Let's discuss releases prior to V8 first (see Figure 27.1). DB2 manages memory efficiently, making use of extended storage when possible. A well-tuned DB2 subsystem requires less than 2 megabytes of virtual storage below the line. The things that affect below-the-line storage are the DSMAX and number of threads using functions (like AMS) that still run below the 16M line.

27

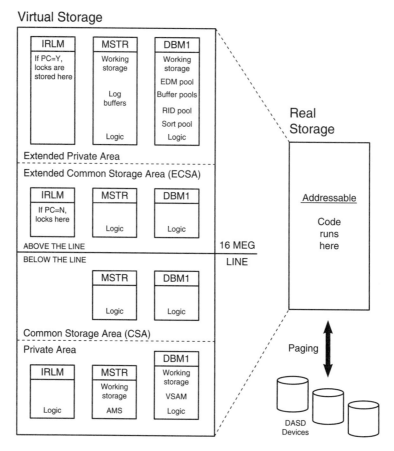

FIGURE 27.1   DB2 memory use (pre-V8).

z/Architecture, DB2 V8, and 64 Bits

V8   One of the biggest impacts of DB2 V8 is the requirement to be running a zSeries machine and z/OS v1.3 or greater. DB2 V8 does not support old hardware, nor does it support OS/390. Owing to these architectural requirements, DB2 will have the ability to support large virtual memory. This means DB2 can now surmount the limitation of 2GB real storage that was imposed due to S/390's 31-bit addressing.

Moving from a 31-bit architecture of past operating systems to a 64-bit architecture allows DB2 to access much more virtual storage. Using z/OS, DB2 can deploy a single large address space of up to 16 exabytes (2^{64} bytes). This architecture replaces both hiperspaces and data spaces. Virtual storage management is improved because it is all in one place and simpler—thereby improving the scalability, availability, and performance of your DB2 subsystems.

V8   Another by-product of this additional storage is that IBM has moved many of DB2's storage areas above the 2GB bar. Refer to Figure 27.2 for an updated look at memory usage by DB2 V8. As of V8, most of the DB2 code now runs above the 2-gigabyte bar. Most of the DSNDBM1 address space, the log manager, parts of DDF, buffer pools, data sharing castout buffers, IRLM locks, the RID pool, sort pools, compression dictionaries, and DBD and OBD objects in the EDM pool have all been moved above the bar.

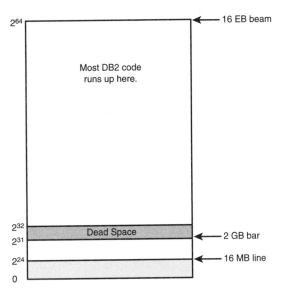

Note: diagram not drawn to scale

FIGURE 27.2   DB2 V8 memory use.

A Rundown of DB2's Memory Structures

Let's examine the primary consumers of memory in a DB2 subsystem and see how we might be able to tune them for better performance.

Buffer Pools   DB2 provides 80 virtual buffer pools and optional hiperpools (pre-V8) for maintaining recently accessed table and index pages in virtual storage. The Buffer Manager component of DB2 manages I/O and the use of buffers to reduce the cost of I/O. If the Buffer Manager can satisfy a GETPAGE request from memory in the buffer pool rather than from disk, performance can increase significantly.

DB2 provides buffer pools as follows:

- 50 buffer pools for 4KB pages (named BP0 through BP49)

- 10 buffer pools for 8KB pages (named BP8K0 through BP8K9)

- 10 buffer pools for 16KB pages (named BP16K0 through BP16K9)

- 10 buffer pools for 32KB pages (named BP32K and BP32K1 through BP32K9)

The size of a buffer pool is specified to DB2 in pages. As of DB2 V8, the maximum total buffer pool size is 1 terabyte.

27

Tuning DB2 buffer pools is a critical piece of overall DB2 subsystem tuning. Strategies for effective buffer pool tuning are presented in Chapter 28, "Tuning DB2's Components," in the section on DB2 subsystem tuning.

In addition to the buffer pools, DB2 creates a RID pool and a sort pool.

Sort Pool   RIDs processed during the execution of list prefetch are stored in the RID pool. Remember that hybrid joins and multiple-index access paths use list prefetch. The RID pool should be increased as your application's use of list prefetch and multiple-index access paths increase.

The size of the RID pool can be explicitly specified using the MAXRBLK DSNZPARM parameter. The RID pool can range in size from 128K to 10 GB. The default is 8000K. Of course, you can set the RID pool to 0 too, which has the effect of disabling the RID pool, causing DB2 to avoid access paths and join methods that require RID pool storage.

> **CAUTION**
>
> Do not set the RID pool to 0. It is almost always better to allow DB2 to determine when it makes sense to use the RID pool for accessing data than to arbitrarily disable the RID pool.

V8 As of DB2 V8, 25% of the RID pool is located below the 2-GB bar and 75% is located above the 2-GB bar.

Sort Pool   The sort pool, sometimes called a *sort work area,* is used when DB2 invokes a sort. Before I discuss the sort pool, examine the DB2 sorting process, which is shown in Figure 27.3. The RDS (Relational Data Services) component of DB2 uses a tournament sort technique to perform internal DB2 sorting.

The tournament sort works as follows:

- Rows to be sorted are passed through a tree structure like the one in Figure 27.3. A row enters the tree at the bottom. It is compared to rows already in the tree, and the lowest values (for ascending sequence) or the highest values (for descending sequence) are moved up the tree.

- When a row emerges from the top of the tree, it is usually placed in an ordered set of rows in memory. Sometimes, however, a value emerges from the top of the tree but does not fit into the current ordered set because it is out of range.

- When a row does not fit into the current ordered set, the complete ordered set of rows is written to a logical work file. This ordered set is then called a *run.*

- Logical work files are located in the buffer pool. As logical work files grow, sometimes they are written to physical work files. DB2 uses the DSNDB07 database to store physical work files.

- After all the rows have passed through the tree, the accumulated runs are merged, forming a sorted results set. This set is returned to the requester, completely sorted.

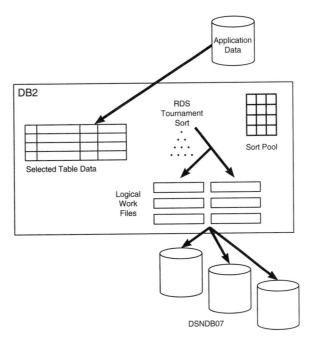

FIGURE 27.3 How DB2 sorts.

How, then, does the sort pool affect RDS sorting? As the sort pool becomes larger, so does the tree used for the tournament sort. As the tree becomes larger, fewer runs are produced. As fewer runs are produced, less data must be merged and the likelihood of using DSNDB07 diminishes. The result is a more efficient sort process.

You can use the following formula to estimate an efficient sort pool for each process:

```
32000 * (12 + sort key length + sort data length + 4)
```

Of course, each process will have a different optimal sort pool size because the length of the sort key and the length of the data to be sorted will vary.

Each concurrent sort operation is assigned a sort pool. The sort work area can range in size from a minimum of 240K to a maximum of 128 MB. The size of the sort pool can be explicitly specified using the SRTPOOL DSNZPARM parameter. If the sort pool is not explicitly specified, its default value is 2000K.

TUNING STRATEGY

As with all DB2 parameters, it is better to explicitly specify RID and sort pool sizes to allow them to default.

EDM Pool   The EDM pool is used to maintain DBDs, cursor tables (for plans), package tables, the authorization cache, and the dynamic statement cache needed by executing SQL statements. The size of the EDM pool is specified in the DSNZPARMs and must be determined before starting DB2. To estimate the size of the EDM pool, you must have the following information:

- The maximum number of concurrently executing plans and packages

- The average plan and package size

- The average cache size for plans

- The number of concurrently accessed DBDs

- The average DBD size

For new DB2 subsystems, letting the DB2 installation process use default values to calculate the size of the EDM pool is best. For existing DB2 subsystems, you can arrive at the average plan and package sizes by issuing the following SQL queries. For the average plan size, use this query:

```
SELECT   AVG(PLSIZE)
FROM     SYSIBM.SYSPLAN
```

For the average package size, use this query:

```
SELECT   AVG(PKSIZE)
FROM     SYSIBM.SYSPACKAGE
```

Add the two averages and divide by 2 to arrive at the total average plan and package size.

TUNING STRATEGY

Binding with the ACQUIRE(USE) option results in smaller plan sizes than binding with ACQUIRE(ALLOCATE). Additional code is stored with the plan for ACQUIRE(ALLOCATE). To reduce the amount of storage used by plans and packages in the EDM pool, specify ACQUIRE(USE) at bind time.

However, plan size usually should not be the determining factor for the specification of the ACQUIRE parameter. Instead, follow the guidelines presented in Chapter 13, "Program Preparation."

Another factor influencing the overall size of plans is the authorization cache. You can associate an authid cache for each plan by setting the size in the CACHESIZE parameter of the BIND command.

TUNING STRATEGY

Binding with the CACHESIZE(0) option also results in smaller plan sizes. However, the caching of authids enhances performance. So, once again, plan size should not be the determining factor in setting CACHESIZE either. The default cache size is 1024KB, which is probably overkill for many shops. Use the formula specified in Chapter 13 to calculate an appropriate CACHESIZE for each plan—instead of relying on the default.

NOTE

Authids are not checked for plans that can be executed by PUBLIC. Avoid specifying a CACHESIZE for these plans.

For the average size of the plan authorization ID cache, use the following query:

```
SELECT   AVG(CACHESIZE)
FROM     SYSIBM.SYSPLAN;
```

Package authorization caching is a system-wide option. Caching is either enabled or disabled for the entire subsystem and a global cache is used. Therefore, package authorization caching does not have an impact on package size.

To arrive at the average DBD size, you must know the average number of columns per table and the average number of tables per database. A general formula for calculating the average DBD size follows:

```
average DBD size = [(average # of tables per database) x 1K]
                 + [(average # of columns per table) x .5K]
```

You can use the following queries to arrive at the average number of tables per database and the average number of columns per table. First, to determine the average number of tables per database, issue the following query:

```
SELECT   COUNT(*) / COUNT(DISTINCT(DBNAME))
FROM     SYSIBM.SYSTABLES
WHERE    TYPE = 'T';
```

You can use the following query to arrive at the average number of columns per table:

```
SELECT   AVG(COLCOUNT)
FROM     SYSIBM.SYSTABLES
WHERE    TYPE = 'T';
```

To arrive at the average number of concurrent plans, packages, and DBDs, you would be wise to accumulate a series of DB2 accounting statistics for your peak processing time. Use these figures to estimate the number of concurrent plans.

Determining the average number of concurrent packages is not easy. You must completely understand your particular DB2 implementation to be successful at determining this number. Asking the following questions can help:

- How many plans use packages instead of simply DBRMs? Issue the following two queries to determine this information:

  ```
  SELECT   COUNT(DISTINCT PLANNAME)
  FROM     SYSIBM.SYSPACKLIST;

  SELECT   COUNT(*)
  FROM     SYSIBM.SYSPLAN
  WHERE    OPERATIVE = 'Y'
  AND      VALID IN('Y','A');
  ```

- On average, how many versions of a package are permitted to remain in the DB2 Catalog? How many are used?

To determine the average number of concurrent DBDs, you must understand each application's database use. If an application that typically uses three databases is much more active than another that uses 12 databases, you must factor this information into your EDM pool sizing strategy. Obtaining this information can be difficult, so you might need to estimate. A general calculation for the EDM pool size follows:

```
EDM Pool Size = [(((#CPP) + (#TPP/4)) x PP-AVG) +
                (((#CPP) + (#TPP/4)) x C-AVG)  +
                ((#DBD) x DBD-AVG) + 50K] x 1.25
```

Value	Description
#CPP	Number of concurrent plans and packages
#TPP	Total number of plans and packages
#DBD	Total number of concurrently used databases
PP-AVG	Average size of all plans and packages
C-AVG	Average authorization cache size
DBD-AVG	Average authorization cache size

The systems programmer calculates the size of the EDM pool during DB2 installation based on estimates of the values discussed in this section. The installation process for DB2 contains the preceding algorithm. The calculation used by the DB2 installation process is only as good as the information supplied to it. The default values (calculated by DB2 during the installation process) are adequate for most shops if correct estimates were input.

As DB2 use expands, however, the EDM pool should expand proportionally. The size of the EDM pool can be explicitly specified using the EDMPOOL DSNZPARM parameter.

As your DB2 usage patterns change, plan and package sizes can grow, necessitating EDM pool growth. For example, using DEGREE(ANY) instead of DEGREE(1) increases plan and package sizes.

TUNING STRATEGY

Overestimate the size of the EDM pool. Having EDM pool memory available as the number of DB2 plans, packages, and databases increases can be better than reacting to a problem after it occurs. Periodically monitor the number of plans, packages, and databases in conjunction with usage statistics, and increase the EDM pool as your DB2 use increases.

Additionally, as more applications are made operational, or as more concurrent users start to access existing applications, EDM pool usage will increase.

TUNING STRATEGY

Prior to DB2 V8, if your DSNDBM1 is storage-constrained you can move some of the EDM pool into a data space. This is particularly helpful if you use dynamic statement caching. You can move some EDM storage into a data space by specifying a non-zero value for EDMPOOL DATA SPACE SIZE on the DSNTIPC installation panel.

V8 As of DB2 V8, this option is not available because data spaces are no longer supported. Of course, more memory is available due to z/OS and the ability of the EDM pool to utilize space above the 2GB bar.

> **TUNING STRATEGY**
>
> Because cached dynamic statements are stored in a separate pool in DB2 V8, re-evaluate your EDM pool storage needs. You might be able to decrease the size of the EDM pool after you move to DB2 V8.

V8 DB2 V8 separates the EDM pool into separate storage areas as follows:

The main *EDM pool* for managing CTs and PTs in use, SKCTs and SKPTs for the most frequently used applications, and cache blocks for your plans that have caches.

The *EDM DBD cache* for the DBDs in use and DBDs referred to by the SKCTs and SKPTs for the most frequently used applications.

The *EDM statement cache* for the skeletons of the most frequently used dynamic SQL statements, if your system has enabled the dynamic statement cache.

DB2 Working Storage   DB2 working storage is memory used by DB2 as a temporary work area. The best way to estimate the working storage size for DB2 is to separate the number of concurrent DB2 users into users of dynamic SQL and users of static SQL. Dynamic SQL uses more working storage (but possibly less of the EDM pool) than static SQL. Estimate approximately 25KB per static SQL user and 75KB per dynamic SQL user. Additionally, DB2 itself uses about 600K. Therefore, you can estimate DB2 working storage usage by using the following:

```
(concurrent static SQL users x 25K) +
(concurrent dynamic SQL users x 75K) + 600K
```

> **TUNING STRATEGY**
>
> You cannot explicitly tune the amount of memory used by concurrent static and dynamic SQL. Implicit control over the number of users can be established by the DSNZPARM values specified for IDFORE, IDBACK, and CTHREAD.

DB2 Code   The DB2 code itself requires approximately 4,300KB of storage. This value is inflexible.

IRLM   Locks are maintained in memory by the IRLM. This capability enables DB2 to process a lock request quickly and efficiently without a physical read.

> **TUNING STRATEGY**
>
> If the IRLM start-up parameters specify PC=Y, the locks are stored in the private address space for the IRLM. PC=N stores the locks in expanded memory, so this specification is more efficient than PC=Y.
>
> As of DB2 V8 all locks are stored in the private address space for the IRLM. As such, this option is not available as of V8.

The IRLM uses approximately 250 bytes per lock. This number is constant whether you are using row locks or page locks, so keep that in mind if you are considering row-level locking. You will likely consume much more storage with row locking because DB2 will probably have to lock more rows than it would pages (depending on the number of rows per page for the table space).

Open Data Sets   Each open VSAM data set requires approximately 1.8KB for the VSAM control block that is created. Refer to Chapter 5, "Data Definition Guidelines," for a discussion of the CLOSE parameter for DB2 table spaces and indexes and its effect on performance.

TUNING STRATEGY

Use segmented table spaces with multiple tables to reduce the amount of memory used by open data sets. When each table is assigned to a unique table space, DB2 must manage more open data sets—one for each table space and table combination. As the number of tables in a table space increases, DB2 must manage fewer open data sets. (All considerations for multi-table table spaces, as outlined in Chapter 5, still apply.)

TUNING STRATEGY

The memory cost per open data set, approximately 1.8K, is small in comparison to the performance gains associated with leaving the data sets open to avoid VSAM open and close operations. Favor using CLOSE YES for most of your table spaces and indexes. Doing so leaves data sets open until the maximum number of open data sets is reached. At this point, DB2 chooses the least recently used data sets to close. You might want to consider specifying CLOSE NO for your most critical objects so that other objects are closed before your most critical objects.

Total Memory Requirements   By adding the memory requirements, as specified in the preceding sections, for the EDM pool, buffer pools, RID pool, sort pool, working storage, open data sets, and IRLM for each DB2 subsystem, you can estimate the memory resources required for DB2. If insufficient memory is available, consider limiting the availability of DB2 until more memory can be procured.

TUNING STRATEGY

DB2 uses virtual and real storage. DB2's performance increases as you assign more memory. If you intend to have very large DB2 applications, do not be stingy with memory.

Tuning CPU Use

Tuning CPU use is a factor in reducing DB2 resource consumption and providing an efficient environment. The major factors affecting CPU cost are as follow:

- Amount and type of I/O
- Number of GETPAGE requests
- Number of columns selected in the SQL statement
- Number of predicates applied per SQL statement

The following paragraphs offer additional information about each of these factors, including suggested tuning strategies.

By reducing physical I/O requests, you decrease CPU consumption. Similarly, the use of sequential prefetch can decrease CPU cost because more data is returned per physical I/O.

> **TUNING STRATEGY**
>
> Encourage the use of sequential prefetch when every (or almost every) row in a table will be accessed. You can do so by coding SELECT statements without predicates, by coding SELECT statements with minimal predicates on columns that are not indexed, or sometimes, by specifying a large number in the OPTIMIZE clause (for example, OPTIMIZE FOR 1000000 ROWS). Because the OPTIMIZE FOR *n* ROWS clause was originally designed to reduce the estimated number of rows to be retrieved (not to increase that number), this trick does not always work.

Each GETPAGE request causes the Data Manager to request a page from the Buffer Manager, which causes additional CPU use.

> **TUNING STRATEGY**
>
> If possible, serialize data requests in static applications so that requests for the same piece of data are not duplicated. If a program requires the same data more than once, try to arrange the processes that act on that data to be contiguous, such that a single I/O is required instead of multiple I/Os. For example, if an employee's department number is required in three separate parts of a transaction, select the information once and save it for the other two times.

As the number of selected columns increases, DB2 must do more work to manipulate these columns, thereby using excess CPU.

> **TUNING STRATEGY**
>
> Code each SELECT statement (even ad hoc SQL) to return only columns that are absolutely needed.

As your number of predicates increases, DB2 must do more work to evaluate the predicates and ensure that the data returned satisfies the requirements of the predicates.

> **TUNING STRATEGY**
>
> Avoid coding redundant predicates. Use your knowledge of the application data in coding SQL. For example, if you know that employees must have an EDLEVEL of 14 or higher to hold the title of MANAGER, use this knowledge when you're writing SQL statements. The EDLEVEL predicate in the following query should not be coded because it is redundant, given the preceding qualification:
>
> ```
> SELECT    EMPNO, LASTNAME
> FROM      DSN8610.EMP
> WHERE     JOB = 'MANAGER'
> AND       EDLEVEL >= 14;
> ```
>
> Document the removal of redundant predicates in case policy changes. For example, if managers can have an education level of 10, the EDLEVEL predicate is no longer redundant and must be added to the query again. Because tracking this information can be difficult, you should avoid removing predicates that are currently redundant but that might not always be so.

27

Tuning I/O

I/O is probably the single most critical factor in the overall performance of your DB2 subsystem and applications. This factor is due to the physical nature of I/O: it is limited by hardware speed. The mechanical functionality of a storage device is slower and more prone to breakdown than the rapid, chip-based technologies of CPU and memory. For this reason, paying attention to the details of tuning the I/O characteristics of your environment is wise.

What is I/O? Simply stated, I/O is a transfer of data by the CPU from one medium to another. *I* stands for input, or the process of receiving data from a physical storage medium. *O* stands for output, which is the process of moving data to a physical storage device. In every case, an I/O involves moving data from one area to another.

In the strictest sense of the term, an I/O can be a movement of data from the buffer pool to a working storage area used by your program. This type, however, is a trivial I/O with a lower cost than an I/O requiring disk access, which is the type of I/O you must minimize and tune.

The best way to minimize the cost of I/O is to use very large buffer pools. This way, you can increase the possibility that any requested page is already in memory, thereby tuning I/O by sometimes eliminating it. In general, I/O decreases as the size of the buffer pools increases. This method, however, has drawbacks. Buffer pools should be backed up with real and virtual memory, but your shop might not have extra memory to give DB2. Also, DB2 basically takes whatever memory you give it and almost always can use more.

> **NOTE**
>
> Of course, another way to minimize the cost of I/O is to utilize faster hardware. IBM's Enterprise Storage System (ESS), sometimes referred to as SHARK, can process data requests faster than older disk storage devices (such as 3380 or 3390 DASD units). The majority of improvements in ESS performance come from improvements to the bus architecture, higher parallelism, improved disk interconnection technology, and increased ESCON channel attachments.

Even with large buffer pools, data must be read from the disk storage device at some point to place it in the buffer pools. Tuning I/O, therefore, is wise.

The number of all reads and writes makes up the I/O workload incurred for any single resource. Therefore, the cost of I/O depends on the disk device, the number of pages retrieved per I/O, and the type of write operation.

The characteristics of the disk device that contains the data being read include the speed of the device, the number of data sets on the device, the proximity of the device to the device controller, and concurrent access to the device. You can improve performance by moving DB2 data sets to disk devices with faster retrieval rates. Consider the following estimates for retrieving a single page from different types of devices:

Device	Retrieval Cost
3380	.020 to .028 seconds per page
3390	.015 to .020 seconds per page
Solid State	.004 to .006 seconds per page

Obviously, a solid-state device offers better performance because it lacks the mechanical aspects of 3380 and 3390 DASD units.

The second factor affecting I/O cost is the number of pages retrieved per I/O. As I indicated in the preceding section, sequential prefetch can increase the number of pages read per I/O. Sequential prefetch also functions as a read-ahead engine. Reads are performed in the background, before they are needed and while other useful work is being accomplished. This way, I/O wait time can be significantly reduced.

Refer to the following average response times. (Note that all times are approximate.) A single page being read by sequential prefetch can be two to four times more efficient than a single page read by synchronous I/O.

Device	Sequential Prefetch	Sequential Prefetch (per page)	Synchronous Read
3380	80ms	2.5ms	25ms
3390	40ms	1.5ms	10ms

Better response times can be achieved with modern storage devices. In a document titled "DB2 for OS/390 Performance on IBM Enterprise Storage Server," IBM has published a prefetch rate of 11.8 MB/second with ESS and 5.8 MB/second with RAMAC-3.

The third factor in I/O cost is the type of write operation: asynchronous versus synchronous. DB2 can not only read data in the background but also write data in the background. In most cases, DB2 does not physically externalize a data modification to disk immediately following the successful completion of the SQL DELETE, INSERT, or UPDATE statement. Instead, the modification is externalized to the log. Only when the modified page is removed from DB2's buffers is it written to disk. This process is called an asynchronous, or deferred, write. Synchronous writes, on the other hand, are immediately written to disk. DB2 tries to avoid them, and it should. If you ensure that sufficient buffers are available, synchronous writes can be avoided almost entirely.

Several types of I/O must be tuned. They can be categorized into the following five groups:

Application I/O

Internal I/O

Sort I/O

Log I/O

Paging I/O

In the sections that follow, you will examine each of these types of I/O.

Application I/O
Application I/O is incurred to retrieve and update application data. As DB2 applications execute, they read and modify data stored in DB2 tables. This process requires I/O.

27

You can apply the following strategies to tune all five types of I/O covered here, not just application I/O. They are of primary importance, however, for application I/O.

> **TUNING STRATEGY**
>
> Tune I/O by increasing the size of the buffer pools. With larger buffer pools, application data can remain in the buffer pool longer. When data is in the buffer pool, it can be accessed quickly by the application without issuing a physical I/O.

> **TUNING STRATEGY**
>
> Tune I/O speed by using the fastest disk drives available. For example, replace older 3380 devices with newer, faster 3390 devices, RAMAC, or ESS. Most applications require multiple I/Os as they execute. For each I/O, you can save from 15ms to 40ms with 3390s instead of 3380s. The performance gains can be tremendous for applications requiring thousands (or even millions) of I/Os.

> **TUNING STRATEGY**
>
> For non-SMS users only: Use proper data set placement strategies to reduce disk head contention. To do so, follow these basic rules:
>
> - Avoid placing a table's indexes on the same disk device as the table space used for the table.
> - Analyze the access pattern for each application. When tables are frequently accessed together, consider placing them on separate devices to minimize contention.
> - Limit shared disk. Putting multiple, heavily accessed data sets from different applications on the same device is unwise. Cross-application contention can occur, causing head movement, undue contention, and I/O waits. Be cautious not only of high-use DB2 tables sharing a single volume, but also of mixing DB2 tables with highly accessed VSAM, QSAM, and other data sets.
> - Place the most heavily accessed table spaces and indexes closest to the disk controller unit. The closer a disk device is on the string to the actual controller, the higher its priority will be. The performance gain from this placement is minimal (especially for 3390 devices), but consider this option when you must squeeze out every last bit of performance.
> - Avoid having table space and index data sets in multiple extents. When the data set consists of more than a single extent, excess head movement can result, reducing the efficiency of I/O.
> - Use the data-partitioned secondary indexes to explicitly partition secondary indexes to match partitioned table spaces and distribute the DPSI and table space partitions over multiple devices.
> - Use the PIECESIZE parameter to explicitly distribute non-partitioned table spaces and indexes over multiple devices.
> - Favor allocation of data sets in cylinders.

V8

Another factor impacting the efficiency of accessing DB2 application data is partitioning. When data is partitioned, it is more likely that DB2 can utilize query parallelism to read data.

> **TUNING STRATEGY**
>
> Consider partitioning simple and segmented table spaces to take advantage of DB2's parallel I/O capabilities. Although partitioning is not required, partitioning can help to encourage DB2 to use parallelism.

Internal I/O

DB2 requires internal I/Os as it operates. Different types of data must be read and updated by DB2 as applications, utilities, and commands execute. This type of I/O occurs during the following:

- Recording utility execution information in the DB2 Directory

- Updating the DB2 Catalog as a result of DCL, DDL, or utility executions

- Reading the DB2 Catalog and DB2 Directory when certain DB2 commands (for example, `-DISPLAY DATABASE`) are issued

- Retrieving skeleton cursor tables, skeleton plan tables, and DBDs from the DB2 Directory to enable programs to execute

- Retrieving data from the DB2 Catalog during `BIND`, `REBIND`, and dynamic SQL use

- Miscellaneous DB2 Catalog I/O for plans marked as `VALIDATE(RUN)` and for other runtime needs

- Reading the Resource Limit Specification Table

> **TUNING STRATEGY**
>
> Limit activities that incur internal I/O during heavy DB2 application activity. This way, you can reduce the possibility of application timeouts due to the unavailability of internal DB2 resources resulting from contention.

> **TUNING STRATEGY**
>
> To enhance the performance of I/O to the DB2 Catalog, consider placing the DB2 Catalog on a solid-state device that uses memory chips rather than mechanical disk. Although solid-state devices are often expensive, they can reduce I/O cost significantly. A power outage, however, can cause the DB2 Catalog to be unavailable or damaged. For many shops, this risk might be too great to take. You can find additional tuning strategies for the DB2 Catalog and DB2 Directory in Chapter 28, "Tuning DB2's Components."

Sort I/O

Sorting can cause an I/O burden on the DB2 subsystem. To sort very large sets of rows, DB2 sometimes uses physical work files in the `DSNDB07` database to store intermediate sort results. `DSNDB07` consists of table spaces stored on disk. The use of disk-based work files for sorting can dramatically affect performance.

27

> **TUNING STRATEGY**
>
> Consider placing DSNDB07 on a solid-state device when applications in your DB2 subsystem require large sorts of many rows or the sorting of a moderate number of very large rows.

> **TUNING STRATEGY**
>
> Tune DSNDB07 because you will probably use it eventually. Be sure that multiple table spaces are defined for DSNDB07 and that they are placed on separate disk devices. Furthermore, ensure that the underlying VSAM data sets for the DSNDB07 table spaces are not using multiple extents.

> **TUNING STRATEGY**
>
> If the cost of sorting is causing a bottleneck at your shop, ensure that you are using the following sorting enhancements:
>
> - The microcode sort feature can improve the cost of sorting by as much as 50%. Microcode is very efficient software embedded in the architecture of the operating system. The microcode sort can be used only by DB2 V2.3 and higher and only when DB2 is run on one of the following CPU models: ES/9000 Model 190 and above, ES/3090-9000T, and ES/3090 Models 180J, 200J, 280J, and above.
> - Provide for unlimited logical work files based on the size of the buffer pool. This capability can significantly reduce I/O because more sort data can be contained in memory rather than written out to DSNDB07.
> - Define DSNDB07 in a separate buffer pool and tune it accordingly for sorting. Keep in mind that although most sort operations are sequential, sorting also requires some random processing.

> **TUNING STRATEGY**
>
> Be sure to create DSNDB07 work files appropriately. Define multiple work files of equal size. You should consider allowing these files to go into extents, as well. Secondary extents allow runaway queries to complete. If you would rather have a runaway query fail than have it acquire the storage for sort work files using extents, define the work files without the ability to take extents. If you allow extents, define them on all work files, not just the last one.

Log I/O

Log I/O occurs when changes are made to DB2 data. Log records are written to DB2's active log data sets for each row that is updated, deleted, or inserted. Every modification (with the exception of REORG LOG NO and LOAD LOG NO) is logged by DB2 to enable data recovery. In addition, when you run the RECOVER utility to restore or recover DB2 table spaces, an active log data set (and sometimes multiple archive log data sets) must be read.

For these reasons, optimal placement of DB2 log data sets on disk is critical.

> **TUNING STRATEGY**
>
> Put your log data sets on your fastest disk devices. For example, a shop using 3380 and 3390 devices should place log data sets on 3390 disk volumes with the DASD fast write feature. DASD fast write is a caching technique that significantly enhances the speed of I/O for DB2 log data sets.

The two types of DB2 log data sets are active logs and archive logs. As the active log data sets are filled, DB2 invokes a process called *log offloading* to move information from the active logs to the archive logs. Log offloading can have a severe impact on the throughput of a DB2 subsystem.

TUNING STRATEGY

Ensure that your log data sets are on different volumes and on separate channels. Avoid placing more than one active log data set on the same disk volume. Otherwise, the whole reason for having dual active logs is negated and the overall performance of DB2 will be impaired significantly during the log offloading process.

Optimal utilization of tapes and tape drives is critical for an efficient DB2 log offloading process. Recall from Chapter 23, "Locking DB2 Data," that log offloading is the process of writing entries from the active log to the archive log.

TUNING STRATEGY

Consider making the active log the same size as a full cartridge. When the log is offloaded, the archive will utilize a full cartridge, resulting in fewer wasted tapes.

Of course, if you use disk archives then there is no reason to impose a size limit.

Paging I/O
Paging I/Os occur when memory is over-utilized and pages of storage are relocated temporarily to disk. When needed, they will be read from disk back into main storage. This process causes very high overhead.

TUNING STRATEGY

Avoid paging by fencing the DB2 address spaces as suggested in the section titled "Tuning Memory Use" at the beginning of this chapter.

TUNING STRATEGY

Increase the amount of real and virtual storage for your CPU. When you increase the amount of memory at the system's disposal, paging is less frequent.

In addition to the tuning of I/O at the data set level, you must monitor and tune I/O at the disk device level. The overall performance of I/O depends on the efficiency of each disk volume to which DB2 data sets have been allocated.

TUNING STRATEGY

Consistently monitor each disk volume to ensure that contention is minimal. You can do so with a third-party tool designed to report on the usage characteristics of disk devices. In general, if device contention for any disk volume is greater than 30%, an I/O problem exists. Each shop should analyze its disk usage patterns, reducing contention as much as possible given the shop's budgetary constraints. When contention is high, however, consider moving some data sets on the device to other, less active volumes.

27

Some disk devices offer hardware caching as an option for all data sets stored on the device. In these cases, the actual disk drive can be used to cache data reads. These features are not usually effective for reading DB2 data.

> **TUNING STRATEGY**
>
> Avoid caching for disk volumes containing DB2 application table space and index data sets. The benefits of caching are greatly reduced for most DB2 application processing because of the efficient, asynchronous manner in which DB2 can read data (using sequential prefetch) and write data (using deferred write).

RAMAC Devices

Some of the conventional wisdom regarding data set placement and I/O changes with RAMAC storage devices. A device is not a physical volume, it is a virtual volume that is spread across multiple physical volumes on the RAMAC. For this reason, arm movement is not a concern.

With RAMAC, it is possible that you could place data sets on separate volumes only to have RAMAC place them on the same physical volume. For this reason, consider using SMS to place the data, and use DFDSS to move data sets when contention occurs.

Tuning Various z/OS Parameters and Options

Because z/OS is a complex operating system, it can be difficult to comprehend. In this section, I discuss—in easy-to-understand language—some environmental tuning options for z/OS.

The z/OS environment is driven by the Systems Resource Manager (SRM). The SRM functions are based on parameters coded by systems programmers in the SYS1.PARMLIB library. Three members of this data set are responsible for defining most performance-oriented parameters for MVS: OPT, IPS, and ICS. You can tune the items discussed in this chapter by modifying these members. However, I do not discuss how to set these parameters in this book.

You should not take this type of tuning lightly. z/OS tuning is complex, and a change made to benefit DB2 might affect another z/OS subsystem. All DB2 personnel in your shop (including management, database administration, and DB2, IMS, CICS, and z/OS systems programming) should discuss these types of tuning options before implementing them. Only a trained systems programmer should make these types of changes.

The first item to consider is whether a job is swappable. A *swappable* job can be temporarily swapped out of the system by MVS. When a job is swapped out, it is not processed. It therefore is not using CPU, cannot request I/O, and generally is dormant until it is swapped back into the system. Almost all of your jobs should be swappable so that MVS can perform as it was designed—maximizing the number of jobs that can be processed concurrently with a minimum of resources.

Because the DB2 address spaces, however, are non-swappable, DB2 itself is never swapped out. Therefore, a DB2 application program requesting DB2 functions never has to wait for

DB2 because it has been swapped out. The following list outlines which components of your overall environment can be swappable:

DB2	Non-swappable
CICS	Swappable or non-swappable
IMS	Non-swappable
TSO	Swappable
QMF	Swappable
Application	Swappable

TUNING STRATEGY

When a CICS subsystem is being used to access DB2, it should be defined as non-swappable to enhance response time (and thereby increase the performance) of the DB2/CICS transactions.

Usually, an application address space is swapped out so that z/OS can maintain even control over the processing environment. z/OS might determine that a job should be swapped out for the following reasons:

- Too many jobs are running concurrently for all of them to be swapped in simultaneously. The maximum number of address spaces that can be simultaneously swapped in is controlled by the SRM based on parameters and the workload.

- Another job needs to execute.

- A shortage of memory.

- Terminal wait. A TSO user might be staring at the screen, thinking about what to do next. Online TSO application programs do not need to be swapped in until the user takes another action.

The *dispatching priority* of an address space is a means of controlling the rate at which the address space can consume resources. A higher dispatching priority for an address space translates into faster performance because resources are more readily available to jobs with higher dispatching priorities. Controlling the dispatching priorities of jobs is an important tuning technique.

Normally, SRM controls the dispatching priority. Your shop may be using the Workload Manager (WLM) to control priorities. Systems programmers assign the dispatching priority of different address spaces. To ensure optimal DB2 performance, arrange the dispatching priorities of your DB2-related address spaces as shown in Figure 27.4. Batch application address spaces are generally dispatched below TSO (Long). Some critical batch jobs could be dispatched higher than TSO (Long).

27

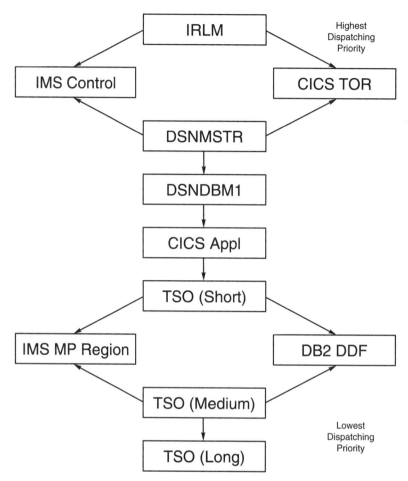

FIGURE 27.4 Dispatching priority hierarchy.

TUNING STRATEGY

Increasing the dispatching priority of batch DB2 application jobs that are critical or long-running increases their performance. However, this increase is at the expense of other jobs running with lower dispatching priorities. Tinkering with the dispatching priorities of application jobs is not a good practice unless it is an emergency. The dispatching priority of an address space can be changed "on–the-fly," but only by authorized personnel.

When you're planning for a high amount of batch activity, ensure that an adequate number of *initiators* is available for the batch jobs. Initiators are essentially servers, under the control of JES, that process jobs as they are queued. In determining whether initiators are available, take the following into account:

- An initiator is assigned to a job class or classes, specified on the job card of your batch JCL. If an initiator is not assigned to the job class that your DB2 jobs will be using, that initiator will not be used.

- The number of initiators available for DB2 job classes dictates the number of DB2 batch jobs that can run concurrently from an MVS perspective. The IDBACK DSNZPARM parameter determines the number of background DB2 jobs that can be run concurrently from a DB2 perspective.

TUNING STRATEGY

Synchronize the value of IDBACK to the number of initiators for the DB2 job classes at your site. If non-DB2 jobs can be run in DB2 job classes, or if the initiator is available also for non-DB2 job classes, the value of IDBACK should be less than the total number of initiators assigned to DB2 job classes.

- Jobs are removed from the job queue for execution by an initiator in order of their selection priority. Selection priority is coded on the job card of your JCL (PRTY). Most shops disable the PRTY parameter and place strict controls on the selection priority of jobs and job classes.

  Note that selection priority is different from dispatching priority. *Selection priority* controls the order in which jobs are queued for processing. *Dispatching priority* controls the resources available to a job after it is executing.

TUNING STRATEGY

Where initiators are at a premium (for example, fewer initiators than concurrent jobs), ensure that the DB2 jobs with the highest priority are assigned a higher selection priority than other DB2 jobs. This way, you can ensure that DB2 jobs are processed in order from most critical to least critical by the system.

Operating system tuning is an important facet of DB2 tuning. After the z/OS environment has been tuned properly, it should operate smoothly with little intervention (from DB2's perspective). Getting to the optimal z/OS environment, however, can be an arduous task.

Tuning z/OS is only one component of DB2 environment tuning. Tuning the teleprocessing environment, discussed next, is vital in achieving proper online performance.

Tuning the Teleprocessing Environment

Tuning your teleprocessing environment is essential to ensure that your online transactions are running in an optimal fashion. DB2 can use any of the three teleprocessors supplied by IBM: CICS, IMS/TM, and TSO. The tuning advice is different for each.

In this section, I do not provide in-depth tuning advice for your teleprocessing environments. An entire book could be devoted to the tuning of CICS, IMS/TM, and TSO. Your shop should ensure that the requisite level of tuning expertise is available. However, you should keep in mind several basic online tuning strategies. The following guidelines are applicable for each teleprocessing environment supported by DB2.

Limit Time on the Transaction Queue   Tune to limit the time that transactions spend on the input queue and the output queue. This way, you can decrease overhead and increase response time.

Design Online Programs for Performance   Ensure that all the program design techniques presented in Chapter 18, "The Doors to DB2," are utilized.

Store Frequently Used Data in Memory   Place into memory as many heavily used resources as possible. For example, consider using data spaces for CICS tables.

Make Critical Programs Resident   Consider making programs for heavily accessed transactions resident to reduce the I/O associated with loading the program. A resident program remains in memory after the first execution, thereby eliminating the overhead of loading it each time it is accessed.

Buffer All Non-DB2 Data Sets   Ensure that all access to non-DB2 data sets (such as VSAM or IMS) is buffered properly using the techniques available for the teleprocessing environment.

CHAPTER **28**

Tuning DB2's Components

After ensuring that the z/OS and teleprocessing environments are tuned properly, you can turn your attention to tuning elements integral to DB2. This chapter discusses the three main DB2 components that can be tuned: the DB2 subsystem, the database design, and the application code. Although many tips and tuning techniques for SQL code already have been presented in Chapters 1 and 2, the additional tuning guidelines in this chapter can be used to augment your application tuning approach.

Tuning the DB2 Subsystem

The first level of DB2 tuning to be discussed in this chapter is at the DB2 subsystem level. This type of tuning is generally performed by a DB2 systems programmer or database administrator. Several techniques can be used to tune DB2 itself. These techniques can be broken down into three basic categories:

- DB2 Catalog tuning techniques
- Tuning DB2 system parameters
- Tuning the IRLM

Each of these tuning methods is covered in the following sections.

Tuning the DB2 Catalog

One of the major factors influencing overall DB2 subsystem performance is the physical condition of the DB2 Catalog and DB2 Directory tablespaces. These tablespaces are not like regular DB2 tablespaces.

> **TUNING STRATEGY**
>
> Ensure that the DB2 Catalog data sets are not in multiple extents. When a data set spans more than one extent, overhead accrues due to the additional I/O needed to move from extent to extent. To increase the size of DB2 Catalog data sets, you must invoke a DB2 Catalog recovery. This procedure is documented in Chapter 6 of the IBM *DB2 Administration Guide*.

> **TUNING STRATEGY**
>
> Institute procedures to analyze the organization of the DB2 Catalog and DB2 Directory table-spaces and indexes. You can use DB2 utilities to reorganize inefficient objects in the DB2 Catalog and DB2 Directory. In-depth information on reorganizing the DB2 Catalog is provided in Appendix H.

> **TUNING STRATEGY**
>
> It also is possible to issue the REBUILD INDEX utility on the DB2 Catalog indexes, which reads the table to rebuild the index, and thereby reorganizes the index, too. You can choose to rebuild the DB2 Catalog indexes when DB2 use grows.

DB2 does not make use of indexes when it accesses the DB2 Catalog for internal use. For example, binding, DDL execution, and authorization checking do not use DB2 indexes. Instead, DB2 traverses pointers, or links, maintained in the DB2 Catalog. These pointers make internal access to the DB2 Catalog very efficient.

The DB2 Catalog indexes are used only by users issuing queries against DB2 Catalog tables. Whether these indexes are used or not is based on the optimization of the DB2 Catalog queries and whether the DB2 optimizer deems that they are beneficial.

> **TUNING STRATEGY**
>
> Execute RUNSTATS on the DB2 Catalog tablespaces and indexes. Without current statistics, DB2 cannot optimize DB2 Catalog queries. Additionally, RUNSTATS provides statistics enabling DBAs to determine when to reorganize the DB2 Catalog tablespaces.

Although it is difficult to directly influence the efficiency of internal access to the DB2 Catalog and DB2 Directory, certain measures can be taken to eliminate obstructions to performance. For instance, follow proper data set placement procedures to reduce DASD head contention.

> **TUNING STRATEGY**
>
> Do not place other data sets on the volumes occupied by the DB2 Catalog and DB2 Directory data sets. Place the DB2 Catalog data sets on different volumes than the DB2 Directory data sets. Place DB2 Catalog tablespaces on different volumes than the indexes on the DB2 Catalog.

> **TUNING STRATEGY**
>
> If you have additional DASD, consider separating the DB2 Catalog tablespaces by function, on distinct volumes.

On volume #1, place SYSPLAN, which is the tablespace used by application programs for binding plans.

On volume #2, place SYSPKAGE, which is the tablespace used by application programs for binding packages. Keep these tablespaces on separate volumes. Because plans can be composed of multiple packages, DB2 may read from SYSPKAGE and write to SYSPLAN when binding plans. Failure to separate these two tablespaces can result in head contention.

On volume #3, place SYSCOPY, which is the tablespace used by utilities. This enhances the performance of DB2 utilities.

On volume #4, place the remaining DB2 Catalog tablespaces. These tablespaces can coexist safely on a single volume because they are rarely accessed in a way that causes head contention. You might choose to separate system-related tablespaces from application-related tablespaces. For example, SYSSEQ, SYSSEQ2, SYSJAVA, SYSJAUXA, SYSJAUXB, and SYSGRTNS are more application-focused and could be placed on a separate device from the other, more system-focused DB2 Catalog tablespaces.

The DB2 Catalog is central to most facets of DB2 processing. It records the existence of every object used by DB2. As such, it is often queried by DBAs, programmers, and ad hoc users. Large queries against the DB2 Catalog can cause performance degradation.

TUNING STRATEGY

Consider isolating the DB2 Catalog tablespaces and indexes in a single buffer pool. This buffer pool must be BP0 because DB2 forces the catalog objects to be created in BP0. To isolate the system catalog objects in BP0, ensure that all other objects are created in other buffer pools (BP1 through BP49, BP8K0 through BP8K9, BP16K0 through BP16K9, BP32K, and BP32K1 through BP32K9).

TUNING STRATEGY

Consider monitoring the SQL access to DB2 Catalog tables and creating additional indexes on tables that are heavily accessed by non-indexed columns.

Additionally, many DB2 add-on tools access the DB2 Catalog as they execute, which can result in a bottleneck. Because the DB2 Catalog provides a centralized repository of information on all objects defined to DB2, it is natural for programmers, analysts, and managers to request access to the DB2 Catalog tables for queries. This can cause contention and reduce performance.

TUNING STRATEGY

Consider making a shadow copy of the DB2 Catalog for programmer queries and use by vendor tools. This reduces DB2 Catalog contention. If most external access to the DB2 Catalog is redirected to a shadow copy, internal access is much quicker. The shadow DB2 Catalog tables should never be allowed to get too outdated. Consider updating them weekly.

To implement this strategy, you must plan a period of inactivity during which the DB2 Catalog can be successfully copied to the shadow tables. Consider using ISOLATION(UR) when unloading the DB2 Catalog rows for movement to the shadow copy. For assistance with implementing this strategy, follow the guidelines presented in Chapter 5, "Data Definition Guidelines," for denormalizing with shadow tables.

> **TUNING STRATEGY**
>
> If you don't use a shadow copy of the DB2 Catalog, consider limiting access to the production DB2 Catalog by allowing queries only through views. You can create views so that users or applications can see only their own data. Additionally, views joining several DB2 Catalog tables can be created to ensure that DB2 Catalog tables are joined in the most efficient manner.

Finally, remember that when DB2 objects are created, DB2 must read and update several DB2 Catalog tables. This results in many locks on DB2 Catalog pages as the objects are being built. To reduce contention and the resultant timeouts and deadlocks, schedule all DDL during off-peak processing periods (for example, in the early morning after the batch cycle but before the first online use, or over the weekend).

> **TUNING STRATEGY**
>
> Consider priming the DB2 Catalog with objects for each new authorization ID that will be used as a creator. This avoids what some people refer to as the "first-time effect." Whenever initial inserts are performed for an authorization ID, additional overhead is involved in updating indexes and pointers. So, for each new authorization ID, consider creating a dummy database, table-space, table, index, synonym, view, package, and plan. As is the case with all DDL, you should do this only at an off-peak time. These objects need never be used and can be dropped or freed after actual DB2 objects have been created for the authorization ID. This is less of a concern for a test DB2 subsystem where performance is a less critical issue.

> **TUNING STRATEGY**
>
> Keep the DB2 Catalog and Directory as small as possible. Do not use the DB2 Catalog to retain historical objects, plans, packages, or recovery information. If any of this information might be beneficial, use a historical copy or version of the DB2 Catalog to retain this information. For example,
>
> - Delete the sample tables that do not apply to the current (and perhaps previous) version of DB2.
> - Be sure to delete the SYSDDF.SYSDDF data sets and objects. These were used by the communications database that was merged with the DB2 Catalog in Version 5.
> - Always delete plans and packages that are not used. For instance, V7 users should delete DSNTEP2 plans that invoke V6 or earlier programs.
> - Delete SYSCOPY rows that are not useful. This is done using the MODIFY RECOVERY utility.

DSNZPARMs

The makeup of the DB2 environment is driven by a series of system parameters specified when DB2 is started. These system parameters are commonly referred to as DSNZPARMs, or ZPARMs for short. The DSNZPARMs define the settings for many performance-related items. Several of the ZPARMs influence overall system performance.

V7 Most of the DSNZPARMs can be modified dynamically using the SET SYSPARM command.

> **NOTE**
>
> Prior to DB2 V3, buffer pool specifications were coded into the ZPARMs. For DB2 V3 and subsequent versions they are set using the `ALTER BUFFERPOOL` command.

A complete listing of DSNZPARM parameters can be found Appendix C of the IBM *DB2 Installation Guide*.

Traces

Traces can be started automatically based on DSNZPARM specifications. Most shops use this feature to ensure that certain DB2 trace information is always available to track performance problems. The DSNZPARM options for automatically starting traces are `AUDITST`, `TRACSTR`, `SMFACCT`, `SMFSTAT`, and `MON`.

> **TUNING STRATEGY**
>
> Ensure that every trace that is automatically started is necessary. Recall from Chapter 24, "Traditional DB2 Performance Monitoring," that traces add overhead. Stopping traces reduces overhead, thereby increasing performance.

DB2 traces can be started by IFCID. The acronym IFCID stands for Instrumentation Facility Component Identifier. An IFCID basically names a single traceable event in DB2. By specifying IFCIDs when starting a trace, you can limit the amount of information collected to just those events you need to trace.

Locking

Lock escalation thresholds are set by the following DSNZPARM options of the system parameters:

NUMLKTS	Maximum number of page or row locks for a single tablespace before escalating them to a tablespace lock
NUMLKUS	Maximum number of page or row locks held by a single user on all table spaces before escalating all of that user's locks to a tablespace lock

> **TUNING STRATEGY**
>
> To increase concurrency, set the NUMLKTS and NUMLKUS thresholds high to minimize lock escalation. For some environments, the default values are adequate (NUMLKTS=1000 and NUMLKUS=10000). However, for a high-volume environment these numbers may need to be adjusted upward to avoid contention problems.

Lock escalation can also be controlled on a tablespace-by-tablespace basis using the `LOCKMAX` parameter. Information on the `LOCKMAX` parameter can be found in Chapter 5. When specified, the `LOCKMAX` parameter overrides `NUMLKTS`.

Logging

The parameters that define DB2's logging features are also specified in the DSNZPARMs. Options can be used to affect the frequency of writing log buffers and the size of the log

28

buffers. The DSNZPARM options that affect DB2 logging are CHKFREQ, INBUFF, and LOGAPSTG.

TUNING STRATEGY

The CHKFREQ parameter indicates how often DB2 takes system checkpoints and it can be specified as either the number of log records written or as a time duration. Restart time is directly affected by how many log records are written after the latest system checkpoint. The more log records, the longer the restart time.

If the value of CHKFREQ is within the range of 200 to 16000000, it indicates the number of log records written before a checkpoint is taken. If CHKFREQ is within the range of 1 to 60, it indicates the number of minutes between checkpoints.

Additionally, DB2 takes a checkpoint when an active log is switched. The active log is switched when it becomes full or the ARCHIVE LOG command is issued.

You can use the SET LOG command or the SET SYSPARM command to change the CHKFREQ parameter dynamically. If you use SET LOG, the value is changed, but only for as long as the DB2 subsystem remains operational. When DB2 shuts down and is restarted, CHKFREQ will reset back to its previous value. If you use SET SYSPARM to change CHKFREQ, the value is changed now and forevermore—even if DB2 is recycled.

DB2 fills log buffers and eventually the log records are written to an active log data set. The write occurs when the buffers fill up, when the write threshold is reached or when the DB2 subsystem forces the log buffer to be written.

TUNING STRATEGY

Many shops simply use the default log output buffer size of 4000K. This is adequate for small shops (those with only one or two small, non-critical DB2 applications). The maximum value for OUTBUFF is 400MB. Shops with large, critical DB2 applications should probably specify a very large OUTBUFF—up to the maximum of 400MB if sufficient memory is available.

By increasing the OUTBUFF size, DB2 can perform better because more logging activity is performed in memory. Log writes can improve because DB2 is less likely to need to wait for a buffer. Log reads can improve because, if the information is in the log buffer, DB2 does not need to read the information from disk storage.

Be aware that when the log buffer is full the entire DB2 subsystem will stop until writes have completed and log buffers are available again.

The LOGAPSTG parameter represents the maximum DBM1 storage that can be used by the fast log-apply process. The default value is 0MB, which means that the fast log-apply process is disabled except during DB2 restart. During DB2 restart, the fast log-apply process is always enabled.

TUNING STRATEGY

Plan for 10MB of storage for each concurrent RECOVER job that you want to have faster log apply processing. So, if you plan on having 3 concurrent RECOVER jobs, specify 30MB for LOGAPSTG.

Timeouts

The amount of time to wait for an unavailable resource to become available before timing out is controlled by the DSNZPARM value, IRLMRWT. When one user has a lock on a DB2 resource that another user needs, DB2 waits for the time specified by IRLMRWT and then issues a -911 or -913 SQLCODE.

> **TUNING STRATEGY**
>
> IRLMRWT controls the amount of time to wait before timing out both foreground and background tasks. Therefore, you must balance a reasonable amount of time for a batch job to wait versus a reasonable amount of time for an online transaction to wait. If this value is too high, transactions wait too long for unavailable resources before timing out. If this value is too low, batch jobs abend with timeouts more frequently. The default value of 60 seconds is usually a reasonable setting.

> **TUNING STRATEGY**
>
> Sometimes it is impossible to find a compromise value for IRLMRWT. Online transactions wait too long to time out, or batch jobs time out too frequently. If this is the case, consider starting DB2 in the morning for online activity with a modest IRLMRWT value (45 or 60 seconds) and starting it again in the evening for batch jobs with a larger IRLMRWT value (90 to 120 seconds). In this scenario, DB2 must go down and come back up during the day. (This might be impossible for shops running 24 hours a day, 7 days a week.)

Additionally, the UTIMOUT parameter can be used to indicate the number of resource timeout cycles that a utility will wait for a drain lock before timing out.

> **TUNING STRATEGY**
>
> The value of UTIMOUT is based on the value of IRLMRWT. If UTIMOUT is set to 6 (which is the default), a utility will wait six times as long as an SQL statement before timing out.

Active Users

The number of active users can be controlled by the DSNZPARM settings, including the following:

CTHREAD	Controls the absolute number of maximum DB2 threads that can be running concurrently
IDFORE	Sets the maximum number of TSO users that can be connected to DB2 simultaneously
IDBACK	Controls the number of background batch jobs accessing DB2
MAXDBAT	Specifies the maximum number of concurrent distributed threads that can be active at one time

> **TUNING STRATEGY**
>
> Use the CTHREAD parameter to ensure that no more than the planned maximum number of DB2 users can access DB2 at a single time. Failure to keep this number synchronized with other DB2 resources can cause performance degradation. For example, if your buffer pools and EDM pool

are tuned to be optimal for 30 users, do not allow CTHREAD to exceed 30 until you have reexamined these other areas.

The same guideline applies for IDFORE to control TSO use, IDBACK to control the proliferation of batch DB2 jobs, and MAXDBAT to control distributed DB2 jobs.

EDM Pool

The size of the EDM pool is specified in the DSNZPARM value named EDMPOOL. The use of the EDM pool and its requirements are described in Chapter 27, " Tuning DB2's Environment," in the section titled "Tuning Memory Use."

Drowning in a Buffer Pool of Tears

The single most critical system-related factor influencing DB2 performance is the setup of sufficient buffer pools. A buffer pool acts as a cache between DB2 and the physical disk storage devices on which the data resides. After data has been read, the DB2 Buffer Manager places the page into a buffer pool page stored in memory. Buffer pools, therefore, reduce the impact of I/O on the system by enabling DB2 to read and write data to memory locations synchronously, while performing time-intensive physical I/O asynchronously.

Through judicious management of the buffer pools, DB2 can keep the most recently used pages of data in memory so that they can be reused without incurring additional I/O. A page of data can remain in the buffer pool for quite some time, as long as it is being accessed frequently. Figure 28.1 shows pages of data being read into the buffer pool and reused by multiple programs before finally being written back to disk. Processing is more efficient as physical I/Os decrease and buffer pool I/Os increase.

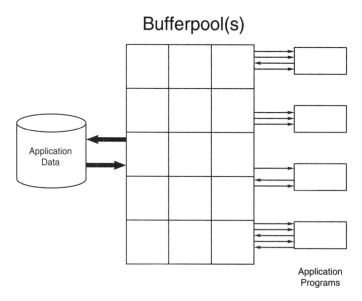

FIGURE 28.1   DB2 buffer pool processing.

How does the buffer pool work? DB2 performs all I/O-related operations under the control of its Buffer Manager component. As pages are read, they are placed into pages in the buffer pool using a hashing algorithm based on an identifier for the data set and the number of the page in the data set. When data is subsequently requested, DB2 can check the buffer pool quickly using hashing techniques. This provides efficient data retrieval. Additionally, DB2 data modification operations write to the buffer pool, which is more efficient than writing directly to DASD.

How does DB2 keep track of what data is updated in the buffer pool? This is accomplished by attaching a state to each buffer pool page: available or not available. An available buffer page meets the following two criteria:

- The page does not contain data updated by an SQL statement, which means that the page must be externalized to disk before another page can take its place.

- The page does not contain data currently being used by a DB2 application.

An unavailable page is one that does not meet one of these criteria because it has either been updated and not yet written to disk, or it is currently in use. When a page is available, it is said to be available for stealing. *Stealing* is the process whereby DB2 replaces the current data in a buffer page with a different page of data. Usually, the least recently used available buffer page is stolen first (but it depends on the stealing algorithm used for the buffer pool). DB2 provide 80 buffer pools to monitor, tune, and tweak.

Although every shop's usage of buffer pools differs, some basic ideas can be used to separate different types of processing into disparate buffer pools. Consult Table 28.1 for one possible buffer pool usage scenario. This is just one possible scenario and is not a general recommendation for buffer pool allocation.

TABLE 28.1   A Possible Buffer Pool Usage Scenario

Buffer Pool	Usage
BP0	Isolate system resources *(DB2 Catalog and Directory, RLST, and so on)*
BP1	Sequential tablespace buffer pool (usually accessed sequentially)
BP2	Sequential index buffer pool (usually accessed sequentially)
BP3	Code tables, lookup tables, and sequential number generation tables
BP4	Indexes for code tables, lookup tables, and sequential number generation tables
BP5	Dedicated buffer pool (for a single, critical tablespace or index)
BP6	Dedicated buffer pool (for an entire application)
BP7	Dedicate to sorting *(DSNDB07)*
BP8	Random tablespace buffer pool (usually accessed randomly)
BP9	Random index buffer pool (usually accessed randomly)
BP10	Reserve for tuning and special testing
BP11-BP49	Additional dedicated buffer pools (per tablespace, index, partition, application, or any combination thereof)
BP8K0	Reserved for DB2 Catalog objects with 8K pages (SYSDBASE, SYSGRTNS, SYSHIST, SYSOBJ, SYSSTR and SYSVIEWS)
BP8K1-BP8K9	Use when 8K tablespaces have been defined

28

TABLE 28.1   Continued

Buffer Pool	Usage
BP16K0	Reserved for DB2 Catalog objects with 16K pages (SYSSTATS)
BP16K1-BP16K9	Use when 16K tablespaces have been defined
BP32Ks	At least one BP32K for large joins; more if 32K tablespaces are permitted; be sure to separate 32K user tablespaces from 32K DSNDB07 tablespaces

I will examine several aspects of this scenario. The first buffer pool, BP0, should be reserved for system data sets such as the DB2 Catalog, QMF control tables, and Resource Limit Specification Tables. By isolating these resources into a separate buffer pool, system data pages will not contend for the same buffer pool space as application data pages.

V8   As of DB2 V8, some of the DB2 Catalog tablespaces require page sizes larger than 4K. These tablespaces use the BP8K0 and BP16K0 buffer pools.

Likewise, a single buffer pool (for example, BP7) can be set aside for sorting. If your environment requires many large sorts that use physical work files, isolating DSNDB07 (the sort work database) in its own buffer pool may be beneficial. This is accomplished by assigning all DSNDB07 tablespaces to the targeted buffer pool (BP7).

Another technique for the allocation of buffer pools is to use separate buffer pools for indexes and tablespaces. This can be accomplished by creating tablespaces in one buffer pool (for example, BP1) and indexes in another (for example, BP2). The idea behind this strategy is to enable DB2 to maintain more frequently accessed data by type of object. For instance, if indexes are isolated in their own buffer pool, large sequential prefetch requests do not cause index pages to be flushed, because the sequential prefetch is occurring in a different buffer pool. Thus, index pages usually remain in memory longer, which increases performance for indexed access.

> **TUNING STRATEGY**
>
> Many organizations do not spend sufficient time tuning their buffer pools. If you do not have the time or the organizational support to highly tune your objects into separate buffer pools, at least separate the tablespaces from the indexes.
>
> If you do nothing else with your buffer pool strategy, separating tablespaces and indexes in different buffer pools can give a nice performance boost for minimal administrative effort.

You can further tune your buffer pool usage strategy by isolating random access from sequential access. Consider using say, BP1 and BP2 for objects that are predominantly accessed sequentially, and say, BP8 and BP9 for randomly accessed objects. It is then possible to further tune the buffer pool parameters so that each type of buffer pool is optimized for the predominant type of access (that is, random or sequential).

Tables providing specialized functions can also be isolated. This is depicted by BP5 and BP6. Because these tables are very frequently accessed, they are often the cause of I/O bottlenecks that negatively impact performance. Creating the tablespaces for these tables in a specialized buffer pool can allow the entire table to remain in memory, vastly improving online performance. Additionally, the isolation of specialized tables into their own buffer pools enables pinpoint tuning for these frequently accessed tables (and indexes). General-purpose tables (and their associated indexes) accessed by multiple programs are good candidates for this type of strategy. Following are some examples:

- Tables used to control the assignment of sequential numbers.

- Lookup tables and code tables used by multiple applications.

- Tables and indexes used to control application-based security.

- Indexes with heavy index-only access. Isolating these indexes in their own buffer pool may enable the leaf pages to remain in memory.

> **TUNING STRATEGY**
>
> Regardless of the number of buffer pools that your shop intends to utilize, you should consider reserving one of the 4K buffer pools for tuning and testing (BP10, in the example). By reserving a buffer pool for tuning, you can ALTER problem objects to use the tuning buffer pool and run performance monitor reports to isolate I/O to the problem objects. The reports can be analyzed to assist in tuning.

It is usually a wise idea to use multiple buffer pools for different types of processing. This should minimize buffer pool page contention. In the example, BP5 is used to isolate one heavily accessed tablespace and/or index in its own buffer pool. Isolating a page set this way can ensure that no other processing will steal its buffer pages. Likewise, you may want to use a single buffer pool per application, such as BP6 in the example. Isolating all of that application's objects into its own buffer pool can eliminate or reduce the instances where one application monopolizes a buffer pool to the detriment of another application using the same buffer pool. It can also make application monitoring easier because all I/O is through a single buffer pool.

The remaining buffer pools (BP11 through BP49) can be used to further isolate specific objects or for further tuning.

The DB2 buffer pools have a huge impact on performance. There are several schools of thought on how best to implement DB2 buffer pools. For example, you may want to consider using separate buffer pools to do the following:

- Separate ad hoc from production

- Isolate QMF tablespaces used for the SAVE DATA command

- Isolate infrequently used tablespaces and indexes

- Isolate tablespaces and indexes used by third-party tools

28

> **CAUTION**
>
> Be careful that you do not allocate too many buffer pools. It is possible to allocate too many buffer pools to adequately manage. Be sure to align your performance needs for multiple buffer pools with your available administrative resources for monitoring and tuning those buffer pools.

One Large Buffer Pool?

The general recommendation from consultants and some IBM engineers in years past was to use only BP0, specifying one very large buffer pool for all DB2 page sets. This strategy turns over to DB2 the entire control for buffer pool management. Because DB2 uses efficient buffer-handling techniques, the theory was that good performance could be achieved using a single large buffer pool.

In the olden days of DB2, this strategy worked fairly well. When only a few, small applications used DB2, it could manage a fairly efficient single buffer pool. Today though, only some very small DB2 implementations can get by with one large buffer pool, using BP0 and letting DB2 do the buffer pool management. The days when most shops employed the single buffer pool strategy are over. As the amount of data stored in DB2 databases increases, specialized types of tuning are necessary to optimize data access. This usually results in the implementation of multiple buffer pools. Why else would IBM provide 80 of them?

> **TUNING STRATEGY**
>
> Avoid using one large DB2 buffer pool. Instead, share the wealth by assigning your DB2 objects to buffer pools based on access type.

If your shop is memory constrained, or you have limited practical experience with DB2 buffer pools, you might want to consider starting with one DB2 buffer pool and then experimenting with specialized buffer pool strategies as you acquire additional memory and practical expertise.

Notes on Multiple Buffer Pool Use

The following guidelines are helpful when allocating multiple buffer pools at your shop.

Ensure That Sufficient Memory Is Available   Before implementing multiple buffer pools, be sure that your environment has the memory to back up the buffer pools. The specification of large buffer pools without sufficient memory to back them up can cause paging. Paging to DASD is extremely nasty and should be avoided at all costs.

Document Buffer Pool Assignments   Be sure to keep track of which DB2 objects are assigned to which buffer pool. Failure to do so can result in confusion. Of course, DB2 Catalog queries can be used for obtaining this information.

Modify Buffer Pools to Reflect Processing Requirements   Defining multiple buffer pools so that they are used optimally throughout the day is difficult. For example, suppose that DSNDB07 is assigned to its own buffer pool. Because sorting activity is generally much higher during the batch window than during the day, buffers assigned to DSNDB07 can go unused during the transaction processing window.

Another example is when you assign tables used heavily in the online world to their own buffer pool. Online transaction processing usually subsides (or stops entirely) when nightly batch jobs are running. Online tables might be accessed sparingly in batch, if at all. This causes the buffers assigned for those online tables to go unused during batch processing.

Unless you are using one large BP0, it is difficult to use resources optimally during the entire processing day. Ask yourself if the performance gained by the use of multiple buffer pools offsets the potential for wasted resources. Quite often, the answer is a resounding "Yes."

DB2 provides the capability to dynamically modify the size of buffer pools using the ALTER BUFFERPOOL command. Consider using ALTER BUFFERPOOL to change buffer pool sizes to reflect the type of processing being performed. For example, to optimize the DSNDB07 scenario mentioned previously, try the following:

- Prior to batch processing, issue the following command: -ALTER BUFFERPOOL BP1 VPSIZE(*max amount*)

- After batch processing, issue the following command: -ALTER BUFFERPOOL BP1 VPSIZE(*min amount*)

The execution of these commands can be automated so that the appropriate buffer pool allocations are automatically invoked at the appropriate time in the batch schedule.

Buffer Pool Parameters

DB2 provides many buffer pool tuning options that can be set using the ALTER BUFFERPOOL command. These options are described in the following paragraphs.

The first parameter, VPSIZE, is arguably the most important. It defines the size of the individual virtual pool. The value can range from 0 to 400,000 for 4K buffer pools, from 0 to 200,000 for 8K buffer pools, from 0 to 100,000 for 16K buffer pools, and from 0 to 50,000 for 32K buffer pools. The total VPSIZE for all buffer pools cannot be greater than 1.6 GB. The minimum size of BP0 is 56 because the DB2 Catalog tablespaces and indexes are required to use BP0.

The capability to dynamically alter the size of a virtual pool enables DBAs to expand and contract virtual pool sizes without stopping DB2. Altering VPSIZE causes the virtual pool to be dynamically resized. If VPSIZE is altered to zero, DB2 issues a quiesce and when all activity is complete, the virtual pool is deleted.

Prior to DB2 V8, virtual buffer pools can be allocated in data spaces. To accomplish this, use the VPTYPE parameter to indicate the type of buffer pool to be used. VPTYPE(DATASPACE) indicates that data spaces are to be used for the buffer pool; VPTYPE(PRIMARY) indicates that the buffer pool is to be allocated as before, in the DB2 database services address space. You should be running in 64 bit mode to take advantage of data space buffer pools.

> **TUNING STRATEGY**
>
> The main reason to implement DB2 buffer pools in data spaces is to relieve storage constraints in DB2's database services (DBM1) address space. Another reason would be to provide greater opportunities for caching very large tablespaces or indexes.
>
> Data space virtual buffer pools are no longer supported as of DB2 V8.

The sequential steal threshold can be tuned using VPSEQT. VPSEQT is expressed as a percentage of the virtual pool size (VPSIZE). This number is the percentage of the virtual pool that

28

can be monopolized by sequential processing, such as sequential prefetch. When this threshold is reached, sequential prefetch will be disabled. All subsequent reads will be performed one page at a time until the number of pages available drops below the specified threshold. The value of VPSEQT can range from 0 to 100, and the default is 80. When VPSEQT is set to 0, prefetch is disabled.

> **TUNING STRATEGY**
>
> If the sequential steal threshold is reached often, consider either increasing the VPSEQT percentage or increasing the size of the associated buffer pool. When sequential prefetch is disabled, performance degradation will ensue.

> **TUNING STRATEGY**
>
> When all of the data from tables assigned to the buffer pool can be stored in the buffer pool, and access is almost exclusively random, specify VPSEQT=0. For example, consider specifying 0 for VPSEQT when a virtual buffer pool is used for small code and lookup tables.

Additionally, the sequential steal threshold for parallel operations can be explicitly set using VPPSEQT. This parallel sequential steal threshold is expressed as a percentage of the nonparallel sequential steal threshold (VPSEQT). The value of VPPSEQT can range from 0 to 100, and the default is 50.

> **TUNING STRATEGY**
>
> Consider isolating data sets that are very frequently accessed sequentially into a buffer pool with VPSEQT set to 95. This enables most of the buffer pool to be used for sequential access.

> **TUNING STRATEGY**
>
> By setting VPPSEQT to 0, you can ensure that parallel I/O will not be available for this virtual pool. *I am not necessarily recommending this, just pointing it out.* If you want to ensure that I/O parallelism is not used for a particular buffer pool, setting VPPSEQT to 0 will do the trick. Use caution and take care before choosing to modify this parameter.

The assisting parallel sequential threshold can be explicitly set using VPXPSEQT. This threshold sets the percentage of the parallel sequential threshold that is available to assist another parallel group member to process a query. The VPXPSEQT sequential threshold is expressed as a percentage of the parallel sequential steal threshold (VPPSEQT). The value of VPXPSEQT can range from 0 to 100, and the default is 0.

To understand the relationship that exists among the buffer pool parameters, refer to Figure 28.2. This diagram depicts the different parameters and thresholds and their relationships to one another.

To better understand the buffer pool parameters, consider the impact of issuing the following command:

```
-ALTER BUFFERPOOL BP1 VPSIZE(2000) VPSEQT(80) VPPSEQT(50) VPXPSEQT(25)
```

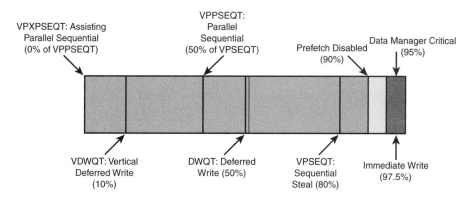

FIGURE 28.2   The relationships among the buffer pool parameters.

The BP1 buffer pool would be set to 8MB (2000 pages each 4KB in size). The sequential steal threshold (VPSEQT) is set to 80% of the buffer pool, which is 6.4MB (1600 pages). The parallel sequential steal threshold (VPPSEQT) is set to 50% of VPSEQT, which is 3.2MB (800 pages). Finally, the assisting parallel sequential steal threshold (VPXPSEQT) is set to 25% of VPPSEQT, which is .8MB (200 pages).

> **CAUTION**
>
> Setting these parameters can be quite confusing because they are set as percentages of other parameters. Take care to ensure that you are specifying the thresholds properly.

Deferred Write

DWQT can be used to specify the deferred write threshold. This threshold is expressed as a percentage of the virtual pool size (VPSIZE). It specifies when deferred writes will begin to occur. When the percentage of unavailable pages exceeds the DWQT value, pages will be written to DASD immediately (not deferred, as normal) until the number of available pages reaches 10% of (DWQT×VPSIZE). The value of DWQT can range from 0 to 100, and the default is 50.

Additionally, VDWQT can be used to set the deferred write threshold per data set. VDWQT is expressed as a percentage of the virtual pool size (VPSIZE). As of DB2 V6, you can express the VDWQT threshold as an integer value instead of a percentage. When the percentage of pages containing updated data for a single data set exceeds this threshold, immediate writes will begin to occur. The value of VDWQT can range from 0 to 90 and the default is 10. This value should be less than DWQT.

> **TUNING STRATEGY**
>
> Hitting either of the deferred write thresholds does not necessarily constitute a problem. Indeed, you can use these parameters to control how DB2 writes data.

28

> Consider setting the deferred write thresholds to enable trickle writing. With trickle writing, DB2 will regularly hit the deferred write threshold to externalize data to disk, instead of deferring writes and externalizing them all in a big bang. The pages that are written will remain in the buffer pool if they are referenced often.

Buffer Pool Page Stealing Algorithm

You can modify the page-stealing algorithm used by DB2 virtual buffer pools using the PGSTEAL parameter. When DB2 removes a page from the buffer pool to make room for a newer page, this is called *page stealing*. The usual algorithm deployed by DB2 uses least-recently-used (LRU) processing for managing buffer pages. In other words, older pages are removed so more recently used pages can remain in the virtual buffer pool.

However, you can choose to use a different, first-in–first-out (FIFO) algorithm. With FIFO, DB2 does not keep track of how often a page is referenced. The oldest pages are removed, regardless of how frequently they are referenced. This approach to page stealing results in a small decrease in the cost of doing a GETPAGE operation, and it can reduce internal DB2 latch contention in environments that require very high concurrency.

> **TUNING STRATEGY**
>
> Use the LRU page-stealing algorithm in most cases. Consider FIFO when the tablespaces and/or indexes assigned to the buffer pool are read once and remain in memory. When the buffer pool has little or no I/O, the FIFO algorithm can provide a performance boost.
>
> Be sure to define objects that can benefit from the FIFO algorithm in different buffer pools from other objects.

Determining Buffer Pool Sizes

Many database analysts and programmers are accustomed to working with buffer pools that are smaller than DB2 buffer pools (for example, IMS and VSAM buffers). DB2 just loves large buffer pools. Each shop must determine the size of its buffer pools based on the following factors:

- Size of the DB2 applications that must be processed

- Desired response time for DB2 applications

- Amount of virtual and real storage available

Remember, though, that DB2 does not allocate buffer pool pages in memory until it needs them. A DB2 subsystem with very large buffer pools might not use them all of the time.

As with the number of buffer pools to use, there are several schools of thought on how best to determine the size of the buffer pool. Actually, buffer pool sizing is more an art than a science. Try to allocate your buffer pools based on your projected workload and within the limitations defined by the amount of real and virtual memory available. Of course, for DB2 V8 you have much more flexibility in creating larger DB2 buffer pools than you had in the past due to the exploitation of 64-bit virtual memory.

The following calculation can be used as a good rough starting point for determining the size of your DB2 buffer pools:

```
[number of concurrent users x 80] +
[(desired number of transactions per second) x (average GETPAGEs per transaction)] +
[(Total # of leaf pages for all indexes) x .70]
```

The resulting number represents the number of 4K pages to allocate for all of your buffer pools. If you are using only BP0, the entire amount can be coded for that buffer pool. If you are using multiple buffer pools, a percentage of this number must be apportioned to each buffer pool you are using. This formula is useful for estimating a buffer pool that balances the following:

- Workload

- Throughput

- Size of the DB2 subsystem

Workload is factored in by the average GETPAGEs per transaction and the number of concurrent users. As workload (in terms of both number of users and amount of resources consumed) increases, so does the number of users and the average GETPAGEs per transaction.

Throughput is determined by the desired number of transactions per second. The size of the buffer pool increases as you increase the desired number of transactions per second. Larger buffer pools are useful in helping to force more work through DB2.

The size of the DB2 subsystem is represented by the number of index leaf pages. As the number of DB2 applications grows, the number of indexes defined for them grows also, thereby increasing the number of index leaf pages as DB2 use expands.

Recommendations for determining some of these values follow. Use the value of CTHREAD to determine the number of concurrent users. If you are sure that your system rarely reaches this maximum, you can reduce your estimate for concurrent users.

To estimate the number of transactions per second, use values from service-level agreement contracts for your applications. If service-level agreements are unavailable, estimate this value based on your experience and DB2-PM accounting summary reports.

To get an idea of overall workload and processing spikes (such as month-end processing), produce accounting summary reports for peak activity periods (for example, the most active two-hour period) across several days and during at least five weeks. Then arrive at an average for total transactions processed during that period by adding the # OCCUR from the GRAND TOTAL line of each report and dividing by the total number of reports you created. This number is, roughly, the average number of transactions processed during the peak period. Divide this number by 7200 (the number of seconds in two hours) for the average number of transactions per second. Then double this number because the workload is probably not evenly distributed throughout the course of the two hours. Also, do not use a number that is less than 10 transactions per second.

You can approximate the average number of GETPAGEs per transaction with the accounting summary or accounting detail reports (such as those provided by DB2 PM). Add all GETPAGEs for all transactions reported, and then divide this number by the total number of transactions reported. Base this estimate on transactions only—including batch programs would cause a large overestimate. Online transactions are generally optimized to read a small amount of data, whereas batch jobs can read millions of pages.

To determine the number of leaf pages for the indexes in your DB2 subsystem, issue the following query:

```
SELECT   SUM(NLEAF)
FROM     SYSIBM.SYSINDEXES;
```

For this query to work properly, RUNSTATS statistics should be up to date and any unused objects should be excluded (using a WHERE clause).

CAUTION

Keep in mind that the formula just discussed for estimating buffer pool requirements should be used as just a very rough guideline. If you have the resources at your disposal, you should carefully analyze your DB2 workload requirements by reviewing each transaction and batch program in conjunction with transaction history and your batch job schedules. You can then create a model for a typical processing day and design your buffer pool strategy to meet that model.

There are also tools on the market that can assist you in setting up and managing your buffer pools. Examples include BMC Software's Pool Advisor and Responsive Systems' Buffer Pool Tool.

DB2 Buffer Pool Guidelines

You can use the following guidelines to ensure an effective DB2 buffer pool specification at your shop.

Be Aware of Buffer Pool Thresholds   Be aware of the following overall effects of the buffer pool thresholds:

Data Manager Threshold	This is referred to as a critical buffer pool. When 95% of a buffer pool's pages are unavailable, the Buffer Manager does a GETPAGE and a release of the page for every accessed row. This is very inefficient and should be avoided at all costs.
Immediate Write Threshold	When 97.5% of a buffer pool's pages are unavailable, deferred write is disabled. All writes are performed synchronously until the percentage of unavailable pages is below 97.5%.

TUNING STRATEGY

Increase the size of your buffer pools when these thresholds are reached:

Data Manager threshold : 95%

Immediate Write threshold (IWTH): 97.5%

It is best to avoid reaching these thresholds because they degrade performance. (The immediate write threshold degrades performance the most.)

Be Generous with Your Buffer Pool Allocations   A buffer pool that is too large is almost always better than a buffer pool that is too small. However, do not make the buffer pool so large that it requires paging to DASD.

Monitor BP0 Carefully   The DB2 Catalog and DB2 Directory are assigned to BP0. This cannot be changed. Therefore, even if other buffer pools are used for most of your application tablespaces and indexes, pay close attention to BP0. A poorly performing DB2 Catalog or DB2 Directory can severely hamper system-wide performance.

V8 As of DB2 V8, similar precautions should be taken with BP8K0 and BP16K0, as these buffer pools also house DB2 Catalog objects.

Allocate BP32K   Specify a 32K buffer pool—even if you have no tablespaces in your system with 32K pages—to ensure that joins requiring more than 4K can operate. If BP32K is not defined, at least with a minimal number of pages, joins referencing columns that add up to 4097 or greater can fail.

The default size of BP32K is 12 pages, which is small, but perhaps a good starting place if you allow large joins. Some shops avoid allocating BP32K to ensure that large joins are not attempted. Avoiding BP32K allocation is also an option, depending on your shop standards.

Be Aware of the 32K Buffer Pool Names   Remember that BP32 and BP32K are two different buffer pools. BP32 is one of the 50 4K buffer pools. BP32K is one of the 10 32K buffer pools. If you miss or add an erroneous *K*, you may wind up using or allocating the wrong buffer pool.

Consider Reserving a Buffer Pool for Tuning   Even if you do not utilize multiple buffer pools, consider using your unused buffer pools for performance monitoring and tuning. When a performance problem is identified, tablespaces or indexes suspected of causing the problem can be altered to use the tuning buffer pool. Then you can turn on traces and rerun the application causing the performance problem. When monitoring the performance of the application, I/O, GETPAGEs, and the usage characteristics of the buffer pool can be monitored separately from the other buffer pools.

Consider Defining a Sort Buffer Pool for DSNDB07   If you assign DSNDB07 to its own buffer pool, consider the appropriate parameters to use. First of all, the VPSEQT parameter is quite useful. Recall that VPSEQT is used to set the sequential steal threshold. Since most activity to DSNDB07 is sequential, VPSEQT should be set very high, to 95 for example. But do not set VPSEQT to 100 because not all sorting activity is sequential.

Furthermore, you can set the immediate write thresholds (DWQT and VDWQT) to the VPSEQT size.

> **NOTE**
>
> Setting the deferred write thresholds is tricky business. If you set them relatively high (for example, same as VPSEQT) you will maintain pages in the pools and avoid writes. However, you may want to specify very low deferred write thresholds to set up trickle write. This avoids the problems that can ensue when DB2 has to write a huge amount of data because the write was deferred. Different options will work for different companies based on your processing requirements.

Finally, it is a good idea to use the BP7 buffer pool for DSNDB07 so as to minimize confusion. Because both end in the number 7, it is easy to remember that one works with the other.

Optimize BP0   BP0 is probably the single most important buffer pool in a DB2 subsystem. The system resources, namely the DB2 Catalog and DB2 Directory objects, are assigned to BP0 and cannot be moved. Therefore, many organizations decide to use BP0 to hold only these resources by failing to assign other objects to BP0. This is a good strategy because placing other objects into BP0 can degrade the performance of processes that access the DB2 Catalog or Directory.

The size of your DB2 subsystem dictates the proper sizing of BP0. Consider starting with a VPSIZE of 2000 pages. Monitor usage of BP0 and increase VPSIZE if access patterns warrant.

The proper specification of VPSEQT, DWQT, and VDWQT will depend on your shop's access patterns against the DB2 Catalog and Directory.

Converting Active Buffer Pool to Use Data Space   For DB2 V7, you can use data spaces for virtual buffer pools. To convert an active DB2 virtual buffer pool to use a data space, perform the following steps:

1. Delete the active buffer pool by using ALTER BUFFERPOOL to specify VPSIZE(0).

2. Stop all tablespaces and indexes that are using the buffer pool.

3. Issue the ALTER BUFFERPOOL command again specifying VPTYPE(DATASPACE). You will also need to specify the appropriate VPSIZE for the buffer pool.

Start all of the objects that were previously stopped.

The total size of data space virtual buffer pools is limited to 32GB (for 4K page size). This limit is imposed because there is a maximum of 8 million "page manipulation blocks" in the DBM1 address space.

V8 Data space virtual buffer pools are no longer supported as of DB2 Version 8.

Hiperpools

V8 For DB2 V7 and earlier releases, you can use hiperpools to back up your virtual buffer pools. Hiperpools are no longer supported as of DB2 V8, though.

Hiperpools can be considered extensions to the regular buffer pools, which are also referred to as virtual pools. Hiperpools use hiperspaces to extend DB2 virtual buffer pools. Working in conjunction with the virtual pools, hiperpools provide a second level of data caching. When old information is targeted to be discarded from (or, moved out of) the virtual buffer pool, it will be moved to the hiperpool instead (if a hiperpool has been defined for that buffer pool).

Only clean pages will be moved to the hiperpool, though. Clean pages are those in which the data that was modified has already been written back to DASD. No data with pending modifications will ever reside in a hiperpool.

Each of the 80 virtual pools can optionally have a hiperpool associated with it. There is a one-to-one relationship between virtual pools and hiperpools. A virtual pool can have one and only one hiperpool associated with it, but it also can have none. A hiperpool must have one and only one virtual pool associated with it.

Hiperpools are page-addressable, so before data can be accessed by an application, it must be moved from the hiperpool to the virtual pool (which is byte-addressable). Hiperpools are backed by expanded storage only, whereas virtual pools are backed by central storage, expanded storage, and possibly DASD if paging occurs. The hiperpool page control blocks reside in the DBM1 address space and thus contribute to virtual storage constraints.

When you specify a virtual pool without a hiperpool, you are letting the operating system allocate the buffer pool storage required in both central and expanded memory. Keeping this information in mind, consider using hiperpools instead of specifying extremely large virtual pools without a hiperpool.

A good reason to utilize hiperpools is to overcome the 1.6GB limit for all virtual buffer pools (prior to V8). If your buffering needs exceed 1.6GB, you can specify virtual buffer pools up to 1.6GB, with larger hiperpools backing the virtual pools. Of course, you can also consider using data spaces for your virtual pools if you are running in 64 bit mode.

V8 Of course, the maximum buffer pool sizes were increased for DB2 V8 to the limit of the z/OS architecture, which is 1TB. (Also, the term "virtual" buffer pool is obsolete as of DB2 V8; virtual pool, virtual buffer pool, and buffer pool are all synonymous as of DB2 V8.)

28

TUNING STRATEGY

For pre-V8 systems, consider specifying virtual pools that will completely fit in central storage and hiperpools associated with the virtual pools. The DB2 Buffer Manager will handle the movement from expanded to central storage and should be more efficient than simply implementing a single large virtual pool. Of course, you will need to monitor the system to ensure that the virtual pool is utilizing central storage in an optimally efficient manner.

Do not over-allocate hiperpool storage. If you exceed the amount of expanded storage you have available, performance will eventually suffer.

Figure 28.3 illustrates the buffer pool to hiperpool relationship. This diagram outlines the basic functionality of hiperpools and buffer pools. Data is read from disk to central storage in the virtual buffer pool. Over time the data may be moved to the hiperpool. Once moved to the hiperpool, before it can be read again by a DB2 program, it must be moved back to the virtual buffer pool. Hiperpools are backed by expanded storage as a hiperspace. Virtual buffer pools are backed by central and expanded storage, and can possibly page to DASD for auxiliary storage.

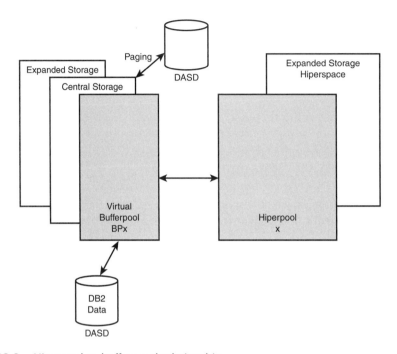

FIGURE 28.3   Hiperpool to buffer pool relationship.

> **CAUTION**
>
> The total of all hiperpools defined cannot exceed 8GB.

Hiperpool Parameters

The ALTER BUFFERPOOL command can be used to tune hiperpool options as well as virtual pool options. The hiperpool parameter options are described in the following paragraphs.

The first option, CASTOUT, indicates whether hiperpool pages are stealable by the operating system. The value can be either YES or NO. Specifying YES enables OS/390 to discard data in the hiperpool if an expanded storage shortage is encountered. A value of NO prohibits OS/390 from discarding hiperpool data unless one of the following occurs:

- The hiperpool is deleted

- Hiperspace maintenance occurs

- Hiperspace storage is explicitly released

Just as VPSIZE controls the size of virtual pools, HPSIZE is used to specify the size of each individual hiperpool. When the size of a hiperpool is altered, it immediately expands or contracts as specified. The value can range from 0 to 2,097,152 for 4K hiperpools, from 0 to 1,048,576 for 8KB hiperpools, from 0 to 524,288 for 16KB hiperpools, and from 0 to 262,144 for 32K hiperpools. The total of all hiperpools defined cannot exceed 8GB.

TUNING STRATEGY

A good starting point for HPSIZE is three times the amount of VPSIZE. If necessary, you can increase HPSIZE from there as you tune your buffer pool and hiperpool usage. Hiperpools allocated with less than three times the associated VPSIZE are usually not very efficient.

Sequential steal thresholds also can be specified for hiperpools, using the HPSEQT parameter. HPSEQT is expressed as a percentage of the hiperpool size (HPSIZE). It specifies the percentage of the hiperpool that can be monopolized by sequential processing, such as sequential prefetch. The value of HPSEQT can range from 0 to 100, and the default is 80.

TUNING STRATEGY

If you know that the majority of your sequential prefetch requests will never be accessed again, you may want to tune your hiperpools to avoid sequential data. Do this by specifying HPSEQT=0. This ensures that only randomly accessed data will be moved to the hiperpool.

There are no deferred write thresholds for hiperpools because only clean data is stored in the hiperpool. Therefore, pages never need to be written from the hiperpool to DASD.

Data Sharing Group Buffer Pools

If data sharing is implemented, group buffer pools are required. A group buffer pool must be defined for each buffer pool defined to each data sharing member. Data is cached from the local buffer pools to the group buffer pools during the processing of a data sharing request.

A page set is said to be GBP-dependent when two or more data sharing group members have concurrent read/write interest in it. The page set is marked as GBP-dependent during the update process and changed pages are written to the group buffer pool. GBP-dependent marking also affects DB2 Catalog and Directory page sets of the shared DB2 catalog. For GBP-dependent page sets, all changed pages are first written to the group buffer pool.

Changed data pages are written to the coupling facility at COMMIT for GBP-dependent page sets. This enables committed data to be immediately available to the other DB2 data sharing group members. It also extends the length of time it takes to commit and therefore makes it important to issue frequent COMMITs in your programs.

The following describes a few typical operations and how a page is passed among the local and group buffer pools. The following scenario is based on a data sharing environment with two member subsystems (DB2A and DB2B):

- An application in DB2A updates a column. The DB2A subsystem checks the coupling facility to determine if it should read the page from the global buffer pools or directly from disk. If DB2A determines that the page is not cached globally, it will read the page(s) from shared DASD and store the page(s) in its local buffer pool—for example, BP6.

28

- An application in DB2B wants to update the same page. A global lock (P-Lock, discussed in Chapter 23, "Locking DB2 Data") is taken indicating to the member that the page is shared. DB2A is notified and writes the changed data page to global buffer pool GBP6.

- DB2B retrieves the page from the global buffer pools and puts it in its own BP6.

- DB2B updates the data page and moves it back to the global buffer pool. The coupling facility invalidates the page contained in the local buffer pool for DB2A.

- If DB2A needs to reread the data page, it will determine that the page has been marked invalid. Therefore, the page is retrieved from global buffer pool GBP6.

The GBPCACHE Parameter

The GBPCACHE clause can be specified on the CREATE and ALTER statement for tablespaces and indexes. GBPCACHE is used to indicate how the global buffer pool is to be used for a particular tablespace or index. There are two options for GBPCACHE: CHANGED and ALL.

If CHANGED is specified, and the tablespace or index has no inter-DB2 read/write interest, the group buffer pool will not be used. When an inter-DB2 read/write interest exists, only changed pages are written to the group buffer pool.

If GBPCACHE is set to ALL, changed pages are written to the group buffer pool. Clean pages are written to the group buffer pool as they are read from the shared disk.

The Castout Process

Changed data is moved from a group buffer pool to disk by means of a castout process. The group buffer pool castout process reads the pages contained in the GBP and writes them to the owning DB2's local buffer, as well as to the physical DASD devices. This process is depicted in Figure 28.4. The castout process moves data from a group buffer pool to DASD through one of the data sharing group members. This is required because there is no direct connection from a coupling facility to DASD.

The coupling facility is still able to update pages during the castout process. The castout process is triggered when:

- The changed page threshold for a page set is reached.

- The total changed page threshold for the group buffer pool is reached.

- The group buffer pool checkpoint is reached.

> **NOTE**
>
> Because the coupling facility may contain data that is more recent than what is contained on the DASD devices, DB2 employs coupling facility recovery mechanisms to recover the data in case of coupling facility failure.

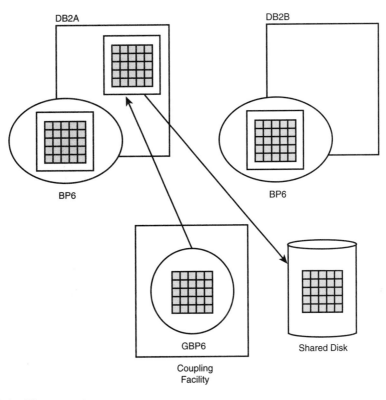

FIGURE 28.4 The castout process.

Data Sharing Buffer Pool Guidelines

Consider the following guidelines when specifying buffer pools for data sharing.

Select Group Buffer Pool Thresholds with Care The castout process can have a negative impact on data sharing performance. Keep castout process execution to a minimum by carefully considering the thresholds that are related to each group buffer pool. You can control the castout process by changing the two group buffer pool thresholds:

- The group buffer pool castout threshold determines the total number of changed pages that can exist in the group buffer pool before castout occurs. DB2 casts out a sufficient amount of data to ensure that the number of changed pages is below the threshold. The group buffer pool castout threshold is specified as a percentage of the total number of pages in the group buffer pool. The default value is 50, which specifies that castout is initiated when the group buffer pool is 50% full of changed pages.

- The class castout threshold also is used to control when data is cast out of a group buffer pool. DB2 internally maps modified data pages belonging to the same table-space, index, or partition to the same castout class queues. A castout class queue is an internal mechanism used by DB2 to control the castout process for groups of page sets. When DB2 writes modified pages to the group buffer pool, it determines

28

how many modified pages are in a particular class castout queue. When the number of modified pages for a castout class queue exceeds the threshold, DB2 casts out data pages from that queue. The castout class threshold is specified as a percentage of the total number of changed pages in the group buffer pool for a given castout class. The default for the class castout is 10, indicating that castout is initiated when 10% of the group buffer pool contains modified pages for the class.

Do Not Underestimate the Size of the Cache Structure   The size of the group buffer pool structure has a major influence on the frequency of castout process execution. This can negatively affect performance.

The total cache structure size affects performance similar to the way that VPSIZE affects the performance of non-group buffer pools (virtual pools). In addition, the less memory allocated to the group buffer pool, the more frequent the castout process.

The number of directory entries also affects performance. A directory entry contains control information for one page regardless of the number of places that page is cached. There is a one-to-one correspondence between cached physical data pages and directory entries. If a page is in the group buffer pool and in the virtual buffer pools of two members, there is only one directory entry for the page. Each directory entry is 208 bytes for 4K pages and 264 bytes for 32K pages. A directory entry is used by the coupling facility to determine where to send cross-invalidation signals when a page of data is changed or when that directory entry must be reused. The higher the write-to-read ratio, the more directory entries are needed.

The final impact on performance is the number of data entries. Data entries are the actual places where the data page resides. The greater the number of distinct pages that are cached, the more directory entries are needed.

Use Partitioned Tablespaces   Design for parallel processing by using partitioned tablespaces for data that is accessed in a data sharing environment. This encourages the use of Sysplex query parallelism. DB2 performs effective parallel processing only when data is partitioned.

Consider Group Buffer Pool Duplexing   Use group buffer pool duplexing to make recovery easier. Without duplexing, your only options for recovery in the event of a group buffer pool failure were to recover the group buffer pool or to rebuild it. With duplexing, a secondary group buffer pool is available on standby in another coupling facility. The secondary group buffer pool can take over if the primary group buffer pool fails.

With a duplexed group buffer pool, you have two allocations of the same group buffer pool that use one logical connection. One allocation is called the primary structure, the other is the secondary structure. The primary structure is used for cross-invalidation and page registration, and it is the structure from which changed data is cast out to DASD. When changes are written to the primary structure, they are written to the secondary structure, as well.

IRLM Tuning Options

Until now, I have covered tuning options for the DB2 database address space and system services address space. You also can tune the IRLM address space.

When the IRLM is started, several parameters can be specified in the JCL for the IRLM. These options can have a significant effect on DB2 performance.

DEADLOK   Indicates when the IRLM executes a deadlock detection cycle. The IRLM must check for deadlocks frequently to avoid long waits for resources that will never be made available.

ITRACE   Indicates whether an IRLM trace will be started.

PC   Indicates where IRLM locks will be stored in memory.

> **TUNING STRATEGY**
>
> A good starting value for the DEADLOK parameter is 15 seconds. However, this parameter should be evenly divisible into the IRLMRWT DSNZPARM value to ensure synchronization between IRLM deadlock detection and DB2 timeout waits.

> **TUNING STRATEGY**
>
> Never issue an IRLM trace for an IRLM used by DB2. Specify ITRACE=NO. The IRLM trace rapidly degrades performance and does not provide much useful information.

> **TUNING STRATEGY**
>
> Specify PC=NO. This guarantees that cross memory services are not used for DB2 locking. Instead, locks are stored in ECSA and are directly addressable. This will optimize the locking performance.
>
> Before using ECSA to store IRLM locks, though, be aware that ECSA is not protected and an erratic system task can potentially overwrite ECSA storage.

Tuning the Database Design

The design of DB2 objects also can be tuned for performance. If changes to DB2 tables, columns, keys, or referential constraints are required, however, the application logic usually must be changed also. Retrofitting application code after it has been coded and tested is not simple.

Several tuning opportunities do not affect application code. When multiple tablespaces are assigned to a DB2 database, locking of the DBD in the DB2 Directory occurs when DDL (ALTER, CREATE, or DROP) is issued for an object in that database. This effectively freezes all access to objects defined to that database.

28

When a high degree of object alteration, creation, and removal occurs in a DB2 database, avoid placing critical production tables in the tablespaces in that database. If they are already in that database, consider moving them to a separate database. This does not involve any application programming changes, but DB2 utility parameters that access tablespaces (such as `DBNAME.TSNAME`) might need to be changed.

Also, if performance is severely degraded, consider denormalization. Several techniques for denormalizing DB2 tables are discussed in Chapter 5.

Be sure to specify proper performance-oriented parameters for all DB2 objects. For an in-depth discussion of these, refer to Chapter 5. A synopsis of these parameters is provided in Table 28.2.

TABLE 28.2   Coding DDL for Performance

DB2 Object	Performance-Oriented DDL Options
Database	Limit DDL against production databases.
Tablespace	In general, use segmented tablespaces.
	Partition tablespaces with very large tables.
	Partition tablespaces to take advantage of parallelism.
	Segment tablespaces for mass delete efficiency.
	Consider simple tablespaces if you need to intermix rows from multiple tables.
	Specify `CLOSE NO`.
	Specify `LOCKSIZE PAGE` to enforce page-level locking and eliminate lock escalation.
	Use `LOCKSIZE ROW` only rarely to enforce row-level locking.
	Specify `LOCKSIZE ANY` to let DB2 handle locking.
	Specify `LOCKSIZE TABLESPACE` for read-only tables.
	Specify free space to tune inserts and delay page splits.
Table	In general, specify one table per tablespace.
	Do not specify an audit parameter unless it is absolutely necessary for the application.
	Avoid `FIELDPROC`s, `EDITPROC`s, and `VALIDPROC`s unless they are absolutely necessary for the application—consider triggers instead.
	Specify `WITH RESTRICT ON DROP` to inadvertent drops.
	Use DB2 referential integrity instead of application referential integrity.
	Use `SEQUENCE` objects instead of `IDENTITY` columns to assign sequential values to a column.
	Use check constraints and triggers instead of application logic to enforce column data values.
View	Do not use one view per base table.
	Use views to enforce security.
	Use views to enforce join criteria.
Alias	Use aliases as globally accessible synonyms.
Index	Create indexes for critical SQL predicates.
	Index to avoid sorts.
	Specify `CLOSE NO`.
	Specify free space to tune inserts.
	Cluster the most frequently used index.

Tuning the Application

As was evident from the DB2 performance tuning pie, tuning the application design provides the single greatest benefit to overall DB2 performance. You can use several methods to accomplish this, each of which is covered in this section. Before proceeding, however, I will review the access paths, particularly the information about filter factors.

Analyzing Access Paths

To determine the actual "behind the scenes" operations being performed by DB2 for each SQL statement, you must analyze the access path chosen for the statement by the DB2 optimizer. An access path, as discussed in Chapter 21, "The Optimizer," is the method DB2 chooses to carry out the data manipulation requested in SQL statements. The DB2 EXPLAIN statement places information about the access paths in a PLAN_TABLE, which can be inspected by a technical analyst. You can use the information in Chapter 25 in conjunction with the access path data to create a complete picture of the operations being performed for each SQL statement.

Is DB2 on its own when making access path determinations? The ideal answer to this question would be "Yes." It would be wonderful if DB2 always had all the information it needed, required no external input, and never chose the wrong access path. However, we do not yet live in this ideal world. DB2 sometimes chooses an inefficient access path over another, more efficient one for the following reasons:

- The statistics might be outdated if RUNSTATS was never run or not run recently. This causes the access paths to be chosen based on incorrect assumptions about the current environment.

- Certain physical parameters are not yet taken into account by the optimizer when it determines access paths. Some examples are differences between physical storage devices (the model of DASD device, or faster devices), the number of data set extents, and COBOL (or other 3GL and 4GL) code.

- Concurrent processes (scheduling) are not considered by the optimizer.

- The DB2 optimizer is prone to the same problems associated with every computer program; it is fallible. (However, given its complexity, its success rate is admirable.)

For these reasons, you may decide to artificially influence the optimizer's decision process. Techniques for accomplishing this are addressed in the next section.

Before I move on, I will survey the factors addressed by the DB2 optimizer. The first consideration is the versions of DB2 that are being used—they should be the same in test and production. Obviously, there are access path techniques available to newer releases of DB2 than were available to older releases.

The optimizer takes the size of the buffer pools into account when determining access paths. As the size of the buffer pools increases, DB2 assumes that read efficiency increases also.

The optimizer also takes into account the type of CPU being used during access path selection. DB2 chooses different access techniques based on the perceived performance of the processor. This is important to remember when modeling SQL in a test DB2 subsystem using production statistics. If the production DB2 subsystem has a different number of buffers or if it runs on a different CPU, the optimizer might choose a different access path in the production environment than it did in the test environment, even if the SQL and the DB2 Catalog statistics are identical.

To get around this, the following measures can be taken:

- When evaluating access paths for SQL statements using production statistics, be sure that the test DB2 subsystem is using the same CPU or a different CPU of the same type. This may be difficult for larger shops with several DB2 subsystems running on various machines, all configured differently.

- Specify test DB2 buffer pools to be the same as the production buffer pools to ensure that access paths do not change as a result of different buffer pool sizes. However, setting test buffer pools as high as production buffer pools can waste memory resources, and setting production buffer pools as low as test buffer pools will degrade performance.

The wisest course of action is simply to realize that access path differences will exist between DB2 subsystems and not to try to avoid access path discrepancies between DB2 subsystems. Running DB2 subsystems with artificial constraints such as those just outlined is counterproductive to optimizing DB2 performance. Just remember that a test access path determined using production statistics does not guarantee that the production access path will be identical. Besides, it is wise to continuously monitor the production access paths for all SQL statements, because they can change when plans or packages are bound or rebound, or when RUNSTATS is run for dynamic SQL.

> **TUNING STRATEGY**
>
> Analyze *all* production DB2 access paths. Some shops analyze only the access paths for static SQL embedded in application programs, but this is inadequate. Develop a plan for analyzing all components of DB2 programs, including the following:
>
> - The structure of the application program to ensure that proper coding techniques are used. Also be sure that otherwise efficient-looking SQL embedded in a program loop does not occur without a proper reason. In other words, a finely-tuned SQL statement inside of a loop that runs two million times is likely to cause performance problems.
>
> - All SQL, whether static or dynamic, embedded in application programs. This includes SQL in online transactions, batch programs, client/server programs, report writers, 4GLs, CASE tools, decision support systems, and packaged applications.
>
> - All regularly executed or critical ad hoc, dynamic SQL. This includes, but is not necessarily limited to, SQL executed by SPUFI, QMF, DSNTIAD, DSNTIAUL, or DSNTEP2, SQL generated by any application system "on the fly," dynamic SQL in packaged applications, SQL generated or submitted using vendor tools, data warehouse queries, and SQL shipped from remote sites, including remote mainframes, minis, and PC workstations.
>
> - All stored procedure and user-defined function programs that contain SQL.

- All SQL in triggers. When a trigger is created DB2 also creates a trigger package but no EXPLAIN data. To EXPLAIN the trigger package you will need to REBIND it specifying EXPLAIN YES.

- Every SQL statement in the DB2 program must be followed by a check of the SQLCODE or SQLSTATE.

If you utilize triggers in your DB2 databases, you need to be aware that code exists within the triggers. This code needs to be examined regularly to ensure that it is optimal given the database design and the application processes that modify the data, causing the trigger to fire. Even if the SQL in the trigger is efficient, other processes performed by the trigger may not be efficient.

Influencing the Optimizer

There are several methods of tuning the system to change access paths or influence access path selection. This section describes several observations on changing the access paths selected by DB2.

The DB2 optimizer is one of the most intricate pieces of software on the market. It does an admirable job of optimizing SQL requests. To achieve this level of success, the optimizer contains a great deal of performance-specific expertise. For example, the optimizer estimates both elapsed times and CPU times when choosing an access path. When a SQL statement is rebound, the optimizer might choose a new access path that increases CPU time but decreases elapsed time. Most shops choose to enhance elapsed time at the expense of additional CPU use because elapsed time has a measurable effect on user productivity. In other words, it is good to trade off CPU cycles for user satisfaction, and the DB2 optimizer attempts to accomplish this. Of course, if both CPU and elapsed time can be reduced, the optimizer will try to do so.

However, the optimizer is not infallible. Sometimes the application analyst understands the nature of the data better than DB2 (at the present time). You can influence the optimizer into choosing an access path that you know is a better one but the optimizer thinks is a worse one. As the functionality and complexity of the optimizer is enhanced from release to release of DB2, the need to trick the optimizer in this way will diminish.

There are five ways to influence the optimizer's access path decisions:

- Standard, DB2-based methods

- Tweaking SQL statements

- Specifying the OPTIMIZE FOR n ROWS clause

- Updating DB2 Catalog statistics

- Using OPTHINT to indicate that an access path in the PLAN_TABLE should be chosen

The next section discusses each of these methods.

Standard Methods

Of all the methods for influencing the DB2 optimizer, standard DB2 methods are the only mandatory ones. Try all the standard methods covered in this section before attempting one of the other methods. There are several reasons for this.

The standard methods place the burden for generating optimal access paths on the shoulders of DB2, which is where it usually belongs. They also use IBM-supported techniques available for every version and release of DB2. Finally, these methods generally provide the greatest gain for the smallest effort.

There are four standard methods for tuning DB2 access paths. The first method is ensuring that accurate statistics are available using the RUNSTATS utility and the BIND or REBIND command. RUNSTATS, which is discussed in detail in Chapter 34, "Catalog Manipulation Utilities," populates the DB2 Catalog with statistics that indicate the state of your DB2 objects, including the following:

Their organization

Clustering information

The cardinality of tablespaces, tables, columns, and indexes

The range of values for columns

All of these factors are considered by the optimizer when it chooses what it deems to be the optimal access path for a given SQL statement.

> **TUNING STRATEGY**
>
> Execute RUNSTATS at least once for every tablespace, table, column, and index known to your DB2 subsystem. Schedule regular RUNSTATS executions for all DB2 objects that are not read-only. This keeps the DB2 Catalog information current, enabling proper access path selection.

The second standard method for tuning DB2 access paths is ensuring that the DB2 objects are properly organized. Disorganized objects, if properly reorganized, might be chosen for an access path. An object is disorganized when data modification statements executed against the object cause data to be stored in a non-optimal fashion, such as non-clustered data or data that exists on a different page than its RID, thereby spanning more than one physical page. To organize these objects more efficiently, run the REORG utility, followed by RUNSTATS and REBIND. In-depth coverage of the REORG utility and guidelines for its use are in Chapter 33, "Data Organization Utilities."

> **TUNING STRATEGY**
>
> Use the DB2 Catalog queries in Chapter 26, "DB2 Object Monitoring Using the DB2 Catalog and RTS," to determine when your DB2 tablespaces and indexes need to be reorganized:
>
> - Reorganize a tablespace when the CLUSTERRATIO of its clustering index falls below 95%. (Schedule this so that it does not affect system performance and availability.)
>
> - Reorganize any index (or index partition) when LEAFDIST is greater than 200. If the value of FREEPAGE for the index is not 0, reorganize only when LEAFDIST is greater than 300. Of course, you should not blindly reorganize indexes when they reach these thresholds. You

should weigh the observed performance degradation against the cost of running the index reorganization jobs before reorganizing your application's indexes.

- Reorganize all DB2 tablespaces and indexes when their data set is in multiple physical extents. Before reorganizing, ensure that space allocations have been modified to cause all data to be stored in a single extent.

You may want to reorganize more frequently than indicated here by creating scheduled REORG jobs for heavily accessed or critical DB2 tablespaces and indexes. This limits performance problems due to disorganized DB2 objects and reduces the number of reorganizations that must be manually scheduled or submitted by a DBA or performance analyst.

The third standard method for tuning DB2 access paths is to encourage parallelism. Consider changing simple and segmented tablespaces to partitioned tablespaces to encourage I/O, CPU, and Sysplex parallelism. Furthermore, it may be advantageous to repartition already partitioned tablespaces to better align ranges of values, thereby promoting better parallel access.

The fourth and final standard method for tuning DB2 access paths is ensuring that there are proper indexes by creating new indexes or dropping unnecessary and unused indexes. DB2 relies on indexes to achieve optimum performance.

Analyze the predicates in your SQL statements to determine whether there is an index that DB2 can use. Indexes can be used efficiently by DB2 if the first column of the index key is specified in an indexable predicate in the SQL statement. Refer to Chapter 2, "Data Manipulation Guidelines," for a discussion of indexable and non-indexable predicates. If no index meets these requirements, consider creating one. As you index more columns referenced in predicates, performance generally increases.

Dropping unused indexes is another critical part of application tuning. Every table INSERT and DELETE incurs I/O to every index defined for that table. Every UPDATE of indexed columns incurs I/O to every index defined for that column. If an index is not being used, drop it. This reduces the I/O incurred for data modification SQL statements, reduces RUNSTATS resource requirements, and speeds REORG and RECOVER processing.

Tweaking the SQL Statement

If you do not want to change the DB2 Catalog statistics but the standard methods outlined in the preceding section are not helpful, you might consider tweaking the offending SQL statement. *Tweaking* is the process of changing a statement in a non-intuitive fashion, without altering its functionality.

At times, you may need to disable a specific index from being considered by the optimizer. One method of achieving this is to append OR 0 = 1 to the predicate. For example, consider a query against the EMP table on which two indexes exist: one on EMPNO and one on WORKDEPT. Appending OR 0 = 1 (as shown next) to the WORKDEPT predicate will cause DB2 to avoid using an index on WORKDEPT.

```
SELECT   EMPNO, WORKDEPT, EDLEVEL, SALARY
FROM     DSN8610.EMP
WHERE    EMPNO BETWEEN '000020' AND '000350'
AND      (WORKDEPT > 'A01' OR 0 = 1);
```

28

The OR `0` = 1 clause does not change the results of the query, but it can change the access path chosen.

Another method of tweaking SQL to influence DB2's access path selection is to code redundant predicates. Recall from Chapter 21 that when DB2 calculates the filter factor for a SQL statement, it multiplies the filter factors for all predicates connected with AND.

TUNING STRATEGY

You can lower the filter factor of a query by adding redundant predicates as follows:

Change this statement		To this	
SELECT	LASTNAME	SELECT	LASTNAME
FROM	DSN8810.EMP	FROM	DSN8810.EMP
WHERE	WORKDEPT = :VAR	WHERE	WORKDEPT = :VAR
		AND	WORKDEPT = :VAR
		AND	WORKDEPT = :VAR

The two predicates added to the end are redundant and do not affect SQL statement functionally. However, DB2 calculates a lower filter factor, which increases the possibility that an index on the WORKDEPT column will be chosen. The lower filter factor also increases the possibility that the table will be chosen as the outer table, if the redundant predicates are used for a join.

TUNING STRATEGY

When redundant predicates are added to enhance performance, as outlined in the preceding strategy, be sure to document the reasons for the extra predicates. Failure to do so may cause a maintenance programmer to assume that the redundant predicates are an error and thus remove them.

Another option for getting a small amount of performance out of an SQL statement is to change the physical order of the predicates in your SQL code. DB2 evaluates predicates first by predicate type, then according to the order in which it encounters the predicates. The four types of SQL predicates are listed in the order that DB2 processes them:

Equality, in which a column is tested for equivalence to another column, a variable, or a literal

Ranges, in which a column is tested against a range of values (for example, greater than, less than, or BETWEEN)

IN, where a column is tested for equivalence against a list of values

Stage 2 predicates

TUNING STRATEGY

Place the most restrictive predicates at the beginning of your predicate list. For example, consider the following query:

```
SELECT    LASTNAME
FROM      DSN8810.EMP
WHERE     WORKDEPT = 'A00'
AND       SEX = 'M'
```

The first predicate has a lower filter factor than the second because there are fewer workers in department A00 than there are males in the entire company. This does not increase performance by much, but it can shave a little off a query's processing time.

Before deciding to tweak SQL statements to achieve different access paths, remember that you are changing SQL code in a nonintuitive fashion. For each modification you make to increase performance, document the reasons in the program, the data dictionary, and the system documentation. Otherwise, the tweaked SQL could be maintained after it is no longer required, or modified away when it still is required for performance.

Also remember that the changes could enhance performance for one release of DB2 but result in no gain or decreased efficiency in subsequent releases. Re-examine your SQL for each new version and release of DB2.

OPTIMIZE FOR *n* ROWS

Another method of influencing access path selection is to specify OPTIMIZE FOR *n* ROWS for a cursor SELECT statement. This clause enables programmers to specify the estimated maximum number of rows that will be retrieved.

By indicating that a different number of rows will be returned than DB2 anticipates, you can influence access path selection. For example, consider the following statement:

```
EXEC SQL
    DECLARE OPT_CUR FOR
        SELECT   WORKDEPT, EMPNO, SALARY
        FROM     DSN8810.EMP
        WHERE    WORKDEPT IN ('A00', 'D11')
        OPTIMIZE FOR 5 ROWS
END-EXEC.
```

The number of rows to be returned has been set to 5, even though this query could return more than 5 rows. DB2 formulates an access path optimized for 5 rows. More rows can be retrieved, but performance could suffer if you greatly exceed the estimated maximum.

This type of tuning is preferable to both updating the DB2 Catalog statistics and tweaking the SQL statement. It provides more information to DB2's optimization process, thereby giving DB2 the opportunity to establish a better access path. The crucial point, though, is that DB2 is doing the optimization; no manual updates or artificial SQL constructs are required.

28

TUNING STRATEGY

When using the OPTIMIZE FOR n ROWS clause, make n as accurate as possible. An accurate estimate gives DB2 the best opportunity to achieve optimum performance for the statement and also helps document the purpose of the SQL statement. Using an accurate value for n also positions your application to take advantage of future enhancements to the OPTIMIZE FOR n ROWS clause.

When coding online transactions in which 25 rows (for example) are displayed on the screen, use the OPTIMIZE FOR n ROWS clause, setting n equal to 25.

NOTE

When using OPTIMIZE FOR n ROWS to disable list prefetch, set the value of n to 1. This technique works well to ensure that list prefetch is not used.

CAUTION

DB2 uses the value of n for the block size of a distributed network request. The smaller the value of n, the fewer rows sent across the network for each block. The only exception is that when n=1, DB2 will set the block size to 16.

Changing DB2 Catalog Statistics

When the standard methods of influencing DB2's access path selection are not satisfactory, you can resort to updating the statistics in the DB2 Catalog. Only certain DB2 Catalog statistics can be modified using SQL UPDATE, INSERT, and DELETE statements instead of the normal method using RUNSTATS. This SQL modification of the DB2 Catalog can be performed only by a SYSADM.

Table 28.3 lists the DB2 Catalog statistics that can be modified. You can use this table to determine which DB2 Catalog columns are updateable (using SQL) and which are used by the optimizer during sequential and parallel access path determination. Remember, for parallel queries, the sequential access path is generated and only then is the parallel access strategy generated.

TABLE 28.3   The Updateable DB2 Catalog Statistics

Catalog Table	Column	How Used?	Description
SYSCOLDIST	FREQUENCYF	Y	Percentage that COLVALUE in the column named in NAME occurs
	COLVALUE	Y	Column value for this statistic
	CARDF	Y	Number of distinct values
	COLGROUPCOLNO	Y	The set of columns for the statistics
	NUMCOLUMNS	Y	Number of columns for the statistics
	TYPE	Y	Type of stats: C for cardinality, or F for frequent value
	STATSTIME	N	Indicates the time RUNSTATS was run to generate these statistics

TABLE 28.3 Continued

Catalog Table	Column	How Used?	Description
SYSCOLDISTSTATS	PARTITION	N	The partition to which this statistic applies
	FREQUENCYF	N	Percentage that COLVALUE in the column named in NAME occurs
	COLVALUE	N	Column value for this statistic
	TYPE	N	Type of statistics (cardinality or frequent value)
	CARDF	N	Number of distinct values
	COLGROUPCOLNO	N	The set of columns for the statistics
	KEYCARDDATA	N	Representation of the estimate of distinct values in this partition
	STATSTIME	N	Indicates the time RUNSTATS was run to generate these statistics
SYSCOLSTATS	LOWKEY	P	Lowest value for the column
	LOW2KEY	P	Second lowest value for the column
	HIGHKEY	P	Highest value for the column
	HIGH2KEY	P	Second highest value for the column
	COLCARD	P	Number of distinct values for the column
	COLCARDDATA	P	Number of distinct values for the column
	STATSTIME	N	Indicates the time RUNSTATS was run to generate these statistics
SYSCOLUMNS	LOW2KEY	Y	Second lowest value for the column
	HIGH2KEY	Y	Second highest value for the column
	COLCARDF	Y	Number of distinct values for the column
	STATSTIME	N	Indicates the time RUNSTATS was run to generate these statistics
SYSINDEXES	CLUSTERRATIOF	Y	Percentage of rows in clustered order
	CLUSTERED	N	Indicates whether the tablespace is actually clustered
	FIRSTKEYCARDF	Y	Number of distinct values for the first column of the index key
	FULLKEYCARDF	Y	Number of distinct values for the full index key
	NLEAF	Y	Number of active leaf pages
	NLEVELS	Y	Number of index b-tree levels
	STATSTIME	N	Indicates the time RUNSTATS was run to generate these statistics
SYSINDEXPART	DSNUM	N	Number of data sets
	EXTENTS	N	Number of data set extents
	LEAFFAR	N	Number of leaf pages far from previous leaf page
	LEAFNEAR	N	Number of leaf pages near previous leaf page
	PSEUDO_DEL_ENTRIES	N	Number of pseudo deleted index keys
	SPACEF	N	Disk storage space

28

TABLE 28.3 Continued

Catalog Table	Column	How Used?	Description
SYSINDEXSTATS	CLUSTERRATIOF	N	Percentage of rows in clustered order
	FIRSTKEYCARDF	N	Number of distinct values for the first column of the index key
	FULLKEYCARDF	N	Number of distinct values for the full index key
	FULLKEYCARDDATA	N	Representation of number of distinct values of the full key
	NLEAF	N	Number of active leaf pages
	NLEVELS	N	Number of index b-tree levels
	KEYCOUNTF	N	Number of rows in the partition
	STATSTIME	N	Indicates the time RUNSTATS was run to generate these statistics
SYSLOBSTATS	AVGSIZE	N	Average size of LOB
	FREESPACE	N	Available space in the LOB tablespace
	ORGRATIO	N	Ratio of disorganization for LOB tablespace
SYSROUTINES	IOS_PER_INVOC	Y	Estimated number of I/Os per invocation of the routine
	INSTS_PER_INVOC	Y	Estimated number of instructions per invocation of the routine
	INITIAL_IOS	Y	Estimated number of I/Os for the first invocation of the routine
	INITIAL_INSTS	Y	Estimated number of instructions for the first invocation of the routine
	CARDINALITY	Y	Predicted cardinality of a table function
SYSTABLEPART	DSNUM	N	Number of data sets
	EXTENTS	N	Number of data set extents
	SPACEF	N	Disk storage space
SYSTABLES	CARDF	Y	Number of rows for a table
	NPAGES	Y	Number of pages used by the table
	NPAGESF	Y	Number of pages used by the table
	PCTPAGES	N	Percentage of tablespace pages that contain rows for this table
	PCTROWCOMP	Y	Percentage of rows compressed
	AVGROWLEN	N	Average row length
	SPACEF	N	Disk storage space
	STATSTIME	N	Indicates the time RUNSTATS was run to generate these statistics
SYSTABLESPACE	NACTIVEF	Y	Number of allocated tablespace pages
	STATSTIME	N	Indicates the time RUNSTATS was run to generate these statistics

TABLE 28.3   Continued

Catalog Table	Column	How Used?	Description
SYSTABSTATS	CARDF	P	Number of rows for the partition
	NPAGES	P	Number of pages used by the partition
	NACTIVE	P	Number of active pages in the partition
	PCTPAGES	P	Percentage of tablespace pages that contain rows for this partition
	PCTROWCOMP	P	Percentage (×100) of rows compressed
	STATSTIME	N	Indicates the time RUNSTATS was run to generate these statistics

Legend:

N = Not used by the optimizer

P = Used for parallel path generation

Y = Used by the optimizer

The two predominant reasons for changing DB2 Catalog statistics to influence the access path selection are to influence DB2 to use an index and to influence DB2 to change the order in which tables are joined. In each case, the tuning methods require that you "play around" with the DB2 Catalog statistics to create a lower filter factor. You should keep in mind five rules when doing so.

Rule 1: As first key cardinality (FIRSTKEYCARDF) increases, the filter factor decreases. As the filter factor decreases, DB2 is more inclined to use an index to satisfy the SQL statement.

Rule 2: As an index becomes more clustered, you increase the probability that DB2 will use it. To enhance the probability of an unclustered index being used, increase its cluster ratio (CLUSTERRATIOF) to a value between 96 and 100, preferably 100.

TUNING STRATEGY

To influence DB2 to use an index, adjust the COLCARDF, FIRSTKEYCARDF, and FULLKEYCARDF columns to an artificially high value. As cardinality increases, the filter factor decreases. As the filter factor decreases, the chance that DB2 will use an available index becomes greater. DB2 assumes that a low filter factor means that only a few rows are being returned, causing indexed access to be more efficient. Adjusting COLCARDF, FIRSTKEYCARDF, and FULLKEYCARDF is also useful for getting DB2 to choose an unclustered index because DB2 is more reluctant to use an unclustered index with higher filter factors. You also can change the value of CLUSTERRATIOF to 100 to remove DB2's reluctance to use unclustered indexes from the access path selection puzzle.

Rule 3: DB2's choice for inner and outer tables is a delicate trade-off. Because the inner table is accessed many times for each qualifying outer table row, it should be as small as possible to reduce the time needed to scan multiple rows for each outer table row. The more inner table rows, the longer the scan. But the outer table should also be as small as possible to reduce the overhead of opening and closing the internal cursor on the inner table.

28

It is impossible to choose the smallest table as both the inner table and the outer table. When two tables are joined, one must be chosen as the inner table, and the other must be chosen as the outer table. My experience has shown that as the size of a table grows, the DB2 optimizer favors using it as the outer table in a nested loop join. Therefore, changing the cardinality (CARDF) of the table that you want as the outer table to an artificially high value can influence DB2 to choose that table as the outer table.

Rule 4: As column cardinality (COLCARDF) decreases, DB2 favors the use of the nested loop join over the merge scan join. Lower the value of COLCARDF to favor the nested loop join.

Rule 5: HIGH2KEY and LOW2KEY can be altered to more accurately reflect the overall range of values stored in a column. This is particularly useful for influencing access path selection for data with a skewed distribution.

The combination of HIGH2KEY and LOW2KEY provides a range of probable values accessed for a particular column. The absolute highest and lowest values are discarded to create a more realistic range. For certain types of predicates, DB2 uses the following formula when calculating filter factor:

```
Filter factor = (Value-LOW2KEY) / (HIGH2KEY-LOW2KEY)
```

Because HIGH2KEY and LOW2KEY can affect the size of the filter factor, the range of values that they provide can significantly affect access path selection.

TUNING STRATEGY

For troublesome queries, check whether the distribution of data in the columns accessed is skewed. If you query SYSIBM.SYSCOLDIST, as discussed in Chapter 26, the 10 most frequently occurring values are shown for indexed columns. To be absolutely accurate, however, obtain a count for each column value, not just the top 10:

```
SELECT     COL, COUNT(*)
FROM       your.table
GROUP BY   COL
ORDER BY   COL
```

This query produces an ordered listing of column values. You can use this list to determine the distribution of values. If a few values occur much more frequently than the other values, the data is not evenly distributed. In this circumstance, consider using dynamic SQL, hard coding predicate values, or binding with REOPT(VARS). This enables DB2 to use nonuniform distribution statistics when calculating filter factors.

TUNING STRATEGY

Referring back to the results of the query in the preceding tuning strategy, if a few values are at the beginning or end of the report, consider changing LOW2KEY and HIGH2KEY to different values. DB2 uses LOW2KEY and HIGH2KEY when calculating filter factors. So, even though the valid domain of small integers is –32768 to +32767, the valid range for access path selection is defined by LOW2KEY and HIGH2KEY, which may set the range to +45 to +1249, for example. As the range of values decreases, the filter factor decreases because there are fewer potential values in the range of values.

TUNING STRATEGY

If neither dynamic SQL nor hard-coded predicates are practical, change HIGH2KEY to a lower value and LOW2KEY to a higher value to reduce the range of possible values, thereby lowering the filter factor. Alternatively, or additionally, you can increase COLCARDF, FIRSTKEYCARDF, and FULLKEYCARDF.

Remember that modifying DB2 Catalog statistics is not a trivial exercise. Simply making the changes indicated in this section might be insufficient to resolve your performance problems because of DB2's knowledge of the DB2 Catalog statistics. Some statistical values have implicit relationships. When one value changes, DB2 assumes that the others have changed also. For example, consider these relationships:

- When you change COLCARDF for a column in an index, be sure to also change the FIRSTKEYCARDF of any index in which the column participates as the first column of the index key, and the FULLKEYCARDF of any index in which the column participates.

- Provide a value to both HIGH2KEY and LOW2KEY when you change cardinality information. When COLCARDF is not –1, DB2 assumes that statistics are available. DB2 factors these high and low key values into its access path selection decision. Failure to provide both a HIGH2KEY and a LOW2KEY can result in the calculation of inaccurate filter factors and the selection of inappropriate access paths.

Before deciding to update DB2 Catalog statistics to force DB2 to choose different access paths, heed the following warnings.

First, never change the DB2 Catalog statistics without documenting the following:

- Why the statistics will be modified

- How the modifications will be made and how frequently the changes must be run

- The current values for each statistic and the values they will be changed to

Secondly, be aware that when you change DB2 Catalog statistics, you are robbing from Peter to pay Paul. In other words, your changes might enhance the performance of one query at the expense of the performance of another query.

DB2 maintenance (PTFs, new releases, and new versions) might change the access path selection logic in the DB2 optimizer. As a result of applying maintenance, binding or rebinding static and dynamic SQL operations could result in different access paths, thereby invalidating your hard work. In other words, IBM might get around to correcting the problem in the logic of the optimizer (that you solved using trickery).

Choosing the correct values for the statistics and keeping the statistics accurate can be an intimidating task. Do not undertake this endeavor lightly. Plan to spend many hours changing statistics, rebinding plans, changing statistics again, rebinding again, and so on.

The situation that caused the need to tinker with the statistics in the DB2 Catalog could change. For example, the properties of the data could vary as your application ages. Distribution, table and column cardinality, and the range of values stored could change. If the statistics are not changing because they have been artificially set outside the jurisdiction of RUNSTATS, these newer changes to the data cannot be considered by the DB2 optimizer, and an inefficient access path could be used indefinitely.

> **TUNING STRATEGY**
>
> When DB2 Catalog statistics have been changed to influence access path selection, periodically execute RUNSTATS and rebind to determine if the artificial statistics are still required. If they are, simply reissue the DB2 Catalog UPDATE statements. If not, eliminate this artificial constraint from your environment. Failure to implement this strategy eventually results in inefficient access paths in your environment (as DB2 and your applications mature).

Only a SYSADM can update the DB2 Catalog. SYSADMs have a great amount of authority, so it is generally a good idea to limit the number of SYSADMs in your shop. When the DB2 Catalog needs to be altered, an undue burden is placed on the SYSADMs.

When the DB2 Catalog has been updated using SQL, all subsequent RUNSTATS executions must be followed by a series of SQL statements to reapply the updates to the DB2 Catalog.

> **TUNING STRATEGY**
>
> If possible, give a single production userid SYSADM authority for modifying DB2 Catalog statistics. This userid has the following requirements:
>
> - Should not have online TSO logon capabilities because only batch jobs need to be run using it
> - Should be under the same strict controls placed on production jobs at your site
> - Should be used to run only DB2 Catalog update jobs
>
> A DBA or some other knowledgeable user can then create UPDATE statements to change the DB2 Catalog statistics as desired. A batch job running under the authid for the production SYSADM can then run the UPDATE statements in production. Because the SYSADM userid has no logon capabilities, the possibility for abuse is limited to the controls placed on the production environment (such as who can update production job streams, who can submit them, or what review process is in place).

Using Optimization Hints (OPTHINT) to Force an Access Path

You also can influence access paths using the OPTHINT feature. Actually, though, this method does not "influence" the access path; instead it directs DB2 to use a specific access path instead of determining a new access path using statistics. IBM refers to this process as specifying optimization hints.

> **CAUTION**
>
> The same basic cautions that apply to modifying DB2 Catalog statistics also apply to optimization hints. Only experienced analysts and DBAs should attempt to use optimization hints. However, optimization hints are much easier to apply than updating DB2 Catalog statistics.

Optimization hints are implemented using the PLAN_TABLE. However, before you can use optimization hints, the DB2 DSNZPARM parameter for optimization hints (OPTHINTS) must be set to YES. If it is set to NO, you cannot use optimization hints.

There are two ways to use the PLAN_TABLE to provide an optimization hint to DB2:

- Alter the PLAN_TABLE to use an access path that was previously created by the DB2 optimizer
- INSERT rows to the PLAN_TABLE to create a new access path independently

In general, favor the first method over the second method. It is a difficult task to create an accurate access path in the PLAN_TABLE. If you do not get every nuance of the access path correct, it is possible that DB2 will ignore the optimization hint and calculate an access path at bind time. However, if you use an access path that was originally created by DB2, you can be reasonably sure that the access path will be valid.

> **CAUTION**
>
> Sometimes an access path created for an older version of DB2 will not be valid in a newer version of DB2. Of course, the opposite is true, too. Some access paths for a newer version of DB2 will not work for older versions.

You should consider using optimization hints for all of the same reasons you would choose to modify DB2 Catalog statistics or tweak SQL. The general reason is to bypass the access path chosen by DB2 and use a different, hopefully more efficient, access path.

In addition to this reason, optimization hints are very useful as you migrate from release to release of DB2. Sometimes, a new release or version of DB2 can cause different access paths to be chosen for queries that were running fine. Or perhaps new statistics were accumulated between binds causing access paths to change. By saving old access paths in a PLAN_TABLE, you can use optimization hints to direct DB2 to use the old access paths instead of the new, and perhaps undesirable, access paths due to the new release or statistics.

Always test and analyze the results of any query that uses optimization hints to be sure that the desired performance is being achieved.

Defining an Optimization Hint   To specify that an optimization hint is to be used, you will have to update the PLAN_TABLE. The first step is to make sure that your PLAN_TABLE includes the following columns:

```
OPTHINT              CHAR(8)    NOT NULL WITH DEFAULT
HINT_USED            CHAR(8)    NOT NULL WITH DEFAULT
PRIMARY_ACCESSTYPE   CHAR(1)    NOT NULL WITH DEFAULT
```

For more information on the PLAN_TABLE and a definition of all PLAN_TABLE columns, refer to Chapter 25, "Using EXPLAIN."

To set an optimization hint, you need to first identify (or create) the PLAN_TABLE rows that refer to the desired access path. You will then need to update those rows in the PLAN_TABLE, specifying an identifier for the hint in the OPTHINT column. For example,

```
UPDATE PLAN_TABLE
   SET OPTHINT = 'SQLHINT'
WHERE   PLANNO = 50
AND     APPLNAME = 'PLANNAME';
```

Of course, this is just an example. You may need to use other predicates to specifically identify the PLAN_TABLE rows to include in the optimization hint. Some columns that might be useful, depending on your usage of dynamic SQL and packages, include QUERYNO, PROGNAME, VERSION, and COLLID.

> **CAUTION**
>
> If you change a program that uses static SQL statements, the statement number might change, causing rows in the PLAN_TABLE to be out of sync with the modified application.

You can use the QUERYNO clause in SQL statements to ease correlation of SQL statements in your program with your optimization hints. Statements that use the QUERYNO clause are not dependent on the statement number. To use QUERYNO, you will need to modify the SQL in your application to specify a QUERYNO, as shown in the following:

```
SELECT MGRNO
FROM    DEPT
WHERE   DEPNO = 'A00'
QUERYNO 200;
```

You can then UPDATE the PLAN_TABLE more easily using QUERYNO and be sure that the optimization hint will take effect, as shown in the following:

```
UPDATE PLAN_TABLE
    SET OPTHINT = 'SQLHINT'
WHERE   QUERYNO = 200
AND     APPLNAME = 'PLANNAME';
```

When the PLAN_TABLE is correctly updated (as well as possibly the application), you must REBIND the plan or package to determine if the hint is being used by DB2. When rebinding you must specify the OPTHINT parameter:

```
REBIND PLAN PLANNAME . . . OPTHINT(SQLHINT)
```

Be aware that the optimization hints may not actually be used by DB2. For optimization hints to be used, the hint must be correctly specified, the REBIND must be accurately performed, and the environment must not have changed. For example, DB2 will not use an access path specified using an optimization hint if it relies on an index that has since been dropped.

Use EXPLAIN(YES) to verify whether the hint was actually used. If the hint was used, the HINT_USED column for the new access path will contain the name of the optimization hint (such as SQLHINT in the previous example).

Miscellaneous Guidelines

The following miscellaneous guidelines provide you with useful general tips for improving DB2 performance.

Favor Optimization Hints Over Updating the DB2 Catalog   Optimization hints to influence access paths are less intrusive and easier to implement than changing columns in the DB2 Catalog. However, use optimization hints only as a last resort. Do not use optimization hints as a crutch to arrive at a specific access path. Optimization hints are best used when an access path changes and you want to go back to a previous, efficient access path.

Limit Ordering to Avoid Scanning   The optimizer is more likely to choose an index scan when ordering is important (ORDER BY, GROUP BY, or DISTINCT) and the index is clustered by the columns to be sorted.

Maximize Buffers and Minimize Data Access   If the inner table fits in 2% of the buffer pool, the nested loop join is favored. Therefore, to increase the chances of nested loop joins, increase the size of the buffer pool (or decrease the size of the inner table, if possible).

Consider Deleting Nonuniform Distribution Statistics

To decrease wild fluctuations in the performance of dynamic SQL statements, consider removing the nonuniform distribution statistics (NUDS) from the DB2 Catalog. Although dynamic SQL makes the best use of these statistics, the overall performance of some applications that heavily use dynamic SQL can suffer. The optimizer might choose a different access path for the same dynamic SQL statement, depending on the values supplied to the predicates. In theory, this should be the desired goal. In practice, however, the results might be unexpected.

For example, consider the following dynamic SQL statement:

```
SELECT    EMPNO, LASTNAME
FROM      DSN8810.EMP
WHERE     WORKDEPT = ?
```

The access path might change depending on the value of WORKDEPT because the optimizer calculates different filter factors for each value, based on the distribution statistics. As the number of occurrences of distribution statistics increases, the filter factor decreases. This makes DB2 think that fewer rows will be returned, which increases the chance that an index will be used and affects the choice of inner and outer tables for joins.

These statistics are stored in the SYSIBM.SYSCOLDIST and SYSIBM.SYSCOLDISTSTATS tables and can be removed using SQL DELETE statements.

This suggested guideline does not mean that you should always delete the NUDS. My advice is quite to the contrary. When using dynamic SQL, allow DB2 the chance to use these statistics. Delete these statistics only when performance is unacceptable. (They can always be repopulated later with RUNSTATS.)

Consider Collecting More Than Just the Top Ten NUDS   If non-uniform distribution impacts more than just the top ten most frequently occurring values, you should consider using the FREQVAL option of RUNSTATS to capture more than 10 values. Capture only as many as will prove to be useful for optimizing queries against the non-uniformly distributed data.

DB2 Referential Integrity Use

Referential integrity (RI) is the implementation of constraints between tables so that values from one table control the values in another. Recall that a referential constraint

28

between a parent table and a dependent table is defined by a relationship between the columns of the tables. The parent table's primary key columns control the values permissible in the dependent table's foreign key columns. For example, in the sample table, DSN8810.EMP, the WORKDEPT column (the foreign key) must reference a valid department as defined in the DSN8810.DEPT table's DEPTNO column (the primary key).

You have two options for implementing RI at your disposal: declarative and application. Declarative constraints provide DB2-enforced referential integrity and are specified by DDL options. All modifications, whether embedded in an application program or ad hoc, must comply with the referential constraints.

Application-enforced referential integrity is coded into application programs. Every program that can update referentially constrained tables must contain logic to enforce the referential integrity. This type of RI is not applicable to ad hoc updates.

With DB2-enforced RI, CPU use is reduced because the Data Manager component of DB2 performs DB2-enforced RI checking, whereas the RDS component of DB2 performs application-enforced RI checking. Additionally, rows accessed for RI checking when using application-enforced RI must be passed back to the application from DB2. DB2-enforced RI does not require this passing of data, further reducing CPU time.

In addition, DB2-enforced RI uses an index (if one is available) when enforcing the referential constraint. In application-enforced RI, index use is based on the SQL used by each program to enforce the constraint.

> **TUNING STRATEGY**
>
> DB2-enforced referential integrity is generally more efficient than application-enforced RI. When you build new applications, use DB2-enforced referential integrity and consider retrofitting older applications that require performance tuning.
>
> Declarative RI has the further benefit that it cannot be bypassed, like application-enforced RI.
>
> Triggers also can be used to implement complex RI and data integrity rules. Triggers, like declarative RI, cannot be bypassed by ad hoc SQL. All SQL data modification, whether static or dynamic, planned or ad hoc, must conform to the trigger logic.

> **TUNING STRATEGY**
>
> If no ad hoc updating is permitted, consider using application-based RI in the following two situations:
>
> - If an application program can be written so that a single check is made for a row from the parent table, when multiple inserts to the child table are performed.
>
> - If the application processing needs are such that the parent table is read before inserting the child (even one child), DB2 just repeats the read process that the application must do anyway.
>
> Of course, application-enforced RI still has the negative aspect of not being enforced for ad hoc data modifications.

TUNING STRATEGY

Consider not implementing DB2-enforced or application-enforced RI in the following cases:

- If DB2 tables are built from another system that is already referentially intact
- If application tables are accessed as read-only

General Application Tuning

This chapter has concentrated on some of the more complex methods of tuning your DB2 applications. A wealth of less complex information about building efficient SQL is also available. For this type of general SQL coding advice, and guidelines for coding efficient, performance-oriented SQL (DCL, DDL, and DML), refer to Chapters 2 through 10.

The Causes of DB2 Performance Problems

All performance problems are caused by change. Change can take many forms, including the following:

- Physical changes to the environment, such as a new CPU, new DASD devices, or different tape drives.

- Installing a new version or release of the operating system.

- Changes to system software, such as a new release of a product (for example, QMF, CICS, or GDDM), the alteration of a product (for example, the addition of more or fewer CICS regions or an IMS SYSGEN), or a new product (for example, implementation of DFHSM). Also included is the installation of a new release or version of DB2, which can result in changes in access paths and the utilization of features new to DB2.

- Changes to the DB2 engine from maintenance releases, which can change the optimizer.

- Changes in system capacity. More or fewer jobs could be executing concurrently when the performance problem occurs.

- Environment changes, such as the implementation of client/server programs or the adoption of data sharing.

- Database changes. This involves changes to any DB2 object, and ranges from adding a new column or an index to dropping and re-creating an object.

- Changes to the application development methodology, such as usage of check constraints instead of application logic or the use of stored procedures.

- Changes to application code.

Performance problems are not caused by magic. Something tangible changes, creating a performance problem in the application. The challenge of tuning is to find the source of the change, gauge its impact, and formulate a solution.

28

See Figure 28.5. This hierarchy shows the order of magnitude by which each type of resource can affect DB2 performance. The resource with the highest potential for affecting performance is at the top. This does not mean that the bulk of your problems will be at the highest level. Although the operating system packs the largest wallop in terms of its potential for degrading performance when improperly tuned, it consists of only approximately 5% of the tuning opportunity.

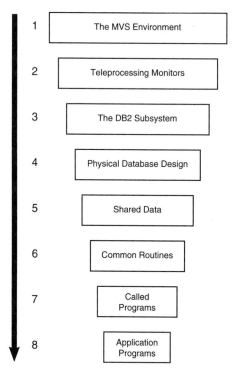

FIGURE 28.5   The tuning hierarchy in terms of impact.

Although the majority of your problems will be application-oriented, you must explore the tuning opportunities presented in the other environments when application tuning has little effect.

The following is a quick reference of the possible tuning options for each environment.

To tune OS/390, z/OS:

Change the dispatching priority.

Modify swappability.

Add memory.

Upgrade CPU.

Implement data sharing.

Use an active performance monitor (enables tuning on the fly).

To tune the teleprocessing environments:

Change the system generation parameters.

Tune the program definition (PSBs and PPT entries).

Modify the Attachment Facility parameters.

Add or change table entries.

Use an active performance monitor (enables tuning on the fly).

To tune the DB2 subsystem:

Modify DSNZPARMs to increase or decrease the number of concurrent users, change lock escalation, increase EDM pool storage, and so on.

Issue SET LOG commands to change log buffers.

Issue ALTER BUFFERPOOL commands to change bufferpool sizes, increase or decrease bufferpool thresholds, and modify associated hiperpools.

Tune the DB2 Catalog, including dropping and freeing objects, executing MODIFY, reorganizing DB2 Catalog tablespaces and indexes, rebuilding the DB2 Catalog indexes, adding indexes to the DB2 Catalog, changing data set placement, moving the DB2 Catalog to a faster DASD device, and implementing data set shadowing.

Perform DSNDB07 tuning.

Use a tool to change DSNZPARMs on the fly.

To tune the DB2 database design:

Modify the logical and physical model.

Modify and issue DDL.

Execute ALTER statements.

Ensure that proper parameters are specified.

Implement table changes.

Partition simple and segmented tablespaces.

Spread non-partitioned objects over multiple devices using PIECESIZE.

Add indexes.

REORG tablespaces.

REORG or REBUILD indexes.

Consider or reconsider data compression.

Denormalize the database design.

To tune shared data:

Denormalize the database design.

Add redundant tables.

28

To tune programs:

Perform SQL tuning.

Use triggers to enforce business rules.

Implement stored procedures and user-defined functions as needed.

Reduce network requests in client/server applications.

Tune the high-level language (such as COBOL or 4GL).

Use a program restructuring tool.

Run RUNSTATS.

Execute EXPLAIN, modify your code, and REBIND.

Use the OPTIMIZE FOR *n* ROWS clause.

Consider activating query parallelism.

Change locking strategies.

Change the DB2 Catalog statistics and REBIND.

Implement optimization hints.

Use a testing tool to provide what if testing and tuning.

Use a tool to sample the application's address space as it executes.

It is important not to confuse the issue, so I will present another tuning hierarchy. Figure 28.6 outlines the order in which DB2 problems should be investigated. Start at the top and work your way down. If you are sure that your MVS environment has not changed, investigate the teleprocessing monitor. Only when you have tried all avenues of tuning at one level should you move to the next. Of course, this process should be used only when the cause of the problem is not obvious. If you just implemented a new application yesterday and the first time it runs problems occur, you most likely can assume the problem is in the new application and begin looking there.

TUNING STRATEGY

Implement at your shop a standard that incorporates tuning hierarchies similar to the ones shown in Figures 28.5 and 28.6.

Document your tuning standard, stating that each component of the DB2 tuning hierarchies should be considered when DB2 performance problems are encountered. Include in the document all the tools that can be used. If possible, get managerial agreement from all areas involved to reduce the friction that can occur when diverse groups attempt to resolve a DB2 tuning problem.

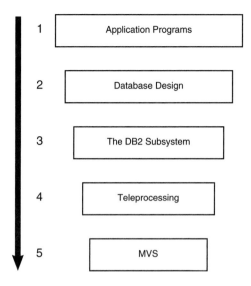

FIGURE 28.6   The tuning review process.

CHAPTER 29

DB2 Resource Governing

In addition to performance monitoring and tuning, actively controlling certain types of SQL can be beneficial. For example, consider a critical decision support query that retrieves hundreds, thousands, or even millions of rows from DB2 tables. If the query is well-planned, the designer will have a good idea of the amount of time necessary to satisfy the request.

As time goes on, however, the performance of the query could degrade for many reasons, such as unorganized indexes and table spaces, additional rows being returned, or outdated RUNSTATS. This degradation could affect the entire system because S-locks are being held and DB2 resources are being monopolized. It would be desirable, therefore, to disallow access on a prespecified basis when performance falls outside an acceptable range.

The Resource Limit Facility

The DB2 Resource Limit Facility (RLF) is a governor that limits specific DB2 resources that can be consumed by dynamic SQL. There are two modes used by the RLF: reactive and predictive. With reactive governing, DB2 will allow the query to begin, but will limit the resources it can consume. With predictive governing, DB2 attempts to determine the resources that will be consumed before the query runs.

With predictive governing, you can stop a statement from executing before it has consumed any resources at all. This is an advantage over the reactive governor, which can stop a dynamic SQL statement only after it has exceeded its limit. With reactive governing, resources are consumed, but no valuable work is completed.

Reactive Governing

With reactive governing, the RLF limits the CPU consumed by dynamic SQL issued by plan name, terminating the requests that exceed the limit and returning a `-905` `SQLCODE` to the requesting program. The RLF also limits dynamic SQL issued by collection name. This effectively limits the dynamic SQL capabilities of all plans and packages of a collection.

Also, the RLF can control when the `BIND` command can be issued. The RLF establishes a means whereby particular plans, packages, or entire collections are unavailable for binding, even to those authorized to issue the `BIND` command. In addition to checking for `BIND` authority, DB2 checks the RLF specifications before allowing a bind.

Predictive Governing

With predictive governing, DB2 determines the cost category for SQL statements at runtime. Recall from Chapter 25, "Using `EXPLAIN`," that DB2 can produce cost estimates for SQL statements and assigns the estimate to one of two categories—category A or category B. You can examine the `COST_CATEGORY` column of the `DSN_STATEMNT_TABLE` to determine whether a given SQL statement falls into category A or B.

Predictive governing can be set up to cause the prepare for a dynamic `SELECT`, `INSERT`, `UPDATE`, or `DELETE` statement to fail if the cost estimate is exceeded. For category A cost estimates where the error threshold is exceeded, DB2 returns a `-495` `SQLCODE` to the application at `PREPARE` time, and the statement is not prepared or executed. If the estimate is in cost category A and the warning threshold is exceeded, a `+495` `SQLCODE` is returned at prepare time, but the prepare is completed, and the application must decide whether to run the statement or not.

Additionally, you can specify what action DB2 should take for cost estimates in category B. The predictive governing process is outlined in Figure 29.1.

The RLF is designed to govern performance based on rows in a table known as a Resource Limit Specification Table (RLST). All resource limits, for both reactive and predictive governing, are defined using a table known as the RLST.

To define the RLST, use the following DDL:

```
CREATE DATABASE DSNRLST;

CREATE TABLESPACE DSNRLSxx
IN DSNRLST;

CREATE TABLE authid.DSNRLSTxx
(AUTHID        CHAR(8)    NOT NULL WITH DEFAULT,
 PLANNAME      CHAR(8)    NOT NULL WITH DEFAULT,
 ASUTIME       INTEGER,
 LUNAME        CHAR(8)    NOT NULL WITH DEFAULT,
 RLFFUNC       CHAR(1)    NOT NULL WITH DEFAULT,
 RLFBIND       CHAR(7)    NOT NULL WITH DEFAULT,
 RLFCOLLN      CHAR(18)   NOT NULL WITH DEFAULT,
 RLFPKG        CHAR(8)    NOT NULL WITH DEFAULT,
```

```
      RLFASUERR       INTEGER,
      RLFASUWARN      INTEGER,
      RLF_CATEGORY_B CHAR(1)   NOT NULL WITH DEFAULT
      )
     IN DSNRLST.DNSRLSxx;

     CREATE UNIQUE INDEX authid.DSNARLxx
     ON authid.DSNRLSTxx
        (RLFFUNC,
         AUTHID DESC,
         PLANNAME DESC,
         RLFCOLLN DESC,
         RLFPKG DESC,
         LUNAME DESC)
     CLUSTER
     CLOSE NO;
```

FIGURE 29.1   The predictive governing process.

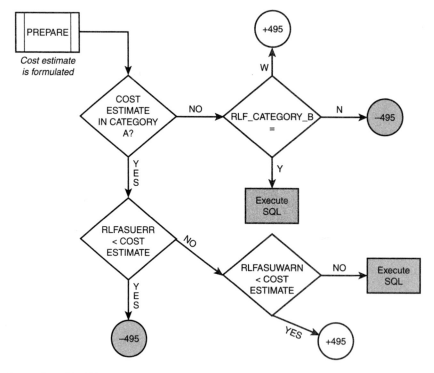

Defining the RLST

A definition of each column in the RLST is provided in Table 29.1.

TABLE 29.1   The Columns of the RLST

Name	Definition
AUTHID	Identifies the primary authorization ID of the user to whom the limit set by this row applies. If blank, this row applies to all primary authorization IDs at the location specified by the LUNAME column.
PLANNAME	Specifies the plan name for which the limit set by this row applies. If blank, this row applies to all plan names at the location specified by the LUNAME column. PLANNAME is valid only when RLFFUNC is blank. If RLFFUNC contains a value, the column must be blank or the entire row is ignored.
ASUTIME	Specifies the maximum number of CPU service units permitted for any single dynamic SQL statement. If NULL, this row does not apply a limit. If less than or equal to 0, this row indicates that dynamic SQL is not permitted.
LUNAME	The logical unit name of the site where the request originated. If blank, this row applies to the local site. If PUBLIC, this row applies to all sites.
RLFFUNC	Indicates the type of resource this row is limiting: *blank* = row governs dynamic SQL reactively by plan name 1 = row governs BIND for plans or packages in collections 2 = row governs dynamic SQL reactively by collection and package names 3 = row disables query I/O parallelism 4 = row disables query CP parallelism 5 = row disables Sysplex query parallelism 6 = row governs dynamic SQL predictively by plan name 7 = row governs dynamic SQL predictively by collection and package names If any other values are in this column, the row is ignored.
RLFBIND	Indicates whether the BIND command is permitted. The value N indicates that BIND is not allowed; any other value means that the BIND command is allowed. Valid only when RLFFUNC equals 1.
RLFCOLLN	Specifies the name of the collection to which this RLF row applies. If blank, this row applies to all packages at the location specified by the LUNAME column. If RLFFUNC is blank, 1, or 6, RLFCOLLN must be blank or the entire row is ignored.
RLFPKG	Specifies the package name for which the limit set by this row applies. If blank, this row applies to all packages at the location specified by the LUNAME column. If RLFFUNC is blank, 1 or 6, RLFPKG must be blank or the entire row is ignored.
RLFASUERR	Specifies the maximum number of CPU service units permitted for any single dynamic SQL statement. If the threshold is exceeded, a -495 SQLCODE is returned to the application. If NULL, this row does not apply a limit. If less than or equal to 0, this row indicates that dynamic SQL is not permitted. Used for predictive governing only (RLFFUNC 6 or 7). Additionally, the dynamic SQL statements must be in cost category A.
RLFASUWARN	Specifies the maximum number of CPU service units permitted for any single dynamic SQL statement. If the threshold is exceeded, a +495 SQLCODE is returned to the application as a warning. If NULL, this row does not apply a limit. If less than or equal to 0, this row indicates that all dynamic SQL will receive a +495 SQLCODE as a warning. Used for predictive governing only (RLFFUNC 6 or 7). Additionally, the dynamic SQL statements must be in cost category A.

29

TABLE 29.1   Continued

Name	Definition
RLF_CATEGORY_B	Specifies the default action to take for category B cost estimates. Used for predictive governing (RLFFUNC 6 or 7). Valid values are as follow:
	blank Execute the dynamic SQL statement.
	Y Prepare and execute the SQL statement.
	N Do not prepare or execute the SQL statement. Return -495 SQLCODE to the application.
	W Complete the prepare, return +495 SQLCODE as a warning to let the application decide whether to execute the dynamic SQL statement or not.

> **CAUTION**
>
> Be sure to make the value of RLFASUWARN less than the value of RLFASUERR. If the warning value is higher, the warning will never be reported because an error will always occur before the warning.

Regulate the impact of dynamic SQL using the RLF. SPUFI, QMF, packaged applications (such as SAP and Peoplesoft), and many vendor-supplied tools use dynamic SQL. Limit usage for these types of tools to reduce the possibility of runaway ad hoc queries that hog system resources.

> **TUNING STRATEGY**
>
> Favor predictive governing over reactive governing to save resources. It is better to know "up front" that a particular query is destined to exceed your service level agreement. That way, you can tune the query and optimize it, instead of having the query fail during processing.

You can create multiple RLSTs, with each controlling resources in a different manner. Some reasons for doing this are as follows:

- To control the same resources in different RLSTs with different limits.

- To control different resources in different RLSTs.

- To eliminate resource control for a plan or package from a certain RLST, thereby removing the limit.

- To control one type of limiting separately from another type; for example, to control binds in one RLST, plans and packages in another, and users in another. However, this is impractical because only one RLST can be active at any given time.

The RLF is started using the START RLIMIT command, which is discussed in Chapter 36, "DB2 Commands." Using this command, a DBA can specify which RLST should be activated for resource limiting.

> **TUNING STRATEGY**
>
> Use several RLSTs to control dynamic SQL access differently during different periods. For example, consider a plan containing dynamic SQL statements that consumes 10 CPU seconds normally but consumes 20 CPU seconds during month-end processing. You can define two RLSTs, one with a limit of 10 and another with a limit of 20. The first RLST is active most of the time, but the DBA can switch the RLF to use the second RLST during month-end processing. This ensures that both normal and month-end processing are controlled adequately.

The QMF Governor

Because QMF uses dynamic SQL, the RLF can be used to govern QMF resource use. To control the usage of QMF, a row would be inserted specifying the following:

- A blank AUTHID (so the limit applies to all users)
- The QMF plan name in the PLANNAME column (for example, for QMF V6 this is most likely QMF610 or something similar)
- The resource limit in ASUTIME

If necessary, multiple rows could be inserted with varying resource limits for different authids.

However, the QMF Governor can govern QMF use independently from DB2 and SQL use. The QMF Governor provides the capability to prompt users or to cancel threads based on excessive resource use. Resource use is either a CPU time limit or a limit based on the number of rows retrieved by a single query.

The operation of the QMF Governor is controlled by rows inserted into a QMF control table named Q.RESOURCE_TABLE. DDL to create this table is shown in the following SQL statement:

```
CREATE TABLE Q.RESOURCE_TABLE
(RESOURCE_GROUP      CHAR(16)  NOT NULL ,
 RESOURCE_OPTION     CHAR(16)  NOT NULL ,
 INTVAL              INTEGER,
 FLOATVAL            FLOAT,
 CHARVAL             VARCHAR(80)
)
IN DSQDBCTL.DSQTSGOV ;
```

Values inserted into the first three columns of this table control QMF resource governing. The IBM-supplied QMF Governor does not use the last two columns, FLOATVAL and CHARVAL.

The following list shows the values that can be supplied for the RESOURCE_OPTION column, indicating the types of QMF governing available:

SCOPE
: Sets the overall QMF resource-governing environment. If a row has RESOURCE_OPTION set to SCOPE, and the row contains a value of 0 in the INTVAL column, governing is enabled. Any other value disables the QMF Governor.

TIMEPROMPT
: Sets the amount of CPU time that can be incurred before prompting users to cancel or continue. If INTVAL is 0, less than 0, or null, prompting does not occur.

TIMELIMIT
: Sets the amount of CPU time that can be incurred before canceling. This is an unconditional cancellation, without a prompt. The INTVAL specified for TIMELIMIT should always be greater than the corresponding TIMEPROMPT value. If INTVAL is 0, less than 0, or null, cancellation does not occur.

TIMECHECK
: Sets the amount of time that must elapse before performing CPU time checks as specified by TIMEPROMPT and TIMELIMIT. If INTVAL is 0, less than 0, or null, time checking does not occur, regardless of the TIMEPROMPT and TIMELIMIT settings.

ROWPROMPT
: Sets the maximum number of rows that can be retrieved before prompting the user to cancel or continue. If INTVAL is 0, less than 0, or null, prompting does not occur.

ROWLIMIT
: Sets the maximum number of rows that can be retrieved before canceling. This is an unconditional cancellation, without a prompt. The INTVAL specified for TIMELIMIT should always be greater than the corresponding TIMEPROMPT value. If INTVAL is 0, less than 0, or null, cancellation does not occur.

When the QMF Governor is set to prompt when reaching a particular threshold, the users are told the amount of CPU time consumed and the number of rows retrieved. This prompt looks like the following:

```
DSQUE00 QMF governor prompt:
Command has run for nnnnnn seconds of CPU times
and fetched mmmmmm rows of data.

==> To continue QMF command press the "ENTER" key.
==> To cancel QMF command type "CANCEL" then press the "ENTER" key.
==> To turn off prompting type "NOPROMPT" then press the "ENTER" key.
```

Users have the choice to continue or cancel their request. Users can request also that additional prompting be disabled. If the request is continued and prompting is not disabled, subsequent prompts are displayed as the limits are reached. Additionally, the QMF Governor might cancel a request if additional limits are met.

> **TUNING STRATEGY**
>
> Use the QMF Governor at least to prompt users when thresholds are bypassed. This enables users to police their own requests. At a minimum, also set a high systemwide cancellation time in case users choose the NOPROMPT option. You can set this with the QMF Governor or the RLF for the QMF plan.

CHAPTER **30**

An Introduction to DB2 Utilities

DB2 utility programs are divided into four broad categories:

- Online utilities
- Offline utilities
- Service aids
- Sample programs

Each of these categories is defined in Part VI, "DB2 Performance Utilities and Commands." A complete description of every utility that makes up each category is also provided. Sample JCL listings are provided for each utility. The job names, data set names, space allocations, and volumes used in the JCL are only examples. The database and tablespace names are from the DB2 sample tables used throughout this book. These names should be changed to reflect the needs of your application.

The online utilities are referred to as *online* because they execute under the control of DB2. They are run using the DSNUTILB program, which is supplied with DB2. DSNUTILB uses the Call Attach Facility (CAF) to run as an independent batch program.

Online utilities operate using control card input. DSNUTILB reads the control card input and then executes the proper utility based on the input. The first word in the control card is the name of the utility to be processed, followed by the other parameters required for the utility.

Generating Utility JCL

In this chapter, all the sample JCL for the online utilities use DSNUPROC, a generic utility procedure supplied with DB2.

IN THIS CHAPTER

- Generating Utility JCL
- Monitoring DB2 Utilities
- Version 7 and the State of IBM DB2 Utilities
- Using LISTDEF and TEMPLATE
- Issuing SQL Statements in DB2 Utilities

Recall from Chapter 18, "The Doors to DB2," that online DB2 utilities can be controlled by DB2I option 8. The DB2I utility panels are shown in Figures 30.1 and 30.2. JCL to execute DB2 utilities can be generated by these DB2I panels.

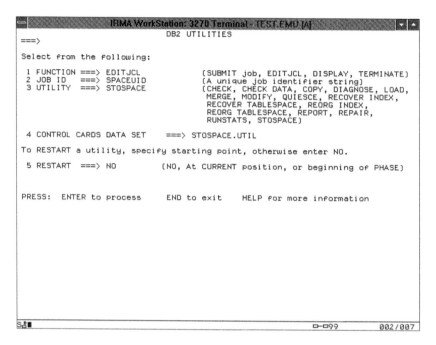

FIGURE 30.1   DB2I utility JCL generation panel 1.

The first panel, shown in Figure 30.1, is set to generate JCL for the STOSPACE utility. The second panel, shown in Figure 30.2, provides additional information used by certain DB2 utilities. If the first panel were set to generate JCL for the COPY, LOAD, or REORG utilities, the second panel would prompt the user to enter data set names required for those utilities.

The DB2I utility JCL generation panels provide four basic options:

SUBMIT	JCL is automatically built to execute the requested DB2 utility, and it is submitted in batch for processing.
EDITJCL	JCL is automatically built and displayed for the user. The user can edit the JCL, if desired, and then submit the JCL.
DISPLAY	The status of a utility identified by JOB ID is displayed online.
TERMINATE	A utility identified by JOB ID is terminated. This cancels a running utility or removes an inactive utility from the DB2 subsystem, thereby disabling future restartability for the utility.

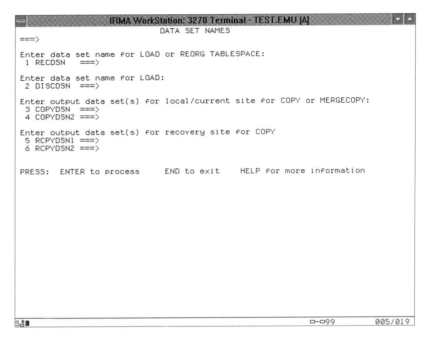

FIGURE 30.2   DB2I utility JCL generation panel 2.

The DISPLAY and TERMINATE options are merely menu-driven implementations of the DB2 -DISPLAY and -TERM commands. The SUBMIT and EDITJCL options provide automated DB2 utility JCL generation and submission. The DB2I utility program provides only rudimentary DB2 utility JCL, however. It works as follows:

1. The user specifies either SUBMIT or EDITJCL and a JOB ID that uniquely identifies a utility.

2. The user specifies one of the supported utilities (see Figure 30.1).

3. The user then specifies on the panel the data set containing the utility control cards to be used. The data set must be pre-allocated.

4. As directed by the panel, the user supplies additional data set names, depending on the selected utility.

5. JCL is generated for the requested utility.

The DB2I utility generator displays the output messages shown in Figure 30.3 when Enter is pressed and the request is processed.

The JCL generated by DB2I for the STOSPACE utility is shown in Figure 30.4. Generating JCL for a utility each time it is required, however, can be cumbersome. Many users create a partitioned data set containing sample utility JCL that they can modify as needed. The examples in Part VI can be used as templates for the creation of DB2 utility JCL for use in your shop.

30

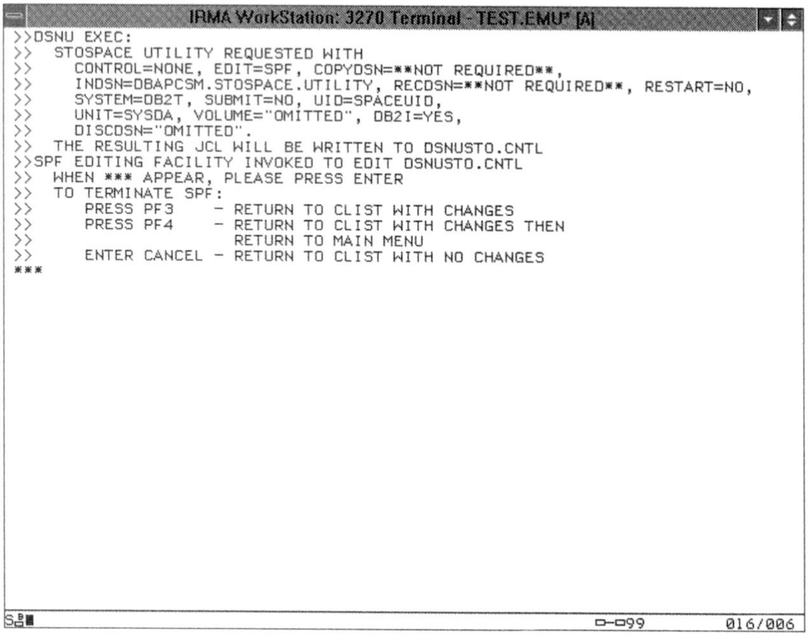

```
┌──────────────────────────────────────────────────────────────────────────┐
│ ▬              IRMA WorkStation: 3270 Terminal - TEST.EMU* [A]       ▼│♦│  │
│>>DSNU EXEC:                                                                │
│>>   STOSPACE UTILITY REQUESTED WITH                                        │
│>>     CONTROL=NONE, EDIT=SPF, COPYDSN=**NOT REQUIRED**,                     │
│>>     INDSN=DBAPCSM.STOSPACE.UTILITY, RECDSN=**NOT REQUIRED**, RESTART=NO,  │
│>>     SYSTEM=DB2T, SUBMIT=NO, UID=SPACEUID,                                 │
│>>     UNIT=SYSDA, VOLUME="OMITTED", DB2I=YES,                               │
│>>     DISCDSN="OMITTED".                                                    │
│>>   THE RESULTING JCL WILL BE WRITTEN TO DSNUSTO.CNTL                       │
│>>SPF EDITING FACILITY INVOKED TO EDIT DSNUSTO.CNTL                          │
│>>   WHEN *** APPEAR, PLEASE PRESS ENTER                                     │
│>>   TO TERMINATE SPF:                                                       │
│>>     PRESS PF3    - RETURN TO CLIST WITH CHANGES                           │
│>>     PRESS PF4    - RETURN TO CLIST WITH CHANGES THEN                      │
│>>                    RETURN TO MAIN MENU                                    │
│>>     ENTER CANCEL - RETURN TO CLIST WITH NO CHANGES                        │
│***                                                                         │
│                                                                            │
│ S▣■                                              □-□99           016/006   │
└──────────────────────────────────────────────────────────────────────────┘
```

FIGURE 30.3   DB2I JCL generation output messages.

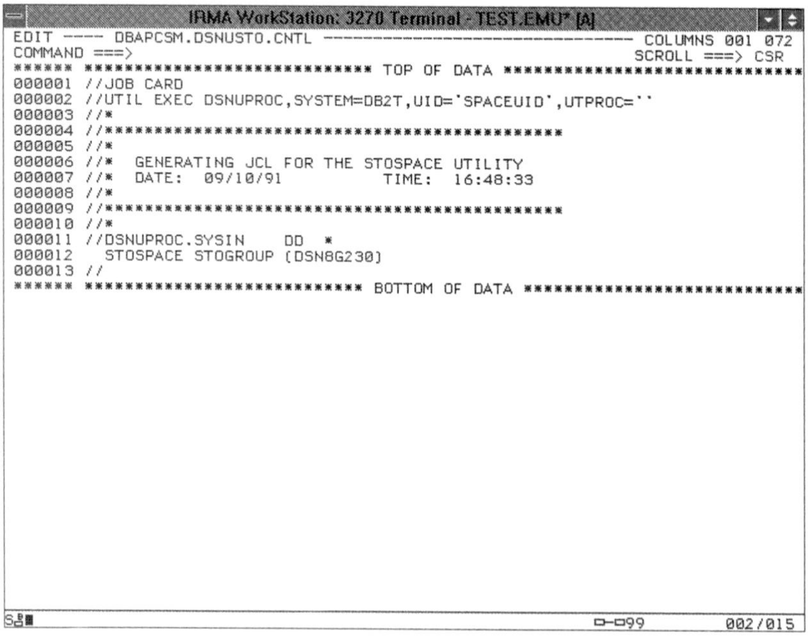

```
┌──────────────────────────────────────────────────────────────────────────┐
│ ▬              IRMA WorkStation: 3270 Terminal - TEST.EMU* [A]       ▼│♦│  │
│ EDIT ---- DBAPCSM.DSNUSTO.CNTL ---------------------------- COLUMNS 001 072 │
│ COMMAND ===>                                              SCROLL ===> CSR   │
│ ****** ************************* TOP OF DATA ****************************** │
│ 000001 //JOB CARD                                                          │
│ 000002 //UTIL EXEC DSNUPROC,SYSTEM=DB2T,UID='SPACEUID',UTPROC=''            │
│ 000003 //*                                                                 │
│ 000004 //*****************************************************              │
│ 000005 //*                                                                 │
│ 000006 //*   GENERATING JCL FOR THE STOSPACE UTILITY                        │
│ 000007 //*   DATE:  09/10/91         TIME:  16:48:33                        │
│ 000008 //*                                                                 │
│ 000009 //*****************************************************              │
│ 000010 //*                                                                 │
│ 000011 //DSNUPROC.SYSIN   DD  *                                             │
│ 000012   STOSPACE STOGROUP (DSN8G230)                                       │
│ 000013 //                                                                  │
│ ****** ************************ BOTTOM OF DATA *************************** │
│                                                                            │
│ S▣■                                              □-□99           002/015   │
└──────────────────────────────────────────────────────────────────────────┘
```

FIGURE 30.4   Generated JCL for the STOSPACE utility.

Each online utility is associated with a utility identifier, or UID, that is passed to DSNUTILB as a parameter to uniquely identify the utility to DB2. Two utilities with the same UID cannot execute concurrently.

The DSNUPROC procedure requires the specification of override parameters to function properly. These parameters should be coded as follows:

LIB   The DB2 link library assigned to your DB2 system. This can be obtained from the database administrator or the system programmer responsible for DB2.

SYSTEM   The DB2 system containing the objects on which the utility will be run.

UID   Identifies the utility to the DB2 system. If this value is blank, the UID defaults to the job name. This enables an analyst or DBA to quickly identify the job associated with a utility. Also, because two identically named MVS jobs cannot run concurrently, two utilities with the same UID cannot run concurrently. This minimizes the possibility of incorrectly restarting or rerunning an abending job.

UTPROC   This value initially should be blank (that is, UTPROC="). This parameter is assigned a value only during restart. A value of 'RESTART(PHASE)' restarts the utility at the beginning of the last executed phase. A value of 'RESTART' restarts the utility at the last or current commit point. The type of restart, PHASE or COMMIT, must be determined by analyzing the type of utility and the abend.

Monitoring DB2 Utilities

Online DB2 utilities can be monitored and controlled using DB2 commands. The DISPLAY and TERM commands can be used for this purpose. For example, the DISPLAY command can be entered as

```
-DISPLAY UTILITY (UID)
```

or

```
-DISPLAY UTILITY (*)
```

> **NOTE**
>
> The -DISPLAY command can be abbreviated to -DIS for simplicity.

The TERM command also can be entered by specifying a wildcard or a UID. The recommendation is to specify a UID when terminating utilities, because an asterisk indicates that every utility known to DB2 should be terminated. Enter the TERM command as

```
-TERM UTILITY (UID)
```

30

The -DISPLAY UTILITY command provides information about the execution status of the utility named by the utility ID. When this command is issued, it returns a screen similar to the one shown in Figure 30.5. This screen lists the following information:

USERID	The user ID of the job performing the utility.
UTILID	The utility ID assigned in the UID parameter on the EXEC card. If the UID parameter is not provided, UTILID is the same name as the jobname.
STATEMENT	The number of the control card containing the utility statement that is being processed (if more than one utility control card is supplied as input to the utility step).
UTILITY	The type of utility that is being executed. For example, if a reorganization is run, UTILITY contains REORG.
PHASE	The phase of the utility being executed. The phases for each utility are discussed in Part VI.
COUNT	A count of the number of records (pages or rows, depending on the utility and phase being monitored) processed by the phase. Count also may be the number of index entries being processed. Count isn't always kept by every utility phase, however.
STATUS	The status of the utility. ACTIVE indicates that the utility is currently active and should not be terminated. If terminated, the utility will abend. STOPPED means that the utility is currently stopped and should be restarted or terminated, depending on the state of the job and the procedures in place for restarting or rerunning.

The TERM command terminates the execution of a DB2 utility. Think carefully before terminating a utility. After a utility is terminated, it cannot be restarted. Instead, it must be rerun, which involves reprocessing.

Five types of online DB2 utilities are provided:

- Data consistency utilities
- Backup and recovery utilities
- Data movement and organization utilities
- Catalog manipulation utilities
- Miscellaneous utilities

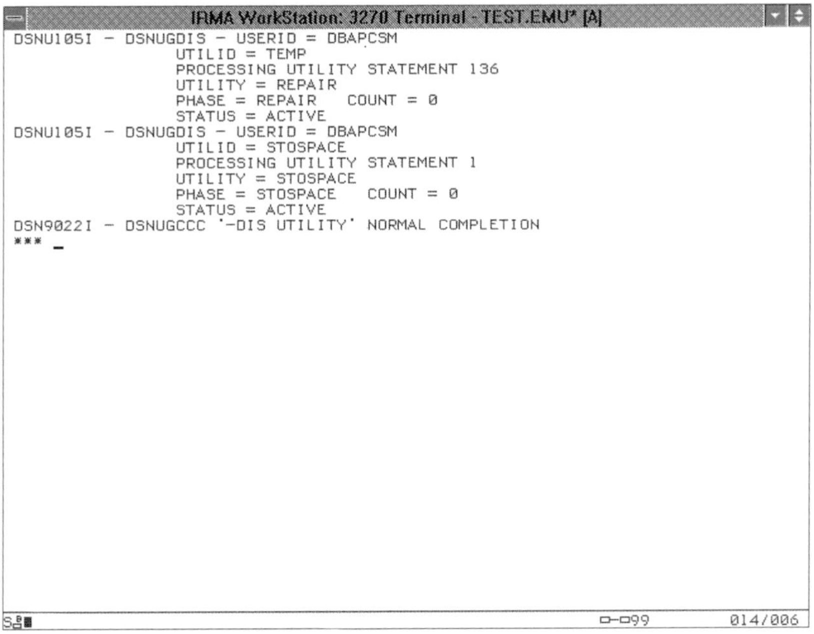

```
░░░░░░░░░░░░░░IRMA WorkStation: 3270 Terminal - TEST.EMU* [A]░░░░░░░░░░▼░░░
DSNU105I - DSNUGDIS - USERID = DBAPCSM
                     UTILID = TEMP
                     PROCESSING UTILITY STATEMENT 136
                     UTILITY = REPAIR
                     PHASE = REPAIR    COUNT = 0
                     STATUS = ACTIVE
DSNU105I - DSNUGDIS - USERID = DBAPCSM
                     UTILID = STOSPACE
                     PROCESSING UTILITY STATEMENT 1
                     UTILITY = STOSPACE
                     PHASE = STOSPACE    COUNT = 0
                     STATUS = ACTIVE
DSN9022I - DSNUGCCC '-DIS UTILITY' NORMAL COMPLETION
*** _
```

FIGURE 30.5   Output from the -DISPLAY UTILITY (*) command.

Version 7 and the State of IBM DB2 Utilities

V7   As of DB2 Version 7, IBM decoupled the core utility functionality from the base DB2 engine and is charging their customers extra if they choose to use IBM's utilities. In all past releases of DB2, core utility functionality came free with the DB2 base product. This is causing confusion and angst for mainframe DB2 users.

This decision was made because IBM wants to use the DB2 utilities as an entry into the database tools market. IBM just recently entered the market for database tools in a big way. By leveraging their installed base for DB2 utilities (which is 100%—remember, they were free), IBM is trying to market additional tools and products like performance monitors, administration tools, and so on.

IBM has competition in the database utility field from companies such as BMC Software, CDB Software, and Computer Associates. These companies thrive by selling more functional, faster utilities than IBM—and they do so by selling products that IBM was giving away for free. Now many organizations are faced with a decision—"Do I buy the IBM utilities or third-party utilities for DB2?"

This is a more difficult question than it appears to be on the surface. First of all, IBM does not sell individual utilities, but suites of utilities. The third-party vendors all sell individual utilities (as well as suites and solutions that include utilities). Additionally, the functionality of the IBM and third-party utilities is not 100% exact. Many of the third-party offerings still provide more functionality at higher speeds than the IBM offerings. But the IBM

30

utilities are still cheaper (though no longer free) than the third-party utilities. Furthermore, only IBM offers certain functionality in certain utilities.

To add to the discomfort, consider that many organizations bought third-party utilities with the comfort level of having the IBM utilities as a backup in case problems were encountered with the third-party products. Additionally, most shops bought only a few of the third-party utilities. Now those shops might have to purchase both the IBM utility suites and the third-party utilities to get the same functionality they had before. So, in essence, IBM is forcing them to buy utility functions twice.

To be fair to IBM, their DB2 utilities are better than they used to be. IBM finally seems to be putting the appropriate development effort into their utilities. Even so, the third-party utilities still provide unique features not available in IBM's utilities. And in many cases, organizations are relying on those features to run their business.

To be critical of IBM, they have been claiming that their DB2 utilities are improved to the point that the IBM stuff is all their customers need since Version 3. This was not true for V3, V4, V5, or V6, and it still is not true for V7 and V8. Many organizations that deal with a lot of data, require 24×7 availability, and/or need to contend with shrinking batch windows need the speed of third-party utilities. Given IBM's utility history, customers have every right to be skeptical about IBM's speed and functionality claims with regard to DB2 utilities.

IBM Utility Packages

 An additional complexity to contend with when trying to understand DB2 utilities is the way that IBM packages their utilities. Prior to V7, all utilities came free with DB2. As of V7, IBM packages the DB2 utilities into four suites, or packages:

- Base utilities—CATMAINT, DIAGNOSE, LISTDEF, OPTIONS, QUIESCE, REPAIR, REPORT, TEMPLATE, and DSNUTILS

- Operational utilities—COPY, LOAD, REBUILD, RECOVER, REORG, RUNSTATS, STOSPACE, and UNLOAD

- Recover and diagnostics utilities—CHECK, COPY, COPYTOCOPY, MERGE, MODIFY, REBUILD, and RECOVER

- Utilities suite—Includes all utilities in both the Operational utilities suite and the Recover and diagnostics utilities suite.

Only the first package, the base utilities, is provided free of charge by IBM. Any of the others must be purchased and licensed before the utilities can be used. This is so, with one exception. IBM permits customers to use any utility to manage DB2 system catalog objects.

Also, to further complicate matters, some utilities are in both suites. For example, COPY is in both the operational utilities suite and the recover and diagnostic utilities suite.

Keep in mind, too, that IBM will not sell just one utility. Instead of allowing customers to purchase individual utilities, IBM sells utilities in the listed packages. If you want to purchase only one specific IBM utility, you are instead forced to purchase an entire suite of utilities—some of which you may not want, or need.

> **NOTE**
>
> In late 2003 IBM decided to stop marketing and selling the Operational Utilities suite and Recover and Diagnostics suite. This means that the only option for IBM utilities at this time is the full Utilities suite. Of course, you still can opt to purchase competitive utilities from another vendor such as BMC Software or Computer Associates.
>
> Additionally, keep in mind that IBM may change its packaging for the utilities at their discretion. Further changes to packaging may have occurred subsequent to the publishing of this book.

So, when a DB2 customer migrates to Version 7, there are some decisions that need to be made. Should you buy IBM utilities or can you go with a third party? And if you go with a third party, can they offer everything that IBM offers? And furthermore, if you need third-party functionality and speed, will you have to buy something from IBM that you do not want or need?

> **CAUTION**
>
> It is my recommendation that all DB2 users purchase the entire DB2 utilities suite from IBM. Then, as needed, you should evaluate which third-party utilities you need to augment the IBM utilities. This is the only reasonable approach. It basically duplicates the "DB2 environment" the way it was before IBM started to charge for their utilities.
>
> Some third-party vendors are selling their utilities as replacements for the IBM utilities. Before you go down that route, make sure that the vendor can supply you with answers to the following questions:
>
> - Is there any functionality the vendor cannot provide that IBM can (for example, does the MODIFY utility clean up SYSLGRNX records)?
> - Will the vendor guarantee a response time for support calls if theirs are the only utilities you own?
> - How will the vendor work with IBM in case of problem situations? IBM has hinted that they will not provide support if the support call requires utility functionality and the customer does not have the IBM utility.

It is confusing, but you must be able to understand all of the options and then make an informed decision about the functionality you need to run your DB2 business.

Using LISTDEF and TEMPLATE

V7 IBM made several improvements to the general useability of DB2 utilities in Version 7. Most of these improvements have been available from third-party ISVs for a number of years, but IBM is now starting to catch up. The biggest V7 utility improvements include the following abilities:

- For one utility to operate on a list of DB2 objects

- To use wildcards to create such lists

- To have DB2 determine which data sets should be allocated

Let's take a look at these new capabilities.

Database Object Lists

V7 A database object list is created using the LISTDEF statement. The purpose of LISTDEF is to allow DB2 utilities to execute against multiple database objects. Traditionally (prior to V7) a DB2 utility was run against a single database object. Each utility required a specific control card to be set up to execute that utility against each database object. Alternatively, a separate utility job could be constructed for each database object. With the LISTDEF statement, the DBA can create a list of database objects that can be submitted to a single utility invocation for execution. So, as of V7, it is very simple to set up one utility execution to run against multiple database objects.

For example, the following statement creates a list named CUSTALL that includes all of the database objects in the CUSTOMER database:

```
LISTDEF CUSTALL INCLUDE TABLESPACES DATABASE CUSTOMER
                INCLUDE INDEXSPACES DATABASE CUSTOMER
```

LISTDEF is not a utility; it is a control statement that can be used within other DB2 utilities. The LISTDEF statement can be used to assign a name to a list of DB2 database objects and previously defined lists of database objects—so, a list can consist of other lists. After the list is defined, it can be used when executing other utilities. Each list must be named and that name can be up to 18 characters in length.

To run a DB2 utility against a list, you have the option of putting the LISTDEF statements in a separate library data set or coding it directly before the DB2 utility control statement that refers to the list. The default DD name for a LISTDEF data set is SYSLISTD, but this can be changed using the OPTIONS LISTDEFDD control statement.

To run LISTDEF as part of a utility execution, the process or user running the utility must have SELECT authority on: SYSIBM.SYSINDEXES, SYSIBM.SYSTABLES, and SYSIBM.SYSTABLESPACE. Of course, the process or user running the utility also must have the requisite authority to execute the utility being used to process the list.

Because LISTDEF is a control statement, not an individual utility, LISTDEF conforms to the concurrency rules for the utility to which the list is being applied. The LISTDEF list is stored until it is referenced by a specific utility, at which time the list is expanded. At that time, the concurrency and compatibility restrictions of the utility being executed apply, with the additional restriction that the catalog tables necessary to expand the list must be available for read-only access.

Creating Lists with LISTDEF

The INCLUDE and EXCLUDE keywords are used to build the list of database objects:

- INCLUDE—Specifies database objects to add to the list

- EXCLUDE—Specifies database objects to remove from the list

The LISTDEF statement can consist of multiple INCLUDE and EXCLUDE clauses. At least one INCLUDE clause must be specified. Furthermore, an INCLUDE clause must be coded before any subsequent EXCLUDE clauses. For most utilities, the INCLUDE and EXCLUDE clauses will be processed in the order they are coded in the LISTDEF statement. Certain specific utilities will modify the order of the list to optimize its processing:

- The CHECK INDEX, REBUILD INDEX, and RUNSTATS INDEX utilities will process all index spaces that are related to a given table space at once, regardless of the order in which the indexes appear in the list.

- The UNLOAD utility will process all specified partitions of a given table space at one time regardless of the order in which the indexes appear in the list.

The list will be built one clause at a time, by adding database objects to the list or removing database objects from the list. Any EXCLUDE statements that try to remove a database object from the list that has not yet been added to the list will cause DB2 to ignore that database object and proceed to the next INCLUDE or EXCLUDE clause. Be aware that a subsequent INCLUDE can return the excluded object to the list.

Furthermore, INCLUDE and EXCLUDE statements can be typed—meaning that they can be set to include or exclude only table spaces or only index spaces. Of course, the typing of INCLUDE and EXCLUDE statements is optional. If the type is not specified, the statement will default to a particular type of object based on the subsequent keywords that are coded. The available keywords for including and excluding database objects from a list include the following:

- DATABASE—To specify table spaces, index spaces, or both from a particular database or databases

- TABLESPACE—To specify table spaces, index spaces, or both for a particular table space or table spaces

- TABLE—To specify table spaces, index spaces, or both from a particular table space or table spaces

- INDEXSPACE—To specify index spaces

- INDEX—To specify index spaces

- LIST—To specify a list of table spaces, index spaces, or both that was previously defined using LISTDEF

Additionally, the PARTLEVEL keyword can be used to specify only certain partitions for inclusion. The PARTLEVEL keyword applies to both table spaces and index spaces, and is

30

ignored for non-partitioned database objects. The PARTLEVEL keyword takes an integer parameter that specifies the partition to be included. Failure to specify the partition number causes a list to be generated that contains one entry for every existing partition of the table space or index space.

Be aware that the only way to exclude a partition is if it was first included explicitly as a partition. For example, the following LISTDEF statement will exclude partition 7 from the list because both statements are coded at the partition level:

```
LISTDEF LST1 INCLUDE TABLESPACE DB.TS1 PARTLEVEL
             EXCLUDE TABLESPACE DB.TS1 PARTLEVEL(7)
```

However, the next LISTDEF statement will not exclude partition 7 from the list, because the INLCUDE statement was specified at the table space level, but the EXCLUDE statement is specified at the partition level:

```
LISTDEF LST2 INCLUDE TABLESPACE DB.TS1
             EXCLUDE TABLESPACE DB.TS1 PARTLEVEL(7)
```

Wildcarding

 The LISTDEF statement can use wildcarding to rapidly specify multiple database objects without having to explicitly name each of the objects. For example, you might specify

```
LISTDEF LST3 INCLUDE TABLESPACE DBXN.*
             EXCLUDE TABLESPACE DBXN.TS2

REORG LIST LST3 . . .
```

This sequence of statements will reorganize all table spaces in the database named DBXN except for the one table space exempted, namely TS2. Furthermore, if a table space is subsequently added to DBXN, the REORG job does not need to be changed. The next time it runs, REORG will query the DB2 Catalog to determine the table spaces that exist in the list name DB1. Since it specifies all table spaces in DBXN, any new table space added to DBXN will automatically be picked up for processing.

The valid wildcard options supported by LISTDEF are as follows:

- The question mark (**?**), which can be used to indicate any single character

- The underscore (**_**), which can be used to indicate any single character

- The percent sign (**%**), which can be used to indicate a string of 0, 1 or many characters

- The asterisk (*****), which can be used to indicate a string of 0, 1 or many characters

These options were chosen by IBM to mimic the wildcarding capability of the SQL LIKE clause. However, the underscore and percent sign characters are commonly occurring characters within database object names, so additional wildcard character options were provided.

> **CAUTION**
>
> Be sure to use the question mark (?) wildcard character instead of the underscore (_) character for pattern-matching in table and index names. For table and index names, the underscore character represents a single occurrence of itself. The underscore can be used as an alternative to the question mark for database, table space, and index space names.

Although wildcarding is a very powerful capability, DB2 does place some limits on its use. For example, it is not permissible to create all-inclusive lists, such as DATABASE * or TABLESPACE *.*.

The bottom line, though, is that the ability to create lists using wildcards greatly eases the task of creating utility jobs.

List Expansion

Lists created using the LISTDEF statement are expanded each time the utility job in which the LISTDEF is included is executed. This is important, because it simplifies the task of creating utility jobs for new database objects. For example, suppose you have a utility job set up to make image copies for every table space within a given database, such as

```
LISTDEF LSTX INCLUDE TABLESPACE DBGL00X1.*

COPY LIST LSTX ...
```

This sequence of commands is set up to copy every table space in the DBGL00X1 database. If you add a new table space to that database you do not need to create a new image copy job or modify the existing job. This is so because the next time the existing job runs the list will be expanded and will now include the new table space—which will cause it to be copied. Lists (and templates), therefore, can greatly simplify the DBA task of creating utility jobs for new database objects.

Referential Integrity and Lists   The RI parameter can be included on the INCLUDE statement to cause all tables that are referentially connected to tables specified in the list to also be included. This relieves the DBA of the burden of manually determining which tables are connected to which. Be advised, however, that the RI parameter cannot be used in conjunction with the PARTLEVEL parameter.

V8

> **NOTE**
>
> Informational referential constraints will be included when using the RI parameter to report on referential table space sets.

LOBs and Lists   Database objects containing LOBs are special and might need to be treated differently than other database objects for utility processing. The LISTDEF statement provides options that enable the DBA to handle database objects that use LOBs differently.

LISTDEF offers three options that can be specified on an INCLUDE or EXCLUDE specification, to indicate how to process the LOB-related objects. The auxiliary LOB relationship can be traversed in either direction:

- From LOB auxiliary table to base table

- From base table to LOB auxiliary table

LOB objects include LOB table spaces, auxiliary tables, indexes on auxiliary tables, and their associated index spaces. Failure to specify one of the following three keyword options will result in DB2 not following the auxiliary relationships, and therefore LOBs will not be filtered from BASE objects in the enumerated list:

- ALL—Indicates that both BASE and LOB objects are to be included in the list. Auxiliary relationships will be followed from all objects resulting from the initial object lookup and both BASE and LOB objects will remain in the final enumerated list.

- BASE—Indicates that only base table spaces and index spaces will be included in the list; that is, no LOB objects will be included for this specific INCLUDE or EXCLUDE. Of course, you can specify a LOB object to begin with, causing LISTDEF to search for the related base objects and only the base objects will be included in the list.

- LOB—Indicates that only LOB table spaces and related index spaces containing indexes on auxiliary tables are to be included in the list. Once again, you can specify that a base object or a LOB object to begin with, but only LOB objects will be included in the list.

Indexes, Lists, and the COPY Utility   An additional consideration for lists built using the LISTDEF statement is the treatment of indexes with regard to the COPY utility. As of DB2 V6 it has been possible to take image copy backups of index spaces to be used for subsequent recovery; previously, indexes had to be rebuilt from table data after table spaces were recovered.

LISTDEF offers the COPY keyword, which can be used to specify whether indexes that are defined as COPY YES (or COPY NO) are to be included or excluded in the list. If the COPY keyword is not coded, all index spaces that satisfy the INCLUDE or EXCLUDE expression, regardless of their COPY attribute, will be included or excluded in the list. If specified, this keyword must immediately follow the INDEXSPACES keyword. If specified elsewhere, the keyword COPY is interpreted as the start of the COPY utility control statement. The COPY keyword can take on one of two values:

- YES—Indicates that index spaces defined with or altered to COPY YES are the only ones to be included in the list.

- NO—Indicates that index spaces defined with or altered to COPY NO are the only ones to be included in the list.

You can use INCLUDE with COPY YES to create a list of index spaces that can be processed by the COPY utility. Or, you can use EXCLUDE with COPY NO to remove index spaces that cannot be processed by the COPY utility from a list of index spaces.

List Usage Guidelines

The whole purpose for using LISTDEF to create lists of database objects is to use those lists when executing DB2 utilities. Once created, the LIST keyword is specified in the utility job in order to process just those objects on the list. The LIST keyword can be used with the following utilities:

- CHECK INDEX—During execution, the database objects in the list will be grouped by related table space for processing.

- COPY—During execution, the database objects in the list will be processed in the order they were specified.

- MERGECOPY—During execution, the database objects in the list will be processed in the order they were specified.

- MODIFY RECOVERY—During execution, the database objects in the list will be processed in the order they were specified.

- MODIFY STATISTICS—During execution, the database objects in the list will be processed in the order they were specified.

- QUIESCE—During execution, the database objects in the list will be processed in the order they were specified.

- REBUILD—During execution, the database objects in the list will be grouped by related table space for processing.

- RECOVER—During execution, the database objects in the list will be processed in the order they were specified.

- REORG—During execution, the database objects in the list will be processed in the order they were specified.

- REPORT—During execution, the database objects in the list will be processed in the order they were specified.

- RUNSTATS INDEX—During execution, the database objects in the list will be grouped by related table space for processing.

- RUNSTATS TABLESPACE—During execution, the database objects in the list will be processed in the order they were specified.

Certain utilities, such as RECOVER and COPY, can process a LIST without a specified database object type. These utilities will derive the database object type to process based on the contents of the list. But other utilities, such as QUIESCE and REORG INDEX, must have the database object type specified before the utility can be executed. For these utilities you must specify an object type in addition to the LIST keyword, for example:

```
QUIESCE TABLESPACE LIST list-name.
```

Additionally, most utilities require output data sets in order to process. You can use the TEMPLATE statement to specify the naming convention and, optionally, the allocation

30

parameters for each output data set type. Templates, like lists, can be reused as long as the naming convention prohibits the specification of duplicate data set names. Although it may be possible to use traditional JCL with certain LISTDEF lists it is not recommended because the JCL quickly becomes unwieldy and impractical to maintain (unless the list of database objects to be processed is quite small).

When used together, LISTDEF and TEMPLATE statements make it easier to develop DB2 utility jobs. Job creation is faster, lists can be coded to capture and process new database objects automatically, and the resulting JCL is easier to maintain because fewer modifications are required when database objects are added to the list.

Previewing the Contents of a List

You can use the OPTIONS PREVIEW control statement to expand the list and see the database objects that will be included in the list before actual processing. The OPTIONS ITEMERROR control statement can be used to alter the handling of errors that might occur during list processing. The OPTIONS LISTDEFDD control statement can be used to switch LISTDEF library data sets between control statements within a job step. The default is LISTDEFDD SYSLISTD.

LISTDEF Example

The example in Listing 30.1 shows the JCL and control statements used to build a list of table spaces to QUIESCE. The list created is named QLIST. This list includes all of the table spaces in database DB1 that begin with the characters "TSL" except for TSLY028A, TSLY066V, and TSLU071X. Also, one table space is included from database DB7, namely TSLU077T.

LISTING 30.1   Image copy JCL

```
//QUIESCE JOB 'USER=NAME',CLASS=A,...
//*******************************************************
//*QUIESCE LISTDEF DD LILSTDEF data sets
//*******************************************************
//STEP1    EXEC  DSNUPROC,UID='DBAPSCM.QUIESCL',
//            UTPROC='',SYSTEM='DB2A'
//LISTDSN DD DSN=JULTU103.TCASE.DATA2,DISP=SHR
//        DD DSN=JULTU103.TCASE.DATA3(MEM1),DISP=SHR
//SYSUT1   DD DSN=JULTU103.QUIESC2.STEP1.SYSUT1,
//        DISP=(MOD,DELETE,CATLG),UNIT=SYSDA,
//        SPACE=(4000,(20,20),,,ROUND)
//SORTOUT DD DSN=JULTU103.QUIESC2.STEP1.SORTOUT,
//        DISP=(MOD,DELETE,CATLG),UNIT=SYSDA,
//        SPACE=(4000,(20,20),,,ROUND)
//SYSIN    DD *

    LISTDEF QLIST INCLUDE TABLESPACE DB1.TSL*
                EXCLUDE TABLESPACE DB1.TSLY028A
                EXCLUDE TABLESPACE DB1.TSLY066V
                EXCLUDE TABLESPACE DB1.TSLU071X
                INCLUDE TABLESPACE DB7.TSLU077T

    QUIESCE LIST QLIST
/*
```

Templates

V7 In order to support database object lists and wildcarding, IBM also had to come up with a way of allocating data sets to support utility processing on a large number of unknown database objects—well, at least unknown at the time the utility JCL was being built. The new TEMPLATE statement accomplishes this.

The purpose of the TEMPLATE statement is to provide DB2 utilities with the basic allocation information necessary to automatically generate and allocate valid data sets that are required for use as DB2 utilities are executed. Traditionally, a DB2 utility is run against a single database object and the JCL is manually prepared with each required data set hard-coded into the JCL job stream. However, with the advent of LISTDEF, DB2 utility jobs can be set up to operate on multiple database objects with a single run. Furthermore, the person developing the JCL has no way to know how many database objects will be processed, so it is not practical to manually allocate data sets to such utility jobs. And due to the nature of the LISTDEF statement, it is possible that a different number of database objects will be processed each time a utility is run using the same list. So, once again, allocating data sets to the JCL in such an environment is impractical, if it is even possible at all.

Like LISTDEF, TEMPLATE is **not** a new utility, but is a new control statement. The TEMPLATE statement lets you allocate data sets, without using JCL DD cards, during the processing of a LISTDEF list. Using TEMPLATE the developer can define the data set naming convention, and specify further allocation parameters such as data set sizing, location, and attributes. The TEMPLATE statement is flexible enough to allow different characteristics for tape and disk data sets. Each TEMPLATE statement generates a named template to be referenced as needed.

To perform the dynamic data set allocation during the utility execution, the TEMPLATE control statement deploys the MVS DYNALLOC macro (SVC 99).

To use a template with a DB2 utility, you have the option of putting the TEMPLATE statements in a separate library data set or directly before the DB2 utility control statements. The default DD name for a TEMPLATE data set is SYSTEMPL, but this can be changed using the OPTIONS TEMPLATEDD control statement.

No additional privileges are required to run TEMPLATE as part of a utility execution. Of course, the process or user running the utility must have the requisite authority to execute the utility for which the template is being used.

Using TEMPLATE

Each TEMPLATE must be named. The TEMPLATE name is limited to eight alphanumeric characters, the first of which must be an alphabetic character (A through Z). After the template name you can specify keywords to control the allocation of tape and disk data sets. Each TEMPLATE statement can apply to either disk or tape, but not both. The UNIT keyword specifies a generic unit name that must be defined on your system. Additional keywords specified for the TEMPLATE statement must be consistent with the unit type specified; that is, valid for tape or disk.

There are three grouping of options that can be specified for a TEMPLATE statement:

- *Common Options*—These options apply to both disk and tape template.

- *Disk Options*—These options apply only to a disk template.

- *Tape Options*—These options apply only to a tape template.

A single TEMPLATE statement can have a set of common options, and then either a set of disk options or a set of tape options.

Common TEMPLATE Options   The following keywords are common options that can be applied to the definition of any TEMPLATE statement:

The UNIT option is used to indicate the device-number, the generic device-type or the group-name to use for allocating the data set.

The DSN option indicates the template for the data set name. The data set name can be created by using any combination of symbolic variables, alphanumeric constants, or national characters. When creating the DSN template follow the same basic rules for using symbolic variables within JCL. Special DB2 symbolic variables are provided that can be used to insert characteristics of the database object, utility, or job that is running. These symbolic variables are summarized in Table 30.1. Each symbolic variable is substituted by its related value at execution time to form an explicit data set name. When used in a DSN expression, the symbolic variable begins with the ampersand sign (&) and ends with a period (.). For example,

```
DSN &DB..&TS..D&JDATE..COPY&ICTYPE.
```

This DSN parameter creates a data set named using

- The database name as the first part,

- The table space name as the second part,

- The character "D" followed by the actual date as the third part,

- And, finally, the word "COPY" followed by the letter "F" (for a full image copy), the letter "C" (for a CHANGELIMIT image copy), or the letter "I" (for an incremental image copy) as the fourth and final part of the name.

The DISP option indicates the disposition of the data set using standard JCL parameters for (status, normal termination, and abnormal termination). The legal values for each are as follows:

- status—NEW, OLD, SHR, MOD.

- normal-termination—DELETE, KEEP, CATLG, UNCATLG.

- abnormal-termination—DELETE, KEEP, CATLG, UNCATLG.

The MODELDCB option indicates the DSN of a model data set that will be used to get the DCB information.

The BUFNO option indicates the number of BSAM buffers to use for data set buffering.

The DATACLAS option indicates the name of the SMS data class to use. If specified, this value must be a valid data class defined to SMS.

The MGMTCLAS option indicates the name of the SMS management class to use. If specified, this value must be a valid management class defined to SMS.

The STORCLAS option indicates the name of the SMS storage class to use. If specified, this value must be a valid storage class defined to SMS.

The RETPD option indicates the retention period for the data set in days. The value must be between 1 and 9999 if specified.

The EXPDL option indicates the expiration date for the data set. The date must be enclosed in single quotes and specified in Julian data format, that is, YYYYDDD.

The VOLUMES option is used to provide a list of volume serial numbers for this allocation. The volume serial numbers are provided in a comma-delimited list and enclosed within parentheses. The first volume on the list must contain sufficient space for the primary allocation of space for the data set.

The VOLCNT option indicates the maximum number of volumes that an output data set might require.

The GDGLIMIT option indicates the number of entries to be created in a GDG base if the DSN specifies a GDG and the GDG base does not already exist. The value of GDGLIMIT can range from 0 to 255, where 0 is a special value to specify that a GDG base should be created if one does not already exist.

TABLE 30.1   DB2 TEMPLATE Symbolics

Parameter	Description
&JOBNAME (or &JO)	The name of the z/OS (or OS/390) job.
&STEPNAME (or &ST)	The name of the z/OS (or OS/390) job step.
&UTILID (or &UT)	The utility id for this utility job (truncated to 8 characters or the first period in the utility ID).
&USERID (or &...)	The userid of the z/OS (or OS/390) job.
&SSID (or &SS)	The DB2 subsystem identifier.
&UTILNAME (or &UN)	The utility name for this utility job (truncated to 8 characters).
&LIST (or &LI)	The name of the list.
&SEQ (or &SQ)	The sequence number of the item in the list being processed.
&JDATE (or &JU)	The Julian date, formatted as YYYYDDD. Must be prefixed with a character number when used (for example, D&JDATE).
&JDAY (or &JD)	The day portion of the Julian date, formatted as DDD. Must be prefixed with a character number when used (for example, D&JDAY).
&TIME	The system time, formatted as HHMMSS. Must be prefixed with a character number when used (for example, T&TIME).
&HOUR (or &HO)	The hour component of the system time, formatted as HH. Must be prefixed with a character number when used (for example, T&HOUR).

30

TABLE 30.1   Continued

Parameter	Description
&MINUTE (or &MI)	The minute component of the system time, formatted as MM. Must be prefixed with a character number when used (for example, T&MINUTE).
&SECOND (or &SC)	The second component of the system time, formatted as SS. Must be prefixed with a character number when used (for example, T&SECOND).
&YEAR	The year, formatted as YYYY. Must be prefixed with a character number when used (for example, Y&YEAR).
&MONTH	The month, formatted as MM. Must be prefixed with a character number when used (for example, M&MONTH).
&DAY	The day of the month, formatted as DD. Must be prefixed with a character number when used (for example, D&DAY).
&DB	The database name.
&TS	The table space name.
&IS	The index space name.
&SN	The space name—either table space or index space depending on which is being processed.
&PART (or &PA)	The partition number—formatted as five digits, left padded.
&ICTYPE (or &IC)	The image copy type—either F for full copy, C for CHANGELIMIT copy, or I for incremental copy.
&LOCREM (or &LR)	The location of the image copy—either L for local copy or R for remote copy.
&PRIBAC (or &PB)	The type of copy—either P for primary copy or B for backup copy.

Disk Options   The following keywords are disk options that can only be applied to the definition of a statement defining a disk TEMPLATE:

The SPACE option indicates the primary and secondary disk space allocation values for the DSN template. The option takes two values, placed between parentheses and separated by a comma: the first is the primary allocation and the second is the secondary allocation.

- CYL—Indicates that allocation quantities are specified in terms of cylinders and allocation will occur in cylinders

- TRK—Indicates that allocation quantities are specified in terms of tracks and allocation will occur in tracks

- MB—Indicates that allocation quantities are specified in terms of megabytes and allocation will occur in records

The PCTPRIME option indicates the percentage of space to be obtained as the primary quantity.

The MAXPRIME option specifies an upper limit on the primary quantity specified using the SPACE parameter (expressed in the units specified on the SPACE parameter).

The NBRSECOND option indicates the division of secondary space allocations. After the primary space is allocated, the remaining space is divided into the specified number of secondary allocations. The NBRSECOND value can range from 1 to 10.

Tape Options   The following keywords are disk options that can only be applied to the definition of a statement defining a disk TEMPLATE:

The UNCNT option indicates the number of devices to be allocated. If a specific device number is coded on the UNIT common option, then UNCNT must be 1 (or not coded).

The STACK option indicates whether output data sets are to be stacked contiguously on tape. Valid values are YES or NO.

The JES3DD option indicates the name of the JCL DD to be used at job initialization time for the tape unit. (JES3 requires that all necessary tape units are pre-allocated by DD statement.)

The TRTCH option indicates the track recording technique (for tape drives with improved data recording capabilities). Valid values are

- NONE—Indicates that TRTCH is eliminated from dynamic allocation

- COMP—Indicates that data is to be written in compacted format

- NOCOMP—Indicates that data in to be written in standard format (that is, not compacted)

TEMPLATE **Examples**

The following statement shows a disk template with an explicit specification of space. The data set name will consist of the database name, the table space name, the name of the utility it was used with, and the time of allocation. Allocation is by cylinder with a primary space of 115 and a secondary of 15:

```
TEMPLATE DISKTMP2 DSN(&DB..&TS..&UTILNAME..T&TIME.)
     SPACE(115,15) CYL
```

This next example shows how to use TEMPLATE in conjunction with LISTDEF. The LISTDEF creates a list of table spaces to COPY. Two templates are specified, one for a disk local copy and one for a tape remote copy. The tape and disk template each specify different UNIT values, the disk template specifies the data set disposition, and the tape template specifies an expiration date of January 2, 2005 (in Julian date format):

```
LISTDEF  COPYLIST INCLUDE TABLESPACE DBGL01.*
                  EXCLUDE TABLESPACE DBGL01.TSNAME
TEMPLATE DISKTMPL UNIT SYSDA
                  DSN(&DB..&TS..COPY&IC.&LR.&PB..D&DATE..T&TIME.)
                  DISP (MOD,CATLG,CATLG)
TEMPLATE TAPETMPL UNIT T35901
                  DSN(&DB..&TS..COPY&IC.&LR.&PB..D&DATE..T&TIME.)
                  EXPDL '2005002'
COPY LIST COPYLIST COPYDDN (DISKTMPL) RECOVERYDDN (TAPETMPL)
     SHRLEVEL REFERENCE
```

30

Testing Options for Lists and Template

It is a good idea to test lists and templates before using them with a utility. Doing so can help to validate the accuracy of the list contents and template specification.

The OPTIONS utility control statement can be used to indicate processing options that apply across many utility executions. By specifying various options you can

- Preview utility control statements.

- Override library names for LISTDEF lists or TEMPLATEs.

- Specify how to handle errors during list processing.

- Alter the return code for warning messages.

- Restore all default options.

The processing options set using the OPTIONS statement remain in effect for the duration of the job step, or until they are overridden by another OPTIONS statement in the same job step.

The OPTIONS control statement requires no specific privileges to be specified. Of course, the process or user running the utility also must have the requisite authority to execute the actual utility that is being executed with the OPTIONS statement.

OPTIONS is not a utility itself, but a control statement used to set up the environment for other utilities to run. The OPTIONS statement is simply stored until it is referenced by a DB2 utility. When the OPTIONS statement is referenced, the list specified for that utility will be expanded and the concurrency and compatibility restrictions of that utility will apply. In addition, the catalog tables necessary to expand the list also must be available for read-only access.

Using OPTIONS

Two keywords can be used in conjunction with OPTIONS: PREVIEW and OFF.

The PREVIEW keyword is similar to the JCL PREVIEW parameter. It is used to check for syntax errors in subsequent utility control cards and will not execute the utilities. For example, PREVIEW can be used in conjunction with LISTDEF to expand a list in order to verify that the proper database objects have been included in the list.

The OFF keyword can be used to restore to the default options. Using OPTIONS OFF will not override the PREVIEW JCL parameter, which, if specified, remains in effect for the entire job step. When specifying OPTIONS OFF, no other OPTIONS keywords may be used.

Issuing SQL Statements in DB2 Utilities

V7 Another new Version 7 utility feature is the EXEC SQL utility control statement. This statement can be used to declare cursors and execute dynamic SQL statements during a DB2 utility execution. The EXEC SQL control statement produces a result table when you specify a cursor. The EXEC SQL control statement executes entirely in the EXEC phase of the utility. The EXEC phase can be restarted if necessary.

The EXEC SQL statement requires no additional privileges to execute. However, EXEC SQL adheres to the same authorization rules as must be followed for executing dynamic SQL using EXECUTE IMMEDIATE.

SQL statements can be used only in conjunction with DB2 utilities that allow concurrent SQL access on a table space with the utility. No other databases are affected when issuing the EXEC SQL statement.

Using EXEC SQL

To use EXEC SQL as a utility control statement, simply code a permissible SQL statement after the EXEC SQL keyword. That SQL statement will be run during the utility execution as a separate thread. When the SQL statement is executed, the specified statement string is parsed and checked for errors. If the SQL statement is invalid, it is not executed and the error condition is reported. If the SQL statement is valid, but an error occurs during execution, that error condition is reported. When an error occurs, the utility terminates.

There are two options when using EXEC SQL to supply an SQL statement to a utility. The first option is for non-SELECT dynamic SQL statements where the SQL is used as input to an EXECUTE IMMEDIATE statement. The following SQL statements can be specified in an EXEC SQL statement for processing by a DB2 utility:

ALTER	RENAME
COMMENT ON	REVOKE
COMMIT	ROLLBACK
CREATE	SET CURRENT DEGREE
DELETE	SET CURRENT LOCALE LC_CTYPE
DROP	SET CURRENT OPTIMIZATION HINT
EXPLAIN	SET CURRENT PATH
GRANT	SET CURRENT PRECISION
INSERT	SET CURRENT RULES
LABEL ON	SET CURRENT SQLID
LOCK TABLE	UPDATE

The second form of SQL permitted within an EXEC SQL utility control statement is a cursor-driven SELECT statement. To use this option simply declare a cursor that is not already declared and specify the SELECT statement to be used in conjunction with the cursor. For example,

```
EXEC SQL
    DECLARE CSR1 CURSOR FOR
      SELECT DEPTNO, DEPTNAME, LOCATION FROM DSN8810.DEPT
ENDEXEC
```

This statement declares a cursor named CSR1 that selects three columns from all of the rows in the DEPT sample table.

30

Why Issue SQL During a Utility?

Once someone learns of this new DB2 capability the next logical question usually is "Why would I want to do that?" Well, there are several good reasons to run SQL in conjunction with a utility.

One possible use is for general purpose SQL that needs to be run and would otherwise be issued using DSNTEP2, SPUFI, or QMF. For example, consider the (perhaps unlikely) scenario where you wish to give every employee a 10% raise. You could use the EXEC SQL utility control statement to perform this task as you run the utility by including the following statement:

```
EXEC SQL
    UPDATE DSN8710.EMP
        SET SALARY = SALARY * 1.10
ENDEXEC
```

Perhaps a more likely scenario will be for DBAs to create the tables required for exception processing in CHECK DATA, or the mapping table and index for running a REORG using SHRLEVEL CHANGE. For example, when running CHECK DATA on the ACT sample table to you might include the following DDL in the utility job using EXEC SQL:

```
EXEC SQL
    CREATE TABLE EXCPT_ACT LIKE DSN8710.ACT
ENDEXEC

EXEC SQL
    ALTER TABLE EXCPT_ACT
      ADD EXCPT_RID CHAR(4)
ENDEXEC

EXEC SQL
    ALTER TABLE EXCPT_ACT
      ADD EXCPT_TS TIMESTAMP
ENDEXEC
```

This effectively creates the exception table and adds the additional columns to the table as needed. Similarly, to create the mapping table for a REORG SHRLEVEL CHANGE, the following DDL can be included in the utility job using EXEC SQL:

```
EXEC SQL
    CREATE TABLESPACE XMAP0001
      IN DBNAME
        USING STOGROUP MAPSG
          PRIQTY 52
          SECQTY 20
          ERASE NO
      LOCKSIZE PAGE
      BUFFERPOOL BP9
      SEGSIZE 8
      CLOSE YES
      COMPRESS NO
ENDEXEC
```

```
EXEC SQL
      CREATE TABLE MAP_TABLE_0001
         (TYPE         CHAR(1) NOT NULL,
          SOURCE_RID   CHAR(5) NOT NULL,
          TARGET_XRID  CHAR(9) NOT NULL,
          LRSN         CHAR(6) NOT NULL)
      IN DBNAME.XMAP0001
ENDEXEC

EXEC SQL
    CREATE UNIQUE INDEX XMAP0001
      ON MAP_TABLE_0001
      (SOURCE_RID ASC,
       TYPE,
       TARGET_XRID,
       LRSN)
ENDEXEC
```

This series of SQL statements effectively creates the table space for the mapping table, the mapping table itself, and the unique index required for the mapping table. Please note that other than the table space needing to be segmented, the exact parameters specified in this example are not etched in stone and can be changed to suit your site's needs. Additionally, if desired, following the REORG an additional step could DROP the mapping table objects. This way the mapping table exists only when it is needed—during the online reorganization process—and it does not hang around consuming extra disk space when it is not required.

DB2's ability to execute SQL statements during a utility job delivers a powerful new capability to the DBA. What used to take multiple steps or jobs might now be able to be accomplished in a single utility step.

CHAPTER **31**

Data Consistency Utilities

Often, the consistency of data in a DB2 database must be monitored and controlled. In the scope of DB2 databases, *consistency* encompasses four things:

- The consistency of reference from index entries to corresponding table rows

- The consistency of reference from LOB entries to corresponding table rows

- The consistency of data values in referential structures

- The consistency of data values conforming to check constraints

- The general consistency of DB2 data sets and data

Recall from previous chapters that a DB2 index is composed of column key values and RID pointers to rows in the DB2 table containing these values. Because the table and index information are in different physical data sets, the information in the index could become invalid. If the index key values or pointers become inconsistent, you would want to be able to pinpoint and correct the inconsistencies. This is the first type of consistency.

When LOB columns are specified in a DB2 table, the data is not physically stored in the same table space as the rest of the data in the table. An auxiliary table is required for each LOB column in the table. The primary table space maintains pointers to the auxiliary table pages where the LOBs are actually stored. Because the primary table data and the LOB data reside in different physical data sets, the pointers in the primary table could become invalid. If the LOB pointers become inconsistent, you would want to be able to pinpoint and correct the inconsistencies. This is the second type of consistency.

The third type of consistency refers to the referential integrity feature of DB2. When a primary-key-to-foreign-key relationship is defined between DB2 tables, a referential structure is created. Every foreign key in the dependent table must either match a primary key value in the parent table or be null. If, due to other utility processing, the referential integrity rules are violated, you must be able to view and possibly correct the violations.

The fourth type of consistency refers to ensuring that data values conform to specific values (or ranges of values). This is implemented using check constraints. A check constraint uses expressions to place specific data value restrictions on the contents of a column. The expression is explicitly defined in the table DDL and is formulated in much the same way that SQL WHERE clauses are formulated. Every data value stored in a column with a check constraint should conform to the pre-defined check constraint expression.

General consistency is the final type of consistency. If portions of DB2 table space and index data sets contain invalid, inconsistent, or incorrect data because of hardware or software errors, you want to be able to correct the erroneous information.

The data consistency utilities are used to monitor, control, and administer these three types of data consistency errors. There are three data consistency utilities (CHECK, REPAIR, and REPORT) with a total of five functions. This chapter describes all of them.

The CHECK Utility

The CHECK utility checks the integrity of DB2 data structures. It has three purposes. The first is to check referential integrity between two tables, displaying and potentially resolving referential constraint violations. The second purpose of the CHECK utility is to ensure that data values conform to the check constraints specified for the table. The third and final purpose is to check DB2 indexes for consistency. This consists of comparing the key values of indexed columns to their corresponding table values, as well as evaluating RIDs in the tables and indexes being checked.

The CHECK DATA Option

The CHECK DATA utility is used to verify the accuracy and integrity of data in DB2 tables.

Referential Integrity Checking

One function of the CHECK DATA option of the CHECK utility checks the status of referential constraints. It is used to validate foreign key values in the rows of a dependent table against primary key values in its associated parent table. For example, consider a referential constraint defined in the DB2 sample tables. The DSN8810.DEPT table has a foreign key, RDE, defined on the column MGRNO. It references the primary key of DSN8810.EMP, which is the EMPNO column. The CHECK DATA utility can be used to verify that all occurrences of MGRNO in the DSN8810.DEPT sample table refer to a valid EMPNO in the DSN8810.EMP sample table.

CHECK DATA can run against a single table space, multiple table spaces, or a single partition of a partitioned table space.

CHECK DATA can delete invalid rows and copy them to an exception table. The CHECK DATA utility resets the check pending status if constraint violations are not encountered or if the utility was run with the DELETE YES option.

The JCL in Listing 31.1 can be used to check data in the DB2 sample tables that contain referential constraints.

LISTING 31.1   CHECK DATA JCL

```
//DB2JOBU  JOB (UTILITY),'DB2 CHECK DATA',MSGCLASS=X,CLASS=X,
//    NOTIFY=USER
//*
//*****************************************************************
//*
//*            DB2 CHECK DATA UTILITY
//*
//*****************************************************************
//*
//UTIL EXEC DSNUPROC,SYSTEM=DSN,UID='CHEKDATA',UTPROC="
//*
//*   UTILITY WORK DATASETS
//*
//DSNUPROC.SORTWK01 DD UNIT=SYSDA,SPACE=(CYL,(5,1))
//DSNUPROC.SORTWK02 DD UNIT=SYSDA,SPACE=(CYL,(5,1))
//DSNUPROC.SORTOUT DD DSN=&&SORTOUT,
//        UNIT=SYSDA,SPACE=(CYL,(5,1))
//DSNUPROC.SYSERR DD DSN=&&SYSERR,
//        UNIT=SYSDA,SPACE=(CYL,(1,1))
//DSNUPROC.SYSUT1 DD DSN=&&SYSUT1,
//        UNIT=SYSDA,SPACE=(CYL,(5,1))
//DSNUPROC.UTPRINT DD SYSOUT=X
//*
//*   UTILITY INPUT CONTROL STATEMENTS
//*        This CHECK DATA statement checks DSN8810.DEPT for
//*        referential constraint violations, deletes all
//*        offending rows, and places them into the exception
//*        table, DSN8510.DEPT_EXCPTN.
//*
//DSNUPROC.SYSIN    DD  *
   CHECK DATA TABLESPACE DSN8D81A.DSN8S81D
   FOR EXCEPTION IN DSN8810.DEPT
         USE DSN8810.DEPT_EXCPTN
   SCOPE ALL     DELETE YES
/*
//
```

> **NOTE**
>
> The sort work data sets need to be assigned in the JCL only if sort work data sets are not dynamically allocated. Additionally, you should consider explicitly defining sort work data sets when checking very large tables.

Check Constraint Checking

The second function of the CHECK DATA option of the CHECK utility checks the status of check constraints. It is used to validate column values against check constraints defined on those columns. For example, consider a check constraint defined on the SALARY column of the DSN8810.EMP table as follows:

```
CONSTRAINT CHECK_SALARY
CHECK (SALARY < 50000.00)
```

All values of the SALARY column must be less than 50000.00 or they are in violation of the check constraint. The CHECK DATA utility can be used to verify that all occurrences of SALARY in the DSN8810.EMP sample table actually contain a valid SALARY conforming to the check constraint.

The columns of a table can contain values that violate the check constraint in the following two circumstances:

1. When a table that already contains data is altered to add a check constraint, enforcement of the constraint depends upon the value of the DB2 CURRENT RULES special register. If the value of the CURRENT RULES register is DB2, check constraint enforcement is deferred during table alteration and the table is placed in a check pending state. If the value of the CURRENT RULES register is STD, check constraint enforcement is immediate. If no rows violate the constraint, the alteration proceeds normally. If existing rows do violate the constraint, the table is placed in a check pending state.

2. When the LOAD utility is executed specifying the ENFORCE NO clause.

The syntax and JCL specification for checking check constraints is the same as that used for checking referential constraints.

LOB Reference Checking

The third function of the CHECK DATA option of the CHECK utility checks the status of LOB references. It is used to validate LOB columns against the LOB pointers to the auxiliary table. Before running CHECK DATA to check LOBs, be sure to first run CHECK LOB to ensure the validity of the LOB table space and run CHECK INDEX or REBUILD INDEX on the auxiliary table index to be sure it is valid.

CHECK DATA can be run against base table spaces only, not LOB table spaces.

The JCL in Listing 31.2 can be used to check data for the DB2 sample table that contains LOB columns.

LISTING 31.2   CHECK DATA JCL (for LOB References)

```
//DB2JOBU  JOB (UTILITY),'DB2 CHECK DATA',MSGCLASS=X,CLASS=X,
//    NOTIFY=USER
//*
//****************************************************************
//*
```

LISTING 31.2   Continued

```
//*          DB2 CHECK DATA UTILITY
//*
//*****************************************************************
//*
//UTIL EXEC DSNUPROC,SYSTEM=DSN,UID='CHEKDATA',UTPROC="
//*
//*  UTILITY WORK DATASETS
//*
//DSNUPROC.SORTWK01 DD UNIT=SYSDA,SPACE=(CYL,(5,1))
//DSNUPROC.SORTWK02 DD UNIT=SYSDA,SPACE=(CYL,(5,1))
//DSNUPROC.SORTOUT DD DSN=&&SORTOUT,
//        UNIT=SYSDA,SPACE=(CYL,(5,1))
//DSNUPROC.SYSERR DD DSN=&&SYSERR,
//        UNIT=SYSDA,SPACE=(CYL,(1,1))
//DSNUPROC.SYSUT1 DD DSN=&&SYSUT1,
//        UNIT=SYSDA,SPACE=(CYL,(5,1))
//DSNUPROC.UTPRINT DD SYSOUT=X
//*
//*  UTILITY INPUT CONTROL STATEMENTS
//*      This CHECK DATA statement checks DSN8810.EMP_PHOTO_RESUME
//*      for LOB reference problems.
//*
//DSNUPROC.SYSIN    DD  *
    CHECK DATA TABLESPACE DSN8D81L.DSN8S81B
    SCOPE AUXONLY    AUXERROR REPORT
/*
//
```

The SCOPE Parameter   The SCOPE parameter is used to set the scope of the rows in the table space that are to be checked. There are four SCOPE options:

PENDING   Indicates that only rows in CHECK PENDING status are to be checked for the specified table spaces, partitions, and tables. The referential integrity check, constraint check, and LOB column check are all performed. If this option is run on a table space that is not in CHECK PENDING status, the table space is ignored.

AUXONLY   Indicates that only the LOB column check is to be performed for table spaces having tables with LOB columns. The referential integrity and constraint checks are not performed.

ALL   Indicates that all dependent tables in the specified table spaces are to be checked. The referential integrity check, constraint check, and the LOB check are performed.

REFONLY   Indicates that all dependent tables in the specified table spaces are to be checked. However, only the referential integrity check and constraint check are performed. The LOB column check is not performed.

> **NOTE**
>
> PENDING is the default option if SCOPE is not specified.

The AUXERROR Parameter   The AUXERROR parameter is used to specify the action to take when LOB reference problems are encountered. There are two options:

REPORT   Indicates that the base table space is set to the auxiliary CHECK PENDING (ACHKP) status.

INVALIDATE   Indicates that the base table LOB column is set to an invalid status. The base table space is set to auxiliary warning (AUXW) status.

For both REPORT and INVALIDATE a LOB column check error is reported with a warning message.

> **NOTE**
>
> REPORT is the default option if AUXERROR is not specified.

CHECK DATA **Phases**   There are six phases of the CHECK DATA utility:

UTILINIT   Sets up and initializes the CHECK DATA utility.

SCANTAB   Extracts keys by index or table space scan and places them in the SYSUT1 DD.

SORT   Sorts the foreign keys using the SORTOUT DD (if the foreign keys were not extracted using an index).

CHECKDAT   Compares the extracted foreign keys to the index entries for the corresponding primary key. This phase also issues error messages for invalid foreign keys.

REPORTCK   Copies the invalid rows to the specified exception table and then deletes them from the source table if the DELETE YES option was chosen.

UTILTERM   Performs the final utility cleanup.

Estimating CHECK DATA **Work Data Set Sizes**

V7 The CHECK DATA utility requires the use of work data sets to accomplish referential constraint checking. Of course, as of DB2 V7 you can set up IBM DB2 utilities to allocate the required data sets dynamically. But this is not required; you may still choose to explicitly allocate utility work data sets. If you choose to do so, the following formulas can help you estimate the sizes of the work data sets required by the CHECK DATA utility. These calculations provide estimated data set sizes. More complex and precise calculations are in the *DB2 Utility Reference* manual. The formulas presented here, however, produce generally satisfactory results.

```
SYSUT1 = (size of the largest foreign key + 13)
     ➥x (total number of rows in the table to be checked)
     ➥x (total number of foreign keys defined for the table)
```

> **NOTE**
>
> If any number is 0, substitute 1.

```
SORTOUT = (size of SYSUT1)
SORTWKxx = (size of SORTOUT) x 2
SYSERR = (number of estimated referential constraint violations) x 60
```

> **NOTE**
>
> Allocate at least one cylinder to the SYSERR data set.

After calculating the estimated size, in bytes, for each work data set, convert the number into cylinders, rounding up to the next whole cylinder. Allocating work data sets in cylinder increments enhances the utility's performance.

CHECK DATA **Locking Considerations**

The CHECK DATA utility can run concurrently with the following utilities: DIAGNOSE, MERGECOPY, MODIFY, REPORT, and STOSPACE.

CHECK DATA, when run specifying DELETE NO, will drain write claim classes for the table space and indexes being processed. When DELETE YES is specified, all claim classes are drained for the table space and indexes impacted.

When CHECK DATA is run against an individual partition, DB2 also drains the write claim class for the logical partition of the (type 2) indexes impacted if DELETE NO is specified. If DELETE YES is specified, DB2 drains all claim classes for the logical partition of the (type 2) indexes being acted upon. Regardless of the other options specified, if the FOR EXCEPTION option is specified, the table space containing the exception table (and any indexes) will have all claim classes drained.

CHECK DATA **Guidelines**

Use CHECK DATA to Ensure Data Integrity   Favor the use of the CHECK DATA utility to reset the check pending status on DB2 table spaces. CHECK DATA is the only way to verify, in an automated fashion and on demand, that DB2 table data is referentially intact and that the data conforms to all check constraints. The alternate methods of resetting the check pending status are as follows:

- Running the REPAIR utility, specifying SET NOCHECKPEND for the appropriate table spaces
- Issuing the START DATABASE command, specifying ACCESS(FORCE)

Neither option ensures data integrity.

Another valid way to reset the check pending status is with the LOAD utility, specifying the ENFORCE CONSTRAINTS option. However, this requires a sequential data set suitable for loading, and this type of data set is not readily available for most application table spaces. Even if a load data set is available, the data it contains might be out of date, and thus of little benefit.

Use SCOPE PENDING   Specify the SCOPE PENDING option when executing the CHECK DATA utility to reduce the amount of work the utility must perform. With the SCOPE PENDING option, CHECK DATA checks only the rows that need to be checked for all tables in the specified table space. This means that only data in check pending is checked. If the table space is not in check pending, the CHECK DATA utility issues a message and terminates processing. This is the most efficient way to execute the CHECK DATA utility because it minimizes runtime by avoiding unnecessary work. The alternative is to specify SCOPE ALL, which checks all dependent tables in the specified table spaces.

Run CHECK DATA When Data Integrity Is Questionable   Execute CHECK DATA after the following:

- Loading a table without specifying the ENFORCE CONSTRAINTS option.

- A check constraint is added to a table and data within an existing row of that table violates the constraint.

- A table is altered to add a check constraint and the CURRENT RULES special register contains DB2.

- When row violations are encountered by the CHECK DATA utility using the DELETE NO option.

- The partial recovery of table spaces in a referential set.

Both situations result in DB2 placing the loaded or recovered table spaces into a check pending status. The CHECK DATA utility is necessary to ensure referentially sound data and to remove the check pending status, permitting future data access.

Bypass CHECK DATA Only When Data Integrity Is Verifiable   After a full recovery of all table spaces in a referential set, you might want to bypass the execution of the CHECK DATA utility. Depending on the order in which the recovery took place, some table spaces are placed in a check pending status. If you have followed the COPY guidelines presented in this book, however, the full recovery of a table space set is referentially sound. In this case, the REPAIR utility specifying the SET NOCHECKPEND option can be used instead of CHECK DATA, because CHECK DATA would be a waste of time.

Define Exception Tables for Tables That Require CHECK DATA   An exception table stores the rows that violate the referential constraint being checked. An exception table should be identical to the table being checked but with the addition of two columns: one column identifies the RID of the offending row, and the other identifies a TIMESTAMP that indicates when the CHECK DATA utility was run.

These two columns can have any name as long as it isn't the same name as another column in the table. The names used in the following example are recommended because they clearly identify the column's use. To avoid ambiguity, use the same column names for all exception tables. The exception table can be created using the following DDL statements:

```
CREATE TABLE
  DSN8810.DEPT_EXCPTN
  LIKE DSN8610.DEPT;
```

```
ALTER TABLE
  DSN8810.DEPT_EXCPTN
  ADD   RID        CHAR(4);

ALTER TABLE
  DSN8810.DEPT_EXCPTN
  ADD   CHECK_TS    TIMESTAMP;
```

The exception table does not need to be empty when the CHECK DATA utility is run because the TIMESTAMP column identifies which execution of CHECK DATA inserted the offending rows.

Do not create a unique index for any exception table. A unique index could cause the CHECK DATA utility to fail because of the insertion of non-unique key values. Non-unique indexes should not pose a problem.

Place the exception tables in a segmented table space. You also can place multiple exception tables in a single segmented table space.

Use DELETE YES for Optimum Automation   Rows that violate the referential constraint can be deleted from the table being checked if the DELETE YES parameter was specified. This is often the preferred method of executing the CHECK DATA utility in a production environment because the elimination of constraint violations is automated. If the deleted rows are needed, they can be retrieved from the exception table.

If DELETE NO is specified instead of DELETE YES, the CHECK DATA utility does not reset the check pending flag, but the rows in violation of the constraint are identified for future action.

A problem can occur, however, when you run the CHECK DATA utility with the DELETE YES option. When a row is deleted from the dependent table, it could cause cascading deletes to one or more dependent tables. This may result in valid data being deleted if the violation is caused by a missing primary key in a parent table. For this reason, you might want to avoid the DELETE YES option. At any rate, exercise caution when checking data with DELETE YES.

Be Aware of Inconsistent Indexes   If rows that appear to be valid are deleted, ensure that the indexes defined for the dependent and parent tables are valid. If data in either index is invalid, the CHECK DATA utility might indicate referential constraint violations, even though there are none. Indexes can be checked for validity using the CHECK INDEX utility (discussed in the next section).

Also, ensure that the parent table contains all expected data. If rows are missing because of improper deletions or partial loads, CHECK DATA will delete the foreign key rows as well (if DELETE YES was specified).

Consider Checking at the Partition Level   CHECK DATA can be executed at the partition level. Choosing to check at the partition level provides the following benefits:

- Pinpoint integrity checking can be performed. If the user has a good idea which partition has a data integrity problem, CHECK DATA can be run on that partition only.

- A regularly scheduled CHECK DATA pattern can be established, whereby a single partition is checked daily (or weekly). This establishes a data-integrity checking process that eventually checks the entire table, but not so frequently as to cause availability problems.

Rerun CHECK DATA After an Abend   The CHECK DATA utility cannot be restarted. If it abends during execution, determine the cause of the abend, terminate the utility, and rerun it. Common causes for CHECK DATA abends are lockout conditions due to concurrent data access and changes to the table being checked (for example, new columns), without corresponding changes to the exception table.

V8 **Do Not Use CHECK DATA for Informational Referential Constraints**   The CHECK DATA utility cannot be used to check *informational referential constraints*. An informational referential constraint is a DB2 DDL constraint that is added as information only (usually to support automatic query rewrite for materialized query tables).

An information referential constraint documents a constraint that is managed programmatically, not by DB2 declarative RI.

> **NOTE**
>
> Some third-party ISVs offer CHECK utilities that can be used to manage user-defined referential constraints. If you are using a CHECK utility other than IBM's, consult the vendor manual to determine whether it handles informational referential constraints.

The CHECK LOB Option

The CHECK LOB utility is used to verify the accuracy and integrity of data in auxiliary table spaces for LOB columns. It can be used to detect structural defects in the LOB table space and invalid LOB values.

After successfully running CHECK LOB, all CHECK PENDING (CHKP) and auxiliary warning (AUXW) statuses will be reset. If exceptions are encountered, CHECK LOB will report on those exceptions only. CHECK LOB cannot be used to fix the exceptions it finds.

The JCL in Listing 31.3 can be used to check data in a DB2 sample auxiliary table that contains LOB columns.

LISTING 31.3   CHECK LOB JCL

```
//DB2JOBU  JOB (UTILITY),'DB2 CHECK LOB',MSGCLASS=X,CLASS=X,
//    NOTIFY=USER
//*
//********************************************************************
//*
//*          DB2 CHECK LOB UTILITY
//*
//********************************************************************
//*
//UTIL EXEC DSNUPROC,SYSTEM=DSN,UID='CHECKLOB',UTPROC="
//*
```

LISTING 31.3   Continued

```
//*  UTILITY WORK DATASETS
//*
//DSNUPROC.SORTWK01 DD UNIT=SYSDA,SPACE=(CYL,(5,1))
//DSNUPROC.SORTWK02 DD UNIT=SYSDA,SPACE=(CYL,(5,1))
//DSNUPROC.SORTOUT DD DSN=&&SORTOUT,
//         UNIT=SYSDA,SPACE=(CYL,(5,1))
//DSNUPROC.SYSERR DD DSN=&&SYSERR,
//         UNIT=SYSDA,SPACE=(CYL,(1,1))
//DSNUPROC.SYSUT1 DD DSN=&&SYSUT1,
//         UNIT=SYSDA,SPACE=(CYL,(5,1))
//DSNUPROC.UTPRINT DD SYSOUT=X
//DSNUPROC.SYSIN      DD  *
    CHECK LOB TABLESPACE DSN8D81L.DSN8S81M
     EXCEPTIONS 0
/*
//
```

CHECK LOB **Phases**

The five phases of the CHECK LOB utility are:

UTILINIT	Sets up and initializes the CHECK LOB utility
CHECKLOB	Scans all active pages of the LOB table space
SORT	Sorts the records from the CHECKLOB phase; reports four times the number of rows sorted
REPRTLOB	Examines records that are produced by the CHECKLOB phase and sorted by the SORT phase, and issues error messages
UTILTERM	Performs the final utility cleanup

CHECK LOB **Locking Considerations**

Any operation or other online utility that attempts to update the same LOB table space cannot be run at the same time as CHECK LOB.

CHECK LOB will drain write claim classes for both the LOB table space and the auxiliary table index being processed.

The EXCEPTIONS **Parameter**

The EXCEPTIONS parameter is used to specify the maximum number of exceptions, which are reported by messages only. If the maximum number of exceptions is exceeded, CHECK LOB will terminate in the CHECKLOB phase.

Specifying EXCEPTIONS 0 indicates that no limit is to be applied to the number of exceptions.

> **NOTE**
>
> If the EXCEPTIONS parameter is not specified, CHECK LOB will use EXCEPTIONS 0 as the default.

The CHECK INDEX **Option**

The CHECK INDEX option of the CHECK utility verifies the consistency of index data and its corresponding table data. This option identifies and reports RID pointer errors for missing index keys and index key mismatches. CHECK INDEX does not correct invalid index entries; it merely identifies them for future correction.

CHECK INDEX can run against an entire index or a single index partition. CHECK INDEX can identify three problems:

- No corresponding row in the table for a given index entry.

- No index entry for a valid table row.

- The data in the indexed columns for the table does not match the corresponding index key for a given matching RID.

Additionally, when checking an auxiliary table index, CHECK INDEX verifies that each LOB is represented by an index entry, and that an index entry exists for every LOB.

To correct errors reported by CHECK INDEX, the user can execute the REBUILD INDEX utility to rebuild the index based on the current table data. Alternatively, the RECOVER INDEX utility can be used to apply an index image copy. If the RECOVER option is chosen, care must be taken to ensure that the recovery results in an index that matches the current state of the data. In general, REBUILD is a better option than RECOVER for fixing index errors.

When mismatch-type errors occur, however, a data analyst who is experienced with the application that contains the problem table or index should research the cause of the anomaly. The predominant causes of invalid indexes are the uncontrolled use of the DSN1COPY utility and the partial recovery of application tables or indexes.

The JCL to execute the CHECK INDEX utility is shown in Listing 31.4.

LISTING 31.4   CHECK INDEX JCL

```
//DB2JOBU  JOB (UTILITY),'DB2 CHECK INDEX',MSGCLASS=X,CLASS=X,
//    NOTIFY=USER
//*
//*****************************************************************
//*
//*          DB2 CHECK INDEX UTILITY
//*
//*****************************************************************
//*
//UTIL EXEC DSNUPROC,SYSTEM=DSN,UID='CHEKINDX',UTPROC="
//*
//*  UTILITY WORK DATASETS
//*
//DSNUPROC.SORTWK01 DD UNIT=SYSDA,SPACE=(CYL,(2,1))
//DSNUPROC.SORTWK02 DD UNIT=SYSDA,SPACE=(CYL,(2,1))
//DSNUPROC.SYSUT1 DD DSN=&&SYSUT1,
//        UNIT=SYSDA,SPACE=(CYL,(2,1)),DCB=BUFNO=20
```

LISTING 31.4 Continued

```
//DSNUPROC.UTPRINT DD SYSOUT=X
//*
//* UTILITY INPUT CONTROL STATEMENTS
//*     The first CHECK INDEX statement checks all indexes
//*     for the named table space.
//*     The next two CHECK INDEX statements check only the
//*     specifically named indexes.
//*
//DSNUPROC.SYSIN    DD  *
   CHECK INDEX(ALL) TABLESPACE DSN8D81A.DSN8S81D
   CHECK INDEX (DSN8810.XACT1)
   CHECK INDEX (DSN8810.XACT2)
/*
//
```

CHECK INDEX Phases

The are five phases of the CHECK INDEX utility:

UTILINIT	Sets up and initializes the CHECK INDEX utility
UNLOAD	Unloads index entries to the SYSUT1 DD
SORT	Sorts the unloaded index entries using SORTOUT DD
CHECKIDX	Scans the table to validate the sorted index entries against the table data
UTILTERM	Performs the final utility cleanup

Estimating CHECK INDEX Work Data Set Sizes

V7 The CHECK INDEX utility requires work data sets to accomplish index checking. Once again, though, as of DB2 V7 you can set up the JCL for CHECK INDEX to allocate the required data sets dynamically. But this is not required; you may still choose to explicitly allocate work data sets for your utility jobs.

The following formulas help you estimate the sizes for the work data sets required by the CHECK INDEX utility. These calculations provide estimated sizes only. More complex and precise calculations can be found in the *DB2 Utility Guide and Reference* manual, but these formulas should produce comparable results:

```
SYSUT1 = (size of the largest index + 13) x (total number of rows in largest index to be
checked)
SORTWKxx = (size of SYSUT1) x 2
```

After calculating the estimated size, in bytes, for each work data set, convert the number into cylinders, rounding up to the next whole cylinder. Allocating work data sets in cylinder increments enhances the utility's performance. This is true for all utilities.

CHECK INDEX Locking Considerations

The CHECK INDEX utility can run concurrently with all utilities except the following:

31

CHECK DATA	LOAD
REBUILD INDEX	RECOVER INDEX
RECOVER TABLESPACE	REORG INDEX
REPAIR REPLACE	REPAIR DELETE
REORG TABLESPACE UNLOAD CONTINUE	
REORG TABLESPACE UNLOAD PAUSE	

V8 CHECK INDEX will drain write claim classes for both the index or index partition and the table space being processed. The partition can be a partition of a partitioning index, a partition of a DPSI, or a logical partition of a (type 2) index.

CHECK INDEX **Guidelines**

Run CHECK INDEX **Only When Needed**   Inconsistencies in DB2 indexes are rare in adequately controlled and administered environments. For this reason, do not regularly schedule the execution of the CHECK INDEX utility for the production indexes in your shop. It usually wastes processing time and increases an application's batch window.

The CHECK INDEX utility should be run only when inconsistent data is observed or when an uncontrolled environment allows (or permits) the liberal use of DSN1COPY or partial recovery.

> **NOTE**
>
> Consider running CHECK INDEX for an entire DB2 subsystem prior to a migration. If a corrupt index exists, you can correct it prior to the migration.

Use CHECK INDEX **After Potentially Dangerous Operations**   Execute CHECK INDEX after a conditional restart or a partial application recovery.

Use CHECK INDEX **on the DB2 Catalog When Necessary**   CHECK INDEX can be used to check DB2 Catalog and DB2 Directory indexes.

> **CAUTION**
>
> If you run CHECK INDEX on either SYSIBM.DSNLUX01 or SYSIBM.DSNLUX02, then CHECK INDEX must be the only utility within the job step.

Check Indexes at the Partition Level When Possible   CHECK INDEX can be run at the partition. Pinpoint integrity checking can be performed if the user knows which index partition has corrupted entries. Running CHECK INDEX on that partition only can save processing time.

Keep in mind, however, that when running CHECK INDEX on a single logical partition of a secondary index, certain types of errors will not be detected. For example, duplicate unique keys might exist across partitions, but if only one partition is being checked the problem will not be found.

Another problem that might go undetected if partition-level checking is being run is out of sequence keys. For example, consider two partitions where the keys are as follows:

Partition 1—1,3,3,5,7

Partition 2—6,8,9

The keys within each partition are in sequence, but the keys for the entire index are out of sequence because the 6 in partition 2 comes after the 7 in partition 1. But if only one partition is being checked, DB2 will not uncover this problem.

Rerun CHECK INDEX **After an Abend**   The CHECK INDEX utility cannot be restarted. If it abends during execution, determine the cause of the abend, terminate the utility, and rerun. The most common cause for CHECK INDEX failure is a timeout because the index is locked out by another user.

Buffer CHECK INDEX **Work Data Sets Appropriately**   Ensure that adequate data set buffering is specified for the work data sets. The BUFNO parameter can be used on the DCB information of JCL DD statements to change buffering. The BUFNO parameter creates read and write buffers in main storage for this data set, thereby enhancing the performance of the utility. The default value for BUFNO is 20.

Ensure that sufficient memory (real or expanded) is available, however, before increasing the BUFNO specification for your CHECK INDEX work data sets.

The REPAIR Utility

The REPAIR utility is designed to modify DB2 data and associated data structures when there is an error or problem.

You can use the REPAIR utility to perform the following tasks:

- Test DBD definitions
- Repair DBDs by synchronizing DB2 Catalog database information with the DB2 Directory DBD definition
- Reset a pending status on a table space or index
- Verify the contents of data areas in table spaces and indexes
- Replace the contents of data areas in table spaces and indexes (using a zap)
- Delete a single row from a table space
- Produce a hexadecimal dump of an area in a table space or index
- Delete an entire LOB from a LOB table space
- Dump LOB pages
- Rebuild OBDs for a LOB table space

REPAIR **Phases**

The REPAIR utility has three phases, regardless of which type of REPAIR is run. These phases are as follows:

UTILINIT	Sets up and initializes the REPAIR utility
REPAIR	Locates and repairs the data or resets the appropriate pending flag
UTILTERM	Performs the final utility cleanup

The REPAIR DBD **Option**

The REPAIR utility can be used to test, maintain, and modify DB2 database information. DB2 maintains database information in the DB2 Catalog SYSIBM.SYSDATABASE table. An object known as a DBD is also maintained in the DB2 Directory in the SYSIBM.DBD01 "table." You can use the REPAIR option with the DBD specification to perform the following functions:

- Test the definition of a DB2 database by comparing information in the DB2 Catalog to information in the DB2 Directory.

- Diagnose database synchronization problems and report differences between the DB2 Catalog information and the DBD stored in the DB2 Directory.

- Rebuild a DBD definition in the DB2 Directory based on the information in the DB2 Catalog.

- Drop an invalid database (if the SQL DROP statement cannot be used because of database inconsistencies). REPAIR DBD can remove the DBD from the DB2 Directory and delete all corresponding rows from the appropriate DB2 Catalog tables.

Listing 31.5 contains sample JCL to REPAIR the DBD for the DSN8D51A sample database.

LISTING 31.5   REPAIR DBD JCL

```
//DB2JOBU  JOB (UTILITY),'DB2 REPAIR DBD',MSGCLASS=X,CLASS=X,
//    NOTIFY=USER
//*
//********************************************************************
//*
//*           DB2 REPAIR UTILITY  : : DBD REPAIR
//*
//********************************************************************
//*
//UTIL EXEC DSNUPROC,SYSTEM=DSN,UID='REPRDBD',UTPROC="
//*
//*  UTILITY INPUT CONTROL STATEMENTS
//*       The first REPAIR statement builds a DBD based on
//*       the DB2 Catalog and compares it to the corresponding
//*       DBD in the DB2 Directory.
//*       The second REPAIR statement reports inconsistencies,
//*       if any exist.
```

LISTING 31.5   Continued

```
//*
//DSNUPROC.SYSIN    DD  *
    REPAIR DBD TEST DATABASE DSN8D61A

    REPAIR DBD DIAGNOSE DATABASE DSN8D81A OUTDDN SYSREC
/*
//
```

REPAIR DBD **Guidelines**

Log All Repairs   Run the REPAIR utility with the LOG YES option. This ensures that all data changes are logged to DB2 and are therefore recoverable.

Consult IBM Before Using DROP **or** REBUILD   Do not issue the REPAIR DBD utility with the DROP or REBUILD option without consulting your IBM Support Center. These options can be dangerous if used improperly.

Use TEST **and** DIAGNOSE **for Error Resolution**   When databases, or their subordinate objects, exhibit peculiar behavior, consider executing REPAIR DBD with the TEST option. If this run returns a condition code other than 0, run REPAIR DBD with the DIAGNOSE option and consult your IBM Support Center for additional guidance.

You should also consider implementing a regularly scheduled REPAIR DBD run to consistently check for problems.

The REPAIR LOCATE **Option**

The LOCATE option of the REPAIR utility zaps DB2 data. The term *zap* refers to the physical modification of data at specific address locations. This form of the REPAIR utility can be used to perform the following functions:

- Delete an entire row from a table space

- Replace data at specific locations in a table space or index

- Reset broken table space page bits

The REPAIR LOCATE utility functions similarly to the IBM AMASPZAP utility. By specifying page locations and offsets, specific RIDs, or key data, you can use the REPAIR utility to alter the data stored at the specified location. Although it generally is not recommended and is not easy, the REPAIR LOCATE utility can sometimes be of considerable help in resolving errors difficult to correct by normal means (that is, using SQL).

The sample JCL provided in Listing 31.6 depicts the REPAIR JCL necessary to modify the data on the third page of the fourth partition at offset 50 for the sample table space DSN8D81A.DSN8S81E.

LISTING 31.6   REPAIR LOCATE JCL

```
//DB2JOBU  JOB (UTILITY),'DB2 REPAIR LOCATE',MSGCLASS=X,CLASS=X,
//    NOTIFY=USER
//*
//********************************************************************
//*
//*       DB2 REPAIR UTILITY  : : LOCATE AND MODIFY DATA
//*
//********************************************************************
//*
//UTIL EXEC DSNUPROC,SYSTEM=DSN,UID='REPRLOCT',UTPROC="
//*
//*  UTILITY INPUT CONTROL STATEMENTS
//*       The REPAIR statement modifies the data on the third
//*       page at offset X'0080' from the value 'SP' to the
//*       value 'ST'.  This update happens only if that location
//*       contains 'SP'.  Additionally, the two characters are
//*       dumped to ensure that the modification is correct.
//*
//DSNUPROC.SYSIN    DD  *
   REPAIR OBJECT
       LOCATE TABLESPACE DSN8D81A.DSN8S81D PAGE X'03'
              VERIFY OFFSET X'0080' DATA 'SP'
              REPLACE OFFSET X'0080' DATA 'ST'
              DUMP OFFSET X'0080' LENGTH 2
/*
//
```

REPAIR LOCATE Locking Considerations

The REPAIR LOCATE utility with the DUMP option takes an S-lock on the table space and an index, if available, during the REPAIR phase. The REPAIR LOCATE utility with the REPLACE option takes a SIX-lock on the table space and any related indexes during the REPAIR phase.

REPAIR LOCATE Guidelines

Log All Repairs   Run the REPAIR utility with the LOG YES option. This ensures that all data changes are logged to DB2 and are therefore recoverable.

Ensure That Adequate Recovery Is Available   Create a backup copy of any table space to be operated on by the REPAIR utility when the intent is to modify data. To make a backup, use the COPY utility or the DSN1COPY service aid utility.

Avoid SVC Dumps When Using REPAIR   When determining the location and values of data to be repaired, use a dump produced only by one of the following methods:

- REPAIR with the DUMP option
- DSN1COPY service aid utility
- DSN1PRNT service aid utility

Do not use an SVC dump, because the information contained therein might not accurately depict the DB2 data as it exists on DASD.

Use VERIFY with REPLACE   When replacing data in a DB2 table space, code the VERIFY option, which ensures that the value of the data being changed is as expected. If the value does not match the VERIFY specification, subsequent REPLACE specifications will not occur. This provides the highest degree of safety when executing the REPAIR utility and also maintains data integrity.

Use REPAIR LOCATE with Caution   REPAIR LOCATE should be used only by a knowledgeable systems programmer or DBA. Familiarity with the MVS utility program AMASPZAP is helpful.

Do Not Use REPAIR on the DB2 Catalog and DB2 Directory   REPAIR LOCATE can be used to modify the DB2 Catalog and DB2 Directory data sets. However, these data sets have a special format and should be modified with great care. It is recommended that REPAIR never be run on these data sets. If you do not heed this warning, be sure to consult the *DB2 Diagnosis Guide and Reference* for the physical format of these data sets before proceeding.

Repair the "Broken" Page Bit When Necessary   Sometimes DB2 erroneously sets the "broken" page bit. If you determine that the page is correct after examining the contents using dumps and the REPAIR utility, you can invoke REPAIR LOCATE with the RESET option to reset the "broken" page bit. However, be absolutely sure that the page in question is accurate before modifying this bit.

Grant REPAIR Authority Judiciously   Remember that REPAIR authority must be granted before anyone can execute the REPAIR utility. However, it is common for many shops to grant REPAIR authority to beginning users or production jobs in order to reset pending flags. Because the REPAIR authority cannot be broken down into which option is needed (that is DBD, LOCATE, or SET), blanket authority to execute any type of REPAIR is given when REPAIR authority is granted. This could be dangerous if an uneducated user stumbles across the ability to zap DB2 table space data.

Remember that REPAIR authority is implicit in the group-level DBCTRL, DBADM, SYSCTRL, and SYSADM authorities.

The REPAIR SET Option

When the REPAIR utility is executed with the SET option, it can be used to reset copy pending, check pending, and recover pending flags. Pending flags can be set at the partition level, as well as at the table space level. For an in-depth discussion of the pending status flags, refer to the section titled "The Pending States" in Chapter 37, "DB2 Utility and Command Guidelines." In general, these flags are maintained by DB2 to indicate the status of table spaces and indexes. When DB2 turns on a flag for a table space or index, it indicates that the object is in an indeterminate state.

When the copy pending flag is set, it indicates that the COPY utility must be used to back up the table space or partition to ensure adequate recoverability. Copy pending status is set when unlogged changes have been made to DB2 table spaces, or when a reference to a full image copy is no longer available in the DB2 Catalog.

The check pending flag indicates that the CHECK DATA utility should be run because data has been inserted into a table containing a referential constraint without ensuring that the data conforms to the referential integrity. The auxiliary check pending flag indicates that there is a problem with a base table reference to a LOB column in an auxiliary table.

The recover pending flag indicates that the table space or the index must be recovered because a utility operating on that object has ended abnormally, possibly causing inconsistent or corrupted data.

The rebuild pending flag indicates that an index does not match the table data and needs to be rebuilt. Sometimes, however, these flags are set by DB2 but the corresponding utility does not need to be run because of other application factors. In this case, the REPAIR SET utility can be run to reset the appropriate pending flag.

Listing 31.7 shows JCL that can be used to reset check pending, copy pending, and recover pending restrictions for the sample table spaces. It also contains a REPAIR statement to reset the recover pending status for an index on one of the sample tables.

LISTING 31.7   REPAIR SET JCL

```
//DB2JOBU  JOB (UTILITY),'DB2 REPAIR SET',MSGCLASS=X,CLASS=X,
//    NOTIFY=USER
//*
//*****************************************************************
//*
//*       DB2 REPAIR UTILITY  : : RESET PENDING FLAGS
//*
//*****************************************************************
//*
//UTIL EXEC DSNUPROC,SYSTEM=DSN,UID='REPRSETP',UTPROC="
//*
//*   UTILITY INPUT CONTROL STATEMENTS
//*     1. The first REPAIR statement resets the copy pending
//*        status for the named table space.
//*     2. The second REPAIR statement resets the check pending
//*        status for two table spaces.
//*     3. The third REPAIR statement resets the recover pending
//*        status for the named table space.
//*     4. The fourth and final REPAIR statement resets the
//*        copy pending status for the named index.
//*
//DSNUPROC.SYSIN    DD  *
    REPAIR SET TABLESPACE DSN8D81A.DSN8S81E  NOCOPYPEND
    REPAIR SET TABLESPACE DSN8D81A.DSN8S81E  NOCHECKPEND
           SET TABLESPACE DSN8D81A.DSN8S81C  NOCHECKPEND
    REPAIR SET TABLESPACE DSN8D81A.DSN8S81R  NORCVRPEND
    REPAIR SET INDEX      DSN8810.XPROJAC1   NORCVRPEND
/*
//
```

REPAIR SET **Guidelines**

Favor the COPY **Utility over** REPAIR SET NOCOPYPEND   To reset the copy pending flag, it is almost always better to run the COPY utility to take a full image copy rather than use REPAIR. Situations contrary to this advice follow:

- Data loaded from a stable source does not need to be copied if the source is maintained. (The data can always be reloaded.) If the data is loaded with the LOG NO option, run REPAIR to reset the check pending condition rather than create an image copy that will never be used.

- When the MODIFY RECOVERY utility is run—deleting the last image copy for a table space—DB2 sets the copy pending flag. If the image copy data set deleted from the SYSIBM.SYSCOPY table is still available, however, recovery to that image copy can be accomplished using the DSN1COPY service aid. This requires manual intervention to recover a table space and is not recommended.

- Test data with a short life span often does not need to be copied because it can be easily re-created. If the copy pending restriction is set for a table of this nature, it is usually quicker to run REPAIR than to create an image copy.

Favor the CHECK DATA **Utility over** REPAIR SET NOCHECKPEND   To reset the check pending flag, it is almost always better to run the CHECK DATA utility to enforce referential constraints rather than use REPAIR. Situations contrary to this advice follow:

- If referential constraint violations are checked by an application program later in a job stream, the REPAIR utility can be run to reset the copy pending restriction. This allows the subsequent deletion of referential constraint violations by the application program. However, the DB2 CHECK DATA utility generally is infallible, and application programs are not, so this scenario should be avoided unless you are retrofitting referential integrity into a system that already exists without it.

- If check pending has been set for a table space containing a table that will have data loaded into it using the LOAD utility (with the REPLACE and ENFORCE CONSTRAINTS options) before data will be accessed, the CHECK DATA utility can be bypassed because the LOAD utility enforces the referential constraints.

Favor the RECOVER **Utility over** REPAIR SET NORCVRPEND   To reset the recover pending flag, it is almost always better to run the RECOVER utility to recover a DB2 table space or index to a time or state rather than use REPAIR.

There is only one situation contrary to this advice. When the LOAD utility abnormally terminates, the recover pending flag is set, and running LOAD REPLACE rather than RECOVER is appropriate. It is never advisable to set the recover pending flag using REPAIR unless the data is not critical and can be lost without dire consequences.

Specify LEVELID **to Use a Down-Level Data Set**   The LEVELID parameter sets the level identifier of the named table space or partition to a new identifier.

You cannot use LEVELID with an open table space or partition, a table space or partition with outstanding in-doubt log records, or pages in the logical page list (LPL).

> **CAUTION**
>
> Actions impacting a down-level data set might cause data integrity and accuracy problems. Use this option at your own risk as IBM will take no responsibility for data problems resulting from the use of down-level data sets.

REPAIR **and Versions**

V8 Recall from Chapter 7, "Database Change Management and Schema Evolution," that DB2 will create new versions of DB2 objects when they are changed using the online schema evolution features of DB2 V8.

The VERSIONS parameter of the REPAIR utility can be used to update the versions of a specific table space or index in the DB2 Catalog and Directory from the version information in the table space or index. Consider using the VERSIONS parameter when you perform the following tasks when you use the OBIDXLAT option of DSN1COPY to move objects from one DB2 subsystem to another.

The REPORT **Utility**

Two types of reports can be generated with the REPORT utility. The first is a table space set report showing the names of all table spaces and tables tied together by referential integrity. This type of report is described in the next section. The second type deals with recovery and is discussed in Chapter 32, "Backup and Recovery Utilities."

The REPORT TABLESPACESET **Option**

The REPORT TABLESPACESET utility generates a report detailing all tables and table spaces in a referential table space set. As you can see in the sample JCL in Listing 31.8, the input to the utility is a single table space. The output is a report of all related table spaces and tables.

LISTING 31.8 REPORT TABLESPACESET JCL

```
//DB2JOBU  JOB  (UTILITY),'DB2 REPORT TS',MSGCLASS=X,
//    NOTIFY=DB2JOBU,USER=DB2JOBU
//*
//****************************************************************
//*
//*           DB2 REPORT TABLESPACESET UTILITY
//*
//****************************************************************
//*
//UTIL EXEC DSNUPROC,SYSTEM=DSN,UID='REPORTTS',UTPROC="
//*
//*  UTILITY INPUT CONTROL STATEMENTS
//*     The REPORT statement generates a report of all objects
```

LISTING 31.8 Continued

```
//*      referentially tied to the named table space
//*
//DSNUPROC.SYSIN   DD  *
   REPORT TABLESPACESET TABLESPACE DSN8D81A.DSN8S81D
/*
//
```

REPORT TABLESPACESET Guidelines

Use REPORT TABLESPACESET Reports for Documentation   The REPORT TABLESPACESET utility is particularly useful for monitoring DB2 objects that are referentially related. DB2 Catalog reports such as those described in Chapter 26, "DB2 Object Monitoring Using the DB2 Catalog and RTS," are also useful but are difficult to structure so that a complete table space set is returned given a table space anywhere in the set.

Rerun the REPORT Utility After Resolving Abends   Run the REPORT TABLESPACESET utility for every table space added to the production DB2 subsystem. Additionally, if referential constraints are added to current application tables, run the REPORT TABLESPACESET utility on their corresponding table spaces immediately after their implementation. Store these reports as documentation for reference.

Periodically run the REPORT TABLESPACESET utility for table spaces that DB2 Catalog queries identify as containing tables defined with referential constraints. Ensure that the QUIESCE utility, when executed against these table spaces, is coded to quiesce *all* table spaces identified by the report—as well as any other table space that is logically related to any table space in the table space set (such as programmatic referential integrity).

> **V8**
>
> **NOTE**
>
> Informational referential constraints will be reported by the REPORT TABLESPACESET utility. Note also that when QUIESCE is used with the TABLESPACESET parameter, it will cause tables connected by both real and informational referential constraints to be quiesced.

If the REPORT utility abends, terminate the utility, if necessary, and rerun it.

The DIAGNOSE Utility

The DIAGNOSE utility is an online utility that can be used to diagnose problems, especially problems with other DB2 utilities. Sample JCL is provided in Listing 31.9.

LISTING 31.9 DIAGNOSE JCL

```
//DB2JOBU  JOB  (UTILITY),'DB2 DIAGNOSE',MSGCLASS=X,CLASS=X,
//         NOTIFY=USER
//*
//*****************************************************************
//*
//*                  DB2 DIAGNOSE UTILITY
//*
//*****************************************************************
```

LISTING 31.9   Continued

```
//*
//UTIL EXEC DSNUPROC,SYSTEM=DSN,UID='DIAGNOSE',UTPROC="
//*
//*  Display all records in the SYSIBM.SYSUTIL DB2 Directory table
//*
//DSNUPROC.SYSIN    DD  *
    DIAGNOSE DISPLAY SYSUTIL
/*
//
```

The DIAGNOSE utility can be used to force dumps for utility abends and format
SYSIBM.SYSUTILX information for printing. It should be used only under instructions and
supervision from an IBM Support Center.

CHAPTER **32**

Backup and Recovery Utilities

The backup and recovery utilities supplied with DB2 are wonderfully complex. They remove much of the burden of database recovery from the DBA or analyst and place it where it belongs: squarely on the shoulders of the DBMS.

Ten forms of backup and recovery are provided by nine DB2 utilities. The following list describes each form of backup and recovery along with the associated DB2 utility for each:

- Backup of all data in a table space, partition, or index (COPY utility)

- Incremental backup of table space data (COPY utility)

- Analyze a table space to determine if a full or incremental backup is required (COPY utility)

- Make a copy of an existing backup copy (COPYTOCOPY utility)

- Merge incremental copies (MERGECOPY utility)

- Full recovery of table space or index data based on the image copy and the log data (RECOVER utility)

- Restoration of a table space or index to an image copy or point in time, referred to hereafter as a partial recovery (RECOVER utility)

- Re-creation of DB2 indexes from table space data (REBUILD utility)

- Record a point of consistency for a table space or a set of table spaces (QUIESCE utility)

- Repair of damaged data (REPAIR utility)

- Report currently available recovery data (REPORT RECOVERY utility)

- Backup and restoration of the entire system (BACKUP SYSTEM and RESTORE SYSTEM)

The COPY Utility

The COPY utility is used to create an image copy backup data set for a complete table space, a single partition of a table space, or a complete index space. It can be executed so that a full image copy or an incremental image copy is created. A *full image copy* is a complete copy of all the data stored in the table space, table space partition, or index being copied. An *incremental image copy* is a copy of only the table space pages that have been modified due to inserts, updates, or deletes since the last full or incremental image copy.

> **CAUTION**
>
> For indexes, only full image copies can be created. Incremental image copies are not permitted for indexes. Furthermore, to be able to copy an index it must have been created with the COPY YES parameter.

The COPY utility utilizes the SYSIBM.SYSCOPY table to maintain a catalog of image copies. Every successful execution of the COPY utility places in this table at least one new row that indicates the status of the image copy. Information stored in the table includes the image copy data set name, the date and time of the COPY, the log RBA at the time of the copy, and the volume serial numbers for uncataloged image copy data sets. This information is read by the RECOVER utility to enable automated table space and index recovery.

The JCL in Listing 32.1 depicts a full image copy for a DB2 table space; the JCL in Listing 32.2 is an incremental image copy. The full image copy takes dual copies, whereas the incremental takes only a single image copy data set.

LISTING 32.1   Image Copy JCL

```
//DB2JOBU JOB (UTILITY),'FULL IMAGE COPY',CLASS=X,MSGCLASS=X,
//         NOTIFY=USER
//*
//*****************************************************************
//*
//*      DB2 COPY UTILITY::FULL COPY
//*
//*****************************************************************
//*
//COPY EXEC DSNUPROC,SYSTEM=DSN,UID='FULLCOPY',UTPROC="
//*
//DSNUPROC.COPY1 DD DSN=CAT.FULLCOPY.SEQ.DATASET1(+1),
//       DISP=(MOD,CATLG),DCB=SYS1.MODEL,
//       SPACE=(CYL,(5,2),RLSE),UNIT=3390
//DSNUPROC.COPY2 DD DSN=CAT.FULLCOPY.SEQ.DATASET2(+1),
//       DISP=(MOD,CATLG),DCB=SYS1.MODEL,
//       SPACE=(CYL,(5,2),RLSE),UNIT=3390
```

LISTING 32.1   Continued

```
//DSNUPROC.SYSIN    DD   *
    COPY TABLESPACE DSN8D881A.DSN8S881D
         COPYDDN (COPY1, COPY2)
         SHRLEVEL REFERENCE
         DSNUM ALL   FULL YES
/*
//
```

LISTING 32.2   Incremental Image Copy JCL

```
//DB2JOBU JOB (UTILITY),'INCREMENTAL COPY',CLASS=X,MSGCLASS=X,
//          NOTIFY=USER
//*
//****************************************************************
//*
//*        DB2 COPY UTILITY :: INCREMENTAL COPY
//*
//****************************************************************
//*
//COPY EXEC DSNUPROC,SYSTEM=DSN,UID='INCRCOPY',UTPROC="
//*
//DSNUPROC.SYSCOPY DD DSN=CAT.INCRCOPY.SEQ.DATASET(+1),
//       DISP=(MOD,CATLG),DCB=SYS1.MODEL,
//       SPACE=(CYL,(2,2),RLSE),UNIT=3380
//DSNUPROC.SYSIN    DD   *
    COPY TABLESPACE DSN8D881A.DSN8S881D SHRLEVEL REFERENCE
         DSNUM ALL   FULL NO
/*
//
```

Listing 32.3 provides sample JCL for taking a full image copy of an index. There are two options that can be used to specify an index in the COPY SYSIN—the INDEX name or the INDEXSPACE name. The INDEX name option requires specifying the index as *creator.index-name*; the INDEXSPACE option requires specifying it as *database.indexspace-name*. Favor using the INDEXSPACE option over the INDEX name. When using the INDEX option DB2 has to resolve the index space name from the index name. If you specify the index space name using the INDEXSPACE option, DB2 will already have the index space name.

> **NOTE**
>
> It is a good practice to limit the index name to 8 characters. By doing so DB2 will use the index name as the index space name, thereby simplifying administration.

LISTING 32.3   Index Copy JCL

```
//DB2JOBU JOB (UTILITY),INDEX COPY',CLASS=X,MSGCLASS=X,
//          NOTIFY=USER
//*
//****************************************************************
//*
```

32

LISTING 32.3   Continued

```
//*         DB2 COPY UTILITY :: INDEX COPY
//*
//**********************************************************************
//*
//COPY EXEC DSNUPROC,SYSTEM=DSN,UID='INDXCOPY',UTPROC="
//*
//DSNUPROC.SYSCOPY DD DSN=CAT.INDXCOPY.SEQ.DATASET(+1),
//       DISP=(MOD,CATLG),DCB=(SYS1.MODEL,BUFNO=20),
//       SPACE=(CYL,(1,1),RLSE),UNIT=3390
//DSNUPROC.SYSIN    DD  *
   COPY INDEXSPACE DSN8D881A.XPROJ1
        SHRLEVEL REFERENCE
/*
//
```

COPY Phases

The COPY utility has three phases:

UTILINIT	Sets up and initializes the COPY utility
REPORT	Reporting for the CHANGELIMIT option
COPY	Copies the table space or index data to the sequential file specified in the SYSCOPY DD statement
UTILTERM	Performs the final utility cleanup

Calculating SYSCOPY Data Set Size

To create a valid image copy, the COPY utility requires that the SYSCOPY data set be allocated. The following formula calculates the proper size for this data set:

```
SYSCOPY = (number of formatted pages) x 4096
```

> **NOTE**
>
> For segmented table spaces, empty formatted pages are not copied. This will reduce the size of the backup data set.

If the table space being copied uses 32K pages, multiply the result of the preceding calculation by 8. The total number of pages used by a table space can be retrieved from the VSAM LISTCAT command or from the DB2 Catalog as specified in the NACTIVEF column in SYSIBM.SYSTABLESPACE. When copying a single partition, use the NACTIVE column in SYSIBM.SYSTABSTATS to estimate the backup size.

If you use the DB2 Catalog statistics, ensure that the statistics are current by running the RUNSTATS utility (discussed in Chapter 34, "Catalog Manipulation Utilities").

After calculating the estimated size in bytes for this data set, convert the number to cylinders, rounding up to the next whole cylinder. Allocating data sets used by DB2 utilities in cylinder increments enhances the utility's performance.

V7 Of course, you can choose to use dynamic allocation and templates as of DB2 V7 instead of manually specifying data sets in your utility JCL.

COPY **Locking Considerations**

Copies running against the different partitions of the same table space can run concurrently. Many other utilities can run concurrently with COPY, as well.

COPY TABLESPACE (whether SHRLEVEL REFERENCE or SHRLEVEL CHANGE) can run concurrently with the following utilities (each accessing the same object):

BACKUP SYSTEM	CHECK INDEX
CHECK LOB	COPY INDEXSPACE
DIAGNOSE	REBUILD INDEX
RECOVER INDEX	REORG INDEX
REPORT	REORG UNLOAD ONLY or UNLOAD EXTERNAL
RUNSTATS INDEX	RUNSTATS TABLESPACE
STOSPACE	UNLOAD
REPAIR LOCATE (KEY, RID, PAGE, DUMP or VERIFY)	

Furthermore, the COPY TABLESPACE utility can run concurrently with REPAIR LOCATE INDEX (PAGE REPLACE) and QUIESCE, but only when specifying SHRLEVEL REFERENCE.

COPY INDEXSPACE (whether SHRLEVEL REFERENCE or SHRLEVEL CHANGE) can run concurrently with the following utilities (each accessing the same object):

BACKUP SYSTEM	CHECK DATA
CHECK INDEX	CHECK LOB
COPY TABLESPACE	DIAGNOSE
RECOVER TABLESPACE	REPORT
RUNSTATS INDEX	RUNSTATS TABLESPACE
STOSPACE	UNLOAD
REORG TABLESPACE UNLOAD ONLY or EXTERNAL	
REPAIR LOCATE (KEY, RID, PAGE, DUMP or VERIFY)	
REPAIR LOCATE TABLESPACE PAGE REPLACE	

Furthermore, the COPY INDEXSPACE utility can run concurrently with QUIESCE, but only when run specifying SHRLEVEL REFERENCE.

The COPY utility with the SHRLEVEL REFERENCE option drains the write claim class for the table space, partition, or index. This enables concurrent SQL read access. When SHRLEVEL CHANGE is specified, the COPY utility will claim the read claim class. Concurrent read and write access is permitted with one exception. A DELETE with no WHERE clause is not permitted on a table in a segmented table space while COPY SHRLEVEL CHANGE is running.

COPY **Guidelines**

You can use the following tips and techniques to ensure that the COPY utility is used effectively at your organization.

Increase Performance Using Inline Copies   The IBM DB2 LOAD and REORG utilities can take inline image copies during regular utility processing. By taking advantage of this capability, overall performance is enhanced because fewer scans of the data are required to produce the image copy data sets.

Balance the Use of Incremental and Full Image Copies   For most application table spaces, favor the creation of full image copies over incremental image copies. The time saved by incremental copying is often minimal, but the additional work to recover using incremental copies is usually burdensome.

To reduce the batch processing window, use incremental image copies for very large table spaces that incur only a small number of modifications between image copy runs. However, base the decision to use incremental image copies rather than full image copies on the percentage of table space pages that have been modified, not on the number of rows that have been modified. The image copy utility reports on the percentage of pages modified, so you can monitor this number. Consider using incremental image copies if this number is consistently small (for example, less than 20%).

You should consider incremental copying as the table space becomes larger and the batch window becomes smaller.

Take Full Image Copies to Encourage Sequential Prefetch   Remember that DB2 utilities requiring sequential data access use sequential prefetch, thereby enhancing utility performance. Thus, full image copies can be quicker than incremental image copies. A full image copy sequentially reads every page to create the image copy. An incremental image copy must check page bits to determine whether data has changed, and then access only the changed pages.

When incremental image copying does not use sequential prefetch, full image copying can be more efficient. Extra time is used because of the additional MERGECOPY step and the potentially inefficient processing (that is, without sequential prefetch). Compare the performance of incremental and full image copies before deciding to use incremental image copies.

Take Full Image Copies for Active and Smaller Table Spaces   Take full image copies for table spaces in which 40% or more of the pages are modified between executions of the COPY utility.

Always take full image copies of table spaces that contain less than 50,000 4K pages. For table spaces with larger page sizes, factor in the page size to arrive at a lower limit—for example, 25,000 8K pages.

Specify SHRLEVEL REFERENCE **to Reduce Recovery Time**   COPY specifying SHRLEVEL REFERENCE rather than SHRLEVEL CHANGE. This reduces the time for table space recovery. See the section titled "RECOVER TABLESPACE Guidelines" later in this chapter.

Running COPY with SHRLEVEL CHANGE can cause uncommitted data to be recorded on the copy. For this reason, recovering to a SHRLEVEL CHANGE copy using the TOCOPY option is not recommended.

An additional reason to avoid SHRLEVEL CHANGE is the impact on the performance of the COPY utility. Because other users can access the table space being copied, the performance of the COPY utility may degrade because of concurrent access. Note, however, that SHRLEVEL REFERENCE has only a performance advantage—not an integrity advantage—over SHRLEVEL CHANGE.

> **CAUTION**
>
> The integrity of SHRLEVEL REFERENCE and SHRLEVEL CHANGE backups are the same if the archive logs exist. In practice, test archive logs are not kept for long periods of time. At any rate, if you are using SHRLEVEL CHANGE be sure to institute a proper retention period for your archive logs to maintain the viability of the backups.

Code JCL Changes to Make COPY Restartable   To make the COPY utility restartable, specify the SYSCOPY DD statement as DISP=(MOD,CATLG,CATLG). When restarting the COPY utility, change the data set disposition to DISP=(MOD,KEEP,KEEP).

Create a Consistent Recovery Point   Be sure to QUIESCE all table spaces in the table space set before copying. Do this even when some table spaces do not need to be copied so you can provide a consistent point of recovery for all referentially related table spaces. Do so by creating a batch job stream with the following steps:

1. START all table spaces in the table space set using ACCESS(UT) or ACCESS(RO). Starting the table spaces in RO mode enables concurrent read access while the COPY is running.

2. QUIESCE all table spaces in the table space set.

3. Execute the COPY utility for all table spaces to be copied.

4. START all table spaces in the table space set using ACCESS(RW).

> **NOTE**
>
> The consistent backup created by this series of steps is ideal for populating a test environment (using DSN1COPY).

Consider Creating DASD Image Copies   Consider using disk rather than tape for image copy SYSCOPY data sets that will remain at the local site for recovery. This speeds the COPY process; disk is faster than tape, and you eliminate the time it takes the operator (or the automated robot tape loader) to load a new tape on the tape drive.

Be sure to verify that the image copy is placed on a separate DASD volume from the table space or index being copied. Failure to do so can result in a disk failure that affects both the data and its image copy. Also, as a failsafe, consider taking dual image copies where one is made to disk and the other is made to tape.

Consider Copying Indexes   The REBUILD process can take a long time to complete for large amounts of data or when multiple indexes exist. As of V6, you can take a full image copy or a concurrent copy of an index. Instead of rebuilding indexes during recovery, you use the RECOVER utility to restore the image copy and apply log records.

> **NOTE**
>
> You must specify the COPY YES parameter when creating an index to be able to use the COPY utility to make image copy backups for the index. The default is COPY NO. Existing indexes can be altered to specify the COPY YES parameter. If the index is defined using COPY YES you can use either the REBUILD method or the COPY and RECOVER method for index recovery.

The following utilities can place an index that was defined with the COPY YES attribute in the informational COPY pending (ICOPY) status:

```
LOAD TABLE (LOG YES or NO)        REBUILD INDEX

REORG TABLESPACE (LOG YES or NO)  REORG INDEX
```

To remove the ICOPY status, create a full image copy of the index after running these utilities.

Synchronize Data and Index Copies   If you decide to use COPY and RECOVER for indexes, instead of rebuilding indexes after recovering table spaces, be sure to keep the data and index backups synchronized. When you COPY a table space, be sure to also COPY any associated indexes defined with COPY YES.

Buffer the SYSCOPY Data Set Appropriately   For large image copies set the BUFNO parameter in the JCL for the SYSCOPY DD statement to a number greater than 20. The BUFNO parameter creates read and write buffers in main storage for the data set, thereby enhancing the performance of the COPY utility. Ensure that sufficient memory (real or expanded) is available, however, before increasing the BUFNO specification for your SYSCOPY data sets.

Favor Dual Image Copies   Take dual image copies for every table space (and index) being copied to eliminate the possibility of an invalid image copy due to an I/O error or damaged tape.

Prepare for disasters by sending additional image copies off-site. It is a wise course of action to take dual offsite copies, in addition to dual local image copies.

Compress Image Copies   To conserve tapes, consider compressing image copies. Use the silo compression if it's available. Additionally, third-party tools are available to compress data on tape cartridges.

Compressing image copy data sets not only saves tapes, but can improve performance. If a backup requires fewer tapes, fewer tape mounts will be required, which should reduce overall elapsed time. The same can be said for the recovery process. If fewer tapes are required to RECOVER, elapsed time should improve.

If your shop does not compress cartridges by default, add the following parameter to the DCB specification for the SYSCOPY DD:

```
DCB=TRTCH=COMP
```

Use CHANGELIMIT **to Help with Copies**   The CHANGELIMIT parameter can be specified on the COPY utility. When CHANGELIMIT is specified, COPY analyzes the number of changed pages since the last copy.

CHANGELIMIT accepts one or two integers (from 0 to 100) as input. Each integer is a percentage. If only one value is specified, an incremental image copy will be created if the percentage of changed pages is greater than 0 and less than the specified value. A full image copy will be created if the percentage of changed pages is greater than or equal to the specified percentage, or if CHANGELIMIT(0) is specified. No image copy will be created if there were no changed pages, unless 0 was specified for the CHANGELIMIT.

If two values are specified, an incremental image copy will be created if the percentage of changed pages is greater than the lowest value specified and less than the highest value specified. A full image copy will be created if the percentage of changed pages is equal to or greater than the highest value specified. No image copy will be created if the percentage of changed pages is outside the range of the low percentage and high percentage specified. If the two percentages happen to be the same, it will follow the rules as if one value was specified, as stated previously. When CHANGELIMIT is specified with COPY, return codes are set as indicated in Table 32.1.

> **CAUTION**
>
> You cannot specify CHANGELIMIT when copying a table space or partition defined as TRACKMOD NO.

TABLE 32.1   COPY/CHANGELIMIT Return Codes

Return Code	Description
1	No CHANGELIMIT percentage is met; no image copy is recommended or taken.
2	The percentage of changed pages is greater than the low CHANGELIMIT value, but less than the high CHANGELIMIT value; incremental copy is recommended or taken.
3	The percentage of changed pages is greater than or equal to the high CHANGELIMIT value; full image copy is recommended or taken.
8	The COPY step failed.

If REPORTONLY is specified, a report of the number of changed pages is produced. Further action can be taken after reviewing the report or checking the return code in the JCL.

Without the REPORTONLY parameter, the COPY utility automatically decides whether or not to take an image copy—if it does take an image copy, the COPY utility determines if the image is to be incremental or full. Consider using the return code to check the type of COPY that was created, and run a MERGECOPY step only if the return code indicates an incremental copy was created.

V7   **Consider Using** LISTDEF **to Copy RI-Related Objects**   The LISTDEF option can be very useful when used with the COPY utility. This is especially so when you need to copy a complete set of referentially related table spaces. You can use the RI parameter on the INCLUDE statement of the LISTDEF to cause all tables that are referentially connected to tables specified in the list to also be included. For example:

```
LISTDEF LSTR1 INCLUDE TABLESPACES
        TABLESPACE DSN8D81A.DSN8S81E  RI
```

This list will include all table spaces that include tables referentially related to any tables in the DSN8S81E table space of the sample database. This is much easier to manage than a job built to explicitly copy each of these table spaces—and it will include any new related table space as soon as it is created.

V8 **Control System Page Placement**   As of DB2 V8, you can use the SYSTEMPAGES parameter to exert some control over the placement of system pages in your image copy data sets. System pages are necessary when using the UNLOAD utility to unload data from an image copy. To ensure that the header, dictionary, and DB2 version system pages are copied at the beginning of the image copy data set, simply code SYSTEMPAGES YES on your COPY utility control card.

Consider Using DFSMS to Make Backup Copies   DFSMS can be utilized in the backup and recovery strategy for DB2 table spaces and indexes. DB2 provides the capability to recover from backup copies of DB2 data sets taken using the concurrent copy feature of DFSMS.

DFSMS is invoked under the control of DB2 using the COPY utility (as of DB2 V4). This simplifies the process of utilizing DFSMS within your DB2 backup and recovery plan. DFSMS is invoked by specifying the CONCURRENT parameter on the COPY utility. The image copy data sets created by the COPY utility and DFSMS are stored in the DB2 Catalog (SYSIBM.SYSCOPY) with an ICTYPE of F and an STYPE of C.

> **NOTE**
>
> An output data set for DFSMS messages must be specified to the DSSPRINT DD card when CONCURRENT copy is specified and the SYSPRINT DD card is defined to a data set.

V8

> **CAUTION**
>
> You cannot use SHRLEVEL CHANGE with CONCURRENT COPY for table spaces having a page size greater than 4K, unless the page size exactly matches the control interval size of the underlying VSAM data set.

V7 **Consider Log Suspension**   As of DB2 V7 (or the V6 refresh), you can issue a SET LOG SUSPEND command to effectively suspend all data modification within a DB2 subsystem. The SET LOG SUSPEND command externalizes log buffers, takes a system checkpoint, updates the BSDS with the highest written RBA, and takes a log write latch to prevent updates. Subsequent writes from the buffer pool are not externalized until the SET LOG RESUME command is issued. This causes the write latch to be released thereby enabling logging and data modification to ensue.

By taking a snapshot of the entire system after issuing the SET LOG SUSPEND command, you will have created a snapshot that can be used for local or remote site recovery with consistent data. Use this technique only in conjunction with external copying technology such as that provided by RVA SnapShot or ESS FlashCopy.

The snapshot copy can be used in the event of a disaster to recover the system to a point of consistency. Alternatively, you can use it to provide a quick, consistent copy of your data point-in-time querying.

However, keep in mind that careful planning is required to minimize application impact of a log suspension. Avoid suspending log activity during periods of heavy data modification.

The COPYTOCOPY Utility

V7 The purpose of the COPYTOCOPY utility, introduced as of DB2 V7, is to permit image copies to be made from existing image copies. The primary benefit is to reduce the amount of time required to run the COPY utility. COPY can be used to take up to four image copies with a single execution of the utility. But with COPYTOCOPY available, instead of using COPY to make four image copy backups, the DBA can use COPY to make a single image copy, and then run COPYTOCOPY to make additional image copies.

COPYTOCOPY can be run against any DB2 image copy data set including inline copies made during the execution of REORG or LOAD. Starting with either the local primary or recovery site primary copy, COPYTOCOPY can make up to three copies of one or more of the following types of copies:

- Local primary
- Local backup
- Recovery site primary
- Recovery site backup

Copies created by COPYTOCOPY can be used by the RECOVER utility just like image copies created using the COPY utility. Both table space and index space copies can be made using the COPYTOCOPY utility. Any DB2 utility process that uses image copy data sets can use the image copies created by COPYTOCOPY. This includes MERGECOPY, UNLOAD, and subsequent runs of COPYTOCOPY. However, keep in mind that image copies created with the CONCURRENT option of the COPY utility are not supported by the COPYTOCOPY utility.

Just like the COPY utility, the COPYTOCOPY utility records information about the image copies that it creates in the SYSIBM.SYSCOPY system catalog table. The COPYTOCOPY utility will insert the values in the DSNAME, GROUP_MEMBER, JOBNAME, AUTHID, DSVOLSER, and DEVTYPE columns as appropriate depending on the copies that are being created.

You cannot run COPYTOCOPY to create additional image copies for certain DB2 Catalog (SYSCOPY in DSNDB06) and DB2 Directory (DSNDB01 and SYSUTILX both in DSNDB01) objects.

To execute COPYTOCOPY, the process or user running the utility must have been granted one of the following privileges:

- SYSADM or SYSCTRL
- IMAGCOPY, DBADM, DBCTRL, or DBMAINT for the database in which the index or table space resides

Processes or users having INSTALL SYSOPR authority can run COPYTOCOPY for table spaces in the DB2 Directory (DSNDB01) and DB2 Catalog (DSNDB06).

COPYTOCOPY **Phases**

COPYTOCOPY creates a new image copy of a table space or an index from an existing image copy. The COPYTOCOPY utility operates in these distinct phases:

UTILINIT	Initialization and setup
CPY2CPY	Copying the image copy
UTILTERM	Cleanup

COPYTOCOPY **Locking and Concurrency**

When COPYTOCOPY is running, the object for which the copy applies is placed in utility restricted read/write state (UTRW). Basically, this will prevent anyone from dropping the object while the COPYTOCOPY utility executes.

Individual data and index partitions are treated as distinct target objects by the COPYTOCOPY utility. Any other utilities operating on different partitions of the same table space or index space can be run concurrently with COPYTOCOPY.

The following utilities cannot be run concurrently on the same object as the COPYTOCOPY utility:

COPY	LOAD
MERGECOPY	MODIFY
RECOVER	REORG INDEX
REORG TABLESPACE	

COPYTOCOPY **Execution**

To run the COPYTOCOPY utility, it is not necessary to provide the explicit data set name of the image copy being copied. Instead, the input to the COPYTOCOPY utility is the name of the table space, index space, or index for which the original copy was made, and an indication of which image copy in the catalog is to be copied. There are three options:

- FROMLASTCOPY—Indicates that the most recent image copy taken for the table space or index space is to be used as input to the COPYTOCOPY utility. The input could be either a full image copy or incremental copy. The utility will retrieve the information from the SYSIBM.SYSCOPY system catalog table.

- FROMLASTFULLCOPY—Indicates that the most recent full image copy taken for the object is to be used as the input to COPYTOCOPY job. Once again, this information is obtained by querying the DB2 Catalog.

- FROMLASTINCRCOPY—Indicates that the most recent incremental image copy taken for the object is to be used as the input to COPYTOCOPY job. FROMLASTINCRCOPY is not valid for index spaces or indexes. If FROMLASTINCRCOPY is specified for an index space or index, COPYTOCOPY will use the last full image copy that was taken for the index, if one is available. Once again, this information is obtained by querying the DB2 Catalog.

Of course, you may choose to specify the data set name for the image copy that is to be copied by the COPYTOCOPY utility. This can be accomplished by using the FROMCOPY clause. When COPYTOCOPY is used in conjunction with a list of objects defined using the LISTDEF statement, the FROMCOPY clause is not valid.

If the FROMCOPY keyword is not used, the COPYTOCOPY utility must determine which specific image copy is to be copied. Before COPYTOCOPY can execute it may have to choose between the local site primary copy, local site backup copy, recovery site primary copy, and recovery site backup copy data sets.

COPYTOCOPY will search image copies in the following order to determine the input data set to be used:

- If you are running COPYTOCOPY at your local site, the search order will be (1) local site primary copy, (2) local site backup copy, (3) recovery site primary copy, (4) recovery site backup copy.

- If you are running the utility at your recovery site, the search order will be (1) recovery site primary copy, (2) recovery site backup copy, (3) local site primary copy, and finally (4) local site backup copy.

If the input data set cannot be allocated or opened, the COPYTOCOPY utility will try to use the next image copy data with the same START_RBA value in SYSIBM.SYSCOPY column, in the search order as indicated previously. When the FROMCOPY keyword is used though, only the explicitly specified data set can be used as the input to COPYTOCOPY.

An example of JCL used to run the COPYTOCOPY utility is depicted in Listing 32.4. This job is used to make a backup local image copy of table space DSN8S71E in database DSN8D71A. This will be either a full or incremental image copy, whichever was last run for this table space.

LISTING 32.4   COPYTOCOPY JCL

```
//DB2JOBU JOB (UTILITY),INDEX COPY',CLASS=X,MSGCLASS=X,
//            NOTIFY=USER
//*
//****************************************************************
//*
//*        DB2 COPYTOCOPY UTILITY
//*
//****************************************************************
//*
//COPY EXEC DSNUPROC,SYSTEM=DSN,UID='C2CTS',UTPROC="
//*
//DSNUPROC.COPY2    DD DSN=COPY002F.IFDY01,UNIT=SYSDA,VOL=SER=CPY02I,
//          SPACE=(CYL,(15,1)),DISP=(NEW,CATLG,CATLG)
```

LISTING 32.4 Continued

```
//DSNUPROC.SYSIN    DD  *
   COPYTOCOPY TABLESPACE DSN8D71A.DSN8S71E COPYDDN(,COPY2)
/*
//
```

COPYTOCOPY **Guidelines**

Deploy the following tips and guidelines as you utilize the COPYTOCOPY utility on your DB2 data.

Avoid Terminating COPYTOCOPY   It is not recommended to use the TERM command to terminate a COPYTOCOPY step. A current restart should be done instead.

If a job step containing more than one COPYTOCOPY statement abends, do not use TERM UTILITY. Instead, you should restart the job from the last commit point using RESTART. If you terminate COPYTOCOPY in this situation you might cause inconsistencies between the ICF catalog and DB2 catalogs when generation data sets (GDGs) are used.

You cannot use RESTART(PHASE) for a COPYTOCOPY job. It is fine to use RESTART(CURRENT) if you do *not* use the -TERM UTILITY command to terminate a COPYTOCOPY execution. When you use RESTART(CURRENT), COPYTOCOPY will restart from the last commit point with the same image copy data set, so be sure to specify the data set disposition to DISP=(MOD,CATLG,CATLG) on the JCL DD statements.

Inline Copy Exception   When using COPYTOCOPY to copy an inline image copy that was made by the REORG utility with the part range option, you will need to specify individual DSNUM for the partitions to be copied. The COPYTOCOPY utility does not support part range. COPYTOCOPY will copy only the specified partition data from the input inline image copy data set into the output image copy data set.

The MERGECOPY **Utility**

The MERGECOPY utility combines multiple incremental image copy data sets into a new full or incremental image copy data set. See Listing 32.5 for sample JCL. The first control card depicts the merging of image copy data sets for the DSN8D81A.DSN8S81D table space into a full image copy. The second control card shows statements that create a new incremental image copy data set for the DSN8D81A.DSN8S81E table space.

LISTING 32.5 MERGECOPY JCL

```
//DB2JOBU JOB (UTILITY), 'MERGECOPY',CLASS=X,MSGCLASS=X,NOTIFY=USER
//*
//****************************************************************
//*
//*        DB2 MERGECOPY UTILITY
//*
//****************************************************************
//*
//COPY EXEC DSNUPROC,SYSTEM=DSN,UID='MERGCOPY',UTPROC="
//*
```

LISTING 32.5   Continued

```
//* UTILITY WORK DATASETS
//*
//DSNUPROC.SYSUT1 DD DSN=CAT.SYSUT1,DISP=(MOD,CATLG,CATLG),
//        UNIT=SYSDA,SPACE=(CYL,(10,1)),DCB=BUFNO=20
//DSNUPROC.SYSCOPY1 DD DSN=CAT.FULLCOPY.SEQ.DATASETD(+1),
//        DISP=(MOD,CATLG),DCB=(SYS1.MODEL, BUFNO=20),
//        SPACE=(CYL,(5,1),RLSE),UNIT=TAPE
//DSNUPROC.SYSCOPY2 DD DSN=CAT.INCRCOPY.SEQ.DATASETE(+1),
//        DISP=(MOD,CATLG),DCB=(SYS1.MODEL, BUFNO=20),
//        SPACE=(CYL,(2,1),RLSE),UNIT=TAPE
//*
//*  UTILITY INPUT CONTROL STATEMENTS
//*      The first MERGECOPY statement creates a new full
//*      image copy for the DSN8D81A.
//*      The second statement creates a new incremental copy
//*      for the named table space.
//*
//DSNUPROC.SYSIN    DD  *
   MERGECOPY TABLESPACE DSN8D81A.DSN8S81D
           DSNUM ALL   NEWCOPY YES
           COPYDDN SYSCOPY1
   MERGECOPY TABLESPACE DSN8D81A.DSN8S81E
           DSNUM ALL    NEWCOPY NO
           COPYDDN SYSCOPY2
/*
//
```

MERGECOPY **Phases**

The MERGECOPY utility runs in three phases:

UTILINIT	Sets up and initializes the MERGECOPY utility.
MERGECOPY	Merges the incremental image copy data sets for the indicated table space and then places the final merged copy (full or incremental) in the data set specified by the SYSCOPY DD statement.
UTILTERM	Performs the final utility cleanup.

Estimating SYSUT1 **and** SYSCOPY **Data Set Sizes**

The MERGECOPY utility sometimes requires the use of the SYSUT1 work data set to merge image copies. If it is impossible to simultaneously allocate all the data sets to be merged, SYSUT1 is used to hold intermediate output from the merge. If not enough tape drives are available (to allocate the incremental copy data sets) when MERGECOPY runs, be sure to allocate a SYSUT1 data set.

The SYSCOPY data set holds the final merged image copy data and must be specified. The space required for this data set is the same as would be required for the SYSCOPY data set for the COPY utility. A merged image copy and a full image copy should be functionally equivalent and therefore should consume the same amount of space.

The following formula should be used to calculate an estimated size for this data set. This calculation is only an estimate. More complex and precise calculations are in the *DB2 Utility Guide and Reference* manual, but this formula should produce comparable results.

```
SYSUT1 = (size of the largest data set to be merged) x 1.5
SYSCOPY = (number of formatted pages) x 4096
```

If the table space being merged uses 32K pages, multiply the result of the SYSCOPY calculation by 8. The total number of pages used by a table space can be retrieved from either the VSAM LISTCAT command or the DB2 Catalog as specified in the NACTIVE column of SYSIBM.SYSTABLESPACE. If you are using the DB2 Catalog method, ensure that the statistics are current by running the RUNSTATS utility (discussed in Chapter 34).

After calculating the estimated size for the data sets, convert the number into cylinders, rounding up to the next whole cylinder. Allocating work data sets in cylinder increments enhances the utility's performance.

Concurrency

Concurrent read and write activity can occur during execution of the MERGECOPY utility. The MERGECOPY utility can run concurrently with any utility except the following:

COPY TABLESPACE	LOAD
MERGECOPY	MODIFY
RECOVER	REORG TABLESPACE
UNLOAD (from the same image copy)	

MERGECOPY Guidelines

When running MERGECOPY, consider using the following techniques and guidelines.

Merge Incremental Copies As Soon As Possible   Directly after the execution of an incremental COPY, run the MERGECOPY utility to create a new full image copy. In this way, the resources to create a new full image copy are used at a non-critical time. If you decide to avoid the creation of full image copies until there is an error, valuable time can be consumed by processing that could have taken place at a less critical time.

Use MERGECOPY to Create Full Image Copies   Specify NEWCOPY YES to produce a new full image copy. NEWCOPY NO can be used to produce a new incremental copy. Favor the creation of new full image copies rather than incremental copies because less work must be performed to correct an error if full table space image copies exist.

Specify the SYSUT1 Data Set   Always specify a data set for SYSUT1 to avoid rerunning MERGECOPY. If SYSUT1 is not specified, the MERGECOPY job might be unable to allocate all the data sets needed for the merge, thereby requiring that MERGECOPY be run again. This must continue until all incremental copies have been merged into a new image copy data set, either full or incremental.

If SYSUT1 is not specified, the output of the MERGECOPY utility indicates whether another merge must be run. MERGECOPY produces a message indicating the number of existing data sets and the number of merged data sets. If these numbers are not equal, rerun the MERGECOPY utility. Again, this can be avoided by specifying a SYSUT1 data set.

Buffer the SYSCOPY and SYSUT1 Data Sets   For large image copies, set the BUFNO parameter in the JCL for the SYSCOPY DD statements to a number greater than 20. The BUFNO parameter creates read and write buffers in main storage for the data set, thereby enhancing the performance of the COPY utility. Ensure that sufficient memory (real or expanded) is available, however, before increasing the BUFNO specification for your SYSCOPY data sets.

Also, consider specifying a larger BUFNO for the SYSUT1 data set if you expect many incremental image copies to be required.

The QUIESCE Utility

The QUIESCE utility is used to record a point of consistency for a table space, partition, table space set, or list of table spaces and table space sets. QUIESCE ensures that all table spaces in the scope of the QUIESCE are referentially intact. It does this by externalizing all data modifications to DASD and recording log RBAs or LRSNs in the SYSIBM.SYSCOPY DB2 Catalog table, indicating a point of consistency for future recovery. This is called a *quiesce point*. Running QUIESCE improves the probability of a successful RECOVER or COPY.

QUIESCE inserts a row with ICTYPE='Q' into SYSIBM.SYSCOPY for each table space quiesced. Additionally, QUIESCE inserts a row with ICTYPE='Q' into SYSIBM.SYSCOPY for any indexes (defined with the COPY YES attribute) associated with the table space(s) being quiesced.

Sample JCL for the QUIESCE utility is in Listing 32.6. This will quiesce all the table spaces for the DB2 sample tables. Of course, as of DB2 V7 you could choose to use LISTDEF and TEMPLATE (as described in Chapter 30, "An Introduction to DB2 Utilities") to simplify this JCL.

LISTING 32.6   QUIESCE JCL

```
//DB2JOBU  JOB (UTILITY),'QUIESCE',CLASS=X,MSGCLASS=X,NOTIFY=USER
//*
//*****************************************************************
//*
//*       DB2 QUIESCE UTILITY
//*
//*       Step 1:  STARTUT:  Start all table spaces in the
//*                table space set in utility-only mode.
//*       Step 2:  QUIESCE:  Quiesce all table spaces in the
//*                table space set.
//*       Step 3:  STARTRW:  Start all table spaces in the
//*                table space set in read/write mode.
//*
//*****************************************************************
//*
//STARTUT EXEC PGM=IKJEFT01,DYNAMNBR=20
//STEPLIB DD DSN=DSN810.DSNLOAD,DISP=SHR
//SYSPRINT DD SYSOUT=*
//SYSTSPRT DD SYSOUT=*
```

LISTING 32.6   Continued

```
//SYSOUT   DD SYSOUT=*
//SYSUDUMP DD SYSOUT=*
//SYSTSIN  DD *
DSN SYSTEM (DSN)
-START DATABASE (DSN8D81A) ACCESS (UT)
END
/*
//QUIESCE EXEC DSNUPROC,SYSTEM=DSN,UID='QUIESCTS',UTPROC=",
//          COND=(0,NE,STARTUT)
//DSNUPROC.SYSIN    DD  *
    QUIESCE TABLESPACE DSN8D81A.DSN8S81C
            TABLESPACE DSN8D81A.DSN8S81D
            TABLESPACE DSN8D81A.DSN8S81E
            TABLESPACE DSN8D81A.DSN8S81R
            TABLESPACE DSN8D81A.ACT
            TABLESPACE DSN8D81A.PROJ
            TABLESPACE DSN8D81A.PROJACT
            TABLESPACE DSN8D81A.EMPPROJA WRITE YES
/*
//STARTRW EXEC PGM=IKJEFT01,DYNAMNBR=20,COND=EVEN
//STEPLIB DD DSN=DSN810.DSNLOAD,DISP=SHR
//*
//SYSPRINT DD SYSOUT=*
//SYSTSPRT DD SYSOUT=*
//SYSOUT   DD SYSOUT=*
//SYSUDUMP DD SYSOUT=*
//SYSTSIN  DD *
DSN SYSTEM (DSN)
-START DATABASE (DSN8D81A) ACCESS (RW)
END
/*
//
```

QUIESCE **Phases**

The QUIESCE utility has three phases:

UTILINIT	Sets up and initializes the QUIESCE utility
QUIESCE	Determines the point of consistency and updates the DB2 Catalog
UTILTERM	Performs the final utility cleanup

QUIESCE **Locking Considerations**

The following utilities can run concurrently with QUIESCE:

CHECK DATA DELETE NO	CHECK INDEX
CHECK LOB	COPY SHRLEVEL REFERENCE (IX or TS)
DIAGNOSE	MERGECOPY
MODIFY	QUIESCE

```
REPORT                                    RUNSTATS

STOSPACE                                  UNLOAD

REORG TABLESPACE UNLOAD (ONLY or EXTERNAL)

REPAIR LOCATE (DUMP or VERIFY)
```

The QUIESCE utility will drain all write claim classes. If WRITE YES is specified, QUIESCE will also drain all write claim classes on an associated partitioning index (or partition), DPSIs, and any non-partitioned indexes. Concurrent read access is permitted during a QUIESCE.

QUIESCE Guidelines

Implement the following guidelines to ensure effective use of the QUIESCE utility.

Run QUIESCE Before COPY   QUIESCE all table spaces in a table space set before copying them. When QUIESCE will be run for a table space in a table space set, QUIESCE every table space in the table space set to ensure data consistency and referential integrity. Of course, if the COPY PENDING flag is on, QUIESCE will fail.

Specify the WRITE Option   Be sure to specify whether changed pages in the buffer pool are to be externalized to disk. Specifying WRITE YES will cause pages in the buffer pool to be written; specifying WRITE NO will not. The default is WRITE YES.

QUIESCE the System Databases Before Copying   QUIESCE all DSNDB01 and DSNDB06 table spaces before copying the DB2 Catalog. Before quiescing these table spaces, consider placing the databases into utility-only mode using the DB2 START command.

Only an Install SYSADM can QUIESCE the DB2 Directory and DB2 Catalog.

Use QUIESCE to Create Interim Points of Recovery   QUIESCE can be used to set up recovery points between regularly scheduled image copies. However, QUIESCE does not replace the need for image copies.

QUIESCE Table Spaces Related by Application RI   Even when table spaces are not tied together using DB2-defined referential integrity but are related by application code, use the QUIESCE utility to ensure the integrity of the data in the tables. This establishes a point of consistency for table spaces that are related but not controlled by the DBMS.

The QUIESCE utility cannot be run on a table space that has a copy pending, check pending, or recovery pending status.

Consider Quiescing Online Table Spaces While Activity Is Low   Run QUIESCE as frequently as possible for table spaces containing tables modified online. This enables the recovery of the table spaces to a point after the last full image copy if there is an error. Do not run the QUIESCE utility during very active periods, however, because it requires a share lock on all the table spaces that it processes. This means that table spaces being processed by QUIESCE cannot be modified until the QUIESCE utility completes.

Code Multiple Table Spaces per QUIESCE   When quiescing multiple table spaces, code the utility control cards with multiple table spaces assigned to one QUIESCE keyword. For example, code this

```
QUIESCE TABLESPACE    DSN8D81A.DSN8S81C
        TABLESPACE    DSN8D81A.DSN8S81D
        TABLESPACE    DSN8D81A.DSN8S81E
```

instead of

```
QUIESCE TABLESPACE    DSN8D81A.DSN8S81C
QUIESCE TABLESPACE    DSN8D81A.DSN8S81D
QUIESCE TABLESPACE    DSN8D81A.DSN8S81E
```

By coding the control cards the first way, you ensure that the quiesce point for all the table spaces is consistent. If the control cards are coded as shown in the second example, the QUIESCE utility is invoked three times, resulting in a different point of consistency for each table space. If you follow the guidelines for starting all table spaces in utility-only mode before running QUIESCE, either QUIESCE option will work. However, getting into the habit of coding the control cards as shown in the first example prevents errors if the start does not finish successfully before the QUIESCE begins to execute.

If the list of table spaces on which the QUIESCE utility is being executed exceeds 1165, it will be terminated with a return code of 8. To QUIESCE groups of more than 1165 table spaces, follow this procedure:

1. Stop all the table spaces before quiescing.

2. Break the table spaces into groups of no more than 1165 table spaces each.

3. Quiesce each group with a single QUIESCE statement. These QUIESCEs can be run in parallel to decrease the overall elapsed time.

4. Start all the table spaces only after all QUIESCE statements have finished.

Consider Using QUIESCE at the Partition Level   The QUIESCE utility can be requested at the partition level. When it makes sense within your environment, consider using this ability to fine tune your backup and recovery strategy.

Consider Using QUIESCE with the TABLESPACESET Parameter   The TABLESPACESET parameter is used to indicate that all of the referentially related table spaces in the table space set are to be quiesced. A table space set is either a group of table spaces tied together with referential integrity or a base table space and all of its LOB table spaces. One table space name is supplied to the TABLESPACESET parameter, and DB2 identifies the rest of the table spaces in the table space set to be quiesced.

The RECOVER Utility

The recovery of DB2 data is an automated process rigorously controlled by the database management system. Figure 32.1 shows the flow of normal DB2 recovery. The standard unit of recovery for DB2 is the table space. As of DB2 V6, indexes can be copied using the COPY utility and recovered using the RECOVER utility. The DB2 COPY utility is used to create an image copy backup. All DB2 image copy data set information is recorded in the DB2 Catalog in the SYSIBM.SYSCOPY table. It is not necessary to keep track of the image copy data sets externally because DB2 manages this information independent of the application code.

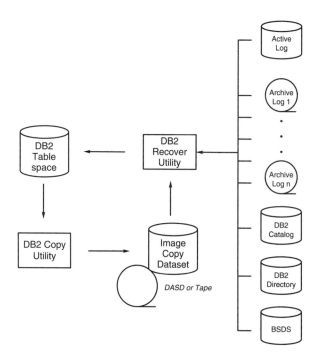

FIGURE 32.1   DB2 recovery.

DB2 is also responsible for keeping a log of all changes made to table spaces. With a few exceptions, all updates are recorded in the DB2 *active log*. When an active log is full, DB2 creates an *archive log*. Many archive logs are created during normal DB2 application processing. All this information is stored in the DB2 Directory's SYSIBM.SYSLGRNX table and the Boot Strap Data Set (BSDS). Refer to Chapter 22, "The Table-Based Infrastructure of DB2," for a complete description of the internal DB2 tables and data sets.

The DB2 RECOVER utility reads all control information pertaining to data recovery and applies the recorded changes contained in the copies and logs, as instructed by the DBMS and the RECOVER utility control parameters.

Basically, the RECOVER utility is used to restore DB2 table spaces and indexes to a specific point in time. You can run two forms of the RECOVER utility: RECOVER TABLESPACE and RECOVER INDEX. Both are discussed in the following sections.

The RECOVER Utility

RECOVER can be used to recover table spaces or indexes by restoring data from an image copy data set and then applying subsequent changes from the log files.

The RECOVER TABLESPACE Utility

The RECOVER TABLESPACE utility restores table spaces to a current or previous state. It first reads the DB2 Catalog to determine the availability of full and incremental image copies, and then reads the DB2 logs to determine interim modifications. The utility then applies the image copies and the log modifications to the table space data set being recovered. The DBMS maintains the recovery information in the DB2 Catalog. This enables the RECOVER utility to automate tasks such as the following:

- Retrieving appropriate image copy data set names and volume serial numbers
- Retrieving appropriate log data set names and volume serial numbers
- Coding the DD statements for each of these in the RECOVER JCL

Data can be recovered for a single page, pages that contain I/O errors, a single partition of a partitioned table space, or a complete table space.

Recovery to a previous point can be accomplished by specifying a full image copy or a specific log RBA. Recovery to the current point can be accomplished by simply specifying only the table space name as a parameter to the RECOVER utility.

Listing 32.6 shows an example of full recovery to the current point for a table space. Listing 32.7 shows the recovery of the same table space to a previous point using the TOCOPY option to specify an image copy, and the recovery of a different table space to a previous point using the TORBA option to specify a log RBA. This applies the log records only up to, not including, the specified RBA. Note that when using the TOCOPY option with GDG datasets, the relative GDG reference is not allowed.

LISTING 32.6   JCL for Full Recovery

```
//DB2JOBU JOB (UTILITY),'FULL RECOVERY',CLASS=X,MSGCLASS=X,
//NOTIFY=USER
//*
//*****************************************************************
//*
//*        DB2 RECOVER UTILITY  ::   FULL RECOVERY
//*
//*****************************************************************
//*
//RCVR EXEC DSNUPROC,SYSTEM=DSN,UID='FULLRECV',UTPROC="
//*
//*   UTILITY INPUT CONTROL STATEMENTS
//*      1. The first RECOVER statement recovers the
//*         DSN8D81A.DSN8S81C table space to the current point
//*         in time.
//*      2. The second RECOVER statement recovers all indexes
//*         in the table space.
//*
//DSNUPROC.SYSIN    DD  *
    RECOVER TABLESPACE DSN8D81A.DSN8S81C DSNUM ALL
    REBUILD INDEX(ALL) TABLESPACE DSN8D81A.DSN8S81C
/*
//
```

LISTING 32.7   JCL for Partial Recovery

```
//DB2JOBU JOB (UTILITY),'PRTL RECOVERY',CLASS=X,MSGCLASS=X,
//          NOTIFY=USER
//*
//*****************************************************************
//*
//*        DB2 RECOVER UTILITY  ::  PARTIAL RECOVERY
//*
//*****************************************************************
//*
//RCVR EXEC DSNUPROC,SYSTEM=DSN,UID='PRTLRECV',UTPROC="
//*
//*   UTILITY INPUT CONTROL STATEMENTS
//*     1. The first RECOVER statement recovers the
//*        DSN8D81A.DSN8S81D table space to the named
//*        image copy data set.
//*     2. The second RECOVER statement recovers the
//*        DSN8D81A.DSN8S81C table space to the specified
//*        log RBA.
//*
//DSNUPROC.SYSIN    DD  *
   RECOVER TABLESPACE DSN8D81A.DSN8S81D
           TOCOPY CAT.FULLCOPY.DATASETD.G0001V00
   RECOVER TABLESPACE DSN8D81A.DSN8S81C
           TORBA X'0000EF2C66F4'
/*
//
```

The RECOVER INDEX (or RECOVER INDEXSPACE) Utility

RECOVER INDEX (or alternatively RECOVER INDEXSPACE) is executed to restore DB2 indexes to a current or previous state. The utility first reads the DB2 Catalog to determine the availability of image copies, and then reads the DB2 logs to determine interim modifications. The utility then applies the image copies and the log modifications to the index space data set of the index being recovered.

RECOVER INDEXSPACE is similar to RECOVER TABLESPACE, except that it operates on DB2 indexes instead of DB2 table spaces. DB2 V6 is the first release of DB2 that enabled recovery of indexes from image copy data sets. The JCL to run the RECOVER INDEXSPACE utility is provided in Listing 32.8.

LISTING 32.8   RECOVER INDEXSPACE JCL

```
//DB2JOBU  JOB (UTILITY),'DB2 RECVR INDEX',MSGCLASS=X,CLASS=X,
//          NOTIFY=USER
//*
//*****************************************************************
//*
//*        DB2 RECOVER INDEXSPACE UTILITY
//*
//*****************************************************************
//*
```

LISTING 32.8   Continued

```
//UTIL EXEC DSNUPROC,SYSTEM=DSN,UID='RCVRINDX',UTPROC="
//*
//*   UTILITY WORK DATASETS
//*
//*
//*   UTILITY INPUT CONTROL STATEMENTS
//*      Recovers the XPROJ1 index from an image copy.
//*
//DSNUPROC.SYSIN    DD  *
    RECOVER INDEXSPACE DSN8D81A.XPROJ1
/*
//
```

> **NOTE**
>
> Prior to V6, all indexes had to be rebuilt from the data, not an image copy. Additionally, prior to DB2 V6, the RECOVER utility performed this index rebuilding. But as of V6, the REBUILD INDEX utility is used to rebuild indexes from table data, not the RECOVER utility.

RECOVER **Phases**

The RECOVER utility has up to six phases:

UTILINIT	Sets up and initializes the RECOVER utility.
RESTORE	Locates and merges all appropriate image copy data sets, after which the table space or index space is restored to the given point using the merged image copy data; processes a list of objects in parallel if you specified the PARALLEL keyword.
RESTORER	For RECOVER with the PARALLEL option, this phase reads and merges the image copies.
RESTOREW	For RECOVER with the PARALLEL option, this phase writes the pages to the object.
LOGAPPLY	Locates outstanding modifications from the log and applies them to the table space or index space being recovered.
UTILTERM	Performs the final utility cleanup.

The RESTORE phase is bypassed if the LOGAPPLY option is specified.

RECOVER **Locking Considerations**

The RECOVER utility can run concurrently with the following utilities:

- DIAGNOSE
- REPORT
- STOSPACE

Additionally, unless RECOVER TOCOPY or TORBA is specified, RECOVER can run concurrently with REORG INDEX and REPAIR LOCATE INDEX.

The RECOVER utility drains all claim classes for the table space, partition, or index being recovered, regardless of the options specified. However, if the ERROR-RANGE option is specified, the locking level is downgraded to a write claim during the UTILINIT phase.

If either the TORBA or TOCOPY option is specified, RECOVER will drain all claim classes for the index or index partition, as well as any non-partitioned index.

RECOVER **Guidelines**

Be sure to implement the following guidelines when you are recovering table spaces.

V7 **Retain Tape Mounts**   When using RECOVER with image copies on one or more tape volumes, you do not need to code JCL statements to retain the tape mounts. You can use the PARALLEL and TAPEUNITS keywords to control the allocation of tape devices for the job. At times RECOVER will not be able to retain all tape mounts causing tapes to be deallocated, even when specifying PARALLEL and TAPEUNITS.

Do Not Specify Work Data Sets   The RECOVER utility does not require work data sets to recover DB2 table spaces and indexes.

Improve Recovery Performance by Avoiding SHRLEVEL CHANGE **Copies**   If RECOVER TABLE-SPACE is used for a table space in which an image copy data set was created with the SHRLEVEL CHANGE specification, the performance of the RECOVER utility degrades. The log RBA stored for an image copy taken with SHRLEVEL CHANGE is at an earlier portion of the log because the table space can be modified during the execution of the COPY utility. Therefore, the RECOVER utility reads the log RBA recorded with the image copy in the SYSIBM.SYSCOPY table and scans the active and archive logs for changes starting with that RBA. Performance can degrade because more log records are read.

Recover SHRLEVEL CHANGE **Copies Appropriately**   Image copies taken using SHRLEVEL CHANGE must be recovered to the current point in time or to a specific point in time using TORBA (not TOCOPY). If a SHRLEVEL CHANGE image copy is recovered using the TOCOPY option, it will be in an indeterminate stage.

Be Aware of Underlying VSAM Data Set Deletions   The underlying VSAM data sets for STOGROUP-defined table spaces are deleted and defined by the RECOVER TABLESPACE utility. If the table space has been user-defined, the corresponding VSAM data set is not deleted.

Recover Multiple Objects with a Single RECOVER   When multiple table spaces must be recovered, code the utility control cards with multiple table spaces assigned to one RECOVER keyword. For example, code this

```
RECOVER TABLESPACE   DSN8D81A.DSN8S81C
        TABLESPACE   DSN8D81A.DSN8S81D
        TABLESPACE   DSN8D81A.DSN8S81E
```

instead of

```
RECOVER TABLESPACE  DSN8D81A.DSN8S81C
RECOVER TABLESPACE  DSN8D81A.DSN8S81D
RECOVER TABLESPACE  DSN8D81A.DSN8S81E
```

Coding the control cards the first way ensures that the archive and active logs are read only once. If the control cards are coded as shown in the second example, the RECOVER TABLESPACE utility runs three times, causing the archive and active logs to be read separately for each invocation of the utility. This reduces CPU time, elapsed time, and time spent waiting for an operator to load the archive tapes.

Consider Restoring in Parallel   If multiple objects are to be recovered, consider using the PARALLEL parameter to restore the objects concurrently. When the PARALLEL option is specified, the RECOVER utility will perform parallel processing during the RESTORE phase. Additionally, you can specify a limit for the number of objects to restore in parallel—for example, PARALLEL(4) indicates that four objects should be restored at a time.

> **NOTE**
>
> If you specify PARALLEL(0) or do not indicate a value (that is, you specify simply PARALLEL), RECOVER will determine the optimal number of objects to process in parallel.

Consider Explicitly Allocating Image Copy Data Sets   DB2 dynamically allocates image copy and log data sets during the execution of the RECOVER utility to minimize an analyst's work during recovery. However, the image copy input to the RECOVER utility can be specified explicitly in the JCL by simply coding a DD statement for each full and incremental image copy to be used. The DD statement can use any name not already used by the RECOVER JCL. DB2 will not dynamically allocate an image copy data set if it finds a DD statement with a matching data set name specified in the RECOVER JCL.

If image copy data sets are explicitly allocated as just described, the UNIT=AFF parameter can be coded to single-thread the image copy input to the RECOVER utility.

Use DB2's Capability to Fall Back to Previous Image Copies   Current point-in-time recovery attempts to allocate the most recent full image copy for processing. If an error is encountered for that image copy, the RECOVER utility uses the previous full image copy.

If a tape image copy data set is unavailable, the operator can reply NO to the tape mount message to cause DB2 to use a previous image copy.

Take Incremental Image Copies to Reduce Log Reading   If incremental image copies exist, the RECOVER TABLESPACE utility attempts to use them to reduce the number of log data sets and records that must be processed to accomplish the recovery.

It is not possible to use COPY to make incremental image copies for indexes, so this guideline is not applicable to indexes.

Remember to Recover Indexes   Execute the REBUILD INDEX utility for all table spaces recovered using the partial recovery options TOCOPY or TORBA. For indexes defined using COPY YES, execute the RECOVER INDEX utility to bring the indexes up to the same point as the table spaces. Failure to REBUILD or RECOVER indexes results in invalid indexes.

Avoid Relative Generation Numbers for GDG Image Copies   The TOCOPY option of the RECOVER TABLESPACE utility is used to explicitly name an image copy data set to which the named table space will be recovered. If the image copy data set is a GDG, the fully qualified data set name must be specified, including the absolute generation and version number. Relative generation number specification is not supported by the RECOVER utility.

Specify a Valid Image Copy Data Set   When the TOCOPY option is used, the image copy data set specified must be recorded in the SYSIBM.SYSCOPY table. If it is not, the recovery fails.

Recover Table Spaces As Appropriate for the Image Copy   Recovery must be processed according to the type of image copy available. For example, if image copies were taken for a partitioned table space at the DSNUM level, RECOVER TABLESPACE must operate at the DSNUM level.

Recover Only Complete Units of Work   Avoid recovering table spaces to an RBA other than an RBA recorded in the SYSIBM.SYSCOPY table as a result of the QUIESCE utility. Recovery to an RBA other than a quiesce point RBA may cause recovery to the middle of a unit of work, resulting in inconsistent data.

Recover Only Consistent Image Copies   Avoid using the TOCOPY option to recover table spaces to an image copy created with SHRLEVEL CHANGE. Doing so can cause data integrity problems because the image copy may reflect partial unit of work changes. Because the table space might have been modified during the execution of the COPY utility, the image copy without the corresponding log changes represents data in an inconsistent state.

Consider Using RECOVER with DFSMS Copies   DB2 provides the capability to recover from backup copies of DB2 data sets taken using the concurrent copy feature of DFSMS. Follow these steps to accomplish this:

1. STOP all table spaces to be recovered.

2. START the objects in utility mode or read-only mode; ACCESS(UT) or ACCESS(RO).

3. Use DFSMS to restore the data sets for the table spaces in question.

4. Use RECOVER with the LOGONLY option to apply only log records and not RESTORE from an image copy.

5. START the table spaces in RW mode.

Consider Using CURRENTCOPYONLY with Concurrent Copies   The CURRENTCOPYONLY parameter can be used to improve the performance of RECOVER while restoring concurrent copies. It specifies that RECOVER should use only the most recent primary copy for each object in the list. The RECOVER utility will build a DFSMSdss RESTORE command for each group of objects associated with the concurrent copy data set name. But if the RESTORE fails, the object fails (and RECOVER will not automatically use the next most recent copy or the backup copy).

Restart the RECOVER Utility As Needed   RECOVER TABLESPACE is a re-startable utility. No special consideration is necessary because work data sets are not required when recovering a table space alone. The utility can be restarted by changing the DSNUTILB JCL parameter to UTPROC=RESTART.

Consult the IBM Manual When Recovering System Table Spaces The DB2 Catalog and DB2 Directory table spaces can be recovered using the RECOVER TABLESPACE utility, but the recovery must be performed in a specific order. Consult the *DB2 Database Administration Guide* for details.

The REBUILD INDEX **Utility**

The REBUILD INDEX utility can be used to re-create indexes from current data. Indexes defined as COPY NO are always recovered from actual table data, not from image copy and log data. If the index is defined as COPY YES, it can be recovered from an image copy or rebuilt from the table data. REBUILD INDEX scans the table on which the index is based and regenerates the index based on the current data. JCL to run the REBUILD INDEX utility is provided in Listing 32.9.

LISTING 32.9   REBUILD INDEX JCL

```
//DB2JOBU  JOB (UTILITY),'DB2 REBUILD IDX',MSGCLASS=X,CLASS=X,
//          NOTIFY=USER
//*
//****************************************************************
//*
//*         DB2 REBUILD INDEX UTILITY
//*
//****************************************************************
//*
//UTIL EXEC DSNUPROC,SYSTEM=DSN,UID='RBLDINDX',UTPROC="
//*
//*  UTILITY WORK DATASETS
//*
//DSNUPROC.SORTWK01 DDUNIT=SYSDA,SPACE=(CYL,(2,1))
//DSNUPROC.SORTWK02 DDUNIT=SYSDA,SPACE=(CYL,(2,1))
//DSNUPROC.SYSUT1 DD DSN=&&SYSUT1,
//        UNIT=SYSDA,SPACE=(CYL,(2,1)),DCB=BUFNO=20
//DSNUPROC.UTPRINT DD SYSOUT=X
//*
//*  UTILITY INPUT CONTROL STATEMENTS
//*    1. The first REBUILD INDEX statement rebuilds the
//*       DSN8810.XPROJ2 index.
//*    2. The second REBUILD INDEX statement rebuilds only
//*       the third partition of the DSN8810.XEMP1
//*       partitioning index.
//*    3. The third and final REBUILD INDEX statement
//*       rebuilds all indexes on all tables in the
//*       DSN8D81A.DSN8S81C table space.
//*
//DSNUPROC.SYSIN    DD  *
    REBUILD INDEX (DSN8810.XPROJ2)
    REBUILD INDEX (DSN8810.XEMP1) DSNUM 3
```

LISTING 32.9   Continued

```
    REBUILD INDEX (ALL) TABLESPACE DSN8D81A.DSN8S81C
/*
//
```

> **NOTE**
>
> The sort work data sets need to be assigned in the JCL only if sort work data sets are not dynami-
> cally allocated. Additionally, you should consider explicitly defining sort work data sets when
> recovering very large indexes.
>
> Rather than explicitly assigning SORTWK files, consider giving DFSORT more responsibility. The
> dynamic default for most shops is DYNALOC=(SYSDA,004). If 4 work files are not enough or the
> SYSDA pool does not have sufficient space, use the SORTNUM DB2 utility clause to increase the
> number of dynamically allocated files and use the SORTDEVT clause to assign the disk pool. Let
> DFSORT assign the primary and secondary allocations.

REBUILD INDEX Phases

There are five phase of the REBUILD INDEX utility:

UTILINIT	Sets up and initializes the REBUILD utility.
UNLOAD	Unloads data from the appropriate table and places it in the data set assigned to the SYSUT1 DD statement (if SORTKEYS is not specified).
SORT	Sorts the unloaded index data.
BUILD	Builds indexes and checks for duplicate key errors. Unique indexes with duplicate key errors are not recovered successfully.
SORTBLD	When the SORTKEYS option is used to invoke parallel index build processing for a simple or segmented table space or table space partition, all activities that normally occur in the SORT and BUILD phases occur in the SORTBLD phase instead.
UTILTERM	Performs the final utility cleanup.

Estimating REBUILD INDEX Work Data Set Sizes

The REBUILD INDEX utility requires work data sets to rebuild DB2 indexes. The following
formulas can help you calculate estimated sizes for these work data sets. More complex
and precise calculations are in the *DB2 Utility Guide and Reference* manual, but these formulas should produce comparable results.

```
SYSUT1 = (size of the largest index key + 13) x (total number of rows in the
➥associated table for the index) x (number of indexes on the table)
SORTWKxx = (size of SYSUT1) x 2
```

> **NOTE**
>
> If any of these numbers is 0, substitute 1.

After calculating the estimated size in bytes for each work data set, convert the number into cylinders, rounding up to the next whole cylinder. Allocating work data sets in cylinder increments enhances the utility's performance.

V7 Of course, you can set up REBUILD to automatically allocate work data sets as of DB2 V7.

REBUILD INDEX **Locking Considerations**

Index rebuilding can run concurrently with the following utilities:

CHECK LOB	DIAGNOSE
MERGECOPY	MODIFY
REPORT	STOSPACE
RUNSTATS TABLESPACE	UNLOAD
COPY TABLESPACE SHRLEVEL REFERENCE	
REORG TABLESPACE (UNLOAD ONLY or UNLOAD EXTERNAL) (without a clustered index)	
REPAIR LOCATE TABLESPACE (PAGE, DUMP, or VERIFY)	
REPAIR LOCATE (RID, DUMP, or VERIFY)	

The REBUILD INDEX utility drains all claim classes for the index being recovered and drains the write claim class for the associated table space.

If REBUILD INDEX is being specified for an individual partition, the utility drains all claim classes for the index partition and the logical partition of a type 2 index. The read claim class is drained for non-partitioned type 2 indexes. Also, this utility will drain write claim classes for the associated table space partition.

REBUILD INDEX **and Index Versions**

V8 Online schema changes (explained in Chapter 7, "Database Change Management and Schema Evolution") can cause multiple versions of a DB2 index to exist in the DB2 Catalog. When a new index version is created, DB2 assigns it the next available version number—which can range from 0 to 15. After DB2 assigns version number 15, it re-assigns version number 1 again, if that version number is not already used. (Version number 0 is reserved for the original definition of the index before any ALTER statements were applied.)

Running REBUILD INDEX causes the version information to be refreshed. In other words, the range of used version numbers for indexes defined with COPY NO is reset. This means that the OLDEST_VERSION column for the index is set to the current version number, indicating that only one version is active. This allows DB2 to reuse all of the other version numbers.

NOTE

LOAD REPLACE, REORG INDEX, and REORG TABLESPACE can also be used to recycle version numbers for indexes defined with COPY NO.

MODIFY RECOVERY can be used to refresh and recycle version numbers for indexes defined with COPY YES, and for table spaces.

REBUILD INDEX **Guidelines**

The following guidelines can be applied to ensure effective usage of the REBUILD INDEX utility.

Avoid SYSUT1 **if Possible**   The SYSUT1 data set is not required to rebuild indexes. By removing SYSUT1 from the JCL, the REBUILD utility will perform faster and will require less work space. However, if SYSUT1 is not included, the REBUILD INDEX utility is not restartable in the UNLOAD phase.

Consider Using CHECK INDEX **Before Rebuilding Large Indexes**   Execute the CHECK INDEX utility for large indexes before running REBUILD INDEX. If CHECK INDEX indicates that the index is invalid, REBUILD INDEX should be run. If CHECK INDEX indicates that the index is valid, however, you can save valuable processing time because CHECK INDEX is faster than REBUILD INDEX.

Be Aware of Underlying VSAM Data Set Deletions   The underlying VSAM data sets for STOGROUP-defined indexes are deleted and defined by the REBUILD INDEX utility. If the index has been user-defined, the corresponding VSAM data set is not deleted.

Reorganize System Indexes Using REBUILD INDEX   Although the DB2 Catalog and DB2 Directory table spaces and indexes can be reorganized, their indexes can be rebuilt which effectively reorganizes these indexes.

Rerun REBUILD INDEX **When Necessary**   REBUILD INDEX is not restartable unless the SYSUT1 data set is specified and cataloged (and SORTKEYS is not specified). If the REBUILD INDEX abends, terminate the utility, correct the cause of the abend, and rerun the utility. Typical causes for REBUILD INDEX abends include the unavailability of the applicable table space and VSAM data set allocation failures.

The REPAIR **Utility**

The REPAIR utility, discussed in Chapter 31, "Data Consistency Utilities," also can be an integral part of data recovery. REPAIR can be used to assist with a recovery if, based on the order and type of recovery attempted, it can be determined that pending flags can be reset with the REPAIR utility rather than another corresponding utility. This may speed recovery when time is critical.

Additionally, if data is damaged or invalid, the REPAIR utility can be used to modify the data.

The REPORT RECOVERY **Utility**

The REPORT RECOVERY utility is the second type of REPORT utility provided by DB2. It can be used to generate a report on table space or index recovery information. The report contains information from the DB2 Directory, the DB2 Catalog, and the BSDS. The input to the utility is either a table space, a single partition of a partitioned table space, or an index.

REPORT RECOVERY has several options, including the following:

- Providing recovery information to the last recoverable point, which is the last execution of a full image copy, LOAD REPLACE LOG YES, or REORG LOG YES

- Providing all recovery information for a table space (or index), not just information to the last recoverable point

- Providing a list of volume serial numbers for the image copy data sets and archive log data sets needed for recovery

The output of REPORT RECOVERY is a report of all related DB2 recovery information, including image copy information, log RBA information, and archive log information needed to recover the requested table space (or index).

The sample JCL in Listing 32.10 produces a report up to the last recoverable point for the sample table space DSN8D81A.DSN8S81C.

LISTING 32.10   REPORT RECOVERY JCL

```
//DB2JOBU  JOB  (UTILITY),'DB2 REPRT RCVRY',MSGCLASS=X,CLASS=X,
//             NOTIFY=USER
//*
//****************************************************************
//*
//*         DB2 REPORT RECOVERY UTILITY
//*
//****************************************************************
//*
//UTIL EXEC DSNUPROC,SYSTEM=DB2T,UID='REPORTRC',UTPROC="
//DSNUPROC.SYSIN    DD  *
   REPORT RECOVERY TABLESPACE DSN8D81A.DSN8S81E
/*
//
```

REPORT RECOVERY Locking Considerations

The REPORT utility is compatible with all other utilities. It functions like any other process that reads DB2 data.

REPORT RECOVERY Guideline

The REPORT RECOVERY utility can be used to determine which data sets will be needed by the RECOVERY utility before recovering a table space. This can be useful when you must determine whether the requisite data sets are still cataloged or available.

Backing Up and Restoring the System

V8 The IBM DB2 COPY and RECOVER utilities are ideal for backing up and recovering DB2 objects, but sometimes recovery needs to be handled at a higher, system level. IBM introduced two new utilities with DB2 V8 to provide a system level, point-in-time recovery: BACKUP SYSTEM and RESTORE SYSTEM.

BACKUP SYSTEM

V8 The BACKUP SYSTEM utility invokes DFSMShsm to copy the disk volumes where DB2 data and the DB2 log reside. The utility can copy data for a single DB2 subsystem (non-data sharing) or a data sharing group. All of the data sets to be copied must be SMS-managed data sets.

BACKUP SYSTEM is ideal for backing up all of the data for a single application, such as SAP R/3 or PeopleSoft.

> **CAUTION**
>
> In a data-sharing environment, if there are any failed or abnormally quiesced members, the BACKUP SYSTEM request fails.

When BACKUP SYSTEM is run, a copy version is created. A copy version is a point-in-time copy of the data maintained by DFSMShsm. Each DB2 system has an associated set of copy pools, one for the databases and another for the logs. Up to 15 copy versions can be maintained. The utility copies the volumes that are associated with the copy pool backup storage group. You can add new volumes to the storage group without having to redefine the copy pool.

Before running the BACKUP SYSTEM utility you must decide if you want a full or data only copy to be made. The default is FULL, which causes the utility to copy both the database copy pool and the log copy pool. Alternatively, you can specify DATA ONLY. This indicates that BACKUP SYSTEM will copy only the database copy pool (and not the log copy pool).

The BACKUP SYSTEM history is recorded in the BSDSs.

To execute BACKUP SYSTEM, the process or user running the utility must have either SYSADM or SYSCTRL authority.

BACKUP SYSTEM Phases

The BACKUP SYSTEM utility has three phases:

UTILINIT	Sets up and initializes the utility
COPY	Copies the data
UTILTERM	Performs the final utility cleanup

BACKUP SYSTEM Concurrency

The BACKUP SYSTEM utility can run concurrently with any other DB2 utility. But only one BACKUP SYSTEM job can be running at any one time.

Keep in mind, too, that the BACKUP SYSTEM utility will wait until the following activities complete before it begins to execute:

- Data sets being extended

- 32K pages being written

- Close page set control log records being written

- Data sets being created or deleted (CREATE or DROP)

- Data sets being renamed (such as during an online reorganization)

BACKUP SYSTEM **Guidelines**

Before running BACKUP SYSTEM, be sure to verify the following:

- All of the data sets to be copied are SMS-managed.

- You are running z/OS V1R5 (or greater).

- Your disk units support ESS FlashCopy.

- You have defined a copy pool for your database data (FULL or DATA ONLY).

- If you plan to also copy the logs, be sure to define a copy pool for your logs.

- You must define an SMS backup storage group for each storage group in the copy pools.

RESTORE SYSTEM

V8 Similar to BACKUP SYSTEM, the RESTORE SYSTEM utility uses DFSMShsm behind the scenes to recover a DB2 subsystem or a data sharing group to a previous point-in-time. RESTORE SYSTEM uses the data that was copied by a previous execution of the BACKUP SYSTEM utility. Remember, all of the data sets that you want to recover must be SMS-managed.

Although DFSMShsm can maintain multiple backup versions of copy pools, you cannot specify a particular backup version to be used by the RESTORE SYSTEM utility. RESTORE SYSTEM always uses the latest version before the log truncation point.

> **NOTE**
> You can specify the log truncation point with the CRESTART SYSPITR option of the DSNJU003 utility. Refer to Chapter 35, "Stand-alone Utilities and Sample Programs," for more information about DSNJU003.

To execute RESTORE SYSTEM, the process or user running the utility must have SYSADM authority.

RESTORE SYSTEM **Phases**

The RESTORE SYSTEM utility has four phases:

UTILINIT	Sets up and initializes the utility
RESTORE	Finds and restores the volume copies (if the LOGONLY option is not specified)
LOGAPPLY	Applies the outstanding log changes to the database
UTILTERM	Performs the final utility cleanup

RESTORE SYSTEM **Concurrency Considerations**

No other utilities can run when RESTORE SYSTEM is running.

RESTORE SYSTEM **Guidelines**

Before running RESTORE SYSTEM, perform the following tasks:

1. Stop DB2.

2. Run DSNJU003 to specify the log truncation point for the point-in-time to which the system is to be recovered. (Note: You must be running in DB2 V8 new function mode.)

3. Start DB2. When the restart completes, DB2 enters system RECOVER-pending and access maintenance mode. During system RECOVER-pending mode, the only action you can take is to run the RESTORE SYSTEM utility.

After running the RESTORE SYSTEM utility job, be sure to take the following steps:

1. Stop and start each DB2 subsystem or member to remove it from access maintenance mode.

2. Issue the DISPLAY UTIL command to check for any utilities that are executing. If any other utilities are running, use the TERM UTIL command to end them.

3. Recover any table space in RECP status and rebuild or recover any index in RECP or RBDP status.

4. If a CREATE TABLESPACE, CREATE INDEX, or data set extension has failed, recover or rebuild any objects in the logical page list.

CHAPTER 33

Data Organization Utilities

The data organization utilities affect the physical data sets of the DB2 objects for which they are run. Rows of data and their sequence are affected by these utilities. The data organization utilities are LOAD, UNLOAD, and REORG. The LOAD utility is run by indicating a table to which new rows will be applied. UNLOAD reads rows from a table and puts them into an output data set. REORG is run at the table space or index level, moving data to optimal locations in the data set.

The LOAD Utility

The LOAD utility is used to accomplish bulk inserts to DB2 tables. It can add rows to a table, retaining the current data, or it can replace existing rows with the new data.

Table Loading Philosophies

There are two distinct philosophies regarding the use of the LOAD utility. The first and generally recommended philosophy takes more time to implement but is easier to support. It requires the reservation of sufficient DASD to catalog the LOAD work data sets in case the LOAD job abends.

The work data sets for the LOAD job are allocated for the DDNAMEs SORTOUT, SYSUT1, SYSERR, and SYSMAP with DISP=(MOD,DELETE,CATLG). This enables the data sets to be allocated as new for the initial running of the REORG job. If the job abends, it catalogs the data sets in case they can be used in a restart. After the step completes successfully, the data sets are deleted. The space for these data sets must be planned and available before the LOAD job runs.

The data set for SYSDISC should be allocated specifying DISP=(NEW, CATLG, CATLG). If there are discards, the LOAD utility returns a RC=4, and it does not abend. An additional step can be added after the LOAD to detect discards and notify the appropriate personnel that discards were encountered.

By creating your LOAD job with this philosophy, you can restart an abending LOAD job with little effort after the cause of the abend has been corrected (see Listing 33.1). You simply specify one of the RESTART options in the UTPROC parameter for DSNUTILB.

LISTING 33.1   LOAD JCL (Restartable)

```
//DB2JOBU  JOB (UTILITY),'DB2 LOAD',MSGCLASS=X,CLASS=X,
//           NOTIFY=USER
//*
//*****************************************************************
//*
//*           DB2 LOAD UTILITY (RESTARTABLE)
//*
//*****************************************************************
//*
//UTIL EXEC DSNUPROC,SYSTEM=DSN,UID='LOADDATA',UTPROC="
//*
//*   UTILITY WORK DATAETS
//*
//DSNUPROC.SORTWK01 DDUNIT=SYSDA,SPACE=(CYL,(2,1))
//DSNUPROC.SORTWK02 DDUNIT=SYSDA,SPACE=(CYL,(2,1))
//DSNUPROC.SORTOUT DD DSN=CAT.SORTOUT,DISP=(MOD,CATLG,CATLG),
//          UNIT=SYSDA,SPACE=(CYL,(2,1))
//DSNUPROC.SYSMAP DD DSN=CAT.SYSUT1,DISP=(MOD,DELETE,CATLG),
//          UNIT=SYSDA,SPACE=(CYL,(2,1)),DCB=BUFNO=20
//DSNUPROC.SYSUT1 DD DSN=CAT.SYSUT1,DISP=(MOD,DELETE,CATLG),
//          UNIT=SYSDA,SPACE=(CYL,(2,1)),DCB=BUFNO=20
//DSNUPROC.SYSDISC DD DSN=CAT.SYSDISC,DISP=(MOD,DELETE,CATLG),
//          UNIT=SYSDA,SPACE=(CYL,(1,1))
//DSNUPROC.SYSERR DD DSN=CAT.SYSERR,DISP=(MOD,DELETE,CATLG),
//          UNIT=SYSDA,SPACE=(CYL,(1,1))
//DSNUPROC.SYSREC00 DD DSN=CAT.LOAD.INPUT.DATASETA,DISP=SHR,DCB=BUFNO=20
//DSNUPROC.UTPRINT DD SYSOUT=X
//*
//*   UTILITY INPUT CONTROL STATEMENTS
//*       The LOAD statement reloads the DSN8810.ACT table
//*
//DSNUPROC.SYSIN    DD  *
   LOAD DATA REPLACE INDDN SYSREC00 LOG NO
   INTO TABLE DSN8810.ACT
       (ACTNO        POSITION ( 1 )  SMALLINT,
        ACTKWD       POSITION ( 3 )  CHAR ( 6 ),
        ACTDESC      POSITION ( 9 )  VARCHAR
       )
/*
//
```

> **NOTE**
>
> The sort work data sets need to be assigned in the JCL only if sort work data sets are not dynami-
> cally allocated. Additionally, you should consider explicitly defining sort work data sets when
> loading very large tables.

The second philosophy is easier to implement but more difficult to support. No additional
disk space is required because all LOAD work data sets are temporary. Therefore, all interim
work data sets are lost when the job abends. See Listing 33.2 for sample JCL.

LISTING 33.2   LOAD JCL (Nonrestartable)

```
//DB2JOBU  JOB (UTILITY),'DB2 LOAD',MSGCLASS=X,CLASS=X,
//    NOTIFY=USER,REGION=3M
//*
//*****************************************************************
//*
//*          DB2 LOAD UTILITY (NON-RESTARTABLE)
//*
//*****************************************************************
//*
//UTIL EXEC DSNUPROC,SYSTEM=DSN,UID='LOADDATA',UTPROC="
//*
//*   UTILITY WORK DATASETS
//*
//DSNUPROC.SORTWK01 DD DSN=&&SORTWK01,
//        UNIT=SYSDA,SPACE=(CYL,(2,1))
//DSNUPROC.SORTWK02 DD DSN=&&SORTWK02,
//        UNIT=SYSDA,SPACE=(CYL,(2,1))
//DSNUPROC.SORTOUT DD DSN=&&SORTOUT,
//        UNIT=SYSDA,SPACE=(CYL,(2,1))
//DSNUPROC.SYSMAP DD DSN=CAT.SYSUT1,DISP=(MOD,CATLG,CATLG),
//        UNIT=SYSDA,SPACE=(CYL,(2,1))
//DSNUPROC.SYSUT1 DD DSN=&&SYSUT1,DCB=BUFNO=10
//        UNIT=SYSDA,SPACE=(CYL,(2,1))
//DSNUPROC.SYSDISC DD DSN=CAT.SYSDISC,DISP=(MOD,CATLG,CATLG),
//        UNIT=SYSDA,SPACE=(CYL,(1,1))
//DSNUPROC.SYSERR DD DSN=&&SYSERR,
//        UNIT=SYSDA,SPACE=(CYL,(1,1))
//DSNUPROC.SYSREC00 DD DSN=CAT.LOAD.INPUT.DATASETD,DISP=SHR,DCB=BUFNO=10
//DSNUPROC.UTPRINT DD SYSOUT=X
//*
//*   UTILITY INPUT CONTROL STATEMENTS
//*      The LOAD statement adds the data in SYSREC00 to
//*      the DSN8810.DEPT table.
//*
//DSNUPROC.SYSIN    DD  *
  LOAD DATA RESUME(YES) ENFORCE CONSTRAINTS LOG NO
  INDDN SYSREC00 INTO TABLE DSN8810.DEPT
      (DEPTNO      POSITION(   1)
                  CHAR(       3),
      DEPTNAME    POSITION(   4)
                  VARCHAR,
      MGRNO       POSITION(  42)
```

LISTING 33.2   Continued

```
                CHAR(        6)   NULLIF(   48)='?',
    ADMRDEPT    POSITION(   49)
                CHAR(        3),
    LOCATION    POSITION(   52)
                CHAR(       16)   NULLIF(   68)='?'         )
/*
//
```

To restart this LOAD job, you must determine in which phase the job abended. If the job abends in any phase of a LOAD REPLACE, you can simply terminate the utility and rerun. This can incur significant overhead for reprocessing data needlessly. If the first philosophy is used, reprocessing is usually avoided.

For a LOAD RESUME(YES), however, if the job abends in any phase other than UTILINIT, you must restore the table space for the table being loaded to a previous point in time. This can be accomplished by running the RECOVER TOCOPY utility or by running a full RECOVER if the LOG NO option of the LOAD utility was specified. After restoring the table space (and possibly its associated indexes), you must correct the cause of the abend, terminate the utility, and then rerun the job. As you can see, this method is significantly more difficult to restart than the first method.

Try to use the first philosophy rather than the second. This makes recovery from error situations as smooth and painless as possible.

Estimating LOAD Work Data Set Sizes

The LOAD utility requires work data sets to load data into DB2 tables. The following formulas can help you calculate estimated sizes for these work data sets. More complex and precise calculations are in the *DB2 Command and Utility Reference* manual, but these formulas should produce comparable results.

```
SORTOUT = (size of the largest index key or foreign key + 14)
         ➡x (total number of rows in the table to be loaded)
         ➡x (total number of indexes defined for the table)
         ➡x (total number of foreign keys in the table) x 1.2
```

> **NOTE**
>
> If any number in the SORTOUT calculation is 0, substitute 1.
>
> The multiplier 1.2 is factored into the calculation to provide a "fudge factor." If you are absolutely sure of your numbers, the calculation can be made more precise by eliminating the additional multiplication of 1.2.

```
SYSUT1 = (size of the largest index key or foreign key + 14)
        ➡x (total number of rows to be loaded to the table)
        ➡x (total number of indexes defined for the table)
        ➡x (total number of foreign keys in the table) x 1.2
```

> **NOTE**
>
> If any number in the SYSUT1 calculation is 0, substitute 1. The multiplier 1.2 is factored into the calculation to provide a "fudge factor." If you are absolutely sure of your numbers, the calculation can be made more precise by eliminating the additional multiplication of 1.2.

```
SORTWKxx = (size of SYSUT1) x 2

 SYSERR = ((number of estimated unique index errors)
      ➥+ (number of estimated data conversion errors)
      ➥+ (number of estimated referential constraint violations)) x 100
```

> **NOTE**
>
> Always allocate the SYSERR data set to be at least 1 cylinder.

```
SYSMAP = (total number of rows to be loaded to the table) x 21
```

> **NOTE**
>
> The SYSMAP data set is required if either of the following is true:
>
> - Discard processing is requested.
> - The table space is segmented or partitioned.

```
SYSDISC = Allocate the SYSDISC data set to be the same size as the data set
      ➥containing the rows to be loaded by the LOAD utility
```

> **NOTE**
>
> The space requirements for SYSDISC may be prohibitive if disk space is at a premium at your shop. Instead of allocating the SYSDISC data set as large as the data being loaded, consider using a small primary quantity and a larger secondary quantity—for example:
>
> SPACE=(CYL,(0,50),RLSE)

> **NOTE**
>
> Although the SYSDISC data set is optional, specifying it is highly recommended to trap records that cannot be loaded.

After calculating the estimated size in bytes for each work data set, convert the number into cylinders, rounding up to the next whole cylinder. Allocating work data sets in cylinder increments enhances the utility's performance.

LOAD **Phases**

There are nine possible phases of the LOAD utility:

UTILINIT	Sets up and initializes the LOAD utility.
RELOAD	Reads the sequential data set specified as input and loads the data to the specified table. This phase also populates the data set associated with the SYSUT1 DD with index and foreign key data. The compression dictionary is rebuilt in this step for COMPRESS

33

	YES table spaces. The copy pending flag is reset at the end of this phase if an inline copy is produced (unless the SORTKEYS parameter is specified).
SORT	Sorts the index and foreign key data using the data sets assigned to the SORTOUT and SORTWKxx DD statements.
BUILD	Builds indexes and identifies duplicate keys, placing the error information in SYSERR. The recovery pending flag is reset for all non-unique indexes. The copy pending flag is reset at the end of this phase if an inline copy is produced unless the SORTKEYS parameter is specified.
SORTBLD	When parallel index build is specified (SORTKEYS), the SORT and BUILD phases are performed in the SORTBLD phase instead.
INDEXVAL	Reads the SYSERR data set to correct unique index violations. The recovery pending flag is reset for all unique indexes.
ENFORCE	Checks foreign keys for conformance to referential constraints and stores the error information in SYSERR. Resets check pending flag for table space.
DISCARD	Reads the SYSERR information to correct referential constraint violations and places the erroneous records in the SYSDISC data set.
REPORT	Sends reports of unique index violations and referential constraint violations to SYSPRINT.
UTILTERM	Performs the final utility cleanup.

> **NOTE**
>
> The SORT phase will be skipped if the RELOAD phase analyzes the data and determines that the SORT phase is not needed.

Creating an Inline Copy During the LOAD

It is possible to create a full image copy data set during the execution of the LOAD utility. This is referred to as an inline COPY. The image copy will be a SHRLEVEL REFERENCE copy.

There are two major benefits of taking an inline copy. The first is that a second pass of the data is not required to create a DB2 image copy. The second benefit is that the table space into which the data is being loaded will not be placed into a copy pending state when inline copy is specified, even if the LOG NO option is specified.

To create an inline copy, use the COPYDDN and RECOVERYDDN keywords. You can specify up to two primary and two secondary copies.

Gathering Inline Statistics During the LOAD

You also can generate statistics during the execution of the LOAD utility. This is referred to as inline RUNSTATS. Up-to-date statistics will be generated during the LOAD instead of requiring an additional RUNSTATS step. To generate inline RUNSTATS, use the STATISTICS keyword. You can gather table space statistics, index statistics, or both.

Discards and Inline RUNSTATS

If you specify both the DISCARDDN and STATISTICS options, the inline statistics collected during the LOAD may be inaccurate. When a row is found with check constraint errors or conversion errors, the row is not loaded into the table, so DB2 will not collect statistics for it. So far, so good.

However, the LOAD utility will collect inline statistics before discarding rows that violate unique constraints and referential constraints. Therefore, when the number of rows that violate RI and unique constraints is high, the statistics could be quite imprecise. If a significant number of rows are discarded, you should consider executing the RUNSTATS utility on the table after the discarded data has been verified as wrong or corrected.

Loading Delimited Input Data Sets

V8 As of DB2 V8, the IBM LOAD utility can load data from an input data set in delimited format. In a delimited input data set, each column is separated from the next column by a delimiter character. Additionally, all the fields in the input data file must be character strings or external numeric values. Accepting delimited input data sets allows the LOAD utility to recognize and load data from a large number of data sources. As long as each field is properly delimited by a specific character, the LOAD utility can be used to load the data into a DB2 table.

CAUTION

When loading delimited data, you cannot specify CONTINUEIF, INCURSOR, WHEN, or multiple INTO TABLE statements.

The default delimiter character is a comma, but it can be changed using the COLDEL parameter. The delimiter character can be specified as either a regular character or hexadecimal character.

CAUTION

When you specify the delimiter character, be sure to verify that the character is specified in the code page of the source data. Furthermore, if the utility control parameter is coded in a different character type than the input file, specify the COLDEL in hex or the result can be unpredictable. For example, specify the delimiter as a hex constant if the utility control statement is coded in EBCDIC and the input data is ASCII or Unicode.

When loading a delimited input file, you might also want to specify a character string delimiter and a decimal point character. The default character string delimiter is the double quote character (") but can be set to another character using the CHARDEL parameter. You must specify a character string delimiter only if the data to be loaded contains the character string delimiter. Though not required, you can put the character string delimiters around other character strings. To load a string containing the character delimiter character, you must double up the character. For example, code the following to LOAD a string containing: He told me "You look well" and I liked it.

`"He told me ""You look well"" and I liked it."`

Finally, you can change the decimal point character, too. This is done using the DECPT parameter. The default is a period, but some countries use a comma. Therefore, you can change the decimal point character to another character of your choice using DECPT.

LOAD **Rerun/Restart Procedures**

The LOAD utility can be restarted. The restart or rerun procedure is determined by the abending phase of the LOAD step. There are two ways to determine the phase in which the abend occurred.

The first method is to issue the DISPLAY UTILITY command to determine which utilities are currently active, stopped, or terminating in the DB2 system. The format of the command is

```
-DISPLAY UTILITY(*)
```

The second method to determine the abending phase is to view the SYSPRINT DD statement of the LOAD step. This method is not as desirable as the first, but it is the only method you can use when the DB2 system is down. At the completion of each phase, DB2 prints a line stating that the phase has completed. You can assume that the phase immediately following the last phase reported complete in the SYSPRINT DD statement is the phase that was executing when the abend occurred.

After determining the phase of the LOAD utility at the time of the abend, follow the steps outlined here to restart or rerun the load. In the following procedures, it is assumed that your LOAD utility processing is generally restartable.

If the abend occurred in the UTILINIT phase

1. Determine the cause of the abend. An abend in this step is usually caused by another utility executing with the same UID or a utility that is incompatible with another utility currently executing.

2. Resolve the cause of the abend. An abend in this phase is probably due to improper job scheduling. Issue the DISPLAY UTILITY command to determine which utilities are currently in process for the DB2 system. Resolve the scheduling problem by allowing conflicting utilities to complete before proceeding to step 3.

   Another possible cause is insufficient sort space. If the SORTWKxx data sets are dynamically added, try to resolve the problem using the following methods:

   - Use the SORTDEVT clause to dynamically create the SORTWKxx data sets someplace else.

   - Use the SORTNUM clause to increase the number of dynamically allocated sort work files.

   - Clean the work packs by deleting or moving extraneous files.

   - Explicitly allocate the appropriate sort work data sets in the JCL.

3. Restart the job at the LOAD step.

If the abend occurred in the RELOAD phase

1. Determine the cause of the abend. An abend in this step is usually caused by insufficient space allocated to the SYSUT1 DD statement. Another cause is that the VSAM data set associated with the table space has run out of available DASD space.

2. Resolve the cause of the abend.

   a. If the problem is an out-of-space abend (B37) on the SYSUT1 DD statement, the data set associated with that DD statement will have been cataloged. Allocate a new data set with additional space, copy the SYSUT1 data set to the new data set, delete the original SYSUT1 data set, and rename the new data set to the same name as the original SYSUT1 data set.

   b. If the problem is an out-of-space abend on the VSAM data set containing the table space being reloaded, contact the DBA or DASD support unit. This situation can be corrected by adding another volume to the STOGROUP being used; using IDCAMS to redefine the VSAM data set, move the VSAM data set, or both; or altering the primary space allocation quantity for the index, the secondary space allocation quantity for the index, or both.

      Restart the job at the LOAD step with a temporary JCL change to alter the UTPROC parameter to RESTART.

   > **CAUTION**
   >
   > Although LOAD can be restarted normally within the RELOAD phase if SORTKEYS is not used, it will restart from the beginning of the RELOAD phase if SORTKEYS is used.

If the abend occurred in the SORT phase

1. Determine the cause of the abend. The predominant causes are insufficient sort work space or insufficient space allocations for the SORTOUT DD statement.

2. Resolve the cause of the abend. If the problem is insufficient space on the sort work or SORTOUT DD statements, simply increase the allocations and proceed to step 3.

3. Restart the job at the LOAD step with a temporary change to alter the UTPROC parameter to RESTART(PHASE).

If the abend occurred in the BUILD phase

1. Determine the cause for the abend. An abend in this step is usually caused by insufficient space allocated to the SYSERR DD statement. Another cause is that the VSAM data set associated with the index space has run out of available DASD space.

2. Resolve the cause of the abend.

   a. If the problem is an out-of-space abend (B37) on the SYSERR DD statement, the data set associated with the DD statement will have been cataloged. Allocate a new data set with additional space, copy the SYSERR data set to the new data

33

set, delete the original SYSERR data set, and rename the new data set to the same name as the original SYSERR data set.

b. If the problem is an out-of-space abend on the VSAM data set containing the index space being reloaded, contact the DBA or DASD support unit. This situation can be corrected by adding another volume to the STOGROUP being used; using IDCAMS to redefine the VSAM data set, move the VSAM data set, or both; or altering the primary space allocation quantity for the index, the secondary space allocation quantity for the index, or both.

3.   a. If LOAD was run using the REPLACE option, restart the job at the LOAD step with a temporary change to alter the UTPROC parameter to RESTART(PHASE).

b. If LOAD was run using the RESUME YES option, the LOAD is not restartable. Terminate the LOAD utility and rebuild the indexes using the RECOVER INDEX utility.

> **NOTE**
>
> When the SORTKEYS parameter is used and the LOAD utility terminates during the RELOAD, SORT, or BUILD phases, both RESTART and RESTART(PHASE) restart from the beginning of the RELOAD phase.

If the abend occurred in the INDEXVAL phase

1. Determine the cause of the abend. Abends in this phase are rare. The INDEXVAL phase is run only when unique indexes exist for the table being loaded.

2. Resolve the cause of the abend.

3. Restart the job at the LOAD step with a temporary JCL change to alter the UTPROC parameter to RESTART(PHASE).

If the abend occurred in the ENFORCE phase

1. Determine the cause for the abend. An abend in this step is usually caused by insufficient space allocated to the SYSERR DD statement. The ENFORCE phase is optional and is not always run.

2. Resolve the cause of the abend. If the problem is an out-of-space abend (B37) on the SYSERR DD statement, the data set associated with that DD statement will have been cataloged. Allocate a new data set with additional space, copy the SYSERR data set to the new data set, delete the original SYSERR data set, and rename the new data set to the same name as the original SYSERR data set.

3. Restart the job at the LOAD step with a temporary change to alter the UTPROC parameter to RESTART.

If the abend occurred in the DISCARD phase

1. Determine the cause for the abend. An abend in this step is usually caused by insufficient space allocated to the SYSDISC DD statement. The DISCARD phase is optional and is not always run.

2. Resolve the cause of the abend. If the problem is an out-of-space abend (B37) on the SYSDISC DD statement, the data set associated with that DD statement will have been cataloged. Allocate a new data set with additional space, copy the SYSDISC data set to the new data set, delete the original SYSDISC data set, and rename the new data set to the same name as the original SYSDISC data set.

3. Restart the job at the LOAD step with a temporary change to alter the UTPROC parameter to RESTART.

If the abend occurred in the REPORT phase

1. Determine the cause for the abend. Abends in the REPORT phase are rare. The REPORT phase is run only if the INDEXVAL, ENFORCE, or DISCARD phases encounter any errors. Sometimes the cause for an abend in this phase is insufficient space allocated to the sort work data sets because the report is sorted by error type and input sequence.

2. Resolve the cause of the abend. If the problem was caused by insufficient space on the sort work or SORTOUT DD statements, simply increase the allocations and proceed to step 3.

3. Restart the job at the LOAD step with a temporary change to alter the UTPROC parameter to RESTART(PHASE).

If the abend occurred in the UTILTERM phase

1. An abend in this phase is unlikely because all the work required for the load has been completed. A problem at this phase means that DB2 cannot terminate the utility.

2. Terminate the DB2 utility by issuing the TERM UTILITY command. The format of the command is

   -TERM UTILITY(UID)

   where UID is obtained from the -DISPLAY UTILITY (*) command.

3. If the LOAD utility work data sets associated with this job were cataloged as a result of the abend, uncatalog them and force the job's completion.

LOAD Locking and Concurrency

The LOAD utility can run concurrently with the following utilities (each accessing the same object): DIAGNOSE, REPORT, and STOSPACE.

The LOAD utility will drain all claim classes for the table space or partition being loaded and any associated indexes, index partitions, and logical index partitions. Furthermore, if the ENFORCE option is specified, LOAD will drain the write claim class for the primary key index.

Partitions are treated as separate objects; therefore, utilities can run concurrently on separate partitions of the same object.

V7 Prior to DB2 V7, to load a partitioned table space by partition, a separate, dedicated LOAD job needed to be set up for each partition. Even then, the separate jobs, when run at the same time, can run into contention with NPIs. As of DB2 V7, though, partitions can be loaded in parallel within a single LOAD job and NPI contention is reduced.

An additional benefit of parallel loading is that the input data need not be broken out into separate data sets. And the same goes for the error data set and mapping data set.

V7 Of course, you can set up your LOAD utility job to load each partition from a separate data set, with a separate discards data set for each partition, too. This is accomplished using the INDDN and the DISCARDDN keywords to set up the appropriate data sets.

> **NOTE**
>
> Be aware that the INDDN and DISCARDDN options can only be specified if the PART keyword is also specified. They cannot be used with segmented or simple table spaces.

The actual number of parallel RELOAD tasks to be run is determined by the number of CPUs, the availability of virtual storage, and the number of available DB2 threads.

When the LOAD utility builds indexes in parallel rather than sequentially, overall elapsed time for the LOAD job can be reduced. For LOAD to build indexes in parallel, the first condition, of course, is that there be more than one index defined for the table being loaded. If that is the case, the SORTKEYS clause must be specified with an estimate for the number of keys, and sort work data sets must be allocated to the LOAD job (either explicitly or dynamically).

Online Loading

V7 As of DB2 V7, you can use the LOAD utility with the SHRLEVEL CHANGE parameter to load data into a table while users concurrently access the existing data. This feature is commonly referred to as an online LOAD resume.

Previously, running the LOAD utility made the table data unavailable. Of course, you could always code a program to insert the data, but that is not very efficient or simple.

Online loading will work using normal SQL INSERTs. The LOAD will perform normal claim processing and no drains. But all normal SQL processing activities will occur. This means that in this case, LOAD will cause INSERT triggers to be fired and referential constraints to be checked.

LOAD **Guidelines**

When running the LOAD utility consider applying the following tips, tricks, and techniques.

Consider Using SORTKEYS   When index keys are not already in sorted order and indexes exist on the table into which data is being loaded, consider using the SORTKEYS keyword. When SORTKEYS is specified, index keys are sorted in memory, rather than being written to work files. This can improve performance by:

- Eliminating the expensive I/O operations to disk

- Reducing the space requirements for the SYSUT1 and SORTOUT data sets

- Reducing elapsed time from the start of the reload phase to the end of the build phase

An estimate of the number of keys to be sorted can be supplied. This is optional, but recommended because the extracted keys will be written to a work data set, minimizing the efficiency gains of using the SORTKEYS parameter. To estimate the number of keys to sort, use the following calculation:

```
Number of Keys = (Total number of rows to be loaded) x
                 [(number of indexes on the table) +
                  (number of foreign keys {unless index exists for the FK}) +
                  ((number of foreign keys participating in multiple
                     relationships) x (number of relationships - 1))
                 ]
```

> **NOTE**
>
> If more than one table is being loaded, the preceding calculation must be repeated for each table—the sum of the results is used.

V7 As of DB2 V7, when loading partitions in parallel along with SORTKEYS DB2 supports multiple RELOAD tasks piping their key/RID pairs to the SORT/BUILD subtasks (one per index). The number of tasks that can be supported is roughly equal to the number of partitions. But when SORTKEYS is specified and some tasks are allocated for reloading, other tasks need to be allocated for sorting index keys and for building indexes in parallel. Thus the number of RELOAD tasks may be reduced in order to improve the overall performance of the entire LOAD job.

Avoid the LOAD Utility for Tables with Triggers   You may wish to avoid using the LOAD utility to add data to any table on which you have defined an INSERT trigger. Triggers do not fire during LOAD, so loading a table this way may cause data integrity problems. Instead, code a program to insert the data as needed because INSERT will cause the trigger to fire appropriately.

> **NOTE**
>
> Of course, this caveat does not apply to an online LOAD resume, because the LOAD utility will perform normal SQL INSERTs, thereby firing triggers as desired.

Consider Serializing Loads for Tables in the Same Database   The LOAD utility is sensitive to concurrent processing. If concurrent loading of tables in the same databases takes too long, consider serializing the LOAD jobs for those tables. Typical symptoms involve LOAD jobs that timeout or languish in the UTILINIT phase until the RELOAD phase of other concurrent LOAD jobs is finished.

> **NOTE**
>
> Consider assigning tables needing to be loaded concurrently to different databases to avoid this problem. Another approach is to assign only one table per database.

Use LOAD to Append or Replace Rows   You can use LOAD to replace data in a table by specifying the REPLACE option. LOAD also can append new data to a table, leaving current data intact, by specifying the RESUME(YES) option. Choose the appropriate option based on your data loading needs.

Use LOAD to Perform Mass Deletes   Use the LOAD utility, specifying an empty input data set (or DD DUMMY), to delete all rows from a non-segmented table space. This is called a *mass delete*. LOAD is usually more efficient than DELETE SQL without a WHERE clause. Specifying the LOG NO option to avoid logging data changes will further enhance the performance of the mass delete. Note, however, the following considerations:

- If multiple tables are assigned to a simple table space, the LOAD utility deletes all rows for all tables in that table space.

- Consider loading a DUMMY data set even for segmented table spaces if a large amount of data must be deleted. Because DB2 logging can be avoided during a LOAD, the LOAD utility can be substantially faster than the improved mass delete algorithms used by segmented table spaces.

Use Fixed Blocked Input   To enhance the performance of the LOAD utility, use a fixed blocked input data set rather than a variable blocked data set.

Buffer the Work Data Sets Appropriately   For large loads, set the BUFNO parameter in the JCL for the SYSUT1 DD statement to a number greater than 20. A BUFNO of approximately 20 is recommended for medium-sized indexes, and a BUFNO between 50 and 100 is recommended for larger tables. The BUFNO parameter creates read and write buffers in main storage for the data set, thereby enhancing the performance of the LOAD utility. The default for BUFNO is 8 for DB2 V3 and 20 for DB2 V4.

Ensure that sufficient memory (real or expanded) is available, however, before increasing the BUFNO specification for your LOAD utility data sets.

Enforce RI During Table Loading When Possible   Favor using the ENFORCE option of the LOAD utility to enforce referential constraints instead of running CHECK DATA after the LOAD completes. It is usually more efficient to process the loaded data once, as it is loaded, than to process the data twice, once to load it and once to check it. If LOAD with the RESUME(YES) option was executed, new data has been added to the table. However, if ENFORCE was not specified and a subsequent CHECK DATA is run, CHECK DATA will check the entire table, not just the new data.

Ensure That LOAD Input Data Sets Are in Key Sequence   Favor sorting the LOAD input data set into sequence by the columns designated in the clustering index. Be sure to sort the data in the appropriate sequence, either ascending or descending, depending on how the index was defined. Otherwise, the LOAD utility does not load data in clustering order, and the table space and indexes will be inefficiently organized.

> **NOTE**
>
> When the index key is null, it should be treated as "high values" for sorting purposes.

If you use DFSORT to sort the input data before loading, consider invoking the SORT DEDUPE option. Doing so not only can decrease the size of the file passed to the LOAD step, but it can minimize or eliminate LOAD discard processing.

Removing duplicates in DFSORT can improve performance because of the different ways that DFSORT and the LOAD utility handle duplicates. When DFSORT encounters duplicates, it sends one of the values to the output file then discards the remaining duplicates. When the LOAD utility encounters duplicates in the input file, it sends all of the duplicates to the discard file. Consider the following code for DFSORT:

```
//SYSIN    DD *
  SORT FIELDS=(1,4,BI,A,5,4,BI,A,9,12,CH,A)
  SUM FIELDS=NONE
/*
```

This code indicates that DFSORT is to sort on three fields. The first starts in position 1 for 4 bytes, the second starts in position 5 for 4 bytes, and the third starts in position 9 for 12 bytes. The first two fields are unsigned binary and the third is character. And the sort is to be ascending for each field. Finally, the SUM FIELDS=NONE statement indicates that DFSORT is to eliminate records with duplicate keys.

Additionally, you can improve performance by removing unneeded records during the DFSORT step, instead of using a WHEN clause on the LOAD utility. Doing so can decrease the size of the file passed to the LOAD step and the DFSORT INCLUDE is more efficient than LOAD WHEN. Consider the following sample DFSORT code:

```
//SYSIN    DD *
  INCLUDE COND=(9,4,CH,EQ,C'CDBD')
/*
```

This code indicates that DFSORT is to start in position 9 and drop the record when the next four bytes equal 'CDBD'. More details on how to use DFSORT can be found in the IBM manual number SC33-4035, *DFSORT Application Programming Guide*.

REORG After Loading When the Input Is Not Sorted   If data is not loaded in clustering sequence, consider following the LOAD with a table space reorganization. This can be performed all the time, which is not recommended, or based on the value of CLUSTER RATIO stored in the DB2 Catalog for the table space and its clustering index. If CLUSTER RATIO is not 100% for a newly loaded table, the REORG utility should be used to cluster and organize the application data.

> **NOTE**
>
> If LOAD is run specifying RESUME(YES) then even if the input is in clustering sequence, the result can be a CLUSTER RATIO less than 100%. It is best to avoid sorting the input in this case. Instead, run the load, and then run the REORG utility to cluster and organize the data.

Favor the Use of LOG NO   Use the LOG NO option unless the table to be loaded is very small. Doing so avoids the overhead of logging the loaded data and speeds load processing. If data is loaded without being logged, however, follow the LOAD utility with a full image copy.

Specify KEEPDICTIONARY for Performance   The LOAD utility will rebuild the compression dictionary for table spaces defined with the COMPRESS YES parameter. Specifying the KEEPDICTIONARY parameter causes the LOAD utility to bypass dictionary rebuilding. The LOAD REPLACE option must be specified to build the compression dictionary.

This will improve the overall performance of the LOAD utility because the CPU cycles used to build the dictionary can be avoided. However, this option should be utilized only when you are sure that the same basic type of data is being loaded into the table. If the type of data differs substantially, allowing the LOAD utility to rebuild the compression dictionary will provide for more optimal data compression.

> **NOTE**
>
> Keeping the compression dictionary can increase work space requirements for the REORG utility. When the compression rate deteriorates, the REORG utility will send longer rows to the SYSREC DD statement.

Avoid Nullable Columns for Frequently Loaded Tables   Loading tables with nullable columns can degrade the LOAD utility's performance. If a table will be loaded frequently (daily, for example), consider reducing or eliminating the number of nullable columns defined to the table to increase the performance of the LOAD utility. This is not always practical or desirable because many program changes may be required to change columns from nullable to NOT NULL or to NOT NULL WITH DEFAULT. Additionally, nullable columns might make more sense than default values given the specification of the application.

Avoid Decimal Columns for Frequently Loaded Tables   Avoid DECIMAL columns for tables that are loaded frequently. Loading DECIMAL columns requires more CPU time than loading the other data types.

Avoid Data Conversion   The LOAD utility automatically converts similar data types as part of its processing. However, try to avoid data conversion, because the LOAD utility requires additional CPU time to process these conversions.

The following data conversions are performed automatically by the LOAD utility:

Original Data Type	Converted Data Type
SMALLINT	INTEGER
	DECIMAL
	FLOAT

Original Data Type	Converted Data Type
INTEGER	SMALLINT
	DECIMAL
	FLOAT
DECIMAL	SMALLINT
	INTEGER
	FLOAT
FLOAT	SMALLINT
	INTEGER
	DECIMAL
CHAR	VARCHAR
	LONG VARCHAR
VARCHAR	CHAR
	LONG VARCHAR
GRAPHIC	VARGRAPHIC
	LONG VARGRAPHIC
VARGRAPHIC	GRAPHIC
	LONG VARGRAPHIC
TIMESTAMP EXT	DATE
	TIME
	TIMESTAMP

Reduce CPU Usage by Explicitly Coding All LOAD Parameters   Explicitly define the input file specifications in the LOAD control cards. Do this even when the data set to be loaded conforms to all the default lengths specified in Table 33.1. This reduces the LOAD utility's CPU use.

TABLE 33.1   Default LOAD Lengths

Column Data Type	Default Length
SMALLINT	2
INTEGER	4
DECIMAL	Column's precision
REAL	4
DOUBLE PRECISION	8
DATE	10
TIME	8
TIMESTAMP	26
CHAR	Column's length
VARCHAR	Column's maximum length
GRAPHIC	Double the column's length

TABLE 33.1   Continued

Column Data Type	Default Length
VARGRAPHIC	Double the column's maximum length
ROWID	Varies
BLOB, CLOB, DBCLOB	Varies

If the input file specifications are not explicitly identified, the LOAD utility assumes that the input data set is formatted with the defaults specified in Table 33.1.

> **NOTE**
>
> You can use the DSNTIAUL sample program, the UNLOAD utility, or REORG UNLOAD EXTERNAL to build LOAD control cards with explicit definitions. The PUNCHDDN keyword is used to specify a data set for the control cards.

For BLOB, CLOB, and DBCLOB data, you must specify the length of the input field in bytes. This length value is placed in a four-byte binary field at the beginning of the LOB value. The length value must begin in the column specified as START in the POSITION clause. The END specification is not used for LOBs.

V8   **Consider Using LOAD Parameters to Edit Data Before Loading**   You can use the STRIP and TRUNCATE parameters of LOAD to tweak graphic and character data before loading. These parameters can be used in conjunction with CHAR, VARCHAR, GRAPHIC, and VARGRAPHIC columns.

The STRIP parameter indicates that LOAD must remove specified characters from the beginning, the end, or both ends of the data prior to loading it. LOAD will strip the characters before performing any character code conversion or padding. If a specific character is not coded, the default is to strip blanks. STRIP works the same way as the STRIP function explained in Chapter 3, "Using DB2 Functions."

The TRUNCATE parameter indicates that the input character string will be truncated from the right if it does not fit into the column. LOAD will truncate the data after any required CCSID translation.

Create All Indexes Before Loading   It is usually more efficient to define all indexes before using the LOAD utility. The LOAD utility uses an efficient algorithm to build DB2 indexes.

If indexes must be created after the data has been loaded, create the indexes with the DEFER YES option and build them later using the REBUILD INDEX utility.

Favor LOAD over INSERT   To insert initial data into a DB2 table, favor the use of the LOAD utility with the REPLACE option over an application program coded to process INSERTs. LOAD should be favored even if the application normally processes INSERTs as part of its design. The initial loading of DB2 table data usually involves the insertion of many more rows than does typical application processing. For the initial population of table data, the LOAD utility is generally more efficient and less error-prone than a corresponding application program, and also maintains free space.

Consider using the LOAD utility with the RESUME(YES) option to process a large volume of table insertions. LOAD is usually more efficient and less error-prone than a corresponding application program that issues a large number of INSERTs.

Do Not Load Tables in a Multi-Table Simple Table Space   Avoid loading tables with the REPLACE option when multiple tables have been defined to a simple table space. The LOAD utility with the REPLACE option deletes all rows in all tables in the simple table space, which is not usually the desired result.

Gather Statistics When Loading Data   If you are loading data into a DB2 table specifying RESUME NO and the REPLACE keyword, you also should use the STATISTICS keyword to gather statistics during LOAD processing. These keywords specify that you are loading a table from scratch and that any previous data will be lost. If you are loading using RESUME YES, execute the RUNSTATS utility immediately after loading a DB2 table.

Accurate statistics are necessary to maintain current information about your table data for access path determination. Of course, access paths for static SQL will not change unless all packages and plans accessing the table are rebound. Any dynamic SQL statements will immediately take advantage of the new statistics.

Consider Loading by Partition   Concurrent loading of multiple partitions of a single table space can be achieved using partition independence. This technique is useful for reducing the overall elapsed time of loading a table in a partitioned table space.

Use Data Contingency Options As Required   The LOAD utility can perform special processing of data depending on the data values in the input load data set. Data contingency processing parameters indicate a field defined in the LOAD parameters or a beginning and ending location of data items to be checked. The data contingency processing parameters follow:

NULLIF	Sets column values to null if a particular character string is found at a particular location—for example: `NULLIF (22) = '?'`
DEFAULTIF	Sets column values to a predefined default value if a particular character string is found at a particular location. For example `DEFAULTIF FIELD = 'DEFLT'`

WHEN	Limits the loaded data to specific records in the load input data set. For example
	
	`LOAD DATA REPLACE`
	`INTO DSN8510.DEPT`
	`WHEN (1 : 3) = 'A00'`

CONTINUEIF	Used when there are record types in the input load data set. Specifies that loading will continue, logically concatenating the next record to the previous input record. For example
	
	`LOAD DATA`
	`INTO DSN8510.EMP`
	`CONTINUEIF (10 : 10) = 'X'`

> **CAUTION**
>
> NULLIF cannot be used with ROWID columns because a ROWID column cannot be null.

Separate Work Data Sets   Spread the work data sets across different physical devices to reduce contention.

Use Caution When Loading ROWID Data   When loading a table with a ROWID column, ensure that the input data is a valid ROWID value. The appropriate way to do this is to load ROWID values that were previously generated by DB2.

If the ROWID is defined with the GENERATED ALWAYS keyword, you cannot load data into that column. Instead, the ROWID value must be generated by DB2.

Handle Floating Point Data   Loading floating point data into DB2 tables requires that you know the format of the data. Two options are available for loading floating point data:

S390   Floating point data is specified in System/390 hexadecimal floating point format. This is the default value. It is also the format in which DB2 stores floating point numbers.

IEEE   Floating point data is specified in IEEE binary floating point format. DB2 expects to find the input numbers in binary floating point format and will convert the data to hexadecimal floating point format as the data is loaded.

> **NOTE**
>
> If a conversion error occurs while converting from binary floating point format to hexadecimal floating point format, DB2 will place the record in the discard file.

Optimize Sort Utility Processing   Be sure to optimize the operation of the sort utility in use at your shop. For example, you can assign additional resources to DFSORT using the following DD statement:

```
//DFSPARM  DD *
HIPRMAX=0,EXCPVR=NONE,SIZE=32768K
```

Additionally, consider using the SORTNUM clause to increase the number of dynamically allocated files and use the SORTDEVT clause to assign the disk pool.

V8 **Be Aware of the Impact of Multi-Level Security on LOAD**   If you use multilevel security to control authorization, the user or process must have write-down privilege to run a LOAD REPLACE on a table space containing a table that has multilevel security with row-level granularity. This allows you to specify values for the security label columns.

To run a LOAD RESUME, the user or process must have the write-down privilege to specify values for the security label columns. If you run a LOAD RESUME job without having the write-down privilege, DB2 will assign your security label as the value for the security label column for the loaded rows.

The UNLOAD Utility

V7 Data in DB2 tables often needs to be moved or copied. For example, you may want to move data to a different DB2 subsystem, from a DB2 table to a sequential file for external processing, or possibly to another relational database system or platform (such as Oracle on Unix or SQL Server on Windows). Certain database schema changes require database objects to be dropped and re-created—and when the object is dropped so is the data, so you need to unload the data before making database object changes. Or, maybe you just want to extract a subset of rows from a table for use as test data.

Prior to V7, DB2 provided two ways of unloading DB2 table data:

- Using SQL SELECT statements issued through DSNTIAUL, DSNTEP2, or perhaps QMF or another application program you have written, or;

- Using the DB2 REORG utility and specifying UNLOAD ONLY, but this method allows you only to reload the data back into the same DB2 table.

These methods were too slow for large quantities of data and too inflexible for most production database requirements. So IBM finally offers a true utility with better speed than DSNTIAUL and much more flexibility than REORG UNLOAD ONLY. The UNLOAD utility performs many of the basic data movement tasks required by DB2 DBAs.

UNLOAD reads data from DB2 tables and externalizes the indicated data to a data set. More than one table or partition for each table space can be unloaded with a single invocation of the UNLOAD utility. The FROM TABLE statement is used to specify the table(s) to be unloaded. Refer to Listing 33.3 for sample unload JCL.

LISTING 33.3   UNLOAD JCL

```
//DB2JOBU  JOB (UTILITY),'DB2 UNLD',MSGCLASS=X,CLASS=X,
//              NOTIFY=USER
//*
//****************************************************************
//*
//*              DB2 UNLOAD UTILITY
//*
//****************************************************************
//*
//UTIL EXEC DSNUPROC,SYSTEM=DSN,UID='UNLDDATA',UTPROC="
//*
//*   UTILITY WORK DATAETS
//*
//DSNUPROC.SYSPUNCH DD DSN=CAT.UNLOAD.SYSPUNCH,DISP=(NEW,CATLG,CATLG),
//         UNIT=SYSDA,SPACE=(TRK,(1,1))
//DSNUPROC.SYSREC DD DSN=CAT.UNLOAD.EMP,DISP=(NEW,CATLG,CATLG),
//         UNIT=SYSDA,SPACE=(TRK,(2,1))
//DSNUPROC.SYSPRINT DD SYSOUT=X
//*
//*   UTILITY CONTROL STATEMENTS
//*      This UNLOAD statement unloads data from DSN8810.EMP
//*
```

33

LISTING 33.3 Continued

```
//DSNUPROC.SYSIN    DD  *
    UNLOAD TABLESPACE DSN8D81A.DSN8S81E
    FROM TABLE DSN8810.EMP
/*
//
```

The UNLOAD utility can unload data from an image copy data set instead of from the actual, live DB2 table space data set. This is accomplished using the FROMCOPY option. Unloading from an image copy can be beneficial because the live data will be unaffected—meaning no locks are taken on the live data nor is any data read from the actual table space data set on disk. So, the performance and availability of applications running against the live data is unaffected by the concurrent unload operation. Of course, when unloading from an image copy the freshness of the data may be an issue. If subsequent updates, inserts, and deletes were processed against the table after the image copy was taken, those modifications will not be captured in the unloaded data because they were not made to the image copy data set—only to the live data itself.

Let's look at an example. The following sample code unloads data from the image copy backup data set named CAT.FULLCOPY.SEQ.DATASET1:

```
UNLOAD TABLESPACE DSN8D81A.DSN8S81E
    FROMCOPY DSN=CAT.FULLCOPY.SEQ.DATASET1
    PUNCHDDN SYSPUNCH UNLDDN SYSREC
```

The table owner is always permitted to use UNLOAD against a table. Otherwise, before a process or user can execute the UNLOAD utility, one of the following privileges must already exist or have been granted to the user or process:

- SELECT privilege on the table(s)
- DBADM authority for the database
- SYSADM authority
- SYSCTRL authority (only for DB2 Catalog tables)

UNLOAD **Phases**

The UNLOAD utility operates in three distinct phases as it reads data from DB2 tables and externalizes the indicated data to a data set:

UTILINIT	Sets up and initializes the UNLOAD utility.
UNLOAD	Reads the data (in a single pass) and unloads formatted records to sequential data sets. If UNLOAD is processing a table space or partition, DB2 takes internal commits to enable the UNLOAD process to be restarted in case operation should halt in this phase.
UTILTERM	Performs the final utility cleanup.

UNLOAD **Termination and Restart Issues**

If the UNLOAD utility is terminated using the TERM UTILITY command during the unload phase, the unloaded data is not erased. However, the output data will be incomplete and will remain that way unless you restart the UNLOAD or delete the data set.

When the source is one or more table spaces, you can restart the UNLOAD job at the partition level or at the table space level when data is unloaded from multiple table spaces using the LIST option. When you restart a terminated UNLOAD job, processing begins with the table spaces or partitions that had not yet been completed. For a table space or partitions that were being processed at termination, UNLOAD resets the output data sets and processes those table space or partitions again. When the source is one or more image copy data sets (FROMCOPY or FROMCOPYDDN was specified), UNLOAD always starts processing from the beginning.

UNLOAD **Locking Considerations**

The level of concurrent activity against a table that is being unloaded depends on the parameters and options being used by the UNLOAD utility.

For an UNLOAD with SHRLEVEL REFERENCE, the write claim class is drained for the table space or partition being unloaded and concurrent SQL readers are allowed. When unloading with SHRLEVEL REFERENCE, the following utilities are incompatible when run on the same target database object:

- CHECK DATA DELETE YES

- LOAD (SHRLEVEL NONE and SHRLEVEL CHANGE)

- RECOVER (all options)

- REORG TABLESPACE UNLOAD CONTINUE or PAUSE

- REPAIR LOCATE KEY, RID DELETE, or REPLACE

- REPAIR LOCATE TABLESPACE PAGE REPLACE

For an UNLOAD with SHRLEVEL CHANGE, a claim read is taken for the table space or partition being unloaded and concurrent SQL readers and writers are allowed. When unloading with SHRLEVEL CHANGE, the same utilities are incompatible with the exception of LOAD SHRLEVEL CHANGE, which is permitted.

For an UNLOAD of an image copy, a claim read is taken for the table space or partition being unloaded and concurrent SQL readers and writers are allowed. When unloading from an image copy, only the COPY-related utilities (MERGECOPY and MODIFY RECOVERY) are incompatible to be run concurrent with the UNLOAD.

UNLOAD **Guidelines**

When running the UNLOAD utility consider applying the following tips, tricks, and techniques.

Automatically Generate LOAD **Control Statements**   The UNLOAD utility can generate LOAD control statements that can be used by the LOAD utility for reloading the unloaded data back into a DB2 table. Use the PUNCHDDN option to specify a DD name for a data set (or template) to define one or more data set names to store these generated LOAD utility control statements.

Specify the Unload Data Encoding Scheme   The UNLOAD utility can specify the encoding scheme to use for the unloaded data. Four options are provided:

- EBCDIC—the unloaded data will be in EBCDIC format.

- ASCII—the unloaded data will be in ASCII format.

- UNICODE—the unloaded data will be in Unicode format.

- CCSID (n1, n2, n3)—the unloaded data will be in the format specified by the three coded character set identifiers. The first integer (n1) specifies the CCSID for SBCS data. The second integer (n2) specifies the CCSID for mixed data. And the third integer (n3) specifies the CCSID for DBCS data. This option is not applied to data with a subtype of BIT.

Bit strings are not converted when using any of these four options—they remain as bit strings. These four options are mutually exclusive and only one can be specified for each UNLOAD execution. If one of these options is not specified, the unloaded data will be formatted using the encoding scheme of the source data.

Handle Floating Point Data   When floating point data is being unloaded the FLOAT parameter should be used to identify the format in which unloaded floating point numbers should be stored. There are two options:

S390	Binary floating point data is written to unloaded records in System/390 hexadecimal floating point format. This is the default value.
IEEE	Binary floating point data is written in IEEE floating point format. This option requires OS/390 V2 R6 or higher with a G5 or better processor.

Use Parameters to Limit UNLOAD **Data**   Not every UNLOAD execution will require every row to be unloaded from the requested table(s). Numerous reasons and situations exist where it might make sense to unload only a subset of the total rows. Three options are provided, making it very flexible to specify a limited number of rows to unload: LIMIT, SAMPLE, and WHEN.

The LIMIT parameter can be used to limit the number of rows to be unloaded by the UNLOAD utility.

The SAMPLE parameter can be used to unload a sampling of the data in the table being unloaded instead of the entire table. The SAMPLE parameter takes a decimal condition that specifies the percentage of rows to be sampled. For example, the following parameter indicates that 15.055% of the rows in the table should be unloaded:

SAMPLE 15.055

The precision of the decimal condition is ddd.dddd where the value must be between 0 and 100 (inclusive). Sampling is applied per individual table.

> **CAUTION**
>
> If the rows from multiple tables are unloaded with sampling enabled, the referential integrity between the tables will likely be lost.

Finally, the WHEN parameter can be used to supply SQL predicates to the UNLOAD utility such that only certain data is unloaded. For example, the following condition will cause only rows where the SALARY is greater than 50,000 to be unloaded:

```
WHEN (SALARY > 50000)
```

V8 **Be Aware of the Impact of Multilevel Security on** UNLOAD   If you use RACF with multilevel security to control access to DB2, be aware of the potential impact it can have on the UNLOAD utility. When unloading from tables protected using multilevel security with row-level granularity, you may not unload all of the rows depending on your security label. A row is unloaded only if your security label dominates the data's security label. If your security label does not dominate the data security label, the row is not unloaded—and DB2 will not inform you of this. For more information about multilevel security and security labels refer back to Chapter 10, "DB2 Security and Authorization."

The REORG Utility

The REORG utility can be used to reorganize DB2 table spaces and indexes, thereby improving the efficiency of access to those objects. Reorganization is required periodically to ensure that the data is situated in an optimal fashion for subsequent access. Reorganization reclusters data, resets free space to the amount specified in the CREATE DDL, and deletes and redefines the underlying VSAM data sets for STOGROUP-defined objects.

There are three types of reorganizations supported by the DB2 REORG utility:

- When REORG is run on an index, DB2 reorganizes the index space to improve access performance and reclaim fragmented space.

- When REORG is run on a regular (non-LOB) table space, DB2 reorganizes the data into clustering sequence by the clustering index, reclaims fragmented space, and optimizes the organization of the data in the table space.

- When REORG is run on a LOB table space, DB2 removes embedded free space and tries to make LOB pages contiguous. The primary benefit of reorganizing a LOB table space is to enhance prefetch effectiveness.

Proper planning and scheduling of the REORG utility is a complex subject. Many factors influence the requirements for executing the REORG utility. The following topics highlight the necessary decisions for implementing an efficient REORG policy in your DB2 environment.

33

Recommended Reorganization Standards

You should develop rigorous standards for the REORG utility because it is one of the most significant aids in achieving optimal DB2 performance. The standard will influence the input to the REORG utility, the REORG job streams, and the rerun and restart procedures for REORG utilities.

As with the LOAD utility, there are two philosophies for implementing the REORG utility. Individual databases, table spaces, and applications can mix and match philosophies. One philosophy, however, should be chosen for every non-read-only table space and index in every DB2 application. Failure to follow a standard reorganization philosophy and schedule will result in poorly performing DB2 applications. The REORG philosophy must be recorded and maintained for each table space and index created.

The philosophies presented here strike a balance between programmer productivity, ease of use and comprehension by operations and control staff, and the effective use of DB2 resources.

Reorganization Philosophies

Two REORG philosophies can be adopted by DB2-based application systems. The first, which is generally the recommended philosophy, is more time consuming to implement but easier to support. It requires that sufficient DASD be reserved to catalog the REORG work data sets if the REORG job abends.

The three work data sets for the REORG job are allocated for the SYSREC, SYSUT1, and SORTOUT DDNAMEs with DISP=(MOD,DELETE,CATLG). This specification enables the data sets to be allocated as new for the initial running of the REORG job. If the job abends, however, it will catalog the data sets for use in a possible restart. After the step completes successfully, the data sets are deleted. The space for these data sets must be planned and available before the REORG job is executed.

The sample REORG JCL in Listing 33.4 follows this philosophy. By creating your REORG job according to this philosophy, you can restart an abending REORG job with little effort after the cause of the abend has been corrected. You simply specify one of the RESTART options in the UTPROC parameter for DSNUTILB.

LISTING 33.4   REORG JCL (Restartable)

```
//DB2JOBU  JOB (UTILITY),'DB2 REORG',MSGCLASS=X,CLASS=X,
//            NOTIFY=USER
//*
//****************************************************************
//*
//*          DB2 REORG UTILITY (RESTARTABLE)
//*
//****************************************************************
//*
//UTIL EXEC DSNUPROC,SYSTEM=DSN,UID='REORGTS',UTPROC="
//*
//*  UTILITY WORK DATASETS
//*
```

LISTING 33.4   Continued

```
//DSNUPROC.SORTWK01 DDUNIT=SYSDA,SPACE=(CYL,(2,1))
//DSNUPROC.SORTWK02 DDUNIT=SYSDA,SPACE=(CYL,(2,1))
//DSNUPROC.SORTOUT DD DSN=CAT.SORTOUT,DISP=(MOD,DELETE,CATLG),
//       UNIT=SYSDA,SPACE=(CYL,(2,1))
//DSNUPROC.SYSUT1 DD DSN=CAT.SYSUT1,DISP=(MOD,DELETE,CATLG),
//       UNIT=SYSDA,SPACE=(CYL,(2,1)),DCB=BUFNO=20
//DSNUPROC.SYSREC DD DSN=OUTPUT.DATASETD,DISP=(MOD,CATLG,CATLG),
//       UNIT=SYSDA,SPACE=(CYL,(15,5)),DCB=BUFNO=20
//DSNUPROC.SYSPRINT DD SYSOUT=*
//DSNUPROC.UTPRINT DD SYSOUT=*
//*
//*   UTILITY INPUT CONTROL STATEMENTS
//*       The REORG statement reorganizes the second partition
//*       of DSN8D81A.DSN8S81E.
//*
//DSNUPROC.SYSIN    DD   *
    REORG TABLESPACE DSN8D81A.DSN8S81E PART 2
/*
//
```

The second philosophy is easier to implement but more difficult to support. No additional DASD is required because all REORG work data sets are defined as temporary. Therefore, upon abnormal completion, all interim work data sets are lost. See Listing 33.5 for sample JCL.

LISTING 33.5   REORG JCL (Nonrestartable)

```
//DB2JOBU  JOB (UTILITY),'DB2 REORG',MSGCLASS=X,CLASS=X,
//           NOTIFY=USER,REGION=0M
//*
//****************************************************************
//*
//*           DB2 REORG UTILITY (NON-RESTARTABLE)
//*
//****************************************************************
//*
//UTIL EXEC DSNUPROC,SYSTEM=DSN,UID='REORGTS',UTPROC="
//*
//*   UTILITY WORK DATASETS
//*
//DSNUPROC.SORTWK01 DDUNIT=SYSDA,SPACE=(CYL,(2,1))
//DSNUPROC.SORTWK02 DDUNIT=SYSDA,SPACE=(CYL,(2,1))
//DSNUPROC.SORTOUT DD DSN=&&SORTOUT,
//       UNIT=SYSDA,SPACE=(CYL,(2,1))
//DSNUPROC.SYSUT1 DD DSN=&&SYSUT1,
//       UNIT=SYSDA,SPACE=(CYL,(2,1)),DCB=BUFNO=20
//DSNUPROC.SYSREC DD DSN=&&SYSREC,
//       UNIT=SYSDA,SPACE=(CYL,(15,5)),DCB=BUFNO=20
//DSNUPROC.SYSPRINT DD SYSOUT=*
//DSNUPROC.UTPRINT DD SYSOUT=*
//*
//*   UTILITY INPUT CONTROL STATEMENTS
```

LISTING 33.5   Continued

```
//*    1. The first REORG statement reorganizes the
//*       named table space.
//*    2. The second REORG statement reorganizes the
//*       named index.
//*
//DSNUPROC.SYSIN    DD  *
REORG TABLESPACE DSN8D81A.DSN8S81D
REORG INDEX (DSN8810.XACT1)
/*
//
```

To restart this REORG job, you must determine in which phase the job failed. If it failed in any phase other than the UTILINIT phase or UNLOAD phase, you must restore the table space being reorganized to a previous point. You can do this by running either the RECOVER TOCOPY utility or a simple RECOVER (if the LOG NO option of the REORG utility was specified).

After restoring the table space (and possibly its associated indexes), you must correct the cause of the abend, terminate the utility, and rerun the job. As you can see, this method is significantly more difficult to restart.

Try to use the first philosophy rather than the second. The first reorganization philosophy makes recovery from errors as smooth and painless as possible.

Reorganization Frequency

The frequency of reorganization is different for every DB2 application. Sometimes the reorganization frequency is different for table spaces and indexes in the same application because different data requires different reorganization schedules. These schedules depend on the following factors:

- Frequency of modification activity (insertions, updates, and deletions)

- Application transaction volume

- Amount of free space allocated when the table space or index was created

The scheduling of reorganizations should be determined by the DBA, taking into account the input of the application development team as well as end-user requirements. The following information must be obtained for each DB2 table to determine the proper scheduling of table space and index reorganizations:

- The data availability requirement to enable effective REORG scheduling.

- The insertion and deletion frequency for each table and table space.

- The number of rows per table.

- An indication of uneven distribution of data values in a table.

- The frequency and volume of updates to critical columns in that table. (*Critical columns* are defined as columns in the clustering index, columns containing variable data, any column used in SQL predicates, or any column that is sorted or grouped.)

Most of this information can be obtained from the DB2 Catalog if the application already exists. For new application table spaces and indexes, this information must be based on application specifications, user requirements, and estimates culled from any existing non-DB2 systems.

Letting REORG Decide When to Reorganize

You can use the OFFPOSLIMIT, INDREFLIMIT, and LEAFDISTLIMIT options of the REORG utility to determine whether a reorganization will be useful. OFFPOSLIMIT and INDREFLIMIT apply to table space reorganization; LEAFDISTLIMIT applies to index reorganization.

The OFFPOSLIMIT parameter uses the NEAROFFPOSF, FAROFFPOSF, and CARDF statistics from SYSIBM.SYSINDEXPART to gauge the potential effectiveness of a REORG. To use OFFPOSLIMIT, specify the clause with an integer value for the REORG. For the specified partitions, the value will be compared to the result of the following calculation:

```
(NEAROFFPOSF + FAROFFPOSF) ? 100 / CARDF
```

If any calculated value exceeds the OFFPOSLIMIT value, REORG is performed. The default value for OFFPOSLIMIT is 10.

The INDREFLIMIT parameter uses the NEARINDREF, FARINIDREF, and CARDF statistics from SYSIBM.SYSINDEXPART to gauge the potential effectiveness of a REORG. To use INDREFLIMIT, specify the clause with an integer value for the REORG. For the specified partitions, the value will be compared to the result of the following calculation:

```
(NEARINDREF + FARINDREF) ? 100 / CARDF
```

If any calculated value exceeds the INDREFLIMIT value, REORG is performed. The default value for INDREFLIMIT is 10.

> **CAUTION**
>
> OFFPOSLIMIT and INDREFLIMIT cannot be used for LOB table spaces. The parameters can be specified for any other type of table space.

You can use the LEAFDISTLIMIT option to allow REORG to determine whether reorganizing an index is recommended. To use LEAFDISTLIMIT, specify the clause with an integer value for the REORG. For the specified index, the value will be compared to the LEAFDIST value in SYSIBM.SYSINDEXPART. If any LEAFDIST exceeds the value specified for LEAFDISTLIMIT, REORG is performed. The default value for LEAFDISTLIMIT is 200.

If the REPORTONLY keyword is specified, a report is generated indicating whether the REORG should be performed or not. The actual REORG will not be performed. You can use the REORG utility in conjunction with REPORTONLY and the INDREFLIMIT and OFFPOSLIMIT keywords for table spaces or the LEAFDISTLIMIT keyword for indexes, to produce reorganization reports. Further information on determining the frequency of reorganization is provided in Part IV, "DB2 Performance Monitoring," and Part V, "DB2 Performance Tuning."

Reorganization Job Stream

The total reorganization schedule should include a RUNSTATS job or step (or use of in-line statistics), two COPY jobs or steps for each table space being reorganized, and a REBIND job or step for all plans using tables in any of the table spaces being reorganized.

The RUNSTATS job is required to record the current table space and index statistics to the DB2 Catalog. This provides the DB2 optimizer with current data to use in determining optimal access paths. Of course, supplying the STATISTICS parameter to the REORG job would cause statistics to be collected during the REORG, and therefore a separate RUNSTATS step would not be needed.

An image copy should always be taken immediately before any table space REORG is run. This ensures that the data is recoverable, because the REORG utility alters the physical positioning of application data. The second COPY job is required after the REORG if it was performed with the LOG NO option.

The second COPY job or step can be eliminated if an inline COPY is performed during the REORG. Similar to the inline COPY feature of LOAD, a SHRLEVEL REFERENCE full image copy can be performed as a part of the REORG. To create an inline copy, use the COPYDDN and RECOVERYDDN keywords. You can specify up to two primary and two secondary copies. When a REORG job runs with the LOG NO option, DB2 turns on the copy pending flag for each table space specified in the REORG (unless inline copy is used). The LOG NO parameter tells DB2 not to log the changes. This minimizes the performance impact of the reorganization on the DB2 system and enables your REORG job to finish faster.

When the LOG NO parameter is specified, you *must* take an image copy of the table space after the REORG has completed and before it can be updated. It is good practice to back up your table spaces after a reorganization anyway. A REBIND job for all production plans should be included to enable DB2 to create new access paths based on the current statistics provided by the RUNSTATS job.

If all the table spaces for an application are being reorganized, each utility should be in a separate job—one REORG job, one RUNSTATS job, one COPY job, and one REBIND job. These common jobs can be used independently of the REORG job. If isolated table spaces in an application are being reorganized, it might be acceptable to perform the REORG, RUNSTATS, COPY, and REBIND as separate steps in a single job. Follow your shop guidelines for job creation standards.

Estimating REORG Work Data Set Sizes

The REORG utility requires the use of work data sets to reorganize table spaces and indexes. The following formulas help you estimate the sizes for these work data sets. More complex and precise calculations are in the *DB2 Utility Guide and Reference* manual, but these formulas should produce comparable results.

```
SYSREC = (number of pages in table space) x 4096 x 1.10
```

> **NOTE**
>
> If the table space being reorganized uses 32K pages, multiply the SYSREC number by 8. The total number of pages used by a table space can be retrieved from either the VSAM LISTCAT command or the DB2 Catalog, as specified in the NACTIVE column of SYSIBM.SYSTABLESPACE. If you use the DB2 Catalog method, ensure that the statistics are current by running the RUNSTATS utility (discussed in Chapter 34, "Catalog Manipulation Utilities").
>
> An additional 10 percent of space is specified because of the expansion of variable columns and the reformatting performed by the REORG UNLOAD phase.

```
SORTOUT = (size of the largest index key + 12)
    ➡x (largest number of rows to be loaded to a single table)
    ➡x (total number of nonclustering indexes defined for each table) x 1.2
```

> **NOTE**
>
> If any number in the SORTOUT calculation is 0, substitute 1. The multiplier 1.2 is factored into the calculation to provide a "fudge factor." If you are absolutely sure of your numbers, the calculation can be made more precise by eliminating the additional multiplication of 1.2.

```
SYSUT1 = (size of the largest index key + 12)
    ➡x (largest number of rows to be loaded to a single table)
    ➡x (total number of nonclustering indexes defined for each table) x 1.2
```

> **NOTE**
>
> If any number in the SYSUT1 calculation is 0, substitute 1. The multiplier 1.2 is factored into the calculation to provide a "fudge factor." If you are absolutely sure of your numbers, the calculation can be made more precise by eliminating the additional multiplication of 1.2.

```
SORTWKxx = (size of SYSUT1) x 2
```

> **NOTE**
>
> If any number in the SORTWKxx calculation is 0, substitute 1.

After calculating the estimated size in bytes for each work data set, convert the number into cylinders, rounding up to the next whole cylinder. Allocating work data sets in cylinder increments enhances the utility's performance.

REORG INDEX **Phases**

The REORG utility consists of the following six phases when run for an index:

UTILINIT	Sets up and initializes the REORG utility.
UNLOAD	Unloads the index and writes the keys to a sequential data set (SYSREC).

33

BUILD	Builds indexes and updates index statistics.
LOG	Only for SHRLEVEL CHANGE; processes the log iteratively to append changes.
SWITCH	Switches access to shadow copy of index space or partition being reorganized (online REORG) with SHRLEVEL REFERENCE or CHANGE.
UTILTERM	Performs the final utility cleanup.

REORG TABLESPACE **Phases**

The REORG utility consists of ten phases when run on a table space:

UTILINIT	Sets up and initializes the REORG utility.
UNLOAD	Unloads the data into a sequential data set (SYSREC) unless NOSYSREC is specified, in which case the data is just passed to the RELOAD phase. If a clustering index exists and either SORTDATA or SHRLEVEL CHANGE is specified, the data is sorted. The compression dictionary is rebuilt in this step for COMPRESS YES table spaces.
RELOAD	Reads the records passed from the UNLOAD phase or from the sequential data set created in the UNLOAD phase, loads them to the table space, and extracts index keys (SYSUT1). Creates a full image copy if COPYDDN, RECOVERYDDN, SHRLEVEL REFERENCE, or SHRLEVEL CHANGE are specified. If SORTKEYS is specified, the index keys are sorted by a subtask.
SORT	Sorts the key entries before updating indexes, if any exist. SYSUT1 is the input to the sort, and SORTOUT is the output of the sort. This phase can be skipped if there is only one key per table, if the data is reloaded in key order, or if the data is reloaded grouped by table. If SORTKEYS is used, passes sorted keys in memory to the BUILD phase
BUILD	Updates any indexes to reflect the new location of records and updates index statistics.
SORTBLD	When parallel index build is specified (SORTKEYS), the SORT and BUILD phases are performed in the SORTBLD phase instead.
LOG	Only for SHRLEVEL CHANGE: processes the log iteratively to append changes to the image copies.
SWITCH	Switches access to a shadow copy of the table space or partition being reorganized (online REORG) with SHRLEVEL REFERENCE or CHANGE.
BUILD2	Corrects nonpartitioning indexes when reorganizing a partition using SHRLEVEL REFERENCE or CHANGE.
UTILTERM	Performs the final utility cleanup.

V7

> **NOTE**
>
> As of DB2 V7, REORG can perform BUILD2 processing in parallel. The maximum number of parallel tasks is controlled by the SRPRMMUP parameter (DSNZPARM).

REORG TABLESPACE Phases for LOB Table Spaces

The REORG utility consists only of three phases when run against a LOB table space:

UTILINIT	Sets up and initializes the REORG utility.
REORGLOB	Rebuilds the LOB table space in place; no LOBs are unloaded or reloaded. The LOB table space is placed in a RECOVER pending state when processing begins and is removed from this state when the REORGLOB phase completes. So, if the REORGLOB phase fails, the LOB table space will be in a RECOVER pending state.
UTILTERM	Performs the final utility cleanup.

REORG Rerun/Restart Procedures

The REORG restart procedure depends on the phase that was running when the failure occurred. There are two ways to determine the phase in which the failure occurred.

The first method is to issue the DISPLAY UTILITY command to determine which utilities are currently active, stopped, or terminating in the DB2 system. The format of the command is

```
-DISPLAY UTILITY(*)
```

The second way to determine the abending phase is to view the SYSPRINT DD statement of the REORG step. This method is not as desirable as the first, but it is the only method you can use when the DB2 system is down. At the completion of each phase, DB2 prints a line stating that the phase has finished. You can assume that the phase immediately following the last phase reported complete in the SYSPRINT DD statement is the phase that was executing when the abend occurred.

After determining the phase of the REORG utility at the time of the abend, follow the steps outlined here to restart or rerun the reorganization. In the following procedures, it is assumed that your REORG processing is restartable.

If the abend occurred in the UTILINIT phase

1. Determine the cause of the abend. An abend in this step is usually caused by another utility executing with the same UID or a utility that is incompatible with another utility currently executing.

2. Resolve the cause of the abend. An abend in this phase is probably due to improper job scheduling. Issue the DISPLAY UTILITY command to determine which utilities are currently in process for the DB2 system. Resolve the scheduling problem by allowing conflicting utilities to complete before proceeding to step 3.

3. Restart the job at the REORG step.

33

If the abend occurred in the UNLOAD phase

1. Determine the cause of the abend. An abend in this step is usually caused by insufficient space allocated to the SYSREC DD statement.

2. Resolve the cause of the abend. If the problem is an out-of-space abend (B37) on the SYSREC DD statement, the data set associated with that DD statement will have been cataloged. Allocate a new data set with additional space, copy the SYSREC data set to the new data set, delete the original SYSREC data set, and rename the new data set to the same name as the original SYSREC data set.

3. Restart the job at the REORG step with a temporary change to alter the UTPROC parameter to RESTART. This restarts the utility at the point of the last commit.

If the abend occurred in the RELOAD phase

1. Determine the cause of the abend. An abend in this phase is usually a Resource Unavailable abend due to another user allocating the table space or the VSAM data set associated with the table space running out of space. Note the SHRLEVEL specified for the REORG.

   When an abend occurs in this phase, the table space will be in recover pending and copy pending status. Associated indexes will be in recover pending status.

2. Resolve the cause of the abend.

   a. If the problem is timeout due to another job or user accessing the table space to be reloaded, determine the conflicting job or user access and wait for it to complete processing before proceeding to step 3.

   b. If the problem is an out-of-space abend on the VSAM data set containing the table space being reloaded, contact the DBA or DASD support unit. This situation can be corrected by adding another volume to the STOGROUP being used; by using IDCAMS to redefine the VSAM data set, move the VSAM data set, or both; or by altering the primary space allocation quantity for the index, the secondary space allocation quantity for the index, or both.

3. a. If the abend was not due to an error in the data set for the SYSREC DD statement, restart the job at the REORG step with a temporary change to alter the UTPROC parameter to RESTART.

   b. If the abend was caused by an error in the data set for the SYSREC DD statement, first terminate the utility by issuing the -TERM UTILITY(*UID*) command. Then recover the table space by executing the Recover table space utility. Next, recreate a temporary copy of the control cards used as input to the REORG step. Omit the control cards for all utilities executed in the step before the abend. This bypasses the work accomplished before the abend. The first card in the new data set should be the utility that was executing at the time of the abend. Finally, restart the job at the REORG step using the modified control cards.

For SHRLEVEL NONE, the table space and indexes are left in recovery pending status. Once the table space is recovered, the REORG job can be rerun. For SHRLEVEL REFERENCE or CHANGE, the data records are reloaded into shadow copies so the original objects are not impacted. The job can be rerun after the utility is terminated.

If the abend occurred in the SORT phase

1. Determine the cause of the abend. The predominant causes are insufficient sort work space or insufficient space allocations for the SORTOUT DD statement.

   When an abend occurs in this phase, the table space will be in copy pending status. Associated indexes will be in recover pending status.

2. Resolve the cause of the abend. If the problem is insufficient space on either the sort work or SORTOUT DD statements, simply increase the allocations and proceed to step 3.

3. Restart the job at the REORG step with a temporary change to alter the UTPROC parameter to RESTART(PHASE).

If the abend occurred in the BUILD phase

1. Determine the cause for the abend. An abend in this step is usually the result of the VSAM data set associated with the index space running out of space.

   When an abend occurs in this phase, the table space will be in copy pending status.

2. Resolve the cause of the abend. If the problem is an out-of-space abend on the VSAM data set containing the index space being reloaded, contact the DBA or DASD support unit. This situation can be corrected by adding another volume to the STOGROUP being used—by using IDCAMS to redefine the VSAM data set, move the VSAM data set, or both—or by altering the primary space allocation quantity for the index, the secondary space allocation quantity for the index, or both.

3. Restart the job at the REORG step with a temporary change to alter the UTPROC parameter to RESTART(PHASE).

For abends in the SORT, BUILD, or LOG phases, the SHRLEVEL option can impact the response:

1. For SHRLEVEL NONE, indexes that were not built will be in recovery pending status. Run REORG with the SORTDATA option or REBUILD INDEX to rebuild these indexes.

   For SHRLEVEL REFERENCE or CHANGE, the records are reloaded into shadow objects, so the original objects have not been affected by REORG. The job can be rerun.

If the abend occurred in the SWITCH phase

1. All data sets that were renamed to their shadow counterparts are renamed back. This leaves the objects in their original state. The job can be rerun. If there is a problem in renaming to the original data sets, the objects are placed in recovery pending

status. The table space can then be recovered using the image copy created by REORG. The indexes must also be recovered.

If the abend occurred in the BUILD2 phase

1. The logical partition is left in recovery pending status. Run REBUILD INDEX for the NPI logical partition to complete the REORG.

If the abend occurred in the UTILTERM phase

1. An abend in this phase is unlikely because all the work required for the reorganization has been completed. A problem at this phase means that DB2 cannot terminate the utility.

   The table space will be in copy pending status.

2. Terminate the DB2 utility by issuing the TERM UTILITY command. The format of the command is

   -TERM UTILITY(*UID*)

   where *UID* is obtained from the -DISPLAY UTILITY (*) command.

3. If data sets associated with the SYSREC, SYSUT1, and SORTOUT DD statements were cataloged as a result of the abend, uncatalog them and force the job to complete.

> **CAUTION**
>
> You cannot restart a REORG on a LOB table space if it is in the REORGLOB phase. Be sure to take a full image COPY of the LOB table space before executing REORG if the LOB table space was defined specifying LOG NO. Failure to do so will place the recoverability of the LOB table space in jeopardy. Any LOB table space defined with LOG NO, will be in COPY pending status after REORG finishes.

Gathering Inline Statistics During the REORG

You can generate statistics during the execution of the REORG utility. This is referred to as inline RUNSTATS. Up-to-date statistics will be generated during the REORG instead of requiring an additional RUNSTATS step.

To generate inline RUNSTATS, use the STATISTICS keyword. You can gather table space statistics, index statistics, or both. By generating statistics during the REORG, you can accomplish two tasks with one I/O (reorganization and statistics collection) and also avoid the need to schedule an additional RUNSTATS step after the REORG.

REORG and the SHRLEVEL Parameter

Similar to the functionality of SHRLEVEL in other DB2 utilities, the SHRLEVEL parameter controls the level of concurrent data access permitted during a REORG. There are three SHRLEVEL options for REORG: NONE, REFERENCE, and CHANGE.

SHRLEVEL NONE indicates that concurrent data reading is permitted while data is being unloaded, but no access is permitted during the RELOAD phase and subsequent phases. This is the default and is the manner in which REORG is executed for all versions of DB2 prior to V5.

SHRLEVEL REFERENCE indicates that concurrent read access is permitted during both the UNLOAD and RELOAD phases of the REORG.

SHRLEVEL CHANGE indicates concurrent read and write access is available throughout most of the reorganization.

Both SHRLEVEL REFERENCE and SHRLEVEL CHANGE require a shadow copy of the object being reorganized.

Using SHRLEVEL CHANGE to Achieve Online Reorganization

Data availability can be greatly enhanced through the use of SHRLEVEL CHANGE when reorganizing table spaces. This option, known as Online REORG or Concurrent REORG, allows full read and write access to the data during most phases of the REORG utility. This is achieved by duplicating the data that is to be reorganized (refer to Figure 33.1). Online REORG takes the following steps:

1. Data is unloaded from the table space, partition, or index during which read and write access is available.

2. Data is reloaded into a shadow copy of the data store being reorganized. Read and write access is still available to the original table space, partition, or index.

3. The log entries recording the changes made to the original data set while the shadow reload was occurring are applied to the shadow. Read and usually write access is still available to the original table space, partition, or index. This step is performed iteratively based upon the conditions specified in MAXRO, DEADLINE, DELAY, and LONGLOG.

4. The original and the copy are swapped so that future access is to the newly reorganized version of the data. Data is unavailable until the swap is accomplished.

5. Read and write access to the data is enabled again.

V7 As of DB2 V7, IBM provides a fast switch option for shadow data sets during an online REORG. The normal process is to swap the data sets by renaming them. But fast switch simply changes which data set DB2 looks at, with no renaming required. The shadow copy that was reorganized is just recorded by DB2 as now being the proper data set to be used. Recall from Chapter 5 the naming convention that is used for all DB2 data sets:

```
vcat.DSNDBx.dddddddd.ssssssss.y0001.znnn
```

The *y0001* component is used with fast switch. DB2 will switch back-and-forth between using i0001 and j0001 for this component of the data set name. The first time your REORG with fast switch enabled, when the REORG completes the j0001 data sets will be in use—and the i0001 data sets will be deleted. The next time you run an online REORG the same thing is done, but then with J data sets becoming I data sets again. Alternating between I and J continues every time you reorganize.

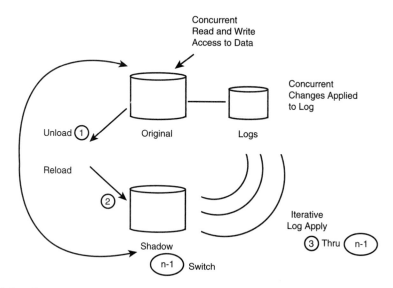

FIGURE 33.1 Concurrent REORG processing.

Set SPRMURNM=1 in DSNZPARM to enable fast switch for all online REORGs. The IPREFIX column of SYSIBM.SYSTABLEPART and SYSIBM.SYSINDEXPART can be queried to determine whether the current active data set uses I or J.

Online REORG Drawbacks

Online REORG should not be used all of the time because there are drawbacks to its use. First and foremost, is the need to have excess disk space to store the shadow copy. The shadow copy typically consumes at least as much space as the object being reorganized. More space may be required because REORG reclaims free space.

Because of the need to apply changes from the log, online REORG is most effectively used when transaction throughput is low and most transactions are of short duration. Furthermore, avoid scheduling REORG with SHRLEVEL CHANGE when low-tolerance applications are executing.

Third-party online reorganization products are available that offer better concurrency during higher volume transaction processing.

The Mapping Table

A mapping table must be specified whenever a SHRLEVEL CHANGE reorganization is run. The mapping table is used by REORG to map between the RIDs of records in the original copy and the like RIDs in the shadow copy. The mapping table must use the following definition as a template:

```
CREATE TABLE table-name
    (TYPE        CHAR(1) NOT NULL,
     SOURCE_RID  CHAR(5) NOT NULL,
```

```
    TARGET_XRID  CHAR(9) NOT NULL,
    LRSN         CHAR(6) NOT NULL
  );
```

Additionally, an index must be created for the mapping table using the following template:

```
CREATE TYPE 2 UNIQUE INDEX index-name
  ON TABLE table-name
  (SOURCE_RID ASC,
   TYPE,
   TARGET_XRID,
   LRSN
   );
```

Be careful when assigning the mapping objects to buffer pools. Do not assign these objects to BP0 or other sensitive buffer pools. For example, do not place mapping objects in the same buffer pool as the objects being reorganized.

Additionally, when running an online REORG when application traffic is high, be sure to adjust the output log buffer (OUTBUF) to be large enough to contain the changes.

Create the table in a segmented table space explicitly set aside for the use of the mapping table. Multiple mapping tables can be created in the segmented table space if concurrent online REORGs are required to be run. One mapping table is required per online REORG execution. Although a single mapping table can be reused for multiple REORGs, they cannot be concurrent REORGs. Consider specifying LOCKSIZE TABLE for the table space containing the mapping table because concurrent tasks will not access the mapping table.

Any name can be used for the mapping table as long as it conforms to the DB2 restrictions on table names. It is wise to create a naming standard to identify mapping tables as such. For example, you may want to name all mapping tables beginning with a prefix of MAP_.

> **CAUTION**
>
> Explicit creation of shadow copy data sets is required only if the object being reorganized uses user-defined VSAM data sets instead of STOGROUPs. This is yet another reason to use STOGROUPs instead of user-defined VSAM.

Online REORG Options

There are several additional options that can be used in conjunction with online REORG. These options are briefly discussed in this section.

MAXRO   The MAXRO option is an integer that specifies the amount of time for the last iteration of log processing for the online REORG. DB2 continues to iteratively apply log records until it determines that the next iteration will take less than the indicated MAXRO value. Of course, the actual execution time for the last iteration may actually exceed the MAXRO value.

Specifying a small positive MAXRO value reduces the length of the period of read-only access, but it might increase the elapsed time for REORG to complete. If you specify a huge positive value, the second iteration of log processing is probably the last iteration.

> **NOTE**
>
> The ALTER UTILITY command can be used to change the value of MAXRO during the execution of an online REORG.

The MAXRO parameter can also be set to DEFER an integer value. The DEFER option indicates that log processing iterations can continue indefinitely. If DEFER is specified, the online REORG will not start the final log processing iteration until the MAXRO value is modified using the ALTER UTIL command.

When DEFER is specified and DB2 determines that the time for the current iteration and the estimated time for the next iteration are both less than five seconds, DB2 will send a message to the console (DSNU362I) indicating that a pause will be inserted before the next log iteration. When running an online REORG specifying DEFER, the operator should scan for DSNU362I messages to determine when to issue an ALTER UTIL command to change the MAXRO value.

The DEFER parameter should always be used in conjunction with LONGLOG CONTINUE.

LONGLOG   The LONGLOG parameter designates how DB2 will react if the number of records that the next log processing iteration is not lower than the number that the previous iterations processed. If this occurs, the REORG log processing may never catch up to the write activity of the concurrently executing transactions and programs.

If LONGLOG CONTINUE is specified, DB2 will continue processing the REORG until the time on the JOB statement expires. When MAXRO DEFER is used in conjunction with LONGLOG CONTINUE, the online REORG continues with read/write access still permitted to the original table space, partition, or index. When the switch to the shadow copy is required, an operator or DBA must issue the ALTER UTIL command with a large integer MAXRO value. CONTINUE is the default LONGLOG value.

If LONGLOG TERM is specified, DB2 terminates reorganization after the delay specified by the DELAY parameter (discussed in the next section).

If LONGLOG DRAIN is specified, DB2 drains the write claim class after the delay specified by the DELAY parameter, thereby forcing the final log processing iteration to happen.

DELAY   The DELAY parameter is used in conjunction with the LONGLOG parameter. It indicates the minimum amount of time before the TERM or DRAIN activity is performed.

DEADLINE   The DEADLINE parameter provides a mechanism for shutting off an online REORG. If DB2 determines that the switch phase will not finish by the deadline, DB2 terminates the REORG.

If DEADLINE NONE is specified, there is no deadline and the REORG can continue indefinitely. This is the default option.

If DEADLINE *timestamp* is specified, the REORG must finish before the specified date and time deadline. This indicates that the switch phase of the log processing must be finished by the timestamp provided.

> **CAUTION**
>
> The timestamp provided to the DEADLINE parameter must be in the future. The REORG will not commence if the date/time combination has already passed.

REORG TABLESPACE **Locking Considerations**

The REORG TABLESPACE utility, regardless of the execution options specified, can run concurrently with the following utilities (each accessing the same object):

- DIAGNOSE
- REPORT

When REORG TABLESPACE is run specifying SHRLEVEL NONE and UNLOAD ONLY, the following additional utilities can be run concurrently:

- CHECK INDEX
- COPY
- QUIESCE
- REBUILD INDEX (only when a clustering index does not exist)
- REORG INDEX (only when a clustering index does not exist)
- REORG SHRLEVEL NONE UNLOAD ONLY
- REPAIR DUMP or VERIFY
- REPAIR LOCATE INDEX PAGE REPLACE (only when a clustering index does not exist)
- RUNSTATS
- STOSPACE

The REORG TABLESPACE utility when run specifying UNLOAD ONLY will drain all write claim classes for the table space or partition being reorganized. Additionally, if a clustering index exists, the REORG utility will drain all write claim classes for the index or partition.

REORG TABLESPACE SHRLEVEL NONE

When REORG TABLESPACE SHRLEVEL NONE is executed with the UNLOAD CONTINUE or UNLOAD PAUSE options, the following locking activity occurs:

- Write claim classes are drained for the table space or table space partition and the associated index or index partition during the UNLOAD phase.
- All claim classes are drained for the table space or table space partition and the associated index or index partition during the RELOAD phase.

- Write claim classes are drained for the logical partition of a nonpartitioned type 2 index during the RELOAD phase.

- For a REORG of a single partition, all claim classes are drained for the logical partition of a non partitioned type 2 index during the RELOAD phase.

REORG TABLESPACE SHRLEVEL REFERENCE

When REORG TABLESPACE SHRLEVEL REFERENCE is executed with the UNLOAD CONTINUE or UNLOAD PAUSE options, the following locking activity occurs:

- Write claim classes are drained for the table space or table space partition and the associated partitioning index and non-partitioned index during the UNLOAD phase.

- All claim classes are drained for the table space or table space partition and the associated partitioning index and non-partitioned type 1 indexes during the SWITCH phase.

- Write claim classes are drained for the logical partition of a non-partitioned type 2 index during the SWITCH phase.

- Write claim classes are drained for the table space or table space partition and the associated partitioning index and non-partitioned type 1 indexes during the UNLOAD phase.

- All claim classes are drained for the logical partition of a non-partitioned type 2 index during the UNLOAD phase.

- All claim classes are drained for the table space or table space partition and the associated partitioning index and nonpartitioned type 1 indexes during the SWITCH phase of a single partition REORG.

- For a REORG of a single partition, the repeatable read class is drained for non-partitioned type 2 index during the SWITCH phase.

REORG TABLESPACE SHRLEVEL CHANGE

When REORG TABLESPACE SHRLEVEL CHANGE is executed with the UNLOAD CONTINUE or UNLOAD PAUSE options, the following locking activity occurs:

- The read claim class is claimed for the table space and associated indexes during the UNLOAD phase.

- The write claim class is drained for the table space and associated indexes during the LOG phase.

- All claim classes are drained for the table space and associated indexes during the SWITCH phase.

REORG INDEX **Locking Considerations**

The REORG INDEX utility is compatible with the following utilities:

- CHECK LOB

- COPY TABLESPACE

- DIAGNOSE

- MERGECOPY

- MODIFY

- RECOVER TABLESPACE (no options)

- RECOVER TABLESPACE ERROR RANGE

- REORG SHRLEVEL NONE UNLOAD ONLY or UNLOAD EXTERNAL
  (only when a clustering index does not exist)

- REPAIR LOCATE RID (DUMP, VERIFY, or REPLACE)

- REPAIR LOCATE TABLESPACE PAGE REPLACE

- REPORT

- RUNSTATS TABLESPACE

- STOSPACE

SHRLEVEL NONE
When REORG INDEX SHRLEVEL NONE is executed, the write claim class is drained for the index or index partition during the UNLOAD phase and all claim classes are drained during both the SORT and BUILD phase. Remember, the SORT phase can be skipped.

SHRLEVEL REFERENCE
When REORG INDEX SHRLEVEL REFERENCE is executed, the write claim class is drained for the index or index partition during the UNLOAD phase—all claim classes are drained during the SWITCH phase.

SHRLEVEL CHANGE
When REORG INDEX SHRLEVEL CHANGE is executed, the read claim class is claimed for the index or index partition during the UNLOAD phase. Additionally, the write claim class is drained during the last iteration of the log processing—all claim classes are drained during both the SWITCH phase.

REORG **Guidelines**

By adhering to the following guidelines, you will ensure efficient and effective reorganization of DB2 table spaces.

Ensure That Adequate Recovery Is Available   Take an image copy of every table space to be reorganized before executing the REORG utility. All image copies taken before the reorganization are marked as invalid for current point-in-time recovery by the REORG utility. These image copies can be used only with the TORBA or TOCOPY options of the RECOVER utility.

Take an image copy of every table space reorganized after using the LOG NO option of the REORG utility. All table spaces reorganized with the LOG NO option are placed into copy pending status.

Analyze Clustering Before Reorganizing   Consider the CLUSTER RATIO of a table space before reorganizing. If the table space to be reorganized is not clustered, specify the SORTDATA parameter. The SORTDATA option causes the data to be unloaded according to its physical sequence in the table space. The data is then sorted in sequence by the clustering index columns.

If the SORTDATA parameter is not specified, the table space data is unloaded using the clustering index, which is highly efficient when the table space is clustered. If the table space is not clustered, however, unloading by the clustering index causes REORG to scan the table space data in an inefficient manner. Refer to Chapter 26, "DB2 Object Monitoring Using the DB2 Catalog and RTS," for DB2 Catalog queries to obtain cluster ratio.

DB2 does not consider a default clustering index to be clustering for the purposes of unloading for a REORG. Only an explicitly created clustering index, if available, will be used.

If the cluster ratio for a table space is less than 90%, consider using the SORTDATA option. When data is less than 90% clustered, unloading physically and sorting is usually more efficient than scanning data. Furthermore, the DBA statistics NEAROFFPOS and FAROFFPOS can be used to judge whether to use the SORTDATA option.

Monitor the results of the REORG utility with and without the SORTDATA option, however, to gauge its effectiveness with different application table spaces.

> **NOTE**
>
> Use of the SORTDATA option can increase the sort work requirements of the REORG utility, especially for tables with long rows and few indexes.

V8   **Rebalance Partitions Using REORG**   As of DB2 V8, you can rebalance table space partitions using the new REBALANCE parameter. Specifying this parameter causes DB2 to rebalance the data such that it is evenly distributed across the partitions. More details on this options can be found in Chapter 7, "Database Change Management and Schema Evolution."

Follow General Reorganization Rules   One rule of thumb for smaller indexes is to reorganize the number of levels is greater than four. For indexes on larger tables four (or more) levels may be completely normal. Other indicators that signify a REORG INDEX is needed are when the LEAFDIST value is large or PSEUDO_DEL_ENTRIES has grown.

Reorganize table spaces when the CLUSTER RATIO drops below 95% or when FARINDREF is large. Reorganizing a large table space as soon as the CLUSTER RATIO is not 100% could produce significant performance gains.

Consider Using SORTKEYS   REORG provides a SORTKEYS parameter similar to the SORTKEYS parameter of LOAD. When more than multiple indexes exist and need to be created, consider using the SORTKEYS keyword. When SORTKEYS is specified, index keys are sorted in parallel with the RELOAD and BUILD phases, thereby improving performance.

An estimate of the number of keys to be sorted can be supplied. To estimate the number of keys to sort, use the following calculation:

```
Number of Keys = (Total number of rows in the table) x
                 [(number of indexes on the table) +
                 (number of foreign keys)]
```

Consider Using NOSYSREC   The NOSYSREC option can be used so that the REORG process does not require unload data set. This can enhance performance because intermediate disk I/O is eliminated. To use the NOSYSREC option, neither the UNLOAD PAUSE nor the UNLOAD ONLY options can be used. Furthermore, you must specify SORTDATA, and SHRLEVEL REFERENCE or SHRLEVEL CHANGE.

However, the NOSYSREC option affects the restartability of the REORG utility. For a SHRLEVEL REFERENCE table space REORG, if an error occurs during the RELOAD phase, you must restart at the UNLOAD phase, effectively unloading all of the data again. This is so because the previously unloaded data has not been saved to disk. Likewise, for a REORG TABLESPACE SHRLEVEL NONE, if an error occurs during the RELOAD phase, a RECOVER TABLESPACE is required. Therefore, it is wise to create an image copy prior to running REORG SHRLEVEL NONE with the NOSYSREC option.

Consider Specifying REUSE   When the REUSE option is used in conjunction with SHRLEVEL NONE, the REORG utility will logically reset and reuse STOGROUP-managed data sets without deleting and redefining them. If REUSE is not specified, the underlying data sets will be deleted and redefined as part of the REORG process. By eliminating the delete and redefine step, you can enhance the overall performance of the reorganization because less work needs to be done. However, if a data set is in multiple extents, the extents will not be released if you specify the REUSE parameter.

Keep in mind that the extents will not be released if you use the REUSE parameter to REORG an object whose data set has multiple extents. Furthermore, if you are reorganizing to increase the primary or secondary storage, using REUSE causes DB2 to not apply any PRIQTY or SECQTY changes.

> **CAUTION**
> The REUSE option is not applicable with a SHRLEVEL REFERENCE or SHRLEVEL CHANGE REORG.

V8 **Use SCOPE PENDING to Reorganize Changed Table Spaces**   Specify SCOPE PENDING to reorganize only those table spaces or partitions that are in a REORG-pending status. Typically, the scope for a REORG TABLESPACE job should be set to SCOPE ALL to reorganize all specified table spaces. However, you might want to reorganize specified table spaces or partitions only if they are in a REORG-pending status (REORP or AREO*). Recall from Chapter 7 that these states can be set when online schema changes are implemented.

> **CAUTION**
>
> If you are reorganizing a partition range using SCOPE PENDING, be sure that a partition adjacent to the specified range is not also in a REORG-pending status. If this is the case, the utility will fail.

Buffer REORG Work Data Sets   Ensure that adequate buffering is specified for the work data set by explicitly coding a larger BUFNO parameter in the REORG utility JCL for the SYSUT1 and SYSREC DD statements. The BUFNO parameter creates read and write buffers in main storage for the data set, thereby enhancing the utility's performance. A BUFNO of approximately 20 is recommended for medium-sized table spaces, and a BUFNO between 50 and 100 is recommended for larger table spaces. However, ensure that sufficient memory (real or expanded) is available before increasing the BUFNO specification for your REORG work data sets.

Specify KEEPDICTIONARY for Performance   The REORG utility will rebuild the compression dictionary for table spaces defined with the COMPRESS YES parameter. Specifying the KEEP-DICTIONARY parameter causes the REORG utility to bypass dictionary rebuilding.

This can improve the overall performance of the REORG utility because the CPU cycles used to build the dictionary can be avoided. However, as the compression ratio deteriorates, the LRECL of the SYSREC data set will get longer. Do not utilize the KEEPDICTIONARY option if the type of data in the table has changed significantly since the last time the dictionary was built. Remember, the dictionary is built at LOAD or REORG time only. If the type of data being stored has changed significantly, allowing the REORG utility to rebuild the compression dictionary will provide for more optimal data compression.

Be Aware of VARCHAR Overhead   The REORG utility unloads VARCHAR columns by padding them with spaces to their maximum length. This reduces the efficiency of reorganizing.

Be Aware of VSAM DELETE and DEFINE Activity   The underlying VSAM data sets for STOGROUP-defined table spaces and indexes are deleted and defined by the REORG utility. If the table space or index data set has been user-defined, the corresponding VSAM data set is not deleted.

Consider Concurrently Reorganizing Partitions   It is possible to execute the REORG utility concurrently on separate partitions of a single partitioned table space. By reorganizing partitions concurrently, the overall elapsed time to complete the REORG should be substantially lower than a single REORG of the entire partitioned table space. However, the overall CPU usage will probably increase. This is usually a satisfactory trade-off however, as elapsed time impacts overall data availability.

Use REORG to Move STOGROUP-Defined Data Sets   The REORG utility can be used to reallocate and move STOGROUP-defined data sets. By altering STOGROUP, PRIQTY, or SECQTY and then reorganizing the table space or index, data set level modification can be implemented. The REUSE option must *not* be specified to ensure that underlying data sets are deleted and redefined.

Use REORG to Archive Data   The REORG utility can be used to delete data from a table in the table space and archive it to a data set. To archive rows during a REORG, use the DISCARD option and the DISCARDDN to indicate a data set to hold the discarded data. The criteria for discarding is specified using the FROM TABLE and WHEN clause.

The table space being reorganized can contain more than one table. You can use the FROM TABLE clause to indicate which tables are to be processed for discards. Multiple tables can be specified. The table cannot be a DB2 Catalog table.

The WHEN clause is used to define the specific criteria for discarding. A selection condition can be coded in the WHEN clause indicating which records in the table space are to be discarded. If the WHEN clause is not coded, no records are discarded.

The WHEN clause is basically an SQL predicate used to specify particular data. It specifies a condition that is true, false, or unknown for the row. When the condition evaluates to true, the row is discarded. For example,

```
REORG TABLESPACE (DSN8D81A.DSN8S81P)
    DISCARD DISCARDDN ARCHDD
    FROM TABLE DSN8810.ACT
    WHEN ACTNO < 100
```

This REORG statement indicates that any row of DSN8810.ACT that contains an ACTNO value less than 100 will be removed from the table and placed in the data set specified by ARCHDD.

> **CAUTION**
>
> Specifying DISCARD potentially can cause a performance degradation for the REORG process. When archiving data using DISCARD, keep in mind that rows are decompressed (if compression is enabled) and any edit routines are decoded. If you specify a DISCARDDN data set, any field procedures on the rows will be decoded, and SMALLINT, INTEGER, FLOAT, DECIMAL, DATE, TIME, and TIMESTAMP columns will be converted to external format.
>
> When not using DISCARD, REORG will bypass all edit routines, field procedures, and validation procedures.

When running a REORG with the DISCARD option on a table involved in a referential constraint, you must run CHECK DATA against any objects placed in a CHECK pending state as a result of the data being archived.

Collect Inline RUNSTATS Using the STATISTICS Option   Collecting statistics during the execution of the REORG utility, referred to as inline RUNSTATS, is preferable to running a subsequent RUNSTATS after every REORG. By specifying the STATISTICS keyword, up-to-date statistics will be generated during the REORG.

Consider Reorganizing Indexes More Frequently Than Table Spaces   The cost of reorganizing an index is small compared to the cost of reorganizing a table space. Sometimes, simply executing REORG INDEX on a table space's indexes can enhance system performance. Reorganizing an index will not impact clustering, but it will do the following:

- Possibly impact the number of index levels.

- Reorganize and optimize the index page layout, removing inefficiencies introduced due to page splits.

- Reset the LEAFDIST value to 0 (or close to 0).

- Reset PSEUDO_DEL_ENTRIES to 0.

- Reduce or eliminate data set extents.

- Apply any new PRIQTY, SECQTY, or STOGROUP assignments.

- Reset free space.

Additionally, reorganizing indexes using SHRLEVEL CHANGE is simpler than reorganizing table spaces online because REORG INDEX SHRLEVEL CHANGE does not use a mapping table. This makes reorganizing indexes with concurrent data access easier to administer and maintain.

Consider Design Changes to Reduce REORG Frequency   You can reduce the frequency of REORG by adding more free space (PCTFREE, FREEPAGE), updating in place to preformatted tables (all possible rows), avoiding VARCHAR, and reorganizing indexes more frequently.

CHAPTER 34

Catalog Manipulation Utilities

The DB2 Catalog and the DB2 Directory are essential to the continuing performance of your DB2 subsystem. This chapter discusses several utilities that can help you keep these system databases and structures in an optimal state.

The CATENFM Utility

The CATENFM utility is used to change the mode of a DB2 V8 subsystem. It can be used to enter enabling-new-function mode and new-function mode. Refer to Appendix G, "DB2 Version 8 Overview," for more details about the modes of DB2 Version 8.

> **NOTE**
>
> All new V8 functionality is unavailable until the DB2 subsystem enters new-function mode.

This utility should only be used by a DBA or system programmer who understands the ramifications of moving from one DB2 V8 mode to another.

The CATMAINT Utility

The CATMAINT utility is used when migrating from one version or release of DB2 to another. It changes the structure of the DB2 Catalog by altering and creating DB2 tables and indexes using the special links and hashes in the DB2 Catalog database. The CATMAINT utility modifies the DB2 Catalog objects in place.

An execution of CATMAINT cannot be partially successful; all the catalog changes are made when the job is successful, or none are made when the job fails.

Only an INSTALL SYSADM as specified in the DSNZPARMs can execute the CATMAINT utility.

CATMAINT **Guidelines**

The guideline presented next should be followed when you are considering CATMAINT usage.

Use CATMAINT **Only As Directed**   The CATMAINT utility should be used only when migrating to a new release of DB2, and then only as directed by IBM in the DB2 release migration procedures.

The DSNJCNVB **Utility**

V8   The DSNJCNVB utility is used to convert the bootstrap data set (BSDS) so that it can support up to 10,000 archive log volumes and 93 active log data sets per log copy.

If you do not convert the BSDS, only 1,000 archive log volumes and 31 active log data sets per log copy can be managed.

The DSNJCNVB utility should be executed as a batch job only when DB2 is not operational. Furthermore, DSNJCNVB can only be run on a DB2 V8 subsystem in new-function mode. Although converting the BSDS is optional, it is highly recommended for large or highly-active DB2 shops.

Expand the Size of the BSDS Before Converting   If you have migrated to V8 from a previous version of DB2, you will need to create a larger BSDS before converting it with DSNJCNVB.

After you have migrated to V8 new-function mode, execute the following steps to prepare to run the DSNJCNVB utility:

1. Rename your existing BSDS copy 1 data set. Be sure to retain your original copy of the BSDS so you can restore it in case of a failure during conversion.

2. Allocate a larger BSDS data set using the VSAM DEFINE statement in installation job DSNTIJIN, using the original BSDS name.

3. Use VSAM REPRO to copy the original data set to the new, larger data set.

4. Repeat steps 1 through 3 for copy 2 of the BSDS (if you are using dual BSDSs).

Finally, after expanding the size of your BSDSs, you can invoke the conversion utility, DSNJCNVB, using the JCL snippet shown in Listing 34.1. The SYSUT1 and SYSUT2 DDNAMEs specify the data sets for copy 1 and copy 2 of the BSDS.

LISTING 34.1   DSNJCNVB JCL

```
//DSNJCNVB EXEC PGM=DSNJCNVB
//STEPLIB  DD    DISP=SHR,DSN=DB2P.SDSNEXIT
//         DD    DISP=SHR,DSN=DB2P.SDSNLOAD
//SYSUT1   DD    DISP=OLD,DSN=DB2P.BSDS01
//SYSUT2   DD    DISP=OLD,DSN=DB2P.BSDS02
//SYSPRINT DD    SYSOUT=*
```

The MODIFY Utility

The MODIFY utility is used to delete rows from DB2 Catalog and DB2 Directory tables.
MODIFY is the clean-up utility. When COPY information in the DB2 Catalog or DB2
Directory is no longer relevant or desirable, MODIFY can be used to delete the unwanted
rows. The MODIFY RECOVERY utility deletes rows related to data recovery from both the DB2
Catalog and DB2 Directory. The MODIFY STATISTICS utility deletes rows related to database
statistics from the DB2 Catalog.

MODIFY Phases

The MODIFY utility uses three phases, regardless of whether recovery or statistical information is being deleted:

UTILINIT	Sets up and initializes the MODIFY utility
MODIFY	Deletes rows from the appropriate DB2 Catalog table(s)
UTILTERM	Performs the final utility cleanup

The MODIFY RECOVERY Utility

The MODIFY RECOVERY utility removes recovery information from SYSIBM.SYSCOPY and
DSNDB01.SYSLGRNX. Recovery information can be removed in two ways. You can delete
rows that are older than a specified number of days, or before a specified date.

You cannot use MODIFY RECOVERY to explicitly remove index copies from the DB2 Catalog.
Index copies are removed implicitly as table space copies are removed. When you run
MODIFY RECOVERY on a table space, the utility also removes SYSIBM.SYSCOPY and
DSNDB01.SYSLGRNX rows that meet the AGE and DATE criteria for related indexes that were
defined with COPY YES.

> **CAUTION**
>
> Records are not removed from SYSLGRNX when you drop a table space. However, if you create a
> new table space and DB2 reuses the DBID and PSID, then the SYSLGRNX records will be deleted.
> But it is a good idea to regularly run MODIFY RECOVERY to remove SYSLGRNX records so that you
> are not stuck with obsolete records after dropping a table space.

The JCL to execute the MODIFY utility with the RECOVERY option is provided in Listing 34.2.
Both the AGE and DATE options are shown.

LISTING 34.2   MODIFY RECOVERY JCL

```
//DB2JOBU  JOB (UTILITY),'DB2 MOD RCV',MSGCLASS=X,CLASS=X,
//         NOTIFY=USER
//*
//*****************************************************************
//*
//*         DB2 MODIFY RECOVERY UTILITY
//*
```

34

LISTING 34.2   Continued

```
//******************************************************************
//*
//UTIL EXEC DSNUPROC,SYSTEM=DSN,UID='MODIRECV',UTPROC="
//*
//*  UTILITY INPUT CONTROL STATEMENTS
//*    1. The first statement deletes all SYSCOPY information
//*       older than 80 days for the named table space.
//*    2. The second statement deletes all SYSCOPY information
//*       with a date before December 31, 1999 for the named
//*       table space.
//*
//DSNUPROC.SYSIN    DD  *
    MODIFY RECOVERY TABLESPACE DSN8D81A.DSN8S81E AGE (80)
    MODIFY RECOVERY TABLESPACE DSN8D81A.DSN8S81D DATE (19991231)
/*
//
```

MODIFY RECOVERY Locking Considerations

The MODIFY RECOVERY utility can run concurrently on the same object with all utilities *except* the following:

- COPY TABLESPACE
- LOAD
- MERGECOPY
- MODIFY RECOVERY
- RECOVER
- REORG

The MODIFY RECOVERY utility will drain write claim classes for the table space or partition being operated upon.

MODIFY RECOVERY Guidelines

When running MODIFY RECOVERY you should consider using the following tips and techniques.

Run MODIFY RECOVERY **Regularly**   The MODIFY RECOVERY utility should be run monthly to eliminate old recovery information stored in SYSIBM.SYSCOPY and DSNDB01.SYSLGRNX. Running this utility more frequently is usually difficult to administer. Running it less frequently causes the recovery tables to grow, affecting the performance of the DB2 CHECK, COPY, LOAD, MERGECOPY, RECOVER, and REORG utilities. Access to other DB2 Catalog tables on the same DASD volumes as these tables also may be degraded.

> **CAUTION**
>
> The MODIFY RECOVERY utility places an X lock on the SYSCOPY table space. As such, run MODIFY RECOVERY when there is little or no concurrent SYSCOPY activity.

Old recovery information must be defined on an application-by-application basis. Usually, DB2 applications run the COPY utility for all table spaces at a consistent time. Sometimes, however, the definition of what should be deleted must be made on a tablespace-by-tablespace basis. One way to define "old recovery information" is anything that is older than the oldest archive log.

> **CAUTION**
>
> MODIFY RECOVERY will delete records from SYSLGRNX only if there are SYSCOPY records to delete. So, if you never took an image copy, SYSLGRNX records were never deleted.
>
> To resolve this situation, start by making image copies of the table spaces in question. The next day, take another image copy of the same table spaces and then run MODIFY RECOVERY specifying DELETE AGE(0). This will delete all but the most recent image copy information from SYSCOPY and SYSLGRNX.

Ensure That Two Full Copies Are Always Available   As a general rule, leave at least two full image copy data sets for each table space in the SYSIBM.SYSCOPY table. In this way, DB2 can use a previous image copy if the most recent one is damaged or unavailable. Additionally, if the full image copy data sets are SHRLEVEL CHANGE, ensure that the log is older than the oldest image copy. If the log does not predate the oldest image, the image copy is not very useful.

Synchronize MODIFY RECOVERY Execution with the Deletion of Log and Copy Data Sets
The MODIFY RECOVERY utility deletes rows from only the SYSIBM.SYSCOPY and DSNDB01.SYSLGRNX tables. It does not physically delete the image copy data sets corresponding to the deleted SYSIBM.SYSCOPY rows, nor does it physically delete the log data sets associated with the deleted DSNDB01.SYSLGRNX log ranges. To delete these data sets, run separate jobs—at the same time that MODIFY RECOVERY is run—using IEFBR14 or IDCAMS. Alternatively, assign an expiration date to the log data sets.

Be Aware of Copy Pending Ramifications   If MODIFY RECOVERY deletes recovery information for a table space such that full recovery cannot be accomplished, the table space is placed in copy pending status.

Be Aware of the Nonstandard DATE Format   Be careful when specifying the DATE option of the MODIFY RECOVERY utility. The data is in the format YYYYMMDD, rather than the standard DB2 date format. If you want October 16, 2002, for example, you must specify it as 20021016 rather than as 2002-10-16.

The MODIFY STATISTICS Utility

The purpose of the MODIFY STATISTICS utility is to remove unwanted, or outdated, statistics history records from the DB2 system catalog tables.

> **NOTE**
>
> Long-time DB2 users might remember the MODIFY STATISTICS utility. It existed in older releases of DB2 to remove non-uniform distribution statistics. With DB2 V7, MODIFY STATISTICS is reintroduced, but with enhanced functionality.

Using MODIFY STATISTICS you can remove rows based on date or age. By specifying a date, MODIFY STATISTICS will remove any historical statistics that are older than that date; by specifying an age, MODIFY STATISTICS will remove any historical statistics that are at least that old. Furthermore, you can target the effects of MODIFY STATISTICS to a table space, an index space, or an index.

It is a good idea to run the MODIFY STATISTICS utility on a regular basis to get rid of old and outdated statistical information in the DB2 Catalog. By deleting outdated information, you can improve performance for processes that access data from the historical statistics tables in the DB2 Catalog.

> **CAUTION**
>
> Be careful not to delete historical statistics that you want to maintain for performance analysis purposes. It can be useful to keep historical statistics to compare the database size and structure information from one period to another. But if you use MODIFY STATISTICS to delete the historical statistics, that information is forever lost and you can no longer use it for such purposes.

The DB2 Catalog tables that contain historical statistics are as follows:

SYSIBM.SYSCOLDIST_HIST	SYSIBM.SYSCOLUMNS_HIST
SYSIBM.SYSINDEXES_HIST	SYSIBM.SYSINDEXPART_HIST
SYSIBM.SYSINDEXSTATS_HIST	SYSIBM.SYSLOBSTATS_HIST
SYSIBM.SYSTABLEPART_HIST	SYSIBM.SYSTABSTATS_HIST
SYSIBM.SYSTABLES_HIST	

Before a process or user can execute the MODIFY STATISTICS utility, one of the following privileges must already exist or have been granted to the user or process:

- DBADM authority for the database
- DBCTRL authority for the database
- DBMAINT authority for the database
- SYSADM authority
- SYSCTRL authority
- Install SYSOPR (only on DB2 Directory and DB2 Catalog table spaces)

The DELETE Option

The DELETE parameter is used to indicate which rows are to be deleted from which DB2 Catalog tables. There are three options that can be specified on the DELETE parameter:

- ALL—Deletes all statistical history rows that are related to the specified database object from all of the DB2 Catalog history tables.
- ACCESSPATH—Deletes only the statistics that are relevant for access path determination for the specified database object from the following DB2 Catalog statistical

history tables: `SYSIBM.SYSINDEXPART_HIST`, `SYSIBM.SYSTABLEPART_HIST`, and `SYSIBM.SYSLOBSTATS_HIST`.

- `SPACE`—Deletes only the space tuning statistics for the specified database object from the following DB2 Catalog statistical history tables: `SYSIBM.SYSINDEXPART_HIST`, `SYSIBM.SYSTABLEPART_HIST`, and `SYSIBM.SYSLOBSTATS_HIST`.

Sample JCL to execute the `MODIFY STATISTICS` utility is provided in Listing 34.3. This job will remove the historical access path statistics for all table spaces in the `GLDB0010` database that are more than 14 days old.

LISTING 34.3   MODIFY STATISTICS JCL

```
//DB2JOBU  JOB (UTILITY),'DB2 MOD RCV',MSGCLASS=X,CLASS=X,
//          NOTIFY=USER
//*
//*****************************************************************
//*
//*          DB2 MODIFY RECOVERY UTILITY
//*
//*****************************************************************
//*
//UTIL EXEC DSNUPROC,SYSTEM=DSN,UID='MODISTAT',UTPROC="
//*
//*   UTILITY INPUT CONTROL STATEMENTS
//*     1. Remove all historical stats over 14 days old
//*        for all table spaces in the GLDB0010 database.
//*
//DSNUPROC.SYSUT1 DD DSN=DB2JOBU. MODISTAT.STEP1.SYSUT1,
//        DISP=(MOD,DELETE,CATLG),
//        UNIT=SYSDA,SPACE=(8000,(200,20),,,ROUND)
//DSNUPROC.SYSERR DD DSN=DB2JOBU. MODISTAT.STEP1.SYSERR,
//        DISP=(MOD,DELETE,CATLG),
//        UNIT=SYSDA,SPACE=(6000,(20,20),,,ROUND)
//DSNUPROC.SORTOUT DD DSN=DB2JOBU. MODISTAT.STEP1.SORTOUT,
//        DISP=(MOD,DELETE,CATLG),
//        UNIT=SYSDA,SPACE=(6000,(20,20),,,ROUND)
//DSNUPROC.SYSIN    DD  *
   LISTDEF GLDB INCLUDE TABLESPACE GLDB0010.*
   MODIFY STATISTICS LIST GLDB
      DELETE ACCESSPATH AGE 14
/*
//
```

MODIFY STATISTICS Guidelines

When developing your `MODIFY STATISTICS` plan, consider following these subsequent tips and techniques.

Run MODIFY STATISTICS As Needed   Use `MODIFY STATISTICS` to pare down the size of the DB2 Catalog. As you execute `RUNSTATS`, the number of historical statistics rows will increase. Over time, the older historical statistics will cease to be of value to you. Be sure to consistently compare the number of historical statistics rows that exist against the number needed for your analysis purposes. And execute MODIFY STATISTICS to maintain the historical statistics at the proper balance for your needs.

Failure to follow this guideline will increase the size of the DB2 Catalog and potentially degrade the performance of RUNSTATS, DDL, and your catalog queries.

Historical Information Is Not Stored for Manual Catalog Changes   Be aware that when you manually insert, update, or delete information into the DB2 Catalog that DB2 will not store historical information for those modifications in the historical DB2 Catalog tables.

Terminate and Restart Issues   It is possible to terminate the MODIFY STATISTICS utility during any of its three phases. And you can then restart the MODIFY STATISTICS utility, too. However, it will restart from the beginning all over again.

The RUNSTATS Utility

The RUNSTATS utility collects statistical information for DB2 tables, table spaces, partitions, indexes, and columns. It can place this information into DB2 Catalog tables or simply produce a report of the statistical information. The statistics in these tables are used for two primary reasons: to provide organizational information for DBAs and to be used as input to the DB2 optimizer during the BIND process to determine optimal access paths for SQL queries. The statistical information can also be queried using SQL. Several sample DB2 Catalog queries were presented in Chapter 26, "DB2 Object Monitoring Using the DB2 Catalog and RTS." The diagram in Figure 34.1 details the functionality of the RUNSTATS utility.

You can use the RUNSTATS utility to

- Produce a statistics report without updating the DB2 Catalog tables

- Update the DB2 Catalog with only DB2 optimizer statistics

- Update the DB2 Catalog with only DBA monitoring statistics

- Update the DB2 Catalog with all the statistics that have been gathered

This flexibility can be useful when you want to determine the effect of RUNSTATS on specific SQL queries—without updating the current useable statistics. Also, if the statistics used by the DB2 optimizer have been modified, RUNSTATS can still be run to gather the DBA monitoring statistics.

V8 Additionally, as of DB2 V8, you can execute RUNSTATS specifying UPDATE NONE and REPORT NO. In this case, RUNSTATS neither reports on, nor updates the statistics in the catalog. This option is available to simply invalidate the dynamic SQL statement cache. Executing RUNSTATS always invalidates the dynamic cache, but prior to V8 you were forced either to update the statistics in the DB2 Catalog or produce a report of the statistics.

Consult Tables 34.1 and 34.2 for a breakdown of the types of statistics gathered by RUNSTATS. The information in this table is accurate as of DB2 V8.

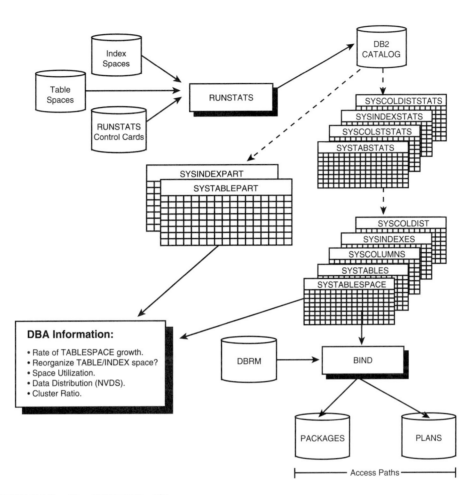

FIGURE 34.1   The RUNSTATS utility.

TABLE 34.1   RUNSTATS Statistics Used to Determine Access Paths

DB2 Catalog Table	Column	Description
SYSIBM.SYSTABLES	CARDF	Number of rows for a table
	NPAGES	Number of pages on which rows of this table appear
	NPAGESF	Total number of pages used by the table
	PCTROWCOMP	Percentage of total active rows that are compressed for this table
SYSIBM.SYSTABSTATS	CARDF	Number of rows in the table space partition
	NPAGES	Number of pages used by the table space partition
SYSIBM.SYSTABLESPACE	NACTIVEF	Number of allocated table space pages (or NACTIVE)

34

TABLE 34.1 Continued

DB2 Catalog Table	Column	Description
SYSIBM.SYSCOLUMNS	LOW2KEY	Second lowest value for the column
	HIGH2KEY	Second highest value for the column
	COLCARDF	Number of distinct values for the column
SYSIBM.SYSCOLDIST	CARDF	Number of distinct values for the column group
	COLVALUE	Nonuniform distribution column value
	FREQUENCYF	Percentage (* 100) that the value in EXITPARM exists in the column
	NUMCOLUMNS	Number of columns associated with the statistics
	COLGROUPCOLNO	Identifies the set of columns associated with the statistics
SYSIBM.SYSINDEXES	CLUSTERRATIOF	Percentage of rows in clustered order (when multiplied by 100)
	CLUSTERING	Whether CLUSTER was specified when the index was created
	FIRSTKEYCARDF	Number of distinct values for the first column of the index key
	FULLKEYCARDF	Number of distinct values for the full index key
	NLEAF	Number of active leaf pages
	NLEVELS	Number of index b-tree levels

TABLE 34.2 RUNSTATS Statistics Used by DBAs for Monitoring and Tuning

DB2 Catalog Table	Column	Description
SYSIBM.SYSTABLESPACE	AVGROWLEN	Average length of the rows for all tables in this table space
SYSIBM.SYSTABLES	AVGROWLEN	Average length of the rows for this table
SYSIBM.SYSTABLES_HIST	AVGROWLEN	Historical average lengths of the rows for this table
SYSIBM.SYSTABLEPART	AVGROWLEN	Average length of the rows for the tables in the table space
	CARDF	Number of rows in the table space or partition; or number of LOBs in the LOB table space
	DSNUM	Number of data sets
	EXTENTS	Number of data set extents
	NEARINDREF	Number of rows between 2 and 16 pages from their original page
	FARINDREF	Number of rows more than 16 pages from their original page
	PAGESAVE	Percentage of pages saved due to data compression
	PERCACTIVE	Percentage of space that contains table rows in this table space

TABLE 34.2   Continued

DB2 Catalog Table	Column	Description
	PERCDROP	Percentage of space used by rows from dropped tables
	SPACE	The currently allocated space for all extents, in K; a value of –1 means the data set was defined using DEFINE NO
	SPACEF	The currently allocated space for all extents, in K
	PQTY	Primary space allocation in 4K blocks for the data set
	SQTY	Secondary space allocation in 4K blocks for the data set (SMALLINT format)
	SQTYI	Secondary space allocation in 4K blocks for the data set (INTEGER format)
SYSIBM.SYSTABLEPARTHIST	AVGROWLEN	Average length of the rows for the tables in the table space
SYSIBM.SYSINDEXES	AVGKEYLEN	Average length of the keys in the index
SYSIBM.SYSINDEXESHIST	AVGKEYLEN	Average historical length of the keys in the index
SYSIBM.SYSINDEXPART	AVGKEYLEN	Average length of the keys in the index
	CARDF	Number of rows referenced by the index or partition
	DSNUM	Number of data sets
	EXTENTS	Number of data set extents
	LEAFDIST	Average distance between successive pages multiplied by 100
	LEAFNEAR	Number of leaf pages located physically near a previous leaf page for successive active leaf pages
	LEAFFAR	Number of leaf pages located physically far from a previous leaf page for successive active leaf pages
	SPACE	The currently allocated space for all extents, in K; a value of –1 means the data set was defined using DEFINE NO
	SPACEF	The currently allocated space for all extents, in K
	PSEUDO_DEL_ENTRIES	Number of pseudo-deleted keys (that is, marked for deletion, but the data has not yet been deleted)
	NEAROFFPOSF	Number of times you must access a near-off page when accessing all rows in indexed order
	FAROFFPOSF	Number of times you must access a far-off page when accessing all rows in indexed order

34

TABLE 34.2   Continued

DB2 Catalog Table	Column	Description
	PQTY	Primary space allocation in 4K blocks for the data set
	SQTY	Secondary space allocation in 4K blocks for the data set (SMALLINT format)
	SQTYI	Secondary space allocation in 4K blocks for the data set (INTEGER format)
SYSIBM.SYSINDEXPART_HIST	AVGKEYLEN	Average historical length of the keys in the index
SYSIBM.SYSLOBSTATS	FREESPACE	Amount of free space in the LOB table space
	ORGRATIO	Ratio of organization for the LOB table space; the greater the value exceeds 1, the less organized the LOB table space

The Two Options for Running RUNSTATS

There are two options for running RUNSTATS: You can collect statistics either at the table space level or at the index level. Additionally, you can execute RUNSTATS at the partition level for both table spaces and indexes (including data-partitioned secondary indexes).

> **NOTE**
>
> When RUNSTATS are collects on a single partition, the partition-level statistics are used to update the aggregate statistics for the entire object.

When collecting statistics at the table space level, you can optionally specify tables, indexes, and specific columns. Listing 34.4 shows RUNSTATS JCL executing the RUNSTATS utility twice: once for the DSN8810.DEPT table space and all its indexes and a second time for the DSN8810.EMP table and several of its columns.

LISTING 34.4   RUNSTATS TABLESPACE JCL

```
//DB2JOBU  JOB (UTILITY),'DB2 RUNSTATS',MSGCLASS=X,CLASS=X,
//           NOTIFY=USER
//*
//****************************************************************
//*
//*            DB2 RUNSTATS TABLESPACE UTILITY
//*
//****************************************************************
//*
//UTIL EXEC DSNUPROC,SYSTEM=DSN,UID='STATSTS',UTPROC="
//*
//*  UTILITY INPUT CONTROL STATEMENTS
//*    1. The first statement accumulates statistics for the
//*       given table space based on the named index columns.
//*    2. The second statement accumulates statistics only for
//*       the named table and columns in the named table space.
//*
```

LISTING 34.4   Continued

```
//DSNUPROC.SYSIN    DD  *
    RUNSTATS TABLESPACE DSN8D81A.DSN8S81D
        INDEX (ALL)     SHRLEVEL REFERENCE
    RUNSTATS TABLESPACE DSN8D81A.DSN8S81E
        TABLE (DSN8810.EMO)
        COLUMN (FIRSTNME,MIDINIT,LASTNAME,SALARY,BONUS,COMM)
        SHRLEVEL REFERENCE
/*
//
```

The other form of RUNSTATS operates at the index level. Listing 34.5 offers sample JCL to execute RUNSTATS for a specific DB2 index.

LISTING 34.5   RUNSTATS INDEX JCL

```
//DB2JOBU   JOB (UTILITY),'DB2 RUNS IX',MSGCLASS=X,CLASS=X,
//          NOTIFY=USER
//*
//*****************************************************************
//*
//*          DB2 RUNSTATS INDEX UTILITY
//*
//*****************************************************************
//*
//UTIL EXEC DSNUPROC,SYSTEM=DSN,UID='STATSIX',UTPROC="
//*
//*   UTILITY INPUT CONTROL STATEMENTS
//*      The RUNSTATS statement accumulates statistics for the
//*      given index.
//*
//DSNUPROC.SYSIN    DD  *
    RUNSTATS INDEX (DSN8810.XEMPPROJACT2)
/*
//
```

RUNSTATS **Phases**

The RUNSTATS utility has three phases:

UTILINIT	Sets up and initializes the RUNSTATS utility
RUNSTATS	Samples the table space data, the index data, or both, and then updates the DB2 Catalog tables with the statistical information
UTILTERM	Performs the final utility cleanup

RUNSTATS **Locking Considerations**

The RUNSTATS utility, regardless of whether it is being run to collect TABLESPACE statistics or INDEX statistics, can operate concurrently with the following utilities:

- CHECK DATA DELETE NO

- CHECK INDEX

- CHECK LOB

- COPY

- DIAGNOSE

- MERGECOPY

- MODIFY RECOVERY

- QUIESCE

- REORG TABLESPACE UNLOAD ONLY

- REPAIR (DUMP or MODIFY)

- REPORT

- RUNSTATS

- STOSPACE

- UNLOAD

Furthermore, RUNSTATS TABLESPACE can operate concurrently with RECOVER INDEX, REBUILD INDEX, REORG INDEX, and REPAIR LOCATE INDEX PAGE REPLACE.

RUNSTATS INDEX can be run concurrently with the following:

- RECOVER TABLESPACE (no options)

- RECOVER ERROR RANGE

- REPAIR LOCATE KEY or RID (DELETE or REPLACE), only if SHRLEVEL CHANGE is specified

- REPAIR LOCATE TABLESPACE PAGE REPLACE

When the RUNSTATS utility is executed with the SHRLEVEL REFERENCE option, it drains write claim classes to the table space, table space partition, index, or index partition. If SHRLEVEL CHANGE is specified, the RUNSTATS utility will claim the read claim class for the object being operated upon; however, no locking occurs if the object is a type 2 index.

DB2 Catalog Tables Updated by RUNSTATS

The actual DB2 Catalog tables and statistics that get updated by RUNSTATS vary depending on the RUNSTATS options specified, primarily the UPDATE option. There are three options that can be specified on the UPDATE parameter:

- ALL—Accumulates and updates all statistics related to the specified database object.

- ACCESSPATH—Accumulates and updates only the statistics that are relevant for access path determination for the specified database object.

- SPACE—Accumulates and updates only the space tuning statistics for the specified database object.

Now, if you execute RUNSTATS TABLESPACE using the UPDATE ALL option, the following DB2 Catalog tables are updated:

- SYSTABLESPACE

- SYSTABLEPART

- SYSTABLES

- SYSTABSTATS

- SYSLOBSTATS

However, if RUNSTATS TABLESPACE is run with the UPDATE ACCESSPATH option, only SYSTABLESPACE, SYSTABLES, and SYSTABSTATS are updated. If RUNSTATS TABLESPACE is run specifying UPDATE SPACE, then SYSTABSTATS, SYSTABLEPART, SYSTABLES, and SYSLOBSTATS are updated.

For RUNSTATS TABLE using either the UPDATE ALL or UPDATE ACCESSPATH option, SYSCOLUMNS and SYSCOLSTATS are updated.

When executing RUNSTATS INDEX using the UPDATE ACCESSPATH option, the following DB2 Catalog tables are updated:

- SYSCOLUMNS

- SYSCOLDIST

- SYSCOLDISTSTATS

- SYSCOLSTATS

- SYSINDEXES

- SYSINDEXSTATS

RUNSTATS INDEX specifying UPDATE SPACE modifies the SYSINDEXPART and SYSINDEXES DB2 Catalog tables. When specifying UPDATE ALL, all seven of these DB2 Catalog tables are updated.

RUNSTATS Guidelines

Use the following tips and techniques to implement effective RUNSTATS jobs at your shop.

Execute RUNSTATS During Off-Peak Hours   RUNSTATS can cause DB2 Catalog contention problems for a DB2 subsystem because it can update the following DB2 Catalog tables:

SYSIBM.SYSCOLDIST	SYSIBM.SYSCOLDIST_HIST
SYSIBM.SYSCOLDISTSTATS	
SYSIBM.SYSCOLSTATS	
SYSIBM.SYSCOLUMNS	SYSIBM.SYSCOLUMNS_HIST
SYSIBM.SYSINDEXES	SYSIBM.SYSINDEXES_HIST
SYSIBM.SYSINDEXPART	SYSIBM.SYSINDEXPART_HIST
SYSIBM.SYSINDEXSTATS	SYSIBM.SYSINDEXSTATS_HIST
SYSIBM.SYSTABLES	SYSIBM.SYSTABLES_HIST
SYSIBM.SYSTABLEPART	SYSIBM.SYSTABLEPART_HIST
SYSIBM.SYSTABLESPACE	
SYSIBM.SYSTABSTATS	SYSIBM.SYSTABSTATS_HIST
SYSIBM.SYSLOBSTATS	SYSIBM.SYSLOBSTATS_HIST

Whenever possible, execute RUNSTATS during an off-peak period to avoid performance degradation.

Execute RUNSTATS **Multiple Times for Long Column Lists**   A limit of 10 columns can be specified per RUNSTATS execution. If you must gather statistics on more than 10 columns, issue multiple executions of the RUNSTATS utility, specifying as many as 10 columns per run.

Of course, if you specify TABLE ALL (which is the default), information will be gathered for all columns of all tables in the table space. The above guidance to run RUNSTATS multiple times should be applied only if you are gathering statistics for more than 10 columns, but fewer than all of the columns.

Be Aware of DB2's Notion of Clustering   Although the calculation of CLUSTER RATIO has not been published by IBM, DB2 does not weigh duplicate values the same as unique values. For example, consider a table with a SMALLINT column that contains the following values in the physical sequence indicated:

1

3

4

95 occurrences of 7

6

9

This would seem to be 99% clustered because 6 is the only value out of sequence. This is not the case, however, because of the complex algorithm DB2 uses for factoring duplicates into the CLUSTER RATIO.

Execute RUNSTATS **After Significant Data Changes**   Run the RUNSTATS utility liberally. The cost of RUNSTATS usually is negligible for small- to medium-size table spaces. Moreover, the payback in optimized dynamic SQL, and static SQL when plans are re-bound using valid statistics, can be significant.

Running RUNSTATS can take longer on larger table spaces, so plan wisely before executing RUNSTATS for very large table spaces and indexes. However, you cannot avoid running RUNSTATS for larger objects because DB2 requires the statistics for formulating efficient access paths, perhaps even more so for larger objects.

Always schedule the running of the RUNSTATS utility for dynamic production data. This gives DB2 the most accurate volume data on which to base its access path selections. Discuss the frequency of production RUNSTATS jobs with your database administration unit.

For volatile tables, be sure to execute the RUNSTATS utility at least monthly.

> **CAUTION**
>
> Be aware that RUNSTATS changes your statistics, which can change your DB2 access paths. If you are satisfied with the performance of your production, static SQL, you should use caution when rebinding those packages and plans against changed statistics.

Favor Using SHRLEVEL REFERENCE   To ensure the accuracy of the statistics gathered by RUNSTATS, favor the use of the SHRLEVEL REFERENCE option. For table spaces that must be online 24 hours a day, however, execute RUNSTATS with the SHRLEVEL CHANGE option during off-peak processing periods.

Use Good Judgment When Scheduling RUNSTATS   Although it may seem best to execute RUNSTATS to record each and every modification to DB2 table data, it is probably overkill. Not every data modification will affect performance. Deciding which will and which won't, however, is an arduous task requiring good judgment. Before running RUNSTATS, analyze the type of data in the table space, the scope of the change, and the number of changes. The overhead of running the RUNSTATS utility and the data availability needs of the application could make it impossible to run the utility as frequently as you want.

It is good practice to execute RUNSTATS in the following situations:

- When new data is loaded into a table
- When a new column is added to a table and is at least partially populated
- When a new index is created
- When a table space or index is reorganized
- When a large number of data modifications have been applied to a particular table (updates, deletions, and/or insertions)
- After recovering a table space or index

Do Not Avoid RUNSTATS Even When Changing Statistics Using SQL   The DB2 optimizer is not perfect. Sometimes, DBAs alter the RUNSTATS information stored in the DB2 Catalog. This should be done only as a last resort.

Also, do not forgo the execution of RUNSTATS after modifying the DB2 Catalog statistics. At the least, RUNSTATS should be run to report on the current statistics, without updating the DB2 Catalog. However, this will make all the DB2 Catalog statistics for the table space outdated, not just the ones that need to be static. Therefore, consider running RUNSTATS to update the DB2 Catalog, regardless of whether the statistics have been modified, but follow the RUNSTATS job with a SQL UPDATE, INSERT, or DELETE statement to make the changes.

Consider Collecting Partition-Level Statistics   RUNSTATS can be executed by partition, thereby collecting statistics for a table space a partition at a time. Employ this technique to collect statistics (over time) while increasing data availability. Additionally, consider collecting RUNSTATS more frequently for volatile partitions, and less frequently for other partitions.

Consider Sampling   The SAMPLE parameter enables the RUNSTATS utility to use sampling methods to collect statistics instead of scanning every row in the table space, tables, and indexes specified. When sampling is specified, the overall resource consumption, CPU time, and elapsed time required by RUNSTATS can be substantially reduced. However, the accuracy of the collected statistics is impacted because only a subset of the rows are read to estimate statistics such as cardinality, high key value, and low key value.

In general, consider sampling only when RUNSTATS takes too much time to execute within the structure of your environment. Additionally, specify as high a sampling percentage as possible because the more data that is sampled, the more accurate the statistics are. For example

```
RUNSTATS TABLESPACE DSN8D51A.DSN8S51D
    TABLE (ALL)    SAMPLE 50
```

This statement causes RUNSTATS to use a sampling rate of 50% for the specified table space and tables.

Consider Collecting Frequent Value Statistics   The KEYCARD and FREQVAL parameters can be used with RUNSTATS to gather frequent value statistics. DB2 typically views any two columns as independent from one another. However, frequent value statistics enable DB2 to capture information about correlated columns. Columns are considered to be correlated with one another when their values are related in some manner. Consider, for example, CITY and STATE columns. If the CITY column is set to CHICAGO it is much more common for the STATE to be set to IL than any other state. However, without frequent value statistics, DB2 would consider Chicago, FL to be just as common as Chicago, IL.

With a multi-column index for CITY and STATE, the RUNSTATS utility can be used to collect frequent value statistics to learn about the correlation between the two columns. For example, consider the following RUNSTATS specification for DSN8810.XEMPPROJACT1 (a unique index on PROJNO, ACTNO, EMSTDATE, and EMPNO):

```
RUNSTATS INDEX DSN8810.XEMPPROJACT1
    KEYCARD
    FREQVAL NUMCOLS 2 COUNT 15
```

This statement causes the cardinality values to be collected for the concatenation of the first and second columns of the index (in this case, PROJNO and ACTNO). The top 15 most frequently occurring values will be collected. These statistics are most useful for queries against columns which are actually correlated in some manner where a matching index scan is used for the columns indicated.

> **NOTE**
>
> The default for NUMCOLS is 1 and the default for COUNT is 15. This means that RUNSTATS will collect the 15 most frequent values for the first key column of the index.
>
> Also, please note that the value for NUMCOLS cannot be larger than the number of columns in the index. If you specify a number greater than the number of indexed columns, RUNSTATS will simply use the number of columns in the index.

V8 **Consider Collecting Column and Column Group Statistics**   You can use the COLUMN keyword of RUNSTATS to collect statistics for non-leading index columns or columns not indexed at all. But sometimes it is necessary to collect statistics for columns as a set, instead of individually. This is accomplished using the COLGROUP keyword.

> **NOTE**
>
> For versions of DB2 prior to V8 IBM provided DSTATS, a separate utility program for accumulating column statistics. For those readers not yet using DB2 V8, DSTATS can be downloaded free-of-charge at the following link:
>
> ftp://www.redbooks.ibm.com/redbooks/dstats/
>
> Be aware, though, that DSTATS does not update the DB2 Catalog. It creates a user work table of data similar to SYSIBM.SYSCOLDIST. A user with SYSADM authority must insert these entries manually into the DB2 Catalog.

Collecting column and column group statistics can greatly improve DB2's ability to correctly formulate access paths—and therefore, improve query performance. This is particularly so for tables accessed frequently in an ad hoc manner. If the application is planned, it is relatively easy to build the correct indexes, and then to capture statistics on those indexes using RUNSTATS. But for ad hoc queries, just about any column can appear in a query predicate. Therefore, consider capturing statistics on non-indexed columns to improve performance.

To collect distribution statistics for non-indexed or non-leading indexed columns, specify the COLGROUP keyword. Simply specify the list of grouped columns using the COLGROUP keyword. This causes RUNSTATS to calculate a single cardinality value for the group of columns.

You can also collect frequency statistics for the grouped columns by specifying FREQVAL with COLGROUP. When using FREQVAL with COLGROUP, you must also specify COUNT *n* to tell RUNSTATS how many frequently occurring values should be collected for the specified group of columns.

34

Additionally, you will need to indicate whether the most frequently occurring values or the least frequently occurring values are to be stored for the group of columns. This is accomplished using one of the following parameters:

- MOST—RUNSTATS will collect the most frequently occurring values for the set of specified columns.

- LEAST—RUNSTATS will collect the least frequently occurring values for the set of specified columns.

- BOTH—RUNSTATS will collect both the most and the least frequently occurring values for the set of specified columns.

Consider Collecting Inline Statistics   Instead of executing RUNSTATS after loading tables, reorganizing table spaces and indexes, or rebuilding indexes, consider collecting statistics as those utilities run. You can use the STATISTICS keyword with LOAD, REBUILD INDEX, and REORG, causing catalog statistics to be collected as part of the utility processing. This eliminates the need to execute RUNSTATS after those utilities.

> **CAUTION**
>
> If you restart a LOAD or REBUILD INDEX utility that uses the STATISTICS keyword, inline statistics collection will not occur. You will need to run RUNSTATS to update the DB2 Catalog statistics after the restarted utility completes.

> **CAUTION**
>
> You cannot collect column group statistics with the STATISTICS keyword. Instead, you must use RUNSTATS.

V7 **Consider Accumulating Historical Statistics**   As of DB2 V7, RUNSTATS can be used to accumulate additional statistics in several DB2 Catalog tables reserved for historical statistics. It is a good idea to accumulate these statistics, especially for very volatile objects, to help analyze data growth over time.

Historical statistics will be accumulated by RUNSTATS when you specify the HISTORY parameter. The following options are available with the HISTORY parameter:

- ALL—Specifies that all the statistics are to be recorded in the DB2 Catalog history tables

- ACCESSPATH—Specifies that only those columns that store statistics used for access path selection are to be recorded in the DB2 Catalog history tables

- SPACE—Specifies that only those columns that store space-related statistics are to be recorded in the DB2 Catalog history tables

- NONE—Specifies that no historical statistics are to be saved in the DB2 Catalog history tables

Of course, RUNSTATS will continue to collect the current statistics regardless of which option is chosen for the HISTORY parameter. But the utility will also record the historical statistics using the follow DB2 Catalog tables:

SYSIBM.SYSCOLDIST_HIST   SYSIBM.SYSCOLUMNS_HIST

SYSIBM.SYSINDEXES_HIST   SYSIBM.SYSINDEXPART_HIST

SYSIBM.SYSINDEXSTATS_HIST   SYSIBM.SYSLOBSTATS_HIST

SYSIBM.SYSTABLEPART_HIST   SYSIBM.SYSTABSTATS_HIST

SYSIBM.SYSTABLES_HIST

These historical statistics can be cleaned up using the MODIFY STATISTICS utility, as detailed earlier in this chapter.

V7   **Consider Collecting Statistics on a List of Objects**   Remember, that as of DB2 V7 you can specify a list of objects to be operated on by IBM utilities. Collecting statistics for a list of objects is accomplished using the LISTDEF statement in conjunction with RUNSTATS. Usage of LISTDEF is covered in Chapter 30, "An Introduction to DB2 Utilities."

Use RUNSTATS to Generate DB2 Statistics Reports   You can use the REPORT YES option, along with the UPDATE NONE option, to use RUNSTATS as a DB2 statistics reporting tool. The REPORT YES option causes RUNSTATS to generate a report of the statistics it collects, and the UPDATE NONE clause signals RUNSTATS to collect the statistics without updating the DB2 Catalog.

The reports, however, will contain information about the actual condition of the DB2 objects for which RUNSTATS was run. The reports will not contain the information as it exists in the DB2 Catalog because the statistics were not updated due to the UPDATE NONE keyword. You can use the report to compare the statistics against the statistics in the DB2 Catalog to determine how the data has changed since the last RUNSTATS was executed.

Use RUNSTATS to Invalidate Statements in the Dynamic SQL Cache   Executing the RUNSTATS utility will invalidate cached dynamic SQL statements. Any cached dynamic SQL statements that access objects for which RUNSTATS is being run will be invalidated.

V8   As of DB2 Version 8, you can run the RUNSTATS utility with both the UPDATE NONE and REPORT NO parameters. This combination of parameters can be used to invalidate dynamic SQL statements without the overhead of running a full RUNSTATS. By specifying both of these parameters, RUNSTATS will not update statistics, nor will it produce a report; instead, just the dynamic SQL cache will be affected.

The STOSPACE Utility

The STOSPACE utility is executed on a STOGROUP or list of STOGROUPs. It populates the DB2 Catalog with table space and index data set DASD usage statistics. These statistics are culled from the appropriate ICF Catalog as indicated in the STOGROUP for which the STOSPACE utility is being executed. All space usage statistics stored in the DB2 Catalog are specified in terms of kilobytes (1024 bytes).

34

JCL to execute the STOSPACE utility for all storage groups known to the DB2 system is in Listing 34.6. The (*) in the JCL can be replaced with either a single STOGROUP name or a list of STOGROUP names separated by commas (enclosed in parentheses).

LISTING 34.6   STOSPACE JCL

```
//DB2JOBU  JOB (UTILITY),'DB2 STOSPACE',MSGCLASS=X,CLASS=X,
//         NOTIFY=USER
//*
//*****************************************************************
//*
//*               DB2 STOSPACE UTILITY
//*
//*****************************************************************
//*
//UTIL EXEC DSNUPROC,SYSTEM=DSN,UID='STOSPACE',UTPROC="
//DSNUPROC.SYSIN    DD  *
   STOSPACE STOGROUP (*)
/*
//
```

STOSPACE **Phases**

The STOSPACE utility has three phases:

UTILINIT	Sets up and initializes the STOSPACE utility.
STOSPACE	Analyzes the VSAM catalog for each table space and index in the indicated STOGROUPs. Space utilization statistics are gathered, and the DB2 Catalog is updated.
UTILTERM	Performs the final utility cleanup.

STOSPACE **Locking Considerations**

The STOSPACE utility can be run concurrently with all utilities.

STOSPACE **Guidelines**

When running the STOSPACE utility, use the following guidelines to ensure effective storage management.

Run STOSPACE Regularly   The STOSPACE utility should be run weekly for STOGROUPs to which highly active table spaces and indexes are assigned. It should be executed at least monthly for *all* STOGROUPs defined to the DB2 system.

Be Aware of DB2 Catalog Updates Caused by STOSPACE   The STOSPACE utility updates the following DB2 Catalog tables and columns:

Table	Column
SYSIBM.SYSSTOGROUP	SPACEF or SPACE, and STATSTIME
SYSIBM.SYSINDEXES	SPACEF or SPACE
SYSIBM.SYSINDEXPART	SPACEF or SPACE

Table	Column
SYSIBM.SYSTABLESPACE	SPACEF or SPACE
SYSIBM.SYSTABLEPART	SPACEF or SPACE

If the storage space value determined by STOSPACE is too large to fit in the SPACE column, the SPACEF column is used.

If the SPACE column in the SYSIBM.SYSSTOGROUP table is 0 after running the STOSPACE utility, consider dropping the STOGROUP, because no objects are currently defined for it. You can issue the following query to determine this:

```
SELECT   NAME, SPACE, SPACEF
FROM     SYSIBM.SYSSTOGROUP
WHERE    SPACE = 0
ORDER BY NAME
```

Be careful, however, if your shop uses DFHSM to automatically migrate inactive data sets to tape. Issue the following query to be sure that no objects have been defined to the STOGROUPs with a SPACE value of 0:

```
SELECT *
FROM    SYSIBM.SYSSTOGROUP ST
WHERE   NOT EXISTS
        (SELECT 1
         FROM    SYSIBM.SYSINDEXPART IP
         WHERE   ST.NAME = IP.STORNAME)
AND     NOT EXISTS
        (SELECT 1
         FROM    SYSIBM.SYSTABLEPART TP
         WHERE   ST.NAME = TP.STORNAME)
```

If no objects are returned by this query, the STOGROUPs previously identified probably can be dropped. There is one more problem, however. If a STOGROUP used as the default storage group for an active database is dropped, future table space and index DDL must explicitly specify a STOGROUP rather than rely on the default STOGROUP for the database. This is not usually a problem because the recommendation is to explicitly specify every parameter when creating DB2 objects. You can use the following query to determine whether a STOGROUP is used as the default STOGROUP for a database:

```
SELECT   NAME
FROM     SYSIBM.SYSDATABASE
WHERE    STGROUP = 'STOGROUP';
```

Monitor DASD Usage   Run the DB2 DASD usage queries (presented in Chapter 26) after successfully running the STOSPACE utility. This helps you monitor DASD used by DB2 objects.

Now that you have your DB2 Catalog in order, look at several other types of DB2 utilities in Chapter 35, "Stand-alone Utilities and Sample Programs."

CHAPTER **35**

Stand-alone Utilities and Sample Programs

In the previous two chapters, you looked at the DB2 online utilities. Several other IBM DB2 "utility" programs are outside this category. (As might be expected, if there are online utilities, there are also offline utilities.) DB2 also provides sample programs that have properties and objectives similar to true DB2 utilities. This chapter discusses each of these remaining types of utilities.

> **NOTE**
>
> Unlike the regular IBM DB2 utilities, the stand-alone utilities and sample programs discussed in this chapter are available to **all** DB2 sites. These offerings are available at no additional cost regardless of whether your company purchases utilities from IBM or a third-party vendor.

The Stand-alone Utilities

The DB2 stand-alone utilities are batch-oriented utilities that perform DB2 administrative activities outside the control of the DB2 subsystem (with the exception of DSN1SDMP). This can be useful if an error makes the DB2 system inactive. For example, stand-alone utilities can be used to copy DB2 data sets and print formatted dumps of their contents without DB2 being active. Every DB2 specialist should have a working knowledge of the stand-alone utilities. The stand-alone utilities are

DSNJLOGF	Log pre-format utility
DSNJU003	Change log inventory utility
DSNJU004	Print log map utility
DSN1CHKR	DB2 Catalog and DB2 Directory verification utility
DSN1COMP	Data compression analysis utility

DSN1COPY	Offline table space copy utility
DSN1SDMP	Dump and trace utility
DSN1LOGP	Recovery log extractor utility
DSN1PRNT	Formatted table space dump utility

Only technical support personnel who understand the intricacies of DB2 logging should use these utilities. As such, only the DB2 systems programmer or DBA who installs and maintains the DB2 system should use these utilities. A brief introduction to these utilities, however, should increase your overall understanding of DB2 logging.

The DB2 Log Preformat Utility (DSNJLOGF)

DSNJLOGF, the DB2 log preformat utility, preformats DB2 active log data sets. The execution of this utility is not mandatory for new active log data sets. However, if DSNJLOGF has not been run prior to the first write activity for the log, DB2 will preformat the log at that time, incurring a delay. Sample JCL is provided in Listing 35.1.

LISTING 35.1   DSNJLOGF JCL

```
//DB2JOBU  JOB (UTILITY),'DSNJLOGF',MSGCLASS=X,CLASS=X,
//           NOTIFY=USER
//*
//******************************************************************
//*      DB2 LOG PREFORMAT
//******************************************************************
//*
//*  Preformat the DB2 active log data sets
//*
//PREF11 EXEC PGM=DSNJLOGF
//SYSPRINT DD SYSOUT=*
//SYSUDUMP DD SYSOUT=*
//SYSUT1   DD  DSN=DSN510.LOGCOPY1.DS01,DISP=SHR
//*
//PREF12 EXEC PGM=DSNJLOGF
//SYSPRINT DD SYSOUT=*
//SYSUDUMP DD SYSOUT=*
//SYSUT1   DD  DSN=DSN510.LOGCOPY1.DS02,DISP=SHR
//*
//PREF21 EXEC PGM=DSNJLOGF
//SYSPRINT DD SYSOUT=*
//SYSUDUMP DD SYSOUT=*
//SYSUT1   DD  DSN=DSN510.LOGCOPY2.DS01,DISP=SHR
//*
//PREF22 EXEC PGM=DSNJLOGF
//SYSPRINT DD SYSOUT=*
//SYSUDUMP DD SYSOUT=*
//SYSUT1   DD  DSN=DSN510.LOGCOPY2.DS02,DISP=SHR
//
```

DSNJLOGF **Guidelines**

Use the following guidelines when running DSNJLOGF.

Use DSNJLOGF   Execute the DSNJLOGF utility instead of allowing DB2 to preformat the active log data set during processing. This will eliminate delays due to log data set preformatting.

Interpret Timestamps in the Log Map Correctly   The timestamps shown in the reports produced by DSNJLOGF can be confusing to interpret properly. Timestamps in the column labeled LTIME are in local time; all other timestamps are in Greenwich Mean Time (GMT).

The Change Log Inventory Utility (DSNJU003)

DSNJU003, better known as the Change Log Inventory utility, modifies the bootstrap data set (BSDS). Its primary function is to add or delete active and archive logs for the DB2 subsystem. Sample JCL to add an archive log data set is provided in Listing 35.2.

LISTING 35.2   DSNJU003 JCL (Change Log Inventory)

```
//DB2JOBU  JOB (UTILITY),'DSNJU003',MSGCLASS=X,CLASS=X,
//         NOTIFY=USER
//*
//*****************************************************************
//*       DB2 CHANGE LOG INVENTORY
//*****************************************************************
//*
//DSNJU003 EXEC PGM=DSNJU003
//SYSUT1   DD   DSN=DB2CAT.BSDS01,DISP=OLD
//SYSUT2   DD   DSN=DB2CAT.BSDS02,DISP=OLD
//SYSIN    DD   *
NEWLOG DSNAME=DB2CAT.FIRST.COPY,COPY1
NEWLOG DSNAME=DB2CAT.SECOND.COPY,COPY2
/*
//
```

DSNJU003 **Utility Guidelines**

Use the following tips when running DSNJU003.

Be Sure DB2 Is Down Before Using DSNJU003   It is best to run the DSNJU003 utility in batch only when DB2 is not running. Although you can run DSNJU003 when DB2 is up and running, the results can be inconsistent.

Use Caution with Data Sharing   Using DSNJU003 to change a BSDS for a data sharing member can cause a log read request from another data sharing member to fail. This will happen when the second member tries to access the changed BSDS before the first member is started.

V8   **Use** DSNJU003 **with** RESTORE SYSTEM   DB2 V8 adds a new option to DSNJU003 so that it can be used in conjunction with the new RESTORE SYSTEM utility. Before running RESTORE SYSTEM, run DSNJU003 with the SYSPITR option to specify the log truncation point for the point in time that you want to use for system recovery. Specify either the log RBA (if you are not data sharing) or the log LRSN (if you are data sharing) to the SYSPITR parameter.

V8 **Consider Using** DSNJU003 **to Rectify** CCSID **Information**   You can use DSNJU003 with the CCSID parameter on a DELETE statement to remove the CCSID information in the BSDS.

> **CAUTION**
>
> This option should only be attempted under direction from IBM technical support and only when the CCSID information in the BSDS is incorrect.

The Print Log Map Utility (DSNJU004)

DSNJU004, also referred to as the Print Log Map utility, is used to list the contents of the BSDS, which includes a status of the logs. All of the following information will be output by DSNJU004:

- Log data set name, log RBA association, and log LRSN for both copies of all active and archive log data sets

- Active log data sets that are available for new log data

- Status of all conditional restart control records in the bootstrap data set

- Contents of the queue of checkpoint records in the BSDS

- The communication record of the BSDS (if one exists)

- Contents of the quiesce history record

- System and utility timestamps

- Contents of the checkpoint queue

- Archive log command history

- BACKUP SYSTEM utility history

- System CCSID information

Sample JCL for DSNJU004 is provided in Listing 35.3.

LISTING 35.3   DSNJU004 JCL (Print Log Map)

```
//DB2JOBU  JOB (UTILITY),'DSNJU004',MSGCLASS=X,CLASS=X,
//             NOTIFY=USER
//*
//*****************************************************************
//*       DB2 PRINT LOG MAP
//*****************************************************************
//*
//DSNJU004 EXEC PGM=DSNJU004
//SYSUT1   DD   DSN=DB2CAT.BSDS01,DISP=SHR
//SYSPRINT DD SYSOUT=*
//
```

DSNJU004 **Utility Guideline**

Use the following tip when running DSNJU004.

Use DSNJU004 **for Documentation**   Run DSNJU004, the print log map utility, before and after running the change log utility. You can use the output of DSNJU004 to document the log change being implemented.

The Catalog Integrity Verification Utility (DSN1CHKR)

DSN1CHKR, the Catalog Integrity Verification utility, verifies the integrity of the DB2 Catalog and DB2 Directory. Sample JCL is provided in Listing 35.4.

LISTING 35.4   DSN1CHKR JCL

```
//DB2JOBU  JOB (UTILITY),'DSN1CHKR',MSGCLASS=X,CLASS=X,
//         NOTIFY=USER
//*
//*****************************************************************
//*       DB2 CATALOG CHECK UTILITY
//*****************************************************************
//*
//*  Verifies the integrity of the SYSPLAN table space
//*
//CHECK EXEC PGM=DSN1CHKR,PARM='FORMAT'
//SYSUT1   DD  DSN=DB2CAT.DSNDBC.DSNDB06.SYSPLAN.I0001.A001,DISP=SHR
//SYSPRINT DD SYSOUT=*
//
```

> **CAUTION**
>
> The SYSUTILX and SYSLGRNX tables are not checkable using DSN1CHKR. This is true even though the predecessors to these tables were checkable (SYSUTIL prior to DB2 V3 and SYSLGRNG prior to DB2 V4).

DSN1CHKR **Guidelines**

Review the following techniques when using DSN1CHKR to verify the integrity of DB2 Catalog table spaces.

Schedule DSN1CHKR **Runs Regularly**   Execute the DSN1CHKR utility for the DB2 Catalog and DB2 Directory weekly to catch problems early, before they affect program development and testing in your test DB2 subsystems or business availability and production processing in your production DB2 subsystems.

Consider Starting the DB2 Catalog in Read-Only Mode   For the results of DSN1CHKR to be 100 percent accurate, DB2 must be down or the table spaces being checked must be started in read-only mode (or stopped). To minimize the outage, consider copying the table spaces to be checked to VSAM files. The VSAM files can be checked instead of the actual DB2 Catalog table spaces. It should take less time to copy the files to VSAM than to check the actual table space data sets. You can also run DSN1CHKR against a copy created using DSN1COPY.

> **CAUTION**
>
> Regardless of the status of the catalog, you must be able to verify that the catalog files being checked do not have pages in the buffer pool that might have been modified.

Take Additional DB2 Catalog Verification Steps   In addition to running DSN1CHKR, consider the following steps to ensure DB2 Catalog integrity:

- Run DSN1COPY with the check option against all DB2 Catalog indexes and table spaces.

- Run the CHECK INDEX utility against all catalog indexes.

Use DSN1CHKR on Valid Table Spaces Only   Several of the DB2 Catalog and DB2 Directory table spaces are not able to be checked using DSN1CHKR. Therefore, be sure to execute DSN1CHKR only on the following system table spaces:

DSNDB01.DBD01

DSNDB06.SYSDBASE

DSNDB06.SYSDBAUT

DSNDB06.SYSGROUP

DSNDB06.SYSPLAN

DSNDB06.SYSVIEWS

The Compression Analyzer (DSN1COMP)

The DSN1COMP utility can be used to analyze DB2 data and approximate the results of DB2 data compression. DSN1COMP can be run on a table space data set, a sequential data set containing a DB2 table space or partition, a full image copy data set, or an incremental image copy data set. It will provide the following statistics:

- Space used with compression

- Space used without compression

- Percentage of bytes saved by using compression

- Total pages required with compression

- Total pages required without compression

- Percentage of pages saved by using compression

- Number of dictionary entries

- Number of dictionary pages required

- Average size of a compressed row

35

> **CAUTION**
>
> DSN1COMP cannot be run against compressed objects. Because the compression dictionary can age, it can be difficult to determine when to replace the dictionary because DSN1COMP cannot be used for this purpose.

Sample DSN1COMP JCL is provided in Listing 35.5. This job reads the VSAM data set for the DSN8D81A.DSN8S81D table space specified in the SYSUT1 DD statement and analyzes the data producing estimated compression statistics.

LISTING 35.5   DSN1COMP JCL

```
//DB2JOBU   JOB (UTILITY),'DB2 DSN1COMP',MSGCLASS=X,CLASS=X,
//            NOTIFY=USER
//*
//*****************************************************************
//*
//*       DB2 DSN1COMP UTILITY
//*
//*****************************************************************
//*
//JOBLIB DD DSN=DSN810.DSNLOAD,DISP=SHR
//DSN1COMP EXEC PGM=DSN1COMP,PARM='ROWLIMIT(20000)'
//SYSPRINT DD  SYSOUT=*
//SYSUDUMP DD  SYSOUT=*
//SYSUT1 DD DSN=DB2CAT.DSNDBC.DSN8D81A.DSN8S81D.I0001.A001,DISP=SHR,AMP=
➥('BUFND=181')
//
```

There are numerous parameters that can be supplied to the DSN1COMP utility. The following are the most commonly used parameters:

- FREEPAGE   Indicates the frequency of inserting a completely blank page when calculating the percentage of pages saved. The default is 0. You should specify the same value used for FREEPAGE in the CREATE TABLESPACE DDL for the table space being analyzed.

- PCTFREE   Specifies the percentage of each page to leave free when calculating the percentage of pages saved. The default is 5. Once again, you should specify the same value used for PCTFREE in the CREATE TABLESPACE DDL for the table space being analyzed.

- FULLCOPY   Indicates that a full image copy is being used as input. If the table space is partitioned, you should also use the NUMPARTS parameter.

- INCRCOPY   Indicates that an incremental image copy is used as input. Once again, for partitioned table spaces, you should also specify the NUMPARTS parameter.

- REORG   Indicates that the estimate should be based on the compression savings achievable by the REORG utility. If REORG is not specified, the estimate is the savings that the LOAD utility would achieve.

- ROWLIMIT   Specifies the maximum number of rows to evaluate to provide the compression estimate. You should use this option to limit the elapsed and processor time required by DSN1COMP.

DSN1COMP **Guidelines**

To ensure effective compression planning, consider the following guidelines as you execute the DSN1COMP utility.

Utilize DSN1COMP **to Plan for Compression**   Execute the DSN1COMP utility for table spaces that are candidates for compression. The statistics provided by this utility can be analyzed to determine whether compression will be cost-effective.

In general, contrast the percentage of pages saved when using compression against the anticipated increase in CPU time to determine whether compression is desirable. The CPU increase should be negligible when DB2 is using hardware compression.

Determine Proper Prefix   Before running DSN1COMP on a table space, first you must determine the actual data set name for the table space to be examined. This information can be found in SYSIBM.SYSTABLEPART; for example:

```
SELECT DBNAME, TSNAME, PARTITION, IPREFIX
FROM    SYSIBM.SYSTABLEPART
WHERE   DBNAME = ?
AND     TSNAME = ?;
```

Substitute the database name and table space name for the DBNAME and TSNAME predicates. Then, use the IPREFIX results to code the appropriate data set name. IPREFIX will contain either an "I" or a "J" depending on which version of the data set is currently active. If IPREFIX contains "J" then the data set should be coded as:

```
//SYSUT1 DD DSN=DB2CAT.DSNDBC.dbname.tsname.J0001.A001,DISP=SHR
```

If IPREFIX contains "I" then the data set should be coded as:

```
//SYSUT1 DD DSN=DB2CAT.DSNDBC.dbname.tsname.I0001.A001,DISP=SHR
```

Use the DSSIZE **Parameter for Large Table Spaces**   The DSSIZE parameter is used to specify the data set size in gigabytes. The preferred method of specifying a large table space is to use the DSSIZE parameter instead of the LARGE parameter.

So, you should specify DSSIZE(4G) or greater to DSN1COMP when you are analyzing a large table space. If you omit DSSIZE, DB2 assumes that the input data set size is 2GB. Of course, if DSSIZE is not specified and the data set is not one of the default sizes, the results of DSN1COMP will be unpredictable.

Use the PAGESIZE **Parameter**   The PAGESIZE parameter of DSN1COMP should be used to specify the page size of the input data set for SYSUT1. Any of the valid page sizes—4K, 8K, 16K, or 32K—are valid. If you specify an incorrect page size, the results of DSN1COMP will be unpredictable.

35

DSN1COMP will try to determine the proper page size if you fail to specify a PAGESIZE value. If DSN1COMP cannot determine the page size, then the utility will fail and an error message will be issued.

The Offline Copy Utility (DSN1COPY)

The Offline Copy utility, better known as DSN1COPY, has a multitude of uses. For example, it can be used to copy data sets or check the validity of table space and index pages. Another use is to translate DB2 object identifiers for the migration of objects between DB2 subsystems or to recover data from accidentally dropped objects. DSN1COPY also can print hexadecimal dumps of DB2 table space and index data sets.

Its first function, however, is to copy data sets. DSN1COPY can be used to copy VSAM data sets to sequential data sets, and vice versa. It also can copy VSAM data sets to other VSAM data sets and can copy sequential data sets to other sequential data sets. As such, DSN1COPY can be used to

- Create a sequential data set copy of a DB2 table space or index data set.

- Create a sequential data set copy of another sequential data set copy produced by DSN1COPY.

- Create a sequential data set copy of an image copy data set produced using the DB2 COPY utility, except for segmented table spaces. (The DB2 COPY utility skips empty pages, thereby rendering the image copy data set incompatible with DSN1COPY.)

- Restore a DB2 table space or index using a sequential data set produced by DSN1COPY.

- Restore a DB2 table space using a full image copy data set produced using the DB2 COPY utility.

- Move DB2 data sets from one disk pack to another to replace DASD (such as migrating from 3380s to 3390s).

- Move a DB2 table space or index space from a smaller data set to a larger data set to eliminate extents. Or, move a DB2 table space or index space from a larger data set to a smaller data set to eliminate wasted space.

> **CAUTION**
>
> If you change the allocation size of a DB2 data set using DSN1COPY, be sure also to change the PRIQTY and SECQTY values for the object to reflect the change in the DB2 Catalog.

DSN1COPY runs as an MVS batch job, so it can run as an offline utility when the DB2 subsystem is inactive. It can run also when the DB2 subsystem is active, but the objects it operates on should be stopped to ensure that DSN1COPY creates valid output.

> **CAUTION**
>
> DSN1COPY performs a page-by-page copy. Therefore, you cannot use DSN1COPY to alter the structure of DB2 data sets. For example, you cannot copy a partitioned tablespace into a simple tablespace.

DSN1COPY does not check to see whether an object is stopped before carrying out its task. DSN1COPY does not directly communicate with DB2.

> **NOTE**
>
> If DB2 is operational and an object is not stopped, DSN1COPY cannot use DISP=OLD for the data set being copied.

Sample DSN1COPY JCL is provided in Listing 35.6. This job reads the VSAM data set for the DSN8D81A.DSN8S81D table space specified in the SYSUT1 DD statement and then copies it to the sequential data set specified in the SYSUT2 DD statement.

LISTING 35.6   DSN1COPY JCL

```
//DB2JOBU  JOB (UTILITY),'DB2 DSN1COPY',MSGCLASS=X,CLASS=X,
//          NOTIFY=USER
//*
//*****************************************************************
//*
//*       DB2 DSN1COPY UTILITY
//*
//*****************************************************************
//*
//JOBLIB DD DSN=DSN810.DSNLOAD,DISP=SHR
//STOPDB EXEC PGM=IKJEFT01,DYNAMNBR=20
//STEPLIB DD DSN=DSN810.DSNEXIT,DISP=SHR
//        DD DSN=DSN810.DSNLOAD,DISP=SHR
//SYSPRINT DD SYSOUT=*
//SYSTSPRT DD SYSOUT=*
//SYSOUT  DD SYSOUT=*
//SYSUDUMP DD SYSOUT=*
//SYSTSIN  DD *
DSN SYSTEM (DSN)
-STOP DATABASE (DSN8D81A) SPACENAM(DSN8S81D)
END
/*
//DSN1COPY EXEC PGM=DSN1COPY,PARM='CHECK'
//SYSPRINT DD  SYSOUT=*
//SYSUDUMP DD  SYSOUT=*
//SYSUT1 DD DSN=DB2CAT.DSNDBC.DSN8D81A.DSN8S81D.I0001.A001,DISP=OLD,AMP=
➥('BUFND=181')
//SYSUT2 DD DSN=OUTPUT.SEQ.DATASET,DISP=OLD,DCB=BUFNO=20
/*
//STARTRW EXEC PGM=IKJEFT01,DYNAMNBR=20,COND=EVEN
//STEPLIB DD DSN=DSN810.DSNEXIT,DISP=SHR
//        DD DSN=DSN810.DSNLOAD,DISP=SHR
//*
//SYSPRINT DD SYSOUT=*
//SYSTSPRT DD SYSOUT=*
//SYSOUT  DD SYSOUT=*
//SYSUDUMP DD SYSOUT=*
//SYSTSIN  DD *
DSN SYSTEM (DSN)
-START DATABASE (DSN8D81A) SPACENAM(DSN8S81D)
```

35

LISTING 35.6   Continued

```
END
/*
//
```

One of the best features of the DSN1COPY utility is its capability to modify the internal object identifier stored in DB2 table space and index data sets, as well as in data sets produced by DSN1COPY and the DB2 COPY utility. When you specify the OBIDXLAT option, DSN1COPY reads a data set specified by the SYSXLAT DD statement. This data set lists source and target DBIDs, PSIDs or ISOBIDs, and OBIDs.

> **CAUTION**
>
> The DSN1COPY utility can only translate up to 500 record OBIDs at a time.

> **NOTE**
>
> DBIDs, PSIDs or ISOBIDs, and OBIDs are internal identifiers used by DB2 internally to uniquely identify database objects.

Each record in the SYSXLAT file must contain a pair of integers separated by a comma. The first integer is the source ID and the second integer is the target ID. The first record in the SYSXLAT file contains the source and target DBIDs. The second record contains the source and target PSIDs or ISOBIDs for indexes. All subsequent records in the SYSXLAT data set are OBIDs for tables.

> **CAUTION**
>
> Be careful with type 2 indexes when using old JCL that worked with type 1 indexes. Only the first two records were required for a type 1 index. For a type 2 index, the SYSXLAT data set must contain the table OBID in addition to the DBID and ISOBID.

For example, assume that you accidentally dropped the DSN8D81A database after the JCL in Listing 35.6 was run. Because this database uses STOGROUP-defined objects, all the data has been lost. However, after re-creating the database, table spaces, tables, and other objects for DSN8D81A, you can restore the DSN8S81D table space using DSN1COPY with the OBIDXLAT option. Consider the sample JCL using this option as shown in Listing 35.7. It is operating on the sequential data set produced in Listing 35.6, copying it back to the data set for the DSN8D81A.DSN8S81D table space. This job translates the DBID for database DSN8D81A from 283 to 201, the PSID for the DSN8S81D table space from 0002 to 0003, and the OBID for the DSN8810.DEPT table from 0020 to 0008.

LISTING 35.7   DSN1COPY JCL (Using the OBIDXLAT Option)

```
//DB2JOBU  JOB (UTILITY),'DB2 DSN1COPY',MSGCLASS=X,CLASS=X,
//         NOTIFY=USER
//*
//****************************************************************
//*
```

LISTING 35.7   Continued

```
//*        DB2 DSN1COPY UTILITY
//*
//*******************************************************************
//*
//JOBLIB DD DSN=DSN810.DSNEXIT,DISP=SHR
//       DD DSN=DSN810.DSNLOAD,DISP=SHR
//DSN1COPY EXEC PGM=DSN1COPY,PARM='OBIDXLAT'
//SYSPRINT DD  SYSOUT=*
//SYSUDUMP DD  SYSOUT=*
//SYSUT1 DD DSN=DB2CAT.DSNDBC.DSN8D81A.DSN8S81D.I0001.A001,DISP=OLD,AMP=
➥(''BUFND=81')
//SYSUT2 DD DSN=DB2CATP.DSNDBC.DSN8D81A.DSN8S81D.I0001.A001,DISP=OLD,AMP=
➥('BUFND=181')
//*
//*  The SYSXLAT input will ::
//*        Translate the DBID 283 (sending) into 201 on
//*        the receiving end.
//*        Translate the OBID 2 (sending) into 3 on the
//*        receiving end.
//*        Translate the PSID 20 (sending) into 8 on the
//*        receiving end.
//*
//SYSXLAT DD *
283  201
2    3
20   8
/*
//
```

The object identifiers for the old objects can be found in two ways. First, you can scan old DBID/PSID/OBID reports. Second, you can use DSN1PRNT to list the first three pages of the copy data set. The object identifiers are shown in the formatted listing produced for those pages. Obtain the new object identifiers using the DB2 Catalog reports listed in Chapter 26, "DB2 Object Monitoring Using the DB2 Catalog and RTS."

DSN1COPY Guidelines

When planning your DSN1COPY jobs, be sure to consult the following tips and guidelines.

Issue the Stop Command Before Running DSN1COPY   Never run the DSN1COPY utility for a DB2 object until it has been explicitly stopped for all access in the appropriate DB2 subsystem. This advice can be ignored if DB2 is not active.

Use DSN1PRNT Instead of DSN1COPY for Hex Dumps   Although DSN1COPY can be used to obtain a hex dump of a DB2 data set, favor the use of DSN1PRNT because it produces a listing that is formatted, and thus easier to use.

Estimate the Size of SYSUT2 Based on 4KB Pages   When the SYSUT2 data set is a sequential data set, estimate its size using the following formula:

```
(Number of pages) × 4096
```

35

Specify the space parameter in cylinders by rounding this number up to the next whole cylinder. If the object being copied uses a page size other than 4KB, use the following formulas:

For 8KB pages, multiply the number by two

For 16KB pages, multiply the number by four

For 32KB pages multiply the number by eight

Also, remember to specify the appropriate PAGESIZE option of DSN1COPY: 4KB, 8KB, 16KB, or 32KB.

The total number of pages used by a table space can be retrieved from the VSAM LISTCAT command or the DB2 Catalog as specified in the NACTIVE column of SYSIBM.SYSTABLESPACE. If you are using the DB2 catalog method, ensure that the statistics are current by running the RUNSTATS utility.

Optimize the BUFND Parameter   The default for the BUFND parameter is 2, which is too low. In order to boost I/O performance, change the BUFND parameter to a larger value. BUFND specifies the number of I/O buffers that VSAM will use for data records.

When using 3390 disk devices, consider coding BUFND=181 which will hold a complete cylinder.

> **CAUTION**
>
> Be sure to provide an adequate region size for your job to use 181 buffers. If the region size for your job is too small to allocate 181 data buffers, your job will fail. The message returned will be a DSN1996I indicating VSAM open error for the data set.

Use the PAGESIZE Parameter   The PAGESIZE parameter of DSN1COPY should be used to specify the page size of the input data set for SYSUT1. Any of the valid page sizes—4K, 8K, 16K, or 32K—are valid. If you specify an incorrect page size, the results of DSN1COPY will be unpredictable.

DSN1COPY will try to determine the proper page size if you fail to specify a PAGESIZE value. If DSN1COPY cannot determine the page size then the utility will fail and an error message will be issued.

Determine Proper Prefix   Before running DSN1COPY on a table space, first you must determine the actual data set name for the table space to be examined. This information in SYSIBM.SYSTABLEPART. For example,

```
SELECT DBNAME, TSNAME, PARTITION, IPREFIX
FROM    SYSIBM.SYSTABLEPART
WHERE   DBNAME = ?
AND     TSNAME = ?;
```

Substitute the database name and table space name for the DBNAME and TSNAME predicates. Then, use the IPREFIX results to code the appropriate data set name. IPREFIX will contain either an "I" or a "J" depending on which version of the data set is currently active. If IPREFIX contains "J" then the data set should be coded as

```
//SYSUT1 DD DSN=DB2CAT.DSNDBC.dbname.tsname.J0001.A001,DISP=SHR
```

If IPREFIX contains "I" then the data set should be coded as

```
//SYSUT1 DD DSN=DB2CAT.DSNDBC.dbname.tsname.I0001.A001,DISP=SHR
```

You must specify the correct fifth level qualifier in the data set name for DSN1COPY to successfully copy the table space data.

Do Not Use DSN1COPY **on Log Data Sets**   Avoid using the DSN1COPY utility on DB2 log data sets because certain options can invalidate the log data.

Use Appropriate Options with LOB **Table Spaces**   You can use DSN1COPY on LOB table spaces, but you cannot specify the SEGMENT or INLCOPY options. Use the LOB keyword to use DSN1COPY with a LOB table space.

Use Appropriate Options with Large Table Spaces   Use the DSSIZE parameter to specify the size of data sets that exceed 2GB (4GB for LOB table spaces). If you fail to specify this parameter, DB2 will assume that the size of the input data set is 2GB. DSN1COPY results will be unpredictable if the DSSIZE parameter is not coded for data sets that exceed 2GB.

When specifying the DSSIZE parameter, the size specified must match exactly the value used when the table space was defined.

You can specify LARGE instead of DSSIZE if the table space was defined with the LARGE parameter. However, it is better to use DSSIZE(4G) instead of LARGE because the LARGE parameter is being phased out in favor of DSSIZE.

V7 **Use Caution When Copying Data with an Identity Column**   When you are using DSN1COPY to copy table data where an identity column exists, you must take extra steps to set up the identity values appropriately. To accomplish this, the following steps should be taken:

1. Be sure to stop the table space on the source DB2 subsystem.

2. Find the sequence information in the DB2 Catalog for the identity column being copied. That information can be retrieved from SYSIBM.SYSSEQUENCES. Add the INCREMENT value to the MAXASSIGNEDVAL to let DSN1COPY assign the next value.

3. Create the table on the target subsystem. On the identity column specification, specify that previously calculate the next value for the START WITH value. Also, be sure to code all of the other attributes of the identity column exactly as coded for the table on the source subsystem.

4. Stop the table space on the target subsystem.

5. Copy the data using DSN1COPY.

6. Restart the table space on the source subsystem with the appropriate level of access.

7. Start the table space on the target subsystem.

The DB2 Dump and Trace Program (DSN1SDMP)

DSN1SDMP is the IFC selective dump utility. Although technically defined by IBM to be a service aid utility, DSN1SDMP is actually a DB2 application program. It must be run under the TSO terminal monitor program, IKJEFT01. DSN1SDMP, unlike the other service aids, can be run only when DB2 is operational.

Using the Instrumentation Facility Interface, DSN1SDMP can write DB2 trace records to a sequential data set named in the SDMPTRAC DD statement. It can also force system dumps for DB2 utilities or when specific DB2 events occur. For shops without a DB2 performance monitor, DSN1SDMP can come in handy in trying to resolve system problems. Sample JCL is shown in Listing 35.8.

LISTING 35.8   DSN1SDMP JCL

```
//DB2JOBU  JOB  (UTILITY),'DSN1SDMP',MSGCLASS=X,CLASS=X,
//         NOTIFY=USER
//*
//*****************************************************************
//*
//*       DB2 FORCE DUMP UTILITY  : :
//*         CONSULT IBM BEFORE RUNNING
//*
//*****************************************************************
//*
//JOBLIB DD DSN=DSN810.DSNLOAD,DISP=SHR
//DUMPER EXEC PGM=IKJEFT01,DYNAMNBR=20
//SYSTSPRT DD  SYSOUT=*
//SYSPRINT DD  SYSOUT=*
//SYSUDUMP DD  SYSOUT=*
//SDMPPRNT DD SYSOUT=*
//SDMPTRAC DD DSN=CAT.TRACE.SEQ.DATASET,
//         DISP=(MOD,CATLG,CATLG),SPACE=(8192,(100,100)),UNIT=SYSDA,
//         DCB=(DSORG=PS,RECFM=VB,LRECL=8188,BLKSIZE=8192)
//SYSTSIN  DD   *
DSN SYSTEM(DSN)
RUN PROGRAM(DSN1SDMP)  PLAN(DSN1SDMP)   -
LIB('DSN810.RUNLIB.LOAD')
END
/*
//SDMPDD   *
CONSULT IBM BEFORE USING
IBM SUPPORT CENTER WILL PROVIDE OPTIONS
/*
//
```

DSN1SDMP Data Sets

SDMPIN	Input parameters to the DSN1SDMP utility
SDMPPRNT	DSN1SDMP output messages
SYSABEND	System dump if DSN1SDMP abends
SDMPTRAC	Output trace records

DSN1SDMP **Guidelines**

You can use the following guidelines as a blueprint for effective DSN1SDMP usage.

Use DSN1SDMP Only As Directed   DSN1SDMP should be used only under instructions from the IBM Support Center.

Be Sure That the User Has the Authority to Run DSN1SDMP   To execute the DSN1SDMP service aid, the requester must have the requisite authority to start and stop the DB2 traces, as well as the MONITOR1 or MONITOR2 privilege.

The Recovery Log Extractor (DSN1LOGP)   DSN1LOGP, otherwise known as the Recovery Log Extractor, produces a formatted listing of a specific DB2 recovery log. When an active log is operated on by DSN1LOGP, an active DB2 subsystem must not be currently processing the log. Any archive log can be processed at any time—whether DB2 is operational or not.

DSN1LOGP produces a detailed or a summary report. The detailed report displays entire log records. The summary report condenses the log records, displaying only the information necessary to request a partial recovery. As such, the detailed report is rarely used. Sample JCL is shown in Listing 35.9.

LISTING 35.9   DSN1LOGP JCL

```
//DB2JOBU  JOB (UTILITY),'DSN1LOGP',MSGCLASS=X,CLASS=X,
//            NOTIFY=USER
//*
//*****************************************************************
//*
//*      DB2 RECOVERY LOG EXTRACTOR
//*
//*****************************************************************
//*
//DSN1LOGP PGM=DSN1LOGP
//SYSPRINT DD SYSOUT=*
//SYSABEND DD SYSOUT=*
//SYSSUMRY DD SYSOUT=*
//BSDS DD DSN=DB2CAT.BSDS01,DISP=SHR
//SYSIN DD *
RBASTART(E300F4)
RBAEND(F40000)
SUMMARY(YES)
/*
//
```

DSN1LOGP **Guidelines**

The following techniques can be used to produce effective log extract reports using the DSN1LOGP service aid.

Do Not Run DSN1LOGP on the Active Log   DSN1LOGP cannot be run on the active log that DB2 is currently using for logging. It can be run on the other active logs as well as on the archive logs. Given this caveat, DSN1LOGP can be run while DB2 is operational.

35

Use the DSN1LOGP Output to Assist in Recovery   You can use the output report produced by the DSN1LOGP service aid utility to determine an appropriate log RBA for partial recovery by the RECOVER TORBA utility. This method should be used only when an appropriate log RBA is available in the SYSIBM.SYSCOPY table as the result of running the QUIESCE utility.

The DB2 Data Set Dump Creator (DSN1PRNT)

The program name for the DB2 Data Set Dump Creator is DSN1PRNT. It can be used to print hexadecimal and formatted dumps of DB2 table space, indexspace, and image copy data sets. It is useful for searching for values and dumping only the pages containing the specified value. Sample JCL is in Listing 35.10.

LISTING 35.10   DSN1PRNT JCL

```
//DB2JOBU  JOB (UTILITY),'DSN1PRNT',MSGCLASS=X,CLASS=X,
//         NOTIFY=USER
//*
//*****************************************************************
//*
//*      DB2 DATA SET DUMP SERVICE AID
//*
//*****************************************************************
//*
//DSN1PRNT PGM=DSN1PRNT,PARM='PRINT,FORMAT'
//SYSPRINT DD SYSOUT=*
//SYSUT1 DD DSN=DB2CAT.DSNDBC.DSN8D81A.DSN8S81D.I0001.A001,DISP=SHR,AMP=
➡('BUFND=181')
//
```

DSN1PRNT Guidelines

Consider the following guidelines when using DNS1PRNT to dump DB2 data sets.

Analyze Problems Using DSN1PRNT Output   Use DSN1PRNT to track down data problems and page errors. By scanning the dump of a DB2 data set, you can view the format of the page and the data on the page.

Be Aware of Potential Errors   If DSN1PRNT encounters an error on a page of a DB2 data set, an error message is printed. If you specified the FORMAT option, the output is not formatted. All pages without errors are formatted.

Use DSN1PRNT for All DB2 Data Set Dumps   Favor the use of DSN1PRNT over other data set dump utilities (such as DSN1COPY) because of the formatting feature of DSN1PRNT.

Run DSN1PRNT Only for Stopped DB2 Objects   When running DSN1PRNT when DB2 is active, be sure that the data set being dumped has been stopped. This ensures that the data being dumped is accurate and unchanging.

Of course, if your shop requires 24×7 availability stopping DB2 is not an option. You can run DSN1PRNT with DB2 up and running, but you will have to live with the possibility of data anomalies.

Be Aware of Data Set Page Sizes   If the object being dumped uses non-4KB pages, remember to specify the PAGESIZE option of DSN1PRNT. Specify the appropriate page size for the data set being printed: 4KB, 8KB, 16KB, or 32KB.

Use the PAGESIZE Parameter   The PAGESIZE parameter of DSN1PRNT should be used to specify the page size of the input data set for SYSUT1. Any of the valid page sizes—4K, 8K, 16K, or 32K—are valid. If you specify an incorrect page size, the results of DSN1PRNT will be unpredictable.

DSN1PRNT will try to determine the proper page size if you fail to specify a PAGESIZE value. If DSN1PRNT cannot determine the page size, then the utility will fail and an error message will be issued.

Use Appropriate Options for LOB Table Spaces   You can use DSN1PRNT with LOB table spaces. To do so, be sure to specify the LOB parameter, and do not specify the INLCOPY parameter.

DB2 Sample Programs

The sample programs are DB2 application programs supplied by IBM with DB2. They are normal DB2 application programs that require precompilation, compilation, linking, and binding, as described in Chapter 13, "Program Preparation." These programs run using the TSO Terminal Monitor Program, IKJEFT01, as described in Chapter 18, "The Doors to DB2." Therefore, you must provide a DB2 system name, a program name, a DB2 load library name, and a plan name for each sample program execution.

You must verify the load library and plan names associated with these programs at your site with your DBA or system administrator. The JCL examples in the following sections specify the default load library, and plan names are the same as the sample program names.

The Dynamic SQL Processor (DSNTEP2)

DSNTEP2 is a PL/I application program that can be used to issue DB2 dynamic SQL statements. The sample JCL in Listing 35.11 demonstrates the capability of this program to issue DCL, DDL, and DML dynamically.

LISTING 35.11   DSNTEP2 JCL

```
//DB2JOBU  JOB (UTILITY),'DB2 SAMPLE SQL',MSGCLASS=X,CLASS=X,
//            NOTIFY=USER
//*
//*****************************************************************
//*
//*       DB2 SAMPLE SQL PROGRAM
//*
```

LISTING 35.11   Continued

```
//*******************************************************************
//*
//JOBLIB DD DSN=DSN810.DSNEXIT,DISP=SHR
//       DD DSN=DSN810.DSNLOAD,DISP=SHR
//BATCHSQL EXEC PGM=IKJEFT01,DYNAMNBR=20
//SYSTSPRT DD   SYSOUT=*
//SYSPRINT DD   SYSOUT=*
//SYSUDUMP DD   SYSOUT=*
//SYSTSIN  DD  *
DSN SYSTEM(DSN)
RUN PROGRAM(DSNTEP2)  PLAN(DSNTEP81)  -
LIB('DSN810.RUNLIB.LOAD')
END
/*
//SYSIN   DD  *
SELECT * FROM SYSIBM.SYSTABLES ;

UPDATE DSN8810.DEPT
SET DEPTNAME = 'CHANGED NAME'
WHERE DEPTNO = 'D01' ;

INSERT INTO DSN8810.ACT
VALUES (129, 'XXXXXX', 'SAMPLE ACCT') ;

DELETE FROM DSN8810.EMP
WHERE SALARY < 1000 ;

CREATE DATABASE TESTNAME
BUFFERPOOL BP12
STOGROUP DSN8G810 ;

GRANT DBADM ON DATABASE TESTNAME TO USERA ;

/*
//
```

Because DSNTEP2 is an application program, it must be compiled, linked, and bound before it can be used. Additionally, because the source code is provided in PL/I, it can be modified easily by a knowledgeable PL/I programmer.

Prior to DB2 V6, you needed to have a PL/I compiler to use DSNTEP2. However, as of V6 IBM now provides both the source code and an object code version of DSNTEP2 with DB2. So, you no longer need a PL/I compiler to use DSNTEP2.

DSNTEP2 can process almost every SQL statement that can be executed dynamically. DSNTEP2 accepts

- The GRANT and REVOKE DCL statements
- The ALTER, COMMENT ON, CREATE, and DROP DDL statements

- The DELETE, INSERT, SELECT, and UPDATE DML statements

- The COMMIT, ROLLBACK, EXEC SQL, EXPLAIN, and LOCK statements

The only important statement that DSNTEP2 does not support is the LABEL ON DDL statement. DSNTEP2 can be modified easily to support this statement (if you have a PL/I compiler).

DSNTEP2 **Guidelines**

The following tips and techniques should be utilized when executing SQL statements using DSNTEP2.

Code DSNTEP2 **Input in the First 72 Bytes of the Input Data Set**   DSNTEP2 reads SQL statements from an input data set with 80-byte records. The SQL statements must be coded in the first 72 bytes of each input record. SQL statements can span multiple input records and are terminated by a semicolon (;). Semicolons are not permitted in the text of the SQL statement.

Be Aware of DSNTEP2 **Error Handling**   Each SQL statement is automatically committed by DSNTEP2. When DSNTEP2 encounters an SQL error, it continues processing the next SQL statement in the input data set. When 10 SQL errors have been encountered, DSNTEP2 ends. If any SQL errors occurred during the execution of DSNTEP2, a return code of 8 is received.

Do Not Rerun Committed Work   To rerun DSNTEP2, remember that all SQL statements that completed with a 0 SQL code were committed. These statements should not be rerun. All SQL statements completed with a negative SQL code must be corrected and reprocessed.

Liberally Comment DSNTEP2 **Input**   Comments can be passed to DSNTEP2 in the SQL statements using two hyphens in columns 1 and 2 or a single asterisk in column 1.

Use DSNTEP2 **to Batch Large Streams of SQL**   Use DSNTEP2 to simulate SPUFI in a batch environment. This can be useful because it enables the execution of dynamic SQL statements from an input data set without monopolizing a TSO terminal as SPUFI does. This can have a significant effect when issuing multiple DDL statements to create DB2 objects.

Prepare DSNTEP2 **For Use**   The DSNTEP2 program must be prepared before it can be run to issue dynamic SQL. If you want to use the source code version of DSNTEP2, you must precompile, compile, link and bind it. You need to bind the object code version of DSNTEP2 before you can use it.

These steps are usually performed by the systems programmer or DBA responsible for installing DB2. Be sure to use the correct plan for DSNTEP2. Sometimes the installer will provide a new plan name for each new version of DB2 and a common technique is to append the version and release number to the plan name, for example DSNTEP81 for DB2 V8.

Consider Changing SYSPRINT **Block Size**   If you plan to execute many statements in a single DSNTEP2 step, consider changing the SYSPRINT BLKSIZE. As delivered by IBM, the block size of SYSPRINT is extremely small. Such a change should be made only by a DBA or system programmer because doing so requires changing the code of DSNTEP2 followed by re-installing the program.

The Dynamic SQL Update Program (DSNTIAD)

DSNTIAD is an assembler application program that can issue the same DB2 dynamic SQL statements as DSNTEP2, with the exception of the SELECT statement. For this reason, it usually is preferable for applications programmers to use DSNTEP2 rather than DSNTIAD.

DSNTAID is written in Assembler language. Because DSNTIAD is a sample program, its source code can be modified to accept SELECT statements. This task is complex and should not be undertaken by a beginning programmer.

Additionally, DSNTIAD supports the LABEL ON statement, whereas DSNTEP2 does not. Also note that DSNTIAD can be a little more efficient than DSNTEP2 because it is written in Assembler. Sample DSNTIAD JCL is provided in Listing 35.12.

LISTING 35.12   DSNTIAD JCL

```
//DB2JOBU  JOB (UTILITY),'DB2 SAMPLE UPD',MSGCLASS=X,CLASS=X,
//          NOTIFY=USER
//*
//****************************************************************
//*
//*         DB2 SAMPLE SQL UPDATE PROGRAM
//*
//****************************************************************
//*
//JOBLIB DD DSN=DSN810.DSNEXIT,DISP=SHR
//       DD DSN=DSN810.DSNLOAD,DISP=SHR
//BATUPSQL EXEC PGM=IKJEFT01,DYNAMNBR=20
//SYSTSPRT DD  SYSOUT=*
//SYSPRINT DD  SYSOUT=*
//SYSUDUMP DD  SYSOUT=*
//SYSTSIN  DD  *
DSN SYSTEM(DSN)
RUN PROGRAM(DSNTIAD) PLAN(DSNTIAD6)  -
LIB('DSN810.RUNLIB.LOAD')
END
/*
//SYSIN   DD  *
UPDATE DSN8810.DEPT
SET DEPTNAME = 'CHANGED NAME'
WHERE DEPTNO = 'D01' ;

INSERT INTO DSN8510.ACT
VALUES (129, 'XXXXXX', 'SAMPLE ACCT') ;

DELETE FROM DSN8510.EMP
WHERE SALARY < 1000 ;
```

LISTING 35.12   Continued

```
CREATE DATABASE TESTNAME
BUFFERPOOL BP12
STOGROUP DSN8G510 ;

GRANT DBADM ON DATABASE TESTNAME TO USERA ;
/*
//
```

DSNTIAD **Guidelines**

Use the following guidelines to ensure the effective execution of SQL using DSNTIAD.

Use DSNTIAD **for DDL**   Consider using DSNTIAD rather than DSNTEP2 to submit batch DDL. Doing so can be a little more efficient but you will not be able to combine SELECT statements in with your DDL.

Control DSNTIAD **Execution Authority**   Consider giving only DBAs and systems programmers the authority to execute DSNTIAD. Allow everyone to execute DSNTEP2 because it provides support for the SELECT statement.

Do Not Comment DSNTIAD **Input**   Unlike DSNTEP2, DSNTIAD does not accept comments embedded in SQL statements.

Be Aware of DSNTIAD **Error Handling**   Each SQL statement is automatically committed by DSNTIAD. When an SQL error is encountered, DSNTIAD continues processing the next SQL statement in the input data set. When 10 SQL errors have been encountered, DSNTIAD ends. If any SQL errors occur during the execution of DSNTIAD, a return code of 8 is received.

Do Not Rerun Committed Work   When rerunning DSNTIAD, remember that all SQL statements that completed with a 0 SQL code were committed. All SQL statements that completed with a negative SQL code need to be corrected and reprocessed.

Prepare DSNTIAD **for Use**   The DSNTIAD program must be prepared before it can be executed. This requires a precompile, compile, link and bind. The systems programmer or DBA responsible for installing DB2 usually performs these steps. Be sure to use the correct plan for DSNTIAD. Sometimes the installer will provide a new plan name for each new version of DB2 and a common technique is to append the version and release number to the plan name, for example DSNTIAD7 for DB2 V7 and DSNTIAD8 for DB2 V8.

Consider Changing SYSPRINT **Block Size**   If you plan to execute many statements in a single DSNTIAD step, consider changing the SYSPRINT BLKSIZE. As delivered by IBM, the block size of SYSPRINT is extremely small. Such a change should be made only by a DBA or system programmer because doing so requires changing the code of DSNTIAD followed by re-installing the program.

The Sample Unload Program (DSNTIAUL)

V7 One option for creating a readable sequential unload data set for DB2 tables (without writing an application program) is the DSNTIAUL sample program. With DB2 V7, though,

IBM now offers a true UNLOAD utility for unloading DB2 data to a sequential data set. Of course, you must first purchase the correct utility package from IBM before you will have the UNLOAD utility available. And, the REORG utility with the UNLOAD ONLY option also can be used to unload data from a DB2 table space. However, DSNTIAUL is still offered as a free-of-charge sample program for unloading data from DB2 tables.

DSNTIAUL is a DB2 application program written in assembler. It is provided free-of-charge with DB2 for z/OS. DSNTIAUL can be used to unload the data from one or more DB2 tables or views into a sequential data set. The LOAD utility then can use this data set. Additionally, DSNTIAUL can produce the requisite control cards for the LOAD utility to load the sequential data set back into the specific DB2 table. Consider the JCL provided in Listing 35.13.

LISTING 35.13   DSNTIAUL JCL

```
//DB2JOBU  JOB (UTILITY),'DB2 SAMPLE UNLD',MSGCLASS=X,CLASS=X,
//            NOTIFY=USER
//*
//****************************************************************
//*
//*         DB2 SAMPLE UNLOAD PROGRAM
//*
//****************************************************************
//*
//JOBLIB DD DSN=DSN810.DSNEXIT,DISP=SHR
//       DD DSN=DSN810.DSNLOAD,DISP=SHR
//UNLOAD   EXEC PGM=IKJEFT01,DYNAMNBR=20,COND=(4,LT)
//SYSTSPRT DD SYSOUT=*
//SYSTSIN  DD *
DSN SYSTEM(DSN)
RUN  PROGRAM(DSNTIAUL) PLAN(DSNTIAU6) -
LIB('DSN810.RUNLIB.LOAD')
/*
//SYSPRINT DD SYSOUT=*
//SYSUDUMP DD SYSOUT=*
//SYSREC00 DD DSN=DEPT.UNLOAD.DATASET,DISP=(,CATLG,DELETE),
//            UNIT=SYSDA,SPACE=(CYL,(1,1)),DCB=BUFNO=20
//SYSPUNCH DD DSN=DEPT.RELOAD.UTILITY.INPUT,DISP=(,CATLG,DELETE),
//            UNIT=SYSDA,SPACE=(TRK,(1,1),RLSE)
//SYSIN     DD *
DSN8810.DEPT
/*
//
```

After running the JCL in Listing 35.13, the DSN8810.DEPT table is unloaded into the data set specified for SYSREC00. The SYSPUNCH data set contains the generated LOAD control cards for loading this data back into the DEPT table. The generated LOAD control cards look like the following:

```
LOAD DATA INDDN SYSREC00 LOG NO INTO TABLE
    DSN8810.DEPT
  (
```

```
DEPTNO        POSITION(      1        )
CHAR(                   3) ,
DEPTNAME      POSITION(      4        )
VARCHAR                          ,
MGRNO         POSITION(      42       )
CHAR(                   6)
        NULLIF(      48)='?',
ADMRDEPT      POSITION(      49       )
CHAR(                   3)
)
```

DSNTIAUL **Guidelines**

When unloading data from DB2 tables using DSNTIAUL, keep the following techniques in mind.

Use DSNTIAUL to Create Unloaded Flat Files   Use DSNTIAUL to produce sequential data sets containing DB2 data from one or more tables. Running DSNTIAUL is significantly easier than coding an application program to extract the desired data.

Use WHERE and ORDER BY with DSNTIAUL   DSNTIAUL can accept WHERE clauses and ORDER BY clauses to limit the data to be unloaded and sort the unloaded data, respectively. However, the combination of the table name and its associated WHERE and ORDER BY clauses cannot exceed 72 total characters.

Use DSNTIAUL to Unload from a View   DSNTIAUL can unload data from DB2 views. When data from multiple tables must be unloaded into a single data set, create a view that joins the two tables and use DSNTIAUL to unload the data from that view.

Use the 'SQL' Parameter   Complete SELECT statements can be specified in SYSIN. This is accomplished by specifying PARMS('SQL') in the SYSTSIN data set. When PARMS('SQL') is specified, the 72-byte restriction is lifted. The largest SQL statement that can be specified is 32,765 bytes.

Keep Your SYSREC Data Sets Synchronized   Unloaded data is placed into a data set associated with the SYSRECxx DD statement. When multiple tables will be unloaded to multiple data sets using DSNTIAUL, be careful when you specify the SYSRECxx data sets. SYSREC00 refers to the first unload utility card, SYSREC01 refers to the second, and so on. Because SYSREC00 is the first DD statement, the number associated with the SYSRECxx DD statement is 1 less than the corresponding input statement being processed.

Unload No More Than 100 Tables with a Single DSNTIAUL Execution   No more than 100 input control cards can be successfully processed by a single execution of the DSNTIAUL utility.

Consider Using LOCK TABLE with DSNTIAUL   The LOCK TABLE statement can be used with DSNTIAUL to create a consistent unload file. By issuing the LOCK TABLE statement, you ensure that no modifications are made to the table during the timeframe of the unload execution.

35

Consider Using DSNTIAUL **for Data Movement and Storage**   You can deploy the DSNTIAUL program for many useful purposes. Any activity that requires bulk movement of data from a DB2 table is ideal for DSNTIAUL. Consider the following uses:

- To migrate data from one DB2 subsystem to another

- To save data when the structure of a table must be changed by dropping and re-creating it

- To copy data before a table structure change is made (because old image copy data sets cannot be applied after a structure change)

- To create a comma-delimited file (other DBMSs can accept a delimited file as input to a load or restore process)

Prepare DSNTIAUL **for Use**   The DSNTIAUL program must be prepared before it can be executed. This requires a precompile, compile, link, and bind. These steps are usually performed by the systems programmer or DBA responsible for installing DB2. Be sure to use the correct plan for DSNTIAUL. Sometimes the installer will provide a new plan name for each new version of DB2 and a common technique is to append the version and release number to the plan name, for example DSNTIAU6 for DB2 V6.

Only Use DSNTIAUL **As a Last Resort**   DSNTIAUL should be used only as a last resort for unloading DB2 data. There are much better options available for DB2 unloading in terms of ease-of-use and speed. DSNTIAUL should be used only by those shops that cannot afford to purchase either the IBM utilities or a faster third party UNLOAD utility.

Interpreting DSNTIAUL, DSNTIAD, and DSNTEP2 Return Codes

There are four possible return codes that can be returned by DSNTIAUL, DSNTIAD, and DSNTEP2. Be sure to examine the return codes shown in Table 35.1 and take appropriate action. If a non-zero return code is received by DSNTIAUL, you may need to re-run DSNTIAUL to unload the desired data.

TABLE 35.1   DSNTIAUL, DSNTIAD, and DSNTEP2 Return Codes

Return Code	Interpretation
0	Successful completion.
4	A warning code was received by an SQL statement. If the statement was a SELECT, DB2 did not perform the unload.
8	An error code was received by an SQL statement. If the statement was a SELECT, DB2 did not perform the unload.
12	The program could not open a data set, an SQL statement returned a severe error (in the -800 or -900 range), or an error was encountered in the SQL message formatting routine.

CHAPTER 36

DB2 Commands

DB2 commands are operator-issued requests that administer DB2 resources and environments. There are six categories of DB2 commands, which are delineated by the environment from which they are issued. These are

- DB2 environment commands
- DSN commands
- IMS commands
- CICS commands
- IRLM commands
- TSO commands

Each of these categories is discussed in this chapter.

DB2 Environment Commands

DB2 environment commands usually are issued either through the DB2I ISPF panels or by batch TSO under the control of the DSN command. However, they can be issued from an MVS console, from IMS/TM using the specialized command /SSR, or from CICS using the specialized CICS command DSNC. The DB2 environment commands can be used to monitor and control DB2 databases, resources, and processing. There are three types of environment commands:

- Information gathering commands
- Administrative commands
- Environment control commands

All DB2 environment commands have a common structure, as follows:

```
cp command operand
```

The *cp* is the command prefix assigned when DB2 is installed. The command prefix identifies a single DB2 subsystem, targeting the command as a DB2 command for a specific DB2 subsystem. The command prefix is built from a combination of the subsystem recognition character concatenated to the DB2 subsystem name. Prior to DB2 V4, only the single character subsystem recognition character was available to identify subsystems. The multi-character command prefix enables more meaningful names to be used. A subsystem recognition character is assigned when DB2 is installed. The default recognition character is a hyphen, but it can be changed by each installation depending on the environment from which the command is issued. The following characters can be used as subsystem recognition characters:

¢	+	;	?
.	¦	-	:
<	!	/	#
(	$	,	@
*	)	%	"
'	=		

A sample DB2 command might be

```
-DB2A DISPLAY DATABASE(DSNDB07)
```

The command specifies that the DSNDB07 database in the DB2A subsystem is to be displayed.

The *command* portion of the environment command is the DB2 command verb. The *operand* is the combination of optional and required keywords and values necessary to successfully issue the command.

Figure 36.1 shows a DB2 environment command, -DISPLAY DATABASE, issued through option 7 of the DB2I panel. The response to that command is shown in Figure 36.2. Listing 36.1 is the JCL needed to issue the same command in a batch job.

LISTING 36.1   JCL to issue I DB2 Command in Batch

```
//DB2JOBC  JOB (COMMAND),'DB2 COMMAND SQL',MSGCLASS=X,CLASS=X,
//            NOTIFY=USER
//*
//****************************************************************
//*
//*       JCL TO ISSUE DB2 COMMAND
//*
```

LISTING 36.1   Continued

```
//******************************************************************
//*
//JOBLIB DD DSN=DSN810.DSNEXIT,DISP=SHR
//       DD DSN=DSN810.DSNLOAD,DISP=SHR
//BATCHCOM EXEC PGM=IKJEFT01,DYNAMNBR=20
//SYSTSPRT DD  SYSOUT=*
//SYSPRINT DD  SYSOUT=*
//SYSUDUMP DD  SYSOUT=*
//SYSTSIN  DD  *
  DSN SYSTEM(DSN)
  - DISPLAY DATABASE (DSNDB06)
  END
/*
//
```

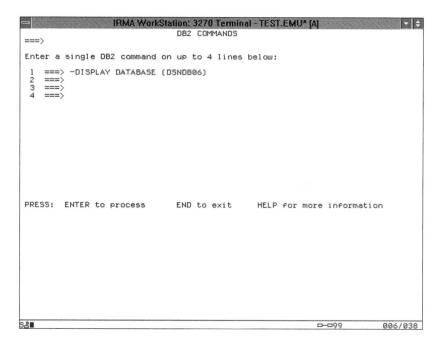

FIGURE 36.1   Issuing a DB2 command through DB2I.

The three types of DB2 environment commands are presented in the following sections.

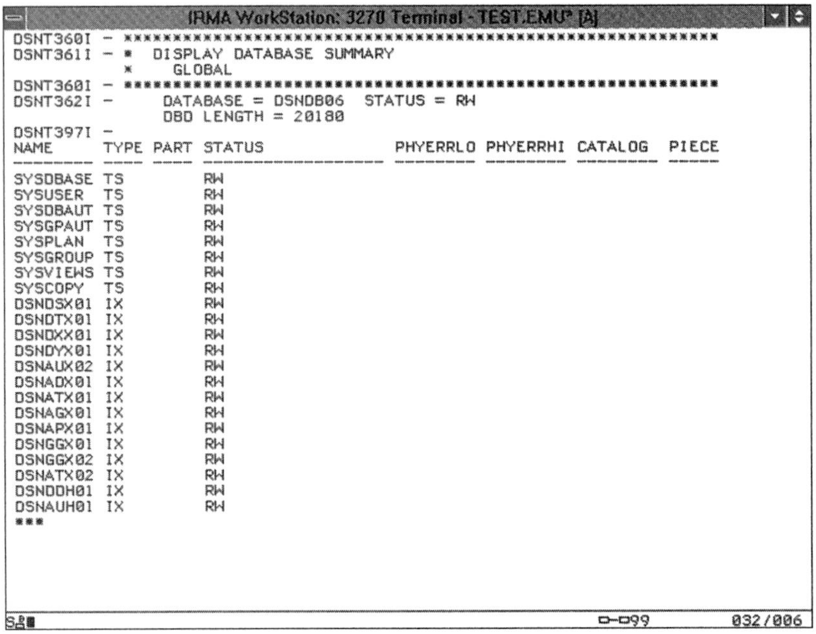

```
┌──────────────────────────────────────────────────────────────────────────────┐
│ ▭               IRMA WorkStation: 3270 Terminal - TEST.EMU² [A]         ▼│◆│
│ DSNT360I - ×××××××××××××××××××××××××××××××××××××××××××××××××××××××××××××××× │
│ DSNT361I - ■  DISPLAY DATABASE SUMMARY                                         │
│           ×      GLOBAL                                                        │
│ DSNT360I - ■■■■■■■■■■■■■■■■■■■■■■■■■■■■■■■■■■■■■■■■■■■■■■■■■■■■■■■■■■■■■■■■■■■■■■ │
│ DSNT362I -     DATABASE = DSNDB06  STATUS = RW                                 │
│                DBD LENGTH = 20180                                              │
│ DSNT397I -                                                                     │
│ NAME     TYPE PART STATUS            PHYERRLO PHYERRHI CATALOG  PIECE           │
│ -------- ---- ---- ----------------- -------- -------- -------- -----           │
│ SYSDBASE TS        RW                                                          │
│ SYSUSER  TS        RW                                                          │
│ SYSDBAUT TS        RW                                                          │
│ SYSGPAUT TS        RW                                                          │
│ SYSPLAN  TS        RW                                                          │
│ SYSGROUP TS        RW                                                          │
│ SYSVIEWS TS        RW                                                          │
│ SYSCOPY  TS        RW                                                          │
│ DSNDSX01 IX        RW                                                          │
│ DSNDTX01 IX        RW                                                          │
│ DSNDXX01 IX        RW                                                          │
│ DSNDYX01 IX        RW                                                          │
│ DSNAUX02 IX        RW                                                          │
│ DSNADX01 IX        RW                                                          │
│ DSNATX01 IX        RW                                                          │
│ DSNAGX01 IX        RW                                                          │
│ DSNAPX01 IX        RW                                                          │
│ DSNGGX01 IX        RW                                                          │
│ DSNGGX02 IX        RW                                                          │
│ DSNATX02 IX        RW                                                          │
│ DSNDDH01 IX        RW                                                          │
│ DSNAUH01 IX        RW                                                          │
│ ■■■                                                                            │
│                                                                                │
│                                                                                │
│                                                                                │
│ S▓■─────────────────────────────────────────────────□─□99────────032/006────  │
└──────────────────────────────────────────────────────────────────────────────┘
```

FIGURE 36.2   Response to the DB2 command issued in Figure 36.1.

Information-Gathering Commands

The information-gathering DB2 environment commands can be used to monitor DB2 objects and resources. They can return the status of DB2 databases, threads, utilities, and traces, as well as monitor the Resource Limit Facility and distributed data locations.

The DISPLAY command is used for information gathering. A description of each of the eight forms of the DISPLAY command follows:

-DISPLAY ARCHIVE	Display input archive log information.
-DISPLAY BUFFERPOOL	Displays the current status of active and/or inactive buffer pools.
-DISPLAY DATABASE	Displays the status and pending information for DB2 databases, table spaces, and indexes. The options that can be used with this command are
	USE—Displays who/what is using resources of these objects
	CLAIMERS—Displays the claims on these objects
	LOCKS—Displays the locks held on these objects
	LPL—Displays the logical page list entries
	WEPR—Displays the write error page range information

V7	`-DISPLAY DDF`	Displays DDF configuration and status information, as well as statistical details on distributed connections and threads.
	`-DISPLAY FUNCTION SPECIFIC`	Displays statistics about external DB2 user-defined functions.
	`-DISPLAY GROUP`	Displays information about the data sharing group.
	`-DISPLAY GROUPBUFFERPOOL`	Displays information about the status of DB2 group buffer pools.
	`-DISPLAY LOCATION`	Displays information for distributed threads.
	`-DISPLAY LOG`	Displays information about the DB2 logs and the status of the log offload task.
	`-DISPLAY PROCEDURE`	Displays information about stored procedures.
	`-DISPLAY RLIMIT`	Displays the status of the Resource Limit Facility, including the ID of the active RLST (Resource Limit Specification Table).
	`-DISPLAY THREAD`	Displays active and in-doubt connections to DB2 for a specified connection or all connections.
	`-DISPLAY TRACE`	Displays a list of active trace types and classes along with the specified destinations for each; consult Chapter 24, "Traditional DB2 Performance Monitoring," for a discussion of DB2 trace types and classes.
	`-DISPLAY UTILITY`	Displays the status of all active, stopped, or terminating utilities.

36

Information-Gathering Command Guidelines

Use the following guidelines when issuing commands to gather information about DB2 and its environment.

Use the `LIMIT` Option to Increase the Amount of Displayed Information   Use the `LIMIT` parameter of the `DISPLAY DATABASE` command to view database object lists greater than 50 lines long. The default number of lines returned by the `DISPLAY` command is 50, but the `LIMIT` parameter can be used to set the maximum number of lines returned to any numeric value. Because 50 lines of output usually is not sufficient to view all objects in a medium-size database, the recommendation is to specify the `LIMIT` parameter as follows:

```
-DISPLAY DATABASE(DSND851A) LIMIT(300)
```

To indicate no limit, you can replace the numeric limit with an asterisk (*).

Use `DISPLAY BUFFERPOOL` to Monitor DB2 Buffer Pools   Use the `DISPLAY BUFFERPOOL` command to display allocation information for each buffer pool. Refer to the example in Listing 34.2 for details of the information provided by `DISPLAY BUFFERPOOL`.

LISTING 34.2   Results of DISPLAY BUFFERPOOL

```
-DISPLAY BUFFERPOOL (BP0)

DSNB401I < BUFFERPOOL NAME BP0, BUFFERPOOL ID 0, USE COUNT 90
DSNB402I < VIRTUAL BUFFERPOOL SIZE = 2000 BUFFERS
                       ALLOCATED      =      2000    TO BE DELETED    =         0
                       IN USE/UPDATED =        12
DSNB403I < HIPERPOOL SIZE = 100000 BUFFERS, CASTOUT = YES
                       ALLOCATED      =    100000    TO BE DELETED    =         0
                       BACKED BY ES   =     91402
DSNB404I < THRESHOLDS -
                       VP SEQUENTIAL       = 80   HP SEQUENTIAL         = 80
                       DEFERRED WRITE      = 50   VERTICAL DEFERRED WRT = 10
                       IOP SEQUENTIAL      = 50
DSNB405I < HIPERSPACE NAMES - @001SSOP
DSN9022I < DSNB1CMD '-DISPLAY BUFFERPOOL' NORMAL COMPLETION
```

Use the DETAIL **Parameter for Buffer Pool Tuning Information**   To produce reports detailing buffer pool usage, specify the DETAIL parameter. Using DETAIL(INTERVAL) produces buffer pool usage information since the last execution of DISPLAY BUFFERPOOL. To report on buffer pool usage as of the time it was activated, specify DETAIL(*).

Listing 36.3 depicts the type of information provided by the DETAIL option of DISPLAY BUFFERPOOL.

LISTING 36.3   Results of DISPLAY BUFFERPOOL

```
-DISPLAY BUFFERPOOL (BP0), DETAIL(INTERVAL)

DSNB401I < BUFFERPOOL NAME BP0, BUFFERPOOL ID 0, USE COUNT 90
DSNB402I < VIRTUAL BUFFERPOOL SIZE = 2000 BUFFERS
                       ALLOCATED      =      2000    TO BE DELETED    =         0
                       IN USE/UPDATED =        12
DSNB403I < HIPERPOOL SIZE = 100000 BUFFERS, CASTOUT = YES
                       ALLOCATED      =    100000    TO BE DELETED    =         0
                       BACKED BY ES   =     91402
DSNB404I < THRESHOLDS -
                       VP SEQUENTIAL       = 80   HP SEQUENTIAL         = 80
                       DEFERRED WRITE      = 50   VERTICAL DEFERRED WRT = 10
                       IOP SEQUENTIAL      = 50
DSNB405I < HIPERSPACE NAMES - @001SSOP
DSNB409I < INCREMENTAL STATISITCS SINCE 05:43:22 DEC 23, 1993
DSNB411I < RANDOM GETPAGE    =      230 SYNC READ I/O ( R) =    180
                       SEQ.   GETPAGE   =      610 SYNC READ I/O ( S) =     20
                       DMTH HIT         =        0
DSNB412I < SEQUENTIAL PREFETCH -
                       REQUESTS         =      124    PREFETCH I/O   =     10
                       PAGES READ       =       69
DSNB413I < LIST PREFETCH -
                       REQUESTS         =        0    PREFETCH I/O   =      0
                       PAGES READ       =        0
DSNB414I < DYNAMIC PREFETCH -
                       REQUESTS         =        0    PREFETCH I/O   =      0
```

LISTING 36.3   Continued

```
                PAGES READ        =           0
DSNB415I < PREFETCH DISABLED -
                NO BUFFER         =           0      NO READ ENGINE =      0
DSNB420I < SYSPAGE UPDATES   =           0  SYS PAGES WRITTEN =      0
                ASYNC WRITE I/O   =           0  SYNC WRITE I/O   =      0
DSNB421I < DWT HIT           =           0  VERTICAL DWT HIT  =      0
                NO WRITE ENGINE   =           0
DSNB430I < HIPERPOOL ACTIVITY (NOT USING ASYNCHRONOUS
                DATA MOVER FACILITY) -
                SYNC HP READS     =         100    SYNC HP WRITES  =    120
                ASYNC HP READS    =           0    ASYNC HP WRITES =      0
                READ FAILURES     =           0    WRITE FAILURES  =      0
DSNB431I < HIPERPOOL ACTIVITY (USING ASYNCHRONOUS
                DATA MOVER FACILITY) -
                HP READS          =         231    HP WRITES       =    263
                READ FAILURES     =           0    WRITE FAILURES  =      0
DSNB440I < I/O PARALLEL ACTIVITY -
                PARALL REQUEST    =           2    DEGRADED PARALL =      0

DSN9022I < DSNB1CMD '-DISPLAY BUFFERPOOL' NORMAL COMPLETION
```

This report can be used to augment buffer pool tuning. Suggested action items are as follows:

- Monitor the read efficiency of each buffer pool using the formula, as presented in Chapter 28, "Tuning DB2's Components" (see the following). The higher the number, the better.

```
(Total GETPAGEs) /     [    (SEQUENTIAL PREFETCH) +
        (DYNAMIC PREFETCH) +
        (SYNCHRONOUS READ)
    ]
```

- If I/O is consistently high, consider tuning the buffer pool to handle the additional workload. For example, you could add virtual pool pages or hiperpool pages.

Use the LIST and LSTATS Parameters for Additional Detail   For additional buffer pool information, the LIST and LSTATS parameters can be specified:

LIST   Lists the open table spaces and indexes within the specified buffer pool(s).

LSTATS   Lists statistics for the table spaces and indexes reported by LIST. Statistical informa-
                tion is reset each time DISPLAY with LSTATS is issued, so the statistics are as of the
                last time LSTATS was issued.

Use LIST, DBNAME, and SPACENAM to Limit Information   Specifying LIST(*) causes DB2 to display all open index spaces and table spaces for the given buffer pool, whether they are currently in use or not. This option can be used in conjunction with the DBNAME and

SPACENAM parameters to display only those specific data sets you are interested in reviewing; for example

```
-DISPLAY BUFFERPOOL(BP0) LIST(*) DBNAME(DSNDB06) SPACENAM(SYSP*)
```

This statement causes only DB2 Catalog table spaces that start with the characters "SYSP" to be displayed. This should display only SYSPLAN and SYSPKAGE.

Use CASTOWNR and GBPDEP for Group Buffer Pool Detail   In a data sharing environment you will need to monitor DB2's usage of group buffer pools. Use the GBPDEP parameter to display only those data sets that are group buffer pool (GPB) dependent. An index space or table space is GBP-dependent if inter-DB2 R/W interest exists in it or changed pages from the object exist in the group buffer pool that have not yet been written to disk.

Additionally, you can use the CASTOWNR parameter to restrict the display to just those data sets for which this DB2 member is the castout owner.

Use DISPLAY LOG to Monitor DB2 Logging   Use the DISPLAY LOG command to display information about the number of logs, their current capacity, the setting of LOGLOAD, and which logs require offloading. Refer to the example in Listing 36.4 for details of the information provided by DISPLAY LOG.

LISTING 36.4   Results of DISPLAY LOG

```
-DIS LOG

DSNJ370I - DSNJCOOA LOG DISPLAY
¦ CURRENT COPY1 LOG = DSNC610.LOGCOPY1.DS03 IS 22% FULL
¦ CURRENT COPY2 LOG = DSNC610.LOGCOPY2.DS03 IS 22% FULL
¦ H/W RBA = 0000039A9F24, LOGLOAD = 150000
¦ FULL LOGS TO OFFLOAD = 2 OF 6, OFFLOAD TASK IS (BUSY,ALLC)
¦ DSNJ371I - DB2 RESTARTED 14:06:23 OCTOBER 22, 2003
¦ RESTART RBA 0000039A8000
¦ DSN9002I - DSNJC001 'DIS LOG' NORMAL COMPLETION
```

Use DISPLAY DATABASE to Monitor DB2 Objects   Use the DISPLAY DATABASE command to monitor the status of table spaces and indexes. The possible status values follow. When a status other than RO or RW is encountered, the object is in an indeterminate state or is being processed by a DB2 utility.

V8	ARBDP	Index is in Advisory Rebuild Pending status; the index should be rebuilt to improve performance (and allow the index to be used for index-only access again).
V8	AREO*	The table space, index, or partition is in Advisory Reorg Pending status; the object should be reorganized to improve performance.
	ACHKP	The Auxiliary Check Pending status has been set for the base table space. An error exists in the LOB column of the base table space.
	AREST	The table space, index space or partition is in Advisory Restart Pending status. If backout activity against the object is not already underway, either issue the RECOVER POSTPONED command or recycle the specifying LBACKOUT=AUTO.

AUXW	Either the base table space or the LOB table space is in the Auxiliary Warning status. This warning status indicates an error in the LOB column of the base table space or an invalid LOB in the LOB table space.
CHKP	The Check Pending status has been set for this table space or partition.
COPY	The Copy Pending flag has been set for this table space or partition.
DEFER	Deferred restart is required for the object.
GRECP	The table space, table space partition, index, index partition, or logical index partition is in the group buffer pool Recover Pending state.
ICOPY	The index is in Informational Copy Pending status.
INDBT	In-doubt processing is required for the object.
LPL	The table space, table space partition, index, index partition, or logical index partition has logical page errors.
LSTOP	The logical partition of a non-partitioning index is stopped.
PSRBD	The entire non-partitioning index space is in Page Set Rebuild Pending status.
OPENF	The table space, table space partition, index, index partition, or logical index partition had an open data set failure.
PSRCP	Indicates Page Set Recover Pending state for an index (non-partitioning indexes).
PSRBD	The nonpartitioning index space is in a Page Set Rebuild Pending status.
RBDP	The physical or logical index partition is in the Rebuild Pending status.
RBDP*	The logical partition of a nonpartitioning index is in the Rebuild Pending status, and the entire index is inaccessible to SQL applications. However, only the logical partition needs to be rebuilt.
RECP	The Recover Pending flag has been set for this table space, table space partition, index, index partition, or logical index partition.
REFP	The table space, index space, or index is in Refresh Pending status.
RELDP	The object has a release dependency.
REORP	The data partition is in the Reorg Pending status.
REST	Restart processing has been initiated for the table space, table space partition, index, index partition, or logical index partition.
RESTP	The table space or index is in the Restart Pending status.
RO	The table space, table space partition, index, index partition, or logical index partition has been started for read-only processing.
RW	The table space, table space partition, index, index partition, or logical index partition has been started for read and write processing.
STOP	The table space, table space partition, index, index partition, or logical index partition has been stopped.

V7 (at REFP)

V7 (at RELDP)

36

STOPE	The table space or index is stopped because of an invalid log RBA or LRSN in one of its pages.
STOPP	A stop is pending for the table space, table space partition, index, index partition, or logical index partition.
UT	The table space, table space partition, index, index partition, or logical index partition has been started for the execution of utilities only.
UTRO	The table space, table space partition, index, index partition, or logical index partition has been started for RW processing, but only RO processing is enabled because a utility is in progress for that object.
UTRW	The table space, table space partition, index, index partition, or logical index partition has been started for RW processing, and a utility is in progress for that object.
UTUT	The table space, table space partition, index, index partition, or logical index partition has been started for RW processing, but only UT processing is enabled because a utility is in progress for that object.
V7 WEPR	Write error page range information.

Use DISPLAY DATABASE **to View Restricted Objects**   By specifying the RESTRICT option on the DISPLAY DATABASE command, only restricted DB2 objects are listed. A database is considered restricted if it is in one of the following states:

- Stopped
- Started for RO or UT processing

A table space or index is considered restricted if it is in one of the following states:

- Stopped
- Started for RO or UT processing
- Being processed by a stopped or active utility
- In a pending state (CHKP, COPY, RECP, or GRECP)
- Contains an LPL or page error range

Use the RESTRICT option to ascertain whether any objects require action to restore them to a useable state.

The ADVISORY option can also be used with DISPLAY DATABASE. Specifying the ADVISORY option on the DISPLAY DATABASE command causes the display to show DB2 objects where read-write access is allowed, but an action needs to be taken on the object. The ICOPY and AUXW statuses are considered ADVISORY states. Finally, you can use the AREST option to identify objects in an advisory restart pending state.

Use DISPLAY DATABASE **to View Objects Being Used**   By specifying the ACTIVE option of the DISPLAY DATABASE command, only table spaces and indexes that have been allocated for use by an application are listed. Use the ACTIVE option to determine the currently allocated objects.

Use DISPLAY DATABASE to Determine Database Usage   The USE option of the DISPLAY DATABASE command displays information on how the database is being used. It returns information on the applications and subsystems to which the database is allocated, the connection IDs, correlation IDs, and authorization IDs for all applications allocated to the displayed table spaces and the LUWID and location of remote threads accessing the database.

Use DISPLAY DATABASE to View Locking Information   Two options of the DISPLAY DATABASE command, LOCKS and CLAIMERS, can be used to view locking details for the database and its associated table spaces. The LOCKS clause displays the applications and subsystems having locks held, waited on, or retained for the specified database as well as the transaction locks for all table spaces, tables, index spaces, and table space partitions being displayed. It will also show drain locks held by running jobs.

The CLAIMERS clause displays the claims on all table spaces, index spaces, and table space partitions whose status is displayed. If the CLAIMERS clause is specified, it overrides both the LOCKS and USE clauses.

Use DISPLAY DATABASE to View the Logical Page List   Pages that are logically in error are written to a special list known as the logical page list (LPL). A logical page error is one that can be corrected without redefining physical devices, for example, caused by a connection problem. The LPL clause can be specified on the DISPLAY DATABASE command to view the logical page errors for the database, table space, or partition. Starting or recovering the object in question can clear logical page errors.

> **NOTE**
>
> If starting the object with the LPL error does not work, DB2 will upgrade the failure to a physical failure. If this occurs, the object must be recovered.

V8 **Simplify the DISPLAY Output Using OVERVIEW**   Consider specifying the OVERVIEW parameter on your DISPLAY command to display each object in the database on its own line. This causes the output to be limited to only the space names and space types that exist in the specified databases. The number of parts will be displayed for any partitioned table spaces and index spaces.

The OVERVIEW keyword cannot be specified with any other parameters or keywords except for SPACENAM, LIMIT, and AFTER.

Use Wildcards to View Multiple Databases   DISPLAY DATABASE can use the asterisk as a wildcard specifier in the operand portion of the command. Consider the following command:

```
-DISPLAY DATABASE (DSN8*)
```

This command lists only the databases that contain the DSN8 characters as the first four characters in their name—the sample database.

Use ONLY **to Display Database Information Without Related Objects**   Normally, the DISPLAY DATABASE command will display information about a database and all of its associated table spaces and indexes. You can use the ONLY option without the SPACENAM( ) keyword to display information about the database, but not the table spaces and indexes in the database.

Use DISPLAY PROCEDURE **to Monitor Stored Procedure Statistics**   The display command can be used to monitor the status of stored procedures. This command will show

- Whether the named procedure is currently started or stopped

- How many requests are currently executing

- The high water mark for concurrently running requests

- How many requests are currently queued

- How many times a request has timed-out

- The WLM environment where the stored procedure executes

Use DISPLAY FUNCTION SPECIFIC **to Monitor UDF Statistics**   The display command can be used to monitor the status of stored procedures. This command displays one output line for each function that a DB2 application has accessed.

- Whether the named function is currently started or stopped, and why

- How many requests are currently executing

- The high water mark for concurrently running requests

- How many requests are currently queued

- How many times a request has timed-out

- The WLM environment where the function executes

Understand the Stored Procedure and UDF Status   When displaying information about stored procedures and UDFs using the DISPLAY PROCEDURE and DISPLAY FUNCTION SPECIFIC commands, a status is returned indicating the state of the procedure or UDF. A procedure or UDF can be in one of four potential states:

STARTED	Requests for the function can be processed
STOPQUE	Requests are queued
STOPREJ	Requests are rejected
STOPABN	Requests are rejected because of abnormal termination

Use DISPLAY UTILITY **to Monitor DB2 Utilities**   The DISPLAY UTILITY command can be used to monitor the progress of an active utility. By monitoring the current phase of the utility and matching this information with the utility phase information, you can determine the relative progress of the utility as it processes.

For example, if the DISPLAY UTILITY command indicates that the current phase of a LOAD utility is the REPORT phase, you know that there is only one more phase and that seven phases have been processed.

> **CAUTION**
>
> The IBM service aid and sample programs will not appear in the DISPLAY UTILITY output.
>
> Many third-party utilities do not show up when -DIS UTIL is issued if they run outside the scope of DB2. Use the display tool provided by the third-party vendor instead.

Use DISPLAY UTILITY to Gauge a Utility's Progress   For the DB2 COPY, REORG, and RUNSTATS utilities, the DISPLAY UTILITY also can be used to monitor the progress of particular phases. The COUNT specified for each phase lists the number of pages that have been loaded, unloaded, copied, or read.

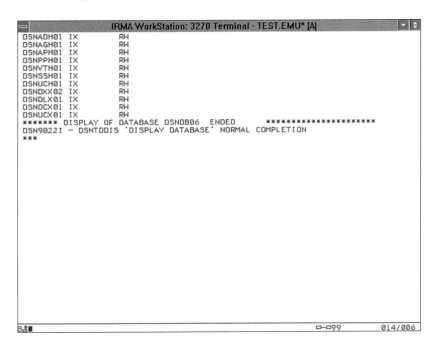

FIGURE 36.3   DISPLAY UTILITY output.

The REORG utility in Figure 36.3 is in the RELOAD phase and has processed nine records. COUNT = *nnn* indicates that *nnn* pages have been unloaded by the REORG utility in the UNLOAD phase. By comparing this number to the number of pages for the table space as found in the NACTIVE column of SYSIBM.SYSTABLESPACE, you can track the progress of the following phases:

Utility	Phase
COPY	COPY
REORG	UNLOAD, RELOAD
RUNSTATS	RUNSTATS

> **NOTE**
>
> You also can check the progress of the CHECK, LOAD, RECOVER, and MERGE utilities using -DIS
> UTIL. The number of rows, index entries, or pages that have been processed are displayed.

Centralize DISPLAY Capability   A centralized area in your organization should have the capability to issue all the information-gathering commands online to effectively administer the DB2 subsystem. This centralized area should be staffed such that support is available when DB2 applications, queries, or utilities are being processed.

Be Wary of the Dynamic Nature of Displayed Information   The information returned by the DISPLAY command is dynamic. As the information is displayed, it may also be changing, making the displayed information inaccurate. Therefore, do not rely solely on information issued by the DISPLAY command unless it can be verified from another source or by multiple executions of the same DISPLAY command. Other sources for verification include online performance monitors and calling end users. Usually, a combination of sources should be consulted before taking any action based on information returned from the DISPLAY command.

Administrative Commands

Administrative commands are provided to assist the user with the active administration, resource specification, and environment modification of DB2 subsystems. Each command modifies an environmental aspect of the DB2 subsystem. The administrative commands are as follows:

-ALTER BUFFERPOOL	Used to alter buffer pool size, thresholds, and CASTOUT attributes for active and inactive buffer pools.
-ALTER GROUPBUFFERPOOL	Used to alter the attributes of group buffer pools.
-ALTER UTILITY	Can change the value of some parameters for the REORG utility.
-ARCHIVE LOG	Forces a DB2 log archival.
-CANCEL THREAD	Cancels a local or distributed DB2 thread
-MODIFY TRACE	Changes the specifications for active DB2 traces.
-RECOVER BSDS	Re-establishes a valid Boot Strap Data Set after an I/O error on the BSDS data set.
-RECOVER INDOUBT	Recovers in-doubt threads that cannot be recovered automatically by DB2 or the appropriate transaction manager.

-RECOVER POSTPONED	Completes backout processing for units of recovery that are left incomplete during an earlier restart (POSTPONED ABORT units of recovery). To be used when automatic resolution was not selected.
-RESET GENERICLU	Purges information stored by VTAM in the coupling facility.
-RESET INDOUBT	Purges information from the "in doubt" thread report (generated by the -DISPLAY THREAD command).
-SET ARCHIVE	Used to set the parameters for log archiving.
-SET LOG	Modifies the checkpoint frequency. The changes that SET LOG makes are temporary; at restart, DB2 again uses the values that were specified when DB2 was installed. The new LOGLOAD value takes effect following the next system checkpoint.
-SET SYSPARM	Modifies DSNZPARM parameters without recycling DB2.
-START DATABASE	Starts a stopped database, table space, table space partition, index, or index partition or changes the status of these objects to RW, RO, or UT.
-START FUNCTION SPECIFIC	Starts an external UDF that is stopped. Not to be used for built-in functions or UDFs that are sourced on another function.
-START PROCEDURE	Starts a stored procedure enabling subsequent execution using the CALL statement.
-START RLIMIT	Starts the Resource Limit Facility with a specific Resource Limit Specification Table (RLST).
-START TRACE	Activates DB2 traces, classes, and IFCIDs; specifies limiting constraints for plans and authids; and specifies the output destination for the activated trace records.
-STOP DATABASE	Stops a database, a table space, or an index and closes the underlying VSAM data sets associated with the stopped object. As of DB2 V3, partitions can be stopped individually.
-STOP FUNCTION SPECIFIC	Stops an external UDF disabling subsequent execution. Not to be used for built-in functions or UDFs that are sourced on another function.
-STOP PROCEDURE	Stops a stored procedure disabling subsequent execution.
-STOP RLIMIT	Stops the Resource Limit Facility.
-STOP TRACE	Stops the specified DB2 traces and classes.
-TERM UTILITY	Terminates the execution of an active or a stopped DB2 utility, releases all the resources that are being utilized by the utility, and cleans up the DB2 Directory.

V7

36

Administrative Command Guidelines

When you issue administrative commands, you are actually changing the DB2 environment. Administrative commands should be used with caution. Review the following guidelines before utilizing administrative commands.

Educate the Users of Administrative Commands   Only an experienced analyst who knows the DB2 commands and their effect on the DB2 subsystem and its components should issue administrative commands. Such control should be accomplished by implementing strict DB2 authorization procedures.

Use ALTER BUFFERPOOL to Dynamically Manage Bufferpools   The ALTER BUFFERPOOL command can be used to dynamically change the size and characteristics of a buffer pool. The following parameters can be used to change the buffer pool using ALTER BUFFERPOOL:

VPSIZE	Size of the virtual buffer pool
HPSIZE	Size of the associated hiperpool
VPSEQT	Virtual pool sequential steal threshold
HPSEQT	Hiperpool sequential steal threshold
VPPSEQT	Virtual pool parallel sequential steal threshold
VPXPSEQT	Virtual pool assisting parallel sequential steal threshold
DWQT	Virtual pool deferred write threshold
VDWQT	Virtual pool vertical deferred write threshold (by data set)
CASTOUT	Hiperpool dirty page discard
VPTYPE	Whether the buffer pool is allocated in the DB2 database services address space (PRIMARY) or in a data space associated with DB2 (DATASPACE)

Use ALTER UTILITY to Impact REORG Processing   The ALTER UTILITY command can be used to change the value of the DEADLINE, MAXRO, LONGLOG, and DELAY parameters for REORG utilities running SHRLEVEL REFERENCE or SHRLEVEL CHANGE. Refer to Chapter 33, "Data Organization Utilities," for more information on the functionality of these parameters.

Use ARCHIVE LOG to Synchronize Disaster Recovery Plans with DB2   Issue the ARCHIVE LOG command to synchronize DB2 log archival and copying with application and DB2 Catalog image copies sent to a remote site for disaster recovery. See Chapter 38, "DB2 Contingency Planning," for further guidance.

Use ARCHIVE LOG to Synchronize New Logs with Shift Changes   Sometimes a new active DB2 log should begin at the commencement of each new operational shift. This can be accomplished with the ARCHIVE LOG command.

Use RECOVER INDOUBT with Caution   The RECOVER INDOUBT command can abort or commit changes made by in-doubt threads. Be cautious before committing in-doubt threads. Most DB2 programs are coded to process updates in commit scopes defined as a unit of work.

The unit of work, as described in Chapter 11, "Using DB2 in an Application Program," is coded as much as possible to maintain data integrity between related tables. If the RECOVER INDOUBT command commits changes for a partial unit of work, the affected tables may not be in a consistent state. If database-enforced referential integrity is *always* used, this is not a concern because the database forces the tables to be in a consistent state. However, very few applications require that every referential constraint be explicitly defined and enforced by DB2.

Avoid Using ACCESS(FORCE)   Issuing the START DATABASE command with the ACCESS(FORCE) option is not recommended because it may cause table spaces or indexes to be in an inconsistent state. ACCESS(FORCE) forces all pending flags (check, copy, and recover) to be reset for the specified object. Never use ACCESS(FORCE) unless you are absolutely sure that the data is in a consistent state for the specified object (for example, after restoring objects using the DSN1COPY service aid utility).

To be safe, never use ACCESS(FORCE). Instead, use the appropriate utility to reset the exception flags.

Ensure That DASD Is Online Before Stopping Databases   The DASD volume for the underlying VSAM data sets for the object that will be started by the START DATABASE command does not need to be online when the START command is issued. Because the STOP DATABASE command closes the underlying VSAM data sets, however, the corresponding volume for that object must be online when the STOP command is issued.

Start and Stop at the Partition Level   The START and STOP commands can be executed for partitioned table spaces and indexes at the partition level. This functionality enhances availability by enabling users to stop only portions of an application (table space or index).

Be Aware of the Time Constraints of the STOP **Command**   The STOP command can be used to close VSAM data sets and cause buffer pages associated with the closed data set to be flushed and forced to DASD. The VSAM close operation may take a while before it is complete, though. The buffers may not be flushed completely to DASD immediately after the STOP DATABASE command completes. Subsequent processing must consider this fact.

Explicitly Start Objects Stopped with the SPACENAM **Parameter**   When a table space or index is explicitly stopped using the SPACENAM parameter of the STOP DATABASE command, it must be explicitly started again before it can be accessed. Starting at the database level will not affect the status of explicitly stopped table spaces or indexes.

Use START PROCEDURE **Before Calling**   The START PROCEDURE command must be issued for each DB2 stored procedure prior to any application calling the stored procedure. Failure to start a stored procedure before trying to execute it with the CALL statement results in the CALL statement failing.

Use the ACTION **Clause When Stopping Stored Procedures**   The stop command disables subsequent executions of the named stored procedure. The ACTION clause can be specified to indicate whether future attempts to run the stored procedure will be entirely rejected [ACTION(REJECT)] or queued [ACTION(QUEUE)] to be run when the stored procedure is started again.

36

Use START RLIMIT **to Vary Resource Limits**   START RLIMIT can use different resource limit specification tables (RLST) with different limits. By specifying the ID parameter, a specific RLST is chosen; for example

```
-START RLIMIT ID=02
```

starts the RLF using the SYSIBM.DSNRLS02 table. This enables different limits to be specified for

- Different times of the day

- Batch and online processing

- Heavy and light ad hoc processing

Use START TRACE **to Specify Trace Destinations**   When issuing the START TRACE command, each type of trace can specify different destinations for the trace output. The following lists destinations for each type of trace:

Trace Destination	Trace Types
GTF	ACCTG, AUDIT, GLOBAL, MONITOR, PERFM, STAT
OP*n*	ACCTG, AUDIT, GLOBAL, MONITOR, PERFM, STAT
OPX	ACCTG, AUDIT, GLOBAL, MONITOR, PERFM, STAT
RES	GLOBAL
SMF	ACCTG, AUDIT, GLOBAL, MONITOR, PERFM, STAT
SRV	ACCTG, AUDIT, GLOBAL, MONITOR, PERFM, STAT

Use START TRACE **to Specify Constraints**   When you issue the START TRACE command, each type of trace can place optional constraints on the data to be collected. The following lists constraints for each type of trace:

Constraint Type	Trace Types
AUTHID	ACCTG, AUDIT, GLOBAL, MONITOR, PERFM
CLASS	ACCTG, AUDIT, GLOBAL, MONITOR, PERFM, STAT
PLAN	ACCTG, AUDIT, GLOBAL, MONITOR, PERFM
RMID	GLOBAL, MONITOR, PERFM

Use No More Than Six Active Traces   Although as many as 32 traces can be active at one time, you should limit the number of active traces to 6 to avoid performance degradation. Add this recommendation to the trace guidelines presented in Chapter 24 to establish the proper controls for issuing DB2 traces.

Be Aware of the Authority Required to Terminate Utilities   To terminate utilities, the issuer of the TERM UTILITY command must meet *one* of the following requirements. The issuer must

- Be the user who initially submitted the utility

- Have SYSADM, SYSCTRL, or SYSOPR authority

If your operational support staff must have the ability to terminate utilities that they did not originally submit, they should be granted SYSOPR authority. However, SYSOPR authority permits the user to start and stop DB2, which is not generally acceptable because the uncontrolled issuing of these commands can wreak havoc on a production system. There is no viable alternative to SYSOPR authority, though, because explicit TERM UTILITY authority is unavailable.

Avoid Using Wildcards When Terminating Utilities   When terminating utilities, explicitly specify the UID to be terminated, rather than use the -TERMINATE UTILITY command to terminate all utilities invoked by your ID. When you explicitly specify what should be terminated, you avoid inadvertently terminating an active utility. After a utility is terminated, it can never be restarted. The utility must be rerun from the beginning and may require data recovery before rerunning.

V7 **Use Caution When Changing System Parameters "On The Fly"**   Changing system parameters can have a dramatic impact on the manner in which your DB2 subsystem operates. Before changing any DSNZPARM system parameters using the SET SYSPARM command, be sure to examine the parameter in–depth and understand the effect the change will have on your DB2 subsystem. Also, be aware that not every system parameter can be changed dynamically. Consult the IBM *DB2 Installation Guide* (Appendix C) for a complete list of system parameters, including information regarding whether or not each parameter can be changed dynamically.

Environment Control Commands

The environment control commands affect the status of the DB2 subsystem and the Distributed Data Facility. These commands commonly are issued only by the DB2 systems programmer, systems administrator, or DBA. A brief description of the environment control commands follows:

-START DB2	Initializes and establishes the DB2 subsystem
-START DDF	Starts the Distributed Data Facility
-STOP DB2	Stops the DB2 subsystem
-STOP DDF	Stops the Distributed Data Facility

Environment Control Command Guidelines

Before issuing environment control commands, be sure to review the following guidelines.

Control the Use of Environment Control Commands   Secure the environment control commands so that they are issued only by technically astute administrative areas.

Verify the Completion of START DB2 **and** STOP DB2   Make sure that the START DB2 command successfully completes by ensuring that access to DB2 is available using DB2I.

36

Another way to verify that the START DB2 command was successful is to make certain that the started tasks for DB2 are active. The default names for these tasks are:

DSNMSTR	DB2 Master Region
DSNDBM1	DB2 Database Region
IRLMPROC	DB2 IRLM

Your installation probably has renamed these address spaces, but the names are probably similar.

Be sure that the STOP DB2 command successfully completes by ensuring that the started tasks for the subsystem being stopped are no longer active.

Verify the Completion of START DDF and STOP DDF   You can check the status of the START DDF and STOP DDF commands by monitoring the status of the DDF address space. (The default name of the DDF address space is DSNDDF.)

Use MODE(FORCE) Sparingly   Exercise caution before stopping the DB2 subsystem with the MODE(FORCE) parameter. The FORCE option terminates all active programs and utilities. As such, in-doubt units of recovery may result by forcing DB2 to stop in this manner. The MODE(QUIESCE) option allows all active programs and utilities to complete before DB2 is stopped.

When DB2 is stopped with MODE(FORCE) or MODE(QUIESCE), only currently executing programs are affected. No new programs or utilities are permitted to run.

DSN **Commands**

DSN commands are actually subcommands of the DSN command. DSN is a control program that enables users to issue DB2 environment commands, plan management commands, and commands to develop and run application programs. DSN commands can be run in the TSO foreground, either directly or indirectly, or in the TSO background. An example of issuing the DSN command processor indirectly in the foreground is through DB2I. (The DB2I panels accomplish most of their functions by issuing DSN commands.) DSN commands can be issued in the background with the IKJEFT01 terminal monitor program.

There are nine DSN commands:

DSN	A command processor that enables the user to issue DB2 environment commands from a TSO session or in a batch job. For example:

```
DSN SYSTEM (DSN)
    - DISPLAY THREAD (*)
END
```

The DSN command processor must be invoked before any DSN command that follows can be issued.

ABEND	Used to request and obtain a dump when problems are suspected with another DSN subcommand. Use this DSN command under the guidance of the IBM Support Center.

BIND   Builds an application plan or package from one or more database request modules.

DCLGEN   Produces the SQL DECLARE TABLE specification and a working storage data declaration section for VS/COBOL, COBOL II, PL/I, or C.

END   Terminates the DSN session and returns the user to TSO.

FREE   Deletes application plans and packages.

REBIND   Rebuilds an application plan or package when SQL statements in a program's DBRM have not been changed. REBIND also can modify the BIND parameters.

RUN   Executes an application program. The program can contain SQL statements, but this is not required.

SPUFI   Executes the SPUFI program. This subcommand can be issued only when processing under ISPF; it cannot be submitted in a batch job.

DSN Command Guidelines

Deploy the following guidelines to ensure effective use of the DSN command.

Use DB2I, Online TSO, or a Batch Job to Invoke DSN   The DSN command processor can be invoked in three ways: from the DB2I panels, online by entering DSN (which enables the user to enter subcommands at the DSN prompt), or in batch, specifying subcommands in the SYSTSIN data set.

In general, it is safest to invoke the DSN commands from the DB2I panels. Some DSN commands such as RUN and BIND, however, may need to be processed in a batch job that invokes the DSN command under the auspices of IKJEFT01. Batch TSO is the only method IBM supplies with DB2 for running a batch DB2 program.

Refer to Chapter 18, "The Doors to DB2," for examples of issuing DSN commands through the DB2I panels.

Use END to Terminate a DSN Command Session   A DSN session is terminated by issuing the END subcommand, by issuing a new DSN command, or by pressing the attention key (PA1) twice in succession.

Use the TEST Option to Trace DSN Problems   If a subcommand or function of the DSN command appears to be functioning improperly, the TEST option can be used to trace DSN commands.

V8   **Use the GROUP Option to Consider Group Attach Processing**   Use the GROUP parameter to indicate that the DSN command should consider group attach processing when the specified system is not active. For example,

```
DSN SYSTEM (DB2) GROUP (YES)
```

IMS Commands

The IMS commands affect the operation of DB2 and IMS/TM. IMS commands must be issued from a valid terminal connected to IMS/TM, and the issuer must have the appropriate IMS authority. Consult the IMS manuals in the following list for additional information on IMS commands:

> SG24-5352, IMS Primer
>
> SC27-1284, IMS V8 Administration Guide: System
>
> SC27-1285, IMS V8 Administration Guide: Transaction Manager
>
> GC27-1301, IMS V8 Messages and Codes, Volume 1
>
> GC27-1302, IMS V8 Messages and Codes, Volume 2
>
> SC27-1304, IMS V8 Operations Guide
>
> SC27-1307, IMS V8 Summary of Operator Commands
>
> GC27-1305, IMS V8 Release Planning Guide

The following IMS commands pertain to DB2:

/CHANGE	Resets in-doubt units of recovery
/DISPLAY	Displays outstanding units of recovery or the status of the connection between IMS/TM and the DB2 subsystem
/SSR	Enables the user to issue DB2 environment commands from an IMS/TM terminal, for example: /SSR -DISPLAY THREAD (*)
/START	Enables the connection between IMS/TM and an active DB2 subsystem
/STOP	Disables the connection between IMS/TM and an active DB2 subsystem
/TRACE	Enables and disables IMS tracing

IMS Command Guidelines

The following techniques are useful when issuing IMS commands that impact DB2.

Control the Use of Critical IMS Commands   The /CHANGE, /START, and /STOP commands should be secured commands. Because these commands can damage IMS/TM transactions that are being processed, they should be avoided during peak processing times. A centralized authority consisting of only systems programmers and DBAs should administer and invoke these commands.

Use /START and /STOP to Refresh the IMS-to-DB2 Connection   The /START and /STOP commands can be used to refresh the IMS to DB2 subsystem connection without bringing down IMS/TM.

Use /TRACE with Caution   The /TRACE command should be issued only by a qualified analyst who understands the ramifications of IMS tracing. This is usually best left to the IMS DBA or systems programmer.

CICS Commands

The CICS commands affect the operation of DB2 and CICS. CICS commands must be issued from a valid terminal connected to CICS, and the issuer must have the appropriate CICS authority.

All CICS commands that pertain to DB2 are prefixed with DSNC. DSNC is a CICS transaction that enables the execution of DB2 commands from a CICS terminal.

The following CICS commands pertain to DB2:

DSNC	Enables the user to issue DB2 environment commands from a CICS terminal. For example: DSNC -DISPLAY THREAD(*) DSNC is also a required prefix for all CICS commands related to DB2.
DSNC DISCONNECT	Enables the user to disconnect DB2 threads.
DSNC DISPLAY	Displays resource and statistical information for CICS transactions that access DB2 data. If more than one page of information is displayed by this command, use the following syntax to page through the information. At the top of the CICS screen, enter P/x, where x is a number indicating which page to display. P/1 displays page 1, P/2 displays page 2, and so on.
DSNC MODIFY	Enables the modification of the message queue destination of the DB2CONN; and the maximum active thread value for the pool, for DSNC commands, or for DB2ENTRY.
DSNC STOP	Disables the CICS attachment to DB2.
DSNC STRT	Enables the CICS attachment to DB2.

36

CICS Command Guidelines

The following techniques are useful when issuing CICS commands that impact DB2.

Control the Use of Critical CICS Commands   The DSNC DISCONNECT, DSNC MODIFY, DSNC STRT, and DSNC STOP commands should be secured commands. Because these commands can damage CICS transactions that are being processed, they should be avoided during peak processing times. A centralized authority consisting of only systems programmers and DBAs should administer and invoke these commands.

Use DSNC DISPLAY PLAN to Monitor DB2 Threads   Use the DSNC DISPLAY PLAN (or DSNC DISPLAY TRANSACTION) command to get information about DB2 threads. For each created thread, the following output is returned:

DB2ENTRY	Name of the DB2ENTRY, *COMMAND for DSNC command calls, or *POOL for pool statistics.
S	Status of the threads where "A" indicates active within a unit of work and "I" indicates that a protected thread is waiting for work.

PLAN   Plan name associated with this thread.

PRI-AUTH   Primary authorization ID for the thread.

SEC-AUTH   Secondary authorization ID for the thread, if one exists.

CORRELATION   Correlation ID for the thread (12 bytes).

Use DSNC DISPLAY STATISTICS **to Monitor DB2 Transaction Information**   Use the DSNC DISPLAY STATISTICS command to obtain statistics for DB2 transactions. The information provided by this command is an accumulation of statistical counters because the CICS attachment to DB2 is activated with the DSNC STRT command. Directly after the DB2 subsystem is attached to CICS, all of these numbers are 0; this should be taken into account in analyzing these statistics. For example, these counters are significantly smaller if the attachment is stopped and started daily instead of once a month.

The DSNC DISPLAY STATISTICS command will provide the following output:

DB2ENTRY   Name of the DB2ENTRY, *COMMAND for DSNC command calls, or *POOL for pool statistics.

PLAN   Plan name associated with this entry. DSNC does not have a transaction associated with it, so PLAN is blank. A string of asterisks indicates that dynamic plan allocation was specified for this entry.

CALLS   Number of SQL executions issued by transactions associated with this RCT entry.

AUTHS   Number of sign-ons for transactions associated with this RCT entry. A sign-on occurs only when a new thread is created or when an existing thread is reused with a new authid or a different plan.

W/P   Number of times any transaction associated with this entry was diverted to the pool or had to wait for an available thread.

HIGH   High-water mark for the number of threads needed by any transaction associated with this entry.

ABORTS   Number of aborts, including both abends and rollbacks, encountered by transactions associated with this entry.

COMMITS   Number of COMMITs executed by transactions associated with this entry.

1-PHASE   Number of single phase commits for transactions associated with this entry.

2-PHASE   Number of two-phase commits for transactions associated with this entry.

TSO Commands

The DB2 TSO commands are CLISTs that can be used to help compile and run DB2 programs or build utility JCL. The TSO commands are issued from a TSO session, either online using ISPF panels or in batch using the IKJEFT01 program. There are two TSO commands:

DSNH	Can be used to precompile, translate, compile, link, bind, and run DB2 application programs written in COBOL, Assembler, FORTRAN, PL/I, or C.
DSNU	Can be used to generate JCL for online DB2 utilities.

IRLM Commands

The IRLM commands affect the operation of the IRLM defined to a DB2 subsystem. IRLM commands must originate from an MVS console, and the issuer must have the appropriate security.

The following IRLM commands pertain to DB2:

MODIFY *irlmproc*,ABEND	Terminates the IRLM identified by *irlmproc* abnormally, regardless of whether any IMS/VS subsystems are controlled by the specified IRLM. Compare this command with the MODIFY *irlmproc*, STOP trace command.
MODIFY *irlmproc*,DIAG	Initiates diagnostic dumps for IRLM subsystems.
MODIFY *irlmproc*,PURGE	Releases IRLM locks retained due to a DB2, IRLM, or system failure.
MODIFY *irlmproc*,SET	Can be used to dynamically set parameters for maximum allowable IRLM amounts for CSA, private storage, and number of trace buffers, as well as number of LOCK LTE entries to be specified on the next connect to the XCF LOCK structure, timeout value for a specified subsystem, and local deadlock frequency.
MODIFY *irlmproc*,START *trace*	Starts internal IRLM traces for the IRLM identified by *irlmproc*. Valid *trace* specifications are ITRACE for internal tracing, GTRACE for GTF tracing, PTBTRACE for PTB buffer tracing, or TRACE to start all three types of traces.
MODIFY *irlmproc*,STATUS	Displays the status of the IRLM identified by *irlmproc*, including information for each subsystem connected to the specified IRLM.
MODIFY *irlmproc*,STOP *trace*	Stops internal IRLM traces for the IRLM identified by *irlmproc*.
START *irlmproc*	Starts the IRLM identified by *irlmproc* using an installation-defined proc.
STOP *irlmproc*	Stops the IRLM identified by *irlmproc*.
TRACE CT, *options*	Stops, starts, or modifies an IRLM diagnostic trace.

IRLM Command Guidelines

The following guidelines offer practical advice for using commands that impact the DB2 IRLM.

36

Stop the IRLM to Stop DB2   The quickest way to bring down a DB2 subsystem is to issue the STOP *irlmproc* command from an MVS console. When the -STOP DB2 command does not terminate the DB2 subsystem quickly enough, consider stopping that DB2 subsystem's IRLM.

Use the STATUS Parameter to Monitor the IRLM   Use the STATUS option of the MODIFY *irlmproc* command to periodically monitor the effectiveness of the IRLM.

CHAPTER 37

DB2 Utility and Command Guidelines

Now you know about each of the DB2 utilities and commands. The specific definitions and usage guidelines presented in the first few chapters of Part VI, "DB2 Utilities and Commands," are certainly helpful, but some general considerations should be discussed. This chapter presents general guidelines for the effective use of DB2 utilities and commands, and it also discusses the pending states.

This chapter presents general advice. Whereas previous chapters presented specific guidelines for each utility, command, or group of utilities or commands, this chapter covers topics that span more than one utility or command.

Utility Guidelines

The following topics provide useful guidance for the development and usage of DB2 utilities.

DB2 Online Utility Return Codes When an online utility runs, a return code is provided indicating the status of the utility execution. If the utility runs to normal completion, the return code is set to 0.

A return code of 4 indicates that the utility completed running, but with warnings. Review the utility output to determine whether some type of reprocessing is required. A warning often indicates a condition that requires no additional consideration.

A return code of 8 means that the utility did not complete successfully. Determine the cause and execute the utility again.

A return code of 12 is an authorization error, which means that the user is not authorized to execute the utility. Either grant the user the proper authority or have an authorized user execute the utility.

DB2 Utility Work Data Sets   Many DB2 online utilities require the allocation of work data sets to complete the task at hand. These work data sets were presented in the first chapters in Part VI. Because a central reference often is handy, the required and optional work data sets for the DB2 online utilities are presented together in Table 37.1. The data sets used by DB2 utilities are listed along the top of the table. The utilities that use these data sets are listed along the left side of the table. Consult the legend to determine the necessity of coding these data sets in the JCL.

TABLE 37.1   Required Utility Data Sets

	SORTOUT	SORTWKxx	SYSCOPY	SYSDISC	SYSERR	SYSMAP	SYSREC	SYSUT1	UTPRINT	SYSIN	SYSPRINT	DSSPRINT
CHECK DATA	R	R			R				O	R	R	
CHECK INDEX	R	R							O	R	R	
CHECK LOB	R	R							O	R	R	
COPY			R							R	R	O
LOAD	X/C/K	R	B	O	O	O	R	R	R	R	R	
MERGECOPY			R						O	R	R	
QUIESCE										R	R	
REBUILD INDEX		R							O	R	R	R
RECOVER										R	R	
REORG INDEX								R		R	R	
REORG TS	X	R	B	D			R	T	R	R	R	

B = Required if the COPYDDN and RECOVERYDDN options are used to make image copies during utility processing
C = Required if referential constraints exist and the ENFORCE CONSTRAINTS option is used
D = Required if the DISCARDDN option is specified to purge data during a REORG
K = Required if the SORTKEYS option is specified with no value or a value of zero
O = Optional (based on utility parameters)
R = Required
T = Required for tables with indexes unless the SORTKEYS option is specified
X = Required if indexes exist

The COPY utility also requires a filter data set containing a list of VSAM data set names when COPY is run with the CONCURRENT and FILTERDDN options.

You also can specify a SYSPUNCH data set for the REORG utility to generate LOAD statement input cards. Additionally, REORG requires a data set to hold the unloaded data unless NOSYSREC or SHRLEVEL CHANGE is specified.

V7   Of course, as of DB2 Version 7, you can use dynamic data set allocation and allow DB2 to allocate the data sets that are required for each utility. Doing so is simple and easier to manage than explicitly coding each data set allocation for each utility. For more details on dynamic data set allocation, refer to Chapter 30, "An Introduction to DB2 Utilities."

DB2 Utility Catalog Contention   DB2 utilities read and update DB2 Catalog and DB2 Directory tables. This can cause contention when multiple utilities are run concurrently.

Table 37.2 lists the DB2 Catalog tables that are either updated or read by the online DB2 utilities. In addition, DB2 utilities update the SYSIBM.SYSUTILX DB2 Directory table.

DB2 utilities rely on claim and drain processing instead of transaction locks to reduce contention and increase availability. SQL statements take claims on resources and utilities take drains.

TABLE 37.2   Utility Contention

Utility	Updates	Reads
CHECK	SYSIBM.SYSCOPY	SYSIBM.SYSCHECKDEP
		SYSIBM.SYSCHECKS
		SYSIBM.SYSCOLUMNS
		SYSIBM.SYSINDEXES
		SYSIBM.SYSINDEXPART
		SYSIBM.SYSTABLES
		SYSIBM.SYSTABLEPART
		SYSIBM.SYSTABLESPACE
COPY	SYSIBM.SYSCOPY	SYSIBM.SYSCOLUMNS
		SYSIBM.SYSINDEXES
		SYSIBM.SYSINDEXPART
		SYSIBM.SYSTABLES
		SYSIBM.SYSTABLEPART
		SYSIBM.SYSTABLESPACE
LOAD	SYSIBM.SYSCOPY	SYSIBM.SYSCHECKDEP
		SYSIBM.SYSCHECKS
		SYSIBM.SYSCOLUMNS
		SYSIBM.SYSINDEXES
		SYSIBM.SYSINDEXPART
		SYSIBM.SYSTABLES
		SYSIBM.SYSTABLEPART
		SYSIBM.SYSTABLESPACE
MERGECOPY	SYSIBM.SYSCOPY	SYSIBM.SYSCOPY
MODIFY RECOVERY	SYSIBM.SYSCOPY	SYSIBM.SYSCOPY
MODIFY STATISTICS	SYSIBM.SYSCOLUMNS	
	SYSIBM.SYSCOLDIST	
	SYSIBM.SYSINDEXES	
	SYSIBM.SYSINDEXPART	
	SYSIBM.SYSLOBSTATS	
	SYSIBM.SYSTABLES	
	SYSIBM.SYSTABSTATS	
	SYSIBM.SYSTABLEPART	
	SYSIBM.SYSTABLESPACE	
QUIESCE	SYSIBM.SYSCOPY	

37

TABLE 37.2   Continued

Utility	Updates	Reads
REBUILD	SYSIBM.SYSCOPY	SYSIBM.SYSCOLUMNS
		SYSIBM.SYSINDEXES
		SYSIBM.SYSINDEXPART
		SYSIBM.SYSTABLES
		SYSIBM.SYSTABLEPART
		SYSIBM.SYSTABLESPACE
RECOVER	SYSIBM.SYSCOPY	SYSIBM.SYSCOLUMNS
		SYSIBM.SYSINDEXES
		SYSIBM.SYSINDEXPART
		SYSIBM.SYSTABLES
		SYSIBM.SYSTABLEPART
		SYSIBM.SYSTABLESPACE
REORG	SYSIBM.SYSCOPY	SYSIBM.SYSCOLUMNS
		SYSIBM.SYSINDEXES
		SYSIBM.SYSINDEXPART
		SYSIBM.SYSTABLES
		SYSIBM.SYSTABLEPART
		SYSIBM.SYSTABLESPACE
REPAIR SET		
	NOCHCKPEND	SYSIBM.SYSTABLES
		SYSIBM.SYSTABLEPART
	NORCVRPEND	DB2 Directory
	NOCOPYPEND	DB2 Directory
RUNSTATS	SYSIBM.SYSCOLDIST	Table spaces and indexes
	SYSIBM.SYSCOLDIST_HIST	being analyzed
	SYSIBM.SYSCOLDISTSTATS	
	SYSIBM.SYSCOLSTATS	
	SYSIBM.SYSCOLUMNS	
	SYSIBM.SYSCOLUMNS_HIST	
	SYSIBM.SYSINDEXES	
	SYSIBM.SYSINDEXES_HIST	
	SYSIBM.SYSINDEXPART	
	SYSIBM.SYSINDEXPART_HIST	
	SYSIBM.SYSINDEXSTATS	
	SYSIBM.SYSINDEXSTATS_HIST	
	SYSIBM.SYSLOBSTATS	
	SYSIBM.SYSLOBSTATS_HIST	
	SYSIBM.SYSTABLES	
	SYSIBM.SYSTABLEPART	
	SYSIBM.SYSTABLEPART_HIST	
	SYSIBM.SYSTABLESPACE	
	SYSIBM.SYSTABLESPACE_HIST	
	SYSIBM.SYSTABSTATS	
	SYSIBM.SYSTABSTATS_HIST	

TABLE 37.2   Continued

Utility	Updates	Reads
STOSPACE	SYSIBM.SYSINDEXES	
	SYSIBM.SYSTABLESPACE	
	SYSIBM.SYSSTOGROUP	
	SYSIBM.SYSTABLEPART	
	SYSIBM.SYSINDEXPART	
UNLOAD		SYSIBM.SYSTABLES
		SYSIBM.SYSCOLUMNS
		Table being unloaded

Partition Level Operation   DB2 online utilities can operate at the table space partition level. The following utilities can be issued for a single partition or for all the partitions of a table space:

- CHECK DATA, CHECK INDEX, and REPAIR data consistency utilities

- COPY, MERGECOPY, QUIESCE, RECOVER, REBUILD INDEX, and REPORT backup and recovery utilities

- LOAD and REORG data organization utilities

- MODIFY and RUNSTATS catalog manipulation utility

Coding Utility Control Cards   All DB2 utility control card input must be contained in 80-character record images. The utility statements must be confined to columns 1 through 72. All input in columns 73 through 80 is ignored by DB2.

Automatically Generate Utility Control Cards   Consider using DB2 Catalog queries to generate utility control card input. By creating standard queries for each utility, you improve the accuracy of the utility input syntax. For example, the following query automatically generates input to the RECOVER utility to invoke full table space recovery for all table spaces in a given database:

```
SELECT   'RECOVER TABLESPACE '  ||  DBNAME  ||
         '.'   ||  NAME  ||  ' DSNUM ALL'
FROM     SYSIBM.SYSTABLESPACE
WHERE    DBNAME = '''DSN8D81A';
```

This query generates RECOVER TABLESPACE control cards for every table space in the sample database. You can formulate queries to automatically create control card input for most of the online utilities.

V7   **Use LISTDEF and TEMPLATE**   In general, the maintenance and execution of DB2 utilities can be greatly simplified by using the LISTDEF and TEMPLATE control statements.

LISTDEF is used to create a database object list such that a DB2 utility can execute against multiple database objects. Wildcards can be used to automatically include objects that conform to specific naming conventions in the list. After a list is created, the utility is run against the list. Using LISTDEF and proper naming conventions, you can create utility jobs that run against all table spaces (for example) in a particular application. When new table spaces are added, if they conform to the naming convention, they will automatically be added to the list—and thereby are automatically added to the utility jobs using that list.

The TEMPLATE statement supports dynamic data set allocation. It provides DB2 utilities with the basic allocation information necessary to automatically generate and allocate valid data sets that are required for use as DB2 utilities are executed. Used in conjunction with LISTDEF, DB2 utility jobs can be set up to operate on multiple database objects with a single run.

Specify the BUFNO JCL Parameter   Various guidelines in Part VI recommend specific BUFNO JCL parameter settings for different utility work data sets. Each installation defines a default number of buffers adequate for the data sets used by most batch jobs. The DB2 utilities, however, can benefit by increasing the work data set buffers. Therefore, if sufficient memory is available to increase the buffering of DB2 utility work data sets, always do so. As of DB2 V4, the default for BUFNO is 20.

Allocate Sufficient Sort Work Space for DFSORT   The CHECK INDEX, LOAD, RECOVER INDEX, and REORG utilities require an external sort routine. DB2 uses an IBM-supplied sort utility named DFSORT. You can use the SORTDEVT and SORTNUM parameters of these utilities to allow the system to allocate the sort work area dynamically. This way, the sort work specification never needs to be adjusted or sized—the system manages the required size.

> **CAUTION**
>
> For very large table spaces requiring a large amount of sort work space, consider explicit allocation of sort work data sets because the system might not be able to allocate large amounts of space during the utility execution.

The SORTDEVT parameter is used to specify the device type for temporary data sets to be dynamically allocated by DFSORT. The SORTNUM parameter specifies the number of temporary data sets to be dynamically allocated by the sort program. If you use SORTDEVT and omit SORTNUM, DFSORT will determine how many data sets to allocate on its own.

> **NOTE**
>
> No sort work space is required when reorganizing type 2 indexes. No sort work space is required when loading a table with no indexes or a single index, when the data to be loaded is in order by the index key.

The SORTWKxx DD statement defines the characteristics and location of the intermediate storage data sets used by DFSORT. Multiple data sets can be allocated for the temporary sort work space required by DFSORT. Specify each sort work data set to a different SORTWKxx DD statement. The xx is a two-digit indicator ranging from 00 to 99. In general, begin with 00 and work your way up. No more than 32 SORTWKxx data sets will be used by DFSORT.

All the data sets allocated to the SORTWKxx DD statements must be allocated on the same media type. Although DFSORT permits the allocation of work data sets to a tape unit, avoid doing this for DB2 utilities because it causes severe performance degradation. Additionally, the SORTWK*xx* DD statements must be allocated on the same type of unit (for example, one SORTWK*xx* data set cannot be allocated to a 3390 device if the others are allocated to 3380 devices).

Specify the SPACE allocation for the SORTWK*xx* data sets in cylinder increments. If you don't, DFSORT will reallocate the data sets in cylinder increments anyway.

For performance, specifying one or two large SORTWK*xx* data sets is preferable to specifying multiple smaller data sets. For more information on DFSORT, consult the *IBM DFSORT Application Programming Guide* (SC33-4035).

When Loading or Reorganizing, Specify LOG NO   To reduce the overhead associated with the LOAD and REORG job, use LOG NO. DB2 logs every modification to DB2 data, except when the LOAD and REORG utilities run with the LOG NO option. When you use LOG NO, however, an image copy must be taken after the successful completion of the LOAD or REORG job.

When Loading or Reorganizing, Perform Inline Utilities   To eliminate the need to run subsequent RUNSTATS and COPY after a LOAD or REORG, use DB2's capability to generate statistics and make image copies as a part of the LOAD or REORG utility.

Use the STATISTICS clause to indicate that inline statistics are to be generated.

Specify COPYDDN data sets (and RECOVERYDDN data sets if off-site copies are desired) to indicate that inline image copies are to be made.

Back Up Data Using the COPY Utility   Use the COPY utility to back up data rather than DSN1COPY. DSN1COPY operates "behind DB2's back." If you always use the COPY utility, DB2 will have an accurate record of all backup data sets.

REBUILD INDEX Versus CREATE INDEX   For very large existing tables, it is quicker to use the REBUILD INDEX utility to build an index than to simply issue a CREATE INDEX statement. REBUILD INDEX is more efficient because it uses an external sort. The REBUILD INDEX utility is designed to rebuild indexes, not initially build them as part of a CREATE statement.

The CREATE INDEX DDL provides the option to defer index population by specifying DEFER YES. This causes an index to be built as an empty shell. After the index is created, it will be put into a rebuild pending status. The REBUILD INDEX utility can then be executed to populate the index. This process is usually much more efficient for indexes on very large tables.

The Pending States

DB2 weaves an intricate web of checks and balances to maintain the integrity of the data housed in its tables. DB2 ensures that image copies, recovers, and referential integrity checks are performed as needed, based on an application's job stream.

For example, if data is loaded into a table with DB2 logging turned off, no further updates can be made to that table until an image copy is made or the table is reloaded with changes logged. If DB2 did not enforce this, valuable application data could be lost because of hardware or software failures. DB2 controls the integrity of its data through the use of exception states, also called *pending flags*.

A table space is in a pending state when the check pending, copy pending, or recover pending flag is set for that table space. There are other table space exception states (as outlined in the previous chapter), but these are the big three.

Why Pending States Occur

A table space's check pending flag is set when

- A check constraint is added to a table and data within an existing row of that table violates the constraint.

- A table is altered to add a check constraint and the CURRENT RULES special register contains 'DB2'.

- A table space with a table or tables containing referential constraints is partially recovered (that is, RECOVER TORBA or RECOVER TOCOPY is run).

- The CHECK DATA utility is run for a table in the table space specifying DELETE NO and referential constraint or check constraint violations are encountered.

- The LOAD utility is run for a table in the table space specifying the ENFORCE NO option and either RI or check constraints exist for any table in the table space.

- A table in the table space is altered to add a new foreign key.

- Any table in a referential set is dropped.

- Any database or table space containing tables in a referential set is dropped.

A table space's copy pending flag is set when

- The REORG utility is run for the table space specifying LOG NO or the LOAD utility is run for a table in the table space specifying LOG NO.

- A table space with a table or tables containing referential constraints is partially recovered (that is, RECOVER TORBA or RECOVER TOCOPY is run).

- The MODIFY utility is run deleting the last full image copy data set from the SYSIBM.SYSCOPY table.

A table space's recover pending flag is set when

- A RECOVER or REORG utility being run for the table space abends.

- A LOAD utility being run for tables in the table space abends.

An index's recover pending (or rebuild pending) flag is set when

- A table space with a table or tables containing referential constraints is partially recovered (that is, RECOVER TORBA or RECOVER TOCOPY is run).

- Abends occur in the REBUILD, RECOVER, REORG, or LOAD utility.

- The index was created specifying DEFER YES.

How to Correct Pending States

The check pending flag for the table space can be reset by

- Running the CHECK DATA utility for the tables in the table space specifying DELETE YES.

- Running the CHECK DATA utility for the tables in the table space specifying DELETE NO if no constraint violations are encountered.

- Running the LOAD utility specifying the ENFORCE CONSTRAINTS option.

- Altering tables in the table space to drop foreign keys and check constraints.

- Running the REPAIR utility specifying SET NOCHECKPEND for the table space or issuing the START command for the table space with the ACCESS(FORCE) parameter. Neither option corrects the problem flagged by the pending state; they merely reset the pending flag.

The copy pending flag for the table space can be reset by

- Running the REORG utility with the LOG YES option or running the LOAD utility with both the REPLACE and LOG YES options.

- Running the COPY utility specifying both the SHRLEVEL REFERENCE and the FULL YES options.

- Running the REPAIR utility specifying SET NOCOPYPEND for the table space or issuing the START command for the table space with the ACCESS(FORCE) parameter. Neither option corrects the problem flagged by the pending state; they merely reset the pending flag.

The recover pending flag for the table space can be reset by

- Running the LOAD utility with the REPLACE option.

- Running a full recovery for the table space.

- Running the REPAIR utility specifying SET NORCVRPEND for the table space or issuing the START command for the table space with the ACCESS(FORCE) parameter. Neither option corrects the problem flagged by the pending state; they merely reset the pending flag.

The recover pending flag for the index can be reset by

- Running the REBUILD INDEX utility for the index.

- Running the RECOVER INDEX utility for the index.

- Running the REPAIR utility specifying SET NORCVRPEND for the index or issuing the START command for the index with the ACCESS(FORCE) parameter. Neither option corrects the problem flagged by the pending state; they merely reset the pending flag.

37

CHAPTER **38**

DB2 Contingency Planning

Contingency planning for disaster recovery is a complex task in the best of situations. Unfortunately, the best of situations does not exist in a DB2 environment. This chapter defines the limitations of DB2 in the framework of disaster recovery and suggests solutions to the problems that these limitations create. This chapter pertains to the recovery of DB2 application data, not to the recovery of the DB2 subsystem (and related data).

Suggestions, cautions, requirements, and techniques are provided to help you create a disaster recovery plan for your DB2 applications.

What Is a Disaster?

It is quite natural for organizations to begin developing a disaster recovery plan before stepping back to analyze the question "What is a disaster?" Without a firm understanding of what type of disasters can occur, it is quite probable that the plan will be incomplete. A good place to start is to define the term *disaster*. The Oxford American dictionary defines a disaster as a "sudden great misfortune." It helps to expand on this, though. My definition follows:

> A *disaster* is any event that has a small chance of transpiring, a high level of uncertainty, and a potentially devastating outcome.

Most of us have witnessed (at least on the news) a disaster situation. Tornadoes, hurricanes, earthquakes, and fires are prime examples of natural disasters. Disasters can also be man-made, such as electric failure, bursting pipes, and war. However, relatively few of us have actually lived through a disaster of the proportion shown on television. But many of us have had our basements flooded or been in an automobile accident. A disaster does not have to have global consequences in order for it to be a disaster to you.

> **NOTE**
>
> Of course, the events of 9/11 are a prime example of a disaster. The businesses located in the World Trade Center experienced a man-made disaster the likes of which we hope never to see again.

Although disasters by their very definition are unpredictable and unlikely, a disaster is something that you must plan for. Insurance companies have made their livelihood on this premise. Every company should have a comprehensive and tested disaster plan that details how to resume business operations in the event of a disaster. Companies with disaster plans will provide a higher degree of customer satisfaction and, in the long run, will be more successful than companies with no plan. Disaster recovery for DB2 should be an integral component of your overall business recovery plan. But to what degree should the disaster planning be taken? Before your company can ascertain the appropriate level of recoverability, you must analyze the risks and determine the objectives.

Determining and Managing Risk

A disaster recovery plan is developed to minimize the costs resulting from losses of, or damages to, the resources or capabilities of your IT facilities. The success of any DB2 disaster recovery plan depends on how well you ascertain the risks involved. First, you must recognize potential disaster situations and understand the consequences of each. How these disasters affect your business is the bottom line reason for contingency planning in the first place. If your shop is on the coast, for example, tornadoes, floods, and hurricanes are more likely to cause problems than snowstorms (unless your are in a Northern area) or earthquakes (unless you are in California).

Each DB2 application must undergo an analysis period whereby the impact of losing the application is evaluated. This can only be accomplished with the input of those individuals who will be affected—the end users.

Risk can be broken up into three categories: financial loss, business service interruption, and legal responsibilities. Within each category, there are varying degrees of risk. Each application has a different impact on the company's bottom line the longer it is unavailable. Consider a bank, for example. Having the demand deposit application unavailable will cause a greater loss than having the human resources application unavailable, not only because deposits will be lost, but because customer trust will diminish.

Similarly, varying degrees of business service interruption and legal responsibilities also will exist. Most applications will be impacted by each of the three risk areas, and each application should be analyzed to determine the level of risk associated with it. The disaster recovery plan needs to factor each of these categories into the mix to determine which applications are most critical.

When developing your disaster recovery plan, remember that business needs are the motivating force behind your planning. It is prudent, therefore, to separate your systems into critical and non-critical applications based on business needs. The task of defining a system as critical has to be made by the area responsible for the business function that the system supports. It is a good idea to rank your applications into classes to determine which applications have the biggest impact if they are not available.

Class 1		Extremely Critical Application. This class of application must be supported with current data and is one of the most important to support immediately. It must be recovered in the first group of applications to be recovered at the disaster site. This group should be limited to 5 or fewer applications to ensure that only the most critical applications are processed first.
Class 2		Business Critical Application. This class of application is important but falls outside the top 5 applications in terms of impact to the business. It must be available at the remote site within the first 2 to 3 days. Typically, it requires current data.
Class 3		Moderately Critical Application. This class of application must be available if the disaster lasts longer than one week. However, its impact to the business is less critical, allowing it to wait for all Class 1 and 2 applications to be recovered first. Its data requirements vary from current, to daily, to possibly weekly.
Class 4		Required Application. This application needs to be supported at the remote site, but it is not critical. Data can be from the last available backup.
Class 5		Non-critical Application. This application need not be supported in the event of a disaster. Very few users will volunteer their applications to be Class 5.

Develop disaster recovery plans first for the critical applications—those in classes 1 through 3. These support the functions that are absolutely necessary should your company experience a disaster. Based upon these rankings, the appropriate backup strategy can be employed for the data (table spaces and indexes) used by each DB2 application.

Non-critical (Class 4 and possibly Class 5) applications should be considered only after complete disaster recovery procedures have been implemented for the critical applications. For some non-critical (pure Class 5) applications, the decision might be made not to develop disaster recovery procedures. This decision is valid only when the system can be lost completely. Obviously, application systems of this type are rare.

If you follow the procedures outlined in this chapter, you will have an exemplary disaster recovery plan for all your applications.

Disaster Recovery Requirements

I have described the reasons why a disaster recovery plan is needed, but what should the goals of this disaster recovery plan be? One part of that plan must deal with the recovery of DB2 data. Most disaster recovery plans are composed of four goals:

- Avoid the loss of data
- Avoid the reprocessing of transactions
- Avoid causing inconsistent data
- Limit the time needed to restart critical application processing

These goals often conflict. For example, how can critical applications be online quickly when they usually consist of large databases? How can the loss of data be avoided when thousands of transactions update DB2 tables every second? Each decision in the plan requires a trade-off to be made.

After you target applications for disaster planning, you then should decide on a disaster recovery strategy. This chapter details four strategies for DB2 disaster recovery planning—the sledgehammer, the scalpel, flashcopy, and DSN1COPY. Each has its strengths and weaknesses. You can choose one strategy or mix and match strategies based on the recovery requirements of each application.

Disaster Strikes

The situation is grim. There has been a devastating fire at your data processing shop. All computer hardware, software, and data at your site has been destroyed. Are you adequately prepared to recover your DB2 data at a remote processing site?

In this section, it is assumed that your data processing shop has planned for remote processing in the event of a disaster. In addition, it is assumed that the operating system software and environment have been recovered successfully. Given these caveats, let's continue with our discussion of DB2 disaster planning.

DB2 disaster recovery happens in two steps: the recovery of the DB2 subsystem and the recovery of the application data. The primary concern of the DBA should be the recovery of the operational data. To accomplish this, however, you must recover your DB2 subsystem first. Therefore, your initial concern should be developing a comprehensive plan for recovering your DB2 subsystem. IBM's *DB2 Administration Guide* covers this topic in depth.

DB2 Recovery Basics

To fully understand DB2 disaster recovery, you must first review basic DB2 recovery procedures and techniques. The standard tools of DB2 recovery are the image copy backup, the DB2 log tapes, and internal DB2 tables and data sets. Refer to Chapter 32, "Backup and Recovery Utilities," (and Figure 32.1) for a discussion of DB2 recovery basics.

The RECOVER utility is invoked to restore the table space data. Depending on your recovery strategy, RECOVER can be used to restore index data, too. DB2 uses all the information it stores in active and archive logs, the DB2 Catalog, the DB2 Directory, and the BSDS to recover data with a minimum of user input. The only input the RECOVER utility requires is the name of the table space (or index) to be recovered. DB2 does the rest. The reduction of user input in a recovery situation lessens the possibility of errors during a potentially hectic and confusing time. The automation of the recovery process, however, is just the circumstance that can complicate offsite DB2 disaster recovery planning.

Strategy #1: The Sledgehammer

This first strategy is referred to as *the sledgehammer* because it is a sweeping, basic approach to application backup and recovery. This strategy should be considered for non–24×7 applications, non-critical applications, and non-volatile applications. It is easy to implement and consists of the following steps:

1. Stop the DB2 subsystem to ensure stable application data. This establishes a system-wide point of consistency.

2. Copy all table spaces using a utility to dump complete DASD volumes. Utilities such as FDR, from Innovation Data Processing, and DFSMS, from IBM, work well.

3. When all DASD volumes containing DB2 data have been successfully copied, restart the DB2 subsystem.

4. Copy the backup tapes and send them offsite.

5. Recovery at the remote site is then performed a complete DASD volume at a time.

There are some problems with this strategy, however. For example, many shops require DB2 to be available 24 hours a day, 7 days a week, so stopping the DB2 subsystem is not an option.

As an alternative to stopping the DB2 subsystem, each application could have a regularly scheduled job to stop only the application. The job would need to QUIESCE the application table spaces, the DB2 Catalog (DSNDB06), and the DB2 Directory (DSNDB01) and then stop each application table space. Note that only an Install System Administrator (SYSADM) can quiesce the DB2 Catalog and DB2 Directory. The complete volume backup could be performed at this point, and, when complete, the application table spaces could be restarted.

An additional problem arises when DB2 data sets are strewn across numerous DASD volumes. If the backup process copies data a complete volume at a time, many non-DB2 data sets that are not required for DB2 recovery will be copied. Most tools that perform complete DASD volume copies can also copy specific data sets, but this complicates the backup process by requiring the user to maintain a list of DB2 data sets as well as a list of DB2 volumes for backing up.

If DFSMS, commonly referred to as *system managed storage*, is used to automate the placement of DB2 table space and index data sets, the location of these data sets is controlled by DFSMS and is dynamic. Therefore, the DB2 table space or index data set being backed up will not consistently remain on the same DASD volume. This further complicates the DASD volume backup strategy.

The sledgehammer strategy is effective for shops willing to trade 24-hour processing capabilities for ease of disaster recovery preparation. But this strategy is not the optimal solution for most DB2 installations because most shops are unwilling to make this trade-off. Shutting down DB2 effectively prohibits the execution of every application that uses DB2 tables. This is usually impossible. Even running the QUIESCE utility affects other applications by forcing a point of consistency on the DB2 Catalog and the DB2 Directory. If you want to avoid these points of contention, choose another strategy.

DFSMS Concurrent Copy

DB2 supports using DFSMS for concurrent copying using the DB2 utilities, as well. The DFSMS concurrent copy function can copy a data set concurrently with other access. DB2 can invoke a DFSMS concurrent copy directly from the DB2 COPY utility. A DFSMS concurrent copy is recorded in the DB2 Catalog SYSIBM.SYSCOPY table with ICTYPE of F and STYPE of C. Likewise, DB2 can automatically restore DFSMS copies using the RECOVER utility. When RECOVER is invoked and a DFSMS copy needs to be part of the recovery, DB2 will invoke the DFDSS RESTORE command to apply the DFSMS concurrent copy.

Of course, the copy can be applied outside the scope of the DB2 RECOVER utility if so desired. To restore the data sets, you can manually apply the DFSMS copies, and then you can use the RECOVER utility for point-in-time recovery in conjunction with the DB2 log.

Strategy #2: The Scalpel

The second strategy uses native DB2 functionality to prepare for disaster recovery. This strategy is called *the scalpel* because it is precise and accurate. It involves the following steps:

1. Produce two or more image copy backups (for each table space), at least one of which must be on tape.

2. Send the tape image copy backup to the remote site. You should do this as soon as possible after the tape has been created to avoid having the tape damaged in a subsequent disaster.

3. Do not back up indexes.

4. Produce a daily report (using DSNTEP2 or QMF) from the SYSIBM.SYSCOPY table and send a copy of the report to the remote site. A sample query that accomplishes this follows:

```
SELECT   DBNAME, TSNAME, DSNUM, TIMESTAMP, ICTYPE,
         ICBACKUP, DSNAME, FILESEQNO, SHRLEVEL, DSVOLSER
FROM     SYSIBM.SYSCOPY
ORDER BY DBNAME, TSNAME, DSNUM, TIMESTAMP
```

A QMF form that can be used with the query is provided in Listing 38.1. The automated running of this query can be accomplished with relative ease by setting up a batch QMF job and sending SYSOUT to a tape data set that can be sent offsite.

LISTING 38.1   QMF Form to be Used with the SYSCOPY Query

```
Total Width of Report Columns: 150

NUM   COLUMN HEADING    USAGE     INDENT   WIDTH    EDIT    SEQ
 1    DATABASE          BREAK1      1        8        C      1
 2    TABLE_SPACE       BREAK2      1        8        C      2
 3    DS_NUM            BREAK3      1        3        L      3
 4    TIMESTAMP                     1        26       C      4
 5    IC_TYPE                       1        4        C      5
 6    IC_BACKUP                     1        2        C      6
 7    DATASET NAME                  1        44       C      7
 8    FIL_SEQ_NO                    1        3        C      8
 9    SHR_LVL                       1        3        C      9
10    VOL SERIAL LIST               1        42       C     10
```

38

This report details all the information available for DB2 to use for recovery. Be sure to synchronize the running of this report with the running of the DB2 Catalog backup sent offsite to ensure that the corresponding offsite DB2 Catalog image copy conforms to the data in this report.

Use Table 38.1 to interpret the value of the ICTYPE column in this report. ICTYPE refers to the type of recovery information recorded in the SYSIBM.SYSCOPY table.

TABLE 38.1   SYSIBM.SYSCOPY ICTYPEs

Type	Description
A	ALTER
B	REBUILD INDEX
D	CHECK DATA LOG(NO)
	(no log records for the range are available for RECOVER)
F	Full image COPY
I	Incremental image COPY
P	Partial recovery point (RECOVER TOCOPY or RECOVER TORBA)
Q	QUIESCE (point of consistency RBA)
R	LOAD REPLACE (LOG YES)
S	LOAD REPLACE (LOG NO)
V	REPAIR VERSIONS
T	TERM UTILITY command
W	REORG (LOG NO)
X	REORG (LOG YES)
Y	LOAD (LOG NO)
Z	LOAD (LOG YES)

5. Use DSNJU004 to produce a BSDS log map report and send a copy of the report to the remote site.

6. Recovery at the remote site is performed a table space at a time. Use REBUILD INDEX to rebuild all indexes. Run CHECK DATA to resolve any constraint violations.

7. For this method of disaster recovery preparation to succeed, the DB2 system data sets must be backed up and sent offsite. Be sure to create offsite backups of the DB2 Catalog, the BSDS, the DB2 Directory, and the archive logs at least daily for volatile systems and at least weekly for all systems, regardless of their volatility.

The scalpel method differs from the sledgehammer in many ways, but perhaps the most important way is its reliance on DB2. Only application data recorded in the DB2 Catalog, the DB2 Directory, and the BSDS can be recovered. For this reason, the scalpel method relies heavily on the capability to recover the DB2 subsystem. Application data is as current as the last backup of the DB2 subsystem—one of the headaches caused by the automation of the DB2 recovery process.

Consider, for example, an application that sends three image copy backups to a remote site daily. One backup is sent offsite in the morning to allow for post-batch recovery, another is sent offsite in the afternoon to allow recovery of all morning transactions, and a third is sent offsite in the evening to allow for recovery of all pre-batch transactions.

However, if only one DB2 Catalog copy is sent offsite daily, for example, after the morning copy but before the afternoon copy, remote recovery can proceed only to the morning copy plus any archive logs sent offsite.

For this reason, try to synchronize your application image copies with your DB2 Catalog backups. Additionally, as mentioned, ensure that the reports at the remote site reflect the status of the DB2 Catalog image copies. Otherwise, you will end up with greater confusion during the disaster recovery scenario, increased data loss, and unusable image copies at your remote site.

The amount of data lost in an offsite recovery depends not only on the synchronization of application table space backups with DB2 Catalog backups but also on the timeliness of the backup of archive logs and the synchronization of the DB2 Catalog backup with the logs. When the DB2 Catalog is backed up to be sent offsite, issue the ARCHIVE LOG command as part of the copy job. Send to the remote site a copy of the archived log that was produced along with the DB2 Catalog image copies.

Additionally, keep at least three image copy backup tapes at your remote site. This provides a satisfactory number of backups if one or more of your image copy tapes is damaged. DB2 automatically falls back to previous image copy backups when a tape is damaged. Changes are applied from the archive logs to re-create the data lost by falling back to the previous image copy.

Note also that updates recorded on the DB2 active logs at the time of the disaster are lost. Recovery can be performed through only the last archive log available at the remote site.

The final consideration for the scalpel method is the creation of the underlying table space and indexspace data sets at the remote site. If you are using native VSAM, you must use AMS to create the data sets before recovering each table space and its related indexes. If you are using STOGROUPs for your production data sets, simply ensure that the STOGROUPs have been altered to point to valid DASD volumes at the remote site. The RECOVER utility creates the underlying VSAM data sets for you.

Strategy #3: DSN1COPY

The third strategy, using DSN1COPY, generally is not recommended because it operates behind the back of DB2 and therefore sacrifices the rigorous control provided by DB2 backup and recovery procedures. Implementing disaster recovery in this manner can be beneficial, however, for a limited number of non-critical applications.

This strategy is close to the sledgehammer approach but a little more complicated. Follow these steps for each DSN1COPY that must be executed:

1. Use the START command with the MODE(RO) option to place all the table spaces to be backed up in read only mode.

2. Issue QUIESCE WRITE(YES) for all the table spaces that will be backed up using DSN1COPY.

3. Execute the DSN1COPY utility for each table space being copied.

4. Start all the table spaces in read-write mode using the START command using the MODE(RW) option.

Recovery at the remote site must be performed using DSN1COPY because these backup data sets are not recorded in the DB2 Catalog. Therefore, each table space and index space data set must be created using AMS before the DSN1COPY can be executed to restore the application data.

This complex and potentially error-prone process should be avoided. If your application data is very stable, however, you might want to avoid recording backups in the DB2 Catalog to simplify your DB2 Catalog maintenance procedures. The MODIFY utility must be executed periodically to clean up the SYSIBM.SYSCOPY table and the SYSIBM.SYSLGRNX table. MODIFY is run specifying a table space and a date range that deletes all image copy and log information for the table space for that date range. Each application must supply the appropriate date range for image copy deletion.

If your date range is unknown, unstable, or random, you might want to avoid using the DB2 Catalog for recovery altogether. You could simply create four DSN1COPY backups every time your (stable) application data changes. Retaining two on-site and sending two offsite should suffice. Remember, this method should be used only for stable data and is not recommended. The most desirable method is to use the DB2 COPY, RECOVER, and REBUILD utilities and to execute the MODIFY utility on a table space by table space basis for each application.

Non-Critical Applications

Sometimes simple DSN1COPY data sets for table spaces in non-critical applications suffice for offsite recovery. These should be taken when DB2 is not operational (or the application has been stopped). Because the application is non-critical, the DSN1COPY might need to be performed less frequently. This decision must be made on an application-by-application basis.

Strategy #4: Suspend, FlashCopy, and Resume

A fourth approach to DB2 disaster recovery makes use of the SET LOG SUSPEND command and FlashCopy or similar disk technology. The SET LOG SUSPEND command allows can be used to temporarily freeze a DB2 subsystem by stopping updates to the log. The logs and data can be quickly copied using IBM's Enterprise Storage Server FlashCopy or equivalent vendor products to produce instant copies.

This technique is gaining popularity in DB2 sites because it minimizes operational disruptions. After shipping tapes, created from the backup copy, to a remote site, DB2 users can implement a simplified disaster recovery scenario, which also reduces the recovery time to that necessary to restore the tape dumps.

Follow these steps to implement this approach:

1. Stop DB2 updates by issuing the -SET LOG SUSPEND command. A DSNJ372I message is issued and will remain on the console until update activity has been resumed.

2. Use FlashCopy to backup all volumes with DB2 data on them. As soon as you see the DSNJ372I message, the DFSMSdss dumps can be started. Be sure to include any ICF Catalogs used by DB2, as well as active logs and BSDSs. Sample JCL follows:

```
//COPYJOB JOB...
//INSTIMG EXEC PGM=ADRDSSU
//SYSPRINT DD SYSOUT=*
//SYSUDUMP DD SYSOUT=V,OUTLIM=3000
//SYSIN DD *
COPY FULL INDYNAM (source) OUTDYNAM (target) DUMPCONDITIONING
/*
```

When the jobs end, the logical relationship has been established.

3. Resume normal DB2 activity by issuing the -SET LOG RESUME command.

4. Make tape copies to send offsite. The tape copy of the secondary volumes can be started as soon as the FlashCopy relationship is established.

> **NOTE**
>
> Normally FlashCopy copies are written to disk. However, you can use FlashCopy to write directly to tape by using the TSO interface to FlashCopy and specifying a mode of NOCOPY. Because the relationship persists until the tape copy is complete, you would be better off to FlashCopy to disk and then copy to tape for offsite disaster copies.

Third Party Solutions

Third party solutions exist that simplify this approach to making instant copies. BMC Software offers Instant Copy and Recover using its COPY PLUS and RECOVER PLUS utilities. Instant Snapshot utilizes the data set snap capabilities of the storage devices. The data sets are "copied" to the same or another device via the snap process. The method used depends upon the technology of the storage vendor. The copied data sets are cataloged with unique names and remain on disk. These data sets are immediately ready and available for recovery or other activities.

Although an Instant Snapshot copy does not require the data to be physically duplicated onto tape or other media, external copies of the data sets created by Instant Snapshot can be created. For example, COPY PLUS can create a copy of an image copy for offsite storage or other purposes from the snapped data sets.

Recovery using the snapped data sets employs the same Instant Snapshot technology. RECOVER PLUS is used to select the appropriate data sets based upon the desired recovery point. Instant Snapshot snaps them back using the storage vendor technology appropriate to the device. The recovery utility's subsequent log apply or other recovery steps begin immediately thereafter. Figure 38.1 depicts this process.

Speed in the restore process is the primary advantage of Instant Snapshot. Testing of the BMC solution has produced results indicating that the snap of a data set requires effectively the same amount of time whether it is one track or two gigabytes. The restore portion of a recovery of a 2GB data set occurred in approximately 12 seconds.

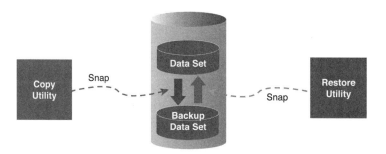

FIGURE 38.1   Instant copy/restore.

Another benefit of the ISV offerings is that they are integrated with offerings from multiple different storage vendors.

The BMC solution is used as an example; other vendors have similar types of offerings.

DB2 Environmental Considerations

Sometimes recovery is targeted to be performed at an alternative site that is already running DB2. This is not advisable. During a disaster, your whole machine will be lost. In addition to DB2, MVS, JES, and TSO, all other system software must be recovered. Your disaster recovery plan will become needlessly complex if you plan to recover to an existing system. Reconfiguring software that is already operational usually is more difficult than bringing everything up from scratch.

> **V8**
>
> **NOTE**
>
> Consider using the BACKUP SYSTEM and RECOVER SYSTEM utilities to help simplify the backup and recovery of you DB2 subsystem and applications for disaster recovery.

If you insist on a plan to recover to a DB2 subsystem that already exists, remember the following. All databases, table spaces, tables, and indexes must be created at the remote site. This could be performed either at the time of the disaster (which is complex and error-prone) or before the disaster (which is easy but consumes resources). With either option, all DB2 objects must exist before the image copy data sets can be restored. This can be accomplished only by using the DSN1COPY service aid with the OBIDXLAT option.

You should maintain a comprehensive report that lists the DBID for each database, the PSID for each table space, and the OBID for each table in both DB2 subsystems. (DBIDs, PSIDs, and OBIDs identify each object to DB2 and are stored in the DB2 Catalog.) A query to produce this report follows:

```
SELECT   S.DBNAME, S.DBID, S.NAME, S.PSID,
         T.CREATOR, T.NAME, T.OBID
FROM     SYSIBM.SYSTABLESPACE   S,
         SYSIBM.SYSTABLES       T
WHERE    S.DBNAME = T.DBNAME
```

```
AND      S.NAME    = T.TSNAME
AND      T.TYPE    = 'T'
ORDER BY S.DBNAME, S.DBID, S.NAME, S.PSID, T.CREATOR, T.NAME;
```

A QMF form to create a formatted report using this query is presented in Listing 38.2. The report generated by this query should be sent to the remote site to assist with disaster recovery. The information can be used as a reference when using DSN1COPY with the OBIDXLAT option. This is the only way to accomplish recovery to a different DB2 subsystem.

LISTING 38.2   QMF Form to be Used with the DBID/PSID/OBID Query

```
Total Width of Report Columns: 61

NUM   COLUMN HEADING     USAGE     INDENT   WIDTH    EDIT    SEQ
 1    DATABASE           BREAK1     1         8        C      1
 2    DBID               BREAK1     1         4        L      2
 3    TABLE_SPACE        BREAK2     1         8        C      3
 4    PSID               BREAK2     1         4        L      4
 5    TABLE_CREATOR                 1         8        C      5
 6    TABLE NAME                    1        18        C      6
 7    OBID                          1         4        L      7
```

Data set management techniques also must be considered. If you allocate VSAM data sets for all production table spaces and indexes, you must use AMS to create the underlying data sets before recovery at the remote site. If you use STOGROUPs, though, the data sets are allocated when the table spaces and indexes are created.

DB2 Contingency Planning Guidelines

When developing your DB2 disaster recovery plan be sure to consider the following tips and techniques.

Plan Before a Disaster Strikes   Ensure that an adequate disaster recovery plan is in place for the DB2 subsystem. This involves backing up system data sets and system table spaces and integrating the timing of the backups with the needs of each DB2 application.

Remember, the absolute worst time to devise a disaster recovery plan is *during* a disaster!

Create a Schedule to Ship Vital Image Copies Offsite Regularly   Remember that the RECOVER utility can recover only with the backup tapes sent to the remote site. Updates on the active log at the time of the disaster are lost, as are all archive logs and image copy backup tapes not sent offsite.

Ensure that every table space has a valid offsite image copy backup.

Do Not Forget to Back Up Other Vital DB2 Data   Copying DB2 table space data is not sufficient to ensure a complete disaster recovery plan. Be sure to back up and send offsite all related DB2 libraries, such as

- Any DB2 DDL libraries that might be required
- JCL and proc libraries

- DBRM libraries

- Application program load libraries

- Libraries and passwords for critical third party DB2 products

- Stored procedure program load libraries

- Application program, stored procedure source code, and copy book libraries

Use SHRLEVEL REFERENCE for Offsite Copies   SHRLEVEL CHANGE means that other processes can read and modify the table space as the COPY is running. SHRLEVEL REFERENCE means that other processes are permitted only to read the table space data during the COPY utility execution.

When running the COPY utility for offsite backup needs:

- Stop concurrent data modification to all table spaces in the table space set using the STOP command or START ... ACCESS(RO).

- Use the SHRLEVEL REFERENCE clause.

If you run COPY with SHRLEVEL CHANGE for an offsite image copy be sure to send the archive logs, or a copy of the archive logs offsite, too. Additionally, ensure that related table spaces are assigned the same quiesce point for recoverability.

Beware of Compression   If your site uses tape-compression software, be sure that the offsite location to be used for disaster recovery uses the same tape-compression software. If it does not, specify the following JCL parm for any offsite image copy data set:

DCB=TRTCH=NOCOMP

Document Your Strategy   Document the backup strategy for each table space (sledgehammer, scalpel, DSN1COPY, or some other internally developed strategy). Document the state of each DB2 application and the DB2 subsystem by producing DB2 Catalog, DB2 Directory, and BSDS reports after producing your offsite backups. Send this information daily to your remote site.

Use an Appropriate Active Log Size   Keep the active log relatively small, but not so small that it affects system performance. Active logging poses a logistical problem. If a disaster strikes, the active log will be lost. Therefore, you will not be able to restore all DB2 data to its state just prior to the disaster. Remember, a disaster implies total loss of your machine or site. At best, data can be restored only back to the last archive log sent offsite. This is one reason to have small active logs, thereby forcing more frequent log archival. If DB2 provided the capability to remote log and remote copy, it would be technically possible to recover data back to its most recent state using remote logs and remote copies.

When the active log is small, consider increasing the maximum number of archive logs for the DB2 subsystem. This maximum is controlled using the MAXARCH DSNZPARM parameter.

V8   As of DB2 V8, the maximum value acceptable for MAXARCH is 10000. The previous maximum was 1000.

Automate Use of the ARCHIVE LOG Command   The ARCHIVE LOG command can be used within a job that is submitted periodically, forcing an archive log and creating a copy of the archive log for offsite recovery. This is an important component of the DB2 disaster recovery plan because the BSDS and the SYSIBM.SYSCOPY table, which play a substantial role in the recovery process, are backed up at log archival time. Be sure to put the appropriate procedures in place to move the archive log copies offsite as soon as feasible after the job completes. A tape that is still sitting in the shop when a disaster strikes will be useless for disaster recovery purposes.

The general recommendation for logging is to enable dual logging—both active and archive. If this is the case, be sure to do one of the following:

- Keep both archive log sets on site, but make a copy of one of the archive log sets and send that copy offsite.

- Keep one archive log set on site and send the second set offsite. This alternative creates a greater exposure to the primary site because only one backup of the logs is available on site.

Copy Each Table Space After an Offsite Recovery   Back up each application's table spaces at the remote site immediately after each application has been recovered.

Validate Your Offsite Recovery   Run a battery of SELECT statements against the recovered application tables to validate the state of the data.

Test Your Offsite Recovery Plan   Test your disaster recovery plan before a disaster occurs. This gives you time to correct problems before it is too late. It is wise to schedule at least yearly disaster recovery tests in which disaster conditions are mimicked. The DB2 environment should be recovered at the offsite location minimally once a year to ensure that the plan is up-to-date and able to be implemented in case of a disaster.

> **CAUTION**
>
> If you fail to test your disaster recovery plan, you are basically planning to fail. Without regularly scheduled disaster recovery testing there is no way to be sure that your plan is up-to-date and workable in the event of a disaster.

38

Appropriate Copying Is Dependent Upon Each Application   DB2 disaster recovery is a complex topic that deserves substantial attention. Each application must be analyzed to uncover its optimal disaster recovery strategy. The frequency of copying will be dependent upon the volatility of the data, the size of the batch window, the length of time allowable for an eventual recovery, and the frequency of log archival.

Include Resumption of Normal Business in Your DR Plan   Be sure to include a section in your disaster recovery plan for returning to "normal" business at a new, real data center. Conducting business from a disaster recovery site can be very costly. A disaster recovery plan with a well-thought-out strategy for resuming normal business practices after the disaster can save time and money.

IN THIS CHAPTER

- DB2 Tools
- DB2 Tools Vendors

CHAPTER **39**

Components of a Total DB2 Solution

DB2, as delivered out of the box, is a relatively complete, full-function relational database management system. An organization can install DB2 as delivered, but it will soon realize that the functionality needed to adequately support large-scale DB2 development is not provided by DB2 alone.

The administration and maintenance of DB2 applications is time-consuming if you use the standard features of the DB2 database management system as supplied by IBM. And, as of DB2 V7, you might have DB2 installed but no utilities for loading, copying, or reorganizing your databases because these tools are no longer supplied with DB2 free-of-charge. Fortunately, a host of tools is available from both IBM and independent third-party vendors that enhance the functionality of DB2. These tools reduce the amount of time, effort, and human error involved in implementing and maintaining a DB2 environment.

DB2 Tools

The sheer number of DB2 add-on tools that are available in the marketplace validates the need for these tools. Most DB2 shops implement one or more add-on tools for DB2. Of these, IBM's QMF is among the most popular. Many more tools from other vendors fill the void for optimizing performance, implementing database changes, and ensuring database recoverability, just to name a few of their capabilities. Table 39.1 provides a rundown of the categories of products.

TABLE 39.1   Categories of DB2 Products

Abbrev	Tool Category Definition
ALT	Tools that administer the SQL necessary to change DB2 objects without losing either authorization or other, dependent objects
AUD	Tools that read the DB2 logs and report on data modification and database changes. May also re-apply SQL from log images.
CAT	Tools that enable panel-driven (or GUI-based) access to the DB2 Catalog without having to code actual SQL queries.
COM	Tools that reduce data storage requirements using compression algorithms.
C/S	DB2-related client/server tools for building applications, connecting databases, or enabling remote access. Includes middleware and gateways.
DBA	Database administration and analysis tools that enable a DBA to determine when to reorganize table spaces and indexes. Useful for implementing proactive tuning.
DES	Database modeling and design tools such as upper CASE tools, entity-relationships diagramming tools, and tools to enable logical to physical model translation.
DSD	Tools that monitor and manage DB2 DASD and space management.
EDT	Tools that provide an ISPF (or GUI-based) editor for accessing, manipulating, and modifying data in DB2 tables. Data is typically displayed using a spreadsheet-like interface and can be modified simply by over-typing (instead of issuing SQL statements).
ETL	Tools that extract, transform, and load data from environment to environment (such as from IMS to DB2). Frequently used in data warehousing projects.
IDX	Tools that analyze your index usage to rate index effectiveness based on SQL statement usage.
INT	Tools that manage and implement data integrity (check constraints) and referential integrity (RI).
MIG	Tools that create and administer the requisite SQL to migrate DB2 objects from one DB2 subsystem to another.
MSC	Miscellaneous tools (do not fit into one of the other categories).
NET	Tools that enable DB2 databases to be connected to the Internet, intranet, and the World Wide Web.
OPR	Operational support tools, such as on-line DB2 standards manuals, change control systems, and schedulers.
PC	PC- and workstation-based DBMSs that mimic DB2 execution such that application development chores can be offloaded from the mainframe.
PLN	Tools that analyze and evaluate the access paths for individual SQL statements and SQL in plans and packages. May also provide suggestions for how to improve the SQL.
PM	DB2 performance monitors.
PRF	DB2 and SQL optimization products that enhance database and application performance.
PRG	Tools that assist the application developer, such as lower CASE tools, 4GLs, SQL generation tools, SQL formatting tools, and application testing tools.
QMF	Tools that augment the functionality and/or enhance the performance of QMF. Examples include query compilers and QMF object administration tools.
QRY	Tools that provide an integrated environment for developing and issuing queries against DB2 tables. May be ISPF- or GUI-based. OLAP tools fall under this category.

39

TABLE 39.1   Continued

Abbrev	Tool Category Definition
REP	Tools that store, manage, and enable access to metadata (such as repositories and data dictionaries).
SEC	Security and authorization tools.
UTL	Tools that generate DB2 utility JCL or enhance DB2 utility functions by providing faster, more efficient execution.

These types of add-on tools can significantly improve the efficiency of DB2 application development. Even IBM is beginning to understand the need for better management tools. IBM provides several DBA tools for free with DB2, including:

- DB2 Control Center: A tool for viewing and managing DB2 databases

- DB2 Development Center: A tool for creating, installing, and testing DB2 stored procedures (previously called DB2 Stored Procedure Builder)

- DB2 Installer: A GUI-based installation assistant

- DB2 Visual Explain: Graphically presents DB2 EXPLAIN output

- DB2 Estimator: A tool for estimating the performance of DB2 applications

- DB2 Warehouse Center: Provides a GUI-driven control center for creating and managing DB2-based data warehoused

Of course, IBM has sold other DB2 tools for a fee such as QMF and DB2-PM for quite some time now. Recently, IBM augmented its portfolio of add-on DB2 tools, and they now compete with the primary DB2 tool vendors such as BMC Software and Computer Associates.

In the following sections, each tool category is described, along with a discussion of desired features. In evaluating products, look for features important to your organization. These lists are not comprehensive, but they provide a good starting point for the evaluation process.

Table Altering Tools

DB2 provides the capability to modify the structure of existing objects using the ALTER DDL statement. The ALTER statement, however, is a functionally crippled statement. Many times DBAs find themselves in a position where it would be nice to be able to alter all the parameters that can be specified for an object; but DB2 does not support this. For example, you can add columns to an existing table (only at the end), but you cannot remove columns from a table. The table must be dropped and then re-created without the columns you want to remove.

V8 Of course, IBM is making in-roads into removing some of these obstacles. DB2 Version 8 provides online schema evolution, whereby more types of changes can be implemented with minimal impact to data availability. For more details on online schema changes refer to Chapter 7, "Database Change Management and Schema Evolution."

Another problem that DBAs encounter in modifying DB2 objects is the cascading drop effect. If a change to a table space mandates its being dropped and re-created (for example, changing the limit keys of a partitioned table space), all dependent objects are dropped when the table space is dropped. This includes the following:

All tables in the table space

All information in SYSCOPY (including image copy information)

All indexes on the tables

Primary and foreign keys

Check constraints

Synonyms and views

Labels and comments

FIELDPROC and EDITPROC assignments

RUNSTATS values

All authorization below the table space level statistics

Ensuring that DDL is issued after the modification to reverse the effects of cascading drops can be a tedious, complex, and error-prone procedure.

Many types of DB2 object alteration cannot be performed using the generic DB2 ALTER statement. Several examples follow:

You cannot change the name of a database, alias, view, column, constraint, table space, or index.

You cannot create a database based on the attributes of an existing database.

You cannot create a table space based on the attributes of an existing table space.

You cannot change the database in which the table space exists.

You cannot change the table space type (for example, changing a simple table space to a segmented or partitioned table space).

You cannot change the SEGSIZE of a segmented table space.

You cannot copy primary and foreign keys using CREATE LIKE; this command creates a new table based on the columns of another table.

You cannot move a table from one table space to another.

You cannot rearrange column ordering.

You cannot add a column into the middle of other columns; only at the end of the table.

You cannot decrease the length of a column (you *can* increase length).

You cannot remove columns from a table.

You cannot change the primary key without dropping and re-creating the primary key.

You cannot add to a table a column specified as NOT NULL.

You cannot add any columns to a table defined with an EDITPROC.

39

You cannot add columns to a table defined with an EDITPROC.

You cannot change a table's EDITPROC or a column's VALIDPROC.

You cannot create a view based on another view.

You cannot add columns to, or remove columns from, a view.

You cannot change the SELECT statement on which the view is based.

You cannot create an index based on another index.

You cannot change the index order (ascending or descending).

You cannot create an alias based on another alias.

You cannot change the location of the alias.

You cannot change the table on which the alias is based.

This list provides the justification needed to obtain an alter tool. Such a tool provides an integrated environment for altering DB2 objects. The burden of ensuring that a change to a DB2 object does not cause other implicit changes is moved from the DBA to the tool.

At a minimum, an alter tool should perform the following functions:

- Maintain tables easily without manually coding SQL.

- Retain or reapply all dependent objects and security affected by the requested alter if a drop is required.

- Retain or reapply all statistical information for dropped objects.

- Navigate hierarchically from object to object, making alterations as it goes.

- Provide panel-driven, or point-and-click modification showing before and after definitions of the DB2 objects before the changes are applied.

- Batch requested changes into a work list that can be executing in the foreground or the background.

- Analyze changes to ensure that the requested alterations do not violate any DB2 DDL rules. For example, if a series of changes is requested and one change causes a subsequent change to be invalid (an object is dropped, for instance), this should be flagged before execution.

- Control the environment in which changes are made.

- Provide for rapid restarts with minimal or no manual intervention required in the event the alter script fails.

- Be capable of monitoring changes as they are applied.

Auditing Tools

An audit is the examination of a practice to determine its correctness. DB2 auditing software therefore should help in monitoring the data control, data definition, and data integrity in the DB2 environment. Several mechanisms provided by DB2 enable the creation of an audit trail, but this trail can be difficult to follow.

The primary vehicle provided by DB2 for auditing is the audit trace. This feature enables DB2 to trace and record auditable activity initiated by specific users. When the DB2 audit trace is activated, the following type of information can be captured to the trace destination:

Authorization failures

Grant and revoke SQL statements

DDL issued against auditable tables

DML issued against auditable tables

Bind requests involving auditable tables

Authorization ID changes requested by the SET CURRENT SQLID statement

Utility executions

An *auditable table* is any table defined to DB2 with the AUDIT clause of the CREATE TABLE statement. There are three options for table auditing: NONE, CHANGES, and ALL. Specifying AUDIT NONE, which is the default, disables table auditing so that the audit trace does not track that table. Specifying AUDIT CHANGES indicates that the first DELETE, INSERT, or UPDATE statement issued against that table in every application unit of work (COMMIT scope) is recorded. AUDIT ALL records the first DML statement of any type accessing this table in each application unit of work. Note, however, that this information is tracked only if the appropriate audit trace is activated. Refer to Chapter 24, "Traditional DB2 Performance Monitoring," for more information on DB2 audit traces.

This information is written to the output trace destination specified for the audit trace. DB2 trace records can be written to GTF, SMF, or an OP buffer. After the information has been written to the specified destination, the problem of how to read this information still exists. If you have DB2-PM, you can run the appropriate audit reports, but even these can be insufficient for true auditing.

An audit tool should provide five important features that DB2's audit tracing capability does not. DB2 auditing requires a trace to be activated, and this can quickly become expensive if many tables must be audited. The first feature an auditing tool should provide is the capability to read the DB2 logs, which are always produced, and report on update activity as needed. This reduces overhead because it uses the regular processing features of DB2 rather than an additional tracing feature, which increases overhead.

The DB2 audit trace records a trace record only for the first statement in a unit of work. The second feature of the auditing tool is reporting all data modification from the DB2 logs.

The DB2 audit trace facility does not record the specifics of the data modification. The third feature of an auditing tool is reporting who (by authorization ID) makes each change, and also showing a before and after image of the changed data.

The fourth feature the auditing tool should provide is the capability to report on the DB2 audit trace data if so desired.

A fifth feature of a DB2 auditing tool is to access the DB2 logs to create redo (or undo) SQL scripts that can be run to re-apply data modifications that occurred during a specific timespan. Although this feature does not provide a true auditing function, it is a common feature since auditing tools by their very nature must access the DB2 logs.

NOTE

Another name for generating undo and redo SQL from the log is transaction recovery. An undo transaction recovery involves generating undo SQL statements to reverse the effect of the transactions in error. To generate undo SQL, the database log is read to find the data modifications that were applied during a given timeframe and

- INSERTs are turned into DELETEs

- DELETEs are turned into INSERTs

- UPDATEs are turned around to UPDATE to the prior value

Redo is a similar form of transaction recovery. But instead of generating SQL for the bad transaction that we want to eliminate, we generate the SQL for the transactions we want to save. Then, we do a standard point in time recovery eliminating all the transactions since the recovery point. Finally, we reapply the good transactions captured in the first step.

Unlike the undo process, which creates SQL statements that are designed to back out all of the problem transactions, the redo process creates SQL statements that are designed to reapply only the valid transactions from a consistent point of recovery to the current time. Because the redo process does not generate SQL for the problem transactions, performing a recovery and then executing the redo SQL can restore the table space to a current state that does not include the problem transactions.

Finally, the auditing tool should provide both standard reports and the capability to create site-specific reports (either from the log or from the DB2 audit trace data).

If your shop has strict auditing requirements, an auditing tool is almost mandatory because of DB2's weak inherent auditing capabilities. Additional things to look for in an auditing tool include the following:

- The tool should consume minimal resources. Before acquiring an auditing tool, determine the estimated I/O and CPU overhead of running the auditing tool to make sure that it will not disrupt your service level agreements for DB2 applications or consume excessive resources.

- The tool should be able to understand DB2 audit trace data and provide formatted reports of the audit trace data, including reports on DDL, DML, and DCL executions.

- Online and batch reporting options should be provided.

- The tool should be able to capture additional information from the DB2 transaction logs.

- Of high importance, the tool should be able to identify the authid of any user that modifies and DB2 data in any table being audited.

- Finally, the tool should be able to read the transaction log and generate undo and redo SQL for transaction recovery.

DB2 Catalog Query and Analysis Tools

The DB2 Catalog contains a wealth of information essential to the operation of DB2. Information about all DB2 objects, authority, and recovery is stored and maintained in the DB2 Catalog. This system catalog is composed of DB2 tables and can be queried using SQL. The data returned by these queries provides a base of information for many DB2 monitoring and administrative tasks.

Coding SQL can be a time-consuming process. Often, you must combine information from multiple DB2 Catalog tables to provide the user with facts relevant for a particular task. This can be verified by reexamining the DB2 Catalog queries presented in Chapter 26, "DB2 Object Monitoring Using the DB2 Catalog and RTS."

Add-on tools can ease the burden of developing DB2 Catalog queries. The basic feature common to all DB2 Catalog tools is the capability to request DB2 Catalog information using a screen-driven interface without coding SQL statements. Analysts can obtain rapid access to specific facts stored in the DB2 Catalog without the burden of coding (sometimes quite complex) SQL. Furthermore, procedural logic is sometimes required to adequately query specific types of catalog information.

Instead of merely enabling data access, many DB2 Catalog tools can do one or more of the following:

- Create syntactically correct DDL statements for all DB2 objects by reading the appropriate DB2 Catalog tables. These statements are generally executed immediately or saved in a sequential data set for future reference or use.

- Modify the "updateable" DB2 Catalog statistical columns using an editor interface (for example, a non-SQL interface).

- Create syntactically correct DCL statements from the DB2 Catalog in the same way that DDL is generated.

- Perform "drop analysis" on an SQL DROP statement. This analysis determines the effect of the cascading drop by detailing all dependent objects and security that will be deleted as a result of executing the DROP.

- Provide a hierarchical listing of DB2 objects. For example, if a specific table is chosen, the tool can migrate quickly up the hierarchy to show its table space and database, or down the hierarchy to show all dependent indexes, views, synonyms, aliases, referentially connected tables, and plans.

- Create and drop DB2 objects, and grant and revoke DB2 security from a screen without coding SQL. Additionally, some tools log all drops and revokes so that they can be undone in the event of an inadvertent drop or revoke execution.

- Specify the ISOLATION clause to access DB2 data using cursor stability, repeatable read, read stability, or uncommitted read processing.

- Serve as a launching point for utilities and commands to be executed.

- Operate on the DB2 Catalog or on a copy of the DB2 Catalog to reduce system-wide contention.

These features aid the DBA in performing his day-to-day duties. Furthermore, a catalog query tool can greatly diminish the amount of time required for a junior DBA to become a productive member of the DBA team.

Compression Tools

A standard tool for reducing DASD costs is the compression utility. This type of tool operates by applying an algorithm to the data in a table so that the data is encoded in a more compact area. By reducing the amount of area needed to store data, DASD costs are decreased. Compression tools must compress the data when it is added to the table and subsequently modified, and then expand the data when it is later retrieved (see Figure 39.1).

Third-party compression routines are specified for DB2 tables using the EDITPROC clause of the CREATE TABLE statement. The load module name for the compression routine is supplied as the parameter to the EDITPROC clause. A table must be dropped and re-created to apply an EDITPROC.

In general, a compression algorithm increases CPU costs while providing benefits in the areas of decreased DASD utilization and sometimes decreased I/O costs. This trade-off is not beneficial for all tables. For example, if a compression routine saves 30% on DASD costs but increases CPU without decreasing I/O, the trade-off is probably not beneficial.

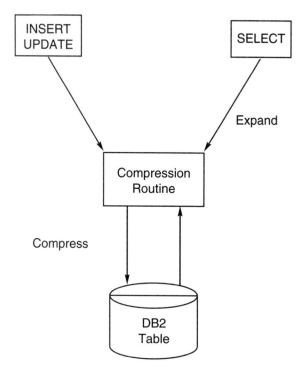

FIGURE 39.1.   A DB2 table compression routine at work.

A compression tool can decrease DASD by reducing the size of the rows to be stored. CPU use usually increases because additional processing is required to compress and expand the row. I/O costs, however, could decrease.

Enhancements to DB2 since V2.3 have made most third-party compression tools of little added value. DB2 provides a basic compression routine called DSN8HUFF. Still most third-party compression tools provide more efficient compression algorithms and advanced analysis to determine the costs and benefits of compression for a specific table. This changed dramatically with DB2 V3. The internal compression capabilities of DB2 since V3 are such that DB2 compression outperforms third-party compression tools. Even when a third-party compression tool can provide benefit to an organization (perhaps because it offers multiple compression routines geared for different types of data), the return on investment is such that most shops typically stick with internal DB2 compression for new tables. The third-party compression tools, however, have not become obsolete. Many organizations refuse to remove software that is working for any number of reasons (from an "if it ain't broken don't fix it" mentality to "not enough cycles to implement such a vast change"). Indeed, most shops are too busy with production work to support the additional effort of removing the third-party EDITPROCs and replacing them with internal DB2 compression.

There are other types of compression tools than those that simply compress DB2 table space data. Some tools compress DB2 image copy backup data sets. These are divided into two camps: those that compress DASD backups and those that compress cartridge backups. This type of compression tool can provide the following benefits:

- Reduced backup storage costs

- Reduced elapsed time for taking backups because fewer tapes must be loaded

- Fewer physical cartridges required (for local and offsite storage)

Another type of compression tool is available from several vendors to compress DB2's archive log data sets. By compressing archive logs, you might be able to fit more archive data sets on DASD, thereby improving the performance of a recovery situation.

DB2-Related Client/Server Tools

Many applications these days span multiple computing environments. This phenomenon is known as client/server processing, and it has proven to be quite successful because it provides a flexible, distributed computing environment. DB2 is a large participant in the client/server plans for many shops. Providing efficient access to large amounts of data, DB2 for z/OS can function as the ultimate database server in a client/server environment.

This being the case, there are many tools on the market that can ease the burden of implementing and administering DB2 in a client/server environment. Middleware products and database gateways that sit between the client workstation and the mainframe enable access to DB2 as a server. These products can provide access to DB2 for z/OS, to DB2 on other platforms, and also to other DBMS server products (Oracle, Microsoft SQL Server, Sybase Adaptive Server Enterprise, Informix, and so on). Additionally, third-party ODBC and JDBC drivers are available to ease workstation access to mainframe DB2 data.

39

Another valid type of client/server tool is a 4GL programming environment that provides seamless access to DB2. These types of products typically split the application workload between the workstation and the server aiding the programmer to rapidly develop DB2 client/server applications.

Database Analysis Tools

DB2 provides only minimal intelligence for database analysis. Usually, a database administrator or performance analyst must keep a vigilant watch over DB2 objects using DB2 Catalog queries or a DB2 Catalog tool. This is not an optimal solution, because it relies on human intervention for efficient database organization, opening up the possibility of human error, forgetting to monitor, and misinterpreting analyzed data.

Fortunately, database analysis tools can proactively and automatically monitor your DB2 environment. This monitoring can perform the following functions:

- Collect statistics for DB2 table spaces and indexes. These statistics can be standard DB2 RUNSTATS information, extended statistics capturing more information (for example, data set extents), or a combination of both.

- Read the VSAM data sets for the DB2 objects to capture current statistics, read RUNSTATS from the DB2 Catalog, read tables unique to the tool that captured the enhanced statistics, or any combination of these three.

- Set thresholds, whereby the automatic scheduling of a REORG utility is invoked based on current statistics. Additional alarm capabilities can be available to take corrective action when database problems are encountered or merely to page the DBA on-call when a problem arises.

- Database analysis tools also can provide a "Swiss-army knife" toolkit for DBAs. Some features to look for include integrity checking, page zapping to fix problems, compression analysis, historical statistics, and interfaces to DB2 utilities and commands.

- Provide a series of canned reports detailing the potential problems for specific DB2 objects.

V7

> **NOTE**
>
> IBM has embarked on a campaign to add intelligence into the DB2 engine and its utilities. For example, with V6 the REORG utility was modified such that it can examine statistics to determine whether or not the reorganization should proceed. Furthermore, a subsequent V7 fix provided the capability for DB2 to collect real-time statistics without manual intervention. This trend will likely continue, and DB2 will become more manageable and self-healing.

Database Modeling and Design Tools

Database modeling and design tools do not have to be unique to DB2 design, although some are. Application development should be based on sound data and process models. The use of a tool to ensure this is a good practice.

Database modeling and design tools may be referred to as CASE tools. CASE, or computer-aided software engineering, is the process of automating the application development life cycle. A CASE tool, such as a data modeling tool, supports portions of that life cycle. A comprehensive checklist of features to look for in a CASE tool is presented in Chapter 14, "Alternative DB2 Application Development Methods." Although CASE tools were very popular in the late 1980s and early 1990s, they have not been in vogue since (though some DB2 applications that were developed in a CASE tool environment still run in production).

Many excellent database design and modeling tools are not specifically designed for DB2 but can be used to develop DB2 applications. Tools developed specifically to support DB2 development, however, add another dimension to the application development effort. They can significantly reduce the development timeframe by automating repetitive tasks and validating the models. If your organization decides to obtain a CASE tool that specifically supports DB2, look for one that can do the following:

- Provide standard features of logical data modeling (such as entity-relationship diagramming and normalization).

- Create a physical data model geared to DB2. This model should support all features of DB2, such as the capability to depict all DB2 objects, referential integrity, VCAT and STOGROUP-defined table spaces, and capacity planning.

- Provide an expert system to verify the accuracy of the physical data model and to suggest alternative solutions.

- Cross-reference the logical model to the physical model, capturing text that supports physical design decisions such as denormalization and the choice of table space type.

- Automatically generate DB2-standard DDL to fully implement the database defined in the physical data model.

- Interface with application development tools and data dictionaries available to the organization.

DASD and Space Management Tools

DB2 provides basic statistics for space utilization in the DB2 Catalog, but the in-depth statistics required for both space management and performance tuning are woefully inadequate. The queries presented in Chapter 26 form a basis for DB2 DASD management, but critical elements are missing.

Monitoring the space requirements of the underlying VSAM data sets to maintain historical growth information can be difficult without a space management tool. When data sets go into secondary extents, performance suffers. Without a DASD management tool, you would have to monitor Real Time Stats or periodically examine LISTCAT output to monitor secondary extents. Both can be time-consuming.

Additionally, the manner in which DB2 allocates space can result in the inefficient use of DASD. Often space is allocated but DB2 does not use it. Although the STOSPACE utility, combined with DB2 queries, provides limited out-of-the-box DASD management, this capability is far from robust. A DASD management tool is the only answer for ferreting out the amount of allocated space versus the amount of used space.

DASD management tools often interface with other DB2 and DASD support tools such as standard MVS space management tools, database analysis tools, DB2 Catalog query and management tools, and DB2 utility JCL generators.

DB2 Table Editors

The only method of updating DB2 data is with the SQL data manipulation language statements DELETE, INSERT, and UPDATE. Because these SQL statements operate on data a set at a time, multiple rows—or even all of the rows—can be affected by a single SQL statement. Coding SQL statements for every data modification required during the application development and testing phase can be time-consuming.

A DB2 table editing tool reduces the time needed to make simple data alterations by providing full-screen edit capability for DB2 tables. The user specifies the table to edit and is placed in an edit session that resembles the ISPF editor. The data is presented to the user as a series of rows, with the columns separated by spaces. A header line indicates the column names. The data can be scrolled up and down, as well as left and right. To change data, the user simply types over the current data.

This type of tool is ideal for supporting the application development process. A programmer can make quick changes without coding SQL. Also, if properly implemented, a table editor can reduce the number of erroneous data modifications made by beginning SQL users.

> **CAUTION**
>
> Remember that the table editor is issuing SQL in the background to implement the requested changes. This can cause a lag between the time the user updates the data and the time the data is committed. Table editor updates usually are committed only when the user requests that the data be saved or when the user backs out of the edit session without canceling.

Remember too that table editors can consume a vast amount of resources. Ensure that the tool can limit the number of rows to be read into the editing session. For example, can the tool set a filter such that only the rows meeting certain search criteria are read? Can a limit be set on the number of rows to be read into any one edit session? Without this capability, large table space scans can result.

A DB2 table editor should be used only in the testing environment. End users or programmers might request that a table editor be made available for production data modification. This should be avoided at all costs. The data in production tables is critical to the success of your organization and should be treated with great care. Production data modification should be accomplished only with thoroughly tested SQL or production plans.

When a table editor is used, all columns are available for update. Thus, if a table editor is used to change production data, a simple mis-keying can cause unwanted updates. Native SQL should be used if you must ensure that only certain columns are updated.

Tested SQL statements and application plans are characterized by their planned nature. The modification requests were well thought out and tested. This is not true for changes implemented through a table editor.

Additionally, tested SQL statements and application plans are characterized by their planned nature. The modification requests were well thought out and tested. This is not true for changes implemented through a table editor.

In addition to simple online browsing and editing of DB2 data using ISPF (or a GUI), the table-editing tool should be able to

- Mimic the functionality of the ISPF editor.

- Provide both single row and multiple row-at-a-time editing options.

- Optionally prompt the user before actually applying any changes to the actual data.

- Cancel accumulated changes of any editing session before exiting.

- Periodically save the changes without exiting the table editor (as an option).

- Propagate referential integrity changes.

- Provide the capability to interface with utilities to copy, load, or unload tables.

- Interface with your DB2 application testing tools.

- Apply filters to rows before displaying them in an editing session.

- Display and save SQL UPDATE, INSERT, and DELETE statements for the accumulated changes of an editing session.

- Issue SQL within an editing session.

- Interface with your program editor.

- Compare data in two tables and show any differences.

Sometimes other DB2 tools, such as a DB2 Catalog query tool, will come with an integrated table editor.

Extract/Transformation/Load (Data Movement) Tools

At times, multiple database management systems coexist in data processing shops. This is increasingly true as shops embark on client/server initiatives. Additionally, the same data (or a subset thereof) might need to be stored in each of the databases. In a multiple DBMS environment, the movement of data from DBMS to DBMS is a tedious task. The need to move data from one environment to another is increasing with the overwhelming acceptance and implementation of data warehouses.

ETL tools ease the burden because the tool understands the data format and environment of each DBMS it works with. The data movement and warehousing tool(s) that a shop chooses depends on the following factors:

- How many DBMS products need to be supported?

- To what extent is the data replicated across the DBMS products?

- What transformations need to occur as the data is moved from one environment to another? For example, how are data types converted for DBMSs that do not support date, time, and timestamp date (or support these data types using a different format)? Or, more simply, do codes in one system need to be transformed into text in another (for example, "A" becomes "Active", and so on).

- Does the data have to be synchronized across DBMS products?

- Is the data static or dynamic?

- If it is dynamic, is it updated online, in batch, or both?

The answers to these questions help determine the type of data conversion tool necessary.

Two basic types of conversion tools are popular in the market today:

Replication tools	These tools extract data from external application systems and other databases for population into DB2 tables. This type of tool can extract data from VSAM, IMS, Sybase, Oracle, flat files, or other structures and insert the data into DB2.
Propagation tools	Inserts data from external applications and other database products into DB2 tables. A propagation tool is similar in function to an extract tool, but propagation tools are active. They constantly capture updates made in the external system, either for immediate application to DB2 tables or for subsequent batch updating. This differs from the extract tool, which captures entire data structures, not data modifications.

Integrity Tools

Referential integrity has been available on DB2 since the early days of DB2 but it can be difficult to administer and implement properly. RI tools eliminate the difficulty by performing one of the following functions:

- Analyzing data for both system- and user-managed referential integrity constraint violations

- Executing faster than the IBM CHECK utility

- Enabling additional types of RI to be supported; for example, analyzing primary keys for which no foreign keys exist and deleting the primary key row

Check constraints for data integrity have been available with DB2 since V4. Tools can help implement and maintain check constraints in the following ways:

- Analyzing data for both system- and user-managed data integrity constraint violations

- Executing faster than the IBM CHECK utility

- Enabling additional types of data integrity to be supported; for example, analyzing the compatibility of check constraints and user-defined DEFAULT clauses

DB2 Object Migration Tools

DB2 does not provide a feature to migrate DB2 objects from one subsystem to another. This can be accomplished only by manually storing the CREATE DDL statements (and all subsequent ALTER statements) for future application in another system. Manual processes such as this are error-prone. Also, this process does not take into account the migration of table data, DB2 security, plans, packages, statistics, and so on.

DB2 object migration tools facilitate the quick migration of DB2 objects from one DB2 subsystem to another. They are similar to a table altering tool but have minimal altering capability (some interface directly with an alter tool or are integrated into a single tool). The migration procedure is usually driven by ISPF panels that prompt the user for the objects to migrate.

Migration typically can be specified at any level. For example, if you request the migration of a specific database, you also could migrate all dependent objects and security. A renaming capability typically is provided so that database names, authorization IDs, and other objects are renamed according to the standards of the receiving subsystem. When the parameters of the migration have been specified completely, the tool creates a job stream to implement the requested DB2 objects in the requested DB2 subsystem.

A migration tool reduces the time required by database administrators to move DB2 databases from environment to environment (for example, from test to production). Quicker turnaround results in a more rapid response to user needs, thereby increasing the efficiency of your business.

Typically, migration tools are the second DB2 tool that an organization acquires (right after a DB2 Catalog query product).

Miscellaneous Tools

Many types of DB2 tools are available. The categories in this chapter cover the major types of DB2 tools, but not all tools can be easily pigeonholed. For example, consider a DB2 table space calculator. It reads table DDL and information on the number of rows in the table to estimate space requirements. A space calculator is often provided with another tool, such as a DASD management tool or a database design and modeling tool.

The number and types of DB2 tools that are available in the market are constantly growing and are limited only by the imagination and ingenuity of the programmers and vendors offering these solutions.

Internet Enabling Tools

The Internet is the hottest technology trend of the past decade. Every organization is looking for ways to increase their competitive advantage by making corporate data available to customers, partners, and employees over the Internet, intranet, and extranets.

39

A specialized category of tools is available to hook DB2 data to the Web. These tools are referred to as Internet-enabling tools. For more information on the Internet and IBM's tools for connecting the Web to DB2, refer to Chapter 17, "DB2 and the Internet."

Operational Support Tools

Many avenues encompass operational support in a DB2 environment, ranging from standards and procedures to tools that guarantee smoother operation. This section describes tools from several operational support categories.

One type of product delivers online access to DB2 documentation. With this tool, you avoid the cost of purchasing DB2 manuals for all programmers, and DB2 information and error messages are always available online. In addition, analysts and DBAs who dial in to the mainframe from home can reference DB2 manuals online rather than keep printed copies at home. IBM's Book Manager is an example of this type of tool.

Another similar type of operational support tool provides online access to DB2 standards and procedures. These tools are commonly populated with model DB2 standards and procedures that can be modified or extended. Tools of this nature are ideal for a shop with little DB2 experience that wants to launch a DB2 project. As the shop grows, the standards and procedures can grow with it.

Products that provide "canned" standards for implementing, accessing, and administering DB2 databases are particularly useful for shops new to DB2. By purchasing an online standards manual, these shops can quickly come up-to-speed with DB2. However, mature DB2 shops can also benefit from these types of products if the third-party vendor automatically ships updates whenever IBM ships a new release of DB2. This can function as cheap training in the new DB2 release. A product containing DB2 standards should fulfill the following requirements:

- Provide online access via the mainframe or a networked PC environment, so all developers and DBAs can access the manual

- Be extensible, so additional standards can be added

- Be modifiable, so the provided standards can be altered to suit prior shop standards (naming conventions, programming standards, and so on)

Tools also exist to enable a better batch interface to DB2. Standard batch DB2 programs run under the control of the TSO terminal monitor program, `IKJEFT01`. Another operational support tool provides a call-attach interface that enables DB2 batch programs to run as a standard MVS batch job without the TSO TMP.

DB2, unlike IMS, provides no inherent capability for storing checkpoint information. Tools that store checkpoint information that can be used by the program during a subsequent restart are useful for large batch DB2 applications issuing many `COMMIT`s.

One final type of operational support tool assists in managing changes. These tools are typically integrated into a change control tool that manages program changes. Change control implemented for DB2 can involve version control, plan and package management, and ensure that timestamp mismatches (SQLCODE -818) are avoided. Some tools can even control changes to DB2 objects.

PC-Based DB2 Emulation Products

Personal computers are pervasive and most data processing professionals have one on their desk. Most end users do, too. As such, the need to access DB2 from the PC is a viable one. However, not everyone needs to do this in a *client/server* environment.

Sometimes, just simple access from a PC will suffice. For this, a PC query tool can be used. Data requests originate from the PC workstation. The tool sends the requests to the mainframe for processing.

When processing is finished, the data is returned to the PC and formatted. These types of tools typically use a graphical user interface with pull-down menus and point-and-click functionality. These features are not available on mainframe products.

Another popular approach to developing DB2 applications is to create a similar environment on the PC. This can be done using a PC DBMS that works like DB2 and other similar PC products that mimic the mainframe (COBOL, IMS/TM, CICS, JCL, and so on). DB2 for Linux, Unix, and Windows is, of course, the most popular PC DBMS in this category, but there are others.

Quite often, tools that can be used in a straight PC environment also can be used in a client/server environment.

Plan Analysis Tools

The development of SQL to access DB2 tables is the responsibility of an application development team. With SQL's flexibility, the same request can be made in different ways. Because some of these ways are inefficient, the performance of an application's SQL could fluctuate wildly unless the SQL is analyzed in-depth by an expert before implementation.

The DB2 EXPLAIN command provides information about the access paths used by SQL queries by parsing SQL in application programs and placing encoded output into a DB2 PLAN_TABLE. To gauge efficiency, a DBA must decode the PLAN_TABLE data and determine whether a more efficient access path is available.

SQL code reviews are required to ensure that optimal SQL design techniques are used. SQL code walkthroughs are typically performed by a DBA, a performance analyst, or someone with experience in SQL coding. This walkthrough must consist of reviews of the SQL statements, the selected access paths, and the program code in which the SQL is embedded. It also includes an evaluation of the RUNSTATS information to ascertain whether production-level statistics were used at the time of the EXPLAIN.

A line-by-line review of application source code and EXPLAIN output is tedious and prone to error, and it can cause application backlogs. A plan analysis tool can greatly simplify this process by automating major portions of the code review process. A plan analysis tool can typically perform the following functions:

39

- Analyze the SQL in an application program, describing the access paths chosen in a graphic format, an English description, or both.

- Issue warnings when specific SQL constructs are encountered. For example, each time a sort is requested (by ORDER BY, GROUP BY, or DISTINCT), a message is presented informing the user of the requisite sort.

- Suggest alternative SQL solutions based on an "expert system" that reads SQL statements and their corresponding PLAN_TABLE entries and poses alternate SQL options.

- Extend the rules used by the "expert system" to capture site-specific rules.

- Analyze at the subsystem, application, plan, package, or SQL statement level.

- Store multiple versions of EXPLAIN output and create performance comparison and plan history reports.

Currently, no tool can analyze the performance of the COBOL code in context along with the SQL that is embedded in it. For example, consider an application program that embeds a singleton SELECT inside a loop. The singleton SELECT requests a single row based on a predicate, checking for the primary key of that table. The primary key value is changed for each iteration of the loop so that the entire table is read from the lowest key value to the highest key value.

A plan analysis tool will probably not flag the SQL statement because the predicate value is for the primary key, which causes an indexed access. It could be more efficient to code a cursor, without a predicate, to retrieve every row of the table, and then fetch each row one by one. This method might use sequential prefetch or query I/O parallelism, thereby reducing I/O and elapsed time, and therefore enhancing performance. Only a trained analyst can catch this type of design problem during a code walkthrough. Plan analysis tools also miss other potential problems, such as when the program has two cursors that should be coded as a one-cursor join. Although a plan analysis tool significantly reduces the effort involved in the code review process, it cannot eliminate it.

Following are some required features for a plan analysis tool:

- It must be capable of interpreting standard DB2 EXPLAIN output and present the information in an easy-to-understand (preferably graphical) format.

- It must automatically scan application source code and PLAN_TABLEs, reporting on the selected access paths and the predicted performance.

- It must be able to provide a historical record of access paths by program, package, plan, or SQL statement.

Performance Monitors

Performance monitoring and tuning can be one of the most time-consuming tasks for large or critical DB2 applications. This topic was covered in depth in Parts V and VI. DB2 performance monitoring and analysis tools support many features in many ways. For example, DB2 performance tools can operate as follows:

- In the background mode as a batch job reporting on performance statistics written by the DB2 trace facility

- In the foreground mode as an online monitor that either traps DB2 trace information using the instrumentation facility interface or captures information from DB2 control blocks as DB2 applications execute

- By sampling the DB2 and user address spaces as the program runs and by capturing information about the performance of the job independent of DB2 traces

- By capturing DB2 trace information and maintaining it in a history file (or table) for producing historical performance reports and for predicting performance trends

- As a capacity planning device by giving the tool statistical information about a DB2 application and the environment in which it will operate

- As an after-the-fact analysis tool on a PC workstation for analyzing and graphing all aspects of DB2 application performance and system-wide DB2 performance

DB2 performance tools support one or more of these features. The evaluation of DB2 performance monitors is a complex task. Often more than one performance monitor is used at a single site. Vendors who sell suites of performance monitors for other system software also frequently offer DB2 performance monitors. Whenever possible, try to utilize a DB2 performance monitor that not only offers full functionality for DB2 monitoring, but also integrates with your other performance monitors that work with DB2 (such as your monitors for CICS, IMS, and z/OS).

For more information on DB2 performance monitoring and tuning, refer to Parts V and VI.

Products to Enhance Performance

Performance is an important facet of DB2 database administration. Many shops dedicate several analysts to tweaking and tuning SQL, DB2, and its environment to elicit every performance enhancement possible. If your shop falls into this category, several tools on the market enhance the performance of DB2 by adding functionality directly to DB2. These DB2 performance tools can interact with the base code of DB2 and provide enhanced performance. Typically, these products take advantage of known DB2 shortcomings.

For example, products exist to perform the following functions:

- Enable DSNZPARMs to be changed without recycling DB2; although DB2 as of V7 offers the ability to change some ZPARM values online, that capacity is not provided for all of the DSNZPARMs, yet.

- Enhance the performance of reading a DB2 page.

- Enhance or augment DB2 buffer pool processing.

Care must be taken when evaluating DB2 performance tools. New releases of DB2 might negate the need for these tools because functionality was added or a known shortcoming was corrected. However, this does not mean that you should not consider performance

39

tools. They can pay for themselves after only a short period of time. Discarding the tool when DB2 supports its functionality is not a problem if the tool has already paid for itself in terms of better performance.

CAUTION

Because these tools interact very closely with DB2, be careful when migrating to a new release of DB2 or a new release of the tool. Extra testing should be performed with these tools because of their intrusive nature.

DB2 Programming and Development Tools

Often times, application development efforts require the population and maintenance of large test beds for system integration, unit, and user testing. A category of testing tools exists to facilitate this requirement. Testing tools enable an application developer or quality assurance analyst to issue a battery of tests against a test base and analyze the results. Testing tools are typically used for all types of applications and are extended to support testing against DB2 tables.

Many other types of tools enhance the DB2 application development effort. These DB2 programming and development tools can perform as follows:

- Compare two DB2 tables to determine the differences. These tools enable the output from modified programs to be tested to determine the impact of code change on application output.

- Enable the testing of SQL statements in a program editor as the programmer codes the SQL.

- Explain SQL statements in an edit session.

- Generate complete code from in-depth specifications. Some tools even generate SQL. When code generators are used, great care should be taken to ensure that the generated code is efficient before promoting it to production status.

- Use 4GLs (fourth-generation languages) that interface to DB2 and extend the capabilities of SQL to include procedural functions (such as looping or row-at-a-time processing).

Due to the variable nature of the different types of DB2 programming tools, they should be evaluated case by case.

QMF Enhancement Tools

A special category of tool, supporting QMF instead of DB2, automatically creates COBOL programs from stored QMF queries. QMF provides a vehicle for the ad hoc development, storage, and execution of SQL statements. When an ad hoc query is developed, it often must be stored and periodically executed. This is possible with QMF, but QMF can execute only dynamic SQL. It does not support static SQL. A method of running critical stored queries using static SQL would be beneficial, because static SQL generally provides better performance than dynamic SQL.

QMF enhancement tools convert the queries, forms, and procs stored in QMF into static SQL statements embedded in a COBOL program. The COBOL program does all the data retrieval and formatting performed by QMF, providing the same report as QMF would. However, the report is now created using static SQL instead of dynamic SQL, thereby boosting performance.

Query Tools

DB2 provides DSNTEP2 and the SPUFI query tool bundled with the DBMS. Most organizations find these inadequate, however, in developing professional, formatted reports or complete applications. It can be inadequate also for inexperienced users or those who want to develop or execute ad hoc queries.

QMF addresses each of these deficiencies. The capability to format reports without programming is probably the greatest asset of QMF. This feature makes QMF ideal for use as an ad hoc query tool for users.

Another important feature is the capability to develop data manipulation requests without using SQL. QMF provides QBE and Prompted Query in addition to SQL. QBE, or Query By Example, is a language in itself. The user makes data manipulation requests graphically by coding keywords in the columns of a tabular representation of the table to be accessed. For example, a QBE request to retrieve the department number and name for all departments that report to 'A00' would look like the construct shown in Figure 39.2.

DSN8610.DEPT	DEPTNO	DEPTNAME	MGRNO	ADMRDEPT
	P.	P.		'A00'

FIGURE 39.2   *DB2 security cascading revokes.*

Prompted Query builds a query by prompting the end user for information about the data to be retrieved. The user selects a menu option and Prompted Query asks a series of questions, the answers to which are used by QMF to build DML. Both QBE and Prompted Query build SQL "behind the scenes" based on the information provided by the end user.

QMF can also be used to build application systems. A QMF application accesses DB2 data in three ways:

- Using the QMF Callable Interface from an application program
- Using the QMF Command Interface (QMFCI) in a CLIST to access QMF
- Using a QMF procedure

Why would you want to call QMF from an application? QMF provides many built-in features that can be used by application programs to reduce development cost and time. For example, QMF can display online reports that scroll not only up and down but also left and right. (Coding left and right scrolling in an application program is not a trivial task.) QMF also can issue the proper form of dynamic SQL, removing the burden of doing so from the novice programmer. Refer to Chapter 12, "Dynamic SQL Programming," for an in-depth discussion of dynamic SQL techniques.

Another benefit of QMF is that you can use inherent QMF commands to accomplish tasks that are difficult to perform with a high-level language such as COBOL. Consider, for example, the following QMF commands:

EXPORT   Automatically exports report data to a flat file. Without this QMF command, a program would have to allocate a data set and read the report line by line, writing each line to the output file.

DRAW   Reads the DB2 Catalog and builds a formatted SQL SELECT, INSERT, UPDATE, or DELETE statement for any table.

SET   Establishes global values for variables used by QMF.

QMF, however, is not the only game in town. Other vendors provide different DB2 table query and reporting tools that can be used to enhance DB2's ad hoc query capabilities. Some of these products are similar in functionality to QMF but provide additional capabilities. They can do the following:

- Use static SQL rather than dynamic SQL for stored queries

- Provide standard query formats and bundled reports

- Provide access to other file formats such as VSAM data sets or IMS databases in conjunction with access to DB2 tables

- Provide access from IMS/TM (QMF is supported in TSO and CICS only)

- Execute DB2 commands from the query tool

Tools that operate on workstations and PCs are becoming more popular than their mainframe counterparts. This is because the PC provides an environment that is more conducive to quickly creating a report from raw data. Using point-and-click, drag-and-drop technology greatly eases the report generation process. Responding to this trend, IBM now offers QMF for Windows, in addition to the traditional QMF for ISPF.

Additionally, data warehousing is driving the creation of tools that enable rapid querying along business dimensions. These tools provide OLAP, or on-line analytical processing. For an overview of data warehousing and OLAP please refer to Chapter 45, "Data Warehousing with DB2."

Finally, fourth-generation languages (4GLs) are gaining more and more popularity for accessing DB2 data. Though not a typical type of DB2 add-on tool, these products provide more functionality than a report writing tool, but with the GUI front-end that makes them easier to use than 3GL programming languages such as COBOL and C. 4GL tools typically work in one of three ways:

- Queries are developed using 4GL syntax, which is then converted "behind the scenes" into SQL queries.

- SQL is embedded in the 4GL code and executed much like SQL embedded in a 3GL.

- A hybrid of these two methods, in which the executed SQL is either difficult or impossible to review.

In general, you should avoid 4GLs that require a hybrid approach. When a hybrid method is mandatory, exercise extreme caution before using that 4GL. These methods are usually difficult to implement and maintain, and they typically provide poor performance.

If you do use a 4GL to access DB2 data, heed the following cautions:

- Many 4GLs provide only dynamic SQL access, which is usually an inefficient way to develop entire DB2 applications. Even if the 4GL provides static SQL access, often the overhead associated with the DB2 interface is high. For this reason, use 4GLs to access DB2 data only for ad hoc or special processing. 4GLs are generally an unacceptable method of developing complete DB2 applications.

- Be wary of using the syntax of the 4GL to join or "relate" DB2 tables. Instead, use views that efficiently join the tables using SQL, then access the views using the 4GL syntax. I was involved in an application tuning effort in which changing a "relate" in the 4GL syntax to a view reduced the elapsed time of a 4GL request by more than 250 percent.

Repositories

A repository stores information about an organization's data assets. Repositories are used to store *metadata*, or data about data. They are frequently used to enhance the usefulness of DB2 application development and to document the data elements available in the data warehouse.

> **What Is Metadata?**
>
> *Metadata* is frequently defined as "data about data." But that is an insufficient definition. Metadata characterizes data. It is used to provide documentation such that data can be understood and more readily consumed by your organization. Metadata answers the **who**, **what**, **when**, **where**, **why**, and **how** questions for users of the data.

In choosing a repository, base your decision on the metadata storage and retrieval needs of your entire organization, not just DB2. Typically, a repository can perform the following functions:

- Store information about the data, processes, and environment of the organization.

- Support multiple ways of looking at the same data. An example of this concept is the three-schema approach, in which data is viewed at the conceptual, logical, and physical levels.

- Support data model creation and administration. Integration with popular CASE tools is also an important evaluation criterion.

- Scan the operational environment to generate metadata from operational systems.

- Store in-depth documentation, as well as produce detail and management reports from that documentation.

- Support change control.

- Enforce naming conventions.

- Generate copy books from data element definitions.

These are some of the more common functions of a data dictionary. When choosing a data dictionary for DB2 development, the following features are generally desirable:

- The data stores used by the repository are in DB2 tables. This enables DB2 applications to directly read the data dictionary tables.

- The repository can directly read the DB2 Catalog or views on the DB2 Catalog. This ensures that the repository has current information on DB2 objects.

- If the repository does not directly read the DB2 Catalog, an interface is provided to ease the population of the repository using DB2 Catalog information.

- The repository provides an interface to any modeling and design tools used.

This section is a brief overview of repositories—an extended discussion of data dictionaries is beyond the scope of this book.

> **NOTE**
>
> Because the DB2 Catalog stores database metadata it can be thought of as a crude data dictionary, but it does not fulfill all of the functionality of a true data dictionary or repository product.

Security Tools

DB2 security is provided internal to DB2 with the GRANT and REVOKE data control language components of SQL. Using this mechanism, authorization is granted explicitly and implicitly to users of DB2. Authorization exits enable DB2 to communicate with other security packages such as IBM's RACF and Computer Associate's Top Secret and ACF2. This eases the administrative burden of DB2 security by enabling the corporate data security function to administer groups of users. DB2 authorization is then granted to the RACF groups, instead of individual userids. This decreases the volume of security requests that must be processed by DB2.

DB2's implementation of security has several problems. Paramount among these deficiencies is the effect of the cascading REVOKE. If an authority is revoked from one user who previously granted authority to other users, all dependent authorizations are also revoked. For example, consider Figure 39.3. Assume that Bob is a SYSADM. He grants DBADM WITH GRANT OPTION to Ron and Dianne. Ron then grants the same to Rick and Bill, as well as miscellaneous authority to Chris, Jeff, and Monica. Dianne grants DBADM WITH GRANT OPTION to Dale, Carl, and Janet. She grants miscellaneous authority to Mike and Sue also. Rick, Bill, Dale, Carl, and Janet now have the authority to grant authority to other users. What would be the effect of revoking Ron's DBADM authority? Chris, Jeff, and Monica would lose their authority. In addition, Rick and Bill would lose their authority, as would everyone who was granted authority by either Rick or Bill, and so on.

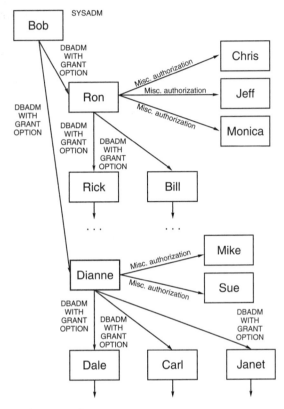

FIGURE 39.3   DB2 security cascading REVOKEs.

This problem can be addressed by a DB2 security add-on tool. These tools typically analyze the effects of a REVOKE. For example, the implications of revoking Ron's DBADM authority would have been clearly displayed, showing all implicit revokes. These tools enable the user to revoke the authority and optionally reassign all dependent authority either by storing the appropriate GRANT statements to reapply the authorizations implicitly revoked or by revoking the authority and automatically reapplying all implicit revokes in the background.

These tools provide other functions. Consider the administrative overhead when DB2 users are hired, quit, or are transferred. Security must be added or removed. A good security tool enables a user to issue a GRANT LIKE command, which can copy DB2 authority from one DB2 object to another or from one user to another. Consider two examples.

Suppose that Ron is transferred to another department. A security tool can assign all of Ron's authority to another user before revoking Ron's authority. Or suppose that a new DB2 table is created for an existing DB2 application, and it requires the same users to access its data as can access the other tables in the application. This type of tool enables a user to copy all security from one table to the new table.

There is one other type of DB2 security product. Rather than augment DB2 security, however, this type of product replaces DB2 security with an external package.

The primary benefit is the consolidation of security. If your organization uses a security package from another vendor rather than RACF for regular data security, security administration for regular data security and DB2 security can be consolidated into a single unit. A second benefit is that the cascading revoke effect can be eliminated because MVS data security packages do not cascade security revocations.

There are some problems with this type of tool, however. For example, these tools do not conform to the rigorous definition of the relational model, which states that the DBMS must control security. Some do not provide all types of DB2 security. For example, INSTALL SYSADM is still required in DB2 for installation of DB2 and DB2 Catalog and Directory recovery.

Keep in mind, too, that for some DB2 security features, such as multilevel security, it is necessary for DB2 to interface with an external security product.

Utility Enhancement Tools

The IBM DB2 COPY, LOAD, RECOVER, REORG, and UNLOAD utilities are notorious for their inefficiency, sometimes requiring more than 24 hours to operate on very large DB2 tables. These utilities are required to populate, administer, and organize DB2 databases.

Several vendors provide support tools that replace the DB2 utilities and provide the same functionality more efficiently. For example, one vendor claims that its REORG utility executes six to ten times faster than the DB2 REORG utility. These claims must be substantiated for the applications at your organization, but enough inefficiencies are designed into the IBM DB2 utilities to make this claim believable.

Before committing to an alternate utility tool, be sure that it conforms to the following requirements:

- Does not subvert the integrity of the data in the DB2 tables.

- Minimally provides the same features as the corresponding DB2 utility. For example, if the DB2 REORG utility can REORG both indexes and tablespaces, the enhanced REORG tool must be capable of doing the same.

- Does not subvert standard DB2 features, when possible. For example, DB2 image copies are maintained in the DB2 Catalog. The enhanced COPY tool, therefore, should store its image copies there as well.

- Provides an execution time at least twice as fast as the corresponding DB2 utility. For example, if the DB2 LOAD utility requires 20 minutes to load a table, the enhanced LOAD tool must load the same table in at least 10 minutes. (This should not be a hard-and-fast rule. Sometimes even a moderate increase in processing time is sufficient to cost-justify a third-party utility tool, especially now that IBM is charging extra for their utilities.)

- Corrects the deficiencies of the standard DB2 utilities, when possible. For example, the DB2 LOAD utility will not load data in sequence by the clustering index. An enhanced tool might provide this capability.

- When testing utility tools from different vendors, ensure that you are conducting fair tests. For example, always reload or recover prior to resting REORG utilities so that you don't skew your results due to different levels of table space organization. Additionally, always run the tests for each tool on the same object with the same amount of data.

> **CAUTION**
>
> IBM utility I/O is charged to the DB2 subsystem. The third-party tool will most likely charge I/O to the batch utility job.

> **CAUTION**
>
> Third-party utility execution usually cannot be monitored using the -DISPLAY UTILITY command. Some ISVs provide an equivalent display capability for their utilities, though.

> **CAUTION**
>
> Some third-party utility products call an IBM utility product for certain features and functionality. Before deciding to completely replace IBM with another vendor's utilities, be sure you understand the limitations that can occur because the IBM utilities will no longer be available.

One last category of DB2 utility tool is the utility manager. This type of tool provides administrative support for the creation and execution of DB2 utility jobstreams. These utility generation and management tools can do the following:

- Automatically generate DB2 utility parameters and JCL, with correct workspace assignments

- Monitor DB2 utility jobs as they execute

- Automatically schedule DB2 utilities when exceptions are triggered

- Assist in the scheduling of DB2 utilities to kick off the most important ones first, or to manage the available batch window

- Restart utilities with a minimum of intervention. For example, if a utility cannot be restarted, the tool automatically issues a -TERM UTIL command and resubmits the utility.

DB2 Tools Vendors

There are a plethora of DB2 tool vendors offering many combinations of products from the categories we just reviewed. Appendix C, "Valid DB2 Data Types" provides an up-to-date listing of the major DB2 ISVs. Each vendor name in Appendix C is accompanied by the type of DB2 add-on tools the company supplies.

Evaluating DB2 Tools Vendors

Although the most important aspect of DB2 tool selection is the functionality of the tool and the way it satisfies the needs of your organization, the nature and stability of the vendor that provides the product is important also. This section provides suggested questions to ask when you are selecting a DB2 tool vendor.

1. How long has the vendor been in business? How long has the vendor been supplying DB2 tools?

2. Does your company have other tools from this vendor? How satisfied are the users of those tools?

3. Are other organizations satisfied with the tool you are selecting? Obtain a list of other organizations who use the same tool, and contact several of them.

4. Does the vendor provide a 24-hour support number? If not, what are its hours of operation? Does the vendor have a toll-free number? If not, how far away is the company from your site? You want to avoid accumulating long distance charges when you are requesting customer support from a vendor. (If an 800 number is not shown in the vendor list, that does not mean that the vendor does not have a toll-free customer support line.)

5. Does the vendor provide a newsletter? How technical is it? Does it provide information on DB2 and the vendor's tools, or just on the vendor's tools? Does the vendor provide a bulletin board service? Can you access it before establishing a relationship with the vendor to evaluate its usefulness? If so, scan some of the questions and reported problems for the tools before committing to the vendor's product.

6. Does this vendor supply other DB2 tools that your organization might need later? If so, are they functionally integrated with this one? Does the vendor supply a full suite of DB2 products or just a few?

7. Does the vendor integrate its tools with other tools? For example, a product that analyzes databases to determine whether a REORG is required should integrate the REORG job with your shop's job scheduler.

8. Does the vendor provide training? Is it on-site training? Does the vendor supply DB2 training as well as training for its tools? Are installation, technical, and user manuals provided free of charge?—How many copies? Is mainframe- or PC-based training available for the vendor's tools?

9. Evaluate the response of the technical support number. Call the number with technical questions at least four times throughout the day: before 8:00 a.m., at noon, just before 5:00 p.m., and again after 9:00 p.m. These are the times when you could find problems with the level of support provided by the vendor. Was the phone busy? Were you put on hold? For how long? When you got a response, was it accurate and friendly? Did the person who answered the phone have to find someone with more technical knowledge? (This can indicate potential problems.)

10. How knowledgeable are the technical support representatives who answer your test calls? Do they know their products inside and out, or do they struggle with the products? Do they know DB2 well (such as a former DBA), or are they unseasoned?

11. Will the vendor answer DB2 questions free of charge in addition to questions about its product? Sometimes vendors will, but they do not advertise the fact. Try it out by calling the technical support number.

12. Does the vendor have a local office? If not, are technicians readily available for on-site error resolution if needed? At what price?

13. Will the vendor deliver additional documentation or error-resolution information by overnight mail? Does it publish a fax number?

14. How are software fixes provided? Electronically? By tape? On the WWW? Is a complete reinstallation required? Are fixes typically accomplished using zaps?

15. How many man hours, on a short notice, is the vendor willing to spend to solve problems? Is there a guaranteed time limit?

16. Is the vendor willing to send a sales representative to your site to do a presentation of the product tailored to your needs?

17. Is the vendor an IBM business partner? How soon will the vendor's tools be modified to support new DB2 releases and versions? Does the vendor participate in IBM's ESP (early ship program) for new DB2 versions and releases?

18. Have the vendor's tools been reviewed or highlighted in any industry publications recently? If so, obtain the publications and read the articles.

19. Will the vendor assist in developing a cost justification? Most tool vendors are eager for your business and will be more than willing to provide cost justification to help you sell upper management on the need for the tool.

20. Does the vendor provide sample JCL to run its product? Skeleton JCL? A panel-driven JCL generator?

21. Does the vendor charge an upgrade fee when the processor is upgraded? How flexible are the terms and conditions for the contract?

22. If the vendor is sold or goes out of business, will the vendor supply the source code of the tool?

23. Is the vendor willing to set a ceiling for increases in the annual maintenance charge?

24. Does the vendor supply database administration tools for other DBMSs used at your shop? Can the same tool, using the same interface, be used to manage multiple databases across multiple operating systems?

25. How does the vendor rank enhancement requests?

These 25 questions provide a basis for evaluating DB2 tool vendors. Judge for yourself which criteria are most important to your organization.

CHAPTER **40**

Organizational Issues

Although you must jump many technical hurdles to use DB2 successfully, the organizational issues of implementing and supporting DB2 are not insignificant. Each corporation must address the organizational issues involved in supporting DB2. Although the issues are common from company to company, the decisions made to address these issues can vary dramatically.

This chapter outlines the issues. Your organization must provide the answers as to how it will support these issues. This chapter can be used in any of the following ways:

- As a blueprint of issues to address for organizations that will implement DB2

- As a checklist for current DB2 users to ensure that all issues have been addressed

- As a resource for programmers who need a framework for accessing their organization's standards and operating procedures

Education

Education is the first issue that should be addressed after your organization decides to implement DB2. Does your organization understand what DB2 is? How it works? For what purposes it is needed at your shop? How it will be used? Without a sound understanding of DB2, its components and features, it is unlikely that you will be able to use DB2 to its best advantage. This basic level of DB2 knowledge can be acquired through a short DB2 fundamentals class for the IT personnel charged with making DB2 a success at your organization.

After addressing the basics of DB2 education, you must deal with ongoing support for DB2 education. This support falls into four categories. The first category of training is a standard regimen of SQL and DB2 programming training to be used by application developers. Every programmer should receive basic training on SQL, education on how to embed SQL in the programming languages they will be using, and possibly a course on using DB2 with CICS or IMS. If this basic level of DB2 education is not required for every DB2 programmer, then DB2 application performance will surely suffer as untrained coders write inefficient and incorrect SQL.

The second category of education support is external training for special needs. This support includes education for database administrators, technical support personnel, and performance analysts. Additionally, your organization needs to plan for ongoing education to keep appropriate personnel up-to-date on new versions and releases of DB2. Although IBM typically offers the earliest courses for new DB2 releases, several third-party vendors such as SML, Inc., YL&A, Inc., and Themis regularly offer release-specific DB2 courses and lectures.

The third category of education is in-house, interactive training in the form of videos, computer-based training, and instructor-led courses. These courses should be used to augment and refresh the formal training given to your DB2 professional staff.

The final category of support is reference material—for example, IBM's DB2 manuals, DB2 books such as this one, vendor-supplied white papers, and industry publications and periodicals. The current IBM manuals for DB2 are listed on the inside back cover of this book. Providing online access to the DB2 and related manuals using Book Manager Library Reader on the mainframe (as shown in Figure 40.1), the workstation (as shown in Figure 40.2), or both is a good idea. Furthermore, most of the DB2 manuals can be downloaded free-of-charge (in Adobe Acrobat format) from IBM's Web site.

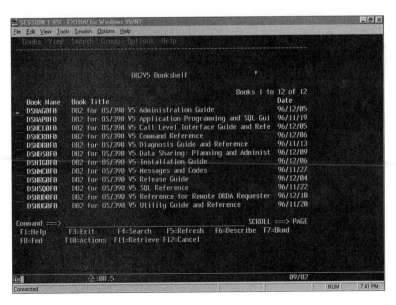

FIGURE 40.1   IBM BookManager Library Reader on the mainframe.

40

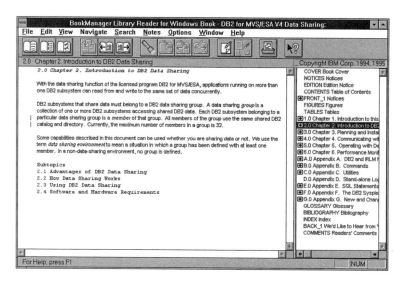

FIGURE 40.2   IBM BookManager Library Reader for Windows.

Vendors are another rich source of DB2 information. The major vendors provide in-depth technical papers on features of DB2 that would be difficult for most shops to research in the same detail. BMC Software, Candle Corporation, Compuware Corporation, Computer Associates, and Quest Software are the best sources for DB2-related white papers.

All of these educational components—in-house education, external education, and industry publications—are useful for learning how you can use DB2 effectively. You would be wise to have a mix of material that supports more than one of the categories outlined previously. In this way, you provide a varied learning environment that meets the needs of all students. This varied learning environment allows each student to learn in the most conducive way for him or her. Plan to provide an on-site library of educational material addressing the following subjects:

Introduction to relational databases

Introduction to DB2 and SQL

Advanced SQL

Programming DB2 using *[your language of choice]*

Programming DB2 in batch

Programming DB2 using TSO, CICS, and IMS

Programming DB2 and the Web

Creating DB2 stored procedures, triggers, and UDFs

Programming DB2 in a distributed environment

Debugging and problem analysis

QMF usage guidelines

You also might want to have an introductory DB2 database administration course to train new DBAs. In addition to this basic education library, plan to provide advanced education for technical DB2 users, such as DBAs, technical support personnel, and technical programmers and analysts. Advanced DBA topics (such as data sharing, performance management, and backup/recovery) should be left to instructor-led training courses because of the complex nature of DB2 database administration.

Additional advanced topics to consider include system administration (for systems programmers) and disaster recovery. Many vendors, including IBM and Themis, offer these classes. Searching for smaller consulting firms and local resources is also prudent; these firms usually provide courses tailored to your installation needs.

The advanced education program should include allocating time to attend area user groups meetings, the annual IBM DB2 Technical Conference, and/or the International DB2 Users Group (IDUG). When DB2 users get together to share experiences at such forums, they uncover undocumented solutions and ideas that would be difficult to arrive at independently.

DB2-Related Industry Periodicals

Another good type of reference material is industry periodicals and publications. Many trade magazines describe database management in general and DB2 specifically. Regular periodical reading can form the basis of a sound, continuing education in DB2 fundamentals.

A listing of recommended industry publications that cover DB2 on a regular basis follows.

> *Advisor* (online magazine)
>
> P.O. Box 469013
>
> Escondido, CA 92046-9963
>
> `http://www.advisor.com`

Data Based Advisor was formerly a print magazine for PC and client/server databases. The *Advisor* Web site has replaced the print publication. It covers many areas of IT, one section of which is database-focused. The site provides regular SQL coverage, but only rarely discusses DB2.

> *Candle Computer Report* (online newsletter)
>
> Candle Corporation
>
> 2425 Olympic Boulevard
>
> Santa Monica, CA 90404
>
> `http://www.candle.com`
>
> Free to customers and potential customers; published monthly

This free online publication from Candle features in-depth technical articles, updates on Candle products, quick tips on how to tune your systems, and technology case studies. Sporadic coverage of DB2.

ComputerWorld (newsweekly)

375 Cochituate Road

Framingham, MA 01701-9494

http://www.computerworld.com

$39.95 per year; published weekly

In-depth data processing newspaper. Frequently contains database-related articles. DB2-specific information is sporadic at best, but the coverage of IT news is outstanding.

The Data Administration Newsletter (newsletter)

Post Office Box 112571

Upper St. Clair, PA 15241

Free with e-mail reminders; published quarterly

http://www.tdan.com

This Web-based newsletter focuses on data administration and database administration topics. Frequently covers issues pertinent to DB2 data and database management.

Data Management Review (magazine)

240 Regency Court

Suite 201

Brookfield, WI 53045

(414) 784-0444

http://www.dmreview.com

http://www.data-warehouse.com

Free to qualified subscribers; published monthly

Interesting publication addressing all types of database management system issues. Highlights include a large product review section, but only occasional DB2-related articles. Recent editorial focus is heavily oriented toward data warehousing topics. On their Web site, you also can subscribe to DM Direct, an email-based newsletter on data management topics.

Datamation (online magazine)

P.O. Box 7529

Highlands Ranch, CO 80163-9329

http://www.datamation.com

Free

Provides coverage of news affecting the data processing community. Sporadic coverage of IBM and DB2. No longer published in hard copy; available only on the Web.

Dbazine.com (Web portal)

http://www.dbazine.com

Free to qualified subscribers; published quarterly

This Web portal offers original content for DBAs—not just for DB2, but for IMS, Oracle, and SQL Server as well—and a vast array of links to technical content on other Web sites.

DB2 Magazine (magazine)

Miller Freeman Publications

P.O. Box 51247

Boulder, CO 80321-1247

http://www.db2mag.com

Free to qualified subscribers; published quarterly

This magazine, sponsored by IBM, provides in-depth, technical articles focused on the DB2 family of products. The Web site has some Web-only content. Very useful for DB2 shops.

DB2 Today (online newsletter)

IBM Corporation

http://www-3.ibm.com/software/data/db2infonews/

Free

This email newsletter, compiled by IBM, provides information and news about DB2, as well as a good number of links to technical DB2 articles. Every DB2 DBA should subscribe to this newsletter.

DB2 Update (technical journal)

Xephon Publications

1301 West Highway 407

Suite 201-450

Lewisville, TX 75067

http://www.xephon.com

$340.00 per year; published monthly

Each issue is devoted to DB2. Provides technical articles on all areas of DB2 administration, design, and development. Each issue contains 20 to 30 pages, with no advertisements. Expensive, but well-worth the cost. Xephon also publishes many other technical journals including ones that focus on MVS and CICS.

IBM System Journal (technical journal)

IBM Corporation

P.O. Box 3033

Southeastern, PA 19398

$49.50 per year; published quarterly

Technical articles written by IBM staff about IBM products and architectures. Sometimes covers DB2 topics. Every IBM shop should subscribe to this journal.

IDUG Solutions Journal (magazine)

IDUG Headquarters

401 N. Michigan Avenue

Chicago, IL 60611-4267

Free to qualified DB2 professionals; published quarterly

This journal is published specifically for the DB2 community and focuses on exclusively on DB2 content across multiple platforms. Published by IDUG.

Information Week (newsweekly)

CMP Publications, Inc.

600 Community Drive

Manhasset, NY 11030

Free to qualified data processing professionals; published weekly

In addition to timely DP news, contains frequent user-focused articles related to DBMS technology.

Intelligent Enterprise (magazine)

Miller Freeman Publications

P.O. Box 51247

Boulder, CO 80321-1247

`http:.//www.intelligententerprise.com`

$39.00 per year; published monthly

A good, general-purpose monthly publication for DBAs and DAs. Provides extensive coverage of all aspects of database development. Contains a regular column by Joe Celko and occasional coverage of DB2. This publication is the result of Miller Freeman combining two prior database-focused publications: *DBMS Magazine* and *Database Programming & Design*.

Z/Journal (magazine)

Thomas Communications

9550 Silkman Street, Suite 415

Dallas, TX 75243

`http://www.zjournal.com`

Free to qualified subscribers; published bi-monthly

Provides in-depth technical articles focusing on all areas of IBM mainframe development. Contains coverage of DB2 in every issue. Also periodically covers WebSphere, CICS, IMS, and other mainframe development issues.

The DB2 Mailing List

Anyone who administers, supports, or writes programs using DB2 should subscribe to the DB2 mailing list. Mailing lists are a sort of community bulletin board. Simply by subscribing to a mailing list, information is sent directly to your e-mail in-box. Details on how to subscribe are provided in Chapter 17, "DB2 and the Internet."

Standards and Procedures

To implement DB2 effectively, you must have a set of standards and procedures that are the blueprint for DB2 development in your organization. *Standards* are common practices that provide an environment that is consistent, efficient, or understandable (for example, a naming standard for DB2 objects). *Procedures* are scripts that outline the way a proscribed event should be handled, such as a disaster recovery plan.

DB2 standards and procedures are usually developed in conjunction with one another and stored in a common place. Standards and procedures are usually part of a corporate-wide (or IT-wide) standards and procedures document. They can be stored in printed format as well as being made available online for easy access. Most organizations publish their standards and procedures on their internal, corporate intranet site on the Web.

Several vendors offer "canned" standards and procedures (both hard copy and online). One such example is Quest Software's DB2 Knowledge Xpert, which is a Windows-based technical resource designed to help developers and DBAs research and solve DB2 problems.

This section describes the items that should be addressed by DB2 standards and procedures.

Roles and Responsibilities

Running DB2 requires a large degree of administrative overhead. Not only must the DB2 subsystem be installed and then maintained, but the functionality of DB2 must also be administered. This work constitutes the bulk of the administrative burden.

A matrix of DB2 functions and who will support them is necessary. The matrix can be at the department level or at the job description level. Table 40.1 shows a sample matrix you can use as a template for your organization.

TABLE 40.1   DB2 Roles and Responsibilities

Role	DA	DBA	PGM	ANL	TS	DSD	SEC	MGT	EU	OPR
Budgeting for DB2		X			X			X	X	X
DB2 Installation		X			X	X	X		X	
DB2 System Support					X					
DB2 System Security					X		X			
System-wide Performance Monitoring		X			X					
System-wide Tuning						X				
DB2 System Backup and Recovery Procedures	X	X	X	X	X	X	X	X	X	X
Hardware Planning					X	X		X		
Capacity Planning		X		X	X				X	
Utility Development		X			X					
Data Analysis	X	X								
DB2 Object Creation		X								
DB2 Database Performance Monitoring										X
DB2 Database Performance Tuning	X	X		X		X				
DB2 Application Design	X	X		X						X
DB2 Program Coding			X	X						
DB2 Program Testing			X	X						
Stored Procedure Coding		X	X	X						
Stored Procedure Testing		X	X	X						
Stored Procedure Support		X	X	X						X
Trigger Coding		X	X	X						
Trigger Testing		X	X	X						
Trigger Support		X	X	X						X
User-defined Function Coding	X	X	X							
User-defined Function Testing	X	X	X							
User-defined Function Support	X	X	X						X	
DB2 Application Security		X					X			
DB2 Application Turnover		X	X	X					X	
DB2 Application Performance Monitoring		X		X	X					
DB2 Application Database Backup and Recovery		X		X					X	X
DB2 Job Scheduling			X	X					X	
DB2 Design Reviews	X	X	X	X	X	X	X	X	X	X
DB2 Tool Selections	X	X	X	X	X	X	X	X		
Implementing DDF		X			X		X			
Distributing DB2 Data	X	X	X	X	X	X	X			

TABLE 40.1   Continued

Role	DA	DBA	PGM	ANL	TS	DSD	SEC	MGT	EU	OPR
DB2 Data Sharing		X			X	X	X	X		X
QMF Installation					X					
QMF Administration		X			X					
QMF Tuning		X		X	X				X	
DA	Data administrator									
DBA	Database administrator									
PGM	Programmer									
ANL	Analyst									
TS	Technical support									
DSD	DASD support									
SEC	Data security									
MGT	Management									
EU	End user									
OPR	Operations									

The matrix in Table 40.1 represents a sampling of roles and responsibilities for the DB2 environment. Each block of the matrix represents a portion of the total responsibility for the given role.

Your organization might have different roles responsible for different areas. Additionally, you might have more categories or a further breakdown of the categories (for example, dividing the *Utilities Development* line into a single line for each utility).

Each position on the matrix should be accompanied by in-depth text as follows:

- A description of the resources encompassing this combination of role and responsibility.

- A definition of the role in terms of what needs to be performed. This information should include a detailed list of tasks and a reference to the supporting organizational procedures that must be followed to carry out these tasks.

- A definition of the responsibility in terms of who should do the tasks. In addition to primary and secondary contacts for the people performing the task, this description should provide a management contact for the department in charge of the responsibility.

Remember, Table 40.1 is only an example. It is not uncommon for DB2 administrative tasks to be assigned to departments or jobs different from the ones shown in the table. Likewise, your organization might identify additional roles that need to be documented. Each shop should have a document appropriately modified to reflect the needs and organization of the company.

This document will eliminate confusion when DB2 development is initiated. Analysts, programmers, and management will have an organized and agreed-on delineation of tasks and responsibilities before the development and implementation of DB2 applications.

40

Based on the roles and responsibilities matrix in use at your shop, you might need to augment or change the following procedures. Certain functions may move to a different area, but all the necessary standards are covered.

Data Administration

A thorough treatment of data administration is beyond the scope of this book, but this section lists some basic guidelines. All DB2 applications must be built using the techniques of logical database design. This design involves the creation of a normalized, logical data model that establishes the foundation for any subsequent development. It documents the data requirements for the organization. Each piece of business data is defined and incorporated into the logical data model. All physical DB2 tables should be traceable to the logical data model.

The data administration standards should outline the following:

- Corporate policies dictating that information is to be managed as a vital business resource

- Who is responsible for creating the logical data model

- How the logical data model will be created, stored, and maintained

- Who is responsible for maintaining and administering the logical data model

- The integration of application data models with an enterprise data model

- Data sharing issues (this does not refer to DB2 data sharing but refers to the sharing of data in general)

- How physical databases will be created from the logical data model

- How denormalization decisions will be documented

- The tools used by the data administrator (modeling tools, data dictionaries, repositories, and so on)

- Rules for data creation, data ownership, and data stewardship

- Metadata management policy

- The communication needed between data administration and database administration to ensure the implementation of an effective DB2 application

Database Administration Guide

A database administration guide is essential to ensure the ongoing success of the DBA function. The guide serves as a cookbook of approaches to be used in the following circumstances:

- Converting a logical model to a physical implementation

- Choosing physical DB2 parameters when creating (or generating) DDL

- DB2 utility implementation procedures and techniques

- DB2 backup and recovery techniques and guidelines—including DB2 disaster recovery procedures

- DB2 application monitoring schedules

- DB2 application and database performance tuning guidelines

This document, although geared primarily for DBA staff, is useful for the programming staff as well. If the program developers understand the role of the DBA and the tasks that must be performed, more effective communication can be established between DBA and application development, thereby increasing the chances of achieving an effective and efficient DB2 application system.

System Administration Guide

The DB2 system administrator is considered to be at a higher level than the database administrator. It is not unusual, though, for a DBA to be the system administrator also. A system administrator guide is needed for many of the same reasons that a DBA guide is required. It should consist of the following items:

- DB2 installation and testing procedures

- Procedures to follow for applying fixes to DB2 (APARs)

- A checklist of departments to notify for impending changes

- Interface considerations (CICS, IMS/TM, TSO, CAF, RRSAF, DDF, and other installation-specific interfaces)

- A DB2 system monitoring schedule

- DB2 system tuning guidelines

- DB2 data sharing policy and implementation

- Procedures for using Workload Manager with DB2

- Procedures for working with z/OS, CICS, WebSphere, and IMS system administrators for issues that span DB2 and other, related system software

- System DASD considerations

Application Development Guide

The development of DB2 applications differs from typical program development. Providing an application development guide specifically for DB2 programmers is therefore essential. It can operate as an adjunct to the standard application development procedures for your organization. This guide should include the following topics:

- An introduction to DB2 programming techniques

- Shop SQL coding standards

- SQL tips and techniques

40

- DB2 program preparation procedures

- Interpretations of SQLCODEs, SQLSTATEs and DB2 error codes

- References to other useful programming materials for teleprocessing monitors (CICS and IMS/TM), programming languages (such as COBOL, Java, and PL/I), interfaces (ODBC), and general shop coding standards

- The procedure for filling out DB2 forms (if any) for database design, database implementation, program review, database migration, and production application turnover

DB2 Security Guide

The DBA unit often applies and administers DB2 security. However, at some shops, the corporate data security unit handles DB2 security. You must provide a resource outlining the necessary standards and procedures for administering DB2 security. It should consist of the following:

- A checklist of the proper authorization to grant for specific situations. For example, if a plan is being migrated to production, it should list the security that must be granted before the plan can be executed.

- A procedure for implementing site-specific security. It must define which tools or interfaces (for example, secondary authorization IDs) are being used and how they are supported.

- An authoritative signature list of who can approve authorization requests.

- Procedures for any DB2 security request forms.

- Procedures for notifying the requester that security has been granted.

- Procedures for removing security from retiring, relocating, and terminated employees.

SQL Performance Guide

The SQL performance guide can be a component of the application development guide, but it should also exist independently. This document should contain tips and tricks for efficient SQL coding. It is useful not only for application programmers but also for all users of DB2 who regularly code SQL.

QMF Guide

If QMF (or another query tool) is in use at your site, a QMF guide must be available. It should contain information from the simple to the complex so that all levels of QMF users will find it useful. This guide should cover the following topics, in increasing order of complexity:

- What QMF is

- Who is permitted to use QMF

- When QMF can be used (such as hours of operation and production windows)

- How to request QMF use

- How to call up a QMF session

- A basic how-to guide for QMF features

- QMF limitations

- References to further documentation (for example, CBT and IBM manuals)

Vendor Tools Guide(s)

It is a good idea to have user guides available for each vendor tool in use at your company. Many of the vendors supply a user's guide that can be used "as is," or augmented with site-specific details such as who is authorized to use the tool, when it can be used, and how it was installed.

Naming Conventions

All DB2 objects should follow a strict naming convention. You learned some basic guidelines for DB2 naming conventions in Chapter 5, "Data Definition Guidelines." This section details the rules to follow in naming a DB2 object.

Make names as English-like as possible. In other words, do not encode DB2 object names, and avoid abbreviations unless the name would be too long otherwise.

Do not needlessly restrict DB2 object names to a limited subset of characters or a smaller size than DB2 provides. For example, do not forbid an underscore in table names, and do not restrict DB2 table names to eight characters or fewer (DB2 allows as many as 128 characters).

Another rule in naming objects is to standardize abbreviations. Use the abbreviations only when the English text is too long.

In most cases, provide a way to differentiate types of DB2 objects. For example, start indexes with *I*, tablespaces with *S*, and databases with *D*. In two cases, however, this approach is inappropriate. You should not constrain tables in this manner; you need to provide as descriptive a name as possible. The second exception is that views, aliases, and synonyms should follow the same naming convention as tables. In this way, DB2 objects that operate like tables can be defined similarly. The type of object can always be determined by querying the DB2 Catalog using the queries presented in Chapter 26, "DB2 Object Monitoring Using the DB2 Catalog and RTS."

Provide naming conventions for the following items:

Databases	STOGROUPs
Table Spaces	Check constraints
Tables	Referential constraints
Global Temporary Tables	Plans

40

Auxiliary Tables	Packages
Indexes	Collections
Views	Versions
Aliases	DBRMs
Synonyms	DBRM Libraries
DCLGEN Members	Transactions
DCLGEN Libraries	Programs
DB2 COPYLIB Members	DB2 Load Libraries
DB2 Subsystems	DB2 Address Spaces
Application DB2 data sets	RCTs
System DB2 data sets	Data sets for DB2 Tools
Locations	Creators
Utility ID	DB2 data sets (tools—general for DB2 subsystem; specific for each tool)
DSNZPARM	RACF groups
DB2 group name	IRLM group name
Location name	Group attach name
DB2 member name	Workfile DB name
User-defined functions	User-defined distinct types
Command prefixes	Triggers

Migration and Turnover Procedures

The minimum number of environments for supporting DB2 applications is two: test and production. Most shops, however, have multiple environments. For example, a shop could have the following DB2 environments to support different phases of the development life cycle:

Unit testing

Integration testing

User acceptance testing

Quality assurance

Education

Having multiple environments requires a strict procedure for migrating DB2 objects and moving DB2 programs and plans from environment to environment. Each shop must have guidelines specific to its environment because all sites do not implement these different environments in the same way. For example, both test and production DB2 could be supported using either a single DB2 subsystem or two DB2 subsystems. (Two are recommended to increase efficiency and turnaround time, but having two is a luxury some smaller shops cannot afford.)

Dual versions of these procedures should exist to describe what is entailed from the point of view of both the requester and the person implementing the request. For the requester, the procedures should include what will be migrated, why and when it will be migrated, who is requesting the migration, and the authorization for the migration. For the person implementing the request, the procedures should include who is responsible for which portions of the migration and a description of the methods used to migrate.

Design Review Guidelines

All DB2 applications, regardless of their size, should participate in a design review both before and after they are implemented. Design reviews are critical for ensuring that an application is properly designed to achieve its purpose.

Design reviews can take many forms. Some of the areas that can be addressed by a design review include the following:

- A validation of the purpose of the application

- An assessment of the logical and physical data models

- A review and analysis of DB2 physical parameters

- A prediction of SQL performance

Before discussing the different types of DB2 design reviews, I must first outline who must participate to ensure a successful review of all elements of the application. The following personnel should engage in the design review process:

AA	Representatives from other applications affected by the application being reviewed (because of the need to interface with the new application, shared data requirements, scheduling needs, and so on)
AD	Application development personnel assigned to this development effort
DA	Data administration representatives
DBA	Database administration representatives
EU	End-user representatives
EUM	End-user management
IC	Information center representatives
MM	MIS management for the new application and all affected applications
OLS	Online support representatives (CICS or IMS/TM unit, or Web support if the application is for the Internet)
OS	Operational support management
TS	Technical support and systems programming representatives

40

Each of these participants does not need to take part in every facet of the design review. Holding more than one design review is best, with each one focusing on an aspect of the design. The scope of each design review should be determined before the review is scheduled so that only the appropriate participants are invited.

You can break down the design review into seven distinct phases, which are described in the following sections.

Phase 1

The first phase of the design review process is the Conceptual Design Review (CDR). This review validates the concept of the application. This review involves a presentation of the statement of purpose as well as an overview of the desired functionality.

A CDR should be conducted as early as possible to determine the feasibility of a project. Failure to conduct a CDR can result in projects that provide duplicate or inadequate functionality—projects that are canceled because of lack of funds, staffing, planning, user participation, or management interest; or projects over budget.

Participants should include AA, AD, DA, DBA, EU, EUM, and MM.

Phase 2

Phase 2 of the design review process is the Logical Design Review (LDR). This phase should be conducted when the first cut of the logical data model has been completed. A thorough review of all data elements, descriptions, and relationships should occur during the LDR. The LDR should scrutinize the following areas:

- Is the model in (at least) third normal form?

- Are all data elements (entities and attributes) required for this application identified?

- Are the data elements documented accurately?

- Are all relationships defined properly?

Failure to hold an LDR can result in a failure to identify all required pieces of data, a lack of documentation, and a database that is poorly designed and difficult to maintain. This failure results in the development of an application that is difficult to maintain. If further data modeling occurs after the logical design review is held, further LDRs can be scheduled as the project progresses.

Participants should include AA, AD, DA, DBA, EU, EUM, and IC.

Phase 3

The third phase of the design review process is the Physical Design Review (PDR). Most DB2 developers associate this component with the design review process. In this phase, the database is reviewed in detail to ensure that all the proper design choices were made. In addition, the DA and DBA should ensure that the logical model was translated properly to the physical model, with all denormalization decisions documented.

In addition, the overall operating environment for the application should be described and verified. The choice of a teleprocessing monitor and a description of the online environment and any batch processes should be provided. Data sharing and distributed data requirements should be addressed during this phase.

At this stage, the SQL that will be used for this application might be unavailable. General descriptions of the processes, however, should be available. From the process descriptions, a first-cut denormalization effort (if required) should be attempted or verified.

Because the PDR phase requires much in-depth attention, it can be further divided. The PDR, or pieces of it, can be repeated before implementation if significant changes occur to the physical design of the database or application.

Participants should include AA, AD, DA, DBA, EU, EUM, IC, MM, OLS, OS, and TS.

Phase 4

Phase 4 is the Organization Design Review (ODR). It is smaller in scope—but no less critical—than the Physical Design Review. This review addresses the enterprise-wide concerns of the organization with respect to the application being reviewed. Some common review points follow:

- How does this system interact with other systems in the organization?

- Has the logical data model for this application been integrated with the enterprise data model (if one exists)?

- To what extent can this application share the data of other applications? To what extent can other applications share this application's data?

- Does the planned application conform to shop guidelines and restrictions for the environment in which it will run? For example, will a new batch program fit within the required batch window? Or, will a new Web program be designed to conform to the organization's design requirements?

- How will this application integrate with the current production environment in terms of DB2 resources required, the batch window, the online response time, and availability?

Participants should include AA, AD, DA, DBA, EU, EUM, IC, MM, OLS, OS, and TS.

Phase 5

Phase 5, the SQL Design Review (SDR), must occur for each SQL statement before production turnover. This phase should consist of the following analyses.

An EXPLAIN should be run for each SQL statement using production statistics. The PLAN_TABLEs should then be analyzed to determine whether the most efficient access paths have been chosen, whether the runtime estimates are within the agreed service level, and to verify function resolution when UDFs are used. If a plan analysis tool is available, the output from it should be analyzed as well.

40

Every DB2 program should be reviewed to ensure that inefficient host language constructs were not used. In addition, efficient SQL implemented inefficiently in loops should be analyzed for its appropriateness. To accomplish this, you will need knowledge of the application language being used, whether it is COBOL, Java, or some other language.

All dynamic SQL should be reviewed whether it is embedded in an application program or earmarked for QMF. The review should include multiple EXPLAINs for various combinations of host variables. Be sure to EXPLAIN combinations of host variable values so that you test both values that are not one of the 10 most frequently occurring values and values that are one of the 10 most frequently occurring values. These values can be determined by running the column occurrence query as presented in Chapter 26.

Different access paths can be chosen for the same query based on differing column value distributions. This needs to be taken into account to determine how best to implement RUNSTATS for tables accessed dynamically.

Suggestions for performance improvements should be made and tested before implementation to determine their effect. If better performance is achieved, the SQL should be modified.

Participants should include AD, DBA, EU, and IC.

Phase 6

Phase 6 is the Pre-Implementation Design Review (Pre-IDR). This phase is simply a review of the system components before implementation. Loose ends from the preceding five phases should be taken care of, and a final, quick review of each application component should be performed.

Participants should include AA, AD, DA, DBA, EU, EUM, IC, MM, OLS, OS, and TS.

Phase 7

The last design review phase is phase 7, the Post-Implementation Design Review (Post-IDR). This phase is necessary to determine whether the application is meeting its performance objectives and functionality objectives. If any objective is not being met, a plan for addressing the deficiency must be proposed and acted on. Multiple Post-IDR phases can occur.

Participants should include AA, AD, DA, DBA, EU, EUM, IC, MM, OLS, OS, and TS.

Operational Support

When you're implementing a DB2 environment, sufficient operational support must be available to administer the environment effectively. *Operational support* is defined as the elements of the organization responsible for supporting, maintaining, and running the applications.

This first major operational concern is the establishment of a staff who can support DB2. You can choose from four approaches to staffing for DB2 support. The first is to develop all DB2 expertise using the existing staff. This approach requires a significant amount of training and can result in slow DB2 implementation as your staff comes up-to-speed with DB2.

The second approach is to hire outside expertise. This approach usually results in a much faster implementation of DB2, but it can breed resentment from your current staff and result in a workplace where it is difficult to accomplish much because of a lack of cooperation between the old staff and the new.

The third approach is to entrust all DB2 development to an outside contracting or consulting firm. This approach is the worst. Although it results in quick development, no one is left to support the application after it is developed.

The fourth and best approach is to combine these strategies. Plan to train your brightest and most eager staff members, while augmenting that staff with several outside experts, temporary consultants, and contract programmers.

> **CAUTION**
>
> Do not fall prey to the classic mistake of over-reliance on consultants. Although consultants can be a crucial component required for success with DB2, be sure to create a conduit for knowledge transfer. Be sure to set up an environment where the consultant is required to share his knowledge and train his replacements. Do not allow a consultant to become irreplaceable.

Expertise (obtained outside or inside the organization) is required in each of the following areas:

Programmers	In addition to basic coding skills, must know SQL coding techniques and the teleprocessing monitor(s) in your shop. Should also have basic Web development skills if Internet applications are being developed.
Systems analysts	Must know DB2 development techniques, data modeling, and process modeling. Should be able to use the CASE tools in your shop.
Data analysts	Must be able to work with data administration and database administration to develop application-level models.
DBA	Must be knowledgeable in all aspects of DB2, with emphasis on the physical implementation of DB2 objects, DB2 utilities, SQL efficiency, and problem solving.
Technical support	Must have basic systems programming skills in addition to an understanding of DB2 installation, DB2 recovery, and day-to-day technical support.
Production control	In addition to basic job scheduling skills, must understand how DB2 is integrated into the organization. Must minimally be able to understand and issue DB2 commands when a problem occurs.
Help desk	Must be able to provide SQL expertise.

Another operational concern is the integration of DB2 standards, policies, procedures, and guidelines with existing (non-DB2) ones. These two sets of standards could conflict. For example, DB2 data sets must conform to a rigid standard, but this standard usually does not agree with the organization's current data set naming standards.

Another operational concern is enabling the production control personnel who submit and monitor production jobs to execute DB2 commands. Enabling operational personnel in this manner could conflict with the current nature of production support as a facilitator and not a doer.

Scheduling of and responsibility for DB2 utilities might pose a problem for your shop. Some utilities lend themselves more toward being developed and supported by a DBA or a technical support area, whereas others are more application-oriented. Sometimes great debates can ensue over who should have responsibility for each utility. There is no hard-and-fast standard that works for every organization. Base your utility standards on the needs, expertise and staffing level of your organization.

Political Issues

The technical hurdles required to support a DB2 environment sometimes pale in comparison to the political issues. Technical problems can always be addressed by a combination of outside expertise, enhanced hardware, add-on tools, and overtime. Political issues are more difficult to overcome because they typically rely on human nature, which is fragile at best.

Of paramount importance to the health of your DB2 support structure is keeping the valuable employees with DB2 skills. Although doing so is not always easy, you can do it by packaging jobs with a healthy mix of job challenge, fair salaries, and merit-based promotions.

When this type of workplace is achieved, however, problems occur when other employees learn that junior personnel with advanced DB2 skills are being paid more than senior personnel without those skills. However, DB2 and SQL skills are in demand in the marketplace, so failure to fairly compensate skilled DB2 employees could result in their leaving. You can take either of two approaches to dealing with the problem, but neither is pleasurable. Either underpay DB2 professionals and risk losing them to firms willing to pay the going rate, or pay the going rate for DB2 expertise and risk possible resentment from the rest of your application development personnel.

Another personnel issue involving DB2 for z/OS is the current IT skills shortage. The demand for IT skills far outpaces the supply. And with DB2 for z/OS, in particular, the problem is troubling. With the client/server boom of a few years ago, many of the folks who learned DB2 in its early days have moved on to other DBMS products (such as Oracle and SQL Server) and platforms (such as Unix and the Web). Finding, and then keeping, employees with DB2 and mainframe skills can be quite difficult.

Following are some other political issues that you must deal with in a DB2 workplace. If 24-hour availability and support is required, your personnel might have to adjust their attitude toward shift work and carrying pagers. Most IT professionals are prepared to be "on call" to resolve production problems.

Often many programmers will clamor for the opportunity to work on DB2 projects for the chance to learn SQL and relational skills. They are aware of the monetary rewards that can result if these skills are added to their repertoire. Choosing which of your valued personnel should be given this chance can be difficult. With the advent of client/server technology and the Internet, many shops now have the opposite problem: skilled DB2 professionals wanting to expand their horizons are looking to move out of the DB2 arena into other projects using newer (and resume-enhancing) technology.

Another type of political problem that you can encounter is the direct opposite of the preceding one: ambivalence. People are sometimes afraid of change, and DB2 forces change on an organization. This change can scare IT personnel and create a resistance movement against DB2 development efforts. This resistance can be assuaged with education and time.

A growing political problem these days is maintaining proper levels of mainframe skills. As the current crop of skilled mainframe technicians retire—or move to other platforms—there is an insufficient supply of new talent to take their place. Let's face it, they just aren't teaching mainframe skills in college any longer. And today's university graduate is more interested in working with the Web, Java, XML, and other, new, "cool" technologies. Fortunately, IBM has augmented DB2 to work with and support most of these newer technologies so it becomes a bit easier to train the non-initiated on mainframe technology.

Finally, many organizations have an "island unto themselves" attitude. This attitude should be avoided regarding DB2 development and support. DB2 is complex and dynamic, which makes it difficult to master. Do not be shy about attending user groups meetings, contracting expert consultants to assist with difficult or critical tasks, or contacting other local companies that have experienced the same problems or developed a similar system. Most DB2 professionals are willing to share their experiences to develop a contact that might be useful in the future. And, by all means, share your experiences with other shops. The more informed everyone is, the better your experience with DB2 will be.

Environmental Support

The organization must ensure that adequate levels of support are available for the online environments of choice (CICS, TSO, IMS/TM, or other in-house teleprocessing monitors). Usually, the addition of DB2 development to these environments adds considerable growth to the number of developers and end users of these monitors. Be sure that this explosion in use is planned and that appropriate staffing is available to support the growth.

Additionally, if performance monitors are unavailable for these environments, the addition of DB2 should cause your organization to rethink its position. When DB2 is added to the puzzle, tracking certain types of performance problems can be nearly impossible without a performance monitor available in each environment.

Tool Requirements

DB2 implementation is not quite as simple as installing DB2 alone. Your organization must budget for not just DB2 but also DB2, QMF, and tools from the categories deemed most important by your organization. As time goes on and DB2 use grows, your organization should plan to acquire more tools. Budgeting for DB2 tools should be an annual process.

40

IN THIS CHAPTER

- What Is DRDA?
- DRDA Functions
- DRDA Architectures and Standards
- The Five DRDA Levels
- Putting It All Together
- Distributed DB2

CHAPTER **41**

DRDA

When speaking about distributed DB2 data, it is necessary to first understand DRDA. DRDA stands for Distributed Relational Database Architecture. It is an *architecture*, developed by IBM, that enables *relational* data to be distributed among multiple platforms. Both like and unlike platforms can communicate with one another. For example, one DB2 subsystem can communicate to another DB2 subsystem (*like*). Alternatively, a DB2 subsystem can communicate with a third-party RDBMS (*unlike*). The platforms need not be the same. As long as they both conform to the DRDA specifications, they can communicate. DRDA can be considered a sort of "universal, distributed data protocol."

This chapter will describe DRDA. Keep in mind that no vendor, not even IBM, has implemented a RDBMS that fully supports all DRDA functionality. Chapter 42, "Distributed DB2," will describe the components of DRDA currently supported by DB2.

What Is DRDA?

DRDA is a set of *protocols,* or rules, that enable a user to access distributed data regardless of where it physically resides. It provides an open, robust heterogeneous distributed database environment. DRDA provides methods of coordinating communication among distributed locations. This allows applications to access multiple remote tables at various locations and have them appear to the end user as if they were a logical whole.

A distinction should be made, however, between the architecture and the implementation. DRDA describes the architecture for distributed data and nothing more. It defines the rules for accessing the distributed data, but it does not provide the actual application programming interfaces (APIs) to perform the access. So DRDA is not an actual program, but is more like the specifications for a program.

41

When a DBMS is said to be DRDA-compliant, all that is implied is that it follows the DRDA specifications. DB2 is a DRDA-compliant RDBMS product.

Benefits of DRDA

DRDA is only one protocol for supporting distributed RDBMS. Of course, if you are a DB2 user, it is probably the only one that matters.

The biggest benefit provided by DRDA is its clearly stated set of rules for supporting distributed data access. Any product that follows these rules can seamlessly integrate with any other DRDA-compliant product. Furthermore, DRDA-compliant RDBMSs support full data distribution including multi-site update. The biggest advantage, however, is that it is available today, and many vendors are jumping on the DRDA-compliance bandwagon.

An alternative to DRDA is to use a *gateway* product to access distributed data. Gateways are comprised of at least two components: one for each distributed location. These parts communicate with one another. As far as DB2 is concerned, a host-based gateway component is necessary. It functions as another mainframe DB2 application. Most gateway products that access DB2 execute using CICS or VTAM. Gateways, however, typically support dynamic SQL only.

Therefore, two more advantages of DRDA surface in the performance arena:

- The removal of the overhead associated with the gateway and its code

- The removal of reliance upon and the inevitable performance degradation associated with it

What About RDA?

Although DRDA is the distributed architecture utilized by DB2, it is not the only architecture in the industry. RDA (Remote Database Access) is a competing set of protocols developed by the ISO and ANSI standard committees.

As a DB2 developer, DRDA will be the method you use to implement distributed data with DB2. However, knowing a bit about RDA cannot hurt.

- RDA was built to work with a standard subset of SQL that is available from DBMS to DBMS. DRDA was built to function with platform-specific extensions to SQL.

- Static SQL can be used with DRDA; with RDA only dynamic SQL is available.

DRDA Functions

Three functions are utilized by DRDA to provide distributed relational data access:

- Application Requester (AR)

- Application Server (AS)

- Database Server (DS)

These three functions inter-operate with one another to enable distributed access (see Figure 41.1).

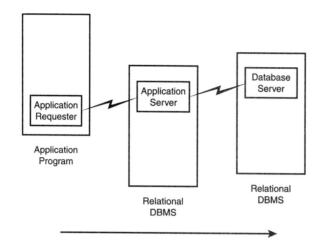

FIGURE 41.1   The three DRDA functions.

Let's further examine these three functions.

Application Requester

The DRDA application requester (AR) function enables SQL and program preparation requests to be requested by application programs. The AR accepts SQL requests from an application and sends them to the appropriate application server (or servers) for subsequent processing. Using this function, application programs can access remote data.

In theory, if all of the data that you are interested in is physically located somewhere else (for example, remote), there may be no need for a local RDBMS, and DRDA does not require the requester to run on a system with a local RDBMS.

For the DB2 Family, the DRDA AR function is implemented using DB2 Connect.

Application Server

The DRDA application server (AS) function receives requests from application requesters and processes them. These requests can be either SQL statements or program-preparation requests. The AS acts upon the portions that can be processed and forwards the remainder to DRDA database servers for subsequent processing. This is necessary if the local RDBMS cannot process the request.

The AR is connected to the AS using a communication protocol called the Application Support Protocol. The Application Support Protocol is responsible for providing the appropriate level of data conversion. This is only necessary when different data representations are involved in the request. An example of this is the conversion of ASCII characters to EBCDIC (or vice versa).

Database Server

The DRDA database server (DS) function receives requests from application servers or other database servers. These requests can be either SQL statements or program preparation requests. Like the application server, the database server will process what it can and forward the remainder on to another database server.

It is important to note that a database server request may be for a component of an SQL statement. This would occur when data is distributed across two subsystems and a join is requested. The join statement is requesting data from tables at two different locations. As such, one portion must be processed at one location; the other portion at a different location.

Because the database servers involved in a distributed request need not be the same, the Database Support Protocol is used. It exists for the following reasons:

- To connect an application server to a database server

- To connect two database servers

Like the Application Support Protocol, the Database Support Protocol is used to ensure compatibility of requests between different database servers.

What Is Returned

When a request is completely processed, the application server must inform the requesting process, the application requester. How is this accomplished?

The AS passes a return code and a result set (if one was produced) back to the AR. The return code is the SQLSTATE (or SQLCODE). A result set is not generated under the following circumstances:

- INSERT

- UPDATE

- DELETE

- SELECT, when no rows qualify

- DCL and DDL requests

This protocol is used unless a cursor is employed. When rows are fetched from a read-only cursor *limited block protocol* can be used. Limited block protocol passes multiple rows across the network at a time, even though one fetch can process only a single row at a time. Limited block protocol enhances overall performance by minimizing network traffic. If the cursor is not read-only (that is, rows can be updated) limited block protocol is not employed.

DRDA Architectures and Standards

In order for DRDA to exist, it relies upon other established protocols (see Figure 41.2). These architectures are examined in the following sections.

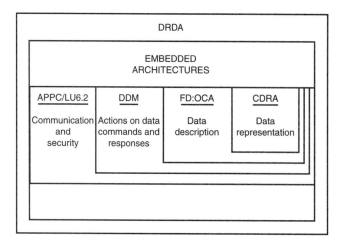

FIGURE 41.2   DRDA's supporting architectures.

Advanced Program-to-Program Communication

Advanced Program-to-Program Communication (APPC) provides peer-level communication support based on LU 6.2 protocols. LU 6.2 is an advanced communication architecture that defines the formats and protocols for communication between functionally equivalent logical units.

APPC/LU 6.2 provides communication and transaction processing facilities needed for cooperative processing and distributed transaction processing.

Distributed Data Management

The Distributed Data Management (DDM) architecture defines facilities for accessing distributed data across a network using APPC and LU 6.2. With DDM, the distributed data to be accessed can reside in either files or relational databases. An RDBMS is implied, however, within the context of DRDA.

Formatted Data: Object Content Architecture

FD:OCA is an architecture that provides for the distribution and exchange of field-formatted data. Using FD:OCA, both the data and its description are packaged together so that any DRDA-compliant DBMS can understand its structure and content.

Character Data Representation Architecture

Character Data Representation Architecture (CDRA) is the architecture utilized to ensure that any symbol or character used on any SAA relational DBMS has the same meaning regardless of the underlying coded character set. CDRA provides a method of unambiguously identifying data from any SAA platform.

CDRA is necessary particularly when data is transferred between a PC workstation (using ASCII code) and a mainframe (using EBCDIC code). Theoretically, CDRA can be extended to support other codes (such as Unicode, a new character encoding scheme gaining support).

The Five DRDA Levels

There are five levels within DRDA. Each level represents an increasing level of distributed support. Additionally, the levels reflect:

- The number of requests and RDBMSs per unit of work

- The number of RDBMSs per request

In order of increasing complexity, the five DRDA levels are

- User-Assisted Distribution

- Remote Request

- Remote Unit of Work (RUW)

- Distributed Unit of Work (DUW)

- Distributed Request

Refer to Table 41.1 for a synopsis of the DRDA levels.

TABLE 41.1   The Five DRDA Levels

DRDA Level	SQL Stmts per UOW	DBMS per UOW	DBMS per SQL stmt
User-Assisted	-	-	-
Remote Request	1	1	1
Remote Unit of Work	>1	1	1
Distributed Unit of Work	>1	>1	1
Distributed Request	>1	>1	>1

The result of moving up the levels is additive. For example, distributed request capability implies distributed unit of work (which in turn implies remote unit of work). The reverse, however, is not implicitly true.

These levels are discussed at greater length in the following sections.

User-Assisted Distribution

User-assisted distribution is the simplest form of data distribution. However, under this DRDA level, the end user is aware of the distribution and participates in accomplishing the distributed access. To accomplish user-assisted distribution, the user must:

- Extract the needed data from the original system

- Load the extracted data to the requesting system

This is an intensive procedure that should not be taken lightly. As it involves replicated data, care must be taken to document the system of record and the date of extraction in case future modification is permitted.

Even given its many limitations, user-assisted distribution is useful for producing snapshot tables and satisfying one-time requests. However, to many, user-assisted distribution is not truly distributed data access. I tend to agree with them.

Oftentimes, user-assisted distribution is not even included in a formal discussion of DRDA. However, I include it here for completeness.

Remote Request

Remote request is the first level of true distribution within DRDA. When a DBMS supports DRDA remote request capability, a single SQL statement can be issued to read or modify a single remote RDBMS within a single unit of work.

Simply stated, remote request enables developers to be operating within one RDBMS, and refer to a different RDBMS. Furthermore, it is possible to utilize remote request capability to access a remote RDBMS, even if a local RDBMS is not being used.

DRDA remote request provides the capability of issuing only one SQL request per unit of work, and only one RDBMS per SQL request.

Remote Unit of Work

The remote unit of work (RUW) DRDA level adds to the functionality of remote request. RUW allows multiple SQL statements. However, the SQL can only read and/or modify a single remote RDBMS within a single unit of work.

To clarify, within the scope of a commit, RUW can access only one RDBMS.

So, DRDA remote unit of work provides the capability of issuing multiple SQL requests per unit of work, but still can access only one RDBMS per SQL request.

Distributed Unit of Work

Distributed unit of work (DUW) builds onto the functionality of remote unit of work. More than one RDBMS can be accessed per unit of work.

Simply stated, DRDA DUW enables multiple SQL statements to read and/or modify multiple RDBMSs within a single unit of work. However, only one RDBMS can be specified per SQL statement.

As with any unit of work, all of the SQL statements within the commit scope either succeed or fail. This requires a two-phase commit protocol to be established. Distributed two-phase commit is functionally equivalent to the two-phase commit DB2 performs when executing under CICS or IMS/TM. When a DUW program issues a COMMIT, the two-phase commit protocol must synchronize the COMMIT across all affected platforms.

Distributed Request

DRDA distributed request capability enables complete data distribution. Using distributed request, the DUW restriction of one RDBMS per SQL statement is removed. Additionally, multiple SQL requests, both distributed and non-distributed, can be contained within a single unit of work.

Simply stated, distributed request enables a single SQL statement to read and/or update multiple RDBMSs at the same time.

There are no RDBMS products that currently provide DRDA distributed request capability.

Putting It All Together

Consider a scenario where three remote processing locations are set up, each with a RDBMS: Pittsburgh, Chicago, and Jacksonville. Let's examine how each of the four DRDA options could access distributed data from these locations (see Figure 41.3).

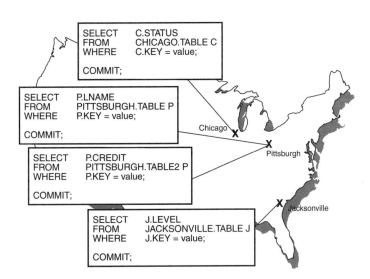

FIGURE 41.3   DRDA remote request.

Consider a situation whereby we need to access specific columns from tables at each remote location. Furthermore, assume that the requests are emanating from Chicago.

Refer to Figure 41.3 for a depiction of remote request distributed access. In this scenario, we can access only a single RDBMS from a single location in a single unit of work. The request for the Chicago table is a local request; the Pittsburgh and Jacksonville requests are remote. Each request is within a single unit of work (indicated by the COMMIT).

Remote unit of work functionality is depicted in Figure 41.4. Contrast this diagram with remote request. Instead of a single statement per unit of work, multiple statements can be issued (see the Pittsburgh example).

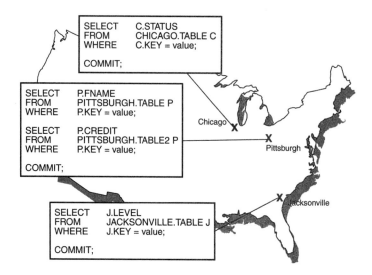

FIGURE 41.4   DRDA remote unit of work.

Distributed unit of work enables multiple RDBMSs per unit of work. This is shown in Figure 41.5.

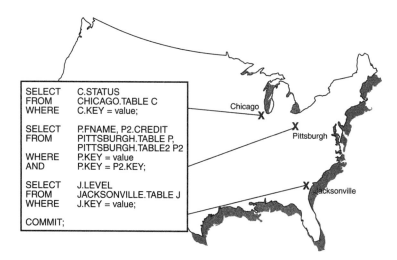

FIGURE 41.5   DRDA distributed unit of work.

All four tables from all three locations can be accessed within one unit of work using DRDA DUW functionality.

Finally, Figure 41.6 depicts distributed request. Using distributed request, multiple RDBMSs from multiple locations can be accessed using a single SQL statement. In this scenario, the application requester sends a request to the Chicago application server, which in turn sends the request to the Chicago database server. It processes what it can and passes it to one of the other database servers (in, say, Pittsburgh), and so on.

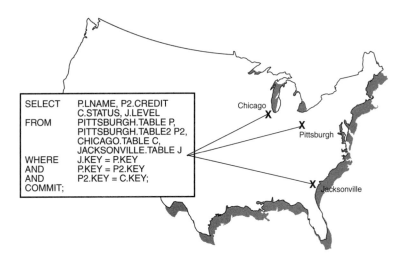

```
SELECT    P.LNAME, P2.CREDIT
          C.STATUS, J.LEVEL
FROM      PITTSBURGH.TABLE P,
          PITTSBURGH.TABLE2 P2,
          CHICAGO.TABLE C,
          JACKSONVILLE.TABLE J
WHERE     J.KEY = P.KEY
AND       P.KEY = P2.KEY
AND       P2.KEY = C.KEY;
COMMIT;
```

FIGURE 41.6   DRDA distributed request.

Distributed DB2

Remember, though, this chapter has covered the DRDA framework only. It has not discussed actual implementation in DB2. For this information, read Chapter 42 and Chapter 43, "DB2 Connect."

CHAPTER **42**

Distributed DB2

In the preceding chapter, I discussed DRDA from a purely theoretical perspective. DB2 distributes data following the DRDA architecture. However, you will find major differences in some aspects of DB2's implementation of distributed data.

Distributing Data Using DB2

DB2 can distribute data following three of the DRDA levels: remote request, remote unit of work, and distributed unit of work. As of DB2 V6, distributed request capability is not available. Additionally, DB2 V6 supports application requester and application server functions. The database server function is not available under DB2 V6.

DB2 also provides the capability to access distributed data using a non-DRDA private protocol. This capability was introduced to DB2 prior to the existence of DRDA.

The Basics

The Distributed Data Facility (DDF) is required for accessing distributed data through DB2. The DDF is an optional DB2 address space. Recall from Chapter 20, "DB2 Behind the Scenes," that the other address spaces are the DBAS, SSAS, and IRLM, as well as optional stored procedure address spaces using WLM.

The Communication Database

Distributed DB2 connections are defined using system tables defined to DB2. Connection information is stored in the DB2 Catalog in the Communications Data Base tables, or CDB. The DDF reads the CDB to perform authid name translations and to map DB2 objects to VTAM objects. The CDB exists in a separate table space in the DB2 Catalog, named SYSDDF.

In a distributed environment, each DB2 subsystem is identified by a unique location name of up to 16 characters. A location can be explicitly accessed using CONNECT or three-part table names.

V8

> **CAUTION**
>
> The DB2 Catalog provides up to 128 bytes for the location name, but only the first 16 bytes are actually used.

42

There are seven CDB tables stored in a single table space (SYSDDF):

SYSIBM.IPLIST	Associates multiple IP addresses to a given LOCATION.
SYSIBM.SYSLOCATIONS	Maps location names to VTAM LUNAMEs. Contains a row for each remote DB2 subsystem to which SQL statements can be sent.
SYSIBM.SYSLULIST	Assigns LUNAMEs to locations.
SYSIBM.SYSLUMODES	Defines session/conversation limits.
SYSIBM.SYSLUNAMES	Defines the attributes of LUNAMEs. Contains a row for each remote DB2 to which SQL statements can be sent or from which SQL statements can be received.
SYSIBM.SYSMODESELECT	Defines the mode for an individual user.
SYSIBM.SYSUSERNAMES	Translates local usernames.

Distributed Terms

In addition to the DRDA terms from the preceding chapter, I use the following terms in the remainder of this chapter:

- A *location* is a single DB2 subsystem. Locations are also called *sites* or *instances*.

- A *unit of work* describes the activity that occurs between commits. It is also called a *unit of recovery* or *commit scope*.

- A *request* is a single SQL statement.

In the remainder of this chapter, I describe the data distribution options that exist for DB2 for z/OS and OS/390.

DB2 Support for the DRDA Levels

DB2 provides support for distributed requests using three of the DRDA levels: remote request, remote unit of work, and distributed unit of work.

Remote Request

Applications can implement remote request capability by issuing a single request to a single location within a single unit of work. This approach is the easiest but least flexible method of coding distributed DB2 access.

Remote Unit of Work

To utilize RUW within an application program, these rules must be followed:

- Each request must be for a single location.

- Each unit of work can contain multiple requests.

- Each unit of work must access data from a single location only.

A single application program can access data from multiple locations using RUW but not within the same unit of work. The programmer must be cognizant of this fact and therefore code the program appropriately.

Distributed Unit of Work

An application utilizes DUW if these rules are followed:

- Each request must be for a single location.

- Each unit of work can contain multiple requests.

- Each unit of work can access data at multiple locations.

DB2 supports both private protocol DUW and full DRDA DUW.

Methods of Accessing Distributed Data

You should note that the developer of a distributed application does not have to know the descriptions of remote request, RUW, and DUW. Ensuring that the application does not access multiple locations within a single request is sufficient. DB2 handles the distributed access based on the nature of the request(s).

Of course, an informed programmer is an efficient programmer. To enhance performance, application developers should be aware of the location at which the data to be accessed exists.

A DB2 application developer has two choices for the manner in which distributed data is accessed:

- Application-directed access

- System-directed access

In the following sections, you will examine these two methods of distributed data access.

Application-Directed Data Access

Application-directed data access is the more powerful of the two options. With this access, explicit connections are required. Furthermore, application-directed distributed access conforms to the DRDA standard.

Establishing Connections

When implementing application-directed distribution, the application must issue a `CONNECT` statement to the remote location, prior to accessing data from that location. Consider this example:

```
CONNECT TO CHICAGO;
```

This statement connects the application to the location named `CHICAGO`. The connection must be a valid location, as defined in the `SYSIBM.LOCATIONS` (or `SYSBM.SYSLOCATIONS`) table. Multiple locations can be connected at once. For example, an application can issue the following:

```
CONNECT TO CHICAGO;
        .
        .
        .
CONNECT TO JACKSONVILLE;
        .
        .
        .
CONNECT TO PITTSBURGH;
```

In this scenario, three connections have been established—one each to Chicago, Jacksonville, and Pittsburgh. The `CONNECT` statement causes a VTAM conversation to be allocated from the local site to the specified remote location. Therefore, if the preceding example were to be issued from Seattle, three VTAM conversations would be established:

- One from Seattle to Chicago
- One from Seattle to Jacksonville
- One from Seattle to Pittsburgh

However, only one connection can be active at any one time. You use the `SET CONNECTION` statement to specify which connection should be active. Now look at this example:

```
SET CONNECTION PITTSBURGH;
```

This statement sets the active connection to Pittsburgh. Additionally, the `SET CONNECTION` statement places the previously active connection into a dormant state.

In all the preceding examples (for both `CONNECT` and `SET CONNECTION`), you could have used a host variable in place of the literal, as in this example:

```
SET CONNECTION :HV;
```

This statement sets the active connection to be whatever location was stored in the host variable at the time the statement was executed.

Releasing Connections

After it is established, a connection is available for the duration of the program unless it is explicitly released or the `DISCONNECT BIND` option was not set to `EXPLICIT` (which is the default).

Connections are explicitly released using the RELEASE statement, as shown here:

```
RELEASE PITTSBURGH;
```

This statement releases the connection to the Pittsburgh location. Valid options that can be specified on the RELEASE statement are

- A valid location specified as a literal or a host variable

- CURRENT, which releases the currently active connection

- ALL, which releases all connections

- ALL PRIVATE, which releases DB2 private connection and is discussed in the next section

The DISCONNECT BIND option also affects when connections are released. You can specify this option for plans only. It applies to all processes that use the plan and have remote connections of any type. The following DISCONNECT parameters are valid:

EXPLICIT	This option is the default. It indicates that only released connections will be destroyed at a COMMIT point.
AUTOMATIC	This option specifies that all remote connections are to be destroyed at a COMMIT point.
CONDITIONAL	This option specifies that all remote connections are to be destroyed at a COMMIT point unless a WITH HOLD cursor is associated with the conversation.

System-Directed Data Access

In addition to application-directed distribution, DB2 also provides system-directed access to distributed DB2 data. The system-directed access is less flexible than application-directed access because of it is viable for DB2-to-DB2 distribution only, and connections cannot be explicitly requested (instead connections are implicitly performed when distributed requests are initiated).

Although system-directed access does not conform to DRDA, it does provide the same levels of distributed support as application-directed access—remote request, RUW, and DUW. System-directed access is requested using three-part table names, as shown in this example:

```
SELECT  COL1, COL2, COL7
FROM    PITTSBURGH.OWNER.TABLE
WHERE   KEY = :HV;
```

Issuing this request causes an implicit connection to be established to the Pittsburgh location. DB2 determines the location by using the high-level qualifier of the three-part name. This type of distribution is called system-directed because the system (DB2), not the application, determines to which location to connect.

Optionally, you can create an alias for the three-part table name. The alias enables users to access a remote table (or view) without knowing its location. Here's an example:

```
CREATE ALIAS EMP
FOR PITTSBURGH.OWNER.EMPLOYEE;

SELECT COL1, COL2
FROM   EMP;
```

The first statement creates the alias EMP for the EMPLOYEE table located in Pittsburgh. The second statement requests the data from the Pittsburgh EMPLOYEE table using the alias, EMP. Note that the three-part name is avoided.

Three-Part Name Support with DRDA

Applications (running DB2 V6 and later) can use three-part names to access distributed data and still use DRDA. Applications that used private protocol distribution can now use DRDA protocol with no program code or database naming changes.

To use DRDA protocol with three-part names, you must BIND a package at each location that is specified in a three-part name and then BIND a package or plan at the local location specifying the DBPROTOCOL(DRDA) BIND option. You do not need to re-code any logic, nor do you need to rename any database objects.

> **CAUTION**
>
> IBM will eventually phase out private protocol distribution in a subsequent release of DB2. IBM continues to support private protocol distribution to provide support for legacy applications written using the private protocol before DRDA support was provided. Now that DB2 provides the ability to use DRDA with three-part names, private protocol distribution will not likely be supported by IBM much longer. And even though IBM still supports private protocol, it is no longer being enhanced. Therefore, you should avoid implementing new applications using private protocol distribution.

Converting Private Protocol to DRDA   To convert an application that uses private protocol distribution to use DRDA instead, follow these steps:

1. First you must determine the locations that are accessed by the application. To do this, you can look for SQL statements in the application that access three-part names. The first component of the three-part name is the location name. If the application uses aliases, you can query the DB2 Catalog to determine the location of the alias using the following SQL SELECT statement:

   ```
   SELECT LOCATION, CREATOR, NAME, TBCREATOR, TBNAME
   FROM   SYSIBM.SYSTABLES
   WHERE  NAME = 'alias name'
   AND    TYPE = 'A';
   ```

   If the application uses dynamic SQL instead of static SQL, simply BIND packages at all remote locations that users access using three part names.

2. Using the list of locations obtained in step 1, BIND a package at each of the locations. You can also BIND a package locally (optionally, you can just use the DBRM).

NOTE

If the application combines application-directed and system-directed access by using a CONNECT to get to a remote location, and then three-part names to get yet another location, you must BIND a package specifying DBPROTOCOL(DRDA) at the first remote location and another package at the third location.

---

3. BIND all remote packages into a plan with the local package or DBRM. Use the DBPROTOCOL(DRDA) option when issuing the BIND for this plan.

4. Ensure that all aliases are accurate. When using private protocol distribution, aliases are resolved at the location that issues the request. However, for DRDA distribution, aliases are resolved at the location where the package is executed. So, you will need to create additional aliases at remote locations when switching from private protocol to DRDA.

5. If you use the resource limit facility (RLF) to control distributed requests, you will need to ensure that the RLF settings are applied correctly. When using private protocol, distribution plan names are provided to the RLF to govern SQL access. When using DRDA, you must specify package names instead of plan names.

   Refer to Chapter 29, "DB2 Resource Governing," for additional information on the RLF.

System-Directed Versus Application-Directed

Which is better: system-directed or application-directed? Both have their benefits and drawbacks. For a short comparison of the two methods, refer to Table 42.1.

TABLE 42.1 System-Directed Versus Application-Directed Access

	Application-Directed	System-Directed
Explicit connections	Yes	No
Three-part table names	No	Yes
Can issue DCL	Yes	No
Can issue DDL	Yes	No
Can issue DML	Yes	Yes
Static SQL using packages	Yes	No
Dynamic SQL at the server	No	Yes
DB2 to any server	Yes	No
DB2 to DB2	Yes	Yes
Open DRDA protocol	Yes	Yes
DB2 Private protocol	No	Yes
Distributed request support	No	No
Read and update at remote locations from CAF	Yes	Yes
Read and update at remote locations from TSO	Yes	Yes
Read and update at remote locations from CICS	Yes	Yes
Read and update at remote locations from IMS/TM	Yes	Yes

Regardless of the relative merits of system-directed versus application-directed distribution, favor application-directed distribution because it is IBM's strategic direction for DB2 data distribution.

Packages for Static SQL

Static SQL is supported in distsributed applications by packages. To access remote locations using SQL embedded in an application program, the program must be precompiled and then bound into a package. The application program calls the SQL API, which executes the package at the RDBMS.

If the application program requires access to multiple RDBMSs, multiple packages must be bound, one at each location. Packages enable a request originating from one location to execute static SQL at remote locations. Of course, dynamic SQL is also supported using system-directed distribution.

Two-Phase Commit

Distributed two-phase commit enables application programs to update data in multiple RDBMSs within a single unit of work. The two-phase commit process coordinates the commits across the multiple platforms. The two-phase commit provides a consistent outcome, guaranteeing the integrity of the data across platforms, regardless of communication or system failures.

Two-Phase Commit Terminology

A syncpoint tree is built by the coordinator of a unit of work. The syncpoint tree determines which process is in control of the commit/abort decision.

Each node in the syncpoint tree is the coordinator of its own resources and of the nodes below it on the syncpoint tree. Additionally, a node is a participant of the node directly above it in the syncpoint tree.

Figure 42.1 shows an example of a syncpoint tree. In this example, DB2V is the coordinator for DB2W, DB2X, and DB2Y. In addition, DB2W is the coordinator for DB2Z.

Keep these terms in mind as I discuss the two-phase commit process in this chapter.

What Are the Two Phases?

The two phases in the two-phase commit process are

1. Preparation

2. Actual commit

The first phase is the preparation phase. Each participant in the two-phase commit process is informed to get ready to commit. The preparation phase uses the *presumed abort* protocol. All affected modifications at all locations within the unit of work therefore are rolled back if an error is encountered.

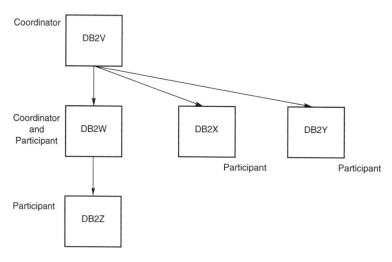

FIGURE 42.1   A two-phase commit syncpoint tree.

Each participant informs the coordinator when it has successfully written the appropriate log records and is therefore ready to commit (or roll back) all changes. Usually, this process is followed by a commit. However, if any participant fails to commit, the coordinator may need to back out all changes for all participants.

During phase 1, each participant returns a "vote" on whether commit can proceed. Each participant returns one of the following votes:

YES	The participant and all dependent nodes are ready for COMMIT or ABORT processing.
READ-ONLY	The participant and all dependent nodes are read-only and do not need to participate in the two-phase commit process.
NO	One or more nodes in the syncpoint tree failed to return a YES or READ-ONLY vote. A communication failure or error is recorded as a NO vote.

If all votes are READ-ONLY, a COMMIT is not necessary because no updates were performed. If all the votes are YES and READ-ONLY, the COMMIT can be processed. If any vote is NO, the unit of work is rolled back.

After all the participants are ready to commit, phase 1 is complete. Therefore, the second phase—the actual commit—is initiated. During phase 2, success is presumed, even in the case of system failure. Because all participants have elected to continue the commit, success can be presumed with no danger of data integrity violations.

The actual commit phase is implemented as a series of communications between the coordinator and its subordinate participants.

The coordinator specifies that each participant that voted YES is free to permanently record the changed data and release all held locks. When the participant successfully completes this work, it responds back to the coordinator indicating that it has successfully committed the unit of work. The coordinator then logs that the participant has success-fully committed.

Additionally, a process called *resynchronization* occurs during phase 2. Resynchronization resolves in-doubt logical units of work. An in-doubt logical unit of work has passed phase 1 but has not passed phase 2. This situation is typically caused by communication failures.

When a communication failure occurs causing in-doubt LUWs, locks may be held, causing system timeouts and deadlocks. For this reason, waiting for the automatic DB2 resynchro-nization may not be feasible. Therefore, you also can initiate resynchronization manually. You do so by using the `RECOVER INDOUBT` command, as in this example:

```
RECOVER INDOUBT ACTION(COMMIT) ID(1031)
```

This command schedules a commit for the threads identified by the correlation ID of 1031. The `ACTION` parameter can be either `COMMIT` or `ABORT`. The decision whether to commit or abort must be made by the analyst issuing the `RECOVER`. For this reason, manual resynchronization should be initiated only when absolutely necessary. Automatic DB2 resynchronization is generally more efficient and accurate.

When resynchronization is complete for all the two-phase commit participants, the two-phase commit is complete.

Multi-Site Updating
The presence of the two-phase commit process within DB2 enables multi-site updating capability. The two-phase commit occurs when data at more than one remote location is modified (`INSERT`, `UPDATE`, and/or `DELETE`).

The two-phase commit process ensures that data at all remote locations is consistent and recoverable.

A multi-site update is possible, regardless of how you attach to DB2:

- CAF
- CICS
- IMS/TM
- TSO

One-Phase or Two-Phase Commit
Two-phase commit is optional. However, if you need to implement applications that perform multi-site updates within a single unit of work, two-phase commit is mandatory. The `SYNCLVL=SYNCPT` parameter must be specified on the VTAM `APPL` definition statement to configure DB2's communication support for two-phase commit.

Distributed Thread Support
Successive versions of DB2 have provided enhanced thread support specifically to increase the performance and functionality of distributed applications.

Inactive DBATS

To optimize performance of distributed processing, DB2 inactivates database access threads (DBATs) as needed instead of disconnecting them. Without this capability, each thread would have to repeatedly connect, process, and then disconnect. This would generate a significant amount of overhead.

A DBAT becomes inactive when *all* the following are true:

- A commit or rollback was the last task performed.

- No locks are being held by the thread.

- The package being executed was bound specifying RELEASE(COMMIT).

- INACTIVE was specified for the DDF THREAD install parameter.

Inactive DBATs become active when they receive a message from VTAM. When the remote application shuts down, the thread is disconnected.

Keep in mind that the existence of inactive threads may cause the number of concurrent DB2 threads to increase substantially. The overall maximum number of concurrent threads (MAXDBAT + CONDBAT) can be 25,000, of which only 2,000 (CTHREAD + MAXDBAT) can be active. Refer to Table 42.2 for a synopsis of the affected DSNZPARMs.

TABLE 42.2   Thread Parameters

Definition	DSNZPARM
Local Threads	CTHREAD
Active DBATs	MAXDBAT
Inactive DBATs	CONDBAT

Database Connection Pooling

DB2 V6 added support for database connection pooling. In prior DB2 releases, when an application requester established a connection to DB2, a connection to the DB2 database was also established. For V6 and later releases, DB2 maintains a pool of database connections that can be reused to process requests from DRDA application requesters. The connection pool enables DB2 to support up to 150,000 DRDA connections to DB2. The connections in the pool are DBATs, referred to as type 2 inactive threads.

DB2 supports two types of inactive threads—type 1 and type 2. Type 2 inactive threads are only available for DRDA connections and use less storage than type 1 inactive threads. Type 2 inactive threads use a pool of DBATs that can be switched among connections as needed.

If you have a requirement to support more inbound remote connections than you have database access threads, you should consider using DDF inactive thread support. The following sections provide information on inactive thread support.

DB2 favors making inactive threads type 2. However, certain scenarios prohibit type 2 inactive threads. After a COMMIT or ROLLBACK, DB2 determines whether a thread can become inactive, and, if it can, whether it can become a type 1 or type 2 inactive thread. Refer to Table 42.3 for a breakdown of when inactive threads can be type 2 or not.

TABLE 42.3   Type 1 and Type 2 Inactive Threads

Condition	Thread can be Type 1	Thread can be Type 2
A hop to another location	Yes	Yes
A connection using DB2 private-protocol access	Yes	No
A package that is bound specifying RELEASE(COMMIT)	Yes	Yes
A package that is bound specifying RELEASE(DEALLOCATE)	No	Yes
A held cursor or a held LOB locator	No	No
A package that is bound specifying KEEPDYNAMIC(YES)	No	No

When a "Yes" is listed for a condition in Table 42.3, the thread can become inactive as the indicated type of inactive thread when a COMMIT is issued. After a ROLLBACK, a thread can become inactive, even if it had open cursors defined WITH HOLD or a held LOB locator because ROLLBACK closes all cursors and LOB locators.

If a thread is eligible to become a type 2 inactive thread, the thread is made inactive and the DBAT is eligible to be used by another connection. If the thread must become a type 1 inactive thread, DB2 first determines that the number of inactive threads will not exceed the installation limit set in DSNZPARMs. If the limit is not exceeded, the thread becomes inactive; if the limit would be exceeded, the thread remains active. If too many active threads exist, DB2 may terminate the thread and its connection.

Miscellaneous Distributed Topics

The following assortment of tips might prove to be helpful as you develop your distributed DB2 applications.

Workstation DB2

In addition to DB2 for z/OS, IBM also provides versions of DB2 for Linux, Unix and Windows (LUW). Of course, these DB2 implementations are not 100-percent compatible with DB2 for z/OS. Also, each DB2 uses SQL, but different SQL features are provided by each. For example, DB2 for LUW supports the EXCEPT clause for performing relational division and the INTERSECT clause for performing relational intersection. DB2 for z/OS does not.

The workstation DB2 products do not internally support DRDA. An additional product, DB2 Connect, which is covered in Chapter 43, provides DRDA support.

DDF Suspend and Resume

V7 If you ever tried to make changes to your database structures in a distributed environment prior to DB2 V7, you probably had some trouble. It can be difficult to maintain your distributed databases, because the DDF DRDA server holds locks preventing you from running DDL. DB2 V7 provides relief with modifications to the STOP DDF and START DDF commands.

A simple STOP DDF command causes locks to be released, but it also causes all remote connections to be lost. DB2 V7 adds a new parameter to the STOP DDF command called MODE(SUSPEND). Issuing a stop with this parameter suspends all DDF activity and enables your DDL to be run. When the maintenance is complete, the START DDF command will return DDF processing to normal.

DB2 Version 8 Distribution Improvements

`V8` IBM delivered a few nice improvements to distributed data support in DB2 for z/OS as of Version 8.

`V8` **Database Aliases**   One of these new features is the ability to specify a *database alias* for distributed connections. This is important because there is a basic difference in the way that distributed data is accessed by DB2 for z/OS and DB2 LUW. When you connect to DB2 for z/OS you address the entire DB2 subsystem by using its location name. With DB2 LUW however, access is by its database name. So the database name of the DB2 LUW system you want to connect to must be specified in the LOCATION column of the SYSIBM.LOCATIONS CDB catalog table (when the requester is DB2 for z/OS). Prior to DB2 V8, a one-to-one mapping was enforced between location name and database name. And there was no way to access multiple DB2 LUW databases that have the same name—even if they reside on different machines.

With DB2 V8, the DBALIAS column is added to SYSIBM.LOCATIONS to fix this problem. You can use the DBALIAS column to point your SELECT statement to the real database name on DB2 LUW that you want to connect to. You continue to specify the LOCATION name as the first qualifier of your three-part table name in your SELECT statement. The mapped LINKNAME links you to the corresponding entry in SYSIBM.IPNAMES, which provides the correct TCP/IP address for the workstation you want to access.

`V8` **Server Location Aliases**   DB2 V8 also allows you to define up to eight alias names in addition to the location name for a DB2 data-sharing group. Each *location alias* is an alternative name that a requester can use to access a DB2 subsystem. Location alias names are defined using the change log inventory (DSNJU003) utility. All that is required is adding the location alias names to your BSDS data sets on each member of the data sharing group. The syntax is as follows:

```
DDF ALIAS = aliasname
```

After running DSNJU003, the BSDS will store the location alias names that have been specified for the DB2 subsystem.

`V8` **TCP/IP Network Member Routing**   Finally, prior to DB2 V8 remote TCP/IP connections were typically set up to automatically balance connections across all members of a data sharing group. This is not always the desired setup, though. DB2 V8 enables you to setup *member routing* in a TCP/IP network. To route requests from certain DB2 for z/OS requesters to specific members of a data sharing group, combine the server location alias feature with the new CDB table SYSIBM.IPLIST.

Combining DRDA and Private Protocol Requests

By combining CONNECT statements and SQL statements that access three-part tables names, you can issue application-directed and system-directed requests from within a single unit of work. However, having a system-directed and an application-directed request to the same location is not possible. The requests must be to different locations.

Consider the following piece of code:

```
CONNECT TO JACKSONVILLE;
     .
     .
     .
SELECT COL7
INTO    :HV7
FROM    DEPT;
     .
     .
     .
SELECT COL1, COL2
INTO    :HV1, :HV2
FROM    CHICAGO.OWNER.EMPLOYEE;
     .
     .
     .
COMMIT;
```

The application connects to Jacksonville using application-directed access (CONNECT). At the Jacksonville location, the DEPT table is accessed. Within the same unit of work, a request is made for Chicago data using system-directed access (three-part table name).

DB2 Versions and Distribution

Distributed connectivity can be set up among multiple DB2 subsystems all running different versions if you so desire. Furthermore, you can access different release levels of DB2 within a single unit of work.

Developing Client/Server Applications

Client/server processing is popular development methodology for accessing remote data. DB2 is an ideal candidate for functioning as the server in the client/server framework. It can accept requests from multiple IBM and non-IBM RDBMS products.

ASCII Server Support

IBM mainframes use a different encoding scheme for alphanumeric characters than most other computers. The IBM encoding scheme is known as EBCDIC. When non-IBM computers communicate with IBM computers it is necessary to translate the EBCDIC encoding scheme to ASCII, the standard encoding scheme used by these other devices.

DB2 enables an entire subsystem, a database, a table space, or a table to be defined to use ASCII instead of EBCDIC. You can enhance performance by creating ASCII objects for

42

distributed applications because characters will not need to be converted to EBCDIC when communicating with other ASCII servers.

Before creating ASCII objects, consider the following caveats:

- You can specify a different encoding scheme for DB2 objects using the CCSID parameter of the CREATE DATABASE, CREATE TABLESPACE, CREATE GLOBAL TEMPORARY TABLE, or CREATE TABLE statement.

- The encoding scheme of an object cannot be altered after the object is created.

- z/OS applications that display ASCII encoded data actually receive the data as EBCDIC, but sort the data using the ASCII collating sequence.

V8 Another alternative, Unicode, is becoming increasingly popular. DB2 for z/OS is being used as the server in more and more large, client/server applications. Unicode makes it easier for multi-national organizations to manage data in a global environment where different languages require different code sets. DB2 V8 is engineered to use and take advantage of Unicode. As of V8, DB2 can convert any SQL statement to Unicode before parsing and as a result, all characters parse correctly. Additionally, the V8 DB2 Catalog has been re-engineering in Unicode.

Native TCP/IP Support

DB2 provides native TCP/IP support for distributed connections. Previous versions of DB2 supported TCP/IP requesters, but only with additional software and configuration. TCP/IP enables direct connections to DB2 from client applications without the overhead and expense of the additional software.

You can choose to use SNA, TCP/IP, or mixed networks for distributed DB2 applications.

DB2 Connect

Applications that run on a non-zSeries platform require a gateway to access DB2 for z/OS data. IBM's DB2 Connect product can be used to enable applications that run on a Linux, Unix, or Windows environment to access mainframe DB2 data.

DB2 Connect is an add-on product from IBM that implements DRDA Application Requester functionality for DB2. Using DB2 Connect, applications executing on non-mainframe platforms can transparently access DB2 for z/OS and OS/390 databases. For example, an application running on a Windows workstation can use DB2 Connect to access DB2 data from the mainframe.

Of course, DB2 Connect is not the only gateway product on the market. Other popular gateway products exist for connecting DB2 for z/OS to client/server applications, such as Neon Systems' Shadow Direct gateway and the Oracle Transparent Gateway. But this chapter will discuss DB2 Connect, because it is the most popular of the available options for DB2 for z/OS and OS/390.

> **NOTE**
>
> DB2 Connect V8 is the most recent version of IBM's gateway product for DB2. Be sure to run this latest version of DB2 Connect to take advantage of the latest and greatest features.

An Overview of IBM DB2 Connect

DB2 Connect provides fast, transparent read/write access to all DB2 family servers, not just z/OS and OS/390. You can use DB2 Connect in conjunction with IBM DB2 Relational Connect to obtain transparent, consolidated access to Oracle, Sybase, Microsoft SQL Server and Informix databases, too.

DB2 Connect forwards SQL statements submitted by application programs to host database servers. DB2 Connect can forward almost any valid SQL statement. DB2 Connect fully supports the common IBM SQL, as well as the DB2 for z/OS and OS/390, DB2 for VSE and VM (formerly SQL/DS), and DB2 for iSeries implementations of SQL.

> **CAUTION**
>
> To maintain portability and database independence, restrict the SQL in your applications using DB2 Connect to common IBM SQL. If you use features supported only on a specific DB2 platform, your applications will not be easily portable to another platform.

DB2 Connect implements the DRDA architecture as discussed in Chapter 42, "Distributed DB2." By exploiting the DRDA architecture, DB2 Connect offers a well-performing, cost-effective solution.

DB2 Connect provides support for distributed requests across databases and DBMS platforms. For example, you can join tables across different DB2 for z/OS subsystems or even code a UNION between a DB2 table and an Oracle table. Currently, only members of the DB2 Family and Oracle are supported for distributed request. Distributed request provides location transparency for database objects.

DB2 Connect supports *multi-site update*. Also known as *distributed unit of work* (*DUW*) and *two-phase commit*, multi-site update enables applications to update data in multiple remote database servers with guaranteed integrity. You can update any mix of supported database servers. For example, your application can update several tables in DB2 on Windows, a DB2 for z/OS table, and a DB2 for AS/400 database, all within a single transaction.

DB2 Connect can be used to bring Web applications and host data together. DB2 Connect provides broad support for developing and deploying applications using the latest Web technologies, helping you in many cases to reduce development time and the cost of ownership for applications and enhancements. Whether you are developing Web applications using Java, .NET, or ASP, DB2 Connect can be used to supply enterprise data to your application server.

Other beneficial features of DB2 Connect include:

- Support for both static and dynamic SQL

- Static SQL profiling for converting ADO, ODBC, DB2 CLI and JDBC applications to static SQL

- Special optimized catalog for ADO, ODBC, DB2 CLI and JDBC applications to make access even faster

- Resource management functions, such as connection pooling and connection concentrator, for building large-volume, enterprise Web applications

- Federated database support for transparent access to DB2 and other data sources

- The ability to prioritize SQL requests submitted by DB2 Connect applications using the dynamic load balancing and fail-over capabilities of Workload Manager

- Support for authentication schemes and single sign-on capability using Kerberos and Microsoft Active Directory

- Encryption of user IDs and passwords to protect them from becoming compromised

- Integration with IPSec and SSL security protocols

Additionally, IBM provides the following utilities to help administer DB2 Connect:

- The Command Line Processor (CLP) is used to issue SQL statements against a DB2 for z/OS (or AS/400) database server database. It sends the SQL statements to the database that you specify.

- The DB2 Control Center lets you administer and monitor DB2 Connect servers. The DB2 Command Center also provides a graphical interface to the Command Line Processor.

- Import and export utilities enable you to load, import, and export data from a file on a workstation to the mainframe, and vice versa.

- The database system monitor is used to view system connections.

Supported Platforms

DB2 Connect supports a variety of the most popular DBMS environments, server operating systems, and client operating systems, enabling you to create viable, efficient distributed applications. DB2 Connect supports DB2 as the host DBMS in the following environments: z/OS, OS390, AS/400, VSE and VM, as well as SQL/DS V3.5.

DB2 Connect supports the following server platforms: Windows NT, Windows 2000, IBM OS/2, Sun Solaris, HP-UX, SCO Unix, IBM AIX, Linux, and Linux for IBM S/390.

The client platforms supported by DB2 Connect include Windows NT (32-bit), Windows 95 (32-bit), Windows 98 (32-bit), Windows XP (32-bit) Home and Professional, Windows 2000, IBM OS/2 (32-bit), HP-UX, SCO UnixWare (V5.2), Sun Solaris, Silicon Graphics IRIX, IBM AIX, and Linux.

Additionally, DB2 Connect is in compliance with most of the popular standards and interfaces including DCE security, ODBC, JDK 1.3, JDBC, SQLJ, ADO, ADO.NET, and OLE DB (among others).

Packaging and Editions of DB2 Connect

IBM offers several connection solutions under the DB2 Connect brand. If you decide to use DB2 Connect to hook up your applications to DB2 for z/OS, you will need to choose how you will connect them. The actual package or edition of DB2 Connect to use depends on your environment and needs. There are four different editions of DB2 Connect:

- DB2 Connect Personal Edition (DB2 Connect PE)

- DB2 Connect Enterprise Edition (DB2 Connect EE)

43

- DB2 Connect Application Server Edition (DB2 Connect ASE)

- DB2 Connect Unlimited Edition (DB2 Connect UE)

These editions offer similar features, but with some important differences, including how connections are made, pricing, and usability for different purposes. DB2 Connect Personal Edition provides direct connectivity to host databases, whereas DB2 Connect Enterprise Edition provides indirect connectivity that allows clients to access host (zSeries and iSeries) DB2 databases through the DB2 Connect server. The other packages are variations of PE and EE.

The following sections will outline the benefits and uses for each of the DB2 Connect editions.

DB2 Connect Personal Edition
Using DB2 Connect PE, applications running on Windows (or Linux) personal workstations are able to access data from a host DB2 server on zSeries or iSeries. It can also be used to connect to a DB2 server on Linux, Unix, or Windows. DB2 Connect PE is typically used for two-tier applications where an intermediate server is not used. The connection is a direct connection from the workstation to the server.

DB2 Connect PE is not designed to act as a connectivity server and cannot accept inbound requests for data. However, because DB2 Connect PE provides a direct connection to host-based DB2 data sources using TCP/IP or SNA, it is useful when processing large result sets.

Figure 43.1 depicts the basic setup using DB2 Connect PE. DB2 Connect PE is installed on the workstation to enable a direct connection to DB2 on a zSeries or iSeries host. To establish a network connection the workstation has to be set up for APPC, TCP/IP or MPTN.

> **NOTE**
>
> TCP/IP connectivity requires connecting to a host running DB2 for OS/390 V5 or later, DB2 for AS/400 V4.2 or later, or DB2 for VM V6.1 or later.

You do not need to have DB2 UDB installed on workstation with DB2 Connect. Indeed, no DBMS at all is required on the workstation; DB2 Connect serves data to the workstation from a DB2 host server.

DB2 Connect Enterprise Edition (EE)
DB2 Connect EE can be used as a mid-tier gateway server for many users requiring host database access. In this environment, as shown in Figure 43.2, clients connect to the host server over a DB2 Connect EE gateway. DB2 Connect EE is running on a server and the clients access host DB2 servers over the DB2 Connect EE server. SNA Communications Support is required only where native TCP/IP connectivity is not available.

> **NOTE**
>
> TCP/IP connectivity requires connecting to a host running DB2 for OS/390 V5 or later, DB2 for AS/400 V4.2 or later, or DB2 for VM V6.1 or later.

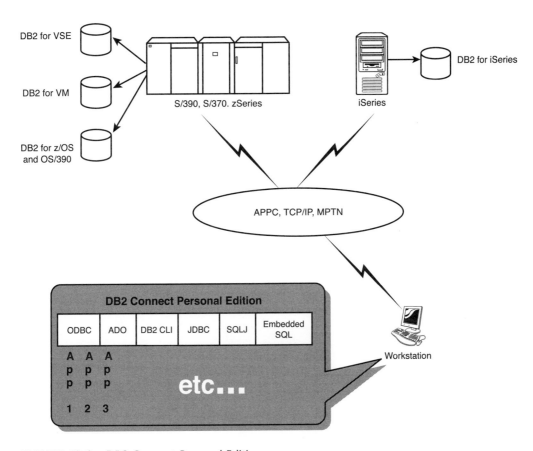

FIGURE 43.1   DB2 Connect Personal Edition.

In this example, you could replace the DB2 Connect server with a DB2 UDB Enterprise Server Edition that has the DB2 Connect Server Support component installed.

Connections to the DB2 Connect EE gateway are configured the same way that connections to distributed DB2 servers are configured.

DB2 Connect EE is a good choice for fat client applications and those applications requiring additional resource management and administration capabilities not provided by DB2 Connect PE.

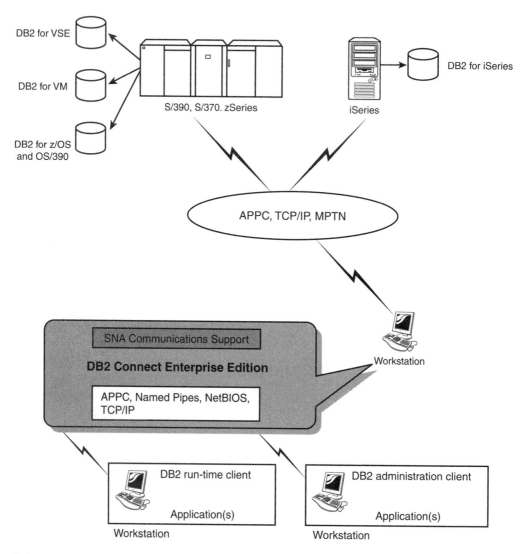

FIGURE 43.2 DB2 Connect Enterprise Edition.

DB2 Connect EE is licensed based on the number of users accessing the server. Users can be either registered or concurrent. A *registered user* is identified by name as using one or more DB2 Connect EE servers. A *concurrent user* is a measure of the number of people that are using the same DB2 Connect EE server at the same time. For concurrent usage, the number of individuals (not processes or connections) using the server at any point-in-time cannot exceed the maximum for which you are licensed.

Choosing a licensing method can be a confusing and difficult task. To clarify, suppose Craig and Beth both need to access a table on a DB2 for z/OS subsystem. If you purchase a single concurrent user license then both Craig and Beth can use the license, but they cannot use it at the same time. On the other hand, if you purchase a registered user license for Craig, then Beth cannot use it at all. Of course, this gets more complicated as the number of users increases and workload varies.

Licensing becomes even more difficult, if not impossible to determine for Web-based applications. As such, IBM makes only the registered user model available for Web-based applications using DB2 Connect EE. This can become very expensive very quickly. Fortunately, IBM provides other options in the DB2 Connect Application Server Edition and DB2 Connect Unlimited Editions.

DB2 Connect Application Server Edition
The technology used in the DB2 Connect ASE product is the same as that used in DB2 Connect EE. DB2 Connect ASE is designed for large-scale, demanding environments, but offers more attractive licensing terms and conditions. DB2 Connect ASE license charges are based on the size of the number of processors available to the application servers where the application is running. Number of users, size of the DB2 Connect server, or size of the DB2 database server on the mainframe does not affect license charges.

DB2 Connect Unlimited Edition
The final packaging option for DB2 Connect is the DB2 Connect Unlimited Edition product. This package is well suited for organizations that require extensive DB2 Connect usage. DB2 Connect UE basically offers unlimited deployment of DB2 Connect PE and DB2 Connect ASE throughout an organization. The licensing for DB2 Connect UE is based on the size of the mainframe database server; it is not affected by either the number of users nor the number of processors available to the application servers.

DB2 Connect UE is ideal for organizations with a large mixture of application types and needs.

DB2 Connect EE Thread Pooling
The most resource-intensive prospect of using DB2 Connect to access mainframe data from a workstation is establishing connections. In an active distributed environment hundreds, or perhaps thousands of client applications are connecting to and disconnecting from the host through the DB2 Connect server. Doing so consumes overhead as processing time is spent establishing and dropping connections.

To reduce this overhead, DB2 Connect EE uses thread pooling techniques that minimize the resources required on the DB2 for z/OS database servers. Efficiency is gained by concentrating the workload from all applications into a much smaller set of connections.

This is known as thread pooling, and there are two techniques at the disposal of DB2 Connect: connection pooling and connection concentrator.

The default technique used by DB2 Connect EE is *connection pooling.* It allows reuse of an established connection infrastructure for subsequent connections. When a DB2 Connect instance is started, a pool of coordinating agents is created. When a connection request comes in, an agent is assigned to this request. The agent will connect to the DB2 server and a thread will be created. When the application issues a disconnect request, the agent will not pass this request along to the DB2 server. Instead, the agent is put back in to the pool.

The agent in the pool still owns its connection to the DB2 server and the corresponding DB2 thread. When another application issues a connect request, this agent is assigned to this new application.

Connection concentrator extends the features of connection pooling by improving load balancing in parallel Sysplex configurations. With connection concentrator, DB2 uses a more sophisticated approach to reducing resource consumption for very high volume OLTP applications. This function can dramatically increase the scalability of your DB2 for z/OS and DB2 Connect solution, while also providing for transaction-level load balancing in DB2 for z/OS data sharing environments.

With connection pooling one application has to disconnect before another one can reuse a pooled connection. Rather than having the connection become free for use by another client at client disconnect, connection concentrator allows re-use of a server task when an application performs a COMMIT or ROLLBACK. The following conditions must be met when a client application reaches a COMMIT point to enable connection concentrator to reuse an agent:

- There can be no cursors using WITH HOLD for the connection. Transactions that do not close WITH HOLD cursors will be assigned a dedicated agent and hence will not be able to take full advantage of connection concentrator.

- There can be no declared global temporary tables having the ON COMMIT PRESERVE ROWS option.

- Packages bound using the KEEPDYNAMIC YES option might not have been referenced.

Be sure that there are enough agents available in the connection pool to contain all active clients. Doing so enables connection concentrator to avoid unnecessary connection reuse outside of the load balancing process.

Whereas connection pooling helps reduce the overhead of database connections and handle connection volume, connection concentrator helps increase scalability. With connection pooling, a connection is only available for reuse after the application owning the connection issues a disconnect. This is not helpful for two-tier client/server applications where users do not disconnect all day long. Additionally, if the application server in a multi-tier application establishes database connections at server start up time and does not release them until the application server is shut down, connection pooling is not helpful. Connection pooling improves overall performance, though, for Web and client/server implementations having a greater number of connections and disconnections.

Connection concentrator allocates host database resources only for the duration of each SQL transaction while keeping user applications active. This allows for configurations where the number of DB2 threads and the resources they consume can be much smaller than if every application connection had its own thread.

To summarize: keep in mind that the main difference between connection pooling and connection concentration is when the connection breaks. Connection pooling breaks the connection at disconnect, whereas connection concentration breaks the connection at the COMMIT point (after maximum logical agents is met).

DB2 Connect Guidelines

Consider applying the advice in the following guidelines to optimize your usage of DB2 Connect.

Choose DB2 Connect PE for Single Workstation Solutions   DB2 Connect PE can be a good choice for two-tier client/server applications running on desktop workstations that need to access data from mainframe DB2 databases. However, the personal edition is not suitable for deployment on multi-user systems and application servers.

If you have two people who share a workstation, DB2 Connect PE is a viable solution, because each person uses the workstation individually. That is, they cannot both use the workstation at the same time. Only one connection is required at any time for both of these users so only one license of DB2 Connect PE is required.

On the other hand, if you set up five workstations as dumb terminals making connections to a DB2 for z/OS server, you would need ten licenses of DB2 Connect PE. Of course, you could use DB2 Connect EE instead, too.

Favor DB2 Connect EE for Multi-User Solutions   DB2 Connect EE is the required solution when a middle tier connectivity server is required. DB2 Connect EE is suitable for environments where the number of concurrent users can be easily determined. However, DB2 Connect UE and ASE are preferable to EE for Web-based applications and multi-tier client/server applications where the number of concurrent users is difficult, or impossible, to determine. This is so mostly due to the cost of licensing.

Setting Up the DDF for z/OS   You must set up the DDF as an application server to connect distributed applications to DB2 for z/OS and OS/390. There are two ways of doing this:

- INSERT the LUNAME of the remote system into the SYSIBM.LUNAMES table.

- INSERT the LUNAME, SYSMODENAME, USERSECURITY, ENCRYPTPSWDS, MODESELECT, and USERNAMES values into the SYSIBM.SYSLUNAME table.

Be sure to perform a DDF update to the Boot Strap Data (BSDS) after making one of these changed. Because DDF will try to connect to VTAM you must ensure that VTAM is active when the DDF starts.

Configure Distributed Threads   Use the DSNZPARM CMTSTAT to control the behavior of distributed threads. CMTSTAT specifies whether a DDF thread is made active or inactive after it successfully commits or rolls back and holds no cursors. Consider setting CMTSTAT to INACTIVE because inactive connections consume less storage. A thread can become inactive only if it holds no cursors, has no temporary tables defined, and executes no statements from the dynamic statement cache.

If you specify ACTIVE, the thread remains active. Although this can improve performance it consumes system resources. If your installation supports a large number of connections, specify INACTIVE.

V8 DB2 supports two different types of inactive threads:

- An inactive DBAT, previously called a type 1 inactive thread, has the same characteristics as inactive threads prior to DB2 V8. This type of thread remains associated with the connections, but DB2 minimizes the thread's storage use as much as possible.

- An inactive connection, previously called a type 2 inactive thread, uses less storage than an inactive DBAT. In this case, the connections are disassociated from the thread. The thread can be pooled and reused for other connections, new or inactive. This provides better resource utilization because there are typically a small number of threads that can be used to service a large number of connections.

Although inactive connections are preferable to inactive DBATs, not every thread can become an inactive connection. If a thread is to become inactive, DB2 tries to make it an inactive connection. If DB2 cannot make it an inactive connection, it tries to make it an inactive DBAT. If neither attempt is successful, the thread remains active.

Increasing Data Transfer Rates   In addition to blocking of rows for a query result set, DB2 can also return multiple query blocks in response to an OPEN or FETCH request to a remote client (such as DB2 Connect). Instead of repeatedly sending requests to DB2 for z/OS requesting one block of data at a time, DB2 Connect can optionally request that the server send back some number of extra query blocks. These extra query blocks allow the client to minimize network traffic, thereby improving performance. DB2 Connect can be set up to request extra query blocks from a mainframe DB2 server by default.

Use the EXTRA BLOCKS SRV parameter on the DB2 DDF installation panel to enable support for extra query blocks. The minimum value for this parameter is 0 and the maximum is 100. Favor keeping the parameter set to the default value, which is 100.

On the client side, you activate support on a cursor or statement basis. It is controlled by a query rowset size for a cursor, or the value of *n* in the OPTIMIZE FOR *n* ROWS clause or FETCH FIRST *n* ROWS ONLY clause.

Specify Character Data Types Cautiously   When character data is accessed using DB2 Connect, the choice of CHAR versus VARCHAR will impact performance. VARCHAR is more efficient if the length varies significantly. If the size of data does not vary much, CHAR is more efficient because each VARCHAR column requires two bytes of length information to be transmitted along with the data.

Of course, DB2 Connect transmission performance is but one consideration when choosing a data type. Refer to Chapter 5 for additional considerations.

BIND **the DB2 Connect Utilities**   DB2 Connect comes with several utilities that use embedded SQL, and therefore their programs must be bound to a database server before they can be used with that system. The list of bind files required by these utilities is contained in the following ddcsmvs.1st file for DB2 for z/OS and OS/390.

> **NOTE**
>
> If you do not use the DB2 Connect utilities, you do not have to BIND their programs to each of your DB2 for z/OS database servers.

If DB2 Connect Enterprise Edition is installed, the DB2 Connect utilities must be bound to each database server once from each type of client platform, before they can be used with that system. For example, if you have 5 Windows clients and 4 Linux clients connecting to DB2 for z/OS using DB2 Connect EE, then BIND the programs in ddcsmvs.1st from one of the Windows clients, as well as from one of the Linux clients, and then from the DB2 Connect server.

> **CAUTION**
>
> If all the clients are not at the same service level, you might need to BIND from each client for each particular service level.

BIND **Your Application Programs Properly**   Every application program that uses embedded SQL must be bound to each database from which it must access data.

Beware of SQLCODE **and** SQLSTATE **Differences**   Different IBM relational DBMSs will not always produce the same SQLCODE values for the same, or similar errors. This can be troublesome in distributed applications. There are two ways of handling this situation:

- Use SQLSTATE instead of SQLCODE. The SQLSTATE values have the same basic meaning across the IBM's DBMS products.

- Use SQLCODE mapping.

DB2 Connect can map SQLCODEs and tokens from each IBM mainframe or iSeries server to your appropriate DB2 UDB system. You can specify your own SQLCODE mapping file if you want to override the default mapping or you are using a non-IBM database server that does not have SQLCODE mapping.

SQLCODE mapping is enabled by default. If you want to turn off SQLCODE mapping, specify NOMAP in the parameter string of the DCS directory or the DCE routing information object.

43

CHAPTER **44**

Distribution Guidelines

In the preceding three chapters, we examined both the distributed architecture employed by DB2 and the manner in which the architecture is implemented. In this chapter, we will review some practical guidelines to follow as you develop distributed DB2 applications.

Distribution Behind the Scenes

Distributed DB2 requests are carried out through the Distributed Data Facility (DDF). The DDF is implemented as an address space in the same manner as the other DB2 address spaces: DBAS, SSAS, and IRLM. Refer to Chapter 20, "DB2 Behind the Scenes," for additional information on these three address spaces.

To more fully understand the workings of distributed data, see Figure 44.1 for a brief description of the components of the DDF.

The DDF is composed of four components:

DCRM	Distributed Communication Resource Manager
DRDS	Distributed Relational Data System
DDIS	Distributed Data Interchange System
DTM	Distributed Transaction Manager

The DCRM manages the interfaces to other resources with which the DDF must interact. The DCRM is the component that actually manages the connections (see Figure 44.2). The DCRM of the requester creates conversations to communicate to the server. The DCRM of the server accepts requests and creates a database access thread (DBAT) to handle distributed requests.

Three different managers within the DCRM enable you to perform these tasks: the conversation manager, the queue manager, and the VTAM manager.

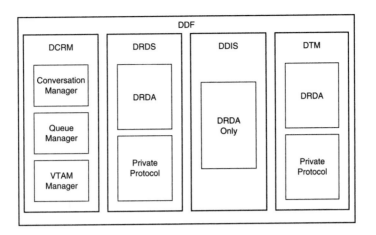

FIGURE 44.1   The Distributed Data Facility.

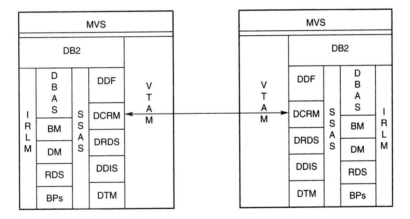

FIGURE 44.2   Distributed communication.

Connections are managed by the *conversation manager (CM)*. The CM is responsible for managing the receipt of messages from remote clients and sending messages from the server back to the requester. Furthermore, the CM manages the creation and termination of connections to support DRDA and private protocol requests.

The *queue manager (QM)* creates and routes work requests for allied agents. Requests from allied agents are queued by the QM and then routed for further processing.

The third and final component of the DCRM is the *VTAM manager*. The CM uses the VTAM manager to communicate with other DBMSs in the network. This component reads the CDB to determine how communication resources are to be used by DDF.

The second component of the DDF is the *Distributed Relational Data System (DRDS)*. It performs tasks similar to those performed by the RDS (in the DBAS). For private protocol requests, the DRDS receives remote requests and invokes the local DCRM to communicate with the remote server DCRM. The server DCRM receives the request and passes it to the RDS of the server. For DRDA requests, the DRDS enables the requester to perform remote binds. The bind request is passed to the server, which uses its DRDS to kick off the bind.

The *Distributed Data Interchange System (DDIS)* is the third component of the DDF. It is used only for DRDA requests. The DDIS performs object mapping of remote objects. Object mapping occurs at both the requester and server.

The final DDF component is the *Data Transaction Manager (DTM)*. As its name implies, the DTM manages distributed transactions. It performs tasks such as monitoring for errors, controlling commits and aborts, and managing recovery.

A firm understanding of the functionality embedded within each of these components can help the application developer or database analyst more fully comprehend the underlying operations required for supporting a distributed environment.

Block Fetch

DB2 employs a method of reducing network communication known as *block fetch*. Communication over the network can be the largest bottleneck in a distributed application. If the number of messages sent over the network can be reduced, performance can be significantly increased.

If block fetch were not utilized when an application accessed rows of data, each one would have to be passed over the network as a single message. One row equates to one message. When block fetch is invoked, the retrieved rows are grouped into a large *block* of data. This block of data is stored in a buffer called the *message buffer*. The message buffer, after it is filled, is transmitted over the network as a single message. Thus, block fetch allows large blocks of data (instead of many single messages) to be transferred.

Figure 44.3 shows the difference between blocked and unblocked data access. Obviously, the amount of network communication diminishes when blocks of data are transmitted instead of single rows of data.

Coding Cursors to Encourage Block Fetch

Block fetch can be used only by read-only cursors. If data can be updated through the cursor, DB2 must send the data over the network one row at a time.

Sometimes, DB2 cannot properly determine whether a cursor is read-only. This type of cursor is called an *ambiguous cursor*. However, there are techniques you can use when coding cursors in an application program to ensure that read-only cursors are known to DB2 to be read-only. These types of cursors are called *unambiguous cursors*.

You can ensure that a cursor is unambiguous in three ways: using the FOR READ ONLY (or FOR FETCH ONLY) clause, using certain SQL constructs, or when the semantics dictate that the cursor is not updateable.

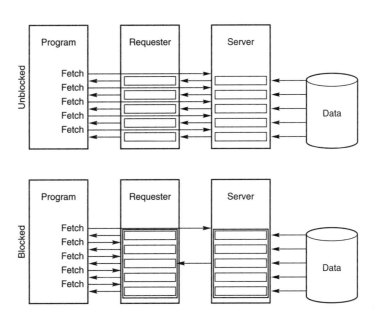

FIGURE 44.3   Block fetch.

FOR READ ONLY **(or** FOR FETCH ONLY**)**   You can append the FOR READ ONLY (or FOR FETCH ONLY) clause to a cursor to indicate that the cursor is read-only. As a rule of thumb, always specify FOR READ ONLY when a distributed query is identified as being read-only. Even if the query is read-only by nature (see the next section), it is still best to code the cursor using FOR READ ONLY, thereby ensuring that the cursor is unambiguous and can utilize block fetch.

> **NOTE**
>
> The FOR READ ONLY clause provides the same function as FOR FETCH ONLY. The FOR READ ONLY construct is preferable to the FOR FETCH ONLY construct because it is ODBC-compliant.

Cursors That Are Read-Only by Nature   Certain cursors, by definition, are always read-only. Any of the following conditions causes a read-only cursor:

- Joining tables
- Specifying the DISTINCT keyword in the first SELECT clause
- Using either UNION or UNION ALL
- Specifying a subquery, where the same table is specified in the FROM clauses of both the subquery and the outer query
- Using a scalar function in the first SELECT clause
- Using either a GROUP BY or HAVING clause in the outer SELECT clause
- Specifying an ORDER BY clause

Even though these conditions cause the cursor to be read-only, you should still specify the `FOR READ ONLY` clause. Doing so enhances clarity and is helpful for documentation purposes.

Semantically Non-Updateable Cursors   Certain types of cursors are semantically not updateable, even when not defined using `FOR READ ONLY` or `FOR FETCH ONLY`. They are read-only cursors because they are included within an application program that avoids updates. This type of cursor exists within a program that conforms to the following guidelines:

- No static `DELETE WHERE CURRENT OF` statements

- No static `UPDATE WHERE CURRENT OF` statements

- No dynamic SQL

Avoid Ambiguous Cursors   Avoiding ambiguous cursors greatly reduces the administrative burden of identifying updateable and read-only cursors. Likewise, it makes tuning easier because the identification of cursors that are candidates for block fetch becomes easier.

Avoiding ambiguous cursors is simple. To do so, you should establish a global shop standard that requires the specification of the `FOR` clause on *every* cursor. Read-only cursors should specify the `FOR FETCH ONLY` clause. Updateable cursors should specify the `FOR UPDATE OF` clause.

Data Currency

Block fetch is used as the default for *ambiguous* cursors if the package or plan was bound with the `CURRENTDATA(NO)` parameter. `CURRENTDATA(NO)` indicates that data currency is not a prerequisite for this package or plan, thereby enabling DB2 to use block fetch.

To disable block fetch for ambiguous cursors, specify `CURRENTDATA(YES)`. However, doing so is not generally recommended.

To determine which plans and packages were bound with `CURRENTDATA(NO)`, issue the following queries against the DB2 Catalog:

```
SELECT   NAME, CREATOR, BOUNDTS, EXPREDICATE
FROM     SYSIBM.SYSPLAN P
ORDER BY NAME;

SELECT   COLLID, NAME, VERSION, CREATOR,
         BINDTIME, DEFERPREP
FROM     SYSIBM.SYSPACKAGE
ORDER BY COLLID, NAME, VERSION;
```

For plans, when the `EXPREDICATE` column is set to B, blocking is enabled. For packages, when the `DEFERPREP` column is set to B, blocking is enabled. In both cases, a value of C indicates that `CURRENTDATA(YES)` was specified.

Specify `CURRENTDATA(NO)`   Binding packages and plans with the `CURRENTDATA(NO)` parameter encourages the use of block fetch. This use, in turn, should enhance the overall performance of distributed queries. The DB2 default value for the CURRENTDATA option is CURRENTDATA(YES).

Limited Versus Continuous Block Fetch

The two types of block fetch are limited and continuous. Each method of block fetching has its benefits and drawbacks.

Limited Block Fetch   *Limited block fetch* can be used by application-directed DRDA units of work. Refer to Figure 44.4. When limited block fetch is used, synchronous processing occurs.

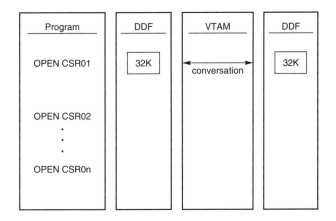

FIGURE 44.4   Limited block fetch.

Limited block fetch uses a single conversation to facilitate communication between the requester and the server subsystems.

Continuous Block Fetch   Continuous block fetch operates asynchronously. Only system-directed, private-protocol units of work can use it. Each open cursor is assigned a separate conversation when continuous block fetch is used. Refer to Figure 44.5.

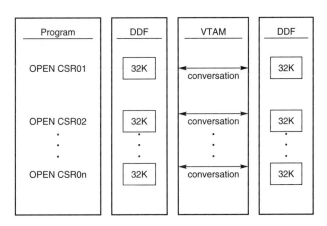

FIGURE 44.5   Continuous block fetch.

Each open cursor has a buffer area on both the server and the requester. The server continues to fill its buffers with results and transmit them to the requester until it reaches VTAM pacing limits. In other words, the server continues processing behind the scenes.

When a sufficient number of conversations are not available to DB2 (one per open cursor), processing reverts to limited block fetch.

A Comparison of Continuous and Limited Block Fetch   The big question is "Which is the better type of block fetch: continuous or limited?" The answer, of course, is "It depends." You must consider the following two trade-offs.

In general, continuous block fetch is more efficient than limited block fetch because fewer messages must be transmitted. However, limited block fetch consumes fewer resources than continuous block fetch because each cursor does not require a conversation.

Programs can use static SQL when they use application-directed DRDA distributed requests. Therefore, static SQL is available only with limited block fetch. So, the performance gain that can be achieved by continuous block fetch through a reduction in network traffic can be mitigated or even eliminated by the requirement to use dynamic SQL.

For a synopsis of the trade-offs between continuous and limited block fetch, refer to Table 44.1.

TABLE 44.1   Distributed Trade-Offs

Continuous Block Fetch	Limited Block Fetch
Resource-Intensive	Network-Intensive
System-Directed	Application-Directed
Private DB2 Protocol	Open DRDA Protocol
DB2 to DB2 Distribution Only	Open Distribution to any DRDA-Compliant RDBMS
Dynamic SQL	Static SQL

Dynamic Cursor Pre-Open

In certain situations, DB2 automatically adds an OPEN cursor request to the PREPARE statement. By anticipating that a cursor is to be opened and doing so, DB2 optimizes performance by avoiding VTAM overhead.

To take advantage of dynamic cursor pre-open, the statement being prepared must be a SELECT statement, no parameter markers can be used, and the connection must be a DRDA connection.

Distributed Performance Problems

Recall the definition of performance given in Part IV. Performance in a distributed environment also can be defined in terms of throughput and response time. The requester and the server each place a different degree of emphasis on these two aspects.

The server views performance primarily in terms of throughput. Remember that throughput is the amount of work that can be done in a unit of time.

The requester views performance more in terms of response time. Response time is more visible to the end user. Recall that response time is the amount of time required to accomplish a predefined set of work.

Analyzing Distributed Throughput

When analyzing the throughput of a given distributed DB2 implementation, you must examine each component of the implementation. Failure to analyze every component may result in an overall performance degradation caused by a single weak link.

The combination of all components used to process a transaction is called the *throughput chain*. A sample throughput chain can include a combination of the following components:

- Requester hardware
- Local/requester operating system (Linux, AIX, z/OS, and so on)
- Local DB2
- Network operating system
- Actual network (or LAN)
- Middleware (or gateway)
- Mainframe
- z/OS
- Server DB2
- DASD

Each link in the chain may be necessary to complete a given transaction. The best throughput that any given configuration can achieve is always confined by the slowest component on the chain.

To achieve optimal performance, you should spend more tuning and optimization effort on the weaker links in the throughput chain.

Factors Affecting Throughput   The three biggest factors affecting throughput in a distributed environment are hardware, contention, and availability.

The processing speed of the *hardware* used in the distributed environment has a big impact on throughput. Factors such as processor speed (MIPS), available memory, physical configuration, and DASD speed have an impact on the throughput component of performance.

When the demand for a particular resource is high, *contention* results. When two or more processes attempt to utilize a particular resource in a conflicting manner, contention degrades overall performance. In a distributed environment, the number of locations that can utilize a resource increases; thus, contention problems usually increase.

The final factor is *availability*. In a distributed environment, multiple computing platforms are used. If one of these platforms breaks down or becomes otherwise unavailable (such as with a communication problem), throughput is affected. Depending on application design, throughput may

- Increase, if transactions continue to be processed. Work targeted for the unavailable component must be saved so that it can be applied later when the unavailable component becomes available.

- Decrease, if logic has not been coded to handle unavailable components, and transactions start to "hang."

- Become nonexistent, if all work is suspended until the unavailable component is made available again.

> **NOTE**
>
> Plan for periods of resource unavailability in a distributed environment and code distributed DB2 application programs accordingly.

Analyzing Distributed Response Time

Response time is typically easier to comprehend than throughput. Usually, a throughput problem comes to light as a result of a complaint about response time.

End users are the typical bearers of bad news about response-time problems. As the actual patrons of the system, they understand its basic performance patterns. When response time suffers, end users tend to voice their dissatisfaction quickly.

Online performance monitoring tools and performance reports are other means of gauging response-time problems.

General Distributed Performance Guidelines

When developing distributed DB2 applications, implement the following techniques to ensure optimal performance.

Standard DB2 Performance Tuning Techniques   Follow standard DB2 performance tuning techniques, as outlined in Part V, "DB2 Performance Tuning."

Minimize the SQL Result Set   Be sure to access only the data that is actually required by the application. Do not access more data than is necessary and filter it out in the application program. Although this tip is a standard SQL tuning rule of thumb, it is particularly applicable in a distributed environment. When fewer rows qualify, less data is sent over the communication lines. And remember, network-related problems tend to be a significant obstacle in distributed environments.

Use OPTIMIZE FOR *n* ROWS   Client programs can use the OPTIMIZE FOR *n* ROWS clause to optimize the retrieval of a large number of rows. To retrieve multiple query blocks on each network transmission, specify a large value for *n*, in the OPTIMIZE FOR *n* ROWS clause for queries that must return a large number of rows. Favor this technique if your application has the following qualities:

- A large number of rows are fetched from read-only queries

- The cursor is not closed before all of the result set is fetched

- No additional SQL statements are issued to the DB2 server while the cursor remains open

- Only one cursor at a time is open and being fetched from that is defined with the OPTIMIZE FOR n ROWS clause

This can result in a reduced number of network transmission, and therefore, enhanced performance.

Distributed Buffer Pool   The buffer pool that will hold the distributed data, after it has been sent from the server to the client, is the buffer pool in which the CDB is defined. Ensure that adequate space has been allocated to accommodate distributed data access in the aforementioned buffer pool.

> **NOTE**
>
> As of DB2 V5, the CDB tables were moved to the DB2 Catalog. This means that these tables must use BP0.

DDF Dispatching Priority   When DB2 is used as a database server in a distributed environment, the dispatching priority of the DDF address space should be reanalyzed.

The general recommendation made in Chapter 27, "Tuning DB2's Environment," (see Figure 27.3) is to code the dispatching priority of DSNDDF on a par with IMS MP regions (below short-running TSO requests but above medium-running TSO requests). However, in a distributed environment with critical distributed transactions, consider changing the dispatching priority of DSNDDF to a higher position in the hierarchy. Refer to Figure 44.6.

You should set the dispatching priority of DSNDDF so that it is not so high as to affect overall system performance but not so low as to degrade the performance of distributed DB2 requests.

In general, higher dispatching priorities should be reserved for I/O-bound applications. Because DSNDDF is a low CPU consumer, setting a higher DPRTY may prove to be advantageous.

> **CAUTION**
>
> Ensure that a higher DSNDDF dispatching priority does not cause excessive resource consumption. If you decide to experiment with the dispatching priority of DSNDDF, thoroughly test different priority hierarchies in your shop until you're satisfied that DDF is at an appropriate level.

Tuning VTAM Parameters   Before you implement distributed DB2 applications, buy your VTAM systems programmer lunch! (Most system programmers have a ravenous appetite; buy them food, and they'll be your friends for life.)

44

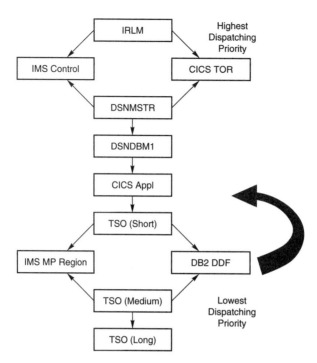

FIGURE 44.6 Distributed dispatching priority hierarchy.

The performance of DB2 in a distributed environment depends heavily on ensuring that the appropriate VTAM parameters are coded for the type of distributed applications to be implemented. The following VTAM parameters are important—pacing rate, VTAM delay, and conversation queuing:

If the VTAM *pacing rate* is set high, and your application retrieves multiple rows, the communication channels can become flooded, consuming an inordinate amount of system resources.

Avoid the VTAM DELAY parameter when your application is coded to retrieve single rows. The DELAY parameter causes a planned wait that would impede performance.

Queuing of conversations can greatly increase response time. Consider increasing CONVLIMIT if the number of queued conversations is high. Likewise, if the number of queued conversations is very low or zero, consider decreasing CONVLIMIT. Start the DB2 global trace, IFCID 167, to collect information on queued conversation requests.

The number of conversations that a remote DB2 subsystem can handle is controlled in the SYSIBM.LUMODES table. You use the CONVLIMIT column of LUMODES to set the limit of conversations per DB2 subsystem (in the LUNAME column) per VTAM logon mode (in the MODENAME column).

For a change to CONVLIMIT to take place, the DDF address space must be recycled. Whenever you're making these types of changes, be sure to keep your VTAM systems programmer in the loop, because setting these values overrides the VTAM DSESLIM parameter, and the VTAM systems programmer usually has a much better idea (than a DB2 DBA or analyst) of what these numbers should be.

Distributed Database Design Issues

When you're designing databases in a distributed environment, follow the standard database design rules of thumb provided in Chapter 5, "Data Definition Guidelines." However, you might need to take a more rigorous approach regarding denormalization. For more information, refer to the exhaustive discussion of denormalization in Chapter 5.

Denormalization can be a useful technique in a distributed environment. In the following sections, I discuss several methods of distributed denormalization. Along the way, I make references to the denormalization types already discussed to clarify the distributed denormalization concepts.

Fragmentation

Fragmentation is a specialized form of distributed denormalization that resembles split tables. To implement fragmentation, a table must be separated into separate parts, or fragments. Each fragment is then stored at a different location. Fragmentation can enhance performance because each fragment can be stored at the location that accesses it most frequently.

As with split tables, fragmentation avoids data duplication. Each fragment must contain a logical subset of the data.

Multiple fragments can be created from a single source table. The methodology used to determine where and how to split the table depends on the data access needs of the distributed applications that must access the data.

Two types of fragmentation can be implemented: horizontal and vertical. *Horizontal fragmentation* splits the data by rows, whereas *vertical fragmentation* splits the data by columns. Tables are horizontally fragmented using ranges of values to create distinct fragments. Tables can be vertically fragmented by assigning specific columns to specific fragments.

Vertical fragmentation requires a certain amount of data duplication because the key column(s) must be stored at each site to defragment the data. Without the redundant key stored at each location, joining the tables back together so that the data returned is the unfragmented, original data would be impossible.

Ensure Lossless Joins and Unions   You must take care to ensure that fragmentation is accomplished such that defragmenting the tables does not result in additional data or a loss of data.

For horizontal fragmentation, rows must be wholly contained within one, and only one, fragment. In other words, the result of selecting all rows from every fragment and combining them together using UNION ALL must provide the same result as a SELECT of all rows from the original, unfragmented table:

```
SELECT   *
FROM     FRAGMENT1
UNION ALL
SELECT   *
FROM     FRAGMENT2
UNION ALL
SELECT   *
FROM     FRAGMENTn;
```

Of course, this statement cannot be successfully executed until DB2 supports distributed request capability.

For vertical fragmentation, only the key columns can be duplicated in multiple fragments. The key columns must reside in every fragment. Even when no data is actually associated with a particular key for a particular fragment, a row must be stored in the fragment for that key to facilitate defragmentation. Nulls (or default values) can be used to indicate that the other columns contain no valid data for the particular key at that particular location.

Simply stated, the result of joining all fragments together should provide the same result as selecting from the original, unfragmented table:

```
SELECT   F1.KEY, F1.COL1, F2.COL2, Fn.COLn
FROM     FRAGMENT1  F1,
         FRAGMENT2  F2,
         FRAGMENTn  Fn
WHERE    F1.KEY = F2.KEY
AND      F2.KEY = Fn.KEY;
```

If certain keys are not included, an outer join must be used. Until such time, because DB2 provides native outer join support, always propagating keys across locations is wise.

Replication

Another type of distributed denormalization is *replication*. In its implementation, it is similar to mirror tables.

When data is replicated, redundant data is stored at multiple distributed locations. Because replication causes copies of the data to be stored across the network, performance can be enhanced (because distributed access is eliminated or reduced).

Replication can be implemented simply by copying entire tables to multiple locations. Alternatively, replicated data can be a subset of the rows and/or columns. The general rule of thumb is to copy only what is needed to each remote location.

Furthermore, each replica should contain accurate, up-to-date information. Whenever possible, you should update all replicated copies at the same time. This way, you can eliminate the administrative burden of having to know the state of each replica. Additionally, replication transparency is ensured when the data is accurate at each location.

To achieve optimal performance, you should always read from the closest replica. A replica may not exist at every location. By always reading from the closest replica (which supports the current requirements), you can enhance performance by reducing the communication path.

You can tune replicas independently of one another. Different clustering strategies, different indexes, and different table space parameters might be appropriate at different locations.

Finally, do not create more replicas than are required. The more replicas, the more complicated the process of updating them.

Snapshots

Similar to mirror tables, *snapshot tables* are read-only copies of tables. Snapshot tables also are similar to replicas, but the data currency requirements for each snapshot table can differ. Data in snapshot tables usually represents a "point in time" and is not accurate up to the second.

Decision-support applications typically use snapshot tables. Snapshots are most useful for optimizing performance when data does not have to be entirely accurate.

As with the other types of distributed denormalization, snapshots tend to optimize performance when they are stored at the location that accesses them most frequently.

You can create multiple snapshot tables—each representing a different "point in time." The number of snapshots required depends on the nature of the data and the needs of the applications that must access them.

To achieve optimal performance, always read from the closest snapshot. A snapshot may not exist at every location. By always reading from the closest replica (which supports the current requirements), you can enhance performance by reducing the communication path.

Be sure to send all updates to the *system of record,* which is the master table (or tables) that always contains accurate, up-to-date information. Application updates should never be made to snapshots, only to the system of record. The snapshot tables need to be refreshed periodically with data from the system of record. You should develop a reliable, systematic method of refreshing snapshot data.

By their very nature, snapshot tables do not contain up-to-the-second information. Ad hoc users, programmers, and anyone else requiring access to snapshot tables need to be informed of the following:

- The data is not current; for current data, the system of record should be accessed.

- The date and time for which the data is accurate.

- The next scheduled refresh date and time.

Distributed Data Placement

A key aspect of distributed performance and functionality lies in the application of proper data placement techniques. To perform proper data placement, you should understand the manner in which each piece of data is accessed within the distributed environment. Analyzing which application or program accesses the data is not sufficient. Analyzing is merely one portion of the distributed data placement puzzle. You also need to analyze and understand the access patterns from each location on the network.

Normal data placement revolves around a single subsystem. The access patterns of programs and applications are recorded; based on that information, portions of the data are placed on DASD devices. Access-based data placement still must be done in the distributed environment. However, location access patterns must be analyzed also. Based on these patterns, portions of data can be placed at the appropriate locations within the distributed network.

The primary goal of distributed data placement is to optimize performance by reducing network transmission costs. Each piece of data should be stored at the location that accesses it most frequently. For example, storing Pittsburgh data at the Pittsburgh server makes more sense than storing it at the Chicago server. Such decisions are easy to make. Problems arise when

- A location has no server

- The frequency of access is (relatively) evenly divided between two or more servers

If the location does not have a server, place the data to the closest location on the network. For example, Pittsburgh data would be better stored in Cleveland than in Chicago, because Cleveland is physically closer to Pittsburgh than Chicago. For scenarios too close to call, the best approach is to choose a location and monitor performance. If performance is not up to par, consider migrating the data to another location.

Distributed Optimization

Optimization in DB2 is usually a clear-cut matter. The DB2 optimizer is a state-of-the-art optimizer that, more often than not, can be relied upon to produce properly optimized access paths for SQL statements. The rule of thumb is to code as much work as possible into the SQL and let the optimizer figure out the best way to access the data. However, in a distributed environment, optimization is not quite so simple.

To understand this difference, consider a distributed implementation of the DB2 sample tables PROJ, PROJACT, and ACT. A project (PROJ) can have many activities, and each activity (ACT) can be a part of many projects. The PROJACT table resolves the many-to-many relationship. For more information on these tables, refer to Appendix D, "DB2 Sample Tables."

Assume that the PROJ and PROJACT tables exist at one location (say, Pittsburgh), and the ACT table exists at a different location (say, Chicago).

The task at hand is to retrieve a list of documentation activities for projects started after January 1, 2000. If DB2 provides distributed request support, the following query would satisfy this request:

```
SELECT   A.ACTNO, A.ACTDESC
FROM     ACT      A,
         PROJ     P,
         PROJACT  J
WHERE    A.ACTNO = J.ACTNO
```

```
AND     J.PROJNO = P.PROJNO
AND     A.ACTKWD = "DOC"
AND     P.PRSTDATE > "01/01/2000";
```

However, DB2 does not provide distributed request. Therefore, issuing this particular join is not possible. Lacking distributed request, what is the best way to satisfy this request? You can optimize this three-table join in (at least) six different ways:

- Join PROJ and PROJACT at Pittsburgh, selecting only projects starting after January 1, 2000. For each qualifying row, move it to Chicago to be joined with ACT to see whether any design activities exist.

- Join PROJ and PROJACT at Pittsburgh, selecting only projects starting after January 1, 2000. Then move the entire result set to Chicago to be joined with ACT, checking for design activities only.

- At Chicago, select only design activities from ACT. For each of them, examine the join of PROJ and PROJACT at Pittsburgh for post-January 1, 2000 projects.

- Select only design activities from ACT at Chicago. Then move the entire result set to Pittsburgh to be joined with PROJ and PROJACT, checking for projects started after January 1, 2000 only.

- Move ACT to Pittsburgh and proceed with a local three-table join.

- Move PROJ and PROJACT to Chicago and proceed with a local three-table join.

Determining which of these six optimization choices will perform best is a difficult task. Usually, performing multiple smaller requests to a remote location is worse than making a single larger request to the remote location. In general, the fewer messages, the better performance will be. However, this rule of thumb is not always true. Try different combinations at your site to arrive at the optimal method of performing distributed queries. The optimal choice will depend on the following:

- The size of the tables

- The number of qualifying rows

- The type of distributed request being made

- The efficiency of the network

Distributed Security Guidelines

Several techniques can enhance the security of distributed DB2 implementations. The following guidelines will assist the developer in securing distributed DB2 data.

Come-From Checking

At times, ensuring that a specific userid has the appropriate authorization to access distributed data is not sufficient. Using the CDB tables, you can use DB2 to institute what is known as *come-from checking*. When come-from checking is established, the requesting location and requesting userid are checked in combination.

Suppose that userid DBAPCSM exists at several locations: CHICAGO, JACKSONVILLE, and PITTSBURGH. By populating the SYSIBM.USERNAMES table appropriately, you can implement come-from checking to effectively disable specific combinations of userid and location.

By inserting the appropriate rows into SYSIBM.LUNAMES and SYSIBM.USERNAMES, you can implement come-from checking to enable a specific user to access data from any location or to enable any user to access data from a specific location. By default, come-from checking is not implemented. Analysis and specific action must be taken to use come-from checking.

Come-from checking is particularly useful when multiple authids may be logging in from multiple locations. Additional control is available with come-from checking.

Authid Translation

Another possibility in a distributed environment is to translate authids automatically for distributed requests. One authid can be translated to another completely different authid.

Authids can be translated by the requesting location, the server location, both locations, or neither location.

Inbound authid translation happens when authids are translated by the server. This term is used because the authid is not changed until it is received by the server (as an inbound request). By contrast, *outbound authid translation* is performed by the requester, prior to the request being sent.

Consistent Authids   You can use authid translation to implement consistent authids for each user on the network, regardless of location. Consider, for example, a situation in which authids are assigned so that they are unique across the network. Perhaps the location is embedded in the name. So, maybe DBA**P**CSM exists in Pittsburgh; DBA**J**CSM, in Jacksonville; and DBA**C**CSM, in Chicago.

Authid translation can be used to convert any of these valid authids to a single, consistent authid such as DBACSM. Doing so greatly reduces the administrative burden of implemented distributed security.

Network Specific Authids   Sometimes assigning all requests from a single location the same consistent authid is useful. If you impose outbound authid translation, all outbound requests can be translated to one specific authid, thereby reducing complexity (of course, at the expense of security).

Password Encryption   If outbound authid translation is implemented, DB2 requires that a valid password is sent along with each authid. If you choose this option, be sure to encrypt the passwords in the SYSUSERNAMES CDB table using one of the following methods:

- Specify Y in the ENCRYPTPSWDS column of the SYSLUNAMES table (for that LU).

- Code an EDITPROC on SYSUSERNAMES to encrypt the password.

Miscellaneous Security Guidelines

Utilize the following security guidelines as you develop distributed DB2 applications.

PUBLIC AT ALL LOCATIONS   If a particular table is to be made accessible by anyone on the network—regardless of authid or location—security can be granted specifying PUBLIC AT ALL LOCATIONS. Of course, it is applicable to only the INSERT, UPDATE, DELETE, and SELECT table privileges.

Miscellaneous Distributed Guidelines

Keep the following guidelines in mind as you implement distributed DB2 applications and databases.

Favor Type-2 Connections   Application-directed distribution is implemented using the CONNECT statement. DB2 supports two different types of CONNECTs:

- Type 1 CONNECT: Multiple CONNECT statements cannot be executed within a single unit of work.

- Type 2 CONNECT: Multiple CONNECT statements can be executed within a single unit of work.

Type 2 CONNECTs allow updates to be made to multiple locations within a single unit of work. If you connect to a system using a type 1 CONNECT, or if the system is at a level of DRDA that does not support two-phase commit, you can update at only one system within a single unit of work. Only one type 1 CONNECT statement is permitted within a single unit of work; however, multiple type 2 CONNECT statements can be executed within a single unit of work.

The type of CONNECT being utilized is determined by a precompiler option and the type of processing being performed by the program.

First, DB2 provides a precompiler option to set the type of connect: CONNECT. Specifying CONNECT(1) indicates that the program is to use type 1 CONNECTs; CONNECT(2), which is the default, specifies type 2 CONNECTs are to be used.

Second, the type of connect to be used can be determined by the type of processing within your application. If the first CONNECT statement issued is a type 1 CONNECT, type 1 CONNECT rules apply for the duration of the program. If a type 2 CONNECT is executed first, type 2 CONNECT rules apply.

Choose Appropriate Distributed Bind Options   Several bind parameters affect the distributed environment. Ensuring that the proper parameters are used when binding plans and packages can greatly influence the performance of distributed applications. Refer to Table 44.2.

44

TABLE 44.2   Distributed Bind Parameter Recommendations

Parameter	Recommendation	Default	Applies*
CURRENTDATA	CURRENTDATA(NO)	CURRENTDATA(YES)	B
DEFER	DEFER(PREPARE)	NODEFER(PREPARE)	P
CURRENTSERVER	"it depends"	local DBMS	P
SQLRULES	"it depends"	SQLRULES(DB2)	P
DISCONNECT	DISCONNECT(EXPLICIT)	DISCONNECT(EXPLICIT)	P
SQLERROR	"it depends"	SQLERROR(NOPACKAGE)	K

The Applies column indicates whether the parameter applies to plans (P), packages (K), or both (B).

Review the information in Table 44.2. Block fetch is used as the default for *ambiguous* cursors if the package or plan was bound with the CURRENTDATA(NO) parameter. CURRENTDATA(YES) is not recommended because block fetch would be disabled.

When system-directed dynamic access is requested, specifying DEFER(PREPARE) causes only a single distributed message to be sent for the PREPARE, DESCRIBE, and EXECUTE statements. A plan bound specifying DEFER(PREPARE) generally outperforms one bound as NODEFER(PREPARE). The default, of course, is NODEFER.

The CURRENTSERVER parameter specifies a connection to a location before the plan is executed. The server's CURRENTSERVER register is set to the location specified in the CURRENTSERVER option, and a type 1 CONNECT is issued. This way, the connection can be established prior to making a request. However, debugging an application without an explicit CONNECT is more difficult.

If adherence to the ANSI/ISO standards for remote connection is essential, you should bind using SQLRULES(STD). The ANSI/ISO standard does not allow a CONNECT to be issued against an existing connection, whereas DB2 does. Always specify SQLRULES(DB2) if conformance to the ANSI/ISO standard is not required.

The DISCONNECT parameter determines when connections are to be released. Three options exist: EXPLICIT, AUTOMATIC, and CONDITIONAL. Refer to Chapter 42, "Distributed DB2," for a discussion of these parameters.

Finally, the SQLERROR option indicates what is to happen when SQL errors are encountered when binding a package. If SQLERROR(CONTINUE) is specified, a package is created even if some of the objects do not exist at the remote location. This way, the package can be bound before objects are migrated to a remote location. The default, SQLERROR(NOPACKAGE), is the safer option.

Remove the Distributed Factor   A wise first step when investigating an error within a distributed environment is to remove the remote processing from the request and try again.

Trying to execute the request directly on the server instead of from a remote client eliminates potentially embarrassing problem scenarios. For example, consider an application in which two DB2 subsystems, DB2S and DB2R, are connected via DDF. An application executing from DB2R is unsuccessful in requesting data from DB2S. The recommended first step in resolving the problem is to ensure that the same request executes properly on DB2S as a *local* request.

Distributed problem determination should ensue only if the request is successful.

Maintain a Problem Resolution Log   Keep a written record of problems encountered in the distributed environment. You should establish and strictly maintain this problem resolution log. You should include every unique problem, along with its solution, in the log. A sample problem resolution log form is shown in Figure 44.7.

Distributed Problem Resolution Log

Problem Number:		Date of Problem:
Application Identifier(s):		Reported By:
Type of Problem:	Codes	
☐ ABEND ☐ Performance ☐ Enhancement ☐ Logic Error ☐ Network ☐ Other ( )		Date Resolved: Resolved By: Time Required to Solve:
DB2 Subsystems Involved:		
Other RDBMSes Involved:		
Description of Problem:		
Description of Resolution:		

FIGURE 44.7   Distributed problem resolution log.

For optimum effectiveness, the log should be automated for ease of maintenance. Anyone involved in distributed problem determination should be permitted to access and update the log. The log should be readily available and stored in a central location. If you review past problems, you can more easily resolve current problems and avoid future problems.

CHAPTER 45

Data Warehousing with DB2

Data warehousing is not a particularly new idea. The basic idea behind data warehousing is one that has been performed by IT professionals throughout the years: enabling end users to have access to corporate operational data to follow and respond to business trends. You might be tempted, therefore, to shrug off data warehousing as another of the many industry buzzwords that rise and fall every few years. However, doing so would be a mistake.

The true benefit of data warehousing lies not with the conceptual components embodying the data warehouse, but in the combination of these concepts into a single, unified implementation that is novel and worthwhile. Consider the typical IT shop. Data is stored in many locations, in many different formats, and is managed by many different DBMSs from multiple vendors. It is difficult, if not impossible, to access and use data in this environment without a consistent blueprint from which to operate. This blueprint is the data warehouse.

Data warehousing enables an organization to make information available for analytical processing and decision-making. The data warehouse defines the manner in which data

- Is systematically constructed and cleansed (or scrubbed)

- Is transformed into a consistent view

- Is distributed wherever it is needed

- Is made easily accessible

- Is manipulated for optimal access by disparate processes

In this chapter, I provide a basic overview of data warehousing concepts and terms. However, I do not provide comprehensive coverage of all that is implied by data warehousing.

Additionally, I provide useful guidelines for developers who are building data warehouses using DB2. Some of the guidelines are generally applicable to any RDBMS; however, many of them are tailored specifically to DB2 for z/OS.

Defining the Basic Terms

Although data warehousing is a pervasive term, used throughout the IT industry, there is a lot of misunderstanding as to what a data warehouse actually is. This section will provide a good introductory treatment of data warehousing and the terminology used when discussing data warehouses.

What Is a Data Warehouse?

A *data warehouse* is best defined by the type and manner of data stored in it and the people who use that data. The data warehouse is designed for decision support providing easier access to data and reducing data contention. It is separated from the day-to-day OLTP applications that drive the core business. A data warehouse is typically read-only with the data organized according to the business rather than by computer processes. The data warehouse classifies information by subjects of interest to business analysts, such as customers, products, and accounts. Data in the warehouse is not updated; instead, it is inserted (or loaded) and then read multiple times.

Warehouse information is historical in nature, spanning transactions that have occurred over the course of many months and years. For this reason, warehouse data is usually summarized or aggregated to make it easier to scan and access. Redundant data can be included in the data warehouse to present the data in logical, easily understood groupings.

Data warehouses contain information that has been culled from operational systems, as well as possibly external data (such as third-party point-of-sale information). Data in the data warehouse is stored in a singular manner for the enterprise, even when the operational systems from which the data was obtained store it in many different ways. This fact is important because the analyst using the data warehouse must be able to focus on using the data instead of trying to figure out the data or question its integrity.

A typical query submitted to a data warehouse is: "What was the total revenue produced for the central region for product 'x' during the first quarter?"

To summarize, a data warehouse is a collection of data that is

- Separate from operational systems

- Accessible and available for queries

- Subject-oriented by business

- Integrated and consistently named and defined

- Associated with defined periods of time

- Static, or non-volatile, such that updates are not made

45

Operational Data Versus the Data Warehouse

The purpose and intent of a data warehouse differ substantially from operational databases supporting OLTP and production systems, such as order entry, shipping, and inventory control (see Table 45.1). Operational databases are typically used by clerical or line workers doing the day-to-day business of an organization. Additionally, operational data is atomic in nature, continually changes as updates are made, and reflects only the current value of the last transaction.

TABLE 45.1   Operational Data Versus Warehouse Data

Operational Data	Warehouse Data
Atomic	Summarized
Production Support	Analytical
Application-Oriented	Subject-Oriented
Current	Historical
Dynamic	Static

What Is a Data Mart?

The term *data mart* is used almost as often as the term *data warehouse*. But how is a data mart different from a data warehouse? A data mart is basically a departmental data warehouse defined for a single (or limited number of) subject area(s).

Data in data marts need not be represented in the corporate data warehouse, if one even exists. Breadth of data in both data marts and corporate data warehouses should be driven by the needs of the business. Therefore, unless the departmental data is required for enterprise-wide analysis, it may not exist in the corporate data warehouse.

A data mart is not necessarily smaller in size than an enterprise data warehouse. It may be smaller, but size is determined based on business needs. Departmental analysis at the business unit level may require more historical information than cross-department, enterprise-wide analysis.

What Is an Operational Data Store?

An Operational Data Store (ODS) provides a centralized view of near real-time data from operational systems. The ODS is optional in a data warehousing environment. If used, it is populated from multiple operational databases or may be used directly as the data store for multiple operational applications. The ODS can then be used as a staging area for data warehouse population (as shown in Figure 45.1).

An ODS is a collection of data that is

- Used by operational systems
- Subject-oriented by business
- Integrated and consistently named and defined
- Current, up-to-date (as opposed to historical)

- At the detail level (as opposed to summarized)

- Dynamic, or volatile, to support operational systems

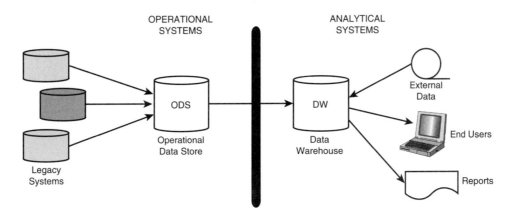

FIGURE 45.1 The Operational Data Store.

What Is OLAP?

OLAP stands for On-Line Analytical Processing. OLAP technology is often used in conjunction with a data warehouse. OLAP technology enables high-level end users (analysts, managers executives, and so on) to derive intelligence from data through interactive and iterative access to multiple views of information (typically stored in a data warehouse).

OLAP uses a multidimensional view of detail, summary, and aggregate data to access information for further analysis. The key term here is *multidimensional*. A dimension is a structural attribute viewed as similar by the end user. For example, months, quarters, years, and so on make up a time dimension; likewise, all cities, regions, countries, and so on could comprise a geography dimension.

Simply stated, a dimension is a modifier of the basic fact that must be analyzed. Examples of facts include sales figures, expenses, and inventory on hand. Multiple dimensions affect the value of these facts. For example, sales differ by geography (for example, sales region), time (for example, first quarter), product (for example, widgets versus flanges), and any other number of factors.

OLAP is characterized by dynamic multidimensional analysis, enabling complex calculations applied across dimensions, across components of a dimension, and/or through hierarchies. Additionally, OLAP provides analysis and trending capabilities over time, subsetting of data, drill-down through varying levels of detail, reach-through to operational data, and methods for comparing different analytical views of data.

OLAP calculations are usually more complex than simple data summarization and aggregation. For example, the following is a typical OLAP query: "What would be the effect on net revenue if account maintenance fees for demand deposit accounts went up by 3% in conjunction with a customer affinity program that reduced the fee by 1% for every additional account held by the customer?" Answering this question is not simple.

The technology used to store the aggregate data on which OLAP operates can be relational or a proprietary multidimensional format. If the data is stored in a relational database, such as DB2, the term *ROLAP*, or Relational OLAP, is used; if a multidimensional database is deployed, such as Essbase (which IBM has licensed from Hyperion Software and delivered as the DB2 OLAP Server), the term *MOLAP*, or Multidimensional OLAP, is used.

This introduction covers the basics of OLAP but is necessarily brief. To cover OLAP in depth could take an entire book.

Designing a Data Warehouse

When you're designing a data warehouse, be sure to drive the project from a plan. This plan should include methods to accomplish each of the following components of data warehouse development:

- Document the business drivers in the marketplace, spearheading the need for a data warehouse.

- Secure an executive sponsor to ensure the overall success of the project.

- Define the scope of the data stored in the data warehouse in terms of subject areas.

- Document the business reasons for the data warehouse; they are typically related to the business drivers in terms of reacting to the identified market trends.

- Develop a detailed analysis of the requirements. Plan to produce a prototype of the data warehouse before proceeding into full-scale development.

- Define the facts and dimensions required. Determine the source systems for acquiring the data that will be populated into the data warehouse. You can have internal and external sources.

- Describe the technology used including client and server hardware, operating systems, DBMS, networking software, data transformation tools, repository technology, middleware, message queuing system, query tools, and other software.

- Define the development approach taken. Is the project staged into smaller manageable projects with defined deliverables? Is it an iterative process with clear milestones? Or is it a monolithic development endeavor? (Try to avoid these endeavors if possible.)

- Document the resources available and the roles they will be assuming for the project.

- Develop a project timeline and document status of the project as it progresses.

Many of these steps are similar to any application development project that is undertaken. However, the success of the data warehouse is contingent on all of these steps being planned and implemented in a consistent and manageable fashion.

Several design issues, however, are somewhat unique to the data warehouse including metadata management and developing star and snowflake schemas.

The Role of Metadata

When you're designing a data warehouse, incorporating repository technology into the plans is a good idea. In addition to the standard role of a repository (storing the metadata and the data model for the corporation), it can act a single, centralized store to assist in the movement of data into the data warehouse. Furthermore, a repository can help end users as they access data by providing definitions of all data elements stored in the data warehouse.

Alas, many shops do not own a repository. Even worse, some of them that do own a repository neglect the product, causing it to become "shelfware." There it sits on the shelf, and the metadata in the product is either outdated, inaccurate, or non-existent. This lack of use does not negate the value of repository products; it simply depicts the cavalier attitude that many organizations take toward their data. If you own a repository, the single most important thing that you can do to enhance the value of your data is to keep the metadata in the repository up-to-date. Doing so requires a lot of effort, a budget, and most of all, commitment.

Refer to Figure 45.2 for a synopsis of the role a repository can play in data warehousing and how it fits in with the other, traditional duties of the repository.

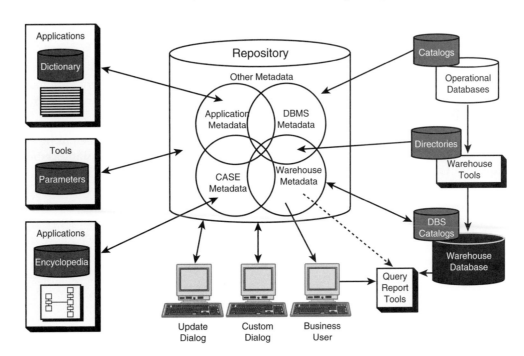

FIGURE 45.2 The role of the repository.

Star Schema

The *star schema* concept is common within a data warehousing environment. The star schema is also sometimes called a star-join schema, data cube, or multidimensional schema. The name *star schema* comes from the pattern formed by the data model when it is graphically depicted (refer to Figure 45.3).

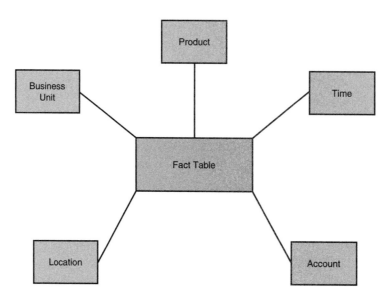

FIGURE 45.3   Star schema.

Typically, a central fact table stores the primary business activity at the center of the star. The dimensions that affect the activity encircle the fact table. You can think of them as the points of the star.

The DB2 optimizer understands and supports the star schema. In practice, when using databases designed with the star schema, users need to join the tables of the star together frequently. Consider the following example of a star join using the example star schema in Figure 45.3:

```
SELECT F.FACT, A.ACCTNO, T.TIME_PERIOD, P.PRODUCT_NAME, B.BUS_UNIT, L.LOCATION
FROM    FACT_TABLE       F,
        ACCOUNT_TABLE    A,
        TIME_TABLE       T,
        PRODUCT_TABLE    P,
        BUSUNIT_TABLE    B,
        LOCATION_TABLE   L
WHERE   F.ACCT = A.ACCT
AND     F.TIME = T.TIME
AND     F.PROD = P.PROD
AND     F.BU   = B.BU
AND     F.LOC  = L.LOC;
```

This SQL statement represents a star join. Each of the five points of the star is joined back to the central fact table. If the fact table is very large, it is inefficient for DB2 to process this as a series of nested loop joins. Because the first join combines the large fact table with a small dimension table, each subsequent join also involves the large amount of data from the fact table. DB2 can detect this situation and invoke a star join technique.

When a star join is deployed, the DB2 optimizer will choose to implement Cartesian products for the dimension tables. In the previous example, DB2 would join together the five dimension tables, ACCOUNT_TABLE, TIME_TABLE, PRODUCT_TABLE, BUSUNIT_TABLE, and LOCATION_TABLE, even though there were no join predicates to combine them. This is why a Cartesion product is required. But, because the FACT_TABLE is usually many times larger than the dimension tables, processing the fact table only once against the Cartesian product of the fact tables can enhance query performance.

> **NOTE**
>
> As many as six dimension tables (five prior to DB2 V6) can be joined as a Cartesian product for a star join in DB2.

DB2 will not automatically deploy this star join technique for star schema joins. A star join will be used only when the DB2 optimizer determines that the star join will outperform other access path options.

> **NOTE**
>
> The star join itself is not a join method, such as nested loop, merge scan, and hybrid joins. DB2 will use the other join methods to accomplish the star join when a star join is chosen as the access path. Do not confuse a star join as a join method.

A variation on this theme is the snowflake schema, in which the dimension tables can have additional relationships. In essence, in a snowflake schema, each dimension table is a mini-star itself.

Once again, in this section I provide only a basic introduction to the star schema. For in-depth coverage, I recommend Ralph Kimball's excellent book, *The Data Warehouse Toolkit: The Complete Guide to Dimensional Modeling, Second Edition* (2002, John Wiley & Sons, ISBN 0-471-20024-7).

Populating a Data Warehouse

After you design the data warehouse, you must move the appropriate data into it. You can use several methods to populate the data warehouse. Some methods, such as replication, propagation, and creating snapshots are relatively simple; others, such as various data transformation techniques, are more involved.

Replication Versus Propagation

You learned about replication in Chapter 44, "Distribution Guidelines." To review, when data is replicated, one data store is copied to one or more locations. Replication can be implemented simply by copying entire tables to multiple locations. Alternatively, replicated data can be a subset of the rows and/or columns.

You can tune replicas independently of one another. Different clustering strategies, different indexes, and different table space parameters might be appropriate at different locations.

Propagation, on the other hand, is the migration of only changed data. Typically, propagation is implemented by scanning the transaction log and applying the results of the INSERT, UPDATE, and DELETE statements to another data store. Figure 45.4 shows the difference between replication and propagation.

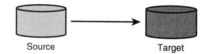

♦ Replication copies all of the data from a source
to a target
    ● the data may be cleansed/modified along the way

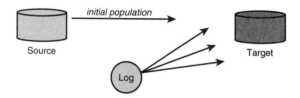

♦ Propagation copies just the changes

FIGURE 45.4   Replication versus propagation.

Data warehouses can use both of these techniques to remain consistent with source data stores. Initial population of a data warehouse can be achieved by replication and subsequent population of changes by either replication (if the data is very dynamic) or propagation of changes only.

Snapshots

Snapshots, also discussed in Chapter 44, are read-only copies of entire tables. A snapshot table is useful in a data warehouse only when the entire table is needed in exactly the same format as is used in the operational environment.

Because data warehouses are integrated and optimized for query, you should not use snapshots very often. However, there is a major exception. The most popular type of data warehouse is an exact copy of the operational database duplicated for analytical querying. This type of data warehouse consists entirely of snapshot tables. The major benefit of the operational database copy is its ease of implementation. The drawbacks are myriad, including lack of integration, data not optimized for query, much of the data is codified and not easy to access, and so on. Yet, because of the relative simplicity of creating copies of operational tables, this type of data warehouse is sure to prosper.

Data Transformation

Data transformation is the process of modifying data as it is moved from the operational and external sources to the target data warehouse or data mart. The four basic types of data transformation follow:

- Simple transformation

- Aggregation and summarization

- Data cleansing (or scrubbing)

- Integration

In the following sections, you examine each of these types.

Simple Transformation

Simple transformation is the underlying component of each of the other three types of data transformation. It can also stand on its own.

A simple data transformation occurs on a single field. No additional analysis is performed as to the impact of the transformation on any other field that may be related to the transformed field. Examples of simple transformations include:

- Replacing a coded value with a decoded, easy-to-understand value

- Replacing default values with relational NULLs

- Changing the data type of a field to a more appropriate type (for example, from CHAR(6) to DATE)

Aggregation and Summarization

Data stored in data warehouses is usually summarized and aggregated at some level because of the vast size of most data warehouses coupled with the analytical processing that occurs on the warehouse data. Although summarization and aggregation are sometimes used interchangeably, you will find a subtle difference between the two.

Summarization is the addition of like values along one or more business dimensions. An example of summarization is adding up detail revenue values by day to arrive at weekly totals (or by week to arrive at monthly totals, by month to arrive at quarterly totals, and so on).

Aggregation refers to a summarization coupled with a calculation across different business elements. An example of aggregation is the addition of bimonthly salary to monthly commission and bonus to arrive at monthly employee compensation values.

Depending on the data requirements of the warehouse, both summarization and aggregation can be deployed during data transformation. Summarization and aggregation are typically used for the following reasons:

- They are required when the lowest level of detail stored in the data warehouse is at a higher level than the detail arriving from the source. This situation occurs when data warehouse queries do not require the lowest level of detail or sometimes when sufficient disk space is not available to store all the data for the time frame required by the data warehouse.

- They can be used to populate data marts from the data warehouse where the data mart does not require the same level of detail as is stored in the warehouse.

- They can be used to roll up detail values when the detail is removed from the warehouse because it is not being used or because it has aged past its useful life in the data warehouse.

Therefore, the data warehouse can consist of detail data as well as multiple levels of summarized and aggregated data across multiple dimensions. For example, revenue is stored at the detail level, as well as by month and by quarter, and also by product group and product type.

V8

> **NOTE**
>
> DB2 offers Materialized Query Tables, or MQTs, that can be used to simplify data aggregation and summarization. MQTs are discussed in detail later in this chapter.

Data Cleansing

Before data is moved to the data warehouse, it almost always must be cleansed (or scrubbed). Do not take this statement lightly. The true scope of a data cleansing project is enormous. Much of production data is dirty, and you don't even want to consider what work cleaning it up would take. By "dirty," I mean that it does not conform to proper domain definitions or "make sense." The age old adage "garbage in, garbage out" still applies, and you can do nothing about it short of analyzing and correcting the corporate data. Failure to do so results in poorly made business decisions.

Basically, the two types of data cleansing are value validation and reformatting.

Value Validation   Value validation is the process of ensuring that each value that is sent to the data warehouse is accurate. You've probably had that experience in which you look at the contents of one of your major flat files or database structures and intuitively know that the data is incorrect. No way could that employee be born in 1995. You know your company doesn't hire toddlers (even if some of your coworkers seem to act like children)! And that next record looks bad, too. How could she have been born in 1978 but hired in 1977. Most companies don't hire unborn embryos.

All too often, these types of data integrity problems are glossed over. "No one would actually take that information seriously, would they?" Well, maybe people won't, but computerized systems will. That information can be summarized, aggregated, and/or manipulated in some way, and then populated into another data element. And when that data element is moved into the data warehouse, analytical processing will be performed on it that can affect the way your company does business. What if warehouse data is being analyzed to overhaul hiring practices? That data may make an impact on the business decisions if enough of the hire and birth dates are inaccurate.

Small data discrepancies can become statistically irrelevant when large volumes of data are averaged. But averaging is not the only analytical function that is employed by analytical data warehouse queries. What about sums, medians, max/min, and other aggregate and scalar functions? Even further, can you actually prove that the scope of your data problems is as small as you think it is? The answer is probably "no."

And the preceding is just one small example of the scope of the data integrity violations that many application systems allow to be inserted into production data stores. Some of the integrity violations may seem to be inexcusable. For example, you probably have discovered the SEX column (or field) that is supposed to store M or F. Frequently, you might see SEX data that defies imagination—everything from * to ! to a blank. These designations typically do not refer to a third sex; they are incorrect data values. Shouldn't programmatically forcing the values to be either M or F be a simple matter? The short answer is "yes," but this answer simplifies the matter too much. Many systems were designed to record this information, if available, but not to force the user to enter it. If you are a telephone marketer, the reasons for this are clear. Not everyone wants to reveal personal information, and acquiring the information independently is not always an easy matter. However, the organization would rather record incomplete information than no information.

The organization is correct in wanting incomplete information over nothing. However, one problem is still ignored. The true problem is that a systematic manner of recording "unknown" values was not employed. Every program that can modify data should be forced to record a special "unknown" indicator if a data value is not readily available at the time of data entry. Most relational DBMS products allow data columns to store a "null," indicating "unknown" or "unavailable" information. Pre-relational DBMS products and flat files do not have this option. However, you can choose some specific, standard default value. The trick is to *standardize* on the default value.

One of the key components of value validation should be the standardization of "unknown" values. This process can be tedious. The primitive examples outlined in the preceding paragraphs use data elements with a domain of two valid values. Most data elements have domains that are considerably more complex. Determining which are valid values and which are not can be difficult for someone who is not intimately aware of the workings of the application systems that allowed the values to be inserted in the first place. Is 1895-01-01 a valid date for a field or is it a default for an "unknown" value?

Nineteenth century dates may be valid for birth dates, stock issuance dates, account inception dates, publication dates, and any number of other dates with long periods of "freshness." Just because the program allows it to be put there, though, that does not mean it is actually a valid date. A user can easily type 1895 instead of 1995. If the data entry program is not intelligent enough to trap these types of errors, the systems will insert dirty data into production data stores. This type of data integrity problem is the most difficult to spot. Likely, only the business person who understands the data and the business requirements can spot these types of problems.

A similar scenario can occur for future dates. Is 2112-01-01 a valid date? Or did the user type 2112 instead of 2002? Once again, you need to know the type of data that is valid for the application. Future dates can be valid for long-term contracts, deeds, pre-need burial contracts, or any number of other dates having long term validity.

Reformatting   The format of data in the source system does not always conform to the desired format of data in the data warehouse. For example, you might choose to store addresses as they would appear on an envelope, as opposed to storing them as a group of separate address lines or atomic address fields (that is, city, state, ZIP). Other examples include the formatting of orders with associated items or the formatting of any type of data to look like forms used by the analysts accessing the data warehouse.

Automating Data Transformation   Data transformation is typically implemented using a third-party tool that eases the definition and implementation of the various forms of transformation. However, creating home-grown programs to perform data transformation is possible, though time consuming. When you're deciding which approach to use, keep the following five questions in mind:

- What is the time frame for the project, and is it possible to create all the data transformation programs necessary in the time allotted with the available staff?

- What is the budget for the data warehouse project, and how much do the third-party tools cost? Keep in mind that a data transformation tool, once acquired, can be used across multiple projects. Also, be sure to factor in the cost of maintaining homegrown data transformation programs before analyzing the cost of a third-party solution.

- What is the size of the data warehouse being implemented? If it is very small, a tool may not be cost justifiable. If it is large, however, a tool could be less costly than a homegrown solution.

- What other data warehouse projects are on the horizon, and can the cost of the tool be spread across multiple projects? Vendors usually provide discounts when you purchase software in volume.

- What are the skills of the data warehouse development staff? The more savvy the team, the less need you have for a third-party data transformation tool.

As for the cleansing process, you truly cannot avoid human interaction completely when attempting to clean dirty data. The best approach is to clean the data at the source. If you don't clean the data there, dirty data will continue to be stored in the organization and sent to the data warehouse. Of course, the data transformation tool can catch and correct some of these values, but it is impractical to assume that all data anomalies can be captured if they are not corrected at the source.

Integration

The fourth, and final, type of data transformation is integration. Integration can be the most difficult component of the transformation process.

Data warehouses are populated with data from multiple sources, both local and remote; internal and external. Integration is the process of rationalizing data elements received from multiple disparate sources. It is possible that a single data element in the data warehouse can be populated from more than one source. For example, competitive pricing information might be received from multiple research firms. One firm might store the data in a decimal format, another in an integer format, and yet another in decimal format, but with more significant digits. Before the pricing data can be moved to the data warehouse, it must be modified to conform to a single definition.

Another integration problem can occur when data from multiple sources must be combined into a single data element in the data warehouse. This frequently takes the form of a calculated or derived result.

The different types of integration that you might encounter are indeed impossible to predict. Data elements in different applications, systems, and organizations will follow different business rules, be impacted by different administration and coding practices, and, in general, be different. Therefore, you must implement flexible integration procedures to be prepared for the many different data types and formats that you will encounter when populating your data warehouse.

Accessing the Data Warehouse

After you design the data warehouse, you can use data access tools (also known as business intelligence tools) to access the data. You can use many types of data access tools, including the following:

- GUI or Web-based database query tools
- Complex report writers
- OLAP tools that analyze data along dimensions
- Data mining tools
- CASE tools
- Program generation tools

Most data warehouses deploy only the first three categories of data access tools for end-user querying and analysis. Additionally, data mining is gaining acceptance. *Data mining* is the practice of automatic and systematic analysis of data to find patterns and trends. The topic of data mining is beyond the scope of this book.

Managing the Data Warehouse

After the data warehouse environment is built and users rely on it for their data analysis needs, you must be prepared to manage the environment like any other mission-critical

45

application. Managing implies creating a systems management plan for the data warehouse that should include the plans to support the following.

Operations

- 24 × 7 support (help desk)
- Automation
- Chargeback
- Capacity planning
- Securing access

Administration

- Maintenance of database structures
- Data availability
- Backup and recovery

Performance Management

- Proactive automation
- Predictive performance modeling
- Server performance optimization
- Network performance optimization
- Database performance optimization

Additionally, you should manage change throughout the application life cycle for operational systems that can affect the warehouse because they are data sources, as well as for any application that accesses warehouse data directly.

The Big Picture

Now that you have learned about the basics of data warehousing, I will tie all this information together with a single picture. Figure 45.5 displays all the core components of a data warehouse environment.

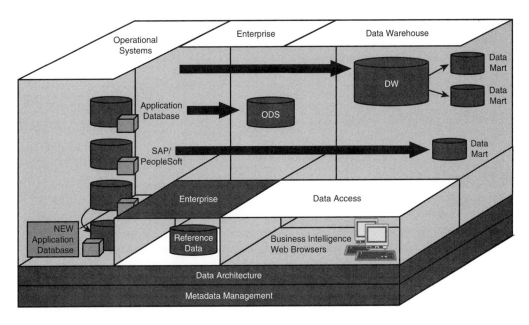

FIGURE 45.5   Data warehousing: the big picture.

DB2 Data Warehouse Center

V7   As of V7, DB2 comes with a new data warehousing management tool called the DB2 Data Warehouse Center. Integrated into DB2 Control Center, the Data Warehouse Center can be used to design data warehouses, register and access data sources, define data extraction and transformation processes, populate data warehouses, automate and monitor Data Warehouse Center operations, and manage and exchange metadata using a DB2-based metadata store (see Figure 45.6).

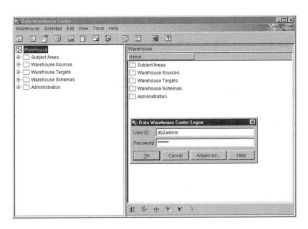

FIGURE 45.6   DB2 Data Warehouse Control Center.

The DB2 Data Warehouse Manager makes it easier to use DB2 for data warehousing and business intelligence applications. Some of the predominant capabilities provided by DB2 Data Warehouse Manager include

- The capability to control and govern warehouse queries

- Help for data cleansing, generating key columns, generating period tables, and inverting and pivoting tables

- Statistical transformers for business intelligence operations such as subtotals, rollups, cubes, moving averages, and regression

- Data replication to allow heterogeneous data movement between data warehouse sources and targets

Data extraction from DB2, ODBC, and OLE DB data sources can be controlled using the Data Warehouse Center. ODBC drivers for Informix, Oracle, Microsoft SQL Server, and Sybase are included with the Data Warehouse Center. Of course, when used in combination with IBM's DataJoiner data can be extracted from many additional data sources (such as NCR Teradata, IMS, and VSAM).

In short, it can be significantly easier for technicians to deploy useful data warehouses on DB2 using the Data Warehouse Manager tool.

Other IBM Data Warehousing Solutions

IBM offers many other data warehousing products that work with DB2 for z/OS and facilitate the creation, management, and use of DB2 as a platform for data warehouses, data marts, and data mining.

One of IBM's main add-on products for DB2 data warehouse development is the DB2 Warehouse Manager, which extends the capabilities of Data Warehouse Center. Of course, products other than the basic Data Warehouse Center are not provided free-of-charge; they must be purchased at an additional cost from IBM.

Other IBM data warehousing products include

- **DB2 DataPropagator**, or DPROP for short, which is used to populate and update data warehouse information. It does so by capturing data changes from the DB2 logs and applying those changes to a DB2-managed data warehouse.

- **DB2 OLAP Server**, which provides financial, mathematical, and statistical functions and runs as an analytical engine in the middle tier of a three-tier client/server configuration.

- **DB2 Intelligent Miner Scoring**, which enables in-house applications and third-party tools to use simple SQL statements to invoke a data mining model stored in a DB2 database.

- **DB2 Intelligent Miner for Data**, which provides data mining algorithms, data visualization capabilities, and can be used to develop models for deployment into DB2 Intelligent Miner Scoring.

- **DB2 Intelligent Miner for Text**, which provides the capability to extract, index, analyze, and categorize information from text sources, such as documents and Web pages.

IBM also partners with providers of query and reporting tools for business intelligence, as well as offering its own QMF for developing data warehouse queries. For a comprehensive overview of the data warehousing facilities offered by IBM, I recommend that you read Ralph Michael L. Gonzales' book, *IBM Data Warehousing* (2003, John Wiley & Sons, ISBN 0-471-13305-1).

Materialized Query Tables

V8 DB2 Version 8 offers a new capability called **Materialized Query Tables**, or **MQTs**. Although not exclusively for data warehousing, MQTs can be used to greatly improve the elegance and efficiency of DB2-based data warehouses. An MQT can be thought of as a view that has been materialized—that is, a view whose data is physically stored instead of virtually accessed when needed. Each MQT is defined as a SQL query, similar to a view. But the MQT pre-computes the query results and stores the data. Subsequent user queries that require the data can re-use the data from the MQT instead of re-computing it, which can save time and resources.

> **NOTE**
>
> Materialized query tables are sometimes referred to as automatic summary tables (ASTs) because this used to be the name of this feature on DB2 for Linux, Unix, and Windows platforms.

Why Use MQTs?

V8 The primary use for MQTs is to optimize the performance of complex queries. Complex queries can be poor performers, because DB2 might have to access thousands of rows across multiple tables using multiple methods. By materializing the complex query into an MQT and then accessing the materialized results, the cost of materialization is borne only once—when the MQT is refreshed.

So, you might consider using MQTs for your existing queries that are most complex and inefficient. Another approach is to consider using MQTs instead of denormalization (when denormalization is required). Simply implement the fully normalized base tables and then build MQTs where you would have denormalized. Then you get the best of both worlds—fully normalized tables to ensure data integrity during modification and MQTs for efficient querying.

Potential Drawbacks of MQTs

But there are potential drawbacks to using MQTs. These problems cross the spectrum from data currency to resource consumption to administration.

45

First of all, MQTs are not magic; they need to be refreshed when the data upon which they are based changes. Therefore, the underlying data should be relatively static or, failing that, your queries should be satisfied with somewhat out-of-date data. If neither of these situations is the case, MQTs might not be a reasonable solution because the materialized data will need to be constantly refreshed.

Additionally, MQTs consume disk storage. If your shop is storage-constrained, you might not be able to create many MQTs. Remember, an MQT will query underlying tables and then physically store that data. The tradeoff for MQTs is using more disk space in return for more efficient queries.

Finally, keep in mind that MQTs need to be maintained. If data in the underlying base table(s) changes, then the MQT must periodically be refreshed with that current data. If the MQT is not used often enough, the cost and effort of maintaining the MQT may exceed the benefit in terms of performance.

How to Create MQTs

V8 There are two methods for creating an MQT: You can create it from scratch using CREATE TABLE or you can modify an existing table into an MQT using ALTER TABLE.

The first method uses the CREATE TABLE statement using syntax that has been augmented to look like a view definition. Consider the following, for example:

```
CREATE TABLE DEPT_SAL
  (DEPT, TOTAL_SALARY, TOTAL_BONUS, TOTAL_COMM, TOTAL_COMPENSATION, EMPLOYEES)
AS
  (SELECT   WORKDEPT, SUM(SALARY), SUM(BONUS) SUM(COMM),
            SUM(SALARY+BONUS+COMM), COUNT(*)
   FROM     DSN8810.EMP
   GROUP BY WORKDEPT)
DATA INITIALLY DEFERRED
REFRESH DEFERRED
MAINTAINED BY SYSTEM
DISABLE QUERY OPTIMIZATION;
```

Let's examine each section of this DDL. First of all, we are creating a table named DEPT_SAL. The first set of parameters is the list of column names. This list is optional; DB2 will use the original names of the columns from the subsequent query if no list of names is provided. In such a scenario, every expression, constant, or function must be named using an AS clause.

The actual SELECT statement that defines this MQT follows. So far, so good—this statement looks very much like a CREATE VIEW statement, except we are creating a table.

> **NOTE**
>
> If the SELECT statement defining the MQT references any CAST functions or user-defined functions, the owner of the MQT must have the EXECUTE privilege on those functions.

After the SELECT statement, there are several parameters that define the nature of the MQT.

Refreshable Table Options

When you create an MQT there are several options available to specify how the data is to be populated and refreshed into the MQT. Population is deferred for MQTs defined for DB2 for z/OS. There are other options, though, for DB2 on other platforms. That is why there are two parameters for deferring data population even though this is currently the only choice. These parameters are

>   DATA INITIALLY DEFERRED—This options indicates that data will not be inserted into the MQT when it is first created. Instead, either the REFRESH TABLE statement or INSERT statements must be used to populate data into the MQT.

>   REFRESH DEFERRED—This option indicates that data in the table can be refreshed at any time using the REFRESH TABLE statement. The data in the table only reflects the result of the query as a snapshot at the time when the REFRESH TABLE statement is processed or when it was last updated for a user-maintained materialized query table.

Furthermore, you can specify whether the MQT is to be maintained by the system or the user. These options are

>   MAINTAINED BY SYSTEM—Indicates that the MQT is maintained by the system. This option is the default and it means that the MQT does not allow LOAD, INSERT, UPDATE, DELETE, or SELECT FOR UPDATE statements. The REFRESH TABLE statement is used to populate data in the MQT.

>   MAINTAINED BY USER—Indicates that the MQT is maintained by the user. The user can execute LOAD, INSERT, DELETE, UPDATE, SELECT FOR UPDATE, or REFRESH TABLE statements to populate the MQT.

Query Optimization Options

The CREATE statement also provides parameters to specify how DB2 uses the MQT for query optimization. Basically, there are two choices: You will either enable or disable query optimization. The choice you make will impact the type of SELECT that can be used by the MQT being defined.

The default option is ENABLE QUERY OPTIMIZATION. When this option is chosen, the MQT can be used for query optimization. However, if the SELECT statement used to define the MQT does not satisfy the following restrictions of query optimization, an error will occur:

-   The SELECT statement must be a subselect. This means you can specify a SELECT, a FROM, a WHERE, a GROUP BY, and HAVING. You cannot specify a UNION or UNION ALL, though.

-   The subselect cannot reference a scalar or table UDF with the EXTERNAL ACTION or NON-DETERMINISTIC attributes

-   The subselect cannot use the RAND built-in function.

-   The subselect cannot contain any predicates that include subqueries.

-   The subselect cannot contain a nested table expression or view that requires materialization.

45

- The subselect cannot contain a join using the INNER JOIN syntax.

- The subselect cannot contain an outer join.

- The subselect cannot contain a special register.

- The subselect cannot contain a scalar fullselect.

- The subselect cannot contain a row expression predicate.

- The subselect cannot contain sideway references.

- The subselect cannot contain table objects with multiple CCSID sets.

- If the subselect references a view, the fullselect in the view definition must follow all of the previous rules.

Optionally, you can specify DISABLE QUERY OPTIMIZATION. Of course, this means that the MQT cannot be used for query optimization, but it can be queried directly. When query optimization is disabled, be aware of the following restrictions on the SELECT statement in the MQT:

- It cannot reference a temporary table—neither created nor declared.

- It cannot reference another MQT.

Attribute Copy Options

When an MQT is created, column attributes are not inherited from the underlying columns of the SELECT statement. The MQT creator must specify how to handle IDENTITY columns and default values.

The attributes of IDENTITY columns in an MQT can either be inherited or not by specifying either of the following:

- EXCLUDING IDENTITY COLUMN ATTRIBUTES

- INCLUDING IDENTITY COLUMN ATTRIBUTES

If neither is specified, the default is to exclude IDENTITY column attributes. When you choose to include IDENTITY column attributes, be sure that your SELECT statement maps existing columns to the IDENTITY column such that the attributes can continue to be used correctly.

The default value specification for columns can be controlled by specifying one of the following:

- EXCLUDING COLUMN DEFAULTS—Indicates that column defaults will not be inherited from the source table. The default values of the column of the new table are either null or there are no default values. If the column can be null, the default is the null value. If the column cannot be null, there is no default value, and an error occurs if a value is not provided for a column on INSERT for the new table.

- INCLUDING COLUMN DEFAULTS—Indicates that column defaults will be inherited from the source table. However, columns that are not updatable will not have a default defined.

- USING TYPE DEFAULTS—Indicates that the default values depend on the data type as delineated in Table 45.2.

TABLE 45.2 Default Data Types

Data Type	Default Value
Numeric	0
Fixed-length string	Blanks
Varying-length string	A string of length 0
Date	Current Date
Time	Current Time
Timestamp	Current Timestamp

Inheriting FIELDPROCs   The MQT will inherit an existing FIELDPROC from a column in the SELECT-list if that column can be mapped directly to a column of a base table or a view in the FROM clause.

WITH NO DATA

When the WITH NO DATA clause is used to define an MQT the table actually ceases to be an MQT. Using WITH NO DATA means that the table is not populated with the results of the query. Instead, the SQL statement is used to define the columns of the new table.

> **NOTE**
>
> To maintain compatibility with DB2 running on other platforms, the clause DEFINTION ONLY can be used as a synonym for WITH NO DATA.

The SELECT statement used when creating a table specifying the WITH NO DATA clause cannot contain any of the following:

- Host variables

- Parameter markers

- Any references to remote objects

- A ROWID column (or a column with a distinct type based on a ROWID)

- Any columns having a BLOB, CLOB, or DBCLOB data type (or a distinct type based on any of these data types)

- PREVIOUS VALUE or NEXT VALUE expressions

- An INSERT statement in the FROM clause

45

Converting an Existing Table into an MQT

V8   Some shops implemented DB2 tables to operate as a type of materialized query table prior to DB2 V8. After migrating to V8, it makes sense for these shops to consider converting these existing tables into MQTs to take advantage of automatic query rewrite and the automated refresh features built in to DB2. An existing table can be converted to an MQT using the ALTER TABLE statement and the ADD MATERIALIZED QUERY clause. For example

```
ALTER TABLE DEPT_SAL
  ADD MATERIALIZED QUERY
  (SELECT   WORKDEPT, SUM(SALARY), SUM(BONUS) SUM(COMM),
            SUM(SALARY+BONUS+COMM), COUNT(*)
    FROM    DSN8810.EMP
   GROUP BY WORKDEPT)
DATA INITIALLY DEFERRED
REFRESH DEFERRED
MAINTAINED BY USER;
```

This ALTER statement causes the existing DEPT_SAL table to be converted into an MQT. It defines the query to be used, as well as the additional MQT parameters. Note that we used the MAINTAINED BY USER to allow on-going user maintenance tasks to continue to work. Of course, we can now use the REFRESH TABLE statement, too.

After converting the table to an MQT, its data will remain the same until the user refreshes it.

MQT Population and Maintenance

V8   As of DB2 V8, when an MQT is created, data is not initially populated into the table. The manner in which data is added to the MQT depends on the MAINTAINED BY option, as previously discussed. Most MQTs will be maintained by the system, and as such, data will be populated when the REFRESH TABLE statement is executed. The REFRESH TABLE statement is implemented "behind the scenes" by DB2 using DELETE, INSERT, and UPDATE, so MQTs follow DATA CAPTURE and AUDIT rules.

If the MQT is specified as MAINTAINED BY USER though, it can be refreshed using the LOAD utility, INSERT, UPDATE and DELETE statements, as well as the REFRESH TABLE statement.

The REFRESH TABLE statement is easy to understand and execute. You simply specify the name of the MQT to refresh, and DB2 automatically rebuilds the data for the MQT using the SELECT statement upon which the MQT was defined. For example, to refresh the sample table we have been using, you would issue the following:

```
REFRESH TABLE DEPT_SAL;
```

Running this statement causes DB2 to delete all rows in the MQT, runs the SELECT statement in the MQT, inserts the results into the MQT, and updates the DB2 catalog to modify the timestamp and cardinality metadata for the MQT. Keep in mind, though, that this all happens as one unit-of-work. So, either the entire refresh is completed, or it fails—there will be no in-between state. Also, all of the changes made by the REFRESH TABLE statement are logged.

The SELECT will run with the same isolation level that was in effect at the time the CREATE TABLE statement for the MQT was issued. This is important because it can impact the results of the SELECT; but the isolation level of the MQT also impacts automatic query rewrite, which is discussed next.

Automatic Query Rewrite

Up until now we have merely discussed how MQTs can be used to simplify the propagation of data from multiple tables into a physical query table. But MQTs are much more useful because the DB2 optimizer understands them.

Your queries can continue to reference the base table. But during access path selection, the optimizer will examine your query to determine whether your table(s) can be replaced by an MQT to reduce the query cost.

The process undertaken by the DB2 optimizer to recognize when an MQT can be used and then rewrite the query to use the MQT is called **automatic query rewrite**, or **AQR**.

For AQR to be invoked for a query, the result that query must be derivable from the MQT definition. The query need not match the SELECT in the MQT definition exactly. When the query can be resolved using the MQT, the query and the MQT are said to **match**. When DB2 finds a match, the submitted query is rewritten by the optimizer to use the MQT.

By using AQR, MQTs can be utilized without the user having to rewrite his SQL statements—instead DB2 rewrites any SQL statement that matches. The goal is to reduce query execution cost. After the optimizer uses AQR to rewrite the query, it will compare the access path of the rewritten query against the original access path, and the one with the lowest cost will be run.

An EXPLAIN will show whether AQR was invoked to use an MQT. If the final query plan comes from a rewritten query, the PLAN_TABLE will show the new access path using the name of the matched MQTs in the TNAME column. Additionally, the TABLE_TYPE column will be set to M to indicate that an MQT was used.

> **NOTE**
> You can also determine whether AQR was used through IFCID 0022, which contains the mini-plan performance trace record.

How to Encourage AQR

Many factors can influence whether AQR is considered for use by the optimizer. A big factor is the way in which you build your MQTs and write your queries. But other factors are involved including database design and some new special registers.

MQT DDL for AQR   The query optimization options discussed previously in this chapter will be a big determining factor in whether DB2 will consider the MQT for AQR. Fortunately, the default is ENABLE QUERY OPTIMIZATION, which specifies that the MQT can be exploited by AQR. However, if you specify DISABLE QUERY OPTIMIZATION, the MQT will not be considered for AQR.

45

The Impact of REFRESH TABLE **on AQR**　Additionally, the optimizer is somewhat aware of the freshness of system-maintained MQTs. AQR will be used for a system-maintained MQT only if a REFRESH TABLE has occurred. Of course, the MQT may not be up-to-date, but DB2 knows that the MQT was refreshed at least once.

The time between refreshes is recorded in the REFRESH_TIME column of the SYSIBM.SYSVIEWS table in the DB2 Catalog.

No such restriction exists when using user-maintained MQTs. Because such an MQT is user maintained, DB2 cannot know whether the data is fresh or not, nor will DB2 maintain the REFRESH_TIME data in the DB2 Catalog. Therefore DB2 does not restrict user-maintained MQTs usage for AQR if the MQT is defined with the ENABLE QUERY OPTIMIZATION specification.

Special Registers　There are new special registers in DB2 V8 that can be set to control AQR. These special registers are CURRENT REFRESH AGE and CURRENT MAINTAINED TABLE TYPES FOR OPTIMIZATION:

> CURRENT REFRESH AGE—Used to control how "fresh" the MQT data must be for it to be considered for AQR. The refresh age of an MQT is the time between the current timestamp and the time that REFRESH TABLE was last run for this MQT. This special register can be set to the following values:
>
> > 0—Indicates that DB2 will not consider AQR for any MQTs. A zero in this register means that only current MQTs are considered by AQR. But DB2 V8 does not support immediately refreshed MQTs, so AQR will not be used.
> >
> > ANY—Indicates that all MQTs are considered by AQR.

> **NOTE**
>
> You can set the REFSHAGE DSNZPARM to specify a default value for CURRENT REFRESH AGE to be used across the DB2 subsystem (or on the CURRENT REFRESH AGE field of the DSNTIP4 panel during installation).

> CURRENT MAINTAINED TABLE TYPES FOR OPTIMIZATION—Indicates the type of MQTs to be considered by AQR; that is system-maintained, user-maintained, or both. This special register can be set to the following values:
>
> > ALL—Indicates that all MQTs will be considered by AQR.
> >
> > NONE—Indicates that no MQTs will be considered by AQR.
> >
> > SYSTEM—Indicates that only system-maintained MQTs will be considered by AQR.
> >
> > USER—Indicates that only user-maintained MQTs will be considered by AQR.

> **NOTE**
>
> You can set the MAINTYPE DSNZPARM to specify a default value for CURRENT MAINTAINED TABLE TYPES FOR OPTIMIZATION to be used across the DB2 subsystem (or on the CURRENT MAINT TYPES field of the DSNTIP4 panel during installation).

Keep in mind, too, that MQTs having the DISABLE QUERY OPTIMIZATION specification are never eligible for AQR, regardless of the setting of CURRENT MAINT TYPES.

Types of Queries Supported by AQR   Only certain specific types of queries can be impacted by AQR. As of DB2 V8, only queries that are dynamically prepared and read only can be rewritten by AQR. Static SQL cannot be rewritten by AQR to use MQTs. If you wish to use an MQT in static SQL, you will have to manually code the SQL to access the MQT. AQR cannot be used.

The DB2 optimizer considers AQR at the query block level. So each block of a query might be rewritten. For a query block to be rewritten to use an MQT it must *not* contain an outer join, the RAND function, or a user-defined scalar or table function with the EXTERNAL ACTION or NON-DETERMINISTIC attribute. Furthermore, SELECT statements in an INSERT or on the SET condition of an UPDATE are not considered for AQR.

Additionally, only MQTs that have an isolation level equal to or higher than the query isolation level will be considered during the AQR process.

Let's look at a quick example. Remember our sample MQT from before:

```
CREATE TABLE DEPT_SAL
  (DEPT, TOTAL_SALARY, TOTAL_BONUS, TOTAL_COMM, TOTAL_COMPENSATION, EMPLOYEES)
AS
  (SELECT   WORKDEPT, SUM(SALARY), SUM(BONUS) SUM(COMM),
            SUM(SALARY+BONUS+COMM), COUNT(*)
   FROM     DSN8810.EMP
   GROUP BY WORKDEPT)
DATA INITIALLY DEFERRED
REFRESH DEFERRED
MAINTAINED BY SYSTEM
ENABLE QUERY OPTIMIZATION;
```

Now, assume that we submit the following query:

```
SELECT   DEPT, AVG(SALARY+BONUS+COMM)
FROM     DSN8810.EMP
GROUP BY WORKDEPT;
```

Obviously, AQR should be able to rewrite this query to utilize the DEPT_SAL MQT. This is so because the query conforms to the rules for AQR, and the information requested is a subset of the information in the MQT.

The Impact of Database Design on AQR   AQR relies on referential constraints defined between tables to help determine whether a query can be rewritten or not. The referential constraints are used by AQR when the MQT contains extra tables that are not referenced by the query.

In many shops, though, DB2 RI is not used. However, most databases have some form of referential integrity—and if it is not defined to DB2, it is maintained by the application.

V8 *Informational referential constraints* are introduced in DB2 V8 to assist AQR. An information referential constraint is not maintained by DB2 during INSERT, UPDATE, and DELETE

45

processing or by the LOAD and CHECK utilities. But the AQR process will consider the constraint to help determine whether queries can be rewritten.

If you have tables where referential integrity is maintained programmatically, seriously consider building information referential constraints when you build MQTs on those tables.

An informational referential constraint can be defined using either CREATE TABLE or ALTER TABLE. It is defined like a normal constraint, but with the NOT ENFORCED keyword. For example, the following column DDL extract defines an information referential foreign key constraint for the MGRNO column to the EMPNO of the EMP table:

```
. . .
MGRNO CHAR(6) NOT NULL,
  CONSTRAINT MGREMP FOREIGN KEY (EMPNO)
  REFERENCES EMP NOT ENFORCED,
. . .
```

> **CAUTION**
>
> Although informational referential constraints are not enforced by DB2 in most contexts, they are used by the QUIESCE and REPORT TABLESPACESET utilities. Additionally, when using LISTDEF with the RI option, information referential constraints will be considered.

ALTER and Query Rewrite

The ALTER TABLE statement can be used to change the MQT's setting to specify whether query rewrite is enabled or disabled. If you alter an MQT to specify ENABLE QUERY OPTIMIZATION then that MQT is immediately eligible for query rewrite. This is so even if the MQT is empty, so be cautious.

Usually, the proper course of action will be to ALTER the table to an MQT with query optimization disabled. Then the MQT should be refreshed—and only then, when the data is accurate, should query optimization be enabled for the MQT.

> **NOTE**
>
> You can also use the ALTER TABLE statement to change an MQT into a base table.

MQT Guidelines

V8 Consider the following guidelines as you implement materialized query tables in your shop.

Enable Query Optimization After Creation

Create user-maintained MQTs with query optimization initially disabled. After the MQT is populated, enable the table for query optimization. If you create the table initially enabled for query optimization, DB2 might rewrite queries to use the empty MQT. And though the query would run quickly, you would not get the desired results.

As Always, Avoid SELECT *

If you create an MQT using SELECT *, the columns of the MQT will be determined at the time the MQT is created. To avoid confusion, always explicitly list the columns in the SELECT-list of the MQT definition.

Avoid Defining MQTs with HAVING

Consider leaving the HAVING clause off of MQTs defined with GROUP BY. Creating an MQT with a HAVING clause is rarely worth the effort. Generally, the HAVING clause reduces the usefulness, and therefore the benefit of the MQT.

An MQT that aggregates data using GROUP BY can be queried for all values grouped. Specifying HAVING will reduce the amount data that can be queried.

Create Indexes on MQTs

DB2 can use indexes to optimize data retrieval from a materialized query table. Build indexes on your MQTs based on their access characteristics and usage patterns.

Use Segmented Table Spaces for MQTs

Consider standardizing on segmented table spaces for your MQTs. This is wise because REFRESH TABLE will perform better if the MQT is stored in a segmented table space. When REFRESH TABLE is executed to populate an MQT, DB2 uses a mass delete to clear the existing data from the MQT. A mass delete also is more efficient for segmented table spaces because of its more efficient use of the space map.

Consider Running EXPLAIN on your REFRESH TABLE Statements

You can run an EXPLAIN on the REFRESH TABLE statement to analyze the access paths used to populate the MQT with data. The PLAN_TABLE output will contain rows for INSERT with the SELECT in the MQT definition.

MQTs Cannot Be Unique

Although most DB2 table characteristics can be applied to MQTs, you cannot specify unique constraints or unique indexes on them. Additionally, because an MQT cannot have a unique key, you cannot make an MQT the parent table in a referential constraint.

Monitor BIND Time with MQTs

Be aware that it might take longer to BIND plans and packages when MQTs are in use. Queries referencing tables on which MQTs are defined can experience increased BIND time due to the DB2 Catalog access and additional processing required during the automatic query rewrite phase.

General Data Warehouse Guidelines

Be sure to understand and apply the following general guidelines when you work on a data warehouse project. These guidelines, though not specific to DB2, are beneficial for building effective data warehouses.

45

Do Not Implement a Data Warehouse As a Panacea   Many data warehouse development projects begin with "pie in the sky" expectations. One of the biggest problems with a data warehouse project is a situation in which the data warehouse is viewed as a "magic bullet" that will solve all of management's information problems.

To alleviate these types of problems, you should manage expectations by securing an executive sponsor, limiting the scope of the project, and implementing the data warehouse in stages (or possibly by implementing multiple data marts for each department).

Incorporate All Three Sides of the Pyramid   When you're developing a data warehouse, be sure to include tools, people, and methods in your warehouse blueprint. Refer to Figure 45.7. A successful data warehouse requires

- People, including full-time employees, subject matter expert consultants, long-term partners, and short-term product support personnel.

- Methods, well-developed policies and procedures for data warehouse planning, architecture, construction, management, and on-going production support.

- Tools, to facilitate data movement, transformation, replication, propagation, data cleansing, business intelligence and querying, and metadata management.

Too often, the focus is solely on the tools component. To be successful, a data warehouse project requires more than just tools. You need careful planning and implementation (methods) as well as a means to learn from the efforts of others (people) through mentoring, consulting, education, seminars, and user groups.

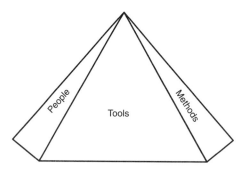

FIGURE 45.7   The data warehousing pyramid of success.

Do Not Mix Operational Needs into the Data Warehouse Project   When a data warehousing project is first initiated, it may have a mixture of operational and analytical/informational objectives. This mixture is a recipe for disaster. Redefine the project to concentrate on non-operational, informational needs only. The primary reason for the existence of the data warehouse in the first place is to segregate operational processing from reporting.

Do Not Underestimate the Complexity of Implementing a Data Warehouse   Moving data into a data warehouse is a complex task. Detailed knowledge of the applications accessing the source databases that feed the data warehouse must be available. Be sure to allot development time for learning the complexities of the source systems. Frequently, the systems documentation for the production system is inadequate or non-existent.

Additionally, be sure to analyze the source data to determine what level of data scrubbing is required. As I mentioned earlier, this process can be an immense, time-consuming task.

Prepare to Manage Data Quality Issues Constantly   Maintaining data quality will be an ongoing concern. Both the end users and the data warehouse construction and maintenance team are responsible for promoting and fostering data quality. Data problems will be discovered not only throughout the development phase of the data warehouse, but throughout the useful life of the data warehouse.

Be sure to establish a policy for how data anomalies are to be reported and corrected before the data warehouse is made generally available to its end users. Additionally, be sure to involve the end users in the creation and support of this policy; otherwise, it is doomed to fail. The end users understand the data better than anyone else in the organization, including the data warehouse developers and DBAs.

Do Not Operate in a Vacuum   As business needs change, operational systems change. When operational data stores change, the data warehouse will be affected as well. When a data warehouse is involved, however, both the operational database and the data warehouse must be analyzed for the impact of changing any data formats. This is true because the data warehouse stores historical data that you might not be able to change to the new format. Before the change is made to the operational system, the data warehouse team must be prepared first to accept the new format as input to the data warehouse, and second, to either maintain multiple data formats for the changed data element or to implement a conversion mechanism as part of the data transformation process. Conversion, however, can result in lost or confusing data.

Prepare to Tackle Operational Problems During the Data Warehousing Project   You will encounter problems in operational systems that feed the data warehouse. These problems may have been in production for years, running undetected. The data warehousing project will uncover many such errors. Be prepared to find them and have a plan for handling them.

Only three options are available:

- Ignore the problem with the understanding that the problem will exist in the data warehouse if not corrected.

- Fix the problem in the operational system.

- If possible, fix the problem during the data transformation phase of data warehouse population.

Of course, the second and third options are the favored approaches.

Determine When Data Is to Be Purged   Even in the data warehouse environment, when certain thresholds are reached, maintaining certain data in the data warehouse does not make sense. This situation may occur because of technology reasons (such as reaching a

45

capacity limit), regulatory reasons (change in regulations or laws), or business reasons (restructuring data, instituting different processes and so on).

Plan to arrange for methods of purging data from the data warehouse without dropping the data forever. A good tactic is to prepare a generic plan for offloading warehouse data to tape or optical disk.

If you create a data warehouse without a data purging plan, be prepared to manage very large databases as the data warehouse grows uncontrollably. Several vendors (Princeton Softech and IBM) offer products that assist with purging and archiving data from DB2 databases. You might want to consider such a product if you have a significant need to archive DB2 data.

Consider Using Denormalization Strategies   Experiment with denormalized tables. Because the data warehouse is a read-only database, you should optimize query at the expense of update. Denormalization takes care of this situation. Analyze the data access requirements of the most frequent queries, and plan to denormalize to optimize those queries.

Refer to Chapter 5, "Data Definition Guidelines," for an in-depth discussion on the types of denormalization.

Be Generous with Indexes   The use of indexes is a major factor in creating efficient data retrieval. You usually can use indexes more liberally in the read-only setting of the data warehouse. Remember, though, you must make a trade-off between data loading and modification and the number of indexes, as shown in Figure 45.8.

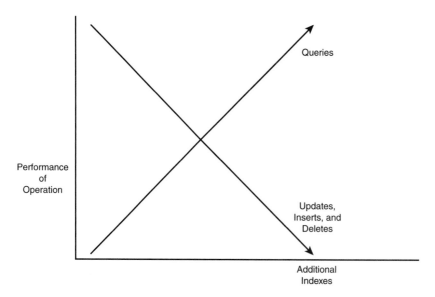

FIGURE 45.8   Indexes and the performance of query versus modification.

These indexes do not have to be the same indexes that exist in the operational system, even if the data warehouse is nothing more than an exact replica or snapshot of the operational databases. You should optimize the indexes based on the access patterns and query needs of the decision support environment of the data warehouse.

Back Up the Data Warehouse   Putting in place a backup and recovery plan for data warehouses is imperative. Even though most of the data comes from operational systems originally, you cannot always rebuild data warehouses in the event of a media failure (or a disaster). As operational data ages, it is removed from the operational databases, but it may still exist in the data warehouse. Furthermore, data warehouses often contain external data that, if lost, may have to be purchased again (creating a financial drain).

Follow "The 10 Steps to Clean Data"   The following list is a short compendium of the top 10 things you can do to ensure data quality in your data warehouse environment:

1. Foster an understanding for the value of data and information within the organization. In short, treat data as a corporate asset. What does this mean? Consider the other assets of your organization. The capital assets ($) are modeled using a chart of accounts. Human resources (personnel) are modeled using management structures, reporting hierarchies, and personnel files. From building blueprints to item bills of material, every asset that is truly treated as an asset is modeled. If your corporation does not model data, it does not treat data as an asset and is at a disadvantage.

   Acceptance of these ideals can be accomplished through lobbying the users and managers you know, starting an internal newsletter, circulating relevant articles and books throughout your company, and treating data as a corporate asset yourself. A great deal of salesmanship, patience, politics, and good luck will be required, so be prepared.

2. Never cover up data integrity problems. Document them and bring them to the attention of your manager and the users who rely on the data. Usually, the business units using the data are empowered to make changes to it.

3. Do not underestimate the amount of time and effort that will be required to clean up dirty data. Understand the scope of the problem and the process required to rectify it. Take into account the politics of your organization and the automated tools that are available. The more political the battle, the longer the task will take. The fewer tools available, the longer the task will be. Even if you have tools, if no one understands them properly, the situation will probably be worse than having no tools at all as people struggle to use what they do not understand.

4. Understand what is meant by "data warehouse" within the context of your projects. What is the scope of the "warehouse": enterprise or departmental? What technology is used? If OLAP is a component of the environment, is it ROLAP or MOLAP?

5. Educate those people implementing the data warehouse by sending them to courses and industry conferences, purchasing books, and encouraging them to read periodicals. A lack of education has killed many potentially rewarding projects.

45

6. Physically design the data stores for the data warehouse differently than the similar, corresponding production data stores. For example, the file and table structures, indexes, and clustering sequence should be different in the warehouse because the data access requirements are different.

7. You will often hear that denormalization is desirable in the data warehouse environment, but proceed with caution. Because denormalized data is optimized for data access, and the data warehouse is "read-only", you might think that denormalization is a natural for this environment. However, the data must be populated into the data warehouse at some point. Denormalized data is still difficult to maintain and should be avoided if performance is acceptable.

8. Understand the enabling technologies for data warehousing. Replication and propagation are different technologies with different availability and performance effects on both the production (OLTP) and the warehouse (OLAP) systems.

9. Only after you understand the basics should you delve into the more complex aspects of data warehousing such as implementing an ODS, very large databases, or multidimensional databases.

10. Reread steps 1 through 9 whenever you think you are overworked, underpaid, or both!

Data in the warehouse is only as good as the sources from which it was gleaned. Failure to clean dirty data can result in the creation of a data outhouse instead of a data warehouse.

DB2-Specific Data Warehousing Guidelines

DB2 offers specific features and functionality that can be exploited for data warehousing. The guidelines in this section should be used as rules of thumb when you're designing, implementing, and using your DB2-based data warehouse.

Use Good DB2 Database Design Techniques   Use the DB2 DDL design techniques presented in Chapter 5 in conjunction with the guidelines presented in this chapter to ensure an optimal DB2 data warehouse implementation.

Ensure Read-Only Data   Create the data warehouse as a decision support vehicle. The data should be periodically updated and summarized. If your design calls for a data warehouse in which all the data is modified immediately as it is changed in production, you need to rethink your data warehouse design.

Consider starting DB2 data warehouse databases as ACCESS(RO) to ensure read-only access. Doing so has the additional effect of eliminating locking on the read-only databases. When the data warehouse is refreshed, the databases have to be restarted in read/write mode.

Consider Using Dirty Reads   Because the data warehouses are read-only in nature, locking is not truly required. You can specify ISOLATION(UR) for all plans, packages, and queries used in the data warehouse environment. With ISOLATION(UR), DB2 will take fewer locks, thereby enhancing performance. However, DB2 might read uncommitted data when

`ISOLATION(UR)` is specified. This should not be a major concern in the read-only data warehouse.

> **CAUTION**
>
> Just a reminder that all of your indexes must be Type 2 indexes before you can use `ISOLATION(UR)`. If you are running DB2 V7 or V8 this should not be a problem.

Avoid Referential Integrity, Triggers, and Check Constraints   Because data is cleansed and scrubbed during the data transformation process, implementing data integrity mechanisms such as referential integrity (RI), triggers, and check constraints on data warehouse tables is not efficient. Even without a comprehensive cleansing during data transformation, the data in the warehouse will be as good as the data in the source operational systems (which should utilize RI and check constraints).

> **NOTE**
>
> Triggers can be useful in data warehouses as a reporting or auditing tool, but not as a data integrity tool. For example, you might create a trigger that records a log containing the time-stamp of the last change to data in the data warehouse. This log then can be queried by users to determine the freshness of the data in the warehouse.

Encourage Parallelism   Consider using partitioned table spaces and specifying `DEGREE(ANY)` to encourage I/O, CPU, and Sysplex parallelism. Parallelism helps to reduce overall elapsed time when accessing large databases such as those common in a data warehouse.

Consider partitioning simple and segmented table spaces to take advantage of DB2's parallelism features. Additionally, consider repartitioning partitioned table spaces to take full advantage of DB2 parallelism based on the usage patterns of your data warehouse access.

Consider Data Compression   DB2's hardware-based data compression techniques are optimal for the data warehousing environment. Consider compressing tables that are infrequently accessed to save disk space. Furthermore, consider compressing all tables if possible.

V8   **Utilize Materialized Query Tables**   MQTs can be used to greatly improve the elegance and efficiency of DB2-based data warehouses. Recall that an MQT is basically a query whose data is stored physically for reuse by future queries.

Queries that can utilize MQTs can experience a significant reduction in elapsed time. This is especially the case for often-repeated queries that aggregate the same, or related data.

Refer back to the previous section on Materialized Query Tables for more details on their usage and benefits.

45

Index

Communications Database (CDB), 770, 1290-1291

comparison operators

  IS NOT DISTINCT FROM, 100

  UDTs, 155

compatibility

  access paths strategy, 763-765

  claims/drains, 797

  page locks, 789

  row locks, 791

  table space locks, 788

COMPILE_OPTS column, 560

compiling applications, 459

complex statements, 77, 414

  Cartesian products, 87

  clustered columns, 86

  columns, 90-91

  denormalization, 84

  exception reporting, 88

  existence tests, 82-83

  explicit inner joins, 87

  explicit outer joins, 87

  flexibility, 94

  IN lists, 79

  indexed columns, 86

  joins, 78, 85

    rows, 84

    subqueries, compared, 85-86

    table limits, 83

  left outer joins, 88

  multi-row fetches, 94

  outer joins, 88-90

  predicate transitive closure, 79-80

  result sets, limiting, 81

  rows

    counting, 83

    expressions, 93

    scalar fullselects, 93

    search criteria, 87

    sorting joins, 86

    subqueries, 78

    table expressions, 78, 91-92

    Top Ten, 80-81

    unions, 78

COMPRESS parameter, 192-193

compressing

  columns, 231

  data, 46, 1369

  disaster recovery, 1226

  image copies, 1055

  plan tables, 882

  planning, 1161

  table spaces, 192-193

Compression Analyzer utility (DSN1COMP), 1159-1161

compression

  dictionaries, 704

  tools, 1236-1237

CompressType UDF, 343

Computer Associates, PDF 1400

computer-aided software engineering. *See* **CASE**

ComputerWorld, **1262**

Compuware Corporation, PDF 1400

COMTHREADLIMIT parameter, 643

CONCAT function, 116

concentrators (connection), 1312

concurrency

  copying, 1074, 1218

  packages, 925

  plans, 925

  users, 1311

  utilities

    BACKUP SYSTEM, 1080

    COPY, 1052

    COPYTOCOPY, 1059

    LOAD, 1093-1094

    MERGECOPY, 1063

    online applications, 428

    QUIESCE, 1065

    REBUILD INDEX, 1077

    RECOVER, 1071

    REORG, 1128

    RESTORE SYSTEM, 1082

    RUNSTATS, 1144

    STOSPACE, 1152

    UNLOAD, 1105

conditional table access, 654

Connect (DB2). *See* **DB2 Connect**

CONNECT statement, 1333

CONNECTERROR parameter, 640

CONNECTION parameter, 661

connections

  application-directed distribution, 1293-1294

  attributes, 640-641

  concentrators, 1312

  DB2, 508-509

  Net.Data, 576

How can we make this index more useful? Email us at indexes@samspublishing.com

dirty reads, **47**

  BIND statements, 491-493

  data warehouses, 1368

  isolation levels, 784-786

DISABLE PARALLEL parameter, 149

DISABLE parameters, 499-500

DISABLE QUERY OPTIMIZA-TION parameter, 1356

disabling

  environments, 500

  index access, 74

  list prefetch, 74, 428

  parallel, 149

disaster recovery

  active log sizes, 1226

  application classes, 1216

  archiving, 1227

  backups, 1225

  compression, 1226

  copying, 1227

  documentation, 1226

  DSN1COPY, 1221-1222

  environments, 1224-1225

  instant copies/restore, 1223-1224

  normal business return, 1227

  offsite copies, 1226

  offsite recovery validation, 1227

  planning, 1225

  QMF forms, 1225

  RECOVER utility, 1217

  recovery basics, 1217

  requirements, 1216-1217

  risks, 1215

  scalpel, 1219-1221

SET LOG SUSPEND command, 1222-1223

shipping image copies off-site, 1225

sledgehammer, 1217-1219

synchronizing, 1194

table spaces, 1227

testing, 1227

disasters, 1214-1215

DISCONNECT parameter, 1294, 1334

disks

  COPY utility image copies, 1054

  devices, 930

  options, 1018

  volumes, 204

DISP option, 1016

dispatching priorities, 937-938, 1325

DISPLAY BUFFERPOOL command, 1183-1184

DISPLAY command, 1182, 1192, 1200

  OVERVIEW parameter, 1189

  resource status, viewing, 858

DISPLAY DATABASE command, 1186-1190

  ACTIVE parameter, 1188

  CLAIMERS/LOCKS clauses, 1189

  RESTRICT parameter, 1188

  USE parameter, 1189

  wildcards, 1189

DISPLAY FUNCTION SPECIFIC command, 1190

DISPLAY GROUP command, 693

DISPLAY LOG command, 1186

DISPLAY PROCEDURE command, 1190

DISPLAY UTILITY command, 1190-1191

  LOAD utility, 1090

  utilities, monitoring, 1004

DISTINCT keyword, 59-60

DISTINCT TYPE class privileges, 350

distinct type names, 272

Distributed Communication Resource Manager (DCRM), 1316

Distributed Computing Environment (DCE), 363

Distributed Data Facility Services (DDFS), 717

Distributed Data Facility. *See* **DDF**

Distributed Data Interchange System (DDIS), 1318

Distributed Data Management (DDM), 1284

Distributed Relational Data System (DRDS), 1317

Distributed Relational Database Architecture. *See* **DRDA**

Distributed Unit of Work (DUW), 1286, 1292

distributing

  cursors, 511

  data

    accessing, 1292-1296

    ASCII support, 1303

    binding options, 1333-1334

    block fetches, 1318-1322

    CDB, 1290-1291

G

GENERATE_UNIQUE function, 117

generate_unique() UDFs, 345

GETDIAGNOSTICS statement

application programs, 373-376

combined information, 376

condition information, 375

connection information, 375-376

statement information, 374

GETHINT function, 117

GetInstruments UDF, 342

GetTrackNames UDF, 342

GETVARIABLE function, 117

global data buffering, 686-689

buffer pools, 687

group buffer pool duplexing, 688-689

updating/reading data, 687

global locks, 799-800

managing, 686

structures, 800

global traces, 814-816, 821

GoldenGate Software Inc., PDF 1401

Google Web site, 596

governors, 439

predictive, 439, 993

QMF, 997-998

reactive, 439, 993

RLF, 992-997

GRANT statements, 349-350

granting

authorities, 351

privileges, 349-350

public access, 350-351

security, 351

GRAPHIC data type, 35, 138

GRAPHIC function, 117

GREATEST function, 117

GRECP status (Group buffer pool recovery pending), 692

GROUP ATTACH name, 684

group attach processing, 1199

Group buffer pool recovery pending (GRECP) status, 692

GROUP BY clause, 29, 90

GROUP MEMBER column, 868, 877

GROUP parameter, 1199

group-level authorizations, 36

group-level names, 689

group-level security, 352

groups, 29

authorities, 351

buffer pool duplexing, 688-689, 695-696

buffer pools, 1186

columns, 90

data sharing, 683-684

creating, 690

global locks, 799-800

hierarchical locks, 800

L-locks, 801

monitoring, 693

P-locks, 801

like programs, 487

MVS performance, 621

repeating, 239-240

storage, 161, 199

buffer pools, 162

default, 202

defining, 199-200

disk volumes, 204

navigational queries, 892

SMS, 201-202

user-defined VSAM data sets, 203

volumes, assigning, 700

transactions, 646

GROUP_MEMBER column, 140

GSE U.K. DB2 Working Group Web site, 591

GTF (Generalized Trace Facility), 819

GUI workstations, 851

Gupta Technologies, LLC, PDF 1401

H

handling errors

applications, 376-378

DSNTEP2 utility, 1173

DSNTIAD, 1175

error codes, 378

error trapping statement, 379-380

HAVING clause, 29

column function results, 130

MQTs, 1363

WHERE clause, compared, 29-30

header pages, 704

Height UDF, 342

help desk, 1277

hex dumps, 1165

HEX function, 117

How can we make this index more useful? Email us at indexes@samspublishing.com

How can we make this index more useful? Email us at indexes@samspublishing.com

RUNSTATS, 882

versions

7, 861

8, 863

PLANEXITNAME parameter

CICS pool thread attributes, 642

CICS thread operation attributes, 644

PLANI RCT INIT macro parameter, 632

PLANNAME column, 995

planning

DDL execution, 274

disaster recovery, 1215-1217, 1225

active log sizes, 1226

application classes, 1216

archiving, 1227

backups, 1225

compression, 1226

copying, 1227

documentation, 1226

DSN1COPY, 1221-1222

environments, 1224-1225

instant copies/restore, 1223-1224

normal business return, 1227

offsite recovery validation, 1227

offsite copies, 1226

QMF forms with DBID/PSID/OBID queries, 1225

RECOVER utility, 1217

recovery basics, 1217

requirements, 1216-1217

risks, 1215

scalpel, 1219-1221

SET LOG SUSPEND command, 1222-1223

shipping image copies offsite, 1225

sledgehammer, 1217-1219

table spaces, 1227

testing, 1227

SQL, 13

PLANNO column, 865

plans, 483

analysis tools, 1245-1246

authority query, 906

authorizations, 355, 925

average size query, 924

BCT, 856

BIND, 804

BINDCT, 856

binding, 474, 489, 610

cache size, 496

CICS, 653

concurrent query, 925

creating, 474

defined, 474

dependency queries, 901

disaster recovery plans, 1194

dynamic, 651-652

freeing, 611

information, storing, 475

managing, 651-652

names, 272, 380-382

packages, compared, 475

parallel, 753

production, 882

rebinding, 55, 611

security, 905

sequential, 753

PLAN_NAME session variable, 362

platforms

DB2 Connect supported, 1307

multiple, 517

PLN tools, 1245-1246

PLNEXIT ENTRY macro parameter, 636

PLNEXIT POOL macro parameter, 638

PLNPGME ENTRY macro parameter, 636

PLNPGME POOL macro parameter, 638

PLNPGMI RCT INIT macro parameter, 632

PLNXTR1 RCT INIT macro parameter, 633

PLNXTR2 RCT INIT macro parameter, 633

PM (Performance Monitor), 822

monitoring reference, 847-849

report sets, 822-823

accounting. *See* accounting report sets

audit, 822, 836-837

explain, 837

I/O activity, 822, 837-839

locking, 823, 839

record trace, 823, 839

SQL trace, 823, 840

statistics, 823, 840-844

summary, 823, 844

T

Y - Z

year timestamp unit, 124

Yevich, Lawson, and
  Associates Web site, 587

Z/Journal, 1265

z/OS

  DDF for, 1313

  memory, tuning, 920

  monitoring, 858

  SRM, 936

  tuning, 918, 936-939, 988